What they're saying about

The Complete Guide to Bed & Breakfasts, Inns & Guesthouses ...

... all necessary information about facilities, prices, pets, children, amenities, credit cards and the like. Like France's Michelin...

—New York Times

Definitive and worth the room in your reference library.

—Los Angeles Times

... innovative and useful ...

—Washington Post

A must for the adventurous ... who still like the Hobbity creature comforts.

—St. Louis Post-Dispatch

What has long been overdue: a list of the basic information of where, how much and what facilities are offered at the inns and guesthouses.

—San Francisco Examiner

Standing out from the crowd for its thoroughness and helpful cross-indexing ...

—Chicago Sun Times

A quaint, charming and economical way to travel—all in one book.

—Waldenbooks (as seen in USA Today)

Little descriptions provide all the essentials: romance, historical landmarks, golf/fishing, gourmet food, or, just as important, low prices. Take your pick!

—National Motorist

For those travelling by car, lodging is always a main concern ... The Complete Guide to Bed & Breakfasts, Inns & Guesthouses provides listings and descriptions ....

—Minneapolis Star & Tribune

... the most complete compilation of bed and breakfast data ever published.

—Denver Post

Unique and delightful inns ...

—Detroit Free Press

... lists more than 260 places in California alone ...

—Oakland Tribune

... I've got just the book for you ... settle back and picture yourself lapping discount luxury.

—Washington Times

The book may give ... readers everything they ever wanted to know ...

—Dallas Morning News

A state-by-state and city-by-city guide ... researched listings ... an impressive number.

—San Francisco Chronicle

... comprehensive ...

—Atlanta Journal

It is a good basic resource for inn fanciers.

—Indianapolis Star

... a worthwhile addition to libraries.

—Library Journal

... a concise guide. .thousands of hotels, inns & guesthouses ...

—Los Angeles Herald-Examiner

... access to more than 10,000 private guesthouses ...

—Chicago Tribune

... the best so far.

—Whole Earth Review

The joy of the Complete Guide to BBIG is that it compromises neither description nor practical info ... an essential reference.

—Midwest Book Review

... excellent guide book.

—Focus, Philadelphia, PA

... well coded and full of practical information.

—Diversion

THE COMPLETE GUIDE TO

BED &
BREAKFASTS,
INNS & GUESTHOUSES
IN THE UNITED STATES AND CANADA

PAMELA LANIER

Other Books By Pamela Lanier

All-Suite Hotel Guide	(Lanier Publishing Int., Ltd.)
Elegant Small Hotels	(Lanier Publishing Int., Ltd.)
Condo Vacations: The Complete Guide	(Lanier Publishing Int., Ltd.)
Golf Resorts: The Complete Guide	(Lanier Publishing Int., Ltd.)
Golf Resorts International	(Lanier Publishing Int., Ltd.)
22 Days in Alaska	(John Muir Publications)
Bed & Breakfast Cookbook	(Running Press)
Cinnamon Mornings	(Running Press)

For further information, please contact:
  The Complete Guide to Bed & Breakfasts,
    Inns and Guesthouses
  P.O. Box 20467
  Oakland, CA 94620-0467

1992 edition. First printing

ISBN 0-89815-453-7

Distributed to the book trade by:
  Ten Speed Press
  P.O. Box 7123
  Berkeley, CA 94707

Cover by Jim Wood

Design & Production by J.C. Wright

Typeset by Futura Graphics

Printed in the United States of America on recycled paper

Innkeeper Survey
Innsider Magazine
April, 1988

For J. C. Dolphin Valdes

Acknowledgements

Corrine Rednour and George Lanier for your help, love, and support—thank you.

For Leslie Chan, Judy Berman and Christy Johnson, Project Coordinators, who gave their all to this update, many many thanks.

To my friends who were so generous with their time and skills:

Venetia Young, Carol McBride, Marianne Barth, Vincent Yu, Madelyn Furze, Rus Quon, Terry Lacey, John Garrett, Chris Manley, Mary Kreuger, Mr. Wiley, Adele Novelli, Ruth Young, Mrs. Gieselman (the best English teacher ever), Mary Institute, Ingrid Head, Sumi Timberlake, Marvin Downey, Marguerite Tafoya, Peggy Dennis, Judy Jacobs, Derek Ng, Katherine Bertolucci, Margaret Callahan, Mary Ellen Callahan, Glenna Goulet and Jane Foster.

Special thanks to Richard Paoli

To the great folks in the Chambers of Commerce, State and Regional Departments of Tourism, I am most grateful.

To the innkeepers themselves who are so busy, yet found the time to fill out our forms and provide us with all sorts of information, I wish you all great success.

Contents

Reservation Service Organizations ———— 503

B&B Inns with Special Features ———— 523

VOTE

FOR YOUR CHOICE OF
INN OF THE YEAR

Did you find your stay at a Bed & Breakfast, Inn or Guesthouse listed in this Guide particularly enjoyable? Use the form in the back of the book or just drop us a note and we'll add your vote for the "Inn of the Year."

The winning entry will be featured in the next edition of **The Complete Guide to Bed & Breakfasts, Inns and Guesthouses in the U.S. and Canada.**

Please base your decision on:

- Helpfulness of Innkeeper
- Cleanliness • Amenities
- Quality of Service
- Decor • Food

Look for the winning Inn in the next Updated & Revised edition of **The Complete Guide to Bed & Breakfasts, Inns and Guesthouses in the U.S. and Canada.**

1992 INN OF THE YEAR

THE LAMPLIGHT INN
LAKE LUZERNE, NEW YORK

In 1984, Gene and Linda Merlino followed a whim and purchased a turn-of-the-century Victorian mini-mansion. Using their expert building, decorating and business skills, the Merlino's converted the aging home, with its grand wrap-around porch, four fireplaces, oak woodwork and twelve-foot beamed ceilings into the exquisite Lamplight Inn.

Gene and Linda do seem to have a magic touch. Each guest room is uniquely decorated in antiques with the personal touches that guests most appreciate. They've received accolades from the local historical society for their renovation work, which successfully blends the original Victorian elegance with modern convenience.

Guests appreciate the "exquisite decor," the "attention to details," and, of course, the "sensational breakfasts" which are served on a spacious sunporch with a view of the Adirondack Mountains. More importantly, though, our readers remark on the warm hospitality and graciousness of the innkeepers, Gene and Linda, who, one visitor wrote, "are the warmest people you can imagine."

INNS OF THE YEAR
HONOR ROLL

1985 Joshua Grindle Inn,
      Mendocino CA

1986 Carter House, Eureka, CA

1987 Governor's Inn, Ludlow, VT

1988 Seacrest Manor, Rockport, MA

1989 Wedgewood Inn,
      New Hope, PA

1990 The Veranda, Senoia, GA

1991 Kedron Valley Inn,
      South Woodstock, VT

Introduction

There was a time, and it wasn't so long ago, when bed and breakfast inns were a rarity in the United States. Travelers made do at a hotel or motel; there was no alternative. The few bed and breakfast inns were scattered across the rural areas of New England and California. They were little known to most travelers; often their only advertisement was by word of mouth.

But in a few short years that has changed, and changed in a way that could only be called dramatic. There has been an explosion in the number of bed and breakfast inns. Today, inns can be found in every state, and often in cities; they have become true alternatives to a chain motel room or the city hotel with its hundreds of cubicles.

This sudden increase in bed and breakfast inns started less than two decades ago when Americans, faced with higher costs for foreign travel, began to explore the backroads and hidden communities of their own country.

Other factors have influenced the growth and popularity of bed and breakfast inns. Among them, the desire to get away from the daily routine and sameness of city life; the desire to be pampered for a few days; and also the desire to stay in a place with time to make new friends among the other guests.

The restored older homes that have become bed and breakfast inns answer those desires. The setting most often is rural; the innkeepers provide the service—not a staff with name tags—and the parlor is a gathering place for the handful of guests. They are a home away from home.

The proliferation of these inns as an alternative lodging has created some confusion. It's been difficult to find—in one place—up-to-date and thorough information about the great variety of inns.

Some books published in the past five or six years have tried to provide this information. But those books focused on one region of the country or named too few inns. While some earlier books gave detailed descriptions of the inns, few bothered to provide information about the type of breakfast served, whether there are rooms for non-smokers, and such things as whether the inn offered free use of bicycles or whether it had a hot tub.

An effort to collect as much information about as many inns as possible in one book has been overdue. Now that has been remedied. You hold a copy of the result in your hands.

Richard Paoli,
Travel Editor
San Francisco Examiner

How to Use this Guide

Organization

This book is organized alphabetically by state and, within a state, alphabetically by city or town. The inns appear first. More inns are listed after the featured inns, alphabetically. At the back of the guide are listings of the reservation service organizations serving each state and inns with special characteristics.

Three Types of Accommodations

Inn: Webster's defines an inn as a "house built for the lodging and entertainment of travelers." All the inns in this book fulfill this description. Many also provide meals, at least breakfast, although a few do not. Most of these inns have under 30 guest rooms.

Bed and Breakfast: Can be anything from a home with three or more rooms to, more typically, a large house or mansion with eight or nine guest accommodations where breakfast is served in the morning.

Guest House: Private homes welcoming travelers, some of which may be contacted directly but most of which are reserved through a reservation service organization. A comprehensive list of RSOs appears toward the back of this guide.

Breakfasts

We define a **full breakfast** as one being along English lines, including eggs and/or meat as well as the usual breads, toast, juice and coffee.

Continental plus is a breakfast of coffee, juice, and choice of several breads and pastry and possibly more.

Continental means coffee, juice, bread or pastry

Meals

Bear in mind that inns that do not serve meals are usually located near a variety of restaurants.

Can We Get a Drink?

Those inns without a license will generally chill your bottles and provide you with set-ups upon request.

Prices

We include a price code to give you an idea of each inn's rates. Generally, the coded prices indicate a given lodging's lowest priced double room, double occupancy rate as follows:

$—under $50 $$—$50-$75 $$$—$75 plus

Appearing to the right of the price code is a code indicating the type of food services available:

B&B: Breakfast included in quoted rate

EP (European Plan): No meals

MAP (Modified American Plan): Includes breakfast and dinner

AP (American Plan): Includes all three meals

All prices are subject to change. Please be sure to confirm rates and services when you make your reservations.

Credit Cards and Checks

If an establishment accepts credit cards, it will be listed as VISA, MC or AmEx, etc. Most inns will accept your personal check with proper identification, but be sure to confirm when you book.

Reservations

Reservations are essential at most inns, particularly during busy seasons, and are appreciated at other times. Be sure to reserve, even if only a few hours in advance, to avoid disappointment. When you book, feel free to discuss your requirements and confirm prices, services and other details. We have found innkeepers to be delightfully helpful.

Most inns will hold your reservation until 6 p.m. If you plan to arrive later, please phone ahead to let them know.

A deposit or advance payment is required at some inns.

Children, Pets and Smoking

Children, pets, smoking and physical handicaps present special considerations for many inns. Whether or not they can be accommodated is generally noted as follows:

	Yes	Limited	No
Children	C-yes	C-ltd	C-no
Pets	P-yes	P-ltd	P-no
Smoking	S-yes	S-ltd	S-no
Handicapped	H-yes	H-ltd	H-no

Accessibility for the Handicapped

Because many inns are housed in old buildings, access for handicapped persons in many cases is limited. Where this information is available, we have noted it as above. Be sure to confirm your exact requirements when you book.

Big Cities

In many big cities there are very few small, intimate accommodations. We have searched out as many as possible. We strongly advise you to investigate the guest house alternative, which can provide you with anything from a penthouse in New York to your own quiet quarters with a private entrance in the suburbs. See our RSO listings at the back of the book.

Farms

Many B&Bs are located in a rural environment, some on working farms. We have provided a partial list of farm vacation experiences. What a restorative for the city-weary. They can make a great family vacation—just be sure to keep a close eye on the kids around farm equipment.

Bathrooms

Though shared baths are the norm in Europe, this is sometimes a touchy subject in the U.S.A. We list the number of private baths available directly next to the number of rooms. Bear in mind that those inns with shared baths generally have more than one.

Manners

Please keep in mind when you go to an inn that innkeeping is a very hard job. It is amazing that innkeepers manage to maintain such a thoroughly cheerful and delightful presence despite long hours. Do feel free to ask your innkeepers for help or suggestions, but please don't expect them to be your personal servant. You may have to carry your own bags.

When in accommodations with shared baths, be sure to straighten the bathroom as a courtesy to your fellow guests. If you come in late, please do so on tiptoe, mindful of the other patrons visiting the inn for a little R&R.

Name of inn
Street address and zip code
Phone number
Name of innkeeper
Dates of operation

Price and included meals
Numbers of rooms and private baths
Credit cards accepted
Travel agent commission ●
Limitations:
  Children (C), Pets (P)
  Smoking (S), Handicapped Access (H)
Foreign languages spoken

Name of city or town

Extra charge for breakfast

ANYPLACE

Any Bed & Breakfast
Any Street, ZIP code
555-555-5555
Tom & Jane Innkeeper
All year

$$ B&B
8 rooms, 6 pb
Visa, MC ●
C-12+ /S-ltd/P-no/H-ltd
French, Spanish

Full breakfast ($)
Lunch, dinner
sitting room
library, bicycles
antiques

Large Victorian country house in historic village. Hiking, swimming and golf nearby. Old-fashioned comfort with modern conveniences.

Description given by the innkeeper about the original characteristics of his establishment

Meals and drinks
Amenities

Sample Bed & Breakfast Listing

6 How to Use this Guide

Ejemplo de una entrada para las posadas con cama & desayuno

Ciudad o pueblo nombre

Nombre de la posada
Dirección
Teléfono
Fechas de temporada

Precio del alojamiento
Qué comidas van incluídas
Número de cuartos y número de cuartos
con baño privado
Tarjetas de crédito aceptables
Agente de viaje comisión •
Limitaciones:
   niños (C); animales domésticos (P);
   prohibido fumar (S); entradas para
   minusválidos (H)
Se habla idiomas extranjeros

Comidas y bebidas
Entretenimientos

ANYPLACE ────────────────────────────────

Any Bed & Breakfast $$ B&B   Full breakfast ($)
Any Street, ZIP code   8 rooms, 6 pb   Lunch, dinner
555-555-5555   Visa, MC •   sitting room
Tom & Jane Innkeeper   C-12+ /S-ltd/P-no/H-ltd   library, bicycles
All year   French, Spanish   antiques

Large Victorian country house in historic village. Hiking, swimming and golf nearby. Old-fashioned comfort with modern conveniences.

Descripción proporcionada por el dueño de
la posada sobre las características
especiales y originales de establecimiento

Mode d'emploi

   Prix des chambres Repas
   inclus ou non
   Nombre de chambres et
   chambres avec salle de bain
   privées
   Cartes de crédit acceptées

Nom de ville

Repas, boissons possibles

Commodités

ANYPLACE ────────────────────────────────

Any Bed & Breakfast $$ B&B   Full breakfast ($)
Any Street, ZIP code   8 rooms, 6 pb   Lunch, dinner
555-555-5555   Visa, MC •   sitting room
Tom & Jane Innkeeper   C-12+ /S-ltd/P-no/H-ltd   library, bicycles
All year   French, Spanish   antiques

Large Victorian country house in historic village. Hiking, swimming and golf nearby. Old-fashioned comfort with modern conveniences.

Nom de l'auberge
Addresse
Téléphone
Dates d'ouverture s'il n'y
   a pas de dates ouvert
   toute l'année

Restrictions—
   Enfants (C); Animaux (P);
   Fumeurs (S); Handicappés (H)
On parle les langues étrangères

L'aubergiste décrit ce qui rend
son auberge unique

Erläuterung der Eintragungen der Unterkunfsstätte

Name der Stadt oder
Ortschaft

Name der Unterkunft
Adresse
Telefon-Nummer
Zu welcher
Jahreszeit offen?

Preis für die Unterkunft, und
welche Mahlzeiten im Preis
einbegriffen sind
Reisebüro-Kommission ●
Anzahl der Zimmer, und wieviel mit
eigenem
Badezimmer (=pb)
Beschränkungen in Bezug auf
Kinder, Haustiere, Rauchen,
oder für Behinderte geeignet
(yes=ja; ltd=beschränkt;
no=nicht zugelassen)
Man spricht Fremdsprachen

Was für ein Frühstück?
Andere Mahlzeiten und Bars

Was gibt's sonst noch?

ANYPLACE

Any Bed & Breakfast	$$ B&B	Full breakfast ($)
Any Street, ZIP code	8 rooms, 6 pb	Lunch, dinner
555-555-5555	Visa, MC ●	sitting room
Tom & Jane Innkeeper	C-12+ /S-ltd/P-no/H-ltd	library, bicycles
All year	French, Spanish	antiques

Large Victorian country house in historic village. Hiking, swimming and golf nearby. Old-fashioned comfort with modern conveniences.

Beschreibung des Gastwirts, was an
diesem Gästehaus einmalig oder
besonders bemerkenswert ist

旅館名
住所
都市又は町の名　電話番号
利用期間。

朝食のタイプ
その他の設備
昼食、夕食、アルコールのサービス

ANYPLACE

Any Bed & Breakfast	$$ B&B	Full breakfast ($)
Any Street, ZIP code	8 rooms, 6 pb	Lunch, dinner
555-555-5555	Visa, MC ●	sitting room
Tom & Jane Innkeeper	C-12+ /S-ltd/P-no/H-ltd	library, bicycles
All year	French, Spanish	antiques

Large Victorian country house in historic village. Hiking, swimming and golf nearby. Old-fashioned comfort with modern conveniences.

Alabama

MENTONE

Mentone Inn B&B	$$ B&B	Full breakfast
P.O. Box 284, Hwy 117, 35984	15 rooms, 15 pb	Afternoon tea
205-634-4836	C-ltd/S-no/P-no/H-no	Catering
Amelia Kirk		sitting room
End April–end October		video, spa, sun deck

Country mountain hideaway, antiques. Relax. Near shops, restaurants, golfing, hiking, trail rides. Fly into Ft. Payne airport. On Alabama Historical Register.

MONTGOMERY

Red Bluff Cottage	$$ B&B	Full breakfast
P.O. Box 1026, 36101	4 rooms, 4 pb	Deep porches
551 Clay St.	●	gazebo, gardens
205-264-0056 FAX:262-1872	C-yes/S-no/P-no/H-no	
Mark & Anne Waldo		
All year		

Two-story raised cottage in historic district. Panoramic view of river plain and state capitol. Family antiques, gazebo and gardens.

More Inns ...

Blue Shadows B&B Box 432, Rural Route #2, Greensboro, 36744 205-624-3637
Brunton House 112 College Ave., Scottsboro, 35768 205-259-1298
Dancy-Polk House 901 Railroad St. N.W., Decatur, 35601 205-353-3579
Hill-Ware Dowdell Mansion Lafayette, 205-864-7861
Malaga Inn 359 Church St., Mobile, 36602 205-438-4701
Noble-McCaa-Butler House 1025 Fairmont, Anniston, 36201 205-236-1791
Rutherford Johnson House P.O. Box 202, Main St., Franklin, 36444 205-282-4423
Victoria 1604 Quintard Ave., Anniston, 36201 205-236-0503
Wandlers Inn B&B 101 Shawnee Dr. N.W., Huntsville, 35806 205-895-0847

Alaska

FAIRBANKS

Alaska's 7 Gables B&B	$ B&B	Full gourmet breakfast
P.O. Box 80488, 99708	11 rooms, 4 pb	Comp. refreshments
4312 Birch Lane	Visa, MC ●	Sitting room, library
907-479-0751 FAX:479-2229	C-yes/S-ltd/P-ask/H-yes	Cable TV, phone in room
Paul & Leicha Welton	Spanish, German	bikes, jacuzzis, canoes
All year		

Spacious Tudor estate with floral solarium entrance and waterfall. Each room follows a stained glass icon theme. 4 apartments, conference/reception room. Excellent location.

GUSTAVUS

Glacier Bay Country Inn	$$$ AP	Full breakfast
P.O. Box 5, 99826	8 rooms, 7 pb	All meals included
Mile 1.5 Tong Rd.	●	Library, sitting room
907-697-2288 FAX:697-2289	C-yes/S-no/P-no/H-no	bicycles, hiking
Al & Annie Unrein		Glacier Bay yacht tours
All year		

Idyllic homestead blends comfortable country living with the Alaskan wilderness. Yacht tours of Glacier Bay. A fisherman's dream, traveler's paradise, professional's retreat.

Gustavus Inn	$$$ AP	Full breakfast
P.O. Box 60, 99826	12 rooms, 3 pb	Lunch & dinner included
1 mi. Gustavus Rd.	●	Bar, tea, bicycles
907-697-2254 FAX:697-2291	C-yes/S-ltd/P-ltd/H-ltd	fishing poles
JoAnn & David Lesh	French, Spanish	courtesy van
All year		

Your home in Glacier Bay features garden fresh produce and local seafood in a family-style homestead atmosphere. Kayaking; Glacier Bay tours.

WASILLA

Yukon Don's B&B Inn	$$ B&B	Continental plus
HC 31 5086, 99654	6 rooms	Restaurant nearby
2221 Macabon	●	Sitting room
907-376-7472	C-yes/S-no/P-yes/H-no	library
Don Tanner, Diane/Art Mongeau		exercise room
All year		

Extraordinary view; 30-year Alaskan resident; great collection of Alaskana; each room has unique Alaskan decor. "One of the Top 50 Inns in America"—Inn Times, July 1991

More Inns ...

1260 Inn Mile 1260 Hwy, Via Tok, 99780 907-778-2205
42nd Avenue Annex 410 W. 42nd Ave., Anchorage, 99503 907-561-8895
A Log Home B&B 2440 Sprucewood St., Anchorage, 99508 907-276-8527
Adams House B&B 700 W. 21st, #A, Anchorage, 99508 907-274-1944
Admiralty Inn 9040 Glacier Hwy., Juneau, 99801 907-789-3263

Glacier Bay Country Inn, Gustavus, AK

Afognak Wilderness Lodge Seal Bay, 99697 907-486-6442
Alaskan Comfort 2182 Stanford Dr., Anchorage, 99508 907-258-7500
Alaskan Hotel 167 S. Franklin, Juneau, 99801 800-327-9347
All The Comforts of Home 12531 Turk's Turn St., Anchorage, 99516 907-345-4279
Anchorage Eagle Nest Hotel 4110 Spenard Rd. (BB), Anchorage, 99503 907-243-3433
Annie McKenzie's Boardwalk P.O. Box 72, Seldovia, 99663 907-234-7816
Arctic Circle Hot Springs P.O. Box 69, Central, 99730 907-520-5113
Aurora House B&B 562 E. 3rd., Nome, 99762 907-443-2700
B&B Inn—Juneau 1802 Old Glacier Hwy, Juneau, 99801 907-463-5855
B&B at Bev & John's Box 75269, Fairbanks, 99707 907-456-7351
B&B—Valdez Box 442, Valdez, 99686 907-835-4211
Beachcomber Inn Box 1027, Petersburg, 99833 907-772-3888
Bear Creek Camp/Youth Hstl Box 1158, Haines, 99827 907-766-2259
Beaver Bend B&B 231 Iditarod, Fairbanks, 99701 907-452-3240
Bunk House Inn Box 3100-VP, Soldotna, 99669 907-262-4584
Cache Inn Lodge Box 441-VP, Haines, 99827 907-766-2910
Camp Denali Box 67—RD, Denali National Park, 99755 907-683-2290
Carlo Creek Lodge Box 890, Denali National Park, 99755 907-683-2512
Chistochina Trading Post Mile 32, Tok/Slann Hwy, Gakona, 99586 907-822-3366
Chugach View B&B 1639 Sunrise Dr., Anchorage, 99508 907-279-8824
Clarke B&B Box 1020, Wrangell, 99686 907-874-2125
Country Garden 8210 Frank St., Anchorage, 99518 907-344-0636
Country Style B&B P.O. Box 220986, Anchorage, 99522 907-243-6746
Daniels Lake Lodge B&B Box 2939—BW, Kenali, 99611 907-776-5578
Darbyshire House B&B 528 "N" St., Anchorage, 99501 907-279-0703
Dawson's B&B 1941 Glacier Hwy, Juneau, 99801 907-586-9708
Denali Cabins Box 427—TD, Denali National Park, 99755 907-683-2643
Denali Crow's Nest P.O. Box 700, Denali National Park, 99756 907-683-2321
Driftwood Inn 135 W. Bunnell Ave., Homer, 99603 907-235-8019
Evergreen Lodge HC 1 Box 1709 GennAllen, Lake Louise, 99588 907-822-3250
Fairview Inn P.O. Box 379-VP, Talkeetna, 99676 907-733-2423
Favorite Bay Inn P.O. Box 101, Angoon, 99820 907-788-3123
Fay's B&B P.O. Box 2378, Anchorage, 99510 907-243-0139
Fireweed Lodge Box 116-VP, Klawock, 99925 907-755-2930
Fort Seward B&B House #1, Box 5, Haines, 99827 907-766-2856
Golden North Hotel P.O. Box 431, Skagway, 99840 907-983-2294
Goldstream B&B P.O. Box 80090, Fairbanks, 99708 907-455-6550
Grandview Gardens B&B 1579 Sunrise Dr., Anchorage, 99508 907-277-7378
Green Bough Inn 3832 Young St., Anchorage, 99508 907-562-4636
Halibut Cove Cabins P.O. Box 1990, Homer, 99603 907-296-2214
Hatcher Pass Lodge Box 2655-BB, Palmer, 99645 907-745-5897
Heger Haus B&B P.O. Box 485, Petersburg, 99833 907-772-4877
Hidden Inlet Lodge Box 3047-VP, Ketchikan, 99901 907-225-4656
High Tide Originals Main St., Seldonia, 99663 907-234-7850
Hillcrest Haven 1455 Hillcrest Dr., Anchorage, 99503 907-274-3086
Homer B&B/Seekins P.O. Box 1264, Homer, 99603 907-235-8996
Iniakeek Lake Lodge Box 80424, Fairbanks, 99701 907-479-6354
Internat'l Riverside Inn Box 910-VP, Soldotna, 99669 907-262-4451
Irene's Inn Box 538-VP, Skagway, 99840 907-983-2520
Jotel Halsingland P.O. Box 1589, Haines, 99827 907-766-2000
Juneau Hostel 614 Harris St., Juneau, 99801 907-586-9559
Kachemak Bay Wilderness Box 956-VP, Homer, 99603 907-235-8910
Kantishna Roadhouse Box 397-TD, Denali National Park, 99755 907-345-1160
Karras B&B 230 Akogwanton St., Sitka, 99835 907-747-3978
Lake House P.O. Box 1499, Valdez, 99686 907-835-4752
Lakewood Inn 984 Ocean Dr., #1, Homer, 99608 907-235-6144
Louie's Place-Elfin Cove P.O. Box 020704, Juneau, 99802 907-586-2032
Magic Canyon Ranch 40015 Waterman Rd., Homer, 99603 907-235-6077
Manley Lodge 100 Landing Rd.-VP, Manley Hot Springs, 99756 907-672-3161
Mary's Bed & Breakfast Box 72, Skagway, 99840 907-983-2875

Mat-Su Resort Bogard Rd.—Mile 1.3, Wasilla, 99687 907-376-3228
Mullins House 526 Seward St., Juneau, 99801 907-586-2959
Oceanview Manor B&B Box 65, 490 Front St., Nome, 99762 907-443-2133
Paxson Lodge 1185 TD Richardson Hwy, Paxson, 99737 907-822-3330
Pilot's Row B&B 217 East 11th Ave., Anchorage, 99501 907-274-3305
Puffin's B&B P.O. Box 3, Gustavus, 99826 907-697-2260
Quiet Place Lodge Box 6474, Halibut Cove, 99603 907-296-2212
Reflection Pond B&B Mile 11 Petersville Rd., Trapper Creek, 99683 907-733-2457
Reluctant Fisherman Inn Box 150, Cordova, 99574 907-424-3272
River Beauty B&B P.O. Box 525, Talkeetna, 99676 907-733-2741
Sadie Cove Wilderness Ldge Box 2265-VP, Homer, 99603 907-235-7766
Scandia House P.O. Box 689, Petersburg, 99833 907-772-4281
Seldovia Rowing Club Inn P.O. Box 41, Bay St., Seldovia, 99663 907-234-7614
Sheep Mountain Lodge Star Route C, Box 4890, Palmer, 99645 907-745-5121
Silver Bow Inn 120 Second St., Juneau, 99801 907-586-4146
Sitka Youth Hostel P.O. Box 2645, Sitka, 99835 907-747-6332
Skagway Inn P.O. Box 13, Skagway, 99840 907-983-2289
Soldotna B&B 399 Lover's Lane, Soldotna, 99669 907-262-4779
Sophie Station Hotel 1717 University Ave., Fairbanks, 99701 907-479-3650
Stage Stop, The P.O. Box 69, Tok, 99780 907-883-5338
Summer Inn B&B P.O. Box 1198, Haines, 99827 907-766-2970
Summit Lake Lodge P.O. Box 1955, Fairbanks, 99707 907-822-3969
Swiss Chalet B&B P.O. Box 1734, Seward, 99664 907-224-3939
Tenakee Inn 167 S. Franklin, Juneau, 99801 907-586-1000
Tolovan B&B 4538 Tolovan, Fairbanks, 99701 907-479-6004
Totem Inn P.O. Box 648 BB, Valdez, 99686 907-835-4443
Trapper Creek B&B P.O. Box 13068, Trapper Creek, 99683 907-733-2220
Tutka Bay Lodge Box 960 F, Homer, 99603 907-235-3905
Twister Creek Union Talkeetan Span, Talkeetna, 99676 907-258-1717
Waterfall Resort P.O. Box 6440, Ketchikan, 99901 800-544-5125
Weathervane House SRD 9589x, Palmer, 99645 907-745-5168
Whaler's Cove Lodge Box 101-VP, Angoon, 99820 907-788-3123
Wild Iris Inn P.O. Box 73246, Fairbanks, 99707 907-479-4062
Wild Rose B&B Box 665, Homer, 99603 907-235-8780
Willard's Moose Lodge SRA Box 28, Homer, 99603 907-235-8830
Wilson's Hotel P.O. Box 969, Bethel, 99559 907-543-3841
Wind Valley Lodge Box 354-VP, Skagway, 99840 907-983-2236
Wright's Bed & Breakfast 1411 Oxford, Anchorage, 99503 907-561-1990
Yes Bay Lodge Yes Bay, 99950 907-247-1575

Arizona

AJO ——

Mine Managers House B&B	$$ B&B	Full breakfast
One Greenway Rd., 85321	5 rooms, 5 pb	Snacks, tea, ice cream
602-387-6505 FAX:387-5051	Visa, MC ●	Sitting room, library
Jean & Micheline Fournier	C-ask/S-ltd/P-no/H-yes	tennis courts, hot tubs
All year		coin laundry, gift shop

Copper Mine Manager's Hilltop Mansion, circa 1919, overlooks town and Open Pit Mine. Near Organ Pipe National Monument. Generous Southwestern hospitality.

12 Arizona

BISBEE ——————————————————————

The Greenway House
401 Cole Ave., 85603
602-432-7170
Joy O'Clock, Dr. George Knox
All year

$$$ B&B
8 rooms, 8 pb
Visa, MC
C-12+/S-ltd/P-no/H-yes

Continental plus
Comp. wine, snacks
Sitting room, library
billiard room, A/C
game room, barbecues

Picturesque copper mining town in mile-high setting. Luxury accommodations in 1906 mansion. Craftsman architecture, furnished with antiques.

FLAGSTAFF ——————————————————————

Birch Tree Inn
824 W. Birch Ave., 86001
602-774-1042
S & E Znetko, D & R Pettinger
All year

$$ B&B
5 rooms, 3 pb
Visa, MC ●
C-yes/S-no/P-no/H-no

Full breakfast
Afternoon tea, snacks
Sitting room, piano
pool table, bicycles
tennis court nearby

Comfortable, country charm; savory, down-home, hearty breakfasts. A four season retreat in the magnificent beauty of Northern Arizona.

PHOENIX ——————————————————————

Maricopa Manor
P.O. Box 7186, 85013
15 W. Pasadena Ave.
602-274-6302
Mary Ellen, Paul Kelley
All year

$$ B&B
5 rooms, 5 pb
●
C-yes/S-yes/H-yes

Continental plus
Comp. wine
Sitting room
library
hot tubs

Old World charm, elegant urban setting. Central and Camelback, close to everything. Luxury suites, secluded, gardens, patios, and palm trees.

Westways "Private" Resort
P.O. Box 41624, 85080
602-582-3868
Darrell Trapp
All year

$$$ B&B
6 rooms, 6 pb
Visa, MC, Disc ●
C-yes/S-yes/P-no/H-ltd
French, Spanish

Full breakfast
Welcome refreshment
Library, sitting room
hot tub, tennis courts
swimming pool, bicycles

Deluxe small oasis resort with Southwest contemporary decor. Golf, tennis, swimming, bicycling and exercise equipment available. Beautiful desert landscape.

PRESCOTT ——————————————————————

Lynx Creek Farm B&B
P.O. Box 4301, 86302
555 Onyx Dr.
602-778-9573
Greg & Wendy Temple
All year

$$ B&B
2 rooms, 2 pb
Visa, MC
C-yes/S-no/P-ltd/H-no
Spanish

Full breakfast
Comp. wine, appetizers
Bicycles, pool
hot tubs
recreation nearby

Charming retreat on 25-acre apple farm. Spacious, antique-filled suites. Beautiful views and climate. Huge gourmet breakfasts include our own fruits and vegetables.

The Marks House Inn
203 E. Union, 86303
602-778-4632
Harold & Dottie Viehweg
All year

$$$ B&B
5 rooms, 5 pb

Full breakfast
Afternoon tea
Comp. hors d'ouevres

Queen Anne featuring hand-painted murals, antiques and city views. One room has a copper tub! 1 block to famous Whiskey Row.

Maricopa Manor, Phoenix, AZ

PRESCOTT

Prescott Pines Inn B&B
901 White Spar Rd., 86303
Hwy 89 South
602-445-7270 800-541-5374
Jean Wu, Michael Acton
All year

$ EP
13 rooms, 13 pb
Visa, MC ●
C-ltd/S-ltd/P-no/H-ltd
some French & German

Full breakfast $4
Kitchenettes, gardens
Sitting room, library
porches, ceiling fans
games, patio with BBQ

Country-Victorian rooms in 4 guesthouses, including one chalet for up to 8 people, all under Ponderosa pines near National Forest. Gourmet breakfasts. Ideal 4-season climate.

SCOTTSDALE

Casa de Mariposa
6916 E. Mariposa, 85251
602-947-9704
Jo & James Cummings
All year

$$ EP/B&B
1 rooms, 1 pb
Visa, MC ●
C-ask/S-no/P-no/H-no

Full breakfast (1st day)
Refrigerator w/drinks
50s theme family room
heated swimming pool
His & Her golf clubs

Located in old Sunkist orchard just minutes away from downtown. Private suite with deluxe king canopy bed, private bath, kitchenette, private entrance.

SEDONA

"A Touch of Sedona" B&B
595 Jordan Rd., 86336
602-282-6462
Dick & Doris Stevenson
All year

$$$ B&B
4 rooms, 4 pb
Visa, MC ●
C-ask/S-ltd/P-no/H-no

Full breakfast
Afternoon tea
Snacks

Eclectic elegance ... furnished with stained-glass lamps, antiques, but with a mix of contemporary. Just walking distance to uptown. Homemade breads.

Briar Patch Inn
Star Route 3, Box 1002, 86336
Hwy 89A N., Oak Creek Cyn
602-282-2342
Jo Ann & Ike Olson
All year

$$$ B&B
15 rooms, 15 pb
Visa, MC ●
C-yes/S-ltd/P-no/H-ltd
German

Full breakfast
Comp. beverages & snacks
Sitting room, library
creek swimming, patios
hiking, bird-watching

A magical oasis in Oak Creek Canyon along spring-fed waters of Oak Creek. Knowledgeable, caring staff. Rustic cabins, fireplaces, shaded patios, Indian influence. A real gem.

SEDONA

Graham's B&B Inn
P.O. Box 912, 86336
150 Canyon Circle Dr.
602-284-1425
Bill & Marni Graham
Except January

$$$ B&B
5 rooms, 5 pb
Visa, MC
C-yes/S-no/P-no/H-no

Full breakfast
Afternoon refreshments
Sitting room, games
golf nearby
hot tub, swimming pool

Comfortable elegance amidst Arizona's spectacular red rock country. Choose early American, antique, art deco, contemporary or Southwest-style room decor. Mobil Four-Star.

Rose Tree Inn
376 Cedar St., 86336
602-282-2065
Rachel M. Gillespie
All year

$$ EP
4 rooms, 4 pb
Visa, MC •
C-yes/S-yes/P-no/H-no

Kitchenettes
In-room coffee & tea
Patios, library
courtyard, jacuzzi
bicycles

Sedona's "best-kept secret"! Quaint, quiet accommodations nestled in a gorgeous English garden environment within walking distance of "Old Town."

Saddle Rock Ranch B&B
P.O. Box 10095, 86336
602-282-7640
All year

$$$ B&B
3 rooms, 3 pb
•
C-14+/S-no/P-no/H-no
Spanish, French, Italian

Full Breakfast
Comp. wine, snacks
Sitting room, library
jacuzzi, pool
view decks, hiking

History. Romance. Antiques. Elegance. Old West movie ranch. Antique-filled rooms feature native rock, adobe, timber beams, fireplaces. Magnificent views, gardens, wildlife.

Sirapu Lodge
P.O. Box 552, 86336
65 Piki Drive
602-282-2833
Lea Pace, Vincent Mollan
All year

$$ B&B
5 rooms, 3 pb
C-7+/S-no/P-yes/H-no

Full breakfast
Comp. tea, cider
Sitting room
library, hiking tours
massage technician

Spacious rooms surround guests with influences of northern Arizona's Native Americans. Enjoy a full Southwest breakfast in our country setting. Guided hiking tours.

Slide Rock Cabins
Star Route 3, Box 1140, 86336
602-282-6900
Mike & Milena Pfeifer Smith

$$$ B&B
4 rooms, 4 pb
Visa, MC
C-no/S-ask/P-no/H-ltd
Slovenian

Continental breakfast
No TV or phones
Easy access to the creek
hosts pleased to advise
you on local activities

In spectacular Oak Creek Canyon. Cabins have a full kitchen, fireplace, jacuzzi tub, & decks. All but one have open lofts. Romantic getaways are Slide Rock Cabins' specialty!

Slide Rock Lodge
Star Route 3, Box 1141, 86336
Hwy 89A, Oak Creek Canyon
602-282-3531
Bogomir & Milena Pfeifer
All year

$$ B&B
24 rooms, 24 pb
Visa, MC
C-yes/S-ltd/P-no/H-no
Slovenian (Yugoslavia)

Continental breakfast
Comp. coffee & pastry
Picnic area, BBQ grills
fireplaces
no TV or phones

20 comfortable, clean, knotty pine paneled rooms, some with fireplaces. Advance reservations recommended.

TUCSON ───────────────────────────────────────

El Presidio B&B Inn	$$$ B&B	Full elaborate breakfast
297 N. Main Avenue, 85701	4 rooms, 4 pb	Afternoon tea, snacks
602-623-6151	●	Complimentary wine
Patti & Jerry Toci	C-no/S-no/P-no/H-no	kitchenettes, phones, TV
All year except July		sitting room, library

Historic Victorian adobe with Old-Mexico ambiance. Spacious suites open to large court-yards, gardens, fountains. Antique decor. Walk to restaurants, museums, sights.

June's B&B	$ B&B	Continental plus
3212 W. Holladay St., 85746	3 rooms	Sitting room, piano
602-578-0857	C-no/S-no/P-no/H-no	swimming pool
June Henderson		art studio
All year		

Mountainside home with pool. Majestic towering mountains. Hiking in the desert. Sparkling city lights. Beautiful backyard & patio. Owner's artwork for sale in her art studio.

La Posada del Valle Inn	$$$ B&B	Continental plus (wkdys)
1640 N. Campbell Ave., 85719	5 rooms, 5 pb	Full breakfast (wkends)
602-795-3840	Visa, MC ●	Afternoon tea
Charles & Debbi Bryant	C-17+/S-no/P-no/H-no	library, sitting room
All year	Spanish	courtyard, patios

Elegant 1920s inn nestled in the heart of the city, offering gourmet breakfast, afternoon tea; catering available for special functions.

The Lodge on the Desert	$ EP/B&B/MAP/AP	Continental plus
306 North Alvernon, 85711	40 rooms, 40 pb	Restaurant, bar
602-325-3366	Visa, MC, AmEx, DC, CB ●	All meals available
Schuyler W. Lininger	C-yes/S-yes/P-ask/H-yes	sitting room, library
All year	French	swimming pool, games

A garden resort hotel established over fifty years ago, with the atmosphere of a Mexican ranch house. Relax! Play ping-pong, shuffleboard, darts, croquet or swim in the pool.

Peppertrees B&B Inn	$$ B&B	Full gourmet breakfast
724 E. University Blvd., 85719	6 rooms	Picnic lunch to go
602-622-7167	●	Afternoon tea, catering
Marjorie G. Martin	C-ltd/S-no/P-no/H-no	library, TV, VCR
All year		walk to restaurants

A warm and friendly territorial home furnished with antiques, serving memorable gourmet breakfasts. Easy walk to Univ. of Arizona, downtown, shopping. On the old trolley line.

More Inns ...

Adobe Inn—Carefree Elbow Bend & Sidewinder, Carefree, 85377 602-488-4444
Arizona Inn 2200 E. Elm St., Tucson, 85719 602-325-1541
Arizona Mountain Inn 685 Lake Mary Rd., Flagstaff, 86001 602-774-8959
B&B in Arizona 5995 E. Orange Blossom, Phoenix, 85018 602-994-3759
Benson's B&B 4016 N. LaJolla Dr., Prescott, 86314 602-772-8358
Bisbee Inn 45 Oklahoma, Box 18, Bisbee, 85603 602-432-5131
Brimstone Butterfly 940 N. Olsen, Tucson, 85719 602-322-9157
Cathedral Rock Lodge SR 2, Box 836, Red Rock, Sedona, 86336 602-282-7608
Cedar B&B 425 W. Cedar, Flagstaff, 86001 602-774-1636
Charlotte White & Assoc.s P.O. Box 15828, Phoenix, 85060 602-230-8668
Cochise Hotel Box 27, Cochise, 85606 602-384-3156
Cone's Tourist Home 2804 W. Warner Rd., Chandler, 85224 602-839-0369

Desert Yankee 1615 N. Norton Ave., Tucson, 85719 602-795-8295
Dierker House B&B 423 W. Cherry, Flagstaff, 86001 602-774-3249
Garland's Oak Creek Lodge P.O. Box 152, Hwy 89A, Sedona, 86336 602-282-3343
Gerry's B&B 5150 37th Ave, Phoenix, 85019 602-973-2542
Grapevine Canyon Ranch P.O. Box 302, Pearce, 85625 602-826-3185
Grapevine Canyon Ranch P.O. Box 302, Pearce, 85625 602-826-3185
Guest House Inn 3 Guest House Rd., Ajo, 85321 602-387-6133
Hacienda del Sol Ranch 5601 N Hacienda del Sol, Tucson, 85718 602-299-1501
Hotel Vendome 230 Cortez St., Prescott, 86301 602-776-0900
Inn at Castle Rock P.O. Box 161, Bisbee, 85603 602-432-7195
Kay El Bar Ranch Box 2480, Wickenburg, 85358 602-684-7593
L'Auberge de Sedona Resort P.O. Box B,
   Sedona, 86336 602-282-7131
La Madera Ranch & Resort 9061 E.
   Woodland Rd., Tucson, 85749 602-749-2773
Lantern Light Inn 3085 W. Hwy 89A, Sedona,
   86336 602-282-3419
Manager's House Inn #1 Greenway Dr., Ajo,
   85321 602-387-6505
Myer's Blue Corn House 4215 E. Kilmer,
   Tucson, 85711 602-327-4663
Ramsey Canyon Inn 85 Ramsey Canyon Rd.,
   Hereford, 85615 602-378-3010
Rancho De Los Caballeros Box 1148,
   Wickenburg, 85358 602-684-5484
Tanque Verde Ranch Route 8, Box 66,
   Tucson, 85748 602-296-6275
Triangle L Ranch B&B P.O. Box 900, Oracle,
   85623 602-896-2804
Valley 'O the Sun B&B P.O. Box 2214,
   Scottsdale, 85252 602-941-1281
Villa Galleria B&B 16650 E. Hawk Dr.,
   Fountain Hills, 85268 602-837-1400
Walking L Ranch RR 4, Box 721B, Flagstaff,
   86001 602-779-2219

Ridgeway House, Eureka Springs, AR

Arkansas

BRINKLEY

Great Southern Hotel	$ B&B	Full breakfast
127 W. Cedar, 72021	4 rooms, 4 pb	Lunch & dinner (Mon-Sat)
501-734-4955	AmEx, Visa, MC	Victorian tearoom
Stanley & Dorcas Prince	C-no/S-yes/P-no/H-yes	banquet & meeting rooms
All year		exercise room, sauna

Restored in true Victorian elegance, featuring serene dining and rooms that reflect a quaint homey atmosphere reminiscent of bygone days.

EUREKA SPRINGS

Bridgeford House
263 Spring St., 72632
501-253-7853
Michael & Denise McDonald
All year

$$ B&B
4 rooms, 4 pb
Visa, MC
C-12+/S-no/P-no/H-no

Full breakfast
Coffee in rooms
Sitting room
garden, flowers in rooms
3 private porches

An 1884 antique-filled Victorian cottage located on a quiet tree-lined street in the historic district. Close to shops.

Brownstone Inn
75 Hillside, 72632
501-253-7505
Connie
March–December

$$ B&B
4 rooms, 4 pb
Visa, MC
C-yes/S-ltd/P-yes/H-yes

Full breakfast
Comp. mineral water
Sitting room
color cable TV

The original facade of the Ozarka Water Company currently houses nostalgic antique-filled guest rooms overlooking a well-kept yard.

Crescent Cottage Inn
211 Spring St., 72632
501-253-6022
Ron & Brenda Sue Bell
All year

$$ B&B
5 rooms, 5 pb
Visa, MC
C-no/S-no/P-no/H-no

Full breakfast
Coffee on verandas
Sitting room, verandas
2 rooms with whirlpool
all queen-size beds

In the historic part of Eureka Springs. Completely restored 3-story Victorian, built in 1881 by the first Arkansas governor. Rooms have TV, telephone and queen-size bed.

Dairy Hollow House
515 Spring St., 72632
501-253-7444
N. Shank, C. Dragonwagon
All year

$$$ B&B
6 rooms, 6 pb
Visa, MC, AmEx, Dis, CB •
C-yes/S-no/P-no/H-no
some French

Full breakfast to room
Restaurant, dinner
Beverage upon check-in
sitting room, hot tub
fireplaces in rooms

Restored Ozark farmhouse. Great breakfasts, fireplaces, hot tub. Six course "NouveauZarks" dinners. Murder mystery weekends. Best Inn Awards, 1989 & 1990.

Heart of the Hills Inn
5 Summit, 72632
62 Business
501-253-7468
Jan Jacobs Weber
All year

$$ B&B
5 rooms, 5 pb
Visa, MC
C-yes/S-no/P-no/H-no

Full gourmet breakfast
Comp. beverage, dessert
Sitting room
porches, antiques
cottage, crib

Victorian charm in Victorian town; great breakfasts on deck or sun room; Southern hospitality; TV and bath in each suite.

Heartstone Inn & Cottages
35 Kingshighway, 72632
501-253-8916
Iris & Bill Simantel
February–mid December

$$ B&B
9 rooms, 9 pb
Visa, MC •
C-yes/S-yes/P-no/H-no

Full gourmet breakfast
Comp. beverages
Sitting room, cable TVs
wedding gazebo, decks
massage/reflexology

Award-winning inn. Antique furnishings, private baths, and entrances. Some queen beds. Historic district. Near all attractions. "Best breakfast in the Ozarks"–NY Times 1989.

18 Arkansas

EUREKA SPRINGS

Ridgeway House
28 Ridgeway Street, 72632
501-253-6618
Linda Kerkera
All year

$$ B&B
4 rooms, 2 pb
Visa, MC, AmEx •
C-yes/S-no/P-no/H-no

Full breakfast
Guest kitchens
Comp. wine, snacks
sitting room
porches & decks

"Fun, Fancy & Formal" sumptous breakfasts, homemade dessert every evening, luxurious rooms, wide porches & decks. Prepare to be pampered—all my guests are V.I.P.'s!!

Scandia B&B Inn
P.O. Box 166, 72632
33 Avo, Hwy 62 West
501-253-8922 800-523-8922
Cindy Barnes, Marty Lavine
All year

$$ B&B
7 rooms, 7 pb
Visa, MC
C-yes/S-yes/P-no/H-yes

Full breakfast
Tea & homemade treats
Sitting room
woodland patio
hot tub

Delightful cottages feature private baths, televisions, designer bed and bath linens, and woodland views. Gourmet breakfast served with crystal and china.

HEBER SPRINGS

Anderson House Inn
P.O. Box 630, 72543
201 E. Main
501-362-5266
Larry & Sandy Anderson
February–November

$ B&B
16 rooms, 16 pb
Visa, MC
C-yes/S-ltd/P-no/H-no

Continental plus
Afternoon tea
Sitting room
city park across street
with tennis courts

Country inn furnished in American antiques available for purchase. Quilts, iron beds. Porch and upstairs balcony overlooks park. Summer paradise for water sports and fishing.

HOT SPRINGS

Fox Pass Inn
P.O. Box 933, 71902
107 Fox Pass
501-624-6622
Betty Robertson
All year

$ B&B
3 rooms, 3 pb
Visa, MC •
C-6+/S-no/P-no/H-no

Full breakfast
Sitting room, 52" TV
organ

Sun room and deck overlooking 2 acres in the city, near downtown and thermal baths. TV in each bedroom. Childcare available

Vintage Comfort B&B Inn
303 Quapaw Ave., 71901
501-623-3258
Helen R. Bartlett
All year

$$ B&B
4 rooms, 4 pb
Visa, MC •
C-6+/S-no/P-no/H-no

Full breakfast
Comp. wine & beverages
Sitting room
antique reed organ

1903 Queen Anne home decorated with antiques, soft, light colors; featuring Southern hospitality. Romantic atmosphere ideal for weddings and honeymoons.

HOT SPRINGS NAT'L PARK

Dog Wood Manor
906 Malvern Ave., 71901
501-624-0896 405-321-0099
Lady Janie Wilson
All year

$$ B&B/EP
5 rooms, 5 pb
Visa, MC •
C-yes/S-yes/P-yes/H-no

Continental breakfast
Bar service, comp. wine
Sitting room, fireplace
transportation provided
to spa & racetrack

1884 Victorian mansion features period antiques and decorative embellishments, wraparound porch, original lead glass windows, original & finished woodwork.

HOT SPRINGS NAT'L PARK

Williams House B&B Inn	$$ B&B	Full breakfast
420 Quapaw St., 71901	6 rooms, 4 pb	Spring water, iced tea
501-624-4275	Visa, MC, AmEx, Optima	Sitting rooms, fireplace
Mary & Gary Riley	•	piano, picnic tables
All year	C-4+/S-ltd/P-ask/H-no	BBQ, hiking trail maps

Williams House shows Victorian flair for convenience and elegance. Your home away from home, nestled in Oachita Mountains. Romantic atmosphere. Mystery weekends.

LITTLE ROCK

Dr. Witt's Quapaw Inn	$$ B&B	Continental plus (wkday)
1868 S. Gaines, 72206	4 rooms, 2 pb	Full breakfast (wkend)
501-376-6873	Visa, MC •	Comp. wine & snacks
Dottie & Charlie Woodwind	C-yes/S-no	library, Victorian organ
All year		airport pickup

Everyone is welcome at this charming, friendly country inn located in the Historic District. Queen-size beds, Victorian antiques, bird-watcher's paradise.

MOUNTAIN VIEW

The Commercial Hotel	$ B&B	Continental plus
P.O. Box 72, 72560	8 rooms, 3 pb	Bakery on premises
Peabody at Washington St.	AmEx	Sitting room
501-269-4383	C-yes/S-no/P-no/H-no	porch
Todd & Andrea Budy		entertainment
All year, Nov-Mar res.		

Restored country inn on historic Courthouse Square; close to Ozark Folk Center and Blanchard Springs Caverns. Old-time music on our porch. Breakfast served daily.

The Inn at Mountain View	$ B&B	Full breakfast
P.O. Box 812, 72560	9 rooms, 9 pb	Sitting room, sun room
307 Washington St.	Visa, MC, Disc •	music room, antiques
501-269-4200	C-6+/S-no/P-no/H-no	evening live folk music
All year	Spanish	

Luxuriously refurbished Victorian home; antiques, fireplace, music and sun rooms. Large front porch overlooks historic courthouse square; famous country breakfast.

PINE BLUFF

Margland II, III and IV	$$ B&B	Full breakfast
P.O. Box 8594, 71611	6 rooms, 6 pb	Comp. wine, tea, snacks
703 W. 2nd	Visa, MC, AmEx •	Sitting room, jacuzzi
501-536-6000 501-534-0201	C-yes/S-yes/P-no/H-yes	cable TV
Wanda Bateman		
All year		

Elegant curves and soothing colors on the outside and luxurious furnishings inside. Each suite upstairs has its own character.

WOOSTER

Patton House B&B Inn	$$ B&B	Full breakfast
P.O. Box 61, 72181	3 rooms, 1 pb	6-acre yard
Highway 25	Visa, MC •	Wraparound front porch
501-679-2975	C-yes/S-yes/P-ltd/H-no	upstairs balcony
Mary Lee Patton Shirley		library porch, TV, VCR
All year		

Rural Victorian hideaway furnished mostly in antiques. Full buffet breakfast. Sausage souffle inn specialty. Nearby restaurants, parks, antique stores, other shopping.

More Inns . . .

5 Ojo Inn 5 Ojo, Eureka Springs, 72632 501-253-6734
5-B's, The P.O. Box 364, Des Arc, 72040 501-256-4789
Anna's House P.O. Box 58, Gilbert, 72636 501-439-2888
Bass Haven Resort HCR 1, Box 4480E, Eureka Springs, 72632 417-858-6401
Bell Spring Cottage Roiute 1, Box 981, Eureka Springs, 72632 501-253-8581
Betty Robertson's B&B P.O. Box 933, Hot Spring Nat'l Park, 71902 501-624-6622
Blue John's Log Cabin 303 P. Square, B'ville, Eureka Springs, 72632 501-423-3478
Bonnybrooke Cottages Route 2, Box 335A, Eureka Springs, 72632 501-253-6903
Carol's Place HCR 31, Box 78, Jasper, 72641 501-446-5144
Carriage House 75 Lookout Lane, Eureka Springs, 72632 501-253-8310
Cliff House Inn Scenic Ark., Highway 7, Jasper, 72641 501-446-2292
Coach House Inn 140 S. Main, Eureka Springs, 72632 501-253-8099
Cobblestone Guest Cottage 29 Ridgeway, Eureka Springs, 72632 501-253-8105
Corn Cob Inn Route 1, Box 183, Everton, 72633 501-429-6545
Cottage Inn Route 2, Box 429, Eureka Springs, 72632 501-253-5282
Crescent Moon P.O. Box 429, Eureka Springs, 72632 501-253-9463
Dogwood Inn B&B U.S. 62, Garfield, 72732 604-287-4213
Edwardian Inn 317 S. Biscoe, Helena, 72342 501-338-9155
Elmwood House 110 Spring, Eureka Springs, 72632 501-253-7227
Enchanted Cottages 18 Nut St., Eureka Springs, 72632 501-253-6790
Eton House 1485 Eton, Fayetteville, 72703 501-521-6344
Eureka Springs & Arkansas P.O. Box 310, Eureka Springs, 72632 501-253-9623
Flatiron Flats 25 Spring St., Eureka Springs, 72632 501-253-9434
Fletcher's Devil's Dive HCR 01, Box 8/23N, Eureka Springs, 72632 417-271-3396
Four Winds B&B 3 Echols St., Eureka Springs, 72632 501-253-9169
Greenwood Hollow Ridge 23 S. Greenwood Hollow, Eureka Springs, 72632 501-253-5283
Hammons Chapel Farm 1 mile of Ark. 5, Romance, 72136 501-849-2819
Hidden Valley Guest Ranch Rural Rt. 2, Box 45, Eureka Springs, 72632 501-253-9777
Hillside Cottager 23 Hillside, Eureka Springs, 72632 501-253-8688
Johnson's Hilltop Cabin Route 1, Box 503, Eureka Springs, 72632 501-253-9537
Lake Chalet, Inn Eureka Springs, 72632 501-253-9210
Lake Lucerne Resort P.O. Box 441, Eureka Springs, 72632 501-253-8085
Lazee Daze Route 1, Box 196, Eureka Springs, 72632 501-253-7026
Lookout Cottage 12 Lookout Circle, Eureka Springs, 72632 501-253-9545
Magnolia Guest Cottage 180 Spring St., Eureka Springs, 72632 501-253-9463
Maple Ridge 2 First St., Eureka Springs, 72632 501-253-5220
Maplewood B&B 4 Armstrong St., Eureka Springs, 72632 501-253-8053
May House 101 Railroad Ave., Clarksville, 72830 501-754-6851
McCartney House 500 S. 19th St., Fort Smith, 72901 501-782-9057
Merry Go Round Cottage 412 N. 8th, Fort Smith, 72901 501-783-3472
Miss Annie's Garden Cottages c/o 24 Armstrong, Eureka Springs, 72632 501-253-8356
New Orleans Hotel 63 Spring St., Eureka Springs, 72632 501-253-8630
Oak Crest Cottages Route 2, Box 26, Eureka Springs, 72632 501-253-9493
Oak Tree Inn Vinegar Hill, 110 W., Heber Springs, 72543 501-362-6111
Old Homestead, The 82 Armstrong, Eureka Springs, 72632 501-253-7501
Old Washington Jail P.O. Box 157, Washington, 71862 501-983-2790
Palace Hotel & Bathhouse 135 Spring St., Eureka Springs, 72632 501-253-7474
Piedmont House 165 Spring St., Eureka Springs, 72632 501-253-9258
Primrose Place 39 Steele St., Eureka Springs, 72632 501-253-9818
Red Bud Valley Resort RR 1, Box 500, Eureka Springs, 72632 501-253-9028
Red Raven Inn P.O. Box 1217, Hwy 14 S, Yellville, 72687 501-449-5168
Redbud Manor 7 Kings Hwy, Eureka Springs, 72632 501-253-9649
Riverside Resort Route 2, Box 410/62E, Eureka Springs, 72632 601-423-3116
Riverview Resort RR 2 Box 475, Eureka Springs, 72632 501-253-8367
Roadrunner Inn Route 2, Box 158, Eureka Springs, 72632 601-253-8166
Rock Cabins 10 Eugenia, Eureka Springs, 72632 501-253-8659
Rosewood Guest Cottage One Kings Highway, Eureka Springs, 72632 501-253-7674
Rustic Manor Route 4, Box 66, Eureka Springs, 72632 501-253-8128

School House Inn 15 Kansas St., Eureka Springs, 72632 501-253-7854
Shady Rest Cottages One Magnetic, Eureka Springs, 72632 501-253-8793
Singleton House B&B 11 Singleton, Eureka Springs, 72632 501-253-9111
Sleepy Hollow Inn 92 S. Main, Eureka Springs, 72632 501-253-7448
Spider Creek Resort Route 2, Box 418, Eureka Springs, 72632 501-253-9241
Stillmeadow Farm Route 1, Box 434-D, Hot Springs, 71913 501-525-9994
Sweet Seasons Cottages P.O. Box 642, Eureka Springs, 72632 501-253-7603
Tanyard Springs Route 3, Box 335, Morrilton, 72110 501-727-5200
Tatman-Garret House P.O. Box 171, Eureka
  Springs, 72632 501-253-7617
Thomas Quinn Guest House 815 N. "B" St., Fort
  Smith, 72901 501-782-0499
Valais-Hi 33 Van Buren, Eureka Springs, 72632
  501-253-5140
Washington Street B&B 1001 South
  Washington, Siloam Springs, 72761
  501-524-5669
White Flower Cottage 62 Kings Hwy, Eureka
  Springs, 72632 501-253-9636
White River Lodgge & Rest. Route 2, Box 400,
  Eureka Springs, 72632 501-253-8596
White River Oaks B&B Rt. 2, Box 449, Eureka
  Springs, 72632 501-253-9033

Gatehouse Inn, Pacific Grove, CA

California

AHWAHNEE ─────────────────────────────────

Ol-Nip Gold Town B&B Inn	$$$ B&B	Full breakfast
49013 Highway 49, 93601	7 rooms, 7 pb	Restaurant, bar
Nipinnawasee	Visa, MC, AmEx, DC, CB	Sitting room, comp. wine
209-683-2155	●	hot tubs, bicycles
Wild Paul & Kyong Chin	C-yes/S-yes/P-ask/H-yes	views of High Sierra
All year	Korean	

Relive the Wild West; dinner shows; breakfast holdups; a trip to the time of Doc Holiday, Jessie James and Gold Rush Days. Close to Yosemite.

ALAMEDA ─────────────────────────────────

Garratt Mansion	$$ B&B	Full breakfast
900 Union St., 94501	6 rooms, 3 pb	Cookies, hot/cold drinks
510-521-4779	●	Sitting room
Royce & Betty Gladden	C-yes/S-no/P-no/H-no	phones in 4 rooms
All year		bicycles

An elegant Victorian in a quiet island community just 20 min. from downtown San Francisco, offering personalized attention.

ALAMEDA

Webster House B&B Inn
1238 Versailles Ave., 94501
415-523-9697
Andrew & Susan McCormack
All year

$$$ B&B
4 rooms, 2 pb
•
C-ltd/S-ltd

Full breakfast
Comp. champagne, tea
Snacks, library
deck, sun porch
waterfall, garden, games

22nd City Historical Monument. Quaint, enchanting Gothic Revival Cottage is the oldest house in Alameda. Walk to beach, windsurfing, shops, golf. San Francisco 20 min. away.

ALBION

Fensalden Inn
P.O. Box 99, 95410
33810 Navarro Ridge Rd.
707-937-4042
Scott & Frances Brazil
All year

$$$ B&B
7 rooms, 7 pb
Visa, MC •
C-ltd/S-ltd/P-ltd/H-ltd

Full breakfast
Wine & hors d'oeuvres
Sitting room
parlor, library
library

On 20 acres of Mendocino Coast. Historic country inn with spectacular ocean views—and only ten minutes from the village of Mendocino. One bungalow sleeps 4.

AMADOR CITY

Culbert House Inn
P.O. Box 54, 95601
10811 Water St.
209-267-0750
Paul & Theresa Rinaldi
All year

$$ B&B
4 rooms, 4 pb
Visa, MC
C-ltd

Full breakfast
Comp. aftn. refreshment
Sitting room
bicycles
garden

Elegant Victorian home decorated in French country style. Full breakfast each morning. Situated in historic town with antique and craft shops. Restaurants nearby.

Mine House Inn
P.O. Box 24, 95601
14125 Hwy 49
209-267-5900
Peter Daubenspeck
All year

$$ B&B
7 rooms, 7 pb
•
C-yes/S-yes/P-no/H-no
Portuguese

Continental breakfast
Sitting room
Art gallery
swimming pool
gift shop

Former Keystone Gold Mining Company office building, all rooms furnished in Victorian antiques. Relive a night from the gold rush days.

ANAHEIM

Anaheim Country Inn
856 S. Walnut St., 92802
714-778-0150 800-755-7801
Lois Ramont, Marilyn Watson
All year

$$ B&B
8 rooms, 4 pb
Visa, MC •
C-12+/S-ltd/P-no/H-no

Full breakfast
Comp. beverages & snacks
Sitting room
organ, hot tub

Large historic house near Disneyland. Garden & trees, off-street parking, antiques, warm homey atmosphere. Complimentary appetizers before dinner.

ANGELS CAMP

Cooper House B&B Inn
P.O. Box 1388, 95222
1184 Church St.
209-736-2145
Chris Sears
All year

$$$ B&B
3 rooms, 3 pb
Visa, MC •
C-6+/S-no

Full breakfast
Comp. beverages & snacks
Sitting room
veranda, gazebo, patio
air conditioned

Elegant inn located in the heart of the Mother Lode. Quiet garden setting near historic downtown. Beautiful county with unique attractions.

Apple Lane Inn, Aptos, CA

ANGWIN—NAPA VALLEY

Forest Manor	$$$ B&B	Continental plus
415 Cold Springs Rd., 94508	3 rooms, 3 pb	Comp. beverages & snacks
707-965-3538	Visa,MC ●	Jacuzzi, refrig., limo
Harold & Corlene Lambeth	C-12+/S-ltd/P-no/H-no	sitting room, piano
All year	Thai, French	organ, 53′ pool & spa

Beautiful secluded 20-acre English Tudor forested estate in Napa Wine Country. Massive carved beams, fireplaces, decks, air-conditioning, game rooms.

APTOS

Apple Lane Inn	$$$ B&B	Full breakfast
6265 Soquel Dr., 95003	5 rooms, 3 pb	Comp. cookies & milk
408-475-6868	Visa, MC ●	Sitting room, library
Doug & Diana Groom	C-no/S-ltd/P-no/H-no	player piano
All year		Weddings to 175 people

Victorian farmhouse furnished with beautiful antiques offers country charm. Quiet, yet close to everything, including fine restaurants. Romantic Victorian gazebo.

Bayview Hotel B&B Inn	$$$ B&B	Continental plus
8041 Soquel Dr., 95003	8 rooms, 8 pb	Restaurant
408-688-8654	Visa, MC ●	Lunch, dinner
Katya & James Duncan	C-5+/S-no/P-no/H-no	sitting room
All year	French, Italian	2-room suite available

1878 California Victorian furnished with lovely antiques; near beaches, hiking trails, bicycle routes, golf, tennis, fishing, antique shops and restaurants.

24 California

APTOS ──────────────────────────────

Mangels House	$$$ B&B	Full breakfast
P.O. Box 302, 95001	5 rooms, 2 pb	Comp. wine, piano
570 Aptos Creek Rd.	Visa, MC ●	Sitting room, fireplace
408-688-7982	C-12+/S-ltd/P-no/H-no	table tennis and darts on
Jacqueline Fisher	French, Spanish	back porch
All year exc. Christmas		

Casual elegance in country setting, only 5 minute drive to Hwy 1. On 4 acres of private lawn and woodland, on edge of Redwood State Park. 1 mi. from beach, golf, Monterey Bay.

ARCATA ──────────────────────────────

Plough and the Stars Inn	$$$ B&B	Full breakfast
1800 27th St., 95521	5 rooms, 3 pb	Comp. wine
707-822-8236	Visa, MC	Common rooms, sun room
Melissa & Bill Hans	C-12+/S-yes/P-ltd/H-ltd	flower & herb gardens
February–mid December		croquet lawn, hot tub

1860s farmhouse on two acres of pastoral grounds; casual, country atmosphere; first-class hospitality. Redwoods, seashore, wildlife marsh minutes away.

AUBURN ──────────────────────────────

The Lincoln House B&B Inn	$$ B&B	Full breakfast
191 Lincoln Way, 95603	3 rooms, 3 pb	Afternoon tea
916-885-8880	●	Swimming pool
Howard & Ginny Leal	C-yes/S-ltd	
All year		

Our storybook inn amplifies the charm of the Gold Country. Enjoy a full breakfast in our dining room with a majestic view of the Sierras.

Power's Mansion Inn	$$$ B&B	Continental plus
164 Cleveland Ave., 95603	13 rooms, 13 pb	Comp. wine, snacks
916-885-1166	●	Deluxe amenities
Tony & Tina Verhaart	C-yes/S-no/P-no/H-yes	fireplaces, patios/decks
All year	French, Spanish	terry robes

1885 mansion, ten thousand sq. ft. built from gold-mining fortune. Has elegance of detailed restoration and antique furnishings with queen beds and central air and heat.

AVALON ──────────────────────────────

Gull House	$$$ B&B	Continental plus
P.O. Box 1381, 90704	5 rooms, 4 pb	Comp. fruit basket
344 Whitley Ave.	●	Refrigerator, whirlpool
213-510-2547	C-no/S-yes/P-no/H-no	pool, BBQ, all king beds
Bob & Hattie Michalis		taxi to boat terminal
April–October		

Deluxe suites in quiet residential area. Breakfast on patio. Beach, sights & activities on this beautiful island. Perfect for couples. Make reservations well in advance.

BAYWOOD PARK ──────────────────────────────

Baywood B&B Inn	$$$ B&B	Continental plus
1370 Second St., 93402	15 rooms, 15 pb	Restaurant, lunch
805-528-8888	C-yes/S-no/P-no/H-yes	Comp. wine
John & Pam Cutmore	British	sitting room, fireplaces
All year		bay views, 11 suites

Bayfront Inn on South Morro Bay. 15 unique rooms ... each with its own personality. Suites have many amenities. Near Hearst Castle, San Luis Obispo, Montano De Oro State Park.

BENICIA

Captain Dillingham's Inn	$$ B&B	Full buffet breakfast
145 East "D" St., 94510	10 rooms, 9 pb	Comp. wine, snacks, etc.
707-746-7164 800-544-2278	Visa, MC, AmEx, DC, CB ●	Sitting room
Denny Demac-Steck	C-yes/S-yes/P-no/H-yes	library
All year		jacuzzis in 8 rooms

Dillingham's, centered in Benicia's historic waterfront district, offers jacuzzi-equipped accommodations in a lush garden atmosphere.

BERKELEY

Flower Garden B&B	$$ B&B	Full breakfast
2341 5th. St., 94710	Visa, MC, AmEx, Disc ●	Afternoon tea
510-644-9530	C-yes/S-yes/P-yes	Sitting room
J. C. Wright	French, Spanish	library, bicycles
All year		comp. wine

Charming, private Victorian near UC Campus, all transport and San Francisco Bay. Flowers, flowers and country charm in-town! 3rd. night 50% off.

Gramma's Inn & Gardens	$$$ B&B	Full breakfast
2740 Telegraph, 94705	40 rooms, 38 pb	Evening wine & cheese
510-549-2145 FAX:549-1085	Visa, MC ●	Sunday brunch $
Barry Cleveland	C-6+/S-ltd/P-no/H-yes	Full in-house catering
All year		sitting room, piano

Two beautiful turn-of-the-century mansions with lovely gardens. Individual guest rooms with antique furnishings, color TV. Close to UC Berkeley; 20 min. to San Francisco.

BIG BEAR CITY

Gold Mountain Manor B&B	$$$ B&B	Full breakfast
P.O. Box 2027, 92314	7 rooms, 3 pb	Comp. beverages, snacks
1117 Anita	●	Sitting room, pool table
714-585-6997	C-12+/S-ltd/P-ltd/H-no	library, hot tub
Conny Ridgway, Donna Doran	French	tennis, sauna, nearby
All year		

Escape to the delights of this magnificent, historic and very romantic 1920s log mansion featured in Ralph Lauren ads. Gourmet country breakfast. Near National Forest.

BIG BEAR LAKE

Knickerbocker Mansion	$$$ B&B	Full breakfast
Box 3661, 92315	10 rooms, 8 pb	"Grandma's kitchen"
869 S. Knickerbocker	●	Sitting room
714-866-8221	C-yes/H-yes	library
Phyllis Knight		hot tubs
All year		

Peaceful retreat at a historic inn; pampering & spoiling. Hiking, water sports, skiing or reading & quiet meditation in a forest setting.

BIG SUR

Deetjen's Big Sur Inn	$$ EP	Full breakfast menu $
Hwy 1, 93920	20 rooms, 13 pb	Restaurant, dinner
408-667-2377	C-ltd/S-yes/P-no/H-no	Wine and beer $
Bettie Sue Walters	Spanish, French	piano
All year		on National Register

Old Norwegian-style rustic inn on the wild Big Sur coast. Redwood canyon hiking, beaches nearby. Candlelight and classical music accompany delicious meals.

BISHOP

The Matlick House
1313 Rowan Lane, 93514
619-873-3133
Nanette Robidart
All year

$$ B&B
4 rooms, 4 pb
•
C-no/S-ltd/P-no

Full breakfast
Picnic lunches
Wine & hors d'oeuvres
sitting room
bicycles

1906 ranch house; antiques throughout; picturesque views of the eastern Sierra Nevadas. Minutes from skiing, fishing, hiking & other outdoor sports.

BODEGA BAY

Bodega Harbor Inn
1345 Bodega Ave., 94923
707-875-3594
Linda Richards
All year

$ B&B
22 rooms, 22 pb
Visa, MC
C-yes/S-yes/H-yes

Continental breakfast
Cable TV
5 rooms with fireplaces
5 rooms with hot tubs

Charming coastal inn furnished with antiques; view of bay. Vacation homes, fireplaces and hot tubs available. Near fishing, golfing, horseback riding.

BOONVILLE

Bear Wallow Resort
P.O. Box 533, 95415
23000 Mountain View Rd.
707-895-3335
Bob & Roxanne Hedges
All year

$$ EP
8 rooms, 8 pb
Visa, MC
C-yes/S-yes/P-yes/H-no

Restaurant
Steak House Fri & Sat
Kitchens in cottages
library, lodge
hot tub, swimming pool

Romantic secluded cottages on 40 acres of redwoods; fireplace, kitchen, sherry, queen bed, beamed ceiling, deck, view, private, quiet.

Toll House Restaurant/Inn
P.O. Box 268, 95415
15301 Hwy. 253
707-895-3630
Barbara McGuinness
All year

$$$ B&B
5 rooms, 3 pb
Visa, MC, Disc •
C-ltd/S-no/P-no/H-yes

Full 4-course breakfast
Restaurant, dinner
Comp. wine, full bar
sitting room, library
hot tub, piano

Mendocino wine country. Flocks of sheep, deer & wild pigs—540 acres of pastures. Built in 1912 in the Bell Valley. The folk language Boonthing began here.

BRENTWOOD

Diablo Vista B&B
2191 Empire Ave., 94513
510-634-2396
Myra & Dick Hackett
All year

$$ B&B
2 rooms, 2 pb
C-8+/S-no/P-no/H-yes
Spanish

Full breakfast
Comp. wine
Library, bicycles
hot tub, swimming pool
TV, stereo, gazebo

Country peace, open air, fabulous breakfast. Miles of trails for bikes, walking or running. Garden and orchard on premises. True re-creation.

BRIDGEPORT

Cain House
P.O. Box 454, 93517
11 Main Street
619-932-7040
Marachal L. Myers
All year

$$$ B&B
6 rooms, 6 pb
Visa, MC, AmEx •
S-no/P-no/H-no

Full breakfast
Comp. wine, cheese
Sitting room
tennis courts

The grandeur of the eastern Sierras is the perfect setting for evening wine and cheese. Complimentary full breakfast included.

CALISTOGA ——————————————————————————

"Culver's", A Country Inn
1805 Foothill Blvd, 94515
707-942-4535
Meg & Tony Wheatley
All year

$$$ B&B
7 rooms
Visa, MC ●
C-12+/S-ltd/P-no/H-yes

Full breakfast
Comp. sherry, beverages
Fresh fruit, piano
living room w/fireplace
pool, hot tub, sauna

Comfortable, elegant Victorian home circa 1875, restored historical landmark in Napa Valley. Easy access to wineries, spas, gliding, ballooning, restaurants.

Calistoga Wayside Inn
1523 Foothill Blvd., 94515
707-942-0645 800-845-3632
Deborah & Leonard Flaherty
February–December

$$$ B&B
3 rooms, 3 pb
Visa, MC, AmEx ●
C-ltd

Full breakfast
Afternoon tea
Comp. wine & sherry
sitting room, library
hot tubs

1920s Spanish-style home with wooded yard, fountains and fish pond. Gourmet breakfast served on patio in the summer. Bicycles and jacuzzi.

Calistoga's Wishing Well
2653 Foothill Blvd., 94515
Hwy 128
707-942-5534
Marina & Keith Dinsmoor
All year

$$$ B&B
3 rooms, 3 pb
Visa, MC ●
C-yes/S-no/P-no/H-yes
Russian

Full country breakfast
Complimentary wine
Hors d'oeuvres
fireplace, hot tubs
swimming pool, bikes, TV

Elegant country farmhouse on four historical areas. Full breakfast served on deck overlooking orchard or poolside with view of Mount Saint Helena.

Mount View Hotel
1457 Lincoln Ave., 94515
707-942-6877
Terri Rose
All year

$$$ B&B
34 rooms, 34 pb
Major credit cards ●
C-yes/S-yes/P-no/H-yes

Full breakfast
Lunch, dinner, bar
Jacuzzi, swimming pool
mesquite BBQ, golf
tennis, entertainment

An Art Deco dream in all its European elegance. The only full-service hotel in Calistoga.

Pink Mansion
1415 Foothill Blvd., 94515
707-942-0558
Jeff Seyfried
All year

$$$ B&B
5 rooms, 5 pb
Visa, MC ●
C-12+/S-no/P-no/H-yes
Spanish

Full breakfast
Lunch, dinner
Comp. wine with cheese
library, parlor
A/C, bicycles

Restored 1875 home combines turn-of-the-century elegance with modern amenities to provide our wine country travelers with old-fashioned comfort.

Quail Mountain B&B
4455 N. St. Helena Hwy, 94515
707-942-0316
Don & Alma Swiers
All year

$$$ B&B
3 rooms, 3 pb
Visa, MC ●
C-no/S-no/P-no/H-no

Full breakfast
Dinner, comp. wine
Sitting room, library
hot tub, pool, gardens
vineyards, private decks

Secluded, wooded, luxury country estate close to wineries, restaurants, spas, gliding, ballooning. Rooms individually decorated with art work and antiques.

CALISTOGA ──────────────────────────────

Scarlett's Country Inn	$$$ B&B	Full breakfast
3918 Silverado Tr., 94515	3 rooms, 3 pb	Comp. wine & cheese
707-942-6669	●	Sitting room
Scarlett Dwyer	C-yes/S-yes/P-no/H-no	air conditioning
All year	Spanish	swimming pool

Secluded French country farmhouse overlooking vineyards in famed Napa Valley. Breakfast served by woodland swimming pool. Close to spas and wineries.

Silver Rose Inn	$$$ B&B	Continental plus
351 Rosedale Rd., 94515	5 rooms, 5 pb	Comp. wine, snacks
707-942-9581	Visa, MC, AmEx ●	Fireplace, jacuzzi
Sally & J. Paul Dumont	C-no/S-no/P-no/H-no	swimming pool, library
All year	French	sitting room

Quiet elegance in a country setting. Walk or jog through adjacent vineyards & enjoy Calistoga's famous mud & mineral baths. Guests are welcomed with a bottle of wine.

Trailside Inn	$$$ B&B	Continental plus
4201 Silverado Trail, 94515	3 rooms, 3 pb	Comp. wine/mineral water
707-942-4106	AmEx, Dis ●	Fireplace, kitchens
Randy & Lani Gray	C-yes/S-yes/P-no/H-no	library, A/C
All year		private decks

1930s farmhouse comfortably decorated with quilts and antiques. Each suite has private entrance, 3 rooms plus bath, fireplace, A/C. Each suite sleeps up to four people.

Zinfandel House	$$ B&B	Full breakfast
1253 Summit Dr., 94515	3 rooms, 2 pb	Comp. wine
707-942-0733	C-no/S-no/P-no/H-no	Library
Bette & George Starke		sitting room
All year		hot tub

Beautiful home situated on wooded hillside overlooking vineyards and mountains. Lovely breakfast served on outside deck or in dining room.

CAMBRIA ──────────────────────────────

Beach House B&B	$$$ B&B	Continental plus
6360 Moonstone Beach Dr,	7 rooms, 7 pb	Aftn. tea, comp. wine
93428	Visa, MC ●	Sitting room, fireplace
805-927-3136	C-ltd/S-no/P-no/H-no	patios, 3 outside decks
Penny Hitch & Kern		mountain bikes
MacKinnon		
All year		

Oceanfront home with antique oak furniture, queen and king-size beds, ocean views. Visit Hearst Castle, beach, wineries, shops. Rural atmosphere, gorgeous sunsets.

Cambria Landing Inn	$$$ B&B	Continental plus
6530 Moonstone Beach Dr,	20 rooms, 20 pb	Comp. wine/champagne
93428	Visa, MC, Disc ●	Hot tubs
805-927-1619	C-yes/S-yes/P-no/H-yes	oceanfront rooms
Kern MacKinnon		
All year		

Romantic country inn setting on an ocean bluff across from rocky beaches. Oceanfront rooms with TV, refrigerators, VCR, private decks/patios, fireplaces & "breakfast in bed"!

CAMBRIA

Pickford House B&B
2555 MacLeod Way, 93428
805-927-8619
Anna Larsen
All year

$$ B&B
8 rooms, 8 pb
Visa, MC •
C-y/S-ltd/P-no/H-yes

Full breakfast
Afternoon wine
Hors d'oeuvres, cookies
sitting room
piano, hot tub

All rooms named after silent film-era stars and furnished with genuine antiques. Full breakfast included. All rooms have showers, TV and tubs. Homemade fruit breads and cakes.

CAPITOLA-BY-THE-SEA

Inn at Depot Hill
P.O. Box 1934, 95010
250 Monterey Ave.
408-462-3376
Suzie Lankes
All year

$$$ B&B
8 rooms, 8 pb
Visa, MC, AmEx •
S-no/P-no/H-yes
Croatian

Full breakfast
Aftn. tea/hors d'oeuvres
Evening dessert & wine
sitting room, library
private garden patios

Near a sandy beach, stately 1901 railway station lavishly offers Orient-Express-style sophisticated charm, timeless beauty, and upscale classical European elegance.

CARLSBAD

Pelican Cove Inn
320 Walnut Ave., 92008
619-434-5995
Robert & Celeste Hale
All year

$$$ B&B
8 rooms, 8 pb
Visa, MC •
C-12+/S-yes/H-yes

Continental plus
Comp. sherry
Beach nearby
beach chairs, towels
picnic baskets

Feather beds and fireplaces in every room. Jacuzzis in 2 rooms. Private tiled baths, private entries, fruit, flowers and candy also in every room. Complimentary Amtrak pickup.

CARMEL

Cobblestone Inn
P.O. Box 3185, 93921
Junipero btwn 7th & 8th
408-625-5222
Ms. Charlie Aldinger
All year

$$$ B&B
24 rooms, 24 pb
AmEx, Visa, MC •
C-yes/S-ltd/P-no/H-no

Full breakfast
Wine & hors d'oeuvres
Sitting room
terrace, bicycles
picnics avail.

Charming country inn nestled in English garden. Each room has a fireplace and country decor, turndown service, beverages and morning paper. Member of Four Sisters' Inns.

Happy Landing Inn
P.O. Box 2619, 93921
Monte Verde at 5th & 6th
408-624-7917
R. & C. Ballard, D. Stewart
All year

$$$ B&B
7 rooms, 7 pb
Visa, MC
C-12+/S-no/P-no/H-yes

Full breakfast
Comp. sherry
Sitting room
Gazebo, gardens, pond
Honeymoon cottage avail.

Hansel & Gretel cottages in the heart of Carmel, like something from a Beatrix Potter book. Surrounds a central flowering garden; breakfast is served in your room.

Holiday House
P.O. Box 782, 93921
Camino Real at 7th Ave.
408-624-6267
Dieter & Ruth Back
All year

$$$ B&B
6 rooms, 4 pb
C-14+/S-ltd/P-no/H-no
German

Full breakfast
Afternoon sherry
Colorful garden
sitting room, library

Lovely inn personifying Carmel charm, in quiet residential area. A short walk to beautiful Carmel beaches, quaint shops, restaurants. Ocean views, beautiful garden.

CARMEL ————————————————————————————————————

The Homestead
P.O. Box 1285, 93921
8th & Lincoln Sts.
408-624-4119
Betty Colletto
All year

$$ EP
12 rooms, 12 pb
C-yes/S-yes

Comp. coffee in rooms
4 cottages w/kitchens
2 cottages w/fireplaces

A unique inn nestled in the heart of Carmel. Rooms and cottages with private baths, some kitchens & fireplaces. Reasonably priced and close to town.

Lincoln Green Inn
P.O. Box 2747, 93921
Carmelo btwn 15th & 16th
408-624-1880 800-262-1262
Jewell Brown
All year

$$$ B&B
4 rooms, 4 pb
Visa, MC, AmEx •
C-yes/S-yes/P-yes/H-yes

Continental breakfast
Comp. tea
English garden

Four charming English country-style cottages set in a formal English garden behind a white picket fence; nestled in a quaint residential area near ocean.

San Antonio House
P.O. Box 3683, 93921
San Antonio at Ocean & 7th
408-624-4334
Jeanne Goodwin
All year

$$$ B&B
4 rooms, 4 pb
Visa, MC, AmEx •
C-12+/S-no/P-no/H-no

Continental plus
Comp. tea
Sitting room, fireplaces
flower gardens, patios
private entrances

Private 2- and 3-room suites decorated with antiques and art. One block from famous Carmel Beach. Sounds of surf and sense of yesteryear melt tensions away.

Sandpiper Inn-At-the-Beach
2408 Bay View Ave., 93923
408-624-6433
Graeme MacKenzie
All year

$$$ B&B
15 rooms, 15 pb
Visa, MC
C-12+/S-ltd/P-no/H-no
French, German

Continental plus
Coffee, tea, sherry
Library, flowers
fireplace lounge
tennis, golf, bicycles

Fifty yards from Carmel Beach. European-style country inn, filled with antiques and fresh flowers. Ocean views, fireplaces, garden.

Sea View Inn
P.O. Box 4138, 93921
Camino Real at 11th & 12th
408-624-8778
Marshall & Diane Hydorn
All year

$$$ B&B
8 rooms, 6 pb
Visa, MC
C-12+/S-no/P-no/H-no

Continental plus
Afternoon tea & coffee
Comp. evening wine
sitting room
library, garden

A small, intimate, cozy Victorian inn, located near the village and the beach. Enjoy breakfast and evening wine served by the fireside, or relax in secluded garden.

Stonehouse Inn
P.O. Box 2517, 93921
8th below Monte Verde
408-624-4569
Barbara Cooke
All year

$$$ B&B
6 rooms
Visa, MC •
C-14+/S-no/P-no/H-no

Continental plus
Comp. port & cookies
Sitting room
fireplace
bicycles

Historic Carmel house built in 1906, traditional Bed & Breakfast. Within walking distance of shopping, restaurants, beach.

CARMEL ─────────────────────────────

Sunset House
P.O. Box 1925, 93921
Camino Real at Ocean & 7th
408-624-4884
Gee Gee & De Emory
All year

$$$ B&B
3 rooms, 3 pb
Visa, MC
C-no/S-yes/P-no/H-no

Continental plus
Living room

An elegant small inn. Woodburning fireplaces, ocean views. Romantic, quiet, homelike surroundings. Breakfast served in your room. A magnificent garden.

───

Tally Ho Inn
P.O. Box 3726, 93921
Monte Verde at 6th St.
408-624-2232
Barbara & Erven Torell
All year

$$$ B&B
14 rooms, 14 pb
Visa, MC, AmEx ●
C-yes/S-yes/P-no/H-no
some French

Continental plus
Afternoon tea, brandy
Floral garden, sun deck
fireplaces, ocean views
close to beach

This English country inn has bountiful gardens with sweeping ocean views from individually appointed rooms and sun decks. Former home of cartoonist Jimmy Hatlo.

───

Vagabond's House Inn
P.O. Box 2747, 93921
4th & Dolores
408-624-7738 800-262-1262
Honey Jones
All year

$$$ B&B
11 rooms, 11 pb
Visa, MC ●
C-12+/S-yes/P-yes/H-no
French

Continental plus
Sitting room w/fireplace
library, courtyard
2 blocks to downtown

Antique clocks and pictures, quilted bedspreads, fresh flowers, plants, shelves filled with old books. Sherry by the fireplace; breakfast served in your room.

CARMEL VALLEY ─────────────────────

Valley Lodge
P.O. Box 93, 93924
8 Ford Rd.
408-659-2261 800-641-4646
Peter & Sherry Coakley
All year

$$$ B&B
35 rooms, 35 pb
Visa, AmEx, MC, Disc. ●
C-yes/S-yes/P-yes/H-yes
French, Spanish

Continental plus
Comp. newspaper
Library, hot tub, sauna
pool, fitness center
conference facilities

Quiet location, lovely grounds. A romantic setting for lovers of privacy, nature, hiking, golf, tennis, swimming, riding—and just plain lovers. Cozy fireplace cottages.

CAZADERO ──────────────────────────

Cazanoma Lodge
P.O. Box 37, 95421
1000 Kidd Creek Rd.
707-632-5255
Randall C. Newman
March—November

$$$ B&B
5 rooms, 5 pb
Visa, MC, AmEx ●
C-yes/S-yes/P-ltd/H-yes

Continental plus
Comp. wine, bar
Swimming pool
entertainment
hiking trails

Secluded lodge on 147 acres of Redwood Forest. Two creeks, trout pond and waterfall. Near the ocean and beautiful Russian River.

CLIO ──────────────────────────────

White Sulphur Springs B&B
P.O. Box 136, 96106
2200 Hwy 89 S.
916-836-2387
T & L. Vanella, D & K. Miller
All year

$$ B&B
7 rooms, 4 pb
Visa, MC ●
C-12+/S-ltd/P-no/H-no

Full breakfast
Comp. refreshments
Piano, pump organ
parlor, library area
swimming pool

Rich antique furnishings abound. Breakfast in a spacious dining room, relax in an Olympic-size pool of soothing mineral waters. Two miles south of Clio.

CLOVERDALE ────────────────────────────

Vintage Towers B&B Inn
302 N. Main St., 95425
707-894-4535
Garret Hall, Jim Mees
All year exc. December

$$$ B&B
8 rooms, 6 pb
Visa, MC ●
C-10+/S-ltd/P-ask/H-yes

Full breakfast
Afternoon snacks
4 sitting rooms, piano
bicycles, gazebo
veranda & gardens

A towered mansion on the national register, on a quiet tree-lined street in a wine country town. Walk to river, wineries and fine dining.

Ye Olde Shelford House
29955 River Rd., 95425
707-894-5956 800-833-6479
Ina & Al Sauder
All year

$$$ B&B
6 rooms, 4 pb
Visa, MC, Dis ●
C-yes/S-ltd/P-no/H-no

Full breakfast
Comp. beverages, snacks
Sitting rm, rec. room
hot tub, pool, bicycles
antique car wine tour

Stately 1880s Victorian, genuine antiques, wraparound porch overlooking vineyards. Delicious breakfast in formal dining room or porch. "Surry & Sip" ride to wineries.

COLOMA ────────────────────────────

The Coloma Country Inn
P.O. Box 502, 95613
345 High St.
916-622-6919
Alan & Cindi Ehrgott
All year

$$$ B&B
5 rooms, 3 pb
●
C-no/S-no/P-no/H-no
Spanish, French

Continental plus
Comp. wine, beverages
Sitting room, bicycles
Victorian tea for groups
near Gold Disc. State Pk

Country Victorian built in 1856, set among rose and flower gardens and pond on 5 acres. Half a block to Sutter's Mill and American River. Balloon flight packages available.

COLUMBIA ────────────────────────────

City Hotel
P.O. Box 1870, Main St., 95310
209-532-1479
Tom Bender
All year

$$ B&B
9 rooms, 9 pb
Visa, MC, AmEx ●
C-yes/S-ltd/P-no/H-no

Continental plus
French restaurant
Sitting room, piano
Anchor Steam beer on draft
in saloon

Historical location in a state-preserved Gold Rush town; 9 antique-appointed rooms; small elegant dining room and authentic saloon.

Fallon Hotel
P.O. Box 1870, 95310
Washington St.
209-532-1470
Tom Bender
All year

$$ B&B
14 rooms, 14 pb
Visa, MC ●
C-no/S-ltd/P-no/H-yes

Continental plus
Sitting room
rose garden
avail. for receptions

Restored Victorian hotel, full of antiques in state-preserved Gold Rush town. Elegant and intimate. Near Yosemite. Many historic family fun events throughout the year.

CORONADO ────────────────────────────

Coronado Village Inn
1017 Park Pl., 92118
619-435-9318
Pete & Betsy Bogh
All year

$$ B&B
14 rooms, 14 pb
Visa, MC, AmEx ●
C-14+/S-yes/P-no/H-no

Continental plus
Afternoon tea
Sitting room, library
bicycles, DD phones, TV
airport shuttle

A delightful small "European" hotel in the heart of the village. Half a block to fine dining and shopping. One block to the large, sandy beach of the Pacific Ocean.

DAVENPORT

New Davenport B&B Inn
31 Davenport Ave., 95017
P.O. Box J
408-425-1818 408-426-4122
Bruce & Marcia McDougal
All year

$$ B&B
12 rooms, 12 pb
Visa, MC, AmEx
C-ltd/S-no/P-no/H-yes

Full breakfast
Restaurant, gift shop
Champagne on arrival
sitting room
gallery

Charming ocean-view rooms decorated with antiques, handcrafts and ethnic treasures. Complimentary champagne. Artist/owners. Beach access.

DAVIS

University Inn
340 "A" St., 95616
916-756-8648
Lynda & Ross Yancher
All year

$$ B&B
4 rooms, 4 pb
Visa, MC, AmEx, Dis, DC
●
C-yes/S-no/P-no/H-yes

Continental plus
Comp. beverages
2 sitting areas
bicycles
airport shuttle

A great taste of Davis, ten steps from the University. Design your own breakfast. Private parking, quiet location. Rooms with private bath, private phone, TV & refrigerator.

DORRINGTON

Dorrington Hotel
P.O. Box 4307, 95223
3431 Hwy 4209-795-5800
Bonnie Saville
All year

$$ B&B
5 rooms
Visa, MC

Continental breakfast
lt. family style dinner
Restaurant
complimentary wine

A history connoisseur's inn with charm, comfort and elegance. Features antique filled rooms in a historical setting with gracious accommodations and fine dining.

DULZURA

Brookside Farm B&B Inn
1373 Marron Valley Rd., 91917
619-468-3043
Edd & Sally Guishard
All year

$$ B&B
10 rooms, 10 pb
MC, Visa ●
C-no/S-ltd/P-no/H-ltd

Full breakfast
4-course dinner by RSVP
Hot tub
piano

Quaint farmhouse nestled in mountain setting with stream. Handmade quilts and rugs, fireplace and farm animals. Gourmet dinners Friday & Saturday.

ELK

Elk Cove Inn
P.O. Box 367, 95432
6300 S. Hwy. 1
707-877-3321
Hildrun-Uta Triebess
All year

$$$ B&B
15 rooms, 10 pb
C-12+/S-no/P-no/H-ltd
Ger., Span., Fr., Ital.

Full breakfast
Dinner included Saturday
Comp. sherry or port
Bar, sitting room, deck
piano, library, stereo

1883 Victorian—original old-fashioned country inn, outstanding dramatic ocean views; specializing in German and French cuisine and personal service.

Harbor House Inn
P.O. Box 369, 95432
5600 S. Hwy 1
707-877-3203
Dean & Helen Turner
All year

$$$ MAP
10 rooms, 10 pb
C-16+/S-ltd/P-no/H-no
French, Spanish

Full breakfast
Full dinner, wine list
Sitting room, piano
fireplaces, parlor stove
gardens, private beach

Spectacular north coast vistas of the sea. Renowned country gourmet cuisine. Wine lover's paradise. Rooms include original artwork, fireplaces or parlor stoves, and decks.

ENCINITAS

InnCline B&B
121 N. Vulcan Ave., 92024
619-944-0318
Richard & Kirsten Cline
All year

$$$ B*B
4 rooms, 4 pb
•
C-yes/S-yes/P-no/H-no

Continental plus
Comp. wine & cheese
Wet bar, kitchenette
sitting room
near beach and tennis

North San Diego comtemporary B&B; Southwestern decor; ocean view; complete privacy or companionship. Romantic double showers. Ideal for groups. Hospitality plus. Willkommen.

EUREKA

A Weaver's Inn
1440 "B" St., 95501
707-443-8119
Bob & Dorothy Swendeman
All year

$$ B&B
4 rooms, 2 pb
Visa, MC •
C-yes/S-no/P-ask/H-no

Full breakfast
Afternoon tea or coffee
Sitting room
hot tub in one room
Japanese garden

Stately 1883 home of weaver; quiet, spacious flower/herb garden; full breakfast; afternoon tea; historic town in heart of Redwoods.

Carter House
1033 Third St., 95501
707-442-1390 707-444-8062
Mark & Christi Carter
All year

$$$ B&B
7 rooms, 4 pb
Visa, MC, AmEx •
C-10+/S-ltd/P-no/H-no
Spanish, French

Full 4-course breakfast
Dinner (by reservation)
Wine, hors d'oeuvres
sitting rooms, gardens
corporate rates

New Victorian. Enjoy wines & appetizers before dinner, cordials or teas & cookies at bedtime. Warm hospitality; award-winning breakfasts. OUR 1986 INN OF THE YEAR.

The Daly Inn
1125 H Street, 95501
704-445-3638
Gene & Sue Clinesmith
All year

$$$ B&B
5 rooms, 3 pb
Visa, MC, AmEx •
C-12+/S-ltd/P-no/H-no

Full breakfast
Afternoon tea, snacks
Complimentary wine
sitting room, library

A beautifully restored turn of the century mansion. One of Eureka's finest examples of Victorian elegance. Should not be missed.

Elegant Victorian Mansion
1406 "C" St., 95501
707-444-3144
Doug & Lily Vierra
All year

$ B&B
4 rooms, 1 pb
Visa, MC •
C-no/S-no/P-no/H-no
French, Dutch, German

Full breakfast
Lunch, snacks
Sauna, massage, croquet
parlors, cable TV, bikes
antique automobiles

"Victorian opulence, grace and grandeur—easily the most elegant home in Eureka. Spirited and eclectic innkeepers share the regal splendor of a national historic landmark."

The Hotel Carter
301 "L" St., 95501
707-444-8062 707-445-1390
Mark & Christi Carter
All year

$$ B&B
20 rooms, 20 pb
Visa, MC, AmEx •
C-yes/S-yes/P-no/H-yes

Continental plus
Dinner (by reservation)
Wine & hors d'oeuvres
sitting room
Belle House rooms avail.

Luxury full-service small hotel; attentive staff. Sophisticated blend of Old World elegance and modern amenities; antiques and art, in-room phones. Intimate hotel of quality.

EUREKA ————————————————————————

Old Town B&B Inn $$$ B&B   Full country breakfast
1521 Third St., 95501   6 rooms, 3 pb   Afternoon refreshments
707-445-3951   Visa, MC, AmEx ●   Comp. wine
Leigh & Diane Benson   C-10+/S-no/P-no/H-no   sitting room w/fireplace
All year   therapeutic massage $

Historic 1871 home, graciously decorated with antiques. Historical landmark. Original home of the Williams Carson family. Cats in residence. Close to Old Town.

FERNDALE ————————————————————————

Gingerbread Mansion $$$ B&B   Continental plus
400 Berding St., 95536   9 rooms, 9 pb   Afternoon tea & cake
P.O. Box 40   Visa, MC ●   4 guest parlors
707-786-4000   C-10+/S-no/P-no/H-no   library w/fireplace
Ken Torbert   Port., Span., Fr., Jap.   English gardens, bikes
All year

Northern California's most photographed inn! Large, elegant rooms, Victorian splendor, twin clawfoot tubs ("his & her bubble baths"). Fairy tale village. Turndown w/chocolate.

Shaw House B&B $$ B&B   Continental plus
P.O. Box 1125, 95536   5 rooms, 2 pb   Comp. beverages & snacks
703 Main St.   ●   Sitting room, library
707-786-9958   C-15+/S-ltd/P-no/H-no   organ, gazebo, yard
Norma & Ken Bessingpas
All year

Ferndale's elegant inn—first house built in Ferndale (1854). Antiques, fresh flowers, wine; join other guests in library, parlor, enclosed deck.

FISH CAMP ————————————————————————

Karen's B&B Yosemite Inn $$$ B&B   Full breakfast
P.O. Box 8, 93623   3 rooms, 3 pb   Afternoon tea, snacks
1144 Railroad Ave.   ●   Sitting room, library
209-683-4550 800-346-1443   C-yes/S-ltd/P-no/H-no   private baths
Karen Bergh   individual heat
All year

Enjoy cozy country comfort, nestled in the pines. Two miles from Yosemite National Park. Skiing, golfing, horseback riding, fine dining. AAA rated.

FORT BRAGG ————————————————————————

Avalon House $$ B&B   Full breakfast
561 Stewart St., 95437   6 rooms, 6 pb   Comp. sherry/port
707-964-5555   Visa, MC, AmEx, Disc ●   Fireplaces in rooms
Anne Sorrells   C-yes/S-ltd/P-no/H-no   whirlpool tubs in rooms
All year

1905 Craftsman house in a quiet neighborhood close to ocean and Skunk Train Depot. Fireplaces. Romantic Mendocino Coast retreat.

Grey Whale Inn $$ B&B   Full buffet breakfast
615 N. Main St., 95437   14 rooms, 14 pb   Comp. tea, lounge
707-964-0640 800-382-7244   Visa, MC, AmEx ●   Sitting room, pool table
John & Colette Bailey   C-12+/S-yes/P-no/H-yes   TV theater room w/VCR
All year   conference room

Historic north coast landmark. Comfortably furnished, some antiques. Ocean view suites/rooms, wheelchair suite, three kitchens. Extensive art collection.

FORT BRAGG

Pudding Creek Inn
700 N. Main St., 95437
707-964-9529
Garry & Carole Anloff
All year exc. January

$$ B&B
10 rooms, 10 pb
Visa, MC •
C-ltd/S-ltd/P-no/H-no

Full breakfast
Comp. coffee, tea
Victorian parlor
lush garden
gift shop

1884 Victorian built by Russian count. Enclosed garden court—fuchsias, begonias, ferns. Country gift shop. Restaurants, beaches, tennis courts nearby.

FREESTONE

Green Apple Inn
520 Bohemian Hwy., 95472
707-874-2526
Rogers & Rosemary Hoffman
All year

$$$ B&B
4 rooms, 4 pb
Visa, MC •
C-6+/H-yes
Spanish

Full breakfast
Complimentary wine
Sitting room w/fireplace
bicycles

1860 farmhouse in a sunny meadow backed by redwoods. Located in a designated historic village near coast and wine country.

FREMONT

Lord Bradley's Inn
43344 Mission Blvd., 94539
Mission San Jose
415-490-0520
Keith & Anne Medeiros
All year

$$ B&B
8 rooms, 8 pb
Visa, MC •
C-no/S-ltd/P-ltd/H-yes
Spanish

Continental plus
Comp. tea
Sitting room

Adjacent to historic Mission San Jose de Guadalupe; nestled below Mission Peak. Kite fliers' paradise; Victorian antiques and decorations; gourmet breakfasts.

GEORGETOWN

American River Hotel
P.O. Box 43, 95634
Main at Orleans St.
916-333-4499 800-245-6566
M. & W. Collin, H. Linney
All year

$$ B&B
18 rooms, 12 pb
Visa, MC, AmEx •
P-no/H-yes

Full breakfast
Evening refreshments
Barbecue, games, aviary
player piano, bicycles
hot tubs, swimming pool

An enchanting setting for weddings, honeymoons, anniversaries, corporate getaways or just a weekend away from the world. Dove aviary, putting green, mini-driving range.

GEYSERVILLE

Campbell Ranch Inn
1475 Canyon Rd., 95441
707-857-3476
Mary Jane & Jerry Campbell
All year

$$$ B&B
5 rooms, 5 pb
Visa, MC, Dis •
C-10+/S-no/P-no/H-no

Full breakfast from menu
Eve. dessert/tea/coffee
Sitting room, piano
tennis court, bicycles
pool, hot tub spa

35-acre rural setting in heart of Sonoma County's wine country with tennis court, swimming pool & spa. Private cottage unit. Fresh flowers, evening dessert, and homemade pie.

Hope-Merrill/Hope-Bosworth
P.O. Box 42, 95441
21253/38 Geyserville Ave.
707-857-3356
Robert & Rosalie Hope
All year

$$ B&B
12 rooms, 7 pb
Visa, MC, AmEx •
C-ask/H-ltd

Full country breakfast
Picnic lunches
Beer & wine license
sitting room, library
swimming pool

Victorians in the heart of Sonoma County's wine country. Old-fashioned hospitality; delicious food. Unique Stage-A-Picnic in the vineyards. Award-winning restoration.

North Coast Country Inn, Gualala, CA

GLEN ELLEN

Jack London Lodge
13740 Arnold Drive, 95442
707-996-6306
All year

$$ B&B
22 rooms, 22 pb
Visa, MC
C-yes/S-yes/P-no/H-no

Continental breakfast
(weekends & summer)
Restaurant, bar service
swimming pool

The lodge is located on the tree-lined Sonoma Creek in a quaint wine country village near Jack London State Park.

GRIDLEY

McCracken's B&B Inn
1835 Sycamore Lane, 95948
916-846-2108
Diane McCracken
All year

$ B&B
5 rooms, 5 pb
Visa, MC, AmEx, Dis ●
S-no/P-no/H-no

Full breakfast
Complimentary wine
Afternoon tea, snacks
sitting room, bicycles
porch, garden

1912 farmhouse, furnished in antiques. Lavish gourmet breakfast, cozy rooms, private baths. Near Sutter Buttes, Gray Lodge Wildlife Area—hiking, birding, photography.

GUALALA

Gualala Hotel
P.O. Box 675, 95445
39301 S. Hwy. 1
707-884-3441
Howard Curtis
All year

$ B&B
19 rooms, 5 pb
Visa, MC, AmEx, Disc
C-yes/S-yes/P-no/H-no

Continental breakfast
Dinner
Sitting room
piano

Historic 1903 hotel, overlooking the ocean, furnished with original antiques. Extensive wine shop, family-style meals.

North Coast Country Inn
34591 S. Highway 1, 95445
707-884-4537
Loren & Nancy Flanagan
All year

$$$ B&B
4 rooms, 4 pb
Visa, MC, AmEx ●
C-12+/S-no/P-no/H-no

Full breakfast to room
Wet bar in all rooms
Hot tub, library, gazebo
antique shop, fireplaces
beach access

A cluster of weathered redwood buildings on a forested hillside overlooking the Pacific Ocean. Close to golf, tennis and riding facilities. Antique shop at inn.

GUALALA ───────────────────────────────────

The Old Milano Hotel $$$ B&B   Full breakfast
38300 Hwy 1, 95445   9 rooms, 3 pb   Gourmet dining Wed-Sun
707-884-3256   Visa, MC   Houseblend coffee & tea
Leslie L. Linscheid   C-16+/S-no/P-no/H-ltd   sitting room
All year   hot tub, wine parlor

Lavishly refurbished inn on 3 acres of grounds. Breathtaking views of Mendocino coast. Near beaches and river, hiking, swimming, cycling.

GUERNEVILLE ───────────────────────────────

Estate Inn $$$ BB   Full breakfast
13555 Highway 116, 95446   10 rooms, 10 pb   Dinner, Beer & wine ($)
707-869-9093   Amex, Visa, MC, •   Sitting room, library
Darryl Motter and James Caron   C-no/S-yes/P-no/H-yes   Bicycle, hot tub, pool
All year   Conference fac., direct
                                                            phones

A grand mission-style mansion hidden among the redwoods where the standard is time-honored and uncompromising.

───

Ridenhour Ranch House Inn $$ B&B   Full gourmet breakfast
12850 River Rd., 95446   8 rooms, 5 pb   Dinner $ weekends
707-887-1033   Visa, MC •   Comp. port or sherry
Diane & Fritz Rechberger   C-10+/S-ltd/P-no/H-yes   picnic lunches, hot tub
Exc. January & February   sitting room, fireplace

Country inn on the Russian River in the heart of the lush and lovely Sonoma wine country. Adjacent to historic Korbel Champagne Cellars. Fresh flowers.

HALF MOON BAY ─────────────────────────────

Cypress Inn Miramar Beach $$$ B&B   Full breakfast
407 Mirada Rd., 94019   8 rooms, 8 pb   Afternoon tea
415-726-6002 800-83-BEACH   Visa, MC, AmEx •   Comp. snacks
Victoria Platt, Michael Fogli   C-yes/S-ltd/P-no/H-yes   sitting room
All year   hot tubs

Beachfront luxury—spectacular views from each room. Deck, fireplaces, gourmet breakfast. 5 miles of sandy beach. Fine dining, shopping, golf and jazz nearby.

───

Mill Rose Inn $$$ B&B   Full breakfast
615 Mill St., 94019   6 rooms, 6 pb   Comp. tea, wine
415-726-9794   major credit cards •   Sitting room, cable TV
Eve & Terry Baldwin   C-12+/S-no/P-no/H-no   fireplaces & spas in rms
all year   French, Spanish, German   VCR & phones

Exquisitely appointed flower-filled rooms and suites with private bath, entrance. English country rose garden by the sea. Oriental rugs, European antiques.

───

Old Thyme Inn $$ B&B   Full breakfast
779 Main St., 94019   7 rooms, 7 pb   Comp. wine
415-726-1616   Visa, MC, AmEx, Disc •   Library
Simon & Anne Lowings   C-ltd/S-ltd/P-yes/H-no   sitting room
All year   French   herb garden

1890 Victorian with herb garden on historic Main Street. Some private baths with large whirlpool tubs, fireplaces. Great breakfasts.

HALF MOON BAY

San Benito House	$$ B&B	Continental plus
356 Main St., 94019	12 rooms, 9 pb	Lunch, dinner, bar
415-726-3425	credit cards ok •	Sauna, sun deck
Carol Mickelsen, Greg Regan	C-no/S-yes/P-no/H-no	croquet, gardens
All year	Portuguese	

A romantic bed and breakfast just south of San Francisco. Historic inn, gourmet restaurant, western-style saloon and garden-deli cafe.

Zaballa House	$$$ B&B	"All-you-can-eat"
324 Main St., 94019	9 rooms, 9 pb	Full breakfast
415-726-9123 800-77-BNB4U	Visa, MC, AmEx, Dis •	Comp. wine and beverages
Sharon Tedrow	C-ltd/S-no/P-yes/H-no	sitting room
All year		gardens

First house built in town (1859). Garden setting by creek. Fireplaces, double whirlpool baths. On same block as two fine restaurants. Friendly and knowledgeable innkeeper.

HEALDSBURG

Camellia Inn	$$ B&B	Full breakfast
211 North St., 95448	9 rooms, 7 pb	Comp. beverage & snacks
707-433-8182	Visa, MC •	Sitting room
Del & Ray Lewand	C-ltd/S-yes/P-no/H-ltd	swimming pool, 2 rooms w/
All year		fireplace & jacuzzi

Elegant Italianate Victorian built in 1869, near Sonoma's finest wineries—beautifully restored and furnished with antiques, oriental rugs.

Frampton House B&B	$$ B&B	Full breakfast
489 Powell Ave., 95448	3 rooms, 3 pb	Snacks, comp. wine
707-433-5084	Visa, MC •	Library, sitting room
Paula S. Bogle	C-yes/S-no/P-no/H-no	hot tub, sauna, pool
All year	Spanish	bicycles, entertainment

An escape from the ordinary. Emphasis on privacy and service. Centrally located for wine country and Sonoma coast. Lavish breakfast.

Grape Leaf Inn	$$$ B&B	Full breakfast
539 Johnson St., 95448	7 rooms, 7 pb	Comp. wine & cheese
707-433-8140	Visa, MC •	Jacuzzi tub/showers for
Karen Sweet	C-12+/S-no/P-no/H-no	two in five guest rooms
All year		

Victorian elegance amidst Sonoma County's finest wineries. Generous full breakfast, complimentary premium wines, all private baths, and more!

Haydon House	$$$ B&B	Full breakfast
321 Haydon St., 95448	8 rooms, 4 pb	Comp. wine, snacks
707-433-5228	Visa, MC •	Two parlors
Keiu & Tom Woodburn	C-12+/S-ltd/P-no/H-no	organ
January—mid December		Victorian cottage

Intimate, beautifully restored & furnished Queen Anne in heart of wine country. Well known for abundant country-style breakfast. Attention to detail is our hallmark.

HEALDSBURG

Healdsburg Inn
P.O. Box 1196, 95448
116 Matheson St.
707-433-6991
Genny Jenkins
All year

$$$ B&B
9 rooms, 9 pb
Visa, MC
C-7+/S-ltd/P-no/H-no

Full breakfast
Comp. wine, eve. dessert
Champagne brunch
(wkend)
rooftop garden, gallery
2 gift shops, fireplaces

Individually appointed Victorian rooms decorated with antiques and sunrise/sunset colors. Centrally located overlooking old town plaza. Breakfast served on airy roof garden.

Madrona Manor—Country Inn
P.O. Box 818, 95448
1001 Westside Rd.
707-433-4231 800-258-4003
John H. & Carol J. Muir
All year

$$$ B&B
21 rooms, 21 pb
Visa, MC, AmEx, DC, CB
●
C-yes/S-yes/P-ltd/H-yes
Spanish

Full breakfast
Gourmet restaurant
Music room, robes
antique rosewood piano
swimming pool, billiards

Circa 1881, furnished with antiques. All rooms with private baths. Carriage house. Wine country, canoeing, bicycling, historical points of interest. February "daffodil" month.

Raford House
10630 Wohler Rd., 95448
707-887-9573
Gina & Vince Velleneuve
All year

$$$ B&B
7 rooms, 5 pb
Visa, MC ●
C-ltd/S-ltd/P-no/H-ltd

Full breakfast
Comp. wine

Victorian farmhouse overlooks the vineyards of Sonoma County. Country setting just a half hour away from San Francisco. County historical landmark.

HOMEWOOD

Rockwood Lodge
P.O. Box 226, 95718
5295 W. Lake Blvd.
916-525-5273
Louis M.Reinkens
All year

$$$ B&B
4 rooms, 2 pb
Visa, MC ●
C-no/S-no/P-no/H-no

Continental plus
Comp. cordials & sweets,
wine
Sitting room, game room

"Old Tahoe" estate nestled in pine forest; Lake Tahoe within 100 feet. Breakfast served in guest rooms. Many fine appointments.

HOPE VALLEY

Sorensen's Resort
14255 Hwy 88, 96120
916-694-2203 800-423-9949
John & Patty Brissenden
All year

$ EP/$$$ B&B
23 rooms, 23 pb
Visa, MC ●
C-yes/S-no/P-ltd/H-ltd

Full breakfast $
Comp. coffee, tea, cocoa
Sitting room, bicycles
hot tub, sauna, gazebo
hiking, fishing

Cozy creekside cabins nestled in Alps of California. Close to Tahoe & Kirkwood, X-C skiing. Full moon river rafting. Water color, fly tying & rod building courses.

INVERNESS

Blackthorne Inn
P.O. Box 712, 94937
266 Vallejo Ave.
415-663-8621
Susan Wigert
All year

$$$ B&B
5 rooms, 2 pb
Visa, MC ●
C-no/S-ltd/P-no/H-no

Full breakfast
Comp. tea, dessert
Wet bar sink area
sitting room w/fireplace
hot tub

Sunset Magazine (April 1983) describes the Blackthorne Inn as "a carpenter's fantasy, with decks, hot tub, fireman's pole, and spiral staircase."

INVERNESS

Dancing Coyote Beach
P.O. Box 98, 94937
12794 Sir Francis Drake
415-669-7200
Kay Ramsey
All year

$$$ B&B
3 rooms, 3 pb
Visa, MC
C-yes/P-no/H-no

Continental plus
Coffee & tea
Popcorn poppers
fireplace, kitchen, deck
living room, library

The best of both worlds ... Privacy while being catered to. Three lovely, fully equiped cottages nestled among pines on secluded beach. A unique bed & breakfast.

Fairwinds Farm B&B
P.O. Box 581, 94937
82 Drake's Summit
415-663-9454
Joyce H. Goldfield
All year

$$$ B&B
1 rooms, 1 pb
C-yes/S-no/P-no/H-no
Sign language

Continental plus
Desserts and snacks
Full kitchen, library
TV, VCR and movies
hot tubs, garden w/pond

One large cottage sleeps 6. Ridge-top cottage adjoins 68,000-acre National Seashore. Ocean view from hot tub. Fireplace, garden with ponds and swing. Barnyard animals.

Rosemary Cottage
Box 619, 75 Balboa Ave., 94937
415-663-9338
Suzanne Storch
All year

$$$ B&B
1 rooms, 1 pb
C-yes/S-yes/P-no/H-no

Full breakfast
Comp. tea, coffee
Kitchen
fireplace
decks, garden

Charming, romantic French country cottage nestled in secluded garden with dramatic forest views. Close to beaches; families welcome.

Ten Inverness Way B&B
P.O. Box 63, 94937
10 Inverness Way
415-669-1648
Mary E. Davies
All year

$$$ B&B
4 rooms, 4 pb
●
C-ltd/S-ltd/P-no/H-no
French, Spanish

Full breakfast
Comp. sherry
Sitting room
library, piano
hot tub (by appointment)

A classic bed and breakfast inn for lovers of handmade quilts, hearty breakfasts, great hikes and good books.

INVERNESS (PT.REYES STN)

Marsh Cottage
P.O. Box 1121, 94956
12642 Sir Francis Drake
415-669-7168
Wendy Schwartz
All year

$$$ B&B
1 rooms, 1 pb
C-yes/S-no/P-no/H-no

Full breakfast
Comp. coffee/tea/wine
Full kitchen
sitting room, fireplace
porch, sun deck

Cheerful, carefully appointed private cottage along bay. Kitchen, fireplace, antiques; extraordinary setting for romantics and naturalists. Near Inverness village.

IONE

The Heirloom
P.O. Box 322, 95640
214 Shakeley Lane
209-274-4468
Pat Cross, Melisande Hubbs
All year

$$ B&B
6 rooms, 4 pb
●
C-12+/S-no/P-no/H-yes

Full gourmet breakfast
Comp. Wine/Beverages
Dinner, sitting room
piano, bicycles, croquet
fireplaces, balconies

Petite 1863 colonial mansion—private garden setting, verandas, fireplaces, heirloom antiques, French country breakfast, comfort, gracious hospitality. Private dinners.

Marsh Cottage, Inverness, CA

ISLETON

Delta Daze Inn
P.O. Box 607, 95641
20 Main Street
916-777-7777
Smiling Shirley & Happy Frank
All year

$$$ B&B
12 rooms, 12 pb
Visa, MC, AmEx ●
C-8+/S-ltd/P-no/H-yes

Continental plus
Afternoon tea, snacks
Comp. ice cream fountain
sitting room, library
bicycles

Happy Frank & Smiling Shirley's inn is "the experience of the Delta" and the magic of the 1920's. Old-fashioned ice cream parlor. Stained glass windows. Delta theme rooms.

JACKSON

The Wedgewood Inn
11941 Narcissus Rd., 95642
209-296-4300 800-WEDGEWD
Vic & Jeannine Beltz
All year

$$$ B&B
6 rooms, 6 pb
Visa, MC, Disc ●
C-no/S-no/P-no/H-no

Full gourmet breakfast
Snacks, cheese, beverage
Sitting room, porch
formal English garden
gazebo, fountains

Charming replica Victorian tucked away on wooded acreage. Antique decor, queen-size beds, porch swing, gardens, wood burning stoves. One of InnTimes readers' Top 50 Inns 1991.

JAMESTOWN

Historic National Hotel
P.O. Box 502, Main St., 95327
209-984-3446
Stephen & Pamela Willey
All year

$$$ B&B
11 rooms, 5 pb
Visa, MC, Disc ●
C-yes/S-ltd/P-yes/H-no
Spanish, French

Continental plus
Full restaurant, bar
Champagne brunch
Sundays
library, antiques
courtyard dining

Restored 1859 hotel in cneter of Gold Rush town. Original saloon. Lots of outdoor activities. Outstanding restaurant; recognized in Bon Appetit. Near Yosemite.

JENNER

Murphy's Jenner Inn
P.O. Box 69, 95450
10400 Coast Hwy 1
707-865-2377 800-732-2377
Jenny Carroll
All year

$$ B&B
11 rooms, 11 pb
Visa, MC •
C-yes/S-no/P-no/H-yes

Continental plus
Comp. teas & aperitifs
Port & sherry available
sitting room
pvt. separate cottages

Coastal retreat inn—antiques, lots of character, peaceful, romantic, river and ocean views. Sunset weddings by the sea, wineries, redwoods nearby, 8 beautiful sandy beaches.

JULIAN

Julian Gold Rush Hotel
P.O. Box 1856, 92036
2032 Main St.
619-765-0201
Steve & Gig Ballinger
All year

$$ B&B
18 rooms, 5 pb
Visa, MC, AmEx •
C-yes/S-yes/P-no/H-no

Full breakfast
Afternoon tea
Sitting room, library
piano, cottage

Sole surviving 1897 hotel in southern Mother Lode of CA, restored to its full glory in genuine American antiques. National Register. "State of CA Point of Historical Interest"

KERNVILLE

Kern River Inn B&B
P.O. Box 1725, 93238
119 Kern River Dr.
619-376-6750
Mike Meehan & Marti Andrews
All year

$$$ B&B
6 rooms, 6 pb
Visa, MC •
C-12+/S-no/P-no/H-yes

Continental plus
Afternoon tea
Comp. wine, snacks
riverviews, fireplaces
whirlpool tubs

Brand new country inn on the Kern River. Mountain setting. Fishing, golf, skiing, antique shops, giant redwoods. Year-round getaway.

The Wedgewood Inn, Jackson, CA

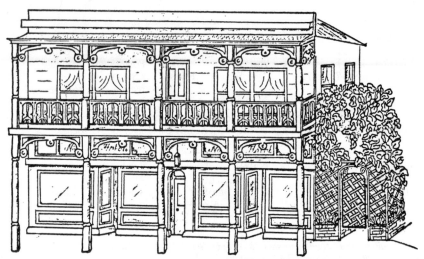

The Historic National Hotel, Jamestown, CA

KLAMATH ————————————————————————————————

Requa Inn	$$ B&B	Full breakfast
451 Requa Rd., 95548	15 rooms, 15 pb	Restaurant, dinner
707-482-8205	Visa, MC, AmEx	Afternoon tea
Paul & Donna Hamby	C-no/S-no/P-no/H-no	sitting room
March–October		

Located on majestic Klamath River in Redwood National Park. A relaxing, romantic retreat. Stroll through woods, swim, boat, or fish. Wonderful dining.

LA JOLLA ————————————————————————————————

The B&B Inn at La Jolla	$$$ B&B	Continental plus
7753 Draper Ave., 92037	16 rooms, 15 pb	Comp. wine & cheese
619-456-2066	Visa, MC ●	Sitting room, library
Betty P. Albee	C-no/S-ltd/P-no/H-yes	tennis courts nearby
All year	Spanish	ocean 1 block away

Our charming historic home pampers you with garden ambience, oceanfront strolls, art museum meanderings, quaint shops, restaurants and nearby tennis courts.

Windansea Beach B&B	$$$ B&B	Full breakfast
PO Box 91223, San Diego, 92169	3 rooms, 2 pb	Comp. fruit, beverages
619-456-9634	●	Sitting room, library
Sherry Cash	C-13+/S-no/P-no/H-no	tennis courts 1 block
All year		ocean & beaches 1 block

Walk to ocean, beaches, shopping and restaurants. Magazine quality guest rooms. Quiet. So much to see and do. Alternates between Continental and full breakfast each morning.

LAGUNA BEACH ————————————————————————————

Carriage House	$$$ B&B	Continental plus
1322 Catalina St., 92651	10 rooms, 10 pb	Comp. wine, cheese,
714-494-8945	●	fruit in room
Dee, Vernon & Tom Taylor	C-yes/S-yes/P-ltd/H-no	courtyard
All year		ocean swimming

Colonial New Orleans-style carriage house with central brick courtyard, tropical landscaping. Six suites each with sitting room, bedroom, bath.

LAGUNA BEACH

Casa Laguna Inn
2510 Coast Hwy, 92651
714-494-2996 800-233-0449
Kevin Henry
All year

$$$ B&B
20 rooms, 20 pb
Visa, MC, AmEx, DC ●
C-yes/S-yes/P-no/H-no

Continental plus
Wine, appetizers, etc.
Sitting room
library, entertainment
heated swimming pool

Panoramic ocean views and Spanish architecture. Gardens, heated pool, landmark "Bell Tower." Continental plus breakfast, tea/wine, light snacks, live music.

Eiler's Inn
741 South Coast Hwy, 92651
714-494-3004
Henk & Annette Wirtz
All year

$$$ B&B
12 rooms, 12 pb
Visa, MC, AmEx
C-ltd/S-yes/P-no/H-no
German, French, Dutch

Continental plus
Comp. wine
Sitting room
courtyard

Romantic country inn, ocean half block, walking distance to village. Courtyard and fountain where breakfast, wine and cheese are served.

LAKE ARROWHEAD

Bluebelle House B&B
P.O. Box 2177, 92352
263 S. State Hwy 173
714-336-3292
Rick & Lila Peiffer
All year exc. Dec 24–27

$$$ B&B
5 rooms, 3 pb
Visa, MC
C-no/S-no/P-no/H-no

Full breakfast
Evening hors d'oeuvres
Comp. wine, sitting room
library, darts on deck
private beach club

Enjoy elegant but cozy European decor in an Alpine setting. Immaculate housekeeping, exquisite breakfasts, warm hospitality. Near lake, village, shops, restaurants.

The Carriage House B&B
P.O. Box 982, 92352
472 Emerald Dr.
714-336-1400
Lee & Johan Karstens
All year

$$$ B&B
3 rooms, 3 pb
Visa, MC ●
C-no/S-no/P-no/H-no
Dutch

Full breakfast
Comp. wine, snacks
Sitting room
large deck with swing
room w/private balcony

Our home is furnished in French country style and is very warm and cozy. Five-minute walk to lake. Feather beds with down comforters. Gourmet breakfasts. We pamper our guests.

Chateau Du Lac
P.O. Box 1098, 92352
911 Hospital Rd.
714-337-6488
Jody & Oscar Wilson
All year

$$$ B&B
6 rooms, 4 pb
Visa, MC, AmEx ●
C-no/S-no/P-no/H-no

Full breakfast
Comp. wine, tea, snacks
Dinner by appointment
sitting room, library
hot tubs in room

The Chateau du Lac overlooks a beautiful view of Lake Arrowhead. It's a warm and friendly place to stay. We do weddings, showers, and birthday parties, too.

Eagles Landing B&B
P.O. Box 1510, Blue Jay, 92317
27406 Cedarwood
714-336-2642
Dorothy & Jack Stone
All year

$$$ B&B
4 rooms, 4 pb
MC, Visa ●
C-16+/S-no/P-no/H-no

Full breakfast
BBQ brunch (Sun), wine
Picnic area, boat rides
Catered dinner in suite
sitting room, fireplace

Enjoy home-style hospitality in an atmosphere reminiscent of a cozy European mountain inn. Decks overlook beautiful Lake Arrowhead. Year-round fun. Private beach club.

Forbestown Inn, Lakeport, CA

LAKE ARROWHEAD

Romantique Lakeview Lodge $$$ B&B		Continental breakfast
P.O. Box 128, 92352	9 rooms, 9 pb	Restaurants nearby
28051 Hwy 189	Visa, MC, AmEx ●	Sitting room, library
714-337-6633	C-ltd/S-ltd/P-no/H-yes	TV, VCR & movies in room
Kurt & Bonnie Campbell		suites w/pool for groups
All year		

Furnished with original antiques, crystal, lace, luxurious baths. Nestled in mountains at beautiful Lake Arrowhead. Breathtaking panoramic view. Walk to restaurants and shops.

LAKE ARROWHEAD–SKYFOREST

Storybrook Inn	$$$ B&B	Full breakfast
P.O. Box 362, 92385	10 rooms, 10 pb	Elaborate social hour
28717 Hwy 18	Visa, MC, AmEx ●	Aftn. tea, snacks
714-336-1483	H-yes	Picnic lunch, dinner
Kathleen & John Wooley	some French, Italian	library, hot tubs
All year		

Great escape to an elegant mountain inn by Lake Arrowhead. Nine charmingly decorated rooms with antiques and private baths. Separate rustic 1930s cabin also available.

LAKEPORT

Forbestown Inn	$$$ B&B	Full breakfast
825 Forbes St., 95453	4 rooms, 1 pb	Aftn. tea, comp. wine
707-263-7858	Visa, MC ●	Turn-down chocolates
Buzz & Jan Bruns	C-12+/S-no/P-no/H-no	sitting room, library
All year		pool, airport pick-up

Quaint Victorian Inn; redecorated in decorator fabrics and American antiques; beautiful gardens; block from Clear Lake; walking distance to town, wineries; country breakfast.

LEMON COVE

Lemon Cove B&B Inn
33038 Sierra Dr., 93244
Hwy 198
209-597-2555
Patrick & Kay Bonette
All year

$$ B&B
7 rooms, 5 pb
Visa, MC
C-no/S-no/P-no/H-no
Spanish

Large country breakfast
Afternoon tea & cookies
Sitting room
pool, whirlpool
gazebo, courtyard

Near Sequoia National Park, a country home nestled in fragrant orange groves. Delicious plantation breakfast served in elegant room. Gazebo available for weddings.

LITTLE RIVER

The Victorian Farmhouse
P.O. Box 357, 95456
7001 N. Hwy 1
707-937-0697
George & Carol Molnar
All year

$$$ B&B
10 rooms, 7 pb
●
C-10+/S-ltd/P-no/H-no
Hungarian

Continental plus
Comp. wine & sherry
Sitting room
7 rooms w/fireplace

Built in 1877; short walk to the ocean. Enjoy deer, flower gardens, creek, or sitting in our small orchard. Quiet atmosphere.

LOS ALAMOS

Union Hotel
P.O. Box 616, 93440
362 Bell St.
805-344-2744
Dick Langdon
All year

$$$ B&B
22 rooms, 9 pb
C-no/S-yes/H-no

Full breakfast
Restaurant, dinner, bar
Sitting room, library
hot tubs, pool, billards
tours in 1918 tour car

Step back in time ... choose your own world, either the ambiance of the old hotel or the house of make-believe. Then experience it.

LOS ANGELES

Channel Road Inn
219 Channel Rd., 90402
Santa Monica
213-459-1920 FAX:454-9920
Kathy Jensen, Diana Rodgers
All year

$$$ B&B
14 rooms, 14 pb
Visa, MC ●
C-yes/S-yes/P-no/H-yes
Spanish, French, German

Continental plus (wkdys)
Full breakfast (Sunday)
Aftn. tea, comp. wine
sitting room, library
bicycles, hot tubs

Elegant historic home converted to luxury inn. Located one block from the sea and furnished in period antiques. Historic and intimate ... so romantic. Outstanding location.

Eastlake Victorian Inn
1442 Kellam Ave., 90026
213-250-1620
Murray Burns, Planaria Price
All year

$$ B&B
8 rooms, 7 pb
●
C-12+/S-ltd/P-no/H-no
French

Full breakfast
Comp. wine, fruit basket
Sitting room, gazebo
morning paper, garden
occas. chamber concerts

1887 elegant Victorian, authentic antiques, hilltop historic residential district three min. from downtown L.A. Best central location; hot air balloon flights.

Salisbury House B&B
2273 W. 20th St., 90018
213-737-7817 800-373-1778
Sue & Jay German
All year

$$$ B&B
5 rooms, 3 pb
Visa, MC, AmEx ●
C-10+/S-ltd/P-no/H-no

Full gourmet breakfast
Comp. tea, shortbread
Sitting room

Experience the ultimate in bed and breakfast luxury and turn-of-the-century charm. Has been used as location for movies and commercials.

MALIBU

Malibu Beach Inn
22878 Pacific Coast Hwy, 90265
310-456-6444
Dan Ferrante
All year

$$$ B&B
47 rooms, 47 pb
Visa, MC, AmEx •
C-yes/S-yes/P-no/H-yes
Spanish

Continental plus
Comp. wine, snacks
On the beach
horse & jet ski rentals
fishing, water sports

Right on the beach. All rooms beautifully decorated in mission style: Mexican tile, textured stucco, fireplaces, private balconies with ocean view, honor bar, remote TV, VCR.

MAMMOTH LAKES

Snow Goose Inn
P.O. Box 946, 93546
57 Forest Trail
619-934-2660 800-874-7368
L. Johnson, B. & C. Roster
All year

$$ B&B
20 rooms, 20 pb
Visa, MC, AmEx •
C-yes/S-yes/P-no/H-no

Full breakfast
Comp. wine, appetizers
Sitting room
bicycles
hot tubs

Winter ski resort/Sierra's summer getaway. European-style deluxe mountain bed and breakfast. Offering special ski packages midweek.

MARINA DEL REY

Marina B&B
P.O. Box 11828, 90295
310-821-9862
Peter & Carolyn Griswold
All year

$$ B&B
1 rooms, 1 pb
•
C-12+/S-no/P-no/H-no

Continental plus
Afternoon tea
Rooftop garden & dining
view of marina
bicycles

Our large suite is located across from Marina. 10 min. from LA Internat'l Airport. Walk to Restaurant Row. All southern California's major attractions within 50 min. drive.

MARIPOSA

Meadow Creek Ranch B&B Inn
2669 Triangle & Hwy 49S, 95338
800-955-3843 209-966-3843
Bob & Carol Shockley
All year

$$$ B&B
4 rooms, 1 pb
Visa, MC, AmEx, •
C-ltd/S-ltd/P-no/H-no
Spanish

Full breakfast
Comp. appetizers
Sitting room
airport pickup
antiques

Originally an 1858 stagecoach stop on the Golden Chain Highway. Front door to Yosemite National Park. Furnished with European and country antiques.

Oak Meadows, too B&B
P.O. Box 619, 95338
5263 Hwy 140 N.
209-742-6161 Frank Ross, Karen Black
All year

$$ B&B
6 rooms, 6 pb
Visa, MC •
C-yes/S-no/P-no/H-noFrench, some German

Continental plus
Sitting room

Relax in luxury. Located in town. Near Yosemite. Rooms decorated with brass beds and hand-made quilts. All private baths.

Pelennor B&B
3871 Hwy 49 South, 95338
209-966-2832
Dick & Gwen Foster
All year

$ B&B
4 rooms
•
C-yes/S-ltd/P-ltd/H-ltd

Full breakfast
Kitchen
Sitting room
spa & lap pool

Quiet country accommodations at economical rates. Enjoy the stars while listening to a tune on the bagpipes.

McCLOUD

Joanie's B&B
P.O. Box 924, 96057
417 Laundale Court
916-964-3106
Joanie Smith
All year

$ B&B
4 rooms, 2 pb
C-no/S-no/P-no/H-yes

Continental plus
Sitting room, library
Piano, bicycles, games,
guests have the run of the
house

Log-built home with spacious guest rooms near fishing, golfing, hiking, skiing, boating. Located at the base of Mount Shasta.

McCloud Guest House
P.O. Box 1510, 96057
606 W. Colombero Dr.
916-964-3160
The Leighs & The Abreus
All year

$$$ B&B
5 rooms, 5 pb
Visa, MC
C-no/S-ltd/P-no/H-no

Continental plus
Restaurant, dinner
Evening sherry
antique pool table
library, bicycles

Completely restored 1907 country inn & restaurant near Mt. Shasta. Warm, country inn charm. Former guests include: President Hoover, Jean Harlow and the Hearst Family.

Stoney Brook Inn
P.O. Box 1860, 96057
309 W. Colombero
916-964-2300 800-369-6118
All Year

$ B&B
17 rooms, 13 pb
Visa, MC
C-y/S-n/P-n/H-n

Continental Plus
Restaurant nearby
Sitting room, library
therapeutic massage
golf, river nearby

Restored historic "community style" inn with cozy, homey character. Closest to Mt. Shasta skiing, waterfalls, fishing, hiking. Available for individual/group retreats.

MENDOCINO

Agate Cove Inn B&B
P.O. Box 1150, 95460
11201 N. Lansing St.
707-937-0551 800-527-3111
Jake/Sallie McConnell-Zahavi
All year

$$$ B&B
10 rooms, 10 pb
Visa, MC, AmEx
C-12+/S-ltd/P-no/H-no

Full country breakfast
Comp. sherry in room
Common room w/antiques
spectacular ocean views
whale watching Dec–Mar

Romantic cottages with fireplaces and spectacular ocean views. Full country breakfast served overlooking ocean in 1860s farmhouse. Beautifully landscaped garden. Winter rates.

Brewery Gulch Inn
9350 Coast Highway 1, 95460
707-937-4752
Anne Saunders
All year

$$$ B&B
5 rooms, 4 pb
Visa, MC, AmEx ●
C-no/S-no/P-no/H-no

Full country breakfast
Sitting room
Fireplaces
down pillows
gardens

Brewery Gulch is an unhurried authentic pre-Victorian farm surrounded by two acres of flowers and tree gardens. Full country breakfast served when you want it.

The Headlands Inn
P.O. Box 132, 95460
Howard St. at Albion St.
707-937-4431
Pat & Rod Stofle
All year

$$$ B&B
5 rooms, 5 pb
S-no/P-no/H-ltd
some Spanish

Full breakfast to room
Aftn. tea, mineral water
Comp. paper, 2 parlors
antique piano, organ
English-style garden

Restored 1868 Victorian home with unusual period antiques in picturesque Mendocino Village. All rooms have private baths, fireplaces, fruit, Q/K beds. Many have ocean views.

MENDOCINO ───────────────────────────────────

John Dougherty House
P.O. Box 817, 95460
571 Ukiah St.
707-937-5266
David & Marion Wells
All year

$$$ B&B
6 rooms, 6 pb
●
C-ltd/S-no/P-no/H-no

Continental plus
Comp. wine
Sitting room, verandas
ocean views
tennis nearby

Historic 1867 house in Village centre; antiques, all private baths, English garden, large verandas with ocean views; quiet peaceful nights; walk to shops and dining.

Joshua Grindle Inn
P.O. Box 647, 95460
44800 Little Lake Rd.
707-937-4143
James & Arlene Moorehead
All year

$$$ B&B
10 rooms, 10 pb
C-no/S-no/P-no/H-yes

Full breakfast
Comp. sherry, min. water
Sitting room
piano

Historic country charm in coastal village of Mendocino. Antiques, fireplaces, private baths. Near shops, galleries, restaurants. OUR 1985 INN OF THE YEAR!

MacCallum House Inn
P.O. Box 206, 95460
45020 Albion St.
707-937-0289
Melanie & Joe Reding
All year

$$ B&B
20 rooms, 8 pb
Visa, MC ●
C-yes/S-yes/P-no/H-no

Continental breakfast
Restaurant, bar
Sitting room

The MacCallum House provides friendly, personal attention to guests in a handsome, authentically restored Victorian home in the village of Mendocino.

Mendocino Village Inn
P.O. Box 626, 95460
44860 Main St.
707-937-0246
Sue & Tom Allen
All year

$$ B&B
12 rooms, 10 pb
Visa, MC
C-10+/S-no/P-no/H-no
Spanish, Japanese

Full breakfast
Comp. wine, truffles
Sitting room
library

Hummingbirds, Picassos, Navajo rugs, fireplaces, French roast coffee, Vivaldi, four-poster beds, migrating whales, scones, fuchsias, 12-foot ceilings. Newly restored.

Sea Rock B&B Inn
P.O. Box 286, 95460
11101 North Lansing St.
707-937-5517
Gretchen McEvoy
All year

$$ B&B
18 rooms, 18 pb
Visa, MC, AmEx
C-yes/S-ltd/H-yes

Full breakfast
Afternoon tea
Private beach
bicycles
garden

Country cottages furnished in Laura Ashley Victorian. Spectacular garden & white water views. Private beach. Buffet breakfast. Hospitality, a speciality.

Stanford Inn by the Sea
P.O. Box 487, 95460
Hwy 1, Comptche-Ukiah Rd.
707-937-5026 800-331-8884
Joan & Jeff Stanford
All year

$$$ B&B
25 rooms, 25 pb
Visa, MC, AmEx, CB, DC ●
C-yes/S-yes/P-yes/H-yes
French, Spanish

Continental plus
Wine, organic vegetables
Pool, hot tub, sauna
decks, nurseries, llamas
bicycles, canoe rentals

A truly elegant country inn in a pastoral setting. All accommodations with ocean views, fireplaces, decks, antiques, four-posters and TVs.

MENDOCINO ───────────────────────

Whitegate Inn	$$ B&B	Full breakfast
P.O. Box 150, 95460	5 rooms, 5 pb	Complimentary wine
499 Howard St.	C-13+/S-no/P-no/H-no	Sitting room
707-937-4892		organ
John & Patricia Valletta		deck with gazebo
All year		

Located in historic Mendocino, one of the town's more elegant homes, all rooms furnished with antiques.

MENDOCINO (LITTLE RIVER) ───────────────────

Stevenswood Lodge	$$$ B&B	Full gourmet breakfast
P.O. Box 170, 95460	10 rooms, 10 pb	Bar service, comp. wine
8211 N Hwy 1-Little River	Visa, MC, ●	Coffee, snacks
800-421-2810	C-yes/S-no/P-no/H-yes	sitting room, library
Robert & Vera Zimmer		lounge, conference room
All year		

Distinctive ocean view suites in "old growth" forest. Beach access, fireplaces, fine art decor, gallery. Mendocino's only AAA four diamond rating.

MILL VALLEY ─────────────────────────

Mountain Home Inn	$$$ B&B	Full breakfast
810 Panoramic Hwy, 94941	10 rooms, 10 pb	Lunch, dinner
415-381-9000	Visa, MC ●	Jacuzzis
Lynn Saggese	C-ltd/S-yes/P-no/H-yes	hiking trails
All year		telephones in rooms

Two-and-a-half-million-dollar restored classic California luxury inn. Adjacent to parklands, Muir Woods. Panoramic S.F. Bay views; jacuzzis, fireplaces, terraces.

MONTARA ─────────────────────────

Goose & Turrets B&B	$$$ B&B	Full 4-course breakfast
P.O. Box 370937, 94037	5 rooms, 5 pb	Afternoon tea, snacks
835 George St.	Visa, MC, AmEx ●	Sitting room w/woodstove
415-728-5451	C-yes/S-no/P-no	gardens
Raymond & Emily Hoche-Mong	French	airport/harbor pickup
All year		

Solitude. Bonhomie. Cozy down comforters, towel warmers, and fantastic breakfasts. 30 minutes from San Francisco; 0.5 mile from Pacific Ocean. 20 min. from S.F. Int'l Airport.

MONTEREY ─────────────────────────

Del Monte Beach Inn	$ B&B	Continental plus
780 Munras, 93940	18 rooms, 2 pb	Fresh fruit, cocoa, tea
1110 Del Monte Blvd.	Visa, MC ●	Sitting room
408-649-4410	C-yes/S-yes/P-no/H-no	
Lisa & Ken Hardy	Spanish	
All year		

Quaint English-style bed & breakfast ideally located near the heart of Monterey. Across the boulevard from beautiful Monterey Bay.

Jabberwock	$$$ B&B	Full breakfast
598 Laine St., 93940	7 rooms, 3 pb	Sherry & hors d'ouevres
408-372-4777	C-no/S-ltd/P-no/H-no	Sitting room
Jim & Barbara Allen	Spanish, French, Danish	sun porch
All year		

Once a convent, this Victorian home is above Cannery Row. Sherry on the sun porch overlooking Monterey Bay, gardens & waterfalls. Near Monterey Bay Aquarium.

MOSS BEACH

Seal Cove Inn
221 Cypress Ave., 94038
415-728-7325
Karen & Rick Herbert

$$$ B&B
10 rooms, 10 pb
Visa, MC, AmEx •
C-yes/S-no/P-no/H-yes

Full breakfast
Comp. wine, snacks
Afternoon tea
2 rooms have jacuzzis
private terraces

A romantic European-style country inn on the coast south of San Francisco. Ten charming guest rooms, all with fireplaces, overlook wildflowers, cypress trees and ocean.

MOUNT SHASTA

Mount Shasta Ranch B&B
1008 W.A. Barr Rd., 96067
916-926-3870
Mary & Bill Larsen
All year

$$ B&B
10 rooms, 4 pb
Visa, MC, AmEx •
C-yes/S-no/P-no/H-no

Full breakfast
Afternoon tea
Comp. wine, snacks
sitting room, hot tubs
library

Affordable elegance in historical setting. Enjoy the country charm of the Main Lodge, Cottage and Carriage House. Nearby lake fishing, year-round golf and winter skiing.

MURPHYS

Dunbar House, 1880
P.O. Box 1375, 95247
271 Jones St.
209-728-2897
Barbara & Bob Costa
All year

$$$ B&B
4 rooms, 4 pb
Visa, MC •
C-10+/S-no/P-no/H-no

Full country breakfast
Comp. bottle of wine
Sitting room
wood-burning stoves
clawfoot tubs

Restored 1880 home with historical designation located in Murphys, Queen of the Sierra. Walking distance to Main Street. A place to be pampered.

NAPA

Beazley House
1910 First St., 94559
707-257-1649 707-257-1051
Jim & Carol Beazley
All year

$$$ B&B
9 rooms, 9 pb
MC, Visa •
C-12+/S-ltd/P-no/H-yes

Full gourmet breakfast
Comp. wine, wine list
Private spas/fireplaces
entertainment
sitting room, library

The Beazley House is a Napa landmark. Relax in old-fashioned comfort. Breakfast, complimentary sherry. Personal wine tour orientation. Recently renovated.

Churchill Manor
485 Brown St., 94559
707-253-7733
Joanna Guidotti
All year exc. Christmas

$$ B&B
8 rooms, 8 pb
Visa, MC, AmEx •
C-yes/S-ltd/P-no/H-ltd

Full breakfast
Comp. wine, tea, snacks
Sitting room, pianos
sauna, side garden
croquet, bicycles

Grand beyond compare, this 1889 mansion, filled with antiques and surprises, is listed on the National Historic Register. Weekday, off-season discounts.

Country Garden Inn
1815 Silverado Trail, 94558
707-255-1197 FAX:255-3112
Lisa & George Smith
All year

$$$ B&B
13 rooms, 9 pb
Visa, MC, AmEx •
C-no/S-no/P-no/H-yes

Full breakfast
Comp. wine, tea, dessert
Sitting room
private jacuzzis & decks
rose garden, terrace

The Country Garden, on 1.5 acres of woodland riverside property is decorated in a very English style with antiques and heirlooms, and of course, true English hospitality.

NAPA ———————————————————————————————————————

Crossroads Inn
6380 Silverado Trail, 94558
707-944-0646
Sam & Nancy Scott
All year

$$$ B&B
3 rooms, 3 pb
Visa, MC •
C-no/S-no/P-no/H-no

Continental plus
Comp. wine, host bar
Aftn. tea, eve. brandies
library, game room, deck
hot tubs, bikes, gardens

Sweeping Napa Valley views; custom 2-person spas; complete privacy; king-sized beds, wine bars and full baths complement each suite.

Hennessey House
1727 Main Street, 94559
707-226-3774
A. Weinstein, L. Zemann
All year

$$$ B&B
9 rooms, 9 pb
Visa, MC, AmEx, Diners •
C-no/S-no/P-no/H-no

Full breakfast
Comp. wine
Sitting room
sauna, swimming pool
near the Wine Train

1889 Queen Anne Victorian with the original architectural details. Antiques, feather beds. Next door to the winery, tasting room and restaurant.

La Belle Epoque
1386 Calistoga Ave., 94559
707-257-2161
Claudia & Merlin Wedepohl
All year

$$$ B&B
6 rooms, 6 pb
Visa, MC, AmEx •
C-yes/S-no/P-no/H-no

Full breakfast
Comp. wine, snacks
Sitting room, wine
tasting room and cellar

Historic Victorian bejeweled in stained glass, antique furnishings, gourmet breakfasts by the fireside. Walk to wine train depot, restaurant and shops.

La Residence Country Inn
4066 Saint Helena Hwy., 94558
707-253-0337
All year

$$$ B&B
20 rooms, 18 pb
Visa, MC •
C-yes/S-no/P-no

Full breakfast
Complimentary wine
Sitting room
swimming pool, hot tub
two acres of grounds

For the sophisticated traveler who enjoys an elegant yet intimate style, La Residence is the only choice in Napa Valley.

Old World Inn
1301 Jefferson St., 94559
707-257-0112
Daine M. Dumaine
All year

$$$ B&B
8 rooms, 8 pb
Visa, MC, AmEx •
C-16+/S-no/P-no/H-no

Continental plus
Comp. wine & cheese
Afternoon tea
evening dessert buffet
sitting room, jacuzzi

Run with Old World hospitality by its English innkeepers, this Victorian inn is uniquely decorated throughout in bright Scandinavian colors.

Stahlecker House B&B Inn
1042 Easum Dr., 94558
707-257-1588
Ron & Ethel Stahlecker
All year

$$$ B&B
3 rooms, 3 pb
Visa, MC, AmEx •
C-ltd/S-ltd/P-no/H-no

Full candlelight breakfast
Beverages & cookies
Sitting room, fireplaces
piano, antiques, sundeck
ping-pong, croquet

A secluded, romantic, quiet, country inn located just minutes from wineries, the Wine Train & fine restaurants. The entire inn & beautiful gardens open to guests.

NAPA ————————————————————————————

Sybron House
7400 St. Helena Hwy, 94558
Yountville
707-944-2785
Sybil & Ron Maddox
All year

$$$ B&B
3 rooms, 3 pb
•
C-no/S-no/P-no/H-no

Continental plus
Comp. wine
Hot tub
tennis courts
sitting room, piano

New Victorian on hill commanding best view of Napa Valley. First-class tennis court and spa.

Trubody Ranch B&B
5444 St. Helena Hwy, 94558
707-255-5907
Jeff & Mary Page
Exc. Christmas & January

$$$ B&B
2 rooms, 2 pb
Visa, MC •
C-no/S-no/P-no/H-no

Continental plus
Sitting room
air conditioned rooms

1872 Victorian home & water tower nestled in 120 acres of family-owned vineyard. Stunning views from the water tower rooms.

NEVADA CITY ————————————————————

Downey House B&B
517 W. Broad St., 95959
916-265-2815 800-258-2815
Miriam Wright
All year

$$ B&B
6 rooms, 6 pb
Visa, MC •
C-12+

Full breakfast
Comp. wine, soft drinks,
Coffee, cookies, fruit
common area, veranda
library, garden

Light, comfortable view rooms. Lovely garden and terrace. Very near fine restaurants, shops, theaters, galleries, museums and outdoor recreational facilities.

Grandmere's Inn
449 Broad St., 95959
916-265-4660
Louise Jones
All year

$$$ B&B
7 rooms, 7 pb
Visa, MC
C-ltd/S-no/P-no/H-ltd

Full breakfast
Dinner by arrangement
soft drinks, cookies
sitting room

Historic landmark with country French decor in the heart of Nevada City. Lovely grounds suitable for weddings and private parties.

The Red Castle Inn
109 Prospect St., 95959
916-265-5135
C. & M. Weaver, E. Brotman
All year

$$ B&B
8 rooms, 6 pb
Visa, MC •
C-12+/S-ltd/P-no/H-no

Full buffet breakfast
Comp. beverages/desserts
Victorian high tea
parlor, antique organ
flowers in every room

State Historic Landmark 4-story brick mansion. Elegant, homey, lush grounds, a nature lover's dream. Vegetarian breakfasts and horse & buggy rides available.

NEWPORT BEACH ————————————————

Doryman's Inn
2102 W. Oceanfront, 92663
714-675-7300
Michael Palitz
All year

$$$ B&B
10 rooms, 10 pb
Visa, MC, AmEx, DC, CB •
C-no/S-yes/P-no/H-ltd

Continental plus
Restaurant
Parlour
patio, roof deck
bicycles, ocean

Ten individually decorated Victorian bedrooms, appointed with marble sunken bathtubs, fireplaces, brass, French glass fixtures. A truly romantic inn.

NEWPORT BEACH

The Little Inn on the Bay | $$$ B&B | Continental plus
617 Lido Park Dr., 92663 | 30 rooms, 30 pb | Comp. wine, eve. snack
714-673-8800 | Visa, MC, AmEx, DC ● | Library, pool
Herrick Hanson | C-yes/S-yes/P-no/H-no | comp. bay cruise
All year | Spanish | comp. bicycles

All the warmth & charm of an 1800s New England country inn. Complimentary bay cruise & bicycles. Walk to beach & quaint shops. Continental breakfast, wine & hors d'oeuvres.

NIPTON

Hotel Nipton | $ B&B | Continental breakfast
HCI, Box 357, 92364 | 5 rooms | Lunch, dinner, snacks
72 Nipton Rd. | Visa, MC ● | Comp. brandy
619-856-2335 | C-yes/S-yes/P-no/H-no | sitting room, hot tub
Roxanne & Gerald Freeman | Spanish | horse trails
All year

19th-century desert hideaway with antiques; home cooked breakfast served in our cafe next door; in east Mojave Desert national scenic area; horses stay for free.

OCCIDENTAL

Heart's Desire Inn | $$$ B&B | Continental plus
P.O. Box 857, 95465 | 8 rooms, 8 pb | Comp. evening sherry
3657 Church St. | Visa, MC, AmEx ● | Sitting room, library
707-874-1311 | C-no/S-no/P-no/H-yes | courtyard garden, aviary
J. Wulfsberg, H.& J. Selinger | German | bicycles, tennis nearby
All year

Renovated 1867 Victorian with European ambience. Rooms feature antique furnishings, goose down comforters, elegant appointments, private baths. Sumptuous breakfasts.

ORLAND

Inn at Shallow Creek Farm | $ B&B | Continental plus
Route 3, Box 3176, 95963 | 4 rooms, 2 pb | Sitting room, library
916-865-4093 | ● | near recreational lake
Kurt & Mary Glaeseman | C-no/S-ltd/P-no/H-no
All year | French, German, Spanish

Known for its gracious country hospitality, the inn offers peaceful surroundings, antique furnishings, gourmet breakfasts and farm-fresh produce.

OROVILLE

Jean Pratt's Riverside B&B | $ B&B | Full breakfast
P.O. Box 2334, 95965 | 7 rooms, 7 pb | Comp. wine
45 Cabana Drive | Visa, MC ● | River waterfront
916-533-1413 | C-ask/S-ltd/P-ltd/H-yes | deck overlooking river
Jean Pratt | | canoes, lawn games
All year | | hiking & birdwatching

Waterfront hideaway on 5 acres. Near I-5, Sacramento, Feather River Canyon, Gold Era historical sites, Oroville Dam, golfing, fishing. Gold panning on premises.

PACIFIC GROVE

Centrella Hotel | $$$ B&B | Full breakfast
612 Central Ave., 93950 | 26 rooms, 25 pb | Tea/wine/hors d'oeuvres
408-372-3372 800-233-3372 | Visa, MC, AmEx ● | Parlor, dining room
J.R. Megna | C-ltd/S-ltd/P-no/H-yes | beveled glass, gardens
All year | Italian | Monarch butterflies

Restored Victorian—award winner for interior design. Ocean, lovers' point and many attractions of the Monterey Peninsula. Fireplaces in suites. Take a trip back in time.

The Little Inn on the Bay, Newport Beach, CA

PACIFIC GROVE

Gatehouse Inn	$$$ B&B	Continental plus
225 Central Ave., 93950	8 rooms, 8 pb	Afternoon tea
408-649-8436	Visa, MC, AmEx ●	Comp. wine & cheese
Kent & Joyce Cherry, A. Young	C-12+/S-no/P-no/H-yes	sitting room, binoculars
	Spanish	near ocean and downtown

Historic 1884 seaside Victorian home, distinctive rooms, stunning views, private baths, fireplaces, delicious breakfasts, afternoon wine and cheese. Centrally located.

Gosby House Inn	$$$ B&B	Full gourmet breakfast
643 Lighthouse Ave., 93950	22 rooms, 20 pb	Wine and hors d'oeuvres
408-375-1287	AmEx, Visa, MC ●	Sitting room
Suzi Russo-Paulhus	C-yes/S-ltd/P-no/H-no	bicycles
All year		

Romantic Victorian mansion. Antique furniture, cheerful pastel fabrics and fireplaces abound. Enjoy turndown service and morning paper. Part of Four Sisters' Inns.

Green Gables Inn	$$$ B&B	Full breakfast
104 Fifth St., 93950	11 rooms, 7 pb	Wine and hors d'oeuvres
408-375-2095	AmEx, Visa, MC ●	Sitting room, bathrobes
Jillian Brewer	C-ltd/S-ltd/P-no/H-no	bicycles, newspapers
All year		coffee/breakfast in room

Spectacular Victorian mansion with views of Monterey Bay. Individually decorated rooms with antiques and beautiful fabrics. The most romantic inn around.

PACIFIC GROVE

The Martine Inn
255 Ocean View Blvd., 93950
408-373-3388
Marion & Don Martine
All year

$$$ B&B
19 rooms, 19 pb
Visa, MC, AmEx ●
C-yes/S-yes/P-no/H-yes
Italian, Russian, Span.

Full breakfast
Picnic basket lunches
Comp.wine/hors d'oeuvres
sitting room, game room
bicycles, conf. room

12,000-square-foot mansion on Monterey Bay. Elegant museum quality American antiques. Breakfast served on old Sheffield silver, crystal, Victorian china, and lace.

Old St. Angela Inn
321 Central Ave., 93950
408-372-3246 800-873-6523
Don & Barbara Foster
All year

$$$ B&B
8 rooms, 5 pb
Visa, MC, AmEx ●
C-16+/S-no/P-no/H-no

Full breakfast
Comp. wine/port, cookies
Solarium, gardens
hot tub

Intimate Cape Cod elegance overlooking Monterey Bay; walking distance to ocean and beaches, aquarium, Cannery Row. Champagne breakfast. Restored church rectory.

Roserox Country Inn
557 Ocean View Blvd., 93950
408-373-7673
Dawn Vyette Browncroft
All year

$$$ B&B
8 rooms, 4 pb
●
C-ltd/S-ltd/P-no/H-no

Full breakfast
Comp wine/hors d'oeuvres
Bar, library, horseshoes
croquet, bicycles
sitting room w/fireplace

Intimate historic Victorian on shores of the Pacific. Honeymoon Suite, antique brass beds, feather quilts, clawfoot tubs. Breakfast in bed. Spectacular ocean views.

Seven Gables Inn
555 Ocean View Blvd., 93950
408-372-4341
The Flatley Family
All year

$$$ B&B
14 rooms, 14 pb
●
C-12+/S-no/P-no/H-no
French, Spanish

Full breakfast
High tea
Grand Victorian parlor
aquarium tickets
ocean views in rooms

Family-run, grand Victorian mansion at the very edge of Monterey Bay. Fine antique furnishings throughout. Incomparable ocean views from all rooms. Gardens.

PALM SPRINGS

Casa Cody B&B Country Inn
175 S. Cahuilla Rd., 92262
619-320-9346
Frank Tysen, Therese Hayes
All year

$ B&B
17 rooms, 17 pb
Visa, MC, AmEx ●
C-ask/S-ask/P-ask/H-yes
French, Dutch, German

Continental breakfast
Library, bicycles
hot tubs, swimming pools
hiking, horseback riding

Romantic, historic hideaway in the heart of Palm Springs Village. Rooms, one or two bedrooms with kitchens and wood-burning fireplace. Beautifully restored in Santa Fe style.

Villa Royale Inn
1620 Indian Trail, 92264
619-327-2314 800-245-2314
C. Murawski, Robert E. Lee
All year

$$$ B&B
31 rooms, 31 pb
Visa, MC, AmEx ●
C-no/S-yes/P-no/H-yes

Continental plus
Restaurant, bar service
Comp. wine on arrival
full room service
tennis courts, 2 pools

Rooms & villas decorated as different European countries on 3.5 acres of flowering gardens. Private patios, spas, fireplaces, poolside gourmet dinners. Villas, hotel rooms.

PALO ALTO

The Victorian on Lytton
555 Lytton Ave., 94301
415-322-8555
Maxwell & Susan Hall
All year

$$$ B&B
10 rooms, 10 pb
Visa, MC ●
C-15+/S-no/P-no/H-yes

Continental
Comp. appetizers,
port & sherry
occasional entertainment

A lovely Victorian built in 1895 offering a combination of forgotten elegance with a touch of European grace. Near Stanford University, charming shops, cafes.

PETALUMA

Cavanagh Inn
10 Keller St., 94952
707-765-4657
Billie Erkel
All year

$$ B&B
7 rooms, 5 pb
AmEx ●
C-yes/S-no/P-no/H-no

Full breakfast
Afternoon tea, snacks
Sitting room, library
whirlpool tub
kitchen in cottage

Elegant Victorian and charming cottage. Within 2 blocks of historic downtown Petaluma and River. 35 minutes to San Francisco, wine country or ocean coast.

PHILO

Philo Pottery Inn
P.O. Box 166, 95466
8550 Hwy 128
707-895-3069
Sue & Barry Chiverton
All year

$$$ B&B
5 rooms, 3 pb
Visa, MC
C-8+/S-ltd/P-no/H-ltd

Full breakfast
Comp. sherry, eve. tea
Homemade cookies
library, sitting room
pottery gallery

1888 redwood stagecoach stop—country antiques and English garden—near Anderson Valley Wineries and restaurants. Philo Pottery Gallery. 20 minutes to Mendocino coast.

PLACERVILLE

The Chichester House
800 Spring St., 95667
916-626-1882 800-831-4008
Bill & Doreen Thornhill
All year

$$$ B&B
3 rooms, 3 pb
●
C-no/S-no/P-no/H-no
Dutch, Portuguese

Full gourmet breakfast
Comp. soft drinks, mixes
Parlor, pump organ
large library
queen-size beds

Feel pampered in our elegant 1892 Victorian home filled with antique family treasures. Gourmet breakfasts served above our gold mine. Vintage travel museum. BBINC Member.

Combellack-Blair House
3059 Cedar Ravine, 95667
916-622-3764
Al & Rosalie McConnell
All year

$$$ B&B
2 rooms
C-no/S-no/P-no/H-no

Continental plus
Comp. tea, coffee
Baked goods
sitting room

Elaborate 1895 Queen Anne Victorian furnished in genuine antiques. Original stained glass windows and free-standing spiral staircase.

River Rock Inn
1756 Georgetown Dr., 95667
916-622-7640
Dorothy Irvin
All year

$$ B&B
4 rooms, 2 pb
●
C-yes/S-ltd/P-no/H-ltd

Full breakfast
Comp. sherry
Sitting room
hot tub, TV lounge
antiques

Relax on the 110' deck overlooking the American River, fish and pan for gold in the front yard. Quiet and beautiful.

Cavanagh Inn, Petaluma, CA

POINT REYES STATION

The Country House
P.O. Box 98, 94956
65 Mañana Way
415-663-1627
Ewell McIsaac
All year

$$$ B&B
3 rooms, 3 pb
●
C-yes/S-no/P-no/H-no
French

Full breakfast
Afternoon tea
Sitting room, library
beautiful garden & view

Country house charm in secluded English garden and orchard, overlooking valley and Inverness Ridge. Fireplaces, easy chairs, antiques and great food.

Cricket Cottage
P.O. Box 627, 94956
18 Cypress Rd.
415-663-9139
Penelope Livingston
All year

$$$ B&B
1 rooms, 1 pb
C-yes/P-ltd/H-yes

Full breakfast
Comp. sparkling juice
Library, hot tubs
private garden
Franklin fireplace

A garden cottage with private hot tub. Cozy, romantic furnishings; original art. Located near Point Reyes National Seashore and Tomales Bay Headlands.

Holly Tree Inn
3 Silverhills Rd., 94956
415-663-1554
Diane & Tom Balogh
All year

$$$ B&B
5 rooms, 5 pb
Visa, MC ●
C-ltd/S-ltd/P-no/H-no

Hearty country breakfast
Comp. refreshments
Sitting room
fireplaces, hot tub

Romantic country inn on 19 acres in a coastal valley near San Francisco. Breakfast by the curved hearth. Herb gardens. Also a cottage in the woods near the waterfront.

POINT REYES STATION

Jasmine Cottage	$$$ B&B	Full breakfast
P.O. Box 56, 94956	1 rooms, 1 pb	Comp. teas & coffee
11561 Coast Route 1	C-yes/S-no/P-yes/H-no	Large naturalist library
415-663-1166		picnic area, patio
Karen Gray		surrounded by gardens
All year		

Secluded country cottage sleeps four. Completely furnished, fully equipped kitchen, writing desk, library, woodburning stove, queen-sized bed, sun room, patio, garden.

Knob Hill	$$ B&B	Continental plus
P.O. Box 1108, 94956	2 rooms, 2 pb	
40 Knob Hill Rd.	●	
415-663-1784	C-yes/S-no/P-no	
Janet Schlitt		
All year		

Custom designed cottage; cozy private room; deck, garden; spectacular views of the Inverness Ridge; direct access to the National Seashore.

Thirty-Nine Cypress	$$$ B&B	Full breakfast
P.O. Box 176, 94956	3 rooms, 1 pb	Sitting room
39 Cypress Way	●	hot tub w/great view
415-663-1709	C-no/S-no/P-no/H-yes	bicycle
Julia Bartlett	French	
All year		

Antiques, original art, oriental rugs, spectacular view! Close to beaches, 140 miles of hiking trails. Horseback riding arrangements available.

QUINCY

The Feather Bed	$$ B&B	Full breakfast
P.O. Box 3200, 95971	6 rooms, 6 pb	Sitting room, gazebo
542 Jackson St.	Visa, MC, AmEx ●	Victorian garden
916-283-0102	C-13+/S-no/P-no/H-no	fountain, bicycles
Chuck & Dianna Goubert		
All year		

Country Victorian in forested surroundings, relaxing our specialty, antiques in individually decorated rooms, located on Heritage Walk. Recreation area.

RED BLUFF

Buttons and Bows B&B	$$ B&B	Full breakfast
427 Washington St., 96080	3 rooms	Sitting room, comp. wine
916-527-6405	●	Library, hot tubs
Elizabeth & Marvin Johnson	C-no/S-no/P-no/H-no	near golf, pool, fishing
All year		and boating

1882 Victorian house, part of Victorian walking tour. Close to unique shops. Full breakfast in formal dining room. Near Lassen National Park, Mount Shasta and Trinity Alps.

The Faulkner House	$$ B&B	Full breakfast
1029 Jefferson St., 96080	4 rooms, 1 pb	Complimentary sherry
916-529-0520	MC, Visa, AmEx ●	Sitting room
Mary Klingler	C-no/S-no/P-no/H-no	bicycles
All year		

1890s Queen Anne Victorian furnished in antiques. Screened porch on quiet street, hiking and skiing nearby. Visit Ide Adobe or Victorian Museum, Sacramento River.

REDDING

Palisades Paradise B&B
1200 Palisades Ave., 96003
916-223-5305
Gail Goetz
All year

$$ B&B
2 rooms
Visa, MC ●
C-yes/S-ltd/P-no/H-ask

Full breakfast (wkends)
Continental plus (wkdys)
Comp. wine, snacks, TV
fireplace, porch swing
hot tubs, garden spa

Breathtaking view of Sacramento River, mountains, and city from a secluded contemporary home in Redding. Gateway to the Shasta-Cascade Wonderland.

REDONDO BEACH

Ocean Breeze Inn
122 S. Juanita Ave., 90277
310-316-5123
Norris & Betty Binding
All year

$ B&B
2 rooms, 2 pb
C-yes/S-ltd/P-ltd/H-ltd

Continental breakfast
Comp. fruit, flowers
Bicycles, whirlpool
TV, airport pickup
senior discounts

Large, luxurious rooms. Quiet neighborhood. Private entrance, bath with 6-foot spa. Near beach, L.A. Airport, Disneyland and all attractions; good restaurants, shopping.

REEDLEY

Reedley Country Inn B&B
43137 Rd 52, 93654
209-638-2585
All year

$$ B&B
4 rooms, 4 pb
Visa, MC
C-9+/S-no/P-no/H-yes

Full breakfast
Complimentary wine
Hot tub
bicycles
3500 rosebushes

Reedley Country Inn is a working plum farm where guests will find a quiet and restful atmosphere. Bicycles are available to ride to King River, where innertubing is popular.

SACRAMENTO

Amber House B&B Inn
1315–22nd St., 95816
916-444-8085 800-755-6526
Michael & Jane Richardson
All year

$$$ B&B
8 rooms, 8 pb
Visa, MC, AmEx ●
C-no/S-ltd/P-no/H-no

Full gourmet breakfast
Comp. wine, tea, coffee
4 suites with jacuzzi
tandem bicycle, private
phones, airport pickup

Luxury guest rooms offer ultimate comfort for the business traveler and the perfect setting for a romantic escape. Phones, cable TV, in-room jacuzzis, breakfasts in room.

Aunt Abigail's B&B Inn
2120 "G" St., 95816
916-441-5007
Susanne & Ken Ventura
All year

$$ B&B
5 rooms, 5 pb
credit cards accepted ●
C-ltd/S-no/P-no/H-no

Full breakfast
Comp. beverages
Secluded garden, piano
sitting rooms, fireplace
hot tub, games

Grand old mansion in the heart of the State Capitol. Large and comfortable, delicious breakfasts, air conditioned. Ideal for business travelers and romantic escapes.

Bear Flag Inn
2814 "I" St., 95816
916-448-5417
Jim & Linda Anderson
All year

$$$ B&B
5 rooms, 5 pb
Visa, MC ●
C-ask/S-no/P-no/H-no

Full breakfast
Comp. refreshments
Sitting room, fireplace
shaded garden, bicycles
deck with hammock

A charming 1910 California Craftsman nestled in a tree-lined residential area in downtown Sacramento. Elegant rooms with all the amenities for business and leisure travelers.

62 California

SAINT HELENA ────────────────────────────────────

Ambrose Bierce House
1515 Main St., 94574
707-963-3003 707-963-7756
Jane Hutchings Gibson
All year

$$$
4 rooms, 2 pb
AmEx ●
C-no/S-yes/P-no/H-no

Continental plus
Comp. sherry
Bicycles
sitting room

History and wine country charm combined amid brass beds and claw foot tubs; complimentary bottle of Ambrose Bierce wine.

Bartels Ranch/Country Inn
1200 Conn Valley Rd., 94574
707-963-4001 800-932-4002
Jami E. Bartels
All year

$$$ B&B
3 rooms, 3 pb
Visa, MC, AmEx, Disc ●
C-ask/S-yes/P-no/H-yes
Spanish, German

Hearty continental plus
Catered lunch & dinner
Comp. wine/fruit/cheese
library, sauna, jacuzzi
darts, horseshoes, golf

Elegant, secluded romantic wine country estate. Award-winning accommodations. 10,000-acre views; entertainment room, fireplace, billiards, bicycles. Champagne under the stars.

Bylund House B&B Inn
2000 Howell Mtn. Rd., 94574
707-963-9073
Bill & Diane Bylund
All year

$$$ B&B
2 rooms, 2 pb
●
C-no/S-ltd/P-no/H-no

Continental plus
Wine & hors d'oeuvres
Sitting room
swimming pool
bicycles

Elegant wine country villa designed by owner-architect, located in secluded valley with sweeping views. Two very private rooms with views, balconies and European feather beds!

Cinnamon Bear B&B
1407 Kearney St., 94574
707-963-4653
Genny Jenkins, Brenda Cream
All year

$$$ B&B
3 rooms, 3 pb
Visa, MC ●
C-10+/S-ltd/P-no/H-no

Full breakfast
Sitting room, piano
fireplace
classical music or swing

Homesick for a visit to your favorite aunt's house? Bring your teddy and come to the Napa Valley wine country.

Creekside Inn
945 Main St., 94574
707-963-7244
J. Nicholson, V. Toogood
All year

$$$ B&B
3 rooms
C-no/S-no/P-no/H-no

Full breakfast
Sitting room

Country French atmosphere in the very heart of St. Helena, yet peacefully sheltered. White Sulphur Creek ripples past secluded rear patio garden.

Deer Run Inn
3995 Spring Mountain Rd, 94574
707-963-3794
Tom & Carol Wilson
All year

$$$ B&B
3 rooms, 3 pb
●
C-no/S-no/P-no/H-no

Continental plus
Comp. wine
Library
swimming pool
horseshoes, Ping Pong

Romantic, cozy country hideaway, furnished in antiques, wrapped in treed deckings on four acres of forest. Situated in the heart of the Napa Valley wine country.

SAINT HELENA ─────────────────

Elsie's Conn Valley Inn
726 Rossi Rd., 94574
707-963-4614
Elsie Asplund Hudak
All year

$$$ B&B
3 rooms, 1 pb
AmEx, Visa, MC ●
C-ltd/S-ltd/P-no/H-no
Finnish

Continental plus
Comp. wine, fruit basket,
cheese
library, sitting room,
fireplace
extensive gardens & yard

Peaceful country hideaway, vineyards, lake trails. Genuine antiques. Continental plus breakfast served indoors or in the garden.

Erika's—Hillside
285 Fawn Park, 94574
707-963-2887
Erika Cunningham
All year

$$ B&B
3 rooms, 2 pb
●
C-ltd/S-ltd/P-no/H-no
German

Continental breakfast
Comp. sparkling water
Sitting room

Enjoy a peaceful and romantic retreat nestled on a hillside overlooking the Silverado Trail with inspiring views of the Napa Valley and its vineyards.

Harvest Inn
One Main St., 94574
707-963-9463   800-950-8466
All year

$$$ B&B
54 rooms
Visa, MC, AmEx, Disc. ●
C-yes/S-yes/P-yes/H-yes
Spanish

Continental breakfast
Bar service, snacks
Hot tubs
swimming pool

Cozy English Tudor cottages are set amidst 7 acres of lovely gardens; an anniversary or honeymoon paradise.

Hilltop House B&B
P.O. Box 726, 94574
9550 St. Helena Rd.
707-944-0880
Annette Gevarter
All year

$$$ B&B
3 rooms, 3 pb
Visa, MC ●
C-12+/S-no/P-no/H-yes

Full breakfast
Comp sherry after dinner
Guest refrigerator
sitting room, hot tub
hiking trails

A secluded mountain hideaway in a romantic setting on 135 acres of unspoiled wilderness, offers a hang glider's view of the Mayacamas Mountains.

The Ink House B&B
1575 St. Helena Hwy., 94574
707-963-3890
Ernie Veniegas, Jim Annis
All year

$$$ B&B
4 rooms, 4 pb
●
C-no/S-no/P-no/H-no

Continental plus
Sherry, brandy available
Parlor, 3 sitting rooms
concert grand piano
bicycles

Private, in beautiful St. Helena, antiques, fireplace, TVs, VCRs. Rooftop observatory with views of vineyards and valley hills.

Shady Oaks Country Inn
399 Zinfandel Lane, 94574
707-963-1190
Lisa & John Wild-Runnells
All year

$$ B&B
4 rooms, 4 pb
AmEx, Visa, MC ●
C-6+/S-yes/P-no/H-yes

Full gourmet breakfast
Picnic basket
Wine & hors d'oeuvres
library, bicycles
garden, croquet

Romantic and secluded on two acres among the finest wineries in Napa Valley. Elegant ambience; country comfort. Full champagne breakfast.

64 California

SAINT HELENA ─────────────────────────────────────

Wine Country Inn | $$$ B&B | Continental plus buffet
1152 Lodi Lane, 94574 | 25 rooms, 25 pb | Patios, balconies
707-963-7077 | Visa, MC ● | swimming pool
James Smith | C-12+/S-yes/P-no/H-yes | whirlpool
Exc. December 12-26

Beautiful country inn furnished with antiques and nestled in the heart of the wine country.

SAN DIEGO ─────────────────────────────────────

The Balboa Park Inn | $$$ B&B | Continental plus
3402 Park Blvd., 92103 | 25 rooms, 25 pb | Dinner, lunch
619-298-0823 FAX:294-8070 | Visa, MC, AmEx, DC ● | Terrace
Edward Wilcox | C-yes/S-yes/P-no/H-ltd | bicycles, whirlpools
All year | Spanish | tennis & pool nearby

Charming inn with 25 romantic suites. Directly across from Balboa Park/zoo/museums/theatre. Newly upgraded theme suites have private baths and luxury features.

The Britt House 1887 | $$$ B&B | Full breakfast
406 Maple St., 92103 | 10 rooms, 1 pb | Formal afternoon tea
619-234-2926 800-624-7236 | Visa, MC, AmEx ● | Sitting room, piano
Elizabeth L. Lord | C-ltd/S-ltd/P-no/H-ltd | sauna
All year

Queen Anne Victorian home with 2-story stained glass windows. Homemade breakfast and afternoon tea. Two blocks from Balboa Park. Available for small parties & weddings.

Carole's B&B Inn | $$ B&B | Continental plus
3227 Grim Ave., 92104 | 8 rooms, 3 pb | Comp. wine & cheese
619-280-5258 619-280-7162 | ● | Sitting room
C. Dugdale, M. O'Brien | C-no/S-yes/P-no/H-no | swimming pool
All year | | player piano, cable TV

Historical site, antiques, large pool. Close to zoo, Balboa Park. Centrally located. Friendly, congenial atmosphere. House built in 1904 and tastefully redecorated.

The Cottage | $ B&B | Continental breakfast
3829 Albatross St., 92103 | 2 rooms, 2 pb |
619-299-1564 | Visa, MC ● |
Carol & Robert Emerick | C-yes/S-no/P-no/H-no |
All year

Relaxation in a garden setting with turn-of-the-century ambiance is offered in a residential downtown San Diego neighborhood.

Harbor Hill Guest House | $$ B&B | Continental breakfast
2330 Albatross St., 92101 | 5 rooms, 5 pb | Kitchens on each level
619-233-0638 | ● | Large sun deck & garden
Dorothy A. Milbourn | C-yes/S-yes/P-no/H-no | barbecue
All year | | rooms with harbor views

Private entrances each level, guest kitchens, continental breakfast. Close to Balboa Park, zoo, museums, Sea World, Old Town, harbor, shopping, theater. Families welcome.

SAN DIEGO

Heritage Park B&B Inn
2470 Heritage Park Row, 92110
619-295-7088
Don & Angela Thiess
All year

$$$ B&B
9 rooms, 5 pb
Visa, MC •
C-14+/S-no/P-no/H-yes
Spanish

Full breakfast
Picnics, dinners, wine
Sitting room, library
bicycles
vintage films

Beautifully restored 1889 Queen Anne mansion in historic Old Town. Tantalizing breakfasts. Film classics shown nightly, antiques, romantic candlelight dinners.

Monets Garden
7039 Casa Lane, 91945
619-464-8296
Michael McConnell
All year

$ B&B
5 rooms, 1 pb
Visa, MC, AmEx
C-yes/S-ltd/P-no/H-no

Continental plus
3 full kitchens
Sitting room, library
laundry, large TV & VCR
botanical garden

Enjoy a gourmet breakfast, antiques, art, private patios and Beautyrest mattresses with feather topping. Central location. Easy freeway and trolly access.

Surf Manor & Cottages
P.O. Box 7695, 92167
3949 LaCresta Dr.
619-225-9765
Jerri Grady
All year

$$ B&B
7 rooms, 7 pb
•
C-yes/S-yes/P-no/H-no

Self-catered full brkfst
Kitchens
Stocked refrigerator
living rooms

Charming one- and two-bedroom suites. Oceanfront apartments and quaint beach cottages. Antiques and country prints. Near all of San Diego's attractions.

SAN FRANCISCO

Alamo Square Inn
719 Scott St., 94117
415-922-2055 800-345-9888
Wayne M. Corn, Klaus E. May
All year

$$$ B&B
5 rooms
Visa, MC, AmEx •
C-ltd/S-ltd/P-no/H-no
German, French

Full breakfast
Comp. tea, wine
Sitting room
bicycles
entertainment (harpist)

Fine restoration of a magnificent mansion. Graced by European furnishings and Oriental rugs, flowers from the garden and host committed to excellence.

Albion House Inn
135 Gough St., 94102
415-621-0896
Jan Robert de Gier
All year

$$ B&B
8 rooms, 8 pb
Visa, MC, AmEx •
C-yes/S-yes/P-no/H-no
Spanish

Full breakfast
Comp. wine
Sitting room

An elegant city hideaway conveniently located near the Opera House, just moments away from Union Square and other tourist attractions.

Amsterdam Hotel
749 Taylor St., 94108
415-673-3277 800-637-3444
Harry
All year

$$ B&B
30 rooms, 22 pb
Visa, MC, AmEx •
C-yes/S-yes/P-no/H-no

Continental breakfast
Sitting room, library
sunny patio
color TV & phones in rms

Located on Nob Hill. Quality accommodations and friendly service provided at modest rates. A little bit of Europe in America. Near Union Square, Financial District, Cable Car.

SAN FRANCISCO

Archbishop's Mansion Inn
1000 Fulton St., 94117
415-563-7872 800-543-5820
Kathleen Austin
All year

$$$ B&B
15 rooms, 15 pb
Visa, MC, AmEx •
C-ltd/S-no/P-no/H-no

Continental plus
Comp. wine, tea, coffee
Sitting room, piano
reception & conference
facilities

Historic French chateau. Luxurious lodging in the "Belle Epoque" style. "Arguably the most elegant, in-city small hotel on the West Coast if not the USA," USA TODAY.

Art Center B&B
1902 Filbert at Laguna, 94123
415-567-1526 800-821-3877
Helvi & George Wamsley
All year

$$ B&B
5 rooms, 5 pb
Visa, MC •
C-ltd/S-no/P-no/H-no
Finnish

Stocked kitchen
Picnic lunch, kitchens
Studio room, art gallery
art classes, city tours
enclosed patio, gardens

Art shows, classes, garden art, upstairs workroom & art materials. We offer an Art Package that includes 3 days lodging, museum tour, buffet. Suites with whirlpool & easels.

Casa Arguello B&B
225 Arguello Blvd., 94118
415-752-9482
Emma Baires, Marina McKenzie
All year

$$ B&B
5 rooms, 5 pb
C-7+/S-no/P-no/H-no
Spanish

Continental plus
Sitting room, TV

An elegant townhouse near Golden Gate Park, the Presidio, Golden Gate Bridge, 10 min. to Union Square.

Casita Blanca
330 Edgehill Way, 94127
415-564-9339
Joan Bard
All year

$$$ B&B
2 rooms, 1 pb
•
C-ltd/S-yes/P-no/H-no
Spanish

Continental breakfast
Two-night minimum
Homes avail. in Tahoe,
Maui, Palm Desert, and
Carmel. Request brochure

Casita Blanca is a detached cottage in a secluded forest area. View of Golden Gate. Fireplace, patio, completely furnished. Other homes in California & Hawaii available.

The Chateau Tivoli
1057 Steiner St., 94115
415-931-1934 800-228-1647
Rodney Karr, Willard Gersbach
All year

$$$ B&B
7 rooms, 5 pb
Visa, MC, AmEx •
C-yes/S-ltd/P-no/H-no

Continental plus (wkday)
Full breakfast (wkend)
Comp. wine, aftn. tea
double parlors
library

A stay at the Victorian townhouse, Chateau Tivoli, provides guests a time travel experience back to San Francisco's Golden Age of Opulence, the 1890s.

Edward II B&B Inn
3155 Scott St. St., 94123
at Lombard St.
415-922-3000
Bob & Denise Holland
All year

$$ B&B
31 rooms, 20 pb
Visa, MC •
C-yes/S-ltd/P-no/H-no
Spanish, Italian

Continental plus
Italian dinner, pub
Parlour, conference room
luxury suites available
phones & cable TV in rms

Perched atop a delightful Italian restaurant and an old English- style pub. Full refurbished 1914 European-style hotel in San Francisco's Marina district. Suites w/whirlpool.

SAN FRANCISCO —————————————————————————

The Garden Studio
1387 Sixth Ave., 94122
415-753-3574
Alice & John Micklewright
All year

$$ EP
1 rooms, 1 pb
C-yes/S-no/P-no/H-no
French

Coffee
Garden, private entrance
full kitchen
TV, radio

On lower level of charming Edwardian home; 2 blocks from Golden Gate Park. Studio opens to garden, has private entrance, private bath, fully equipped kitchen, queen-sized bed.

The Golden Gate Hotel
775 Bush St., 94108
415-392-3702 800-835-1118
John & Renate Kenaston
All year

$$ B&B
23 rooms, 14 pb
Visa, MC, AmEx, DC ●
C-yes/S-yes/P-ltd/H-no
German, French

Continental breakfast
Afternoon tea
Sitting room
sightseeing tours

Charming turn-of-the-century hotel. Friendly atmosphere. Antique furnishings, fresh flowers. Ideal Nob Hill location. Corner cable car stop.

Grove Inn
890 Grove St., 94117
415-929-0780 800-829-0780
Klaus & Rosetta Zimmermann
All year

$$ B&B
16 rooms, 9 pb
Visa, MC, AmEx ●
C-yes/S-ltd/P-no/H-no
Italian, German

Continental breakfast
Sitting room
bicycles
laundry

Turn-of-the-century Victorian, fully restored, simply furnished. Community kitchen, refrigerator. Part of Alamo Square Historic district.

The Inn San Francisco
943 S. Van Ness Ave., 94110
415-641-0188 800-359-0913
Marty Neely, Connie Wu
All year

$$$ B&B
22 rooms, 17 pb
Visa, MC, AmEx ●
C-12+/S-yes/P-no/H-no

Continental plus
2 sitting rooms, library
Sun deck, gazebo, garden
hot tub, phones, TV's
off-street parking

A grand 27-room 1872 Victorian mansion furnished in 19th-century antiques. Garden room, hot tub, fresh flowers in rooms. Rooms with jacuzzi, fireplace available.

The Inn at Union Square
442 Post St., 94102
415-397-3510 800-288-4346
Brooks Bayly
All year

$$$ B&B
30 rooms, 30 pb
Visa, MC, AmEx ●
C-yes/S-no/P-no/H-yes
French, Spanish

Continental
Comp. wine, aftn. tea
Hors d'oeuvres
comp. shoe shine & paper
turn-down, meeting room

Rooms are individually decorated with Georgian furniture and warm colorful fabrics by noted San Francisco interior designer Nan Rosenblatt.

Inn on Castro
321 Castro St., 94114
415-861-0321
Joel M. Roman
All year

$$$ B&B
5 rooms, 5 pb
Visa, MC, AmEx
C-no/S-ltd/P-no/H-no
Spanish, Italian, French

Continental plus
Comp. tea, wine
Sitting room
bicycles

Restored Victorian, lush contemporary interiors, filled with an abundance of art, accessories, plants, flowers, and especially friendliness.

68 California

Jackson Court
2198 Jackson St., 94115
at Buchanan St.
415-929-7670
Patricia Cremer
All year

$$$ B&B
10 rooms, 10 pb
Visa, MC, AmEx
C-12+/S-yes/P-no/H-no
Spanish

Continental breakfast
Comp. sherry
Sitting room

An elegant brick mansion built in 1901 in the heart of San Francisco, distinguished by its luxurious amenities and attention to comfort and hospitality.

The Mansions Hotel
2220 Sacramento St., 94115
415-929-9444
Tracy Pritikin/Pore
All year

$$$ B&B
29 rooms, 29 pb
Visa, MC, AmEx, DC •
C-yes/S-yes/P-yes/H-no

Full breakfast
Dinner, tea, wine
Sitting room, pianos
park next door
Mansion Magic Concerts

Breakfast in bed, fresh flowers in your room, nightly concerts, billiard room, Bufano Gardens, superb dining. San Francisco landmark. Close to all S.F. main attractions.

Moffatt House
431 Hugo St., 94122
Near 5th avenue
415-661-6210 FAX:564-2480
Ruth Moffatt
All year

$ B&B
4 rooms
•
C-yes/S-yes/P-yes/H-no
Spanish, French, Italian

Continental plus
Hot beverages, kitchen
Tennis, bicycles nearby
Japanese Tea Garden tkt.
runner's discount

Walk to Golden Gate Park's major attractions from our Edwardian home. Safe location for active, independent guests. Excellent public transportation.

The Monte Cristo
600 Presidio Ave., 94115
415-931-1875
George
All year

$$ B&B
14 rooms, 12 pb
Visa, MC, AmEx •
C-no/S-yes/P-no/H-yes
French, Spanish

Continental plus
Comp. tea, wine
Parlor w/fireplace
phones, TV

1875 hotel-saloon-bordello, furnished with antiques. Each room uniquely decorated—Georgian four-poster, Chinese wedding bed, spindle bed, etc.

No Name Victorian B&B
Box 349, 94101
847 Fillmore Street
415-931-3083
Susan & Richard Kreibich
All year

$$$ B&B
5 rooms, 3 pb
Visa, MC, AmEx •
C-yes/S-no/P-no/H-no
German

Full breakfast
Afternoon tea, snacks
Comp. wine, sitting room
tennis courts
hot tubs

Victorian in the heart of San Francisco. Enjoy the great hospitality of the innkeepers and the city.

Nolan House
1071 Page St., 94117
415-863-0384 800-SF-NOLAN
T. Beaver, T. Sockett
All year

$$$ B&B
6 rooms, 4 pb
Visa, MC •
C-yes/S-ltd/P-no/H-no

Full breakfast
Comp. wine at check-in
Cordials & mints
sitting room
feather beds, parking

Classic Victorian hospitality in tastefully restored "Painted Lady." Antique furnishings. Walking distance to Golden Gate Park and Haight-Ashbury District.

SAN FRANCISCO ─────────────────────────────────────

Obrero Hotel & Restaurant
1208 Stockton St., 94133
415-989-3960
Bambi McDonald
All year

$ B&B
12 rooms
C-ltd/S-no/P-no/H-no
Fr., Ger., It., Canton.

Full European breakfast
Basque dinners

Friendly slice of life in bustling Chinatown adjacent to North Beach, within walking distance of Union Square and Fisherman's Wharf.

Petite Auberge
863 Bush St., 94108
415-928-6000
Mr. Rich Revaz
All year

$$$ B&B
26 rooms, 26 pb
AmEx, Visa, MC ●
C-yes/S-ltd/P-no/H-no

Full breakfast
Wine and hors d'oeuvres
Sitting room
near Cable Car line

Romantic French country inn near Union Square in San Francisco. Turndown service, robes, afternoon wine and hors d'oeuvres. Honeymoon packages. One of the Four Sisters' Inns.

The Queen Anne Hotel
1590 Sutter St., 94109
415-441-2828
Richard L. Shaw, CHA
All year

$$$ B&B
Visa, MC, AmEx, DC ●
C-yes/S-yes/P-no/H-yes

Continental breakfast
Cream sherry, cookies
Catering available
banquet & meeting fac.
sitting room, library

A charming full-service Bed & Breakfast-style hotel that has recently celebrated its 100th anniversary as a Victorian landmark in San Francisco.

Red Victorian Inn B&B
1665 Haight St., 94117
415-864-1978
Sally McReynolds, John Drake
All year

$$ B&B
18 rooms
Visa, MC, AmEx ●
C-ltd/S-no/P-no/H-no
Spanish, German

Continental plus
Afternoon tea, popcorn
Meditation room, massage
peace gallery parlor
transformational art

Near Golden Gate Park in colorful Haight-Ashbury, our "New Age" hotel welcomes creative thinkers and globally conscious, friendly people. Global Family Networking Center.

Stanyan Park Hotel
750 Stanyan St., 94117
415-751-1000
Brad Bihlmeyer
All year

$$$ B&B
36 rooms, 36 pb
All major credit cards ●
C-yes/S-yes/P-no/H-yes
Spanish

Continental plus
Comp. afternoon tea
restaurant & bar
next door

Listed on the National Register of Historic Places. Completely renovated Victorian hotel at the east border of Golden Gate Park at the geographical center of San Francisco.

Victorian Inn on the Park
301 Lyon St., 94117
415-931-1830 FAX:931-1830
W. & L. Benau, S. & P. Weber
All year

$$$ B&B
12 rooms, 12 pb
Visa, MC, AmEx ●
C-ltd/S-yes/P-no/H-no

Continental plus
Comp. wine
Homemade breads, cheeses
parlor, library
TV on request

1897 Queen Anne Victorian—near Golden Gate Park, downtown. Each room has antiques, flowers, beautiful comforters, down pillows, phones and private baths. A historic landmark.

SAN FRANCISCO

The Washington Square Inn
1660 Stockton St., 94133
415-981-4220 800-388-0220
Brooks Bayly
All year

$$$ B&B
15 rooms, 11 pb
Visa, MC, AmEx •
C-yes/S-no/P-no/H-no

Continental plus
Comp. wine & beer
Sitting room
furnished with English and
French antiques

In San Francisco's North Beach—the essence of San Francisco. Near all attractions and many fine restaurants.

White Swan Inn
845 Bush St., 94108
415-775-1755
Rich Revaz
All year

$$$ B&B
26 rooms, 26 pb
Visa, MC, AmEx •
C-yes/S-ltd/P-no/H-no
Fr., Cantonese, Tagalog

Full breakfast
Hors d'oeuvres, wine
Library, sitting room
English garden
near Cable Car line

English garden inn, in cosmopolitan San Francisco; built in 1908. Business conference facilities; country breakfast; afternoon appetizers. Special services.

SAN GREGORIO

Rancho San Gregorio
Route 1, Box 54, 94074
5086 La Honda Rd.
415-747-0810
Bud & Lee Raynor
All year

$$ B&B
5 rooms, 4 pb
Visa, MC •
C-yes/S-ltd

Full country breakfast
Comp. beverages, snacks
Sitting room, library
antiques, gazebo
gardens, orchards

California Mission-style coastal retreat; serene; spectacular views of wooded hills; friendly hospitality; hearty breakfast; 40 miles south of San Francisco. Near Año Nuevo.

SAN JOSE

The Hensley House
456 N. 3rd St., 95112
408-298-3537
Sharon Layne, Bill Priest
All year

$$$ B&B
5 rooms, 5 pb
Visa, MC, AmEx •
C-ask/S-no/P-no/H-no

Full breakfast
Lunch/dinner by reserv.
Comp. wine, tea, snacks
sitting room, library
whirlpool in one room

Elegant city Queen Anne Victorian, close to everything. Gourmet breakfast. Business services, FAX, phone, PC, conference, meetings, airport service. Historic Register.

SAN JOSE/SAN MARTIN

Country Rose Inn—A B&B
455 Fitzgerald Ave. #E, 95021
San Martin/Gilroy, 95046
408-842-0441
Rose M. Hernandez
All year

$$$ B&B
5 rooms, 5 pb
Visa, MC •
C-no/S-no/P-no/H-no
Spanish

Full breakfast
Comp. tea, wine, cheese
Sitting room, library
grand piano, horseshoes
porch, shuffle board

Rural, secluded B&B featuring serenity, antiques. Near Gilroy Garlic Festival, county airport, ballooning, hiking, bicycling. Pivotal to Yosemite, San Francisco, Monterey.

SAN LUIS OBISPO

Adobe Inn
1473 Monterey St., 93401
805-549-0321
Michael & Ann Dinshaw
All year

$ B&B
15 rooms, 15 pb
Visa, MC, AmEx •
C-yes/S-ltd/P-no/H-yes

Full breakfast
Picnic baskets
Afternoon tea (Thur-Sat)
fireplaces in most rooms
wine tours, travel arr.

Cozy, comfortable and congenial southwestern-style inn. Located in the heart of this charming town. Fireplaces. Near Hearst Castle, beaches, wine tours, restaurants.

SAN LUIS OBISPO ───────────────────────────────────

Apple Farm Inn	$$$ EP	Restaurant
2015 Monterey St., 93401	67 rooms, 67 pb	All meals served
805-544-6100 800-255-2040	Visa, MC, AmEx ●	Swimming pool, hot tubs
Bob & Katy Davis	C-yes/S-yes/P-no/H-yes	gift shop, mill house
All year		working water wheel

Memorable lodging experience; uniquely appointed rooms—canopy beds, fireplaces, turrets, cozy window seats. Working water wheel. Mill house. Rated Four Diamond.

Arroyo Village Inn	$$$ B&B	Full breakfast
407 El Camino Real, 93420	7 rooms, 7 pb	Picnic lunch w/notice
Arroyo Grande	Visa, MC, AmEx ●	Wine & hors d'oeuvres
805-489-5926	C-10+/S-no/P-no/H-no	sitting room, library
John & Gina Glass		large parlour
All year		

In the heart of California's scenic Central Coast; charming Laura Ashley decor; scrumptious breakfasts. Convenient to golf, beach, wineries, Hearst Castle.

Garden Street Inn	$$$ B&B	Full breakfast
1212 Garden St., 93401	13 rooms, 13 pb	Comp. wine, snacks
805-545-9802	Visa, MC, AmEx	Sitting room, library
Dan & Kathy Smith	C-16+/S-ltd/P-no/H-yes	fireplaces, board games
		hot tubs, decks

1887 Victorian lovingly restored. Romantic get-away in the heart of an old-fashioned downtown. Antiques, expansive decks, jacuzzis, homemade breakfast, genuine hospitality.

SAN RAFAEL ───────────────────────────────────

Casa Soldavini	$$ B&B	Continental plus
531 "C" St., 94901	3 rooms, 2 pb	Afternoon tea, snacks
415-454-3140	●	Sitting room, piano
Linda Soldavini, Dan Cassidy	C-no/S-no/P-yes/H-no	TV, VCR, patio w/swinglush
All year		gardens, bicycles

1932 winemaker's home, nestled in a quaint Italian neighborhood near Mission San Rafael. Close to everything. Enjoy 1930s movies & melodies or just relax on our front porch.

SANTA BARBARA ───────────────────────────────────

The Arlington Inn	$$ B&B	Full breakfast
1136 De La Vina St., 93101	Visa, MC, AmEx ●	Comp. wine, snacks
805-428-3912	C-yes/S-yes/P-no/H-no	
Lorry Ortner		
All year		

Located in downtown historic district. Walking distance to shops and restaurants. Complimentary full breakfast, afternoon wine and cheese. European hospitality.

B&B at Valli's View	$$ B&B	Full breakfast
340 N. Sierra Vista, 93108	2 rooms, 2 pb	Comp. wine
805-969-1272	●	Train/airport pickup
Valli & Larry Stevens	C-yes/P-ltd/H-yes	garden swing, patios
All year		deck, mountain views

A secluded home nestled in Montecito foothills provides peace and tranquillity, yet near city. Gourmet breakfast on patio or by fireplace.

The Garden Street Inn, San Luis Obispo, CA

SANTA BARBARA ─────────────────────────

Bath Street Inn	$$ B&B	Full breakfast
1720 Bath St., 93101	7 rooms, 7 pb	Evening refreshments
805-682-9680 800-788-BATH	Visa, MC, AmEx ●	Sitting & dining rooms
Susan Brown, Joanne Thorne	C-12+/S-no/P-no/H-no	TV room, library
All year		bicycles

Luxurious 3-story Victorian, panoramic views, balconies, brick courtyards. Lovely gardens create country inn environment; blocks from downtown.

The Bayberry Inn B&B	$$$ B&B	Full gourmet breakfast
111 W. Valerio St., 93101	8 rooms, 8 pb	Sparkling cider, cheeses
805-682-3199	Visa, MC ●	Sitting room, fireplaces
Keith Pomeroy	C-no/S-no/P-no/H-yes	piano, bicycles
All year		jacuzzi, garden, croquet

A gracious in-town bed & breakfast inn within walking distance to shops, fine restaurants and entertainment, only 1.5 miles to beach. Fireplaces.

SANTA BARBARA ────────────────────────────────

Blue Quail Inn & Cottages
1908 Bath St., 93101
805-687-2300
Jeanise Suding Eaton
All year exc. Dec 24-25

$$ B&B
9 rooms, 7 pb
Visa, MC ●
C-ltd/S-ltd/P-no/H-no

Full breakfast
Picnic lunches, cider
Comp. wine, eve. sweets
sitting room, garden
brick patio, bicycles

Guest rooms, suites and private cottages filled with country charm in a delightfully quiet and relaxing country setting. Close to town and beaches. Scrumptious full breakfast.

Cheshire Cat Inn
36 W. Valerio St., 93101
805-569-1610 FAX:682-1876
C. Dunstan, M. Goeden
All year

$$$ B&B
12 rooms, 12 pb
●
C-14+/S-no/P-no/H-no

Continental plus
Comp. wine (Sat. eve)
Library, sitting room
bicycles, hot tub
cooking school

Victorian elegance, uniquely decorated in Laura Ashley and English antiques; private baths, jacuzzis, balconies, fireplaces, gardens; convenient location, parking.

Harbour Carriage House
420 W. Montecito St., 93101
805-962-8447 800-594-4633
Kimberly Pegram
All year exc. Dec 24-25

$$$ B&B
9 rooms, 9 pb
●
C-no/S-no/P-no/H-no

Full breakfast
Comp. wine, refreshments
fireplaces, balconies
spa tubs, mountain views

Harbour Carriage House—An Inn by the Sea. Simply elegant country French atmosphere in the main house and carriage house. 2 blocks from beach.

Long's Seaview B&B
317 Piedmont Rd., 93105
805-687-2947
LaVerne Long
All year

$$ B&B
1 rooms, 1 pb
C-12+/S-no/P-no/H-no

Full breakfast
King size bed
Gardens, patio

Home with a lovely view, furnished with antiques. Quiet neighborhood. Full breakfast served on the patio. Homemade jams and fresh fruits.

Ocean View House
P.O. Box 20065, 93102
805-966-6659
Carolyn & Bill Canfield
All year

$$ B&B
2 rooms, 1 pb
C-yes/S-ltd/P-ltd/H-no

Continental plus
Stocked refrigerator
Beach towels & chairs
2 room suite available
w/ den, private entry

Breakfast on the patio while viewing sailboats and the Channel Islands. Private home in a quiet neighborhood. $10 extra for single night stay. Fruit trees in yard.

Old Yacht Club Inn
431 Corona Del Mar Dr., 93103
805-962-1277
N.Donaldson, S.Hunt, L.Caruso
All year

$$$ B&B
9 rooms, 9 pb
Visa, MC, AmEx ●
S-ltd/P-no/H-no
Spanish

Full breakfast
Dinner (weekends)
Comp. evening beverage
beach chairs & towels
bicycles

A 1912 California classic. Beautifully decorated antique-filled rooms. Gourmet breakfast. Dinner on weekends. Half block to beautiful beach.

SANTA BARBARA ──────────────────────────────

The Parsonage
1600 Olive St., 93101
805-962-9336
Hilde Michelmore
All year

$$$ B&B
6 rooms, 6 pb
●
C-no/S-ltd/P-no/H-no
German

Full breakfast
Comp. wine
Sitting room

A beautifully restored Queen Anne Victorian. An atmosphere of comfort, grace and elegance; with ocean and mountain views. Close to shops, dining, sightseeing.

Sandman at the Beach
18 Bath St., 93101
805-963-4418 800-433-3097
Mike & Becky Montgomery
All year

$$ B&B
20 rooms, 22 pb
Visa, MC, AmEx, Dis, En ●
C-yes/S-yes/P-ask/H-yes
French, Spanish, Arabic

Continental breakfast
Aftn. tea, comp. wine
Sitting room, hot tub
beach towels, umbrellas

Spanish-style villa, quiet, charming. One block from beach. Courtyard jacuzzi. Several units with fireplaces and kitchens.

Simpson House Inn
121 E. Arrellaga, 93101
805-963-7067
G. & L. Davies, G. Wilson
All year

$$$ B&B
10 rooms, 10 pb
Visa, MC ●
C-yes/S-ltd/P-no/H-yes
Spanish, French, Danish

Full breakfast
Comp. wine, beverages
Sitting room, library
verandas, gardens
grounds, bicycles

1874 Victorian estate secluded on an acre of English gardens. Elegant antiques, art. Delicious leisurely breakfast on verandas. Walk to historic downtown.

Villa Rosa
15 Chapala St., 93101
805-966-0851
Beverly Kirkhart, Annie Puetz
All year

$$$ B&B
18 rooms, 18 pb
Visa, MC, AmEx ●
C-14+/S-yes/P-no/H-no
Spanish

Continental breakfast
Comp. wine/fruit/cheese
Roses & chocolate, pool
terry robes, 2 lounges
masseuse, conf. room

Traditional Spanish building renovated with the ingredients of sophisticated Santa Fe-New Mexico decor, casual elegance in the Santa Barbara tradition.

SANTA CLARA ──────────────────────────────

Madison Street Inn
1390 Madison St., 95050
408-249-5541
Ralph & Theresa Wigginton
All year

$$ B&B
5 rooms, 3 pb
Visa, MC, AmEx ●
C-yes/S-ltd/P-no/H-no
French

Full breakfast
Lunch, dinner w/notice
Comp. wine & beverages
library, sitting room
hot tub, bicycles, pool

Santa Clara's only inn! A beautiful Victorian; landscaped gardens. Eggs Benedict is a breakfast favorite. Close to Winchester Mystery House. Weekend dinner package.

SANTA CRUZ ──────────────────────────────

Babbling Brook Inn
1025 Laurel St., 95060
408-427-2437 800-866-1131
Helen King
All year

$$$ B&B
12 rooms, 12 pb
Visa, MC, AmEx, Disc ●
C-no/S-ltd/P-no/H-ltd

Full buffet breakfast
Comp. wine, refreshments
Picnic baskets
phone & TV in rooms
romantic garden gazebo

Secluded inn among waterfalls, gardens, gazebo, Laurel Creek, pines and redwoods. Complimentary wine, fireplaces. 12 rooms in country French decor; private bathrooms; decks.

SANTA CRUZ

Chateau Victorian, B&B Inn
118 First St., 95060
408-458-9458
Franz & Alice-June Benjamin
All year

$$$ B&B
7 rooms, 7 pb
Visa, MC, AmEx
C-no/S-no/P-no/H-no
German

Continental plus
Comp. wine & cheese
Sitting room
2 decks, patio
fireplaces in rooms

One block from the beach and the boardwalk, in the heart of the Santa Cruz fun area. All rooms have queen-size beds with private bathrooms.

Cliff Crest B&B Inn
407 Cliff Street, 95060
408-427-2609
Bruce & Sharon Taylor
All year

$$$ B&B
5 rooms, 5 pb
Visa, MC, AmEx ●
C-no/S-no/P-no/H-yes

Full gourmet breakfast
Evening wine & tidbits
Sitting room, library

Romantic Victorian mansion. Five unique rooms w/private baths, fireplaces, solarium, belvedere, breakfast in bed. One block to beach, boardwalk.

The Darling House
314 W. Cliff Dr., 95060
408-458-1958
Darrell & Karen Darling
All year   ●

$$$ B&B/MAP
8 rooms, 2 pb
Visa, MC, AmEx ●
C-ltd/S-ltd/P-no/H-ltd

Continental plus
Comp. dinner-wknite pkg.
Beverage, orchids in rm.
library, hot tub spa
double size bathtubs

1910 ocean side mansion with beveled glass, Tiffany lamps, Chippendale antiques, open hearths and hardwood interiors. Walk to beach.

Pleasure Point Inn
2-3665 East Cliff Dr., 95062
408-475-4657
Margaret & Sal Margo
All year

$$$ B&B
3 rooms, 3 pb
Visa, MC ●
C-12+

Continental plus
Comp. wine & cheese
Fireplace in suite
fishing charters
day cruises on yacht

On beach, overlooking beautiful Monterey Bay. Walk to beach & shopping village. Rooms include private bath, sitting room & deck. Motor yacht available for fishing or cruises.

SANTA CRUZ—BEN LOMOND

Chateau Des Fleurs
7995 Hwy 9, 95005
408-336-8943
Lee & Laura Jonas
All year

$$$ B&B
3 rooms, 3 pb
Visa, MC, AmEx, Disc
C-no/S-no/P-no/H-no

Full breakfast
Comp. wine, library
Sitting room, organ
antique piano, hiking,
swimming, tennis nearby

A Victorian mansion once owned by the Bartlett (pear) family, this inn is spacious, special, sensational, historic, quiet, unforgettable, surrounded by evergreens & wineries.

SANTA ROSA

Gee-Gee's B&B Home
7810 Sonoma Hwy 12, 95409
707-833-6667
Gerda Heaton-Weisz
All year

$$ B&B
4 rooms, 1 pb
●
C-no/S-no/P-no/H-no
French, German

Full breakfast
Comp. refreshments, wine
Sitting room, fireplace
TV, decks, RV parking
bicycles, swimming pool

Comfortable home on one acre in the Valley of the Moon—enchanting country setting. One mile to renowned wineries, golf course, horseback riding, jogging/hiking trails.

SANTA ROSA ———————————————————————————————————

Pygmalion House B&B $$ B&B Full breakfast
331 Orange St., 95401 5 rooms, 5 pb Sparkling cider & snacks
707-526-3407 ● Sitting room, fireplace
Lola L. Wright C-10+/S-ltd/P-no/H-no television
All year central A/C & heat

Delightfully restored Queen Anne cottage central to Northern California wine country, San Francisco Bay area and North Coast resort areas.

Vintner's Inn $$$ B&B Continental plus
4350 Barnes Rd., 95403 44 rooms, 44 pb Restaurant, bar
707-575-7350 Visa, MC, AmEx, DC ● Sitting room
Cindy Young C-yes/S-yes/P-no/H-yes hot tubs, wine touring
All year Spanish nearby tennis, pool

European-styled country inn surrounded by a 50-acre vineyard. Antique furniture, conference facilities. Home of John Ash & Co. Restaurant. AAA Four Diamond rating.

SAUSALITO ————————————————————————————————————

Butterfly Tree $$$ B&B Full breakfast
P.O. Box 790, 94965 3 rooms, 3 pb Comp. wine, tea
20 Sunset Way C-ask/S-no/P-no/H-no Sitting room, library
415-383-8447 Spanish nature walk to ocean
Karla Andersdatter herb garden, butterflies
All year

Secluded retreat for special occasions. Within recreational area and Muir Woods. Ocean view. Walk to beach, 30 min. from San Francisco. Monarch butterflies are winter guests.

SAUSALITO ————————————————————————————————————

Casa Madrona Hotel $$$ B&B Continental breakfast
801 Bridgeway, 94965 34 rooms, 34 pb Restaurant
415-332-0502 800-288-0502 Visa, MC, AmEx ● Wine & cheese hour
John Mays C-yes/S-yes/P-no/H-ltd outdoor dining
All year German, French, Spanish spa

Casa Madrona offers the privacy and coziness of a European country inn with individually decorated rooms, spectacular views of S.F. Bay & yacht harbor.

Sausalito Hotel $$$ B&B Continental plus
16 El Portal, 94965 15 rooms, 9 pb Adjacent to ferry
415-332-4155 FAX:332-3542 Visa, MC, AmEx ● walk to shops, harbors
Liz MacDonald, Gene Hiller C-ltd/S-yes/P-ltd/H-no restaurants
All year

Intimate European-style hotel furnished in Victorian antiques. Rooms have color TVs and phones. Located in heart of Sausalito and adjacent to San Francisco ferry.

SEAL BEACH ————————————————————————————————————

Seal Beach Inn & Gardens $$$ B&B Lavish full breakfast
212–5th St., 90740 23 rooms, 23 pb Comp. wine and cheese
213-493-2416 Visa, MC, AmEx ● Fruit, tea, coffee
Marjorie Bettenhausen C-ltd/S-ltd/P-no/H-no sitting rooms, library
All year swimming pool

Charming French Mediterranean inn, antique street lights, ornate fences, brick courtyard, private pool, exquisite gardens, near Disneyland & Long Beach.

SOMERSET

Fitzpatrick Winery Lodge
7740 Fairplay Rd., 95684
209-245-3248 209-245-6838
Brian & Diana Fitzpatrick
All year

$$ B&B
4 rooms, 4 pb
Visa, MC
C-yes/S-no/P-no/H-ltd

Full breakfast
Plowman's lunch
Comp. wine, bar service
sitting room, hot tub
therapeutic massage

Handmade log lodge atop a hill at 2500-foot elevation with spectacular views overlooking El Dorado's wine country. Country charm and Irish hospitality.

SONOMA

Sonoma Chalet B&B
18935 Fifth St. W., 95476
707-938-3129 707-996-0190
Joe Leese
All year exc. Christmas

$$$ B&B
7 rooms, 4 pb
Visa, MC, AmEx •
C-ltd/S-ltd/P-ltd/H-no

Continental plus
Comp. sherry, tea/coffee
Sitting room, fireplaces
wood burning stoves
garden, spa, bicycles

Swiss-style chalet & country cottages located in the beautiful Sonoma Valley. Romantic, antique filled rooms. Wonderful country farm setting near historic plaza and wineries.

Sonoma Hotel
110 W. Spain Street, 95476
707-996-2996
Dorene & John Musilli
All year

$$ B&B
17 rooms, 5 pb
Visa, MC, AmEx •
C-yes/S-yes

Continental breakfast
Comp. wine, snacks
Restaurant, bar
lunch, dinner
garden patio

Vintage hotel nationally acclaimed; bed & breakfast ambiance, exceptional dining amidst antiques or on the garden patio.

SONOMA

Victorian Garden Inn
316 E. Napa St., 95476
707-996-5339
Donna J. Lewis
All year

$$$ B&B
4 rooms, 3 pb
Visa, MC, AmEx •
C-ltd/S-ltd/P-no/H-no
Spanish

Continental plus
Sitting room
piano
swimming pool

Secluded, large 1870 Greek revival farmhouse. Antiques, private entrances, fireplaces, Victorian rose gardens, winding paths, near plaza. Gracious hospitality.

SONOMA—GLEN ELLEN

JVB Vineyards B&B
P.O. Box 997, 95442
14335 Hwy 12
707-996-4533
Jack/Beverly Babb, M. Fleming
All year

$$$ B&B
2 rooms, 2 pb
•
C-no/S-no/P-no/H-no

Full breakfast
Comp. wine
Library
hot tub
wine country

Two private Mexican-style guest cottages near historic Sonoma. Adobe, red tile roof and floors, overlooking our vineyard. Fantastic homemade waffles.

SONORA

Barretta Gardens Inn
700 S. Barretta St., 95370
209-532-6039
Bob & Betty Martin
All year

$$$ B&B
5 rooms, 5 pb
Visa, MC, AmEx
C-yes/S-ltd/P-no/H-no

Full breakfast
Comp. beverages
Sitting rooms, library
fireplace, solarium
porches, parking lot

Our turn-of-the-century Victorian overlooks Sonora and Sierra Foothills. Admire glowing sunsets. Antique furnishings, terraced gardens, whirlpool bath for two. Near Yosemite.

SONORA ───

Lavender Hill B&B
683 S. Barretta St., 95370
209-532-9024
Alice J. Byrnes
All year

$$ B&B
4 rooms, 2 pb
C-no/S-ltd/P-no/H-no

Full breakfast
Comp. coffee or tea
Sitting room
porch swing

Restored Victorian in historic Gold Country. Antique furnishings, lovely grounds, porch swing and unmatched hospitality. Walk to town. Near Yosemite.

Lulu Belle's B&B
85 Gold St., 95370
209-533-3455
Janet & Chris Miller
All year

$$$ B&B
5 rooms, 5 pb
Visa, MC, AmEx, Dis ●
C-yes/S-ltd/P-no/H-ltd
German, Spanish

Full breakfast
Comp. beverages, snacks
Library, music room, A/C
hot tub, bicycles
phone and TV available

Historic 106-year-old Victorian with beautiful gardens and Lulu Belle's famous hospitality. Enjoy nearby theater, antiquing, boating, horseback riding and Gold Rush towns.

Oak Hill Ranch B&B
P.O. Box 307, Tuolumne, 95379
18550 Connally Lane
209-928-4717
Sanford & Jane Grover
All year

$$ B&B
5 rooms, 3 pb
C-ltd/S-no/P-no/H-yes

Full gourmet breakfast
Comp. tea, coffee
Bicycles, gazebo
player piano, organ
sitting room, fireplaces

"For a perfect sojourn into the past," spacious rural Victorian on 56 acres, near three state parks and Yosemite. 3000 ft. elevation in California Gold Country.

The Ryan House
153 S. Shepherd St., 95370
209-533-3445
Nancy & Guy Hoffman
All year

$$$ B&B
3 rooms, 3 pb
Visa, MC ●
C-yes/S-no/P-no/H-no

Full breakfast
Aftn. tea, comp. wine
Sitting room
queen-sized beds
2 parlors

Gold Rush romance in historic Mother Lode, close to fine dining and antique shops—we make you kindly welcome!!!

Serenity
15305 Bear Club Dr., 95370
209-533-1441 800-426-1441
Fred & Charlotte Hoover
All year

$$$ B&B
4 rooms, 4 pb
Visa, MC, AmEx, Disc ●
C-no/S-ltd/P-no/H-no

Full breakfast
Comp. tea/wine/lemonade
Sitting room, library
queen/twin beds, veranda
beautiful grounds

Enjoy relaxed elegance in 19th-century-styled home. Large rooms, library, veranda, and 6 acres of wooded grounds with pines, wildflowers and wildlife add to the ambiance.

Via Serena Ranch
18007 Via Serena Dr., 95370
209-532-5307
Beverly Ballash
All year

$$ B&B
3 rooms
C-15+/S-no/P-no/H-no

Full breakfast
Sitting room
Large deck
electric blankets
air conditioning

In the heart of the Mother Lode country, a tourist bonanza; situated among tall pines and oaks. 3 miles from Sonora yet far from the city lights. A western welcome awaits all.

SOQUEL

Blue Spruce B&B Inn
2815 Main St., 95073
408-464-1137
Pat & Tom O'Brien
All year

$$$ B&B
5 rooms, 5 pb
Visa, MC, AmEx •
C-12+/S-no/P-no
Spanish

Full breakfast
Comp. wine, snacks
Sitting room
in-room spas and
gas fireplaces

Offering the flavor of yesterday with the luxury of today—walk to gourmet dining, quality antiques, local wineries. Explore the Monterey Bay from nearby Santa Cruz to Carmel

STINSON BEACH

Casa Del Mar
P.O. Box 238, 94970
37 Belvedere Ave.
415-868-2124
Rick Klein
All year

$$$ B&B
5 rooms, 5 pb
Visa, MC, AmEx •
C-yes/S-no/P-no/H-no

Full breakfast
Comp. wine, juice,
Hors d'oeuvres
sitting room, library
garden, near ocean

Romantic ocean views; historic garden; delicious breakfasts; colorful artwork; and you can hear the waves break all day long.

SUTTER CREEK

Gold Quartz Inn
15 Bryson Dr., 95685
209-267-9155 800-752-8738
Wendy Woolrich
All year

$$$ B&B
24 rooms, 24 pb
Visa, MC •
S-no/P-no/H-yes

Full breakfast
Afternoon tea, beverages
Food catered for groups
porch, picnics, A/C
TV in rm, conference rm.

Tucked away in charming Gold Country town. Step back 100 years. Rooms are decorated with antique furniture, prints and charming small touches, and have private porches.

TAHOE CITY

Chaney House
P.O. Box 7852, 96145
4725 W. Lake Blvd.
916-525-7333
Gary & Lori Chaney
All year

$$$ B&B
4 rooms, 2 pb
•
C-yes/S-no/P-no/H-no

Full breakfast
Sitting room, bicycles
private beach and pier

Unique stone lakefront home. Gourmet breakfast on patios overlooking the lake in season. Private beach and pier. Close to ski areas.

Cottage Inn at Lake Tahoe
P.O. Box 66, 95730
1690 W. Lake Blvd.
916-581-4073
P.& C. Brubaker, J.& S. Kreft
All year

$$$ B&B
15 rooms, 15 pb
Visa, MC, DC, JVC •
C-yes/S-no/P-no/H-yes

Full breakfast
Aftn. tea, comp. wine
Sitting room
sauna, fireplaces
access to private beach

Romantic lakeside cottages in Old Tahoe Pinegrove. Scandinavian decor, fluffy comforters, soft towels and knotty pine interiors. Enjoy cider by the big rock fireplace.

Mayfield House B&B
P.O. Box 5999, 95730
236 Grove St.
916-583-1001
Cynthia & Bruce Knauss
All year

$$ B&B
6 rooms
Visa, MC •
C-10+/S-ltd/P-no/H-yes

Full breakfast
Comp. wine, brandy
cheese & crackers

Within walking distance to shops and restaurants—each room individually decorated—"spit-spat" clean—convenient shuttle to skiing.

TAHOMA

The Captain's Alpenhaus
P.O. Box 262, 96142
6941 W. Lake Blvd.
916-525-5000
Joel Butler & Phyllis Butler
All year

$ B&B
14 rooms, 12 pb
Visa, MC, AmEx •
C-yes/S-yes/P-ltd
Spanish

Full breakfast
Restaurant, bar
Sitting room, pool
hot tubs, Ping-Pong
volleyball, horseshoes

Our European-style country inn, gourmet quality restaurant with an "Alpine" bar, fireplace. Across the street from Lake Tahoe and only minutes from Sierra ski resorts.

TEMPLETON

Country House Inn
91 Main St., 93465
805-434-1598
Dianne Garth
All year

$$ B&B
5 rooms, 1 pb
•
C-12+/S-no/P-no/H-no

Full breakfast
Comp. refreshments
Picnic lunches w/notice
dining & sitting room
player piano

Home built in 1886 by founder of Templeton. 6 spacious bedrooms with antiques, fresh flowers, beautiful gardens. Near 6 wineries, Hearst Castle.

TWAIN HARTE

Twain Harte's B&B
P.O. Box 1718, 95383
18864 Manzanita Dr.
209-586-3311
Gene & Barbara Morales
All year

$$ B&B
6 rooms, 2 pb
Visa, MC
C-yes/S-yes/P-no/H-yes

Full breakfast
Comp. refreshments
Sitting room, piano

Quaint mountain hideaway in wooded setting. Close to winter and summer recreation. Antique furnished and near fine dining. Family suite available.

UKIAH

Vichy Springs Resort
2605 Vichy Springs Rd., 95482
707-462-9515
Gilbert & Marjorie Ashoff
All year

$$$ B&B
14 rooms, 14 pb
Visa, MC, AmEx, DC, CB •
C-yes/S-no/P-no/H-yes
Spanish

Continental plus
Restaurant, lunch/dinner
Sitting room, library
mineral baths, pool
sauna, 700-acre ranch

Vichy Springs is a true historic country inn—quiet, elegant, and charming. The baths are incomparable memories for a lifetime.

VALLEY FORD

Inn at Valley Ford
P.O. Box 439, 94972
14395 Hwy 1
707-876-3182
N. Balashov, S. Nicholls
All year

$$ B&B
4 rooms
Visa, MC •
C-no/S-ltd/P-no/H-ltd
French

Continental plus
Comp. tea
Hot tub
bicycles
sitting room

Comfortable Victorian farmhouse furnished with antiques, books and flowers. Located in rolling, pastoral hills, minutes from the Pacific and Sonoma Wine Country.

VENTURA

"La Mer"
411 Poli St., 93001
805-643-3600
Gisela Flender Baida
All year

$$$ B&B
5 rooms, 5 pb
Visa, MC •
C-14+/S-no/P-no/H-no
German, Spanish

Bavarian full breakfast
Comp. wine or champagne
Picnic baskets, library
therapeutic massages
antique carriage rides

Authentic European style in old Victorian. Ocean view. Three blocks to beach. Private entrances and private baths. Complimentary wine.

VENTURA

Bella Maggiore Inn
67 S. California St., 93001
805-652-0277 800-523-8479
Thomas Wood
All year

$$ B&B
32 rooms, 32 pb
AmEx, Visa, MC •
C-13+/S-yes/P-no/H-no

Full breakfast
Comp. wine, snacks
Sitting room, piano
spas in some rooms
garden courtyard

Walk to beach from historic landmark inn. Enjoy European elegance—garden courtyard, chandeliers, antiques, original artwork, grand piano in lobby.

VOLCANO

St. George Hotel
P.O. Box 9, 95689
16104 Pine Grove-Volcano
209-296-4458
Charles & Marlene Inman
Wed-Sun, mid-Feb–Dec

$$ EP/$$$ MAP
20 rooms, 6 pb
C-ltd/S-no/P-ltd/H-ltd

Full breakfast
Dinner included, bar
Sitting room
pianos
meeting facilities

Elegant Mother Lode hotel built in 1862. Maintains a timeless quality. Quiet, uncommercialized town.

WALNUT CREEK

The Mansion at Lakewood
1056 Hacienda Dr., 94598
510-945-3600
Mike & Sharyn McCoy
All year

$$$ B&B
7 rooms, 7 pb
Visa, MC, AmEx •
C-12+/S-no/P-no/H-no

Continental plus
Afternoon tea, snacks
Sitting room, library
suite with fireplace &
jacuzzi

19th-century country retreat for the 20th-century urban traveler. Elegantly restored 1861 estate with 3 acres of gardens. 7 extraordinary rooms. Hospitality unsurpassed!

WEST COVINA

Hendrick Inn
2124 E. Merced Ave., 91791
818-919-2125
Mary & George Hendrick
All year

$ B&B
4 rooms, 1 pb
C-5+/S-yes/P-no/H-no
Spanish spoken

Full breakfast
Dinner with notice
Extra meals optional
deck area, jacuzzi, pool
library, bicycles

Featured in Life magazine and NY Times Travel. Beautifully decorated ranch home features a jacuzzi, swimming pool, large porch and deck. Close to popular attractions.

WESTPORT

DeHaven Valley Farm
39247 N. Hwy 1, 95488
707-961-1660
J. & K. Tobin, Diane Markley
All year

$$$ B&B
8 rooms, 6 pb
Visa, MC •
C-yes/S-no/P-no

Full breakfast
Restaurant, lunch
4-course dinner Wed-Sat
sherry/tea, sitting room
library, hot tubs

1885 farmhouse and cottages on 20 acres of hills, meadows and streams, next to Pacific Ocean. Horses, donkeys, sheep and more. Explore Mendocino, tide pools, redwood forests.

Howard Creek Ranch
P.O. Box 121, 95488
40501 N. Hwy 1
707-964-6725
Charles/Sally Lasselle Grigg
All year

$$ B&B
8 rooms, 5 pb
C-ltd/S-ltd/P-ltd/H-ltd
German, Italian, Dutch

Full ranch breakfast
Comp. tea, sitting room
Piano, pool, hot tub
sauna, massage by resv.
horses, a working ranch

Historic farmhouse filled with collectibles, antiques & memorabilia, unique health spa with privacy and dramatic views adjoining a wide beach. Award-winning flower garden.

Howard Creek Ranch, Westport, CA

WHITTIER

Coleen's California Casa
P.O. Box 9302, 90608
11715 S. Circle Dr.
310-699-8427
Coleen Davis
All year

$$ B&B
3 rooms, 3 pb
●
C-yes/S-yes/P-ltd/H-yes
some Spanish

Full gourmet breakfast
Lunch & dinner on requ.
Comp. wine, tea, snacks
sitting room, patio
jacuzzi in suite

Beautifully decorated hillside home with sweeping view and lush landscaping. Wine & cheese await your return from sightseeing. Just 5 minutes from the 605 freeway.

WILLIAMS

Wilbur Hot Springs
Star Route, 95987
916-473-2306
Richard & Ezzie Davis
All year

$$ EP
15 rooms, 2 pb
Visa, MC
C-ltd/S-ltd/P-no/H-ltd

Kitchen privileges
Sitting room, piano
swimming pool, hot tub
entertainment

A peaceful rural retreat; no traffic, clean air, incredibly starry nights; naturally hot mineral baths; large country kitchen; turn-of-the-century hotel.

WINDSOR

Country Meadow Inn
11360 Old Redwood Hwy, 95492
707-431-1276
Barry & Sandy Benson-Weber
All year

$$$ B&B
5 rooms, 5 pb
Visa, MC ●
C-yes/S-ltd/P-no/H-yes

Full breakfast
Refreshments, wet bar
Sitting room, library
games, hot tubs in room
pool, Victorian garden

Informal country setting. Romantic and comfortable. Fireplaces, whirlpool tubs, decks, flower gardens, swimming and a freshness that extends to the abundant gourmet breakfast.

YOUNTVILLE ————————————————————————————————

Burgundy House Country Inn	$$$ B&B	Full breakfast
P.O. Box 3156, 94599	5 rooms, 5 pb	Comp. wine
6711 Washington St.	●	Air conditioned
707-944-0889	C-no/S-no/P-no/H-no	Mobil 4-star rated
Dieter & Ruth Back	French, German	
All year		

1870 rustic country French stone house with Old World appeal. Furnished with country antiques. Perfect location in beautiful Napa Valley.

Oleander House	$$$ B&B	Full breakfast
P.O. Box 2937, 94599	4 rooms, 4 pb	Comp. soft drinks
7433 St. Helena Hwy	credit cards accepted ●	Sitting room, spa, patio
707-944-8315	C-no/S-no/P-no/H-no	near ballooning, tennis,
John & Louise Packard	Spanish	golf, dining, shops
All year		

Country French charm. Antiques. Spacious rooms with brass beds, private decks, fireplaces, central A/C, and Laura Ashley fabrics and wallpapers. Beautiful rose garden.

YUBA CITY ————————————————————————————————

Harkey House B&B	$$ B&B	Continental plus
212 C Street, 95991	3 rooms, 1 pb	Dinner, tea, wine
916-674-1942	●	Sitting room, piano
Bob Jones, Lee Limonoff-Jones	C-yes/S-ltd/P-ltd/H-no	fireplaces, spa, hot tub
All year		basketball, bicycles

1864 dwelling of former sheriff. Patio, pool, spa and garden for your relaxation.

More Inns . . .

7th Street Inn 525 Seventh St., Petaluma, 94952 707-769-0480
Adelaide Inn 5 Adelaide Place, San Francisco, 94102 415-441-2261
Alder House 105 Vision Rd., Box 6, Inverness, 94937 415-669-7218
Alta Mira Continental Htl P.O. Box 706, Sausalito, 94966 415-332-1350
Altamira Ranch Box 875, 6878 Hwy 82, Basalt, 81621 303-927-3309
American Family Inn P.O. Box 349, San Francisco, 94101 415-931-3083
Anaheim B&B 1327 S. Hickory, Anaheim, 92805 714-533-1884
Anderson Creek Inn P.O. Box 217, Boonville, 95415 707-895-3091
Andrews Hotel 624 Post St., San Francisco, 94109 415-563-6877
Ann Marie's Lodging 410 Stasel St., Jackson, 95642 209-223-1452
Annie Horan's B&B 415 W. Main St., Grass Valley, 95945 916-272-2418
Ansonia B&B Inn 711 Post St., San Francisco, 94109 415-673-2670
Appleton Place B&B Inn 935 Cedar Ave., Long Beach, 90813 213-432-2312
Arbor Guest House 1436 G St., Napa, 94559 707-252-8144
Ark, The P.O. Box 273, Inverness, 94937 415-663-9338
Au Relais Inn 681 Broadway, Sonoma, 95476 707-996-1031
Auberge du Soleil 180 Rutherford Hill Rd., Rutherford, 94573 707-963-1211
Aurora Manor 1328 16th Ave., San Francisco, 94122 415-564-2480
Austin Street Cottage 739 Austin St., Sonoma, 95476 707-938-8434
B&B Accomm. in Berkeley 2235 Carleton St., Berkeley, 94704 415-548-7556
B&B San Juan P.O. Box 613, San Juan Bautista, 95045 408-623-4101
B.G. Ranch & Inn 9601 N. Hwy 1, Mendocino, 95460 707-937-5322
Baker Inn 1093 Poli St., Ventura, 93001 805-652-0143
Bale Mill Inn 3431 N St. Helena Hwy., Saint Helena, 94574 707-963-4545
Ballard Inn 2436 Baseline, Ballard, 93463 805-688-7770
Bartels Ranch/Country Inn 1200 Conn Valley Rd., Saint Helena, 94574 707-963-4001
Bayside Boat & Breakfast 49 Jack London Square, Oakland, 94607 415-444-5858

Bayview House 1070 Santa Lucia Ave., Baywood Park, 93402 805-528-3098
Bear River Mt. Farm 21725 Placer Hills Rd., Colfax, 95713 916-878-8314
Bear Valley Inn P.O. Box 33, Olema, 94950 415-663-1777
Bed & Breakfast Inn 4 Charlton Court, San Francisco, 94123 415-921-9784
Bedside Manor P.O. Box 93, Oakland, 94604 415-452-4550
Bell Creek B&B 3220 Silverado Tr., Saint Helena, 94574 707-963-2383
Bell Glen Eel River Inn 70400 Highway 101, Leggett, 95455 707-925-6425
Belle de Jour Inn 16276 Healdsburg Ave., Healdsburg, 95448 707-433-7892
Belvedere Inn 727 Mendocino Ave., Santa Rosa, 95401 707-575-1857
Best House B&B 1315 Clarke St., San Leandro, 94577 415-351-0911
Big Canyon Inn P.O. Box 1311, Lower Lake, 95457 707-928-5631
Big Canyon Inn 11750 Big Canyon Rd., Middletown, 95461 707-928-5631
Big Yellow Sunflower B&B 235 Sky Oaks, Angwin, 94508 707-965-3885
Black Surrey Inn 1815 Silverado Tr., Napa, 94558 707-255-1197
Blackberry Inn 44951 Larkin Rd., Mendocino, 95460 707-937-5281
Blue Heron Inn B&B 390 Kasten St, Box 1142, Mendocino, 95460 707-937-4323
Blue Lantern Inn 34343 St. of Blue Lant., Dana Point, 92629 714-661-1304
Blue Rose Inn 520 N. Main St., Fort Bragg, 95437 707-964-3477
Blueroses P.O. Box 338, Manchester, 95459 707-882-2240
Bock's B&B 1448 Willard St., San Francisco, 94117 415-664-6842
Bolinas Villa 23 Brighton Ave., Bolinas, 94924 415-868-1650
Boonville Hotel Hwy 128, P.O. Box 326, Boonville, 95415 707-895-2210
Boulder Creek B&B 4572 Ben Hur Rd., Maiposa, 95338 209-742-7729
Bowen's Pelican Lodge P.O. Box 35, Westport, 95488 707-964-5588
Brandy Wine Inn 1623 Lincoln Ave., Calistoga, 94515 707-942-0202
Brannan Cottage Inn 109 Wapoo Ave., Calistoga, 94515 707-942-4200
Briar Rose B&B Inn 897 E. Jackson St., San Jose, 95112 408-279-5999
Bridgeport Hotel Main St., Bridgeport, 93517 619-932-7380
Briggs House 2209 Capitol Ave., Sacramento, 95816 916-441-3214
Brinkerhoff B&B Inn 523 Brinkerhoff Ave., Santa Barbara, 93101 805-963-7844
Brookhill Box 1019, 17655 Hwy 17S, Cobb, 95426 707-928-5029
Brookside Vineyard B&B 3194 Redwood Rd., Napa, 94558 707-944-1661
Bullard House B&B Inn 256 E. 1st Ave., Chico, 95926 916-342-5912
Burbank/Belair 941 N. Frederic, Burbank, 91505 818-848-9227
Burley B&B 6500 San Miguel Rd., San Diego, 92002 619-479-9839
Burlingame B&B 1021 Balboa Ave., Burlingame, 94010 415-344-5815
Butterfield B&B P.O. Box 1115, Julian, 92036 619-765-2179
Calderwood 25 W. Grant St., Healdsburg, 95448 707-431-1110
Calistoga Inn 1250 Lincoln Av., Calistoga, 94515 707-942-4101
Calistoga Silver Rose Inn P.O. Box 1376, Healdsburg, 95448 707-942-9581
Camelot Resort P.O. Box 467 4th & Mill, Guerneville, 95446 707-869-2538
Camino Hotel P.O. Box 1197, Camino, 95709 916-644-7740
Candlelight Inn 1045 Easum Dr., Napa, 94558 707-257-3717
Carolyn's B&B Homes P.O. Box 943, Coronado, 92118 207-548-2289
Carriage House B&B 325 Mesa Road, Point Reyes Station, 94956 415-663-8627
Carriage House Inn P.O. Box 1900, Carmel, 93921 408-625-2585
Carter Hotel 301 L St, Eureka, 95501 415-444-8062
Casa Tropicana 610 Avenida Victoria, San Clemente, 92672 714-492-1234
Cavanagh Cottage B&B 10 Keller St, Petaluma, 94952 707-765-4657
Cedar Creek Inn P.O. Box 1466, Alpine, 92001 619-445-9605
Chalet Bernensis 225 St. Helena Hwy, Saint Helena, 94574 707-963-4423
Chalet de France SR Box 20A, Kneeland PO, Eureka, 95549 707-443-6512
Chalet on the Mount 4960 Usona Rd., Mariposa, 95338 209-966-5115
Chalfant House 213 Academy St., Bishop, 93514 619-872-1790
Charlaine's Bay View B&B 44 Sierra Vista Dr., Monterey, 93940 408-655-0177
Chateau, The 4195 Solano Ave., Napa, 94558 707-253-9300
Chestelson House 1417 Kearney St., Saint Helena, 94574 707-963-2238
Chihuahua Valley Inn P.O. 99, Warner Springs, 92086 714-7669779
Chihuahua Valley Inn 30247 Chihuahua Valley, Aquanga, 92302 714-766-9779

Christiana Inn Box 18298, South Lake Tahoe, 95706 916-544-7337
Christmas House B&B Inn 9240 Archibald Ave., Rancho Cucamonga, 91730 714-980-6450
Christy Hill Inn Box 2449, Olympic Valley, 95730 916-583-8551
Circle Bar B Guest Ranch 1800 Refugio Rd., Galeta, 93117 805-968-1113
Clementina's Bay Brick 1190 Folsom St., San Francisco, 94103 415-431-8334
Cleone Lodge 24600 N Hwy. #1, Fort Bragg, 95437 707-964-2788
Clocktower Inn, The 181 E. Santa Clara St., Ventura, 93001 805-652-0141
Colfax's Guest House Redwood Ridge Rd., Boonville, 95415 707-895-3241
Colonial Inn P.O. Box 565, Fort Bragg, 95437 707-964-9979
Colonial Terrace Inn P.O. Box 1375, Carmel, 93921 408-624-2741
Comfort B&B 1265 Guerrero St., San Francisco, 94110 415-641-8803
Commodore International 825 Sutter St. at Jones, San Francisco, 94109 415-885-2464
Consciousness Village Box 234, Sierraville, 96126 916-994-8984
Coombs Residence Inn 720 Seminary St., Napa, 94559 707-257-0789
Cooper's Grove Ranch 5763 Sonoma Mountain Rd, Santa Rosa, 95404 707-571-1928
Cora Harschel 8 Mariposa Ct., Burlingame, 94010 415-697-5560
Coronado Victorian House 1000 Eighth St., Coronado, 92118 619-435-2200
Cort Cottage P.O. Box 245, Three Rivers, 93271 209-561-4671
Country Bay Inn 34862 S. Coast Hwy, Capistrano Beach, 92624 714-496-6656
Country Cottage 291 1st St. East, Sonoma, 95476 707-938-2479
Country Cottage 2920 Grand Ave., Box 26, Los Olivos, 93441 805-688-1395
Country Inn 632 N. Main St., Fort Bragg, 95437 707-964-3737
Court Street Inn 215 Court St., Jackson, 95642 209-223-0416
Courtside 14675 Winchester Blvd., Los Gatos, 95030 408-395-7111
Courtyard B&B 334 W. St. Charles, San Andreas, 95249 209-754-1518
Cowper Inn 705 Cowper St., Palo Alto, 94301 415-327-4475
Crane's Nest 319 W. 12th St., Long Beach, 90813 213-435-4084
Creekside Inn & Resort P.O. Box 2185, Guerneville, 95446 707-869-3623
Creekwood 850 Conn Valley Rd., Saint Helena, 94574 707-963-3590
Crocker Country Inn 26532 River Rd., Cloverdale, 95425 707-894-3911
Crown B&B Inn 530 S. Marengo, Pasadena, 91101 818-792-4031
Crystal Rose Victorian Inn 7564 St. Helena Hwy, Napa, 94558 707-944-8185
Cypress House P.O. Box 303, Mendocino, 95460 707-937-1456
Danish Country Inn 1455 Mission Drive, Solvang, 93463 000-688-2018
Darken Downs Equestre-Inn Star Route Box 4562, San Miguel, 93451 805-467-3589
Delphinus B&B Berkeley Marina, Berkeley, 94530 415-527-9622
Dick & Shirl's B&B 4870 Triangle Rd., Mariposa, 95338 209-966-2514
Doll House B&B 118 School St., Willits, 95490 707-459-4055
Dolores Park Inn 3641—17th St., San Francisco, 94114 415-621-0482
Dolphin's Home P.O. Box 3724, Olympic Valley, 95730 916-581-0501
Domike's Inn 220 Colfax Ave., Grass Valley, 95945 916-273-9010
Donnymac Irish Inn 119 N. Meridith, Pasadena, 91106 818-440-0066
Dorris House B&B P.O. Box 1655, Alturas, 96101 916-233-3786
Down Under Inn 157 15th St., Pacific Grove, 93950 408-373-2993
Drakesbad Guest Ranch Warner Valley Rd., Chester, 96020 (916) Drakes
Driver Mansion Inn 2019 21st Street, Sacramento, 95818 916-455-5243
Dry Creek Inn 13740 Dry Creek Rd., Auburn, 95603 916-878-0885
Eagle House Victorian Inn 139 2nd St., Eureka, 95501 707-442-2334
Eagle's Nest B&B 41675 Big Bear Blvd., Big Bear Lake, 92315 714-866-6465
East Brother Light Station 117 Park Place, Point Richmond, 94801 415-233-2385
Eden Valley Place 22490 Mt. Eden Rd., Saratoga, 95070 408-867-1785
Edgemont Inn 1955 Edgemont St., San Diego, 92102 619-238-1677
El Dorado Inn 405 First St. W., Sonoma, 95476 707-996-3030
Elm House 800 California, Napa, 94559 707-255-1831
Elms 1300 Cedar St., Calistoga, 94515 707-942-9476
Emperor Norton Inn 615 Post St., San Francisco, 94109 415-775-2567
Estate Inn 13555 Highway 116, Guerneville, 95446 707-869-9093
Fairview Manor P.O. Box 74, Ben Lomond, 95005 408-336-3355
Farallone Hotel 1410 Main, Montara, 94037 415-728-7817

Farmhouse 300 Turpin Rd., Saint Helena, 94574 707-944-8430
Farmhouse Inn 7871 River Rd., Forest Ville, 95436 707-887-3300
Fay Mansion Inn 834 Grove St., San Francisco, 94117 415-921-1816
Fern Grove Inn 16650 River Rd., Guerneville, 95446 707-869-9083
Ferndale Inn P.O. Box 887, Ferndale, 95536 707-786-4307
Ferrando's Hideaway P.O. Box 688, Point Reyes, 94956 415-663-1966
Figs Cottage 3935 Rhodes Ave., Studio City, 91604 818-769-2662
Fleming Jones Homestead 3170 Newtown Rd., Placerville, 95667 916-626-5840
Flume's End B&B 317 S. Pine St., Nevada City, 95959 916-265-9665
Fools Rush Inn 7533 N. Highway 1, Little River, 95456 707-937-5339
Foothill House 3037 Foothill Blvd, Calistoga, 94515 707-942-6933
Forest Lodge Ocean Ave. and Torres, Carmel-By-The-Sea, 95903 408-624-7023
Forster Mansion Inn 27182 Ortega Hwy., San Juan Capistrano, 92675 714-240-7414
Foxes in Sutter Creek Box 159, 77 Main St., Sutter Creek, 95685 209-267-5882
Freitas House Inn 744 Jackson St., Fairfield, 94533 707-425-1366
French Hotel 1538 Shattuck Ave., Berkeley, 94709 415-548-9930
Furtado's Hideaway P.O. Box 650, Boonville, 94515 707-895-3898
Gables B&B Inn 4257 Petaluma Hill Rd., Santa Rosa, 95404 707-585-7777
Gaige House 13540 Arnold Dr., Glen Ellen, 95442 707-935-0237
Gasthaus zum Baren 2113 Blackstone Dr., Walnut Creek, 94598 415-934-8119
Gate House Inn 1330 Jackson Gate Rd., Jackson, 95642 209-223-3500
Geralda's B&B 1056 Bay Oaks Dr., Los Osos, 93402 805-528-3973
Gerda W. Ray 1130 Shotwell St., San Francisco, 94110 415-821-3025
Glass Beach B&B Inn 726 N. Main St., Fort Bragg, 95437 707-964-6774
Glenborough Inn B&B 1327 Bath St., Santa Barbara, 93101 805-966-0589
Glendeven 8221 N. Hwy 1, Little River, 95456 707-937-0083
Glenelly Inn 5131 Warm Springs Rd., Glen Ellen, 95442 707-996-6720
Golden Haven Hot Springs 1713 Lake St., Calistoga, 94515 707-942-6793
Golden Ore House B&B 448 S. Auburn St., Grass Valley, 95945 916-272-6870
Goodman House 1225 Division St., Napa, 94559 707-257-1166
Graeagle Lodge P.O. Box 38, Blairsden, 96103 916-836-2511
Grand Cottages 809 S. Grand Ave., San Pedro, 90731 213-548-1240
Granny's Garden B&B 7333 Hwy. 49 N., Mariposa, 95338 209-377-8342
Granny's House P.O. Box 31, Weaverville, 96093 916-623-2756
Gray Whale Upstairs 12781 Sir Francis Drake, Inverness, 94937 415-669-1330
Green Dolphin Inn P.O. Box 132, Elk, 95432 707-877-3342
Green Lantern Inn P.O. Box 2619, Carmel, 93921 408-624-4392
Greenwood Lodge P.O. Box 172, Elk, 95432 707-877-3422
Greenwood Pier Inn P.O. Box 36, Elk, 95432 707-877-9997
Guest House 120 Hart Lane, Arroyo Grande, 93420 805-481-9304
Gunn House 286 S. Washington, Sonora, 95370 209-532-3421
Halbig's Hacienda 432 S. Citrus Ave., Escondido, 92927 619-745-1296
Hanford House P.O. Box 1450, Sutter Creek, 95685 209-267-0747
Happy Medium P.O. Box 10, Midpine, Midpine, 95345 209-742-6366
Harbin Hot Springs P.O. Box 782, Middletown, 95461 707-987-2477
Hartley House Inn 700—22nd St., Sacramento, 95816 916-447-7829
Helen K Inn 2105—19th St., Bakersfield, 93301 805-325-5451
Heritage House Little River, 95456 707-937-5885
Heritage Inn 978 Olive St., San Luis Obispo, 93401 805-544-2878
Heuer's Victorian Inn 1302 "E" St., Eureka, 95501 707-445-7334
Hidden Oak 214 E. Napa St., Sonoma, 95476 707-996-9863
Hidden Valley B&B 9582 Halekulani Dr., Garden Grove, 92641 714-636-8312
Hideaway Cottages 1412 Fairway, Calistoga, 94515 707-942-4108
Highland Dell Inn 21050 River Blvd, Monte Rio, 95462 800-767-1759
Hill House B&B 2504 A. St., San Diego, 92102 619-239-4783
Hill House Inn P.O. Box 625, Mendocino, 95410 707-937-0554
Hilltop at Truckee Box 8579, Hwy. 267, Truckee, 95737 916-587-2545
Holbrooke Hotl/Purcell Hse 212 W. Main St., Grass Valley, 95945 916-273-1353
Homestead Guest Ranch B&B P.O. Box 13, Midpines, 95345 209-966-2820

Hopland House B&B Inn P.O. Box 310, Hopland, 95449 707-744-1404
Horseshoe Farm Cottage P.O. Box 332, Point Reyes Station, 94956 415-663-9401
Hotel California 1316 S. Coast Hwy, Laguna Beach, 92651 714-497-1457
Hotel Charlotte Route 120, Groveland, 95321 209-962-6455
Hotel Leger P.O. Box 50, Mokelumne Hill, 95245 209-286-1401
Hotel Louise 845 Bush St., San Francisco, 94108 415-775-1755
Hotel San Maarten 696 S. Coast Hwy, Laguna Beach, 92651 714-494-9436
Hotel St. Helena 1309 Main St., Saint Helena, 94574 707-963-4388
Hotel Villa Portofino P.O. Box 127, Avalon, 90704 213-510-0555
House of a 1000 Flowers P.O. Box 369, Monte Rio, 95421 707-632-5571
Huckleberry Springs Inn P.O. Box 400, Monte Rio, 95462 707-865-2683
Hudson 1740 N. Hudson Ave., Hollywood, 90028 213-469-5320
Imperial Hotel P.O. Box 195, Amador City, 95601 209-267-9172
Ingleside Inn 200 W. Ramon Rd., Palm Springs, 92262 619-325-0046
Inn at Mt. Ada P.O. Box 2560, Avalon, 90704 213-510-2030
Inn at Saratoga 20645 Fourth St., Saratoga, 95070 617-232-8144
Inn at Two Twenty Two 222 W. Valerio, Santa Barbara, 93101 805-687-7216
Inn at the Opera 333 Fulton St., San Francisco, 94102 415-836-8400
Inn on Summer Hill 2520 Lillie Ave., Santa Barbara, 93067 805-969-9998
Inverness Valley Inn 13275 Sir Francis Drake, Inverness, 94937 415-669-7250
Iris Inn 1134 "H" St., Eureka, 95501 707-445-0307
Irish Cottage 5623 Taft Ave., La Jolla, 92037 619-454-6075
Irwin Street Inn 522 N. Irwin, Hanford, 93230 209-584-9286
Isis Oasis Lodge 20889 Geyserville Ave., Geyserville, 95441 707-857-3524
James Blair House 2985 Clay St., Placerville, 95667 916-626-6136
Jamestown Hotel P.O. Box 539, Jamestown, 95327 209-984-3902
Janet Kay's P.O. Box 3874, Big Bear Lake, 92315 800-243-7031
Jeffrey Hotel P.O. Box 4, Coulterville, 95311 209-878-3400
Jeter Victorian, The 1107 Jefferson, Red Bluff, 96080 916-527-7574
John Muir Inn, The 1998 Trower Ave, Napa, 94558 707-257-7220
Judy's Ranch House 701 Rossi Rd., Saint Helena, 94574 707-963-3081
Julian Lodge P.O. Box 1930, Julian, 92036 619-765-1420
Julian White House, The 3014 Blue Jay Dr., Julian, 92036 619-765-1764
Kate Murphy's Cottage 43 France St., Sonoma, 95476 707-996-4359
Keating House Inn 2331 Second Ave., San Diego, 92101 619-239-8585
Kenton Mine Lodge P.O. Box 942, Alleghany, 95910 916-287-3212
Kim DuBois 15 Malibu Court, Clayton, 94517 415-672-4400
Kingsburg's Swedish Inn 401 Conejo St., Kingsburg, 93631 209-897-1022
L'Auberge du Sans-Souci 25 W. Grant St., Healdsburg, 95448 707-431-1110
La Casa Inglesa B&B 18047 Lime Kiln Rd., Sonora, 95370 209-532-5822
La Chaumiere 1301 Cedar St., Calistoga, 94515 707-942-5139
La Hacienda Inn 18840 Los Gatos Road, Los Gatos, 95030 408-354-9230
La Maida House 11154 La Maida St., North Hollywood, 91601 818-769-3857
Lady Anne Victorian Inn 902–14th St., Arcata, 95521 707-822-2797
Lakeside House P.O. Box 7108, Tahoe City, 95730 916-683-8796
Lakeview Lodge P.O. Box 189, Lake Arrowhead, 92352 714-337-6633
Lamplighters 7724 E. Cecilia St., Downey, 90241 213-928-8229
Larkmead Country Inn 1103 Larkmead Ln., Calistoga, 94515 707-942-5360
Le Petit Chateau 1491 Via Soledad, Palm Springs, 92262 619-325-2686
Le Petit Manoir 468 Noe St., San Francisco, 94114 415-864-7232
Le Spa Francais 1880 Lincoln Ave., Calistoga, 94515 707-942-4636
Lemon Tree Inn 299 W. Santa Paula St., Santa Paula, 93060 805-525-7747
Lewiston B&B P.O. Box 688, Lewiston, 96052 916-778-3385
Lion's Head Guest House Box 21203, El Cajon, 92021 619-463-4271
Lodge at Manual Mill P.O. Box 998, Arnold, 95223 209-795-2622
Los Gatos Hotel 31 E. Main St., Los Gatos, 95030 408-354-4440
Los Laureles Lodge 300 Carmel Valley Rd., Carmel Valley, 93924 408-659-2233
Los Olivos Grand Hotel 2860 Grand Ave., Los Olivos, 93441 805-688-7788
Lost Whale Inn 3452 Patrick's Point Dr, Trinidad, 95570 707-677-3425

Lucia Lodge Big Sur, 93920 408-667-2391
Lyon Street B&B 120 Lyon St., San Francisco, 94117 415-552-4773
MacLean House P.O. Box 651, Inverness, 94937 415-669-7392
Magnolia Hotel P.O. Box M, Yountville, Napa, 94599 707-944-2056
Magnolia House 222 S. Buena Vista St, Redlands, 92373 414-798-6631
Maison Bleue French B&B P.O. Box 51371, Pacific Grove, 93950 408-373-2993
Majestic, The 1500 Sutter St., San Francisco, 94109 415-441-1100
Mama Moon Gardens P.O. Box 994, Mendocino, 95460 707-937-4234
Manka's Inverness Lodge P.O. Box 126, Inverness, 94937 415-669-1034
Marina Inn 3110 Octavia St., San Francisco, 94123 415-928-1000
Marlahan House 9539 North Hwy 3, Fort Jones, 96032 916-468-5527
Masonic Manor 1468 Masonic Ave., San Francisco, 94117 415-621-3365
Mavilla Inn P.O. Box 2607, Avalon, 90704 213-510-1651
Melitta Station Inn 5850 Melita Rd., Santa Rosa, 95409 707-538-7712
Mendocino Hotel P.O. Box 587, Mendocino, 95460 707-937-0511
Mendocino Tennis Club/Ldge 43250 Little Lake Rd., Mendocino, 95460 707-937-0007
Merritt House 386 Pacific St., Monterey, 93940 408-646-9686
Millefiori Inn 444 Columbus, San Francisco, 94133 415-433-9111
Mission Ranch 26270 Dolores, Carmel, 93923 408-624-6436
Monte Verde Inn P.O. Box 3373, Carmel, 93921 408-624-6046
Monterey, The 406 Alvarado St., Monterey, 93940 408-375-3184
Morey Mansion B&B Inn 190 Terracina Blvd., Redlands, 92373 714-793-7970
Mountain Home Ranch 3400 Mountain Home, Calistoga, 94515 707-942-6616
Mountain View Inn P.O. Box 2011, Truckee, 95734 916-587-5388
Mountainside 3955 Deer Lake Park Rd., Julian, 92036 619-765-1295
Mountainside B&B P.O. Box 165, Kelsey, 95643 916-626-0983
Murphy's Inn 318 Neal St., Grass Valley, 95945 916-273-6873
Murphys Hotel P.O. Box 329, 457 Main, Murphys, 95247 209-728-3444
Nancy & Bob's Inn P.O. Box 386, Sutter Creek, 95685 209-267-0342
Napa Inn 1137 Warren St., Napa, 94559 707-257-1444
Napa Valley Railway Inn 6503 Washington St., Yountville, 94559 707-944-2000
Narrow Gauge Inn 48571 Hwy. 41, Fish Camp, 93623 209-683-7720
Narrows Lodge 5670 Blue Lake Rd., Upper Lake, 95485 707-275-2718
Nethercott Inn P.O. Box 671, Middletown, 95461 707-987-3362
Norden House Box 94, Norden, 95724 916-426-3326
O'Hagin's Guest House P.O. Box 126, Sebastopol, 95472 707-823-4771
O'Neill's Private Accom. 11801 Sharon Dr., San Jose, 95129 408-996-1231
O'Rourke Mansion 1765 Lurline Rd., Colusa, 95932 916-458-5625
Oak Knoll Inn 2200 E. Oak Knoll Ave., Napa, 94558 707-255-2200
Oakbridge Manor 9525 Oakridge Place, Chatsworth, 91311 818-998-7547
Oakridge Manor B&B 9525 Oakridge Pl., Chatsworth, 91311 818-998-7547
Oceanview Lodge 1141 N. Main St., Fort Bragg, 95437 707-964-1951
Ojai B&B 921 Patricia Ct., Ojai, 93023 805-646-8337
Ojai Manor Hotel 210 E. Matilija, Ojai, 93023 805-646-0961
Olallieberry Inn 2476 Main St., Cambria, 92008 805-927-3222
Old Auburn Inn 149 Pleasant, Auburn, 95603 916-885-6407
Old Monterey Inn 500 Martin St., Monterey, 93940 408-375-8284
Old Oak Table 809 Clemensen Ave., Santa Ana, 92701 714-639-7798
Old Victorian Inn 207 W. Acacia St., Stockton, 95203 209-462-1613
Ole Rafael B&B 528 C St., San Rafael, 94901 415-453-0414
Olema Inn P.O. Box 37, Olema, 94950 415-663-9559
Olive House 1604 Olive St., Santa Barbara, 93101 805-962-4902
Oliver House Country Inn 2970 Silverado Tr., Saint Helena, 94574 707-963-4089
Olson Farmhouse B&B 3620 Road B, Redwood Valley, 95470 707-485-7523
Orca Inn 31502 N. Hwy 1, Fort Bragg, 95437 707-964-5585
Osprey Hill Box 1307, Mendocino, 95460 707-937-4493
Overview Farm B&B Inn 15650 Arnold Dr., Sonoma, 95476 707-938-8574
Pacific Bay Inn 520 Jones St., San Francisco, 94102 800-445-2631
Pacific Heights Inn 1555 Union St., San Francisco, 94123 415-776-3310

Palm B&B 10382 Willow St., Jamestown, 95327 209-984-3429
Palms of Chico 1525 Dayton Rd., Chico, 95726 916-343-6868
Panama Hotel & Restaurant 4 Bayview St., San Rafael, 94901 415-457-3993
Partridge Inn 521 First St., Davis, 95616 916-753-1211
Patrick Creek Lodge Gasquet, 95543 Dial 0 Idlew
Pelican Inn 10 Pacific Way, Muir Beach, 94965 415-383-6000
Pensione San Francisco 1668 Market St., San Francisco, 94102 415-864-1271
Piety Hill Inn 523 Sacramento St., Nevada City, 95959 916-265-2245
Pillar Point Inn 380 Capristrano Rd., Princeton By-The-Sea, 94018 415-728-7377
Pine Beach Inn P.O. Box 1173, Fort Bragg, 95437 707-964-5603
Pine Hills Lodge P.O. Box 701, Julian, 92036 619-765-1100
Pine Street Inn 1202 Pine St., Calistoga, 94515 707-942-6829
Pines Inn P.O. Box 250, Carmel-By-The-Sea, 93921 408-624-3851
Pismo Landmark B&B 701 Price St, Pismo Beach, 93449 805-773-5566
Plantation House 1690 Ferry St., Anderson, 96007 916-365-2827
Plum Tree Inn 307 Leidesdorff St., Folsom, 95630 916-351-0116
Point Arena Lighthouse Box 11, Point Arena, 95468 707-882-2777
Point Reyes Seashore Lodge 10021 Hwy 1, Olema, 94950 415-663-9000
Portofino Beach Hotel 2306 W. Oceanfront, Newport Beach, 92663 714-673-7030
Prager Winery B&B 1281 Lewelling Lane, Saint Helena, 94574 707-963-3713
Prospect Park Inn 1110 Prospect St., La Jolla, 92037 619-454-0133
Quince Street Trolley P.O. Box 7654, San Diego, 92167 619-226-8454
Quinta Quetzalcoati P.O. Box 27, Point Richmond, 94807 415-235-2050
Rachel's Inn Box 134, Mendocino, 95460 707-937-0088
Raffles Palm Springs Hotel 280 Mel Ave., Palm Springs, 92262 619-320-3949
Ranch at Somis 6441 La Cumbre Rd., Somis, 93066 805-987-8455
Rancho Caymus Inn P.O. Box 78, Rutherford, 94573 707-963-1777
Red Lion Inn 222 N. Vineyard Rd., Ontario, 91764 714-983-0909
Red Rooster Ranch P.O. Box 554, Los Olivos, 93441 805-688-8050
Restful Nest B&B 4274 Buckeye Creek Rd., Mariposa, 95338 209-742-7127
Richardson House P.O. Box 2011, Truckee, 95734 916-587-5388
Richardson's Resort P.O. Box 9028, South Lake Tahoe, 95731 916-541-1777
Riley's B&B 1322-24 6th Ave., San Francisco, 94122 415-731-0788
Rio Villa Beach Resort 20292 Hwy 116, Monte Rio, 95462 707-865-1143
River Lane Resort 16320 First St., Guerneville, 95446 707-869-2323
River Ranch P.O. Box 197, Tahoe City, 95730 916-583-4264
Robin's Nest P.O. Box 1408, San Andreas, 95249 209-754-1076
Robles del Rio Lodge 200 Punta Del Monte, Carmel Valley, 93924 408-659-3705
Rock Haus Inn 410—15th St., Del Mar, 92014 619-481-3764
Rockhaven 7774 Silverado Trail, Napa, 94558 707-944-2041
Rockridge B&B 5428 Thomas Ave., Oakland, 94618 415-655-1223
Rose Victorian Inn 789 Valley Rd., Arroyo Grande, 93420 805-481-5566
Roseholm 51 Sulphur Mt. Rd., Ventura, 93001 805-649-4014
Rosi's of Rutherford B&B P.O. Box 243, Rutherford, 94573 707-963-3135
Roundhedge Inn 159 N. Whipple St., Fort Bragg, 95437 707-964-9605
Roundstone Farm P.O. Box 217, Olema, 94950 415-663-1020
Rupley House Inn P.O. Box 1709, Placerville, 95667 916-626-0630
Saddleback Inn 300 S. State Hwy 173, Lake Arrowhead, 92352 714-336-3571
Saint Orres P.O. Box 523, Gualala, 95445 707-884-3303
Salt Point Lodge 23255 Coast Hwy 1, Jenner, 95450 707-847-3234
San Clemente Hideaway 323 Cazador Lane, San Clemente, 92672 714-498-2219
San Diego Hideaway 8844 Alpine Ave., San Diego—La Mesa, 92041 619-460-2868
San Luis Bay Inn Box 188, Avila Beach, 93424 805-595-2333
Sanford House 306 S. Pine, Ukiah, 95482 707-462-1653
Santa Maria Inn 801 S. Broadway, Santa Maria, 93454 805-928-7777
Santanella House 12130 Hwy. 116, Guerneville, 95446 707-869-9488
Schlageter House P.O. Box 1202, Mariposa, 95338 209-966-2471
Scotia Inn P.O. Box 248, Scotia, 95565 707-764-5683
Scott Valley Inn P.O. Box 261, Etna, 96027 916-467-3229

Sea Coast Hideaways 21350 N. Coast Hwy 1, Jenner, 95450 707-847-3278
Sea Gull Inn P.O. Box 317, Mendocino, 95460 707-937-5204
Sea Ranch Lodge P.O. Box 44, Sea Ranch, 95497 707-785-2371
Sea and Sand Inn 201 W. Cliff Dr., Santa Cruz, 95060 408-427-3400
Seacrest Inn P.O. Box 128, Avalon, 90704 213-510-0196
Sears House Inn Main St., P.O. Box 844, Mendocino, 95460 707-937-4076
Seventh St. Inn, The 525 Seventh St., Petaluma, 94952 707-769-0480
Shadow Mountain Ranch 2771 Frisius Rd., Julian, 92036 619-765-0323
Shenandoah Inn 17674 Village Dr., Plymouth, 95669 209-245-4491
Sherman House 2160 Green Street, San Francisco, 94123 415-563-3600
Sierra B&B Box 221, Midpines, 95345 209-966-5478
Sierra Nevada House P.O. Box 268, Coloma, 95613 916-622-5856
Sierra Shangri-La P.O. 285, Route 49, Downieville, 95936 916-289-3455
Skyview II 2156 Becky Place, San Diego, 92104 619-584-1548
Sonora Inn 160 S. Washington, Sonora, 95370 209-532-7468
Sovereign at Santa Monica 205 Washington Ave., Santa Monica, 90403 800-331-0163
Spanish Villa Inn 474 Glass Mtn. Rd., Saint Helena, 94574 707-963-7483
Spencer House 1080 Haight St., San Francisco, 94117 415-626-9205
Spray Cliff P.O. Box 403, Laguna Beach, 92677 714-499-4022
Spring Creek Inn 15201 Hwy 299 W., Box 1, Shasta, 96087 916-243-0914
Spring Oaks, B&B Inn 2465 Spring Oak Drive, Running Springs, 92382 714-867-9636
St. Francis Yacht Club P.O. Box 349, San Francisco, 94101 415-931-3083
Star Route Inn 825 Olema-Bolinas Rd., Bolinas, 94924 415-868-2502
Stevens House 917 3rd St., Eureka, 95501 707-444-8062
Stewart-Grinsell House 2963 Laguna St., San Francisco, 94123 415-346-0424
Stillwater Cove Ranch Jenner, 95450 707-847-3227
Stonetree Ranch 7910 Sonoma Mt. Rd., Glen Ellen, 95442 707-996-8173
Stoney Brook Inn P.O. Box 1860, McCloud, 96057 916-964-2300
Strawberry Creek Inn P.O. Box 1818, Idyllwild, 92349 714-659-3202
Strawberry Lodge Hwy 50, South Lake Tahoe, 95720 916-659-7200
Strout House 253 Florence Ave., Sebastopol, 95472 707-823-5188
Summer House B&B 216 Monterey Way, Capitola Valley, 95010 408-475-8474
Summerland Inn 2161 Ortega Hill Rd,B12, Summerland, 93067 805-969-5225
Sundial Lodge P.O. Box J, Carmel, 93921 408-624-8578
Sunflower House 243 Third St., Solvang, 93463 805-688-4492
Sunnyside Inn 435 E. McKinley, Sunnyvale, 94086 408-736-3794
Sunset B&B Inn P.O. Box 1202, Sunset Beach, 90742 213-592-1666
Sutter Creek Inn P.O. Box 385, Sutter Creek, 95685 209-267-5606
Suzanne Multout 449 N. Detroit St., Los Angeles, 90036 213-938-4794
Swan-Levine House 328 S. Church St., Grass Valley, 95945 916-272-1873
Switzerland Haus P.O. Box 256, Big Bear Lake, 92315 714-866-3729
Sycamore House 99 Sycamore Ave., Mill Valley, 94941 415-383-0612
Tall Timber Chalets 1012 Darms Lane, Napa, 94558 707-252-7810
Tamarack Lodge Retreat P.O. Box 69, Mammoth Lakes, 93546 619-934-2442
Tanglewood House 250 Bonnie Way, Glen Ellen, 95442 707-996-5021
Taylor's Estero Vista Inn P.O. Box 255, Bodega, 94922 707-876-3300
Ten Aker Wood P.O. Box 208, Cazadero, 95421 707-632-5328
Terrace Manor 1353 Alvarado Terrace, Los Angeles, 90006 213-381-1478
Thatcher Inn 13401 Hwy. 101, Hopland, 95449 707-744-1890
Theodore Woolsey House 1484 E. Ojai Ave., Ojai, 93023 805-646-9779
Thistle Dew Inn 171 W. Spain St., Sonoma, 95476 707-938-2909
Thomas' White House Inn 118 Kale Rd., Bolinas, 94924 415-868-0279
Thorn Mansion P.O. Box 1437, San Andreas, 95249 209-754-1027
Tiffany Inn 1323 De la Vina, Santa Barbara, 93101 805-963-2283
Timberhill Ranch Resort 35755 Hauser Bridge Rd., Cazadero, 95421 707-847-3258
Tomales Country Inn 25 Valley St., Tomales, 94971 707-878-9992
Top O'The World Lodge 4614 Cavedale Road, Glen Ellen, 95442 707-938-4671
Tree House Bed & Breakfast P.O. Box 1075, Point Reyes Station, 94956 415-663-8720
Trinidad B&B P.O. Box 849, Trinidad, 95570 707-677-0840

Trojan Horse Inn 19455 Sonoma Hwy, Sonoma, 95476 707-996-2430
Union Hotel 401 First St., Benicia, 94510 707-746-0100
Union Street Inn 2229 Union St., San Francisco, 94123 415-346-0424
Upham Hotel & Garden Cttgs 1404 De La Vina St., Santa Barbara, 93101 805-962-0058
Valley Knoll Vineyard Highway 29, Saint Helena, 94574 707-963-7770
Valley View Citrus Ranch 14801 Ave. 428, Orosi, 93647 209-528-2275
Venice Beach House, The 15 30th Ave., Venice, 90291 213-823-1966
Victorian Hotel 2520 Durant Ave., Berkeley, 94704 415-540-0700
Villa Idalene P.O. Box 90, Julian, 92036 619-765-1252
Villa St. Helena 2727 Sulphur Springs Av, Saint Helena, 94574 707-963-2514
Villa d'Italia 780 Mission Canyon Rd., Santa Barbara, 93105 805-687-6933
Village Inn P.O. Box 850, Monte Rio, 95462 707-865-2304
Vineyard House P.O. Box 176, Coloma, 95613 916-622-2217
Vineyard Inn P.O. Box 368, Sonoma, 95476 707-938-2350
Vista Grande B&B 4160 Vista Grande Way, Mariposa, 95338 209-742-6206
Volcano Inn P.O. Box 4, Volcano, 95689 209-296-4959
Washington Street Lodging 1605 Washington St., Calistoga, 94515 707-942-6968
Watermans, A B&B 12841 Dunbar Rd., Glen Ellen, 95442 707-996-8106
Webber Place 6610 Webber St., Yountville, 94599 707-944-8384
West Adams B&B Inn 1650
    Westmoreland Blvd., Los
    Angeles, 90006 213-737-5041
Westport Inn B&B Box 145,
    Westport, 95488 707-964-5135
Whale Watch Inn by the Sea
    35100 Hwy 1, Gualala, 95445
    707-884-3667
Wharf Road B&B 11 Wharf Rd.,
    Bolinas, 94924 415-868-1430
White Ranch 707 White Lane,
    Saint Helena, 94574 707-963-4635
Wick's 560 Cooper Ave., Yuba
    City, 95991 916-674-7951
Wildasinn House, The 26 Lupin
    St., Box 8026, Mammoth Lakes,
    93546 619-934-3851
Wilkum Inn P.O. Box 1115,
    Idyllwild, 92349 714-659-4087
Willow Spgs. Country Inn 20599
    Kings Ct., Soulsbyville, 95372
    209-533-2030
Willows B&B Inn 710—14th St., San
    Francisco, 94114 415-431-4770
Willows, The 15905 River Rd, Box
    465, Guerneville, 95446
    707-869-3279
Windrose Inn 1407 Jackson Gate
    Rd., Jackson, 95642 209-223-3650
Wine Country Cottage 400
    Meadowood Ln., Saint Helena,
    94574 709-963-0852
Wine Way Inn 1019 Foothill Blvd.,
    Calistoga, 94515 707-942-0680
Wool Loft 32751 Navarro Ridge Rd.,
    Albion, 95410 707-937-0377

The Nolan House, San Francisco, CA

Ye Olde South Fork Inn P.O. Box 731, North Fork, 93643 209-877-7025
Yesterhouse Inn 643 Third St., Napa, 94559 707-257-0550
Zaca Lake P.O. Box 187, Los Olivos, 93441 805-688-4891
Zane Grey Pueblo Hotel P.O. Box 216, Avalon, 90704 213-510-0966

Colorado

ALAMOSA

Cottonwood Inn B&B
123 San Juan Ave., 81101
719-589-3882
Julie/George Mordecai-Sellman
All year

$$ B&B
5 rooms, 2 pb
Visa, MC •
C-12+/S-ltd
Spanish

Full breakfast
Library
Neutrogena soaps/creams
turn-down service

Charming inn. Artwork and antiques adorn cozy guest rooms. Biking, hiking, dune walking, fishing, bird-watching, skiing. Historically furnished dining room. Gourmet breakfast.

ASPEN

Hearthstone House
134 E. Hyman St., 81611
303-925-7632
Irma Prodinger
Summer & winter

$$$ B&B
17 rooms, 17 pb
Visa, MC, AmEx •
C-5+/S-ltd/P-no/H-no
French, German

Full breakfast
Afternoon tea
Hot tub, bed turndown
service, sitting room,
fireplace, herbal bath

The preferred place to stay! Distinctive lodge with the hospitality and services in the finest tradition of European luxury inns.

Innsbruck Inn
233 W. Main St., 81611
303-925-2980
Karen & Heinz Coordes
6/1–10/15, 11/23–4/15

$$ B&B
30 rooms, 30 pb
Visa, MC, AmEx, DC, CB
•
C-yes/S-yes/P-no/H-no
German

Continental plus
Comp. wine (winter)
Afternoon tea (winter)
sitting room, library
hot tub, sauna, pool

Tyrolean charm and decor; located at ski shuttle stop, 4 blocks from malls. Sunny breakfast room, generous buffet, apres-ski refreshments, fireside lobby.

Snow Queen Victorian Lodge
124 E. Cooper St., 81612
303-925-8455 303-925-6971
Norma Dolle, Larry Leduigham
All year

$$ B&B
8 rooms, 5 pb
AmEx, Visa, MC •
C-yes/S-yes/P-no/H-no
Spanish

Continental breakfast
Weekly party
Parlor w/fireplace
TV, outdoor hot tub
walk to ski lifts

Quaint Victorian ski lodge with a friendly atmosphere. Variety of reasonably priced rooms, most with private bath. One kitchen unit. Rooms named after silver mines in town.

Ullr Lodge
520 W. Main St., 81611
303-925-7696
Anthony Percival
All year

$$ EP/B&B
25 rooms, 25 pb
Visa, MC, AmEx, DC, Ch •
C-yes/S-yes/P-no/H-no
Dutch, Flemish

Continental breakfast
Full breakfast (winter)
Hot tubs, sauna
swimming pool (summer)
sitting room

Small European-style lodge offering rooms and condominiums. Free shuttle to ski route. Walking distance to music festival and Aspen Institute.

BOULDER

Boulder Victorian Historic
1305 Pine St., 80302
303-938-1300
Jacki Myers, Kristen Peterson
All year

$$$ B&B
7 rooms, 7 pb
Visa, MC, AmEx •
C-yes/S-no/P-no/H-ltd

Continental plus
Afternoon tea, snacks
Sitting room, patio
deck, steam showers
nearby health club

Victorian grandeur in downtown Boulder. Brass beds with down comforters; fine period antiques; evening desserts & cappucino served in elegant parlor after a night on the town.

Briar Rose B&B Inn
2151 Arapahoe Ave., 80302
303-442-3007
Bob & Margaret Weisenbach
All year

$$ B&B
11 rooms, 6 pb
Visa, MC, AmEx •
C-yes/S-ltd/P-yes/H-no
Polish, Tibetan

Full breakfast
Comp. sherry, port
High tea—chamber music
poetry, drama readings
bicycles

Entering the Briar Rose is like entering another time when hospitality was an art and the place for dreams was a feather bed. Three rooms with fireplaces.

Pearl Street Inn
1820 Pearl St., 80302
303-444-5584 800-232-5949
Yossi Shem-Avi
All year

$$ B&B
7 rooms, 7 pb
Visa, MC, AmEx, Diners •
C-yes/S-yes/P-yes/H-no
French

Continental plus
Comp. wine & tea, bar
Sitting room
entertainment
TV in most rooms

A rare combination of a European inn and luxury hotel. Near Boulder's pedestrian mall. Refreshing breakfast and evening bar in garden courtyard.

BRECKENRIDGE

Williams House B&B
P.O. Box 2454, 80424
303 N. Main St.
303-453-2975
Diane Jayres, Fred Kinat
All year exc. May & Oct

$$ B&B
3 rooms, 1 pb
AmEx •
C-no/S-no/P-no/H-no

Continental plus
Apres-ski treat
Afternoon tea, deck
sitting room, sun room
TV, VCR, mountain views

Charming historic home decorated in antiques and lace curtains. Enjoy mountain views in sun room or the romantic fireplace in parlor. Walk to shuttles, shops, restaurants.

BUENA VISTA

Adobe Inn
P.O. Box 1560, 81211
303 N. Hwy 24
719-395-6340
Marjorie, Paul & Mike Knox
All year

$$ B&B
5 rooms, 5 pb
Visa, MC
C-yes/S-no/P-no/H-no
some Spanish

Full gourmet breakfast
Comp. beverages
Restaurant, sitting room
library, piano, solarium
2 suites, jacuzzi

Santa Fe-style adobe hacienda. Indian, Mexican, antique, wicker & Mediterranean rooms. Indian fireplaces. Gourmet breakfast. Jacuzzi. Majestic mountain & river scenery.

CARBONDALE

Ambiance Inn B&B
66 N. 2nd Street, 81623
303-963-3597
Norma & Robert Morris
All year

$$ B&B
4 rooms, 4 pb
Visa, MC •
C-yes/S-ltd/P-no/H-no

Full breakfast
Dinner with reservation
Restaurant, coffee, tea
sitting room, library
ski, fish, golf nearby

Modern chalet home, vaulted ceilings, each large room has unique personality. 1 block to downtown Carbondale, 35 minutes to Aspen, centrally located for a mountain experience.

The Holden House, Colorado Springs, CO

CARBONDALE

The Biggerstaff House B&B
0318 Lions Ridge Rd., 81623
303-963-3605
Jack & Jane E. Van Horn
All year exc. May & Nov.

$$ B&B
4 rooms, 1.5 pb
Visa, MC ●
C-12+/S-no/P-no/H-no

Full breakfast
Afternoon tea, snacks
Sitting room, library
lounge w/mountain view
balconies off 2 bedrooms

Conveniently located in the Aspen Roaring Fork Valley to all summer activities and 5 winter ski areas. Gold medal trout fishing at the Frying Pan & Roaring Fork Rivers.

COLORADO SPRINGS

Holden House—1902 B&B Inn
1102 W. Pikes Peak Ave., 80904
719-471-3980
Sallie & Welling Clark
All year

$$ B&B
5 rooms, 5 pb
Visa, MC, AmEx, Disc ●
C-no/S-no/P-no/H-no

Full gourmet breakfast
Comp. beverages/cookies
Sitting room w/TV
living room
fireplace

Charming 1902 Victorian home filled with antiques and family heirlooms. Located in historic "Old Colorado City" area. Close to restaurants and shops. Friendly resident cat.

CRESTED BUTTE

Cristiana Guesthaus
P.O. Box 427, 81224
621 Maroon Ave.
303-349-5326
Rosie & Martin Catmur
All year

$$ B&B
21 rooms, 21 pb
Visa, MC, AmEx, Disc ●
C-yes/S-ltd/P-no/H-no

Continental plus
Comp. hot beverages
Sitting room
hot tub, sauna

Close to historic downtown. Relaxed, friendly atmosphere. Enjoy the hot tub, sauna, sun deck, and homebaked breakfast served in our cozy lobby. Superb mountain views.

CRESTED BUTTE ──

Purple Mountain Lodge $ B&B Full breakfast (winter)
P.O. Box 897, 81224 5 rooms, 3 pb Cont. breakfast (summer)
714 Gothic Ave. Visa, MC, SkiAm, DC ● Sitting room
303-349-5888 C-yes/S-yes/P-no/H-no
Walter & Sherron Green Swiss
Summer & winter

*Victorian home in historic town. Relax by the massive stone fireplace in the living room;
breakfast with view of Mt. Crested Butte.*

DENVER ──

Castle Marne $$$ B&B Full gourmet breakfast
1572 Race St., 80206 9 rooms, 9 pb Aftn. tea, sitting room
303-331-0621 800-92-MARNE Visa, MC, AmEx ● Library, gift shop
The Peiker Family S-no/P-no/H-no game room w/pool table
All year Spanish, Hungarian computer, fax, copier

*Castle Marne, luxury urban inn. Minutes from airport, convention center, business district,
shopping, fine dining. Local and National Historic Structure. Office for guests.*

Queen Anne Inn $$ B&B Continental plus
2147 Tremont Place, 80205 10 rooms, 10 pb Lunch, dinner avail
Clements Historic Dist. Visa, MC, AmEx ● Comp. wine, beverages
303-296-6666 800-432-INNS C-15+/S-no/P-no/H-no sitting room, faxes
Ann & Chuck Hillestad bicycles, flower garden
All year

*Colorado's most award winning inn (15 formal awards). Located in beautiful, residential
1870s district in heart of downtown. Fresh flowers, original art, chamber music.*

DILLON (SILVERTHORNE) ────────────────────────────────

Blue Valley Guest House $$ B&B Continental plus
Blue River Rt. 26R, 80435 3 rooms, 1 pb Complimentary beverages
28 Summit Drive Visa, MC ● Living room, grand piano
303-468-5731 800-530-3866 C-ltd/S-no/P-no/H-no rock fireplace, TV
Alice & George Lund bicycles, hot tub
All year

*Delightful high country inn. Mountain wild flowers adorn antique heirlooms. Friendly, helpful
hospitality. Trout fishing, shopping, hiking, 4 major ski areas nearby.*

DURANGO ──

Blue Lake Ranch $$$ B&B Full European breakfast
16919 State Hwy 140, 81326 1 rooms, 1 pb Afternoon tea
Hesperus ● Sitting room, sauna
303-385-4537 C-ltd/S-no/P-no/H-no bicycles, lake, gardens
D. Alford & S. Isgar, M.D. Cabin is available
May–September

*Victorian farmhouse surrounded by gardens of flowers, vegetables and herbs. Spectacular
lake & mountain views, trout-stocked lake, meals of homegrown ingredients.*

Country Sunshine B&B $$ B&B Full breakfast
35130 Hwy. 550 N., 81301 5 rooms, 3 pb Afternoon tea
303-247-2853 Visa, MC, AmEx, Disc ● Comp. wine, snacks
Michael & Faith C-yes/S-no/P-yes/H-ask sitting room
All year library

*Spacious ranch-style house on 3 acres of Pine Oak forest. Abundant wildlife, skiing, fishing,
golf, mountain biking, hot springs.*

DURANGO

Riverhouse B&B
495 Animas View Dr., 81301
303-247-4775
Crystal Carroll
Exc. Oct 15–Nov 15, Apr

$$ B&B
6 rooms, 6 pb
Visa, MC •
C-yes/S-no/P-no/H-no

Full gourmet breakfast
Comp. wine, juice/snacks
Massage & hypnosis sess.
exercise room available
snooker table, fish pond

Enjoy breakfast in spacious 928 sq. ft. skylighted atrium. View the Animas River Valley. Hear the haunting whistle of historic narrow-gauge train. Special menus available.

Scrubby Oaks B&B Inn
P.O. Box 1047, 81302
1901 Florida Ave.
303-247-2176
Mary Ann Craig
All year

$$ B&B
7 rooms, 3 pb
•
C-yes/S-no/P-no/H-no

Full breakfast
Complimentary snacks
Sitting room, library
games, pool table, TV
sauna, close to skiing

On 10 acres overlooking Animas Valley & surrounding mountains. Rooms furnished w/antiques, artwork & good books. Near Durango-Silverton train, Mesa Verde & Purgatory Ski Area.

ESTES PARK

Anniversary Inn
1060 Mary's Lake Rd., 80517
Moraine Route
303-586-6200
Don & Susan Landwer
All year

$$ B&B
4 rooms, 1 pb
•
C-no/S-no/P-no/H-no

Full gourmet breakfast
Lunch, tea, snacks
Sitting room, library
"Sweetheart" cottage

Turn-of-the-century log house, moss-rock fireplace. Hearty breakfast served on wraparound porch. Half-mile to Rocky Mountain National Park.

FRISCO

Lark B&B
P.O. Box 1646, 80443
109 Granite St., at 1st
303-668-5237
Mark & Roberta Fish
All year

$$ B&B
3 rooms, 3 pb
Visa, MC, AmEx •
C-12+/S-no/P-no/H-yes

Full breakfast
Lunch & dinner on requ.
Snacks
sitting room
bicycles, hot tubs

Pleasant European-style B&B. Centrally located to Summit ski areas and Vail. Gourmet breakfast, apres ski and hot tub.

GRAND JUNCTION

Gate House B&B
2502 N. First St., 81501
303-242-6105
Rhonda & Garrett McClary
All year

$ B&B
4 rooms, 2 pb
Visa, MC •
C-10+

Full breakfast
Library

The Gate House is elegantly decorated and has beautiful surroundings. We serve gourmet breakfasts. Centrally located to area attractions.

Junction Country Inn B&B
861 Grand Ave., 81501
303-241-2817
Karl & Theresa Bloom
All year

$ B&B
4 rooms, 2 pb
Visa, MC, AmEx •
C-yes/S-no/P-no/H-no

Full breakfast
Snacks
Sitting room, library
local historical coll.

Wonderful, antique-filled home located in historic district. Comfortable, friendly and relaxing. Walking distance to shops, restaurants, museum, sports stadium.

GUNNISON

Mary Lawrence Inn
601 N. Taylor, 81230
303-641-3343
Tom & Les Bushman
All year

$ B&B
5 rooms, 3 pb
Visa, MC ●
C-yes/S-no/P-no/H-no

Full breakfast
Sack lunch ($)
Sitting room
many books
tandem bicycles

Our renovated home is inviting and comfortable; delectable breakfasts. Gunnison country offers marvelous outdoor adventures; super Crested Butte ski package.

LIMON

Midwest Country Inn
795 Main St, P.O. Box X, 80828
719-775-2373
Harold & Vivian Lowe
All year

$ EP
32 rooms, 32 pb
Visa, MC, AmEx ●
C-yes/S-yes/P-no/H-no

Coffee & tea available
Restaurant—1 block
Sitting room, gift shop
"listening" waterfall
and "watching" fountain

Beautiful rooms, oak antiques, stained glass, elegant wallpapered bathrooms, near I-70, 1.5 hours from Denver and Colorado Springs. Train rides available Saturday evenings.

LOVELAND

The Lovelander B&B Inn
217 W. 4th St., 80537
303-669-0798
M. & B. Wiltgen, S. Strauss
All year

$$ B&B
9 rooms, 9 pb
Visa, MC, AmEx, Disc ●
C-10+/S-no/P-no/H-ltd

Full gourmet breakfast
Comp. beverages
Meeting & reception ctr.
sitting room, library
1 whirlpool/deluxe room

Victorian grace and old-fashioned hospitality from the heart of the Sweetheart City: a community of the arts. Gateway to the Rockies.

MANITOU SPRINGS

Two Sisters Inn
Ten Otoe Place, 80829
719-685-9684
Sharon Smith, Wendy Goldstein
All year

$$ B&B
5 rooms, 3 pb
Visa, MC ●
C-ltd/S-no/P-no/H-no

Full gourmet breakfast
Comp. wine, snacks
Picnic lunches
Sitting room
library

Gracious Victorian nestled at base of Pikes Peak in historic district. Honeymoon cottage in garden. Mineral springs, quaint shops, restaurants.

MINTURN

Eagle River Inn
P.O. Box 100, 81645
145 N. Main St.
303-827-5761 800-344-1750
Beverly Rude
Exc. May & mid-October

$$$ B&B
12 rooms, 12 pb
Visa, MC, AmEx ●
C-12+/S-no/P-no/H-no

Continental plus
Comp. wine & cheese
Sitting room, patio
hot tub, backyard
conference/banquet room

Quiet mountain inn nestled alongside the Eagle River minutes from Vail Ski Resort. Furnished in southwest decor. Romantic riverside setting catering especially to couples.

OURAY

St. Elmo Hotel
P.O. Box 667, 426 Main, 81427
303-325-4951
Dan & Sandy Lingenfelter
All year

$$ B&B
9 rooms, 9 pb
Visa, MC ●
C-yes/S-ltd/P-no/H-no

Full breakfast
Restaurant, sitting room
Comp. wine, coffee, tea
piano, outdoor hot tub
sauna, meeting room

Hotel & Bon Ton Restaurant surrounded by beautiful, rugged 14,000-ft. peaks. Furnished with antiques, stained glass & brass; honeymoon suite. Hot springs, jeeping, X-C skiing.

Two Sisters Inn, Manitou Springs, CO

PAGOSA SPRINGS ———————————————————————————

Davidson's Country Inn	$ B&B	Full breakfast
Box 87, 81147	10 rooms, 3 pb	Afternoon teas
2 miles East Hwy 160	Visa, MC ●	Library, sitting room
303-264-5863	C-yes/S-no/P-ltd/H-no	game room, horseshoes
Evelyn & Gilbert Davidson		cottage available
All year		

Enjoy restful country charm in the heart of the Rocky Mountains. Cozy inn is furnished with antiques and family heirlooms. Group rates for 12 or more.

PUEBLO ———————————————————————————————

Abriendo Inn	$$ B&B	Full gourmet breakfast
300 W. Abriendo Ave., 81004	7 rooms, 7 pb	Comp. wine, snacks
719-544-2703	Visa, MC, AmEx, DC ●	Cater groups for lunch
Kerrelyn M. Trent	C-7+/S-ltd/P-no/H-no	and dinner
All year		sitting room

A classic B&B on the National Register of Historic Places. The comfortable elegance and luxury of the past. Taste-tempting breakfasts. Nearby attractions & recreational areas.

RED CLIFF

The Pilgrim's Inn
P.O. Box 151, 81649
101 Eagle Street
303-827-5333
Michael & Mary Wasmer
All year

$$ B&B
4 rooms, 2 pb
Visa, MC ●
C-yes/S-no/P-no/H-no

Full breakfast
Afternoon tea, snacks
Restaurants nearby
sitting room, library
hot tub alongside creek

Newly restored Victorian home filled w/antiques, Asian art, photographs & paintings of local artists. Ideal location for nordic & alpine skiing, bicycling, hiking & camping.

SILVERTON

The Alma House
P.O. Box 780, 81433
220 E. 10th St.
303-387-5336 303-249-4646
Don & Jolene Stott
Mem. Day–Labor Day

$ EP
10 rooms, 1 pb
Visa, MC, AmEx, Disc ●
C-yes/S-no/P-no/H-no

Comp. coffee, tea
Sitting room
Color TVs in rooms
in-house movies
honeymoon suite

Completely restored 1898 Colorado mountain town hotel featuring soft water, huge towels, clock-radio, cable color TV, Beautyrest Queen in each room. Beautiful views.

Teller House Hotel
P.O. Box 2, 81433
1250 Greene St.
303-387-5423 800-387-5423
Fritz Klinke & Loren Lew
All year

$ B&B
9 rooms
credit cards accepted ●
C-yes/S-ltd/P-no/H-ltd

Full breakfast
Lunch, dinner, bar
Piano in 1 room
Bakery on premises, ski
rentals, lift discounts

Step back 100 years in the heart of the San Juan Mountains. Victorian-era lodging in the "Mining Town that Never Quit", narrow gauge railroad.

TELLURIDE

Johnstone Inn
P.O. Box 546, 81435
403 W. Colorado Ave.
303-728-3316 800-752-1901
Bill Schiffbauer
Ski season & summer

$$ B&B
8 rooms, 1 pb
Visa, MC, AmEx ●
C-10+/S-no/P-no/H-no

Full breakfast
Comp. wine in ski season
Sitting room, library
color TV, games

Gracefully restored Victorian inn furnished in antiques. Close to town & ski lifts. Homemade bread & muffins, refreshments. History, charm and hospitality.

San Sophia
330 W. Pacific Ave., 81435
P.O. Box 1825
303-728-3001 800-537-4781
Dianne & Gary Eschman
All year

$$$ B&B
16 rooms, 16 pb
Visa, MC, AmEx ●
C-10+/S-no/P-no/H-no

Full breakfast
Comp. wine, beer, snacks
Sitting room, library
hot tubs, dining deck
ski storage, boot dryers

Elegant new inn with all luxurious rooms. Gourmet breakfast; spectacular views of surrounding mountains. One block from historic downtown district.

WINTER PARK

Beau West B&B
P.O. Box 3156, 80482
148 Fir Dr.
303-726-5145 800-473-5145
Greg Baca, Susan Mutersbaugh
Nov 20-Apr 20, June-Sept

$$ B&B
3 rooms, 2 pb
Visa, MC ●
C-yes/S-no/P-no/H-no

Continental plus
Sitting room
library
hot tubs

Your bed and breakfast stay includes a dreamy bedroom, gourmet continental breakfast, fireplace and jacuzzi – all at our slopeside location!

More Inns . . .

1894 Victorian P.O. Box 9322, Colorado Springs, 80932 719-630-3322
1899 Inn 314 S. Main, La Veta, 81055 303-742-3576
7-W Guest Ranch 3412 County Rd. 151, Gypsum, 81637 303-524-9328
Allenspark Lodge Colorado Hwy. 7—Bus., Allenspark, 80510 303-747-2552
Alpen Hutte 471 Rainbow Dr., Box 91, Silverthorne, 80498 303-468-6336
Alpina Haus 935 E. Durant, Aspen, 81611 800 24A-SPEN
Altamira Ranch Box 875, 23484 Hwy. 82, Basalt, 81621 303-927-3309
Ambiance Inn 66 N. 2nd. St., Carbondale, 81623 303-963-3579
Angelmark B&B 50 Little Pierre Ave., Winter Park, 80482 303-726-5354
Annabelle's B&B 382 Vail Circle, Dillon, 80435 303-468-8667
Aspen Canyon Ranch 13206 Country Rd. #3, Parshall, 80468 303-725-3518
Aspen Lodge & Guest Ranch Longs Peak Route 7, Estes Park, 80517 303-586-8133
Aspen Ski Lodge 101 W. Main St., Aspen, 81611 303-925-3434
Avalanche Ranch 12863 Hwy 133, Redstone, 81623 303-963-2846
Baker's Manor 317 Second St., Ouray, 81427 303-325-4574
Baldpate Inn P.O. Box 4445, Estes Park, 80517 303-586-6151
Balloon Ranch Box 41, Del Norte, 81132 303-754-2533
Bar Lazy J Guest Ranch Box N, Parshall, 80468 303-725-3437
Bear Creek Inn P.O. Box 1797, Telluride, 81423 303-728-6681
Bear Pole Ranch Star Rt. 1, Box BB, Steamboat Springs, 80487 303-879-0576
Black Forest B&B 11170 Black Forest Rd., Colorado Springs, 80908 719-495-4208
Blue Sky Inn 719 Arizona St., Buena Vista, 81211 303-395-8865
Brass Bed Inn 926 E. Durant, Aspen, 81611 303-925-3622
Brewery Inn B&B P.O. Box 473, Silver Plume, 80476 303-674-5565
Brumder Hearth P.O. Box 1152, Crested Butte, 81224 303-349-6253
Cambridge Club Hotel 1560 Sherman, Denver, 80203 303-831-1252
Cedar' Edge Llamas B&B 2169 Hwy. 65, Cedaredge, 81413 303-856-6836
Christopher House B&B 821 Empire St., Box 241, Silverton, 81433 303-387-5857
Cinnamon Inn B&B, The 426 Gunnison Ave., Lake City, 81235 303-944-2641
Claim Jumper 704 Whiterock, Box 1181, Crested Butte, 81224 303-349-6471
Cleveholm Manor 0058 Redstone Blvd., Redstone, 81623 303-963-2526
Cliff House Lodge 121 Stone St., Morrison, 80465 303-697-9732
Columbine Lodge P.O. Box 267, Green Mountain Falls, 80819 719-684-9062
Copper Horse Guest House 328 W. Main, Aspen, 81611 303-925-7525
Cottenwood House P.O. Box 1208, Estes Park, 80517 303-586-5104
Coulter Lake Guest Ranch P.O. Box 906, Rifle, 81650 303-625-1473
Crawford House Box 775062, Steamboat Springs, 80477 303-879-1859
Crest House 516 S. Division St., Sterling, 80751 303-522-3753
Crystal Lodge Lake City, 81235 303-944-2201
Dahl Haus B&B 122 S. Oak St., Box 695, Telluride, 81435 303-728-4158
Damn Yankee B&B Inn, The 100 6th Ave., Ouray, 81427 800-842-7512
Deer Valley Ranch Box Y, Nathrop, 81236 303-395-2353
Deer Valley Resorts P.O. Box 796, Bayfield, 81122 303-884-2600
Delaware Hotel 700 Harrison Ave., Leadville, 80461 303-486-1418
Diamond J Guest Ranch 26604 Frying Pan Rd., Meredith, 81642 303-927-3222
Dove Inn 711—14th St., Golden, 80401 303-278-2209
Drowsy Water Ranch Box 147A, Granby, 80446 303-725-3456
E.T.'s B&B 1608 Sage Lane, Paonia, 81428 303-527-3300
Eastholme Box 98, 4445 Haggerman, Cascade, 80809 719-684-9901
Echo Manor Inn 3366 Hwy 84, Pagosa Springs, 81147 303-264-5646
Elizabeth St. Guest House 202 E. Elizabeth St., Fort Collins, 80524 303-493-2337
Emerald Manor P.O. Box 3592, Estes Park, 80517 303-586-8050
Engelmann Pines 1035 Cranmer, Winter Park, 80482 303-726-4632
Fireside Inn P.O. Box 2252, Breckenridge, 80424 303-453-6456
Fool's Gold B&B P.O. Box 603, Silverton, 81433 303-387-5879
Forest Queen Hotel Box 127, 2nd & Elk Ave., Crested Butte, 81224 303-349-5336
Golden Rose Hotel P.O. Box 127, 102 Main, Central City, 80427 303-825-1413
Great Sand Dunes Inn 5303 Hwy 150, Mosca, 81146 719-378-2356

Griffin's Hospitality Hse 4222 N Chestnut, Colorado Springs, 80907 303-599-3035
Hackman House B&B Box 6902, Woodland Park, 80866 719-687-9851
Harbor Hotel P.O. Box 4109, Steamboat Springs, 80477 800-543-8888
Hardy House B&B Inn P.O. Box 0156, Georgetown, 80444 303-569-3388
Hearthstone Inn 506 North Cascade, Colorado Springs, 80903 719-473-4413
Helmshire Inn 1204 S. College, Fort Collins, 80524 303-493-4683
Hideout 1293–117 Rd., Glenwood Springs, 81601 303-945-5621
Historic Redstone Inn 82 Redstone Blvd., Redstone, 81623 303-963-2526
Home Ranch Box 822, Clark, 80428 303-879-1780
Hotel Lenado 200 S. Aspen St., Aspen, 81611 303-925-6246
House on the Hill P.O. Box 770598, Steamboat Springs, 80477 303-879-1650
Imperial Hotel 123 N. Third St., Cripple Creek, 80813 303-689-2713
Inn At Raspberry Ridge 5580 Country Rd. 3, Marble, 81623 303-963-3025
Inn at Rock 'n River P.O. Box 4644, Estes Park, 80517 303-443-4611
Inn at Steamboat 3070 Columbine Dr., Steamboat Springs, 80477 303-879-2600
Jackson Hotel 220 S. Main St., Poncha Springs, 81242 303-539-3122
Kaiser House, The 932 Cooper Ave., Glenwood Springs, 31602 303-945-8827
Katies Korner P.O. Box 804, Colorado Springs, 80901 303-630-3322
Kelsall's Ute Creek Ranch 2192 County Rd. 334, Ignacio, 81137 303-563-4464
Lark, The P.O., Box 1646, 80443 303-668-5237
Lazy H Ranch Box 248, Allenspark, 80510 303-747-2532
Leadville Country Inn 127 E. 8th St, Box 1989, Leadville, 80461 719-486-2354
Little Red Ski Haus 118 E. Cooper, Aspen, 81611 303-925-3333
Little Southfork B&B 15247 County Rd. 22, Dolores, 81323 303-882-4259
Lodge at Cordillera P.O. Box 1110, Edwards, 81632 303-926-2200
Logwood 35060 US Hwy 550, Durango, 81301 303-259-4396
MacTiernan's San Juan 2882 Highway 23, Ridgway, 81432 303-626-5360
Magpie Inn, The 1001 Spruce St., Boulder, 80302 303-449-6528
Manor B&B, The 317 2nd St., Ouray, 81427 303-325-4574
Mar Dei's Mountain Retreat P.O. Box 1767, Frisco, 80443 303-668-5337
Meadow Creek B&B Inn 13438 US Hwy 285, Pine, 80470 303-838-4167
Merritt House B&B 941 E. 17th Ave., Denver, 80218 303-861-5230
Midway Inn 1340 Hwy 133, Hotchkiss, 81419 303-527-3422
Molly Gibson Lodge 120 W. Hopkins, Aspen, 81611 303-925-2580
Moss Rose B&B P.O. Box 910, Lake City, 81235 303-366-4069
Mountain House B&B 905 East Hopkins, Aspen, 81611 303-920-2550
Mountain Mansion Inn B&B P.O. Box 1229, Leadville, 80461 719-486-0655
Mountain Weavery 1119 E. Ptarmigan Rd., Vail, 81657 303-476-5539
New Sheridan Hotel P.O. Box 980, Telluride, 81435 303-728-4351
Nordic Inn P.O. Box 939, Crested Butte, 81224 303-349-5542
North Fork Ranch Box B, Shawnee, 80475 303-838-9873
On Golden Pond B&B 7831 Eldridge, Arvada, 80005 303-424-2296
Orchard House, The 3573 E-1/2 Road, Palisade, 81526 303-464-0529
Outlook Lodge P.O. Box 5, Green Mountain Falls, 80819 719-684-2303
Parrish's Country Squire 2515 Parrish Rd., Berthoud, 80513 303-772-7678
Peaceful Place B&B 1129 Manitou Ave., Manitou Springs, 80829 719-685-1248
Pennington's Mnt. Vllg Inn 100 Pennington Court, Telluride, 81435 303-728-5337
Penny's Place 1041 County rd. 307, Durango, 81301 303-247-8928
Pennys Place 1041 County Rd. 307, Durango, 81301 303-247-8928
Pikes Peak Paradise Box 5760, Woodland Park, Colorado Springs, 80866 719-687-6656
Pomegranate Inn Box 1368, Aspen, 81612 800-525-4012
Poor Farm Country Inn 8495 C.R. 160, Salida, 81201 719-539-3818
Portland Inn 412 W. Portland, Box 32, Victor, 80860 719-689-2102
Pueblo Hostel & Cantina P.O. Box 346, Ridgway, 81432 303-626-5939
Red Crags B&B 302 El Paso Blvd, Manitou Springs, 80829 719-685-1920
Riversong P.O. Box 1910, Estes Park, 80517 303-586-4666
Royal Pine Inn B&B P.O. Box 4506, Pagosa Springs, 81157 800-955-0274
Salina House 365 Gold Run, Boulder, 80302 303-442-1494
Sardy House 128 E. Main St., Aspen, 81611 303-920-2525
Scandinavian Lodge Box 5040, Steamboat Village, 80449 303-879-0517

Seventh Ave. Manor 722 E. 7th Ave., Denver, 80203 303-832-0039
Silverheels Box 367, 81 Buffalo Dr., Dillon, 80435 303-468-2926
Ski Tip Lodge Box 38, Keystone, 80435 303-468-4202
Sky Valley Lodge Box 2153, Steamboat Springs, 80477 303-879-5158
Skyline Guest Ranch 7214 Highway 145, Telluride, 81435 303-728-3757
Snow Goose Box 722, 687 Garfield, Meeker, 81641 303-878-4532
Sue's Guest House P.O. Box 483, Cascade, 80809 303-684-2111
Sunnymede B&B 106 Spencer Ave., Manitou Springs, 80829 719-685-4619
Sweetwater Creek Ranch 2650 Sweetwater Rd., Gypsum, 81637 303-524-7949
Talbott House 928 Colorado Ave., Glenwood Springs, 81601 303-945-1039
Tall Timber Box 90G, Durango, 81301 303-259-4813
Tarado Mansion Route 1, Box 53, Arriba, 80804 719-768-3468
The Inn at Rock 'n River P.O. Box 829, US Hwy 36, Lyons, 80540 800-448-4611
Tipple Inn 747 S. Galena St., Aspen, 81611 800-321-7025
Trailshead Lodge P.O. Box 873, Lead, 57754 605-584-3464
Trout City Inn Box 431, Buena Vista, 81211 719-495-0348
Tudor Rose B&B Box 1995, 429 Whiterock, Crested Butte, 81224 303-349-6253
Tumbling River Ranch Grant, 80448 303-838-5981
Two-Ten Casey P.O. Box 154, 210 Casey, Central City, 80427 303-582-5906
Vagabond Inn B&B P.O. Box 2141, Durango, 81301 303-259-5901
Victoria Oaks Inn 1575 Race St., Denver, 80206 303-355-1818
Victorian Inn 2117 W. 2nd Ave., Durango, 81301 303-247-2223
Victorian Veranda B&B P.O. Box 361, Eaton, 80615 303-454-3890
Vista Verde Guest Ranch Box 465, Steamboat Springs, 80477 303-879-3858
Wanek's Lodge at Estes P.O. Box 898, Estes Park, 80517 303-586-5851
Waunita Hot Springs Ranch 8007 Country Rd. 877, Gunnison, 81230 303-641-1266
Weisbaden Spa & Lodge Box 349, Ouray, 81427 303-325-4347
Wind River Ranch P.O. Box 3410, Estes Park, 80517 303-586-4212
Winding River Resort P.O. Box 629, Grand Lake, 80447 303-627-3215
Windsor Hotel B&B Inn P.O. Box 762, Del Norte, 81132 719-657-2668
Woodland Hills Lodge P.O. Box 276, Woodland Park, 80863 800-621-8386
Wyman Hotel 1371 Greene St., Silverton, 81433 303-387-5372
Ye Ole Oasis 3142 "J" Road, Box 609, Hotchkiss, 81419 303-872-3794

Connecticut

BOLTON

Jared Cone House	$$ B&B	Full breakfast
25 Hebron Rd., 06043	3 rooms, 1 pb	Sitting room
203-643-8538	C-yes/S-no/P-no/H-no	bicycles
Jeff & Cinde Smith		canoe available
All year		

Enjoy the charm of our home with scenic views of the countryside; spectacular foliage; berry farms; antiquing. Full breakfast featuring our own maple syrup when available.

BRISTOL

Chimney Crest Manor B&B	$$$ B&B	Full breakfast
5 Founders Dr., 06010	4 rooms, 4 pb	All rooms are suites
203-582-4219	Visa, MC ●	Sitting room, piano
Dante & Cynthia Cimadamore	C-ltd/S-ltd/P-no/H-no	wading pool, 3 mi. to
All year		Hershey, Lake Compounce

32-room Tudor mansion located in historical area of Bristol. Six fireplaces. Twenty minutes from Hartford, Litchfield and Waterburg. Unique architecture. Balloon packages.

CLINTON

Captain Dibbell House
21 Commerce St., 06413
203-669-1646
Helen & Ellis Adams
All year exc. January

$$ B&B
3 rooms, 3 pb
Visa, MC •
C-12+/S-ltd/P-no/H-no

Full breakfast
Comp. refreshments
Sitting room, gazebo
bicycles, horseshoes
beach chairs & towels

Our 1866 sea captain's Victorian offers comfortable lodging and home-baked savories to guests while they discover the charms of our coastal towns.

DEEP RIVER

Riverwind Inn
209 Main St., 06417
203-526-2014
Barbara Barlow, Bob Bucknall
All year

$$$ B&B
8 rooms, 8 pb
Visa, MC
C-no/S-yes/P-no/H-no

Full breakfast
Comp. sherry
8 common rooms
piano, classic British
limousine service

Furnished in country antiques. Smithfield ham with breakfast, fireplace in dining room. New England charm and southern hospitality.

EAST HADDAM

Bishopsgate Inn
P.O. Box 290, 06423
7 Norwich Road
203-873-1677
Dan & Molly Swartz
All year

$$$ B&B
6 rooms, 6 pb
C-6+/S-yes/P-no/H-ltd

Full breakfast
Comp. wine
Dinner
piano, sauna
sitting room

1818 colonial home with 6 charming guest rooms, open fireplaces, period pieces and fine antiques, near famous Goodspeed Opera House.

ESSEX

The Griswold Inn
36 Main Street, 06426
203-767-1776
William Winterer
All year

$$$ B&B
25 rooms, 25 pb
Visa, MC, AmEx
C-yes/S-yes/P-ask/H-yes

Continental breakfast
Restaurant, bar service
Lunch & dinner available
sitting room, library

Located in center of historic Essex; renowned marine art collection; entertainment nightly from Griswold Inn Banjo Band to Cliff Haslem's Sea Chantys.

GLASTONBURY

Butternut Farm
1654 Main St., 06033
203-633-7197
Don Reid
All year

$$ B&B
4 rooms, 2 pb
Visa, MC, AmEx
C-yes/S-ltd/P-no/H-no

Full breakfast
Comp. wine, chocolates
Piano, 8 fireplaces
sitting rooms, library
bicycle

An 18th-century jewel furnished with period antiques. Attractive grounds with herb gardens and ancient trees, dairy goats and prize chickens. 10 minutes from Hartford.

IVORYTOWN

Copper Beech Inn
46 Main St., 06442
203-767-0330
Eldon & Sally Senner
All year exc. Mondays

$$$ B&B
13 rooms, 13 pb
major credit cards
C-ltd/S-yes/P-no/H-yes

Continental plus
Lunch, dinner, bar
Piano, TV, Jacuzzi
bicycles, gardens
porcelain gallery

A hostelry where even a short visit is a celebration of good living. The only 4-star restaurant in Connecticut. The feel of the entire inn is country elegance.

LITCHFIELD

Tollgate Hill Inn
P.O. Box 1339, 06759
Route 202 & Tollgate Rd.
203-567-4545
Frederick J. Zivic
Exc. 3 weeks in March

$$$ EP/MAP
20 rooms, 20 pb
•
C-yes/S-yes/P-yes/H-no

Continental breakfast
Lunch, dinner, bar
Sitting room
piano, tennis
weekend entertainment

Restored 1745 inn listed on National Register of Historic Places. Luncheon, dinner, cocktails, overnight accommodations in beautifully decorated guest rooms.

MIDDLEBURY

Tucker Hill Inn
96 Tucker Hill Rd., 06762
203-758-8334
Susan & Richard Cebelenski
All year

$$ B&B
4 rooms, 2 pb
Visa, MC •
C-yes/S-ltd/P-no/H-no

Full breakfast
Hot & cold drinks
Sitting room
library
TV room

Large colonial-style inn near the Village Green. Our period rooms are large and spacious. Hearty full-course breakfast. Convenient to sights and sports.

MYSTIC

The Adams House
382 Cow Hill Rd., 06355
203-572-9551
Maureen/Ron Adams,
Laura Miner
All year

$$ B&B
7 rooms, 7 pb
Visa, MC
C-no/S-no/P-no/H-no

Continental plus
Comp. wine/cheese w/tour
Sitting room, TV room
fireplaces
flower beds

1790 home; 3 fireplaces; private setting; in-ground swimming pool; approximately 1.5 miles from downtown Mystic. Surrounded by lush greenery and flower beds.

Charley's Harbour Inne
RFD #1, Box 398, 06355
Edgemont St.
203-572-9253
C. Lecouras, R. Morehouse
All year

$ EP
5 rooms, 5 pb
none
C-yes/S-yes/P-yes/H-no
Greek

Kitchen privileges
Sitting room
canoe and row boats
cable TV, A/C

Small inn plus 3-room cottage on Mystic River. Walk to seaport & all attractions. Waterfront tables, cable TV, kitchen privileges, canoeing and boating.

Comolli's Guest House
36 Bruggeman Place, 06355
203-536-8723
Dorothy Comolli
All year

$$$ B&B
2 rooms, 1 pb
C-no/S-yes/P-no/H-no

Continental breakfast
Kitchen privileges
TV in rooms

Country setting on top of dead-end street overlooking Mystic seaport; immaculate and quiet. Within walking distance of everything.

Inn at Mystic
Junction Rts. 1 & 27, 06355
203-536-9604
All year

$$$ EP
68 rooms, 68 pb
Visa, MC, AmEx, DC •
C-yes/S-yes/P-no/H-yes
French, Spanish

Restaurant, bar
Sitting room
Tennis, hot tubs
swimming pool
boating available

Overlooking Mystic Harbor and Sound. Varied accommodations with antiques, reproductions, canopied beds, balconies, fireplaces, jacuzzis, gourmet restaurant, tennis, boating.

MYSTIC

The Palmer Inn
25 Church St., Noank, 06340
203-572-9000
Patricia White Cornish
All year

$$$ B&B
6 rooms, 6 pb
Visa, MC
C-no/S-ltd/P-no/H-no

Continental plus
Comp. sherry, tea
Sitting room
bicycles, games
fireplaces, flowers

Elegant 1907 mansion with antique furnishings. Quiet charm of New England fishing village, 2 miles to historic Mystic. Thanksgiving & Victorian Christmas weekends.

Red Brook Inn
P.O. Box 237, 06372
2800 Goldstar Hwy
203-572-0349
Ruth Keyes
All year

$$$ B&B
9 rooms, 9 pb
Visa, MC
C-9+/S-no/P-no/H-no

Full breakfast
Comp. wine, tea, cider
Sitting room, library
bicycles, patio
whirlpool

The inn strikes a nice balance between authentic handsome furnishings and comfort. Surrounded by wooded acres, convenient to old New England sights.

NEW LONDON

Queen Anne Inn
265 Williams St., 06320
203-447-2600 800-347-8818
M. Beatty, Ray/Julie Rutledge
All year

$$$ B&B
9 rooms, 9 pb
Visa, MC, AmEx, Dis, DC
●
C-12+/S-ltd/P-no/H-no

Full buffet breakfast
Comp. tea, refreshments
Sitting room, hot tub
sauna, nearby tennis
massage, health club

Elegant lodging near the historically rich Mystic-Groton-New London waterfront resort area. Tennis, massage, health & racquet club are available nearby for a small fee.

NEW MILFORD

The Homestead Inn
5 Elm St., 06776
203-354-4080
Rolf & Peggy Hammer
All year

$$ B&B
14 rooms, 14 pb
Visa, MC, AmEx ●
C-no/S-no/P-ltd/H-ltd

Continental plus
Sitting room, piano
front porch, gardens
near trout fishing

Small country inn in picturesque New England town next to village green, near shops, churches, restaurants, antiques, galleries, hiking, crafts.

NEW PRESTON

Boulders Inn
Lakeshore Rd., Route 45, 06777
203-868-0541
Lilla & Kees Adema
All year

$$$ B&B
17 rooms, 17 pb
Visa, MC, AmEx ●
C-ask/S-yes/P-no/H-yes
German, Dutch, French

Full breakfast
Restaurant, bar, dinner
Sitting room, bicycles
tennis, private beach
boats, hiking trail

Exquisitely furnished country inn in spectacular location, overlooking Lake Waramaug. Dining with lakeview from inside dining room or outside terraces.

The Inn on Lake Waramaug
107 North Shore Road, 06777
203-868-0563 800-LAKE-INN
David Kane
All year

$$$ MAP
25 rooms, 25 pb
Visa, MC, AmEx, DC ●
C-yes/S-yes/P-no/H-yes

Full breakfast
Luncheon, dinner, bar
Pool, sauna, tennis
sitting room, piano
entertainment

Authentic colonial (1790) restored and furnished with pine and cherry antiques. Complete resort, private beach, indoor pool, Showboat Cruises, sleigh rides.

106 Connecticut

NORFOLK

Blackberry River Inn
Route 44, 06058
203-542-5100
Kim & Bob Zuckerman
All year

$$$ B&B
19 rooms, 9 pb
Visa, MC, AmEx, DC ●
C-yes/S-yes/P-no/H-ltd

Continental plus buffet
Restaurant, bar
Sitting room, library
hot tub, tennis courts
skiing/fishing/canoeing

A 225-year-old Colonial inn in rural northwest Connecticut serving fine continental country cuisine. 19 rooms, some with fireplaces. A great country getaway!

Manor House
P.O. Box 447, Maple Ave, 06058
203-542-5690
Hank & Diane Tremblay
All year

$$ B&B
9 rooms, 9 pb
Visa, MC ●
C-12+/S-ltd/P-no/H-ltd
French

Full breakfast (to room)
Comp. tea, coffee, cocoa
Sitting room, library
piano, sun porch, gazebo
bicycles, gardens, lake

Historic Victorian mansion furnished with genuine antiques, on 5 acres. Romantic and elegant bedrooms, several with fireplaces. Sleigh & carriage rides. Concert series.

Mountain View Inn
Route 272, 06058
203-542-5595
Michele Sloane
All year

$$ B&B
10 rooms, 7 pb
Visa, MC, AmEx ●
C-yes/S-yes/P-ltd/H-yes

Full breakfast (ex. Sun)
Gourmet restaurant
Lunch, tea, dinner, bar
sitting room, piano
outdoor dining deck

Romantic 1875 Victorian country inn located in picture perfect village. Central to musical concerts, antiquing, skiing and hiking.

NORWALK

Silvermine Tavern
194 Perry Ave., 06850
203-847-4558
Frank Whitman, Jr.
All year

$$$ B&B
12 rooms, 12 pb
Visa, MC, AmEx, DC ●
C-yes/S-yes/P-no/H-no

Continental
Restaurant, bar
Lunch, dinner
sitting room

Charming 225-year-old country inn only an hour from New York City. Decorated with hundreds of antiques. Overlooking the Tranquil Millpond.

OLD GREENWICH

Harbor House Inn
165 Shore Rd., 06870
203-637-0145
Dolly Stuttig
All year

$$
23 rooms, 17 pb
●
C-yes/S-yes/P-no/H-no

Breakfast
Kitchen facilities
Sitting room, piano
large lobby, bicycles
tennis court, near beach

A lovely guest house with a large lobby, filled with Persian rugs & a piano. Guest use of kitchen. Refrigerators, color TVs, coffee makers in rooms, maidservice M-F.

OLD LYME

Bee and Thistle Inn
100 Lyme St., 06371
203-434-1667
Bob & Penny Nelson
All year

$$$ EP
11 rooms, 9 pb
Visa, MC, AmEx ●
C-yes/S-yes/P-no/H-no

Lunch, dinner, bar
Bicycles
2 parlors, piano
harpist Saturdays

An inn on 5.5 acres in historic district. On the Lieutenant River set back amidst majestic trees. Sophisticated country cuisine.

OLD LYME

Old Lyme Inn
P.O. Box 787, 06371
85 Lyme St.
203-434-2600
Diana Field Atwood
All year

$$$ B&B
13 rooms, 13 pb
major credit cards ●
C-yes/S-yes/P-ltd/H-yes

Continental plus
Lunch, dinner
Sitting room
telephones & TV in rooms
banister porch

An 1850 Victorian inn in Old Lyme's historic district. Restaurant was given three stars by the New York Times on three separate visits. Empire and Victorian furnishings.

OLD MYSTIC

The Old Mystic Inn
58 Main St., Box 634, 06372
203-572-9422
Mary & Peter Knight
All year

$$$ B&B
8 rooms, 8 pb
Visa, MC, AmEx ●
C-6+/S-no/P-no/H-no

Full country breakfast
Afternoon tea
Sat. eve. wine & cheese
sitting room
bicycles

Located minutes from Mystic Seaport and Aquarium, this charming inn offers a complete country breakfast to guests.

PLAINFIELD

French Renaissance House
550 Norwich Rd., Rt. 12, 06374
203-564-3277
Lucile & Ted Melber
All year

$$ B&B
4 rooms, 1 pb
Visa, MC, DC
C-yes/S-no

Full breakfast
Comp. wine & beverages
Sitting room, library
near antique shops and
restaurants

1871 Victorian French Renaissance Second Empire architecture; listed on Historic Register. Large rooms; rounded arched windows; high ceilings; charming atmosphere.

POMFRET

Clark Cottage, Wintergreen
Box 94, Rt. 44 & 169, 06258
203-928-5741
Doris & Stanton Geary
All year

$$ B&B
5 rooms, 3 pb
Visa, MC ●
C-yes/S-no/P-no/H-no

Full breakfast
Restaurant nearby
Aftn. tea, comp. wine
sitting room, library
screened porch, bicycles

1890 cottage on 4 acres of lawn, extensive flower and rose gardens, and vegetable gardens overlooking an undeveloped valley which is magnificent when the leaves turn.

PORTLAND

The Croft
7 Penny Corner Rd, 06480
203-342-1856
Elaine Hinze
All year

$$ B&B
2 rooms, 2 pb
Visa, MC ●
C-yes/S-no/P-no/H-no

Full breakfast
Farm fresh eggs, tea
TV, phone, dining area
in suites, one w/kitchen
living room & pvt. entry

An 1822 colonial country home located in central Connecticut, convenient to Wesleyan University. Open fields, barns and an herb garden. Golf and skiing nearby.

PUTNAM

Felshaw Tavern
Five Mile River Rd., 06260
203-928-3467
Herb & Terry Kinsman
All year

$$$ B&B
2 rooms, 2 pb
●
C-yes/P-no/H-no

Full breakfast
Comp. wine
Sitting room, library
5 miles to golf, tennis,
and swimming

Noble center-chimney Colonial, built as tavern in 1742, lovingly restored, antiques, rich in history. In rural setting, accessible to Boston, Providence, Hartford, Worcester.

RIDGEFIELD

West Lane Inn	$$$ B&B	Continental breakfast
22 West Lane, 06877	20 rooms, 20 pb	Full breakfast $
203-438-7323	Visa, MC, AmEx, DC	Comp. whiskey or julep
M. M. Mayer	C-yes/S-yes/P-no	bicycles, tennis nearby
All year	Spanish	

Colonial elegance framed by majestic old maples and flowering shrubs. Breakfast served on the veranda. Always a relaxing atmosphere.

SALISBURY

The White Hart	EP	Restaurant, bar
P.O. Box 385, 06068	26 rooms, 26 pb	Lunch/Dinner available
The Village Green	Visa, MC, AmEx, DC, CB ●	Weekends and summer
203-435-0030	C-yes/S-yes/P-yes/H-ltd	sitting room
Juliet & Terry Moore	Span, Swedish, Fr, Germ	Afternoon tea
All year		

19th century gracious inn and restaurants. "chinz covered dream of an inn" — Berkshire Magazine, rated "excellent" by NY Times.

SIMSBURY

Simsbury 1820 House	$$$ B&B	Continental plus
731 Hopmeadow St., 06070	34 rooms, 34 pb	Lunch, dinner
203-658-7658 800-TRY-1820	Visa, MC, AmEx ●	Restaurant, bar
Kelly Hohengarten	C-yes/S-yes/P-no/H-yes	sitting room
All year		picnic hampers

A graciously restored 19th-century mansion of 34 rooms in period decor, all with 20th-century amenities. Noted dining room serves daily. Brochure available.

TOLLAND

Tolland Inn	$$ B&B	Continental plus
P.O. Box 717, 06084	7 rooms, 5 pb	Comp. wine, tea
63 Tolland Green	Visa, MC, AmEx	Sitting room
203-872-0800	C-ltd/S-no/P-no/H-no	
Susan & Steve Geddes Beeching		
All year		

Historic inn on New England village green. Short drive from I-84; convenient to Hartford, Sturbridge, Brimfield and University of Connecticut.

WOODBURY

Curtis House, Inc.	$ EP	Continental breakfast $
506 Main St. South, 06798	18 rooms, 12 pb	Luncheon, dinner, bar
203-263-3394	major credit cards ●	
The Hardisty Family	C-yes/S-yes/P-no/H-yes	
All year exc. Christmas		

Connecticut's oldest Inn, most rooms with canopied beds, in heart of antique country.

More Inns ...

1741 Saltbox Inn P.O. Box 677, Kent, 06757 203-927-4376
Alexander's B&B 17 Rhynus Rd., Sharon, 06069 800-727-7592
Applewood Farms Inn 528 Col. Ledyard Hwy., Ledyard, 06355 203-536-2022
Austin's Stonecroft Inn 17 Main St., East Haddam, 06423 203-873-1754
B&B at Laharan Farm 350 Route 81, Killingworth, 06417 203-663-1706
Barnes Hill Farm B&B Route 37, Sherman, 06784 203-354-4404
Barney House 11 Mountain Spring Rd., Farmington, 06032 203-677-9735
Birches Inn West Shore Rd., New Preston, 06777 203-868-0229

Captain Stannard House 138 S. Main St., Westbrook, 06498 203-399-7565
Chester Bulkley House B&B 184 Main St., Wethersfield, 06109 203-563-4236
Cobbie Hill Farm Steele Rd (off Rte. 44), New Hartford, 06057 203-379-0057
Cumon Inn 130 Buckland Rd., South Windsor, 06074 203-644-8486
Dolly Madison Inn 73 W. Wharf Rd., Madison, 06443 203-245-7377
Elms Inn 500 Main St., Ridgefield, 06877 203-438-2541
Evie's Turning Point Farm Rte 45, Cornwall Bridge, Warren, 06754 203-868-7775
Farmhouse on the Hill 418 Gurleyville Rd., Storrs, 06268 203-429-1400
Fife'n Drum Inn Main St., Route 7, Kent (Litchfield Hills), 06757 203-927-3509
Fowler House P.O. Box 340, Plains Rd, Moodus, 06469 203-873-8906
Gelston House Goodspeed Landing, East Haddam, 06423 203-873-1411
Greenwoods Gate B&B Inn P.O. Box 662, Norfolk, 06058 203-542-5439
Hawley Manor Inn 19 Main St., Newtown, 06470 203-426-4456
Hayward House Inn 35 Hayward Ave., Colchester, 06415 203-537-5772
Hedgerow House Box 265, Thompson, 06227 203-923-9073
Highland Farm B&B Highland Ave., New Hartford, 06057 203-379-6029
Homestead Inn 420 Field Point Rd., Greenwich, 06830 203-869-7500
Hopkins Inn Hopkins Rd., New Preston, 06777 203-868-7295
Inn at Chapel West 1201 Chapel St., New Haven, 06511 203-777-1201
Inn at Chester 318 W. Main St., Chester, 06412 203-526-4961
Inn at Woodstock Hill Box 98, Plaine Hill, South Woodstock, 06267 203-928-0528
Killingworth Inn 249 Rt. 81, Killingworth, 06417 203-663-1103
Lasbury's B&B 24 Orchard St., Stonington Village, 06378 203-535-2681
Madison Beach Hotel 94 West Wharf Road, Madison, 06443 203-245-1404
Maples Inn 179 Oenoke Ridge, New Canaan, 06840 203-966-2927
Mayflower Inn Route 47, Washington, 06793 213-868-0515
Old Babcock Tavern 484 Mile Hill Rd.,Rt.31, Tolland, 06084 203-875-1239
Old Riverton Inn P.O. Box 6, Rt. 20, Riverton, 06065 203-379-8678
Parsonage B&B 18 Hewlett St., Waterbury, 06710 203-574-2855
Provincial House 151 Main St., Winsted, 06098 203-379-1631
Randall's Ordinary P.O. Box 243, North Stonington, 06359 203-599-4540
Samuel Watson House Route 193, Thompson, 06277 203-923-2491
Sandford/Pond House P.O. Box 306, Bridgewater, 06752 203-355-4677
Saybrook Point Inn 2 Bridge St., Old Saybrook, 06475 800-243-0212
Shore Inne 54 E. Shore Rd., Groton Long Point, 06340 203-536-1180
Stanton House Inn 17 Mead Ave., Greenwich, 06830 203-869-2110
Stephen Potwine House, The 84 Scantic Rd., East Windsor, 06088 203-623-8722
Stonecroft Inn 17 Main St., East Haddam, 06423 203-873-1754
Stonehenge Inn P.O. Box 667, Ridgefield, 06877 203-438-6511
Under Mountain Inn 482 Under Mountain Rd., Salisbury, 06068 203-435-0242
Wake Robin Inn Route 41, Lakeville, 06039 203-435-2515
Wake Robin Inn Route 41, Lakeville, 06039 203-435-2515
Weaver's House P.O. Box 336, Route 44, Norfolk, 06058 203-542-5108
Whaler's Inn P.O. Box 488, Mystic, 06355 800-243-2588
Whispering Winds Inn 93 River Rd., East Haddam, 06423 203-526-3055
Winterbrook Farm Beffa Rd., Staffordville, 06076 203-684-2124
Yankee Pedlar Inn 93 Main St, Torrington, 06790 203-489-9226
Yesterday's Yankee Route 44 East, Box 442, Salisbury, 06068 203-435-9539

Delaware

LAUREL

Spring Garden
RD 1, Box 283A, 19956
Delaware Ave. Extended
302-875-7015
Gwen North
All year

$$ B&B
6 rooms, 2 pb
•
C-10+/S-ltd/H-yes
Spanish

Full breakfast
Comp. wine, snacks
Bar service set-ups
sitting room, library
bicycles, historic tours

Get away to a Colonial National Registry country plantation home near Atlantic beaches & Chesapeake Bay. State Tourism Award for Excellence in Hospitality.

MILFORD

Towers B&B
101 N.W. Front St., 19963
302-424-0321 800-366-3814
Michael Real
All year

$$$ B&B
6 rooms, 4 pb
Visa, MC •
C-12+/S-ltd/P-no/H-no
Spanish

Full breakfast
Afternoon tea
Comp. wine
sitting room
library, bicycles

A whimsical Victorian dream. Unique Steamboat Gothic Victorian mansion. Suites with fireplaces, furnishings in the French Victorian manner. Rehoboth and beaches nearby.

NEW CASTLE

David Finney Inn
216 Delaware St., 19720
P.O. Box 207
302-322-6367 800-334-6640
Judith S. Piser
All year

$$ B&B
17 rooms, 17 pb
Visa, MC, AmEx, Disc •
C-yes/S-yes/P-no/H-yes
Spanish

Continental breakfast
Luncheon, dinner
Bar, piano
living room, bike paths
entertainment

Restored 1685 inn in unique historic village 35 minutes south of Philadelphia. Thirteen rooms, four suites, private baths. Gourmet restaurant, tavern.

Jefferson House B&B
5 The Strand, 19720
302-323-0999 302-322-8944
C. Bechstein, Dr. Rosenthal
All year

$$ B&B
3 rooms, 3 pb
•
C-yes/S-yes

Full breakfast
Restaurant, lunch/dinner
Afternoon tea, jacuzzi
room w/porch river view
one room with kitchen

Charming 200-year-old riverfront hotel, center of historic district. Furnished with antiques or in a country motif. Original wood floors & millwork. William Penn landed here.

William Penn Guest House
206 Delaware St., 19720
302-328-7736
Irma & Richard Burwell
All year

$ B&B
4 rooms
C-no/S-no/P-no/H-no
Italian

Continental breakfast
Living room

This house was built about 1682, and William Penn stayed overnight! Restored and located in the center of the Square.

REHOBOTH BEACH

Corner Cupboard Inn	$$$ MAP/B&B	Full breakfast
50 Park Ave., 19971	18 rooms, 18 pb	Dinner included
302-227-8553	Visa, MC, AmEx	Restaurant
Elizabeth G. Hooper	C-yes/S-yes/P-yes/H-no	sitting room, piano
All year		beach

The inn that was in before inns were in! Fifty years at 50 Park Ave. as a summer retreat for Baltimore and Washington. B&B mid-Sept. to Mem. Day, MAP otherwise.

Tembo B&B	$$ B&B	Continental plus
100 Laurel St., 19971	6 rooms, 1 pb	Use of kitchen
Don & Gerry Cooper	C-12+/S-no/P-ask/H-no	Sitting room w/fireplace
All year		A/C, enclosed porch
		refrigerator in rooms

Warm hospitality in cozy beach cottage furnished with antiques, fine art, braided rugs. Short walk to beach, quality shops, restaurants. Nonsmoking.

WILMINGTON

A Small Wonder B&B	$$ B&B	Full breakfast
213 W. Crest Rd., 19803	2 rooms, 2 pb	Choice of comp. beverage
302-764-0789	Visa, Mc, AmEx ●	Sitting room, library
Dot & Art Brill	C-9+/S-ltd/P-no/H-no	music room, rec. room
All year		VCR, TV, pool, hot tub

Well-appointed, traditional suburban home. Award-winning landscaping. Very close to I-95, museums, corporations, colleges, historical sites. National award for B&B hospitality.

More Inns ...

Addy Sea P.O. Box 275, Bethany Beach, 19930 302-539-3707
Beach House, The 15 Hickman St., Rehoboth Beach, 19971 302-227-7074
Biddles B&B 101 Wyoming Ave., Dover, 19901 302-736-1570
Buckley's Tavern 5812 Kennett Pike, Centreville, 19807 302-656-9776
Gladstone Inn 3 Olive Ave., Rehoboth Beach, 19971 302-227-2641
Homestead Guests 721 Garfield Pkwy, Bethany Beach, 19930 (302)539-724
Lord & Hamilton Seaside In 20 Brooklyn Avenue, Rehoboth Beach, 19971 302-227-6960
Lord Baltimore Lodge 16 Baltimore Ave., Rehoboth Beach, 19971 302-227-2855
Noble Guest House B&B 33 S. Bradford St., Dover, 19901 302-674-4084
O'Connor's Guest House B & 20 Delaware Avenue, Rehoboth Beach, 19971 302-227-2419
Pleasant Inn Lodge 31 Olive Ave. @ 1st St., Rehoboth Beach, 19971 302-227-7311
Savannah Inn B&B 330 Savannah Rd., Lewes, 19958 302-645-5592
Sea-Vista Villas Box 62, Bethany Beach, 19930 302-539-3354
Victorian Rose B&B 22 Church St, Selbyville, 19975 302-436-2558

District of Columbia

WASHINGTON

Adams Inn	$ B&B	Continental plus
1744 Lanier Pl. NW, 20009	11 rooms, 6 pb	Coffee, tea, donuts
202-745-3600	Visa, MC, AmEx ●	Sitting room
Gene & Nancy Thompson	C-yes/S-no/P-no/H-no	library, TV lounge
All year		gardens, deck

Restored Edwardian townhouse; enjoy charm and quiet of residential street in the heart of the famous Adams-Morgan neighborhood. Shops and restaurants nearby. Walk to zoo.

WASHINGTON

Capitol Hill Guest House
101 Fifth St. NE, 20002
202-547-1050
Mark Babich
All year

$$ B&B
10 rooms
Visa, MC, AmEx ●
C-8+/S-no/P-no/H-no

Continental breakfast
Sitting room
maid service daily
comp. sherry in sitting room

Formerly home to US Congressional pages. Turn-of-the-century Victorian rowhouse with original woodwork and appointments. Ten moderately priced rooms in historic district.

Connecticut-Woodley House
2647 Woodley Rd. NW, 20008
202-667-0218
Ray Knickel
All year

$$ EP
15 rooms, 7 pb
C-yes/S-yes/P-no/H-no

Restaurants nearby
Convention ctr. nearby
TV lounge, A/C
laundry facilities
family rates

Comfortable, convenient, and inexpensive accommodations. Walk to restaurants, shops, Metro, bus transportation, Smithsonian museums, and other points of interest.

The Embassy Inn
1627 16th St. NW, 20009
1842–16th St. NW
202-234-7800 800-423-9111
Susan Stiles
All year

$$ B&B
38 rooms, 38 pb
Visa, MC, AmEx, DC, CB ●
C-yes/S-yes/P-no/H-no
Spanish

Continental breakfast
Comp. wine
Afternoon tea, snacks
sitting room
walk to Metro

Relaxing and friendly haven near Metro, White House, restaurants and shops with knowledgeable and helpful staff. Colonial style decor in renovated 1920's boarding house.

The Kalorama Guest House
1854 Mintwood Place NW, 20009
202-667-6369
Michael Gallagher
All year

$$ B&B
50 rooms, 50 pb
Visa, MC, AmEx, DC ●
C-yes/S-yes/P-no/H-no

Continental plus
Comp. wine, lemonade
Sitting room
conference room avail.

Charming European-style bed & breakfast in six turn-of-the-century townhouses. Period art, furnishings, brass beds, plants, outdoor landscaped garden, and hospitality.

Kalorama House/Woodley Prk
2700 Cathedral Ave., NW, 20008
202-328-0860
Michael Gallagher
All year

$$ B&B
19 rooms, 12 pb
MC, Visa, AmEx, DC ●
C-yes/S-yes/P-no/H-no

Continental breakfast
Comp. wine, lemonade
Parlor, sun room
24-hour message service
free local phone calls

Victorian townhouse decorated in period furnishings. Antique-filled, spacious rooms. Beautiful sun room for your morning breakfast. Charming, unique & inexpensive.

Morrison-Clark Inn
1015 "L" St. N.W., 20001
202-898-1200
Lorraine Lucia
All year

$$$ B&B
54 rooms, 54 pb
Visa, MC, AmEx ●
C-yes/S-yes/P-no/H-yes
Spanish

Continental plus
Restaurant, bar
Sitting room

The perfect urban oasis for visitors to downtown Washington. Victorian decor is alive in D.C.'s finest historic inn. Award-winning fine dining restaurant

WASHINGTON

The Reeds
P.O. Box 12011, 20005
c/o Bed & Breakfast, Ltd.
202-328-3510
Robin Nelson
All year

$$ B&B
6 rooms, 1 pb
•
C-ltd/S-yes/P-no/H-no
French, Spanish

Continental breakfast
Sitting room, gardens
library, Victorian porch
piano, antiques

Spacious rooms with wood-burning fireplaces and crystal chandeliers bring a bit of the Nineteenth Century to historic downtown Washington.

Swiss Inn
1204 Massachusetts NW, 20005
202-371-1816 800-955-7947
Ralph Nussbaumer
All year

$$ EP
7 rooms, 7 pb
Visa, MC, AmEx •
C-no/S-no/P-no/H-no
French, German, Italian

Kitchenettes
Library
Air conditioning

Within walking distance to White House and Convention Center; all air-conditioned. Suites have private baths and fully equipped kitchenettes.

The Windsor Inn
1842 16th St., NW, 20009
202-667-0300 800-423-9111
Susan Stiles
All year

$$ B&B
46 rooms, 46 pb
Visa, MC, AmEx, DC, CB •
C-yes/S-yes/P-no/H-no
French, Spanish

Continental breakfast
Comp. sherry, snacks
TV, radio alarm clock in
rooms

Relaxing and charming haven in heart of nation's capitol. Art deco flair. Close to Metro and many restaurants. 11 blocks north of White House. Friendly and helpful staff.

More Inns ...

B&B Accom. of Washington
  3222 Davenport St. NW,
  Washington, 20008
  202-363-8909
Castlestone Inn 1918 17th St.
  NW, Washington, 20009
  202-483-4706
Meg's International House
  1315 Euclid St., NW,
  Washington, 20009
  202-232-5837
Victorian Accommodations
  1304 Rhode Island Av NW,
  Washington, 20005 202-234-6292

Elizabeth Pointe Lodge, Amelia Island, FL

Florida

AMELIA ISLAND

1735 House
584 S. Fletcher Ave., 32034
904-261-5878 800-872-8531
Gary A. & Emily S. Grable
All year

$$$ B&B
5 rooms, 5 pb
Visa, MC, AmEx •
C-yes/S-yes/P-no/H-no

Continental plus
Comp. newspaper
In-room coffee service
beach towels
surf cast fishing

White frame house overlooking Atlantic Ocean. Breakfast served with morning paper. Stay in suites (up to 4) or lighthouse (up to 6). Golf, tennis, fishing, riding, sailing.

Florida House Inn, Amelia Island, FL

AMELIA ISLAND

Elizabeth Pointe Lodge
P.O. Box 1210, 32034
98 S. Fletcher Ave.
904-277-4851
David & Susan Caples
All year

$$$ B&B
20 rooms, 20 pb
Visa, MC, AmEx •
C-yes/S-yes/P-no/H-yes

Full breakfast
Comp. wine, snacks
Sitting room, library
bicycles, oceanfront

Reminiscent of a turn-of-the-century lodge; oceanfront on a small Florida barrier island; bike to historic seaport village nearby. Hearty breakfast, newspaper, fresh flowers.

Florida House Inn
P.O. Box 688, 32034
22 S. Third St.
904-261-3300 800-258-3301
Bob & Karen Warner
All year

$$ B&B
12 rooms, 12 pb
Visa, MC, AmEx •
C-yes/S-no/P-no/H-yes
some Spanish

Full breakfast
Restaurant, bar
Sitting room, library
bicycles, near beaches,
golf, tennis, fishing

Florida's oldest continually operating tourist hotel, circa 1857, in 50-block historic district. Country antiques, quilts, wide shady porches, courtyard with fountain.

BIG PINE KEY

The Barnacle
Route 1 Box 780A, 33043
Long Beach Rd.
305-872-3298
Wood & Joan Cornell
All year

$$ B&B
4 rooms, 4 pb
•
C-no/S-yes/P-no/H-no
French

Full breakfast
Comp. wine
Hot tub, bicycles
fishing poles
refrigerators

Barefoot living with panache. Secluded area on ocean in fabulous Florida Keys. Private cottage and efficiency unit.

BRADENTON BEACH

Duncan House B&B	$$ B&B	Full breakfast
1703 Gulf Dr., 34217	4 rooms, 4 pb	Comp. wine
813-778-6858	Visa, MC, AmEx •	Sitting room
Becky Ann Kern	C-ltd/S-no/P-no/H-no	sun deck
All year		turn-down service

Turn-of-the-century Victorian. Located on beautiful Anna Maria Island. Steps away from white sandy beaches.

CEDAR KEY

Historic Island Hotel	$$$ B&B	Full gourmet breakfast
P.O. Box 460, Main St., 32625	10 rooms, 6 pb	Full menu, cafe
904-543-5111	Visa, MC	Natural foods restaurant
Marcia Rogers	C-yes/S-no/P-no/H-ltd	comp. wine, draft beer
All year	Spanish	sitting & dining room

1850 Jamaican architecture in historic district. Antiques. Gourmet natural foods specializing in original recipes, seafood and vegetarian, poppy-seed bread. Murals.

COCOA

Colonial River House	$ B&B	Continental plus
607 N. Indian River Dr., 32922	5 rooms	Snacks
407-632-8780	•	Swimming, crabbing
Dan Haddad	C-12+/S-no/P-no/H-no	clamming, and fishing
All year		boat & equipment rental

Traditional two-story Colonial on the Indian River. Art gallery ambience. 8 miles from beach, 15 minutes from Space Center. Walk to quaint Cocoa Village.

CORAL GABLES

Hotel Place St. Michel	$$$ B&B	Continental breakfast
162 Alcazar Ave., 33134	28 rooms, 28 pb	Lunch, dinner, bar, deli
305-444-1666	Visa, MC, AmEx, DC, CB •	Sitting room, piano
Stuart Bornstein, A. Potamkin	C-yes/S-yes/P-no/H-no	entertainment
All year	Fr, Span, Ger, It, Port	

Charming small European-style hotel filled with English & French antiques, featuring the best service and friendly atmosphere. Award-winning restaurant.

DAYTONA BEACH

Captain's Quarters Inn	$$ B&B	Full breakfast
3711 S. Atlantic Ave., 32127	25 rooms, 25 pb	Lunch, comp. wine
904-767-3119	Visa, MC, AmEx •	Cheese, crackers
Becky Sue Morgan & Family	C-yes/S-yes/P-ask/H-yes	turn-down service
All year		heated pool, bicycles

Daytona's first new B&B inn, directly on the world's most famous beach. Old-fashioned coffee shop. Unique antique shoppe, all-suite inn, private balconies. AAA "excellent."

Live Oak Inn	$$ B&B/MAP	Continental plus
444-448 South Beach St., 32114	16 rooms, 16 pb	Restaurant, bar service
904-252-4667	Visa, MC, Dis •	Comp. wine, tea, snacks
Vinton Day Fisher	S-no/P-ask/H-yes	sitting room, library
All year		jacuzzis, massage avail.

Daytona's only Historic Registry inn. Early Florida antiques. A Romantic setting: marina, river & garden views, fine dining. Close to airport, beach, speedway, pool, golf.

EDGEWATER

The Colonial House
110 E. Yelkca Terrace, 32132
904-427-4570
Eva Brandner
All year

$ B&B
5 rooms, 4 pb
•
C-7+/S-yes
German, French, Italian

Full breakfast
Comp. snacks on arrival
Guest refrigerator, A/C
washing machine, TV
pool, hot tub

Colonial-style home with year-round heated pool and hot tub close to one of Florida's finest beaches and attractions.

FORT MYERS

Drum House Inn
2135 McGregor Blvd., 33901
813-332-5668
Jim & Shirley Drum
All year

$$$ EP
6 rooms, 6 pb
C-no/S-no/P-no/H-yes

Continental plus
Comp. wine, snacks
Sitting room
library
bicycles

Romantic Florida style. Uniquely decorated with antiques and period furniture. Walk to Ford & Edison homes. Shopping and restaurants nearby.

HIGH SPRINGS

Bloomsbury
P.O. Box 2567, 32643
30 N.E. First Ave.
904-454-4040
Sheila Barksdale
All year

$$$ B&B
4 rooms, 2 pb
Visa, MC, Disc
C-yes/S-ltd/P-yes/H-yes
Russian

Continental plus
Sitting room
Bicycles

English-run stylish Victorian house. Convenient downtown location near restaurant, antique shops. Swimming, canoeing, cave-diving at nearby warm-water spring.

HOLLYWOOD

Maison Harrison House
1504 Harrison St., 33020
604-922-7319
Donald Dupere, Andre Garneau
All year

$ B&B
6 rooms, 6 pb
•
C-no/S-yes/P-no/H-no
French

Continental plus
Sitting room, A/C
Color cable TV
private decks, hot tubs
exercise facility, BBQ

Mediterranean elegance in a tropical setting. Completely restored with style and charm, relax and enjoy the French hospitality.

HOLMES BEACH

Harrington House B&B
5626 Gulf Dr., 34217
813-778-5444
Jo & Frank Davis
All year

$$$ B&B
5 rooms
Visa, MC •
C-12+/S-no/P-no

Full gourmet breakfast
Comp. iced tea, popcorn
Sitting room
bicycles
swimming pool

Charming restored 1920s style home reflects a "casual elegance" on the beach. Antiques, balconies, great rooms, swimming pool, peace and quiet. Near major attractions.

JACKSONVILLE

1217 On the Bouelvard
1217 Boulevard St., 32206
904-354-6959
Virginia & Charles Kelly
September–July

$$ B&B
3 rooms, 3 pb
C-yes/S-no/P-no/H-no

Continental plus
Comp. wine, snacks
Afternoon tea
sitting room
tennis court

Enjoy Southern hospitality in a restored Colonial Revival home; located in historic Springfield, minutes from downtown riverfront shops and restaurants.

JACKSONVILLE

House on Cherry Street
1844 Cherry St., 32205
904-384-1999
Carol Anderson
All year

$$ B&B
4 rooms, 4 pb
Visa, MC •
C-9+/S-yes/P-no/H-no

Full breakfast
Comp. wine, snacks
Sitting room
air conditioned
porch, bicycles

In historic Riverside, a restored colonial house filled with period antiques, decoys, four poster beds and country collectibles. On beautiful St. John's River.

Judge Gray's House
2814 St. Johns Ave., 32611
800-654-3095 904-388-4248
Bill Edmonds
All year

$ B&B
3 rooms, 3 pb
•
C-10+/S-ltd/P-no/H-no
some Spanish

Continental plus
Comp. wine, tea
Sitting room, library
verandas, swing, hammock
TV, phone in room, A/C

1911 Queen Anne home in historic Riverside. Antiques, art. Off-street parking. Near downtown, I-10, I-95, shopping, parks, tennis, golf.

KEY WEST

Blue Parrot Inn
916 Elizabeth St., 33040
305-296-0033
Rick Scrabis, Ed Lowery
All year

$$$ B&B
9 rooms, 9 pb
Visa, MC, AmEx, Disc
C-no/S-yes/P-no/H-no

Continental plus
Library
swimming pool
A/C, private bath

Classic Bahamian Conch house built in 1884 with major renovations in 1989. In the heart of Old Town Key West. Walk to beaches, shopping, restaurants, clubs.

Curry Mansion Inn
511 Caroline St., 33040
305-294-5349 800-253-3466
Edith & Albert Amsterdam
All year

$$$ B&B
15 rooms, 15 pb
Visa, MC, AmEx •
C-yes/S-yes/P-yes/H-yes
Fr., Span., Ger., Ital.

Continental plus
Full bar/snacks 5pm-7pm
Sitting room, library
swimming pool, billiards
private beach club

Landmark Victorian mansion with new poolside guest wing. Every amenity. Magnificent antiques, fabulous breakfast, daily cocktail party w/music, beach club. All complementary.

Duval House
815 Duval St., 33040
305-294-1666
Richard Kamradt
All year

$$$ B&B
27 rooms, 25 pb
Visa, MC, AmEx
C-15+/S-yes

Continental plus
2 apts. with kitchenette
Sitting room
TV lounge, sun decks
swimming pool, gardens

A restored guest house (circa 1885) offering fine lodging. Ideally located in historic Old Key West. Tropical gardens and a laid-back atmosphere. Walk to beaches, restaurants.

Eden House
1015 Fleming St., 33040
305-296-6868 800-533-KEYS
Michael Eden
All year

$$$ EP
41 rooms, 41 pb
Visa, MC, AmEx •
C-yes/S-yes/P-no/H-no
some Spanish

Restaurant, cafe
Free happy hour
Swimming pool
snorkeling, scuba diving
sailing & jet ski nearby

In old Key West. Ceiling fans and white wicker. Sip a cool drink under our poolside gazebo, lounge on the veranda or dine in our garden cafe. Join us on a sunset sail.

KEY WEST ─────────────────────────────────────

Heron House
512 Simonton St., 33040
305-294-9227 800-937-5656
Fred Geibelt
All year

$$ B&B
23 rooms, 21 pb
Visa, MC, AmEx •
C-15+/S-yes/P-no/H-yes

Continental plus
Gardens, sun deck
gym, swimming pool

Old island charm situated in location central to all the main tourist attractions. Pool, sun deck, gardens and gym.

Key West B&B/Popular House
415 William St., 33040
305-296-7274
Jody Carlson
All year

$$ B&B
7 rooms, 2 pb
Visa, MC, AmEx •
S-yes

Continental plus
Sitting room
hot tubs, sauna
sun deck

In the heart of the Historic Preservation District, a 100-year-old Victorian located within walking distance to everything. Sun deck, sauna, jacuzzi for your relaxation.

Merlinn Guesthouse
811 Simonton St., 33040
305-296-3336
Pat Hoffman
All year

$$ B&B
18 rooms, 18 pb
Visa, MC, AmEx •
C-yes/S-yes/P-yes/H-yes

Full breakfast
Comp. rum punch, snacks
Sitting room
library, garden
swimming pool

Magical, secluded retreat in the heart of Old Town. Homemade quiche and muffins. You'll love the leisurely breakfast in the lush, tropical oriental garden.

Nassau House
1016 Fleming St., 33040
305-296-8513 800-545-3907
Greg Henley
All year

$$ B&B
6 rooms, 6 pb
Visa, MC, AmEx •
C-ltd/S-yes/P-no/H-no
Continental breakfast

Full kitchens in units
Air conditioning
Tropical lagoon pool with
waterfall

Located in "Old Town." Six intimate units all fully furnished with white wicker furniture, plants, A/C, color cable TV, private deck. Pool is lagoon style with waterfall.

Palm's of Key West—Resort
820 White St., 33040
305-294-3146 800-558-9374
Terence Clarkson
All year

$$$ B&B
21 rooms, 21 pb
Visa, MC •
C-ltd/S-yes/P-no/H-ltd
French, German, Dutch

Continental breakfast
Complimentary wine
Swimming pool, phones
sitting room, room TVs
fans, A/C

Very relaxed, very quiet and very private 100-year-old house in Old Town. All rooms are poolside, completely restored and furnished with antiques.

Seascape
420 Olivia St., 33040
305-296-7776
Alan Melnick
All year

$$ B&B
5 rooms, 5 pb
Visa, MC, AmEx
C-no/S-yes/P-no/H-no

Continental breakfast
Comp. wine (in season)
Heated pool-spa
sun decks, wicker
A/C, TVs, Bahama fans

Built in 1889, listed on National Historic Register. Intimate pool in tropical garden setting. Sun decks. Royal blue and white wicker motif. Center of Old Town Key West.

KEY WEST

The Watson House
525 Simonton St., 33040
305-294-6712
Ed Czaplicki, Joe Beres
All year

$$$ B&B
3 rooms, 3 pb
Visa, MC, AmEx •
C-no/S-yes/P-no
Spanish

Continental breakfast
Veranda, heated spa
Swimming pool, gardens
cable TV, phones, A/C
wicker/rattan furniture

Small, quaint award-winning inn with fully furnished guest suites in a lush, tropical garden setting. Located in the Historic Preservation District.

Whispers B&B Inn
409 William St., 33040
305-294-5969
Les & Marilyn Tipton
All year

$$ B&B
6 rooms
Visa, MC, AmEx
C-no/S-ltd/P-no/H-no

Full gourmet breakfast
Ceiling fans, porches
Rooms have A/C and TVs
walking distance to all
activities

Historic Register. Victorian old town inn. Owner-occupied, serving gourmet breakfasts in our tropical garden. Beer or wine on arrival. Antiques throughout. Quiet and romantic.

Wicker Guesthouse
913 Duval St., 33040
305-296-4275
Mark & Libby Curtis
All year

$$ EP
15 rooms, 1 pb
Visa, MC •
C-yes/S-yes/P-ltd/H-no
French, Spanish, Italian

Fully equipped kitchens
For guest use, coffee
Sitting room
jacuzzi
therapeutic massage

Ideally located, comfortable and friendly atmosphere. Complimentary coffee and tea served. Guest kitchen, living room, TV, sundecks and jacuzzi.

KISSIMMEE

Unicorn Inn
8 S. Orlando Ave., 34741
407-846-1200
Janet & Roy Timbrell
All year

$$ B&B
7 rooms, 7 pb
•
C-yes/S-yes/P-no/H-no

Full breakfast
TV in rooms
coffee makers
in all rooms

Located in beautiful downtown Kissimmee, minutes from Disney World, Gatorland Zoo, Wet & Wild Boardwalk & baseball and a whole lot more.

LAKE HELEN

Clauser's Bed & Breakfast
201 E. Kicklighter Rd., 32744
904-228-0310
Marge & Tom Clauser
All year

$$ B&B
2 rooms, 2 pb
Visa, MC •
C-no/S-no/P-no/H-no

Full breakfast
Comp. wine, snacks, tea
Sitting room, library
verandas, gardens
rockers, bicycles

1880s Victorian home in tranquil country setting. Nominated for National Register. Magnificent trees, heirlooms, quilts, linens and lace. "Everybody's grandmother's house."

LAKE WALES

Chalet Suzanne Country Inn
P.O. Drawer AC, 33859
US Hwy 27 & CR 17A
813-676-6011 800-288-6011
Carl & Vita Hinshaw
All year

$$$ B&B
30 rooms, 30 pb
Major credit cards •
C-yes/S-yes/P-yes/H-ltd
German, French

Continental breakfast
Restaurant, lounge
Comp. sherry in room
pool on lake, airstrip
3 rooms w/pvt. jacuzzi

Unique country inn centrally located for Florida attractions. Gourmet meals; award-winning restaurant. Ranked one of 10 most romantic spots in Florida. A memorable experience.

120 Florida

LAUDERDALE BY THE SEA

Breakaway Guest House
4457 Poinciana, 33308
305-771-6600
All year

B&B
41 rooms, 41 pb
Visa, MC ●
C-yes/S-yes/P-no/H-yes

Continental breakfast
BBQ, picnic tables
Library, courtyard
playground/park, pool
shuffle board, tennis

Relax poolside enjoying ocean breezes in our old Florida hideaway. Cook in! Ocean, tennis, fishing pier, shops, restaurant steps away.

MARATHON

Hopp-Inn Guest House
5 Man-O-War Dr., 33050
305-743-4118
Joe & Joan Hopp
October–August

$$ B&B
5 rooms, 5 pb
●
C-yes/S-yes/P-no/H-ltd
German

Full breakfast
Televisions
Bahama fans
air conditioning

Three rooms with private entrances and baths. Located on the ocean with tropical plants and many palm trees. Two ocean view villas sleep 2-6.

MAYO

Jim Hollis River Rendevous
Route 2, Box 60, 32066
904-294-2510
Rosa Falconer, Jim Hollis
All year

$ EP
23 rooms, 24 pb
Visa, MC, AmEx, DC
C-yes/S-yes/P-ltd/H-yes

Full breakfast $
Restaurant, bar
Hot tubs, steam room
natural spring, bicycles
game room, canoe rentals

Nestled on the beautiful Suwannee River–a unique experience for a hideaway. "Once is not enough."

MIAMI

Miami River Inn
118 SW S. River Dr., 33130
305-325-0045 800-HOTEL89
Sallye G. Jude
All year

$$ B&B
41 rooms, 39 pb
Visa, MC ●
C-yes/S-yes/P-no/H-no
Spanish

Continental breakfast
Aftn. tea, comp. wine
Sitting room, library
hot tubs, pool, croquet
table games, telephone

A cluster of historic buildings, carefully restored and furnished in period. Right next to downtown Miami but a world apart.

MIAMI BEACH

Penguin Hotel
1418 Ocean Dr., 33139
305-534-9334
The Sakson Family
All year

$$ B&B
44 rooms, 44 pb
Visa, MC, AmEx ●
C-yes/S-yes/P-no/H-no
Spanish, German, French

Continental plus
Bar service
Sitting room
beach chairs, towels
restaurants nearby

Magnificent beachfront location in the heart of the Art Deco district. Newly restored, family-run, fabulous nearby restaurants and nightlife.

MICANOPY

Herlong Mansion
P.O. Box 667, 32667
402 N.E. Cholokka Blvd.
904-466-3322
H.C. (Sonny) Howard, Jr.
All year

$$$ B&B
6 rooms, 6 pb
Visa, MC ●
C-yes/S-no/P-no/H-no

Continental plus (wkdys)
Full breakfast (wkends)
Aftn. tea, comp. wine
sitting room
library

Twenty antique and craft shops one block away. Historic Greek Revival house, circa 1845. Moss draped oaks, pecans and dogwoods.

NAPLES

Inn by the Sea
287–11th Ave. S., 33940
813-649-4124
Elise Sechrist Orban
All year

$ B&B
6 rooms, 5 pb
Visa, MC •
C-16+/S-no/P-no/H-no

Continental plus
Sitting room
Bicycles
beach just 700 feet away

Tropical beach house just 700 feet from beach. Walk to fabulous shopping, art galleries, restaurants. Located in Old Naples Historic District.

ORLANDO

PerriHouse B&B
10417 State Road 535, 32836
407-876-4830 800-780-4830
Nick & Angi Perretti
All year

$$ B&B
9 rooms, 9 pb
AmEx •
C-yes/S-ltd

Continental plus
Complimentary wine
Private entrance to room
swimming pool, jacuzzi

A private & secluded country estate on 20 acres conveniently nestled right in Disney's "backyard". All Orlando & Disney attractions minutes away. Boutique shopping nearby.

PENSACOLA

Liechty's Homestead Inn
7830 Pine Forest Rd., 32526
904-944-4816
Neil & Jeanne Liechty
All year

$$ B&B
6 rooms, 6 pb
AmEx, Visa, MC •
C-12+/S-no/P-no/H-no

Full 6-course breakfast
Dessert, ice cream, pie
Sitting room

Featuring Lancaster Pennsylvania Amish-Mennonite recipes at our restaurant. Our rooms have wood floors, poster beds, fireplaces and garden tubs.

RUSKIN

Ruskin House B&B
120 Dickman Dr. S.W., 33570
813-645-3842
Dr. Arthur M. Miller
All year

$ B&B
4 rooms, 1 pb
Visa, MC
C-5+/S-ltd/P-ask/H-yes
French, some Spanish

Continental plus
Full breakfast (arrange)
Sitting room, library
health club nearby ($)

Gracious 1910 waterfront home with period (1860-1920) antiques, between Tampa & Sarasota on west coast. Three minutes from I-75. Friendly!

SAINT AUGUSTINE

Carriage Way B&B
70 Cuna St., 32084
904-829-2467 800-648-2888
Frank & Karen Burkley-Kovacik
All year

$$ B&B
9 rooms, 9 pb
Visa, MC •
C-yes/S-no/P-no/H-no
French

Continental plus
Lunch/dinner/tea/snacks
Comp. wine, Sat. dessert
piano, catering, picnics
Honeymoon brkfast in bed

1883 Victorian home in heart of historic district furnished with antiques and reproductions. Clawfoot bathtubs. Casual, leisurely atmosphere. "Special touches" available.

Casa De La Paz
22 Avenida Menendez, 32084
904-829-2915
Sandy Upchurch
All year

$$ B&B
6 rooms, 6 pb
Visa, MC, AmEx, Disc •
C-8+/S-no/P-no/H-no
French

Full breakfast
Comp. sherry, champagne
Sitting room, library
room service, courtyard
veranda, carriage tours

On the bayfront in the Historic District, this elegant Mediterranean-style home (1915) offers the finest accommodations in a beautiful, central location.

SAINT AUGUSTINE

Castle Garden B&B
15 Shenandoah St., 32084
404-829-3839
Bruce & Joyce Kloeckner
All year

$$ B&B
4 rooms, 4 pb
Visa, MC, AmEx •
C-yes/S-no/P-no/H-no

Full breakfast
Snacks, comp. wine
Sitting room
bicycles, fresh flowers
chocolates on pillows

St. Augustine's only Moorish Revival dwelling, former Castle Warden Carriage House, built 1800's. Restored, antiques, lush landscape, beautiful gardens, quiet hideaway.

The Kenwood Inn
38 Marine St., 32084
904-824-2116
The Constant Family
All year

$$ B&B
15 rooms, 15 pb
Visa, MC, Disc
C-6+/S-no/P-no/H-no

Continental breakfast
Sitting room, piano
swimming pool
walled in courtyard

Lovely old 19th-century Victorian inn located in historic district of our nation's oldest city. Walk to attractions; beautiful beaches 5 minutes away.

Old City House Inn & Rest.
115 Cordova St., 32084
904-826-0113
Robert & Alice Compton
All year

$$ B&B
5 rooms, 5 pb
Visa, MC, AmEx
C-yes/S-no/P-no/H-no

Full breakfast
Restaurant, bar
Comp. wine
veranda, bicycles
6 mi. to beach

Newly renovated Colonial Revival house in heart of nation's oldest city. Queen-size beds and private entrances. Five-star restaurant. Walk to historical attractions, shops.

Southern Wind B&B
18 Cordova St., 32084
904-825-3623
Jeanette & Dennis Dean
All year

$$ B&B
7 rooms, 7 pb
Visa, MC, AmEx
C-yes/S-no/P-no/H-ltd

Full breakfast
Comp. wine
Sitting room
large verandas
cable TV, bicycles

On the Carriage Trail through historic district, Southern Wind offers an elegant 1916 columned masonry home with exceptional buffet breakfast. Separate guest inn for families.

St. Francis Inn
279 St. George St., 32084
904-824-6068
Marie Register
All year

$ B&B
11 rooms, 11 pb
Visa, MC •
C-yes/S-yes/P-no/H-no

Continental plus
Iced tea & lemonade
Sunday nite music,
free passes to Oldest House,
bicycles

Built in 1791, located in Historic District, one block west of the "Oldest House in USA." New owner, many improvements.

Victorian House B&B
11 Cadiz St., 32084
904-824-5214
Daisy Morden
All year

$$ B&B
6 rooms, 6 pb
Visa, MC
C-ltd/S-yes/P-no/H-no

Continental plus
Sitting room

Located in the heart of the historic area. Enjoy canopy beds, stenciled walls. Explore the charm of St. Augustine from the Victorian House.

SAINT AUGUSTINE

Westcott House
146 Avenida Menendez, 32084
904-824-4301
Ruth Erminelli
All year

$$$ B&B
8 rooms, 8 pb
Visa, MC •
C-ltd/S-ltd/P-no/H-no

Continental plus
Comp. wine, brandy
Sitting room
3 Victorian porches
courtyard

Built in 1880s, beautifully decorated Victorian home furnished w/European antiques, located in historic district overlooking Matanzas Bay for a breathtaking view.

SAINT PETERSBURG

Bayboro House on Tampa Bay
1719 Beach Dr. SE, 33701
813-823-4955
Gordon & Antonia Powers
All year

$$ B&B
4 rooms, 4 pb
Visa, MC •
C-no/S-ltd/P-no/H-no

Continental plus
Comp. wine/cocktails
Veranda
player piano

Walk out the door to sunning and beachcombing from a turn-of-the-century Queen Anne house. Florida B&B-ing at its best. 1991 St. Petersburg Historical Preservation Award.

TARPON SPRINGS

Spring Bayou Inn
32 W. Tarpon Ave., 34689
813-938-9333
Ron & Cher Morrick
December 15–August 15

$$ B&B
5 rooms, 3 pb
C-no/S-no/P-ask/H-no

Continental breakfast
Comp. wine
Parlor, library
fireplace, front porch
baby grand piano

Elegant Victorian with modern conveniences. Walk to shops, bayou, restaurants, sponge docks. Golf, beaches, tennis, and fishing nearby.

VENICE

Banyan House
519 S. Harbor Dr., 34285
813-484-1385
Chuck & Susan McCormick
All year

$$ B&B
9 rooms, 7 pb
C-12+/S-ltd/P-no

Continental plus
Sitting room
bicycles, hot tubs
swimming pool

Historic Mediterranean-style home. Enormous banyan tree shades courtyard, pool and spa. Centrally located to shopping, restaurants, beaches and golfing.

WINTER GARDEN

Casa Adobe
P.O. Box 770707, 34777
S/R 535, Lake Buena Vista
407-876-5432
Lorrie Nassofer
All year

$$ B&B
3 rooms, 2 pb
•
C-yes/S-yes/P-yes/H-yes

Continental plus
Afternoon tea/snacks
Comp. wine, hot tubs
library, pool, bikes
Horseback riding

Lakefront estate and country hideaway located on the Butler Chain of Lakes—just minutes from Disney World and all central Florida attractions.

ZOLFO SPRINGS

Double M Ranch B&B
Route 1, Box 292, 33890
813-735-0266
Mary Jane & Charles Matheny
All year

$$ B&B
1 rooms, 1 pb
C-no/S-no/P-no/H-no

Continental plus
Sitting room
Pool table, ranch tour
nearby golf, canoeing,
fishing, and riding

4,500-acre citrus and cattle ranch in central Florida. Peaceful, quiet, with wildlife and numerous golf courses nearby. 2 night minimum, call 6-9pm EST.

More Inns ...

Alexander's 1118 Fleming St., Key West, 33040 305-294-9919
Alpen Gast Haus 8328 Curry Ford Rd., Orlando, 32822 305-277-1811
Angelina 302 Angela St., Key West, 33040 305-294-4480
Artist House 534 Easton St., Key West, 33040 305-296-3977
Authors 725 White St., Key West, 33040 305-296-3977
Avonelle's 4755 Anderson Rd., Orlando, 32806 305-275-8733
Bailey House P.O. Box 805, Fernandina Beach, 32034 904-261-5390
Bay View House Rt 1, Box 2120, Santa Rosa Beach, 28734 904-267-1202
Big Ruby's Guesthouse 409 Appelrouth Lane, Key West, 33040 305-296-2323
Borg's 712 Amelia St., Key West, 33040 305-296-3671
Brass Key Guesthouse 412 Frances St., Key West, 33040 305-296-4719
Briercliff 1523 Briercliff Dr., Orlando, 32806 407-894-0504
Cabbage Key Inn Cabbage Key, 33924 813-283-2278
Casa Adobe P.O. Box 770707, Winter Garden, 34777 407-876-5432
Casa Alhambra B&B Inn 3029 Alhambra St., Fort Lauderdale Beach, 33304 305-467-2262
Cavalier Hotel/Cabana Club P.O. Box 1157, Miami Beach, 33139 305-534-2135
Chelsea House 707 Truman Ave., Key West, 33040 305-296-2211
Coconut Grove Guest House 817 Fleming St., Key West, 33040 305-296-5107
Colours Key West 410 Fleming St., Key West, 33040 305-294-6977
Coquina Inn B&B 544 S. Palmetto, Daytona Beach, 32114 904-254-4969
Cottages 1512 Dennis St., Key West, 33040 305-294-6003
Courtyard at Lake Lucerne 211 N. Lucerne Cir. E, Orlando, 32801 407-648-5188
Crown Hotel 109 N. Seminole Ave., Inverness, 32650 904-344-5555
Cypress House 601 Caroline St., Key West, 33040 305-294-6969
DeLand Country Inn 228 W. Howry Ave., DeLand, 32720 904-736-4244
Doll House B&B 719 S.E. 4th St., Ocala, 32671 904-351-1167
E.H. Gato Jr. Guesthouse 1327 Duval St., Key West, 33040 305-294-0715
Early House 507 Simonton St., Key West, 33040 305-296-0214
East Lake B&B 421 Old East Lake Rd., Tarpon Springs, 34689 813-937-5487
Eaton Lodge 511 Eaton St., Key West, 33040 305-294-3800
Ellie's Nest 1414 Newton St.,, Key West, 33040 305-296-5757
Essex House 1001 Collins Ave., Miami Beach, 33139 305-534-2700
Feller House 2473 Longboat Dr., Naples, 33942 813-774-0182
Five Oaks Inn 1102 Riverside Dr., Palmetto, 34221 813-723-1236
Florida Suncoast B&B 119 Rosewood Dr., Palm Harbor, 34685 813-787-3500
Fogarty House 227 Duval St., Key West, 33040 305-296-9592
Fortnightly Inn 377 E. Fairbanks Ave., Winter Park, 32789 407-645-4440
Garden House 329 Elizabeth St., Key West, 33040 305-296-5368
Gasparilla Inn Boca Grande, 33921 813-964-2201
Gibson Inn P.O. Box 221, Apalachicola, 32320 904-653-2191
Gideon Lowe House 409 William St., Key West, 33040 305-294-5969
Hibiscus House P.O. Box 2612, West Palm Beach, 33402 407-863-5633
Hollinsed House 611 Southard St., Key West, 33040 305-296-8031
Homeplace, The 501 Akron, Stuart, 34994 407-220-9148
Island City House Hotel 411 William St., Key West, 33040 305-294-5702
Jean Hutchison 811 N.W. 3rd Ave., Delray Beach, 33444 407-276-7390
Jules' Undersea Lodge P.O. Box 3330, Key Largo, 33037 305-451-2353
Key West Style P.O. Box 078581, W. Palm Beach, 407-848-4064
La Belle Francaise 101 Oriole Ct, Royal Palm Beach, 33411 407-793-3550
Lake Weir Inn Rt. 2, 12660 SE Hwy 25, Ocklawaha, 32179 904-288-3723
Lakeside Inn Box 1390, Mount Dora, 32757 800-556-5016
Lamp Post House 309 Louisea St., Key West, 33040 305-294-7709
Lemon Bay B&B 12 Southwind Dr., Englewood, 33533 813-474-7571
Lighthouse Court 902 Whitehead St., Key West, 33040 305-294-9588
Marquesa Hotel 600 Fleming St., Key West, 33040 305-292-1919
Mary Lee B&B 717 Sunlit Court, Brandon, 33511 813-653-3807
Meadow Marsh 940 Tildenville School, Orlando, 32787 305-656-2064

Mermaid & The Alligator 729 Truman Ave., Key West, 33040 305-294-1894
New World Inn 6000 South Palafox St., Pensacola, 32501 904-432-4111
Nick and Ann Perretti 8151 N.W. 12th Ct., Coral Springs, 33071 305-752-2355
Norment-Parry Inn 211 N. Lucerne Cir. E., Orlando, 32801 407-648-5188
North Hill Inn 422 N. Baylen St., Pensacola, 32501 904-432-9804
Oasis Guest House 823 Fleming St., Key West, 33040 305-296-2131
Old Town Garden Villas 921 Center St., Key West, 33040 305-294-4427
Orange Springs One Main St., Box 550, Orange Springs, 32682 904-546-2052
Orchid House 1025 Whitehead St., Key West, 33040 305-294-0102
Peppermill B&B 625 East Washington St., Monticello, 32344 904-997-4600
Phillippi Crest Inn 2549 Ashton Rd., Sarasota, 34231 813-924-2396
Pilot House Guest House 414 Simonton St., Key West, 33040 305-294-8719
Pines of Key West 521 United St., Key West, 33040 305-296-7467
Pink Camellia 145 Avenue E, Apalachicola, 32320 904-653-2107
Rainbow House 525 United St., Key West, 33040 305-292-1450
Rinaldi House 502 Lake Ave., Orlando, 32801 407-425-6549
Robin Dodson 11754 Ruby Lake Rd., Orlando, 32819 305-239-0109
Rod & Gun Club P.O. Box G, Everglades City, 33929 813-695-2101
Sea Isle Resort 915 Windsor Lane, Key West, 33040 305-294-5188
Seaside Inn Daytona Beach, 800-874-3215
Seminole Country Inn 15885 Warfield Blvd., Indiantown, 33456 305-597-3777
Seven Sisters Inn 820 SE Fort King St., Ocala, 32671 904-867-1170
Simonton Court 320 Simonton St., Key West, 33040 305-294-6386
Spencer Home B&B 313 Spencer St., Orlando, 32809 407-855-5603
Sprague House 125 Central Ave., Crescent City, 32012 904-698-2430
Sunbright Manor 606 Live Oak, De Funiak Springs, 32433 904-892-0656
Sunrise Sea House B&B 39 Bay Dr., Bay Point, Key West, 33040 305-745-3525
Sunshine 508 Decatur Ave., Pensacola, 32507 904-455-6781
Sweet Caroline 529 Caroline St., Key West, 33040 305-296-5173
Tilton Hilton 511 Angela St., Key West, 33040 305-294-8697
Tropical Inn 812 Duval St., Key West, 33040 305-294-9977
Wakulla Springs & Lodge One Springs Dr., Wakulla, 32305 904-561-7215
Walden House 717 Caroline St., Key West, 33040 305-296-7161
West Palm Beach B&B PO Box 8581, West Palm Beach, 33407 407-848-4064
Westwinds 914 Eaton St., Key West, 33040 305-294-3860
Windsong Garden 5570-4 Woodrose Court, Fort Myers, 33907 813-936-6378
Yearling Cabins Route 3, Box 123, Hawthorne, 32640 904-466-3033

House on Cherry Street, Jacksonville, FL

Georgia

ATLANTA

Beverly Hills Inn
65 Sheridan Dr. N.E., 30305
404-233-8520 800-331-8520
Mit & Hima Amin
All year

$$$ B&B
18 rooms, 18 pb
Visa, MC, AmEx ●
C-yes/S-yes/P-no/H-no

Continental plus
Comp. wine, courtyard
Sitting room, library
piano, health club priv.
London taxi shuttle

Charming city retreat, fine residential neighborhood. Close to Lenox Square, Historical Society and many art galleries. 15 min. to downtown. Shuttle to nearby attractions.

Shellmont B&B Lodge
821 Piedmont Ave. NE, 30308
404-872-9290
Edward & Debbie McCord
All year

$$$ B&B
4 rooms, 4 pb
Visa, MC, AmEx ●
C-ltd/S-ltd/P-no/H-yes

Continental plus
Beverages, chocolates
Sitting room
bicycles
near restaurants

Classic Victorian home; guest suites; private baths; authentic furnishings; magnificent woodwork. Located near historic district. National Register; City Of Atlanta Landmark.

Woodruff B&B Inn
223 Ponce de Leon Ave., 30308
404-875-9449 800-473-9449
Joan & Douglas Jones
All year

$$$ B&B
11 rooms, 6 pb
●
C-yes/S-yes/P-no/H-no

Full Southern breakfast
Comp. soda
Sitting room
hot tubs, porches
movies/TV in parlor

Southern hospitality in the heart of Atlanta! Old Victorian home, formerly a bordello. Antiques, full Southern breakfast, hot tubs, hot-air ballooning available.

BRUNSWICK

Brunswick Manor
825 Egmont St., 31520
912-265-6889
Claudia and Harry Tzucanow
All year

$$ B&B
9 rooms, 8 pb
personal checks ●
C-yes/S-ltd/P-ltd/H-ltd
some Spanish

Full gourmet breakfast
Comp. wine, high tea
Sitting room, library
bicycles, tennis courts
airport pick-up

Elegant Olde Towne historic inn, 1886, near Golden Isles. Gourmet breakfasts; high tea each afternoon. Boat chartering available. Gracious hospitality. Airport pick-up.

Rose Manor Guest House
1108 Richmond St., 31520
at Hanover Square
912-267-6369
Rachel Rose
All year

$ B&B
5 rooms, 3 pb
●
C-yes/S-ltd/P-no/H-no
some French

Full breakfast
Picnic lunch, high tea
Evening cordials
library, English gardens
bicycles, croquet

Southern Victorian, elegantly restored, resplendent English gardens, gracious amenities. Historic Port City, World's Shrimp Capital, gateway to Georgia's Golden Isles.

CLARKESVILLE

Glen-Ella Springs Inn
Route 3, Box 3304, 30523
Bear Gap Rd.
404-754-7295 800-552-3479
Barrie & Bobby Aycock
All year

$$ B&B
16 rooms, 16 pb
Visa, MC, AmEx ●
C-ltd/S-yes/P-no/H-yes

Continental plus
Lunch, dinner, beverages
Restaurant, conf. room
sitting room, library
pool, hiking, gardens

100-year-old inn in northeast Georgia. Award-winning restoration in 1987. Gourmet dining room features fresh seafood, prime rib and many specialties.

Habersham Hollow Inn
Route 6, Box 6208, 30523
404-754-5147
C.J. & Maryann Gibbons
All year

$$ B&B
4 rooms, 4 pb
Visa, MC
C-yes/S-ltd/P-yes

Continental plus
Dinner, comp. wine
Hiking, fishing
white water rafting
horseback riding

Five minutes to Helen. Elegant country inn. King-size four-poster beds. Secluded, cozy, fireplace cabins located on the grounds.

CLAYTON

English Manor Inns
P.O. Box 1605, 30525
US Hwy. 76 East
800-782-5780
Susan & English Thornwell
All year

$$ B&B/$$$ AP
60 rooms, 60 pb
Visa, MC ●
C-yes/S-yes/P-yes
French, Spanish, German

Full breakfast
Sunday brunch, high tea
Dinner, comp. wine
setups, pool, hot tubs
tennis courts, croquet

Seven inns, all furnished in exquisite antiques, reflecting the charm of an earlier era with all the amenities of today.

COMMERCE

The Pittman House
103 Homer St., 30529
404-335-3823
Tom & Dot Tomberlin
All year

$ B&B
4 rooms, 2 pb
Visa, MC, Dis ●
C-yes/S-no/P-no/H-no

Full breakfast
Snacks
Sitting room
library
tennis court nearby

The Pittman House is a restored 1890 Colonial with wrap-around rocking porch. Completely furnished with antiques. Great sports & shopping nearby.

DAHLONEGA

Smith House
202 S. Chestatee St., 30533
404-864-3566 800-852-9577
The Welches
All year

$ EP
18 rooms, 18 pb
Visa, MC, AmEx
C-yes/S-yes/P-no/H-ltd

Continental breakfast
Restaurant
Country store
sitting room

All-you-can-eat family-style dining for over 50 years. A stay at Smith House Inn is one of old-fashioned nostalgic character.

DARIEN

Open Gates B&B
Box 1526, Vernon Square, 31305
Exit 10, I-95
912-437-6985
Carolyn & Philip Hodges
All year

$$ B&B
5 rooms, 3 pb
●
C-ask/S-no/P-no/H-no

Full breakfast
Boxed lunch, comp. wine
Library, Steinway piano
bicycles, pool, antiques
sailing, boat tours

Timber baron's gracious home on oak-shaded historic square. Access to untrammeled barrier islands, including Sapelo and the Altamaha Delta rice culture.

FERNANDINA BEACH

Greyfield Inn
P.O. Drawer B, Florida, 32034
Cumberland Island
904-261-6408
Mary Jo & Oliver Ferguson
All year

$$$ AP
9 rooms, 1 pb
Visa, MC
C-yes/S-ltd/P-no/H-no

Full breakfast
Lunch & dinner included
Bar
sitting room, Bar
hot tub, bicycles

House built 1904 for Margaret Carnegie. Original furnishings and unspoiled island—no telephone, TV, etc. Beach. Seafood; everything homemade.

GAINESVILLE

The Dunlap House
635 Green St., 30501
404-536-0200
Rita & Jerry Fishman
All year

$$$ B&B
11 rooms, 11 pb
Visa, MC, AmEx ●
C-ask/S-yes/P-no/H-yes
Spanish

Continental plus
Comp. wine, tea
Sitting room, bicycles
wedding/meeting facil.

Luxurious historic accommodations. Breakfast in bed or on the veranda. Restaurant and lounge across the street. Lodging and dining excellence.

HAMILTON

Wedgwood B&B
P.O. Box 115, 31811
Hwy 27 & Mobley Drive
404-628-5659
Janice Neuffer
March—December

$$ B&B
3 rooms, 1 pb
●
C-ask

Full breakfast
Comp. beverages & snacks
Living room, library
den with TV & VCR
bicycle, gazebo

Callaway Gardens is 6 miles north. Your hostess makes you feel at home in this beautiful 1845 southern home.

HELEN

Hilltop Haus B&B
P.O. Box 154, 30545
Chattahoochee St.
404-878-2388
Frankie Allen
All year

$ B&B
2 rooms, 2 pb
C-ltd/S-ltd/P-no/H-yes

Full country breakfast
Afternoon coffee
Bicycles
sitting rooms
with fireplaces

Located within walking distance of alpine village, Helen. Country-style breakfast with buttermilk biscuits, Appalachian Trail nearby.

MACON

1842 Inn
353 College St., 31201
912-741-1842 800-336-1842
Aileen Hatcher
All year

$$$ B&B
22 rooms, 22 pb
Visa, MC, AmEx ●
C-yes/S-yes/H-yes

Continental plus
Tea, coffee, bar service
Morning paper, whirlpool
turn-down/bedtime sweets
overnight shoeshines

Antebellum mansion and Victorian cottage furnished with fine antiques. All rooms have private baths, air conditioning and color televisions.

SAINT SIMONS ISLAND

Little St. Simons Island
P.O. Box 1078, 31522
912-638-7472
Debbie McIntyre
Mid-February—November

$$$ AP
12 rooms, 12 pb
Visa, MC ●
C-yes/S-yes/P-no/H-ltd

Full breakfast
Meals & activities incl.
Swimming pool
sitting room
bicycles, horses

A 10,000-acre undeveloped barrier island with early 1900s lodge and guest cottages. Southern cuisine. Professional naturalists and activities included.

SAUTEE ───────────────────────────────

The Stovall House
Route 1, Box 1476, 30571
Hwy 225 North
404-878-3355
Ham Schwartz
All year

$$ B&B
6 rooms, 6 pb
C-yes/S-yes/P-no/H-ltd
Spanish

Continental breakfast
Restaurant
Lunch, dinner
sitting room

Award-winning restoration of 1837 farmhouse on 28 serene acres; mountain views; a country experience. One of top 50 restaurants in Georgia. National Register.

SAVANNAH ───────────────────────────────

Ballastone Inn
14 E. Oglethorpe Ave., 31401
912-236-1484 800-822-4553
Richard Carlson, Tim Hargus
All year

$$$ B&B
18 rooms, 18 pb
Visa, MC, AmEx ●
C-no/S-yes/P-no/H-yes

Continental plus
Comp. sherry, cognac
Full service bar
elevator, VCRs
parlor, courtyard

Closest B&B inn to the Savannah Riverfront. 1835 mansion with beautiful antiques and courtyard. Fireplaces, jacuzzis. Recommended by the New York Times, Gourmet, and Brides.

Bed & Breakfast Inn
117 W. Gordon St., 31401
at Chatham Sq.
912-238-0518 FAX:233-2537
Robert McAlister, Pamela Gray
All year

$ B&B
7 rooms, 4 pb
Visa, MC ●
C-yes/S-yes/P-ltd/H-no
German, French, Spanish

Full homestyle breakfast
Sitting room
Library, garden

Restored 1853 Federal-style townhouse in heart of historic Savannah; amidst museums, restaurants & antique shops; walk to major attractions. Personalized hospitality.

East Bay Inn
225 East Bay St., 31401
912-238-1225 800-634-5488
Tricia Patterson
All year

$$$ B&B
28 rooms, 28 pb
Visa, MC, AmEx, DC, CB ●
C-yes/S-yes/P-no/H-yes

Continental breakfast
Lunch, dinner, bar
Eve. wine or beer
turn-down service
piano, library

Overlooking the historic waterfront of Savannah, the East Bay Inn epitomizes the grandeur and maritime prominence that was 1850s Savannah, rich in tradition.

Eliza Thompson House
5 W. Jones St., 31401
912-236-3620 800-348-9378
Lee & Terri Smith
All year

$$$ B&B
25 rooms, 25 pb
Visa, MC, AmEx ●
C-yes/S-yes/P-no/H-yes

Continental plus
Champagne on arrival
Evening cordials/sweets
imported wine daily
parlor, concierge

Regally restored home in the heart of the Historic District. Elegant parlor, beautifully landscaped courtyard with splashing fountains. Serene.

Foley House Inn
14 W. Hull St., 31401
912-232-6622 800-647-3708
Susan Steinhauser
All year

$$$ B&B
20 rooms, 20 pb
Visa, MC, AmEx ●
C-yes/S-yes/P-no/H-no

Continental plus
Comp. port, sherry, tea
Hot tub, newspaper
shoes shined on request
VCR & film lib. in rooms

A restored antebellum mansion, furnished with antiques, 5 jacuzzi rooms, in-room video disc players. Turndown service, fireplace rooms. Truly the best of two worlds.

SAVANNAH

Forsyth Park Inn
102 W. Hall St., 31401
912-233-6800
Virginia & Hal Sullivan
All year

$$$ B&B
10 rooms, 10 pb
Visa, MC, AmEx ●
C-yes/S-yes
some French

Continental breakfast
Comp. wine
Sitting room
tennis courts, hot tubs
piano music nightly

An elegantly restored Victorian mansion in the historic district. Rooms feature fireplaces, whirlpool tubs, antiques and 16-foot ceilings.

The Gastonian
220 E. Gaston St., 31401
912-232-2896 800-322-6603
Hugh & Roberta Lineberger
All year

$$$ B&B
13 rooms, 13 pb
Visa, MC, AmEx ●
C-no/S-no/P-no/H-yes

Full Southern breakfast
Comp. wine & fruit
Twin parlors
bicycles
hot tub

1868 southern elegance! Completely furnished with antiques, Persian rugs, whirlpool baths. Hot tubs on the sun deck. Luxurious. Mobil 4-Star; AAA 4-Diamond.

Jesse Mount House
209 W. Jones St., 31401
912-236-1774 800-347-1774
H. Crawford, L. Bannerman
All year

$$$ B&B
2 rooms, 2 pb
●
C-yes/S-yes/P-ltd/H-yes

Continental plus
Comp. sherry and candies
Garden with fountains
full kitchen, bicycles
room phones, cable TV

Circa 1854 elegant Greek Revival house. Two luxurious 3-bedroom suites for one to six persons in a party. Cable TV. Rare antiques, gilded harps.

Liberty Inn 1834
128 W. Liberty St., 31401
912-233-1007 800-637-1007
Frank & Janie Harris
All year

$$$ B&B
7 rooms, 7 pb
Visa, MC, AmEx ●
C-yes/S-yes/P-no/H-yes

Continental breakfast
Comp. cordial, coffee
Twin parlor
hot tub, spa
A/C, kitchenettes

1834 inn located in heart of historic Savannah, near the waterfront and shops. Garden, super spa, parking, continental breakfast. Peach cordial in each suite.

Olde Harbour Inn
508 E. Factors Walk, 31401
912-234-4100 800-553-6533
Pamela L. Barnes
All year

$$ B&B
24 rooms, 24 pb
Visa, MC, AmEx ●
C-yes/S-yes/P-no/H-ltd

Continental plus
Comp. wine, cheese,
crackers & ice cream
sitting room, library
kitchens in suites

Our traditionally renovated inn, built in 1892, offers spacious suites complete with kitchens and river views in Savannah's Historical District.

Presidents'-Quarters
225 E. President St., 31401
912-233-1600 800-233-1776
Muril L. Broy
All year

$$$ B&B
16 rooms, 16 pb
Visa, MC, AmEx, DC ●
C-yes/S-ltd/P-no/H-yes

Continental plus
Comp. wine, aftn. tea
Ltd. bar, sandwiches
sitting room, courtyard
jacuzzi, swimming pool

Newly restored 1885 home in the heart of Historic District offering jacuzzi bathtubs, gas log fireplaces, period reproductions. Deluxe but affordable accommodations.

Evans House, Thomasville, GA

SAVANNAH

Pulaski Square Inn
203 W. Charlton St., 31401
912-232-8055 800-227-0650
Mr & Mrs. J.B. Smith
All year

$ B&B
9 rooms, 5 pb
Visa, MC, AmEx ●
C-yes/S-yes/P-no/H-ltd

Continental breakfast
Sitting room
fireplaces

Distinctive inn on a lovely square in historic downtown. Continental breakfast in room or garden. Beautiful antiques, oriental rugs, fireplaces.

Remshart-Brooks House
106 W. Jones St., 31401
912-234-6928
Anne & Ewing Barnett
All year

$$ B&B
1 rooms, 1 pb
●
C-12+/S-yes/P-no/H-ltd

Continental plus
Sherry in room
Sitting room
terrace garden

Experience the charm and hospitality of historic Savannah while being "at home" in the garden suite of Remshart-Brooks House—built in 1854.

SENOIA

The Veranda
252 Seavy St., Box 177, 30276
404-599-3905
Jan & Bobby Boal
All year

$$$ B&B
8 rooms, 8 pb
Visa, MC, AmEx ●
C-ltd/S-ltd/P-no/H-yes
German

Full breakfast
Lunch, dinner by res.
Library, conference fac.
sitting room, organ
tennis courts nearby

Historic inn furnished with antiques, fascinating collections of Victorian memorabilia. Delicious meals, beautifully served in an Old South setting. OUR 1990 INN OF THE YEAR.

THOMASVILLE

Evans House B&B
725 S. Hansell St., 31792
912-226-1343
Lee Puskar
All year

$$ B&B
4 rooms, 4 pb
●
C-yes/S-no/P-ask/H-no

Full breakfast
Comp. wine, snacks
Bicycles

Restored Victorian home located in Parkfront historical district across from Paradise Park. Walking distance of historic downtown, tours, antique shops and restaurants.

More Inns . . .

118 West 118 W. Gaston St., Savannah, 31401 912-234-8557
17 Hundred 90 Inn 307 E. President St., Savannah, 31401 912-236-7122
217 Huckaby Box 115, Parrott, 31777 912-623-5545
A Place Away 110 Oglethorpe St., Andersonville, 31711 912-924-1044
Amy's Place 217 W. Cuyler St., Dalton, 30720 404-226-2481
Anapauo Farm Star Route, Box 13C, Lakemont, 30522 404-782-6442
Ansley Inn 253 Fifteenth St. NE, Atlanta, 30309 404-872-9000
Arden Hall 1052 Arden Dr. SW, Marietta, 30060 404-422-0780
Augusta House P.O. Box 40069, Augusta, 30904 404-738-5122
Barrister House 25 W. Perry St., Savannah, 31499 912-234-0621
Beachview Bed & Breakfast 537 Beachview Dr., Saint Simons Island, 31522 912-638-9424
Beggar's Bush-Cane Miller 615 Mud Creek Rd., Albany, 31707 912-432-9241
Blackmon B&B 512 N. Alexander Ave., Washington, 30673 404-678-2278
Blueberry Hill Rt. 1, Box 253, Hoboken, 31542 912-458-2605
Boat House 383 Porter St., Madison, 30650 404-342-3061
Brady Inn 250 N. 2nd St., Madison, 30650 404-342-4400
Bramlette B&B 255 Clarkewoods Rd., Athens, 30607 404-546-9740
Buckley's Cedar House Route 10, Box 161, Ringgold, 30736 404-935-2619
Burns-Sutton House P.O. Box 992, Clarkesville, 30523 404-754-5565
Burress B&B Box 201, Warm Springs, 31830 404-655-2168
Carriage Stop Inn/Antiques 1129 Georgia Ave., Macon, 31201 912-743-9740
Carrie L. Corrion 1675 Roswell, ND, #1027, Marietta, 30062 404-565-9425
Charlton Court 403 Charlton St. E., Savannah, 31401 912-236-2895
Charm House Inn Box 392, Highway 441, Clarkesville, 30523 404-754-9347
Coleman House 323 N. Main St., Swainsboro, 30401 912-237-2822
Colley House B&B, The 210 S. Alexander Ave., Washington, 30673 404-678-7752
Comer House 2 East Taylor St., Savannah, 31401 912-234-2923
Cottage Inn,The Box 488, Hwy. 49N, Americus, 31709 912-924-9316
Country Hearth Inn 301 Main St., St. Simons Island, 31522 800-673-6323
Culpepper House B&B 35 Broad St., Senoia, 30276 404-599-8182
Deer Creek B&B 1304 S. Broad St., Thomasville, 31792 913-226-7294
Dillard House Inn P.O. Box 10, Dillard, 30537 404-746-5349
Dodge Hill Inn 105 9th Ave. NE, Eastman, 31023 800-628-3778
Durham's B&B 130 Beaver Trail, Winterville, 30683 404-742-7803
Early Hill 1580 Lick Skillet Rd., Greensboro, 30648 404-453-7876
Edenfield House Inn Box 556, Swainsboro, 30401 912-237-3007
Elderberry Inn B&B Home 75 Dalton St., Ellijay, 30540 404-635-2218
Evans House, The 206 Miller St., Fort Valley, 31030 912-922-6691
Forest Hills Mt. Resort Route 3, Dahlonega, 30533 404-864-6456
Gaubert Bed & Breakfast 521 Oglethorpe, Saint Simons Island, 31522 912-638-9424
Georgia's Guest B&B 640 E. 7th St., Waynesboro, 30830 404-554-4863
Goodbread House, The 209 Osborne St., St. Marys, 31558 912-882-7490
Gordon Street Inn 403 W. Gordon St., Thomaston, 30286 404-647-5477
Gordon-Lee Mansion 217 Cove Rd., Chickamauga, 30707 404-375-4728
Greystone Inn 214 E. Jones St., Savannah, 31401 912-236-2442
Haslam-Fort House 417 E. Charlton St., Savannah, 31401 912-233-6380
Hearn Academy Inn Box 639, Cave Spring, 30124 404-777-8865
Helendorf Inn P.O. Box 305, Helen, 30545 404-878-2271
Helmstead, The 1 Fargo Rd., Homerville, 31634 912-487-2222
Holly Ridge Country Inn Rt. 2, Box 356, Washington, 30673 404-285-2594
Hotel Warm Springs B&B Inn Box 351, Warm Springs, 31830 404-655-2114
Hunter House B&B 1701 Butler Ave., Tybee Island, 31328 912-786-7515
Inman Park B&B 100 Waverly Way NE, Atlanta, 30307 404-688-9498
Jenny May & Sapp's B&B 229 Broad St., Buena Vista, 31803 912-649-7307
Karen R. Herman 1185 Grimes Bridge Rd., Roswell, 30075 800-533-4332
King's on the March 1776 Demere Rd., Saint Simons Island, 31522 912-638-1426
LaPrade's Route 1, Hwy 197N, Clarkesville, 30523 404-947-3312

Lake Rabun Inn Lakemont, 30552 404-782-4946
Laurel Ridge P.O. Box 338, Dahlonega, 30533 404-864-7817
Layside B&B 611 River St., Blakely, 31723 912-723-8932
Lee Street 1884 622 S. Lee St., Americus, 31709 912-924-1290
Liberty B&B Inn 108 W. Liberty St., Washington, 30673 404-678-3107
Little Blue House Box 566, Warm Springs, 31830 404-655-3633
Magnolia Place Inn 503 Whitaker St., Savannah, 31401 912-236-7674
Magnolia Plantation U.S. 80, Danville, 31017 912-962-3988
Marlow House/Stanley House 192 Church St., Marietta, 30060 404-426-1887
Merriwood Country Inn Rt. 6, Box 50, Americus, 31709 912-924-4992
Moon River B&B 715 Mt. Zion Rd., Resaca, 30735 404-629-4305
Morris Manor, The 425 Timberlane Dr., Americus, 31709 912-924-4884
Mountain Top Inn Rt. 147, Pine Mountain, 31822 800-533-6376
Mountain Top Lodge Route 7, Box 150, Dahlonega, 30533 404-864-5257
Mulberry, The 601 E. Bay St., Savannah, 31401 912-238-1200
Myon B&B 128 1st St., Tifton, 31793 912-382-0959
Neel House 502 S. Broad St., Thomasville, 31792 912-228-6500
Oglethorpe Inn 836 Greene St., Augusta, 30901 404-724-9774
Old Home Place 764 Union Grove Church, Adairsville, 30103 404-625-3649
Old Winterville Inn 108 S. Main St., Winterville, 30683 404-742-7340
Olena's Guest House Route 26, Montezuma, 31063 912-472-7620
Olmstead B&B Pembroke Dr., Washington, 30673 404-678-1050
Parrott-Camp-Soucy Home 155 Greenville St., Newman, 30263 404-253-4846
Pinefields Plantation Rt. 2, Box 215, Moultrie, 31768 912-985-2086
Plains B&B Inn, The 100 W. Church St., Plains, 31780 912-824-7252
Planters inn 29 Abercorn St., Savannah, 31499 912-232-5678
Quail Country B&B 1104 Old Monticello Rd., Thomasville, 31792 913-226-7218
Quailridge B&B Box 155, Norman Park, 31771 912-985-7262
Rivendell 3581 S. Barnett Shoals, Watkinsville, 30677 404-769-4522
River Street Inn 115 E. River St., Savannah, 31499 912-234-6400
Riverview Hotel 105 Osborne St., Saint Marys, 31558 912-882-3242
Robert Toombs Inn 101 South State St., Lyons, 30436 912-526-4489
Royal Colony Inn 29 Abercorn St., Savannah, 31401 912-232-5678
Rusharon P.O. Box 273, Cleveland, 30528 404-865-5173
Simmons-Bond Inn 130 W. Tugaloo, Toccoa, 30577 800-533-7693
Statesboro Inn 106 South Main St., Statesboro, 30458 912-489-8628
Stone-Conner House 575 College St., Macon, 31302 912-745-0258
Suite Revenge 400 W. Main St., Marshallville, 31057 912-967-2252
Susina Plantation Inn Route 3 Box 1010, Thomasville, 31792 912-377-9644
Swift Street Inn 1204 Swift St., Perry, 31069 912-987-3428
Tate House Box 33, Tate, 30177 404-735-3122
Timmons House 407 E. Charlton St., Savannah, 31401 912-233-4456
Towering Oaks B&B Lodge #5 Box 5172, Cleveland, 30528 404-865-6760
Twin Oaks 9565 E. Liberty Rd., Villa Rica, 30180 404-459-4374
VIP B&B 501 N. Dr., Dublin, 31021 912-275-3739
Victoria Barie House 321 E. Liberty St., Savannah, 31499 912-234-6446
Victorian Village 1841 Hardeman Ave., Macon, 31302 912-743-3333
Water Oak Cottage 211 S. Jefferson St., Washington, 30673 404-678-3605
West Fields B&B Rt. 3, Box 728, Thomson, 404-595-3156
Whitfield Inn 327 W. Main St., Thomaston, 30286 404-647-2482
Whitworth Inn 6593 McEver Rd., Flowery Branch, 30542 404-967-2386
Willow Lake Rt. 4, Box 117, Thomasville, 31792 913-226-6372
Woodall House 324 W. Main St., Thomaston, 30286 404-647-7044
Woodhaven Chalet Route 1, Box 39, Sautee, 30571 404-878-2580
Worley Homestead Inn 410 W. Main St., Dahlonega, 30533 404-864-7002
York House P.O. Box 126, Mountain City, 30068 404-746-2068
'417' Haslam-Fort House 417 E. Charlton St., Savannah, 31401 912-233-6380

Hawaii

HAIKU, MAUI

Halfway to Hana House	$$ B&B	Continental plus
P.O. Box 675, 96708	1 rooms, 1 pb	Afternoon tea, snacks
100 Waipio Rd.	●	Studio has mini-kitchen
808-572-1176	C-no/S-no/P-no/H-no	patio, flower gardens
Gail Pickholz	Some French, Pidgeon	fruit trees
All year	Eng	

Tropical hideaway with 180° wraparound ocean view, colorful setting, near freshwater pools, biking and hiking. Delicious aloha breakfast on patio with Hawaiian coconut pudding.

HANALEI, KAUAI

B&B and Beach—Hanalei	$$ B&B	Continental plus
Bay	4 rooms, 4 pb	Restaurant nearby
P.O. Box 748, 96714	●	Sitting room, library
5095 Opelu Rd.	C-yes/S-no/P-no/H-no	television, coolers &
808-826-6111		snorkel equip. available
Carolyn Barnes		
All year		

Steps to famous Hanalei Bay. Breakfast in view of 1000 foot waterfalls. Antiques and rattan. Hike Na Pali, snorkel, golf, kayak, windsurf, fish and sail.

HONOLULU, OAHU

Manoa Valley Inn	$$$ B&B	Continental breakfast
2001 Vancouver Dr., 96822	8 rooms, 5 pb	Comp. wine, aftn. tea
99-969 Iwaena St. Aiea HI	Visa, MC, AmEx, CB ●	Sitting room
808-947-6019 800-634-5115	C-14+/S-ltd/P-no/H-no	conference room
Mapuana Schneider		tour/dining information
All year		

Hawaii's intimate country inn located in lush Manoa Valley, two miles from Waikiki Beach. Daily afternoon fresh tropical fruits, wine & cheese tastings on the shady lanai.

KAILUA-KONA

Akamai B&B	$$ B&B	Stocked refrigerator
172 Kuumele Pl., 96734	2 rooms, 2 pb	Restaurant, lunch/dinner
808-261-2227 800-642-5366	●	Afternoon tea, snacks
Diane Van Ryzin	C-7+/S-yes/P-no/H-yes	swimming pool
All year	French	

Hawaiian style B&B. Walking distance to beautiful beach. Private entrance to fully furnished studio. Private poolside garden lanai.

Kailua Plantation House	$$$ B&B	Continental plus
75-5948 Alii Dr., 96740	5 rooms, 5 pb	Restaurants nearby
808-329-3727	Visa, MC, AmEx ●	Sitting room
Lisa Berger	C-12+/S-no/P-no/H-no	dipping pool, hot tubs
All year	French	private baths & lanais

Hawaii's most elegant oceanfront bed & breakfast. Situated atop a promontory of black lava rocks less than one mile from the quaint town of Kailua-Kona.

KANEOHE, OAHU

Emma's Guest Rooms
47-600 Hui Ulili St., 96744
808-239-7248 FAX:239-7224
Emma Sargeant, Stan Sargeant
All year

$ EP
3 rooms, 3 pb
MC, Visa, AmEx, Disc ●
C-yes/S-no/P-no/H-no
German

Guest kitchenette
Dining room, library
TV lounge

Cool windward location, private entrance, fully equipped kitchen, tropical garden view dining, convenient shopping, beaches and all Oahu island attractions.

KAPAA, KAUAI

Kay Barker's B&B
P.O. Box 740, 96746
3rd St. off Crossley Rd.
808-822-3073 800-835-2845
Gordon Barker
All year

$$ B&B
4 rooms, 4 pb
●
C-yes/S-yes/P-no/H-yes

Continental plus
Sitting room, library
restaurant, tennis,
beaches & river 10 min.

Lovely home in a garden setting, with mountain and pasture views. Ten minutes from beaches, restaurants, golf, tennis and shopping.

Orchid Hut
6402 Kaahele St., 96746
808-822-7201
Norm & Leonora Ross
All year

$$ B&B
1 rooms, 1 pb
●
C-no/S-no/P-no/H-no
French,Danish,Indonesian

Continental plus
Separate 3-room cottage
Kitchenette
sitting room
beach mats & towels

Charming, private, modern cottage. Spectacular view of Wailua River. Beautiful tropical landscaping. Convenient to beaches, restaurants, shopping. 3-day minimum.

KOLOA, KAUAI

Poipu B&B Inn
2720 Hoonani Rd., 96756
RR1, Box 308B
808-742-1146 800-552-0095
Dotti Cichon, B. Young
All year

$$ B&B
7 rooms, 7 pb
Visa, MC, AmEx, DC, CB ●
C-yes/S-no/P-no/H-ltd
French, German

Continental plus
Afternoon tea, snacks
Sitting room, lanais
tennis & pool free
video library, cable TV

Romantic restored 1933 plantation house with the charm of old Hawaii. Also oceanfront condo, cottages, homes. Furnished in white wicker, pine antiques and carousel horses.

LAWAI, KAUAI

Victoria Place
P.O. Box 930, 96765
3459 Lawai Loa Lane
808-332-9300
Edee Seymour
All year

$$ B&B
4 rooms, 4 pb
●
C-15+/S-no/H-yes

Continental plus
Lunch & dinner nearby
Large library, pool
lanai overlooking mtns.
beach mats, snorkel gear

Jungle and ocean views—all rooms open onto pool—near beaches, golf course, tennis. We pamper: flowers, popcorn, homemade muffins and aloha.

MAKAWAO, MAUI

Haleakala B&B
41 Manienie Rd., 96768
808-572-7988
Mara Marin
All year

$$ EP
4 rooms, 3 pb
●
C-no/S-no/P-no/H-no

Coffee
Sitting room

Beautiful country home on two acres on slopes of Haleakala. Inspiring views. Near all Maui's "special" places. Aloha to you. ...

136 Hawaii

POIPU, KAUAI

Gloria's Spouting Horn	$$ B&B	Continental plus
4464 Lawai Road, 96756	4 rooms, 4 pb	Wine coolers on arrival
808-742-6995		beach mats
Gloria & Robert Merkle		& towels provided
All year		

Oceanfront accommodations with surf 40 ft. away; relax in hammocks under coco palms on secluded beach. Charming cottage antiques. Romantic Tea House. Tropical breakfast.

PRINCEVILLE, KAUAI

Hale 'Aha	$$$ B&B	Continental plus
P.O. Box 3370, 96722	4 rooms, 4 pb	Restaurant nearby
3875 Kamehameha	●	Library, hot tubs
808-826-6733 800-826-6733	C-no/S-no/P-no/H-no	bicycles, on golf course
Herb & Ruth Bockelman		tennis court nearby
All year		

New, affordable luxury. Peaceful resort area with ocean, mountains, waterfalls, lush hiking trails, hidden beaches, rivers. Plus helicopters, snorkeling, boating & shopping.

VOLCANO

Kilauea Lodge	$$$ B&B	Full breakfast
P.O. Box 116, 96785	19 rooms, 19 pb	Lunch, dinner
808-967-7366	Visa, MC, AmEx	Restaurant, full bar
Lorna & Albert Jeyte	C-ask/S-no/P-no/H-no	sitting room, bicycles
All year	German	Volcanoes National Park

Mountain lodge with full service restaurant. 6 rooms with fireplace. One mile from spectacular Volcanoes National Park. 28 miles from Hilo.

More Inns ...

Adriennes B&B Paradise RR 1, Box 8E, Captain Cook, 96704 808-328-9726
Aha Hui Hawaiian Box 10, Hawi, 96719 808-889-5523
Alohaland Guest House 98-1003 Oliwa St., Aiea, 96701 808-487-0482
B&B Waikiki Beach P.O. Box 89080, Honolulu, 96830 808-923-5459
Bed, Breakfast & Beach PO Box 748, Hanalei, 96714 808-826-6111
Carson's Volcano Cottage P.O. Box 503, Volcano, 97685 808-967-7683
Coconut Inn 181 Hui Rd. "F", Napili, Maui, 96761 808-669-5712
Fern Grotto Inn 4561 Kuamoo Rd, Wailua, Kauai, 96746 808-822-2560
Guesthouse at Volcano P.O. Box 6, Volcano, 96785 808-967-7775
Haikuleana B&B Inn 69 Haiku Rd., Haiku, Maui, 96708 808-575-2890
Hale Honua Ranch P.O. Box 347, Kealakekua, 96750 808-328-8282
Hale Kipa O Kiana RR 2, Box 4874, Kalapana Shores, 96778 808-965-8661
Hale Pau Kala 33 Kalaka Pl., Kailua, 96734 808-261-3098
Hale Plumeria B&B 3044 Hollinger St., Honolulu, Oahu, 96815 808-732-7719
Hamakua Hideaway P.O. Box 5104, Kukuihaele, 96727 808-775-7425
Hawaii Kai 876 Ka'ahue St., Hononlulu, 96825 808-395-8153
Hawaii's Best B&Bs P.O. Box 563, Kamuela, 96743 808-885-4550
Hawaiian B&B 876 Kaahue St., Honolulu, 96825 808-395-5183
Heavenly Hana Inn P.O. Box 146, Hana, Maui, 96713 808-248-8442
Homer & Mahina Maxey B&B 1277 Mokulua Dr., Kailua, 96734 808-261-1059
Hotel Hana Maui Maui, 96713 808-248-8211
John Guild Inn 2001 Vancouver Dr., Honolulu, 96822 808-947-6019
Kahala Hibiscus Inn 1030 Kealaolu Ave., Honolulu, 96816 808-732-5889
Kaia Ranch & Co. P.O. Box 404, Hana, Maui, 96713 808-248-7725
Kalani Honua Box 4500, Ocean Hwy 137, Pahoa, 96778 808-965-7828
Keapana B&B 5620 Keapana Rd., Kapaa, Kauai, 96746 800-822-7968
Kula Lodge RR 1 Box 475, Kula, Maui, 96790 808-878-2517
Lahaina Hotel 127 Lahainaluna Rd., Lahaina, Maui, 96761 808-661-0577
Mahi Ko Inn General Delivery, Kilauea, 96754 800-458-3444

Mahina Kai P.O. Box 699, Anahola, Kauai, 96703 808-822-9451
Manago Hotel Box 145, Captain Cook, 96704 808-323-2642
Pacific-Hawaii B&B 19 Kai Nani Pl., Kailua, Oahu, 96743 808-262-6026
Paradise Inn B&B 4540 Fernandes Rd., Kapaa, 96746 808-822-4104
Paradise Place HCR 9558, Keaau, 96749 808-966-4600
Pau Hana Inn P.O. Box 546, Kaunakakai, Molokai, 96748 800-367-8047
Plantation Inn 174 Lahainaluna Rd., Lahaina, Maui, 96761 800-433-6815
Randy Rosario 6470 Kawaihau Rd., Kapaa, Kauai, 96746 808-822-1902
Volcano Heart Chalet P.O. Box 404, Big Island, 96713 808-248-7725
Whaler's Way B&B 541 Kupulau Dr, Kihei, Maui, 96753 808-879-7984

Idaho

COEUR D'ALENE

Greenbriar Inn
315 Wallace, 83814
208-667-9660
Kris McIlvenna, Bob McIlvenna
All year

$$ B&B
7 rooms, 4 pb
Visa, MC, AmEx ●
C-yes/S-no/P-no/H-no
French

Full 4-course breakfast
Gourmet dining by resv.
Comp. wine, catering
library, hot tub
tandem bikes, canoes

Coeur d'Alene's only historic residence, 4 blocks from lakefront, shopping area. Gourmet cuisine, antiques, down comforters. European-style country inn.

IRWIN

McBride's B&B Guesthouse
P.O. Box 166, 83428
102 Valley Dr.
208-483-4221
Deanna & Craig McBride
All year

$ B&B
1 rooms, 1 pb
Visa, MC ●
C-yes/S-yes/P-yes

Full country breakfast
Comp. wine
Beautiful yard, grill
maid service daily
hiking, fishing, hunting

Private guest house in a high mountain valley. Year-round sportsman's paradise with easy access to Snake River, Tetons, Yellowstone Park.

LEWISTON

Carriage House B&B
611–5th St., 83501
208-746-4506
Chuck & Nancy Huff
All year

$$ B&B
2 rooms, 2 pb
Visa, MC
C-12+/S-no/P-no/H-no

Full breakfast
Refreshments, seltzers
Snacks, gift shop
indoor spa, bicycles
private courtyard

European country guest house; historical neighborhood; tastefully appointed w/antiques; elegant suites; sumptuous breakfasts; near Snake River and Scenic Hells Canyon Tours.

MOSCOW

Beau's Butte
702 Public Ave., 83843
208-882-4061
Joyce & Duane Parr
All year

$ B&B
2 rooms, 1 pb
C-12+/S-no/P-no/H-no

Full breakfast
Comp. beverage, snacks
Sitting room
fireplace, sun room
hot tubs, TV, VCR

Tranquil country setting, convenient to university. Locally crafted country decor; fantastic views; scrumptious breakfasts.

138 Idaho

NORTH FORK ————————————————————————————————

Indian Creek Guest Ranch $$$ B&B Full breakfast
HC 64 Box 105, 83466 4 rooms, 4 pb Meals served
208-394-2126 • Comp. beverages
Jack & Theresa Briggs C-yes/S-yes/P-yes/H-no sitting room, piano
April–October horseback, jeep trips

Restful small mountain ranch. We never take more than ten people at a time. Private baths; homegrown and homemade foods.

POCATELLO ————————————————————————————————

Holmes Retreat B&B $$ B&B Full gourmet breakfast
178 N. Mink Creek Rd., 83204 10 rooms, 10 pb Comp. lemonade, tea
208-232-0336 Visa, MC, AmEx, DC • Sitting room with plants
Shirley & Acel Holmes C-yes/S-ltd/P-ltd/H-yes piano, garden w/fountain
All year library, nature walk

6.4 acres nestled in the mountains, beside scenic Mink Creek. Bird-watcher's paradise! Fishing in creek, croquet, volleyball. Special bed turndown service. Gracious hosts.

SHOUP ————————————————————————————————

Smith House B&B $ B&B Full breakfast
49 Salmon River Rd., 83469 5 rooms, 1 pb Comp. wine & snacks
208-394-2121 Visa, MC • Sitting room, library
Aubrey & Marsha Smith C-yes/S-no/P-yes/H-no hot tubs, organ
All year gift shop, float trips

Rustic, country setting with all the comforts of home. Enjoy sightseeing, hunting, hiking or just relaxing. Delicious breakfasts!

STANLEY ————————————————————————————————

Idaho Rocky Mtn. Ranch $$$ B&B Full breakfast
HC 64, Box 9934, 83278 21 rooms, 21 pb Picnic lunch, dinner
208-774-3544 Visa, MC Restaurant, beer & wine
Bill & Jeana Leavell C-yes/S-no/P-ask/H-no sitting room, library
June–Sept, Nov–April Spanish natural hot springs pool

Historic log lodge and cabins; spectacular mountain scenery; gourmet dining in rustic atmosphere; extensive outdoor activities, natural hot springs pool.

More Inns . . .

Bitterroot Mountain Inn 403 Main Street, Wardner, 83837 208-786-1771
Blackwell House 820 Sherman Ave., Coeur d'Alene, 83814 208-664-0656
Bonnie's B&B Box 258, Plummer, 83851 208-686-1165
Busterback Ranch Star Rt., Ketchum, 83340 208-774-2217
Coeur d'Alene B&B 906 Foster Ave., Coeur d'Alene, 83814 208-667-7527
Comfort Inn Box 984, Hailey, 83333 208-788-2477
Cottage B&B, The 318 N. Hayes, Moscow, 83843 208-882-0778
Cricket on the Hearth 1521 Lakeside Ave., Coeur d'Alene, 83814 208-664-6926
Ellsworth Inn 715 3rd Ave. S., Hailey, 83333 208-788-2298
Gables, The 916 Foster Ave., Coeur d'Alene, 83814 208-664-5121
Gregory's McFarland House 601 Foster Ave., Coeur d'Alene, 83814 208-667-1232
Harpers Bend River Inn Rt. 2, Box 7A, Lenore, 83541 208-486-6666
Hillcrest House 210 Hillcrest Dr., Pinehurst, 83850 208-682-3911
Home Place 415 W Lake Hazel Rd., Meridian, 83642 208-888-3857
Hotel McCall 1101 N. Third St., McCall, 83638 208-634-8105
Idaho City Hotel P.O. Box 70, Idaho City, 83631 208-392-4290
Idaho Country Inn 134 Latigo, Saddle Hill, Ketchum, 83340 208-726-1019
Idaho Heritage Inn 109 W. Idaho, Boise, 83702 208-342-8066
Inn the First Place 509 N. 15th St., Coeur d'Alene, 83814 208-667-3346
Jameson B&B 304 Sixth St., Wallace, 83873 208-556-1554

Knoll Hus P.O. Box 572, Saint Maries, 83861 208-245-4137
Lift Haven Inn Box 21, 100 Lloyd Dr., Ketchum, 83340 208-726-5601
Looking Glass Guest Ranch HC-75, Box 32, Kooskia, 83539 208-926-0855
MaryAnne's HCR 1, Box 43E, Harrison, 83833 208-245-2537
Old McFarland Inn 227 S. First Ave., Sandpoint, 83864 208-265-0260
Osprey Cove B&B 8680 Sunnyside Rd., Sandpoint, 83864 208-265-4200
Peacock Hill 1245 Joyce Rd., Moscow, 83843 208-882-1423
Peg's B&B Place P.O. Box 144, Harrison, 83833 208-689-3525
Pine Tree Inn 177 King St., Box 1023, Wallace, 83873 208-752-4391
Powderhorn Lodge Box 3970, Ketchum, 83340 208-726-3107
Redfish Lake Lodge P.O. Box 9, Stanley, 83278 208-774-3536
River Birch Farm P.O. Box 87, Laclede, 83841 208-263-4033
River Street Inn P.O. Box 182, Sun Vlly, Ketchum, 83353 208-726-3611
River Street Inn P.O. Box 182, Sun Valley, 83353 208-726-3611
Riverside B&B Highway 55, Horseshoe Bend, 83629 208-793-2408
Riverside Inn B&B 255 Portneuf Ave., Lava Hot Springs, 83246 208-776-5504
Rolling Hills B&B Rt. 1, Box 157, Potlatch, 83855 208-668-1126
Sheep Creek Ranch 717–3rd St., Lewiston, 83501 800-248-1045
Shiloh Rose 3414 Selway Dr., Lewiston, 83501 208-743-2482
Sunrise 2730 Sunrise Rim Rd., Boise, 83705 208-345-5260
Tulip House 403 S. Florence St., Grangeville, 83530 208-983-1034
Twin Peaks Inn 2455 W. Twin Rd., Moscow, 83843 208-882-3898
Van Buren House, The 220 N. Van Buren, Moscow, 83843 208-882-8531
Warwick Inn, The 303 Military Dr., Coeur d'Alene, 83814 208-765-6565
Whitaker House 410 Railroad Ave, #10, Sandpoint, 83864 208-263-0816

Illinois

CARLYLE

Country Haus B&B	$$ B&B	Full breakfast
1191 Franklin, 62231	4 rooms, 4 pb	Evening snacks
618-594-8313	Visa, MC, AmEx	Sitting room with TV
Ron & Vickie Cook	C-3+/S-no/P-no/H-no	library, hot tubs
All year		phone jacks in rooms

Informal country hospitality. 1890's Eastlake home. Family-style breakfast. One mile from Carlyle Lake. Chosen for 1994 Olympic Festival sailing.

EVANSTON

The Homestead	$$ EP	Comp. coffee
1625 Hinman Ave., 60201	35 rooms, 35 pb	French restaurant
708-475-3300	C-yes/S-yes/P-no/H-ltd	
David T. Reynolds		
All year		

Historic residential neighborhood; two blocks from Lake Michigan & Northwestern Univ.; 30 minutes from downtown Chicago by car or rail; French restaurant serves dinner.

GALENA

Comfort Guest House	$$ B&B	Continental plus
1000 Third St., 61036	3 rooms, 2 pb	Sitting room w/fireplace
815-777-3062	Visa, MC	front porch
Dave & Sandy Miller	C-14+/S-ltd/P-no/H-no	
All year		

Riverfront town, home of Ulysses S. Grant. 1856 guest house. Stroll to downtown antique shops. Quilts, country breakfasts. Golf, skiing, biking nearby.

140 Illinois

GALENA ─────────────────────────────────

Stillman's Country Inn
513 Bouthillier, 61036
815-777-0557
Bill & Pamela Lozeau
All year

$$ B&B
5 rooms, 5 pb
Visa, MC
C-ltd/S-yes/P-no/H-no
German

Continental breakfast
Victorian dining rooms
Lounges, entertainment
whirlpool rooms
cable TV in rooms

Stillman Manor Estate, 1858. General Grant was a regular guest. Antiques and fireplaces, crystal, porcelain. Riverboats.

GENEVA ─────────────────────────────────

Oscar Swan Country Inn
1800 W. State St., 60134
708-232-0173
Nina & Hans Heymann
All year

$$$ B&B
7 rooms, 4 pb
Visa, MC ●
C-yes/S-no/P-no/H-no
German

Full breakfast
Comp. snacks & beverages
Sitting room, library
tennis courts, pool
X-C skiing on 7 acres

Country hideaway on 7 private acres. Fireplaces, cozy kitchen, hearty breakfast, wonderful River Town, antiques, bike paths. The New England of the Midwest.

NAPERVILLE ─────────────────────────────

Harrison House B&B
25 W 135 Essex Ave., 60540
26 N. Eagle
708-420-1117 709-355-4665
Dawn Dau, Lynn Harrison
All year

$$$ B&B
4 rooms, 2 pb
Visa, MC, AmEx ●
S-ltd
Spanish

Full breakfast (wkends)
Continental breakfast
Comp. wine, tea, snacks
Sitting room, bicycles
tennis & pool nearby

25 miles west of Chicago. Walk to quaint shops, restaurants. Antique guest rooms; Victorian Room has jacuzzi. Scrumptious breakfast and gracious hospitality.

ROCK ISLAND ────────────────────────────

The Potter House
1906 – 7 Ave., 61201
309-788-1906 800-747-0339
Nancy & Gary Pheiffer
All year

$ B&B
4 rooms, 3 pb
Visa, MC ●
C-yes

Full breakfast
Afternoon tea
Library
tennis courts, pool &
restaurant nearby

Historic landmark, circa 1907. Close to Mississippi River attractions. Breakfast served in mahogany paneled dining room or elegant sunporch.

WHEATON ────────────────────────────────

The Wheaton Inn
301 W. Roosevelt Road, 60187
708-690-2600
Jackie & Ogden Andrews
All year

$$$ B&B
16 rooms, 16 pb
Visa, MC, AmEx, DC, Dis ●
C-yes/S-yes/P-ask

Full breakfast
Bar Service (some)
Comp. wine, snacks
sitting room, library
near golf, tennis, etc.

Elegant but homey atmosphere in the Williamsburg tradition, 10 rooms with fireplaces, 6 with whirlpools. Weekend getaways or corporate traveler's delight.

WINNETKA ───────────────────────────────

Chateau des Fleurs
552 Ridge Rd., 60093
708-256-7272
Sally H. Ward
All year

$$$ B&B
3 rooms, 3 pb
Visa ●
C-12+/S-no/P-no/H-no

Continental plus
Afternoon tea, snacks
Grand piano, 50" TV
VCR with movies, bikes
jacuzzis in 2 rms, pool

Beautiful French country home furnished in rare antiques. Lovely views of magnificent trees, English gardens. Located near private road for walking or jogging. Close to train.

More Inns...

Aldrich Guest House 900 Third St., Galena, 61036 815-777-3323
Annie Tique's Hotel 378 Main St., Marseilles, 61341 815-795-5848
Aunt Zelma's Country Guest RR 1, Box 129, Tolono, 61880 217-485-5101
Avery Guest House B&B 606 S. Prospect St., Galena, 61036 815-777-3883
Barb's B&B 606 S. Russell, Champaign, 61821 217-356-0376
Barber House Inn 410 W. Mason, Polo, 61064 815-946-2607
Bedford House Route 20 West, Galena, 61036 815-777-2043
Belle Aire Mansion Route 20 West, Galena, 61036 815-777-0893
Bennett Curtis House 302 W. Taylor, Grant Park, 60940 815-465-6025
Bertram Arms–B&B RR #3, Box 243, Robinson, 62454 618-546-1122
Better 'n Grandma's 102 S. Meyers, Rantoul, 61866 217-893-0469
Brick House B&B P.O. Box 301, Goodfield, 61742 309-965-2545
Bundling Board Inn 222 E. South St., Woodstock, 60098 815-338-7054
Carr Mansion Guest House 416 E. Broadway, Monmouth, 61462 309-734-3654
Charles & Barbara Pollard 2633 Poplar, Evanston, 60201 312-328-6162
Chestnut Mountain Resort 8700 W. Chestnut Rd., Galena, 61036 800-435-2914
Colonial Inn Rock & Green Sts., Grand Detour, 61021 815-652-4422
Corinne's B&B Inn 1001 S. 6th St., Springfield, 62703 217-527-1400
Corner George Inn Corner of Main & Mill, Maeystown, 62256 618-458-6660
Corner Nest B&B 3 Elm St., P.O. Box 22, Elsah, 62028 618-374-1892
Curly's Corner RR 2, Box 590, Arcola, 61910 217-268-3352
Davidson Place B&B 1110 Davidson Dr., Champaign, 61820 217-356-5915
DeZoya House 1203 Third St., Galena, 61036 815-777-1203
Die Blaue Gaus 95265 Route 59, Naperville, 60565 312-355-0835
Favorite Brother Inn, The 106 E. Columbia, Arthur, 61911 217-543-2938
Grandview Guest Home 113 S. Prospect St., Galena, 61036 815-777-1387
Green Tree Inn P.O. Box 96, Elsah, 62028 618-374-2821
Haagen House B&B 617 State St., Alton, 62002 618-462-2419
Hamilton House B&B Inn 500 W. Main St., Decatur, 62522 217-429-1669
Hellman Guest House 318 Hill St., Galena, 61036 815-777-3638
Hobson's Bluffdale Eldred-Hillview Rd, Eldred, 62027 217-983-2854
Hotel Nauvoo Route 96, Town Center, Nauvoo, 62354 217-453-2211
Hyde Park House 5210 S. Kenwood, Chicago, 60615 312-363-4595
Inn-on-the-Square 3 Montgomery St., Oakland, 61943 217-346-2289
Ironhedge Inn B&B 305 Oregon, West Dundee, 708-426-7777
La Petite Voyageur B&B 116 E. South St., Dwight, 60420 815-584-2239
Maggie's Bed & Breakfast 2102 North Keebler Road, Collinsville, 62234 618-344-8283
Mansion of Golconda P.O. Box 339, Golcanda, 62938 618-683-4400
Maple Lane 3115 Rush Creek Rd., Stockton, 61085 815-947-3773
Mars Avenue Guest Home 515 Mars Ave., Galena, 61036 815-777-3880
Mischler House 718 South 8th St., Springfield, 62703 217-523-3714
Mississippi Memories B&B Box 291, Riverview Hght, Nauvoo, 62354 217-453-2771
Mother's Country Inn 349 Spring St., Galena, 61036 815-777-3153
Old Church House Inn Mossville, 309-579-2300
Olde Brick House, The 502 North High Street, Port Byron, 61275 309-523-3236
Parley Lane B&B Route 1, Box 220, Nauvoo, 62354 217-453-2277
Pine Hollow Inn 4700 N. Council Hill Rd, Galena, 61036 815-777-1071
Pleasant Haven B&B 201 E. Quincy, Box 51, Pleasant Hill, 62366 217-734-9357
Queen Anne Guest House 200 Park Ave., Galena, 61036 815-777-3849
River Rose Inn 1 Main Street, Elizabeth Town, 62931 618-287-8811
River View Guest House 507 E. Everett, Dixon, 61021 815-288-5974
Robert Scribe Harris House 713 S. Bench St., Galena, 61036 815-777-1611
Round-Robin Guesthouse 231 East Maple Avenue, Mundelein, 60060 312-566-7664
Ryan Mansion Inn Route 20 West, Galena, 61036 815-777-2043
Seacord House 624 N. Cherry St., Galesburg, 61401 309-342-4107
Stage Coach Inn 41 W. 278 Whitney Rd., Saint Charles, 60174 312-584-1263
Standish House 540 W. Carroll St., Lanark, 61048 815-493-2307
Stillwaters Country Inn 7213 W. Buckhill Rd., Galena, 61036 312-528-6313

Stolz Home RR 2, Box 27, Gibson City, 60936
217-784-4502
Suprenaut B&B 304 W. Second St.,
Momenca, 60954 815-472-3156
Sweet Basil Hill Farm 15937 W. Washington
St., Gurnee, 60031 708-244-3333
Thelma's Bed & Breakfast 201 South
Broadway, West Salem, 62476 618-456-8401
Toad Hall B&B House 301 N. Scoville Ave.,
Oak Park, 60302 708-386-8623
Top O' The Morning B&B 1505–19th Ave.,
Rock Island, 61201 309-786-3513
Victoria's B&B 201 N. Sixth St., Rockford,
61107 815-963-3232
Victorian Inn B&B 702–20th St., Rock Island,
61201 309-788-7068
Victorian Mansion 301 High St., Galena, 61036 815-777-0675
Welcome Inn 506 W. Main St., Oblong, 62449 618-592-3301
Wright Farmhouse RR 3, Carthage, 62321 217-357-2421

Waterford B&B, Goshen, IN

Indiana

BEVERLY SHORES

Dunes Shore Inn	$ B&B	Continental plus
Box 807, 46301	12 rooms	Fruit, cider & cookies
Lakeshore County Rd.	Visa, MC	Library, sitting room
219-879-9029	C-yes/S-ltd/P-no/H-no	outdoor grill, tables
Rosemary & Fred Braun	German	bicycles
All year		

Located one block from Lake Michigan and surrounded by the National Lakeshore and Dunes State Parks, this inn is an oasis for nature lovers. One hour from Chicago.

CHESTERTON

Gray Goose Inn	$$ B&B	Full breakfast
350 Indian Boundary Rd., 46304	5 rooms, 5 pb	Comp. beverages, snacks
219-926-5781	Visa, MC, AmEx, Disc ●	Sitting room
Timothy Wilk, Chuck Ramsey	C-12+/S-ltd/P-no/H-no	telephone in rooms
All year		bicycles, boats

In Dunes Country. English country house on private wooded lake. Charming guest rooms, private baths, fireplaces, gourmet breakfast. Near interstates.

CONNERSVILLE

Maple Leaf Inn B&B	$ B&B	Continental plus
831 N. Grand Ave., 47331	4 rooms, 4 pb	Snacks
317-825-7099	Visa, MC	Sitting room
Gary & Karen Lanning	C-yes/S-ltd/P-no/H-no	bicycles
All year		

1860s home furnished with antiques; pictures by local artists; nearby are antique shops, state parks, nature trails, restored canal town.

CORYDON

Kinter House Inn
101 S. Capitol Ave., 47112
812-738-2020
Mary Jane Bridgwater
All year

$$ B&B
16 rooms, 16 pb
Visa, MC, AmEx, DC •
C-yes

Full breakfast
Comp. coffee, tea, cider
Tennis courts
golf arrangements
swimming

National Historic Registry. 14 guest rooms in Victorian and country decor. Full breakfast. Located in downtown historic Corydon. 2 miles south of I-64.

CRAWFORDSVILLE

Davis House
1010 W. Wabash Ave., 47933
317-364-0461
Janice Stearns
All year

$$ B&B
3 rooms, 3 pb
Visa, MC, AmEx •
C-yes/S-yes/P-no/H-no

Continental plus
Comp. beverages & snacks
Sitting room
library

Victorian mansion with country atmosphere near canoeing, hiking, and historical sites. Complimentary snacks. Homemade coffee cakes and breads for breakfast.

EVANSVILLE

Brigadoon B&B Inn
1201 S.E. Second St., 47713
812-422-9635
Katelin Forbes
All year

$ B&B
4 rooms, 2 pb
Visa, MC, AmEx •
C-yes/S-no/P-yes/H-yes

Full breakfast
Stained glass
Library, sitting room
meeting rooms for parties,
etc.

Romantic, lace-filled, river city Victorian. Picket fence, gingerbread porch, parquet floors, four fireplaces. Hearty breakfast, homemade breads.

GOSHEN

The Checkerberry Inn
62644 County Road 37, 46526
219-642-4445
John & Susan Graff
All year exc. January

$$$ B&B
12 rooms, 12 pb
Visa, MC, AmEx •
C-yes/S-ltd/H-yes

Continental plus
Lunch/dinner, restaurant
Sitting room, library
tennis court, pool
croquet court

European-style country inn surrounded by Amish farmland, 100 acres of fields and woods. French country cuisine, luxuriously comfortable decor.

Waterford B&B
3004 S. Main St., 46526
219-533-6044
Judith Forbes
All year

$ B&B
4 rooms, 2 pb
C-8+/S-ltd/P-no/H-no

Full breakfast
Sitting room
library
shuffleboard court

1854 brick Italianate home on the national historic register. Located on SR 15 with 2 acres of nicely landscaped gardens.

GREENCASTLE

Walden Inn
P.O. Box 490, 46135
2 Seminary Square
317-653-2761
Matthew O'Neill
All year exc. Christmas

$$$ EP
Visa, MC, AmEx, DC •
C-yes/S-yes/P-no/H-yes

Breakfast, lunch, dinner
Restaurant, pub, library
bicycles, pool, sauna
tennis, golf, canoeing
meeting facilities

A warm and unpretentious atmosphere with distinctive cuisine and personalized service. Guest rooms comfortably furnished with Amish furniture. Near quaint shops, restaurants.

HAGERSTOWN

Teetor House
300 West Main St., 47346
317-489-4422
Jack & Joanne Warmoth
All year

$$ B&B
4 rooms, 4 pb
Visa, MC ●
C-yes/S-ltd

Full breakfast
Lunch & dinner (groups)
Comp. soft drinks
sitting room, library
tennis courts, pool

Elegance and charm in a peacefully rural setting near unique shops and restaurants. Air conditioned. 5 miles from I-70. Golf courses nearby. Horse and buggy rides available.

HUNTINGTON

Purviance House B&B
326 S. Jefferson, 46750
219-356-4218 219-356-9215
Jean Gernand
All year

$ B&B
3 rooms, 2 pb
C-yes/S-no/P-no/H-no

Continental plus
Lunch & dinner by res.
Comp. wine, tea, snacks
sitting room, library
kitchen privileges

Lovingly restored 1859 National Register house furnished with antiques, offers warm hospitality and homey comforts. Historic and recreational areas nearby.

INDIANAPOLIS

The Hoffman House
P.O. Box 906, 46206
545 E. 11th St.
317-635-1701
Laura A. Arnold
May—Oct/Nov—Apr wkends

$$ B&B
2 rooms
Visa, MC ●
C-12+/S-no/P-no/H-no

Continental plus
Sitting room
Guest pass to athletic
club with pool, squash,
racquetball, sauna, etc.

The Hoffman House is a B&B homestay built in 1903, located in heart of downtown Indianapolis. Close to State Capitol, central business district and major cultural activities.

Nuthatch B&B
7161 Edgewater Place, 46240
317-257-2660
Joan H. Morris
All year

$$ B&B
2 rooms, 2 pb
C-12+/S-ltd/P-no/H-no

Full breakfast
Tea, cookies, snacks
Sitting room, deck
picnic table, swing
canoe rental nearby

1920s country French architecture in a resort river setting minutes from downtown Indianapolis. Breakfast is a home-cooked celebration.

KNIGHTSTOWN

The Lavendar Lady B&B
130 W. Main St., 46148
317-345-5400
Clyde & Judith Larrew
All year

$$ B&B
3 rooms, 3 pb
Visa, MC
C-ask/S-no/P-no/H-no

Full breakfast
Complimentary wine
High tea by request - $5

The Lavendar Lady has been restored to her original charm & warmth. Each room uniquely decorated. Antique shops, excursion train rides & golf are but some of the attractions.

Old Hoosier House
7601 S. Greensboro Pike, 46148
317-345-2969
Tom & Jean Lewis
All year

$$ B&B
4 rooms, 3 pb
●
C-yes/S-ltd/P-no/H-no

Full breakfast
Cheese, snacks, dessert
Sitting room
library, bicycles
special golf rates

1840 country home near Indianapolis; popular antique area; comfortable homey atmosphere; delicious breakfasts on patio overlooking Royal Hylands Golf Club.

LA GRANGE

The 1886 Inn
212 W. Factory St., 46761
219-463-4227
The Billman Family
All year

$$ B&B
3 rooms, 3 pb
Visa, MC
C-yes/S-no/P-no/H-no

Continental plus
Sitting room
bicycles

Step back in time to the 19th-century style of living at this 1886 brick inn. Only 10 minutes from Shipshewana Auction and Flea Market in Indiana's Amish country.

METAMORA

Publick House
P.O. Box 202, 47030
28 Duck Creek Crossing
317-647-6729
P. Breuer, N. Becker
April–December

$$ B&B
4 rooms, 4 pb
Visa, MC ●
C-ltd/S-ltd/P-no/H-yes

Full breakfast
Set-ups
Snacks
canal boat & steam engine
train rides

Circa 1850 frontier architecture in a historic arts and crafts canal town featuring operating aqueduct and grist mill. Over 100 crafts and gift shops.

MIDDLEBURY

Bee Hive B&B
P.O. Box 1191, 46540
51129 CR 35, Bristol
219-825-5023
Herb & Treva Swarm
All year

$$ B&B
3 rooms, 1 pb
Visa, MC
C-yes/S-no/P-no

Full breakfast
Comp. wine, refreshments
Sitting room
restaurant nearby
guest cottage available

A country home in a relaxing atmosphere. Located in Amish Country with plenty of local attractions. Ski trails nearby. Easy access to Indiana Toll Road.

Patchwork Quilt Inn
11748 CR 2, 46540
219-825-2417
Maxine Zook
All year

$$ B&B
9 rooms, 9 pb
C-12+/S-no/P-no/H-no

Full breakfast
Lunch, dinner available
Sitting room
piano, Amish tours
gift shop

Prepare to be pampered in gracious country home. In Amish country. Near Shipshewana Flea Auction. Closed Sundays.

Varns Guest House
P.O. Box 125, 46540
205 S. Main St.
219-825-9666
Carl & Diane Eash
All year

$$ B&B
5 rooms, 5 pb
Visa, MC
C-ltd/S-no/P-no/H-no

Continental plus
Sitting room, fireplace
Whirlpool tub in 1 room
wraparound porch w/swing
TV, golfing, A/C

Beautifully restored turn-of-the-century home in Amish community features modern luxury. Many country shops and fine dining nearby.

MISHAWAKA

Beiger Mansion Inn
317 Lincoln Way East, 46544
219-256-0365
Ron Montandon, Phil Robinson
All year

$$ B&B
10 rooms, 4 pb
Visa, MC, AmEx, Disc ●
C-yes/S-no/P-no/H-no

Full gourmet breakfast
Restaurant, lunch
Comp. wine, snacks
bicycles, rooms with A/C
art gallery, gift shop

22,000-square-foot mansion built in 1903; perfect example of neoclassical limestone architecture. Close to restaurants, golf, U. Notre Dame. Art gallery with gift shop.

MORGANTOWN

The Rock House
380 W. Washington St., 46160
812-597-5100
George & Donna Williams
All year

$ B&B
6 rooms, 4 pb
C-yes/S-ltd/P-no

Full breakfast
Afternoon tea, snacks
Sitting room, antiques
available for groups
murder mystery dinners

Circa 1894. Unusual Victorian home built of concrete block embedded with treasures: dishes, doorknobs, dice, marbles! Located at "The Gateway to Brown County."

NASHVILLE

Allison House Inn
P.O. Box 546, 47448
90 S. Jefferson St.
812-988-0814
Bob & Tammy Galm
All year

$$$ B&B
5 rooms, 5 pb
C-6+/S-no/P-no/H-no

Continental plus
Library
sitting room

In the heart of Brown County, the center for the arts and craft colony. Coziness, comfort and charm.

PERU

Rosewood Mansion Inn
54 N. Hood, 46970
317-472-7151
Zoyla & Carm Henderson
All year

$$ B&B
9 rooms, 9 pb
Visa, MC, AmEx, DC ●
C-ltd/S-ltd/H-no
Spanish

Full breakfast
Lunch/dinner on request
Comp. beverages & snacks
sitting room, library
bicycles, swimming pool

Quiet, elegant surroundings. Large, comfortable guest rooms. Gourmet breakfast. Many nearby attractions. Three blocks from downtown. We cater to businessmen. Six suites.

SHIPSHEWANA

Green Meadow Ranch
7905 W. 450 N., 46565
219-768-4221
Paul & Ruth Miller
Exc. January & February

$$ B&B
7 rooms
C-ltd/S-no/P-no/H-no
Penn. Dutch

Continental plus
Sitting room

Country home decorated with antiques, near famous flea market in Amish area. Miniature horses and donkeys, folk art.

SOUTH BEND

The Book Inn
508 West Washington, 46601
219-288-1990
Peggy & John Livingston
All year

$$$ B&B
5 rooms, 5 pb
Visa, MC, AmEx ●
C-no/S-no/P-no/H-no

Continental plus
Sitting room
Library
quality used bookstore
located downstairs

Designers Showcase Second Empire urban home. Twelve foot ceilings, irreplaceable butternut woodwork, comfortable antiques & fresh flowers welcome you.

Queen Anne Inn
420 W. Washington, 46601
219-234-5959
Pauline & Bob Medhurst
All year

$$ B&B
5 rooms, 5 pb
Visa, MC, AmEx ●
C-yes/S-ltd/P-no/H-no

Full breakfast
Snacks, tea
Sitting room, library
phones, TV in rooms
conference room (15-25)

Relax in a charming 1893 Victorian home with Frank Lloyd Wright influence—near city center and many good restaurants. A Victorian getaway is offered. Business rates available

SYRACUSE

Anchor Inn B&B
11007 N. State Rd. 13, 46567
219-457-4714
Robert & Jean Kennedy
All year

$$ B&B
7 rooms, 3 pb
Visa, MC
C-yes/S-no/P-no/H-no

Full breakfast
Comp. coffee and tea
Adjacent to golf course
Across from Lake Wawasee

Turn-of-the-century home filled with period furniture. Close to Amish communities & several antique shops. Many lakes in the area & adjacent to 18-hole public golf course.

TIPPECANOE

Bessinger's Hillfarm B&B
4588 SR 110, 46570
219-223-3288
Wayne & Betty Bessinger
All year

$ B&B
2 rooms, 2 pb
C-10+/S-no/P-no/H-no

Full breakfast
Lunch, dinner
Sitting room, ponds
wildlife, birdwatching
X-C skiing, canoeing

Bessinger's Hillfarm Wildlife Refuge is a comfortable log home, overlooking water area with many islands. Hiking, canoeing, X-C skiing, fishing, swimming, or plain relaxing.

WASHINGTON

Mimi's House
101 W. Maple St., 47501
812-254-5562 812-254-5562
David & Stuart Graham
All year

$ B&B
6 rooms, 4 pb
C-yes/S-yes/P-no/H-yes

Continental breakfast
Library
Common room
TV, Ping-Pong

A truly unique home, filled with furnishings and memorabilia of the Graham family, noted glass, truck and auto manufacturers. Experience 1920s and 1930s. On National Register.

Bessinger's B&B, Tippecanoe, IN

148 Indiana

WESTFIELD ——————————————————————————

Country Roads Guesthouse	$ B&B	Continental plus
2731 West 146th St., 46074	1 rooms, 1 pb	Kitchen fireplace
317-846-2376	C-yes/S-no/P-no/H-no	Sitting room, antiques
N. A. Litz		basketball, volleyball
All year		swimming pool, bicycles

100 year-old farmhouse and barn set on 4 acres. Good location for jogging & biking. Close to antique shops, historic sites and fine restaurants.

More Inns ...

1900 House, The 50777 Ridgemoor Way, Granger, 46530 219-277-7783
Abode B&B 107 N. Eddy St., South Bend, 46617 219-234-8583
Amish Acres, Inc. 160 W. Market, Wappanee, 46550 219-773-4188
Atwater Century Farm B&B RR 4, Box 307, Lagrange, 46761 219-463-2743
Autumnwood B&B 165 Autumnwood Lane, Madison, 47250 812-265-5262
Barn House 10656 E. 63rd St., Indianapolis, 46236 317-823-4898
Bob & Arlene Mast 26206 CR 50, Nappanee, 46550 219-773-4714
Brick Inn 1540 Bloomington St., Greencastle, 46135 317-653-3267
Brick Street Inn 175 S. Main St., Zionsville, 46077 317-873-5895
Camel Lot 4512 W. 131st St., Westfield, 46074 317-873-4370
Candlelight Inn 503 E. Fort Wayne St., Warsaw, 46580 219-267-2906
Candlewyck Inn 331 W. Washington Blvd., Fort Wayne, 46802 219-424-2643
Chestnut Hill Log Home B&B RR 4, Box 295, Hoover, Nashville, 47448 812-988-4995
Cliff House B&B 122 Fairmount Dr., Madison, 47250 812-265-5272
Clifty Inn P.O. Box 387, Madison, 47250 812-265-4135
Columbus Inn 445 Fifth St., Columbus, 47201 812-378-4289
Coneygar 54835 C.R. 33, Middlebury, 46540 219-825-5707
Country B&B 27727 CR 36, Goshen, 46526 219-862-2748
Country Homestead Guest Ho Route 1, Box 353, Richland, 47634 812-359-4870
Cragwood Inn B&B 303 N. Second St., Decatur, 46733 219-728-9388
Creekwood Inn Route 20-35, Michigan City, 46460 219-872-8357
De'Coy's B&B 1546 W. 100 N., Hartford City, 47348 317-348-2164
Driftwood P.O. Box 16, Plymouth, 46563 219-546-2274
Duneland Beach Inn 3311 Potawatomi, Michigan City, 46360 219-874-7729
Elderberry Inn 411 W. First St., Madison, 47250 812-265-6856
Essenhaus Country Inn 240 US 20, Middlebury, 46540 219-825-9471
Flower Patch B&B 16263 CR 22, Goshen, 46526 219-534-4207
Four Seasons Farm B&B RR 1, Box 385, Wolcottville, 46795 219-854-3993
Friendliness With A Flair 5214 E. 20th Place, Indianapolis, 46218 317-356-3149
Fruitt Basket Inn B&B 116 W. Main St., North Manchester, 46962 219-982-2443
Grandview Guest House Box 311, Grandview, 47615 812-649-2817
Gunn Guest House 904 Park Ave., Winona Lake, 46590 219-267-2023
Haven B&B P.O. Box 798, Washington, 46501 812-254-7770
Heritage House 705 W. Second St., Madison, 47250 812-265-2393
Hill Top Country Inn 1733 CR 28, Auburn, 46706 219-281-2529
Hilltop House B&B 88 W. Sinclair St., Wabash, 46992 219-563-7726
Home B&B 21166 Clover Hill Ct., South Bend, 46614 219-291-0535
Indiana Amish Country B&B 1600 W. Market St., Nappanee, 46550 219-773-4188
Inter Urban Inn 503 S. Harrison, Alexandria, 46001 317-724-2001
Jamison Inn 1404 N. Ivy Rd., South Bend, 46637 219-277-9682
Jelley House Country Inn 222 S. Walnut St., Rising Sun, 47404 812-438-2319
Koontz House B&B 7514 N. Hwy 23, Koontz Lake, 46574 219-586-7090
Lafayette Street B&B 723 Lafayette St., Columbus, 47201 812-372-7245
Lake Breeze RR 5, Box 169A, Syracuse, 46567 219-457-5000
Lakeside Haven 63070 Lakeside Dr., Goshen, 46526 219-642-3678
Lanning House 206 E. Poplar St., Salem, 47167 812-883-3484
Manor House 612 E. 13th St., Indianapolis, 46202 317-634-1711

Maple Hill RR 3, Box 76, Middletown, 47356 317-354-2580
Mary's Place 305 Eugene Dr., PBx 428, Middlebury, 46540 219-825-2429
Mayor Wilhelm's Villa 428 N. Fifth St., Vincennes, 47591 812-882-9487
McGinley's Vacation Cabins Route 3, Box 332, Nashville, 47448 812-988-7337
Milburn House 707 E. Vistula St., Bristol, 46507 219-848-4026
Millwood House 512 West St., Madison, 47250 812-265-6780
Olde McCray Mansion Inn 703 E. Mitchell St., Kendallville, 46755 219-347-3647
Open Hearth B&B 56782 SR 15, Bristol, 46507 219-825-2417
Pairadux Inn 6363 N. Guilford Ave., Indianapolis, 46220 317-259-8005
Pheasant Country B&B 900 E. 5th St., Fowler, 47944 317-884-0908
Plain & Fancy SR 135 N., RR 3, Box 62, Nashville, 47448 812-988-4537
Quilt Haven 711 Dittemore Rd., Bloomington, 47404 812-876-5802
Retreat House 8223 W. 550 North, North Salem, 46165 317-676-6669
River Belle B&B, The P.O. Box 669, Hwy 66, Grandview, 47615 812-649-2500
Sandy Hollow Inn B&B 935 Sandy Hollow Dr., Portland, 47371 219-726-9444
Seasons P.O. Box 187, Nashville, 47448 812-988-2284
Snapp Inn Route 3, Box 102, Limestone, 37681 615-257-2482
Solomon Mier Manor 508 S. Cavin St., Ligonier, 46767 219-894-3668
Story Inn P.O. Box 64, Nashville, 47448 812-988-6516
Sugar Creek B&B 901 W. Market St., Crawfordsville, 47933 317-362-4095
Sunset House RR 3, Box 127, Nashville, 47448 812-988-6118
Swiss Hills B&B RR 3, Box 315, Vevay, 47043 812-427-3882
Sycamore Spring Farm Box 224, Churubusco, 46723 219-693-3603
Thorpe House Clayborne St., Metamora, 47030 317-647-5425
Timberidge B&B 16801 SR 4, Goshen, 46526 219-533-7133
Victoria House Route 4, Box 414, Nashville, 47448 812-988-6344
Victorian Guest House 302 E. Market, Nappanee, 46550 219-773-4383
Victorian House RR1 Box 27, Roachdale, 46172 317-522-1225
Warren Cabin B&B 1161 Church St., Corydon, 47112 812-738-2166
Weavers Country Oaks RR 4, Box 193H, Lagrange, 46761 219-768-7191
White Hill Manor 2513 E. Center St., Warsaw, 46580 219-269-6933
Wingfield's Inn B&B 526 Indian Oak Mall, Chesterton, 46304 702-348-0766
Ye Olde Scotts Inn RR 1, Box 5, Leavenworth, 47137 812-739-4747
Yount's Mill Inn 3729 Old State Rd. 32 W, Crawfordsville, 47933 317-362-5864
Zimmer Frei Haus 409 N. Main St., Monticello, 47960 219-583-4061

Iowa

ATLANTIC ————————————————————————————————————

Chestnut Charm B&B $$ MAP   Full breakfast
1409 Chestnut St., 50022   5 rooms, 3 pb   Sitting room, piano
712-243-5652   Visa, MC •   A/C, sun rooms, antiques
Bruce & Barbara Stensvad   C-no/S-no/P-no/H-no   fountained patio
All year

Enchanting 1898 Victorian mansion on large estate. Be pampered in elegance. Gourmet dining. Experience beauty and fantasy with someone special.

CALMAR ────────────────────────────────────

Calmar Guesthouse $ B&B   Full breakfast
RR 1, Box 206, 52132   5 rooms, 1 pb   Sitting room
319-562-3851   C-yes/S-ltd/P-no/H-no
Lucille B. Kruse   German
All year

Beautiful, fully restored Victorian. Breakfast served in formal dining room. Near Norwiegan Museum. Bily Clocks, Luther College, NITI College, golf, canoeing, fishing.

COUNCIL BLUFFS ────────────────────────────

Robin's Nest Inn B&B $ B&B   Full breakfast
327–9th Ave., 51503   4 rooms   Dinner upon request
712-323-1649   Visa, MC   Aftn. tea & refreshments
Dorethea Smith, Wendy Storey   C-yes/S-no/P-no/H-no   sitting room, TV
All year   weekend theme packages

Stately brick Victorian with romantic country furnishings; country breakfast, fresh breads and pastries; walking distance to historic Dodge house and Haymarket square.

DUBUQUE ────────────────────────────────────

Redstone Inn $$ EP/$$$ B&B   Full breakfast (suites)
504 Bluff St., 52001   15 rooms, 15 pb   Comp. champagne (suites)
319-582-1894   Visa, MC, AmEx ●   Afternoon tea Jun-Oct
Mary Kay Hurm   C-yes/S-yes/P-no/H-no   sitting room
All year   hot tub, hair dryers

Genuine antique furniture used throughout this professionally decorated chateau-style inn. Located in center of the Cathedral National Register District.

The Richards House $ B&B   Full breakfast
1492 Locust St., 52001   5 rooms, 4 pb   Snacks
319-557-1492   Visa, MC, AmEx ●   Sitting room, antiques
Michelle Delaney   C-yes/S-ltd/P-ask/H-no   concealed TV's, phones
All year   fireplaces

1883 Stick-style Victorian mansion with over 80 stained-glass windows. Seven varieties of woodwork and period furnishings. Working fireplaces in guest rooms.

Stout House B&B $$ B&B   Full breakfast
504 Bluff St. (mail), 52001   6 rooms, 6 pb   Comp. brandy or soda
1105 Locust St.   Visa, MC, AmEx ●   Library
319-582-1890   C-yes/S-yes/P-no/H-no   sitting room
Jodi & Roland Emond
All year

Romanesque stone mansion, former home of archbishop, highlighted by gleaming wood, stained glass, library, original art. Near tourist attractions in historic Dubuque.

GREENFIELD ────────────────────────────────

The Wilson Home $$$ B&B   Full breakfast
RR1, Box 132, 50849   2 rooms, 2 pb   Sitting room, library
515-743-2031   ●   Indoor swimming pool
Wendy & Henry Wilson   C-yes/S-ltd/P-no   challenging golf course
January 15–October 15   tennis nearby

Spacious guestrooms open directly onto indoor pool area set in Iowa's rolling countryside. Easily accessible from Des Moines or Omaha. Near Iowa Aviation Preservation Center.

La Corsette Maison, Newton, IA

HOMESTEAD

Die Heimat Country Inn
Main St., 52236
Amana Colonies
319-622-3937
Don & Sheila Janda
All year

$ B&B
19 rooms, 19 pb
Visa, MC
C-yes/S-yes/P-no/H-no

Full breakfast
Occasional beverages
Sitting room
shaded yard
wooden glider

Stay overnight at our century-old restored inn. All rooms have private baths furnished with Amana furniture and antiques. Colony restaurants and wineries nearby.

KEOSAUQUA

Mason House/Bentonsport
RR 2, Box 237, 52565
319-592-3133
Sheral & Bill McDermet
All year

$ B&B
10 rooms, 2 pb
C-yes/S-no/P-no/H-yes

Full breakfast
Dinner by reservation
Comp. snacks
Sitting room, parlor
canoeing

1846 steamboat era inn located in National Historic District. Peaceful escape to bygone era. Potter and blacksmith shops—next block.

NEWTON

La Corsette Maison Inn
629 First Ave. E., 50208
515-792-6833
Kay Owen
All year

$$ B&B
4 rooms, 4 pb
Visa, MC ●
C-yes/S-no/P-ask/H-no

Full breakfast
Gourmet dinner
Restaurant
sitting room

Turn-of-the-century mission-style mansion. Charming French bedchambers, beckoning hearths. 30 minutes from Des Moines on I-80. Near I-35. Gourmet Dining 4½ star rating.

PRINCETON

The Woodlands
P.O. Box 127, 52768
319-289-3177 319-289-4661
The Wallace Family
All year

Full breakfast
Lunch, dinner available
Snacks, sitting room
library, bicycles, pool
near Mississippi River

Secluded woodland escape nestled among pines on 26 acres of forest and meadows ... an elegant breakfast by the pool or a cozy fireplace ... skiing, fishing, golf, nature trails.

More Inns . . .

Apple Orchard Inn B&B RR 3 Box 129, Missouri Valley, 51555 712-642-2418
Babi's B&B Route 1, South Amana, 52334 319-662-4381
Cloverleaf Farm Route 2, Box 140A, Fort Atkinson, 52144 319-534-7061
Decker House Inn 128 N. Main, Maquoketa, 52060 319-652-6654
English Valley B&B RR 2, Montezuma, 50171 515-623-3663
FitzGerald's Inn P.O. Box 157, Lansing, 52151 319-538-4872
Hancock House 1105 Grove Terrace, Dubuke, 52001 319-557-8989
Hannah Marie Country Inn RR 1, Hway. 71 S., Spencer, 51301 712-262-1286
Happy Hearth B&B 400 W. Washington, Fairfield, 52556 515-472-9386
Heritage House RR 1, Leighton, 50143 515-626-3092
Historic Harlan Hotel 122 N. Jefferson St., Mount Pleasant, 52641 319-385-3126
Hotel Brooklyn 154 Front St., Brooklyn, 52211 515-522-9229
Inn at Stone City Anamosa, 52205 319-462-4733
Juniper Hill Farm 15325 Budd Rd., Dubuque, 52001 319-582-4405
LaVerne & Alice Hageman Route 2, Box 104, Fort Atkinson, 52144 319-534-7545
Lansing House Box 97, 291 N. Front St, Lansing, 52151 319-538-4263
Larson House B&B 300 N. 9th St., Fort Dodge, 50501 515-573-5733
Little House Vacations Elkader, 52043 319-783-7774
Loy's B&B RR 1, Box 82, Marengo, 52301 319-642-7787
Lucille's B&B RR 1, Box 55, Williamsburg, 52361 319-668-1185
Monarch, The 303 Second Street, Le Claire, 52753 319-289-3011
Mont Rest 300 Spring St., Bellevue, 52031 319-872-4220
Montgomery Mansion 812 Maple Ave., Decorah, 52101 319-382-5088
Old World Inn, The 331 S. Main St., Spillville, 52168 319-562-3739
Orval & Diane Bruvold Route 1, Decorah, 52101 319-382-4729
Rainbow H. Lodging House RR 1, Box 89, Elk Horn, 51531 712-764-8272
River Oaks Inn B&B 1234 E. River Dr., Davenport, 52803 319-326-2629
Spring Side Inn P.O. Box 41, RR 2, Bellevue, 52031 319-872-5452
Strawtown Inn & Lodge 1111 Washington St., Pella, 50219 515-628-2681
Summit Grove Inn 1426 S. Seventh St., Stuart, 50250 515-523-2147
Taylor Manor 919 Washington St., Cedar Falls, 50613 309-266-0035
Terra Jane, The Route 5, Box 69, Council Bluffs, 51503 712-322-4200
Terra Verde Farm Route 1, Box 86, Swisher, 52338 319-846-2478
Travelling Companion 4314 Main St., Elk Horn, 51531 712-764-8932
Usher's 711 Corning, Red Oak, 51566 712-623-3222
Victorian B&B Inn P.O. Box 249, Avoca, 51521 712-343-6336
Victorian House 508 E. 4th St., Tipton, 52772 319-886-2633
Walden Acres B&B RR 1, Box 30, Adel, 50003 515-987-1567

Kansas

COLUMBUS —————————————————————————————

Meriwether House B&B	$ B&B	Continental breakfast
322 W. Pine, 66725	7 rooms	Sitting room
316-429-2812 316-674-3274	Visa, MC	
M. Meriwether, L. Simpson	C-yes/S-no/P-no/H-ask	
All year		

Cottage home close to downtown. Furnished with antiques. Decorator shop within. Lace,
wallpaper, and many decorating items for sale.

CONCORDIA

Crystle's B&B
508 W. 7th St., 66901
913-243-2192
Carrie & Jim Warren-Gully
All year

$ B&B
5 rooms, 1 pb
Visa, MC
C-yes/S-no/P-no/H-no
Spanish

Full breakfast
Comp. tea, lemonade
Sitting room, library
tennis, swimming pool, and
golf nearby

Hospitality and charm overflowing! A beautiful 1880 home with original antiques decorating unique and creative rooms. Enjoy a breakfast and discover historic Concordia.

COUNCIL GROVE

The Cottage House
25 N. Neosho, 66846
316-767-6828 800-727-7903
Connie Essington
All year

$$ B&B
26 rooms
Visa, MC, AmEx, DC, Dis ●
C-yes/S-yes/P-ltd/H-yes

Continental breakfast
Restaurant
Sitting room, sauna room
6 rooms w/whirlpool tubs
near Hays House Restaur.

Beautifully renovated Victorian hotel with all of the modern comforts. Lovely antique furnishings. Located in historic "Birthplace of the Santa Fe Trail."

TONGANOXIE

Almeda's B&B Inn
220 S. Main, 66086
913-845-2295
Almeda & Richard Tinberg
All year

$ B&B
7 rooms, 1 pb
C-ltd/S-ltd/P-no/H-no

Continental plus
Comp. cold drinks
Sitting room
organ, all rooms A/C
suite available

Dedicated as a historical site in 1983; in the '30s was the inspiration for the movie "Bus Stop." Decorated in country style with many antiques. Close to golf courses & pool.

TOPEKA

Heritage House
3535 SW Sixth Ave., 66606
913-233-3800
Betty & Don Rich
All year

$$ B&B
14 rooms, 14 pb
Visa, MC, AmEx, DC, Dis ●
C-yes/S-no/P-no/H-no

Full breakfast
Lunch, dinner
Restaurant, bar service
sitting room
conference room

Historic inn with individually designed rooms. Gourmet meals served in sun room. City charm close to park and zoo. Wine and liquor.

WICHITA

Inn at Willowbend
3939 Comotara, 67226
316-636-4032
Gary & Bernice Adamson
All year

$$$ B&B
22 rooms, 22 pb
Visa, MC, AmEx, Dis, DC ●
C-yes/S-yes/P-no/H-yes

Full breakfast
Complimentary wine
Bar service
sitting room, library
hot tubs in suites

A traditional bed and breakfast with modern conveniences located on a championship golf course.

Inn at the Park
3751 E. Douglas, 67218
316-652-0500
Cindy Cline
All year

$$$ B&B
12 rooms, 12 pb
Visa, MC, AmEx ●
C-no/S-no/P-no/H-yes
Spanish

Continental plus
Afternoon tea
Sitting room
library, hot tubs
tennis and pool nearby

A 1910 mansion, nestled on the edge of a park. 12 uniquely decorated suites. Close to fine dining, theater, business, shopping. Ideal for vacationers and corporate travelers.

WICHITA _____

Max Paul ... An Inn	$$ B&B	Continental plus
3910 E. Kellogg, 67218	14 rooms, 14 pb	Sitting room, library
316-689-8101	Visa, MC, AmEx, DC	Group & conf. facilities
Roberta & Jill Eaton	C-ask/S-yes/P-no/H-no	hot tub, pool
All year		tennis nearby

Feather beds and antique furniture; fireplaces, decks, exercise/jacuzzi room opens on gardens and pond; close to park, shops and restaurant.

More Inns ...

Balfours' House B&B Abilene, 67410 913-263-4262
Barn B&B Inn RR 2, Box 87, Valley Falls, 66088 913-945-3303
Braddock Ames B&B P.O. Box 892, Syracuse, 67878 316-384-5218
Butterfield B&B Hays, 67601 913-628-3908
Caney B&B Hwy 75, Caney, 67333 316-879-5478
Cimarron Hotel & Restauran P.O. Box 633, Cimarron, 67835 316-855-2244
Clyde Hotel 420 Washington, Clyde, 66938 913-446-2231
Country Quarters Route 5, Box 80, Fort Scott, 66701 316-223-2889
Dauddy Haus Route 2, Box 273, Haven, 67543 316-465-2267
Dodds House B&B Hwy 75S, Holton, 66436 913-364-3172
Flower Patch 610 Main, Atwood, 67730 913-626-3780
Fort's Cedar View RR 3, Box 120B, Ulysses, 67880 316-356-2570
Goodnite at Irene's 703 S. 6th, Atwood, 67730 913-626-3521
Halcyon House 1000 Ohio, Lawrence, 66044 913-841-0314
Haven of Rest Marion, 66861 316-382-2286
Hawk House B&B Inn 307 W. Broadway, Newton, 67114 316-283-2045
Heritage Inn 300 Main, Halstead, 67056 316-835-2118
Hollyrood House B&B Route 1, Box 47, Holyrood, 67450 913-252-3678
Holste Homestead Ludell, 67744 913-626-3522
Home on the Range Atwood, 67730 913-626-9309
Hotel Josephine 5th & Ohio, Holton, 66436 913-364-3151
Hunters Leigh B&B 4109 E. North St., Salina, 67401 913-823-6750
Huntington House 324 S. Main, Fort Scott, 66701 316-223-3644
Jones Sheep Farm B&B Peabody, 66866 316-983-2815
Kansas City B&B P.O. Box 14781, Lenexa, 66215 913-888-3636
Kimble Cliff B&B 6782 Anderson Ave., Manhattan, 66502 913-539-3816
Kirk House 145 W. 4th Ave., Garnett, 66032 913-448-5813
Lear Acres-B&B on a Farm Rt. 1 Box 31, Bern, 66408 913-336-3903
Little Bit Like Home 323 E. Greeley, Tribune, 67879 316-376-4776
Loft B&B Osborne, 67473 913-346-5984
Lois' B&B Beloit, 67420 913-738-5869
Long's Country Inn 801 W. 54th. Ave., Manhattan, 66502 913-776-3212
Peaceful Acres B&B Route 5, Box 153, Great Bend, 67530 316-793-7527
Pomeroy Inn Hill City, 67642 913-674-2098
Pork Palace Ludell, 67744 913-626-9223
Rock House B&B 201 Dogwood, Wakefield, 67487 913-461-5732
School House Inn 106 E. Beck, Melvern, 66510 913-549-3473
Schumann Gast Haus 615 S. "B" St., Arkansas City, 67005 316-442-8220
Spillman Creek Lodge Sylvan Grove, 67481 913-277-3424
Stuewe Place 617 Nebraska, Alma, 66401 913-765-3636
Sunbarger Guest House RR 1, Cassoday, 66842 316-735-4499
Swedish Country Inn 112 W. Lincoln, Lindsborg, 67456 913-227-2985
Thistle Hill B&B Route 1, Box 93, Wakeeney, 67672 913-743-2644
Victorian Memories 314 N. 4th, Burlington, 66839 316-364-5752
Victorian Reflections 303 N. Cedar, Abilene, 67410 913-263-7774
Woody House B&B Route 1, Box 156, Lincoln, 67455 913-524-4744

Kentucky

BARDSTOWN

Jailer's Inn	$$ B&B	Continental breakfast
111 W. Stephen Foster, 40004	5 rooms, 5 pb	Comp. wine & cheese
505-348-5551	Visa, MC ●	Sitting room
Fran McCoy	C-yes/S-ltd/H-yes	landscaped courtyard
March–December		roses, gazebo

Jailer's Inn was once a jail (1819–74), then a jailer's residence (1874–1987), and is now completely remodeled and attractively decorated with antiques and heirlooms.

Talbot Tavern/McLean House	$$ B&B	Continental breakfast
107 W. Stephen Foster, 40004	11 rooms, 11 pb	Lunch, dinner, bar
Court Square	Visa, MC, AmEx, DC	Entertainment
502-348-3494	C-yes/S-yes/P-no/H-no	gift shop
The Kelley Family		
All year		

1779 stone inn, one of first hostelries west, each room original, fireplaces, antiques. Wall paintings done by guest Prince Louis Phillipe of France.

FRANKFORT

Olde Kantucke B&B Inn	$ B&B	Continental plus
210 E. Fourth St., 40601	4 rooms, 3 pb	Afternoon tea
502-227-7389	Visa, MC, AmEx ●	Sitting room, ceiling fans,
Patty Smith	C-15+/S-yes/P-no/H-no	clawfoot tubs
All year		

Cheerful, old-fashioned boarding house atmosphere in historic district of Frankfort, which is nestled among the rolling hills of the Bluegrass region.

Taylor-Compton House	$$ B&B	Continental plus
419 Lewis St., 40601	2 rooms	Living room & den
502-227-4368	C-yes/S-no/P-yes/H-no	TV, movies
Barri Christian		near shops, restaurants
March–mid December		

Elegant Victorian residence located next to Old Capitol Building and near historic specialty shops. Furnished with period antiques. Relive history!

GEORGETOWN

Breckinridge House B&B	$$ B&B	Full breakfast
201 S. Broadway, 40324	2 rooms, 2 pb	Antique shop
502-863-3163	Visa, MC ●	Two suites with
Annette & Felice Porter	C-ask/S-yes/P-no/H-no	sitting room, kitchen,
All year		private bath & antiques

Charming Georgian home was the residence of John Breckinridge, one of the leading Confederate generals. Two suites. Homemade breads, pecan rolls, bacon and eggs, fresh fruit.

Four Seasons Country Inn, Glasgow, KY

GEORGETOWN

Log Cabin B&B
350 N. Broadway, 40324
502-863-3514
Janis & Clay McKnight
All year

$$ B&B
2 rooms, 1 pb
C-yes/S-yes/P-yes/H-yes

Continental plus
Complete kitchen
Entire cabin filled with
interesting amenities
fireplace, A/C, porch

Authentic log cabin (1809); antique furnishings, complete kitchen, 2 bedrooms, fireplace, air conditioning; located 2 miles north of Lexington, 1.7 miles off I-75.

GLASGOW

Four Seasons Country Inn
4107 Scottsville Rd., 42141
502-678-1000
Henry Carter
All year

$$ B&B
17 rooms, 17 pb
Visa, MC, AmEx, DC, Dis
●
C-yes/S-yes/P-no/H-yes

Continental breakfast
Snacks
Sitting room
swimming pool

Charming Victorian-style inn built new in 1989. Modern conveniences and amenities with warm country furnishings and atmosphere.

LOUISVILLE

Old Louisville Inn
1359 S. Third St., 40208
502-635-1574
Marianne Lesher
All year

$$ B&B
11 rooms, 8 pb
Visa, MC ●
C-yes/S-ltd/P-no/H-no

Continental plus
Afternoon tea
Sitting room, library
bicycles, tennis 1 block
hot tub in one room

"Your home away from home." Wake up to the aroma of freshly baked breads and muffins and Southern hospitality.

MIDDLESBOROUGH

The RidgeRunner
208 Arthur Heights, 40965
606-248-4299
Susan Richards, Irma Gall
All year

$$ B&B
6 rooms, 2 pb
Visa, MC
C-no/S-no/P-no/H-no

Full breakfast
Comp. tea, refreshments
Sitting room
library
porch

Charming and lovingly restored Victorian mansion. Lovely woodwork, pocket doors, interesting windows, spacious porch. Breathtaking views of mountains. Antique furnishings.

Old Louisville Inn, Louisville, KY

OWENSBORO

WeatherBerry B&B
2731 W. Second St., 42301
502-684-8760
Bill & Susan Tyler
All year

$$ B&B
3 rooms, 3 pb
Visa, MC ●
C-ask/S-no/P-no/H-no

Full breakfast
Snacks
Sitting room, library
Day Lily garden
weather station replica

Charming and elegant Victorian farmhouse, circa 1840. Antiques, full Kentucky breakfast, weather station replica, Day Lily garden, convenient to downtown.

PADUCAH

Paducah Harbor Plaza B&B
201 Broadway, 42001
502-442-2698
Beverly & David Harris
All year

$ B&B
4 rooms
Visa, MC, AmEx
C-yes/S-no/P-no/H-no

Continental plus
Snacks, catered food
Sitting room
library

Restored Victorian turn-of-the-century European plan hotel. Lovely antique furnishings. Located in historic district. One block from American Quilter's Society Museum.

VERSAILLES

Shepherd Place
31 Heritage Rd., 40383
U.S. 60 Lexington
606-873-7843
Marlin & Sylvia Yawn
All year

$$ B&B
2 rooms, 2 pb
Visa, MC
C-yes/S-no/P-no/H-no

Full breakfast
Complimentary snacks
Sitting room
fleeces, wools
hand knits for sale

Pre-Civil War home. Spacious bedrooms. Private baths. Stroll the grounds, help feed the sheep or relax in the porch swing. Full home-cooked Kentucky breakfast.

More Inns . . .

Amos Shinkle Townhouse 215 Garrard St., Corington, 41011 606-431-2118
B&B at Sills Inn 270 Montgomery, Versailles, 40383 800-526-9801

Beaumont Inn 638 Beaumont Dr., Harrodsburg, 40330 606-734-3381
Boone Tavern Hotel CPO 2345, Berea, 40404 606-986-9358
Bowling Green B&B 659 E. 14th Ave., Bowling Green, 42101 502-781-3861
Broadwell B&B Route 6, Box 58, Cynthiana, 41031 606-234-4255
Canaan Land Farm B&B 4355 Lexington Rd., Harrodsburg, 40330 606-734-3984
Davis House B&B, The R # 2, Box 21A1, Kuttawa, 42055 502-388-4468
Doe Run Inn Route 2, Brandenburg, 40108 502-422-2982
Ehrhardts B&B 285 Springwell Dr., Paducah, 42001 502-554-0644
Glenmar B&B Rt. 1, Box 682, Springfield, 40069 606-284-7791
Olde Bethlehem Academy Elizabethtown, 42701 502-862-9003
Rokeby Hall 318 S. Mill St., Lexington, 40508 606-254-5770
Shadwick House 411 S Main St., Somerset, 42501 606-678-4675
Victorian Secret B&B 1132 S. First St., Louisville, 40203 502-581-1914

Louisiana

JEANERETTE

B&B on Bayou Teche | $ B&B | Continental plus
2148½ W. Main St., 70544 | 1 rooms, 1 pb | Kitchenette, freezer
on Hwy 182 | ● | Laundry facilities
Warren & Barbara Patout | C-yes/S-yes/P-no/H-yes | barbecue pit, canoe
All year | French | TV, radio, phone, A/C

Guest cottage with kitchen on scenic highway 182—130 miles west of New Orleans. Near many tourist attractions. Weekly rates.

MONROE

Boscobel Cottage | $$ B&B | Full plantation brkfast
185 Cordell Lane, 71202 | 2 rooms, 2 pb | Comp. wine, snacks
318-325-1550 | Visa, MC ● | Sitting room, porches
Kay & Cliff LaFrance | C-yes/S-yes/P-yes/H-no | antique comforts
All year

1820 Cottage listed on National Register. Lovely country hideaway facing Ouachita River. Stay in historic chapel or garconniere. Serene beauty. All creature comforts.

NAPOLEONVILLE

Madewood Plantation House | $$$ B&B/MAP | Full breakfast (map)
Route 2, Box 478, 70390 | 8 rooms, 8 pb | Cont. breakfast (B&B)
4250 Hwy 308 | ● | Dinner, wine & cheese
504-369-7151 | C-yes/S-ltd/P-ltd/H-no | sitting room, piano
Keith & Millie Marshall | some French | canopied beds
All year

Greek Revival mansion. Canopied beds, antiques, fresh flowers, wine and cheese, dinner by candlelight in formal family dining room.

NEW ORLEANS

A Hotel—The Frenchmen | $$$ B&B | Full breakfast
417 Frenchmen Street, 70116 | 25 rooms, 25 pb | Lunch, snacks
504-948-2166 800-831-1781 | Visa, MC, AmEx ● | Bar, sitting room
Mark Soubie, Jr. | C-no/S-yes/P-no/H-yes | hot tubs, swimming pool
All year | | sun deck, books

Each of the rooms is decorated with period furniture, ceiling fan & high ceiling. Classically served Frenchmen breakfast on silver trays in your room, or poolside patio.

NEW ORLEANS ───────────────────────

Columns Hotel
3811 St. Charles Ave., 70115
504-899-9308
Claire & Jacques Creppél
All year

$$ B&B
20 rooms, 10 pb
Visa, MC, AmEx, DC •
C-yes/S-yes/P-no/H-yes
Spanish

Continental breakfast
Lunch, dinner, bar
Piano

Jazz every Wednesday in ballroom—no charge. Historic register. Garden District, near Audubon Zoo, Universities. Victorian lounge in Esquire's "Top 100."

Cornstalk Hotel
915 Royal St., 70116
504-523-1515
Debi & David Spencer
All year

$$$ B&B
14 rooms, 14 pb
Visa, MC, AmEx
C-yes/S-yes/P-no/H-no
French, German

Continental breakfast
Comp. tea, wine, paper
Stained-glass windows
oriental rugs
fireplaces

Small, elegant hotel in heart of French Quarter. All antique furnishings. Complimentary wine/liqueurs upon check-in. Recent renovation.

The Dusty Mansion
2231 Gen. Pershing, 70115
504-895-4576
Cynthia Tomlin Riggs
All year

$ B&B
4 rooms, 2 pb
•
C-yes/S-yes/P-no/H-no
Spanish, French

Continental plus
Sunday champagne brunch
Comp. wine, beverages
sitting room
pool table, sun deck

Charming turn-of-the-century home, spacious, comfortable. Near St. Charles Street Car; easy access to French Quarter. Southern hospitality!

Hotel Ste. Helene
508 Rue Chartres, 70130
504-522-5014
Regina Farrell
All year

$$ B&B
16 rooms, 16 pb
Visa, MC, AmEx, DC •
C-yes/S-yes/P-no/H-yes
Spanish

Continental breakfast
Afternoon tea
Elevator
swimming pool

Preferred location in the heart of the French Quarter. Intimate European style guest house, custom designed rooms, gracious hospitality. Breakfast served by the pool.

Lafitte Guest House
1003 Bourbon St., 70116
504-581-2678 800-331-7971
John Maher, Robert Guyton
All year

$$ B&B
14 rooms, 14 pb
Visa, MC, AmEx •
C-yes/S-yes/P-no/H-ltd

Continental breakfast
Wine & hors d'oeuvres
Sitting room
balconies, courtyard
queen & king-size beds

This fine French manor building greets you with elegance and tradition. Fine antique pieces and reproductions. In the heart of the French Quarter and liveliness of Bourbon St.

Lamothe House
621 Esplanade Ave., 70116
504-947-1161 800-367-5858
Carol Chauppette
All year

$$$ B&B
20 rooms, 20 pb
Visa, MC, AmEx •
C-yes/S-yes/P-no/H-no

Continental breakfast
Pralines, comp. beverage
Sitting room, courtyard
newspaper, parking
AAA 4-Diamond rating

An elegantly restored historic old mansion located on the eastern boundary of the French Quarter. This old mansion surrounds a romantic courtyard.

160 Louisiana

Marquette House
2253 Carondelet St., 70130
504-523-3014
Steve & Alma Cross
All year

$ EP
12 rooms, 12 pb
Visa, MC ●
C-yes/S-no/P-no/H-no

Laundry, kitchenettes
12 suites in brick bldg.
Sitting rooms, veranda
garden-patio, fountain
Television in some rooms

12 guest suites in pre-Civil War brick building. Beautiful garden-patio area with fountain. Kitchenettes in each room. Off-street parking.

Nine-O-Five Royal Hotel
905 Rue Royal St., 70116
504-523-0219
Mr. J. Morell
All year

$$$ EP
14 rooms, 14 pb
C-yes/S-yes/P-no/H-no

Kitchens in all rooms
Three suites

Quaint guest house built in the 1890s, located in the French Quarter. Nicely furnished, antiques, high ceilings. Kitchenettes and Southern charm.

Rue Dumaine
P.O. Box 70523, 70172
731 Rue Dumaine
504-581-2802
Clydia Ann Davenport
All year

$$$ B&B
1 rooms, 1 pb
●
C-no/S-no/P-no/H-no
French, Spanish

Continental plus
Separate guesthouse
Snacks, beverages
private patio, fireplace
balcony, piano

Private entrance to your exclusive hideaway built in 1824 and filled with antiques and every amenity. Heart of French Quarter.

Soniat House
1133 Chartres St., 70116
504-522-0570 800-544-8808
Rodney Smith
All year

$$$ EP
24 rooms, 24 pb
Visa, MC, AmEx ●
C-yes/S-yes/P-no/H-no
Spanish

Continental breakfast-$
Bar service
Jacuzzis

A private hotel in the residential area of the French Quarter, furnished in period antiques offering modern amenities. 1991 One of 10 Best Small Hotels in America—Traveler.

Terrell Mansion
1441 Magazine St., 70130
504-524-9859 800-878-9859
Harry Lucas
All year

$$$ B&B
9 rooms, 9 pb
Visa, MC, AmEx ●
C-yes/S-yes/P-no/H-no
French

Continental breakfast
Complimentary wine
Selection of cocktail
sitting room

An elegant mansion completely furnished in period antiques. Easy access to French Quarter and the finest dining places.

NEW ROADS

Pointe Coupee B&B
Office 605 E. Main St., 70760
504-638-6254
Rev. & Mrs. Miller Armstrong
All year

$$ B&B
14 rooms
●
C-yes/S-ltd/P-ltd/H-yes

Full breakfast
Kitchen facilities
Comp. soft drinks
sitting room

Overnight accommodations in three restored homes in downtown New Roads, near beautiful False River and scenic, historic Point Coupee Parish.

SAINT FRANCISVILLE ─────────────────────────────────

Barrow House	$$$ B&B	Continental breakfast
P.O. Box 1461, 70775	5 rooms, 3 pb	Full breakfast $5
524 Royal St.	●	Dinner (res), comp. wine
504-635-4791	C-8+/S-yes/P-no/H-no	sitting room, bicycles
Lyle & Shirley Dittloff		cassette walking tours
All year		

Circa 1809, located in historic district. Rooms with balconies and period antiques. Cassette walking tours for guests. Honeymoon packages. Arnold Palmer golf course nearby.

SHREVEPORT ─────────────────────────────────────

2439 Fairfield, A B&B	$$$ B&B	Full breakfast
2439 Fairfield Ave., 71104	4 rooms, 4 pb	Sitting room, library
318-424-2424	Visa, AmEx ●	Hot tubs, fountain
James R. Harris, Jr.	C-no/S-no/P-no/H-no	private garden, gazebo
All year		balconies

Victorian elegance, Southern charm in the most fabulous Victorian home. Decorated in English antiques, down bedding, Amish quilts, lovely gardens. Corporate rates available.

Fairfield Place B&B	$$$ B&B	Full breakfast
2221 Fairfield Ave., 71104	6 rooms, 6 pb	Sitting room
318-222-0048	Visa, MC, AmEx ●	
Jane Lipscomb	C-ltd/S-ltd/P-ltd/H-no	
All year		

Casually elegant 1900s inn. European and American antiques, gourmet breakfast. Ideal for business travelers and tourists.

WHITE CASTLE ────────────────────────────────────

Nottoway Plantation Inn	$$$ B&B	Full breakfast
P.O. Box 160, 70788	13 rooms, 13 pb	Restaurant, comp. wine
Lousiana Hwy 1	Visa, MC ●	Swimming pool
504-545-2730	C-yes/S-yes/P-no/H-ltd	sitting room
Cindy Hidalgo, Faye Russell	French	piano, tennis nearby
All year exc. Christmas		

Fresh flowers in your room, chilled champagne, a wake-up call consisting of hot sweet potato biscuits, coffee and juice delivered to your room. Also a guided tour of mansion.

More Inns . . .

Annabelle's House B&B 1716 Milan, New Orleans, 70115 504-899-0701
Asphodel Village Rt. 2, Box 89 Hwy 68., Jackson, 70748 504-654-6868
Bedico Creek Inn 665 C C. Rd, Ponchatoula, 70454 504-845-8057
Bois de Chenes Inn 338 N. Sterling St., Lafayette, 70501 318-233-7816
Bougainvillea House 841 Bourbon St., New Orleans, 70116 504-525-3983
Camellia Cove 205 West Hill St, Washington, 70589 318-826-7362
Chimes Cottages 1360 Moss St., New Orleans, 70152 504-525-4640
Columns on Jordan 615 Jordan, Shreveport, 71101 318-222-5912
Cottage Plantation Route 5, Box 425, Saint Francisville, 70775 504-635-3674
Dauzat Guest House 337 Burgundy St., New Orleans, 70130 504-524-2075
De La Morandiere P.O. Box 327, Washington, 70589 318-826-3510
Delta Queen Steamboat Co. Robin Street Wharf, New Orleans, 70130 800-543-1949
Estorge House 427 N. Market St., Opelousas, 70570 318-948-4592
Estorge-Norton House 446 E. Main St., New Iberia, 70560 318-365-7603
French Quarter Maisonnette 1130 Chartres St., New Orleans, 70116 504-524-9918
Glencoe Plantation P.O. Box 178, Wilson, 70789 504-629-5387
Grenoble House Inn 329 Dauphine St., New Orleans, 70112 504-522-1331
Hedgewood Hotel 2427 St. Charles Ave., New Orleans, 70130 504-895-9708

Historic B&B Home P.O. Box 52257, New Orleans, 70152 800-749-4640
Homeplace Rt 2, Box 76A, Bunkie, 71322 318-826-7558
Hotel Maison de Ville 727 Toulouse St., New Orleans, 70130 504-561-5858
Hotel Villa Convento 616 Ursulines St., New Orleans, 70116 504-522-1793
Josephine Guest House 1450 Josephine St., New Orleans, 70130 504-524-6361
La Chaumiere 202 S Main St, Washington, 70589 318-826-3967
Longpre Garden's Gsthouse 1726 Prytania, New Orleans, 70130 504-561-0654
Mechling Guesthouse 2023 Esplanade, New Orleans, 70116 504-943-4131
Milbank—Historic House 102 Bank St., Box 1000, Jackson, 70748 504-634-5901
Mouton Manor Inn 310 Sidney Martin Rd, Lafayette, 70507 318-237-6996
Myrtles Plantation P.O. Box 1100, Hwy 61, Saint Francisville, 70775 504-635-6277
Noble Arms Inn 1006 Royal St., New Orleans, 70116 504-524-2222
Oak Alley Plantation Route 2 Box 10, Hwy. 18, Vacherie, 70090 504-265-2151
Old Castillo Hotel, The 220 Evangeline Blvd, St. Martinville, 70582 318-394-4010
Old Lyons House 1335 Horridge St., Vinton, 70668 318-589-2903
Old World Inn 1330 Prytania, New Orleans, 70130 504-566-1330
Parkview Guest House 7004 St. Charles, New Orleans, 70118 504-861-7564
St. Charles Guest House 7635 St. Charles, New Orleans, 70130 504-523-6556
St. Francisville Inn P.O. Box 1369, Saint Francisville, 70775 504-635-6502
Tezcuco Plantation Village 3138 Hwy. 44, Darrow, 70725 504-562-3929
Viroqua Heritage Inn 220 E. Jefferson, Viroqua, 54665 608-637-3306

Maine

BAR HARBOR

Black Friar Inn
10 Summer St., 04609
207-288-5091
Barbara & Jim Kelly
May—October

$$$ B&B
6 rooms, 6 pb
Visa, MC
C-12+/S-no/P-no/H-no

Full breakfast
Aft. tea & refreshments
Sitting room
fly fishing trips

Rebuilt in 1981 with architectural finds from Mt. Desert Island. Furnished with antiques, Victorian & country flavor. Near Acadia National Park. Walk to shops & restaurants.

Castlemaine Inn
39 Holland Ave., 04609
207-288-4563 800-338-4563
T. O'Connell, N. O'Brien
All year

$$$ B&B
12 rooms, 12 pb
Visa, MC, AmEx
C-10+/S-ltd/P-no

Continental plus buffet
Sitting room w/fireplace
2 day minimum July,
August & holidays

The inn is nestled on a quiet side street in Bar Harbor village, surrounded by the magnificent Acadia National Park. Rooms are well-appointed. AAA 3-Diamond rating.

Cleftstone Manor
92 Eden St., 04609
207-288-4951
Pattie & Don Reynolds
April—October

$$$ B&B
16 rooms, 14 pb
Visa, MC
C-8+/S-no/P-no/H-no
Spanish

Continental plus buffet
Comp. tea, wine & cheese
Sitting room, library
games, formal gardens
restaurant nearby

Recapture a timeless splendor in our charming Victorian 33-room "cottage" amidst formal gardens. Lavish breakfast buffet. Lace curtains, goose-down comforters. Safe journey.

BAR HARBOR ————————————————————————————

Graycote Inn
40 Holland Ave., 04609
207-288-3044
William & Darlene DeMao
May–November

$$$ B&B
10 rooms, 10 pb
Visa, MC
C-yes/S-ltd/P-no/H-no

Full breakfast
Comp. wine & snacks
Sitting room, fireplaces
king or queen-size beds
fireplaces, balconies

This elegantly restored Victorian inn is located near Acadia National Park and Frenchman's Bay. Numerous shops & fine restaurants are within walking distance.

Hearthside B&B
7 High St., 04609
207-288-4533
Barry & Susan Schwartz
All year

$$$ B&B
9 rooms, 9 pb
Visa, MC
C-10+/S-no/P-no/H-no

Continental plus
Comp. wine, cookies
Evening refreshments
porch, patio
parlor with fireplace

Small, gracious hostelry in a quiet in-town location; elegant & comfortable; furnished with a blend of antiques & traditional furniture. Visit Bar Harbor & Acadia Nat'l Park.

Ledgelawn Inn
66 Mount Desert St., 04609
207-288-4596 800-274-5334
Michael & Nancy Cloud
April–November

$$$ B&B
33 rooms, 33 pb
MC, Visa, AmEx ●
C-yes/S-yes/P-no/H-no

Continental plus
Bar service, comp. tea
Sitting room, library
piano, pool, sauna
modern exercise room

A graceful turn-of-the-century mansion with lots of charm, antiques, sitting areas, fireplaces, hot tub; in a quiet location only 5 minutes walk to downtown.

Manor House Inn
106 West St., 04609
207-288-3759
Mac Noyes
May–mid-October

$$$ B&B
14 rooms, 14 pb
Visa, MC, AmEx
C-8+/S-no/P-no/H-no

Continental plus
Afternoon tea
Sitting room, fireplaces
swimming pool, piano
gardens, tennis courts

Many special touches. Restored Victorian, National Register, antique furniture. Rooms have Victorian bedroom, parlor and bath. Pool, tennis courts, near Acadia National Park.

Mira Monte Inn
69 Mt. Desert St., 04609
207-288-4263 800-553-5109
Marian Burns
Early May–late October

$$$ B&B
11 rooms, 11 pb
Visa, MC, AmEx ●
C-yes/S-yes/P-no/H-ltd

Continental plus
Comp. wine & cheese
Juice, snacks
Sitting room, piano
phones, A/C in some rms

Renovated Victorian estate; period furnishings, fireplaces, one-acre grounds; quiet, in-town location, two king beds, walk to waterfront.

Ridgeway Cottage Inn
11 High St., 04644
207-288-9511
All year

$$ B&B
6 rooms, 4 pb
Visa, MC
C-no/S-no/P-no/H-no

Full breakfast
Complimentary wine
Sitting room
walk to the sea

The Ridgeway is a Victorian home on a tree-lined street in a quiet residential section of Bar Harbor. Guests can park at the inn and walk to nearby restaurants and shops.

BAR HARBOR

Town Guest House
12 Atlantic Ave., 04609
207-288-5548 800-458-8644
May—October

$$$ EP/B&B
9 rooms, 9 pb
Visa, MC, AmEx ●
C-yes/S-no/P-no/H-no

Continental plus
Sitting room

Victorian inn offers old-fashioned comfort with modern conveniences. Enjoy period furniture, marble sinks, porches, working fireplaces, private baths in our gracious rooms.

BASS HARBOR

Bass Harbor Cottages
Country Inn
P.O. Box 40, 04653
Rt. 102 A
207-244-3460
Constance L. Howe
All year

$ EP
3 rooms, 3 pb
Visa, MC
C-yes/S-no/P-no/H-no

Kitchen available
TVs in cottages
porch overlooks harbor
near Acadia Nat'l Park

Our small, intimate inn offers privacy, tranquility & views of the harbor. A staircase leads to the water's edge.

Pointy Head Inn
HCR 33, Box 2A, 04653
Route 102A
207-244-7261
Doris & Warren Townsend
Mid-May—October

$$ B&B
5 rooms, 1 pb
●
C-ltd/S-no/P-no/H-no

Full breakfast
Sitting room
porch & deck
piano & 2 organs

Located on Bass Harbor, adjacent to Acadia National Park. Hearty breakfast on deck overlooking harbor. Half hour to Bar Harbor.

BATH

Fairhaven Inn
RR 2, Box 85, 04530
N. Bath Rd.
207-443-4391
George & Sallie Pollard
All year

$$ B&B
6 rooms, 4 pb
C-yes/S-yes/P-no/H-no

Full breakfast
Tea, soda, sitting room
Piano, library, bicycles
hiking trail, X-C skiing
winter snowshoeing

Old country inn surrounded by 27 acres of meadows, woods, lawns. Antique bed sets, quilts, etc. Hiking, swimming, golf nearby. Gourmet breakfasts available.

The Inn at Bath
969 Washington St., 04530
207-443-4294
Nicholas Bayard & T.A. Finley
All year

$$ B&B
5 rooms, 5 pb
Visa, MC, AmEx ●
C-7+/S-ltd/P-no/H-no
Italian, French, Spanish

Full breakfast
Comp. wine, aftn. tea
Sitting room, Library
Fireplaces, Bicycles
Beach chairs and towels

Historical elegance—comfortable Greek Revival inn with water views & antiques. Centered in the architecturally rich "City of Ships" near Maritime Museum, L.L.Bean & Freeport.

BELFAST

Northport House B&B Inn
197 Northport Ave., 04915
207-338-1422 800-338-1422
P. Mankevetch, M.L. Wood
All year

$ B&B
8 rooms, 5 pb
Visa, MC
C-yes/S-no/P-no/H-no

Full breakfast
Afternoon tea,
Desserts, tea cakes
sitting room

Old Victorian house (circa 1873) in coastal community. Rooms are spacious and tastefully decorated in period pieces. Enjoy a large American gourmet breakfast each morning.

The Inn at Bath, Bath, ME

BELFAST

The Jeweled Turret Inn
16 Pearl St., 04915
207-338-2304 800-696-2304
Carl & Cathy Heffentrager
All year

$$ B&B
7 rooms, 7 pb
●
C-yes/S-ltd/P-no/H-no

Full breakfast
Afternoon tea & dessert
Sitting rooms, parlors
antiques
tennis & pool nearby

Intimate, charming, romantic. Unique architectural features; turrets, verandas, fireplaces, beautiful woodwork. Walk to town, shops & harbor. On National Register.

BETHEL

The Chapman Inn B&B
P.O. Box 206, 04217
Church & Broad Sts.
207-824-2657
Sandra & George Wight
All year

$ B&B
10 rooms, 4 pb
Visa, MC, AmEx ●
C-yes/S-yes/P-ltd/H-no

Full breakfast
Comp. coffee or tea
Sauna, cable TV
sitting room, VCR
gameroom, private beach

In heart of historic district. Large, sunny rooms. Breakfast featuring fresh fruits and whole grains. Recreation nearby. Family and weekly rates, also dorm facilities.

The Hammons House
P.O. Box 16, Broad St., 04217
207-824-3170
Sally Rollinson
All year

$$ B&B
4 rooms
Visa, MC
C-yes/S-no/P-no/H-no
German

Full breakfast
Comp. wine, sitting room
Porches, art gallery
patio, conservatory
antique shop (June-Oct)

Comfort and elegance of historic circa 1859 home; antique furnishings, beautiful gardens, delicious breakfasts. Convenient to restaurants, shops, skiing, golf.

BINGHAM

Mrs. G's B&B	$$ B&B	Full breakfast
P.O. Box 389, 04920	4 rooms, 2 pb	Dinner by reservation
Meadow St.	●	Comp. wine
207-672-4034	C-yes/S-yes/P-no/H-no	horseshoes, badminton
Frances Gibson	Italian	nearby tennis
May–October		

Old Victorian home with rocking chairs on front porch. Walking distance to churches, shopping, restaurants. Situated on scenic Kennebec River. A lovely loft can hold 10.

BLUE HILL

Blue Hill Farm Country Inn	$$ B&B/MAP	Continental plus
Route 15, Box 437, 04614	7 rooms, 7 pb	Dinner (MAP)
207-374-5126	Visa, MC ●	Comp. wine
Jim & Marcia Schatz	C-12+/S-no/P-no/H-no	sitting room
All year		piano, library

In continuous operation since 1840; nestled in picturesque village at head of Blue Hill Bay; mouthwatering Down East cooking. Special fall & winter packages.

BOOTHBAY HARBOR

Admiral's Quarters Inn	$$ EP/B&B	Continental breakfast
105 Commercial St., 04538	7 rooms, 7 pb	Comp. coffee
207-633-2474	Visa, MC	Unsurpassed harbor view
Jean & George Duffy	C-12+/S-yes/P-no/H-ltd	and sea views
May–October		decks

Commanding a view of the Harbor unsurpassed by all, this large old sea captain's house has pretty rooms, private baths and decks for viewing.

Captain Sawyer's Place	$$ B&B	Continental plus
87 Commercial St., 04538	10 rooms, 10 pb	Complimentary wine, tea
207-633-2290	Visa, MC	
Doreen Gibson	C-12+	
Mid-May–October		

A warm Victorian sea captain's home, overlooking the bustling harbor. A few stops away from fine shops and restaurants.

Hilltop Guest House	$ B&B	Continental breakfast
44 McKown Hill, 04538	6 rooms, 3 pb	
207-633-2941 207-633-3839	C-yes/S-yes/P-yes/H-no	
The Mahrs		
All year		

Sits atop McKown Hill overlooking town & harbor; walk to all activities. Parking in our lot.

Kenniston Hill Inn	$$ B&B	Full breakfast
Route 27, P.O. Box 125, 04537	10 rooms, 10 pb	Comp. brandy
207-633-2159 800-992-2915	Visa, MC ●	Sitting room
David & Susan Straight	C-14+/S-no/P-no/H-no	bicycles
All year		

200-year-old colonial on 4 acres of gardens, lawns and woods. Quilts and fresh flowers. A full gourmet breakfast.

BOOTHBAY HARBOR

The Anchor Watch
PO Box 102, 3 Eames Rd., 04538
207-633-2284
Diane Campbell
All year

$$ B&B
4 rooms, 4 pb
●
C-12+/S-yes/P-no/H-no

Continental breakfast
Efficiency appt. avail.
Fresh strawberries from
courtyard (in season)
3 rooms with ocean views

Scenic shore; winter ducks feed near the rocks; flashing lighthouses; lobstermen hauling traps, 5-minute walk to restaurants, shops, boats.

The Atlantic Ark Inn
64 Atlantic Ave., 04538
207-633-5690
Donna Piggott
May–October

$$ B&B
6 rooms, 6 pb
●
C-ltd/S-ltd/P-no/H-no

Full breakfast
Comp. wine or sherry
Iced tea, iced coffee
freshly baked breads
sitting room

Quaint and intimate, this small inn offers lovely harbor views, antiques, oriental rugs, mahogany beds, private baths, gourmet breakfasts, flowers, wine. Short walk to town.

The Howard House
Route 27, 04538
207-633-3933 207-633-6244
Jim & Ginny Farrin
All year

$ B&B
15 rooms, 15 pb
●
C-yes/S-yes/P-no/H-ltd

Full breakfast buffet
Nonsmoking rooms avail.
Private balconies

Unique chalet design on 20 wooded acres; sparkling clean modern rooms with private balconies; one mile from downtown Boothbay Harbor.

The Seafarer Guest House
38 Union St., 04538
207-633-2116
Olga Carito
April 1–November 1

$$ B&B
5 rooms, 2 pb
●
C-12+/S-no/P-no/H-no
Italian

Continental plus
Lunch (on request, $)
Comp. tea, beverages
doll collection

Grand old Victorian sea captain's home; head of harbor; magnificent, majestic view; close to center. Antiques, doll collection add charm throughout house.

BRIDGTON

Tarry-a-While B&B Resort
RD 2, Box 68, 04009
Highland Ridge Rd.
207-647-2522
Hans & Barbara Jenni
May–October

$$$ B&B
36 rooms, 26 pb
C-yes/S-yes/P-no/H-no
German

Continental plus buffet
Sitting room, library
3 sandy beaches
free canoes, pedal boats
rowboats, tennis, bikes

Several cottages with 4 B&B rooms each. Rooms with private baths have A/C, heaters. Recreation Hall. Schloss–Victorian with majestic views. Restaurant–Switzer Stubli.

The Noble House
P.O. Box 180, 04009
37 Highland Rd.
207-647-3733
Dick & Jane Starets
All year

$$ B&B
9 rooms, 6 pb
●
C-yes/S-ltd/P-no/H-no

Full breakfast
Comp. cream sherry
Sitting room, library
baby grand piano, organ
canoe, lake, lawn games

Majestic turn-of-the-century home on beautiful Highland Lake; four-season activities; antique and craft shops, summer theater, skiing, family suites, personal attention.

BROOKSVILLE

Breezemere Farm Inn	$$$ B&B	Full breakfast
P.O. Box 290, 04617	14 rooms, 10 pb	Dinner (Mon, Wed, Fri)
Breezemere Rd.	Visa, MC ●	Complimentary wine
207-326-8628	C-ltd/S-ok/P-ltd/H-no	sitting room, gameroom
Joe & Linda Forest		bicycles, boating
Mem. Day–Columbus Day		

Unrivaled scenic beauty–coves, islands, ledges, trees, unparalleled nature–bald eagles, seals, tidal life. Fine eating, sparkling accommodations. 7 cottages available.

BRUNSWICK

Samuel Newman House	$$ B&B	Continental plus
7 South St., 04011	7 rooms	Comp. tea
207-729-6959	Visa, MC	Sitting room
John & Jana Peirce	C-yes/S-no/P-no/H-no	airport limo service
All year		no smoking policy

A handsome federal-style house built in 1821, next to Bowdoin College, near the coast; 10 miles from Freeport. Airport limo service from Portland Airport.

CAMDEN

A Little Dream	$$$ B&B	Full breakfast
66 High St., 04843	6 rooms, 4 pb	Comp. sherry
207-236-8742	Visa, MC, AmEx	Sitting room
Joanna Ball, Bill Fontana	C-no/S-no/P-no/H-no	antique books
All year	Italian, some Fr. & Ger.	

Lovely luxury B&B in a turn-of-the-century turreted Victorian. Rooms with waterview, decks, or fireplace. Featured in Country Inns Magazine & Glamour Magazine.

Abigail's B&B	$$$ B&B	Full breakfast
8 High St., 04843	3 rooms, 3 pb	Afternoon tea
207-236-2501	Visa, MC ●	Sitting room
Edward & Donna Misner	C-yes/S-no/P-no/H-no	Porch, library
All year		Near hiking/golf/tennis

Historic Federal with country elegance and hospitality. Walk to harbor, shops, restaurants. Parlors with fireplaces and a wicker filled porch.

Blackberry Inn	$$ B&B	Full gourmet breakfast
82 Elm St., 04843	8 rooms, 8 pb	Comp. wine & cheese
207-236-6060	Visa, MC	Sitting room, library
Edward & Vicki Doudera	C-yes/S-no/P-no/H-no	A/C, fireplaces
All year	French, Italian	outdoor courtyard

A wonderfully ornate Victorian home furnished in period style; a short stroll from Camden's harbor, shops and restaurants.

Camden Harbour Inn	$$$ B&B	Full breakfast from menu
83 Bayview St., 04843	22 rooms, 22 pb	Dinner, bar service
207-236-4200	MC, Visa, AmEx, Dis	Parlour, porch, patio
Sal Vella, Patti Babij	C-ltd/S-yes/P-no/H-yes	lounge with fireplace
All year		meeting facilities

Historic 1874 Victorian inn with spectacular panorama of harbor, bay and mountains. Fine dining; cocktails in the Thirsty Whale. Meeting facilities. Winter weekend specials.

CAMDEN

Camden Maine Stay Inn
22 High Street, 04843
207-236-9636
P. & D. Smith, D. Robson
All year

$$ B&B
8 rooms, 4 pb
Visa, MC ●
C-6+/S-yes/P-no/H-no
French

Full breakfast
Comp. tea, wine, cakes
2 parlors w/fireplaces
piano, TV room
deck

Built in 1802, the inn is situated in the high street historic district on two acres of lovely grounds only two blocks from the harbor and village center.

Edgecombe-Coles House
HCR 60 Box 3010, 04843
64 High St.
207-236-2336
Terry & Louise Price
All year

$$$ B&B
6 rooms, 6 pb
Visa, MC, AmEx, DC ●
C-8+/S-yes/P-no/H-no

Full breakfast
Comp. eve. port, sherry
Sitting room, piano
library, bicycles
tennis courts

Distinctive country inn with breathtaking views of Penobscot Bay. Antique furnishings, private baths, hearty breakfasts. Maine's most beautiful seaport.

Goodspeed's Guest House
60 Mountain St., 04843
207-354-8077
The Goodspeeds & the Smalls
June–October

$$ B&B
8 rooms, 1 pb
C-10+/S-yes/P-no/H-no

Continental breakfast
Sitting room
bicycles
library

Quiet location, large grounds, only 5 blocks from harbor. Restored farm house with antique furniture, clock collection, stained glass and plank floors.

Hartstone Inn
41 Elm St., 04843
207-236-4259
Sunny & Peter Simmons
All year

$$ EP/B&B
10 rooms, 10 pb
Visa, MC, AmEx, Disc ●
C-13+/S-yes/P-no/H-no

Full breakfast
Dinner, picnic sails
Comp. tea, cookies
sitting room, fireplaces
library, TV room

Stately Victorian inn, centrally located in picturesque village, steps away from harbor. Hearty breakfasts, romantic dinners, friendly, relaxed atmosphere.

Hawthorn Inn
9 High St., 04843
207-236-8842
Pauline & Bradford Staub
All year

$$ B&B
9 rooms, 9 pb
Visa, MC ●
C-10+/S-no/P-no/H-no

Full breakfast
Afternoon tea
2 sitting rooms
piano, hot tub in suites
volleyball

Refurbished Victorian home with light, airy rooms. Views of either harbor or mountains. Just a 5-minute walk to shops and restaurants.

Mansard Manor
5 High Street, 04843
207-236-3291
Ted & Lori O'Neil
April–December

$$ B&B
3 rooms, 3 pb
C-yes/S-no/P-no/H-no

Full breakfast
Afternoon tea, cider
Lemonade, snacks
sitting room, deck

Lovely historic Victorian located just steps from village, harbor and mountains. Elegant antique furnishings, delectable breakfast. Quiet, romantic seaside getaway.

CAMDEN

Swan House
49 Mountain St. (Rt 52), 04843
207-236-8275
Chrysanthe Soukas
May–October

$$$ B&B
6 rooms, 2 pb
Visa, MC •
C-8+/S-no/P-no/H-ltd

Full breakfast
Sitting room
outdoor gazebo

Located in a quiet neighborhood, a short walk from Camden's Harbor. Hearty breakfasts and country antiques. Enjoy the private backyard gazebo.

Windward House B&B
6 High St., 04843
207-236-9656
Jon & Mary Davis
All year

$$ B&B
5 rooms, 5 pb
Visa, MC
C-10+/S-no/P-no/H-no

Full gourmet breakfast
Comp. port, sherry
Sitting rooms
library
garden room

In Harbor Village; spacious historic 1854 colonial fully restored, beautifully decorated, furnished with fine antiques. Gracious hospitality. Full gourmet breakfast.

CASTINE

Holiday House
P.O. Box 215, 04421
Perkins St.
207-326-4335
Sara & Paul Brouillard

$$$ B&B
9 rooms, 7 pb
•
C-yes

Continental plus
Complimentary tea
Large public rooms
housekeeping cottage

An Edwardian Mansion, c. 1893, built on the waterfront. Beautiful ocean-front guest rooms, expansive porches & a prime location.

The Manor
Box 276, 04421
Battle Ave.
207-326-4861
Sara & Paul Brouillard
All year exc. Christmas

$$$ B&B
12 rooms, 10 pb
Visa, MC •
C-yes/S-yes/P-ltd/H-no
French, Spanish

Continental plus
La Conque Restaurant/bar
Sitting room, library
lounge, billiard room
piano, bicycles, cottage

Elegant turn-of-the-century mansion. Very quiet, yet close to restaurants and shops. Gourmet dining on-site, 5 acres of lawns. National Register.

CENTER LOVELL

Center Lovell Inn
Route 5, 04016
207-925-1575
Bill & Susie Mosca
May–Oct 21, Dec 20-Feb

$$$ EP/MAP
11 rooms, 7 pb
Visa, MC, AmEx •
C-ltd/S-no/P-no/H-yes
Italian, French, Spanish

Full breakfast
Dinner, bar
Sitting room
antique shop in barn

Country inn, family oriented, surrounded by White Mountain National Forest, near Saco River for canoeing, Kezar Lake, foliage, Fryeburg Fair.

CHEBEAGUE ISLAND

Chebeague Island Inn
P.O. Box 492, South Rd., 04017
207-846-5155 207-774-5891
Wendy & Kevin Bowden
May–September

$$ EP
22 rooms, 15 pb
Visa, MC •
C-yes/S-yes/P-no/H-no
French, Italian

Full breakfast
Lunch, dinner, bar
Sitting room, piano
porch, bicycles
nature walks, ferry

Beautiful island retreat. Wraparound porch overlooking Casco Bay. Local seafood and other specialties served. Remote yet convenient.

DAMARISCOTTA

Brannon-Bunker Inn
HCR 64 Box 045E, 04543
#45 Route 129
207-563-5941
Jeanne & Joe, Mike/Beth/Jamie
All year

$$ B&B
9 rooms, 4 pb
Visa, MC •
C-yes/S-no/P-no/H-ltd

Continental plus
Kitchen facilities
Sitting room
porch
antique shop on premises

Country B&B; charming rooms furnished with antiques; close to all mid-coast recreational facilities including ocean, beach, boating & golf; antiquing!

DEER ISLE

Pilgrim's Inn
Main St., 04627
207-348-6615
Jean & Dud Hendrick
Mid-May—mid-October

$$$ B&B/MAP
13 rooms, 8 pb
•
C-yes/S-no/P-yes/H-no

Full breakfast
Supper, tea, coffee, bar
Sitting room, piano
bicycles, library
deck, patio grill area

Idyllic location on Deer Isle. Elegant yet informal colonial inn, creative cuisine, rustic antique-furnished barn. Commons rooms with 8' fireplaces.

DENNYSVILLE

Lincoln House Country Inn
Routes 1 & 86, 04628
207-726-3953
Mary & Jerry Haggerty
All year

$$$ MAP
11 rooms, 8 pb
Visa, MC, AmEx •
C-yes/S-yes/P-no/H-no

Full breakfast
Dinner included
Bar, comp. wine
sitting room
piano

A lovingly restored colonial with 95 acres of hiking, birding and fishing. Centerpiece of north-eastern corner of coastal Maine. Internationally acclaimed. National Register.

EAST BOOTHBAY

Five Gables Inn
P.O. Box 75, 04544
Murray Hill Rd.
207-633-4551
Ellen & Paul Morissette

$$ B&B
15 rooms, 15 pb
•
C-12+/S-no/P-no

Full breakfast
Sitting room
Fireplaces, games
wraparound veranda
pool & boating nearby

Charm and elegance of old Victorian decor and the convenience of spotless facilities. All 15 rooms have views of the bay. Each room has unique furnishings and a private bath.

EASTPORT

Todd House
1 Capen Av, Todd's Head, 04631
207-853-2328
Ruth M. McInnis
All year

$ B&B
7 rooms, 3 pb
C-yes/S-ltd/P-yes/H-yes

Continental plus
Sitting room
Library, fireplace
yard with barbecue
picnic facilities

Step into the past in our revolutionary-era Cape with wide panorama of Passamaquoddy Bay. Breakfast in common room before huge fireplace.

ELIOT

High Meadows B&B
Route 101, 03903
207-439-0590
Elaine Raymond
April—December

$$ B&B
5 rooms, 3 pb
C-no/S-yes/P-no/H-no

Full breakfast
Afternoon wine, tea
Sitting room
Barn available for
parties and weddings

1736 colonial house in the country. Walking & cross-country ski trails. 6.5 miles to historic Portsmouth, New Hampshire; shopping, theater & fine dining.

Atlantic Seal B&B, Freeport, ME

FREEPORT

181 Main Street B&B
181 Main St., 04032
207-865-1226
Ed Hassett
All year

$$$ B&B
7 rooms, 7 pb
Visa, MC ●
C-no/S-ltd/P-no/H-no
French

Full breakfast
Comp. coffee, tea, etc.
Sitting room
library
in-ground pool

Cozy, antique-filled 1840 cape, in town, with ample parking, hearty breakfasts. Walk to L.L. Bean and luxury outlets.

Bagley House
RR 3, Box 269C, 04032
207-865-6566
Sigurd A. Knudsen, Jr.
All year

$$$ B&B
5 rooms, 5 pb
Visa, MC, AmEx ●
C-yes/S-no/P-no/H-no

Full breakfast
Lunch picnics on request
Sitting room, library
X-C skiing (winter)
6-acre yard, barbecue

Peace, tranquillity and history abound in this magnificent 1772 country home. A warm welcome awaits you. Minutes from downtown Freeport.

Country at Heart B&B
37 Bow St., 04032
207-865-0512
Roger & Kim Dubay
Exc. Thanksgiving, Xmas

$$ B&B
3 rooms
●
C-yes/P-no/H-no

Full breakfast
Afternoon tea, snacks
Sitting room, fireplace
walk to many restaurants

Enjoy a stay in our 1870 home in one of 3 country decorated rooms. Handsome crafts, antiques and reproduction furnishings. 2 blocks from L.L. Bean & dozens of outlet stores.

FREEPORT

Harraseeket Inn
162 Main St., 04032
207-865-9377 800-342-2415
The Gray Family
All year

$$$ B&B
6 rooms, 6 pb
Visa, MC, AmEx ●
C-10+/S-ltd/P-no/H-no

Full breakfast
Restaurant, tavern
Afternoon tea, library
sitting rooms, fireplace
ballroom, dining rooms

Luxury B&B. Private baths (jacuzzi or steam), cable TV, elegant Maine buffet country break-fast. Two blocks north of L.L. Bean. Walk to famous factory outlet shops.

Isaac Randall House
5 Independence Dr., 04032
207-865-9295
Jim & Glynrose Friedlander
All year

$$ B&B
8 rooms, 6 pb
C-yes/S-ask/P-ask/H-ask
Spanish, French

Full breakfast
Comp. beverages/snacks
Sitting room, library
dining porch, piano
A/C in all rooms

A gracious country inn circa 1823, elegantly and comfortably furnished with antiques. Pond, woods, picnic areas. Walk to L.L. Bean.

Kendall Tavern B&B
213 Main St., 04032
207-865-1338
Jim Whitley, J.D. Ragan
All year

$$$ B&B
7 rooms, 7 pb
Visa, MC
C-no/S-no/P-no/H-no

Full breakfast
Sitting room
hot tubs

Walk to L.L. Bean, outlet shops, and fine dining. Close to many points of interest along beautiful Maine coast.

White Cedar Inn
178 Main St., 04032
207-865-9099
Phil & Carla Kerber
All year

$$ B&B
6 rooms, 4 pb
Visa, MC
C-10+/S-no/P-no/H-no

Full breakfast
Outdoor grill
Sitting room
picnic table
brick patio

Recently restored 100-year-old home with large uncluttered antique-furnished rooms. Located just 2 blocks from L.L. Bean.

FRYEBURG

Admiral Peary House
9 Elm St., 04037
207-935-3365 800-237-8080
Nancy & Ed Greenberg
May 15—Oct, Dec 15—Mar

$$$ B&B
4 rooms, 4 pb
Visa, MC ●
C-ltd/S-no/P-no/H-no
French

Full breakfast
High tea
Sitting room, library
bicycles, tennis courts
hot tubs, billiards, A/C

Charming historical home in a picturesque White Mountain village. Clay tennis court, skiing, canoeing, hiking, spacious grounds and perennial gardens.

HARPSWELL (SOUTH)

Harpswell Inn
RR1 Box 141, 04079
141 Lookout Point Rd.
207-833-5509
Susan & Bill Menz
All year

$$ B&B
12 rooms
Visa, MC ●
C-ltd/S-no/P-no/H-no
Danish, Swedish, German

Full breakfast
Great rooms
Murder weekends
bicycles
3 bedroom cottage avail.

Lush lawns slope to the sea, private dock. Enjoy boating, swimming, bicycling, or just relax & unwind. Gourmet restaurants & Bowdoin College nearby. Freeport shopping 25 min.

ISLE AU HAUT

The Keeper's House
P.O. Box 26, 04645
207-367-2261
Jeff & Judi Burke
May–October

$$$ AP
4 rooms
C-yes/S-no/P-no/H-no
Spanish

Full breakfast
Lunch, dinner included
Snacks
hiking
ocean swimming

Operating lighthouse station on remote unspoiled island within Acadia National Park. Tiny fishing village, primitive spectacular natural surroundings. Arrive on mailboat.

KENNEBUNK

Arundel Meadows Inn
P.O. Box 1129, 04043
Route 1, Arundel
207-985-3770
Mark Bachelder, Murray Yaeger
All year

$$$ B&B
7 rooms, 7 pb
Visa, MC
C-12+/S-no/P-no/H-ltd

Full gourmet breakfast
Afternoon tea
Set-ups, library
sitting room

Rooms individually decorated with art, antiques. Some with fireplaces; all with private baths. Gourmet breakfasts and teas. Near shops and beaches.

Sundial Inn
P.O. Box 1147, 04043
48 Beach Ave.
207-967-3850
All year

$$ B&B
34 rooms, 34 pb
Visa, MC, AmEx
C-no/S-ltd/P-no/H-yes
French

Continental plus
Afternoon tea (winter)
Sitting room
whirlpool tubs
beach

Directly on Kennebunkport beach. Completely renovated with country Victorian antiques and designer linens. Beautiful ocean views. An elevator for your convenience.

KENNEBUNKPORT

The 1802 House B&B Inn
Locke St., Box 646 A, 04046
207-967-5632
Pat O'Connor, Pat Ledda
All year

$$ B&B
8 rooms, 8 pb
Visa, MC, AmEx •
C-12+/S-yes/P-no/H-no

Full breakfast
Comp. tea, cider, or
lemonade
hearthside sitting room

One of Kennebunkport's most popular inns; charming colonial decor, located next to a beautiful 18-hole golf course. Some working fireplaces. Honeymoon suite.

Captain Fairfield Inn
P.O. Box 1308, 04046
Pleasant & Green Sts.
207-967-4454
Bonnie & Dennis Tallagnon

$$$ B&B
9 rooms, 9 pb
Visa, MC •
C-10+/S-ltd/P-no/H-no
some French

Full breakfast
Afternoon tea
Sitting room, library
lovely park-like gardens
and grounds, bicycles

Beautiful Federal 1813 sea captain's mansion. Walking distance to town and sea. Some rooms have fireplaces. Chef-owner prepares wonderful breakfasts.

The Captain Lord Mansion
P.O. Box 800, 04046
Pleasant & Green Sts.
207-967-3141 800-522-3141
Bev Davis, Richard Litchfield
All year

$$$ B&B
16 rooms, 16 pb
Visa, MC, Disc
C-12+/S-ltd/P-no/H-no

Full breakfast
Afternoon tea, sweets
Snacks, gift shop
sitting room, piano
beach towels, umbrellas

An intimate Maine coast inn with working fireplaces in 11 guest rooms. Furnished with genuine antiques. Many activities and sights abound. AAA 4-Diamond. Mobil 3-Star.

KENNEBUNKPORT

The Chetwynd House Inn
P.O. Box 130, 04046
Chestnut St.
207-967-2235
Susan Knowles Chetwynd
All year

$$ B&B
4 rooms, 2 pb
●
C-16+/S-ltd/P-no/H-no
French, Italian

Full multi-course brkfst
Complimentary tea
Sitting room, library

Pristine rooms. Handsome, lovely furnishings. Antique pieces. Rich mahogany and cherry woods. Poster beds. Tea tables. Outstanding for guest reunions.

The Dock Square Inn
P.O. Box 1123, 04046
Temple St.
207-967-5773
Frank & Bernice Shoby
March–December

$$$ B&B
6 rooms, 6 pb
Visa, MC
C-10+/S-ltd/P-no/H-no
Italian

Full gourmet breakfast
Goodies always available
Sitting room
bicycles
color cable TV

Gracious Victorian country inn—former shipbuilder's home located in the heart of historic Kennebunkport village. Warm congenial atmosphere.

English Meadows Inn
141 Port Road, 04043
Route 35
207-967-5766
Charlie Doane
April–October

$$ B&B
15 rooms, 5 pb
C-10+/S-no/P-yes/H-no
French

Full breakfast
Afternoon tea, lemonade
Room service for brkfst
sitting room, piano
airport/station pickup

1860 Victorian farmhouse; real country setting. Stroll to beaches, town, restaurants. Inn furnished throughout with antiques and local artworks. Extra-special breakfasts.

Inn at Harbor Head
RR 2, Box 1180, 04046
Pier Rd., Cape Porpoise
207-967-5564
Dave & Joan Sutter
All year exc. November

$$$ B&B
5 rooms, 5 pb
Visa, MC ●
C-12+/S-no/P-no/H-no

Full gourmet breakfast
Comp. sherry/port in rm.
Sitting room, library
down comforters
whirlpool tubs

Waterfront inn on Cape Porpoise Harbor. Rated "Excellent" by the American Bed & Breakfast Assoc. "A special retreat, a perfect escape—welcoming hospitality and superb food."

The Inn on South Street
P.O. Box 478A, 04046
South St.
207-967-5151 207-967-4639
Eva Downs
February–December

$$$ B&B
4 rooms, 4 pb
AmEx ●
C-10+/S-no/P-no/H-no
German, Spanish, Russian

Full breakfast
Comp. tea, wine, juice
Sitting room
fireplace, garden
apartment suite avail.

Enjoy beautifully appointed rooms in a romantic 19th-century home. Convenient, quiet location. Sumptuous breakfast, fireplaces, gardens, fresh flowers.

The Kennebunkport Inn
P.O. Box 111, 04046
One Dock Square
207-967-2621 800-248-2621
Rick & Martha Griffin
All year

$$ EP
34 rooms, 34 pb
Visa, MC, AmEx ●
C-yes/P-no/H-no
French

Continental/full($)
Restaurant, dinner My-Oc
Victorian pub
pool, color TV
golf & tennis nearby

Classic country inn in old sea captain's home. All rooms with private baths & color TV. Gourmet dining, turn-of-the-century bar, piano bar. Located in historic district.

Kilburn House
P.O. Box 1309, 04046
6 Chestnut St.
207-967-4762
Samuel Minier
May 15–October

$$ B&B
6 rooms, 2 pb
Visa, MC
C-yes/S-no/P-no/H-no

Continental plus
Afternoon tea
Sitting room

Kilburn House is located in the historic village of Kennebunkport, Maine, a colonial town with picturesque fishing port and colonial homes.

Kylemere House, 1818
P.O. Box 1333, 04046
South St.
207-967-2780
Mary & Bill Kyle
April 15–December 15

$$ B&B
5 rooms, 3 pb
AmEx, Visa, MC •
C-12+/S-ltd/P-no/H-no

Full gourmet breakfast
Comp. wine, beverages
Sitting rm., porch, lawn
featured in Glamour 4/90
Regis & Kathie Lee Show

Charming federal inn in historic area located within a short walk to shops and beach. Warm, inviting rooms, traditional hospitality and "down east" breakfast.

Maine Stay Inn & Cottages
P.O. Box 500-AL, 04046
34 Maine St.
207-967-2117 800-950-2117
Carol & Lindsay Copeland
All year

$$$ B&B
17 rooms, 17 pb
Visa, MC, AmEx •
C-yes/S-yes/P-no/H-no
some French & German

Full breakfast
Afternoon tea, snacks
Sitting room, lawn games
swing set, garden
wraparound porch

Victorian inn known for exceptional warmth, hospitality and great breakfasts. Elegant inn rooms, charming garden cottages, spacious lawn, porch, and fireplaces.

Ocean View
72 Beach Ave., 04043
207-967-2750 207-967-2681
Carole & Bob Arena
April–October

$$$ B&B
9 rooms, 9 pb
C-no/S-ltd/P-no/H-no

Continental plus
Comp. coffee, tea, fruit
Sitting room, library
exclusive boutique
steps to sandy beach

Oceanfront rooms with sight, sounds & smell of Atlantic at our doorstep. Rooms are well coordinated, cheerful, fresh flowers everywhere. Steps to beach, shopping, galleries.

Old Fort Inn
P.O. Box M, 04046
Old Fort Ave.
207-967-5353 800-828-3678
Sheila & David Aldrich
Mid-April–mid-December

$$$ B&B
16 rooms, 16 pb
Visa, MC, AmEx •
C-ltd/S-ltd/P-no/H-no

Continental plus
Sitting room, piano
Cable TV, phone in room
tennis, swimming pool
jacuzzi tubs, bicycles

A luxurious resort in a secluded charming setting. The inn has yesterday's charm with today's conveniences. Within walking distance to the ocean.

Welby Inn
P.O. Box 774, Ocean Ave, 04046
207-967-4655
David & Betsy Rogers-Knox
All year

$$$ B&B
7 rooms, 7 pb
AmEx
C-10+/S-no/P-no/H-no

Full breakfast
Eve. homemade Amaretto
Guest pantry
sitting room, piano
bicycles

Gracious turn-of-the-century home in historic Kennebunkport. Walk to beach, marina and shops. Deep-sea fishing and harbor cruises available.

KENNEBUNKPORT

White Barn Inn
P.O. Box 560C, 04046
Beach St.
207-967-2321 207-967-5331
L. Bongiorno & C. Hackett
March–December

$$$ B&B
24 rooms, 24 pb
Visa, MC, AmEx ●
C-yes/S-yes/P-no/H-ltd

Continental plus
Dinner, bar, aftn. tea
Fireplaces in some rooms
entertainment, bicycles
near beach & town square

Elegant Queen Anne antiques & reproductions. Dining room set with pewter silver & linen. Architecturally preserved barn. Casual elegance. Recipient of 1983 Silver Spoon award.

KINGFIELD

The Herbert
P.O. Box 67, 04947
Main St., Rts 27 & 16
207-265-2000 800-THE-HERB
Bud Dick
All year

$ (Apr-Nov) EP
31 rooms, 31 pb
Visa, MC, AmEx, DC, Enr ●
C-yes/S-ltd/P-yes/H-no

Continental (wkdys)
Sunday brunch, aftn. tea
Restaurant, bar
sitting room, library
bikes, tennis, sauna

Cozy spot with jacuzzis, lazy dogs and great food. Huge wine list. Relaxing any season for any reason. Skiing, golf and theatre. Packages available.

KITTERY

Melfair Farm B&B
11 Wilson Rd., 03904
207-439-0320
Claire Cane
March–December

$$ B&B
5 rooms, 1 pb
●
C-10+/S-yes/P-no/H-no
French

Full breakfast
Comp. iced tea, lemonade
Large sitting room
piano, TV
amid 9 countryside acres

1871 New England farmhouse, pastoral setting. Minutes from fine shopping, beaches. Theater, gourmet dining in nearby historical Portsmouth, New Hampshire.

NAPLES

The Augustus Bove House
RR 1, Box 501, 04055
Corner of Rts. 302 & 114
207-693-6365
David & Arlene Stetson
All year

$ B&B
12 rooms, 5 pb
Visa, MC, AmEx ●
C-yes/S-ltd/P-yes/H-ltd

Full breakfast
Honeymoon tray
Comp. coffee, tea
sitting room
veranda, lawn

Recently restored, the Augustus Bove House offers authentic colonial accomodations in a relaxing atmosphere. Located between two lakes and 20 min. from mountains for skiing.

Inn at Long Lake
P.O. Box 806, 04055
207-693-6226
Irene & Maynard Hincks
All year

$$ B&B
16 rooms, 16 pb
Visa, MC, AmEx, Disc ●
C-yes/S-ltd/P-no/H-no
Some french, spanish

Continental plus
Afternoon tea
Comp. wine
sitting room, library
tennis court

Restored 16-room inn nestled in Sebago Lakes region, close to year-round activities, shopping, fine dining. Mid-week discount packages. Romantic elegance, Maine hospitality.

Lamb's Mill Inn
Box 676 Lamb's Mill Rd., 04055
207-693-6253
Laurel Tinkham, Sandy Long
All year

$$$ B&B
6 rooms, 6 pb
●
C-yes/S-no/P-no/H-no

Full breakfast
Afternoon tea, snacks
Sitting room, library
hot tubs, outside stone
fire pit & gas grills

Charming small country inn, 1/2 mile from Naples Village, in heart of western Maine's lakes & mountains region, "ewe hike, ewe bike, ewe ski, ewe zzzz...."

NEW HARBOR

Bradley Inn
HC61, Box 361, 04554
Route 130 Pemaquid Pt. Rd
207-677-2105 207-677-3367
Bill & Cathy Tracy
March–December

$$$ B&B
13 rooms, 13 pb
Visa, MC, AmEx
C-yes/S-no/P-no/H-yes

Continental plus
Restaurant, bar service
Sitting room, library
tennis court, bicycles

Lovely Pemaquid Point garden setting, moments to lighthouse, beach, numerous activities. Freshly renovated, excellent dining, quiet bar, water views.

Gosnold Arms
HC 61, Box 161, 04554
Route 32, Northside Rd.
207-677-3727
The Phinney Family
Mid-May–October

$$$ B&B
26 rooms, 19 pb
Visa, MC
C-yes/S-ltd/P-no/H-ltd

Full breakfast
Dinner
Cocktails
sitting room
small wharf

Charming country inn and cottages. All-weather dining porch overlooking harbor. Beaches, lobster pounds, parks nearby.

NEWCASTLE

The Captain's House B&B
P.O. Box 242, 04553
19 River Rd.
207-563-1482
Joe Sullivan & Susan Rizzo
All year

$$ B&B
5 rooms
C-yes/S-yes/P-no/H-no

Full breakfast from menu
Comp. tea
Dinner (winter)
sitting room

Spacious colonial home overlooking the Damariscotta River offers sunny rooms furnished with antiques and delicious full Maine breakfast. Omelettes a specialty.

Crown 'N' Anchor Inn
P.O. Box 17, River Rd., 04553
207-563-8954
J. Barclay, J. & M. Forester
All year

$$ B&B
4 rooms, 1 pb
Visa, MC ●
C-12+/S-no/P-no/H-no

Full breakfast
Afternoon tea
Sitting room
library
bicycles

Restored Greek Revival house with fine Victorian antiques and commanding water views. Gourmet breakfast by candlelight. Walk to village.

Mill Pond Inn
RFD1, Box 245, 04553
Route 215, Damariscotta
207-563-8014
Bobby & Sherry Whear
All year

$$ B&B
5 rooms, 5 pb
Visa, MC
C-5+/S-yes/P-no/H-ltd

Full breakfast
Comp. wine, sitting room
Swimming/boating in lake
canoe for guests
hammock, horseshoes

Small, private inn with a water view from four rooms, across the road from Damariscotta Lake.

The Newcastle Inn
River Rd., 04553
207-563-5685
Ted & Chris Sprague
All year

$$$ B&B
15 rooms, 15 pb
●
C-ltd/S-no/P-no/H-ltd

Gourmet 4-course brkfast
Evening reception bar
Dinner, aftn. beverages
sitting room w/fireplace
screened-in porch

Fine dining and a pampering environment in an intimate, full-service, country inn on the Damariscotta River.

OGUNQUIT

Gorges Grant Hotel
P.O. Box 2240, Route 1, 03907
207-646-7003

B&B/MAP
56 rooms, 56 pb
Visa, MC, AmEx, others ●
C-yes/S-yes/P-no/H-yes

Full breakfast$
Restaurant, bar
Hot tubs
indoor & outdoor pool

Elegant, small, modern hotel operated with an inn flavor. Located in Ogunquit near (within a short trolley ride) one of the world's best beaches.

Hartwell House
P.O. Box 393, 03907
118 Shore Road
207-646-7210 800-235-8883
T & J Kolva, J & T Hartwell
All year

$$$ B&B
17 rooms, 17 pb
Visa, MC, AmEx ●
C-14+/S-no/P-no/H-no

Continental plus
Tea/lemonade (sometimes)
Swimming, tennis avail.
air conditioning
golf privileges, fishing

Elegantly furnished in early American & English antiques. Set amid 2 acres of sculpted gardens, perfect for relaxing. Swim, stroll, fish, golf.

High Tor
Frazier Pasture Rd., 03907
207-646-8232
Julie O'Brien, Cleda Wiley
June–October

EP
2 rooms, 2 pb
C-8+/S-no/P-no/H-no

Refrigerator, coffee,
TV in rooms
above Marginal Way
park and walk everywhere

Quiet, secluded guest house directly on ocean. Wide verandas, private grounds. Panoramic Atlantic views from every window. Footpath to sandy beaches and coves.

Morning Dove B&B
P.O. Box 1940, 03907
30 Bourne Lane
207-646-8762
Peter & Eeta Sachon
All year except Nov-Jan

$$ B&B
6 rooms, 4 pb
Visa, MC, Amex
C-12+/S-yes/P-no/H-no

Continental plus
Comp. wine, chocolates
Victorian porch
near tennis, golf
off season packages

1860s farmhouse featuring modern baths, airy rooms, authentic antiques, fresh flowers. Walk to beaches, Perkins Cove, playhouse and art galleries, trolley.

PEMAQUID

Little River Inn
HC 62, Box 178, 04558
Route 130
207-677-2845
Kristina de Khan
All year

$$ B&B
6 rooms, 2 pb
Visa, MC
C-yes/S-yes/P-no/H-no

Continental plus
Sitting room
River fishing, forest
near beach, restaurants,
New Harbor, canoe rental

1840 Cape farmhouse by the Pemaquid River with view to the cove. Select a traditional room or one of the rustic gallery rooms. Delicious country breakfast.

PORTLAND

Inn on Carleton
46 Carleton St., 04102
207-775-1910
Susan Holland
All year

$$$ B&B
7 rooms, 3 pb
C-ltd/S-no/P-no/H-no

Continental plus
Comp. tea
Sitting room

Restored Victorian townhouse in Portland's West End historic district—close to city museums, shops, restaurants and waterfront.

PROSPECT HARBOR

Oceanside Meadows Inn
P.O. Box 90, Route 195, 04669
207-963-5557
Norm & Marge Babineau
All year

$$ B&B
7 rooms, 1 pb
Visa, MC
C-yes/S-no/P-yes/H-no

Full breakfast
Lunch, dinner
Sitting room
library, games, VCR
ocean & sandy beach

Charming 19th-century home; sandy beach and ocean across street; beautiful gardens. One hour from Bar Harbor and Acadia National Park.

ROCKPORT

Sign of the Unicorn House
P.O. Box 99, 04856
191 Beauchamp Ave.
207-236-4042 207-236-8789
Howard & Winnie Easton Jones
All year

$$$ B&B
4 rooms, 2 pb
●
C-yes/S-ltd/P-no/H-yes

Full gourmet breakfast
Comp. hors d'ouevres
Beverages, sitting rm.
piano, workshops
small group meditation

Decorated in Carllarsen Swedish style! Centrally located. Howard makes museum-quality Nantucket Lightship baskets. Antiquing trips. Reunions/anniversaries/weddings/retreats.

SEARSPORT

Homeport Inn
Route 1, E. Main St., 04974
207-548-2259
Dr. & Mrs. George F. Johnson
All year

$$ B&B
11 rooms, 7 pb
Visa, MC, AmEx, DC, CB ●
C-yes/S-ltd/P-no/H-yes

Full breakfast
Tea, wine, English pub
Soda fountain, garden
antique shop, ocean view
bicycles, golf, tennis

Listed on the Historic Register. Ideal mid-coast location for an extended stay to visit coast of Maine. Victorian cottage also available by the week.

Thurston House B&B Inn
P.O. Box 686, 04974
8 Elm St.
207-548-2213
Carl & Beverly Eppig
All year

$ B&B
4 rooms, 2 pb
●
C-6+/S-no/P-no/H-ltd

Full breakfast
Snacks (sometimes)
Sitting room
library, shade garden
tennis courts nearby

Circa 1830 Colonial in quiet village setting. Easy stroll to everything, including Maritime Museum, tavern, beach park on Penobscot Bay.

William & Mary Inn
U.S. Rte. 1, PO Box 813, 04974
207-548-2190
William & Mary Sweet
May 1 – February 1

$$ B&B
3 rooms, 3 pb
●
C-yes/S-no/P-no

Full breakfast
Afternoon tea, snacks
Complimentary wine
sitting room
library

Circa 1830 sea captain's house furnished elegantly with antiques. Bedrooms have poster beds, fireplaces, private baths. Walk to the ocean.

SOUTH FREEPORT

Atlantic Seal B&B
P.O. Box 146, 25 Main, 04078
207-865-6112
Capt. Thomas & Gaila Ring
All year

$$ B&B
3 rooms, 2 pb
personal checks ●
C-8+/S-no/P-no/H-no

Full breakfast
Lunch on island cruise
Comp. wine, snacks, tea
rowboats, beach nearby
island boat excursions

Enjoy lovely harbor views, friendly downeast hospitality, our hearty sailor's breakfast and exciting cruises. Five minutes from Freeport's outlet stores.

Albonegon Inn, Southport, Capitol Island, ME

SOUTHPORT

Albonegon Inn
Capitol Island, 04538
207-633-2521
Kim & Bob Peckham
July–mid October

$$ B&B
15 rooms, 3 pb
Visa, MC
C-yes
Spanish

Continental breakfast
Afternoon tea
Sitting room, piano
tennis court
beaches

A very special place to relax. On a private island, perched on the edge of the ocean. Spectacular views! Hike, bird-watch, swim, beachcomb, tennis, sail. Golf nearby.

SOUTHWEST HARBOR

Harbour Woods
P.O. Box 1214, Main St., 04679
207-244-5388
M. Eden, J. Paviglionite
All year

$$ B&B
3 rooms, 3 pb
C-no/S-no/P-no/H-no

Full breakfast
Snacks
Sitting room
Acadia National Park
hiking/swimming/cruises

Gracious and comfortable. Spacious rooms with harbor or garden views. Thick towels, fresh flowers, candlelight, soft music, imaginative breakfasts.

Island House
P.O. Box 1006, 04679
Clark Point Rd.
207-244-5180
Ann R. Gill
May–October

$$ B&B
5 rooms, 1 pb
●
C-12+/S-no/P-no

Full breakfast
Comp. beverages
Sitting room/fireplace
library, large garden
fishing docks, harbor

The Island House, a gracious, restful, seacoast home on the quiet side of Mount Desert Island. An efficiency apartment available. Near wharves; 5 min. to Acadia National Park.

SOUTHWEST HARBOR ────────────────────────────────

Kingsleigh Inn · $$ B&B · Full breakfast
P.O. Box 1426, 04679 · 8 rooms, 8 pb · Afternoon tea
100 Main St. · Visa, MC · Sitting room w/fireplace
207-244-5302 · C-8+/S-ltd/P-no/H-no · library
Nancy & Tom Cervelli
All year

A cozy intimate inn overlooking the harbor. Filled with many antiques, wing-back chairs and four-poster beds. Rooms with harbor views.

Lindenwood Inn · $$ B&B · Full breakfast
P.O. Box 1328, 04679 · 8 rooms, 3 pb · Guest cottage available
Clark Point Rd. · ● · Sitting room
207-244-5335 · C-12+/S-no/P-no/H-no · harpsichord, fireplace
Gardiner & Marilyn Brower · · TV, decks
All year

A friendly, cozy restored sea captain's home on the quiet side of Mount Desert Island. Stroll to shops, wharf, restaurants. Enjoy the island's many attributes year-round.

Penury Hall · $ B&B · Full breakfast
Main St., Box 68, 04679 · 3 rooms · Comp. wine, coffee, tea
207-244-7102 · C-ltd/S-yes/P-no/H-no · Sitting room, sauna
Toby & Gretchen Strong · · picnic day sails
All year · · canoe & windsurfer avail

Comfortable rambling Maine home for us and our guests. Decor reflects hosts' interests in art, antiques, books, gardening, sailing. Water sports paradise.

SPRUCE HEAD ────────────────────────────────

Craignair Inn · $$ B&B · Full breakfast
Clark Island Rd., 04859 · 16 rooms · Restaurant, coffee & tea
207-594-7644 · Visa, MC ● · Wine service, parlor
Norman & Terry Smith · C-yes/S-yes/P-yes/H-no · library, flower garden
All year · · coastal activities

Area is alive with history of quarrying days. Located on 4 acres of shorefront. Swimming in abandoned granite quarry is delightful. The old church and store still stand.

STONINGTON ────────────────────────────────

Burnt Cove B&B · $$ B&B · Continental plus
RFD 1, Box 2905, 04681 · 2 rooms · Box lunches
Whitman Rd. · Visa, MC
207-367-2392 · C-12+/S-no/P-no/H-no
Bob Williams, Diane Berlew
May–October

Waterfront location on Penobscot Bay island; working lobster wharves; multitude of birds; nature conservancy trails; shops, restaurants; fishing village.

SUNSET ────────────────────────────────

Goose Cove Lodge · $$$ B&B/MAP · Continental plus (B&B)
Goose Cove Rd., 04683 · 21 rooms, 21 pb · Full bkfst./dinner (MAP)
Deer Isle · ● · BYOB, sitting rm, piano
207-348-2508 · C-yes/S-ltd/P-no/H-yes · bicycles, entertainment
George Pavloff · French, German, Spanish · beaches, sailboats
May–mid-October

Rustic retreat—sand beaches, rocky shores, spruce forest with moss-covered trails and open ocean at the End of Beyond. B&B in the spring and fall. MAP in the summer.

SURRY ————————————————————

Surry Inn
P.O. Box 25, Route 172, 04684
207-667-5091
Peter Krinsky
All year

$$ B&B
13 rooms, 11 pb
Visa, MC
C-5+/S-yes/P-no/H-ltd
Fr., Rus., Ger., Czech.

Full breakfast
Dinner, bar, comp. tea
Canoes, private beach
croquet, horseshoes
sitting room, library

Coastal country inn offering excellent cuisine, rolling lawns, private beach, spectacular sunsets, stenciled walls, New England charm and comfort.

TENANTS HARBOR ————————————————————

East Wind Inn
P.O. Box 149, 04860
One Mechanic St.
207-372-6366 FAX:372-6320
Tim Watts
All year

$$ EP
26 rooms, 12 pb
Visa, MC ●
C-12+/S-yes/P-ask/H-ltd

Full breakfast $
Comp. beverages
All meals, sitting room
entertainment, piano
conference room

Authentic country inn. Fishing boats unload at wharf. Antiques, telephones, color TV and piano. Productive meeting site with well-equipped conference rooms.

VINALHAVEN ————————————————————

Fox Island Inn
P.O. Box 451, 04863
Carver St.
207-863-2122
Anita Kellogg
May—October

$ B&B
10 rooms, 1 pb
C-5+/S-ltd/P-no/H-no

Continental breakfast
Sitting room
piano

A restored century-old townhouse on an unspoiled Maine island. A short walk to the picturesque harbor and fishing village of Vinalhaven.

WALDOBORO ————————————————————

The Blackford Inn
P.O. Box 817, 04572
164 Friendship St.
207-832-4714
All year

$$ B&B
3 rooms, 1 pb
Visa, MC
C-yes

Full breakfast
Sitting room
Wrap-around porch with
a river view
Reserv. req. Oct-May

Enjoy a healthy breakfast by the fireplace in our tin ceiling dining room before setting out to discover mid-coast Maine.

WATERFORD ————————————————————

The Waterford Inne
P.O. Box 149, 04088
Chadbourne Rd.
207-583-4037
Barbara/Rosalie Vanderzanden
Exc. Mar, Apr, Thkgv. wk

$$ EP
10 rooms, 7 pb
C-yes/S-yes/P-ask/H-no

Full breakfast $
Dinner, afternoon tea
Sitting room
library

Country inning at its best! The hospitality, food and lovely surroundings will bring you back again and again.

WELD ————————————————————

Kawanhee Inn Lakeside
Route 142, Webb Lake, 04285
207-585-2243 207-778-4306
Marti Strunk
June—October 15

$$ EP
10 rooms, 5 pb
●
C-yes/S-ltd/P-no/H-yes

Full service restaurant
Tennis courts
lake beach, bicycles
sitting room, piano

Rustic lodge and cabins on crystal-clear Webb Lake. Cathedral pines, field stone fireplaces, hiking, tennis, canoe, fishing, golf, dining.

WEST BOOTHBAY HARBOR

The Lawnmeer Inn
Box 505, 04575
207-633-2544
Frank Kelley
May—October

$$ EP
32 rooms
Visa, MC ●
C-yes/S-yes/P-ask/H-no
some French

Full breakfast $
Dinner
Restaurant, bar
sitting room
library

"The only thing that we overlook is the water."

WEST GOULDSBORO

Sunset House
HCR 60, Box 62, 04607
Route 186
207-963-7156
Carl & Kathy Johnson
All year

$$ B&B
7 rooms
Visa, MC
C-12+/S-no/P-no/H-no

Full breakfast
Double parlor, sunporch
Fresh water pond for
swimming, fishing
great biking

Late Victorian country farm inn on the coast; water views; beautiful sunsets. Short distance to Acadia National Park. Observe bald eagle, osprey, loons in natural environment.

YORK

Dockside Guest Quarters
P.O. Box 205, 03909
Harris Island Rd.
207-363-2868
The David Lusty Family
Memorial Day—mid-Oct

$$ EP
21 rooms, 19 pb
Visa, MC ●
C-yes/S-no/P-ltd/H-ltd
German

Continental plus $
Lunch, dinner, bar room
Restaurant, sitting room
porches, lawn
marina, boat rentals

Beautifully scenic location along edge of harbor, looking out over blue waters. Ocean beaches nearby, walk to historic district. AAA 3-Diamonds. June bargain calender.

Dockside Guest Quarter, York, ME

YORK HARBOR

York Harbor Inn
P.O. Box 573, 03911
York St., Route 1A
207-363-5119 800-343-3869
Joseph & Garry Dominguez
All year

$$ B&B
32 rooms, 26 pb
Visa, MC, AmEx •
C-yes/S-yes/P-no/H-ltd

Continental plus
Lunch, dinner, bar
Sitting room, piano
bicycles, ocean swimming
conf./banquet facilities

Quiet, authentic country inn (circa 1637) listed in National Register of Historic Places; overlooks the ocean and York Harbor Beach. Air conditioning and phones in rooms.

YORK–CAPE NEDDICK

The Cape Neddick House
1300 Rt. 1, P.O. Box 70, 03902
207-363-2500
Dianne Goodwin & Family
All year

$$ B&B
6 rooms, 1 pb
•
C-9+/S-ltd/P-no/H-no

Full breakfast
Comp. wine, tea, coffee
Parlor & living room
bicycles, guitar
horseshoes, picnic area

Coastal country 4th-generation Victorian home. Close to beaches, antiques, outlet shops, boutiques. Cultural & historic opportunities. Award-winning Apple Butter Nut Cake.

More Inns . . .

Aaron Dunning House 76 Federal St., Brunswick, 04011 207-729-4486
Admiral's Inn 70 S. Main St., Ogunquit, 03907 207-646-7093
Admiral's Loft 97 Main St., Ogunquit, 03907 207-646-5496
Alewife House 1917 Alewive Rd., Rt 35, Kennebunk, 04043 207-985-2118
Alfred M. Senter B&B Box 830, South Harpswell, 04079 207-833-2874
Allen's Inn 279 Main St., Sanford, 04073 207-324-2160
Arcady Down East South St., Blue Hill, 04614 207-374-5576
Artemus Ward House Waterford, 04088 207-583-4106
Artists Retreat 29 Washington St., Eastport, 04631 207-853-4239
Atlantean Inn 11 Atlantic Ave., Dept., Bar Harbor, 04609 207-288-3270
Bakers B&B Route 2, Box 2090, Bethel, 04217 207-824-2088
Bakke B&B RD#1,Box 505A,Foster Pt, West Bath, 04530 207-442-7185
Bass Harbor Inn Shore Rd., Bass Harbor, 04653 207-244-5157
Bay Ledge Inn and Spa 1385 Sand Point Rd., Bar Harbor, 04609 207-288-4204
Bayview Inn 111 Eden St. (Route 3), Bar Harbor, 04609 207-288-5861
Bayview Inn B&B RR4, 2131 Webhannet Dr., Wells Beach, 04090 207-646-9260
Beauport Inn P.O. Box 1793, Ogunquit, 03907 207-646-8680
Bedside Manor Guest House HCR 35 Box 100, Thomaston, 04861 207-354-8862
Belmont, The 6 Belmont Ave., Camden, 04843 207-236-8053
Ben-Loch Inn RFD #1 Box 1020, Dixmont, 04932 207-257-4768
Bennetts 3 Broadway, York Beach, 03910 207-363-5302
Berwick Box 261, Ogunquit, 03907 207-646-4062
Bethel Inn and Count P.O. Box 26, Bethel, 04217 800-654-0125
Bittersweet Inn Clarks Cove Rd., Walpole, 04573 207-563-5552
Blue Harbor House 67 Elm St., Camden, 04843 207-236-3196
Blue Hill Inn P.O. Box 403, Blue Hill, 04614 207-374-2844
Blue Shutters 6 Beachmere Pl., Ogunquit, 03907 207-646-2163
Blue Water Inn Beach St., Ogunquit, 03907 207-646-5559
Boothbay Harbor Inn 37 Atlantic Ave. Box 4, Boothbay Harbor, 04538 207-633-6302
Breakwater Inn Ocean Ave., Kennebunkport, 04046 207-957-3118
Brick Farm B&B RFD 1, Skowhegan, 04976 207-474-3949
Bristol Inn, The Upper Round Pond Rd., Newcastle, 000-563-1125
Broad Bay Inn & Gallery P.O. Box 607, Main St., Waldoboro, 04572 207-832-6668
Buck's Harbor Inn P.O. Box 268, South Brooksville, 04617 207-326-8660
Bufflehead Cove P.O. Box 499, Kennebunkport, 04046 207-967-3879
Canterbury House P.O. Box 881, York Harbor, 03911 207-363-3505
Cap'n Frost's B&B 241 W. Main St., Thomaston, 04861 207-354-8217
Captain Jefferds Inn Box 691, Kennebunkport, 04046 207-967-2311

Carleton Gardens 43 Carleton St., Portland, 04102 207-772-3458
Carriage House Inn P.O. Box 238, Searsport, 04974 207-548-2289
Castine Inn P.O. Box 41, Main St., Castine, 04421 207-326-4365
Cedarholm Cottages Star Route, Lincolnville, 04849 207-236-3886
Channelridge Farm 358 Cross Point Rd., North Edgecomb, 04556 207-882-7539
Charmwoods Naples, 04055 207-693-6798
Chestnut House 69 Chestnut St., Camden, 04843 207-236-6137
Claibern's B&B P.O. Box B, Oxford, Otisfield, 04270 207-539-2352
Claremont Southwest Harbor, 04679 207-244-5036
Clarion Nonantum Inn Ocean Ave., Box 2626, Kennebunkport, 04046 207-967-4050
Clark Perry House 59 Court St., Machias, 04654 207-255-8458
Clipper Ship Guest House 46 N. Main St., Ogunquit, 03907 207-646-9735
College Club Inn P.O. Box 617, US Rt. 1, Searsport, 04974 207-548-6575
Colonial Winterport Inn Rt. 1A Main St, Box 525, Winterport, 04496 207-223-5307
Copper Light B&B Box 67, Port Clyde, 04855 207-372-8510
Cornish Inn P.O. Box 266, Cornish, 04020 207-625-8501
Country Cupboard RFD 1, Box 1270, Kingfield, 04947 207-265-2193
Country Squire B&B RR 1 Box 178 Mighty, Gorham, 04038 207-839-4855
Coveside Five Islands, 04546 207-371-2807
Crab Apple Acres Inn Route 201, The Forks, 04985 207-663-2218
Crescent Beach Inn Route 77, Cape Elizabeth, 04107 207-799-1517
Crocker House Country Inn Hancock Point Rd., Hancock Point, 04640 207-422-6806
Dark Harbor House Inn Box 185, Islesboro, 04848 207-734-6669
Davis Lodge Route 4, Rangeley, 04970 207-864-5569
Douglass Place Route 2, Box 90, Bethel, 04217 207-824-2229
Dove B&B 16 Douglas St., Brunswick, 04011 207-729-6827
East River B&B P.O. Box 205 High St., East Machias, 04630 207-255-8467
Edwards Harbourside Inn Stage Neck Rd., York Beach, 03910 207-363-3037
Eggemoggin Inn RFD Box 324, Deer Isle, 04650 207-348-2540
Elfinhill P.O. Box 497, Newcastle, 04553 207-563-1886
Elizabeth's B&B HC 61, Box 004, Damariscotta, 04543 207-563-1919
Elms B&B 84 Elm St., Route 1, Camden, 04843 207-236-6250
English Robin Route 1, Box 194, Kennebunkport, 04046 207-967-3505
Ewenicorn Farm B&B 116 Goodwin Rd., Rt. 10, Eliot, 03903 207-439-1337
Farm House RR 1, Box 656, Kennebunkport, 04046 207-967-4169
Farmhouse Inn P.O. Box 496, Rangeley, 04970 207-864-5805
Feather Bed Inn Box 65, Mount Vernon, 04352 207-293-2020
Flakeyard Farm RFD 2, Kennebunkport, 04046 207-967-5965
Four Seasons Inn P.O. Box 390, Bethel, 04217 207-824-2755
Foxcroft B&B 25 W. Main St., Dover-Foxcraft, 04426 207-564-7720
Gazebo, The P.O. Box 668, Rt. 1 N., Ogunquit, 03907 207-646-3733
Glad II 60 Pearl St., Bath, 04530 207-443-1191
Glidden House RR 1 Box 740, Newcastle, 04553 207-563-1859
Gracie's B&B 52 Main St., Thomaston, 04861 207-354-2326
Green Acres Inn RFD #112, Canton, 04221 207-597-2333
Green Shutters Inn P.O. Box 543, Boothbay Harbor, 04538 207-633-2646
Green Woods R.F.D. No. 2, Lincolnvile, 04849 207-338-3187
Greenville Inn P.O. Box 1194, Greenville, 04441 207-695-2206
Grey Gull Inn 321 Webhannet Dr., Wells, 04090 207-646-7501
Grey Havens Inn Box 82, Five Islands, 04546 207-371-2616
Grey Rock Inn Northeast Harbor, 04662 217-276-9360
Gundalow Inn 6 Water Street, Kittery, 03904 207-439-4040
Harbor Hill Inn Box 280, Winter Harbor, 04693 203-963-8872
Harbor Inn P.O. Box 538A, Kennebunkport, 04046 207-967-2074
Harbor Lights Home Route 102, Southwest Harbor, 04679 207-244-3835
Harborgate B&B RD 2-2260, Brunswick, 04011 207-725-5894
Harbour Towne Inn 71 Townsend Ave., Boothbay Harbor, 04538 207-633-4300
Harbour Watch B&B R.F.D. 1 Box 42, Kittery Point, 03905 207-439-3242
Harbourside Inn Northeast Harbor, 04662 207-276-3272
Harriet Beecher Stowe Hse 63 Federal St., Brunswick, 04011 207-725-5543

Haven, The RR 4 Box 2270, Wells, 04090 207-646-4194
Heathwood Inn Bar Harbor, 800-582-3681
Higgins Beach Inn Scarborough, 04074 207-883-6684
High Tide Inn Camden, 04843 207-236-3724
Hiram Alden Inn 19 Church St., Belfast, 04915 207-338-2151
Holbrook House 74 Mt. Desert St., Bar Harbor, 04609 207-288-4970
Holbrook Inn B&B 7 Holbrook St., Freeport, 04032 207-865-6693
Home Port Inn 45 Main St., Lubec, 04652 207-733-2077
Homestead Inn B&B P.O. Box 15, York Beach, 03910 207-363-8952
Homewood Inn P.O. Box 196, Yarmouth, 04096 207-846-3351
Horatio Johnson House 36 Church St., Belfast, 04915 207-338-5153
Hosmer House B&B 4 Pleasant St., Camden, 04843 207-236-4012
Hugel Haus B&B 55 Main St., Lubec, 04652 207-733-4965
Inn at Canoe Point Box 216C, Route 3, Hulls Cove, 04644 207-288-9511
Inn at Cold Stream Pond P.O. Box 76, Enfield, 04433 207-732-3595
Inn at Harmon Park York St. & Harmon, York Harbor, 03911 207-363-2031
Inn at Parkspring 135 Spring St., Portland, 04072 207-774-1059
Island B&B Box 275,Ltl. Cranberry, Isleford, 04646 207-244-9283
Island Inn On the Harbor, Monhegan Island, 04852 207-596-0371
Island Watch B&B P.O. Box 1359, Southwest Harbor, 04679 207-244-7229
Islesboro Inn Islesboro, 04848 207-734-2222
Jo-Mar B&B on the Ocean P.O. Box 838, York Beach, 03910 207-363-4826
John Peters Inn P.O. Box 916, Blue Hill, 04614 207-374-2116
Juniper Hill Inn Route 1 North, Ogunquit, 03907 207-646-4501
Kedarburn Inn Route 35, Box 61, Waterford, 04088 207-583-6182
Kennebunk Inn 45 Main St., Kennebunk, 04043 207-985-3351
King's Inn P.O. Box 92, West Bethel, 04286 207-836-3375
L'Auberge Country Inn P.O. Box 21, Bethel, 04217 207-824-2774
Lake Brook Guest House RR 3, Box 218, Kennebunkport, 04046 207-967-4069
Lake House Routes 35 & 37, Waterford, 04088 207-583-4182
Lake Sebasticook B&B 8 Sebasticook Ave., Newport, 04953 207-368-5507
Laphroaig B&B Rt. 15, Box 67, Deer Isle Village, 04627 207-348-6088
Le Domaine Restaurant/Inn P.O. Box 496, US Rt. 1, Hancock, 04640 207-422-3395
Le Vatout Route 32, Box 375, Waldoboro, 04572 207-832-4552
Leisure Inn 19 School St., Ogunquit, 03907 207-646-2737
Letteney Farm Vacations RFD 2, Box 166A, Waldoboro, 04572 207-832-5143
Lighthouse Inn Box 249, Nubble Rd., York Beach, 03910 207-363-6072
Lilac Inn Box 1325, 3 Ridge Rd., York Beach, 03910 207-363-3930
Linekin Village B&B Route 65, Box 776, East Booth Bay, 04544 207-633-3681
Lodge 19 Yates, Biddefordpool, 04006 617-284-7148
Londonderry Inn Route 3, Belmont Ave., Belfast, 04915 207-338-3988
Longville Inn P.O. Box 75, Lincolnville Beach, 04849 207-236-3785
Lord Camden Inn 24 Main St., Camden, 04843 207-236-4325
Maples Cottage Inn 16 Roberts Ave., Bar Harbor, 04609 207-288-3443
Marimor Motor Inn 66 Shore Rd., Ogunquit, 03907 207-646-7397
Markert House P.O. Box 224, Glidden, Newcastle, 04553 207-563-1309
McGilvery House P.O. Box 588, Searsport, 04974 207-548-6289
Medomak House Box 663, Friendship, Waldoboro, 04572 207-832-4971
Middaugh B&B 36 Elm St., Topsham, 04086 207-725-2562
Middlefield Farm B&B Bristol Mills, 04539 207-529-5439
Migis Lodge Route 302, South Casco, 04077 207-655-4524
Mill Pond House Box 640, Tenants Harbor, 04860 207-372-6209
Monhegan House Monhegan, 04852 207-594-7983
Moonshell Inn Island Ave., Peaks Island, 04081 207-766-2331
Moosehorn B&B Route 1, Box 322, Baring, 04694 207-454-8883
Mountainside B&B P.O. Box 290, Bridgton, 04009 207-647-5091
Nautilus B&B 7 Willow Ave., Box 916, York Beach, 03910 207-363-6496
New Meadows Inn Bath Rd., West Bath, 04530 207-443-3921
Newagen Seaside Inn Box H, Southport Island, Cape Newagen, 04552 207-633-5242
Norridgewock Colonial Inn Upper Main St, Rt 2 &20, Norridgewock, 04957 207-634-3470

Norseman Inn HCR-61 Box 50, Bethel, 04217 207-824-2002
North Woods B&B 55 N. High St., Bridgton, 04009 207-647-2100
Northern Pines Health Rsrt Raymond, 04071 207-655-7624
Norumbega Inn 61 High St., Route 1, Camden, 04843 207-236-4646
Oakland House Herricks Rd., Sargentville, 04673 207-359-8521
Ocean House Box 66, Port Clyde, 04855 207-372-6691
Ocean Point Inn Shore Rd., East Boothbay, 04544 207-633-4200
Ogunquit House P.O. Box 1883, Ogunquit, 03907 207-646-2967
Old Cape of Bristol Mills P.O. Box 129, Rte. 130, Bristol Mills, 04539 207-563-8848
Old Granite Inn 546 Main St., Rockland, 04841 207-594-7901
Old Parsonage Inn P.O. Box 1577, Bucksport, 04416 207-469-6477
Old Red Farm Desert of Maine Rd., Freeport, 04032 207-865-4550
Old Tavern Inn P.O. Box 445, Litchfield, 04350 207-268-9317
Old Village Inn 30 Main St., Ogunquit, 03907 207-646-7088
Olde Berry Inn Kennebunk Rd., Box 2, Alfred, 04002 207-324-0603
Olde Rowley Inn P.O. Box 87, North Waterford, 04267 207-583-4143
Oliver Farm Inn Box 136 Old Route 1, Nobleboro, 04555 207-563-1527
Overview, The RD 2, Box 106, Lubec, 04652 207-733-2005
Owl and The Turtle 8 Bay View St., Camden, 04843 207-236-4769
Oxford House Inn 105 Main St., Fryeburg, 04037 207-935-3442
Pachelbel Inn 20 Roberts Ave, Bar Harbor, 04609 207-288-9655
Penobscot Meadows Inn M.A.: 90 Northport Ave., Belfast, 04915 207-338-5320
Pentagoet Inn P.O. Box 4, Main St., Castine, 04421 207-326-8616
Pointed Fir B&B Paradise Rd., Box 745, Bethel, 04217 207-824-2251
Pomegranate Inn 49 Neal St., Portland, 04102 297-772-1006
Port Gallery Inn P.O. Box 1367, Kennebunkport, 04046 207-967-3728
Pressey House-1850 85 Summer St., Oakland, 04963 207-465-3500
Primrose Cottage Inn 73 Mt. Desert St., Bar Harbor, 04609 207-288-4031
Pulpit Harbor Inn Crabtree Point Rd., North Haven Island, 04853 207-867-2219
Purple Sandpiper House R.R. #3 Box 226, Wells, 04090 207-646-7990
Red House HC 60 Box 540, Lincolnville, 04849 207-236-4621
Ricker House P.O. Box 256, Cherryfield, 04622 207-546-2780
River House B&B HCR 35, Box 119, Thomaston, 04861 207-354-8936
Roaring Lion Main St., P.O. Box 756, Waldoboro, 04572 207-832-4038
Rock Gardens Inn Sebasco Estates, 04565 207-389-1339
Rosemary Cottage Russell Ave., Rockport, 04856 207-236-3513
Schooners Inn & Restaurant P.O. Box 1121, Kennebunkport, 04046 207-967-5333
Scotland Bridge Inn P.O. Box 521, York, 03909 207-363-4432
Sea Chimes B&B RD 1, Shore Rd., Cape Neddick, 03902 207-646-5378
Seafair Inn Box 1221, Ogunquit, 03907 207-646-2181
Seaside Inn Gooch's Beach, Kennebunkport, 04046 207-967-4461
Sebago Lake Lodge White Bridge Rd., North Windham, 04062 207-892-2698
Sebasco Lodge Sebasco Estates, 04565 207-389-1161
Senter B&B Route 123, South Harpswell, 04079 207-833-2874
Shady Maples RFD #1, Box 360, Bar Harbor, 04609 207-288-3793
Shepard Hill B&B Shepard Hill Rd., Union, 04862 207-785-4121
Shining Sails Inc. Box 344, Monhegan Island, 04852 207-596-0041
Sign of the Owl Route 1 Box 85, Lincolnville, 04849 207-338-4669
Songo B&B Songon Locks Rd., Naples, 04055 207-693-3960
Southside-by the Harbor Southside Rd.,Rt.1,Box, New Harbor, 04554 207-677-2991
Spouter Inn, The Box 176, Lincolnville Beach, 04849 207-789-5171
Stacked Arms B&B RR 2, Box 146, Wiscasset, 04578 207-882-5436
Stonewycke Inn P.O. Box 589, Searsport, 04974 207-548-2551
Stratford House Inn 45 Mt. Desert St., Bar Harbor, 04609 207-288-5189
Strauss Haus Shore Rd., Ogunquit, 03907 207-646-7756
Sudbury Inn Lower Main St., Bethel, 04217 207-824-2174
Sugarloaf Inn Carrabassett Valley, Carrabassett Valley, 04947 207-237-2701
Sullivan Harbor Farm Route 1, Sullivan, 04682 207-422-3591
Summer Place RFD 1 Box 196, York, 03909 207-363-5233
Sunday River Inn Sunday River Rd., Bethel, 04217 207-824-2410

Terrace By the Sea 11 Wharf Lane, Ogunquit, 03907 207-646-3232
The Tides 119 West Street, Bar Harbor, 04609 207-288-4968
Thistle Inn P.O. Box 176, Boothbay Harbor, 04538 207-633-3541
Thomas Inn & Playhouse P.O. Box 128, South Casco, 04077 207-655-7728
Thornhedge Inn 47 Mt. Desert St., Bar Harbor, 04609 207-288-5398
Three Stanley Avenue P.O. Box 169, Kingfield, 04947 207-265-5541
Tide Watch Inn Pine St., P.O. Box 94, Waldoboro, 04572 207-832-4987
Tides Inn By-The-Sea 737 Goose Rocks Beach, Kennebunkport, 04046 207-967-3757
Time & Tide B&B RR 1 Box 275B, Surry, 04684 207-667-3382
Tolman House Inn P.O. Box 551, Tolman Rd, Harrison, 04040 207-583-4445
Topside McKown Hill, Boothbay Harbor, 04538 207-633-5404
Trebor Inn P.O. Box 299, Guilford, 04443 207-876-4070
Trellis House P.O. Box 2229, Ogunquit, 03907 207-646-7909
Vicarage East Ltd Box 368A, West Harpswell, 04079 207-833-5480
Victoria's B&B 58 Pine St., Ellsworth, 04605 207-667-5893
Victorian House Route 26, Poland Spring, 04274 207-998-2169
Village Cove Inn P.O. Box 650, Kennebunkport, 04046 207-967-3993
Waldo Emerson Inn 108 Summer St, Kennebunk, 04043 207-985-7854
Walker Wilson House 2 Melcher Place, Brunswick—Topsham, 04086 207-729-0715
Welch House 36 McKown St., Boothbay Harbor, 04538 207-633-3431
Weld Inn Box 8, Weld, 04285 207-585-2429
Weld Inn, The P.O. Box 8, Weld, 04285 207-585-2429
Weskeag Inn Route 73, P.O. Box 213, South Thomaston, 04858 207-596-6676
Westgate B&B 18 West St., Boothbay Harbor, 04538 207-633-3552
Weston House B&B 26 Boynton St., Eastport, 04631 207-853-2907
Westways on Kezar Lake Box 175, Route 5, Center Lovell, 04016 207-928-2663
Whaleback Inn B&B Box 162, Pepperrell Rd., Kittery Point, 03905 207-439-9560
Whitehall Inn Rt. 1 N. at 52 High St., Camden, 04843 207-236-3391
Widow's Walk Box 150, Stratton, 04982 207-246-6901
Wild Rose of York 78 Long Sands Rd., York, 03909 207-363-2532
Windward Farm Young's Hill Rd., Washington, 04574 207-845-2830
Winter's Inn P.O. Box 44, Kingfield, 04947 207-265-5421
Wooden Goose Inn P.O. Box 195, Cape Neddick, 03902 207-363-5673
Yardarm Village Inn Box 773, 130 Shore Rd., Ogunquit, 03907 207-646-7006
Yellow House B&B Water St., Box 732, Damariscotta, 04543 207-563-1388
Yellow Monkey Guest House 44 Main St., Ogunquit, 03907 207-646-9056
Youngtown Inn Route 52, Lincolnville, 04849 207-763-3037

Maryland

ANNAPOLIS ————————————————————————————————

College House Suites	$$$ B&B	Continental plus
One College Ave., 21401	2 rooms, 2 pb	Suite has sitting room,
Historic District	●	bedroom and private bath
301-263-6124		courtyard
Don Wolfrey, JoAnne Wolfrey	C-no/S-no/P-no/H-no	
All year		

Elegant suites in historic Annapolis. Walk to Colonial Harbor, U.S. Naval Academy, historic sites. Featuring private courtyard entrance, fireplace, Laura Ashley decor.

ANNAPOLIS

Gibson's Lodgings
110 Prince George St., 21401
301-268-5555
Claude & Jeanne Schrift
All year

$$ B&B
20 rooms
●
C-ltd/S-ltd/P-no/H-yes

Continental breakfast
Comp. evening wine
Piano, conference fac.
daily maid service
parking

Located in historic district, near City Docks, adjacent to U.S. Naval Academy. Antique furnishings throughout. Offstreet parking. Daily maid service. Unique conf. facilities.

Mary Rob B&B
243 Prince George St., 21401
301-268-5438 301-261-2764
Col. Rob Carlson, Mary Taylor
All year

$$$ B&B
4 rooms, 3 pb
●
C-ask/S-no/P-no/H-no

Full breakfast
Snacks, near restaurants
Sitting room, library
bicycles, cable TV
phone in room, jacuzzi

Victorian Italianate Villa in heart of Annapolis historic district. Beautifully decorated with antiques and reproductions. Breakfast to order. Beautyrest mattresses.

Prince George Inn B&B
232 Prince George St., 21401
301-263-6418
Bill & Norma Grovermann
All year

$$$ B&B
4 rooms, 2 pb
●
C-ltd/S-ltd/P-no/H-no

Full breakfast
Refrigerator, teas
Parlor, screened porch
central heat and A/C

A 100-year-old Victorian brick townhouse lovingly furnished with period antiques. Located in Historic District near Naval Academy and City Dock.

Shaw's Fancy B&B
161 Green St., 21401
301-263-0320
Jack House, Lilith Ren
All year

$$$ B&B
3 rooms, 2 pb
●
C-10+/S-ltd/P-no/H-no

Continental plus
Teas, juices, cakes
Hot tubs, garden
air conditioning
health club privileges

Whimsical Victorian in the heart of historic Annapolis. Walk to naval academy, shops, restaurants. Gourmet breakfast in our lovely garden, or sherry on the porch swing.

William Page B&B Inn
8 Martin St., 21401
301-626-1506
Robert Zuchelli, Greg Page
All year

$$$ B&B
5 rooms, 3 pb
●
C-no/S-no/P-no/H-no

Continental plus
Afternoon tea, snacks
Wet bar set-up
sitting room
tennis and pool nearby

Circa 1908, furnished in genuine antiques and period reproductions. Featuring suite with private bath and whirlpool. Free off-street parking.

BALTIMORE

Admiral Fell Inn
888 S. Broadway, 21231
301-522-7377 800-292-4667
Dominik Eckenstein
All year

$$$ B&B
37 rooms, 37 pb
Visa, MC, AmEx ●
C-yes/S-yes/P-no/H-yes
German, French, Spanish

Continental breakfast
Lunch, dinner, bar
Entertainment, hot tub
cruises, parking
free van service

Beautiful urban inn located on the water in historic Fells Point section. Many activities within easy reach. Traditional Southern hospitality. Jacuzzis in 3 rooms.

BALTIMORE

Betsy's B&B

1428 Park Ave., 21217	$$$ B&B	Full breakfast
301-383-1274	3 rooms, 3 pb	Hot tub (by reservation)
Betsy Grater	Visa, MC, AmEx ●	piano, TV, bicycles
All year	C-yes/S-ltd/P-no/H-no	swim club privileges

This charming 100-year-old townhouse has a hallway floor laid in alternating oak and walnut strips, 6 carved marble fireplaces and handsome brass rubbings.

Celie's Waterfront B&B

1714 Thames St., 21231	$$$ B&B	Continental plus
410-522-2323	7 rooms, 7 pb	Refrigerators
Celie Ives	Visa, MC, AmEx, Disc ●	Private garden, A/C
All year	C-10+/S-no/P-no/H-yes	bedroom fireplaces
		whirlpool, parking

New antique-filled urban inn overlooking the water in maritime community of Fells Point. Minutes to Harbor Place by antique trolley or water taxi. Spectacular roof deck views.

Paulus Gasthaus

2406 Kentucky Ave., 21213	$$ B&B	Full breakfast
301-467-1688	2 rooms, 1 pb	Comp. sherry in room
Lucie & Ed Paulus	●	Sitting room
All year	C-ltd/S-no/P-no/H-no	outdoor patio
	German, some French	near golf, fitness trail

Best of two worlds: Tudor-style European home, lovely residential neighborhood, free parking. Quality accommodations, Gemuetlichkeit, near Inner Harbor.

Shirley-Madison Inn

205 W. Madison St., 21201	$$$ B&B	Continental breakfast
301-728-6550	27 rooms, 27 pb	Comp. evening sherry
Stanley Gondzar	Visa, MC, AmEx, DC ●	Tea, sitting room
All year	C-yes/S-yes/P-no/H-no	library
		courtyard/backyard

Elegant 1880 Victorian mansion furnished with Victorian & Edwardian antiques. Short walk to Inner Harbor, cultural corridor, financial district. Charming & hospitable.

Society Hill Hotel

58 W. Biddle St., 21201	$$$ B&B	Continental breakfast
301-837-3630	15 rooms, 15 pb	Restaurant, comp. wine
Kate C. Hopkins	Visa, MC, AmEx ●	Pianist
All year	C-yes/S-yes/P-ltd/H-no	van service throughout
		Baltimore City

Baltimore's first "urban inn." All guest rooms decorated with antiques, Victorian furniture. Fresh flowers, homemade candies.

Twin Gates B&B Inn

308 Morris Ave., 21093	$$$ B&B	Full gourmet breakfast
Baltimore—Lutherville	5 rooms, 5 pb	Comp. wine, tea
301-252-3131 800-635-0370	●	Free winery tours
Gwen & Bob Vaughan	C-no/S-no/P-no/H-no	library
All year		

Elegant Victorian mansion in serene northern suburb. Twenty minutes to convention center, Harbor Place and National Aquarium. Excellent seafood restaurants, free winery tours.

BERLIN

Atlantic Hotel Inn & Rest.
2 N. Main St., 21811
301-641-3589
Stephen T. Jacques
All year

$$ B&B
16 rooms, 16 pb
Visa, MC ●
C-yes/S-yes/H-yes

Continental breakfast
Afternoon tea, cheese
Restaurant, bar, dinner
sitting room, library
lounge, parlor

Restored Victorian hotel, circa 1895, centrally located in historic Berlin. 16 bedrooms with antique furnishings, private baths and air-conditioning. Fine dining.

CHESTERTOWN

The White Swan Tavern
231 High St., 21620
301-778-2300
Mary Susan Maisel
All year

$$$ B&B
5 rooms, 5 pb
C-yes/S-yes/P-no/H-ltd

Continental breakfast
Comp. wine, eve. sherry
Comp. fruit basket
sitting room, terrace
bicycles

18th-century inn nestled in Maryland's historic eastern shore. Genuine antiques, homemade continental breakfast, tea, complimentary wine & fruit.

CUMBERLAND

Inn at Walnut Bottom
120 Greene Street, 21502
301-777-0003
Sharon Ennis Kazary
All year

$$ B&B
12 rooms, 10 pb
Visa, MC, AmEx
C-yes/S-no/P-no/H-ltd

Full breakfast
Restaurant
Afternoon tea, snacks
sitting room, library
TV room, bicycles

Charming traditional country inn and Arthur's Restaurant. Beautiful mountain city with scenic railroad, historic district & extraordinary recreation area. Family atmosphere.

FREDERICK

Spring Bank—A B&B Inn
7945 Worman's Mill Rd., 21701
301-694-0440
Ray & Beverly Compton
All year

$$$ B&B
6 rooms, 1 pb
Visa, MC, AmEx, Disc ●
C-no/S-no/P-no/H-no

Continental breakfast
Comp. wine
Double parlors, library
view from observatory
10 acres for roaming

On National Register of Historic Places. Antiques. Near Baltimore, Washington, D.C., and Civil War battlefields. Exceptional dining in Frederick Historic District 2 mi. away.

HAGERSTOWN

Beaver Creek House B&B
20432 Beaver Creek Rd., 21740
301-797-4764
Don & Shirley Day
All year

$$ EP/B&B
5 rooms, 3 pb
●
C-no/S-no/P-no/H-no

Full breakfast
Afternoon tea, snacks
Comp. sherry in room
sitting room, library
restaurants nearby

Antique-filled Victorian country home near I-70 and 81. Clean, hospitable, relaxed; near historic sites, golf, antique and outlet shopping.

Lewrene Farm B&B
RD3, Box 150, 21740
Downsville Pike
301-582-1735
Lewis & Irene Lehman
All year

$ B&B
6 rooms, 3 pb
C-yes/S-no/P-no/H-no
Spanish, some German

Full breakfast
Bedside snack, piano
Sitting room, whirlpool
gazebo, large farm
conference facility

Quiet farm, cozy colonial home with fireplace, antiques, candlelight breakfasts, Historic Antietam Battlefield, Harper's Ferry, outlets, restaurants, I-81 & I-70 nearby.

HAVRE DE GRACE

Spencer–Silver Mansion
200 S. Union Ave., 21078
410-939-1097
Jim & Carol Nemeth
All year

$$ B&B
4 rooms, 1 pb
•
C-yes/S-ltd/P-no/H-no
German

Full breakfast
Sitting room with TV
Two parlors, fireplace
porch, reading nook
free guided tours

In the heart of the historic district, our 1896 mansion takes visitors back to the turn of the century. Antique-filled Victorian-style rooms and informative hosts.

Vandiver Inn
301 S. Union Ave., 21078
301-939-5200
Mary McKee
All year

$$ B&B/$$$ MAP
10 rooms, 10 pb
Visa, MC, AmEx •
C-no/S-yes/P-no/H-no

Continental plus
Sitting room, TV
Melodian, porches
bicycles, tennis
Chesapeake Bay cruises

Large detached Queen Anne cottage in historic town of Havre de Grace, nestled by the Chesapeake Bay. Complimentary country breakfast. Dinner on Friday & Saturday nights.

NEW MARKET

National Pike Inn
P.O. Box 299, 21774
9 W. Main St.
301-865-5055
Tom & Terry Rimel
All year

$$$ B&B
4 rooms, 2 pb
Visa, MC
C-10+/S-ltd/P-no/H-no

Continental plus
Basket of fruit, snacks
Coffee, tea, sitting rm
private garden courtyard
shopping, tennis, golf

Our Colonial decor and warm hospitality will make your stay memorable! Explore historic architecture, antique shopping, and dine in excellence—all within walking distance.

The Strawberry Inn
P.O. Box 237, 21774
17 Main St.
301-865-3318
Jane & Ed Rossig
All year

$$ B&B
5 rooms, 5 pb
C-8+/S-yes/P-no/H-yes

Continental plus
Sitting room
Gazebo, air conditioning
tennis nearby
small conference facil.

A country inn where the proprietor is host to his guests. A place of gracious hospitality, peace and quiet. Breakfast served to your room at your requested time.

OAKLAND

Red Run Inn
Route 5, Box 268, 21550
301-387-6606
Ruth M. Umbel
All year

$$ B&B
5 rooms, 5 pb
Visa, MC, AmEx •
C-yes/S-yes/P-no/H-no

Continental plus
Lunch, dinner, bar
Comp. wine, sitting room
tennis, entertainment
swimming pool

Tourist area, four season resort: skiing, water sports, fall foliage, fishing. The old barn dates back to the 1940s.

OLNEY

Thoroughbred B&B
16410 Batchlr Forest Rd, 20832
Batchellor's Forest Rd.
301-774-7649
Helen M. Polinger
All year

$$ B&B
9 rooms, 3 pb
Visa, MC •
C-12+/S-no/P-no/H-ltd

Full breakfast
Sitting room, library
Hot tubs, pool table
swimming pool
tennis courts nearby

Champion racehorses have been bred & raised here. 175 acres of rolling hills. 12 miles from Washington, D.C., & 6 miles to Metro. Five lovely rooms plus a 4-bedroom farmhouse.

OXFORD ─────────────────────

Robert Morris Inn	$$$ EP/B&B	Full breakfast (W-Sun) $
P.O. Box 70, 21654	33 rooms, 33 pb	Continental (M-Tu)
314 N. Morris St.	Visa, MC ●	Restaurant, bar service
301-226-5111	C-no/S-yes/P-no/H-ltd	
Jay, Wendy & Ken Gibson		
All year		

Historic Chesapeake Bay romantic inn located in charming Oxford, MD. Featuring the best crab cakes on the eastern shore. Tennis, fishing, boating, and golfing all nearby.

SAINT MICHAELS ─────────────────────

Kemp House Inn	$$ B&B	Continental plus
412 Talbot St., 21663	8 rooms, 3 pb	Private cottage avail.
P.O. Box 638	Visa, MC ●	Bicycles
301-745-2243	C-yes/S-yes/P-yes/H-no	queen-sized beds
Steve & Diane Cooper		
All year		

1805 Georgian house with four-poster beds and working fireplaces in historic eastern shore village; close to restaurants, museums, harbor.

Parsonage Inn	$$$ B&B	Continental plus
210 N. Talbot (Rt. 33), 21663	7 rooms, 7 pb	Comp. ice tea, tea
301-745-5519	Visa, MC ●	Parlor, library
Sharon & Dave Proctor	C-yes/S-no/H-yes	bicycles
All year		

Unique brick Victorian, part of historic district. Walking distance to maritime museums, shops, gourmet restaurants. Working fireplaces and Laura Ashley linens.

Wades Point Inn On The Bay	$$ B&B	Continental plus
P.O. Box 7, 21663	24 rooms, 14 pb	Sitting room
Wades Point Rd.	Visa, MC	Screened porches
301-745-2500	C-yes/S-ltd/P-no/H-yes	fishing & crabbing dock
Betsy & John Feiler		biking, golf, tennis
March–December		

Georgian Colonial for those seeking the splendor of the country and the serenity of the Bay. 120 acres for relaxation and recreation. Sightseeing in nearby historic towns.

SNOW HILL ─────────────────────

The River House Inn	$$$ B&B	Full breakfast
201 E. Market St., 21863	5 rooms, 5 pb	Lunch, dinner, snacks
301-632-2722	Visa, MC ●	Comp. wine/tea, porches
Susanne & Larry Knudsen	C-yes/S-no/P-no/H-no	A/C, fishing, boating
All year		country club golf

Come relax at our elegant 1860s riverfront country home in historic Snow Hill. Enjoy Maryland's eastern shore, beaches and bay.

TANEYTOWN ─────────────────────

Glenburn	$$ B&B	Full breakfast
3515 Runnymede Rd., 21787	3 rooms, 2 pb	Refrigerator, kitchen
301-751-1187	●	2 bdr. cottage w/kitchen
Elizabeth & Robert Neal	C-yes/S-ltd/P-no/H-no	swimming pool, porches
All year		golf, A/C

Georgian house with Victorian addition, antique furnishings, featured in Maryland House & Garden Pilgrimage. Historic rural area close to Gettysburg.

TILGHMAN ISLAND

Black Walnut Point Inn
P.O. Box 308, 21671
Black Walnut Rd.
301-886-2452
M. Thomas Ward, Brend C. Ward
All year

$$$ B&B
7 rooms, 5 pb
C-no/S-ltd/P-no/H-yes

Continental plus
Comp. wine
Sitting room, bicycles
tennis, pool, shoreline
57-acre wildlife reserve

The inn at the end of the road. Key West sunsets. Hammocks by the bay. Quiet and peaceful.

VIENNA

Nanticoke Manor House
P.O. Box 248, 21869
Church St. @ Water St.
301-376-3530
William & Barbara Fearson
All year

$$ B&B
6 rooms, 3 pb
Visa, MC •
C-10+/S-no/P-no/H-no

Cont. plus, full avail $
Comp. wine & cheese
Restaurant, dinner avail
sitting room, library
piano, croquet, bicycles

Victorian inn overlooking colonial port on Maryland Eastern Shore. Authentically restored & furnished. Fireplaces, spiral staircase. Near wildlife refuges.

The Tavern House
P.O. Box 98, 21869
111 Water St.
301-376-3395
Harvey & Elise Altergott
All year

$$ B&B
3 rooms
Visa, MC •
C-12+/S-yes
Spanish, German

Full breakfast
Aftn. tea, comp. wine
Sitting room
tennis courts nearby

Restored Colonial tavern on Nanticoke River. Simple elegance; stark whites, detailed woodwork. Looking out over river and marshes. Great for bicycling and bird-watching.

More Inns . . .

1876 House P.O. Box 658, Oxford, 21654 301-226-5496
Agora 824 E. Baltimore St., Baltimore, 21202 301-234-0515
Annapolis B&B 235 Prince George Sr., Annapolis, 21401 301-269-0669
Bay View B&B 2654 Ogleton Rd., Annapolis, 21403 301-268-0781
Bolton Hill B&B 1534 Bolton St., Baltimore, 21217 301-669-5356
Broom Hall B&B 2425 Pocock Rd., Fallston, 21047 301-557-7321
Capt. & Ms J's Guest House P.O. Box 676, Solomons, 20688 301-326-3334
Castle P.O. Box 578, Route 36, Mount Savage, 21545 301-759-5946
Charles Inn 74 Charles St., Annapolis, 21401 301-268-1451
Country Inn P.O. Box 397, McHenry, 21541 301-387-6694
Davis House P.O. Box 759, Solomons Island, 20688 301-326-4811
Eagles Mere B&B 102 E. Montgomery, Baltimore, 21230 301-332-1618
Elmwood c. 1770 B&B P.O. Box 220, Princess Anne, 21853 301-651-1066
Flyway Lodge Rt.1, Box 660, US Rt.21, Chestertown, 21620 301-778-5557
Freeland Farm 21616 Middletown Rd., Freeland, 21053 301-357-5364
Glasgow Inn 1500 Hambrooks Blvd., Cambridge, 21613 301-228-0575
Governor's Ordinary P.O. Box 156, Vienna, 21869 301-376-3530
Great Oak Manor Route 2 Box 766, Chestertown, 21620 301-778-5796
Hambleton Inn 202 Cherry St., Box 299, Saint Michaels, 21663 301-245-3350
Harrison's Country Inn P.O. Box 310, Tilghman, 21671 301-886-2123
Hayland Farm 5000 Sheppard Ln., Ellicott City, 21043 301-531-5593
Heart of Annapolis B&B 185 Duke of Gloucester, Annapolis, 21404 301-267-2309
Hill's Inn 114 Washington Ave., Chestertown, 21620 301-778-NINS
Imperial Hotel 208 High St., Chestertown, 21620 301-778-5000
Inn at Antietam P.O. Box 119, Sharpsburg, 21782 301-432-6601
Inn at Buckeystown 3521 Buckeystown Pike, Buckeystown, 21717 301-874-5755
Inn at Mitchell House Box 329, R.D. 2, Chestertown, 21620 301-778-6500

Inn at Perry Cabin Saint Michaels, 21663 301-745-5178
Inwood Guest House Box 378, Route 1, Cascade, 21719 301-241-3467
Jonah Williams Inn 101 Severn Ave., Annapolis, 21403 301-269-6020
Judge Thomas House 1893 195 Willis St., Westminster, 21157 301-876-6686
Kent Manor Inn Kent Island, Box 815, Stevensville, 21666 301-643-5757
Kitty Knight House Route 213, Georgetown, 21930 301-648-5777
Marameade, The 2439 Old National Pike, Middletown, 21769 301-371-4214
Maryland Inn Church Circle, Annapolis, 21401 800-638-8902
Matoaka Cottages P.O. Box 124, Saint Leonard, 20685 301-586-0269
Middle Plantation Inn 9549 Liberty Rd., Frederick, 21701 301-898-7128
Mulberry House 111 W. Mulberry St., Baltimore, 21201 301-576-0111
Newel Post, The 3428 Uniontown Rd., Uniontown, 21157 301-775-2655
Piper House B&B Inn Antietam Battlefield, Sharpsburg, 21782 301-797-1862
Quality International 10750 Columbia Pike, Silver Spring, 20901 301-236-5032
Radcliffe Cross Route 3, Box 360, Chestertown, 21620 301-778-5540
Reynolds Tavern 4 Church Cr., Annapolis, 21401 800-638-8902
Robert Johnson House 23 State Cir., Annapolis, 21401 800-638-8902
Rosebud Inn 4 N. Main St., Woodsboro, 21798 301-845-2221
Sarke Plantation Inn 6033 Todd Point Rd., Cambridge, 21613 301-228-7020
Snow Hill Inn 104 E. Market St., Snow Hill, 21863 301-632-2102
Society Hill–Gov't House 1125 North Calvert St., Baltimore, 21202 301-752-7722
Society Hill–Hopkins 3404 St. Paul St., Baltimore, 21218 301-235-8600
Sophie Kerr House Route 3, Box 7-B, Denton, 21629 301-479-3421
State House Inn 15 State Cir., Annapolis, 21401 800-638-8902
Strawberry Factory Route 20, Gratitude, Rock Hall, 21661 301-639-7468
Tidewater Inn Dover & Harrison St., Easton, 21601 301-822-1300
Trailside Country Inn US 40, Flintstone, 21530 301-478-2032
Tran Crossing 121 E. Patrick St., Frederick, 21701 301-663-8449
Turning Point Inn 3406 Urbana Pike, Frederick, 21701 301-874-2421
Two Swan Inn P.O. Box 727, Saint Michaels, 21663 301-745-2929
Tyler-Spite House 112 W. Church St., Frederick, 21701 301-831-4455
Upsteam Guest House 3604 Dustin Rd, Box 240, Burtonsville, 20866 301-421-9163
Victoriana Inn 205 Cherry St., Box 449, Saint Michaels, 21663 301-745-3368
Washington Hotel & Inn Somerset Ave., Princess Anne, 21853 301-651-2525
Westlawn Inn 7th St. & Chesapeake, North Beach, 20714 301-855-8410
Westminster Inn 5 South Center St., Westminster, 21157 301-876-2893
Winchester Country Inn 430 S. Bishop St., Westminster, 21157 301-876-7373
Winslow Home 8217 Caraway St., Cabin John, 20818 301-229-4654

Betsy's B&B, Baltimore, MD

Massachusetts

ATTLEBORO

Col. Blackinton Inn
203 N. Main St., 02703
508-222-6022
Allana Schaefer
All year

$$ B&B
16 rooms, 11 pb
Visa, MC, AmEx, CB, Dis •
C-yes/S-ltd/P-no/H-yes
German

Full breakfast
Afternoon tea, snacks
Bar service, library
2 sitting rooms
walking

Featuring secluded garden terrace, viewing park-like cemetery and the Bungay River. Ideal for touring and business travel in southeastern Massachusetts.

Emma C's B&B
18 French Farm Rd., 02703
508-226-6365
Caroline & Jim Logie
All year

$$ B&B
3 rooms, 1 pb
AmEx •
C-yes/S-no/P-ask/H-no
some Spanish

Full breakfast
Comp. refreshments
Sitting room, bicycles
swimming pool, golf
A/C in rooms, color TV

Enjoy the warmth of this "country Colonial" home. Minutes from Wheaton College, Brown University, Great Woods, and La Salette Shrine.

AUBURN

Capt. Samuel Eddy House
609 Oxford St. S., 01501
508-832-5282 508-832-3149
Jack & Carilyn O'Toole
All year

$$ B&B
5 rooms, 5 pb
Visa, MC •
C-yes/S-ltd/P-no/H-no

Full breakfast
Dinner by reservation
Restaurant, aftn. tea
sitting rm, country shop
gardens, swimming pool

1765 Homestead, restored to its original era. Antiques, beehive fireplaces, queen canopies, bed chambers with private baths. Herb gardens & shop. Close to Boston & Sturbridge.

BARNSTABLE

Charles Hinkley House
P.O. Box 723, 02630
Rt 6A, Olde King's Hwy
508-362-9924
Les & Miya Patrick
All year

$$$ B&B
4 rooms, 4 pb
•
C-no/S-no/P-no/H-yes

Full breakfast
Comp. sherry
Sitting room
4 rooms with fireplaces
on National Register

Intimate country inn where great expectations are quietly met. Fireplace suites with four-poster beds. Short stroll from Cape Cod Bay. "Most photographed inn in Cape Cod."

Cobb's Cove Inn
P.O. Box 208, 02630
31 Powder Hill Rd.
508-362-9356
Evelyn Chester, Henri Jean
All year

$$$ B&B
6 rooms, 6 pb
•
C-no/S-ltd/P-no/H-no
French

Full breakfast
Dinner, comp. wine, tea
Whirlpool tubs, robes
toiletries, piano
sitting room, library

Secluded getaway inn for couples. Two fabulous honeymoon suites with water views. Located on Cape Cod's unspoiled North Shore overlooking Cape Cod Bay.

Billerica B&B, Billerica, MA

BARNSTABLE

Thomas Huckins House
P.O. Box 515, 02630
2701 Main St., Route 6A
508-362-6379
Burt & Eleanor Eddy
All year

$$$ B&B
3 rooms, 3 pb
Visa, MC
C-6+/S-yes/P-no/H-no

Full breakfast
Sitting room
fireplaces

B&B in historic 1705 house on Cape Cod's picturesque northside. Fireplaces, antiques, canopy beds, privacy and charm. Walk to ocean and village.

BASS RIVER

Captain Isaiah's House
33 Pleasant St., 02664
508-394-1739
Alden & Marge Fallows
Late June–early Sept

$ B&B
8 rooms, 2 pb
C-5+/S-yes/P-no/H-no

Continental breakfast
Sitting room
fireplaces
whale watching nearby

Charming, restored old sea captain's house in historic Bass River area. Most rooms have fireplaces. Continental breakfast with home-baked breads, coffee cake.

BOSTON

Beacon Hill B&B
27 Brimmer St., 02108
617-523-7376
Susan Butterworth
All year

$$$ B&B
3 rooms, 3 pb
●
C-yes/S-no/P-no/H-no
French

Full breakfast
Restaurants nearby
Sitting room
garage nearby

1869 Victorian townhouse. Fireplaces, riverview. Gas-lit, historically preserved downtown neighborhood. Boston Common, "Cheers" bar, Freedom Trail, Convention Center easy walk

BOSTON

The Emma James House
47 Ocean St., 02124
617-288-8867 617-282-5350
Vicki, Bob, Moo, Michael
All year

$$ B&B
6 rooms, 2 pb
●
C-yes/S-no/P-no/H-no

Continental plus
Tea and coffee
Guest breakfast kitchen
library with television
grocery stores nearby

Grand yet comfortable Victorian home. 15 minutes by subway to downtown Boston, 45-minute drive to Cape Cod. Children welcome.

BOSTON (BROOKLINE)

Beacon Inn
665 Salem St., Malden, 02148
1087 & 1750 Beacon St.
617-566-0088
Maureen Keaney
All year

$ EP
25 rooms, 6 pb
Visa, MC ●
C-yes/S-yes/P-no/H-no

Lobby fireplaces
original woodwork

Large, comfortable furnished, sunny rooms provide pleasant accommodations at a surprisingly affordable price. Near subway line.

BREWSTER

Bramble Inn
P.O. Box 807, 02631
2019 Main St., Route 6A
508-896-7644
Ruth & Cliff Manchester
April–December

$$$ B&B
8 rooms, 8 pb
●
C-12+/S-yes/P-no/H-ltd

Continental plus
Lunch, dinner
Sitting room
near beach, tennis

Romantic country inn in historic district of Cape Cod. Beach, tennis courts, and close to golf, fishing, and museums.

Captain Freeman Inn
15 Breakwater Rd., 02631
508-896-7481
Barbara & John Mulkey
All year

$$ B&B
12 rooms, 9 pb
Visa, MC, AmEx, Disc ●
C-12+/S-no/P-no/H-no

Full breakfast
Sitting room
bicycles
swimming pool

A quiet country inn in a charming old sea captain's mansion; spacious rooms, canopy beds and romantic porch. 3 luxury suites with fireplace, TV, A/C, refrigerator and jacuzzi.

Isaiah Clark House
Box 169, 02631
1187 Main St.
508-896-2223
C. DiCesare, R. Griffin
Mid-February–December

$$ B&B
5 rooms, 5 pb
Visa, MC ●
C-12+/S-ask/P-no/H-no
French, Italian

Full breakfast
Comp. tea and snacks
Library, sitting room
cable TV, records, tapes
bicycles, Rose Cottage

Charming 1780 captain's house set on five lush acres. Air conditioned rooms. Near the beach and all the Cape attractions. Warm New England hospitality.

Old Sea Pines Inn
2553 Main St., 02631
P.O. Box 1026
508-896-6114
Stephen & Michele Rowan
April–December 22

$ B&B
14 rooms, 9 pb
Visa, MC, DC, CB ●
C-9+/S-yes/P-no/H-no
Italian, German

Full breakfast
Beverage on arrival
Restaurant
sitting room w/fireplace
parlor, deck

Newly redecorated turn-of-the-century mansion furnished with antiques. Near beaches, bicycle trails, quality restaurants and shops.

BREWSTER

The Old Manse Inn
P.O. Box 839, 02631
1861 Main St.
508-896-3149
Sugar & Doug Manchester
March–December

$$ B&B
9 rooms, 9 pb
Visa, MC, AmEx ●
C-yes/S-yes/P-no/H-yes

Full breakfast
Gourmet dinner, bar
Aftn. tea, coffee
library, patio
garden, rooms with A/C

Enjoy the salt air from your room in this antique sea captain's home. Walk to Cape Cod's attractions. Dining by reservation; award-winning food.

BROOKLINE

Anthony's Town House
1085 Beacon St., 02146
617-566-3972
Barbara Anthony
All year

$ EP
14 rooms
●
C-yes/S-yes/P-no/H-no

Turn-of-the-century brownstone townhouse; spacious rooms in a Victorian atmosphere; family-operated for over 50 years; conveniently located in trolley line; 10 min. to Boston.

CAMBRIDGE

Irving House at Harvard
24 Irving St., 02138
617-547-4600
Rachael Solem
All year

$ B&B
44 rooms, 8 pb
Visa, MC, AmEx ●
C-yes/S-no/P-ask/H-ltd
Spanish, some French

Continental plus
Sitting room
library
bicycles

Friendly accommodations in the heart of Cambridge.

CAPE COD–BARNSTABLE

Ashley Manor
P.O. Box 856, 02630
3660 Old Kings Hwy(Rt 6A)
508-362-8044
Fay & Donald Bain
All year

$$$ B&B
6 rooms, 6 pb
Visa, MC, AmEx ●
C-no/S-ask/P-no/H-no

Full gourmet breakfast
Comp. wine/sherry/port
Flowers, fruit, snacks
sitting room, croquet
bicycles, tennis court

1699 mansion in the historic district; rooms and suites have antiques, fireplaces and private baths; walk to beach, village and harbor. Fresh flowers and candy in rooms.

CHATHAM

Bradford Inn & Motel
P.O. Box 750, 02633
26 Cross St.
508-945-1030 800-CHATHAM
William P. & Audrey E. Gray
All year

$$$ B&B
25 rooms, 25 pb
Visa, MC, AmEx, Disc ●
C-8+/S-yes/P-no

Full breakfast from menu
Snacks, restaurant, bar
Sitting room, library
heated swimming pool
tennis courts nearby

Located off Main St., within Chatham's Historic District. Abundant amenities: fireplaces, 4-poster canopy beds, A/C, refrigerator, cable TV. Rated 3 Diamond-AAA/3 Star-Mobile.

Captains House of Chatham
369-377 Old Harbor Rd., 02633
508-945-0127
David & Cathy Eakin
February 15–November

$$$ B&B
14 rooms, 14 pb
Visa, MC, AmEx
C-12+/S-ltd/P-no/H-no

Continental plus
Comp. afternoon tea
Sitting room
boat trips
AAA 4-Diamond (1987)

Antiques & Williamsburg wallpapers. Charming guest rooms have 4-poster beds, fireplaces. Private 2-acre estate of lawns and gardens. Quiet and elegant.

CHATHAM

Cranberry Inn at Chatham
359 Main St., 02633
508-945-9232 800-332-4667
Richard Morris, Peggy DeHan
March–mid-December

$$$ B&B
14 rooms, 14 pb
●
C-12+/S-ltd/P-no/H-no

Continental plus
Tap Room, liquor license
Rooms w/phone, TV, A/C
patio, front porch
poster beds, suites

Conveniently located in the heart of Chatham's picturesque seaside village and historic district. Relaxed and intimate atmosphere, beautifully decorated with antiques.

Cyrus Kent House Inn
63 Cross St., 02633
508-945-9104 800-338-5368
Richard T. Morris
March 15–December 15

$$$ B&B
10 rooms, 10 pb
Visa, MC, AmEx ●
C-12+/S-yes/P-no/H-no

Continental plus
Sitting room, fireplaces
Porch, deck, gardens
ample parking, phones
art & antique gallery

A sea captain's house reborn in the heart of the quaint seaside village of Chatham. Award-winning restoration. Picturesque stroll to Main St. shops, beaches and restaurants.

Moses Nickerson Inn
364 Old Harbor Rd., 02633
508-945-5859 800-628-6972
Elsie & Carl Piccola
All year

$$$ B&B
7 rooms, 7 pb
Visa, MC, AmEx ●
C-14+/S-yes/P-no/H-no

Full breakfast
Comp. wine, cheese/fruit
Sitting room near beach
fresh flowers, antiques
turndown service

Elegant sea captain's home built in 1839. Canopy beds, fireplaces, romantic and quiet. Walk to village and beaches. Glass-enclosed breakfast room overlooking garden.

Old Harbor Inn
22 Old Harbor Rd., 02633
508-945-4434
Sharon & Tom Ferguson
All year

$$$ B&B
6 rooms, 6 pb
Visa, MC, AmEx
C-14+/S-ltd/P-no/H-no

Continental plus
Restaurants nearby
Sitting room
sun room, deck
near golf, boating

English country decor. Queen/Twin beds. Delectable buffet breakfast. Walk to quaint seaside village attractions. Pleasurable memory-making awaits. AAA 3-Diamond; member ABBA.

CONCORD

The Colonial Inn
48 Monument Square, 01742
508-369-9200 800-370-9200
Jurgen Demisch

$$$ B&B/MAP
54 rooms, 54 pb
Visa, MC, AmEx, DC, Dis ●
C-yes/S-yes/P-no/H-yes
Spanish

Restaurant, bar
All meals available
Sitting room
complete fitness club -
3 mi. away–$10 fee

The National Register Colonial Inn dates back to 1716. We feature 54 distinctive rooms w/private bath, color TV & A/C. Full-service dining & entertainment. Walk to shops.

Hawthorne Inn
462 Lexington Rd., 01742
508-369-5610
Gregory Burch, Marilyn Mudry
All year

$$$ B&B
7 rooms, 7 pb
●
C-yes/S-ltd/P-no/H-no

Continental plus
Tea & coffee at check-in
Sitting room
yard, small pond, garden
bicycles

On the "Battle Road" of 1775, furnished with antiques, quilts and artwork with the accent on New England comfort and charm.

COTUIT

Salty Dog Inn
451 Main St., 02635
Cape Cod
508-428-5228
Jerry & Lynn Goldstein
All year

$ B&B
5 rooms, 1 pb
Visa, MC •
C-12+/S-no/P-no

Continental plus
Picnic tables
Parlor
bicycles
tennis nearby

Restored Victorian retaining the charm of turn-of-the-century homes. In the quiet seaside town of Cotuit, near the excitement of Hyannis and Falmouth and island boats.

CUMMINGTON

Cumworth Farm
RR 1, Box 110, 01026
Route 112
413-634-5529
Mary & Edward McColgan
All year

$$ B&B
6 rooms
C-yes/S-ltd

Full breakfast
Afternoon tea
Comp. wine, snacks
sitting room
piano, bicycles

Big, 200-year-old farmhouse; sugarhouse on premises; sheep; berries—pick your own in season. Close to cross-country skiing, hiking trails. Quiet getaway.

Windfields Farm
RR 1, Box 170, 01026
Windsor Bush Rd.
413-684-3786
Carolyn & Arnold Westwood
Exc. March & April

$$ B&B
2 rooms
C-12+/S-no/P-no/H-no

Full breakfast
Comp. wine, tea, cider
Sitting room, piano
library, fireplace
swimming pond, gardens

Secluded Berkshire Hills homestead. Family heirlooms. Equidistant to Tanglewood, Williamstown, Northampton. Hiking, skiing, swimming. Organic gardens/maple syrup/eggs/berries.

CUTTYHUNK

Allen House Inn
P.O. Box 27, Main St., 02713
508-996-9292
Nina Brodeur, Margo Solod
Memorial Day—Oct 5

$$$ B&B
15 rooms, 3 pb
Visa, MC
C-yes/S-no/P-no/H-no
French

Continental breakfast
Lunch, dinner, BYOB
Sitting room, cottages
boat rental
fishing guides

A tiny island with quiet beaches. Enjoy fresh seafood and Atlantic breezes drifting through your open windows.

DEERFIELD

Yellow Gabled House B&B
307 N. Main St., 01373
Deerfield—South
413-665-4922
Edna Julia Stahelek
All year

$$ B&B
3 rooms, 1 pb
•
C-10+

Full breakfast
Sitting room, library
Antiques, gardens
tennis nearby
carriage rides arranged

Old country house in the heart of historical and cultural area. 1.5 miles from crossroads of I-91, Rt. 116, Rt. 5 & 10. 4 miles to Historical Deerfield. Near 5-college area.

DENNIS

Isiah Hall B&B Inn
152 Whig St., 02638
508-385-9928 800-736-0160
Marie & Dick Brophy
Mid-March—October

$$ B&B
11 rooms, 10 pb
AmEx, Visa, MC •
C-7+/S-yes/P-no/H-ltd

Continental plus
Comp. tea & coffee
Library, gift shop
2 sitting rooms, gardens
innkeeping seminars

Enjoy our relaxing country ambience and hospitality in the heart of Cape Cod. Walk to beach, village, Playhouse and restaurants, from quiet residential neighborhood.

DENNISPORT

Rose Petal B&B
P.O. Box 974, 02639
152 Sea St.
508-398-8470
Dan & Gayle Kelly
All year

$ B&B
4 rooms
Visa, MC ●
C-yes/S-ltd/P-no/H-no
some French

Full breakfast
Comp. wine, snacks
Guest refrg. on sunporch
gas grill, lawn furnit.
sitting room, TV, piano

Inviting 1872 home, attractive yard, lovely accommodations, superb breakfasts with homemade pastries. In residential neighborhood, few blocks to sandy beach or Village center.

EAST ORLEANS

The Farmhouse
163 Beach Rd., 02653
508-255-6654
Dot Standish
All year

$ B&B
8 rooms, 4 pb
Visa, MC
C-6+/S-yes/P-no/H-no

Continental plus
Sitting room
oceanview deck
picnic tables

19th-century farmhouse beautifully restored. Enjoy a unique blend of country life in a seashore setting. Short walk to Nauset Beach, breakfast on deck with ocean view.

Nauset House Inn
P.O. Box 774, 02643
143 Beach Rd.
508-255-2195
D & L Johnson, C & J Vessella
April–October

$$ EP
14 rooms, 8 pb
Visa, MC
C-12+/S-ltd/P-no/H-no

Full breakfast $
Wine & hors d'oeuvres
Commons room
piano, conservatory
dining room

Intimate 1810 inn, unique turn-of-the-century conservatory, warm ambience, a short walk to the sea.

The Parsonage
P.O. Box 1501, 02643
202 Main St.
508-255-8217
Ian & Elizabeth Browne
All year

$$ B&B
7 rooms, 7 pb
Visa, MC ●
C-6+/S-no/P-no/H-no

Continental plus
Guest refrigerator
Appetizers, parlor
piano, dining room
patio

Experience a 1770 antique-furnished Cape home. Savor breakfast on the patio, walk to restaurants. Biking, golfing, tennis, fishing, Nauset beach nearby. Warm, friendly hosts.

Ship's Knees Inn
P.O. Box 756, 02643
186 Beach Rd.
508-255-1312
Nancy & Carl Wideberg
All year

$ B&B
25 rooms, 11 pb
●
C-12+/S-yes/P-no/H-no

Continental breakfast
Sitting room
swimming pool
tennis courts

A restored sea captain's house; surrounded by the charm of yesterday while offering the convenience of today.

EAST SANDWICH

Wingscorton Farm Inn
Olde Kings Hwy, Rt. 6A, 02537
11 Wing Blvd.
508-888-0534
All year

$$$ B&B
4 rooms, 4 pb
Visa, MC, AmEx ●
C-yes/S-yes/P-yes/H-yes

Full breakfast
Picnic basket lunch
Dinner, comp. wine
library, bicycles
private ocean beach

A special retreat for couples seeking a private, intimate getaway. Eclectic mix of antiquity and modern conveniences in a setting of a working New England farm. Private beach.

The Penny House, Eastham–North, MA

EASTHAM

The Over Look Inn	$$$ B&B	Full breakfast
P.O. Box 771, 02642	8 rooms, 8 pb	Dinner occasional
3085 County Rd., Route 6	●	Afternoon tea, library
508-255-1886 800-356-1121	C-12+/S-ltd/P-no/H-ask	sitting room, bicycles
The Aitchison Family		tours, rentals, packages
All year		

Victorian country inn within walking distance of Cape Cod National Seashore. Bike paths & nature trails. Delicious breakfast; tranquil wooded setting. Cottage available.

The Whalewalk Inn	$$$ EP/B&B	Full gourmet breakfast
220 Bridge Rd., 02642	12 rooms, 12 pb	Comp. hors d'ouevres
508-255-0617	●	Bar, sitting room, patio
Carolyn & Richard Smith	C-12+/S-yes/P-no/H-no	fireplaces, lawn games
April–November		rooms, suites, cottage

Restored 1830s whaling master's home. Elegance and hospitality. Uniquely decorated. Located on quiet road near bay and ocean. Minutes to beaches, bike trails, Orleans Village.

EASTHAM–NORTH

Penny House Inn	$$ B&B	Full breakfast
P.O. Box 238, 02651	12 rooms, 12 pb	Comp. wine, aftn. tea
4885 County Rd., Rte 6	Visa, MC ●	Sitting room
508-255-6632	C-no/S-yes/P-no/H-no	library, fireplace
Bill & Margaret Keith	French	gathering place
All year		

Experience the original Cape Cod charm and serenity of this 1751 bow roof rambling Cape conveniently located near all National Seashore Park activities.

EDGARTOWN

The Arbor	$$$ B&B	Continental breakfast
P.O. Box 1228, 02539	10 rooms, 8 pb	Comp. wine, beverages
222 Upper Main St.	Visa, MC ●	Parlor, fresh flowers
508-627-8137	C-12+/S-ask/P-no/H-no	garden, courtyard
Peggy Hall		lovely cottage available
May–October		

Turn-of-the-century home in historic Edgartown. Walk to town & harbor. Rooms are delightfully and typically New England. Enchanting one-bedroom cottage available by the week.

EDGARTOWN

Captain Dexter House
P.O. Box 2798, 02539
35 Pease's Point Way
508-627-7289
Russ Wilson, Marchel Kowalski
All year

$$$ B&B
11 rooms, 11 pb
Visa, MC, AmEx ●
C-12+/S-ltd/P-no/H-no

Continental plus
Comp. wine
Hot cider (winter)
lemonade (warm weather)
sitting room

Lovely 1840s home; romantic antique-filled guest rooms with canopied beds and working fireplaces. Expansive landscaped gardens. Near the harbor, shops and restaurants.

The Chadwick Inn
P.O. Box 1035, 02539
67 Winter St.
508-627-4435 508-627-5656
Peter & Jurate Antioco
All year

$$ B&B
21 rooms, 21 pb
Visa, MC, AmEx ●
C-8+/S-yes/P-no/H-yes
French

Continental plus
Comp. wine
Sitting room
library

In stately Edgartown Historic District, 1840s Greek Revival buildings, gardens, brick courtyard. Rooms furnished with antiques, canopy beds, fireplaces and terraces.

Colonial Inn of Marthas
P.O. Box 68, 02539
38 N. Water St.
508-627-4711 800-627-5701
Linda Malcouronne
April–December

$$$ B&B
Visa, MC, AmEx ●
C-yes/S-yes/P-no/H-yes
Portuguese

Continental plus
Restaurant, bar
Sitting room, library
near tennis, riding
golf, sailing, fishing

Overlooking the harbor, this charming and lovingly refurbished inn offers affordable luxury. Steps away from museums, galleries, shops, beach. We invite you to be our guests!

Edgartown Inn
P.O. Box 1211, 02539
56 N. Water St.
508-627-4794
Susanne Chlastawa-Faraca
April–October

$$$ EP
22 rooms, 13 pb
C-yes/S-yes
French

Full breakfast $

192 year old historic inn where Nathaniel Hawthorne, Daniel Webster & John Kennedy stayed. Serving homemade cakes and breads for breakfast in the garden.

Governor Bradford Inn
128 Main Street, 02539
508-627-9510
Kimberley & Bill Johnson
All year

$$ B&B
16 rooms, 16 pb
Visa, MC, AmEx, DC ●
C-no/S-yes/P-no/H-yes

Continental breakfast
Full breakfast $
Comp. wine, aftn. tea
sitting room
library

A gracefully restored whaling captain's home in the seaport village of Edgartown, on the island of Martha's Vineyard. Spacious rooms have king-size poster or brass beds.

Point Way Inn
P.O. Box 128, 02539
104 Main St.
508-627-8633
Ben & Linda Smith
All year

$$$ B&B
15 rooms, 15 pb
Visa, MC, AmEx ●
C-yes/S-yes/H-ltd

Continental plus
Comp. wine/lemonade/tea
Honor bar, snacks
sitting room, library
croquet, gardens, gazebo

Located near center of town; 11 rooms with working fireplaces. Inn is a former whaling captain's mansion. A complimentary courtesy car is available to guests.

EDGARTOWN

Shiverick Inn	$$$ B&B	Continental plus
P.O. Box 640, 02539	10 rooms, 10 pb	Comp. tea or coffee
Peases Point Wy—Pent Ln.	Visa, MC, AmEx ●	Sitting room, library
508-627-3797	S-ltd	dining room, parlor
Claire & Juan del Real		formal garden, bicycles
All year		

Exquisitely restored 19th-century mansion offering one-of-a-kind suites and guest rooms with fireplaces, library, formal parlor and garden.

The Victorian Inn	$$ B&B	Full breakfast (in-seas)
P.O. Box 947, 02539	14 rooms, 14 pb	Comp. tea & sherry
24 South Water St.	Visa, AmEx	Afternoon refreshments
508-627-4784	C-yes/S-yes/P-yes/H-no	library, sitting room
Katherine Appert	Spanish, French	eve. turn-down service
All year		

Restored Whaling Captains's Mansion. Antique filled rooms, fresh flowers, night service, harbor views. Near beaches, shops & harbor. Noteworthy service.

ESSEX

George Fuller House	$$ B&B	Full breakfast
148 Main St., 01929	5 rooms, 5 pb	Comp. coffee, tea
508-768-7766	Visa, MC, AmEx ●	Sitting room, fireplaces
Cindy & Bob Cameron	C-yes/S-ltd/P-no/H-no	learn to sail/charter in
All year		30-foot yacht (midweek)

Federalist-style with antique furnishings, four fireplaces, color TV, marsh view. Located near antique shops and seafood restaurants. 30-foot yacht for sailing/charters.

FAIRHAVEN

Edgewater B&B	$$ B&B	Continental breakfast
2 Oxford St., 02719	5 rooms, 5 pb	Comp. tea, coffee
508-997-5512	●	Sitting room
Kathy Reed	C-4+/S-yes/P-no/H-no	library
All year		spacious lawns

Gracious waterfront mansion overlooking Bedford Harbor. Spacious accommodations; 2 suites w/fireplaces. 5 min. from I-195. Close to historic areas, beaches, factory outlets.

FALMOUTH

Captain Tom Lawrence House	$$ B&B	Full gourmet breakfast
	6 rooms, 6 pb	Comp. tea
75 Locust St., 02540	Visa, MC	Sitting room, library
508-540-1445	C-12+/S-yes/P-no/H-no	piano, TV
Barbara Sabo-Feller	German	porch, large yard
All year		

Newly redecorated Victorian captain's home close to village center, beaches, golf and island ferries. Quiet atmosphere. Breakfast with homemade bread from organic grain.

Mostly Hall B&B Inn	$$$ B&B	Full gourmet breakfast
27 Main St., 02540	6 rooms, 6 pb	Coffee, tea, sherry
508-548-3786	C-16+/S-no/P-no/H-no	Sitting room, piano
Caroline & Jim Lloyd	German	gazebo, veranda, porch
Mid Feb—mid Jan		bicycles, gardens

Falmouth's first summer residence built in southern style for New Orleans bride. Spacious corner rooms. Queen-sized four-poster canopy beds. Near beaches, shops, ferries.

FALMOUTH

The Palmer House Inn
81 Palmer Ave., 02540
508-548-1230 800-472-2632
Ken & Joanne Baker
All year

$$$ B&B
8 rooms, 8 pb
Visa, MC, AmEx •
C-12+/S-no/P-no/H-no

Full gourmet breakfast
Afternoon tea & snacks
Sitting room, piano, TV
bicycles, open porches
tennis & golf nearby

Step back in time to Grandmother's day in this charming Victorian. Antiques; gourmet breakfast; bicycles; near shops, beaches, restaurants, island ferries. Let us pamper you.

Peacock's Inn on the Sound
P.O. Box 201, 02540
508-457-9666
Bud & Phyllis Peacock
All year

$$$ B&B
10 rooms, 10 pb
Visa, MC •
C-12+/S-ltd/P-no/H-no

Full gourmet breakfast
Snacks, sitting room
Library, cable TV, bikes
country-style dining rm.
golf, tennis, ferry

Oceanfront B&B, country cottage charm, large spacious rooms with spectacular ocean views, fireplaces, providing rest and relaxation or endless activities. Steps away to beach.

Village Green Inn
40 W. Main St., 02540
508-548-5621
Linda & Don Long
All year

$$ B&B
5 rooms, 5 pb
C-16+/S-no/P-no/H-no

Full gourmet breakfast
Seasonal beverages
Comp. wine, guest parlor
fireplaces, open porches
piano, cable TV, bikes

Gracious old Victorian ideally located on Falmouth's historic green. Enjoy 19th-century charm and warm hospitality in lovely spacious rooms. Delightful breakfast served.

FALMOUTH – CAPE COD

Grafton Inn
261 Grand Ave. S., 02540
508-540-8688 FAX:540-1861
Liz & Rudy Cvitan
April–November

$$$ B&B
11 rooms, 9 pb
Visa, MC •
C-16+/S-no/P-no/H-yes
Croatian

Full breakfast
Comp. wine & cheese
Sitting room
bicycles, cottage
porch

Oceanside—on the beach; panoramic view; delectable croissants from France. Convenient to ferry, shops, restaurants. Gallery throughout.

GREAT BARRINGTON

Baldwin Hill Farm B&B
RD 3, Box 125, 01230
Baldwin Hill Rd, Egremont
413-528-4092
Richard & Priscilla Burdsall
All year

$$ B&B
4 rooms, 1 pb
Visa, MC •
C-10+/S-no/P-no/H-no

Full country breakfast
Afternoon tea, snacks
2 sitting rooms, library
screened porch, pool
fireplace, X-C skiing

Spacious Victorian farmhouse. 360 degree views of mountains. 500 acres for nature hikes. Restaurants nearby. Hiking, tennis, golf, boating, fishing. Friendly and elegant.

Round Hill Farm
17 Round Hill Rd., 01230
413-528-3366
Thomas & Margaret Whitfield
All year

$$ B&B
8 rooms, 3 pb
Visa, MC, AmEx •
C-16+/S-no/P-ltd/H-no
French

Full breakfast
Apartments,300-acre farm
Parlor, library
swimming hole, porches
trout stream, X-C skiing

A haven for nonsmokers; classic New England hilltop guest house on dirt road; porches; privacy; the Berkshire Hills year-round. Jogging, bicycling, X-C skiing from the door.

Seekonk Pines, Great Barrington, MA

GREAT BARRINGTON

Seekonk Pines Inn
142 Seekonk Cross Rd., 01230
413-528-4192
Linda & Christian Best
All year

$$ B&B
6 rooms, 4½ pb
C-yes/S-no/P-no/H-no
German

Full breakfast
Hot cider, beverages
Sitting room, bicycles
swimming pool, piano
kitchenette for guests

Country estate; close to Tanglewood, skiing, hiking. Hosts are artists/singers. Original artwork, homemade jams, produce for sale. Low-fat and low-cholesterol diets. Peaceful.

Turning Point Inn
RD 2 Box 140, 01230
3 Lake Buel Rd.
413-528-4777
Shirley, Irving & Jamie Yost
All year

$$$ B&B
6 rooms, 1 pb
MC, Visa
C-yes/S-no/P-no/H-no

Full breakfast
Comp. tea, coffee, juice
4-room cottage with bath
piano, fireplaces
bicycles, cottage

We offer a natural environment: whole grain vegetarian breakfast; no smoking; hiking, skiing; comfort in 18th-century inn near Tanglewood, next to ski slopes.

HARWICH PORT

Bayberry Shores
255 Lower County Rd., 02646
508-432-0337 800-272-4343
The Van Gelders, Mary Clayton
All year

$$ B&B
3 rooms, 3 pb
Visa, MC, AmEx ●
C-yes/S-yes/H-ltd

Continental plus
Cable TVs, refrigerators
Fireplaced common room
brick terrace with BBQ
free tennis & pool near

Brickfront traditional home only 350 yards from beach. Spacious rooms with twin or king beds, wicker and country florals. Babysitting available. Efficiency with fireplace.

HARWICH PORT ──────────────────────────

Harbor Breeze	$$ B&B	Continental plus
326 Lower County Rd., 02646	8 rooms, 8 pb	Refrigerators, cable TVs
508-432-0337 800-272-4343	Visa, MC, AmEx ●	Common area
David & Kathleen Van Gelder	C-yes/S-yes/P-ask/H-ltd	w/microwave
March–November		picnic area, free tennis
		pool, walk to beach

Walk to harbor, beach, shops, dining. Guest rooms each with private entrance around a garden courtyard–country casual atmosphere perfect for families.

Harbor Walk Guest House	$ B&B	Continental plus
6 Freeman St., 02646	6 rooms, 4 pb	Canopy beds
508-432-1675	●	library, sitting room
Preston & Marilyn Barry	C-ltd/S-no/P-ltd/H-no	tennis & ocean nearby
May–October	some French	

Victorian charmer, featuring antiques, homemade quilts and queen canopy beds. Walk to beach and most photographed harbor on Cape Cod. Summer sports paradise.

Inn on Bank Street	$$ B&B	Continental plus
88 Bank St., 02646	6 rooms, 6 pb	Comp. tea, coffee, juice
508-432-3206	Visa, AmEx ●	Sitting room, fireplace
Arky & Janet Silverio	C-ltd/S-ltd/P-no/H-yes	TV, piano, library
April–mid November	Italian, Spanish	sun porch

The right place to get away to. Peaceful, private, comfortable and friendly. Walk to ocean beach, shops, restaurants and movie theater.

HARWICH PORT, CAPE COD ──────────────────────

Dunscroft By-the-Sea	$$$ B&B	Full breakfast
24 Pilgrim Rd., 02646	8 rooms, 8 pb	Comp. wine, juices
508-432-0810 800-432-4345	●	Library, piano
Alyce & Wally Cunningham	C-12+/S-ltd/P-no/H-no	sun porch, brick terrace
All year		mile-long private beach

Located 300 feet from a beautiful private beach on Nantucket Sound; walk to restaurant and shops. Exclusive residential area. Honeymoon cottage, romance package available.

HYANNIS ──────────────────────────

Elegance By-The-Sea	$$ B&B	Full breakfast
162 Sea St., 02601	6 rooms, 6 pb	Afternoon tea avail.
508-775-3595	Visa, MC, AmEx ●	Queen-size canopy beds
Clark & Mary Boydston	C-no/S-no/P-no/H-no	sitting room
All year	French	bicycle rentals

Victorian captain's home offers hearty New England breakfast and romantic antique-furnished guest rooms. Walk to beach, golf or boats to Nantucket or Martha's Vineyard.

Inn on Sea Street	$$ B&B	Full breakfast
358 Sea St., 02601	5 rooms, 3 pb	Fruit & cheese
508-775-8030	Visa, MC, AmEx	Sitting room
Lois Nelson, J.B. Whitehead	C-16+/S-yes/P-no/H-no	library
April–November		

Elegant Victorian inn, steps from the beach and Kennedy Compound. Antiques, canopy beds, fireplace, home-baked delights. Full gourmet breakfast, fruit and cheese.

HYANNIS

Sea Breeze Inn
397 Sea St., 02601
508-771-7213
Patricia Battle
All year

$ B&B
14 rooms, 12 pb
•
C-yes/S-yes/P-no/H-no

Continental breakfast
Kitchen privileges
Sitting room
bicycles
cable TV

Quaint, nautical atmosphere, private setting, beach & Hyannisport Harbor 900 ft., near center of Hyannis. All Cape Cod towns & points of interest within 1 hour.

LEE

Haus Andreas
RR1, Box 435, 01238
Stockbridge Rd.
413-243-3298
Gerhard & Lilliane Schmid
All year

$$ B&B
7 rooms, 5 pb
Visa, MC
C-10+/S-yes/P-no/H-no
French, German

Continental plus
Guest pantry, library
Heated pool, tennis
bicycles, lawn sports
sitting room, piano

Historic revolutionary setting, heated pool, golf, tennis, luxury, comfort, local fine restaurants. Complimentary breakfast. Relax in Old World charm.

LENOX

Birchwood Inn
P.O. Box 2020, 01240
7 Hubbard St.
413-637-2600
Joan, Dick & Dan Toner
All year

$$ B&B
12 rooms, 10 pb
Visa, MC •
C-8+/S-ltd/P-no/H-ltd

Full breakfast
Comp. tea, wine & cheese
Sitting room, library
6 fireplaces
lake nearby

This 200 year old colonial is on the historic register. Beautifully appointed, fireplaces, full breakfast. Guided hiking/biking tours. Weekend dinner packages

Blantyre
P.O. Box 995, Rt. 20, 01240
413-637-3556 413-298-3806
Ann Fitzpatrick
Mid May—early November

$$$ B&B
23 rooms, 23 pb
Visa, MC, AmEx, DC •
C-no/S-yes/P-no/H-yes
French, German

Continental plus
Restaurant, bar
Comp. wine, snacks
tennis, pool, hot tubs
croquet, bikes, hiking

A gracious country house hotel surrounded by 85 acres of grounds. The hotel has a European atmosphere and exceptional cuisine.

Brook Farm Inn
15 Hawthorne St., 01240
413-637-3013
Bob & Betty Jacob
All year

$$ B&B
12 rooms, 12 pb
Visa, MC •
C-15+/S-no/P-no/H-no

Continental plus
Comp. tea with scones
Library, sitting room
swimming pool, garden

100-year-old-inn with the grace of its Victorian past and comfort of the present. There is poetry here: 650 volumes and 60 poets on tape with players available.

Cornell Inn
197 Main St., 01240
413-637-0562
David Rolland
All year

$$ B&B
9 rooms, 9 pb
Visa, MC •
C-12+/S-yes/P-no/H-no

Continental plus
Comp. wine, snacks
Afternoon tea, bar
sitting room

We have cross-country skiing and hiking in our backyard; luxury suites with kitchens, jacuzzis, fireplaces. Special weekend packages.

LENOX ——————————————————————————————

Forty-Four St. Ann's Ave. | $$$ B&B | Continental plus
P.O. Box 718, 01240 | 3 rooms, 3 pb | Sitting room
44 St. Ann's Ave. | C-no/S-yes/P-no/H-no | porches—1 screened
617-637-3381 | French | spacious yard w/flowers
Barbara & Milton Kolodkin
Memorial Day—Labor Day

Close to Tanglewood (a village). Air-conditioned rooms; elegant breakfasts; quiet location; professional, knowledgeable hosts who help you enjoy the Berkshires.

The Gables Inn | $$ B&B | Continental plus
103 Walker St., 01240 | 17 rooms, 17 pb | Comp. wine
413-637-3416 | Visa, MC, AmEx | Sitting room, library
Mary & Frank Newton | C-13+/S-yes/P-no/H-no | tennis courts
All year | Spanish | swimming pool

Built in 1885, this gracious "cottage" was the home of Edith Wharton at the turn of the century. Lovingly furnished in period style.

Garden Gables Inn | $$ B&B | Continental plus
P.O. Box 52, 01240 | 12 rooms, 12 pb | Comp. port and sherry
141 Main St. | Visa, MC | Library, bicycles, pool
413-637-0193 | C-12+/S-ltd/P-no/H-no | whirlpool, tennis court
Mario & Lynn Mekinda | German, French | sitting room
All year

This 220-year-old gabled inn is located in the center of Lenox on four wooded acres. Furnished with antiques. One mile to Tanglewood and many other attractions.

Gateways Inn | $$$ B&B | Continental plus
71 Walker St., 01240 | 8 rooms, 8 pb | Dinner, Restaurant, bar
413-637-2532 | Visa, MC, AmEx, DC | Sitting room
Vito Perulli, Brenda Mayberry | C-12+/S-no/P-no/H-no | telephones in room
All year | French, German, Italian | tennis, pool nearby

Chef-owned Gateways Inn is Berkshire's only four-star restaurant. Elegant, luxurious townhouse in heart of Lenox.

Rookwood Inn | $$ B&B | Continental plus buffet
P.O. Box 1717, 01240 | 16 rooms, 16 pb | Afternoon tea & cakes
19 Old Stockbridge Rd. | MC, AmEx ● | Sitting room
413-637-9750 | C-yes/S-no/P-no/H-no | library, verandas
Tom & Betsy Sherman | | fireplaces, lawn
All year

Our elegant, country Victorian Painted Lady offers a relaxing stay, wonderful beds, antique filled rooms, and unique buffet breakfast. Quiet, near dining, shopping, etc.

Underledge Inn | $$ B&B | Continental plus
76 Cliffwood St., 01240 | 9 rooms, 9 pb | Sitting room
413-637-0236 | Visa, MC | library, piano
Marcie & Cheryl Lanoue | C-10+/S-ltd/P-no/H-no | 5 fireplaces
May—November

Underledge offers elegance and country charm. Large parlour bedrooms with fireplaces, decorated with an air of bygone days. Breakfast in unique solarium.

Rookwood Inn, Lenox, MA

LENOX

Village Inn
P.O. Box 1810, 01240
16 Church St.
413-637-0020 800-253-0917
Clifford Rudisill, Ray Wilson
All year

$
31 rooms, 29 pb
Visa, MC, AmEx, Diners ●
C-6+/S-yes/P-no/H-yes
Spanish, French, German

Restaurant, bar
Jacuzzi, frplc. in suite
Sitting room, library
lakes, mountain trails
parks & museums nearby

Historic 1771 inn reflecting charm and warmth of colonial New England. Rooms individually furnished in country antiques. Afternoon tea with homemade scones. American cuisine.

Walker House Inn
74 Walker St., 01240
413-637-1271
Richard & Peggy Houdek
All year

$$ B&B
8 rooms, 8 pb
C-8+/S-no/P-ask/H-ltd
Spanish, French

Continental plus
Comp. wine, aftn. tea
Sitting room, piano
library video theatre
opera/film wkends, bikes

We make our guests feel like special pampered friends. Lovely country atmosphere on 3 acres. Walk to shops, restaurants. 100-inch video screen where films and plays are shown.

Whistler's Inn
5 Greenwood St., 01240
413-637-0975
Richard & Joan Mears
All year

$$$ B&B
11 rooms, 11 pb
Visa, MC, AmEx ●
C-no/S-no/P-no/H-no
Spanish, Polish, French

Full breakfast
Comp. sherry, tea/coffee
Sitting room, piano
library, bicycles
air conditioned

Elegant, antique-filled Tudor mansion; cozy library and French salon with Steinway piano. Home-baked breads and muffins. Old World charm. Lake nearby.

LEXINGTON

Halewood House
2 Larchmont Lane, 02173
617-862-5404
Carol Halewood
All year

$$ B&B
2 rooms
●
C-6+/S-no/P-no/H-no

Continental plus
Snacks
Sitting room
near tennis, swimming,
restaurants, shopping

Well-decoazted rooms, large modern bath. Excellent food. New England charm and architecture. Walking distance to historic sights. Near route 95.

LOWELL

Sherman-Berry House
163 Dartmouth St., 01851
508-459-4760 FAX:459-4760
Susan Scott, David Strohmeyer
All year

$$ B&B
2 rooms
●
C-yes/S-no/P-no/H-no

Full breakfast
Lemonade, treats
Sitting room, library
bikes, computer, copier
fax

Step back into 1893—Queen Anne Victorian, stained glass, antiques, player piano and tandem bicycle. Near Lowell Historical Park. Easy access to Boston.

MARBLEHEAD

Harborside House
23 Gregory St., 01945
617-631-1032
Susan Blake
All year

$$ B&B
2 rooms
C-10+/S-no/P-ltd/H-no

Continental plus
Bedside Harbor Sweets
Living room w/fireplace
deck overlooking harbor
period dining room

c. 1850 colonial home offers antiques & modern amenities. Homemade baked goods. Sunny breakfast porch overlooks harbor. Close to historic sites, shops, beaches & restaurants.

Spray Cliff on the Ocean
25 Spray Ave., 01945
508-744-8924 800-626-1530
Richard & Diane Pabich
All year

$$$ B&B
5 rooms, 5 pb
Visa, MC, AmEx, DC ●
C-yes/S-no/P-no/H-no

Continental plus
Comp. wine, sherry
Sitting room, gardens
walk to beach
suite w/ fireplace, deck

English Tudor mansion set high above the Atlantic. Views extend forever. Elegant bedrooms, cozy relaxed atmosphere; garden terrace. Come unwind.

MARTHA'S VINEYARD

Ashley Inn
P.O. Box 650, Edgartown, 02539
129 Main St., Edgartown
508-627-9655
Jude Cortese, Fred Hurley
All year

$$$ B&B
10 rooms, 8 pb
Visa, MC, AmEx ●
C-10+/S-yes/P-no/H-no

Continental breakfast
Sitting room
tea room, grounds
badminton, hammock

Attractive 1800s sea captain's home with country charm, decorated with period antiques, brass and wicker. A leisurely stroll to shops, beaches, fine foods.

The Bayberry
P.O. Box 654, 02575
Old Courthouse, W.Tisbury
508-693-1984
Rosalie Powell
All year

$$$ B&B
5 rooms, 3 pb
Visa, MC ●
C-12+/S-no/P-no/H-ltd

Full gourmet breakfast
Comp. tea, wine
Sitting room, gardens
piano, croquet, hammock
beach pass and towels

Gourmet breakfast served before fireplace in charming country home on historic Martha's Vineyard Island. Antique furnishings, canopy beds, warm friendly atmosphere.

MARTHA'S VINEYARD

Thorncroft Inn
P.O. Box 278, 02568
278 Main St.
508-693-3333
Karl & Lynn Buder
All year

$$$ B&B
19 rooms, 19 pb
●
C-12+/S-ltd/P-no/H-no

Full breakfast
Afternoon tea
Evening turndown service
morning paper at door
3.5 acres of grounds

Romantic, noncommercial atmosphere; fine antiques; private baths; fireplaces; central air-conditioning; luxury suites with jacuzzi; balconies; canopied four-poster beds.

NANTUCKET

Brant Point Inn
6 N. Beach St., 02554
508-228-5442
Peter & Thea Kaizer
All year

$$$ B&B
8 rooms, 8 pb
Visa, MC, AmEx
C-3+/S-yes

Continental breakfast
Sitting room, porch
Belgium fireplace
fishing charters arrang.

Ideally located, this post & beam inn is minutes from Nantucket's finest beaches & the historic town. All modern amenities to assure a relaxing & comfortable visit. Welcome!

Centerboard Guest House
P.O. Box 456, 02554
8 Chester St.
508-228-9696
R. Reid, M., L. Wasserman
All year

$$$ B&B
7 rooms, 7 pb
Visa, MC, AmEx ●
C-12+/S-no/P-no/H-no

Continental plus
Comp. refreshments
Beach towels
library, sitting room
suite, jacuzzi

A Victorian guest house of quiet country elegance; lovingly renovated and restored in 1986-87; located in historic district, Nantucket Center; beaches nearby.

The Century House
10 Cliff Rd., 02554
508-228-0530
Gerry Connick & Jean Heron
All year

$$ B&B
9 rooms, 9 pb
●
C-ask/S-ltd/P-no/H-no
Fr, Rus, Ger, Jap, Chi

Continental plus
Happy hour setups
Afternoon tea, munchies
sitting room, veranda
H. Miller player piano

Historic sea captain's B&B inn serving Nantucket travelers since the mid-1800s; minutes to beaches, restaurants, galleries, shops; antique appointments, Laura Ashley decor.

Corner House
P.O. Box 1828, 02554
49 Centre St.
508-228-1530
John & Sandy Knox-Johnston
April 15–December

$$ B&B
14 rooms, 14 pb
Visa, MC ●
C-8+/S-ltd/P-no/H-ltd
French, German

Continental plus
Afternoon tea
Sitting rooms, conf. fac
screen porch w/wicker
secluded garden terrace

Especially charming and attractive antique-furnished 18th-century B&B inn in the heart of Nantucket's historic district, near wharf, shops, museums, beaches.

Eighteen Gardner St. Inn
18 Gardner St., 02554
508-228-1155
Roger & Mary Schmidt
April–October 15

$$ B&B
10 rooms, 10 pb
●
C-yes/S-yes/P-no/H-no

Continental breakfast
Complimentary wine
Sitting room

Restored 1835 whaling captain's home. Queen-sized canopy beds; antiques; fireplaces. Original floor boards & period wallpapers. "Casual elegance & attentive service."

NANTUCKET

La Petite Maison
132 Main St., 02554
508-228-9242
Holli Martin
April 15–January 15

$$ B&B
4 rooms, 1 pb
MC, Visa
C-8+/S-yes/H-ltd
French

Continental plus
Afternoon tea
Sitting room
dining room w/fireplace

Charming, antique-furnished European-style guest house in a quiet town location. Continental breakfast served on the sun porch; peaceful garden; friendly atmosphere.

Martin's Guest House
61 Centre Street, 02554
508-228-0678
Channing & Ceci Moore
All year

$$$ B&B
13 rooms, 9 pb
Visa, MC, AmEx
C-yes/S-yes/P-no/H-no

Continental plus
Complimentary sherry
Sitting room

Stately 1803 Mariner's home in Nantucket's historic district. Four-poster canopy beds, 13 airy rooms. Spacious living room, dining room, verandah.

Quaker House Inn & Rest.
5 Chestnut St., 02554
508-228-0400 508-228-9156
Caroline & Bob Taylor
Memorial Day–September

$$$ EP
9 rooms, 9 pb
Visa, MC ●
C-ltd/S-ltd/P-no/H-no

Full breakfast $
Restaurant
Dinner, beer, wine
sitting room

Located in the heart of Nantucket's historic district. Guest rooms have private baths, queen-size beds, and decorated in 19th-century antiques. Charming candlelit dinners.

Stumble Inne
109 Orange St., 02554
508-228-4482
The Condon Family
All year

$$$ B&B
13 rooms, 10 pb
Visa, MC, AmEx ●
C-yes/S-yes/P-no/H-no

Continental plus
Afternoon tea
Sitting room
spacious grounds
parking

Nantucket's friendliest bed & breakfast. Delightful Laura Ashley decor. Hearty continental breakfast in our gracious dining room. Walk to Nantucket activities and sites.

The Woodbox Inn
29 Fair St., 02554
508-228-0587
Dexter Tutein
June–mid-October

$$$ EP
9 rooms, 9 pb
C-yes/S-yes/P-ltd/H-yes
French, German

Full breakfast $
Dinner
Sitting room
fireplaces

"Probably the best place to stay on Nantucket." Oldest inn (1709) in Nantucket, furnished with period antiques. Breakfast 8:30-10:30; dinner—continental cuisine—7 and 9 p.m.

NANTUCKET ISLAND

Cobblestone Inn
5 Ash St., 02554
508-228-1987
Robin Hammer-Yankow
All year

$$ B&B
5 rooms, 5 pb
●

Continental plus
Living room
sun porch, yard

Circa 1725 home on a quiet cobblestoned street in Nantucket's historic district. Relax in our yard/sun porch/living room. Walk to shops, museums, restaurants. Open year-round.

NEW MARLBOROUGH

The Old Inn on the Green
Star Route 70, Route 57, 01230
413-229-3131 800-752-1896
B. Wagstaff & L. Miller
All year

$$$ B&B
16 rooms, 12 pb
Visa, MC ●
C-yes/S-yes/P-no/H-yes
French, German, Span-ltd

Continental plus
Restaurant, bar
Dinner (Fri-Sun)
five public rooms
nearby whirlpools

1760 colonial inn on historic landmark register. 3 public rooms downstairs. Parlor, dining room, old tavern. Inn furnished with antiques.

NEWBURYPORT

The Windsor House
38 Federal St., 01950
508-462-3778
Judith & John Harris
All year

$$$ B&B/MAP
6 rooms, 3 pb
Visa, MC ●
C-yes/S-yes/P-yes/H-no

Full English breakfast
Aftn. tea, evening meal
Common rooms, organ

Federalist mansion/ship's chandlery in restored historic seaport furnished in period antiques; explore our shops, museums, beaches and wildlife refuge.

NEWTON

Sage and Thyme B&B
P.O. Box 91, 02160
65 Kirkstall Rd.
617-332-0695
Edgar & Hertha Klugman
All year

$$ B&B
2 rooms
●
C-yes/S-no/P-no/H-no
Ger., Ital., Sp., Fr.

Full breakfast
Comp. coffee, juice
A/C in rooms

Classic colonial in a quiet neighborhood. Downtown Boston only 5 miles away. Outstanding breakfasts and congenial hosts and cats.

NORTHAMPTON

The Knoll
230 N. Main St., 01060
413-584-8164
Leona (Lee) Lesko
All year

$ B&B
3 rooms
C-no/S-no/P-no/H-no

Full breakfast

Large Tudor house in quiet rural setting on 16 acres. Near 5 colleges: Smith, Amherst, Mt. Holyoke, University of Massachusetts, Hampshire.

NORTHFIELD

Northfield Country House
P.O. Box 617, 01360
School St.
413-498-2692
Andrea Dale
All year

$$ B&B
7 rooms
C-10+/S-yes/P-no/H-no

Full gourmet breakfast
Dinner (by reservation)
Sitting room, piano
X-C skiing, tennis court
swimming pool

English manor house softened by firelight and flowers. Personally decorated bed chambers with antiques. 3 rooms with romantic fireplaces. Center of New England activities.

OAK BLUFFS

The Oak House
P.O. Box 299CG, 02557
Seaview & Peguot Aves.
508-693-4187
Betsi Convery-Luce
May—mid-October

$$$ B&B
10 rooms, 10 pb
Visa, MC ●
C-10+/S-yes/P-no/H-no

Continental breakfast
Afternoon tea
Sitting room, piano
sun porch, near beach
bicycles

Romantic Victorian inn on the beach. Richly restored 1872 Governor's home. Oak paneling, wide porches, balconies, leaded windows, water views. Walk to ferry, town, sights.

PETERSHAM

Winterwood at Petersham
P.O. Box 176, 01366
North Main Street
508-724-8885
Jean & Robert Day
All year

$$$ B&B
5 rooms, 5 pb
Visa, MC, AmEx •
C-yes/S-yes/P-no/H-no

Continental plus
Restaurant
Bar service
sitting room, library
fireplaces

Sixteen-room Greek revival mansion—built as private summer home—on National Register of Historic Homes. Beautifully appointed and professionally decorated.

PLAINFIELD

Rolling Meadow Farm
H.C. 15A Pleasant St., 01070
415-634-2166
Marie Grull
All year

$$ B&B
3 rooms, 1 pb
C-yes/S-no/P-no/H-no
German

Full breakfast
Boxed lunches available
Family room, decks
near shopping, skiing
flea markets & festivals

Enjoy spacious, comfortable rooms with balconies & European hospitality in our chalet in the Berkshire Hills. Special breakfasts.

PLYMOUTH

Morton Park Place
1 Morton Park Rd., 02360
508-747-1730 800-698-1730
James & Janine Smith
All year

$ B&B
4 rooms, 2 pb
Visa, MC •
C-yes/S-yes/P-no/H-no
Spanish

Continental breakfast
Sitting room

One mile from Routes 3 and 44; Victorian charm in a park setting; 5 minutes from downtown and the waterfront. Individual rooms or suites available.

PRINCETON

The Harrington Farm
178 Westminster Rd., 01541
508-464-5600 800-736-3276
Victoria Morgan, John Bomba
All year

$$ B&B
8 rooms, 1 pb
Visa, MC •
C-yes/S-no/P-ltd/H-no
German

Full farm breakfast
Lunch, dinner
Tea, coffee, snacks
sitting room
bicycles

1763 farmhouse on western slope of Mt. Wachusett. A century of innkeeping tradition, full farm breakfast, skiing, hiking, breathtaking sunsets.

PROVINCETOWN

Bradford Gardens Inn
178 Bradford St., 02657
508-487-1616
M. Susan Culligan
April—December

$$ B&B
12 rooms, 12 pb
Visa, MC, AmEx •
C-ask/S-ltd/P-no/H-no
French

Full gourmet breakfast
Sitting room, fireplace
townhouses available
landscaped gardens
maid service

1820 Colonial antique-filled inn. Most rooms and cottages have fireplaces. Situated in beautiful gardens. Within a short walk to town center. Exceptionally clean & friendly.

Cape Codder Guest House
570 Commercial St., 02657
508-487-0131
Deborah Dionne
Mid-April—October

$ B&B/EP
14 rooms, 1 pb
Visa, MC
C-yes/S-ltd/P-ask/H-ltd

Continental breakfast
Daily maid service
Private sandy beach
sun deck, seaside garden
1 apt. with private bath

Old-fashioned comfort in quiet area; private beach, sun deck; whale-watching and bicycling nearby; informal friendly atmosphere; resident marine biologists!

PROVINCETOWN

Fairbanks Inn
90 Bradford St., 02657
508-487-0386
Don Graichen
All year

$$ B&B
14 rooms, 7 pb
Visa, MC, AmEx ●
C-no/S-yes/P-no/H-yes

Continental breakfast
Library, sitting room
sun deck, patio
porch

A 1776 sea captain's house. Seven bedrooms with original working fireplaces. Warm, congenial atmosphere with typical New England charm.

Land's End Inn
22 Commercial St., 02657
508-487-0706
David Schoolman
All year

$$$ B&B
14 rooms, 10 pb
C-no/S-yes/P-no/H-no

Continental breakfast
Sitting room
panoramic views
near shops, restaurants

Victorian summer house set high on a hill overlooking Provincetown with panoramic views of Cape Cod. With a homelike and friendly atmosphere. Oriental wood carvings, antiques.

Rose and Crown Guest House
158 Commercial St., 02657
508-487-3332
Sam Hardee
All year

$$ B&B
8 rooms, 5 pb
●
C-yes/S-yes/P-no/H-ltd

Continental breakfast
Comp. wine in room
Sitting room

A relaxed, elegant 1780s captain's house. Rooms feature antiques in a homey atmosphere. An unusual eclectic living room is featured.

Somerset House
378 Commercial St., 02657
508-487-0383
Don & Sandy

$$ B&B
13 rooms, 10 pb
Visa, MC, AmEx
C-yes/S-yes/P-no/H-no

Continental breakfast
Library, antiques
original paintings
lithographs

An historic 3 story Victorian house built in 1850. Located in the center of town, across the street from the beach. Many plants and flowers enhance the decor.

REHOBOTH

Perryville Inn
157 Perryville Rd., 02769
508-252-9239
Betsy & Tom Charnecki
All year

$$ B&B
5 rooms, 4 pb
Visa, MC, AmEx ●
C-yes/S-ltd/P-no/H-no

Continental plus
Comp. wine, tea, coffee
2 sitting rooms
piano, balloon rides
bicycles

Newly renovated 19th-century spacious farmhouse in quiet country setting. Centrally located between Boston, Newport, Providence. On National Register of Historic Homes.

ROCKPORT

Addison Choate Inn
49 Broadway, 01966
508-546-7543
Peter & Chris Kelleher
All year

$$$ B&B
10 rooms, 10 pb
●
C-14+/S-ltd/P-no/H-yes
German

Continental breakfast
Afternoon iced tea
Swimming pool
sitting room
library

Remarkably fine small country inn. Cruise the coast on our private yacht the "Sweetwater." Antiques, flowers, a surprise on your pillow!

ROCKPORT

Beach Knoll Inn
30 Beach St., 01966
508-546-6939
Diane & Terry Golden
All year

$$ EP
15 rooms, 15 pb
●
C-yes/S-yes/P-no/H-no

Fully equipped kitchens
Air conditioning
Family beach 1 block
water views

Historic seaside rooms, apartments, cottage with Colonial atmosphere. Reproduction and antique furnishings. Overlooking beach, short walk to shops, restaurants, recreation.

The Inn on Cove Hill
37 Mt. Pleasant St., 01966
508-546-2701
John & Marjorie Pratt
April–October

$ B&B
11 rooms, 9 pb
C-16+/S-no/P-no/H-no

Continental breakfast
(in bed Spring & Fall)
Canopy beds
antiques, garden
panoramic view, porch

This 18th-century inn overlooks a historic harbor. Breakfast is served on fine china in the garden or in your room. Short walk to shops, Art Association, rocky seafront.

Mooringstone for Nonsmokrs
12 Norwood Ave., 01966
508-546-2479 508-546-1095
David & Mary Knowlton
May–October

$$ B&B
3 rooms, 3 pb
Visa, MC, AmEx
C-no/S-no/P-no

Continental plus
Aftn. tea, snacks
Air conditioning
cable TV, refrigerators
restaurants nearby

Quiet, central to beach and shops. Comfortable A/C ground floor rooms. Cable TV, parking, refrigerators. Daily, weekly and off-season rates, without a room tax.

Old Farm Inn
291 Granite St., 01966
Route 127, Pigeon Cove
508-546-3237 800-233-6828
The Balzarini Family
April–December

$$ B&B
13 rooms, 13 pb
Visa, MC ●
C-yes/S-yes/P-no/H-ltd

Continental plus
Comp. sherry, port
Sitting room, bicycles
2 bedroom house avail.
queen or king beds

Relax by the fire, nap under a tree, wander on the rocky coastline. Unwind at our friendly, cozy, country farmhouse. Cottage with 2 bedrooms also available.

Pleasant Street Inn
17 Pleasant St., 01966
508-546-3915 800-541-3915
Roger & Lynne Norris
All year

$$$ B&B
8 rooms, 8 pb
Visa, MC, AmEx ●
C-6+/S-yes/P-no

Continental plus
Sitting room
veranda

A recently renovated inn situated on a knoll overlooking the village; within walking distance to shops, restaurants, beaches and galleries.

Rocky Shores Inn/Cottages
65 Eden Rd., 01966
508-546-2823 800-348-4003
Gunter & Renate Kostka
April–October

$$ B&B (Inn)
22 rooms, 22 pb
●
C-10+/S-ltd/P-no/H-no
German

Continental plus
Sitting room
rooms with ocean views
walk to beaches

Inn and cottages with unforgettable views of Thatcher Island lights and open sea. Inn has 7 fireplaces & beautiful woodwork. Complimentary breakfast included for inn guests.

ROCKPORT

Sally Webster Inn
34 Mt. Pleasant St., 01966
508-546-9251
The Webster Family
May–Oct, Feb–Apr wknds

$$ B&B
6 rooms, 6 pb
Visa, MC
C-16+/S-yes/P-no/H-no

Continental breakfast
Comp. wine for special
occasions
sitting room, piano

Historic, colonial home built in 1832. Antique decor. Walk to village and sea. Welcome to the charm of yesteryear.

Seacrest Manor
131 Marmion Way, 01966
508-546-2211
L. Saville, D. MacCormack, Jr
Exc. December–February

$$$ B&B
8 rooms, 6 pb
C-ltd/S-ltd/P-no/H-no
some French

Full breakfast
Afternoon tea
Library, sitting room
gardens, sun deck
bicycles

Decidedly small, intentionally quiet inn. Beautiful peaceful setting; lovely gardens overlooking woods and sea. Famous full breakfast included. OUR 1988 INN OF THE YEAR!

Yankee Clipper Inn
P.O. Box 2399, 01966
96 Granite St.
508-546-3407 800-545-3699
Bob & Barbara Ellis
All year exc. Dec 24-27

$$$ B&B
27 rooms, 27 pb
●
C-yes/S-ltd/P-no/H-no

Full breakfast
Gourmet dinner
Sitting room, weddings
small conference fac.
swimming pool, bicycles

Beautiful oceanfront grounds in picturesque Rockport. Accommodations in 3 converted estate buildings. Rooms furnished in antiques and named after clipper ships.

SAGAMORE BEACH

Widow's Walk B&B
152 Clark Rd., 02562
508-888-3888
Frank & Priscilla Hennessey
May–December

$$ B&B
3 rooms, 2 pb
C-yes/S-no/P-ask/H-yes

Full breakfast
Dinner, snacks
Comp. wine, sitting room
bicycles, tennis
beach equipment

Our country cape-style home offers wide plank floors, fireplace, sitting room, full gourmet breakfast, backyard tennis courts. 100 yards to sandy beach.

SALEM

Amelia Payson Guest House
16 Winter St., 01970
508-744-8304
Ada & Donald Roberts
All year

$$$ B&B
4 rooms, 4 pb
Visa, MC, AmEx
C-12+/S-no

Continental plus
Restaurant nearby

Beautifully decorated rooms in an elegantly restored 1845 Greek Revival-style home; five-minute stroll finds restaurants, museums, shopping and train station.

Coach House Inn
284 Lafayette St., 01970
508-744-4092 800-688-8689
Patricia Kessler
All year

$$ B&B
11 rooms, 10 pb
Visa, MC, AmEx
C-yes/S-yes/P-no/H-no

Continental breakfast

Return to elegance. Enjoy the intimacy of a small European-type inn. Victorian fireplaces highlight the charming decor of each room.

SALEM

The Salem Inn
7 Summer St., 01970
508-741-0680 800-446-2995
Diane & Richard Pabich
All year

$$$ B&B
23 rooms, 23 pb
Major credit cards •
C-yes/S-yes/P-no/H-no

Continental plus
Comp. wine, restaurant
Private garden, phones
color TV, A/C, courtyard
special packages avail.

Spacious, luxuriously appointed rooms in elegantly restored Federal mansion. Some efficiencies & suites. In the heart of historic district, fine restaurants, gift shop.

Stephen Daniels House
One Daniels St., 01970
at 55 Essex St.
508-744-5709
Catherine Gill
All year

$$$ B&B
5 rooms, 3 pb
C-yes/S-yes/P-yes/H-no

Continental breakfast
Comp. tea
Sitting rooms
walk-in fireplaces
private garden, bicycles

300-year-old house furnished with canopy beds, antiques throughout, fireplaces in every room. Lovely flower-filled shady English garden, private for guests.

The Stepping Stone Inn
19 Washington Sqaure N., 01970
508-741-8900 800-338-3022
Paula Bradbury
March—December

$$$ B&B
8 rooms, 8 pb
Visa, MC, AmEx, DC •
C-yes/S-yes/P-ltd

Continental plus
Afternoon tea
Sitting room
private functions avail.

Step into the past at our elegant inn located in Heritage Trail; breakfast in a candlelit dining room; 8 unique guest rooms; rated "best" by The Washington Post.

SANDWICH

Captain Ezra Nye House
152 Main St., 02563
508-888-6142 800-388-2278
Harry & Elaine Dickson
All year

$$ B&B
6 rooms, 4 pb
Visa, MC, AmEx •
C-6+/S-no/P-no/H-no
Spanish

Full breakfast
Comp. wine
Sitting room, library
2 canopy beds
working fireplaces

1829 Federal home in the heart of historic Sandwich; nearby museums, antique shops, the ocean and world-famous Heritage Plantation.

Isaiah Jones Homestead
165 Main St., 02563
508-888-9115 800-526-1625
Steve & Kathy Catania
All year

$$ B&B
4 rooms, 4 pb
Visa, MC, AmEx, Disc •
S-no

Continental plus
Afternoon tea
Lemonade, iced tea
gift shop, phone avail.
room with whirlpool tub

Victorian B&B; 4 rooms all with private baths & queen-sized beds, furnished with museum-quality antiques. Breakfast & afternoon tea or bedside goodies. Deluxe room.

Village Inn at Sandwich
P.O. Box 951, 02563
4 Jarves St.
508-833-0363 800-922-9989
Patricia & Winfried Platz
April—December 23

$$ B&B
6 rooms, 6 pb
Visa, MC, AmEx •
C-no/S-no/P-no/H-no
German

Continental plus
Comp. wine
Feather comforters
wraparound porch
rocking chairs

1830s Federal-style home in the heart of the village. Wraparound porch surrounded by fragrance of roses. Walking distance to boardwalk, beach and restaurants.

SCITUATE

The Allen House
18 Allen Place, 02066
617-545-8221
Christine & Iain Gilmour
April–Feb.

$$ B&B
4 rooms, 2 pb
Visa, MC, AmEx ●
C-16+/S-no/P-no/H-no
French, German, Spanish

Full breakfast
Afternoon tea
Sitting room

Gourmet cook-owner serves "Fantasy Breakfast" on Victorian porch overlooking harbor in unpretentious fishing town 25 miles south of Boston.

SOUTH CHATHAM

Ye Olde Nantucket House
P.O. Box 468, 02659
2647 Main St.
508-432-5641
Norm Anderton
All year

$$ B&B
5 rooms, 5 pb
Visa, MC ●
C-8+/S-yes

Continental plus
Homebaked goods

Delightful 19th-century home with friendly, informal atmosphere. Close to Nantucket Sound beach. Fresh breads, muffins and crepes daily.

SOUTH EGREMONT

Weathervane Inn
Route 23, Main St., 01258
413-528-9580
The Murphys
All year

$$$ B&B/MAP
10 rooms, 10 pb
Visa, MC ●
C-7+/S-yes/P-no/H-yes

Full breakfast
Bar, dinner by menu
Cordial in room
sitting room, library
swimming pool

The Murphy family warmly greets you at the Weathervane, a 200-year-old hostelry with modern amenities. Hearty breakfasts and superb dining will make your stay memorable.

SOUTH YARMOUTH

Four Winds
345 High Bank Rd., 02664
508-394-4182
Mary & Walt Crowell
All year

$$ B&B
5 rooms, 4 pb
C-yes/S-yes

Continental plus
Fireplaced parlour
fishing, swimming, golf
tennis, shopping nearby

Four Winds is a 1712 sea captain's home in historic South Yarmouth near saltwater beaches and golf courses.

STERLING

Sterling Inn
P.O. Box 609, 01564
Rt. 12 near Sterling Ctr.
508-422-6592 508-422-6333
Mark & Patricia Roy
All year

$ B&B
6 rooms, 4 pb
Visa, MC, AmEx
C-ltd/S-ltd/P-no/H-ltd

Continental breakfast
Lunch, dinner, bar
Afternoon cheese & fruit
sitting room, piano
entertainment

Turn-of-the-century setting, unique to the area. Near skiing. Private dining rooms. One hour to Boston.

STOW

Amerscot House
61 West Acton Rd., 01775
508-897-0666
Doreen Gibson
All year

$$$ B&B
3 rooms, 3 pb
Visa, MC, AmEx ●
C-yes/S-no/P-no/H-no

Full breakfast
Comp. sherry, tea
1 suite is available w/
sitting room, bedroom
bath and jacuzzi

Early American farmhouse c. 1734. Antiques, quilts, fresh flowers. Enjoy apple orchards, golf, select stores or the historic sites of Concord/Boston.

STURBRIDGE

Sturbridge Country Inn
P.O. Box 60, 01566
530 Main St.
508-347-5503
Mr. MacConnell
All year

$$$ B&B
9 rooms, 9 pb
Visa, MC, AmEx ●
C-yes/S-yes/P-no/H-yes

Continental breakfast
Restaurant, bar
Lunch, dinner
comp. champagne
hot tubs

Close to Old Sturbridge Village lies our grand Greek Revival structure. Each room has period reproductions, fireplaces, and whirlpool tubs.

SUDBURY

Checkerberry Corner B&B
5 Checkerberry Circle, 01776
508-443-8660
Stuart & Irene MacDonald
All year

$$ B&B
3 rooms
●
C-yes

Full breakfast
Afternoon tea, snacks
Sitting room

Charming colonial home located in heart of historic minutemen country; minutes from Concord, Lexington, Wayside Inn; easy access to Boston.

TOWNSEND

Wood Farm
40 Worcester Rd., 01469
508-597-5019
Debra Jones, Jim Mayrand
All year

$ B&B
4 rooms
C-ltd/S-no/P-ltd/H-no
French, Spanish

Full breakfast
Sitting room
gardens, bicycles
box stalls for horses

Restored 1716 Cape in antique country; country breakfast at working sheep farm; warm conversation by the hearth. Wooded trails and waterfall. Special theme weekends.

TRURO

Parker House
P.O. Box 1111, 02666
Route 6-A, Truro Center
508-349-3358
Stephen Williams
All year

$$ B&B
2 rooms
C-no/S-no/P-no/H-no

Continental breakfast
Ocean and bay beaches
national park
tennis

A warmly classic 1850 Cape house with many antiques. Close to beaches and charm of Wellfleet and Provincetown.

VINEYARD HAVEN

Lothrop Merry House
P.O. Box 1939, Owen Prk, 02568
508-693-1646
Mary & John Clarke
All year

$$$ B&B
7 rooms, 4 pb
Visa, MC
C-yes/S-no/P-no/H-no

Continental breakfast
Beach front
Terrace
boat cruises
canoe, sailing

Charming 18th-century guest house. Harbor, view, beach front. Walk from ferry. Fireplaces, antiques. Home-baked continental breakfast served.

WARE

Wildwood Inn
121 Church St., 01082
413-967-7798
F. Fenster, R. Watson
All year

$ B&B
7 rooms, 4 pb
Visa, MC, AmEx ●
C-6+/S-no/P-no/H-no

Full breakfast
Lemonade, cider
Sitting room, canoe
tennis courts
swimming hole

Relax! American primitive antiques, heirloom quilts, firm beds. Enjoy Sturbridge, Deerfield, Amherst. Canoe, swim, bike, hike. We'll spoil you. A.B.B.A. approved!

WELLFLEET

The Inn at Duck Creeke
Main St., Box 364, 02667
617-349-9333
Robert P. Morrill
Mid-May-mid-October

$$ B&B
25 rooms, 17 pb
Visa, MC, AmEx
C-yes/S-yes/P-no/H-ltd

Continental breakfast
Dinner, bar
Entertainment
3 porches & lobby

Cozy Sea Captain's house in coastal fishing village. Close to beaches and Audobon Sanctuary. Overlooks salt marsh and duck pond.

WEST BARNSTABLE

Honeysuckle Hill
591 Main St., 02668
508-362-8418 800-441-8418
Bob & Barbara Rosenthal
All year

$$$ B&B
3 rooms, 3 pb
Visa, MC, AmEx, Disc ●
C-ltd/S-yes/P-ltd/H-ltd
French, Italian

Full gourmet breakfast
Afternoon tea & pastries
Great room, TV, library
croquet, bicycles, piano
cookies by bed

Charming Victorian inn with feather beds, full country breakfasts, afternoon teas and homemade cookies at bedside. Near lovely Sandy Neck beach.

WEST FALMOUTH

Sjöholm B&B Inn
P.O. Box 430, 02574
17 Chase Rd.
508-540-5706
Barbara Eck
All year

$$ B&B
15 rooms, 5 pb
C-5+/S-ltd/P-no/H-no

Full breakfast buffet
Sitting room
TV, porch
near warm water beaches

1750s restored farmhouse in quiet, country setting. Spectacular warm water beaches and golf nearby. Close to gourmet dining and ferries to Martha's Vineyard.

WEST HARWICH

Cape Cod Sunny Pines B&B
P.O. Box 667, 02671
77 Main St.
508-432-9628 800-356-9628
Eileen & Jack Connell
April–November

$$$ B&B/MAP
6 rooms, 6 pb
Visa, MC ●
C-12+/S-ltd/P-no/H-no

Gourmet Irish breakfast
Restaurant, bar
Comp. wine, tea
porch, A/C, cable TV
pool, spa, gardens

Irish hospitality in Victorian ambiance. Gourmet Irish breakfast by candlelight and Irish music. Relax in the New Claddagh Tavern and tearoom. Central Cape Cod location.

Lion's Head Inn
P.O. Box 444, 02671
186 Belmont Rd.
800-321-3155
Fred, Deborah & Ricky Denton
All year

$$ B&B
6 rooms, 6 pb
Visa, MC ●
C-ltd/S-yes/P-no/H-ltd

Full gourmet breakfast
Complimentary tea, wine
Sitting room w/fireplace
swimming pool, patio
private woods, cottages

Built as a Cape half-house in 1800; former sea captain's home; charming inn with a sense of history; furnished in period antiques; central Cape Cod location. Walk to beach.

WOODS HOLE

The Marlborough
320 Woods Hole, Box 238, 02543
508-548-6218
Patricia Morris
All year

$$ B&B
5 rooms, 5 pb
●
C-2+/S-no/P-ltd/H-no
some French

Full gourmet breakfast
Dinner (off season)
Afternoon tea, wine
sitting room, A/C, pool
paddle tennis court

Charming inn located close to island ferries and cozy day trips to all of southeast New England. Antique shop on premises.

YARMOUTH PORT ————————————————————————

Colonial House Inn	$$ MAP	Continental plus
Rt. 6A, 277 Main St., 02675	21 rooms, 21 pb	Restaurant, bar
Old Kings Hwy.	Visa, MC, AmEx, DC ●	Dinner included, tea
508-362-4348 800-999-3416	C-yes/S-yes/P-no/H-yes	library, sitting room
Malcolm J. Perna		jacuzzi, fitness ctr.
All year		

Large guest rooms are individually decorated and furnished with antiques. Charming view of our grounds and adjacent historic homes. Indoor heated pool. Conference center (150).

Crook' Jaw Inn	$$$ MAP	Full breakfast
186 Main St., Route 6A, 02675	7 rooms, 7 pb	Dinner included
508-362-6111 800-255-2813	Visa, MC, AmEx	Sitting room
Don Spagnolia	C-yes/S-yes/H-yes	library
All year	French, Italian, Spanish	small weddings

Wedgewood Inn	$$$ B&B	Full breakfast
83 Main St., 02675	6 rooms, 6 pb	Afternoon tea
508-362-5157	Visa, MC, AmEx, DC ●	Common room
Milt & Gerrie Graham	C-10+/S-ltd/P-no/H-ltd	porches
All year		

Romantic country inn located in historic area of Cape Cod. Near beaches and fine restaurants. Antiques, fireplaces, screened porches, wide board floors, canopy beds.

More Inns . . .

10 Mugford Street B&B 10 Mugford St., Marblehead, 01945 617-631-5642
1777 Greylock House 58 Greylock St., Lee, 01238 413-243-1717
1797 House Charlemont Rd., Buckland, 01338 413-625-2697
A Cambridge House B&B Inn P.O. Box 211, Cambridge, 02140 617-491-6300
AMC–Bascom Lodge P.O. Box 686, Lanesboro, 01237 413-743-1591
Acorn House 240 Sea St., Hyannis, 02601 617-771-4071
Alpine Haus Mashapaung Rd., Box 782, Holland, 01550 413-245-9082
Amherst 30 Amherst Ave., Falmouth, 02540 617-548-2781
Amity House 15 Cliffwood St., Lenox, 01240 413-637-0005
Anchor Inn 66 Centre St., Nantucket, 02554 508-228-0072
Anchorage 122 South Shore Dr., Bass River, 02664 617-398-8265
Anderson-Wheeler Homestead 154 Fitchburg Turnpike, Concord, 01742 617-369-3756
Another Place Inn 240 Sandwich St., Plymouth, 02360 548-746-0126
Apple Tree Inn 224 West St., Lenox, 01240 413-637-1477
Arey's Pond Relais P.O. Box 1387, East Orleans, 02653 508-240-0599
Asheton House 3 Cook St., Provincetown, 02657 617-487-9966
Ashfield Inn P.O. Box 129, Main St., Ashfield, 01330 413-628-4571
Ashley's B&B 6 Moon Hill Rd., Lexington, 02173 617-862-6488
Attleboro House 11 Lake Ave., Oak Bluffs, 02557 617-693-4346
Autumn Inn 259 Elm St., Northampton, 01060 413-584-7660
B&B Above the Rest 50 Boatswains Way, #105, Boston, 02150 617-884-7748
B&B with Barbara & Bo 15 Three Rivers Rd., Wilbraham, 01095 413-596-6258
Bacon Barn Inn 3400 Main St, Barnstable, 02630 508-362-5518
Baird Tavern B&B Old Chester Rd., Blandford, 01008 413-848-2096
Barnaby Inn P.O. Box 151, West Harwich, 02671 508-432-6789
Beach House 61 Uncle Stephen's Rd., West Dennis, 02670 617-398-8321
Beach House Inn 4 Braddock Lane, Harwich Port, 02646 508-432-4444
Beach Plum Inn Box 98, Menemsha, 02552 617-645-9454
Beachside N. Beach St., Nantucket Island, 02554 617-228-2241
Beacon Hill B&B 2 106 Chestnut St., Boston, 02108 617-227-7866
Bed & Breakfast One Hawes Rd., Box 205, Sagamore Beach, 02562 508-888-1559

Bed 'n B'fast 44 Commercial St., Provincetown, 02657 508-487-9555
Beechwood Inn 2839 Main St., Barnstable, 02630 508-362-6618
Belvedere B&B Inn 167 Main St., Bass River, 02664 508-398-6674
Berkshire Thistle B&B, The Rte. 7, P.O. Box 2105, Stockbridge, 01262 413-298-3188
Bernardston Inn Church St., Bernardston, 01337 413-648-9282
Billerica B&B 88 Rogers St., Billerica, 01862 508-667-7317
Bleu Auberge 5 Scar Hill Rd., Boylston, 01505 617-869-2666
Blue Door, The 20 East St., Middleton, 01949 508-777-4829
Blue Shutters Inn 1 Nautilus Rd., Gloucester, 01930 617-281-2706
Bow Roof House 59 Queen Anne Rd., Chatham, 02633 617-945-1346
Brass Lantern 11 N. Water St., Nantucket, 02554 508-228-4064
Bread & Roses Star Route 65, Box 50, Great Barrington, 01230 413-528-1099
Brookfield House Inn P.O. Box 796, West Brookfield, 01585 617-867-6589
Brookline Manor Guest Hous 32 Centre St., Brookline, 02146 617-232-0003
Bull Frog B&B Box 210, Star Route, Ashfield, 01330 413-628-4493
By-the-Sea Guests 57 Chase Ave., Box 50, Dennisport, 02639 617-398-8685
Cable House 3 Narwood Ave., Rockport, 01966 508-546-3895
Cambridge House B&B, A 2218 Massachusetts Ave, Cambridge, 02140 617-491-6300
Candlelight Inn 53 Walker St., Lenox, 01240 413-637-1555
Canterbury Farm B&B Fred Snow Rd., Becket, 01223 413-623-8765
Captain Dexter House P.O. Box 2457, Vineyard Haven, 02568 508-693-6564
Captain Lysander Inn Ltd. 96 Commercial St., Provincetown, 02657 617-487-2253
Captain Sylvester Baxter 156 Main St., Hyannis, 02601 508-775-5611
Captain's Quarters 85 Bank St., Harwich Port, 02646 800-272-4343
Carl & Lottie Sylvester 9 South St., Williamsburg, 01096 413-268-7283
Carlisle House Inn 26 N. Water St., Nantucket, 02554 508-228-0720
Carriage House 4 Ray's Court, Nantucket Island, 02554 617-228-0326
Carver House 638 Main St., Centerville, 02632 617-775-9414
Centennial House 94 Main St., Northfield, 01360 413-498-5921
Centuryhurst Antiques B&B P.O. Box 486, Sheffield, 01257 413-229-8131
Chalet d'Alicia B&B E. Windsor Rd., Peru, 01235 413-655-8292
Chamberlain P.O. Box 187, Sturbridge, 01566 617-347-3313
Charlotte Inn S. Summer St., Edgartown, 02539 617-627-4751
Chatham Town House Inn 11 Library Lane, Chatham, 02633 508-945-2180
Chestnut House 3 Chestnut St., Nantucket Island, 02554 617-228-0049
Circuit House Box 2422, 150 Circuit A, Oak Bluffs, 02557 617-693-5033
Cliff Lodge B&B 9 Cliff Rd., Nantucket, 02554 617-228-9480
Cliffside Beach Club P.O. Box 449, Nantucket, 02554 617-228-0618
Cliffwood Inn 25 Cliffwood St., Lenox, 01240 413-637-3330
Col. Ebenezer Crafts Inn P.O. Box 187, Sturbridge, 01566 508-347-3313
Colonel Ashley Inn RR #1 Box 142, Bow Wow, Sheffield, 01257 413-229-2929
Colonel Roger Brown House 1694 Main St., Concord, 01742 508-369-9119
Colonial House Inn 207 Sandwich St., Plymouth, 02360 617-746-2087
Commonwealth Inn P.O.Box 251, Fiskdale, Sturbridge—Fiskdale, 01566 508-347-5503
Coonamesset Inn Falmouth, 508-548-2300
Copper Beech Inn 497 Main St., Box 67, Centerville, 02632 617-771-5488
Country Comfort 15 Masonic Ave., Shelburne Falls, 01370 413-625-9877
Country Cricket Inn Huntington Rd., Rt. 112, Worthington, 01098 413-238-5366
Country Inn Acres Inc. 86 Sisson Rd., Harwich Port, 02646 617-432-2769
Country Motor Lodge P.O. Box 187, Sturbridge, 01566 617-347-3313
Crosswinds Inn 140 Bradford St., Provincetown, 02657 508-487-3533
Daggett House P.O. Box 1333, Edgartown, 02539 508-627-4600
Dalton House 955 Main St., Dalton, 01226 413-684-3854
Dillingham House 71 Main St., Sandwich, 02563 508-833-0065
Dockside Inn Box 1206, Oak Bluffs, 02557 617-693-2966
Dolphin Guest House 10 N. Beach St., Nantucket, 02554 617-228-4028
Durant Sail Loft Inn One Merrill's Wharf, New Bedford, 02740 508-999-2700
East Country Berry Farm 830 East St., Lenox, 01240 413-442-2057
Easton House Box 1033, Nantucket, 02554 617-228-2759

Eden Pines Inn Eden Rd., Rockport, 01966 508-546-2505
Edgartown Heritage Hotel 227 Upper Main St., Edgartown, 02539 617-627-5161
Egremont Inn P.O. Box 418, South Egremont, 01258 413-528-2111
Elm Arch Inn Elm Arch Way, Falmouth, 02540 617-548-0133
Elms, The P.O. Box 895, West Falmouth, 02574 508-540-7232
Fair Gardens 27 Fair St., Nantucket, 02554 617-228-4258
Farmhouse State Rd., Martha's Vineyard, 02568 617-693-5354
Field Farm Guest House 554 Sloan Rd., Williamstown, 01267 413-458-3135
Forest Way Farm Route 8A (Heath), Charlemont, 01339 413-337-8321
Four Ash Street 4 Ash St., Nantucket, 02554 617-228-4899
Four Chimneys 38 Orange St., Nantucket, 02554 508-228-1912
Four Chimneys Inn 946 Main St., Dennis, 02638 617-385-6317
Franklin Burr Homestead HC63 B196, Kinne Brook, Worthington, 01098 413-238-5826
Gazebo B&B Edgartown Rd., Vineyard Haven, 02568 617-693-6955
General Rufus Putnam House 344 Main St., Rt. 122-A, Rutland, 01543 508-886-4256
Gingerbread B & Brunch RR 2 Box 542A Stafford, Charlton, 01507 617-248-7940
Gladstone Inn 219 Grand Ave. S., Falmouth, 02540 508-548-9851
Golden Goose P.O. Box 336, Tyringham, 01264 413-243-3008
Goss House B&B 61 Pine Lane, Barnstable, 02630 617-362-8559
Grandmother's House RR1 Box 37, Colrain, 01340 413-624-3771
Hanover House Box 2107, Vineyard Haven, 02568 617-693-1066
Harborview Hotel Edgartown, Martha's Vineyard, 508-627-4333
Hastings By the Sea 28 Worcester Ave., Falmouth, 02540 617-548-1628
Hawthorn House 2 Chestnut St., Nantucket, 02554 617-228-1468
Heritage, The Buffington Hill Rd., Worthington, 01098 413-238-4230
Hidden Brook RR 1, Box 238C, Cummington, 01026 413-634-5653
High Haven House Box 289, Summer St., Vineyard Haven, 02568 617-693-9204
Hill Gallery Cole St., Cummington, 01026 413-238-5914
Hillbourne House B&B Route 28, Box 190, South Orleans, 02662 617-255-0780
Hilltop B&B Truce Rd., Conway, 01341 413-369-4928
House On Main Street 1120 Main St., Williamstown, 01267 413-458-3031
House of the Seven Gables 32 Cliff Rd., Nantucket, 02554 617-228-4706
House on the Hill P.O. Box 51, 968 Main, South Harwich, 02661 617-432-4321
Hussey House—1795 15 N. Water St., Nantucket, 02554 617-228-0747
India House 37 India St., Nantucket, 02554 617-228-9043
Inn Yesterday Huntington Rd., Rt. 11, Worthington, 01098 413-238-5529
Inn at Cummington Farm VII RR 1, Box 234, Cummington, 01026 413-634-5551
Inn at Fernbrook 481 Main St., Centerville, 02632 508-775-4334
Inn at Seven Winter St. Seven Winter St., Salem, 01970 617-745-9520
Inn at Stockbridge Stockbridge, 01262 413-298-3337
Inn of the Golden Ox 1360 Main, Brewster, 02631 617-896-3111
Ivy Lodge 2 Chester St., Nantucket, 02554 617-228-6612
James & Ellen Allen B&B 60 Nickerson Ln., Box 22, Cotuit, 02635 617-428-5702
Jared Coffin House 29 Broad St., Nantucket, 02554 508-228-2405
Joshua Sears Manor 4 Summer St & Route 6A, Yarmouthport, 02675 508-362-5000
Katama Guest House RFD #108,166 Katama Rd., Edgartown, 02539 617-627-5158
Kingsleigh 1840/ A B&B 32 Park St., Lee, 01238 413-243-3317
Lambert's Cove Country Inn Box 422, RFD, Vineyard Haven, 02568 508-693-2298
Lamplighter Inn 26 Bradford St., Provincetown, 02657 508-487-2529
Langhaar House P.O. Box 191, Southfield, 01259 413-229-2007
Lantana House 22 Broadway, Rockport, 01966 508-546-3535
Le Jardin 777 Coldspring Rd., Williamstown, 01267 413-458-8032
Le Languedoc Inn 24 Broad St., Nantucket, 02554 617-228-2552
Leiden Tree Inn 26 King St., Rockport, 01966 508-546-2494
Liberty Hill Inn 77 Main St., Route 6A, Yarmouth Port, 02675 508-362-3976
Lighthouse Inn West Dennis, 02670 508-398-2244
Lindsey's Garrett 38 High St., Marblehead, 01945 617-631-2653
Littlejohn Manor Newsboy Monument, Rt 23, Great Barrington, 01230 413-528-2882
Manor House 57 Maine Ave., West Yarmouth, 02673 617-771-9211

Mariners Cove B&B 15 Seconsett Pt. Rd., Waquoit, 02536 508-548-3821
Meeting House Inn 40 Meeting House Way, Edgartown, 02539 508-627-8626
Menemsha Inn North Road, Box 38, Menemsha, 02552 617-645-2521
Merrell Tavern Inn Route 102, Main St., South Lee, 01260 413-243-1794
Moorings Lodge 207 Grand Ave. S., Falmouth, 02540 617-540-2370
Morrill Place Inn 209 High St., Newburyport, 01950 617-462-2808
Nantucket Landfall 4 Harbor View Way, Nantucket, 02554 617-228-0500
Narragansett House 62 Narragansett Ave., Oak Bluffs, 02557 617-693-3627
Nashua House Kennebee and Park Ave., Oak Bluffs, 02557 617-693-0043
Nesbitt Inn 21 Broad St., Nantucket Island, 02554 617-228-0156
New Boston Inn Routes 57 & 8, Sandisfield, 01255 413-258-4477
No. 10 Bed & Breakfast 10 Cross St., Harwich Port, 02646 508-432-9313
Oak Bluffs Inn P.O. Box 4277, Oak Bluffs, 02557 508-693-7171
Ocean Gold Cape Cod B&B 74 Locust Lane, Route 2, East Brewster, 02631 617-255-7045
Ocean Side Inn Main St., Box 2700, Vineyard Haven, 02568 617-693-1296
Old Cape House 108 Old Main St., Bass River, 02664 617-398-1068
Old Hundred House 1211 Craigville Beach R, Centerville, 02632 617-775-6166
Old Silver Beach B&B 3 Cliffwood Lane, Box 6, West Falmouth, 02574 617-540-5446
Olde Captain's Inn 101 Main St., Route 6, Yarmouth Port, 02675 508-362-4496
Olde Jenkins Guest House Rte. 122, Barre, 01005 508-355-6444
Olde Lamplighter Church St., Stockbridge, 01262 413-298-3053
One Centre Street Inn 1 Centre St., Yarmouth Port, 02675 508-362-8910
Orchards, The Williamstown, 01267 800-225-1517
Osterville Fairways Inn 1198 Race Ln., Marstons Mill, 02648 617-428-2747
Outlook Farm Route 66, Westhampton, 01027 413-527-0633
Over Look Inn P.O. Box 771, Eastham, 02642 508-255-1886
Parker Guest House 4 East Chestnut St., Nantucket, 02554 617-228-4625
Parson Hubbard House Old Village Rd., Shelburne Falls, 01370 413-625-9730
Periwinkle Guest House 9 N. Water St., Nantucket, 02554 617-228-9267
Peterson's B&B 226 Trotting Park, East Falmouth, 02536 508-540-2962
Pistachio Cove 229 County Rd., Lakeville, 02347 617-763-2383
Pleasant Pheasant B&B 296 Heath St., Chestnut Hill, 02167 617-566-4178
Queen Anne Inn 70 Queen Anne Rd., Chatham, 02633 617-945-0394
Ramsey House 203 W. Park St., Lee, 01238 413-243-1598
Red Bird Inn P.O. Box 592, New Marlborough, 01230 413-229-2433
Red Inn 15 Commercial St., Provincetown, 02657 617-487-0050
River Bend Farm 643 Simonds Rd., Williamstown, 01267 413-458-5504
Roberts House India & Centre Sts., Nantucket Island, 02554 617-228-9009
Rockport Lodge 61 South St., Rockport, 02108 508-546-2090
Rose Cottage 24 Worcester,Rts 12 & 1, West Boylston, 01583 617-835-4034
Rueben Joy Guest House 107 Main St., Nantucket, 02554 617-228-6612
Safe Harbor Guest House 2 Harbor View Way, Nantucket, 02554 508-228-3222
Salt Marsh Farm B&B 322 Smith Neck Rd., South Dartmouth, 02748 508-992-0980
Scott House Hawley Rd., Buckland, 01338 413-625-6624
Sea Street B&B 9 Gregory St., Marblehead, 01945 617-631-1890
Seafarer Inn 86 Marmion Way, Rockport, 01966 508-546-6248
Seafarer Motel Main St., Chatham, 02633 617-432-1739
Seven Sea Street Inn 7 Sea St., Nantucket, 02554 508-228-3577
Seven South St.—The Inn 7 South St., Rockport, 01966 508-546-6708
Ship's Inn Box 1483, Oak Bluffs, 02557 617-693-2760
Ships Inn 13 Fair St., Nantucket, 02554 508-228-0040
Shiretown Inn N. Water St., Box 921, Edgartown, 02539 800-541-0090
Shiverick Inn, The Martha's Vineyard, 508-627-3797
Simmons Homestead Inn P.O. Box 578, Hyannis Port, 02647 508-778-4999
Six Water Street P.O. Box 1295, Sandwich, 02563 508-888-6808
Soft Breezes Inn 158 Corporation Rd., Dennis, 02638 508-385-5246
South Wind Box 810, Vineyard Haven, 02568 617-693-5031
Spring Cottage B&B Suites 98 Orange Street, Nantucket, 02554 508-325-4644
Squaheag House RR #1, Northfield, 01360 413-498-5749

Stagecoach Hill Inn Route 41, Sheffield, 01257 413-229-8585
Staveleigh House P.O. Box 608, Sheffield, 01257 413-229-2129
Steep Acres Farm 520 White Oaks Rd., Williamstown, 01267 413-458-3774
Stonehedge B&B 119 Sawyer Hill Rd., Berlin, 01503 617-838-2574
Strawberry Banke Farm B&B on Skyline Trail, Middlefield, 01243 413-623-6481
Strawberry Hill P.O. Box 718, Lenox, 01240 413-637-3381
Stump Sprouts Guest Lodge West Hill Rd., West Hawley, 01339 413-339-4265
Sudbury B&B 3 Drum Lane, Sudbury, 01776 617-443-2860
Summer House P.O. Box 313, S. Bluff, Siasconset, 02564 508-257-9976
Sunny Pines B&B Inn 77 Main St, West Harwich, 02671 508-432-9628
Sunnyside Farm 11 River Rd., Whately, 01093 413-665-3113
Sunset Inn 142 Bradford St., Provincetown, 02657 617-487-9810
Suzannah Flint House 98 Essex St., Salem, 01970 508-744-5281
Ted Barbour 88 Rogers St., North Billrtivs, 01862 617-667-7317
Ten Lyon Street Inn 10 Lyon St., Nantucket, 02554 617-228-5040
Terrace Gardens Inn 539 Main St., Centerville, 02632 617-775-4707
Terrace Townehouse 60 Chandler St., Boston, 02116 617-350-6520
Thorncorft Inn Martha's Vineyard, 508-693-3333
Thornewood Inn 453 Stockbridge Rd., Great Barrington, 01230 413-528-3828
Tirnanoag–McKenna Place Chester Rd., Blandford, 01008 413-848-2083
Tisbury Inn Vineyard Haven, Martha's Vineyard, 508-693-2200
Tuck Inn 17 High St., Rockport, 01966 617-546-6252
Tuckerman House 45 William St, Box 194, Vineyard Haven, 02568 617-693-0417
Tuckernuck Inn 60 Union St., Nantucket, 02554 508-228-4886
Twelve Center Guest House 12 Center St., Provincetown, 02657 617-487-0381
Twin Maples 106 South St., Williamsburg, 01098 413-268-7925
Two-Sixty-Four Sandwich St 264 Sandwich St., Plymouth, 02360 508-747-5490
Unique B&B Under Mountain, Box 7, Sheffield, 01257 413-229-3363
Victoria House 5 Standish St., Provincetown, 02657 617-487-1319
Victorian 583 Linwood Ave., Whitinsville, 01588 617-234-2500
Victorian Inn at Harwich P.O. Box 340, Harwich, 02645 508-432-8335
Wake Up On Pleasant Street 31 Pleasant St., Nantucket, 02554 617-228-0673
Wave's Landing Guest House 158 Bradford St., Provincetown, 02657 617-487-9198
Wayside Inn South Sudbury, 01776 617-443-8846
West Moor Inn Off Cliff Rd., Nantucket, 02554 617-228-0877
Whale Inn Rt. 9, Main St., Box 6, Goshen, 01032 413-268-7246
Wharf Cottages New Whale St., Nantucket Island, 02554 617-228-4620
Wheatleigh Inn Lenox, 01240 413-637-0610
White Horse Inn B&B 378 South St, Rts 7 & 2, Pittsfield, 01201 413-443-0961
White Wind Inn 174 Commercial St., Provincetown, 02657 508-487-1526
William Wood House 71 Perry St., Brookline, 02146 617-566-2237
Williams Guest House 136 Bass Av., Gloucester, 01930 617-283-4931
Williamsville Inn Route 41, West Stockbridge, 01266 413-274-6118
Windamar House 568 Commercial St., Provincetown, 02657 617-487-0599
Windflower Inn Route 23, Box 25, Great Barrington, 01230 413-528-2720
Wingate Crossing R 28A,190 N Falmouth Hy, North Falmouth, 02556 617-540-8723
Winsor House Inn P.O. Box 287 SHS, Duxbury, 02331 617-934-0991
Winstead, The 328 Bank St., Harwich, 02645 508-432-4586
Worthington Inn Route 143, Old North Rd, Worthington, 01098 413-238-4441
Wyndemere House 718 Palmer Ave., Falmouth, 02540 617-540-7069
Yankee Pedlar Inn 1866 Northampton St., Holyoke, 01040 413-532-9494

Michigan

ANN ARBOR

The Urban Retreat
2759 Canterbury Rd., 48104
313-971-8110
Andrè Rosalik, Gloria Krys
All year

$$ B&B
2 rooms, 1 pb
C-no/S-yes/P-no/H-no

Full breakfast
Comp. snacks, bar
Sitting room, library
patio, picnic area
gardens, bicycles, A/C

Charming 1850s ranch home on quiet tree-lined street; furnished with antiques; adjacent to 127-acre meadowland park; minutes from major universities.

BAY CITY

Stonehedge Inn B&B
924 Center Ave., 48708
517-894-4342
Ruth Koerber, John Kleekamp
All year

$$ B&B
7 rooms
Visa, MC, AmEx ●
C-yes/S-yes/P-no/H-no

Continental plus
Comp. wine, tea, snacks
Sitting room
library
bicycles

Elegant journey into the past; 1889 English Tudor home has original stained glass windows, nine fireplaces and a magnificent open staircase. Breakfast in formal dining room.

BROOKLYN

Chicago Street Inn
219 Chicago St., 49230
517-592-3888
Karen & Bill Kerr
All year

$$ B&B
4 rooms, 4 pb
Visa, MC
C-13+/S-ltd/P-no

Continental plus
Sitting room

1886 Queen Anne Victorian home, furnished with antiques. Located in quiet village in the foothills of the Irish hills. Antique shops and hiking trails nearby.

CHARLEVOIX

Bridge Street Inn
113 Michigan Ave., 49720
616-547-6606
Vera & John McKown
All year

$$ B&B
9 rooms, 3 pb
●
C-no/S-no/P-no/H-no

Continental plus
Close to beaches,
restaurants, shopping,
& boating

Recapture the grace and charm of a gentler era in this ca. 1895 colonial revival home. 3 stories decorated with unique and interesting antiques. Each room has different decor.

FENNVILLE

Hidden Pond Farm
P.O. Box 461, 49408
5975–128th Ave.
616-561-2491
Priscilla & Larry Fuerst
All year

$$$ B&B
2 rooms, 2 pb
C-13+/S-ltd/P-no/H-no

Full breakfast
Snacks
Sitting room, library
guest use of home
bicycles

28 acres of wooded, ravined land for your relaxation. Full gourmet breakfast. Beaches, Saugatuck, Holland & Fennville 10 minutes away. Lovely quiet retreat.

Morningside, Frankfort, MI

FLINT ───────────────────────────

Avon House B&B
518 Avon St., 48503
313-232-6861
Arletta Minore
All year

$ B&B
3 rooms
C-yes/S-yes/P-no/H-no

Full breakfast
Formal dining room
Sitting room, A/C
Stienway grand piano
extended stay rates

Enchanting Victorian home built in the 1880's. Filled with warm natural woodwork, window benches & antiques. Walk to downtown, cultural center, museums, performing arts, etc.

FRANKFORT ───────────────────────

Morningside B&B
Box 411, 219 Leelanau, 49635
616-352-4008
Shirley Choss
All year

$$ B&B
4 rooms, 4 pb
●
C-yes/S-no/P-no/H-no

Full breakfast
Sitting room
library

Queen Anne Victorian, furnished with antiques. Short walk to beach, lighthouse, pier, shops, marinas, restaurants. South entrance Sleeping Bear Park.

GLEN ARBOR

Sylvan Inn
6680 Western Ave., 49636
P.O. Box 648
616-334-4333
Jenny & Bill Olson
May–February

$$ B&B
14 rooms, 7 pb
Visa, MC •
C-ltd/S-no/P-no/H-yes

Continental plus
Sitting room
hot tubs
sauna

Luxuriously renovated 1885 historic inn situated in the heart of Sleeping Bear National Lakeshore. Easy access to fine dining, shopping, swimming, biking, skiing.

HOLLAND

Dutch Colonial Inn
560 Central Ave., 49423
616-396-3664
Bob & Pat Elenbaas
All year

$$ B&B
5 rooms, 5 pb
Visa, MC, AmEx
C-yes/S-no/P-no/H-no

Full breakfast
Afternoon tea, snacks
Sitting room
bicycles
whirlpool tubs

Lovely 1928 Dutch Colonial home. Touches of elegance and antiques. Air-conditioned. Whirlpool tubs for two in private baths; hideaway suite.

McIntyre B&B
13 E. 13th St., 49423
616-392-9886
Russ & Betty Jane McIntyre
All year

$$ B&B
3 rooms, 1 pb
C-5+/S-no/P-no/H-no

Continental breakfast
Afternoon tea, coffee
Sitting room with TV
near Hope College

Beautifully maintained home built in 1906. Antiques throughout. Air-conditioned rooms. Excellent beds. Off-street parking. Continental breakfast. Warm hospitality.

LAKESIDE

The Pebble House
15093 Lakeshore Rd., 49116
616-469-1416
Jean & Ed Lawrence
All year

$$$ B&B
8 rooms, 6 pb
C-12+/S-yes/P-no/H-ltd

Full breakfast
Library room, pergolas
Screen house w/hammocks
fireplace, bicycles
tennis courts, walkways

Ca. 1910 decorative block & beach pebble house. Arts & Crafts furniture & decorative items. Fireplace, woodstove, rocking chairs and a lake view. Like going home to Grandma's.

LEXINGTON

Governor's Inn B&B
P.O. Box 471, 48450
7277 Simons St.
313-359-5770
Bob & Jane MacDonald
Memorial Day–late Sept

$ B&B
3 rooms, 3 pb
C-12+/S-yes/P-no/H-no

Continental plus
Sitting room

Governor's Inn recreates the atmosphere of a turn-of-the-century summer home—wicker, iron beds, rockers on the shady porch.

LUDINGTON

B&B at Ludington
2458 S. Beaune Rd., 49431
616-843-9768
Grace & Robert Schneider
All year

$ B&B •
4 rooms, 1 pb
Major credit cards •
C-yes/S-no/P-yes/H-yes
French, Spanish

Full country breakfast
Afternoon tea
Sitting room
piano, hot tub
creek & trout pond

Two miles from Lake Michigan, we have 125 acres for hiking, skiing, snowshoeing (showshoes provided). Homey atmosphere yet excellent privacy. Also room in remodeled barn loft.

LUDINGTON

The Inn at Ludington
701 E. Ludington Ave., 49431
616-845-7055
Diane Shields
All year

$$ B&B
6 rooms, 4 pb
Visa, MC, AmEx •
C-yes/S-ltd/P-no/H-no

Full breakfast
Box lunch available
Sitting room
library
fresh flowers

1889 Queen Anne Victorian mansion furnished w/treasured antiques & cherished collectibles. Near beach, shopping, restaurants, X-C skiing. "Dickens' Christmas" weekends in Dec.

MACKINAC ISLAND

Haan's 1830 Inn
P.O. Box 123, 49757, Huron St.
906-847-6244 414-248-9244
The Haan Family
Mid-May–mid-October

$$$ B&B
7 rooms, 5 pb
C-yes/S-ltd/P-no/H-no

Continental plus
Parlor, porches
antique furnishings

Restored Greek Revival home on Historic Register. Across street from Hennepin Bay. 4 blocks from Fort Mackinac and downtown. Featured in Summer 1990 Innsider Magazine.

MANISTEE

Inn Wick-A-Te-Wah
3813 Lakeshore Dr., 49660
616-889-4396
Marge & Len Carlson
All year

$$ B&B
4 rooms, 1 pb
Visa, MC •
C-ltd/S-ltd/P-no/H-no

Full breakfast
Comp. wine, fruit
Snacks, sitting room
inner tubes, bicycles
sunfish (sailing)

Gorgeous view to Portage Lake and Lake Michigan Channel. All water sports, golf, and snow skiing nearby. Lovely, airy rooms with period furnishings.

MARQUETTE

Michigamme Lake Lodge
2403 US 41 West, 49855
906-225-1393 906-339-4400
Frank & Linda Stabile
All year

$$$ B&B
9 rooms, 6 pb
Visa, MC •
C-no/S-no/P-no/H-no

Continental plus
Afternoon tea
Sitting room, porch
gift shop, canoes
1700 ft. of lake & beach

On the lake, sandy beach, canoes, stroll gardens and birch groves. Built in the 1930s. Quiet and secluded. Furnished with antiques. On National and State Register.

NEW BUFFALO

Sans Souci Euro Inn
19265 S. Lakeside Rd., 49117
616-756-3141 FAX:756-5511
Angelika Siewert & family
All year

$$$ B&B
8 rooms, 8 pb
Visa, MC, AmEx •
C-ltd/S-ltd/P-no/H-yes
German, Spanish

Full buffet breakfast
Fireplaces, whirlpools
TV, VCR, audio systems
private lakes, swim/fish
near Lake Michigan, golf

Exceptional accommodations in 88/89 converted farmbuildings. Contemporary warm eurodecor. Privacy. Reunite, meet here. "A little piece of heaven!"

PORT HURON

Victorian Inn
1229 7th St., 48060
313-984-1437
Lennie Smith
All year

$$ B&B
4 rooms, 2 pb
Visa, MC, AmEx, Disc
C-13+/S-yes/P-no/H-no

Continental plus
Restaurant, pub
Lunch, dinner
near museum, downtown
civic center, marina

The Victorian Inn features fine dining with creative cuisine and guest rooms presenting a timeless ambiance in authentically restored Victorian elegance.

PORT SANILAC

Raymond House Inn
111 S. Ridge St., 48469
313-622-8800
Shirley Denison
May–October

$ B&B
7 rooms, 7 pb
●
C-12+/S-ltd/P-no/H-no

Full breakfast
A/C in most rooms
sitting room
pottery studio

112-year-old Victorian home furnished in antiques; on Lake Huron; marina, boating, salmon fishing, swimming; owner-artist's gallery. New studio of handmade pottery.

SAUGATUCK

Kemah Guest House
633 Pleasant, 49453
616-857-2919
Cindi & Terry Tatsch
All year

$$$ B&B
5 rooms
Visa, MC ●
Spanish

Continental plus
Non-alcoholic socials
Sitting room
library

Turn-of-the-century mansion sports a combination of Old World flavor, art deco and a splash of southwestern airiness.

The Kingsley House B&B
626 W. Main, Fennville, 49408
616-561-6425
David & Shirley Witt
All year

$$ B&B
5 rooms, 5 pb
●
C-8+/S-no

Full breakfast
Comp. tea, cocoa, coffee
Sitting rooms, frplcs.
bicycles, porch swing
one jacuzzi suite

Elegant Queen Anne Victorian home, built in 1886. Country setting near beaches, cross-country skiing. Truly an unforgettable experience. Family antiques.

The Park House
888 Holland St., 49453
616-857-4535 800-321-4535
Lynda & Joe Petty
All year

$$$ B&B
7 rooms, 7 pb
Visa, MC ●
C-12+/S-yes/P-no/H-yes

Continental plus
Soft drinks, juice
Sitting room, TV
3rd floor game loft
suites w/jet tub, frplc.

Country home with New England charm; built in 1857. National Historic Register Home. Near town, Lake Michigan beaches, paddleboat rides, dinner cruises, X-C skiing, golf.

Red Dog B&B
P.O. Box 956, 49453
132 Mason St.
616-857-8851
D.Indurante/K.Richter/G.Kott
All year

$$ B&B
6 rooms, 4 pb
Visa, MC ●
C-yes/S-no/P-no/H-no

Continental plus
Sitting room
bicycles

A comfortable place to stay in the heart of Saugatuck. Steps away from restaurants, shopping, golf, beaches, watersports, boardwalk and year-round activities.

Twin Gables Country Inn
P.O. Box 881, 49453
900 Lake St.
616-857-4346
Michael & Denise Simcik
All year

$ B&B
10 rooms, 10 pb
Visa, MC ●
C-ltd/S-ltd/P-no/H-yes
Italian, French, Maltese

Continental plus buffet
Refreshments, fireplace
Whirlpool, hot tub, pool
A/C, bicycles, pond
garden park, ski equip.

Country charm overlooking Kalamazoo Lake. 8 charming rooms, each in a delightful theme decor. Short walk to downtown. 3 cottages furnished in antiques also available.

SAUGATUCK

Wickwood Inn
510 Butler St, Box 1019, 49453
616-857-1097
Sue & Stub Louis
All year

$$ B&B
11 rooms, 11 pb
Visa, MC, AmEx ●
C-no/S-yes/P-no/H-yes

Continental breakfast
Comp. hors d'oeuvres
Full Sunday brunch
screened porch, patio
4 common rooms

Truly elegant comfort in stately home on beautiful Lake Michigan yachting harbor. Laura Ashley decor, antiques, stunning common rooms. Featured in 9/86 Glamour Magazine.

SOUTH HAVEN

Old Harbor Inn
515 Williams St., 49090
616-637-8480
Gwen DeBruyn
All year

$$ EP
37 rooms, 37 pb
Visa, MC, AmEx, DC, Dis ●
C-yes/S-yes/P-no/H-yes

Restaurant
Turndown & laundry serv.
Comp. paper, hot tubs
fishing, boating, golf
tennis, beaches, sailing

Nestled on the banks of the Black River, Old Harbor Inn offers guests the charm and grace of a quaint coastal village. Luxury suites, hot tubs, fireplaces, kitchenettes, pool.

Yelton Manor
140 North Shore Dr., 49090
616-637-5220
Elaine & Rob
All year

$$$ B&B
11 rooms, 11 pb
Visa, MC, AmEx
C-16+/S-ltd/P-no/H-no

Full breakfast
Evening hors d'oeuvres
Fireplace in parlor
library, screened porch
jacuzzis in some rooms

Countrylike atmosphere. Walking distance to lake, marina, shops, fine restaurants. 10 charming guest rooms, including a honeymoon suite. Meeting room facility.

TRAVERSE CITY

Linden Lea On Long Lake
279 S. Long Lake Rd., 49684
616-943-9182
Jim & Vicky McDonnell
All year

$$ B&B
2 rooms, 1 pb
●
C-yes/S-no
Spanish

Full breakfast
Comp. wine, snacks
Sitting room
lake frontage, rowboat
sandy beach, raft

Wooded lakeside retreat with private sandy beach, rowboat & raft. Comfortable country furnishings, window seats, antiques & beveled glass throughout. Heavily wooded. Peaceful.

The Victoriana 1898
622 Washington St., 49684
616-929-1009
Flo & Bob Schermerhorn
All year

$$ B&B
4 rooms, 4 pb
Visa, MC ●
C-12+/S-no/P-no/H-no

Full breakfast
Comp. wine, snacks
Afternoon tea
sitting room
library

Touch a lot of history in this classic Victorian furnished with antiques and family heirlooms. Very special breakfast every day.

UNION CITY

The Victorian Villa Inn
601 N. Broadway St., 49094
517-741-7383
Ronald & Sue Gibson
All year

$$$ B&B
10 rooms, 10 pb
Visa, MC ●
C-yes/S-no/P-no/H-no

Continental (wkdays)
Full breakfast (wkends)
Victorian tea, piano
sitting rooms, bicycles
landscaped grounds

Elegantly restored 1876 estate house with romantic accommodations. An opportunity to escape the 20th century. Special Victorian theme weekends.

UNION PIER ───

Pine Garth Inn	$$$ B&B	Full breakfast
P.O. Box 347, 49129	7 rooms, 7 pb	Complimentary wine
15790 Lakeshore Road	Visa, MC •	Afternoon tea, snacks
616-469-1642	C-no/S-no/P-no/H-no	library, TV's, VCR
R. & P. Bulin, S. Marske		video library, bicycles
All year		

Seven beautiful country style rooms overlooking Lake Michigan. Private beach, fireplaces, whirlpool tubs & fabulous country breakfasts. Four season resort area.

More Inns ...

1880 Inn On The Hill 716 E Ludington Ave, Ludington, 49431 616-845-6458
1882 John Crispe House B&B 404 E. Bridge St., Plainwell, 49080 616-685-1293
A Country Place B&B Rt. 5, Box 43, N. Shore, South Haven, 49090 616-637-5523
Alberties Waterfront 18470 Main St-N. Shores, Spring Lake, 49456 616-846-4016
American Inn B&B 312 E Cass St (M-55), Cadillac, 49601 616-779-9000
Arizona East 3528 Thornville Rd, Metamora, 48455 313-678-3107
Arundel House 56 N. Shore Dr., South Haven, 49090 616-637-4790
Atchison House 501 W. Dunlap St., Northville, 48167 313-349-3340
B&B at Lynch's Dream 22177 80th Ave., Evart, 49631 616-734-5989
B&B at The Pines 327 Ardussi St., Frankenmuth, 48734 517-652-9019
Bannicks B&B 4608 Michigan Rd., M-9, Dimondale, 48821 517-646-0224
Bartlett-Upjohn House 229 Stuart Ave, Kalamazoo, 49007 616-342-0230
Batavia Inn 1824 W Chicago Rd, Coldwater, 49036 517-278-5146
Bavarian Town B&B 206 Beyerlein St, Frankenmuth, 48734 517-652-8057
Bay B&B Route 1, Box 136A, Charlevoix, 49720 616-599-2570
Bear & The Bay 421 Charlevoix Ave., Petoskey, 49770 616-347-6077
Bear Haven 2947—4th St., Trenton, 48183 313-675-4844
Bellaire B&B 212 Park St, Bellaire, 49615 616-533-6077
Belvedere House 306 Belvedere Ave., Charlevoix, 49720 616-547-4501
Betsie Valley B&B 4440 US-31 South, Interlochen, 49643 616-275-7624
Big Bay Lighthouse B&B No. 3 Lighthouse Rd., Big Bay, 49808 906-345-9957
Blanche House Inn 506 Parkview, Detroit, 48214 313-822-7090
Blue Country B&B 1415 Holton Rd (M-120), Muskegon, 49445 616-744-2555
Blue Lake Lodge B&B P.O. Box 1, Mecosta, 49332 616-972-8391
Bogan Lane Inn P.O. Box 482, Mackinac Island, 49757 906-847-3439
Bolins' B&B 576 Colfax Ave, Benton Harbor, 49022 616-925-9068
Botsford Inn 28000 Grand River Ave., Framington Hills, 40824 313-474-4800
Boulevard Inn 904 W. Chicago Blvd., Tecumseh, 49286 517-423-5169
Briaroaks Inn 2980 N. Adrian Hwy., Adrian, 517-263-1659
Bridgewalk B&B P.O. Box 577, Central Lake, 49622 616-544-8122
Brockway House B&B 1631 Brockway, Saginaw, 48602 517-792-0746
Brookside Inn US 31, Beulah, 49617 616-882-7271
Cairn House B&B 8160 Cairn Hwy, Elk Rapids, 49629 616-264-8994
Calumet House B&B P.O. Box 126, Calumet, 49913 906-337-1936
Carrington's Country House 43799 60th Ave., Paw Paw, 49079 616-657-5321
Celibeth House B&B Route 1, Box 58A, Blaney Park, 49836 906-283-3409
Centennial Inn 251 Alpers Rd, Lake Leelanau, 49653 616-271-6460
Chaffin's Balmoral Farm 1245 W. Washington Rd., Ithaca, 48847 517-875-3410
Chandelier Guest House 1567 Morgan Rd., Clio, 48420 313-687-6061
Channel View Inn 217 Park, Charlevoix, 49720 616-147-6180
Charter Cottage P.O. Box 661, Northport, 49670 616-386-5534
Chicago Pike Inn 215 E. Chicago St., Coldwater, 49036 517-279-8744
Cider House B&B 5515 Barney Rd., Traverse City, 49684 616-947-2833
Clifford Lake Hotel 561 W. Clifford Lake, Stanton, 48888 517-831-5151
Coleman Corners B&B 7733 Old M-78, East Lansing, 48823 517-339-9360

Colonial House Inn 90 N. State St., Saint Ignace, 49781 906-643-6900
Cottage On The Bay B&B HCR-1, Box 960, Michigamme, 49861 906-323-6191
Country Chalet 723 S. Meridian Rd., Mount Pleasant, 48858 517-772-9259
Country Charm Farm 5048 Conkey Rd, Caseville, 48725 517-856-3110
Country Cottage B&B 135 E. Harbor Hwy., Maple City, 49664 616-228-5328
Country Heritage B&B 64707 Mound Rd., Romeo, 48065 313-752-2879
Country Inn of Grand Blanc 6136 S. Belsay Rd., Grand Blanc, 48439 313-694-6749
Country Place B&B Rt. 5, Box 43, South Haven, 49090 616-637-5523
Cozy Spot 1145 Kalamazoo, Petoskey, 49770 616-347-3869
Creative Holiday Lodge 1000 Calumet St., Lake Linden, 49945 906-296-0113
Crystal Inn B&B 600 Marquette Ave, Crystal Falls, 49920 906-875-6369
Curtis B&B 4262 S. M-76, West Branch, 48661 517-345-1411
Darmon Street B&B P.O. Box 284, Central Lake, 49622 616-544-3931
Dearborn Inn 200301 Oakwood Blvd., Dearborn, 48124 313-271-2700
Delano Inn 302 Cutler, Allegan, 49010 616-673-2609
Doll House Inn 709 E. Ludington Ave., Ludington, 49431 616-843-2286
Double J Resort Ranch P.O. Box 94, Rothbury, 49452 616-894-4444
Duley's State Street Inn 303 State St, Boyne City, 49712 616-582-7855
E. E. Douville House 111 Pine St., Manistee, 49660 616-723-8654
Easterly Inn P.O. Box 366, East Jordan, 49727 616-536-3434
Ellsworth House Dixon, Rt 1 204 Lake St, Ellsworth, 49729 616-588-7001
Essenmacher's B&B 204 Locust Lane, Cadillac, 49601 616-775-3828
Florence B&B P.O. Box 1031, Bay View, 49770 616-348-3322
Fountain Hill 222 Fountain, NE, Grand Rapids, 49503 616-458-6621
Frankenmuth Bender Haus 337 Trinklein St, Frankenmuth, 48734 517-652-8897
Frieda's B&B 13141 Omena Point Rd., Omena, 49674 616-386-7274
Garden Gate B&B 315 Pearl St., Caro, 48723 517-673-2696
Gibson House, The 311 W Washington, Greenville, 48838 616-7546691
Gingerbread House, The P.O. Box 1273, Bay View, 49770 616-347-3538
Gordon Beach Inn 16240 Lakeshore Rd., Union Pier, 49129 616-469-3344
Green Inn 4045 West M-76, West Branch, 48661 517-345-0334
Greencrest Manor 6174 Halbert Rd, Battle Creek, 49017 616-962-8633
Grist Guest House 310 E. Main St., Homer, 49245 517-568-4063
H. D. Ellis Inn 415 W. Adrian, US 223, Blissfield, 49228 517-486-3155
Hall House B&B 106 Thompson St., Kalamazoo, 49007 616-343-2500
Hansen's Guest House 102 W. Adams, Homer, 49245 517-568-3001
Harbor House Inn Harbor & Clinton Sts., Grand Haven, 49417 616-846-0610
Harbour Inn Beach Dr., Harbor Springs, 49740 616-526-2107
Hart House 244 W Park St, Lapeer, 48446 313-667-9106
Hathaway House Blissfield, 517-486-2141
Haus Austrian 4626 Omena Point Rd., Omena, 49674 616-386-7338
Heald-Lear House 455 College Ave, SE, Grand Rapids, 49503 616-451-4859
Helmer House Inn Route 3, County Rd. 417, McMillan, 49853 906-586-3204
Heritage Manor Inn 2253 Blue Star Hwy, Fennville, 49408 616-543-4384
Hibbard Tavern 115 E Summit, Milford, 48042 313-685-1435
Highland Park Hotel B&B 1414 Lake Ave., Grand Haven, 49417 616-842-6483
Highlands, The P.O. Box 101, Leland, 49654 616-256-7632
Hiram D. Ellis Inn 415 W. Adrian St., Blissfield, 49228 517-486-3155
Homestead B&B 9279 Macon Rd., Ann Arbor—Saline, 48176 313-429-9626
Homestead B&B 9279 Macon Rd, Saline, 48176 313-429-9625
Hotel Frankfort Main St., Frankfort, 49635 616-882-7271
House on the Hill P.O. Box 206, Lake St., Ellsworth, 49729 616-588-6304
J. Paules' Fenn Inn 2254 S 58th St, Fennville, 49408 616-561-2836
Jarrold Farm Box 215A, County Rd 643, Cedar, 49621 616-228-6955
Jay's B&B 4429 Bay City Rd., Midland, 48640 517-631-0470
Kalamazoo House 447 W. South St., Kalamazoo, 49007 616-343-5426
Kimberly Country Estate 2287 Bester Rd, Harbor Springs, 49740 616-526-7646
Kirby House, The Box 1174, 294 W.Center, Saugatuck (Douglas), 49453 616-857-2904

Kueffner Haus B&B 176 Parker St, Frankenmuth, 48734 517-652-6839
L'DA RU B&B 4370 N. Spider Lake Rd., Traverse City, 49684 616-946-8999
Lake Street Manor B&B 8569 Lake St. (M-53), Port Austin, 49467 517-738-7720
Lakeview Hills Country Inn P.O. Box 365, Lewiston, 49756 517-786-2000
Lakeview Inn P.O. Box 297, Grand Marais, 49839 906-494-2612
Last Resort B&B Inn 86 N. Shore Dr, South Haven, 49090 616-637-8943
Laurium Manor B&B 320 Tamarack St, Laurium, 49913 906-337-2549
Lavender Hill B&B Rt 1. Box 92, Ellsworth, 49729 616-588-7755
Leelanau Country Inn 149 E. Harbor Highway, Maple City, 49664 616-228-5060
Ludington House 501 E. Ludington Ave., Ludington, 49431 616-845-7769
Macleod House, The Rt 2, Box 943, Newberry, 49868 906-2933841
Main Street B&B 403 E Main St, Harbor Springs, 49740 616-526-7782
Manitou Manor P.O. Box 864, Leland, 49654 616-256-7712
Mapletree Inn B&B Rt. 1, Box 169-F, M-22, Northport, 49670 616-386-5260
Maplewood B&B 15945 Wood Rd., Lansing, 48906 517-485-1426
Maplewood Hotel P.O. Box 1059, Saugatuck, 49453 616-857-1771
Margaret's B&B 230 Arbutus, Box 344, Manistique, 49854 906-341-5147
Marywood Manor 236 Mary St., Saugatuck, 49453 616-857-4771
Masters House B&B 2253 North Shore, Walloon Lake, 49796 616-535-2294
Mayflower B&B Hotel 827 W. Ann Arbor Trail, Plymouth, 48170 313-453-1620
McCann House, The P.O. Box 241, St. James, 49782 616-448-2387
McCarthy's Bear Creek Inn 15230 "C" Dr. N., Marshall, 49068 616-781-8383
McGee Homestead B&B 2534 Alden Nash NE, Lowell, 49331 616-897-8142
Mendon Country Inn 440 W. Main St., Mendon, 49072 616-496-8132
Metivier Inn Box 285, Mackinac Island, 49757 906-847-6234
Montague Inn 1581 S. Washington Ave., Saginaw, 48601 517-752-3939
Morning Glory Inn 8709 Old Channel Trail, Montague, 49437 616-894-8237
Mulberry House 1251 Shiawassee St., Owasso, 48867 517-723-4890
Munro House B&B 202 Maumee St., Jonesville, 49250 517-849-9292
Murphy Inn 505 Clinton Ave., Saint Clair, 48079 313-329-7118
N. Beach Inn & Restaurant 51 North Shore Dr., South Haven, 49090 616-637-6738
National House Inn 102 S. Parkview, Marshall, 49068 616-781-7374
Neahtawanta Inn 1308 Neahtawanta Rd., Traverse City, 49684 616-223-7315
Newnham Inn Box 1106, 131 Giffith S, Saugatuck, 49453 616-857-4249
Norden Hem Resort P.O. Box 623, Gaylord, 49735 517-732-6794
Oak Cove Resort 58881 46th St., Lawrence, 49064 616-674-8228
Oakbrook Inn 7256 E. Court St., Davison, 48423 313-658-1546
Old Lamplighter's Homestay 276 Capital Ave., N.E., Battle Creek, 49017 616-963-2603
Old Mill Pond Inn 202 West 3rd St., Northport, 49670 616-386-7341
Old Octagon House 595–24th Ave, Hudsonville, 49426 616-896-9941
Old Wing Inn 5298 E. 147th Ave., Holland, 49423 616-392-7362
Olde Bricke House P.O. Box 211, Allen, 49227 517-869-2349
Omena Shores B&B P.O. Box 15, Omena, 49674 616-386-7311
Onekama Lake Breeze House, Onekama, 49675 616-889-4969
PJ's B&B 722 N. 29th St., Bilings, 59101 406-259-3300
Parsonage 1908 6 E. 24th St., Holland, 49423 616-396-1316
Pebble Beach 496 Rosedale Ave., Petoskey, 49770 616-347-1903
Pentwater Abbey P.O. Box 735, Pentwater, 49449 616-869-4049
Pentwater Inn P.O. Box 98, Pentwater, 49449 616-869-5909
Pine Ridge N-10345 Old US 23, Fenton, 48430 313-629-8911
Pine Willow B&B 600 Selden Rd, Iron River, 49935 906-265-4287
Pink Palace Farms 6095 Baldwin Rd., Swartz Creek, 48473 313-655-4076
Plum Lane Inn P.O. Box 74, Northport, 49670 616-386-5774
Porches 2297 70th St., Fennville, 49408 616-543-4162
Porches B&B, The 2297 Lakeshore Dr, Fennville, 49408 616-543-4162
Queen Anne's Castle 500 Webster, Traverse City, 49684 616-946-1459
Questover Inn 8510 Lake St., Port Austin, 48467 517-738-5253
Red Geranium Inn 508 E. Main St. (M-72), Harrisville, 48740 517-724-6153

Reynolds House 5259 W Ellsworth Rd, Ann Arbor, 48103 313-995-0301
Richardi House, The 402 N. Bridge St, Bellaire, 49615 616-533-6111
River Haven 9222 St. Joe River Rd., White Pigeon, 49099 616-483-9104
Riverside Inn 302 River St., Leland, 49654 616-256-9971
Rose Brick Inn 124 E. Houghton Ave., West Branch, 48661 517-345-3702
Rosemont Inn 83 Lake Shore Dr., Douglas, 49406 616-857-2637
Ross B&B House 229 Michigan Ave., South Haven, 49090 616-637-2256
Rummel's Tree Haven 41 N. Beck St., Sebewaing, 48759 517-883-2450
Sault Ste. Marie Water Street Inn, The, 140 E. Water St., 49783 906-632-1900
Seascape B&B 20009 Breton, Spring Lake, 49456 616-842-8409
Shack Country Inn, The 2263 W. 14th St., White Cloud, 49349 616-924-6683
Shifting Sands 19343 N. Shore Dr., Spring Lake, 49456 616-842-3594
Silver Creek 4361 US-23, South, Black River, 48721 517-471-2198
South Cliff Inn B&B 1900 Lakeshore Dr., St. Joseph, 49085 616-983-4881
Spring Brook Inn P.O. Box 390, Prudenville, 48651 517-366-6347
Springbrook B&B 28143 Springbrook Dr., Lawton, 49065 616-624-6359
Stafford's Bay View Inn P.O. Box 3 G, Petoskey, 49770 616-347-2771
Stagecoach Stop B&B Box 18, 4819 Leonard Rd, Lamont, 49430 616-677-3940
Stonegate Inn 10831 Cleveland, Nunica, 49448 616-837-9267
Stuart Avenue Inn B&B 405 Stuart Ave., Kalamazoo, 49007 616-342-0230
Summer House P.O. Box 107, State St, Garden, 49835 906-644-2457
Sunrise B&B Box 52, Eastport, 49627 616-599-2706
Sutton's Weed Farm B&B 18736 Quaker Rd, Hudson, 49247 517-547-6302
Sylverlynd 3452 McBride Rd., Owosso, 48667 517-723-1267
Taggart House B&B 321 E. Maple St., Big Rapids, 49307 616-796-1713
Tall Oaks Inn Bed & Breakf Box 6, Grand Beach, New Buffalo, 49117 616-469-0097
Tall Trees Route 2, 323 Birch Rd., Roscommon, 48653 517-821-5592
Terrace Inn 216 Fairview Ave., Bay View, 49770 616-347-2410
Timekeepers Inn 303 Mears Ave., Whitehall, 49461 616-894-5169
Torch Lake B&B 10601 Coy St., Alden, 49612 616-331-6424
Trillium 611 S. Shore Dr., Frankfort, 49635 616-352-4976
Twala's B&B, Torch Lake Rte 2, Box 84B, Central Lake, 49648 616-599-2864
Union Hill Inn 306 Union, Ionia, 48846 616-527-0955
Victoria Resort 241 Oak, South Haven, 49090 616-637-6414
Victorian Splendor 426 N. Washington St., Owosso, 48867 517-725-5168
Village B&B 1135 Fifth Street, Muskegon, 49440 616-726-4523
Village Green P.O. Box 1731, Dearborn, 48121 313-561-6041
Vintage House B&B Box 424, 102 Shabwasung, Northport, 49670 616-386-7228
Walker's White Gull B&B 5926 Hwy M-22, Glen Arbor, 49636 616-334-4486
Walloon Lake Inn P.O. Box 85, Walloon Lake Village, 49796 616-535-2999
Warwickshire Inn 5037 Barney Rd., Traverse City, 49684 616-946-7176
Washington Street Inn 608 Washington St, Grand Haven, 49417 616-842-1075
Webber House 527 James St., Portland, 48875 517-647-4671
Wellman Accommodations 205 Main St., Horton, 49246 517-563-2231
Wellock Inn 404 S. Huron Ave., Harbor Beach, 48441 517-479-3645
West Wind B&B P.O. Box 344, Lexington, 48450 313-359-5772
White Gull Inn P.O. Box 351, Glenn Arbor, 49636 616-334-4486
White Rabbit Inn 14634 Red Arrow Hwy, Lakeside, 49116 616-469-4620
White Rose Country Inn 6036 Barnhart Rd., Ludington, 49431 616-843-8193
Widow's Watch B&B 401 Lake St., Box 27, Harrisville, 48740 517-724-5465
William Clements Inn 1712 Center (M-25), Bay City, 48708 517-894-4600
Winchester Inn 524 Marshall St., Allegan, 49010 616-673-3621
Windermere Inn 747 Crystal Dr., Beulah, 49617 616-882-7264
Wood How Lodge Route 1 Box 44E, Northport, 49670 616-386-7194
Wood's Inn 2887 Newport Rd, Ann Arbor, 48103 313-665-8394
Wooden Spoon B&B 316 W. 7th St., Traverse City, 49684 616-947-0357
Woods & Hearth B&B 950 S. Third St., Niles, 49120 616-683-0876
Yesterday's Inn 518 N. 4th, Niles, 49120 616-683-6079

Minnesota

CANNON FALLS

Quill & Quilt, B&B
615 W. Hoffman St., 55009
507-263-5507
D. Anderson, D. Karpinski
All year

$ B&B
4 rooms, 4 pb
Visa, MC •
C-12+/S-ltd

Full breakfast
Dinner by arrangement
Comp. wine, sitting room
library, cable TV, games
bikes, rec. room, deck

1897 colonial revival home. Four guest rooms, suite with whirlpool. In scenic Cannon River Valley; near biking, hiking, skiing, canoeing. 1 hour from Minneapolis/St. Paul.

GRAND MARAIS

Pincushion Mountain B&B
P.O. Box 181, 55604
Gunflint Trail
800-542-1226
Scott & Mary Beattie
All year except April

$$ B&B
4 rooms, 1 pb
Visa, MC •
C-12+/S-no/P-no/H-no

Full breakfast
Sitting room, deck
Sauna, hiking, biking
cross-country skiing
44 acres

B&B sits on ridge of Sawtooth Mountains overlooking north shore of Lake Superior 1,000 feet below. Hiking, mountain biking, X-C ski trails at doorstep. Bike and ski rentals.

LAKE CITY

Red Gables B&B Inn
403 N. High St., 55041
612-345-2605
Mary & Douglas DeRoos
All year

$$ B&B
4 rooms, 2 pb
Visa, MC •
C-13+/S-ltd/P-no/H-no

Full breakfast
Comp. wine, snacks
Sitting room, library
bicycles
tennis nearby

Graciously restored 1865 Victorian on the shores of the Mississippi River. Enjoy antique decor, quiet elegance and Victorian breakfast. Sailing, swimming, skiing.

LANESBORO

Mrs. B's Lanesboro Inn
P.O. Box 411, 55949
101 Parkway
507-467-2154
Bill Sermeus, Mimi Abell
All year

$$
9 rooms, 9 pb
S-ltd
some Norwegian, Hebrew

Full breakfast
Lunch & dinner by resv.
Comp. sherry, chocolate
sitting room, library
tennis & golf nearby

Nestled deep in Root River Valley; 1872 limestone building in village on National Register. Serene; rural; famous for regional cuisine.

McGREGOR

Savanna Portage Inn
HCR 4, Box 96, 55760
Clyde N. Johnson
All year

$$ B&B
4 rooms, 2 pb
Visa, MC, AmEx, Dis
C-yes/S-no/P-no/H-yes

Complimentary breakfast
Afternoon tea, snacks
sitting room, library
hiking & skiing trails

Southern colonial style home (1977), 14 wooded acres. Spacious, sunny corner rooms, electric heat. Enjoy hiking, skiing, snowmobiling, hunting, fishing or antiquing nearby.

MINNEAPOLIS

Evelo's B&B	$ B&B	Full breakfast
2301 Bryant Ave. S., 55405	3 rooms	TV, refrigerator
612-374-9656	AmEx ●	coffee maker
David & Sheryl Eveb	C-yes/S-no/P-no/H-no	air conditioning
All year		

1897 Victorian, period furnishings. Located on bus line, walk to Guthrie Theater, Minneapolis Art Institute, children's theater. Near historic Lake District.

Nan's B&B	$$ B&B	Full breakfast
2304 Fremont Ave. S., 55405	3 rooms	Sitting room with
612-377-5118	AmEx ●	woodstove
Nan & Jim Zosel	C-yes/S-yes/P-ask/H-no	beautiful porch
All year		

Comfortable urban 1890s Victorian family home; guest rooms furnished in antiques; near the best theatres, galleries and shopping in Minneapolis. Friendly, informative hosts.

NEW PRAGUE

Schumacher's New Prague	$$$ EP	Restaurant, bar
212 W. Main St., 56071	11 rooms, 11 pb	Breakfast, lunch, dinner
612-758-2133 612-445-7285	Visa, MC, AmEx, Disc ●	Comp. wine, piano
John & Kathleen Schumacher	C-no/S-yes/P-no/H-ltd	front porch, gift shop
All year		whirlpools, fireplaces

Eleven European-decorated sleeping rooms named after the months of the year. Restaurant serves Czechoslovakian and German cuisine seven days a week.

SAINT PAUL

Chatsworth B&B	$$ B&B	Continental plus
984 Ashland Ave., 55104	5 rooms, 3 pb	Tea, coffee, cocoa
612-227-4288	C-yes	Sitting room
Donna & Earl Gustafson		library
All year		2 rooms with whirlpools

Peaceful retreat in city near Governor's Mansion. Whirlpool baths, down comforters, lace curtains. Excellent restaurants and unique shops within walking distance.

SPRING VALLEY

Chase's	$$ B&B	Full farm breakfast
508 N. Huron Ave., 55975	5 rooms, 2 pb	Comp. tea
507-346-2850	Visa, MC ●	Library
Bob & Jeannine Chase	C-yes/S-no/P-no/H-no	sitting room
May—October		crochet

Antiques throughout Chase's 19th-century mansion. Sleep in solitude, breakfast in quietness. Scenic southeastern Minnesota bluff country.

STILLWATER

Lowell Inn	$$$ B&B	Full breakfast
102 N. Second St., 55082	21 rooms, 21 pb	Lunch, dinner, bar
612-439-1100	Visa, MC, DC, AmEx ●	Jacuzzi
The Palmer Family	C-yes/S-yes/P-no/H-yes	
All year	German	

Colonial country inn nestled in history-filled Stillwater, Minnesota near the bluff of St. Croix River. Elegant dining and accommodations.

More Inns . . .

1900 Dupont 1900 Dupont Ave. S., Minneapolis, 55413 612-374-1973
Afton House Inn Hwy 95, Afton, 612-436-8883

American House 410 E. Third St., Morris, 56267 612-589-4054
Anchor Inn Hwy. 4, RR, Spring Lake, 56680 218-798-2718
Anderson House 333 W. Main St., Wabasha, 55981 612-565-4524
Archer House 212 Division St., Northfield, 55057 507-645-5661
Asa Parker House 17500 St. Croix Trail, Marine, 612-433-5248
Asa Parker House B&B 17500 St. Croix Trail N, Marine on the St. Croix, 55047 612-433-5248
B&B Lodge Rt. 3, Box 178, Hinckley, 55037 612-384-6052
Basswood Hill's Farm Route 1, Box 331, Cannon Falls, 55009 507-778-3259
Birdwing Spa Litchfield, 55355 612-693-6064
Black Cow Inn, The 535 6th St., Pine City, 55063 612-629-7421
Bluff Creek Inn 1161 Bluff Creek Drive, Chaska, 55318 612-445-2735
Brasie House 2321 Colfax Ave., Minneapolis, 55405 612-377-5946
Breezy Point Resort P.O. Box 70, Breezy Point Place, 56472 218-562-7811
Bunt's B&B Lake Kabetogama, Ray, 56669 218-875-3904
Calumet Inn 104 W. Main, Pipestone, 56164 507-825-5871
Candlelight Inn, The 818 W. 3rd St., Red Wing, 55066 612-388-8034
Canterbury Inn B&B 723 2nd St. SW, Rochester, 55902 507-289-5553
Caribou Lake B&B N512 Co. Rd., Box 156, Lutsen, 55612 218-663-7489
Carousel Rose Inn 217 W. Third St., Carver, 55315 612-448-5847
Carriage House B&B 420 Main, Winona, 55987 507-452-8256
Carriage House B&B 20 Main St., Winona, 55987 507-452-8256
Carrington House B&B Route 5, Box 88, Alexandria, 56308 612-846-7400
Carrolton Country Inn RR 2, Box 139, Lanesboro, 55949 507-467-2257
Cedar Knoll Farm Rt. 2, Box 147, Good Thunder, 56037 507-524-3813
Chase On The Lake Lodge P.O. Box 206, Walker, 56484 218-547-1531
Cherub Hill 101 NW 1st. Ave., Faribault, 55021 507-332-2024
Christopher Inn 201 Mill St., Excelsior, 55331 612-474-6816
Clearwater Lodge 355-B Gunflint Trail, Grand Marais, 55604 218-388-2254
Como Villa 1371 W. Nebraska Ave., St. Paul, 55108 612-647-0471
Cosgrove 228 S. Second St., Le Sueur, 56058 612-665-2763
Country B&B 32030 Ranch Tr., Shafer, 55074 612-257-4773
Country House, The Rt. 3 Box 110, Miltona, 56354 218-943-2928
Dee's Country B&B 210 S. Indian Tr., Afton, 55001 612-436-6964
Dickson Viking Huss B&B 202 E. 4th St., Park Rapids, 56470 218-732-8089
Dorset Schoolhouse P.O. Box 201, Park Rapids, 56470 218-732-1377
East Bay Hotel Box 246, Grand Marais, 55604 218-387-2800
Eden Bed & Breakfast RR 1, Box 215, Dodge Center, 55927 507-527-2311
Ellery House 28 S. 21st Ave. E., Duluth, 55812 218-724-7639
Evergreen Knoll Acres Rt. 1, Box 145, Lake City, 55041 612-345-2257
Fitzger's Inn 600 E. Superior St., Duluth, 55802 218-722-8826
Fountain View Inn 310 N. Washington Ave., Albert Lea, 56007 507-377-9425
Grand Old Mansion 501 Clay St., Mantorville, 55955 507-635-3231
Grand View Lodge Rt. 6, Box 22, Brainerd, 56401 218-963-2234
Grant House Box 87, Rush City, 55069 612-358-4717
Guest House B&B 299 Outer Dr., Silver Bay, 55614 218-226-4201
Gunflint Lodge Box 100 GT, Grand Marais, 55604 800-328-3325
Hallet House P.O. 247, Crosby, 56441 218-546-5433
Hazlewood c/o Thorwood 705 Vermillion, Hastings, 55033 612-437-3297
Heirloom Inn B&B, The 1103 S. Third St, Stillwater, 55082 612-430-2289
Hotel and Zach's 3rd & Johnson, Winona, 55987 507-452-5460
Hudspeth House B&B 21225 Victory Lane, Taylors Falls, 55084 612-465-5811
Hutchinson House B&B 305 NW 2nd St., Faribault, 55021 507-332-7519
Inn At Palisade, The 384 Hwy. 61 E., Silver Bay, 55614 218-226-3505
Inn on the Farm 6150 Summit Dr., N., Brooklyn Center, 55430 612-569-6330
Inn on the Green Rt. 1 Box 205, Caledonia, 55921 507-724-2818
Jacob's Inn 108 2nd Ave. NW, Kasson, 55944 507-634-4920
Jail House, The 109 Houston 3 NW, Preston, 55965 507-765-2504
Kettle Falls Hotel Box 1272, Int'l Falls, Orr, 55771 218-374-3511
Kings Oakdale Park G.H. 6933 232nd Ave NE, Stacy, 55029 612-462-5598
Lakeside B&B 113 W. 2nd St., Graceville, 56420 612-748-7657

Lamb's B&B 29738 Island Lake Rd., St. Joseph, 56374 612-363-7924
Lawndale Farm Rt. 2, Box 50, Herman, 56248 612-677-2687
Le Blanc House 302 University Ave., Minneapolis, 55413 612-379-2570
Lindgren's B&B Co. Rd. 35, W191, Lutsen, 55612 218-663-7450
Log House On Spirit Lake Box 130, Vergas, 56587 218-342-2318
Lowell House RR 2 Box 177, 531 Wood, Old Frontenac, 55026 612-345-2111
Lund's Guest House 500 Winona St. SE, Chatfield, 55923 507-867-4003
Mansion 3600 London Rd., Duluth, 55804 218-724-0739
Mathew S. Burrows 1890 Inn 1632 E. 1st St., Duluth, 55812 218-724-4991
Miller B&B 887 James Ave., St. Paul, 55102 612-227-1292
Murray Street Gardens B&B 22520 Murray St., Excelsior, 55331 612-474-8089
Naniboujou Lodge Star Route 1, Box 505, Grand Marais, 55604 218-387-2688
Nim's Bakketopp Hus RR 2, Box 187A, Fergus Falls, 56537 218-739-2915
Old Jail Company B&B, The 100 Government Rd, Taylors Falls, 55084 612-465-3112
Old Taylors Falls Jail 102 Government Rd., Taylors Falls, 55084 612-465-3112
Outing Lodge at Pine Point 11661 Myeron Rd N, Stillwater, 55082 612-439-9747
Overlook Inn B&B 210 E. Laurel, Stillwater, 55082 612-439-3409
Palmer House Hotel 500 Sinclair Lewis Ave., Sauk Centre, 56378 612-352-3431
Park Row B&B 525 W. Park Row, St. Peter, 56082 507-931-2495
Park Street Inn, The Rt. 1, Box 254, Nevis, 56467] 612-599-4763
Peacecliff HCR 73, Box 998D, Walker, 56484 218-547-2832
Pepin House 120 S. Prairie St., Lake City, 55041 612-345-4454
Peter's Sunset Beach Hotel Rt. 2, Box 118, Glenwood, 56334 612-634-4501
Pillow, Pillar & Pine 419 Main St., Cold Spring, 56320 612-332-6774
Pine Edge Inn 308 First St. SE, Little Falls, 56345 612-632-6681
Pine Springs Inn 448 Center Ave. N., Blooming Prairie, 55917 507-583-4411
Prairie House Round Lake RR 1, Box 105, Round Lake, 56167 507-945-8934
Pratt Taber Inn 706 W. 4th, Red Wing, 55066 612-388-5945
Prior's On Desoto 1522 Desoto St., St. Paul, 55101 612-774-4244
Rahilly House 304 S. Oak St., Lake City, 55041 612-345-4664
Rainy River Lodge Baudette, 56623 218-634-2730
Red Pine B&B 15140 400th St., North Branch, 55056 612-583-3326
River Rose c/o Thorwood 705 Vermillion, Hastings, 55033 612-437-3297
Rivertown Inn B&B 306 W. Olive St., Stillwater, 55082 612-430-2955
Robards House, The 518 Lincoln Ave., Alexandria, 56308 612-763-4073
Rum River Country B&B Rt. 6, Box 114, Princeton, 55371 612-389-2679
Scanlan House B&b 708 Park Ave. S., Lanesboro, 55949 507-467-2158
Schuyten Guest House 257 Third Ave., Newport, 55055 612-459-5698
Sherwood Forest Lodge 7669 Interlachen Rd., Lake Shore-Brainerd, 56401 218-963-2516
Spicer Castle P.O. Box 307, Spicer, 56288 612-796-5870
St. James Hotel 406 Main St., Red Wing, 55066 612-388-2846
Stanford Inn 1415 Superior St., Duluth, 55805 218-724-3044
Stonehouse B&B HCR 2, Box 9, Pequot Lakes, 56472 218-568-4255
Sunnyside at Forestville RR 2, Box 119, Preston, 55965 507-765-3357
Superior Overlook B&B Box 963, Grand Marais, 55604 218-387-1571
Swanson-Johnson Inn Rt. 2, Box 77, Red Wing, 55066 612-388-3276
Thayer Hotel Hwy. 55, Annandale, 55302 612-274-3371
Thorwood Inn 4th & Pine, Hastings, 55033 612-437-3297
Three Deer Haven Hwy 169, Ely, 55731 218-365-6464
Touch Of The Past 102 3rd Ave. SE, Spring Grove, 55974 507-498-5146
Triple L Farm Rt. 1, Box 141, Hendricks, 56136 507-275-3740
Trovall's Inn Box 98, Hwy. 61, Hoveland, 55606 218-475-2344
University Club, The 420 Summit Ave., St. Paul, 55102 612-222-1751
Victorian Bed & Breakfast 620 South High Street, Lake City, 55041 612-345-2167
Victorian Lace Inn 1512 Whitewater Ave., St. Charles, 55972 507-932-3054
Walden Woods B&B Route 1, Box 193, Deerwood, 56444 612-692-4379
Wm. Sauntry Mansion 626 N. Fourth St, Stillwater, 55082 612-430-2653
Woodland Inn, The Rt. 4, Box 68, Sleepy Eye, 56085 507-794-5981
Young's Island Gunflint Tr. 67-1, Grand Marais, 55604 218-388-4487

Mississippi

COLUMBUS

Amzi Love B&B
305 S. 7th St., 39701
601-328-5413
Sid Caradine
All year

$$$ B&B
4 rooms, 2 pb
Visa, MC ●
C-12+/S-ltd/P-no/H-no
Spanish

Full breakfast
Dinner, wine, snacks
Tea, cappucino, expresso
sitting room, bicycles
tour guide available

Occupied by 7th generation Love family. Greek Revival cottage. Original furnishings. Historic Register. Located in Historic district. Fishing, boating on Tenn.-Tom. Waterway.

JACKSON

Millsaps Buie House
628 N. State St., 39202
601-352-0221
J.Fenter/N.Fleming/H. Brewer
All year

$$$ B&B
11 rooms, 11 pb
Visa, MC, AmEx, DC ●
C-12+/S-ltd/H-yes

Full breakfast
Hospitality hr 5:30-6:30
Sitting room
library

Historic house with its eleven guest rooms offers the services of a fine hotel with the warmth of a home. Understated elegance.

LONG BEACH

Red Creek Colonial Inn
7416 Red Creek Rd., 39560
601-452-3080 800-729-9670
Beau & Betty Gray
All year

$$ B&B
7 rooms, 5 pb
●
C-yes/S-ltd/P-ltd

Continental plus
Lunch & dinner (request)
Coffee, soft drinks
afternoon tea, snacks
library, bicycles

Three-story "raised French cottage" with 6 fireplaces, 64-foot porch, and many antiques. Situated amidst 11 acres of live oaks and magnolias near beaches.

LORMAN

Rosswood Plantation
Route 552, 39096
601-437-4215 800-533-5889
Jean & Walt Hylander
Exc. January–February

$$$ B&B
4 rooms, 4 pb
Visa, MC ●
C-yes/S-ltd/P-no/H-ltd

Full breakfast
Comp. wine, mint juleps
Sitting room, piano, TV
Civil War library
pool, whirlpool/spa

Classic 1857 mansion on a working plantation near Natchez. Ideal for honeymoons. Canopied beds, fine antiques, all conveniences. National Register, a Mississippi landmark.

NATCHEZ

The Briars Inn
P.O. Box 1245, 39120
31 Irving Lane
601-446-9654
R.F Canon, Newton Wilds
All year

$$$ B&B
13 rooms, 13 pb
Visa, MC, AmEx ●
C-12+/S-yes/P-no/H-yes

Full 5-course breakfast
Bar service, snacks
Sitting room, library
swimming pool, porch
gardens

Circa 1812, unique retreat into 19th century splendor with modern amenities. National Register. 19 acres of gardens overlooking Mississippi River. Entirely antique-furnished.

Rosswood Plantation, Lorman, MS

NATCHEZ

Hope Farm
147 Homochitto St., 39120
601-445-4848
Ethel G. Banta
All year

$$$ B&B
4 rooms, 4 pb
C-6+/S-yes/P-no/H-no

Plantation breakfast
Comp. refreshments
Sitting room
library

Fine old southern mansion, circa 1775, on 20 acres including 10 acres of formal gardens. Antiques throughout.

Pleasant Hill
310 S. Pearl St., 39120
601-442-7674
Brad & Eliza Simonton
All year

$$$ B&B
5 rooms, 5 pb
Visa, MC ●
C-yes/S-yes/P-no

Full breakfast
Sitting room

Pleasant Hill is a true family antebellum home with antique-filled rooms plus a lovely garden room where breakfast is served.

PORT GIBSON

Oak Square Plantation
1207 Church St., 39150
601-437-4350 800-729-0240
Mr. & Mrs. William Lum
All year

$$ B&B
8 rooms, 8 pb
Visa, MC, AmEx, Dis ●
C-yes/S-ltd/P-no/H-ltd

Full breakfast
Comp. wine & tea
Victorian parlor
piano, TV, courtyard
fountain, gazebo

Antebellum mansion in the town General Ulysses S. Grant said was "too beautiful to burn." Heirloom antiques. Canopied beds. National Register. AAA 4-diamond rated.

VICKSBURG ───

Cedar Grove Mansion-Inn	$$$ B&B	Full breakfast
2300 Washington St., 39180	17 rooms, 17 pb	Comp. wine or soft drink
P.O. Box B, 39181	Visa, MC ●	Cocktails, mint juleps
601-636-2800 800-862-1300	C-yes/S-ltd/H-yes	live music, hot tubs
Ted Mackey	Spanish	pool, formal gardens
All year		

Antebellum mansion, ca. 1840. Exquisitely furnished with many original antiques, including gaslit chandeliers. Four acres of formal garden. Relive "Gone With the Wind."

The Duff Green Mansion	$$$ B&B	Full breakfast
1114 First East St., 39180	7 rooms, 7 pb	Lunch, dinner, bar
P.O. Box 75	Visa, MC, AmEx, Diners ●	Sitting room, library
601-636-6968 800-992-0037	C-yes/S-yes/P-no/H-ltd	turn-down service, pool
Harry Sharp, Alicia Sharp	Spanish	candlelight tours
All year		

Vicksburg's only true mansion, 12,000 sq. ft. of antique-filled rooms. Used as a hospital during the Civil War. Choice of drink on arrival. Two VIP suites. meeting facilities.

More Inns ...

Anchuca 1010 First East St., Vicksburg, 39180 601-636-4931
Antebellum Homes 906–3rd Ave., Columbus, 39701 601-329-3533
Burn, The 712 N. Union St., Natchez, 39120 601-442-1344
Cartney-Hunt House 408 S. 7th St., Columbus, 39701 601-327-4259
Corners, The 601 Klein St., Vicksburg, 39180 601-636-7421
Dunleith 84 Homochitto, Natchez, 39120 601-446-8500
Gray Oaks 4142 Rifle Range Rd., Vicksburg, 39180 601-638-4424
Hamilton Place 105 E. Mason Ave., Holly Springs, 38635 601-252-4368
Linden 1 Linden Pl., Natchez, 39120 601-445-5472
Melrose 136 Melrose Ave., Natchez, 39120 601-446-9408
Monmouth Plantation P.O. Box 1736, Natchez, 39120 601-442-5852
Mount Holly Box 140, Chatham, 38731 601-827-2652
Oliver-Britt House 512 Van Buren Av., Oxford, 38655 601-234-8043
Ravennaside 601 S. Union St., Natchez, 39120 601-442-8015
Silver Street Inn 1 Silver St., Natchez, 39120 601-442-4221
Springfield Plantation Rt. 1 Box 201, Hwy 553, Fayette, 39069 601-786-3802
Tomil Manor 2430 Drummond St., Vicksburg, 39180 601-638-8893

Missouri

ARROW ROCK ───

Borgman's B&B	$ B&B	Continental plus
706 Van Buren, 65320	4 rooms	Lunch, dinner (arranged)
816-837-3350	C-yes/S-no/P-no/H-yes	Sitting room, porch
Kathy & Helen Borgman		victrola
All year		summer repertory theater

Enjoy antiques, crafts, theater, and history in the warmth of this century-old home in historic Arrow Rock, at the head of the Santa Fe Trail.

Borgman's B&B, Arrow Rock, MO

ARROWROCK

Cedar Grove B&B/Antiques
Cedar Grove, 65320
816-837-3441
Kaye & David Perkins
All year

$$ B&B
2 rooms
C-yes/S-ltd/P-no/H-no

Continental plus
Sitting room
library
yard with swing

Visit our lovely guest house where you can relax and enjoy the charm of an historic small Missouri village. Fine antiques, crafts and gift shops within walking distance.

Down Over Inn
602 Main St., 65320
816-837-3268
John & Joy Vinson
April 15–December 15

$ B&B
4 rooms, 4 pb
C-yes/S-yes/P-no/H-yes

Continental plus
Cottage w/kitchen & bath
Sitting room, piano
porch, The Old Library
playpen toys for kids

Distinctively decorated guest cottage and rooms. Enjoy Missouri small-town atmosphere. See "Tom Sawyer" which was filmed in Arrow Rock. Rare & collectable book shop on-site.

BONNE TERRE

1909 Depot
Oak St. at Allen St., 63628
314-731-5003
Catherine & Douglas Goergens
All year

$$$ EP
8 rooms, 8 pb
Visa, MC, Disc
C-yes/S-ltd/P-no/H-no

Continental breakfast
Restaurant, bar
Dinner W-Sat, Lunch Sat.
scuba diving, boat tours
of Bonne Terre Mine

Restored Victorian Train Depot listed as a National Historic Site. Decorated with authentic railroad memorabilia. Train-car suites available.

BRANSON

Branson House B&B
120 4th St., 65616
417-334-0959
Opal Kelly
March–December

$$ B&B
7 rooms, 7 pb
●
C-no/S-ltd/P-no/H-no

Full gourmet breakfast
Comp. wine, cookies
Sitting room
yard, central A/C

Old home furnished with antiques. Breakfast served in the dining room or on the front porch. Overlooking downtown Branson and beautiful lake. Quaint, romantic surroundings.

Gaines Landing B&B
P.O. Box 1369, 65616
521 W. Atlantic St.
800-825-3145
Jeanne D. Gaines
All year

$$ B&B
3 rooms, 3 pb
●
C-no/S-no/P-no/H-no

Full breakfast
Sitting room
Library
swimming pool
spa

Contemporary home featuring a suite with private entrance, bath and hot tub. Two rooms with king size beds, private entrances and bath, swimming pool and spa.

CARTHAGE

Grand Avenue Inn
1615 Grand Ave., 64836
417-358-7265
Dixie & Neal Carter
All year

$$ B&B
4 rooms, 4 pb
Visa, MC ●
C-yes/S-no/P-no/H-no

Full breakfast
Snacks
Sitting room
library

Victorian inn listed in National Register. Furnished in antiques and country charm. Close to Precious Moments Chapel, Red Oak II, Crossroads of America on Historic Route 66.

COLUMBIA–ROCHEPORT

School House B&B
Third & Clark Sts., 65279
314-698-2022
John & Vicki Ott
All year

$$ B&B
8 rooms, 8 pb
Visa, MC ●
C-no/S-no/P-no/H-yes

Full breakfast
Comp. milk & cookies
Outdoor garden courtyard
Sitting room, jacuzzi
bicycle & walking trail

Turn-of-the-century, 3-story schoolhouse. Newly renovated and restored. Near Missouri River Bike Trail, cafes, antique shops, and theater.

HANNIBAL

Fifth Street Mansion
213 S. Fifth St., 63401
314-221-0445 800-874-5661
Donalene & Mike Andreotti
All year

$$ B&B
7 rooms, 7 pb
●
C-yes/S-yes/P-no/H-no

Full breakfast
Complimentary tea
Sitting room
special event weekends

Italianate Victorian brick mansion; National Historic Register home near historic district. Special events like mystery weekends, craft workshops, and art shows.

Garth Woodside Mansion
RR 1 off Route 61, 63401
314-221-2789
Diane & Irv Feinberg
All year

$$ B&B
8 rooms, 8 pb
Visa, MC ●
C-12+/S-ltd

Full breakfast
Comp. tea or hot cider
Library, tour planning
turndown service
guest nightshirts

Mark Twain was a guest at this 39-acre country estate. Original Victorian furnishings, flying staircase. Pampered elegance, hospitality and a relaxing experience awaits you.

HERMANN

Birk's Gasthaus
700 Goethe St., 65041
314-486-2911 800-748-7883
Gloria & Elmer Birk
Exc. Dec 25–Jan 1

$ B&B
9 rooms, 7 pb
Visa, MC ●
C-no/S-no/P-no/H-no

Full breakfast
Comp. coffee
Dining area, lounge
piano, sitting room
porch with gazebo

Original owner owned 3rd largest winery in the world, still in operation. Victorian furnishings, tubs w/gold-plated feet. Mystery Dinner Theater. Grand place to stay.

INDEPENDENCE

Woodstock Inn B&B
1212 W. Lexington, 64050
816-833-2233
Lane & Ruth Harold
All year

$ B&B
11 rooms, 11 pb
Visa, MC
C-yes/S-no/P-no/H-yes
German

Full breakfast
Comp. coffee, tea, etc.
Sitting room
National Frontier Trails
Center 6 blocks away

Enjoy comfort, privacy and tastefully appointed rooms in this century-old renovated bed and breakfast. Individualized breakfasts. Truman, Missouri history sites nearby.

KANSAS CITY

Doanleigh Wallagh Inn
217 E. 37th St., 64111
816-753-2667
Ed & Carolyn Litchfield
All year

$$ B&B
5 rooms, 5 pb
Visa, MC, AmEx ●
C-yes/S-ltd/P-no/H-no

Full breakfast
Pump organ, piano, TV
Facilities for meetings,
parties, weddings
phone & TV in rooms

Located between the Plaza and Crown Center. Georgian style home – European and American antiques, romantic, comfortable elegance, Midwestern hospitality, unpretentious.

Milford House B&B
3605 Gillham Rd., 64111
816-753-1269
Ian & Pat Mills
All year

$$ B&B
4 rooms, 4 pb
Visa, MC, AmEx ●
C-10+/S-no/P-no/H-no

Full breakfast
Afternoon tea, snacks
Sitting room, piano
tennis courts
phones & TVs in rooms

100-year-old home situated in heart of Kansas City. Combination of Queen Anne and Dutch Colonial style. Four luxurious guest rooms. Afternoon tea our specialty!

Southmoreland on the Plaza
116 E. 46th St., 64112
816-531-7979
Penni Johnson, Susan Moehl
All year

$$$ B&B
12 rooms, 12 pb
Visa, MC, AmEx ●
C-13+/S-ltd/P-no/H-yes

Full breakfast
Comp. wine, snacks
Library, frplc, solarium
decks, jacuzzi, croquet
airport shuttle, mod/FAX

Only B&B on Country Club Plaza, Kansas City's cultural, shopping, entertainment area. Elegantly restored Colonial revival; special services for business & vacation traveler.

MOUNTAIN VIEW

Jack's Fork Country Inn
Route 1 Box 347, 65548
Hwy 17
805-934-1000
Exc. December 2 weeks

$ B&B
5 rooms, 5 pb
Visa, MC, Dis
C-yes/S-ltd/P-yes/H-no

Full gourmet breakfast
Gazebo, TV/library room
Sitting room, antiques
swimming pool, hot tubs
canoe trips, hunting

Charming country home with antiques throughout. Gardenlike setting with panoramic views Perfect for the romantically inclined or sports enthusiast.

Jack's Fork Country Inn, Mountain View, MO

PARKVILLE

Down to Earth Lifestyles
12500 N. Crooked Rd., 64152
Route 22
816-891-1018
Lola & Bill Coons
All year

$$ B&B
4 rooms, 4 pb
●
C-yes/S-yes/H-yes

Full breakfast
Drink on arrival, wine
Sitting room, piano
organ, entertainment
indoor heated pool

Unique new earth-contact home designed for guests. Private baths, telephones, indoor pool. Closed-in country setting between Kansas City and airport.

PLATTE CITY

Basswood Country Inn
15880 Interurban Rd., 64079
816-431-5556 800-242-2775
Don & Betty Soper
All year

$$ B&B
7 rooms, 7 pb
Visa, MC ●
C-7+/S-yes/P-no/H-ltd
American Sign Language

Continental plus
Private entrances, decks
Fishing lakes, trails
craft & gift store
shuffleboard, horseshoes

Historic Basswood Lakes; former millionaire's estate. 6 suites plus mother-in-law cottage sleeps 6. Elegant country French; private baths, patios, refrig., microwaves and TV.

SAINT CHARLES

Saint Charles House
338 S. Main St., 63301
314-946-6221
Patricia York
All year

$$$ B&B
3 rooms, 3 pb
C-no/S-no/P-no/H-no

Continental plus
Complimentary snacks
tours, riverboats
trolley rides nearby

In heart of ten block historic area on Missouri River. One elegant suite, two English cottage rooms furnished in fine antiques. Near museums, shops and restaurants.

SAINT JOSEPH

Harding House B&B
219 N. 20th St., 64501
816-232-7020
Glen & Mary Harding
All year

$ B&B
4 rooms, 1 pb
Visa, MC, AmEx ●
C-yes

Full breakfast
Afternoon tea
Comp. wine, tea room
sitting room, library
antique pump organ

Gracious turn-of-the-century home, furnished with antiques, offers you warm hospitality. Famous lemon bread and homemade coffee cakes.

SAINT LOUIS

Coachlight B&B
P.O. Box 8095, 63156
314-367-5870
Susan & Chuck Sundermeyer
All year

$$ B&B
3 rooms, 3 pb
Visa, MC, AmEx ●
C-3+/S-ltd/P-no/H-no

Full breakfast
Comp. refreshments
Sitting room
color TV, A/C
phone in room

1904 World's Fair vintage brick home, Friendly ambiance, charming, beautiful antiques. Generous breakfast. Historic neighborhood; walk to shops, restaurants, galleries.

Lafayette House
2156 Lafayette Ave., 63104
314-772-4429
Sarah & Jack Milligan
All year

$ B&B
4 rooms, 2 pb
●
C-yes/S-yes/P-no/H-no

Full breakfast
Comp. wine, snacks
Sitting room
library, cable TV, VCR
crib available

An 1876 Victorian mansion "in the center of things to do in St. Louis." Air conditioned. We have resident cats. Furnished in antiques but with modern conveniences.

Music Box Inn
703 North Kirkwood Rd., 63122
314-822-0328
Nancy Yablonski
All year

$$ B&B
4 rooms, 4 pb
Visa, MC ●
C-ltd/S-no/P-no/H-no

Full breakfast
Comp. tea, wine
Sitting room
porch, bicycles
flower gardens

Listen to the sounds of antique music boxes; a delightful colonial featured in "Better Homes and Gardens".

Winter House
3522 Arsenal St., 63118
314-664-4399
Kendall/Sarah Lee Winter
All year

$$ B&B
2 rooms, 2 pb
Visa, MC, DC ●
C-12+/S-no/P-no/H-no

Continental plus
Comp. tea
Sitting room
balcony, small deck
near tennis and trails

1897 Richardsonian Romanesque 10-room house with turret. Complimentary tea and live piano on weekends by arrangement. Close to Missouri Botanical Gardens and symphony.

SAINT LOUIS—BONNE TERRE

Mansion Hill Country Inn
11215 Natural Bridge, 63044
Mansion Hill Dr.
314-731-5003 314-358-5311
Douglas & Catherine Goergens
All year

$$$ EP
5 rooms, 2 pb
Visa, MC, Disc
C-yes/S-ltd/H-no

Continental breakfast
Restaurant, dinner W-Sat
Lunch Sat, full pub
sitting room, library
golf, scuba diving

Relaxed getaway in turn-of-the-century English-style mansion on 130 acres with 45-mile view of Ozark Mountain foothills. Fishing, golf, X-C ski, scuba at Bonne Terre Mine.

SPRINGFIELD

Walnut Street Inn	$$ B&B	Full breakfast
900 E. Walnut St., 65806	6 rooms, 6 pb	Dinner with reservation
417-864-6346	Visa, MC ●	Comp. wine & cheese, bar
Karol & Nancy Brown	C-10+/S-no/P-no	high tea, sitting room
All year		tennis nearby

Gracious 1894 Victorian inn in city's historic district. City's showcase home furnished with beautiful antiques. Gourmet breakfast in bed available.

TRENTON

Hyde Mansion B&B	$$ B&B	Full breakfast
418 E. 7th St., 64683	5 rooms, 5 pb	Comp. beverages, snacks
816-359-5631	Visa, MC, AmEx	Sitting room, library
Robert & Carolyn Brown	C-12+/S-ltd/P-no/H-no	Baby Grand piano, patio
All year		screened porch, bicycles

Inviting hideaway in rural America, 1949 mansion refurbished for your convenience. Close to Amish country, serves full breakfast.

WARRENSBURG

Cedarcroft Farm B&B	$ B&B	Full breakfast
Route 3, Box 130, 64093	2 rooms	Lunch, dinner by arrang.
816-747-5728 800-368-4944	Visa, MC, Dis ●	Comp. tea & goodies
Bill & Sandra Wayne	C-yes/S-ltd/P-no/H-no	sitting room, parlor
All year		hiking trails, ponds

Real country hospitality in antique-filled 1867 family farmhouse with 80 acres to roam. Only an hour from Kansas City, Truman Lake. Hosts are Civil War reenactors/historians.

WASHINGTON

Schwegmann House B&B Inn	$$ B&B	Continental plus
438 W. Front St., 63090	9 rooms, 7 pb	Bicycles
314-239-5025	Visa, MC ●	sitting room
Karen Jones	C-yes/S-yes/P-no/H-yes	piano
All year		

A stately pre-Civil War Georgian-style brick residence overlooking the Missouri River in the heart of Missouri's wine country. Antique furnishings and quilts.

Washington House B&B Inn	$$$ B&B	Full breakfast
P.O. Box 527, 63090	4 rooms, 4 pb	Comp. bottle of wine
3 Lafayette	●	Cheese, teas, coffees
314-239-2417	C-yes/H-yes	sitting room
Chuck & Kathy Davis		
All year		

Our historic 1837 inn on the Missouri River features antique furnishings and decor, queen-size canopy beds, river views, country breakfasts. Balcony and terrace on riverside.

More Inns ...

Arthur's Horse & Carriage 601 W. Maple, Independence, 64050 816-461-6814
Augustin River Bluff Farm RR 1, Box 42, New Haven, 63068 314-239-3452
B&B on the Square P.O. Box 320, Carthage, 64836 417-358-1501
Benner House B&B 645 Main St., Historic Weston, 64098 816-386-2616
Boone's Lick Trail Inn 1000 S. Main St., Saint Charles, 63301 314-947-7000
Bordello House 111 Bird, Hannibal, 63401 314-221-6111
Brewer's Maple Lane Farms RR #1, Carthage, 64836 417-358-6312
Country View B&B Route 3, Box 593, Nixa, 65714 417-725-1927
Das Brownhaus 125 E. 2nd St., Hermann, 65041 314-486-3372

Der Klingerbau Inn 108 E. 2d St., Hermann, 65041 314-486-2030
Dome Ridge 14360 N.W. Walker Rd., Kansas City, 64164 816-532-4074
Eminence Cottage & Brkfst P.O. Box 276, Eminence, 65466 314-226-3642
Faust Townhouse 8023 N. Stoddard, Kansas City, 64152 816-741-7480
Frisco House Church & Rella Streets, Hartville, 65667 417-741-7304
Gramma's House Route 3, Box 410, Marthasville, 63357 314-433-2675
Grandpa's Farm Box 476, HCR1, Lampe, 65681 417-779-5106
Hotel Sainte Genevieve Main & Merchant Sts., Sainte Genevieve, 63670 314-883-2737
Inn St. Gemme Beauvais 78 N. Main, Box 231, Sainte Genevieve, 63670 314-883-5744
Lakeview Hills Country Inn One Lakeview Dr., Lewiston, 49756 517-786-2000
Lamplight Inn B&B 207 E. School St., Bonne Terre, 63628 314-358-4222
Loganberry Inn 310 W. 7th St., Fulton, 65251 314-642-9229
Ozark Mountain Country B&B P.O. Box 295, Branson, 65616 417-334-4720
Parkview Farm RR #1, Box 54, Lathrop, 64465 816-664-2744
Pridewell 600 W. 59th St., Kansas City, 64112 816-931-1642
Ramblewood B&B 402 Panoramic Dr., Camdenton, 65020 314-346-3410
Richardson House B&B P.O. Box 227, Jamesport, 64648 816-684-6664
River Country B&B 1900 Wyoming, Saint Louis, 63118 324-965-4328
River's Edge B&B Resort HCR 1, Box 11, Eminence, 65466 314-226-3233
Saint Charles House 338 S Main St, Charles, 63301 314-946-6221
Schmidt Guesthouse 300 Market, Hermann, 65041 314-486-2146
Schuster-Rader Mansion 703 Hall St., Saint Joseph, 64501 816-279-9464
Seven Gables Inn 26 N. Meramec, Saint Louis, 63105 314-863-8400
Shawnee Bluff Route 72, Box 14-2, Lake Ozark, 65049 314-365-2442
Southern Hotel 146 S. Third St., Sainte Genevieve, 63670 314-883-3493
Steiger Haus 1021 Market St., Sainte Genevieve, 63670 314-883-5881
Trisha's B&B 203 Bellevue, Jackson, 63755 314-243-7427
Victorian Guest House #3 Stillwell, Hannibal, 63401 314-221-3093
Wardell Guest House One Wardell Rd., Macon, 63552 816-385-4352
Whip Haven Farm R.R. 1, Box 395, Sullivan, 63080 314-627-3717
William Klinger Inn P.O. Box 29, Hermann, 65041 314-486-5930

Montana

BIG SKY

Lone Mountain Ranch
P.O. Box 69, 59716
Lone Mountain Access Rd.
406-995-4644
Bob/Vivian Schaap, M. Ankeny
All year

$$$ AP
20 rooms, 20 pb
Visa, MC, AmEx •
C-yes/S-no/P-no/H-ltd

All meals included
Winter sleighride dinner
Bar, sitting room, piano
hot tub, jacuzzi, horses
weekly rates

Historic guest ranch offering family vacations and Nordic ski vacations near Yellowstone National Park. Beautiful log cabins with fireplaces, conveniences.

BIGFORK

Burggraf's Countrylane B&B
Rainbow Dr., 59911
on Swan Lake
406-837-4608 406-837-2468
Natalie, R.J. Burggraf & pets
April–January

$$ B&B
3 rooms, 2 pb
Visa, MC •
C-yes/S-ltd/P-no/H-yes

Full breakfast
Comp. wine/cheese/fruit
Picnic baskets avail.
lake, snowmobile rental
boat and canoe rental

True log home nestled in heart of Rocky Mountains; 7 acres on the shores of Swan Lake; panoramic view; complimentary wine & cheese; country breakfast. Boating or canoeing.

BOZEMAN

Sun House B&B
9986 Happy Acres West, 59715
406-587-3651
Richard & Patricia Crowle
All year

$ B&B
3 rooms, 1 pb
Visa, MC •
C-yes/S-no/P-no/H-no

Full breakfast
Comp. wine, soft drinks
Sitting room
library, hot tubs
cross-country ski trails

Quiet, country retreat—a mountain hideaway near fishing, hiking, and skiing.

Silver Forest Inn
15325 Bridger Canyon Rd, 59715
406-586-1882
Kathryn & Richard Jensen
All year

$ B&B
5 rooms, 2 pb
Visa, MC •
C-yes/S-ltd/P-ask/H-no
Spanish

Full breakfast
Catered lunch & dinner
Aftn. tea, comp. wine
sitting room, 2 hot tubs
massage, TV, Ping-Pong

Romantic and historic mountain hideaway with panoramic vistas, year-round recreation, superb skiing, delicious breakfasts and friendly innkeepers.

Voss Inn
319 S. Willson, 59715
406-587-0982
Bruce & Frankee Muller
All year

$$ B&B
6 rooms, 6 pb
Visa, MC, DC •
C-ltd/S-ltd/P-no/H-no

Full breakfast
Afternoon tea, sherry
Sitting room, piano
day trips to Yellowstone

Warmly elegant historic Victorian mansion beautifully decorated with period wallpaper and furniture. Walk to university, museums, restaurants, shopping.

GREAT FALLS

Sovekammer B&B Inn
1109 Third Ave. N., 59401
406-453-6620
Dean & Irene Nielsen
All year

$ B&B
5 rooms, 2 pb
Personal checks •
C-yes/S-no/P-no/H-no

Gourmet Danish breakfast
Gourmet coffee all day
Lunch & dinner (resv.)
sitting room, bicycles
front porch and swing

Colorful, old-fashioned inn in historic downtown. Walk to CM Russell Museum. Perfect stop between Yellowstone and Glacier Park!

Three Pheasant Inn
626 Fifth Ave. N., 59401
406-453-0519
B.J. Morse
All year

$ B&B
5 rooms, 2 pb
Visa, MC, Disc •
S-no/P-no/H-no

Full breakfast
Comp. wine, snacks
Sitting room
library with cable TV
private garden, gazebo

Charming antique-filled Victorian home in the heart of Great Falls. Enjoy our excellent breakfasts, gracious guest rooms and shared sun porches, booklined library and garden.

RED LODGE

Willows Inn
P.O. Box 886, 59068
224 South Platt Ave.
406-446-3913
Elven, Kerry & Carolyn Boggio
All year

$ B&B
6 rooms, 4 pb
Visa, MC •
C-yes/S-no/P-no/H-no
Finnish, Spanish

Continental plus
Comp. aftn. refreshments
TV parlor w/VCR & movies
games/books, local menus
ski racks, sun decks

Charming Victorian, beautifully decorated guest rooms. Delicious homebaked pastries. Spectacular mountain scenery. Yellowstone Park; ski, fish, hike, golf, bike. 2 cottages.

THREE FORKS ——————————————————————————

Sacajawea Inn $ EP   Restaurant, bar service
P.O. Box 648, 59752   34 rooms   All meals available
5 N. Main Street   Visa, MC, AmEx, Dis ●   Library, dining room
406-285-6934   C-yes/S-ltd/P-ask/H-ask   rocking chairs
Jane & Smith Roedel   Spanish, French
All year

Come savor the casual elegance of a bygone era in this 1910 National Historic Landmark.
Excellent fishing, hunting, biking. Between Glacier & Yellowstone Parks.

WHITEFISH ——————————————————————————

Kandahar Lodge $$$ EP/MAP   Full breakfast
P.O. Box 1659, 59937   50 rooms, 50 pb   Restaurant
Big Mountain Rd.   Visa, MC, AmEx, Disc ●   Sitting room
406-862-6098   C-yes/S-yes/P-no/H-no   two hot tubs
Buck & Mary Pat Love   two saunas
All year

Beautiful rock and cedar lodge in Alpine setting. Ski to the door. Close to Glacier Park.
European atmosphere, restaurant. Rustic yet elegant.

More Inns . . .

Bighorn Lodge 710 Bull River Rd., Noxon, 59853 406-847-5597
Bull Lake Guest Ranch 15303 Bull Lake Rd., Troy, 59935 406-295-4228
Camp Creek Inn 7674 Hwy 93 South, Sula, 59871 406-821-3771
Castle B&B 900 S. Baker Ave., Whitefish, 59937 406-862-1257
Chalet, The 1204 — 4th Ave. N., Great Falls, 59401 406-452-9001
Cliff Lake Lodge P.O. Box 573, Cameron, 59720 406-682-4982
Cottonwood Ranch Retreat P.O. Box 1044, Roberts, 59070 406-445-2415
Country Caboose B&B 852 Willoughby Rd., Stevensville, 59870 406-777-3145
Double Arrow Lodge Seeley Lake, 59868 800-468-0777
Duck Inn 1305 Columbia Ave., Whitefish, 59937 406-862-DUCK
Edgewood, The 12 Dakota Ave., Whitefish, 59937 406-862-WOOD
Foxwood Inn Box 404, White Sulphur Springs, 59645 406-547-3918
Goldsmith Inn 809 E. Front, Missoula, 59802 406-721-6732
Grave Creek B&B P.O. Box 551, Eureka, 59917 406-882-4658
Hargrave Cattle House Thompson River Valley, Marion, 59925 406-858-2284
Hibernation House P.O. Box 1400, Whitefish, 59937 406-862-3511
Hidden Hollow Hideaway Box 233, Townsend, 59644 406-266-3322
Huckleberry Inn 1028 3rd Ave. W., Kalispell, 59901 406-755-4825
Johnson's Petty Creek Rnch Mail Box 195, Alberton, 59820 406-864-2111
Lazy K Bar Ranch Box 550, Big Timber, 59011 406-537-4404
Lehrkind Mansion 719 N. Wallace, Bozeman, 59715 406-586-1214
Maxwell's Mountain Home 606 S. Broadway, Red Lodge, 59068 406-446-3052
Mission Mountain B&B RR Box 183 A, Saint Ignatius, 59865 406-745-4331
Nevada City Hotel Nevada City, 59755 406-843-5377
O'Duachain Country Inn 675 Ferndale Dr., Bigfork, 59911 406-837-6851
PJ's B&B 722 N. 29th St., Billings, 59101 406-259-3300
Pitcher Guest House P.O. Box 3450, Red Lodge, 59068 406-446-2859
Ruth's B&B 802 7th. Ave, Polson, 59860 406-883-2460
Schwartz's B&B 890 McCaffery Rd., Bigfork, 59911 406-837-5463
Torch & Toes B&B 309 S. Third Ave., Bozeman, 59715 406-586-7285
Upcountry Inn 2245 Head Lane, Helena, 59601 406-442-1909
Virgelle Merc. Rural Route 1, Loma, 59460 800-426-2926
Whispering Pines Box 36, Huson, 59846 406-626-5664

Nebraska

PAXTON ———————————————————————————————

Gingerbread Inn	$ B&B	Full breakfast
P.O. Box 247, 69155	5 rooms, 2 pb	Lunch for groups
308-239-4265	Visa, MC	Sitting room, library
All year	C-3+/S-no/P-no/H-no	garden with gazebo
		picnic grounds, bikes

Come relax country style. Just off I-80. Restored 1895 home. Genuine antiques. Breakfast served from wood range. Complimentary gingerbread cookies.

More Inns . . .

Bel-Horst Inn Marion at fountain, Belgrade, 68623 308-357-1094
Clown 'N Country RR Box 115, Madrid, 69150 308-326-4378
Fort Robinson Inn Box 392, Crawford, 69339 308-665-2660
Grey Gull 321 Webhannet Dr., Wells, 04090 207-646-7501
My Blue Heaven 1041 5th St., Pawnee City, 68420 402-852-3131
Offutt House 140 N. 39th St., Omaha, 68131 402-553-0951
Plantation House B&B Rt.2, Box 17, Elgin, 68636 402-843-2287
Rogers House 2145 "B" St., Lincoln, 68502 402-476-6961
Spring Lake Ranch H.C. 84, Box 103, Gordon, 69343 308-282-0835
Thompson House Route 1, Brownville, 68321 402-825-6551
Watson Manor Inn 410 S. Sycamore, North Platte, 69103 308-532-1124

Nevada

CARSON CITY ———————————————————————————

Deer Run Ranch B&B	$$$ B&B	Full breakfast
5440 Eastlake Blvd., 89704	2 rooms, 2 pb	Comp. wine, beverages
Washoe Valley	Visa, MC	Snacks, refrigerator
702-882-3643	C-no/S-no/P-ask/H-no	sitting room, library
David & Muffy Vhay	limited Spanish	TV, VCR, private entry
Exc. Thanksgiving & Xmas		

Western ambiance in a unique architect-designed and built ranch house near Reno and Carson City overlooking Washoe Lake. Pond, swimming pool, privacy, great breakfasts.

ELY ———————————————————————————————————

Steptoe Valley Inn	$$ B&B	Full breakfast
P.O. Box 151110, 89315	5 rooms, 5 pb	Juice and cheese
220 E. 11th	Visa, MC, AmEx	Sitting room, library
702-289-8687	C-12+/S-no/P-no/H-no	rose garden, back porch
Jane & Norman Lindley	Spanish	private balconies, TVs
June–September		

Romantic, historic structure near railroad museum, reconstructed 1990. Elegant dining room/library. Rooms have country-cottage decor. Guided backcountry outings.

INCLINE VILLAGE ───────────

Haus Bavaria　　　　　　$$ B&B　　　　　　Full breakfast
P.O. Box 3308, 89450　　　5 rooms, 5 pb　　　Comp. wine
593 N. Dyer Circle　　　　Visa, MC, AmEx ●　Large family room
702-831-6122 800-GO TAHOE　C-10+/S-no/P-no/H-no　TV, fireplace
Bick Hewitt
All year

There is much to do and see in this area, from gambling casinos to all water sports and golf,
hiking, tennis and skiing at 12 different nearby sites.

More Inns ...

B&B South Reno 136 Andrew Lane, Reno, 89511 702-849-0772
Blue Fountain B&B 1590 "B" St., Sparks, 89431 702-359-0359
Breitenstein House Lamoille, 89828 702-753-6356
Edith Palmer's Country Inn Box 756, South B St., Virginia City, 89440 702-847-0707
Elliot Chartz House 412 N. Nevada, Carson City, 89701 702-882-5323
Genoa House Inn P.O. Box 141, 180 Nixon, Genoa, 89411 702-782-7075
Gold Hill Hotel Box 304, Virginia City, Virginia City, 89440 702-847-0111
Hardwicke House P.O. Box 96, Silver City, 89429 702-847-0215
Old Pioneer Garden Inn Star Rt. Unionville #79, Imlay, 89418 702-538-7585
Orchard House 188 Carson St., Genoa, 89411 702-782-2640
Robin's Nest Inn 130 E. Winnemucca, Winnemucca, 89445 702-623-2410
Robric Ranch P.O. Box 2, Yerrington, 89447 702-463-3515
Savage Mansion P.O. Box 445, Virginia City, 89440 702-847-0574
Sierra Spirit Ranch 3000 Pinenut Rd., Gardnerville, 89410 702-782-7011
Windybrush Ranch Box 85, Smith, 89430 702-465-2481

New Hampshire

ANDOVER ───────────

The English House　　　$$ B&B　　　　　　Full breakfast
P.O. Box 162, Main St., 03216　7 rooms, 7 pb　　　Comp. sherry, aftn. tea
Main Street　　　　　　　Visa, MC　　　　　Sitting room
603-735-5987　　　　　　C-9+/S-no/P-no/H-yes　homemade jams
Ken & Gillian Smith　　　French, German　　breads & muffins
All year

Elegant comfort of an old English country house set in the scenic beauty of New England.
Breakfast and afternoon tea are rare treats.

ASHLAND ───────────

Glynn House Victorian Inn　$$ B&B　　　　　　Full breakfast
P.O. Box 819, 03217　　　4 rooms, 4 pb　　　Comp. wine, snacks
43 Highland St.　　　　　●　　　　　　　　Sitting room, bicycles
603-968-3775　　　　　　C-yes/S-yes/P-no/H-no　tennis, lake
Karol & Betsy Paterman　Polish, Russian　　golf & skiing nearby
All year

Fine example of Victorian Queen Anne architecture situated among the lakes and mountains.
Antiques, gourmet breakfasts and hospitality are our specialities.

BARTLETT ────────────────────────────

Country Inn at Bartlett	$$ B&B	Full breakfast
P.O. Box 327, Route 302, 03812	17 rooms, 10 pb	Comp. tea/coffee, snacks
603-374-2353 800-292-2353	Visa, MC, AmEx ●	Sitting room
Mark Dindorf	C-yes/S-ltd/P-ltd	outdoor hot tub
All year		cross-country ski trails

A B&B inn for hikers, skiers and outdoors enthusiasts in the White Mountains. Enjoy mountain hospitality, an outdoor hot tub and expert hiking and trail advice.

The Notchland Inn	$$$ B&B	Full breakfast
Gen'l Delivery, 03812	11 rooms, 11 pb	Dinner, BYOB
Rte. 302, Hart's Location	Visa, MC, AmEx	Sitting room, library
603-374-6131	C-ltd/S-ltd/P-no/H-ltd	hot tubs, sauna
John & Pat Bernardin		cross-country skiing
All year		

A traditional country inn where hospitality hasn't been forgotten. Working fireplaces in every room, gourmet meals and spectacular mountain views. Hiking & swimming nearby.

BETHLEHEM ────────────────────────────

The Mulburn Inn	$$ B&B	Full breakfast
Main St., 03574	7 rooms, 7 pb	Afternoon tea, snacks
603-869-3389	Visa, MC, AmEx, Disc ●	Sitting room
The Burns and the Mulkigians	C-yes/S-no/P-no/H-no	library
All year		wraparound porches

A sprawling summer cottage built in 1913 as a family retreat known as the Ivie House on the Woolworth Estate. Warm, fireside dining with hot, country breakfast.

BRADFORD ────────────────────────────

The Bradford Inn	$$$ MAP (EP/B&B)	Full breakfast
RFD 1 Box 40, Main St., 03221	12 rooms, 12 pb	Restaurant, dinner incl.
603-938-5309 800-669-5309	Visa, MC ●	Sitting room, library
Tom & Connie Mazol	C-yes/S-yes/P-yes/H-yes	bicycles
All year	Arabic	meeting facilities

There's simply "nothing to do," but we have a fireplace, good books, three ski areas, and two lovely lakes nearby. Banquets available. Recent period renovations.

Mountain Lake Inn	$$$ B&B	Full country breakfast
P.O. Box 443, Route 114, 03221	9 rooms, 9 pb	Dinner, tea/coffee/snack
603-938-2136 800-662-6005	●	Sitting room, library
Carol & Phil Fullerton	C-yes/S-yes/P-no/H-no	full screened porch
All year		piano, bicycles

165 acres of beautiful vacationland for any season. Built before the Revolution. Near all ski areas. Private sandy beach.

CAMPTON ────────────────────────────

Mountain Fare Inn	$ B&B	Full breakfast
P.O. Box 553, 03223	8 rooms, 5 pb	Dinner (groups, winter)
Mad River Rd.	●	Snacks, sitting room
603-726-4283	C-yes/S-no/P-ask/H-no	hiking, biking, golf
Susan & Nicholas Preston		X-C & downhill skiing
All year		

1840s white clapboard mountain village home. Truly New Hampshire. We welcome skiers, hikers, travelers to share and fun and beauty. Your hosts are ski coaches at ski resort.

CAMPTON

Osgood Inn B&B
P.O. Box 419, Cross St., 03223
603-726-3543
Dexter & Patricia Osgood
Exc. Thanksgiving & Xmas

$$ B&B
4 rooms
C-yes/S-ltd/P-no/H-no

Full breakfast
Afternoon tea, snacks
Sitting room, gardens
porch, yard, birds
ski area 10 miles

Charming gracious village inn. Close to major ski areas, shops, tourist attractions. Wonderful breakfasts, handmade quilts. Restful and quiet.

CENTRE HARBOR

Red Hill Inn
RFD 1, Box 99M, 03226
Route 25B & College Rd.
603-279-7001
D Leavitt/R Miller/G Strobel
All year

$$ B&B
21 rooms, 21 pb
AmEx, Visa, MC ●
C-ltd/S-yes/P-no/H-no

Full breakfast
Lunch (summer), dinner
Bar, Sunday brunch
library, lake swimming
small conference center

Lovely restored mansion on fifty private acres overlooking Squam Lake (Golden Pond) and White Mountains. Excellent country gourmet cuisine, antiques.

CHOCORUA VILLAGE

The Farmhouse B&B
P.O. Box 14, 03817
Page Hill Rd.
603-323-8707
Kathie & John Dyrenforth
May–October

$$ B&B
4 rooms
C-yes/S-yes/P-no/H-no

Full country breakfast
Comp. aftn. tea, cookies
Sitting room, library
March maple sugaring
screened porch

Country charm, gracious hospitality. Pre-Civil War homestead. Lakes and mountains resort area. Breakfast features our own maple syrup and farm products.

CONWAY

Darby Field Inn
P.O. Box D, 03818
Bald Hill Rd.
603-447-2181 800-426-4147
Marc & Maria Donaldson
All year

$$ MAP
16 rooms, 14 pb
Visa, MC, AmEx ●
C-yes/S-no/P-no/H-no
Spanish

Full breakfast
Dinner, bar
Sitting room, piano
15 miles of X-C skiing
pool, entertainment

Cozy little country inn overlooking the Mt. Washington Valley and Presidential Mountains. Candlelight dinners; surrounding mountains and rivers, ski trails.

EAST ANDOVER

Patchwork Inn
P.O. Box 107, Maple St., 03231
603-735-6426
Brad & Ethelyn Sherman
All year

$$ B&B
8 rooms, 3 pb
Visa, MC ●
C-yes/S-no/P-no/H-no

Full breakfast
Picnic baskets, wine
Set-ups, TV room, piano
gift shop, BBQ grill
lawn games, magic shows

1805 country inn; lakeside village setting, just off beaten path. Close to skiing. Full country breakfast features family-made honey and maple products.

EATON CENTER

The Inn at Crystal Lake
Route 153, Box 12, 03832
603-447-2120 800-343-7336
Walter & Jacqueline Spink
All year

$$ B&B/$$$ MAP
11 rooms, 11 pb
AmEx, MC, Visa ●
C-yes/S-ltd/P-no/H-no

Full country breakfast
Dinner, bar, parlor, TV
Fireplace, lounge, pianos
lake swimming & boats
hiking & X-C ski nearby

Newly restored country inn–Greek revival with Victorian influence. Relaxing ambience, extraordinary international cuisine presented with elegant appeal. Be pampered!

EXETER

Exeter Inn
90 Front St., 03833
603-772-5901
J.H. Hodgins
All year

$$ EP
50 rooms, 50 pb
Visa, MC, AmEx, DC, Dsc
●
C-yes/S-yes/P-yes/H-no
French, Spanish

Restaurant
Lunch, dinner
Afternoon tea, snacks
bar service, sitting rm
library, sauna

Three story brick Georgian-style building; on the campus of Phillips Exeter academy; in the Revolutionary capitol of New Hampshire.

FRANCONIA

Bungay Jar B&B
P.O. Box 15, 03580
Easton Valley Rd.
603-823-7775
Kate Kerivan, Lee Strimbeck
All year

$$ B&B
6 rooms, 4 pb
Visa, MC ●
C-6+

Full breakfast
Dinner for groups by res
Afternoon tea, snacks
library, antiques, sauna
swimming hole, balconies

5.5 miles south of Franconia Village. Crackling fire; mulled cider; popovers; homemade snacks. Mountain views on 8 private, quiet wooded acres with garden walks to river.

Franconia Inn
Easton Rd., 03580
603-823-5542
Alec & Richard Morris
Mem. Day–Oct, 12/15-4/1

$$$ B&B/MAP
35 rooms, 31 pb
Visa, MC, AmEx ●
C-yes/S-yes/P-no/H-no

Full breakfast
Restaurant, full bar
Lounge w/movies, library
bicycles, pool, tennis
piano, sitting room

Located in the Easton Valley–Mount Lafayette and Sugar Hill. Riding stable, ski center. All rooms beautifully decorated. Sleigh rides, horseback riding, soaring.

Horse and Hound Inn
205 Wells Rd., 03580
603-823-5501
Bill Steele, Jim Cantlon
May–March

$$ B&B
12 rooms, 6 pb
●
C-no/S-yes/P-no/H-no

Full breakfast
Restaurant
Dinner 6-9 pm (exc. Tue)
sitting room

Fine traditional inn on a quiet road amid hiking and cross-country trails. Nearest inn to ski lifts. Fine dining, menu changes daily.

Lovett's Inn
Route 18, Profile Rd., 03580
603-823-7761 800-356-3802
Anthony & Sharon Avrutine
Exc. April & November

$$ EP/$$$ MAP
30 rooms, 22 pb
Visa, MC, AmEx ●
C-yes/S-ltd/P-no

Full breakfast
Restaurant, bar, dinner
Afternoon tea, library
sitting room, bicycles
cable TV, X-C skiing

Beautiful 1784 historic inn with fireplaced cottages and gourmet restaurant. Spectacular Franconia Notch. Hiking, swimming, biking, X-C & downhill skiing. Breathtaking views.

GORHAM

Gorham House Inn B&B
P.O. Box 267, 03581
55 Main Street
603-466-2271
Maggie Cook & Ron Orso
All year

$$ B&B
3 rooms
Visa, MC ●
C-yes/S-ltd/P-yes

Full breakfast
Hot or iced tea, snacks
Sitting room
library

1891 Victorian on town common. Closest B&B to White Mountain National Forest & Mount Washington. Fine restaurants, golf, hiking, skiing, sightseeing nearby.

Stillmeadow B&B, Hampstead, NH

GREENFIELD

Greenfield B&B Inn	$$ B&B	Full breakfast
P.O. Box 400, 03047	8 rooms, 4 pb	Lunch (for groups to 12)
Forest Rd., Route 31 N.	Visa, MC ●	Comp. wine, tea, coffee
603-547-6327	C-ltd/S-ltd	sitting room, library
Vic & Barbara		basketball, 3-acre lawn
All year		

Mountain valley Victorian mansion. Bargain antiques. Winter and summer recreation nearby. Romantic comfort for first and second honeymooners.

HAMPSTEAD

Stillmeadow B&B	$$ B&B	Full breakfast (wkends)
P.O. Box 565, 03841	4 rooms, 4 pb	Continental plus (wkdys)
545 Main St.	AmEx	Comp. wine and cookies
603-329-8381	C-yes/S-no/P-no/H-no	croquet, gardens, bikes
Lori & Randy Offord	some Fr.,Ger.,Span.	near lake & X-C skiing
All year		

Discover Southern New Hampshire's best kept secret. Memorable, charming getaway. Inviting Greek Revival Colonial with 5 chimneys and 3 staircases. Close to Sunset Lake.

HAMPTON

The Curtis Field House	$$ B&B	Full breakast
735 Exeter Rd., 03842	3 rooms, 2 pb	Dinner (on request)
603-929-0082	Visa, MC	Afternoon tea
Mary Houston	C-10+/S-ltd/P-no	sitting room, library
Open May–October		tennis courts, pool

Royal Bairy Wills Cape-country setting. Near Phillips Exeter, antiques, historical area, ocean. Full breakfast served on terrace. Lobster dinners on request.

Inn at Elmwood Corners	$$ B&B	Full breakfast
252 Winnacunnet Rd., 03842	7 rooms, 2 pb	Catered dinner by arr.
603-929-0443	Visa, MC ●	Cookies, iced tea
John & Mary Hornberger	C-yes/S-ltd	sitting room/library
All year		wraparound porch

Memorable breakfasts in an 1870 home filled with quilts and country charm. 1.5 miles from the ocean; short walk to a quaint village.

HAMPTON BEACH ——————————————————————————————————————

The Oceanside | $$$ B&B | Continental plus
365 Ocean Blvd., 03842 | 10 rooms, 10 pb | (except July, August)
603-926-3542 | Visa, MC, AmEx, Disc | Bar service
Skip & Debbie Windemiller | C-ltd | sitting room, library
Mid-May–mid-October | | beach chair & towels

Directly across the street from sandy beach; beautiful ocean views. Active, resort-type atmosphere during mid-summer. All rooms recently renovated, many with antiques.

HANCOCK ——

John Hancock Inn | $$ EP | Restaurant, bar service
Main Street, 03449 | 11 rooms, 11 pb | All meals available
603-525-3318 | Visa, MC ● | Sitting room
Linda, Joe & Chris Johnston | C-yes/S-yes/P-no/H-ltd | bicycles
All year | | many activities nearby

Built in 1789, this National Historic Register inn on Main Street is located in one of New Hampshire's most picturesque villages. Try the Shaker Cranberry Pot Roast.

HAVERHILL ——————————————————————————————————————

Haverhill Inn | $$$ B&B | Full breakfast
P.O. Box 95, 03765 | 4 rooms, 4 pb | Comp. sherry, tea
Dartmouth College Hwy | C-8+/S-ltd/P-no/H-ltd | Piano, library
603-989-5961 | French | sitting room
Stephen Campbell | | canoeing
All year

An elegant federal colonial with working fireplaces in every room, and incomparable views of Vermont and New Hampshire hills. Cross-country ski trails, canoeing trips.

HENNIKER ———————————————————————————————————————

Colby Hill Inn | $$$ B&B | Full breakfast
3 The Oaks, 03242 | 16 rooms, 16 pb | Dinner, bar
603-428-3281 | Visa, MC, AmEx | Comp. beverages. cookies
Ellie & John Day | C-6+/S-yes/P-no/H-ltd | sitting room, library
All year | | croquet, badminton, pool

1800 country inn on 5 acres in a quiet village. Antique-filled rooms, smiling hosts, fine dining. Swimming, hiking, skiing, canoeing, kayaking, fishing and cycling all nearby.

———

Meeting House Inn | $$ B&B | Full breakfast
35 Flanders Rd., 03242 | 6 rooms, 6 pb | Lunch, dinner, lounge
603-428-3228 | Visa, MC, AmEx | Hot tub, sauna
J. & B. Davis, P. & C. Bakke | C-yes/S-no/P-no/H-no | bicycles
All year | | sitting room

A country retreat with cozy rooms and attention to detail. "Your place to return to again and again."

HOLDERNESS ——————————————————————————————————————

Inn on Golden Pond | $$$ B&B | Full breakfast
P.O. Box 680, Route 3, 03245 | 9 rooms, 9 pb | Piano
603-968-7269 | Visa, MC ● |
Bill & Bonnie Webb | C-no/S-no/P-no/H-no |
All year

Located on 55 wooded acres across the street from Squam Lake, setting for "On Golden Pond." Close to major attractions, skiing.

HOLDERNESS

The Manor on Golden Pond

Box T, Route 3, 03245	$$$	Dinner, bar
603-968-3348 800-545-2141	29 rooms, 29 pb	Entertainment, pool
Andre R. Lamoureux	Visa, MC, AmEx, CB, DC ●	tennis, canoes, rowboats
All year	C-yes/S-yes/P-no/H-ltd	beach snack bar (summer)
	French, Spanish	

Elegant 1903 English mansion overlooking "Golden Pond." Spectacular views, spacious grounds, private beach, romantic dining. Charming accommodations.

INTERVALE

The Forest—A Country Inn

P.O. Box 37, Route 16A, 03845	$$ B&B	Full breakfast
800-448-3534	13 rooms, 7 pb	Dinner by reservation
Ken & Rae Wyman	Visa, MC, AmEx	Aftn. tea, wine in room
All year exc. April	C-yes/S-no/P-no/H-no	swimming pool, piano, TV
		X-C skiing, skating

Century-old inn furnished with antiques; nestled in peaceful woodlands. Near White Mountains attractions. Sleigh rides, fireplaces. Family rates & packages available.

Wildflowers Guest House

P.O. Box 802, 03845	$$ B&B	Continental plus
N. Main St., (Route 16)	6 rooms, 2 pb	Sitting room
603-356-2224	C-yes/S-yes/P-no/H-no	
Eileen & Dean		
May—October		

Century-old country home offering simplicity and charm of yesteryear; cozy parlor with woodstove; dining room with fireplace.

JACKSON

Dana Place Inn

P.O. Box L, 03846	$$ B&B	Full breakfast
Route 16, Pinkham Notch	18 rooms, 9 pb	Dinner, pub, sitting rm.
603-383-6822 800-537-9276	Visa, MC, AmEx ●	Piano, river swimming
The Levine Family	C-yes/S-yes/P-no/H-no	indoor pool, X-C skiing
All year	French	tennis courts, jacuzzi

A Colonial farmhouse charmingly updated; surprisingly sophisticated in decor and facilities, yet country in personality and hospitality. Outstanding cuisine and a cozy pub.

Ellis River House

P.O. Box 656, Route 16, 03846	$ B&B	Full country breakfast
603-383-9339 800-233-8309	7 rooms, 2 pb	Tea, coffee, cookies
Barry & Barb Lubao & family	Visa, MC ●	Sitting room, atrium
All year	C-yes/S-yes/P-ask/H-ask	cable TV, VCR, whirlpool
	Polish	hot tub, fishing

Turn-of-the-century house overlooking spectacular Ellis River. Working farm; full hearty country breakfast with homemade breads; jacuzzi spa. Trout fishing and X-C skiing.

Inn at Jackson

P.O. Box H, 03846	$$ B&B	Full breakfast
Thorne Hill Rd. & Rt. 16A	8 rooms, 8 pb	Comp. wine
603-383-4321 800-289-8600	Visa, MC, AmEx ●	Fireplace in rooms
Lori Tradewell	C-yes/S-ltd/P-no/H-no	sitting room
All year		library

Spacious and gracious inn overlooking the best of the White Mountains and Jackson village. Away from the hustle and bustle.

Paislay & Parsley, Jackson, NH

JACKSON

Inn at Thorn Hill
Thorn Hill Rd., Box A, 03846
603-383-4242
Peter & Linda LaRose
All year exc. April

$$$ EP/B&B/MAP
20 rooms, 18 pb
Visa, MC, AmEx •
C-12+/S-no/P-no/H-no
Spanish

Full breakfast $
Restaurant, bar service
Sitting room, croquet
horseshoes, tobogganing
downhill/X-C ski, pool

Stanford White designed Victorian era inn; breathtaking views of the White Mountains; candlelight dinners. Perfect getaway for lovers, skiiers, and nature enthusiasts.

Paisley and Parsley B&B
Box 572, 03846
Five Mile Circuit Rd.
603-383-0859 800-248-0859
Bea & Chuck Stone
Dec–Apr, Jun 20–Nov 20

$$ B&B
3 rooms, 3 pb
Visa, MC •
C-10+/S-no/P-no/H-yes
some French

Full breakfast
Afternoon tea, snacks
Sitting room, library
hot tub, bicycles
near skiing, golf, fish

On a hill in mountain village with spectacular view of Mt. Washington. Private phones and entrances. Exceptionally charming new home, folk art, fine antiques, herb garden.

The Village House
P.O. Box 359, Route 16A, 03846
603-383-6666
Robin Crocker
All year

$ B&B
10 rooms, 8 pb
Visa, MC •
C-yes/S-yes/P-no/H-no

Full breakfast (winter)
Cont. plus (spring-fall)
Afternoon snacks
pool, tennis courts
living room w/fireplace

Beautiful village setting on 7 acres. Ten tastefully decorated rooms. Close to fine dining, hiking & golfing. Fantastic cross-country skiing, as well as downhill skiing.

JACKSON VILLAGE

Nestlenook Farm @ River
Dinsmore Rd., 03846
603-383-8071
Robert & Nancy Cyr
All year

$$$ B&B
7 rooms, 7 pb
Visa, MC •
C-12+/S-no/P-no/H-no

Full breakfast
Social hour wine/snacks
Sitting room, bicycles
Pool, skating, X-C ski
Sleigh/horseback rides

Escape into a Victorian fantasy. Seven elegant rooms with canopy beds, 19th century parlor stoves and fireplaces available.

JAFFREY ────────────────────

Benjamin Prescott Inn | $$ B&B | Full breakfast
Route 124 E., 03452 | 11 rooms, 9 pb | Comp. tea, coffee
603-532-6637 | Visa, MC ● | Sitting room
Barry & Jan Miller | C-5+/S-ltd/P-no/H-no | bicycles
All year

Relax ... Indulge ... Less than two hours from Boston, the inn offers the opportunity to reset your pace and explore the Monadnock region.

Galway House B&B | $ B&B | Full breakfast
247 Old Peterboro Rd., 03452 | 2 rooms | Sitting room
603-532-8083 | C-yes/S-no/P-no/H-no | Library, sun deck
Joe & Marie Manning | | recently redecorated
August 15—June | | cross-country skiing

Four season inn run in the "old country tradition"—a warm bed, a warm hearth, a full country breakfast at a moderate price. Woodland setting. The Currier & Ives corner of NH.

Lilac Hill Acres B&B | $$ B&B | Full breakfast
5 Ingalls Rd., 03452 | 6 rooms, 1 pb | Comp. tea
603-532-7278 | C-12+/S-ltd/P-no/H-no | Sitting room
The McNeill's | | piano, pond
All year

Five-star service in a beautiful setting. Enjoy a bit of life on the farm with a warm personal touch. Join us year-round.

JEFFERSON ────────────────────

Applebrook B&B | $$ B&B | Full breakfast
P.O. Box 178, Rt. 115A, 03583 | 8 rooms, 3 pb | Dinner by reservation
603-586-7713 800-545-6504 | Visa, MC, Disc ● | Sitting room
Sandra Conley & Martin Kelly | C-yes/S-no/P-yes/H-no | library
All year | | Dorm avail. for groups

Hike, golf, ski from comfortable Victorian farmhouse. Taste our mid-summer raspberries while enjoying mountain views. Stained glass and goldfish pool.

The Jefferson Inn | $ EP/B&B | Full breakfast
RFD 1, Box 68A, Route 2, 03583 | 10 rooms, 8 pb | Afternoon tea
603-586-7998 800-729-7908 | Visa, MC, AmEx ● | Conference room
Bertie Koelewijn, Greg Brown | C-ltd/S-ltd | swimming pond, tennis
Exc. November & April | Dutch, German, French | 2-bedroom family suite

Uniquely furnished Victorian near Mount Washington; outdoor paradise including hiking, golf, theater, swimming pond; wraparound porch; 360-degree views; evening tea.

LINCOLN ────────────────────

The Red Sleigh Inn B&B | $$ B&B | Full hearty breakfast
P.O. Box 562, 03251 | 8 rooms | Comp. tea, wine
Pollard Rd. | Visa, MC, Discover | Sitting room, library
603-745-8517 | C-10+/S-ltd/P-no/H-no | indoor/outdoor pool
Bill & Loretta Deppe | | sauna, hot tubs, BBQs
All year

The mountains surrounding us abound in ski touring trails. Bedrooms are tastefully decorated with many antiques. Panoramic view of surrounding mountains.

LYME

The Lyme Inn	$$ MAP	Full breakfast
Route 10, On the Common,	14 rooms, 12 pb	Dinner, bar
03768	Visa, MC, AmEx, DC, CB	Sitting room
603-795-2222	C-8+/S-yes/P-no/H-yes	
Fred & Judy Siemons		
All year		

Old country inn furnished in genuine antiques. Small New Hampshire town.

MARLBOROUGH

Peep-Willow Farm	$ B&B	Full breakfast
Bixby St., 03455	3 rooms, 1 pb	Comp. wine
603-876-3807	•	Snacks
Ms. Noel Aderer	C-yes/S-no/P-ask/H-yes	sitting room
All year		

I raise thoroughbred horses—you can help with chores (no riding), watch the colts play and enjoy the view all the way to Vermont's Green Mountains.

MOUNT SUNAPEE

The Blue Goose Inn	$$ B&B	Full breakfast
Route 103 B, Box 117, 03772	5 rooms, 3 pb	Dinner on request
603-763-5519	Visa, MC •	Sitting room, bicycles
Meryl & Ronald Caldwell	C-yes/S-yes/P-no/H-yes	lake, downhill skiing
All year		picnicking, lawn games

Adjacent to Mt. Sunapee State Park; 19th-century farmhouse on 3.5 acres. Picnicking, grill, lawn games, canoe, windsurfer and bikes available. Ideal location near everything.

NEW IPSWICH

Inn at New Ipswich	$$ B&B	Full hearthside brkfast
P.O. Box 208, 03071	6 rooms, 5 pb	Tea, coffee, snacks
Porter Hill Rd.	Visa, MC •	Sitting room, library
603-878-3711	C-8+/S-no/P-no/H-no	game chest, 6 fireplaces
Steve & Ginny Bankuti	Hungarian	screened porch
All year		

Graceful, lovingly maintained 1790 farmhouse; amidst stone walls and fruit trees. Hearty hospitality. Near X-C and downhill skiing, antiquing, concerts, arts & crafts, hiking.

NEW LONDON

New London Inn	$$$ B&B	Full country breakfast
P.O. Box 8, Main St., 03257	30 rooms, 30 pb	All meals available
603-526-2791	Visa, MC	Bar service, library
Jeffrey & Rosemary Follansbee	C-ask/S-yes/P-no/H-no	award-winning gardens
All year		conference facilities

Conveniently located on Main Street in a lovely college town. This 1792 inn offers exceptional fireside dining and charming rooms. Lakes, golf, skiing, all close by.

NEWPORT

Inn at Coit Mountain	$$$ B&B	Full gourmet breakfast
HCR 63, Box 3, Route 10, 03773	5 rooms, 1 pb	Lunch, dinner, tea
603-863-3583 800-367-2364	Visa, MC	Sitting room, library
Dick & Judi Tatem	C-yes/S-ltd/H-yes	sleigh rides
All year		airport pickup

Elegant country home with French charm and rooms with fireplaces. Year-round activities in the Lake/Mount Sunapee region.

NORTH CONWAY —————————————————————

The 1785 Inn
P.O. Box 1785, 03860
Route 16 at Scenic Vista
603-356-9025 800-421-1785
Charlie & Becky Mallar
All year

$$ B&B
13 rooms, 8 pb
Visa, MC, AmEx •
C-yes/S-ltd/P-ltd/H-ltd
French

Full breakfast
Restaurant, lounge, pool
2 sitting rooms, piano
classical guitar Sat-Sun
ski/honeymoon packages

Historic inn at The Scenic Vista overlooking the Saco River Valley and Mt. Washington. Award winning X-C skiing from inn. Has won several food & wine accolades.

The Buttonwood Inn
P.O. Box 1817, 03860
Mt. Surprise Rd.
603-356-2625 800-258-2625
Hugh, Ann & Walter Begley
All year

$ B&B
9 rooms, 3 pb
Visa, MC, AmEx •
C-yes/S-yes/P-no/H-no

Full breakfast
Comp. wine
Sitting room, library
40-foot swimming pool
TV, lawn sports

Tucked away on Mt. Surprise. Quiet & secluded yet only 2 miles from town, excellent dining & shopping. Skiing & all outdoor activities nearby. Apres-ski game room w/fireplace.

Center Chimney—1787
P.O. Box 1220, 03860
River Rd.
603-356-6788
Farley Ames Whitley
All year

$ B&B
4 rooms
C-yes/S-yes/P-no/H-no

Continental plus
Comp. hot cider (winter)
Sitting room, library
cable TV, piano
fireplaces, whirlpool

Charming early Cape, woodsy setting, just off Saco River and Main St. Easy walking to shops, restaurants; year-round sports.

Cranmore Mountain Lodge
P.O. Box 1194, 03860
Kearsarge Rd.
603-356-2044 800-356-3596
Dennis & Judy Helfand
All year

$$ B&B
16 rooms, 5 pb
Visa, MC, AmEx, Dis
C-yes/S-yes/P-no/H-no
Danish

Full breakfast
Dinner, poolside BBQs $
Fireplace room
piano, hot tub
swimming, tennis

Authentic country inn located in the heart of the White Mts. Hearty country breakfast. Tennis court, pool, jacuzzi, tobogganing, skating, cross-country skiing.

Merrill Farm Resort
RFD Box 151, Route 16, 03860
603-447-3866 800-445-1017
Lee & Christine Gregory
All year

$ B&B
Visa, MC, AmEx, DC •
C-yes/S-yes/P-no/H-yes
German

Continental plus
Beverages & cookies
Hot tub, sauna, bicycles
sitting room, library
swimming pool

Let us introduce you to real old-fashioned New England hospitality. A casual country setting with a touch of class.

Nereledge Inn
P.O. Box 547, River Rd., 03860
603-356-2831
Valerie & Dave Halpin
All year

$$ B&B
9 rooms, 3 pb
Visa, MC, AmEx
C-yes/S-no/P-no/H-no

Full breakfast
Dinner, pub, games
2 sitting rooms
piano, Saco River
June fly-fishing school

Cozy 1787 inn, five minutes walk from village, close to skiing areas, fishing, golf, climbing, canoeing. Home-cooked meals including country-style breakfast.

NORTH CONWAY

Old Red Inn & Cottages	$$ B&B	Full breakfast
P.O. Box 467, 03860	17 rooms, 15 pb	Kitchenettes
Route 16 & 302	Visa, MC, AmEx, Disc	Living room w/woodstove
603-356-2642	C-yes/S-yes/P-ltd/H-no	piano, herb garden
Don & Winnie White	French	flower gardens
All year		

Four-season 1810 country inn with 10 cottages and award-winning gardens. Walking distance to village. Spectacular mountain views—Mt. Washington seen from canopied bed suite!

Peacock Inn	$$$ B&B	Full country breakfast
P.O. Box 1012, 03860	18 rooms, 16 pb	Comp. wine/cheese/fruit
Kearsarge Rd.	Visa, MC, AmEx, Disc ●	Sitting room, library
603-356-9041 800-328-9041	C-yes/S-yes/P-no/H-no	bicycles, tennis courts
Claire J. Jackson		sauna, pool, hot tubs
Exc. April & November		

Recapture the romance at our intimate country inn. Enjoy a scrumptious country breakfast while overlooking the mountains. Then relax at the health club or in our indoor pool.

Scottish Lion Inn	$$ B&B	Full breakfast
PO Box 1527, 03860	7 rooms, 7 pb	Lunch, dinner, bar
Rt. 16 1 mi. N. of Conway	Visa, MC, AmEx, Dis	Sitting room, library
603-356-6381 800-258-0370	C-yes/S-yes/P-no/H-no	hot tub, bicycles
Chef Michael & Janet Procopio	Ital., Hawaiin, Phillip.	X-C skiing, hiking
All year exc. Christmas		

A country inn in the Scottish tradition. Over sixty scotches and an American Scottish Highland menu. All attractions are minutes away.

Stonehurst Manor	$$$ MAP	Full breakfast
P.O. Box 1937, Route 16, 03860	25 rooms, 23 pb	Dinner incl., tea/coffee
603-356-3271 800-525-9100	Visa, MC, AmEx	Library, piano, bar
Peter Rattay	C-yes/S-yes/P-no/H-yes	swimming pool, hot tub
All year	German	tennis courts

Turn-of-the-century mansion with old oak and stained glass. Relax by our fireplace in the library. Mount Washington Valley.

Sunny Side Inn	$ B&B	Full breakfast
Seavey St., 03860	11 rooms, 3 pb	Comp. cocoa, cider
603-356-6239	Visa, MC	Living room w/TV
Chris & Mary Lee	C-yes/S-ltd/P-no/H-yes	fireplace, porches
All year	Spanish	

Small casual B&B offers good company by our woodstove or fireplace and hearty breakfasts to start the day right. Walk to town or Mt. Cranmore.

NORTH WOODSTOCK

Wilderness Inn B&B	$ B&B/$$ MAP	Full gourmet breakfast
RFD 1, Box 69, 03262	7 rooms, 5 pb	Dinner with reservation
Route 3 & Courtney Rd.	Visa, MC, AmEx ●	Aftn. tea, cider, cocoa
603-745-3890	C-yes/S-yes/P-no/H-no	swimming hole, 3 porches
Rosanna & Michael Yarnell	Fr.,Ital.,Hindi, Amharic	near Loon & Cannon Mtns.
All year		

"The quintessential country inn." Circa 1912, located in quaint New England town. Inn and rooms furnished with antiques and oriental carpets. 3 miles to Loon Mountain skiing.

NORTH WOODSTOCK

Woodstock Inn
80 Main St., 03262
603-745-3951 800-321-3985
Scott & Eileen Rice
All year

$
17 rooms, 11 pb
Visa, MC, AmEx, Disc
C-yes/S-yes/P-no/H-no

Full breakfast
Restaurant, bar
Lunch, dinner
sitting room

100-year-old Victorian, accented with antiques, glass enclosed petticoat porch. Town's original train station attached to rear of building, serving pub-style lunch and dinner.

NORTHWOOD

Meadow Farm B&B
Jenness Pond Rd., 03261
603-942-8619
Janet & Douglas Briggs
All year

$$ B&B
3 rooms
C-yes/S-ltd/P-ltd/H-no

Full breakfast
Sitting room
Private beach
canoeing
antiquing

Restored charming 1770 colonial home—50 acres of fields, woods. Private beach on lake. Enjoy walks, cross-country skiing. Memorable breakfasts.

ORFORD

White Goose Inn
P.O. Box 17, Route 10, 03777
603-353-4812
Manfred & Karin Wolf
All year

$$$ B&B
15 rooms, 13 pb
Visa, MC
C-8+/S-ltd/P-no/H-no
German

Full breakfast
Sitting room
swimming pond

Classic brick Federalist in country setting near Dartmouth College with 9 fireplaces, stenciled walls, country quilts, spring-fed pond and grazing sheep.

PLYMOUTH

Crab Apple Inn
RR 4, Box 1955, 03264
Route 25
603-536-4476
Carolyn & Bill Crenson
All year

$$ B&B
5 rooms, 5 pb
Visa, MC
C-10+/S-no/P-no/H-no

Full gourmet breakfast
Comp. wine, coffee, tea,
Chocolates, fruit
library, patio, croquet
bicycles, snow shoes

1835 brick federal with elegant guest rooms, down comforters, English gardens, classical music, brook in yard, fireplaces. 15 min. to mountain and lake attractions. Antiquing.

Northway House
RFD 1, US Route 3 North, 03264
603-536-2838
Micheline & Norman
McWilliams
All year

$ B&B
3 rooms
C-yes/S-yes/P-ltd/H-no
French

Full breakfast
Comp. wine
Sitting room
cable TV
near skiing, shops

Hospitality plus awaits the traveler in this charming colonial. Close to lakes and mountains. Gourmet breakfast. Reasonable rates—children welcome.

PLYMOUTH, EAST HEBRON

Six Chimneys
Star Rt., Box 114, 03232
Route 3A, Newfound Lake
603-744-2029
Peter & Lee Fortescue
April 15—March 15

$$ B&B
6 rooms, 4 pb
Visa, MC ●
C-7+/S-ltd/P-no/H-no

Full breakfast
Dinner (winter)
Comp. wine, tea, coffee
sitting room, X-C skiing
hiking trail, beach

A nostalgic trip to a 200-year-old coaching stop—relaxing atmosphere, cozy fires. Awaken to beguiling breakfast aromas. Central location for lake and mountain activities.

PORTSMOUTH

Inn at Strawbery Banke	$$ B&B	Full breakfast
314 Court St., 03801	7 rooms, 7 pb	Sitting room
603-436-7242	Visa, MC, AmEx	outdoor garden
Sarah Glover O'Donnell	C-12+/S-no/P-no/H-ltd	bicycles
All year		

This colonial inn charms travelers with its beautiful rooms & outdoor garden. Located in heart of old Portsmouth with its quaint shops, working port, parks, historical homes.

Martin Hill Inn	$$$ B&B	Full breakfast
404 Islington St., 03801	7 rooms, 7 pb	All rooms have writing
603-436-2287 800-445-2286	Visa, MC ●	tables and sofas or
Jane & Paul Harnden	C-12+/S-no/P-no/H-no	separate sitting areas
All year		

1810 colonial has beautifully appointed rooms with period antiques. Elegant yet comfortable. Walk to downtown Portsmouth and waterfront. Lovely gardens.

RINDGE

Grassy Pond House	$$ B&B	Full breakfast
03461	4 rooms, 3 pb	Tea, coffee, soft drinks
603-899-5166 603-899-5167	personal checks	Sitting room, piano
Carmen Linares, Bob Multer	C-no/S-no/P-no/H-no	pond for boats, fishing
All year		tennis & skiing nearby

1831 homestead nestled among 155 forested acres overlooking pond. Carefully restored, charmingly furnished, clean, comfortable, extensive gardens, Christmas tree farm.

Tokfarm Inn	$ B&B	Continental breakfast
Box 1124, RR 2, 03461	6 rooms	Sitting room w/fireplace
603-899-6646	C-16+/S-no/P-no/H-no	Antique organ
Mrs. W.B. Nottingham	Ger., Fr., Dutch, Span.	hiking trails
April–November		spring-fed pond

Charming century-old hilltop farmhouse on Christmas Tree Farm. Spectacular tri-state view. Cathedral of the Pines and all sports close by.

RYE

The Cable House	$ B&B	Continental plus
20 Old Beach Rd., 03870	7 rooms, 2 pb	Sitting room
603-964-5000	C-2+/S-yes/P-no/H-no	
Katherine Kazakis	Greek	
May 15–September 30		

Named historical site, walk to beach. Landfall of first direct cable between Europe and the USA.

Rock Ledge Manor B&B	$$ B&B	Full breakfast
1413 Ocean Blvd, Rt. 1A, 03870	4 rooms, 4 pb	Sitting room
603-431-1413	C-11+/S-no/P-no/H-no	piano
Norman & Janice Marineau		bicycles
All year		

Seacoast getaway on the ocean, period furnishings, full memorable breakfast served in mahogany-ceilinged breakfast room. Near all NH and ME activities, University of NH.

SNOWVILLE

Snowvillage Inn
Box 176 L, Stuart Rd., 03849
603-447-2818 800-447-4345
Peter, Trudy & Frank Cutrone
All year exc. April

$$ B&B/$$$ MAP
19 rooms, 19 pb
Visa, MC, AmEx
C-ltd/S-ltd/P-ltd/H-ltd
German

Full country breakfast
Dinner, bar, tea/cookies
Sauna, fireplace, piano
tennis court, sitting rm
hike from door, skiing

Seclusion and peace amidst mountain magic. Warm old-country elegance, great food; dine in chalet with breathtaking view of Mt. Washington and glorious sunsets. Lovely gardens.

STRAFFORD

Province Inn
P.O. Box 309, 03884
Province Rd.
603-664-2457
Steve & Corky Garboski
All year

$$ B&B
4 rooms
●
C-yes/S-yes

Full breakfast
Guest refrigerator
Sitting room, library
bicycles, tennis, pool
private lake access

Unspoiled country setting; 120 acres of hiking with waterfall; canoeing on beautiful non-commercial lake. Convenient to seacoast, mountains and lakes.

SUNAPEE

Haus Edelweiss B&B
P.O. Box 609, 03782
13 Maple St.
603-763-2100 800-248-0713
A. & L. Norton- McGonnigal
All year

$ B&B
5 rooms, 1 pb
Visa, MC
C-6+/S-ltd/P-no/H-no
German

Full breakfast
Comp. wine, snacks
Sitting room, TV
front/back sitting porch
books, games, packages

Lovely, spacious Victorian located at Sunapee Harbor, minutes from Mt. Sunapee. Leisurely and unsurpassed breakfasts: traditional, Yankee, Bavarian or continental.

The Inn at Sunapee
P.O. Box 336, 03782
125 Burkehaven Hill Rd.
603-763-4444
Ted and Susan Harriman
May–Oct, Dec–March

$$ B&B/$$$ MAP
22 rooms, 2 pb
Visa, MC ●
C-yes/S-ltd/P-no/H-no

Full breakfast
Restaurant, dinner
Bar service, sitting rm
library, tennis courts
swimming pool, game room

Enjoy our grand mountain views, our chef's sophisticated touch, our delightful rooms, and the pristine lakes and mountains of Sunapee.

WENTWORTH

Hilltop Acres B&B
P.O. Box 32, 03282
East Side & Buffalo Rd.
603-764-5896
Marie A. Kauk
June–October

$$ B&B
6 rooms, 4 pb
Visa, MC
C-yes/S-ltd/P-no/H-no
German

Continental plus
Afternoon tea, snacks
Sitting room, library
lawn games, cable TV
recreation room, piano

Country hospitality; charming, comfortable rooms; large pine-paneled recreation room with antique piano, fireplace; peaceful outdoor setting; pine forest and flowing brook.

Mountain Laurel Inn
P.O. Box 147, 03282
Rt. 25 & Atwell Hill Rd.
603-764-9600 800-338-9986
Don & Diane LaBrie
All year

$$ B&B
6 rooms, 6 pb
Visa, MC
C-ltd/S-no/P-no/H-ltd
French

Full breakfast
Comp. snacks
Afternoon tea
sitting room
air-conditioned

150-year-old Colonial in picturesque New England town on scenic route through White Mountains. Gracious hospitality. King-sized beds.

Mountain Laurel Inn, Wentworth, NH

WEST CHESTERFIELD

Chesterfield Inn
Route 9, 03466
800-365-5515
Judy & Phil Hueber
All year

$$$ MAP
9 rooms, 9 pb
Visa, MC, AmEx, DC ●
S-yes/H-yes

Full breakfast
Dinner, restaurant, bar
Snacks, sitting room
A/C and TV in all rooms
2 rooms have balconies

Featuring opulent guest rooms and exciting cuisine, Chesterfield Inn is located 2 miles east of Brattleboro, VT, the gateway to southern Vermont & New Hampshire.

WINNISQUAM

Tall Pines Inn
P.O. Box 327, Old Rt. 3, 03289
800-722-6870
Ken & Kate Kern
All year

$$ B&B
3 rooms, 1 pb
Visa, MC ●

Full breakfast
Dinner by reservation
Woodstove

Located on Lake Winnisquam, Tall Pines Inn features spectacular lake & mountain views, beach & boat rentals and winter skiing all nearby. A place to come year round.

More Inns . . .

1895 House 74 Pleasant St., Littleton, 03561 603-444-5200
289 Court 289 Court St., Kenne, 03431 603-357-3195
Acorn Lodge P.O. Box 144, Ossipee, 03864 603-539-2151
Ammonoosuc Inn Bishop Rd., Lisbon, 03585 603-838-6118
Aviary Bow Lake, Box 268, Northwood, 03261 603-942-7755
Backside Inn P.O. Box 171, Mount Sunapee, 03772 603-863-5161
Beal House Inn 247 W. Main St., Littleton, 03561 603-444-2661
Bells B&B P.O. Box 276, Bethlehem, 03574 603-869-2647
Bernerhof Inn Box 381, Route 302, Glen, 03838 (603)383-441
Birchwood Inn Route 45, Temple, 03084 603-878-3285
Black Iris B&B P.O. Box 83, Warren, 03279 603-764-9366
Black Swan Inn 308 W. Main St., Tilton, 03276 603-286-4524
Blanche's B&B Easton Valley Rd, Rt116, Easton, 03580 603-823-7061
Blue Heron Inn 124 Landing Rd., Hampton, 03842 603-926-9666
Breezy Point Inn RFD-1, Box 302, Antrim, 03440 603-478-5201
Cannon Mt. Inn and Cottage Easton Rd., Route 116, Franconia, 03580 603-823-9574
Cartway House Inn Old Lakeshore Rd/Gilfor, Laconia, 03246 603-528-1172
Cascade Lodge/B&B Main St., P.O. Box 95, North Woodstock, 03262 603-745-2722

Chase House RR 2, Box 909, Cornish, 03745 603-675-5391
Christmas Farm Inn Route 16B, P.O. Box 176, Jackson, 03846 603-383-4313
Corner House Inn Main St., P.O. Box 204, Center Sandwich, 03227 603-284-6219
Country Options P.O. Box 736, Ashland, 03217 603-968-7958
Country Place RFD 2, Box 342, Tilton, 03276 603-286-8551
Covered Bridge Motor Lodge Box 277B, White Mt. Hwy, Jackson, 03846 603-383-9151
Darby Brook Farm Hill Rd., Alstead, 03602 603-835-6624
Davenport Inn RFD 1 Box 93A, Jefferson, 03583 603-586-4320
David's Inn Bennington Sq., Bennington, 03442 603-588-2458
Dearborn Place Box 997, Route 25, Centre Harbor, 03226 603-253-6711
Delford Inn Centre St., East Sullivan, 03445 603-847-9778
Dexter's Inn & Tennis Club P.O. Box 703 B, Sunapee, 03782 603-763-5571
Dowd's Country Inn On the Common, Lyme, 03768 603-795-4712
Eastman Inn Main St., Conway, 03860 603-356-6707
Edencroft Manor Route 135, Dalton Rd., Littleton, 03561 603-444-6776
Ferry Point House R-1 Box 335, Laonia, 03246 603-524-0087
Fitzwilliam Inn Fitzwilliam, 03447 603-585-9000
Follansbee Inn P.O. Box 92, Keysar St., North Sutton, 03260 603-927-4221
Francestown B&B Main St., Francestown, 03043 603-547-6333
Freedom House B&B Box 338, 1 Maple St., Freedom, 03836 603-539-4815
G Clef B&B 10 Ashbrook Rd., Exeter, 03833 603-772-8850
Gould Farm P.O. Box 27, Jaffrey, 03452 603-532-6996
Gunstock Inn 580 Cherry Valley Rd., Gilford, 03246 603-293-2021
Haley House Farm RFD #1, N. River Rd., Epping, 03857 603-679-8713
Hall's Hillside B&B R.D. #4 Box 3GA72, Gilford, 03246 603-293-7290
Harrisville Squires' Inn Box 19, Keene Rd., Harrisville, 03450 603-827-3925
Hathaway Inn RFD 4, Red Gate Lane, Meredith, 03253 603-279-5521
Helga's B&B 92 Packers Falls Rd., Newmarket, 03857 603-659-6856
Hickory Stick Farm RFD #2, Laconia, 03246 603-524-3333
Hide-Away Lodge P.O. Box 6, New London, Springfield, 03257 603-526-4861
Highlands Inn P.O. Box 118C, Bethlehem, 03574 603-869-3978
Hilltop Inn, The Main St., Route 117, Sugar Hill, 03585 603-823-5695
Historic Tavern Inn P.O. Box 369, Gilmanton, 03237 603-267-7349
Hitching Post B&B RFD #2, P.O. Box 790, Chichester, 03263 603-798-4951
Hitching Post Village Inn Old Route 16, Center Ossipee, 03814 603-539-4482
Hobson House Town Common, Wentworth, 03282 603-764-9460
Home Hill Country Inn RFD 2, Cornish, 03781 603-675-6165
Indian Shutters Inn Route 12, North Charlestown, 03603 603-826-4445
Inn at Crotched Mountain Mountain Rd., Francestown, 03043 603-588-6840
Inn at Danbury Route 104, Danbury, 03230 603-768-3318
Inn at Loudon Ridge Box 195, Loudon, 03301 603-267-8952
Jaffrey Manor Inn 13 Stratton Rd., Jaffrey, 03452 603-532-8069
Kimball Hill Inn P.O. Box 74, Whitefield, 03598 603-837-2284
Kona Mansion Inn Box 458, Centre Harbor, 03226 603-253-4900
Lake Shore Farm 30 Jenness Pond Rd., Northwood, 03261 603-942-5921
Lavender Flower Inn P.O. Box 328, Main St., Center Conway, 03813 603-447-3794
Ledgeland RR1, Box 94, Sugar Hill, 03585 603-823-5341
Leighton Inn 69 Richards Ave., Portsmouth, 03801 603-433-2188
Loch Lyme Lodge RFD 278, Lyme, 03768 603-795-2141
Loma Lodge RFD #1 Box 592, Sunapee, 03782 603-763-4849
Main St. B&B of Franconia Main Street, Franconia, 03580 603-823-8513
Manor on the Park 503 Beech St., Manchester, 03104 603-669-8600
Manor, The Box T, Route 3, Holderness, 603-968-3348
Maple Hedge B&B Box 638, Charlestown, 03603 603-826-5237
Maple Hill Farm RR1 Box 1620, New London, 03257 603-526-2248
Mill Pond Inn 50 Prescott Rd., Jaffrey, 03452 603-532-7687
Monadnock Inn Main St., Box 103, Jaffrey Center, 03454 603-532-7001
Moose Mountain Lodge Moose Mountain, Etna, 03750 603-643-3529

Mount Washington Hotel Bretton Woods, 03575 603-278-1000
Mt. Adams Inn RFD #1, Box 72, Route 3, S. Main St., 03262 603-745-2711
Mt. Cardigan B&B Knowles Hill Rd., Alexandria, 03222 603-744-5803
New England Inn P.O. Box 100, Intervale, 03845 603-356-5541
New England Inn P.O. Box 428, Route 16A, North Conway, 03860 603-356-5541
Noah Cooke Inn Route 2, Box 300, Keene, 03431 603-357-3117
Nostalgia B&B Box 520, Route 1, Northwood, 03261 603-942-7748
Nutmeg Inn Pease Road, RFD 2, Meredith, 03253 603-279-8811
Old Governor's House P.O. Box 524, Sunapee, 03782 603-763-9918
Olde Orchard Inn RR, Box 256, Moultonboro, 03254 603-476-5004
Partridge Brook Inn P.O. Box 151, Westmoreland, 03467 603-399-4994
Pasquaney Inn Star Route 1 Box 1066, Bridgewater, 03222 603-744-2712
Philbrook Farm Inn North Rd., Shelbourne, 03581 603-466-3831
Pinestead Farm Lodge Route 116, RFD 1, Franconia, 03580 603-823-5601
Poplars 13 Grandview St., Claremont, 03743 603-543-0858
Ram in the Thicket Maple St., Milford, 03055 603-654-6440
Riverside Country Inn Route 16A, Box 42, Intervale, 03845 603-356-9060
Schoolhouse Motel P.O. Box 302, North Conway, 03860 800-638-6050
Seven Hearths Inn Old Route 11, Sunapee, 03782 603-763-5657
Sheafe Street Inn 3 Sheafe St., Portsmouth, 03801 603-436-9104
Shepherd's Inn Forest Hills Rd. Rt.142, Franconia, 03580 603-823-8777
Sise Inn 40 Court St., Portsmouth, 03801 603-433-1200
Sleepy Hollow B&B RR #1, Baptist Hill Rd., Canterbury, 03224 603-267-6055
Snowy Owl Inn P.O. Box 407, Waterville Valley, 03215 603-236-8383
Staffords in the Field Box 270, Chocorua, 03817 603-323-7766
Stag Hollow Inn Route 115, Jefferson, 03583 603-586-4598
Stepping Stones B&B RFD #1, Box 208, Wilton Center, 03086 603-654-9048
Stoddard Inn Route 123, Stoddard, 03464 603-446-7873
Stone Rest B&B 652 Fowler River Rd., Alexandria, 03222 603-744-6066
Stonebridge Inn Star Route 3, Box 82, Hillsborough, 03244 603-464-3155
Sugar Hill Inn Route 117 (Sugar Hill), Franconia, 03580 603-823-5621
Suncook House 62 Main St., Suncook, 03275 603-485-8141
Sunset Hill House Sunset Rd., Sugar Hill, 03585 603-823-5522
Tall Pines Inn B&B Old Rt. 3, Belmont, 03289 603-528-3632
Tamworth Inn P.O. Box 189, Main St., Tamworth, 03886 603-323-7721
Thatcher Hill Inn Thatcher Hill Rd., Marlborough, 03455 603-876-3361
Theatre Inn 121 Bow St., Portsmouth, 03801 603-431-5846
Thirteen Colonies Farm RFD Route 16, Union, 03887 603-652-4458
Tilton Manor 28 Chestnut St., Tilton, 03276 603-286-3457
Times Ten Inn Route 103B, Box 572, Sunapee, 03782 603-763-5120
Tin Whistle Inn 1047 Union Av., Laconia, 03246 603-528-4185
Trumbull House Box C-29, Hanover, 03755 603-643-1400
Tuc'Me Inn B&B 68 N. Main St., Wolfeboro, 03894 603-569-5702
Tuckernuck Inn RFD 4, Box 88, Meredith, 03253 603-279-5521
Uplands Inn Miltimore Rd., Antrim Center, 03440 603-588-6349
Victorian B&B 16 Summer St., Rt. 104, Bristol, 03222 603-744-6157
Village Guest House P.O. Box 222, Campton Village, 03223 (603)726-444
Village House @ Sutton Mls P.O. Box 151, Sutton Mills, 03221 603-927-4765
West Ossipee House Covered Bridge House, West Ossipee, 03890 603-539-2874
Westwinds of Hancock P.O. Box 635, Route 1, Hancock, 03449 603-525-4415
Whitney's Inn Route 16B, Jackson, 03846 603-383-6886
Wildcat Inn & Tavern Box T, Main St., Jackson Village, 03846 603-383-4245
Wolfeboro Inn 44 N. Main St., Wolfeboro, 03894 603-569-3016
Woodbound Inn Woodbound Rd., Jaffrey, 03452 603-532-8341
Wyatt House English Inn Route 16, North Conway, 03860 603-356-7977
Wyman Farm RFD 8, Box 437, Concord, 03301 603-783-4467

Josiah Reeve House, Alloway, NJ

New Jersey

ALLOWAY

Josiah Reeve House B&B
P.O. Box 501, 08001
N. Greenwich St.
609-935-5640
Judith & Paul D'Esterre
All year

$$ B&B
4 rooms, 2 pb
Visa, MC
C-16+/S-no/P-no/H-no

Continental plus
Comp. wine, snacks
Sitting room, piano, TV
black marble fireplaces
handpainted mural, bikes

Elegant country retreat furnished with period antiques, circa 1836. 10 fireplaces, spiral staircase. Golf, fishing, Boxwood garden with fountains and patios.

AVON-BY-THE-SEA

Avon Manor
109 Sylvania Ave., 07717
908-988-6326
Jim & Kathleen Curley
All year

$$ B&B
7 rooms, 2 pb
Visa, MC ●
C-yes/S-no/P-no/H-no

Full breakfast
Comp. wine
Sitting room
fireplace

Romantic seaside inn furnished with period antiques and Laura Ashley prints. Full wraparound porch. One block to beach. Air-conditioned.

Cashelmara Inn
P.O. Box 223, 07717
22 Lakeside Ave.
201-776-8727
Martin Mulligan/Mary Wiernasz
All year

$$$ B&B
14 rooms, 14 pb
Visa, MC, AmEx
C-yes/S-no/P-no/H-no

Full breakfast
Comp. wine
Sitting room

Oceanfront, lakeside charming Victorian inn with period antiques. Cozy rooms with private baths. Hearty breakfast served on enclosed oceanside veranda.

The Avon Manor, Avon-by-the-Sea, NJ

BAY HEAD

Bay Head Sands B&B
2 Twilight Rd., 08742
908-899-7016
Mary Stockton Glass/Ken Glass
All year

$$$ B&B
9 rooms, 5 pb
Visa, MC, AmEx
C-ltd/S-yes/P-no/H-no

Full breakfast
Comp. tea—off season
After beach snacks—in season
sitting room, color TV

Friendly, romantic seaside getaway, Laura Ashley prints, antiques, iron beds, delicious home-baked treats. One block from beach. A special place.

Conover's Bay Head Inn
646 Main Ave., 08742
201-892-4664
Carl & Beverly Conover
Exc. wkdys/Dec 15-Feb 15

$$$ B&B
12 rooms, 12 pb
Visa, MC, AmEx ●
C-14+/S-no/P-no/H-no

Full breakfast
Comp. tea Oct-April
Sitting rm., dining rm.
library, parlor, porch
small conference room

Romantic seashore hideaway furnished with antiques, handmade pillows, bedcovers, crocheted washcloths, old family pictures. Quiet town on ocean at the bay head.

BEACH HAVEN

The Magnolia House
215 Centre St., 08008
Long Beach Island
609-492-0398
Dolores Boss, M. & T. Gilmore
Spring, summer, fall

$$ B&B
12 rooms, 12 pb
C-12+/S-no/P-no/H-no

Continental plus
Afternoon tea, sherry
Sitting room
beach tags & chairs
bicycles

Newly restored 120-year-old oceanside Victorian. Park and walk to white sand beaches and all historic Long Beach Island has to offer.

BEACH HAVEN

Victoria B&B
126 Amber St., 08008
609-492-4154
Marilyn & Leonard Miller
All year exc. winter

$$$ B&B
16 rooms, 16 pb
C-no/S-yes/P-no/H-no

Continental plus
Comp. tea, lemonade
served poolside
parlor, porches
beach badges, chairs

The experience of Victoria's gracious hospitality and charming atmosphere will forever be remembered. A B&B fantasy of a time gone by. A variety of activities nearby.

BERNARDSVILLE

The Bernards Inn
27 Mine Brook Rd., 07924
Route 202
908-766-0002
Alice Rochat
All year

$$$ EP
21 rooms, 20 pb
Visa, MC, AmEx, DC
C-yes/S-yes/P-no/H-no
Spanish, German

Continental plus
Restaurant, bar, ent't
snacks, sitting room
near Nat'l Historic Park
& Revolutionary War Site

In the gracious style of a European hotel, the Bernards Inn offers elegant accommodations, exemplary food, and impeccable service in an unhurried atmosphere.

CAPE MAY

Abigail Adams B&B
12 Jackson St., 08204
609-884-1371
Kate Emerson
All year

$$$ B&B
5 rooms, 3 pb
Visa, MC ●
C-16+/S-no/P-no/H-no

Full breakfast
Continental plus (summ.)
Comp. tea
sitting room, porch

Intimate, elegant country charm, ocean views, gourmet breakfast all located in historic Cape May and within 100 feet of beach. Walk to Victorian shopping mall and restaurants.

Angel of the Sea
5 Trenton Ave., 08204
609-884-3369 800-848-3369
Barbara & John Girton
All year

$$$ B&B
27 rooms, 27 pb
Visa, MC, AmEx ●
C-8+/S-no/P-no/H-no

Full breakfast
Lunch, comp. fruit bskt.
Wine, tea, sitting rm.
oceanfront porch
fireplaces, bicycles

Cape May's most luxurious B&B mansion; fabulous ocean views; rooms have private baths, ceiling fans, ocean views, clawfoot tubs; free use of bicycles and all beach equipment.

Barnard-Good House
238 Perry St., 08204
609-884-5381
Nan & Tom Hawkins
April–November 15

$$$ B&B
5 rooms, 5 pb
Visa, MC
C-no/S-ltd/P-no/H-no

Full 4-course breakfast
Wine, snacks (sometimes)
Sitting room
antique organ
A/C in rooms

Victorian splendor in landmark-dotted town. Breakfast is a taste bud thrill … sumptuous, gourmet and lovingly created for you. Awarded best breakfast in N.J.

Bedford Inn
805 Stockton Ave., 08204
609-884-4158
Alan & Cindy Schmucker
March–December

$$ B&B
11 rooms, 11 pb
Visa, MC ●
C-7+/S-no/P-no/H-no

Full breakfast
Comp. sherry, beverages
Sitting room, parlor
set-up service
enclosed sun porch

Elegant 1880 Italianate seaside inn with unusual double staircase; offering lovely, antique-filled rooms and suites. Close to beach and historic shopping district.

CAPE MAY ——————————————————————

Bell Shields House
501 Hughes St., 08204
609-884-8512
Lorraine Bell
February–October

$$$ B&B
6 rooms, 1 pb
C-yes/S-ltd/P-no/H-no

Full breakfast
Sitting room, TV
Wraparound porch
beach passes
parking area

Restored Victorian house in middle of historic district. 2 blocks from beach and Victorian shopping mall. Delicious home-cooked breakfasts. Decorated with antiques.

The Brass Bed Inn
719 Columbia Ave., 08204
609-884-8075
John & Donna Dunwoody
All year

$$ B&B
8 rooms, 6 pb
Visa, MC
C-12+/S-ltd/P-no/H-no

Full breakfast
Afternoon tea & snacks
Sitting room, library
veranda, rocking chairs
near beach, theater

Beautiful brass beds (19th Century), lace curtains, bountiful breakfasts & a friendly welcome hallmark our inn. In the heart of historic district, walk to everything!

Captain Mey's Inn
202 Ocean St., 08204
609-884-7793
C. Fedderman, M. LaCanfora
All year

$$$ B&B
9 rooms, 2 pb
Visa, MC
C-12+/S-ltd/P-no/H-no
Dutch, Italian

Full country breakfast
Comp. wine, refreshments
Victorian parlor
parking, beach equipment
veranda, courtyard

Turn-of-the-century inn with spacious rooms furnished in antiques, private Delft Blue collection, Dutch artifacts, European accents. Evening turndown service with mints.

Carroll Villa
19 Jackson St., 08204
609-884-9619
Pamela Huber, Mark Kulkowitz
February 14–December 31

$$ B&B
23 rooms, 18 pb
Visa, MC ●
C-yes/S-yes/P-no/H-no
German

Full breakfast
Continental (off season)
Restaurant, snacks
sitting room, conf. fac.
garden terrace

Restored 1881 Victorian hotel. Mid-block between ocean and Victorian Mall. Porch and garden dining. European ambience. Full Mad Batter breakfast. Moderate rates.

The Brass Bed Inn, Cape May, NJ

CAPE MAY ——————————————————————————

Colvmns by the Sea
1513 Beach Dr., 08204
609-884-2228
Barry & Cathy Rein
April–December

$$$ B&B
11 rooms, 11 pb
Visa, MC
C-12+/S-ltd/P-no/H-no
German

Full gourmet breakfast
Comp. wine, tea & snacks
Sitting room, hot tub
beach chairs & towels
bicycles free

Large, airy rooms, most with ocean views. Elegant turn-of-the-century mansion, decorated with Victorian antiques. Rockers on veranda. Gourmet breakfast.

Duke of Windsor B&B Inn
817 Washington St., 08204
609-884-1355
Bruce & Fran Prichard
All year

$$ B&B
9 rooms, 7 pb
Visa, MC for deposit
C-12+/S-no/P-no/H-no

Full breakfast
Sitting rooms, veranda
organ, bicycles
Christmas grand tour

Grand in scale and bold in Victorian character. Warm and friendly atmosphere, antiques. Close to beaches, restaurants, shopping area, historical area, tennis courts.

Leith Hall
22 Ocean St., 08204
609-884-1934
Elan & Susan Zingman-Leith
All year

$$$ B&B
7 rooms, 6 pb
C-yes/S-no/P-no/H-no
French, Yiddish

Full breakfast
Afternoon English tea
Sitting room, library
beach chairs, towels
tags available

Elegantly restored 1880s home in the heart of the Victorian district. Only half block from the beach, with ocean views.

Mainstay Inn & Cottage
635 Columbia Ave., 08204
609-884-8690
Tom & Sue Carroll
April–November

$$$ B&B
13 rooms, 9 pb
C-12+/S-no/P-no/H-no

Full breakfst (spr/fall)
Cont. breakfast (summer)
Afternoon tea
piano
3 sitting rooms

Two wealthy 19th-century gamblers spared no expense to build this luxurious villa. Sumptuous Victorian furnishings, garden, afternoon tea.

Poor Richard's Inn
17 Jackson St., 08204
609-884-3536
Richard & Harriett Samuelson
Valentines–New Years

$ B&B
9 rooms, 4 pb
C-ltd/S-yes/P-no/H-no

Continental breakfast
Sitting room
oriental rock garden

Classic gingerbread guest house offers accommodations with eclectic Victorian and country decor; near beach; friendly, unpretentious atmosphere.

Sea Holly B&B Inn
815 Stockton Ave., 08204
609-884-6294
Christy & Chris Igoe
All year

$$$ B&B
8 rooms, 8 pb
Visa, MC, Disc
C-ltd/S-ltd/P-no/H-no

Full breakfast
Comp. sherry, tea, etc.
Sitting room, books
beach equipment and tags
rockers, veranda, bikes

Elegant 3-story 1875 Victorian Gothic; private baths; some ocean view rooms; period antiques; walk to restaurants, shops and beach; known for Christy's breakfast and treats.

CAPE MAY ——————————————————————————————————

Springside
18 Jackson St., 08204
609-884-2654
Meryl & Bill Nelson
All year

$$ EP
4 rooms
Visa, MC
C-5+/S-no/P-no/H-no

Sitting room
Library
King-sized beds
½ block from beach
½ block from mall

1890 Victorian beach house with bright, airy guest rooms with ocean views. Many creature comforts—big beds, ceiling fans, rockers on veranda, books and good music.

The 7th Sister Guesthouse
10 Jackson St., 08204
609-884-2280
JoAnne & Bob Myers
All year

$$$ EP
6 rooms
C-7+/S-yes/P-no/H-no
Spanish, French, German

Guest refrigerator
Sitting room
Piano, library
rooms 100 ft. from beach
near restaurants

Original furniture plus an extensive wicker collection. Paintings by the owner/innkeeper, JoAnne Echevarria Myers, hang throughout. Ocean view rooms wonderfully furnished.

The Abbey
Columbia Ave. at Gurney, 08204
609-884-4506
Jay & Marianne Schatz
April–December

$$$ B&B
14 rooms, 14 pb
Visa, MC
C-12+/S-ltd/P-no/H-no

Continental (summer)
Full brkfast (spr./fall)
Comp. wine, snacks
2 parlors, piano, harp
off-street parking

Elegantly restored villa, with period antiques. Genuine merriment and a warm atmosphere are always present. One block from Atlantic Ocean.

The Albert Stevens Inn
127 Myrtle Ave., 08204
609-884-4717
Diane & Curt Diviney Rangen
All year

$$$ B&B/MAP
6 rooms, 6 pb
Visa, MC, AmEx ●
C-yes/S-no/P-ask/H-no
French

Full breakfast
Comp. Dinner (Nov–Mar)
Evening tea, sherry
Stress-Reduction Center
large, lighted jacuzzi

1889 country Queen Anne Victorian nestled on the quiet side of Cape May. Genuine antiques, crystal and porcelain as well as original artifacts from Dr. Albert Stevens.

The Gingerbread House
28 Gurney St., 08204
609-884-0211
Fred & Joan Echevarria
All year

$$$ B&B
6 rooms, 3 pb
C-7+/S-yes/P-no/H-no

Continental plus
Aftn. tea w/baked goods
Wicker-filled porch
parlor with fireplace
Victorian antiques

The G.B.H. offers period furnished rooms—comfortable accommodations within walking distance to all major sights and restaurants. Half block from the beach.

The Humphrey Hughes House
29 Ocean St., 08204
609-884-4428
Lorraine & Terry Schmidt
All year

$$$ B&B
12 rooms, 12 pb

Full breakfast
Afternoon tea
Sitting room
library
piano

Our inn is one of the most authentically restored bed & breakfast inns. Hospitality, Victorian charm, and casual, yet elegant, creature comforts are the hallmarks of our house.

The Gingerbread House, Cape May, NJ

CAPE MAY

The Mason Cottage
625 Columbia Ave., 08204
609-884-3358
Dave & Joan Mason
May–October

$$ B&B
5 rooms, 3 pb
Visa, MC ●
C-12+/S-no/P-no/H-no

Continental plus
Afternoon tea
Sitting room, veranda
games, reading material
parlor, bike rack

An elegant Victorian Inn located on a quiet, tree-shaded street in the center of the historic district, just a block from the ocean and the Victorian mall.

The Sand Castle
829 Stockton Ave., 08204
609-884-5451
Tracie & Daniel Spinosa
Mid-April–mid-October

$$$ B&B
7 rooms, 1 pb
Visa, MC ●
C-ltd/S-ltd/P-no/H-no

Continental plus
Comp. tea & cookies
Sitting room
Bicycles
beach passes

1873 carpenter gothic with country Victorian decor. Comfortable atmosphere, ocean view from wraparound veranda. Only a short block from the ocean.

White House Inn
821 Beach Ave., 08204
609-884-5329 800-729-7778
Shirley D. Stiles
April–October 20

$$ B&B
8 rooms
●
C-3+/S-ltd/P-no/H-no
some French

Continental plus
Sitting room
Suite w/pvt. bath avail.
porch, ocean view
beach tags

A bed & breakfast inn on the beach with a Victorian atmosphere. Away from the center of the city, yet close to shops, restaurants, everything.

CAPE MAY

Windward House	$$$ B&B	Full breakfast
24 Jackson St., 08204	8 rooms, 8 pb	Comp. wine, tea
609-884-3368	Visa, MC	Library, A/C, parking
Owen & Sandy Miller	C-12+/S-yes/P-no/H-no	ocean view sundeck
All year		bicycles, beach passes

Edwardian shingle cottage; sun and shade porches; spacious antique-filled guest rooms; massive oak doors with stained and leaded glass. All air conditioned rooms.

Wooden Rabbit	$$ B&B	Full breakfast
609 Hughes St., 08204	3 rooms, 3 pb	Afternoon tea
609-884-7293	Visa, MC	Sitting room
Greg & Debby Burow	C-yes/S-no/P-no/H-no	sun room
All year		air-conditioned rooms

Horse-drawn carriages roll through our quiet, shaded neighborhood—colorful Victorian homes; fine restaurants; antiques; sandy beaches. Country ambiance; family hospitality.

Woodleigh House	$$ B&B	Continental plus
808 Washington St., 08204	4 rooms, 4 pb	Comp. wine
609-884-7123	●	Sitting room, porches
Buddy & Jan Wood	C-5+	courtyards, bicycles
All year		1 bedroom apt. available

Nestled in Cape May's historic district, surrounded by porches and courtyards. This attractive example of "Country Victorian" is charmingly hosted.

CHATHAM

Parrot Mill Inn at Chatham	$$$ B&B	Continental breakfast
47 Main St., 07928	11 rooms, 10 pb	Afternoon tea
201-635-7722	Visa, MC, AmEx ●	Sitting room
Betsy Kennedy	C-yes/S-no/P-no/H-no	
All year		

English country elegance. Tastefully decorated bedrooms with private baths, situated ideally near major corporate offices and universities within Morris County area.

CLINTON

Leigh Way	$$ B&B	Continental plus
66 Leigh St., 08809	5 rooms, 3 pb	Restaurant nearby
908-735-4311	Visa, MC, AmEx ●	Sitting room, fireplace
Terry Schlegal	C-no/S-no/P-no/H-no	fishing, sailing
April–December	French	tennis nearby

Lovingly restored inn with cozy fireplace, porch swing and ferns. Authentic Victorian (c. 1862) located in picture-book Clinton, where small town America is alive and well.

CREAM RIDGE

Country Meadows	$$ B&B	Full breakfast
RR#3 Box 3174, 08514	3 rooms	Snacks
Jonathan Holmes Rd.	Visa	Sitting room, library
609-758-9437	C-yes/S-no/P-ltd/H-no	TV/VCR w/family videos
Dick & Carol Connolly		
All year		

Secluded small farm. NE salt box home filled w/antiques & country collectives. Hearty country breakfast. Near historic sites, golf, fishing, horse & auto racing, amusement pk.

DENNISVILLE

Henry Ludlam Inn
1336 Rt. 47, Woodbine, 08270
Cape May County
609-861-5847
Ann & Marty Thurlow
All year

$$$ B&B
6 rooms, 2 pb
●
C-12+/S-ltd/P-no/H-no

Full 4-course breakfast
Picnic baskets, wine
Dinner winter (Sat)
sitting room, fireplaces
piano, gazebo, lake

1804 home overlooking Ludlam Lake. All chambers decorated with antiques, feather beds, fireplaces. Fishing, canoeing, delicious country breakfasts. Fireside picnics in winter.

FLEMINGTON

Cabbage Rose Inn
162 Main St., 08822
908-788-0247
Pam & Al Scott
All year

$$ B&B
5 rooms, 3 pb
Visa, MC, AmEx ●
C-ltd/S-no/P-no/H-no

Continental plus
Afternoon refreshments
Comp. sherry, fireplaces
sitting room, piano
sun porch, gazebo

Victorian romance and roses galore! Walk to fabulous shopping, restaurants and galleries. Nearby wineries, theater, Bucks County, PA, Delaware River. Warmest hospitality.

Jerica Hill—A B&B Inn
96 Broad St., 08822
908-782-8234
Judith S. Studer
All year

$$ B&B
5 rooms, 2 pb
Visa, MC, AmEx
C-12+/S-no/P-no/H-no

Continental plus
Sherry, refreshments
Picnic & wine tours
bicycles
hot air balloon flights

Gracious Victorian in heart of historic Flemington. Spacious, sunny guest rooms, antiques, living room with fireplace, wicker-filled screened porch.

FRENCHTOWN

Old Hunterdon House Inn
12 Bridge St., 08825
201-996-3632
Gloria Cappiello
All year

$$$ B&B
7 rooms, 7 pb
Visa, MC
C-no/S-no/P-no/H-no

Full breakfast
Comp. fruit & cheese
Comp. cordials, desserts
housekeeping service
sitting room

Small town Civil War-era mansion furnished in Victoriana. Distinctive guest rooms and emphasis on special touches for comfort and elegance.

HADDONFIELD

Queen Anne Inn
44 West End Ave., 08033
609-428-2195
Nancy Lynn
All year

$$ B&B
10 rooms
Visa, MC, AmEx ●
C-4+/S-ltd/P-no/H-no

Continental plus
Comp. wine, refreshments
Sitting rooms, porch
laundry facilities
bathrobes

Restored, historic Victorian treasure. Walk to the safe & comfortable Hi-speed line. Be in Philadelphia in 20 min., connections to Atlantic City, NY, etc. Walk to shops, etc.

MONTCLAIR

The Marlboro Inn
334 Grove St., 07042
201-783-5300
Joanna Rees
All year

$$$ B&B
Visa, MC, AmEx, DC ●
C-yes/S-yes/P-no/H-yes
Spanish Italian

Continental breakfast
Full breakfast $
Full menu
sitting room
piano

Turn-of-the-century Tudor mansion on a 3-acre estate, featuring luxury bedrooms and suites, each with private bath. Featuring chefs Eric Gallanter and Peter Gallasch

NORTH WILDWOOD

Candlelight Inn
2310 Central Ave., 08260
609-522-6200
Paul DiFilippo, Diane Buscham
All year exc. January

$$$ B&B
9 rooms, 7 pb
Visa, MC, AmEx, Disc •
C-no/S-no/P-no/H-no
French

Full breakfast
Comp. wine, refreshments
Sitting room, piano
hot tub, sun deck
getaway specials

Seashore B&B with genuine antiques, fireplace, wide veranda. Hot tub and sun deck. Getaway specials and murder mystery parties available. Close to beach and boardwalk.

OCEAN CITY

The Enterprise B&B Inn
1020 Central Ave., 08226
609-398-1698
Steve & Patty Hydock
All year

$$ B&B
11 rooms, 9 pb
Visa, MC •
C-yes/S-yes/P-no/H-no

Full breakfast
Comp. beach tags
Jacuzzi in one room
8 rooms, 3 apartments

A little bit of country at the shore! Home-cooked country breakfast; gingerbread; wicker. 15 minutes to Atlantic City. Rated "One of the Best Inns" (Atlantic City Magazine)

New Brighton Inn
519 Fifth St., 08226
609-399-2829
Daniel & Donna Hand
All year

$$$ B&B
4 rooms, 2 pb
Visa, MC, AmEx
C-10+/S-ltd/P-no/H-no

Full breakfast
Afternoon tea
Sitting room
library, slate patio
bicycles

Magnificently restored seaside Victorian filled with antiques. Close to beach, boardwalk, shopping district, restaurants. A charming and definitely romantic inn.

Northwood Inn B&B
401 Wesley Ave., 08226
609-399-6071
Marj & John Loeper, Rebeca
All year

$$$ B&B
8 rooms, 6 pb
Visa, MC •
C-10+/S-no/P-no/H-no

Continental plus (wkdys)
Full breakfast (wknds)
Aftn. tea/snacks, piano
porches, roof-top deck
game room, beach passes

Elegantly restored 1894 Victorian with 20th-century comforts. Three blocks to beach and boardwalk. Between Atlantic City and Cape May. 1990 Beautification Award winner.

Top o'the Waves
5447 Central Ave., 08226
609-399-0477 FAX:399-6964
Des & Dolly Nunan
All year

$$$ B&B
7 rooms, 7 pb
Visa, MC, AmEx •
C-yes/S-ltd/P-no/H-yes
Italian, some Span.& Fr.

Full breakfast (Summer)
Continental plus (wntr.)
Restaurant, bicycles
access to pool, hot tubs
exercise classes, tennis

Location: on the beach! Lovely sunrises, ocean views, wonderful for relaxation. Service: we care about our guests & give individual attention. Privacy: excellent for writers.

ORANGE GROVE

Cordova
26 Webb Ave., 07756
201-774-3084 212-751-9577
Doris Chernik
Mem. Day–Labor Day

$ B&B
20 rooms, 3 pb
•
C-yes/S-ltd/P-no/H-no
French, Russian

Continental plus
Guest kitchen
Sat. night wine & cheese
sitting room, bicycles
yard, BBQ, picnic tables

This century-old Victorian inn is located in a lovely historic beach community. At Cordova you feel like one of the family, experience Old World charm, many amenities.

PRINCETON

Peacock Inn
20 Bayard Lane, 08540
609-924-1707
Candy Lindsay, Michael Walker
All year

$$$ B&B
17 rooms
Visa, MC, AmEx ●
P-yes/H-ltd
Italian, Czech, French

Full breakfast
Restaurant, bar
Comp. wine, snacks
sitting room, library
garden, bicycles

Peacock Inn is located in Princeton near university & boutiques; gourmet restaurant; abundant history; 1 hour by train to NYC/Philadelphia. Great for meetings or weddings.

SEA GIRT

Holly Harbor Guest House
112 Baltimore Blvd., 08750
908-449-9731 800-348-6999
Kim & Bill Walsh
All year

$$$ B&B
12 rooms
AmEx ●
C-yes/S-no/P-no/H-no
German

Full buffet breakfast
Open porch
ocean swimming
beach badges

Enjoy the friendly atmosphere in our redecorated turn-of-the-century inn nestled in quiet seashore community, eight houses from ocean.

SPRING LAKE

The Chateau
500 Warren Ave., 07762
908-974-2000
Scott Smith
April–November 10

$ EP
35 rooms, 35 pb
●
C-yes/S-yes/P-no/H-ltd

Cont. breakfast to room
Comp. wine
Sitting room
bicycles
cable color TV

Turn-of-the-century inn, nestled between two parks, overlooking lake. Air-conditioning, TV, refrigerators, phones. AAA-rated 3 diamonds.

Ashling Cottage
106 Sussex Ave., 07762
908-449-3553 800-237-1877
Goodi & Jack Stewart
March–December

$$ B&B
10 rooms, 8 pb
C-no/S-ltd/P-no/H-no
German

Continental plus buffet
Complimentary wine
AAA rated 3 diamonds
TV, VCR, sitting room
library, games, bicycles

Victorian gem furnished with oak antiques and solarium breakfast room, a block from the ocean, in a storybook setting.

Johnson House Inn
25 Tuttle Ave., 07762
908-449-1860
H. Gombos & The Desiderios
All year

$$$ B&B
17 rooms, 8 pb
C-yes/S-yes
Hungarian, Finnish

Continental plus
Sitting room with TV

In days of old, the pineapple, a sign of comfort and hospitality, was a welcome sign for friend and weary traveler. Let us re-create that same atmosphere for you.

Normandy Inn
21 Tuttle Ave., 07762
908-449-7172
Michael & Susan Ingino
All year

$$$ B&B
18 rooms, 18 pb
●
C-yes/S-ltd/P-no/H-no

Full breakfast
Comp. wine
Sitting room
bicycles, front porch
side enclosed porch

A country inn at the shore, decorated with lovely Victorian antiques, painted with 5 different Victorian colors. Hearty breakfast included.

SPRING LAKE

Sea Crest By The Sea	$$$ B&B	Continental plus
19 Tuttle Ave., 07762	12 rooms, 12 pb	Afternoon tea
908-449-9031	Visa ●	Sitting room, library
John & Carol Kirby	C-no/S-no/P-no/H-no	bicycles, local trolley
All year		croquet, beach towels

Luxury by the sea; English and French antiques; queen-size beds; one block from beach and boardwalk. Afternoon tea; entertainment by restored player piano. A seaside holiday.

STANHOPE

Whistling Swan Inn	$$ B&B	Full breakfast buffet
P.O. Box 791, 07874	6 rooms, 6 pb	Comp. sherry, cookies
110 Main St.	Visa, MC, AmEx ●	Sitting room
201-347-6369	C-no/S-no/P-no/H-no	clawfoot tubs for two
Joe Mulay & Paula Williams		bicycles
All year		

Northwestern New Jersey's finest Victorian bed and breakfast guest house; 1.5 miles from Waterloo Village, International Trade Zone, 20 miles to Delaware River.

STOCKTON

Stockton Inn, "Colligan's"	$$ B&B	Continental plus
P.O. Box C, 1 Main St., 08559	11 rooms, 11 pb	Restaurant, bar
609-397-1250	Visa, MC, AmEx	Sunday brunch
Andy McDermott, Bruce Monti	C-ltd/S-yes/P-no/H-no	Alfresco dining, also
All year exc. Christmas		8 suites

Unique country inn located in riverside town. Distinctive lodging; garden and fireside dining. 3 miles to Lambertville–New Hope galleries, theaters, antiquing.

Woolverton Inn	$$ B&B	Full breakfast
6 Woolverton Rd., 08559	13 rooms, 4 pb	Self-service tea, snacks
609-397-0802	Visa, MC	Sitting room, library
Louise Warsaw	C-no/S-ltd/P-no/H-yes	piano, fireplaces
All year exc. Dec 20-26	French	bicycles, lawn games

1793 stone manor house set amidst formal gardens & stately trees, overlooking Delaware River Valley, famed for antiques & fine food.

More Inns ...

Alexander's Inn 653 Washington St., Cape May, 08204 609-884-2555
Barnagate B&B 637 Wesley Ave., Ocean City, 08226 609-391-9366
Bayberry Barque B&B Inn 117 Centre St., Beach Haven, 08008 609-492-5216
Bentley Inn, The 694 Main Ave, Bay Head, 08742 201-892-9589
Chestnut Hill on Delaware P.O. Box N, Milford, 08848 201-995-9761
Cliveden Inn 709 Columbia Ave., Cape May, 08204 609-884-4516
Coryell House 44 Coryell St., Lambertville, 08530 609-397-2750
Delsea 621 Columbia Ave., Cape May, 08204 609-884-8540
Dormer House 800 Columbia Ave., Cape May, 08204 609-884-7446
Dormer House International 800 Columbia Ave., Cape May, 08204 609-884-7446
Garden Suite 42 Ridgedale, Madison, 07940 201-765-0233
Green Gables 212 Centre Street, Beach Haven, 08008 609-492-3553
Hanson House 111 Ocean St., Cape May, 08204 609-884-8791
Heirloom B&B Inn 601 Columbia Ave., Cape May, 08204 609-884-1666
Hermitage Guest House 309 First Ave, Asbury Park, 07712 201-776-6665
Hewitt Wellington Hotel 200 Monmouth Avenue, Spring Lake, 07762 908-974-1212
Holly House 20 Jackson St., Cape May, 08204 609-884-7365
Hollycroft 506 North Blvd., South Belmar, 07719 201-681-2254
Hudson Guide Farm Andover, 07821 201-398-2679
Inn @ Lambertville Station 11 Bridge St., Lambertville, 08530 609-397-4400

Jeremiah J. Yercance House 410 Riverside Ave., Lyndhurst, 07071 201-438-9457
John F. Craig House 609 Columbia Ave., Cape May, 08204 609-884-0100
Kenilworth, The 1505 Ocean Ave., Spring Lake, 07762 201-449-5327
Keswick Inn 32 Embury Ave., Ocean Grove, 07756 201-775-7506
Linda Lee 725 Columbia Ave., Cape May, 08204 609-884-1240
Ma Bowman's B&B 156 Harmersville Peck-, Salem, 08079 609-935-4913
Manor House 612 Hughes St., Cape May, 08204 609-884-4710
Manse Inn 510 Hughes St., Cape May, 08204 609-884-0116
Mooring Guest House 801 Stockton Ave., Cape May, 08204 609-884-5425
National Hotel 31 Race St., Frenchtown, 08825 201-996-4871
Northwood Inn 401 Wesley Ave., Ocean City, 08226 609-399-6071
Old Mill Inn P.O. Box 423, Basking Ridge, 07920 201-221-1100
Peacock Inn 20 Bayard Lane, Princeton, 08540 609-924-1707
Perry Street Inn 29 Perry Street, Cape May, 08204 609-884-4590
Pierrot-by-the-Sea B&B 101 Centre St., Beach Haven, 08008 609-492-4424
Pine Tree Inn 10 Main Ave., Ocean Grove, 07756 201-775-3264
Publick House Inn 111 Main St., Box 85, Chester, 07930 201-879-6878
Queen Victoria 102 Ocean St., Cape May, 08204 609-884-8702
Sandpiper Inn 71 Atlantic Ave., Spring Lake, 07762 201-449-6060
Sands B&B Inn 42 Sylvania Ave., Avon-by-the-Sea, 07717 201-776-8386
Seaflower, The 110 Ninth Ave., Belmar, 07719 201-681-6006
Shaloum Guest House 119 Tower Hill, Red Bank, 07701 201-530-7759
St. Rita Hotel 127 Engleside Ave., Beach Haven, 08008 609-492-9192
Stone Post Inn 115 Washington Ave., Spring Lake, 07762 201-449-1212
Studio of John F. Peto 102 Cedar Ave., Island Heights, 08732 201-270-6058
Summer Cottage Inn 613 Columbia Ave., Cape May, 08204 609-884-4948
Victoria House 214 Monmouth Ave., Spring Lake, 07762 201-974-1882
Victorian Lace Inn 901 Stockton Ave., Cape May, 08204 609-884-1772
Victorian Rose 719 Columbia Ave., Cape May, 08204 609-884-2497
Warren Hotel 901 Ocean Ave., Spring Lake, 07762 201-449-8800
Wilbraham Mansion 133 Myrtle Ave., Cape May, 08204 609-884-2046
Winchester Hotel One S. 24 St., Longport, 08403 609-822-0623

New Mexico

ALBUQUERQUE

Casas de Suenos B&B Inn	$$$ B&B	Full gourmet breakfast
310 Rio grande Blvd. SW, 87104	12 rooms, 12 pb	Afternoon tea
505-247-4560	Visa, MC, AmEx, Disc •	Comp. wine, snacks
Ann & Russ Fisher-Ives	S-no/P-no/H-yes	sitting room, library
All year	Spanish	bicycles

Fresh flower arrangements, blooming gardens, and hospitality. Adjoining Albuquerque's famous old town, with museums, theater, fine dining, galleries, shops, nature trails.

Casita Chamisa B&B	$$$ B&B	Continental plus
850 Chamisal Rd. NW, 87107	3 rooms, 2 pb	Homemade coffee cakes
505-897-4644	Visa, MC, AmEx •	Sitting room, patio
Kit & Arnold Sargeant	C-yes/S-no/P-ask/H-no	decks, indoor pool
Exc. Oct. 15 — Nov. 1		near tennis, horses

2 Bedroom country guesthouse and 19th century adobe house 15 minutes to downtown. Near museums, art galleries, aerial tram, Indian petroglyphs, skiing. Archaeologist-owner.

ALBUQUERQUE

Sarabande B&B
5637 Rio Grande Blvd NW, 87107
505-345-4923
B. Vickers, M. Magnussen
All year

$$ B&B
3 rooms, 3 pb
Visa, MC •
C-no/S-no/P-no/H-yes

Full breakfast
Aftn. tea, comp. wine
Tennis courts, bicycles
fireplace, jogging path
near riding & nature ctr

Nestled in the pastoral village of Los Ranchos; the best of old New Mexico charm and country comfort. Linger by the courtyard fountain or reminisce in the country kitchen.

CHIMAYO

La Posada de Chimayo
P.O. Box 463, 87522
#279 County Rd. #0101
505-351-4605
Sue Farrington
All year

$$$ B&B
4 rooms, 4 pb
C-yes/S-yes/P-ask/H-no
Spanish

Full breakfast
Comp. wine
Private sitting rooms
fireplace
hiking

A traditional adobe guest house in beautiful northern New Mexico; brick floors, viga ceilings, corner fireplaces, Mexican rugs. 30 miles to Santa Fe & Taos.

CORRALES

Corrales Inn B&B
P.O. Box 1361, 87048
58 Perea Rd.
505-897-4422
Mary Briault, Laura Warren
All year

$$ B&B
6 rooms, 6 pb
Visa, MC
C-yes/S-yes/P-yes/H-yes
French

Full breakfast
Restaurant (Wed-Sun)
Comp. wine, sitting room
library, hot tubs
horses

Gracious lodgings in rural setting near Albuquerque and the Rio Grande. Large rooms; 2,000-volume library; classical music plays, paintings. Sports and sights nearby.

COSTILLA

Costilla B&B
P.O. Box 186, 87524
Plaza de Arriba, Hwy 196
505-586-1683
Helen Doroshow
All year

$$ B&B
3 rooms, 3 pb
Visa, MC •
C-yes/P-yes/H-yes
Spanish, German

Continental plus
Restaurant, bar
Aftn. tea, comp. wine
sitting room

Minutes from Ski Rio Resort; easy drive from Taos; charming adobe suites with fireplace, surrounded by alpine beauty.

ESPANOLA

Casa Del Rio
P.O. Box 92, 87532
505-753-6049
Eileen & Mel Vigil
All year

$$ B&B
1 rooms, 1 pb
Visa, MC, others •
C-ltd/S-no/P-ltd/H-no
Spanish

Full breakfast
Picnic basket, dinner
Wakeup tray to room

A Gold Medallion certified B&B that offers intimate luxury in a rustic setting; appointed with handmade crafts, rugs, furniture. situated halfway between Taos and Santa Fe.

LAS CRUCES

Lundeen "Inn of the Arts"
618 S. Alameda Blvd., 88005
505-526-3326 FAX:526-3355
Gerald & Linda Lundeen
All year

$ B&B
15 rooms, 15 pb
Visa, MC, AmEx, Dis •
C-yes/S-ltd/P-no/H-no
Spanish

Full breakfast
Comp. coffees & teas
Sitting room
library

Appreciate artistic lodging, rooms decorated representing famous artists, authentic antiques. Full breakfast, afternoon social hour. Theatre nights, Indian Art demonstrations.

LAS VEGAS

Carriage House B&B
925 Sixth St., 87701
505-454-1784
Kera Anderson
All year

$ B&B
5 rooms
Visa, MC •
C-yes/S-ltd/P-yes/H-no

Full breakfast
Sitting room
library
antiques for sale

This 1893 Victorian mansion in historic Las Vegas is also an antique store. Beautifully decorated in period furnishings & decor items. Like the bed? We'll wrap it up for you!

LOS ALAMOS

Orange Street B&B
3496 Orange St., 87544
505-662-2651
Michael & Susanne Paisley
All year

$ B&B
6 rooms, 2 pb
•
C-no/S-no/P-no/H-no

Continental plus
Comp. wine, snacks
Sitting room, cable TV
bicycls for guest's use
tennis, swimming nearby

A delightful inn favoring Santa Fe-style and country charm. Relax & enjoy a delicious breakfast, beautiful views and hiking, bicycling, skiing.

MESILLA

Mesón de Mesilla
P.O. Box 1212, 88046
1803 Avenida de Mesilla
505-525-9212 505-525-2380
Chuck Walker
All year

$$ B&B
13 rooms, 13 pb
Visa, MC, AmEx, DC, Dis •
C-yes/S-yes/P-ask/H-no
Spanish

Full breakfast
Restaurant, lunch (W-F)
Dinner (Tue-Sat), bar
comp. wine, bicycles
swimming pool (in seas.)

Tranquil setting; gourmet breakfasts; restaurant on premises. Walk to old Mesilla Plaza; ride bicycles; swim in season. Quiet Old World charm.

PILAR

The Plum Tree B&B
Box A-1, State Rd. 68, 87531
2886 State Rd. 68
505-758-4696 800-678-7586
Rich Thibodeau
All year

$ B&B
5 rooms, 3 pb
Visa, MC, AmEx •
C-yes/S-ltd/P-ltd/H-yes

Continental plus
Cafe, kitchen
Sitting room, hot tub
sauna, massage therapist
conference room

At the Plum Tree you can hike, bird-watch, rock hunt, swim, X-C ski, raft, learn to kayak, see petroglyphs, study art, enjoy wholesome food. Nature program in the fall.

SANTA FE

Adobe Abode
202 Chapelle, 87501
505-983-3133
Pat Harbour
All year

$$$ B&B
3 rooms, 3 pb
Visa, MC
C-yes/S-yes/P-no/H-no
Spanish

Full breakfast
Snacks, comp. sherry
Sitting room, bicycles
morning paper, cable TV
off-street parking

Restored, historic adobe 3 blocks from the Plaza, with a sophisticated mix of Southwest decor and European touches. Beautiful gourmet breakfast!

Alexander's Inn
529 E. Palace Ave., 87501
505-986-1431
Carolyn Lee/Mary Jo Schneider
All year

$$ B&B
5 rooms, 3 pb
Visa, MC •
C-6+/S-no/P-no/H-no
French

Continental plus
Afternoon tea, beverages
Sitting room w/fireplace
lovely terrace, porches
lilacs & roses in garden

Cozy, quiet and romantic, yet just minutes from the Plaza. Full continental breakfast served by the fireside or on the terrace.

SANTA FE ──

Arius Compound
P.O. Box 1111, 87504
1018½ Canyon Rd.
505-982-2621 800-735-8453
Len & Robbie Goodman
All year

$$ EP
5 rooms, 5 pb
Visa, MC, AmEx, DC, CB
C-yes/S-yes/P-ask/H-no

1 or 2 bedroom suites
Full kitchens
Hot tub

1 & 2 bedroom guest houses on historic adobe compound. Classic Sante Fe charm; corner fireplaces, complete kitchens, garden patios and fountains, fruit trees. Outdoor hot tub.

Canyon Road Casitas
652 Canyon Rd., 87501
505-988-5888 800-279-0755
Trisha Ambrose
All year

$$$ B&B
2 rooms, 2 pb
Visa, MC, AmEx, DC, CB •
C-yes/S-no/P-no/H-ltd
Spanish

Continental plus
Comp. wine, snacks
Guest robes
private walled courtyard
bicycles

Awarded most spectacular B&B in N.M. by Rocky Mountain B&B. Decorated in the finest of Southwestern decor. European down quilts, down pillows, feather beds. Original artwork.

Casa De La Cuma B&B
105 Paseo De La Cuma, 87501
505-983-1717
Al & Norma Tell
All year

$$$ B&B
5 rooms, 2 pb
C-13+/S-ltd/P-no/H-no
Spanish

Continental plus
Comp. beverages
TV, Solarium, garden
patio with barbecue
avail. as rental house

Mountain views! Walking distance to downtown Plaza, shopping, restaurants, galleries, library, museums, banks. City sports facilities across street. Skiing 17 miles.

Dancing Ground of the Sun
711 Paseo de Peralta, 87501
505-986-9797
David & Donna McClure
All year

$$$ B&B
4 rooms, 4 pb
Visa, MC •
C-12+/S-no/P-no/H-no

Continental plus
Afternoon tea, snacks
Full kitchens, suites
fireplaces, newspaper
private phones, cable TV

Renew your spirit in the privacy of an enchanting, immaculate Santa Fe casita. In historical district, 2 blocks to plaza. Skiing 17 miles.

Dunshee's
986 Acequia Madre, 87501
505-982-0988
Susan Dunshee
All year

$$$ B&B
1 rooms, 1 pb
Visa, MC
C-yes/S-no/P-no/H-no

Full breakfast
Homemade cookies, tea
Sitting room
refrig., microwave, TV
patio, porch

Romantic hideaway in adobe home in historic zone, two-room suite furnished with antiques, folk art, fresh flowers, two fireplaces.

El Paradero
220 W. Manhattan, 87501
505-988-1177
Ouida MacGregor, Thom Allen
All year

$$ B&B
14 rooms, 8 pb
Visa, MC •
C-yes/S-ltd/P-ltd/H-ltd
Spanish

Full gourmet breakfast
Comp. tea & snacks
Gourmet picnic lunches
television room
living room, piano

180-year-old adobe in quiet downtown location. Gourmet breakfasts, warm atmosphere, detailed visitor information. True southwestern hospitality.

SANTA FE

Grant Corner Inn
122 Grant Ave., 87501
505-983-6678
Louise Stewart, Martin Walter
All year

$$ B&B
13 rooms, 7 pb
Visa, MC •
C-6+/S-yes/P-no/H-yes
Spanish

Full breakfast
Comp. wine & cheese
Gourmet picnic lunches
private club access (pool,
sauna, tennis)

Elegant colonial home located in the heart of downtown Santa Fe, nine charming rooms furnished with antiques; friendly, warm atmosphere.

Inn of the Animal Tracks
707 Paseo de Peralta, 87501
505-988-1546
Daun Martin
All year

$$$ B&B
5 rooms, 5 pb
Visa, MC, AmEx •
C-yes/S-no/P-no/H-yes

Full breakfast
Lunch ($)
High tea
sitting room

Full of humor and Southwest charm. Historic adobe-style inn. 3 blocks from city's 17th-century Plaza and close to ski slopes. Hearty breakfast and afternoon teas.

Polly's Guest House
410 Camino Don Miguel, 87501
505-983-9481
Ted & Polly Rose
All year

$$ EP
1 rooms, 1 pb
Visa, MC, checks
S-yes/P-ask

House has kitchen
Coffee, tea, staples
Private garden patio
separate telephone
abundant closet space

Adobe casita, comfortably furnished; Southwestern books, nice kitchen, cozy garden patio; Eastside neighborhood. Walk to Plaza, museums, restaurants, shopping, foothills.

Preston House
106 Faithway St., 87501
505-982-3465
Signe Bergman
All year

$ B&B
15 rooms, 7 pb
Visa, MC
C-ltd/S-ltd/P-no/H-no

Continental plus
Afternoon tea
Sitting room
lawn

Historic 100-year-old Queen Anne house on National Register with fireplaces and antiques; quiet location 3 blocks from Plaza.

Sunset House
436 Sunset, 87501
505-983-3523 505-982-3332
Jack & Gloria Bennett
All year

$$ B&B
2 rooms, 2 pb
C-ltd/S-no/P-no/H-no

Continental breakfast
Organ, phone in rooms
pool, track, tennis &
racquetball nearby

Ideal location. 4 blocks from plaza, sports complex, pool, track, tennis, racquetball. Ski area 14 miles. Artistic, friendly atmosphere. Apartments also available.

TAOS

Casa Zia
Box 5497, 87571
513 Zia Dr.
505-751-0697
George Reed
All year

$$ B&B
4 rooms, 4 pb
•
C-yes/S-no/P-no/H-no

Continental plus
Sitting room, library
spa & exercise room
furniture gallery at inn

Host is working artist & furniture designer/finisher. Close to all shops & galleries; best ski slopes in NM within 30 minutes. Emphasis on warm & friendly ambiance.

TAOS

El Rincón B&B
114 Kit Carson, 87571
505-758-4874
Nina C. Meyers, Paul Castillo
All year

$ B&B
12 rooms, 12 pb
Visa, MC, AmEx •
C-yes/S-yes/P-yes/H-yes
Spanish

Continental breakfast
Complimentary wine
VCRs & Stereos in rooms
hot tubs

Historic home in the heart of Taos. Fine art collection and all modern amenities.

Hacienda Del Sol
P.O. Box 177, 87571
109 Mabel Dodge Lane
505-758-0287
John & Marcine Landon
All year

$$ B&B
7 rooms, 5 pb
Visa, MC •
C-yes/S-no/P-no/H-ltd

Continental plus
Comp. wine, snacks
Library, guest robes
fireplaces
outdoor hot tub

180-year-old large adobe purchased as hideaway by Mabel Dodge for Indian husband, Tony. Adjoins vast Indian lands, yet close to Plaza. Tranquillity and mountain views.

The Historic Taos Inn
125 Paseo del Pueblo N., 87571
505-758-2233 800-TAOS-INN
Carolyn Haddock
All year

$$$ B&B
39 rooms, 39 pb
Visa, MC, AmEx, DC •
C-yes/S-yes/P-no/H-ltd
Spanish, French

Continental breakfast
Full service restaurant
Bar, library, hot tubs
musical entertainment
ski (wint.), swim (sum.)

Historic adobe property, a block north of Plaza. Guest rooms feature antiques, handloomed Indian bedspreads, pueblo-style fireplaces, and handcrafted furniture.

La Posada de Taos
P.O. Box 1118, 87571
309 Juanita Lane
505-758-8164
Sue Smoot
All year

$$ B&B
5 rooms, 5 pb
•
C-yes/S-yes/P-yes/H-yes

Full breakfast
Sitting room
piano
Japanese garden

Mountain views from this provincial adobe inn in artists' colony of Taos. Visit Indian pueblos and art galleries. Hearty breakfasts.

Salsa del Salto B&B Inn
M.A.: Box 453, El Prado, 87529
Hwy 150
505-776-2422
Mary Hackett, Dadou Mayer
All year

$$$ B&B
6 rooms, 6 pb
Visa, MC •
C-yes/S-ask/P-no/H-no
French, German, Spanish

Full breakfast
Afternoon tea, snacks
Sitting room, library
bikes, tennis, hot tubs
pool, ski packages

Exquisite Southwest inn perfectly located halfway between historic Taos and Taos Ski Valley. Private pool and tennis court. Gourmet breakfast.

Stewart House Gallery/Inn
P.O. Box 2326, 87571
Ski Valley Rd. (Hwy 150N)
505-776-2913
Mildred & Don Cheek
All year

$$ B&B
6 rooms, 6 pb
Visa, MC •
C-12+/S-no/P-no/H-no

Full breakfast
Sitting room
library, hot tubs
private patios

Mountain views and sunsets. Private patios. Five miles from historic Taos Plaza and world-famous Taos Pueblo. Skiing, fishing, rafting, hiking nearby.

More Inns . . .

Adobe Walls Motel East Kit Carson Rd., Taos, 505-758-3972
Adobe and Roses B&B 1011 Ortega NW, Albuquerque, 87114 505-898-0654
All Season's B&B Swallow Pl., Box 144, Cloudcroft, 88317 505-682-2380
American Artists House 132 Frontier Rd., Taos, 87571 505-758-4446
Amizette Inn P.O. Box 756, Taos Ski Valley, 87525 505-776-2451
Bear Mtn. Guest Ranch P.O. Box 1163, Silver City, 88062 505-538-2538
Blue Star Healing & Vaca. P.O. Box 800, El Prado, 87529 505-758-4634
Broken Drum Guest Ranch Route 2 Box 100, Pecos, 87552 505-757-6194
Brooks Street Inn P.O. Box 4954, Taos, 87571 505-758-1489
Casa Benarides B&B 137 Kit Carson Rd., Taos, 87571 505-758-1772
Casa de Las Chimeneas 405 Cordoba, Box 5303, Taos, 87571 505-758-4777
Casa del Gavilan P.O. Box 518, Cimarron, 87714 505-376-2246
Casa del Rey 305 Rover, Los Alamos, 87544 505-672-9401
Chinguague Compound P.O. Box 1118, San Juan Pueblo, 87566 505-852-2194
Dasburg House & Studio Box 2764, Taos, 87571 505-758-9513
El Western Lodge Box 301, Gilt Edge, Red River, 87558 505-754-2272
Elms P.O. Box 1176, Mesilla Park, 88001 505-524-1513
Galisteo Inn Box 4, Route 69, Galisteo, 87540 505-982-1506
Hacienda de Las Munecas P.O. Box 564, Placitas, 87043 505-867-3255
Hilltop Hacienda 2520 Westmoreland, Las Cruces, 88001 505-382-3556
Hotel Edelweiss P.O. Box 83, Taos, 87571 505-776-2301
Hotel St. Francis 210 Don Gaspar Ave., Sante Fe, 87501 505-983-5700
Inn of the Victorian Bird Box 3235, Arroyo Wyamun, Sante Fe, 87501 505-455-3375
Inn of the Victorian Bird P.O. Box 3235, Santa Fe, 87501 505-455-3375
La Casa Muneca 213 N. Alameda, Carlsbad, 88220 505-887-1891
La Casita Guesthouse P.O. Box 103, Dixon, 87527 505-579-4297
La Posada de Santa Fe 330 E. Palace Ave., Santa Fe, 87501 800-727-5276
Las Palomas Conf. Center P.O. Box 6689, Taos, 87571 505-758-9456
Laughing Horse Inn P.O. 4904, Taos, 87571 505-758-8350
Llewellyn House 618 S. Alameda, Las Cruces, 88005 505-526-3327
Lodge at Cloudcroft P.O. Box 497, Cloudcroft, 88317 505-682-2566
Lone Pine B&B 3065 Arizona Ave., Los Alamos, 87544 505-662-3015
Los Alamos B&B P.O. Box 1212, Los Alamos, 87544 505-662-6041
Los Olmos Guest Ranch P.O. Box 127, Glenwood, 88039 505-539-2311
Mabel Dodge Lujan House P.O. Box 3400, Taos, 87571 505-758-9456
Manzano House 661 Garcia, Santa Fe, 87501 505-983-2054
Monjeau Shadows Inn Bonito Route, Nogal, 88341 505-336-4191
Pine Cone Inn B&B Box 94, 13 Tejano Canyo, Sandia Park, 8k7047 505-281-1384
Plaza Hotel 230 Old Town Plaza, Las Vegas, 87701 505-425-3591
Pueblo Bonito B&B Inn 138 W. Manhattan, Santa Fe, 87501 505-984-8001
Rancho Arriba B&B P.O. Box 338, Truchas, 87578 505-689-2374
Rancho Encantado State Rd. 592, Tesuque, 87501 505-982-3537
Ranchos Ritz B&B P.O. Box 669, Ranchos de Taos, 87557 505-758-2640
Red Violet Inn 344 N. Second St., Raton, 87740 505-445-9778
Sagebrush Inn S. Santa Fe Rd., Hwy 68, Taos, 87571 800-428-3626
Salsa del Salto P.O. Box 453, El Prado, 87529 505-776-2422
Sierra Mesa Lodge P.O. Box 463, Alto, 88312 505-336-4515
Silver River Inn P.O. Box 3411, Farmington, 87499 505-325-8219
Silvertree Inn P.O. Box 1528, Taos, 87571 505-758-3071
Sunrise Springs Rt. 2, Box 203, Santa Fe, 87501 505-471-3600
Vallecitos Retreat P.O. Box 226, Vallecitos, 87581 505-582-4226
Walnut Executive Suite P.O. Box 777, Los Alamos, 87544 505-662-9392
Wortley Hotel Box 96, Lincoln, 88338 505-653-4500
Yours Truly P.O. Box 2263, Corrales, 87048 505-898-7027

New York

ADDISON

Addison Rose B&B $$ B&B   Full breakfast
37 Maple St., 14801   3 rooms, 1 pb   Afternoon tea
607-359-4650   C-no/S-no/P-no/H-no   Antiques
Bill & Mary Ann Peters   near golf, hiking
All year   skiing, lakes & streams

Discover "Victorian elegance in the heart of the country" in this restored, period-furnished "painted lady". Minutes from Corning and Finger Lakes Wineries.

ALBANY

Mansion Hill Inn $$$ B&B   Full breakfast
115 Philip St. at Park, 12202   12 rooms, 12 pb   Restaurant, bar
518-465-2038   Visa, MC, AmEx, DC •   Health club privileges
MaryEllen & Steve Stofelano   C-yes/S-yes/P-yes/H-yes   golf and tennis nearby
All year   Sp., Ital., Ger., Fr.

An urban inn, established in a residential neighborhood. The inn is comprised of three Victorian-era buildings around the corner from Governor's Mansion & Empire State Plaza.

Pine Haven B&B $$ B&B   Continental plus
531 Western Ave., 12203   4 rooms   Dining room w/fireplace
518-482-1574   •   Living room, TV, books
All year   C-12+/S-no/P-no/H-no   board games, antiques
   original oak woodwork

Victorian ambiance in the heart of the city. Century old Victorian in a beautiful residential area of the state's capital. Features iron & brass beds, feather mattresses.

ALEXANDRIA BAY

Bach's Alexandria Bay Inn $$ B&B   Full breakfast
2 Church St., 13607   5 rooms, 5 pb   Aftn. tea, comp. wine
315-482-9697   Visa, MC   Sitting room, library
Virginia & Robert Bach   C-yes/S-ltd/P-no/H-no   boat tours, fishing
All year   Spanish, some French   hiking, antique shopping

A beautiful Victorian inn in the Thousand Islands. Glorious antiques and Laura Ashley bedding fill the guest rooms. Gourmet breakfast served in dining room or lovely porches.

AMENIA

Troutbeck Country Inn $$$ AP   All meals included
Box 26, Leedsville Rd., 12501   31 rooms, 26 pb   Open bar
914-373-9681 FAX:373-7080   AmEx •   Public rooms, piano
J. Flaherty, K. Robinson   C-ltd/S-yes/P-no/H-no   tennis courts, library
All year   Span., Port., Ital., Fr.   year-round swimming pool

Historic English country estate on 422 acres, with indoor and outdoor pools, tennis courts, fine chefs, 12,000 books, lovely grounds. A quiet retreat.

AUBURN

Springside Inn
P.O. Box 327, 13021
Rte. 38 South
315-252-7247
William Dove
All year

$$ MAP
8 rooms, 5 pb
Visa •
C-yes/S-no/P-no/H-no

Continental plus
Dinner included
Restaurant, bar
bicycles, lake
swimming, fishing

Charming guest rooms. Breakfast in a basket prepared for each room. Summer Dinner Theater combines gourmet dining with Broadway entertainment. Wedding receptions & banquets.

AVERILL PARK

Ananas Hus B&B
Route 3, Box# 301, 12018
South Rd., W. Stephentown
518-766-5035
T. Tomlinson/C. Tomlinson
All year

$$ B&B
3 rooms
AmEx
C-12+/S-no/P-no
Norwegian

Full gourmet breakfast
Coffee, tea, iced tea
Sitting room
reading material
exercise bicycle

Hillside ranch home on 30 acres with panoramic view of Hudson River Valley midway between western Massachusetts and Capitol District. Location—South Rd., West Stephen Town

The Gregory House
P.O. Box 401, 12018
Route 43
518-674-3774
Bette & Bob Jewell
All year

$$ B&B
12 rooms, 12 pb
Visa, MC, AmEx, DC, CB •
C-6+/S-yes/P-no/H-no

Continental breakfast
Restaurant (Tues-Sun)
Bar, comp. sherry, pool
common room w/fireplace
direct dial phones in rm

Gracious country charm centrally located—near Albany, Troy, Saratoga, Tanglewood, mountains, lakes and skiing. Vermont and Berkshires 45 min. away.

BAINBRIDGE

Berry Hill Farm B&B
RD1, Box 128, 13733
Ward-Loomis Rd.
607-967-8745
Jean Fowler, Cecilio Rios
All year

$$ B&B
3 rooms, 1 pb
•
C-yes/S-ltd/P-no/H-no
Span, Fr, German, Ital

Full country breakfast
Sitting room, porch
Herb & flower gardens
nature trails, X-C ski
swimming & beaver ponds

Comfortably restored 1820's farmhouse on a hilltop surrounded by acres of woods, meadows and extensive perennial flower gardens. Furnished with antiques. Tennis, golf nearby.

BOLTON LANDING

Hilltop Cottage B&B
P.O. Box 186, 12814
6883 Lakeshore Dr.
518-644-2492
Anita & Charles Richards
All year

$ B&B
4 rooms, 1 pb
C-4+/S-ltd/P-no/H-no
German

Full breakfast

Beautiful Lake George—Eastern Adirondack region. Clean, comfortable. Renovated farmhouse. Walk to beaches, restaurants, marinas. Friendly hosts knowledgeable about area.

BROOKLYN

B&B on the Park
113 Prospect Park West, 11215
718-499-6115
Liana Paolella
All year

$$$ B&B
6 rooms, 4 pb
Visa, MC
C-yes/S-ltd/P-no/H-no
French

Full breakfast
Sitting room
Victorian antiques
stained glass, woodwork

Beautifully appointed 1892 Victorian townhouse—a refuge minutes from Manhattan. Situated in Park Slope, a historic district of Brooklyn. Fabulous full breakfasts.

BURDETT

Red House Country Inn	$$ B&B	Full breakfast
Picnic Area Rd., 14818	6 rooms, 2 pb	Comp. wine, tea, coffee
Finger Lakes Nat'l Forest	Visa, MC, AmEx •	Oversized pool
607-546-8566	C-12+/S-ltd/P-no	sitting room, piano
Joan Martin, Sandy Schmanke		nature trails
All year		

Within national forest; 28 miles of trails. Beautiful rooms in this gorgeous setting. Near famous Watkins Glen, east side of Seneca Lake. Over 30 wineries nearby.

BURLINGTON FLATS

Chalet Waldheim	$$$ B&B	Continental plus
RD 1, Box 51-G-2, 13315	2 rooms	Afternoon tea, snacks
607-965-8803	C-yes/S-no/P-no/H-yes	Complimentary wine
Franzi & Heinz Kuhne	German	sitting room, antiques
May — December		patio, deck, pond

Unique, quiet chalet; authentic antiques; private entrance; 75 acres offer trails; gourmet breakfast; 12 mi. to famous Cooperstown museums, golf & Lake Otsego.

CANANDAIGUA

Lakeview Farm B&B	$ B&B	Full breakfast
4761 Rt. 364, Rushville, 14544	2 rooms	Comp. tea, coffee, A/C
716-554-6973	AmEx •	Sitting room, lounge
Howard & Betty Freese	C-ltd/S-ltd/P-no/H-no	pond, lawn games
All year		walking trails

Two antique-furnished rooms in our country home overlooking Canandaigua Lake. 170 acres, close to beach, restaurants, and all Finger Lakes attractions.

CANDOR

The Edge of Thyme	$$ B&B	Full breakfast
P.O. Box 48, 6 Main St., 13743	6 rooms, 3 pb	Comp. tea, wine
607-659-5155	Visa, MC •	Sitting rms w/fireplaces
Eva Mae, Frank Musgrave	C-yes/S-no/P-no/H-no	piano, indoor games
All year		lawn games

Gracious Georgian home, antiques, gardens, arbor, leaded glass windowed porch. Finger Lakes, Cornell, Ithaca College, Watkins Glen, Corning, wineries nearby.

CAZENOVIA

Brae Loch Inn	$$$ B&B	Continental breakfast
5 Albany St., 13035	12 rooms, 12 pb	Restaurant, bar
315-655-3431 800-655-3431	Visa, MC, AmEx, DC •	Banquet fac., catering
James Grey Barr	C-yes/S-yes/P-no/H-yes	meeting rooms, lounge
All year		phones in all rooms

Victorian inn built in 1805, decorated in Scottish motifs, Victorian antiques, tartan plaids. Waitresses wear kilts and tams. Unique Scottish gift shop.

CHAPPAQUA

Crabtree's Kittle House	$$$ B&B	Continental breakfast
11 Kittle Rd., 10514	11 rooms, 11 pb	Lunch, dinner
914-666-8044	Visa, MC, AmEx, DC	Restaurant, bar
John & Dick Crabtree	C-yes/S-yes/P-yes/H-yes	Snacks
All year	Spanish	

Built in 1790, Crabtree's Kittle House maintains a distinctive blend of country-style comfort. Not to be missed are the dinner specialties of the house.

CHESTERTOWN

Balsam House
Box 171, Friends Lake, 12817
518-494-2828 800-441-6856
Shawn & Alison Green
Exc. April–mid-April

$$$ B&B/MAP
20 rooms, 20 pb
•
C-yes/S-yes/P-no/H-no

Continental plus
Country French cuisine
Entertainment
bicycles, piano

Dramatically restored Victorian country inn, filled with antiques and wicker from 1900s. Fine wine list, superb dining, casual elegance, southern hospitality.

CLARENCE

Asa Ransom House
10529 Main St. (Rt. 5), 14031
716-759-2315
Bob & Judy Lenz
All year exc. January

$$$ B&B
9 rooms, 9 pb
•
C-yes/S-ltd/P-no/H-no

Full breakfast
Dinner, bar, snacks
Sitting room, library
most rooms w/fireplace
herb garden, bicycles

Village inn furnished with antiques, period reproductions; tap room, gift shop, herb garden, regional dishes, homemade breads & desserts. 30 min. from Buffalo & Niagara Falls.

CLAYTON–1000 ISLANDS

Thousand Islands Inn
P.O. Box 69, 13624
335 Riverside Dr.
315-686-3030
Allen & Susan Benas
Memorial Day-late Sept

$$ EP
13 rooms, 13 pb
Visa, MC, DC, CB
C-yes/S-yes/P-no/H-no

Full breakfast $
All meals served
Piano
near public tennis courts
and pool

The last full-service inn in the Islands. 1000 Islands salad dressing originated here in the early 1900s. Original recipe still used. 1987 was our 90th year!

COLD SPRING

Hudson House, Country Inn
2 Main St., 10516
914-265-9355
R. Contiguglia/K. Dennison
All year

$$$ B&B
15 rooms, 13 pb
Visa, MC, AmEx, DC
C-yes/S-yes/P-ltd/H-no

Continental breakfast
All meals available
Bar service
sitting room, A/C
private balconies

Historic landmark completely restored and furnished with pine antiques. Outdoor dining overlooking the Hudson River.

COLDEN

Back of the Beyond
7233 Lower E. Hill Rd., 14033
716-652-0427
Bill & Shash Georgi
All year

$$ B&B
3 rooms
C-yes/S-no/P-no/H-no

Full country breakfast
Comp. wine, snacks
Kitchen, fireplace
pool table, gift shop
swimming pond, X-C ski

Charming mini-estate 50 miles from Niagara Falls, skiing, hiking, organic herb, flower and vegetable gardens. Breakfast served on deck/living room. Private chalet and cabin.

COOPERSTOWN

Angelholm
P.O. Box 705, 13326
14 Elm St.
607-547-2483
George & Carolin
All year

$$ B&B
4 rooms, 2 pb
Visa, MC
C-yes/S-ltd/P-no/H-no

Full breakfast
Sitting room
porch, piano

Historic 1815 colonial in town, with off-street parking. Walking distance to shops, restaurants and Hall of Fame Museum.

Chestnut Street Guest House, Cooperstown, NY

COOPERSTOWN

Chestnut Street Guesthouse	$$ B&B	Continental plus
79 Chestnut St., 13326	3 rooms, 1 pb	Restaurants nearby
607-547-5624	AmEx	Sitting room
John & Pam Miller	C-yes/S-no/P-no/H-no	walk to 3 museums
All year		tennis nearby

Park your car and enjoy the beauty of our delightful village. Warm hospitality and a lovely home await you. Please come share it with us.

Hill & Hollow Farm B&B	$$ B&B	Full breakfast
RD 3, Box 70, 13326	2 rooms	Iced tea, lemonade
State Route 28	Visa, MC, AmEx ●	Sitting room w/fireplace
607-547-2129	C-8+/S-no/P-no/H-no	patio & picnic tables
Carolea & Patrick Rooney		flower & herb gardens
All year		

"Country living" atmosphere, furnished with antiques. Easy reach of Cooperstown museums and nearby colleges. Lovely homecooked breakfasts in stenciled dining room.

The Inn at Cooperstown	$$$ B&B	Continental breakfast
16 Chestnut St., 13326	17 rooms, 17 pb	Sitting room
607-547-5756	Visa, MC, AmEx, DC ●	1986 NY State Historic
Michael Jerome	C-yes/S-yes/P-no/H-yes	Preservation award winner
All year		

Restored Victorian inn providing genuine hospitality; close to Baseball Hall of Fame, Fenimore House and Farmer's Museum; open all year.

COOPERSTOWN

Litco Farms B&B	$$ B&B	Full breakfast
P.O. Box 1048, 13326	4 rooms, 2 pb	Sitting room
Route 28, Fly Creek	•	library, pool
607-547-2501	C-yes/S-yes/P-no/H-no	X-C ski trails
Jim & Margaret Wolff		
All year		

Families and couples enjoy our 20'x40' pool, 70 acres and nature trails. Handmade quilts by our resident quilter. Warm hospitality; marvelous breakfasts are truly memorable.

CORNING

Rosewood Inn	$$$ B&B	Full breakfast
134 E. First St., 14830	6 rooms, 6 pb	Tea & cookies
607-962-3253	Visa, MC •	Sitting room
Dick & Winnie Peer	C-yes/S-ltd/P-ltd/H-ltd	library
All year		A/C in all rooms

Elegantly appointed B&B in the Victorian manner. Walk to downtown Corning, Corning Glass Center, Corning Museum of Glass, theaters, museums and restaurants.

CROTON-ON-HUDSON

Alexander Hamilton House	$$ B&B	Full gourmet breakfast
49 Van Wyck St., 10520	5 rooms, 2 pb	Sitting room
914-271-6737	Visa, MC, AmEx •	Fireplaces, bicycles
Barbara Notarius	C-yes/S-no/P-no/H-no	gardens, swimming pool
All year	French, Russian	bridal chamber w/jacuzzi

1889 Victorian home furnished with oriental rugs, antiques and other treasures. First B&B in Westchester County. Gourmet breakfasts. Close to West Point and NYC by train.

DE BRUCE

De Bruce Country Inn	$$ MAP	Full breakfast
RD 1, Box 286A, 12758	15 rooms, 15 pb	Restaurant, bar, dinner
De Bruce Rd.	•	Library, sauna, pool
914-439-3900	C-yes/S-yes/P-yes/H-no	private preserve
All year	French	trout pond, art gallery

Within the Catskill Forest Preserve with its trails, wildlife, famous trout stream, our turn-of-the-century inn offers superb dining overlooking the valley.

DEPOSIT

White Pillars Inn	$$ B&B	Full gourmet breakfast
82 Second St., 13754	5 rooms, 3 pb	Lunch & dinner by resv.
607-467-4191 607-467-4189	Visa, MC, AmEx, DC, CB •	Comp. wine, desserts
Ms. Najla R. Aswad	C-yes/S-no/P-no/H-no	sitting room, library
All year		portable TVs optional

Lavishly furnished 1820 Greek Revival mansion. Gourmet breakfast is the highlight of your stay. Antiquing, cycling or just a perfect place to do nothing at all.

DOVER PLAINS

Old Drovers Inn	$$$ B&B	Continental plus (wkday)
P.O. Box 675, 12522	4 rooms, 4 pb	Full breakfast (wkend)
Old Route 22	Visa, MC, DC •	Restaurant, bar service
914-832-9311	C-yes/S-yes/P-yes/H-ltd	sitting room, library
Alice Pitcher/Kemper Peacock		near tennis, golf, etc.
All year		

Authentic, early American inn only 75 miles north of NYC. Fireplaces, antiques, beautiful grounds & exquisite food make this the ultimate of romantic experiences.

DRYDEN

Sarah's Dream B&B
P.O. Box 1087, 13053
49 W. Main St., (Rt. 13)
607-844-4321
Judi Williams, Ken Morusty
All year

$$ B&B
7 rooms, 7 pb
Visa, MC, AmEx •
C-10+/S-no/P-no/H-no

Full breakfast
Comp. tea and snacks
Sitting room, library
airport pickup
room trays for weddings

On National Register of Historic Places. 1828 Greek Revival furnished with antiques. Subtly elegant, not pretentious. Nearby: golfing, sailing, skiing, antiquing.

DUNDEE

Country Manor B&B
4798 Dundee-Himrod Rd., 14837
RD 1, Box 16A
607-243-8628
Tricia & Jim Kidd
All year

$$ B&B
3 rooms, 1 pb
C-yes/S-no/P-no/H-no

Full breakfast
Box lunches
Sitting room, library
card, puzzle room
wildlife on 7 acres

Fifteen-room Victorian farmhouse on seven acres, including a ballroom. Full breakfast complemented by homemade jam from fruits grown on the grounds.

EAST HAMPTON

Maidstone Arms
207 Main St., 11937
516-324-5006
Rita & Gary Reiswig
All year exc. February

$$$ B&B
19 rooms, 19 pb
Visa, MC, AmEx •
C-yes/S-yes/P-no/H-no

Continental breakfast
Dinner, bar service
Library
sitting room
entertainment

Country charm, elegant restaurant. Choose one of sixteen rooms and three cottages. Breakfast served on the wicker sun porch.

EAST HAMPTON

Pink House
26 James Lane, 11937
516-324-3400
Sue Calden, Ron Steinhilber
All year

$$$ B&B
5 rooms, 5 pb
Visa
C-5+/S-no/P-no/H-no
Spanish

Full breakfast
Afternoon tea
Sitting room
library
swimming pool

The Pink House offers the romance and quaint country charm of Old East Hampton with an emphasis on special luxuries and personal service.

ELKA PARK

Redcoat's Return
Dale Lane, 12427
518-589-6379 518-589-9858
Tom & Margaret Wright
Nov 23–Mar, May 23–Oct

$$$ B&B
14 rooms, 7 pb
Visa, MC, AmEx
C-yes/S-yes/P-no/H-no

Full breakfast
Dinner, tea
Sitting room
cocktail lounge
gazebo, croquet, patio

Cozy English-style country inn, scenically nestled in the heart of the Catskill Game Preserve. Abundant seasonal activities; excellent cuisine.

ELMIRA

Strathmont — A B&B
740 Fassett Rd., 14905
607-733-1046
Alan & Debra Pedersen
All year

$$$ B&B
4 rooms, 4 pb
Visa, MC, AmEx •
C-14+/S-no/P-no/H-yes

Full breakfast
Afternoon tea
Comp. wine, snacks
sitting room
library, gym

Newly restored 15,000-square-foot French manor estate on 18 acres. Decorated in fine Victorian antiques. Near Finger Lakes wineries, auto racing. An experience of a lifetime.

FLEISCHMANNS

Timberdoodle Inn
Main Street, 12430
914-254-4884
Peggy & Joe Ruff
All year

$$ B&B
7 rooms, 5 pb
Visa, MC •
C-yes/S-ltd/P-yes/H-no

Full breakfast
Sitting room, library
Tennis & pool in village
trout fishing taught by
host (licensed NY Guide)

Sportsman's inn located in High Peaks Catskill Mountains. Fish world-famous trout streams, hike forest preserve trails, ski Belleayre and Hunter slopes.

FLY CREEK

Lost Trolley Farm
RD 1, Box 127, Rt. 28, 13337
607-547-5729
Martha Wenner
Memorial Day–October

$ B&B
2 rooms
C-yes/S-no/P-no/H-no

Full breakfast
Sitting room
library

Four miles from Cooperstown; village of museums. Quiet, homey farmhouse. Families welcome. Hearty breakfast includes special muffins and breads.

FOSTERDALE

Fosterdale Heights House
205 Mueller Rd., 12726
914-482-3369
Roy & Trish Singer
All year

$ B&B
12 rooms, 3 pb
Visa, MC
C-no/S-yes/P-no/H-no

Full breakfast
Dinner, snacks, pond
Sitting room, library
billiard room, piano
X-C skiing, canoeing

Historic 1840 European-style country estate. Catskill Mountains, less than 2 hours from New York City. Gentle, quiet. Bountiful country breakfast.

FULTON

Battle Island Inn
RD #1, Box 176, 13069
315-593-3699
Richard & Joyce Rice
All year

$$ B&B
6 rooms, 6 pb
Visa, MC •
C-yes/S-no/P-no/H-no

Full breakfast
Sitting room
four acres of large
flower and herb gardens

1840s farm estate furnished with period furnishings. Gourmet breakfast served in our elegant Empire Period dining room. Located across from golf course, X-C skiing.

GARRISON

The Bird & Bottle Inn
Route 9, 10524
Old Albany Post Rd.
914-424-3000
Ira Boyar
All year

$$$ B&B/MAP
4 rooms, 4 pb
Visa, MC, AmEx, •
C-ltd/S-ltd/P-no/H-no

Full breakfast
Dinner (MAP), bar

Established in 1761, the inn's history predates the Revolutionary War. Each room has period furniture, a working fireplace and four-poster or canopy bed.

GOWANDA

The Teepee
RD 1, Box 543, 14070
716-532-2168
Max & Phyllis Lay
All year

$$$ B&B
4 rooms
C-yes/S-yes/P-no/H-no

Full breakfast
Bicycles

Operated by Seneca Indians on the Cattaraugus Indian Reservation. Country living, Indian tours, Amish tours. Friendly—do not scalp!

GRAFTON ──

Grafton Inn	$$ B&B	Full breakfast
Rt. 2 & Babcock Lake Rd, 12082	5 rooms	Lunch and dinner by RSVP
518-279-9489	•	Comp. wine, snacks
Elsie & Ken Risedorf	C-yes/H-no	sitting room
All year exc. 12/15–2/1		next to 3,000-acre park

Country farmhouse built in 1794; 20 miles to Williamstown, MA; Bennington, VT; Albany, NY; museums, discount shopping, swimming & skiing nearby.

GREENVILLE ──

Greenville Arms	$$$ B&B	Full breakfast from menu
RD 1, Box 2, 12083	18 rooms, 13 pb	Dinner with reservation
South Street, Route 32	Visa, MC •	Library, piano, pool
518-966-5219	C-ltd/S-ltd/P-no/H-no	guest living rooms
Eliot & Letitia Dalton		art workshops, croquet
All year		

A Victorian country inn in a small village in the Hudson River Valley. The former house of William Vanderbilt settled on 6 acres of established shade trees and gardens.

HADLEY ──

Saratoga Rose Inn	$$ B&B	Full breakfast
4870 Rockwell St., 12835	5 rooms, 5 pb	Restaurant, bar, dinner
518-696-2861 800-942-5025	Visa, MC, AmEx	Comp. wine, library
Nancy & Anthony Merlino	C-no/S-ltd/P-no/H-no	in-room dining, antiques
All year		bicycles

Romantic Victorian inn/restaurant. Near Saratoga, Lake George, skiing, recreational activities. Fireplace or jacuzzi in some rooms. Gourmet meals prepared by owner/chef.

HAMMONDSPORT ──

Another Tyme B&B	$$ B&B	Full breakfast
P.O. Box 134, 14840	3 rooms, 1 pb	Afternoon tea & snacks
7 Church St.	Visa, MC	Comp. wine
607-569-2747	C-yes/S-no/P-no/H-no	sitting room
Carolyn Clark		
All year		

The past is recaptured in the three comfortable guest rooms. The grace and charm of another tyme plus a gourmet breakfast.

Blushing Rose	$$ B&B	Full country breakfast
11 William St., 14840	4 rooms, 4 pb	Comp. wine, beverages
607-569-3402 607-569-3483	C-no/S-no/P-no/H-no	Sitting room
Ellen & Bucky Laufersweiler		bicycles
All year		lake nearby

An 1843 Victorian Italianate located in heart of a historic village. Enjoy museums, wineries, Corning, swimming, boating or just strolling.

HAMPTON BAYS ──

House on the Water	$$$ B&B	Full breakfast
P.O. Box 106, 11946	2 rooms, 2 pb	Comp. coffee & tea
33 Rampasture Rd.	•	Kitchen privileges
516-728-3560	C-no/S-ltd/P-no/H-no	barbecue, windsurfer
Mrs. Ute Lambur	German, Spanish, French	sail/pedal boats, bikes
May–November		

Seven miles to Southampton Village. Museum, art gallery, stores. Short drive to beaches. Breakfast on terrace, relax in garden, kitchen privileges (snacks).

HEMPSTEAD

Country Life B&B
237 Cathedral Ave., 11550
On the Garden City Line
516-292-9219
Richard & Wendy Duvall
All year

$$ B&B
4 rooms, 3 pb
•
C-yes/S-no/P-no/H-no
Spanish, German, French

Full breakfast
Comp. wine
Stereo, patio, backyard
color TV & A/C in rooms

Charming old Dutch colonial; close to New York City, beaches, airports and public transportation, Fifth Avenue of Long Island, tourist sights, Hofstra & Adelphi Universities.

HILLSDALE

Swiss Hutte
Route 23, 12529
MA/NY border
518-325-3333 413-528-6200
Mr. & Mrs. Gert & Cindy Alper
April 15–March

$$$ MAP,EP avail
16 rooms, 16 pb
Visa, MC
C-yes/S-yes/P-yes/H-yes
German

Full breakfast
Lunch, dinner, noon tea
Restaurant, bar service
sitting room
tennis, pool, skiing (W)

Swiss chef and owner. French continental decor. Indoor and outdoor patio dining. Nestled in a hidden valley among firs and hemlocks. All rooms have telephones.

ITHACA

Buttermilk Falls B&B
110 E. Buttermilk Falls, 14850
607-272-6767
Margie Rumsey
All year

$$ B&B
4 rooms, 4 pb
Visa, MC
C-ltd/S-ltd/H-ltd

Full breakfast
Complimentary drink
Afternoon tea, snacks
sitting room, library
swimming pool

Hike the wooded gorge trails, then swim at the base of Buttermilk Falls, just across the street from our 1814 brick homestead. Experience warm hospitality and privacy.

Glendale Farm B&B
224 Bostwick Rd., 14850
607-272-8756
Jeanne Marie Tomlinson
All year

$$ B&B
7 rooms, 4 pb
Visa, MC
C-yes/S-yes/P-yes/H-yes

Full breakfast
comp. sherry
Sitting room
screened porch
organ, piano

Restored Victorian farmhouse furnished with antiques; full country breakfast. Near Buttermilk Falls State Park, in the heart of the Finger Lakes.

Hanshaw House B&B Inn
15 Sapsucker Woods Rd., 14850
607-273-8034
Helen Scoones
All year

$$ B&B
4 rooms, 4 pb
Visa, MC, AmEx
C-yes/S-no/P-no/H-no

Full breakfast
Comp. wine, aftn. tea
Snacks, sitting room
patio, pond, gardens
overlooking woods

Elegantly remodeled 1830s farmhouse overlooking pond and woods. Furnished with antiques, colorful chintzes, goose down comforters. Private baths, air conditioning, gardens.

Peregrine House Inn
140 College Ave., 14850
607-272-0919
Nancy Falconer, Susan Vance
All year

$$ B&B
8 rooms, 4 pb
Visa, MC •
C-12+/P-no

Full breakfast
Afternoon tea
Comp. wine, snacks
sitting room
TV in rooms

1874 Brick Victorian inn furnished with antiques, pretty linens, terry robes. In the heart of city, near Cornell campus. Air conditioned.

ITHACA

Rose Inn
P.O. Box 6575, 14851
813 Auburn Rd., Rt. 34 N.
607-533-7905 FAX:533-4202
Sherry & Charles Rosemann
All year

$$$ B&B
16 rooms, 16 pb
AmEx •
C-10+/S-no/P-no/H-no
German, Spanish

Full breakfast
Gourmet dinner by resv.
Antique shop, parlor
3 suites with jacuzzis
piano, bicycles

1850s Italianate mansion with 3-story circular mahogany staircase. Furnished with period pieces. 20 landscaped acres, orchard. One of Uncle Ben's "Ten Best Inns in America."

ITHACA–GROTON

Austin Manor
210 Old Peruville Rd., 13073
607-898-5786
Michael & Doris Salerno
Exc. Thanksgiving, Xmas

$$ B&B
4 rooms, 2 pb
•
C-yes/S-no/P-no/H-no
some Italian

Full breakfast
Comp. wine
Lunch & dinner sometimes
near tennis & pool

Restored Victorian with 14 spacious rooms, on 185 acres of land. Minutes to all the joys of the Finger Lakes, as well as Cornell Univ., Ithaca College, downtown, wineries.

KEENE

Bark Eater Inn
Alstead Hill Rd., 12942
518-576-2221
Joe–Pete Wilson
All year

$$$ B&B
17 rooms, 4 pb
AmEx •
C-yes/S-yes/P-yes

Full breakfast
Comp. tea, wine
Sitting room
piano

Country inn from the stagecoach days, nestled in quiet valley in heart of Adirondack Mountains. Gracious hosts and gourmet food compliment your stay.

LAKE LUZERNE

The Lamplight Inn B&B
P.O. Box 70, 12846
2129 Lake Ave. (9N)
518-696-5294 800-BNG-INN8
Gene & Linda Merlino
All year

$$ B&B
10 rooms, 10 pb
Visa, MC, AmEx •
C-12+/S-ltd/P-no/H-no

Full breakfast
Comp. tea & coffee
Sitting rm. w/fireplaces
porch w/swing, gardens
lake swimming, bicycles

Romantic 1890 Victorian, 5 fireplaced bedrooms, antiques, comfortable atmosphere. Spacious sun porch breakfast room. Southern Adirondacks. OUR 1992 INN OF THE YEAR!

LAKE PLACID

Highland House Inn
3 Highland Place, 12946
518-523-2377
Teddy & Cathy Blazer
All year

$$ B&B
7 rooms, 7 pb
Visa, MC •
C-yes/S-yes

Full breakfast
Coffee, tea, cocoa
Sitting room
Bicycles, hot tubs, pool
and tennis all nearby

Renowned for blueberry pancakes. Glass enclosed garden dining during the summer. Central village location. Uniquely appealing. Fully efficient country cottage also available.

Interlaken Inn–Restaurant
15 Interlaken Ave., 12946
518-523-3180
Roy & Carol Johnson
Exc. April & November

$$$ MAP
12 rooms, 12 pb
Visa, MC •
C-7+/S-yes/P-no/H-no

Full breakfast, dinner
Restaurant, bar
Comp. wine, high tea
sitting room, croquet
volleyball & badminton

Adirondack inn; heart of Olympic country; quiet setting—half block from Main St. Between Mirror Lake and Lake Placid; some rooms with balconies. Great food!

The Lamplight Inn, Lake Luzerne, NY

LAKE PLACID

South Meadow Farm Lodge	$$ EP	Full breakfast
HCR 1, Box 44, 12946	5 rooms	Trail lunch, farm dinner
Cascade Road	C-yes/S-yes/P-no/H-no	Comp. hot cider (winter)
518-523-9369		sitting room, piano
Tony & Nancy Corwin		swimming pond
All year		

Enjoy the Olympic cross-country ski trails that cross our small farm, the view, our fireplace, and home grown meals.

LIVINGSTON MANOR

R.M. Farm	$$ B&B	Full breakfast
P.O. Box 391, 12758	4 rooms	Comp. tea and coffee
Lenape Lake Rd.	C-yes	Sitting room, library
914-439-5511		lake fishing, X-C skiing
Gina Molinet		hunting, pond swimming
All year		

Charming rooms and panoramic views are yours at this mountaintop farm amidst the Catskill's finest resources. Bird-watching, hunting, swimming, skiing. Bring your own horses.

LOCKPORT

National Centennial House	$$ B&B	Continental plus
111 Ontario St., 14094	3 rooms, 3 pb	Comp. wine, cheese
716-434-8193	C-12+/S-no/P-no/H-no	Afternoon tea
Billie & Marvin Pascoe		sitting room, library
All year		

Gorgeous historic mansion with wonderful black walnut and chestnut woodwork. 1 block from Erie Barge Canal. Superb ambiance. 20 miles from Buffalo, Niagara Falls and Lewiston.

MOUNT TREMPER

Mount Tremper Inn
P.O. Box 51, 12457
Rt. 212 & Wittenberg Rd.
914-688-5329
Lou Caselli, Peter LaScala
All year

$$ B&B
23 rooms
C-no/S-ltd/P-no/H-no

Full breakfast
Elegant parlor, library
game room, reading room
comp. sundries

1850 Victorian mansion with Victorian antiques, classical music, gourmet breakfast, wraparound porch, large fireplace. Near Woodstock and all ski slopes.

MUMFORD

The Genesee Country Inn
P.O. Box 340, 14511
948 George St.
716-538-2500
Glenda Barcklow/Kim
Rasmussen
All year

$$$ B&B
12 rooms, 12 pb
Visa, MC, AmEx, DC •
C-ltd/S-yes/P-no/H-ltd

Full breakfast
Afternoon tea, snacks
Common rooms, fireplaces
some canopy beds, TVs
A/C, fly fishing

17-room 1833 stone mill specializing in hospitality and quiet, comfortable retreats. Unique natural setting—woods, gardens, waterfalls. Near Village-Museum.

NAPLES—SOUTH BRISTOL

Landmark Retreat
6006 Route 21, 14512
716-396-2383
Ann Albrecht, Lottie Benker
All year

$ B&B
6 rooms, 1 pb
Visa, MC •
C-yes/S-yes/P-yes/H-yes
German

Full breakfast
Afternoon tea, snacks
Sitting room, library
gazebo, patios
picnic facilities

Country setting with peaceful scenery and spectacular view of Canandaigua Lake. Near golf, fishing, skiing and wineries. Ideal for workshops.

NEW ROCHELLE

Rose Hill Guest House
44 Rose Hill Ave., 10804
914-632-6464
Marilou Mayetta
All year

$$ B&B
2 rooms

•
C-yes/S-yes/P-ltd/H-no

Continental plus
Comp. wine, tea
Sitting room, library
VCR, cable TV
bicycles

Beautiful Norman Rockwell home 20 minutes from Manhattan or Greenwich. Enjoy the "Big Apple" and country living in one. Biking, horseback riding, golfing, sailing, etc.

NEW YORK

The James House
131 E. 15th St., 10003
212-213-1484
James Hance
All year

$$$ B&B
4 rooms, 3 pb

•
C-ask/S-no/P-ask/H-no
French, Spanish

Continental plus
Guest refrigerator
Sitting room, A/C
maid service
marble bathrooms

A contemporary B&B 2 blocks from Empire State Building. Walk to Broadway theaters, the Village, Macy's. Deluxe facilities (unhosted) designed for sophisticated travelers.

NORTH HUDSON

Pine Tree Inn B&B
P.O. Box 555, Route 9, 12855
518-532-9255
Peter & Pat Schoch
All year

$ B&B
5 rooms
C-6+/S-ltd/P-no/H-no

Full breakfast
Dinner by resv. (winter)
Comp. tea & coffee
sitting room

Adirondack sturdy, converted 1920 hotel, country-comfortable furnishings (circa 1740-1856). Near Schroon Lake, Fort Ticonderoga and Lake Placid.

NORTH RIVER

Garnet Hill Lodge	$$ MAP	Full breakfast
13th Lake Rd., 12856	19 rooms, 19 pb	Dinner incl., bar
518-251-2444	•	Sitting room, piano
George & Mary Heim	C-yes/S-ltd/P-no/H-ltd	tennis courts
Exc. June & November		beach, lake swimming

Mountain retreat with freshly baked breads, cross-country skiing, hiking trails on premises. Alpine skiing and Adirondack Museum nearby.

OGDENSBURG

Maple Hill Country Inn	$$ B&B	Full breakfast
Box 21, Riverside Dr., 13669	4 rooms	Dinner on request
315-393-3961	C-yes/S-yes/P-yes/H-no	Comp. tea, wine, snacks
Marilyn Jones		library, sitting room
All year		winter tours

"More than a nice place to stay." We offer comfortable rooms, views of the St. Lawrence River and a hearty breakfast. Getaway weekends. Antiques & collectibles for sale.

OLIVEREA

Slide Mtn. Forest House	$$ B&B/MAP	Full breakfast
163 Oliverea Rd., 12461	21 rooms, 17 pb	Lunch & dinner avail. $
914-254-5365	Visa, MC	Restaurant, bar, pool
Ralph & Ursula Combe	C-yes/S-yes/P-no/H-no	sitting room, hiking
All year	German	tennis courts, fishing

Fresh air, nature and a touch of Old World charm await you at our German/American-style Catskill Mountains Inn. Congenial informal family atmosphere of a small resort.

PALENVILLE

Palenville House B&B	$$ B&B	Full breakfast
P.O. Box 465, 12463	4 rooms, 2 pb	Comp. snacks, tea, cider
Junction Rts. 23A & 32A	•	Sitting room
518-678-5649	C-5+/S-no/P-no	one deluxe suite with
James Forster, James Poretta		fireplace & whirlpool
All year		

1901 charming Queen Anne home. Close to skiing, hiking, swimming and golfing. 2 hours from New York City. Full breakfast and lots of peace and comfort.

PENN YAN

Heirlooms B&B	$$ B&B	Full breakfast
2756 Coates Rd., 14527	4 rooms, 4 pb	Sitting room, fireplace
315-536-7682	Visa, MC	library, creek
Kathy & Dan Disbrow	C-ask/S-no/P-ask/H-no	stables, horses
All year		

1822 Federal home with view of two lakes, wide pine floors, open stairway; charmingly decorated with grandmother's things, quilts. On 18 acres. Part of underground railroad.

PITTSFORD

Oliver Loud's Inn	$$$ B&B	Continental breakfast
1474 Marsh Rd., 14534	8 rooms, 8 pb	Restaurant & bar
716-248-5200 FAX:248-9970	Visa, MC, AmEx, DC •	Comp. wine/fruit/snacks
Vivienne Tellier	C-12+/S-ltd/P-no/H-yes	sitting room, A/C
All year	French, Spanish	jogging, X-C skiing

English country house charm and service in meticulously restored c. 1810 stagecoach inn on banks of Erie Canal. 12 minutes from downtown Rochester. Major attractions nearby.

RENSSELAER

Tibbitt's House Inn
100 Columbia Turnpike, 12144
Routes 9 & 20
518-472-1348
Herb & Claire Rufleth
All year

$ EP
5 rooms, 1 pb
C-no/S-yes/P-no/H-no

Breakfast from menu $
Dining room, picnic area
Enclosed porch, garden
patio, maid service
one apartment available

Comfortable, 128-year-old, antique-furnished farmhouse, 2 miles from Albany, State Museum, Hudson River, hiking/biking, old Dutch fort.

RICHFIELD SPRINGS

Country Spread B&B
P.O. Box 1863, 13439
23 Prospect St., Rt. 28
315-858-1870
Bruce & Karen Watson
All year

$$ B&B
2 rooms, 2 pb
Visa, MC
C-yes/S-no/P-no/H-no

Full breakfast
Refrigerator, snacks
Sitting room, television
private deck, games

Casual, comfortable hospitality; air conditioned and tastefully decorated. Close to Cooperstown and central New York attractions. Families welcome. Delicious breakfasts await.

ROCHESTER

Dartmouth House B&B
215 Dartmouth St., 14607
716-271-7872 716-473-0778
Ellie & Bill Klein
All year

$$ B&B
2 rooms, 2 pb
AmEx •
C-ltd/S-no/P-no/H-no

Full candlelight brkfast
Complimentary beverages
Sitting room, porches
grand piano, organ
bicycles, A/C, TV

Spacious Tudor home close to everything. Quiet, architecturally fascinating, residential neighborhood. Hosts are well traveled and love people! Great breakfasts!

Strawberry Castle B&B
1883 Penfield Rd., 14526
Penfield
716-385-3266
Cynthia & Charles Whited
All year

$$ B&B
3 rooms
Visa, MC, AmEx •
C-12+/S-yes/P-no/H-no

Continental plus
3 acres of grounds
Sitting room, piano
swimming pool, patio
bicycles

Landmark Victorian mansion on three acres. Large rooms and suites with antique furnishings. Small town advantages with convenience to Finger Lakes area.

ROCHESTER (FAIRPORT)

Woods-Edge B&B
P.O. Box 444, 14450
151 Bluhm Rd.
716-223-8877
Betty Kinsman
All year

$$ B&B
3 rooms, 2 pb
•
C-yes/S-no/P-no/H-no

Full breakfast
Afternoon tea, snacks
Sitting room, library
bicycles, hiking
tennis court

Country hideaway nestled in secluded location of fragrant pines and wildlife. Only 20 minutes from downtown Rochester, near exit 45 of NYS I-90.

ROME

Maplecrest B&B
6480 Williams Rd., 13440
315-337-0070
Diane Saladino
All year

$$ B&B
3 rooms, 1 pb
Visa, MC, AmEx •
C-yes/S-no/P-no/H-no
Italian

Full breakfast
Beverage on arrival
Refrigerator use
sitting room, bicycles
grill, picnic facilities

Modern split-level home. Formal country breakfast. Close to historic locations. Adirondack foliage, lakes, and skiing. Near Griffiss Air Force Base.

SARATOGA SPRINGS

Adelphi Hotel
365 Broadway, 12866
518-587-4688
Gregg Siefker, Sheila Parkert
May–November

$$ B&B
20 rooms, 20 pb
Visa, MC, AmEx
C-yes/S-yes/P-no/H-no

Continental breakfast
Summer dinners, bar
Entertainment
sitting room
library, piano

Charming accommodations. Opulently restored high Victorian hotel located in the historic district of the renowned resort and spa of Saratoga Springs.

Chestnut Tree Inn
9 Whitney Place, 12866
518-587-8681
Cathleen & Bruce DeLuke
Mid-April–October

$$ B&B
10 rooms, 5 pb
Visa, MC
C-yes/S-no/P-no/H-no

Continental breakfast
Afternoon tea, lemonade
Comp. wine, snacks
sitting room, antiques
porch, spas

Restored turn-of-the-century Saratoga guest house. In town; walk to racetrack and downtown. Furnished with antiques. Including large wicker porch.

The Inn on Bacon Hill
200 Wall St., 12871
Schuylerville
518-695-3693
Andrea Collins-Breslin
All year

$$ B&B
4 rooms, 2 pb
Visa, MC •
C-12+/S-no/P-no/H-no

Full breakfast
Comp. wine, tea
Sitting room, piano
library, games
close to ski areas

10 minutes from Saratoga Springs – elegant 1862 restored Victorian. Rural setting, warm hospitality, sumptuous breakfasts, central A/C. Innkeeping course offered.

Saratoga B&B
Out Church St, Route 9N, 12866
518-584-0920
Kathleen & Noel Smith
All year

$$ B&B
4 rooms, 4 pb
Visa, MC, AmEx •
C-yes/S-yes/P-ltd/H-yes
French

Full Irish breakfast
Sitting room
piano, bicycles

1860 Victorian farmhouse on five pine-filled acres. Some rooms with fireplaces, all rooms with private baths. Gracious hosts who will help with touring plans.

Six Sisters B&B
149 Union Ave., 12866
518-583-1173
Kate Benton
All year

$$ B&B
4 rooms, 4 pb
C-ltd/S-no/P-no

Full breakfast
Comp. beverage upon arr.
Sitting room, porch
A/C, restaurant nearby
spa packages

Pictorial 1880s Victorian, located within walking distance of Museum of Racing, antique center, restaurants, downtown. Close to mineral spas and state park.

The Westchester House
P.O. Box 944, 12866
102 Lincoln Ave.
518-587-7613
Bob & Stephanie Melvin
All year

$$ B&B
7 rooms, 7 pb
Visa, MC, AmEx •
C-ltd/S-ltd/P-no/H-no
French, German

Continental plus
Comp. beverages
Sitting room, library
wraparound porch, piano
A/C, games, X-C skiing

Gracious Queen Anne Victorian featuring elaborate chestnut woodwork, antique furnishings and up-to-date comforts. Walk to all that historic Saratoga offers. Gardens.

Saratoga B&B, Saratoga Springs, NY

STONY BROOK ————————————————————————

Three Village Inn	$$$ EP	Restaurant, bar service
150 Main St., 11790	27 rooms, 27 pb	Lunch, dinner, snacks
516-751-0555	Visa, MC, AmEx, DC •	Live piano music Fri-Sun
Lou Miaritis	C-yes/S-yes/P-no/H-yes	sitting room, library
All year exc. Christmas		beaches nearby

Three Village Inn offers historic Colonial charm with magnificent views of Stony Brook Harbor on the Long Island Sound. We offer the finest food, service, and hospitality.

TANNERSVILLE ————————————————————————

Eggery Inn	$$$ B&B/MAP	Full breakfast from menu
County Rd. 16, 12485	15 rooms, 15 pb	Wine list, sitting room
518-589-5363	Visa, MC	Dinner for groups (res.)
Abe & Julie Abramczyk	C-ltd/S-yes/P-no/H-yes	cable TV in rooms
All year		player piano, AAA app.

Majestic setting, panoramic views, dining in a garden setting, homelike personal atmosphere and individualized attention. Near Hunter Mountain ski slopes.

TRUMANSBURG ————————————————————————

Taughannock Farms Inn	$$$ B&B	Continental plus
2030 Gorge Rd. (Rte.89), 14886	7 rooms, 7 pb	Restaurant, bar
at Taughannock Falls Park	C-yes/S-ltd/P-no/H-no	Guest houses, sitting rm
607-387-7711	Dutch, German, French	music box, lake swimming
C. Keith & Nancy A. le Grand		gardens, hiking trails
March 15–December 15		

Majestically situated high on a slope with commanding views of forests & Lake Cayuga. Near 200-foot Taughannock waterfall. Hiking trails, boat rentals, picnic grounds, marina.

VERNON

Lavender Inn
RD #1, Box 325, 13476
NY Route 5
315-829-2440
Lyn Doring, Rose Degni

$$ B&B
3 rooms, 3 pb
Visa, MC, AmEx •
S-ltd/P-no/H-no

Full breakfast
Lunch & dinner available
TV & VCR in parlor, A/C
meeting facilities
herb & flower gardens

1799 Federal style home offers a quiescent respite for the weary traveler. Antiques, quilts, pine plank floors. Craft study weekends taught by hosts. Many activities nearby.

WALLKILL

Audreys Farmhouse B&B Ltd.
RD 1, Box 268A, 12589
914-895-3440
Don & Audrey Leff
All year

$$$ B&B
5 rooms, 4 pb
•
C-yes/S-no/H-no

Full breakfast
Box lunch, kitchen, BBQ
Aftn. tea, comp. brandy
sitting room, library
pool, decks, weddings

1740 elegant, restored farmhouse. All rooms with private baths, feather beds and down comforters. In-ground pool. Magnificent view of mountains. Gourmet breakfasts. Romantic.

WARRENSBURG

Country Road Lodge
HCR 1 Box 227, 12885
Hickory Hill Rd.
518-623-2207
Steve & Sandi Parisi
All year

$$ B&B
4 rooms, 2 pb
•
C-no/S-ltd/P-no/H-no

Full breakfast
AP (December-April)
Sitting room
piano, library

Quiet, idyllic setting along Hudson River at the end of a country road. Discreetly sociable host. No traffic or TV. In the southern Adirondack Mountains, near Lake George, etc

Merrill Magee House
2 Hudson St., 12885
518-623-2449
Ken & Florence Carrington
All year

$$ B&B
13 rooms, 10 pb
Visa, MC, AmEx, Disc •
C-12+/S-yes/P-no/H-yes

Full breakfast
Restaurant, bar, dinner
Comp. coffee, tea, cocoa
sitting room, library
swimming pool, hot tubs

Elegant Victorian setting with decidedly 20th-century comforts. In the center of a charming Adirondack Mountain village.

White House Lodge
53 Main St., 12885
518-623-3640
James & Ruth Gibson
All year

$$$ B&B
5 rooms
Visa, MC
C-7+/S-ltd/P-no/H-no

Continental breakfast
Comp. wine, cookies
Homemade cakes, pies
sitting room, television
front porch

Pre-Civil War mansion, four miles from beautiful Lake George. Eight miles from Gore Mountain. Queen village of the Adirondacks.

WATERLOO

Historic James R. Webster
115 E. Main St., 13165
Routes 5 & 20
315-539-3032
Leonard & Barbara Cohen
All year

$$$ B&B
2 rooms, 2 pb
•
C-no/S-no/P-no/H-no

Continental breakfast
Full breakfast $
Candlelight dinners
sitting rooms in suites

Finger Lakes–pampered honeymoons, two private palatial suites, haute cuisine, European & Asian treasures, marble bathrooms, rare museum collections. Expensive and luxurious.

WELLS

Adirondack Mountain Chalet
G.G. Commons, Box 341, 12190
518-924-2112
Jeffree & Elizabeth

Full kitchen
Sleeps up to 4
Mountain spring water
woodstove, central heat
maps of trails avail.

Relax and renew your spirit. Unique mountain chalet in Adirondack State Park. Accessible by foot or car. Swimming, canoeing, biking, skiing, mountain hiking.

WEST SHOKAN

Haus Elissa B&B
P.O. Box 95, Rt. 28-A, 12494
914-657-6277
Gretchen & Helen Behl
All year

$$ B&B
2 rooms, 1 pb
C-14+/S-ltd/P-no/H-no
German, Dutch, French

Full breakfast
Comp. coffee, juice, tea
Sitting room, sun porch
library, piano
local history library

A blend of Catskill coziness and continental hospitality. Our own German pastries served with breakfast. Near fishing, hiking, skiing, fine dining, Woodstock.

WESTFIELD

The William Seward Inn
RD #2, Box 14, 14787
S. Portage Rd., Rte. 394
716-326-4151
Jim & Debbie Dahlberg
All year

$$$ B&B
10 rooms, 10 pb
Visa, MC •
C-12+/S-no/P-no/H-yes
French

Full gourmet breakfast
Wet bar available
Sitting room
library
bicycles

Country mansion with period antiques; complimentary full gourmet breakfast; close to major antique center, wineries, ski slopes and cross-country, and charming Lake Chatauqua.

Westfield House
P.O. Box 505, 14787
E. Main Rd., Route 20
716-326-6262
Betty & Jud Wilson
All year

$$ B&B
6 rooms, 6 pb
Visa, MC •
C-12+/S-no/P-no/H-yes

Full breakfast
Comp. wine, snacks
Sitting room, bicycles
needlework shop
small meeting facilites

Elegant red brick Gothic Revival inn situated behind maple trees overlooking vineyards. Near antique shops, recreational and cultural activities, and skiing. Special Weekends.

WESTHAMPTON BEACH

1880 Seafield House
P.O. Box 648, 11978
2 Seafield Lane
516-288-1559 800-346-3290
Elsie Collins
All year

$$$ B&B
3 rooms, 3 pb
•
C-no/S-no/P-no/H-no

Full breakfast
Sherry, arrival treat
Sitting room, piano
tennis court, library
swimming pool

Country hideaway with three suites furnished in antiques—gourmet breakfast served in our lovely decorated dining room or enclosed porch overlooking the pool.

WEVERTOWN

Mountainaire Adventures
Route 28, 12886
Glen-Dillon Hill Road
518-251-2194 800-950-2194
Douglas Cole
All year

$$ B&B
8 rooms, 6 pb
Visa, MC •
C-yes/S-yes/P-yes/H-yes

Full breakfast
Comp. hot drinks, videos
Bar, sitting room
bicycles, sauna
hot tubs

Adirondack inn and chalet with mountain views. Near Gore Mountain Ski area and Lake George. Private adventure tours!

More Inns . . .

1770 House 143 Main St., East Hampton, 11937 516-324-1770
1819 Red Brick Inn RD 2, Box 57A, Dandee, 14837 607-243-8844
1870 House B&B 20 Chestnut St., Franklinville, 14737 716-676-3571
21 House Montauk Hwy. Box 149, Amagansett, 11930 800-888-8888
33 South 33 South St., Cuba, 14727 716-968-1387
Abode B&B P.O. Box 20022, New York, 10028 212-472-2000
Adrianna 44 Stewart St., Dolgeville, 13329 315-733-0040
Agnes Hall Tourist Home 94 Center St., Oneonta, 13820 607-432-0655
All Breeze Guest Farm Haring Rd., Barryville, 12719 914-557-6485
Alpine Inn Alpine Rd., Oliverea, 12462 914-254-5026
American House B&B Inn 39 Main St., Geneseo, 14454 716-243-5483
Antrim Lodge Hotel Roscoe, 12776 607-498-4191
Appel Inn Route 146, Altamont, 12009 518-861-6557
Apple Tree B&B, The 49 W. High St, Ballston Spa, 12020 518-885-1113
Arrowhead Ranch Parksville, 12768 914-292-6267
Astoria Hotel 25 Main St., Rosendale, 12472 914-658-8201
At Home in New York P.O. Box 407, New York, 10185 212-247-3294
Auberge des Quatre Saisons Route 42, Shandaken, 12480 914-688-2223
Audrey's B&B 219 Mountain Rest Rd., New Paltz, 12561 914-255-1103
Aurora Inn Main St., Route 90, Aurora, 13026 315-364-8842
Avon Manor, The 109 Slyvania Ave., Avon-By-The-Sea, 07717 201-775-9770
B&B at Twin Fawns 166 Otto Stahl Rd. RD 1, Mt. Vision, 13810 607-293-8009
B&B of Long Island, Inc. P.O. Box 392, Old Westbury, 11568 516-334-6231
B&B of Waterville 211 White St., Waterville, 13480 315-841-8295
Bakers B&B RD 2 Box 80, Stone Ridge, 12484 914-687-9795
Bassett House 128 Montauk Hwy., East Hampton, 11937 516-324-6127
Bay Horse Bed & Breakfast 813 Ridge Road, Lansing, 14882 607-533-4612
Beaverbrook House Duell Rd., Bengall, 12545 914-868-7677
Beaverkill Valley Inn Beaverkill Rd., Lew Beach, 12753 914-439-4844
Bed & Breakfast Sunset Trail, Clinton Corners, 12514 914-266-3922
Beekman Arms Route 9, Rhinebeck, 12572 914-876-7077
Belle Crest House P.O. Box 891, Shelter Island Heights, 11965 516-749-2041
Belleayre Youth Hostel P.O. Box 665, Pine Hill, 12465 914-254-4200
Bellinger Woods 611 W. German St., Herkimer, 13350 315-866-2770
Benn Conger Inn 206 W. Cortland St., Groton, 13073 607-898-5817
Bent Finial Manor 194 Main St, Warrensburg, 12885 518-677-5741
Big Moose Inn, Inc. on Big Moose Lake, Eagle Bay, 13331 315-357-2042
Birch Creek B&B P.O. Box 583, Pine Hill, 12465 914-254-5222
Bivona Hill B&B Academy Rd., Brookfield, 13314 315-899-8921
Blackberry Inn B&B 59 Sentinel Rd., Lake Placid, 12946 518-523-3419
Bluebird B&B 21 Harper St., Stamford, 12167 607-652-3711
Bowditch House 166 N. Ferry Rd., Shelter Island, 11965 516-749-0075
Bowman House 61 Lake St., Hammondsport, 14840 607-569-2516
Box Tree Hotel P.O. Box 477, Purdy's, 10578 914-277-3677
Breinlinger's B&B RD 3, Box 154 W. Hill, Elmira, 14903 607-733-0089
Brewer House Inn 112 E. Main Street, Westfield, 14787 716-326-2320
Brewster Inn 6 Ledyard Av., Cazenovia, 13035 518-655-9232
Brooklyn B&B 128 Kent St, Brooklyn, 11222 718-383-3026
Brown's Village Inn B&B Box 378, Stafford St., Fair Haven, 13064 315-947-5817
Buena Vista Manor Route 9W, Box 144, West Camp, 12490 914-246-6462
Burke's Cottages Lake Shore Dr., Sabael, 12864 516-281-4983
Buttermilk Bear 37 Milligan St., Little Falls, 13365 315-823-3378
Caffrey House Squires Ave., East Quogue, 11942 516-728-1327
Calico Quail Inn Route 44, Box 748, Millbrook, 914-677-6016
Cambridge Inn B&B 16 West Main St, Cambridge, 12816 518-677-5741
Canadarago Lake House E. Lake Rd., Richfield Springs, 13439 315-858-1761
Canaltown B&B 119 Canandaigua St., Palmyra, 14522 315-597-5553
Candlelight Cottages Route 9N Box 133 N, Bolton Landing, 12814 518-644-3321

Captain Hawkins Inn 321 Terryville Rd., Port Jefferson, 11776 516-473-8211
Carriage House Inn Wickham Blvd & Ontario, Sodus Point, 14555 315-483-2100
Castle Hill B&B Box 325, near Route 9D, Wappingers Falls, 12590 914-298-8000
Castle Inn 3220 W. State Rd., Olean, 14760 518-422-7853
Cathedral Farms Inn RD 1, Box 560, Oneonta, 13820 607-432-7483
Catskill Mountain Lane Route 47, Oliverea, 12462 914-254-5498
Cavern View RD 1, Box 23, Howes Cave, 12092 518-296-8052
Cecce Guest House 166 Chemung St., Corning, 14830 607-962-5682
Cedar Beach Bed & Breakfas 642 West Lake Road, Hammondsport, 14840 607-868-3228
Cedar Terrace Resort Upper Main St., Cairo, 12413 518-622-9313
Centennial House 13 Woods Lane, East Hampton, 11937 516-324-9414
Center House Farm B&B Box 64 RD #2, Watkins Glen, 14891 607-535-4317
Chalet Leon 3835 Rt. 414 Box 388, Watkins Glen, 14891 518-546-7171
Champagne's High Peaks Inn Route 73, P.O. Box 701, Keene Valley, 12943 518-576-2003
Chateau L'Esperance Star Rte.–Hwy. 11B, Nicholville, 12965 315-328-4669
Chelsea Pines Inn 317 W. 14th St., New York, 10014 212-929-1023
Chequit Inn 23 Grand Ave., Shelter Island, 11965 516-749-0018
Cherry Valley Ventures 6119 Rt. 20, Lafayette, 13084 518-677-9723
Chesham Place 317 W. Main St., Ilion, 13357 315-894-3552
Chester Inn, The Box 163, Main St, Chestertown, 12817 518-494-4148
Chestnut Grove Inn R.D.7, Box 10, Oswego, 13069 315-342-2547
Chez Renux 229-C Budd Rd., Woodbourne, 12788 914-434-1780
Clinton House 21 W. Park Row, Clinton, 13323 315-853-5555
Cobblestones, The 1160 Routes 5 & 20, Geneva, 14456 315-789-1890
Cold Brook Inn P.O. Box 251, Boicerille, 12412 914-657-6619
Colgate Inn Hamilton, 13346 315-824-2134
Colonial Inn Main Street, Pine Hill, 12465 914-254-5577
Conifer Hill Bed & Breakfa RD 2, Box 309, Route 22, Trumansburg, 14886 607-387-5849
Copper Hood Inn Route 28, Shandaken, 02480 914-688-9962
Copperfield Inn North Creek, 12853 518-251-5200
Corner Birches B&B Guests 86 Montcalm St., Lake George, 12845 518-668-2837
Cottonwood Inn & Motel Route 44, Millbrook, 12545 914-677-3919
Country Hills RD # Box 80, Route 28, Mohawk, 13407 315-866-1306
Country House Box 146, 37 Mill St., Canaseraga, 14822 607-545-6439
Country View B&B 1500 Route 392, Cortland, 13045 607-835-6517
Cozy Cottage 4987 Kingston Rd., Skaneateles (Elbridge), 13060 315-689-2082
Crislip's B&B Rd 1, Bx 57, Ridge Rd, Queensburg, 12804 518-793-6869
Crislip's B&B P.O. Box 57, Glens Falls, 12801 518-793-6869
Dannfield 50 Canada Rd., Painted Post, 14870 607-962-2740
David Harum House 80 S. Main St., Homer, 13077 607-749-3548
Decker Pond Inn 1076 Elmira Rd., Newfield, 14867 607-273-7133
Delamater House 44 Montgomery St., Rhinebeck, 12572 914-876-7077
Delevan House 188 Delevan Avenue, Corning, 14830 607-962-2347
Denonville Inn 1750 Empire Blvd., Webster, 14580 518-671-1550
Don & Sally Kallop B&B off Route 9, Rhinebeck, 12572 914-876-4576
Donegal Manor B&B 117 Main St, Warrensburg, 12885 518-623-3549
East Lake George House 492 Glen St., Glens Falls, 12801 378-656-9452
Eastwood House 45 So. Main St., Castile, 14427 716-493-2335
Edson House 7856 Griswold Circle, Le Roy, 14482 715-758-2340
Eleanor's 3 Washington Ave., South Nyack, 10960 914-353-3040
Ellicottville Inn 4-10 Washington St., Ellicotville, 14731 716-699-2373
Elmshade Guest House 402 S. Albany St., Ithaca, 14850 607-273-1707
Evergreens 1248 Waterloo-Geneva Rd, Waterloo, 13165 315-539-8329
Fala B&B E. Market St., Hyde Park, 12538 914-229-5937
Fannie Schaffer Vegetarian P.O. Box 457 M, Woodridge, 12789 914-434-4455
Finton's Landing 661 E. Lake Rd., Penn Yan, 14527 315-536-3146
Five Acre Farm RD #3, Box 60, Saint Johnsville, 13452 315-733-0040
Five Gables 489 E. Main St., West Winfield, 13491 315-822-5764
Four Seasons B&B 470 W. Lake Rd., Rt.54A, Branchport, 14418 607-868-4686
Fox Run Vineyards B&B 670 Route 14, RD 1, Penn Yan, 14527 315-536-2507

Friends Lake Inn Friends Lake Rd., Chestertown, 12817 518-494-4751
Friendship Manor 349 S. Main St., Albion, 14411 716-589-7973
Frost Haven Resort B&B West Bay Rd., Fair Haven, 13064 315-947-5331
Gables Bed & Breakfast, Th 62 West Main Street, Cobleskill, 12043 315-733-0040
Gasho Inn Route 32, Box M, Central Valley, 10917 914-928-2277
Gates Hill Homestead Off Dugway Road, Brookfield, 13314 315-733-0040
Genesee Falls Hotel P.O. Box 396, Portageville, 14536 716-493-2484
Geneva on the Lake P.O. Box 929, Geneva, 14456 315-789-7190
Glen Atty Farm Box 578, West Shokan, 12494 914-657-8110
Glenora Guests 65 N. Glenora Rd., Dundee, 14837 607-243-7686
Gold Mountain Chalet Tice Road Box 456, Spring Glen, 12483 914-395-5200
Goose Creek Guesthouse 1475 Waterview Dr., Southold, 11971 516-765-3356
Gould 108 Fall St., Seneca Falls, 13148 518-568-5801
Grant Inn Stormy Hill Rd., Grant, 13324 315-826-7677
Green Acres RD 1, Route 474, Ashville, 14710 716-782-4254
Green Gables B&B 24 Wawbeek Ave., Tupper Lake, 12986 518-359-7815
Greenfield Pole Club Birchall Rd., Box 83, Greenfield Park, 12435 916-647-3240
Greenmeadow RD #3, Alder Creek Road, Boonville, 13309 315-733-0040
Greenway Terrace Motel 18-19 Moody Rd., Rte 30, Tupper Lake, 12986 518-359-2852
Gypsy Lady N. Bennington, Rt. 6, Walloomsac, 12090 518-686-4880
Habersham Country Inn 6124 Routes 5 & 20, Canandaigua, 14424 716-394-1510
Halcyon Manor 380 Bay Av., Patchogue, 11772 516-289-9223
Hammertown Inn RD 2, Box 25, Pine Plains, 12567 518-398-7539
Hasbrouck House Inn Route 209, Box 76, Stone Ridge, 12484 914-687-0055
Hedges House 74 James Ln., East Hampton, 11937 516-324-7100
Hellers, The 46C River Rd., Rhinebeck, 12572 914-876-3468
Henry J. Dombrowski 8404 Old Lake Shore Rd., Angola, 14006 716-549-1055
Hickory Grove Inn Rd. 2, Box 898, Cooperstown, 13326 607-547-8100
Hideaway Hotel Huntersfield Road, Prattsville, 12468 518-299-3616
High Meadow B&B 3740 Eager Rd, Jamesville, 13078 315-492-3517
High Woods Inn 7472 Glasco Turnpike, Saugerties, 12477 914-246-8655
Highland Springs Allen Rd., East Concord, 14055 716-592-4323
Highwinds Inn Barton Miners Rd, North River, 12856 518-251-3760
Hillside Inn 518 Stewart Ave, Ithaca, 607-272-9507
Historic Cook House 167 Main St., Newfield, 14867 607-564-9926
Holloway House Routes 5 & 20, East Bloomfield, 14443 716-657-7120
Homestead, The Red Mill Rd., Greenville, 12083 518-966-4474
Horned Dorset Inn Leonardsville, 13364 315-855-7898
Hound & Hare B&B, The 1031 Hanshaw Rd., Ithaca, 14850 607-257-2821
House On Saratoga Lake 143-51 Manning Rd., Ballston Spa, 12020 518-584-5976
House on the Hill Box 86 Old Route 213, High Falls, 12440 914-687-9627
House on the Quarry 7480 Pine Rd., Saugerties, 12477 914-246-8584
Huntting Inn 94 Main St., East Hampton, 11937 516-324-0410
Incentra Village House 32 8th Ave., New York, 10014 212-206-0007
Inn at Belhurst Castle P.O. Box 609, Geneva, 14456 315-789-0359
Inn at Blue Stores Box 99, Star Rt., Rt. 9, Hudson, 12534 518-537-4277
Inn at Edge of the Forest 11 E. Dayton Dr., Corinth, 12822 518-654-6656
Inn at Hobnobbin Farm P.O. Box 176, Route 17, Mayville, 14757 716-753-3800
Inn at Lake Joseph RD 5, Box 85, Forestburgh, 12777 914-791-9506
Inn at Saratoga 231 Broadway, Saratoga Springs, 12866 518-583-1890
Inn at Shaker Mill Farm Cherry Ln., Canaan, 12029 518-794-9345
Inn at the Falls 50 Red Oaks Mill Rd., Poughkeepsie, 12603 914-462-5770
Inn on the Library Lawn #1 Washington St., Westport, 12993 518-962-8666
Iris Farm 162 Hook Rd., Macedon, 14502 315-986-4536
Issac Turner House 739 Main St., Fair Haven, 13064 315-947-5901
James Russell Webster Inn 115 East Main St, Waterloo, 13165 315-539-3032
Jerry's Accommodations 168 Cottage Walk, Ocean Beach, 11770 516-583-8870
Klartag Farms B&B W. Branch Rd., Rushford, 14777 716-437-2946
Lake Keuka Manor 626 W. Lake Rd., Hammondsport, 14840 607-868-3276
Lake Placid Manor Whiteface Inn Rd., Lake Placid, 12946 518-523-2573

Lakeside Terrace B&B RD 1, P.O. Box 197, Dundee, 14837 607-292-6606
Landmark Retreat B&B 6006 Route #21, Naples, 14512 716-396-2383
Lange's Grove Side Rt. 23/P.O. Box 79, Acra, 12405 518-622-3393
Lanigan Farmhouse Box 399, RD 1, Stamford, 12167 607-652-7455
Lanza's Country Inn RD 2, Box 446, Livingston Manor, 12758 914-439-5070
Laurel Hill B&B 2670 Powderhouse Rd., Corning, 14830 607-936-3215
Le Chambord Inn Route 52, Box 3, Hopewell Junction, 12533 914-221-1941
Le Muguet 2553 Church St., Three Mile Bay, 13693 315-649-5896
Leland House 26 E. Main St., Springville, 14141 518-592-7631
Lincklaen House 79 Albany St., Cazenovia, 13035 315-655-8171
Linen'n'Lace B&B Home 659 Chilton Av., Niagara Falls, 14301 518-285-3935
Living Springs Retreat Rt. 3, Bryant Pond Rd., Putnam Valley, 10579 914-526-2800
Locustwood Inn 3563 Route 89, Canoga, 13148 315-549-7132
Longfellow Inn 11 Roberts Ave., Box Y, Chautauqua, 14722 716-357-2285
Ludwig's Kozy Kove Box 866, Cayuga, 13034 315-889-5940
Mansion, The Rt29,W of Saratoga, Rock City Falls, 12863 518-885-1607
Maple Ridge Inn Rt. 372, Rt. 1,Box 391C, Cambridge, 12816 518-677-3674
Maplewood P.O. Box 40, Chichester, 12416 914-688-5433
Margaret Thatchers B&B 9 James St., Box 119, Dryden, 13053 518-844-8052
Margaretville Mountain Inn Margaretville Mountain, Margaretville, 12455 914-586-3933
Marsh House P.O. Box 250, Schoharie, 12157 518-295-7981
Marshfield B&B RR 1, Box 432, Amenia, 12501 914-868-7833
Mary Sweeney B&B "Bantry," Asher Rd., Rhinebeck, 12572 914-876-6640
Maxwell Creek Inn 7563 Lake Road, Sodus, 14551 315-483-2222
Maybrook Lodge #2 P.O. Box 80, Kerhonkson, 12446 914-626-9823
McEnaney's Lincoln Log Route 9, Lake George, 12845 518-668-5326
Merryhart Victorian Inn 12 Front St., Box 363, Marathon, 13803 607-849-3951
Mill House Inn 33 North Main, East Hampton, 11937 516-324-9766
Mill-Garth-Mews Inn P.O. Box 700, Amagansett, 11930 516-267-3757
Millhof Inn Route 43, Stephentown, 12168 518-733-5606
Minerva Hill Lodge Route 28N, Minerva, 12851 518-251-2710
Missert's Bed & Breakfast 66 Highland Ave., Hamburg, 14075 716-649-5830
Mohonk Mountain House Lake Mohonk, New Paltz, 12561 914-255-1000
Montgomery Inn Guest House 67 Montgomery St., Rhinebeck, 12572 914-876-3311
Mulligan Farm B&B 5403 Barber Rd., Avon, 14414 716-226-6412
Muse, The 5681 Middle Road, Horseheads, 14845 607-739-1070
Nana's B&B 54 Old Ford Rd., New Paltz, 12561 914-255-5678
Napoli Stagecoach Inn Napoli Corners, Little Valley, 14755 716-938-6735
New Mohican House Old Rt 23/P.O. Box 79, Acra, 12405 518-622-3393
Nieuw Country Loft 41 Allhuson Rd., New Paltz, 12561 914-LLA-OLD
Nottingham Lodge Bed & Bre 5741 Bristol Valley, Rt, Canandaigua, 14424 716-374-5355
Ocean Beach Inn/Restaurant Bay Walk, Ocean Beach, 11770 516-583-5558
Old Niagara House B&B 337 Buffalo Av., Niagara Falls, 14303 518-285-9408
Old Post House Inn 136 Main St., Southampton, 11968 516-283-1717
One Market Street One Market St., Cold Spring, 10516 914-265-3912
One More Time 141 Tinker St., Woodstock, 12498 914-679-8701
Orchard House Rt. 44/55 Box 413, Clintondale, 12515 914-883-6136
Peirce House B&B 218 S. Albany St., Ithaca, 14850 518-273-8043
Phoenix Inn at River Road RD #3, Box 150, Cooperstown, 13326 607-547-8250
Pig Hill Inn B&B 73 Main St., Cold Spring, 10516 914-265-9247
Pine Hill Arms Pine Hill, 12462 918-254-9811
Plumbush--A Victorian B&B Chautauqua-Stedman Rd., Mayville, 14757 716-789-5309
Pollyanna, The 302 Main Street, Oneida, 13421 315-733-0040
Port Jerry Resort H.C.R. Box 27, Bolton Landing, 12814 518-644-3311
Potter's Resort Jct Rts 28 & 30, Blue Mountain Lake, 12812 518-352-7331
Providence Farm 11572 Hiller Rd., Akron, 14001 716-759-2109
Rainbow Guest House 423 Rainbow Blvd, So., Niagara Falls, 14092 716-282-1135
Ranchouse at Baldwin Baldwin Rd., Ticonderoga, 12883 518-585-6596
Reber's Motel on the Hill 5 Route 97, Barryville, 12719 914-557-8111
Red Coach Inn Two Buffalo Ave., Niagara Falls, 14303 716-282-1459

Red Hook Inn 31 S. Broadway, Red Hook, 12571 914-758-8445
Rhinecliff B&B Box 167,William & Grinn, Rhinecliff, 12574 914-876-3710
Richard M. Hayes Box 537, Bolton Landing, 12814 518-644-5941
Rondout B&B 88 W. Chester St., Kingston, 12401 914-331-2369
Rose Cottage, The 2 Roberts Avenue, Chautauqua, 716-357-5375
Rose Mansion & Gardens 625 Mt. Hope Ave., Rochester, 14620 716-546-5426
Roycroft Inn 40 S. Grove St., East Aurora, 14052 716-652-9030
Runaway Inn Main Street, Fleischmanns, 12430 (914)-5660
Sacks Lodge Saugerties, 12477 914-246-8711
Sage Cottage Box 626, Trumansburg, 14886 607-387-6449
Salt Hill Farm 5209 Lake Rd, Galway, 12074 518-882-9466
Scenery Hill N. Cross Rd., Staatsburg, 12580 914-889-4812
Secret Garden 6071 Malden Tpk., Saugerties, 12477 914-246-3338
Sedgewick Inn Berlin, 518-658-2334
Sedgwick Inn, The Route 22, Berlin, 12022 518-658-2334
Sequoia Inn 7686 N. Jefferson St., Pulaski, 13302 315-298-4407
Serendipity RD 2, Box 1050, Cooperstown, 13326 607-547-2106
Shelter Island Resort 35 Shore Rd., Shelter Island, 11965 518-749-2001
Shepherd's Croft HCR Box 263, Purling, 12470 518-622-9504
Shepherd's Neck Inn Montauk, 516-668-2105
Sherwood Inn 26 W. Genesee St., Skaneateles, 13152 315-685-3405
Silver Waters Guesthouse 8420 Bay St., Sodus Point, 14555 315-483-8098
Simmons Way Village Inn Main St., Route 44, Millerton, 12546 518-789-6235
Sixteen Firs 352 St. Paul Ave., Staten Island, 10304 212-727-9188
Skene Manor Mountain St. off Rt. 4, Whitehall, 12887 518-499-1112
Spruce Lodge B&B 31 Sentinel Rd., Lake Placid, 12946 518-523-9350
Stacey's Country Inn 62 Big Island Rd., Warwick, 10990 914-986-7855
Stagecoach Inn Old Military Rd., Lake Placid, 12946 518-523-9474
Starbuck House B&B 253 Clinton St., Watertown, 13601 315-788-7324
Stockbridge Inn B&B RD 2 Box 536, Cooperstown, 13326 607-547-5069
Stony Water B&B RR#1, Box 69, Elizabethtown, 12932 518-873-9125
Summer House Box 43, 22 Peck Ave., Chautauqua, 14722 216-226-6934
Summerwood B&B P.O. Box 388, Richfield Springs, 13439 315-858-2024
Sunny Side Up B&B RD 1, Box 58, Butler Rd, Plattsburgh, 12901 518-563-5677
Sunrise Inn B&B RD 1 Box 232B, Hancock, 13783 607-865-7254
Tara Farm B&B Kiernan Rd., Campbell Hall, 10916 914-294-6482
The Globe 45 Pearl Street, New Harford, 13413 315-733-0040
The Historian Route 5, Box 224, Nelliston, 13410 315-733-0040
Thendara Inn & Restaurant 4356 East Lake Rd., Canandaigua, 14424 518-394-4868
Thornberry Inn Stony Kill Rd., Canaan, 12029 518-781-4939
Three Bear Inn 3 Broome St., Box 507, Marathon, 13803 518-849-3258
Timothy's B&B Bx. 2500, RR2, Lake George, 12845 518-668-5238
Town & Country B&B P.O. Box 208, Pine St., South Dayton, 14138 716-988-3340
Towpath Inn Route 26 and West Rd., Turin, 13473 315-348-8122
Tummonds House 5392 Walworth/Ontario, Ontario, 14519 315-524-5381
Tunnicliff Inn 34-36 Pioneer St., Cooperstown, 13326 607-547-9611
Twin Forks B&B P.O. Box 657, Hampton Bays, 11946 516-728-5285
Twin Gables of Woodstock 73 Tinker St., Woodstock, 12498 914-679-9479
Two Brooks B&B SR 108, Route 42, Shandaken, 12480 914-688-7101
Valley View Country Rt. 47, Oliverea, 12462 914-254-5117
Victoria Lodge 502 E. Main St., West Winfield, 13941 315-822-6290
Victorian Carriage House 46 William St., Clinton, 13323 315-853-8389
Village Inn B&B 111 S. Erie St., Mayville, 14757 716-753-3583
Village Victorian Inn 31 Center St., Rhinebeck, 12572 914-876-8345
Vrede Landgoed Dug Rd., RD #2, Beaver Dams, 14812 607-535-4108
Wagener Estate B & B 351 Elm St., Penn Yan, 14527 315-536-4591
Washington Inn South Broadway, Saratoga Springs, 12866 518-584-9807
Washington Irving Lodge Route 23A, Tannersville, 12485 518-589-5560
Washington Irving Lodge P.O. Box 675, Rt. 23A, Hunter, 12442 518-589-5560
Way Inn 7377 Salina St., Pulaski, 13142 315-298-6073

Wayside Inn 104 Wilton Rd., Greenfield, 12833 518-893-7249
Welcome Inn B&B 529 Warren Rd., Ithaca, 14850 607-257-0250
West Wind Farm B&B 402A Hornby Rd., Corning, 14830 607-962-3979
What Cheer Hall P.O. Box 417, N. Main, Newport, 13416 316-845-8312
Wheeler B&B RD #2 Box 455, Hammondsport, 14810 607-776-6756
Whistle Wood Farm 11 Pells Rd., Rhinebeck, 12572 914-876-6838
White Inn 52 E. Main St., Fredonia, 14063 716-672-2103
Whiteface Chalet Springfield Rd., Wilmington, 12997 518-946-2207
Whitegate P.O. Box 917, Oxford, 13830 607-843-6965
Wilder Tavern Country Inn 5648 N. Bloomfield Rd., Canandaigua, 14425 716-394-8132
Williams Inn 27 Main St., Hornell, 14843 518-324-7400
Willow Cove 77 S. Glenora Rd., RD 4, Dundee, 14837 607-243-8482
Windswept B&B County Rd. 16, Elka Park, 12427 518-589-6275
Windy Shores B&B 2629 Lake Road, Ontario, 14519 315-524-2658
Woods Lodge Schroon Lodge, 12870 518-532-7529
Woven Waters HC 73 Box 193E Rt. 41, Willet, 13863 607-656-8672
Zeiser's Oak Mtn. Lodge Route 30, Speculator, 12164 518-548-7021

North Carolina

ASHEVILLE

Aberdeen Inn B&B	$$ B&B	Full breakfast buffet
64 Linden Ave., 28801	9 rooms, 9 pb	Comp. wine, aftn. tea
704-254-9336	Visa, MC ●	Dinner Christmas Day
Linda & Ross Willard	C-12+/S-no/P-no/H-no	sitting room, library
All year		cable TV, fireplaces

Comfortable old tree-shaded Colonial. Wraparound porch, fireplaces in three rooms, handmade afghans on the beds. Lovely private grounds & gardens. Near Biltmore and downtown.

Blake House Inn	$$ B&B	Full breakfast
150 Royal Pines Dr., 28704	5 rooms, 5 pb	Restaurant (Wed-Sun)
Arden, South Asheville	Visa, MC	Comp. wine, bar
704-684-1847	C-no/S-no/P-no/H-yes	sitting room, bicycles
Bob, Eloise & Chef P. Roesler		tennis & pool nearby

Mountains cradle our town with a protective embrace. Sip wine and dine in an intimate country inn on the edge of town. Pati, a Cordon Bleu chef, will prepare fabulous meals.

Cairn Brae	$$ B&B	Continental plus
217 Patton Mountain Rd., 28804	3 rooms, 3 pb	Aftn. wine, eve. sherry
704-252-9219	Visa, MC ●	12 minutes from downtown
Edward & Milli Adams	C-6+/S-no/P-no/H-no	
April–November		

Cairn Brae–the Scotish name for "rocky hillside" describes the inn's location on four wooded acres above Asheville. Beautiful views. Woodsy trails.

Cedar Crest Victorian Inn	$$ B&B	Continental plus
674 Biltmore Ave., 28803	10 rooms, 8 pb	Afternoon refreshments
704-252-1389	Visa, MC	Evening beverages/sweets
Jack & Barbara McEwan	C-12+/S-ltd/P-no/H-no	sitting room, piano
All year		A/C, phones, desks

The essence of Victorian, opulent carved woodwork, beveled glass, period antiques. Breakfast and tea on veranda. Four blocks to Biltmore Estate.

ASHEVILLE

Cornerstone Inn
230 Pearson Dr., 28801
704-253-5644
Gary & Nancy Gaither
All year

$$ B&B
3 rooms, 3 pb
●
C-10+/S-no/P-no/H-no

Full breakfast
Comp. tea & soft drinks
Sitting room
A/C and phones in rooms

A historic Dutch Tudor home nestled among hemlocks, Cornerstone Inn combines fine antiques and collectibles to create country elegance.

Dry Ridge Inn
26 Brown, Weaverville, 28787
704-658-3899
John & Karen VanderElzen
All year

$$ B&B
5 rooms, 5 pb
Visa, MC ●
C-yes/S-ltd
Dutch

Full breakfast
Comp. wine
Sitting room
bicycles
gift shop

Convenient to Asheville and Blue Ridge Pkwy. with small town charm. Large comfortable guest rooms; antiques and homemade quilts.

Flint Street Inns
100 & 116 Flint St., 28801
704-253-6723
Rick, Lynne & Marion Vogel
All year

$$$ B&B
8 rooms, 8 pb
Visa, MC, AmEx ●
C-12+/S-yes/P-no/H-no

Full southern breakfast
Comp. wine, cider, etc.
Sitting room, fireplaces
English style garden
A/C, bicycles for guests

Charming, turn-of-the-century-style residences, located in historic district. Comfortable walking distance to town, restaurants, and shops.

The Lion & the Rose
276 Montford Ave., 28801
Montford Historic Dist.
704-255-7673
Jeanne Donaldson
All year

$$$ B&B
4 rooms, 4 pb
Visa, MC ●
C-12+/S-ltd

Full breakfast
Comp. wine, aftn. tea
TV and card rooms
suite available
lovely verandas

Classic, elegantly restored & furnished English Queen Anne 1898 townhome. Full gourmet breakfasts, varied daily. Four deluxe suites. "Pampering" in tasteful Victorian style.

Old Reynolds Mansion
100 Reynolds Heights, 28804
704-254-0496
Fred & Helen Faber
Exc. weekdays Dec–Mar

$ B&B
10 rooms, 7 pb
C-6+/S-yes/P-no/H-no

Continental breakfast
Comp. wine
Afternoon beverages
sitting room, verandas
swimming pool

A restored 1850 antebellum mansion in a country setting. Wide verandas, mountain views, woodburning fireplaces, huge old swimming pool. On the National Register.

The Ray House B&B
83 Hillside St., 28801
704-252-0106
Alice & Will Curtis
All year

$ B&B
4 rooms, 2 pb
C-yes/S-yes/P-ltd/H-no
French

Continental breakfast
Library/music room
grand piano

The Ray House is located in the city, yet hidden among spruces and native trees. Interior has English country home feel.

320 North Carolina

ASHEVILLE

Reed House
119 Dodge St., 28803
704-274-1604
Marge Turcot
May–October

$ B&B
4 rooms, 1 pb
Visa, MC
C-yes/S-yes/P-no/H-no

Continental plus
Comp. wine
Sitting room
piano, pool table
play area for children

Children welcome in our Victorian home in Biltmore: fireplace in your room, breakfast on the porch, relaxing rocking chairs everywhere. Listed in the National Register.

Richmond Hill Inn
87 Richmond Hill Dr., 28806
704-252-7313 800-545-9238
Susan Michel
All year

$$$ B&B
21 rooms, 21 pb
●

Full breakfast
Gourmet restaurant
Extensive library
fresh flowers, phone, TV
conference facilities

Historic Victorian inn built in 1889, magnificently renovated, with gracious service and fine dining in restaurant. Elegant setting for meetings and small weddings. 5 cottages

---

Wright Inn/Carriage House
235 Pearson Dr., 28801
40 Cisco Rd., 28805
704-251-0789
Ed & Barbara Siler, V.Stevens
All year

$$$ B&B
9 rooms, 9 pb
Visa, MC
C-ltd/S-no/P-no/H-no

Full breakfast (inn)
Carriage house
Afternoon tea, snacks
sitting room

The elegantly restored Wright Inn offers the discriminating traveler the opportunity to step back to the peaceful and gracious time at the turn of the century.

BANNER ELK

Archers Inn
Route 2, Box 56-A, 28604
Beech Mt. Parkway
704-898-9004
Joe & Bonny Archer
All year

$$ B&B
14 rooms, 14 pb
Visa, MC ●
C-yes/S-yes/P-no/H-ask

Full breakfast
Dinner available
Library, sitting room
large hot tub for guests
1 room w/pvt. hot tub

Quaint country inn with long-range view and fireplaces in most rooms. Two miles from the ski slopes. Hiking trail on premises.

The Banner Elk Inn B&B
P.O. Box 1953, 28604
Hwy 194 N, Old Turnpike E
704-898-6223
Beverly Lait
All year

$$ B&B
4 rooms, 2 pb
Visa, MC ●
C-yes/S-no/P-yes/H-no
Spanish, German

Full breakfast
Afternoon tea, snacks
Sitting room, antiques
porch w/rocking chairs

Lovely, historic, centrally located, recently renovated, stunning & charming. International atmosphere, antiques. Near Grandfather Mtn., Valle Crucis, Blue Ridge Parkway.

BEAUFORT

The Cedars Inn
305 Front St., 28516
919-728-7036
William & Patricia Kwaak
All year

$$$ B&B
11 rooms, 11 pb
Visa, MC ●
C-ltd/S-ltd/P-no/H-no
Spanish, French

Full breakfast
Restaurant, bicycles
Sail boat, power boats
harbor tours
outer banks ferry

Restored shipbuilder's home c. 1768, in the historic seacoast village of Beaufort on the outer banks.

BEAUFORT

Langdon House
135 Craven St., 28516
919-728-5499
Jimm Prest
All year

$$ B&B
4 rooms, 4 pb
C-12+/S-ltd/P-no/H-no

Full breakfast
Dinner reservations
Refreshments
sitting room, bicycles
fishing & beach supplies

Friends who help you make the most of your visit. Restored 18th-century home in historic seaside hamlet on the outer banks. Wonderful breakfasts—waffles are our specialty!

BELHAVEN

River Forest Manor
600 E. Main St., 27810
919-943-2151
Axson Smith Jr.
All year

$$ B&B
12 rooms, 12 pb
Visa, MC, AmEx, Texaco
C-yes/S-yes/P-no/H-yes

Continental breakfast
Restaurant, full bar
Sitting room, laundry
swimming pool, hot tubs
tennis court, bicycles

A true country inn located on the Intercoastal Waterway. Opened in 1947 as an Inn, restaurant & marina. Each evening a superb smorgasbord is served w/ 75 dishes.

BLACK MOUNTAIN

B&B Over Yonder
Route 1, Box 269, 28711
N. Fork Rd.
704-669-6762
Wilhelmina K. Headley
June 14–October

$ B&B
5 rooms, 5 pb
Visa, MC ●
C-yes/S-ltd

Full breakfast
Tea, coffee, cocoa
Sitting room, library
wildflower gardens
tennis & pool nearby

Secluded and comfortable on wooded hillside. Breakfast of mountain trout served on rock terraces surrounded by wildflowers with views of highest peaks in eastern U.S.

BLOWING ROCK

Maple Lodge B&B
P.O. Box 1120, 28605
Sunset Dr.
704-295-3331
Marilyn Latham
April–February

$$ B&B
8 rooms, 8 pb
C-12+/S-yes/P-no/H-no

Continental plus
Comp. sherry in room
Brunch Thurs-Sun
sitting room, fireplace
piano, tennis courts

"Grandmother's House" flavor. Two parlors, wicker TV room and sun porch for guests. Sherry and fruit bowls in rooms. We are now serving brunch on the sun porch Thurs-Sunday.

Ragged Garden Inn
P.O. Box 1927, 28605
Sunset Dr.
704-295-9703
Joe & Joyce Villani
Exc. January 6–March

$$ B&B
9 rooms, 9 pb
Visa, MC, AmEx
C-12+/S-yes/P-no/H-no

Continental plus
Cottage for family avail
beautiful walled garden

Near Blue Ridge Parkway and majestic Grandfather Mountain. People come here for the fantastic cool summers and the scenery.

BREVARD

Inn at Brevard
410 E. Main St., 28712
704-884-2105
Eileen Bourget
March–December

$$ B&B
13 rooms, 11 pb
C-ltd/S-ltd/P-no/H-no

Full breakfast
Lunch, dinner
Sunday brunch
sitting room, color TV

Antique furnishings, gracious hospitality, restful beauty. Main building recently placed on the National Register of Historic Places.

BREVARD

Womble Inn
301 W. Main St., 28712
704-884-4770
Steve & Beth Womble
All year

$ B&B
6 rooms, 6 pb
C-yes/S-yes/P-no/H-yes

Continental breakfast
Full breakfast $
Sitting room
piano

Gracious atmosphere of antiquity, breakfast served in your room, private baths, near town and Brevard Music Center, wonderful Christmas shop.

BRYSON CITY

Folkestone Inn
767 W. Deep Creek Rd., 28713
704-488-2730
Norma & Peter Joyce
All year

$$ B&B
9 rooms, 9 pb
●
C-yes

Full English breakfast
Comp. snacks, wine
Sitting room, library
porch, rocking chairs
balconies, antiques

Friendly atmosphere and gracious country living. Situated in a peaceful and secluded rural mountain setting. Walk to three waterfalls; hiking; fishing, tubing.

Fryemont Inn
P.O. Box 459, 28713
Fryemont Rd.
704-488-2159 800-845-4879
Sue & George Brown
April–November

$$$ MAP
36 rooms, 36 pb
Visa, MC
C-yes/S-yes/P-no/H-no

Full breakfast
Full dinner included
Library, sitting room
tennis courts
swimming pool

Located on a mountain shelf overlooking the Great Smoky Mountains National Park. A tradition in mountain hospitality since 1923.

Nantahala Village
4 Hwy 19 West, 28713
704-488-2826 800-488-1507
John Burton & Jan Letendre
April – December

$$ EP
54 rooms, 54 pb
Visa, MC, AmEx, Dis ●
C-yes/S-ltd/P-no/H-ltd

Restaurant
All meals available
Sitting room, Rec. hall
tennis court, volleyball
rafting, horsebackriding

Family mountain resort; 200 acres in the Nantahala Mountains, Western N.C., great base for a wide variety of sightseeing activities.

Randolph House Country Inn
P.O. Box 816, 28713
Fryemont Rd.
704-488-3472
Bill & Ruth Randolph Adams
April–November

Please call
6 rooms, 3 pb
Visa, MC, AmEx ●
C-yes/S-yes/P-no/H-yes

Full country breakfast
Dinner, tea on request
Wine, set-ups
sitting room
library, piano

Country inn circa 1895. Original furnishings; located in Smoky Mountains, close to Appalachian trails; whitewater rafting; ruby mines. Country gourmet food.

CASHIERS

High Hampton Inn
P.O. Box 338, Hwy. 107S, 28717
704-743-2411
W. D. McKee
April–October

$$$ AP
all pb
Visa, MC ●
C-yes/S-yes/P-no/H-yes

Full breakfast
Lunch & dinner buffet
Restaurant, library
tennis courts, bicycles
swimming lake, golf

High Hampton is a rustic inn that is also a complete resort. The large lobby has 4 fireplaces. Restaurant; swimming lake; golf course; boating; hiking.

CASHIERS

Millstone Inn
P.O. Box 949, 28717
Hwy 64 West
704-743-2737
Heinz Haibach, Jose Fernandez
Easter–Thanksgiving

$$$ B&B
11 rooms, 11 pb
Visa, MC
C-no/S-yes/P-no/H-no
Spanish, German

Full breakfast
Complimentary sherry
Sitting room, porch
library, games
hiking

Rustic elegance in a romantic setting. Surrounded by native forestland and flora. Breathtaking mountain views. The Millstone Inn exudes privacy.

CHARLOTTE

The Homeplace B&B
5901 Sardis Rd., 28270
704-365-1936
Peggy & Frank Dearien
All year

$$$ B&B
4 rooms, 2 pb
Visa, MC, AmEx •
C-10+/S-no/P-no/H-no

Full breakfast
Refreshments
Evening cookies or cake
sitting room, den w/TV
parlour, screened porch

The Homeplace offers country charm & Victorian elegance on 2.5 acres with wraparound porch, garden gazebo, tin roof, and full homemade breakfast.

The Inn on Providence
6700 Providence Rd., 28226
704-366-6700
Darlene & Daniel McNeill
All year

$$ B&B
5 rooms, 3 pb
Visa, MC
C-12+/S-no/P-no/H-no

Full breakfast
Afternoon tea
Sitting room
library
swimming pool

Experience the grandeur of this large southern homestead and enjoy our attention to detail. Breakfast served on the veranda overlooking the pool.

The Morehead Inn
1122 E. Morehead St., 28204
704-376-3357 FAX:335-1110
W. D. Cochrane, B. D. Spain
All year

$$$ B&B
12 rooms, 12 pb
Visa, MC, AmEx, DC, Ch •
C-ltd/S-ltd/P-no/H-ltd
Span., Fr., Ital., Port.

Continental plus
Comp. wine, tea
Meeting/social functions
piano, whirlpool, bikes
YMCA fitness privileges

Restored estate in historic district; furnished with American & English antiques and art; quiet elegance. Churchill Galleries, an exclusive antique gallery, located on-site.

Still Waters
6221 Amos Smith Rd., 28214
704-399-6299
Janet & Rob Dyer
All year

$$ B&B
3 rooms, 3 pb
Visa, MC
C-yes/S-no/P-no/H-no

Full breakfast
Gazebo, deck
sport court, lake
boat ramp, dock

Log resort home on two wooded acres overlooking Lake Wylie. Near Charlotte downtown and airport. Full breakfast featuring homemade bread.

CHIMNEY ROCK

The Gingerbread Inn
P.O. Box 187, Hwy 74, 28720
704-625-4038
Tom & Janet Sherman
All year

$ B&B
4 rooms
C-yes/S-yes/P-no/H-no

Continental breakfast
Sitting room

Our rooms are furnished with charming country furniture and home-sewn quilts. Relax in rocking chairs on deck overlooking the Rocky Broad River.

CLINTON

Shield House
216 Sampson St., 28328
919-592-2634 800-462-9817
Anita Green, Juanita McLamb
All year

$ B&B
7 rooms, 7 pb
Visa, MC, AmEx •
C-ask/S-ltd/P-no/H-no

Full breakfast
Comp. coffee, sodas
Sitting room
tennis & golf nearby
2-bedroom bungalow avail

Reminiscent of Gone With The Wind. Elegant furnishings; outstanding architectural features. Listed in National Register. I-40 10 miles; I-95 29 miles.

CLYDE

Windsong: A Mountain Inn
120 Ferguson Ridge, 28721
704-627-8059
Donna & Gale Livengood
All year

$$$ B&B
5 rooms, 5 pb
Visa, MC •
C-12+/S-no/P-no/H-no

Full breakfast
Wine, hors d'oeuvres
Lounge with wet bar
pool table, llama herd
tennis courts, pool

Secluded, contemporary rustic log inn set high in the Smoky Mountains. Rooms have fireplaces, tubs and private deck. Breathtaking views. Near National Park and Maggie Valley.

DILLSBORO

Squire Watkins Inn
P.O. Box 430, 28725
Haywood Rd.
704-586-5244
Tom & Emma Wertenberger
All year

$$ B&B
5 rooms, 5 pb
C-12+/S-ltd/P-no/H-no

Full squire's breakfast
Comp. coffee & tea
Sitting room, piano
solarium
porch swing & rockers

Small mountain Bed and Breakfast Inn for lovers of romance, comfort, relaxation, scenic hikes, great breakfasts and small towns.

DURHAM

Arrowhead Inn
106 Mason Rd., 27712
919-477-8430
Jerry, Barbara & Cathy Ryan
January–December 22

$$$ B&B
9 rooms, 5 pb
Visa, MC, AmEx •
C-ask/S-ltd/P-no/H-yes
French

Full breakfast
Comp. tea
Sitting room
piano, patio
air conditioned

1775 manor house offers tasteful period rooms with both private or shared baths. Handicap access. Written up in USA Today, Food, Wine, House & Garden.

The Blooming Garden Inn
513 Holloway St., 27701
919-687-0801 919-688-1401
Dolly & Frank Pokrass
All year

$$$ B&B
5 rooms, 5 pb
Visa, MC, AmEx •
C-yes/S-no/P-no/H-no

Full gourmet breakfast
Comp. wine, tea, snacks
Sitting rooms, library
145 foot porch, antiques
jacuzzis for 2 in suites

Vibrant colors transform this authentically restored Victorian home into a cozy, pleasant, memorable retreat in downtown historic Durham. Gourmet breakfasts. Flower gardens.

EDENTON

Lords Proprietors' Inn
300 N. Broad St., 27932
919-482-3641
Arch & Jane Edwards
All year

$$$ B&B
20 rooms, 20 pb
C-yes/S-yes/P-no/H-no

Full breakfast
Tea, homemade cookies
Sitting room, bicycles
private pool privileges

Three restored houses in the historic district of "the South's prettiest town." Furnished by area antique dealers with all for sale.

The Blooming Garden Inn, Durham, NC

EDENTON

Trestle House Inn
Route 4, P.O. Box 370, 27932
Soundside Rd.
919-482-2282
Peggy & Chuck Gregory
All year

$$ B&B
4 rooms, 4 pb
Visa, MC, AmEx ●
C-9+/S-ltd/P-no/H-no

Continental plus
BYOB, library
Sitting room, billiards
steam, exercise room
shuffleboard, fishing

Peaceful setting overlooking private 20-acre lake and 60 acres of trees. Five miles from historic town of Edenton.

FRANKLIN

Buttonwood Inn
190 Georgia Rd., 28734
704-369-8985
Liz Oehser
May–December

$$ B&B
4 rooms, 3 pb
Visa, MC ●
C-ltd/S-ltd/P-no/H-no

Full breakfast
Sitting room, TV
golf nearby

Completely surrounded by tall pines, small and cozy Buttonwood will appeal to the person who prefers simplicity and natural rustic beauty.

Franklin Terrace
67 Harrison Ave., 28734
704-524-7907 800-633-2431
Ed & Helen Henson
May–October

$ B&B
7 rooms, 7 pb
Visa, MC ●
C-no/S-ltd/P-no/H-no

Continental plus
Comp. refreshments
Antiques & gifts shop

All rooms furnished with antiques. First floor houses dessert shop with cheesecakes, homemade pies & cakes—also antique shop. In town. Beautiful views.

GLENVILLE

Mountain High
Big Ridge Rd., 28736
704-743-3094
Mr. & Mrs. George Carter
July–November

$ B&B
3 rooms, 2 pb
C-no/S-no/P-no/H-no

Full breakfast
Sitting room
our own spring water

High & cool, gorgeous mountain views. White watering and other sports close by. Facilities for artists.

GREENSBORO

Greenwood B&B
205 N. Park Dr., 27401
919-274-6350 800-535-9363
Jo Anne Green
All year

$$ B&B
5 rooms, 3 pb
Visa, MC, AmEx •
C-yes/S-yes/P-no/H-no

Continental plus
Comp. wine/fruit/cookies
Swimming pool
sitting room
cable TV

Three minutes from downtown Greensboro on park in historic district. Chalet-style home built in 1905. TV room, guest kitchen.

HENDERSON

La Grange Plantation Inn
Route 3, Box 610, 27536
Nutbush Road
919-438-2421
Jean & Dick Cornell
All year

$$$ B&B
5 rooms, 5 pb
Visa, MC, AmEx •
C-no/S-no/P-no/H-no

Full breakfast
Parlor, swimming pool
croquet, bird-watching
fishing, hiking trails

Award-winning restoration of nationally registered 18th-centry plantation house on beautiful Kerr Lake near Virginia border. American and English antiques.

HENDERSONVILLE

Claddagh Inn
755 N. Main St., 28792
704-697-7778 800-225-4700
Fred & Marie Carberry
All year

$ B&B
14 rooms, 14 pb
Visa, MC, AmEx, Disc •
C-yes/S-yes/P-no/H-no

Full breakfast
Dinner, comp. tea/sherry
Sitting room, library
TV, phone & A/C in rooms
tennis, shuffleboard

On National Register of Historic Places. Beautiful country inn located in downtown Hendersonville, provides a homelike atmosphere where love and lasting friendships prevail.

Havenshire Inn
Route 13, Box 366, 28739
Cummings Rd.
704-692-4097 FAX:696-8450
C. Findley
All year

$$ B&B
7 rooms, 4 pb
Visa, MC •
C-yes/S-yes/P-no/H-no
Spanish

Continental plus
Aftn. tea, comp. wine
Organ, fitness center
pond, river, canoe
Swedish massage

19th-century English country manor house. Rich furnishings lend to atmosphere of comfortable elegance. Horses; pond, canoeing, fishing, picnicking.

Waverly Inn
783 N. Main St., 28792
704-693-9193 800-537-8195
John & Diane Sheiry
All year

$$ B&B
16 rooms, 16 pb
Visa, MC, AmEx, Disc •
C-yes/S-yes/P-no/H-no

Full breakfast
Comp. wine, beverages
Sitting room, A/C
telephones & TV avail.
tennis courts

A landmark near downtown shopping park, quaint restaurants. On National Register. Beautiful antiques. Spotlessly clean. AAA Approved.

HICKORY

Hickory B&B
464 7th St. SW, 28602
704-324-0548 800-654-2961
Suzanne & Bob Ellis
All year

$$ B&B
5 rooms, 2 pb
C-no/S-no/P-no/H-no

Full country breakfast
Afternoon tea
Library, piano
flowers

A restful night in our home, followed by a specially cooked breakfast, guarantees contentment. Come see us. Decorated with country furnishings & Southern hospitality.

HIGHLANDS

Colonial Pines Inn
Route 1, Box 22B, 28741
Hickory St. at 4½ St.
704-526-2060
Chris & Donna Alley
All year

$$ B&B
7 rooms, 7 pb
Visa, MC •
C-ltd/S-ltd/P-no/H-no

Full breakfast
Afternoon refreshments
Sitting room, kitchen
grand piano
picnic area

Two acres of lawn and trees, close-in, with mountain view from large veranda. Antique furnishings and country charm. Newly renovated guest house with fireplace sleeps four.

The Highlands Inn
P.O. Box 1030, 28741
Corner of 4th & Main Sts.
704-526-5036 704-526-9380
Pat & Rip Benton
April–November

$$ B&B
28 rooms, 28 pb
Visa, MC, AmEx
C-yes/S-yes/P-no/H-yes

Continental plus
Restaurant, lunch
Dinner, comp. snacks
sitting room, library
aviary room, golf priv.

Located in heart of historic Highlands. Close to all outdoor activities. Breathtaking mountain views, waterfalls and beautiful shops. On National Registry of Historic Places.

The Old Edwards Inn
P.O. Box 1778, 28741
Corners of 4th & Main Sts
704-526-5036 704-526-9380
Pat & Rip Benton
April–November

$$ B&B
20 rooms, 20 pb
Visa, MC, AmEx
C-no/S-yes/P-no/H-no

Continental plus
Restaurant, lunch
Dinner, comp. snacks
sitting room, golf priv.
Victorian side yards

Located in the heart of historic Highlands. Close to all outdoor activities. Noted for breathtaking mountain views, waterfalls and beautiful shops. Golf available.

KILL DEVIL HILLS

Ye Olde Cherokee Inn
500 N. Virginia Dare Tr, 27948
919-441-6127
Phyllis & Robert Combs
April–November

$$ B&B
7 rooms, 7 pb
Visa, MC, AmEx, Choice •
C-no/S-ltd/P-no/H-ltd

Continental breakfast
Sitting room
Wraparound porches
overhead ceiling fans
Sr. citizen discount

Beach house with rustic cypress interior. Small, private, quiet. Atlantic Ocean 600 feet away. Near historic sites, shops and restaurants.

LAKE JUNALUSKA

Providence Lodge
207 Atkins Loop, 28745
704-456-6486
Wilma & Ben Cato
June–September

$$ MAP
16 rooms, 8 pb
C-yes/S-no/P-no/H-ltd

Full breakfast
Dinner included
Sitting room, fireplace
porch, clawfoot tubs

A touch of yesterday in an old, very rustic mountain lodge—where our family-style meals are our claim to fame. Near tennis, pool, canoeing, paddleboats, shuffleboard, golf.

LAKE JUNALUSKA

Sunset Inn
300 N. Lakeshore Dr., 28745
704-456-6114 800-733-6114
Wilma Cato, Norma Wright
May 15–October 3

$$ MAP
22 rooms, 19 pb
C-yes/S-yes/P-no/H-ltd

Full breakfast
Dinner included
Sitting room
piano

Charming old inn with astonishing views of lake and Blue Ridge Mountains; large bedrooms; "rocking chair" porches; scrumptious country-style meals.

LAKE LURE

Lodge on Lake Lure
Route 1, Box 529A, 28746
Charlotte Dr.
704-625-2789
Jack & Robin Stanier
April–November

$$$ B&B
11 rooms, 11 pb
Visa, MC, AmEx •
C-12+/S-no/P-no/H-no

Full breakfast
complimentary wine
Sitting room, library
piano, lake swimming
tennis, golf nearby

Adult getaway in the Blue Ridge Mountains. Giant stone fireplace, breathtaking view of mountains and lake. Only public facility actually on Lake Lure.

LAKE TOXAWAY

Earthshine Mountain Lodge
Route 1, Box 216-C, 28747
Route 1, Golden Rd.
704-862-4207
Marion & Kim Boatwright
All year

$$$ AP
9 rooms, 9 pb
•
C-yes/S-no/P-no/H-no

Full breakfast
Lunch, dinner
Comp. set-ups after 5 pm
evening entertainment
hiking, horseback riding

Rustic luxury mountain top lodge. Spectacular views. 70 acres homestead setting. Borders Pisgah National Forest. Perfect for families.

The Greystone Inn
Greystone Lane, 28747
704-966-4700 800-824-5766
Timothy C. Lovelace
May–October

$$$ MAP
22 rooms, 22 pb
Visa, MC, AmEx •
C-yes/S-yes/P-no/H-no

Full breakfast
Gourmet dinner included
Sitting room, piano
swimming, tennis
daily lake tour, jacuzzi

Intimate historic mansion on a large mountain lake. Excellent golf, tennis, sailing, canoeing, water skiing. Country club membership during stay.

LITTLE SWITZERLAND

Big Lynn Lodge
P.O. Box 459, Hwy 226-A, 28749
704-765-4257 800-654-5232
Gale & Carol Armstrong
April 15–October

$$$ MAP
40 rooms, 40 pb
Visa, MC, Disc •
C-yes/S-yes/P-no/H-ltd
German

Full breakfast
Dinner included, fruit
Sitting room, library
player piano lounge
billards, shuffleboard

Old-fashioned country inn. Dinner and breakfast included with room. Cool mountain air. Elevation 3200 ft. Breathtaking view. Come and relax. Suites with whirlpools available.

MANTEO

Tranquil House Inn
P.O. Box 2045, 27954
Queen Elizabeth St.
919-473-1404 800-458-7069
Margaret Buell
All year

$$ B&B
28 rooms, 28 pb
Visa, MC, AmEx •
C-yes/S-yes/P-no/H-yes

Continental plus
Afternoon tea
Comp. wine, snacks
sitting room, library
bicycles

Minutes from the beach but a world apart. We offer accommodations in the tradition of the old Nags Head Inns.

MOUNT AIRY —————

Pine Ridge Inn
2893 W. Pine St, 27030
919-789-5034
Ellen & Manford Haxton
All year

$$ B&B
7 rooms, 5 pb
Visa, MC, AmEx ●
C-yes/S-yes/P-no/H-yes

Full breakfast
All meals available
Comp. tea, wine
sitting room, piano
hot tub, swimming pool

Elegant luxury at foot of Blue Ridge Mountains. A country inn with all the amenities of a grand hotel. All meals available on request.

NAGS HEAD —————

The First Colony Inn
6720 S. Virginia Dare, 27959
919-441-2343 800-368-9390
Richard & Camille Lawrence
All year

$$$ B&B
26 rooms, 26 pb
Visa, MC, Disc ●
C-yes/S-ltd/P-no/H-yes

Continental plus
Aftn. tea, comp. wine
Sitting room, library
verandas, pool, croquet
ocean beach, fishing

With verandas along all four sides. Furnished with antiques, wonderful big beds. Ocean views on second and third floors. Direct ocean access to uncrowded private beach.

NEW BERN —————

The Aerie
509 Pollock St., 28560
919-636-5553 800-849-5553
Lois & Rick Cleveland
All year

$$$ B&B
7 rooms, 7 pb
AmEx, Visa, MC ●
C-yes/S-ltd/P-no/H-no

Full country breakfast
Comp. wine, beverages
Airport pickup
sitting room
player piano

Victorian home one block from Tryon Palace. Walk to shops and restaurants. Superb country breakfast; antique and reproduction furnishings; modern amenities.

Harmony House Inn
215 Pollock St., 28560
919-636-3810
Diane & A.E. Hansen
All year

$$$ B&B
9 rooms, 9 pb
Visa, MC, AmEx ●
C-yes/S-ltd/P-no/H-no

Full breakfast
Comp. soft drinks/juices
Victorian pump organ
parlor, porch with
swings & rocking chairs

Unusually spacious circa 1850 home, rocking chairs on porch, lovely yard. In the historic district, near Tryon Palace, shops, fine restaurants.

The King's Arms Inn
212 Pollock St., 28560
919-638-4409
David & Diana Parks
All year

$$$ B&B
9 rooms, 9 pb
Visa, MC, AmEx ●
C-yes/S-yes/P-no/H-no

Continental plus
Furnished with antiques
fireplaces

In heart of historic district. Delicious hot breakfast. Southern hospitality. Information on sightseeing and dining. Three blocks from Tryon Palace.

New Berne House Inn B&B
709 Broad St., 28560
800-842-7688 919-636-2250
David & Gina Hawkins
All year

$$$ B&B
6 rooms, 6 pb
Visa, MC, AmEx ●
C-yes/S-no/P-yes/H-no

Full gourmet breakfast
Afternoon tea, swing
Library, porch, piano
garden, Tandem bicycle
tours, airport pick-ups

Comfortable elegance and the warmth of southern hospitality in authentically restored B&B. Private, vintage baths; gourmet breakfast. Near Tryon Palace. AAA & AARP discounts.

OCRACOKE ——————————————————————————————

Berkley Center Country Inn	$$ B&B	Continental breakfast
P.O. Box 220, Rt. 12, 27960	11 rooms, 9 pb	Sitting room
919-929-1886	●	bicycles
Ruth & Wes Egan	C-yes/S-yes/P-no/H-yes	
March–November		

Beautifully restored estate on harbor of outer banks fishing village located in U.S. National Seashore. 19 miles of uncommercialized beach.

OLD FORT ——————————————————————————————

The Inn at Old Fort	$ B&B	Continental plus
P.O. Box 1116, 28762	4 rooms, 4 pb	Snacks
W. Main St.	●	Parlor and den
704-668-9384	C-yes/S-ltd/P-no/H-no	cable TV, large porch
Chuck & Debbie Aldridge		
All year		

1880s Victorian cottage furnished with antiques. Large porch for rocking; terraced lawn and gardens; 3.5 acres overlooking Blue Ridge town. Near Asheville, Lake Lure.

PINEBLUFF ——————————————————————————————

Pine Cone Manor B&B	$ B&B	Continental plus
P.O. Box 1208, 28373	4 rooms, 2 pb	Comp. wine
450 E. Philadelphia	Visa, MC	Sitting room, porches
919-281-5307	C-12+/S-yes/P-no/H-yes	whirlpool tub
Virginia Keith		bicycles, woods (paths)
All year		

Comforts of home away from home. Pinehurst Golf Resort area. Early 1900s home; friendly atmosphere; golf courses; horse farms; antiquing and good restaurants nearby.

PISGAH FOREST ——————————————————————————————

Key Falls Inn	$$ B&B	Full breakfast
151 Everett Rd., 28768	5 rooms, 5 pb	Afternoon tea, lemonade
704-884-7559	Visa, MC, AmEx ●	Sitting room, cable TV
P. Grosvenor, J. Fogleman	C-yes/S-ltd/P-no/H-no	VCR, trail to waterfall
All year	Spanish	tennis, pond for fishing

Charming, restored Victorian farmhouse furnished with antiques, on 28 acres near Brevard. Porches, mountain view, waterfall, pond, wooded setting, and sumptuous breakfasts.

The Pines Country Inn	$$ B&B/MAP	Full breakfast
719 Hart Rd., 28768	22 rooms, 19 pb	Dinner (MAP, Wed-Sat)
Pisgah Forest	C-yes/S-yes/P-no/H-ltd	Sitting room
704-877-3131		piano
Tom & Mary McEntire		great biking & hiking
May–October		

Quiet, homey country inn, fantastic view. Accommodations in the Inn or the 4 cabins and cottages. Where you come as our guest and leave as our friend, part of our family.

PITTSBORO ——————————————————————————————

Fearrington House Inn	$$$ B&B	Continental breakfast
2000 Fearrington Vllge., 27312	14 rooms, 14 pb	Lunch, dinner
919-542-2121	Visa, MC ●	Comp. cheese plate
Jenny & R.B. Fitch	C-12+/S-ltd/P-no/H-yes	sitting room
All year		swimming pool

Classic countryside elegance in suites furnished with English antiques. Charming courtyard and gardens. Delicately prepared regional cuisine. Member of Relais & Chateaux.

POLKVILLE

Patterson's Carriage Shop
Hwy 10, P.O. Box 268, 28136
704-538-3929
Lorenzo (Pat)/Nancy Patterson
All year

$ B&B
4 rooms
C-12+/S-no/P-no/H-no

Full breakfast
Dinner by reservation
Sitting room, porch
grounds, carriage shop
horse accommodations

100-year-old farmhouse in quiet country setting. Full country breakfast served with 100% maple syrup. Carriage shop with horse drawn vehicles for sale. Horse grazing pastures.

RALEIGH

Oakwood Inn
411 N. Bloodworth St., 27604
919-832-9712
Diana Newton, Terri Jones
All year

$$$ B&B
6 rooms, 4 pb
Visa, MC ●
C-12+/S-no/P-no/H-no

Full breakfast
Comp. wine, snacks
Bedside treat
sitting room

Charming inn in Victorian home built in 1871. On National Register and furnished with period antiques reflecting charm of yesteryear.

ROBBINSVILLE

Blue Boar Lodge
200 Santeetlah Rd., 28771
704-479-8126
Roy & Kathy Wilson
April–December

$$$ MAP
9 rooms, 9 pb
Visa, MC
C-yes/S-yes/P-no/H-no

Full breakfast
Dinner included
Sitting room, game room
lake swimming
boat rental, fishing

Secluded hideaway in the Smoky Mountains; near beautiful hiking trails and lake activities; family-style meals.

SALISBURY

Rowan Oak House
208 S. Fulton, 28144
704-633-2086 800-786-0437
Ruth Ann & Bill Coffey
All year

$$ B&B
4 rooms, 4 pb
●
C-12+/S-ltd
Spanish

Full breakfast
Comp. wine, snacks
Afternoon tea, library
sitting room, bicycles
jacuzzi tub in one room

"Lavish, luxurious and unique" describes our Queen Anne home with antiques, flowers, porches, gardens, and historic Salisbury's small town atmosphere. AAA approved!

SALUDA

The Orchard Inn
P.O. Box 725, 28773
Highway 176
704-749-5471
Ann & Ken Hough
All year

$$$ B&B
10 rooms, 10 pb
C-no/S-yes/P-no/H-no

Full breakfast
Lunch, dinner, fruit
Library, living room
walking paths

Orchard Inn is a real country inn featuring quiet living with all the comforts and informal elegance of a mountain country house.

SPRUCE PINE

The Fairway Inn
110 Henry Lane, 28777
704-765-4917
Margaret/John Pierce Stevens
May–October

$$ B&B
5 rooms, 5 pb
Visa, MC
C-ltd/S-ltd/P-no/H-no

Full breakfast
Comp. wine & cheese
Sitting room
wake-up service
daily newspaper

Nestled in the Blue Ridge Mountains and overlooking the golf course, we offer attractive rooms and breakfast in your room. Warmth, good cheer, and personalized service.

SPRUCE PINE

Richmond Inn
101 Pine Ave., 28777
704-765-6993
Bill Ansley, Lenore Boucher
All year

$$ B&B
7 rooms, 7 pb
Visa, MC ●
C-yes/S-no/P-no/H-no
French, German

Full breakfast
Comp. tea, wine
Sitting room, piano
stone terrace porch

In the heart of the most spectacular mountain scenery. Close to Blue Ridge Parkway. Luxurious accommodations, Anglo/North Carolinian hosts. Cottages available.

TARBORO

Little Warren B&B
304 E. Park Ave., 27886
919-823-1314
Patsy & Tom Miller
All year

$$ B&B
3 rooms, 3 pb
Visa, MC
C-4+/S-yes/P-no/H-no
Spanish

Full breakfast
Comp. wine, beer, etc.
Sitting room
tennis courts

Large, gracious family home historic district. Complimentary wine, fresh flowers. Choose from full English, American southern or continental breakfast.

TRYON

Mill Farm Inn
P.O. Box 1251, 28782
Hwy. 108 & Howard Gap Rd.
704-859-6992 800-545-6992
Chip & Penny Kessler
All year

$$ B&B
10 rooms, 10 pb
C-yes/S-no/P-no/H-no
French

Continental plus
Sitting porch
large living room

Fine guest inn, including complimentary breakfast—homelike atmosphere, bird-watcher's paradise, plus cultural living experience.

Pine Crest Inn
200 Pine Crest Lane, 28782
800-633-3001 704-859-9135
Jennifer & Jeremy Wainwright
All year

$$ B&B
28 rooms, 28 pb
Visa, MC ●
C-yes/S-yes/P-no/H-no
French

Full breakfast
Lunch Sun, dinner M-Sat
Restaurant, bar, snacks
sitting room, fireplaces
library, club privileges

Peaceful Blue Ridge getaway. Main inn, cabins and cottages on three acres, most with fireplaces. Gourmet restaurant, wine list. Close to golf, tennis. Magnificent sightseeing.

VALLE CRUCIS

Mast Farm Inn
P.O. Box 704, 28691
704-963-5857
Sibyl & Francis Pressly
May–Oct, Dec 26–Mar 15

$$$ MAP
12 rooms, 8 pb
Visa, MC
C-yes/S-no/P-no/H-yes
Portugese

Continental plus
Dinner included
Sitting room
setups

Inn on 18-acre farm in beautiful mountain valley near Boone. Ski, golf, fish, white water rafting. Country cooking. Vegetables from our farm.

WASHINGTON

Pamlico House B&B
400 E. Main St., 27889
919-946-7184
Jeanne & Lawrence Hervey
All year

$$ B&B
4 rooms, 4 pb
Visa, MC ●
C-yes/S-ltd/P-no/H-no

Full breakfast
Restaurant
Sitting room
color TV in room
tennis nearby

Turn-of-the-century home in historic district, three blocks from waterfront. Antique furnishings, elegant guest rooms, wraparound porch.

Belle Meade Inn, Waynesville, NC

WAYNESVILLE

Belle Meade Inn
P.O. Box 1319, 28786
804 Balsam, Hazelwood
704-456-3234
Larry Hanson, William Shaw
April–December

$$ B&B
4 rooms, 4 pb
Visa, MC ●
C-6+/S-no/P-no/H-no

Full breakfast
Afteronn tea, snacks
Library
bicycles
golfing, National Park

Nested in the mountains, this elegant home from yesteryear offers distinctive breakfasts. Golfing, Biltmore House and Smoky Mountain National Park nearby.

Grandview Lodge
809 Valley View Circle, 28786
704-456-5212 800-255-7826
Stan & Linda Arnold
All year

$$$ MAP
15 rooms, 15 pb
●
C-yes/S-yes
Polish, Russian, German

Full breakfast
Dinner incl., lunch
Restaurant (resv)
library, piano, golf
tennis, shuffleboard

Country inn located on rolling land, with an orchard and arbor. Breakfast features homemade jams & jellies. Dinner includes fresh vegetables, freshly baked breads & desserts.

Hallcrest Inn
299 Halltop Circle, 28786
704-456-6457 800-334-6457
Russell & Margaret Burson
June–October

$$ MAP
12 rooms, 12 pb
MC, Visa ●
C-yes/S-ltd/P-no/H-no

Full breakfast
Dinner included
Tea/coffee/cocoa/juice
library, living room

Small country inn in 100-year-old farmhouse with adjacent modular unit. Family-style dining around lazy-susan tables and beautiful view of the mountain.

WAYNESVILLE

Haywood Street House B&B | $ B&B | Continental plus
409 South Haywood St., 28786 | 5 rooms, 1 pb | Snacks
704-456-9831 | C-10+/S-no/P-no/H-no | Sitting room
Lynn & Chris Sylvester | | library
All year | | veranda

Antiques, beautiful wood paneling & mantels; close to area attractions; view the Smoky Mountains from veranda; 1 block to Main Street. Warm hospitality & delightful breakfasts

Heath Lodge | $$$ MAP | Full breakfast
900 Dolan Rd., 28786 | 22 rooms, 22 pb | Dinner included
704-456-3333 800-HEATH-99 | ● | Sitting room, 2 pianos
David & Bonnie Probst | C-yes/S-yes/P-ltd/H-ltd | outdoor deck w/hot tub
Mid April–mid November | Spanish | color TV in rooms

Secluded on a wooded hillside, this mountain inn offers unique lodging with beamed ceilings and country furnishings. Bountiful breakfasts and gourmet dinners.

Palmer House | $$ B&B | Full breakfast
108 Pigeon St., 28786 | 7 rooms, 7 pb | Comp. juice in evening
704-456-7521 | C-yes/S-yes/P-no/H-ltd | Bedtime chocolates
Kris Gillet, Jeff Minick | | sitting room, piano
All year | | book & game library

Rambling old house with small-town charm in the Smoky Mountains. Hiking, golf, skiing nearby. Our bookstore on Main St. offers a 10% discount to guests. Delicious breakfasts.

The Swag | $$$ AP | Full breakfast
Route 2, Box 280-A, 28786 | 12 rooms, 12 pb | Lunch & dinner included
704-926-0430 | Visa, MC | Library, piano, sauna
Deener Matthews | C-ltd/S-yes/P-no/H-ltd | racquetball, hiking
Memorial Day–October | | croquet field above pond

At 5,000 feet, hand-hewn log lodge. Elegant, intimate hideaway. Twelve unique bedrooms, excellent cuisine, breathtaking views. Executive retreat, honeymoon haven.

WILMINGTON

Anderson Guest House | $$ B&B | Full breakfast
520 Orange St., 28401 | 2 rooms, 2 pb | Comp. wine, mixed drinks
919-343-8128 | ● | Afternoon tea
Landon & Connie Anderson | C-yes/S-yes/P-yes/H-no | restaurant nearby
All year | | baby-sitting service

1851 Italianate townhouse; separate guest quarters overlooking private garden. Furnished with antiques, ceiling fans, fireplaces. Drinks upon arrival. Delightful breakfasts.

Catherine's Inn on Orange | $$ B&B | Full breakfast
410 Orange St., 28401 | 3 rooms, 3 pb | Comp. wine, snacks, tea
919-251-0863 800-476-0723 | Visa, MC, AmEx ● | Bar service
Catherine & Walter AcKiss | C-12+/S-no/P-no/H-no | sitting room, library
All year | | swimming pool

In heart of the historical district. Experience the warm gracious hospitality and our tasty breakfasts. Near Wilmington attractions—beaches, shopping, museums, restaurants.

WILMINGTON

The Five Star Guest House
14 N. Seventh St., 28401
919-763-7581
Ann & Harvey Crowther
All year

$$ B&B
3 rooms, 3 pb
Visa, MC, AmEx •
C-ask/S-yes/P-no/H-no

Full breakfast
Comp. wine, snacks, tea
Sitting room
library
piano

Authentically restored, spacious guest rooms furnished with antiques. Private baths feature clawfoot tubs. Breakfast is served in our elegant dining room.

Market Street B&B
1704 Market Street, 28403
919-763-5442
Jo Anne Jarrett
All year

$$ B&B
3 rooms, 3 pb
Visa, MC
C-no/S-no/P-no/H-no

Full breakfast
Sitting room, sun room
central air conditioning
off-street parking

Early 20th century Georgian-style mansion on National Register of Historic Places. Beaches and golfing only minutes away.

WILSON

Miss Betty's B&B Inn
600 W. Nash St., 27893
919-243-4447 800-258-2058
Betty & Fred Spitz
All year

$$ B&B
8 rooms, 8 pb
Visa, MC, Disc
C-no/S-yes/P-no/H-yes

Full breakfast
Afternoon tea
Comp. wine, snacks
3 parlors
air-conditioned

Located in the "antique capital of North Carolina", the main inn (c.1858) and the guest house (c.1910) provide a touch of Victorian elegance and beauty. Peace & tranquillity.

WINSTON–SALEM

Colonel Ludlow Inn
Summit & W. 5th Streets, 27101
919-777-1887
Ken Land
All year

$$ B&B
10 rooms, 10 pb
Visa, MC, AmEx •
C-10+/S-yes/P-no/H-no

Full breakfast
Comp. wine, snacks
Whirlpool tubs, library
sitting room with piano
phones, cable TV, VCR

Historic National Register: Circa 1887; unique guest rooms (private deluxe baths, some with two-person jacuzzi); beautiful antiques. Restaurants, shops walking distance.

Lady Anne's Victorian B&B
612 Summit St., 27101
919-724-1074
Shelley Kirley
All year

$$$ B&B
4 rooms, 3 pb
Visa, MC •
C-11+/S-no/P-no/H-no

Full breakfast
Afternoon tea, snacks
Sitting room, hot tubs
cable TV, stereo, tapes
room refrig., coff. mak.

Beautiful historic Victorian with elegant antiques, delicious breakfasts, evening dessert tray. Romantic suites and rooms. Ideally located from downtown, restaurants, shops.

More Inns ...

Albemarle Inn 86 Edgemont Rd, Asheville, 28807 704-255-0027
Alpine Inn Hwy 226-A, Little Switzerland, 28749 704-765-5380
Applewood Manor 62 Cumberland Circle, Asheville, 28801 704-254-2244
Baird House P.O. Box 749, Mars Hill, 28754 704-689-5722
Bakersville B&B Route 4, Box 427, Bakersville, 28705 704-688-3451
Balsam Lodge P.O. Box 279, Balsam, 28707 704-456-6528
Bath Guest House So. Main St., Bath, 27808 919-923-6811
Bear Creek Lodge Route 1, Box 335, Saluda, 28773 704-749-2272
Beaufort Inn 101 Ann St., Beaufort, 28516 919-728-2600
Bedside Manor Route 1, Box 90A, Sugar Grove, 28679 704-297-1120
Black Mountain Inn 718 Old Hwy. 70, Black Mountain, 28711 704-669-6528
Blackbeard's Lodge P.O. Box 37, Ocracoke, 27960 919-928-3421

Blackberry Inn P.O. Box 965, Black Mountain, 28711 704-669-8303
Bluestone Lodge P.O. Box 736, SR 1112, Valle Crucis, 28691 704-963-5177
Boxley B&B 117 E. Hunter St., Madison, 27025 919-427-0453
Boyette House Box 39, Ocracoke, 27960 919-928-4261
Bridle Path Inn 30 Lookout Rd., Asheville, 28804 704-252-0035
Brookside Lodge P.O. Box 925, Lake Junaluska, 28745 704-456-8897
Brookstown Inn B&B 200 Brookstown Ave., Winston-Salem, 27101 919-725-1120
Brugiss Farm B&B Rt. 1 Box 300, Elk Knob, Laurel Springs, 28644 919-359-2995
Buntie's B&B 322 Houston St., Monroe, 28110 704-289-1155
C.W. Pugh's B&B P.O. Box 427, Wanchese, 27981 919-473-5466
Captains' Quarters 315 Ann St., Beaufort, 28516 919-728-7711
Carefree Cottages Rt. 1 Box 748, Nags Head, 27959 919-441-5340
Carolina B&B 177 Cumberland Ave., Asheville, 28801 704-254-3608
Caroline Inn Box 1110, Chapel Hill, 27514 919-933-2001
Chandler Inn P.O. Box 2156, Highlands, 28741 704-526-5992
Chapel Brook B&B Route 1, Box 290-D, Vilas, 28692 704-297-4304
Chinquapin Inn P.O. Box 145, Penland, 28765 704-765-0064
College Hill B&B 922 Carr St., Greensboro, 27407 919-274-6829
Colonial Inn 153 W. King St., Hillsborough, 27278 919-732-2461
Colony Beach Inn P.O. Box 87, Nags Head, 27959 919-441-3666
Corner Oak Manor 53 St. Dunstan's Rd., Asheville, 28803 704-253-3525
Crepe Myrtle Inn 501 Ocean Dr., Emerald Isle, 28557 919-354-4616
Delamar Inn B&B 217 Turner St., Beaufort, 28516 919-728-4300
Dill House 1104 Arendell St., Morehead City, 28557 919-726-4449
Dillsboro Inn 2 River Rd., Box 490, Dillsboro, 28725 704-586-3898
Dock Street Inn 522 Dock St., Wilmington, 28401 919-763-7128
Doctor's Inn 716 S. Park St., Asheboro, 27203 919-625-4916
Doe Creek Inn Hwy 17, Shallotte, 28459 919-754-7736
Dogwood Inn P.O. Box 70, Hwy 64 &74, Chimney Rock, 28720 704-625-4403
Dosher Plantation House Route 5, Box 100, Southport, 28461 919-457-5554
Echo Mountain Inn 2849 Laurel Park Hwy., Hendersonville, 28739 704-693-9626
Edgewater Inn 10 W. Columbia St., Wrightsville Beach, 28480 919-256-2914
Eli Olive's Inn P.O. Box 2544, Smithfield, 27577 919-934-9823
Esmeralda Inn Box 57, Chimney Rock, 28720 704-625-9105
Fairfield Mountains Route 1, Buffalo Rd., Lake Lure, 28746 704-625-9111
Figurehead Bed & Breakfast 417 Helga St., Kill Devil Hills, 27948 919-441-6929
Forever Christmas Inn 2 Courtland, Box 865, Mountain Home, 28758 704-692-1133
Forsyth, The 305 Walnut St., Waynesville, 28786 704-456-3537
Fourth Ward B&B 523 N. Poplar St., Charlotte, 28202 704-334-1485
Gideon Ridge Inn P.O. Box 1929, Blowing Rock, 28605 704-295-3644
Glendale Springs Inn R 16, Milepost 259, Glendale Springs, 28629 919-982-2102
Governor Eden Inn 304 N. Broad St., Edenton, 27932 919-482-2072
Granville Queen Inn 108 S. Granville Street, Edenton, 27932 919-482-5296
Graystone Guesthouse 100 S. Third St., Wilmington, 28401 919-762-0358
Greenwich Inn 111 W. Washington St., Greensboro, 27401 919-272-3474
Greystone Inn, The Lake Toxaway, 800-824-5766
Griffin-Pace House Rt. 4, Box 300, Hwy 58N, Nashville, 27856 919-459-4746
Hampton Manor 3327 Carmel Rd., Charlotte, 28211 704-542-6299
Hamrick Inn B&B 7787 Hwy 80 South, Burnsville, 28714 704-675-5251
Heather House P.O. Box 61, 102 Church, Hayesville, 28904 704-389-3343
Hemlock Inn Bryson City, 28713 704-488-2885
Henry Weil B&B 200 W. Chestnut St., Goldsboro, 27530 919-735-9995
Heritage Country Inn 7 Bates Branch Rd., Franklin, 28734 704-524-7381
Hidden Crystal Inn School Road, Hiddenite, 28636 704-632-0063
Hillcrest House 209 Hillcrest Rd., Chapel Hill, 27514 919-942-2369
Hilltop House B&B 104 Campbell St., Murphy, 28906 704-837-8661
Historic Woodfield Inn P.O. Box 98, Flat Rock, 28731 704-693-6016
Hoover House 306 Natural Springs Dr., Murphy, 28906 704-837-8734
Hound Ears Lodge and Club P.O. Box 188, Blowing Rock, 28605 704-963-4321
Inlet Inn 601 Front at Queen Sts., Beaufort, 28615 919-728-3600

Inn At Teardrop 175 W. King St., Hillsborough, 27278 919-732-1120
Inn The Pines 1495 W. Connecticut Ave, Southern Pines, 28387 919-692-1632
Inn at Bingham School P.O. Box 267, Chapel Hill, 27514 919-563-5583
Inn at St. Thomas Court 101 S. Second St., Wilmington, 28401 919-343-1800
Inn at the Taylor House Hwy 194, Box 713, Valle Crucis, 28691 704-963-5581
Island Inn Box 7, Ocracoke Island, 27960 919-928-4351
Jarrett House P.O. Box 219, Dillsboro, 28725 704-586-9964
Jason House Inn Granville St., Edenton, 27932 919-482-3400
Jefferson Inn 150 W. New Hampshire, Southern Pines, 28387 919-692-6400
Lake Lure Inn P.O. Box 6, Hwy 74, Lake Lure, 28746 704-625-2525
Lawrences Route 1, Box 641, Lexington, 27292 704-249-1114
Lowe-Alston House B&B 204 Cascade Ave., Winston-Salem, 27127 919-727-1211
Lullwater Farmhouse Inn Route 5, Box 540, Franklin, 28734 704-524-6532
Magnolia Inn Box 266, Pinehurst, 28374 919-295-6900
Melrose Inn 211 Melrose, Tryon, 28782 704-859-9419
Morehead Manor 107 N. 10th St., Morehead City, 28557 919-726-0760
Mountain Springs Cottages P.O. Box 2, Candler, 28715 704-665-1004
Mountain View Lodge P.O. Box 90, Glendale Springs, 28629 919-982-2233
Mountainview Chateau P.O. Box 723, Valle Crucis, 28691 704-963-6593
Mountview Chateau Route 1, Box 426, Banner Elk, 28604 704-963-6593
Murchison House B&B Inn 305 S. 3rd St., Wilmington, 28401 919-343-8580
New England Inn 3726 Providence Rd., Charlotte, 28211 704-362-0005
Nu-Wray Inn P.O. Box 156, Burnsville, 28714 704-682-2329
Oak Ridge Farm B&B Rt. 5, Box 111, HWY 1, Mooresville, 28115 704-663-7085
Oaks, The P.O. Box 1008, Saluda, 28773 704-749-9613
Old House B&B Old US 70, P.O. Box 384, Ridgecrest, 28770 704-669-5196
Old Mill Inn & Antiques P.O. Box 252, Bat Cave, 28710 704-625-4256
Olde Mill House 44 McClure Mill Rd., Franklin, 28734 704-524-5226
Orig. Hickory Nut Gap Inn P.O. Box 246, Bat Cave, 28710 704-625-9108
Oscar's House Box 206, Ocracoke Island, 27960 919-928-1311
Overcarsh House 326 West Eighth St., Charlotte, 28202 704-334-8477
Phelp's House Route 1, Box 55, Highlands, 28741 704-526-2590
Pickett Fence Inn 106 W. Front St., Lillington, 27546 919-893-4382
Pilgrims Rest Inn 600 W. Nash St., Wilson, 27893 919-243-4447
Pilot Knob P.O. Box 1280, Pilot Mountain, 27041 919-325-2502
Pinebridge Inn 101 Pinebridge Ave., Spruce Pine, 28777 704-765-5543
Pines Guest Lodge 1003 Arberdale Dr., Fayetteville, 28304 919-864-7333
Pineview Inn & Conf. Ctr. Route 10,Box 265, Chapel Hill, 27514 919-967-7166
Plaza Manor 511 Martin St., Greensboro, 27406 919-274-3074
Pool Rock Plantation Route 5, Box 62, Henderson, 27536 919-492-6399
Poor Richard Summitt Inn E. Rogers St., Franklin, 28734 704-524-2006
Premier B&B 1001 Johnson St., High Point, 27262 919-889-8349
Red House Inn 412 W. Probart St., Brevard, 28712 704-884-9349
Red Lion Inn Star Route, Box 200, Rosman, 28772 704-884-6868
Red Rocker Inn 136 N. Dougherty St., Black Mountain, 28711 704-669-5991
Reverie 1197 Greenville Hwy, Hendersonville, 28739 704-693-8255
River City B&B 1004 W. Williams Circle, Elizabeth City, 27909 919-338-3337
River's End B&B 120 W. Moore St., Southport, 28461 919-457-9939
Sanderling Inn SR Box 319Y, Duck, 27949 919-261-4111
Scarborough Inn Hwy 64/264, Box 1310, Manteo, 27954 919-473-3979
Scotts Keep B&B 308 Walnut St., Swansboro, 28584 919-326-1257
Ships Timbers B&B Box 10, Ocracoke, 27960 919-928-6141
Shotgun House 406 Ann St., Beaufort, 28516 919-728-6248
Snowbird Mountain Lodge 275 Santeetlah Rd., Robbinsville, 28771 704-479-3433
Snuggle Inn US Hwy 19, P.O. Box 416, Maggie Valley, 28751 704-926-3782
Squire's Vintage Inn Route 2 Box 130R, Warsaw, 28398 919-296-1831
Stone Hedge Inn P.O.Box 366, Tryon, 28782 704-859-9114
Stonehearth Inn P.O. Box 242, Bat Cave, 28710 704-625-4027
Sunshine Inn P.O. Box 528, Sunset Dr, Blowing Rock, 28605 704-295-3487
Tanglewood Manor House P.O. Box 1040, Clemmons, 27012 919-766-0591

Lady Anne's Victorian B&B, Winston-Salem, NC

Tar Heel Inn, The P.O. Box 176, Oriental, 28571 919-249-1078
Todd House 6 Live Oak St., Tabor City, 28463 919-653-3778
Tom Jones B&B Inn P.O. Box 458, Carthage, 28327 919-947-3044
Traub's Inn 116 W. Macon St., Warrenton, 27589 919-257-2727
Trent River Plantation P.O. Box 154, Pollocksville, 28573 919-224-3811
Turby-Villa East Whitehead St., Sparta, 28675 919-372-8490
Wachovia B&B, Inc. 513 Wachovia, Winston-Salem, 27101 919-777-0332
Walker Inn 39 Junaluska Rd., Andrews, 28901 704-321-5019
Way Inn 299 S. Main St., Waynesville, 28786 704-456-3788
West Oak Bed & Breakfast Fryemont Rd., Bryson City, 28713 704-488-2438
Wilsons Tourist Home P.O. Box 47, Robbinsville, 28771 704-479-8679
Windy Oaks Route 7, Box 587, Chapel Hill, 27514 919-942-1001
Woodside Inn Box 197, Milton, 27379 919-234-8646
Worth House—Victorian Inn 412 S. Third St., Wilmington, 28401 919-762-8562

North Dakota

More Inns ...

Farm Comfort, Kemare, 58746 701-848-2433
Jacobson Mansion Route 2, Box 27, Scranton, 58653 701-275-8291
Prairie View B&B Route 2, Box 87, New Salem, 58563 701-843-7236
Triple T Ranch Route 1, Box 93, Stanley, 58784 701-628-2418

Ohio

CENTERVILLE

Yesterday B&B
39 S. Main St., 45459
513-433-0785
Barbara & Tom Monnig
closed varied vacations

$$ B&B
3 rooms, 3 pb
•
C-12+/S-ltd/P-no

Continental plus
Fruit bowl in parlor
Sitting room, porch
one suite available
vintage linen shop

Beautifully restored Victorian home in historic district. Short drive to downtown Dayton, Air Force Museum, King's Island Amusement Park, antique centers.

CHILLICOTHE

Old McDill-Anderson Place
3656 Polk Hollow Rd., 45601
614-774-1770
The Meyers
All year

$$ B&B
4 rooms, 3 pb
Visa, MC
C-ltd/S-no/P-no/H-no

Full breakfast
Afternoon tea, snacks
Sitting room
library

Early farmstead, now a quiet town-edge homestay for visitors to historic sites & outdoor drama. Seasonal breakfasts. Off-season fireplace cooking & renovation seminars.

DANVILLE

The White Oak Inn
29683 Walhonding Rd., 43014
614-599-6107
Joyce & Jim Acton
All year

$$ B&B
10 rooms, 10 pb
Visa, MC •
C-12+/S-no/P-no/H-no

Full breakfast (wkends)
Dinner with notice
Afternoon snacks, sherry
common room, porch
screen house, lawn games

Large country home nestled in wooded area. Outdoor enthusiasts' paradise. Comfortable antique decor; 3 fireplace rooms. Homemade breads, desserts. Near Amish country/antiques.

DAYTON

Prices' Steamboat House
6 Josie St., 45403
513-223-2444
Ron & Ruth Price
All year

$$ B&B
3 rooms, 3 pb
•
C-12+/S-no/P-no/H-no

Full breakfast
Comp. beverages
Sitting room
library
tennis courts

On the National Register, this 1852 Victorian mansion, Steamboat Gothic, is furnished with exquisite antiques and overlooks downtown Dayton.

DELLROY

Pleasant Journey Inn
4247 Roswell Rd. SW, 44620
216-735-2987
Jim & Marie Etterman
All year

$$ B&B
4 rooms, 1 pb
Visa, MC
C-10+

Full breakfast
Iced tea, lemonade
Sitting room

Restored Civil War mansion, furnished with antiques. Country charm close to swimming, boating, tennis and golf. Owners are retired Navy couple.

OLD WASHINGTON

Zane Trace B&B
225 Old National Road, 43768
614-489-5970 301-757-4262
Ruth Wade-Wilson
May–October

$ B&B
4 rooms
C-yes/S-yes/P-no/H-ltd

Continental breakfast
Refrigerator availabe
Sitting room
heated swimming pool
picnics

On historic national trail, this 1859 Victorian brick home has charm a plenty. Near Zane Grey Museum.

PAINESVILLE

Rider's 1812 Inn
792 Mentor Ave., 44077
216-942-2742
Elaine Crane, Gary Herman
All year

$$$ B&B
9 rooms, 8 pb
Visa, MC, AmEx •
C-yes/S-ltd/P-ltd/H-no
Spanish

Continental plus
Restaurant, bar
Sitting room, library
English pub games, bikes
nearby golf, Lake Erie

Living history—authentic stagecoach inn since 1812. Breakfast in bed, restaurant, pub, antiques. We are eager to welcome you & plan explorations of the Ohio Western Reserve.

POLAND

Inn At The Green
500 S. Main St., 44514
Youngstown
216-757-4688
Ginny & Steve Meloy
All year

$$ B&B
4 rooms, 4 pb
Visa, MC •
C-11+/S-no/P-no/H-no

Continental breakfast
Comp. wine
Sitting room, deck
library, patio
garden room

Authentically restored Victorian townhouse in preserved Western Reserve village near Youngstown. Convenient to Turnpike and I-80. Antiques, fireplace, oriental rugs, garden.

PUT-IN-BAY

Le Vent Passant
1539 Langram Road, 43456
419-285-5511
Fred & Eleanor Fether
April–October

$$ B&B
4 rooms, 1 pb
Visa, MC
C-yes/S-no/P-no/H-no

Full breakfast

Relax while viewing everchanging Lake Erie waters from either a rocking chair or swing on a wrap-around porch in the country quiet of South Bass Island.

SANDUSKY

Wagner's 1844 Inn
230 E. Washington St., 44870
419-626-1726
Walt & Barbara Wagner
All year

$$ B&B
3 rooms, 3 pb
Visa, MC •
C-no/S-ltd/P-no/H-no

Continental plus
Comp. wine, chocolates
Billard room with TV
air-conditioning

Elegantly restored Victorian home. Listed on National Register of Historic Places. Near Lake Erie attractions. Air-conditioned rooms.

SPRING VALLEY

3 B's Bed-n-Breakfast
103 E. Race St., 45370
513-862-4278 513-862-4241
Patricia & Herb Boettcher
All year

$ B&B
5 rooms
C-yes/S-yes/P-yes/H-ltd

Full breakfast
Supper, tea, wine
Sitting room
air conditioned
bicycles

Relax in this charming village home—owners are a retired Air Force couple. 20 miles from Dayton's Air Force Museum, King's Island. Choice of Victorian or restored farmhouse.

TIFFIN

Zelkova Inn
2348 S. County Rd. #19, 44883
419-447-4043
Michael Pinkston
All year

$$$ B&B
4 rooms, 2 pb
Visa, MC •
C-yes/S-ltd/P-no/H-no

Continental plus
Dinner by reservation
Aftn. tea, comp. wine
sitting room, library
swimming pool

Nestled in the woods, Zelkova Inn is a blend of grandeur and simplicity. Quiet except for the breeze blowing through the trees.

TOLEDO

Mansion View Inn B&B
2035 Collingwood Ave., 43620
419-244-5676
Matt Jasin
All year

$$ EP/$$$ B&B
4 rooms, 4 pb
Visa, MC •
C-ask/S-ltd/P-no/H-no

Full breakfast
Afternoon tea
Sitting room, library
wedding facilities
self-guided tour broch.

1887 Queen Anne Victorian, listed on National Register. Stunning architecture. Romance and anniversary packages available. One block from Toledo Museum of Art, antiques area.

TROY

Allen Villa B&B
434 S. Market St., 45373
513-335-1181
Robert & June Smith
All year

$$ B&B
5 rooms, 5 pb
Visa, MC, AmEx •
C-12+/S-ltd/P-no

Full breakfast
Comp. wine, aftn. tea
Self-serve snack bar
music room, bicycles
kitchens in carriage hse

1874 restored Victorian mansion with antiques throughout, television, phones, central A/C, 3 wineries, historic town, 15 min. from Dayton Int'l Airport; I-70 and I-75 access.

WEST MILTON

Locust Lane Farm B&B
5590 Kessler Cowlesvlle, 45383
513-698-4743
Ruth Shoup
All year

$ B&B
2 rooms, 1 pb
C-yes/S-no/P-no/H-no

Full breakfast
Afternoon tea
Library, sitting room
screened porch, deck
patio, bicycles

A delightful old home tastefully decorated with antiques. Comfort and hospitality. Country farm setting. Gourmet breakfast served in dining room or screened porch.

ZOAR

Cobbler Shop B&B Inn
P.O. Box 650, House# 22, 44697
2nd & Main Sts.
216-874-2600
Marion "Sandy" Worley
All year

$$ B&B
4 rooms, 2 pb
Visa, MC, AmEx •
C-6+/S-ltd/P-no/H-no

Full breakfast
Comp. wine, snacks, tea
Sitting room

Original structure in historic village, furnished in 18th- and 19th-century antiques; close to local museum and a number of charming shops.

Inn at Cowger House #9
#9 Fourth St., Box 527, 44697
216-874-3542
Mary & Edward Cowger
All year

$$ B&B
3 rooms, 3 pb
•
C-yes/S-yes/P-no/H-no

Full country breakfast
Lunch & dinner by resv.
Entertainment
honeymoon suite with
fireplace & jacuzzi

A little bit of Williamsburg. 1817 log cabin with 2-acre flower garden maintained by the Ohio Historic Society.

More Inns ...

1890 B&B 663 N. Whitewoman St., Coshocton, 43812 614-622-1890

50 Lincoln 50 E. Lincoln St., Columbus, 43215 614-291-5056
Adams Street B&B 175 W. Adams St., Millersburg, 44654 216-674-0766
Aunt Bee's Bed & Breakfast 5538 S. Section Line Rd, Delaware, 43015 614-881-4412
Bayberry Inn B&B 25675 St., Route 41 N., Peebles, 45660 513-587-2221
Beach House 213 Kiwanis Ave., Huron, 44839 419-433-5839
Beatty House S. Shore Dr., Kelley's Island, 43438 419-746-2379
Bells Located in downtown, Logan, 43138 614-385-4384
Birch Way Villa 111 White Birch Way, South Amherst, 44001 216-986-2090
Blackfork Inn 303 N. Water St., Loudonville, 44842 419-994-3252
Bogart's Corner B&B 1403 E. Bogart Rd., Sandusky, 44870 419-627-2707
Buckeye B&B P.O. Box 130, Powell, 43065 614-548-4555
Candle Wick B&B 245 E. Main St., Hillsboro, 45133 513-393-2743
Captain Montague's B&B 229 Center St., Huron, 44839 419-433-4756
Castle Inn 610 S. Court St., Circleville, 43113 614-477-3986
Centennial House 5995 Center St., Box 67, Peninsula, 44264 216-657-2506
Central House 27 W. Columbus St., Pickerington, 43147 614-837-0932
Chillicothe B&B 202 S. Paint St., Chillicothe, 45601 614-772-6848
Cider Mill B&B P.O. Box 441, Zoar, 44697 216-874-3133
Clair E 127 Ohio St., Marietta, 45750 614-374-2233
Coach House Inn B&B, The 304 St. Rt. 113 W., Milan, 44846 419-499-2435
Cricket Lodge B&B Lakeshore Dr., Kelley's Island, 43438 419-746-2263
Deep Woods Cabin B&B Logan, 43133 614-332-6084
Dripping Rock Farm 4247 Roswell Rd. SW, Dellroy, 44620 216-735-2987
Folger's Bantam Farm B&B Route 6, Mitchell Lane, Marietta, 45750 614-374-6919
Frederick Fitting House 72 Fitting Ave., Bellville, 44813 419-886-2863
Glidden House 1901 Ford Dr., Cleveland, 44106 216-231-8900
Governor's Lodge SR 552, Waverly, 45690 614-947-2266
Granville Inn 314 E. Broadway, Granville, 43023 614-587-3333
Haven @ 4th & Park P.O. Box 467, Zoar, 44697 216-874-4672
Hidden Hollow B&B 9340 State Route 5 , Kinsman, 44428 216-876-8686
Hill View Acres B&B 7320 Old Town Rd., East Fultonham, 43735 614-849-2728
House Of Seven Porches,The 331—5th Street, Marietta, 614-373-1767
Howey House 340 N. Bever St., Wooster, 44691 216-264-8231
Inn at Cedar Falls, The 21190 State Rt. 374, Logan, 43138 614-385-7489
Log Cabin 7657 TWP Rd. 234, Logan, 43138 614-385-8363
McNutt Farm II/Outdoorsman 6120 Cutler Lake Rd., Blue Rock, 43720 614-674-4555
Mertz Place, The 240 Mirabeau Street, Greenfield, 45123 513-981-2613
Nevada Comfort B&B Nevada, 614-482-2869
Oak Hill B&B 16720 Park Rd., Mount Vernon, 43050 614-393-2912
Oakwood B&B 226 N. Broadway, Medina, 44256 216-723-1162
Old Island House Inn 102 Madison St., Port Clinton, 43452 419-734-2166
Old Stone House Inn 133 Clemons St., Marblehead, 43440 419-798-5922
Otto Court B&B 5653 Lake Rd., Geneva-On-The-Lake, 44041 216-466-8668
Pickwinn B&B Guesthouse 707 N. Downing St., Piqua, 45356 513-773-8877
Pines Logan, 43133 614-385-7012
Pipe Creek B&B 2719 Columbus Ave., Sandusky, 44870 419-626-2067
Pleasant Valley Lodge 1983 Pleasant Valley Rd, Lucas, 44843 419-892-2443
Portage House 601 Copley Rd., Akron, 44320 216-535-1952
Prospect Hill B&B 408 Boal St., Cincinnati, 45210 513-421-4408
Quiet Country B&B 14758 TWP Rd. 453, Lakeville, 44638 216-378-3882
Rockledge Manor Route 3, Possum Run Rd., Bellville, 44813 419-892-3329
Russell-Cooper House 115 E. Gambier St., Mount Vernon, 43050 614-397-8638
Sanduskian, The 232 Jackson St., Sandusky, 44870 419-626-6688
Slavka's B&B 180 Reinhard Ave., Columbus, 43206 614-443-6076
St. George House 33941 Lorain Rd., North Ridgeville, 44039 216-327-9354
Tudor House P.O. Box 18590, Cleveland, 44118 216-321-3213
Victorian B&B 78 Smith Place, Columbus, 43201 614-299-1656
Weaving Haus P.O. Box 431, Zoar, 77697 216-874-3318
Whispering Pines B&B P.O. Box 340, Dellroy, 44620 216-735-2824
White Fence Inn 8842 Denmanu Rd., Lexington, 44904 419-884-2356

Willowtree Inn 1900 W. State Route 571, Tipp City, 45371 513-667-2957
Wind's Way B&B 3851 Edwards Rd., Newtown, 45244 513-561-1933
Worthington Inn 649 High St., Worthington, 43085 614-885-2600

Oklahoma

GUTHRIE

Harrison House	$$ B&B	Continental plus
124 W. Harrison St., 73044	35 rooms, 35 pb	Comp. wine, snacks
405-282-1000 800-375-1001	AmEx, Visa, MC •	Sitting room, gift shop
Phyllis Murray	C-yes/S-yes/P-ltd/H-yes	bicycles, shoeshines
All year		games, elevator

Turn-of-the-century charm with comfort of elegant 35-room restored hotel. Next to live theater, museums. Breakfast in Victorian parlor. Horseback riding, fishing.

More Inns ...

Clayton Country Inn Route 1, Box 8, Clayton, 74536 918-569-4165
Drake House 617 S. 93rd. E. Ave., Tulsa, 74112 918-835-0752
Edgewater B&B P.O. Box 1746, Grove, 74344 918-786-4116
Grandison B&B 1841 NW 15th, Oklahoma City, 73106 405-521-0011
Memories B&B 120 West Queen, Coalgate, 74538 405-927-3590
Stone Lion Inn B&B 1016 W. Warner, Guthrie, 73044 405-282-0012

Oregon

ASHLAND

Chanticleer Inn	$$$ B&B	Full gourmet breakfast
120 Gresham St., 97520	7 rooms, 7 pb	Refreshments available
503-482-1919	Visa, MC •	throughout the day
Nancy & Jim Beaver	C-ltd/S-no/P-no/H-no	sitting room, fireplace
All year		phones in all rooms, A/C

Fresh country charm, attention to detail. Antiques, fluffy comforters, garden patio, mountain views. Close to theaters. Discount ski lift tickets. Outstanding accommodations.

Cowslip's Belle B&B	$$ B&B	Full breakfast
159 N. Main St., 97520	4 rooms, 4 pb	Comp. tea, coffee
503-488-2901	Visa, MC •	Snacks, library
Jon & Carmen Reinhardt	C-12+/S-no/P-no/H-no	sitting room
All year		airport pick-up

Come enjoy our scrumptious breakfast, cozy down comforters, lovely antiques, stained glass, quilts, 1913 Craftsman home and carriage house.

ASHLAND

Hersey House B&B
451 N. Main St., 97520
503-482-4563
Lynn Savage, Gail Orell
Late April–October

$$$ B&B
4 rooms, 4 pb
Visa •
C-12+/S-ltd/P-no/H-no

Full breakfast
Comp. tea, wine, snacks
Edible flowers w/meal
sitting rm, player piano
balcony, English garden

Elegantly restored turn-of-the-century Victorian with family antiques, china, silver, linens, queen beds, central A/C, lovely English garden. Short walk to theaters.

The Iris Inn
59 Manzanita St., 97520
503-488-2286
Vicki Lamb
All year

$$ B&B
5 rooms, 1 pb
Visa, MC
C-7+/S-no/P-no/H-no
Spanish

Full breakfast
Complimentary wine
Lemonade, iced tea
sitting room
nightly turn-down

Lovely restored 1905 home; spacious, flower-filled yard for relaxing; 4 blocks to Oregon Shakespeare Festival; elegant & creative breakfasts.

Woods House B&B
333 N. Main St., 97520
503-488-1598
Francoise & Lester Roddy
All year

$$ B&B
6 rooms, 6 pb
Visa, MC
C-12+/S-no/P-no/H-no

Full breakfast
Afternoon tea
Comp. sherry
sitting room

Relax in quiet country elegance of 1908 Craftsman-style inn. Spacious gardens. Walk to theaters and restaurants. Skiing at Mount Ashland.

ASTORIA

Grandview B&B
1574 Grand Ave., 97103
503-325-5555 800-488-3250
Charleen Maxwell
All year

$ B&B
8 rooms, 6 pb
Visa, MC, Disc. •
C-10+

Continental plus
Lunch & dinner for conf.
Sitting room
books in room, bicycles
liquor not permitted

Light, airy, cheerful Victorian close to superb Maritime Museum, Lightship, churches, golf, clam-digging, fishing, beaches and rivers. Sleeps 21.

BANDON

Sea Star Guesthous
370–1st Street, 97411
503-347-9632
David & Monica Jennings
All year

$$ B&B
4 rooms, 4 pb
Visa, MC, AmEx
C-yes/S-no/P-no/H-no

Full breakfast
Bistro, all meals avail.
Complimentary wine
kitchens & laundry
decks, skylights

Uniquely designed coastal getaway with European ambiance, located on the harbor in "Old-town". Gourmet breakfast served in our own bistro.

BEND

Farewell Bend B&B
29 N.W. Greeley, 97701
503-382-4374
Lorene Bateman
All year

$$ B&B
3 rooms, 3 pb
Visa, MC
C-no/S-no/P-no/H-no

Full breakfast
Aftn. tea, comp. wine
Sitting room
library, deck
terry bath robes

Restored 70-year-old Dutch Colonial; gourmet breakfast and hand-made quilts. Skiing, fishing, golfing. The recreation center of the Pacific Northwest. Near downtown Bend.

BEND

Gazebo B&B
21679 Obsidian Ave., 97702
503-389-7202
Gale & Helen Estergreen
All year

$ B&B
2 rooms
C-yes/S-no/P-no/H-no

Full breakfast
Snacks
Laundry facilities
VCR, TV

"Inn the country, close to town." Private home, antiques. Beautiful views from garden gazebo. Lakes, mountains, skiing, golf nearby.

BROOKINGS

Chetco River Inn
21202 High Prairie Rd., 97415
503-469-8128 800-327-2688
Sandra Brugger
Exc. Thanksgiving & Xmas

$$$ B&B
3 rooms, 3 pb
Visa, MC
C-12+/S-ltd/P-no/H-no

Full breakfast
Lunch, dinner with resv.
Beverages & cookies
Sitting room, library
games, hiking, river

Relax in peaceful seclusion of our private 35-acre forest, bordered on 3 sides by the Chetco River. Enjoy "Old World" hospitality & "New World" comfort using alternate energy.

Holmes Sea Cove B&B
17350 Holmes Dr., 97415
503-469-3025
Lorene & Jack Holmes
All year

$$$ B&B
3 rooms, 3 pb
Visa, MC
C-ltd/S-no/P-no/H-no

Continental plus
Tea, coffee, cocoa
Trail to private park,
creek and beach
airport pickup

Delightful seacoast hideaway. Three cozy rooms with spectacular ocean views, private entrances, baths. Tasty continental plus breakfast served in rooms.

COOS BAY

Captain's Quarters B&B
P.O. Box 3231, 97420
265 S. Empire Blvd.
503-888-6895
Jean & John Griswold
All year

$ B&B
3 rooms
C-10+/S-no/P-ltd/H-no
Spanish, German

Full breakfast
Snacks, tea, coffee
Sitting room
library
athletic club nearby

1890 Victorian sea captain's home. Bay view, antiques, hotcakes, muffins, local berries and cheeses. Near beaches, boating, crabbing and clamming.

CORVALLIS

Abed & Breakfast at Sparks
2515 SW 45th St., 97333
503-757-7321
Neoma & Herb Sparks
All year

$$ B&B
4 rooms, 2 pb
•
C-8+/S-no/P-no/H-no

Full breakfast
Coffee, tea and soda
Sitting rm., dining rm.
hot tubs, TV, VCR
deck with heated spa

Antique-furnished home in peaceful country setting bordering private golf course. Heated spa, huge decks. Three miles from downtown/OSU.

Madison Inn B&B
660 SW Madison Ave., 97333
503-757-1274
Richard & Paige Down
All year

$$ B&B
7 rooms, 2 pb
Visa, MC
C-yes/S-yes/P-no/H-no

Full breakfast
Comp. wine, juice
2 sitting rooms
piano
guest cottage

Historic Madison inn is ideally located one block from downtown Corvallis and two blocks from Oregon State campus.

Channel House B&B Inn, Depoe Bay, OR

DEPOE BAY

Channel House B&B Inn
P.O. Box 56, 97341
35 Ellingson St.
503-765-2140
Bill & Rachael Smith
All year

$$ B&B
7 rooms, 7 pb
•
C-yes/S-yes/P-ask/H-yes

Full breakfast
Coffee, tea, cookies
Sitting room, fireplaces
whirlpool tubs, mopeds,
whale watching, fishing

A unique oceanfront country inn with deluxe suites featuring private whirlpool tubs. Gourmet seafood restaurant on lower level.

ELMIRA

McGillivray's Log Home B&B
88680 Evers Rd., 97437
503-935-3564
Evelyn R. McGillivray
All year

$ B&B
2 rooms, 2 pb
Visa, MC
C-yes/H-yes

Full breakfast

Enjoy hearty breakfasts in this secluded country home. Rooms feature king beds, private baths, and air-conditioning. 14 miles west of Eugene, Oregon.

EUGENE

Chambers House B&B Inn
1006 Taylor Street, 97402
503-686-4242 800-543-0707
Rhond & John Howard
All year

$$$ B&B
1 rooms, 1 pb
•
C-no/S-no/P-no/H-no
Japanese

Full breakfast
Comp. wine, snacks
Sitting room, piano
turn-down service
hot tubs

This hundred-year-old Victorian on the National Historic Register offers world-class suite accommodations with full, home cooked breakfasts.

Kjaer's House in the Woods, Eugene, OR

EUGENE

Kjaer's House in the Woods
814 Lorane Hwy, 97405
503-343-3234
George & Eunice Kjaer
All year exc. Christmas

$$ B&B
2 rooms, 1 pb
•
C-yes/S-no/P-no/H-no
German

Full breakfast
Afternoon tea, snacks
Sitting room, library

1910 Craftsman home in parklike setting among tall firs. Furnished with antiques and provides urban convenience with suburban tranquillity.

The Lyon and The Lambe
988 Lawrence at 10th, 97401
503-683-3160
Henri & Barbara Brod
All year

$$ B&B
4 rooms, 4 pb
Visa, MC •
C-12+/S-yes/P-ask/H-no
French, German, Portug.

Full gourmet breakfast
Full breakfast (Sunday)
Dinner by prior res.
comp. wine, sitting room
library, bicycles

An elegant home in a quiet neighborhood, only blocks from city's center. Whirlpool bath; continental plus breakfast; congenial hosts.

GOLD BEACH

Heather House B&B
190 11th St., 97444
503-247-2074
Katy & Bob Cooper
All year

$$ B&B
4 rooms, 2 pb
Visa, MC •
C-12+/S-no/P-no/H-no

Full breakfast
Afternoon tea
Sitting room, library
airport pick-up avail.
by arrangement

Enjoy the exceptional climate of Oregon's Southern Coast in this lovely house that offers breathtaking ocean views from most rooms.

GRANTS PASS

Lawnridge House	$ B&B	Full breakfast
1304 NW Lawnridge, 97526	2 rooms, 2 pb	Refrigerator, comp. wine
503-476-8518	•	Filled bookshelves
Barbara Head	C-ltd/S-ltd	secluded deck & porch
All year	Spanish, some French	Alfresco dining

1909 historic home with antique furnishings, canopy beds, fireplace, beamed ceilings, dark wood floors, oriental rugs, color cable TV, phone and air-conditioning

Riverbanks Inn B&B	$$ B&B	Full breakfast
8401 Riverbanks Rd., 97527	5 rooms, 3 pb	Exercise room, decks
503-479-1118	Visa, MC •	Ponds, oriental garden
Myrtle Franklin	C-yes/S-no/P-no/H-no	massage, artists studio
Exc. January & February	some Spanish	Zen House, jacuzzi suite

Woods; paths to the Rogue River; ponds with wild ducks and bass. A restful retreat; fanciful rooms such as Casablanca or Jean Harlow. Also a river cottage and fishing lodge.

LINCOLN CITY

Palmer House B&B Inn	$$$ B&B	Full 3-course breakfast
646 NW Inlet, 97367	3 rooms, 3 pb	Comp. sherry
503-994-7932	Visa, MC •	Dinner service for groups
Malcolm & Sally Palmer	C-no/S-ltd/P-no/H-no	renting entire inn
All year		

Panoramic ocean view, excellent beach access highlight this contemporary inn. Robes, beach towels, kites, perfect breakfasts, elegant decor, super location.

McMINNVILLE

Steiger Haus	$$ B&B	Full breakfast
360 Wilson St., 97128	5 rooms, 5 pb	Comp. wine or beverage
503-472-0821	•	Sitting room, TV, games
Doris & Lynn Steiger	S-no/P-no	decks, terraces
All year	Some German & French	English garden

In the heart of the Oregon wine country. Unique architecture in parklike town setting. Close to gourmet restaurants. Charm and hospitality plus!

MYRTLE CREEK

Sonka's Sheep Station Inn	$$ B&B	Full breakfast
901 NW Chadwick Lane, 97457	4 rooms, 2 pb	Comp. tea, cookies
503-863-5168	Visa, MC	Sitting room
Louis & Evelyn Sonka	C-12+/S-no/P-no/H-no	bicycles
All year		

Working sheep ranch; house furnished in sheep country motif and antiques. Quiet setting along river. Guests may partake of ranch activities as hosts and guests agree.

NEWBERG

Secluded B&B	$ B&B	Full gourmet breakfast
19719 NE Williamson Rd., 97132	2 rooms, 1 pb	Comp. tea & coffee
503-538-2635	•	Living room w/fireplace
Durell & Del Belanger	C-10+/S-no/P-no/H-no	library, A/C, VCR
All year		hiking trails

Located in the heart of wine country! Antiques in every room; gourmet breakfast served; large library. Hiking trails and seasonal wildlife. Air-conditioned home.

NEWPORT

Ocean House B&B
4920 NW Woody Way, 97365
503-265-6158 503-265-7779
Bob & Bette Garrard
Exc. Dec 15–Jan 7

$$ B&B
4 rooms, 4 pb
Visa, MC
C-12+/S-no/P-no/H-no

Full breakfast
Snacks, coffee, tea
Sitting room, library
beach trail, garden
gallery; golf nearby

Near the center of coastal activities and fun, this large comfortable home with beautiful surroundings overlooks gardens and surf. Unforgettable.

NORTH BEND

Sherman House B&B
2380 Sherman Ave., 97459
503-756-3496
Jennifer & Phillip Williams
All year

$$ B&B
3 rooms, 1 pb
AmEx
C-yes/S-yes/P-no/H-no

Full breakfast
Comp. tea
Sitting room
kitchen privileges

A 1903 Pennsylvania Dutch home with extensive flower gardens, furnished with antiques and old toys. Close to shopping, dunes and ocean. Antiques/collectables shop on premises.

OREGON CITY

Jagger House B&B
512 Sixth St., 97045
503-657-7820
Claire Met
All year

$$ B&B
3 rooms, 1 pb
Visa, MC •
C-12+/S-no/P-no/H-no

Full breakfast
Snacks
Sitting room
gazebo in garden
close to 5 museums

Cozy country comfort in 1880 house at "end of Oregon Trail". Antiques, reproductions. Private. Innkeeper is a history/old house buff.

PORT ORFORD

Home by the Sea B&B
P.O. Box 606P, 97465
444 Jackson St.
503-332-2855
Brenda & Alan Mitchell
All year

$$ B&B
2 rooms, 2 pb
Visa, MC
C-no/S-no/P-no/H-no

Full breakfast
Complimentary tea
Refrigerator, laundry
beach access, ocean view
cable TV, phones, spa

Enjoy dramatic views of the ocean and miles of unspoiled public beaches in this quiet fishing village. Tennis and golf nearby.

PORTLAND

General Hooker's B&B
125 SW Hooker, 97201
503-222-4435 FAX:222-4435
Lori Hall
All year

$$ B&B
4 rooms, 1 pb
Visa, MC, AmEx •
C-10+/S-no/P-no/H-no

Continental plus
Comp. wine & beverages
Sitting room, library
A/C, roof deck
cable TV & VCR in rooms

Elegantly refurbished Victorian in quiet, historic neighborhood within walking distance of downtown. Romantic amenities include 7-foot bed and skylight bath in Rose Suite.

MacMaster House
1041 SW Vista Ave., 97205
503-223-7362
Cecilia Murphy
All year

$$$ B&B
6 rooms, 2 pb
Visa, MC, AmEx
C-14+/S-no/P-no/H-no

Full breakfast
Comp. beverages
Sitting room
library
tennis nearby

Historic Colonial mansion near Washington Park. Convenient to rose gardens, cafes, galleries, boutiques. Lovely neighborhood for walking and jogging. Fireplace rooms.

Portland Guest House, Portland, OR

PORTLAND

Portland Guest House — $$ B&B — Full breakfast
1720 N.E. 15th Ave., 97212 — 5 rooms, 3 pb — Comp. beverages
503-282-1402 — Visa, MC, AmEx • — Room phones, antiques
Susan Gisvold — C-ltd/S-no/P-no — jogging routes
All year — bus & light rail tickets

1890 Victorian in historic Irvington. All rooms have vintage linens & great beds. Luscious breakfasts. Closest B&B to Convention Center, Coliseum, Lloyd Center Mall.

ROSEBURG

House of Hunter — $ B&B — Full breakfast
813 S.E. Kane St., 97470 — 4 rooms, 2 pb — Snacks
503-672-2335 — • — Sitting room
Walt & Jean Hunter — C-12+/S-no/P-no/H-no
All year

Restored historic home; mixture of antiques and modern; close to downtown. Awaken to coffee in your room; full breakfast in dining room.

SANDLAKE

Sandlake Country Inn — $$ B&B — Full breakfast
8505 Galloway Rd., 97112 — 3 rooms, 3 pb — Comp. spiced cider
503-965-6745 — Visa, MC • — Sitting room, robes
Margo & Charles Underwood — C-no/S-no/P-no — garden spa, hammock
All year — bikes, cottage w/jacuzzi

Romantic, peaceful hideaway especially designed for making marriage memories. Flowers, antiques. Coastal forest setting. Gourmet breakfasts served in your room or deck.

SHANIKO

Historic Shaniko Hotel
P.O. Box 86, 97057
4th & "E" Sts.
503-489-3441
All year

$$ B&B
18 rooms, 18 pb
Visa, MC •
C-yes/S-no/P-no/H-no

Full breakfast
Lunch, dinner

Historic setting in old wool shipping center and authentic ghost town. Close to fishing. On U.S. Hwy. 97, 40 miles N. of Medras. 56 miles S. of the Columbia River.

YAMHILL

Flying M Ranch
23029 NW Flying M Rd., 97148
503-662-3222 FAX:662-3202
Bryce G & Barbara J Mitchell
All year exc. Dec 24-25

$$ EP
28 rooms, 28 pb
Visa, MC, AmEx •
C-yes/S-ltd/P-ltd/H-yes

Breakfast $
Restaurant, bar
Large swimming pond
tennis court, piano
honeymoon cabin

Rustic & warm log lodge offers dining, dancing, mountain trail rides, camping, fishing, swimming pond, airstrip & wineries nearby. Honeymoon cabin with fireplace, jacuzzi tub.

More Inns . . .

A Gran-Mother's Home 12524 SW Bonnes Ferry, Lake Oswego, 97034 505-244-4361
AHLF House B&B 762 NW 6th St., Grants Pass, 97526 503-474-1381
Adobe Yachats, 97498 503-547-3441
Allenhouse B&B 2606 N.W. Lorejoy St., Portland, 97210 503-227-6841
Arden Forest Inn 261 W. Hersey, Ashland, 97520 503-488-1496
Aristea's Guest House 1546 Charnelton St., Eugene, 97401 503-683-2062
Ashland Guest Villa 634 Iowa St., Ashland, 97520 503-488-1508
Ashland's Main St. Inn 142 W. Main St., Ashland, 97520 503-488-0969
Auberge des Fleurs 39391 SE Lusted Rd., Sandy, 97055 503-663-9449
Auburn Street Cottage 549 Auburn St., Ashland, 97520 503-482-3004
B & G's B&B 711 W. 11th Ave., Eugene, 97402 503-343-5739
Backroads B&B 85269 Lorane Hwy., Eugene, 97405 503-485-0464
Baldwin Inn B&B 126 W. First St., Prineville, 97754 503-447-5758
Bayberry Inn 438 N. Main, Ashland, 97520 503-488-1496
Bayberry Inn 483 N. Main St., Ashland, 97520 503-482-1252
Bed, Bread & Trail Route 1, Box 365, Joseph, 97846 503-432-9765
Bien Venue B&B 95629 Jerry Flat Rd., Gold Beach, 97444 503-247-2335
Big Blue House B&B 53223 Riverview Dr., La Pine, 97739 503-536-3879
Bigelow B&B 308 E. Fourth St., The Dalles, 97058 503-298-8239
Birch Leaf Lodge RR 1, Box 91, Halfway, 97834 503-742-2990
Birch Tree Manor B&B 615 S. Main St., Hwy 11, Milton—Freewater, 97862 503-938-6455
Bird's Nest Inn B&B Yachats, 97498 503-547-3683
Blackberry Inn B&B P.O. Box 188, Seal Rock, 97376 503-563-2259
Blue Haven Inn 3025 Gienger Rd., Tillamook, 97141 503-842-2265
Boarding House 208 N. Holladay Dr., Seaside, 97138 503-738-9055
Campus Cottage B&B Inn 1136 E. 19th Ave., Eugene, 97403 503-342-5346
Cape Cod B&B 5733 SW Dickinson St., Portland, 97219 503-246-1839
Chandler's Bed, Bread, & T Box 639, 700 E. Main, Joseph, 97846 503-432-9765
Chocolates for Breakfast 606 N. Holiday, Seaside, 97138 503-738-3622
Clear Creek Farm B&B Route 1, Box 138, Halfway, 97834 503-742-2238
Cliff Harbor Guest House P.O. Box 769, Bandon, 97411 503-347-3956
Clinkerbrick House 2311 N.E. Schuyler, Portland, 97212 503-281-2533
Columbia Gorge Hotel 4000 Westcliff Dr, Hood River, 97031 800-345-1921
Columbia Hotel 262 1/2 E. Main, Ashland, 97520 503-482-3726
Coos Bay Manor B&B Inn 955 S. Fifth St., Coos Bay, 97420 503-269-1224
Corbett House B&B 7533 SW Corbett Ave., Portland, 97219 503-245-2580
Country Lane B&B P.O. Box Y, Lakeside, 97449 503-759-3869

Country Walrus Inn 2785 E. Main St., Ashland, 97520 503-488-1134
Country Willows Inn 1313 Clay St., Ashland, 97520 503-488-1590
Davidson House 887 Monmouth St., Independence, 97351 503-838-3280
Dragovich House P.O. Box 261, Gates, 97346 503-897-2157
Edinburgh Lodge B&B 586 E. Main St., Ashland, 97520 503-488-1050
Endicott Gardens 95768 Jerry's Flat Rd., Gold Beach, 97444 503-247-6513
Fadden's Inn 326 Main St., Ashland, 97520 503-488-0025
Farm Mini Barn House 7070 Springhill Dr. N., Albany, 97321 503-928-9089
Fellows House 416 S. McLoughlin, Oregon City, 97045 503-656-2089
Floras Lake House P.O. Box 1591, Bandon, 97411 503-347-9205
Fox House Inn 269 "B" St., Ashland, 97520 503-488-1055
Franklin House 1681 Franklin Ave., Astoria, 97103 503-325-5044
Franklin St. Station B&B 1140 Franklin St., Astoria, 97103 503-325-4314
Getty's Emerald Garden B&B 640 Audel Ave., Eugene, 97404 503-688-6344
Gilbert House 341 Beach Dr., Seaside, 97138 503-738-9770
Gile's Guest Haus 690 W. Broadway, Eugene, 97402 503-683-2674
Gracie's Landing 235 S.E. Bay View Ave., Depoe Bay, 97341 503-765-2322
Guest House at Gardiner by 401 Front St., Gardiner, 97441 503-271-4005
Gwendolyn's B&B 735 8th, P.O. Box 913, Port Orford, 97465 503-332-4373
Hackett House 922 State St., Hood River, 97031 503-386-1014
Handmaiden's Inn, The 230 Red Spur Dr., Grants Pass, 97527 503-476-2932
Harbison House 1845 Commercial S.E., Salem, 97302 503-581-8118
Hartman's Hearth 208 N. Holladay Dr., Seaside, 97138 503-738-9055
Heidi Haus 62227 Wallace Rd., Bend, 97701 503-388-0850
Heron Haus 2545 NW Westover Rd., Portland, 97210 503-274-1846
Highland Acres 1350 E. Nevada St., Ashland, 97520 503-482-2170
Highlands B&B 608 Ridge Rd., North Bend, 97459 503-756-0300
Horncroft 42156 Kingston-Lyons Dr, Stayton, 97383 503-769-6287
House at Water's Edge 36 NW Pinecrest Court, Bend, 97701 503-382-1266
Hudson House 37700 Hwy 101 S, Cloverdale, 97112 503-392-3533
Huntington Manor 3555 NW Harrison Blvd., Corvallis, 97330 503-753-3735
Inn Of The Oregon Trail 416 S. McLoughlin, Oregon City, 97045 503-656-2089
Jacksonville Inn P.O. Box 359, Jacksonville, 97530 503-899-1900
John Palmer House 4314 N. Mississippi Ave, Portland, 97217 503-284-5893
Johnson House P.O. Box 1892, Florence, 97439 503-997-8000
Judge Tau Velle House B&B P.O. Box 1630, Jacksonville, 97530 503-899-8938
Key's B&B 5025 SW Homesteader Rd., Wilsonville, 97070 503-638-3722
Lake Creek Lodge Star Route, Sisters, 97759 503-595-6331
Lakecliff Estate B&B P.O. Box 1220, Hood River, 97031 503-386-5918
Lakeside Cottage 234 Pioneer S., Box 26, Lowell, 97452 503-937-2443
Lands Inn B&B Star Route 1, Kimberly, 97848 503-934-2333
Lara House B&B 640 N.W. Congress, Bend, 97701 503-388-4064
Lea House Inn 433 Pacific Hwy., Cottage Grove, 97424 503-942-0933
Lithia Rose Lodging 163 Granite St., Ashland, 97520 503-482-1882
Littlefield House 401 N. Howard, Newberg, 97132 503-538-9868
Livingston Mansion B&B Inn Box 1476, Jacksonville, 97530 503-899-7107
Lorane Valley B&B 86621 Lorane Hwy, Eugene, 97405 503-686-0241
McCall House 153 Oak St., Ashland, 97520 503-482-9296
McCully House Inn 240 E. California St., Jacksonville, 97530 503-899-1942
McKenzie River Inn 49164 McKenzie Hwy, Vida, 97488 503-822-6260
Meadowlark B&B, The 755 E. California St, Jacksonville, 97530 503-899-8963
Mirror Pond House 1054 NW Harmon Blvd., Bend, 97701 503-389-1680
Morical House 668 N. Main St., Ashland, 97520 503-482-2254
Morrison's Rogue River 8500 Galice Rd., Merlin, 97532 503-476-3825
Mountain Shadows B&B Box 147, Welches, 97067 503-622-4746
Mt. Ashland Inn 550 Mt. Ashland Rd., Ashland, 97520 503-482-8707
Mt. Baldy B&B 678 Troll View Rd., Grants Pass, 97527 503-479-7998
Neil Creek House 341 Mowetza Dr., Ashland, 97520 503-482-1334

Nicki's Country Place 31780 Edson Creek, Gold Beach, 97444 503-247-6037
Oak Hill Country B&B 2190 Siskiyou Blvd., Ashland, 97520 503-482-1554
Oak Street Station B&B 239 Oak St., Ashland, 97520 503-482-1726
Oar House 520 SW 2nd St., Newport, 97365 503-265-9571
Oceanaire Rest B&B 95354 Hwy 101, Yachats, 97498 503-547-3782
Old Stage Inn, The 883 Old Stage Rd, Jacksonville, 97530 800-US-STAGE
Oregon Caves Chateau P.O. Box 128, Cave Junction, 97523 503-592-3400
Oregon House Inn 94288 Hwy 101, Yachats, 97498 503-547-3329
Orth House 105 W Main St, Jacksonville, 97530 503-899-1900
Out of the Blue B&B 386 Monmouth St., Independence, 97351 503-838-3636
Owl's View B&B 29585 Owls Ln., Newberg, 97132 503-538-6498
Paradise Ranch Inn 7000 Monument Dr., Grants Pass, 97526 503-479-4333
Parkside 171 Granite St., Ashland, 97520 503-482-2320
Petchekovitch and Son B&B 106 W. 6th St., Port Orford, 97465 503-332-9055
Petera Ahn Reuthlinger 7770 Griffin Creek Rd., Medford, 97501 503-535-7423
Pioneer B&B Star Route, Spray, 97874 503-462-3934
Portland's White House 1914 N.E. 22nd Ave., Portland, 97212 503-287-7131
Powder River B&B HCR 87, Box 500, Baker, 97814 503-523-7143
Pringle House B&B P.O. Box 578, Oakland, 97462 503-459-5038
Queen Anne 125 N. Main St., Ashland, 97520 503-482-0220
Reames House B&B 540 E California St, Jacksonville, 97530 503-899-1868
Redwing, The 115 N. Main St., Ashland, 97520 503-482-1807
Riverside Inn 430 S. Holladay St., Seaside, 97138 503-738-8254
Romeo Inn 295 Idaho St., Ashland, 97520 503-488-0884
Sea Dreamer Inn 15167 McVay Ln. Box 184, Brookings, 97415 503-469-6629
Shrew's House 570 Siskiyou Blvd., Ashland, 97520 503-482-9214
Shutes Lazy S 200 Mowetza Dr., Ashland, 97520 503-482-5498
Sleepy Hollow B&B 4320 Stearns Lane, Oakland, 97462 503-459-3401
Stange Manor 1612 Walnut, La Grande, 97850 503-963-2400
State House B&B 2146 State St., Salem, 97301 503-588-1340
State Street Inn 1005 State St., Hood River, 97031 503-386-1899
Steamboat Inn Steamboat, 97447 503-496-3495
Stone House 80 Hargadine St., Ashland, 97520 503-482-9233
Sylvia Beach Hotel 267 N.W. Cliff St., Newport, 97365 503-265-5428
Tennyson Manor P.O. Box 825, Rogue River, 97537 503-582-2790
Tern Inn B&B 3663 S. Hemlock, Box 95, Cannon Beach, 97110 503-436-1528
This Olde House B&B 202 Alder St., Coos Bay, 97420 503-267-5224
Thompson's B&B By the Lake 1420 Wild Plum Ct., Klamath Falls, 97601 503-882-7938
Three Capes B&B 1685 Maxwell Mnt. Rd., Oceanside, 97134 503-842-6126
Treon's Country Homestay 1819 Colestin Rd., Ashland, 97520 503-482-0746
Tu Tu Tun Lodge, The 96550 N. Bank Rogue, Gold Beach, 97444 503-247-6664
Under the Greenwood Tree 3045 Bellinger Lane, Medford, 97501 503-776-0000
Victoriana B&B 606 12th Ave., Seaside, 97138 503-738-8449
Walker House 811 First Ave., Seaside, 97138 503-738-5520
Wallowa Lake Lodge Joseph, 97846 503-432-4082
Ward House B&B 516 Redwood St., Box 86, Brookings, 97415 503-469-5557
Washington Inn 1002 NW Washington Blvd, Grants Pass, 97526 503-476-1131
Waverly Cottage 305 N. Grape, Medford, 503-779-4716
Wedgwood Inn 563 SW Jefferson Ave., Corvallis, 97333 503-758-7377
Wheeler's B&B Box 8201, Coburg, 97401 503-344-1366
Williams House Inn 608 W. 6th St., The Dalles, 97058 503-296-2889
Willowbrook Inn B&B 628 Foots Creek Rd., Gold Hill, 97525 503-582-0075
Wilson House Inn, The 746 N.W. Sixth St, Grants Pass, 97526 503-479-4754
Wimer Street Inn 75 Wimer St., Ashland, 97520 503-488-2319
Winchester Inn 35 S. 2nd St., Ashland, 97520 503-488-1113
Wolf Creek Tavern P.O. Box 97, Wolf Creek, 97497 503-866-2474
Woods B&B, The 428 Oakview Dr., Roseburg, 97470 503-672-2927
Youngberg Hill Farm B&B 10660 Youngberg Hill Rd, McMinnville, 97128 503-472-2727

Pennsylvania

ADAMSTOWN

Adamstown Inn
P.O. Box 938, 19501
62 W. Main St.
215-484-0800 800-594-4808
Tom & Wanda Berman
All year

$$ B&B
4 rooms, 2 pb
Visa, MC •
C-12+/S-ltd/P-no/H-no

Continental plus
Afternoon tea, snacks
Sitting room
jacuzzi's in 2 rooms
public tennis and pool

Small charming Victorian inn located in the antique district and Pennsylvania Dutch country-side. Minutes from Reading/Lancaster factory outlets. Morning coffee & tea at door.

AIRVILLE

Spring House
Muddy Creek Forks, 17302
717-927-6906
Ray Constance Hearne
All year

$$ B&B
5 rooms, 3 pb
•
C-yes/S-no/P-no/H-yes
Spanish

Full breakfast
Comp. wine, tea, cookies
Sitting room, piano
bicycles
creek swimming

Restored 18th-century stone house in pre-Revolutionary river valley settlement near Lancaster, York. Feather beds, gourmet country breakfast. Hiking, fishing, wineries.

ALLENTOWN

Coachaus
107-111 N. Eighth St., 18101
215-821-4854 800-762-8680
Barbara Kocher/Francine Danko
All year

$$$ B&B
24 rooms, 24 pb
Visa, MC, AmEx, DC, CB •
C-ltd/S-ltd/P-ltd/H-no

Full breakfast
Comp. wine
Sitting room
TV, room phones
air conditioning, FAX

Lovingly restored, graciously appointed; blessed with amenities of the finest hotels. Fine dining, shops, theater nearby. 1-, 2-, and 3-bedrooms with private bath and kitchen.

Glasbern
RD 1 Box 250, Fogelsvlle, 18051
Pack House Rd.
215-285-4723
Beth & Al Granger
All year

$$$ B&B
23 rooms, 23 pb
Visa, MC, AmEx •
C-ltd/S-yes/P-no/H-ltd

Full breakfast
Lunch, dinner, bar
Fireplaces, conf. room
hiking trails
pool, 16 whirlpools

A simple elegance pervades this 19th-century bank barn, situated in a hidden pastoral valley. Creatively renovated. 100 acres of trails, streams, and ponds.

BEDFORD

Bedford House
203 W. Pitt St., 15522
814-623-7171
Lyn & Linda Lyon
All year

$ B&B
8 rooms, 8 pb
Visa, MC, AmEx, Dis
C-12+/S-no/P-no/H-yes

Full breakfast
Afternoon tea
Sitting rm, library nook
Frplc. in 5 guestrooms
tennis, golf nearby

The in-town B&B. C. 1800 brick Federal near shops, restaurants, churches. Located halfway between Pittsburgh & Harrisburg, PA Turnpike exit 11.

BIRD-IN-HAND

Greystone Manor B&B
P.O. Box 270, 17505
2658 Old Philly Pike
717-393-4233
Sally Davis
All year

$$ B&B
13 rooms, 13 pb
Visa, MC •
C-ltd/S-ltd/P-no/H-no

Continental breakfast
Lobby, A/C
color cable TV
quilts & crafts shop

Victorian mansion and carriage house located on 2 acres close to Amish farms. Unique, air-conditioned rooms with private baths. Quilts & crafts shop in basement.

Village Inn
2695 Old Philadelphia, 17505
Box 253
717-293-8369
Richmond & Janice Young
All year

$$ B&B
11 rooms, 11 pb
Visa, MC, AmEx, Disc
C-yes/S-ltd/P-no/H-no

Continental plus
Evening snacks
Sitting room
bus tour of Dutch Cntry.
hot tubs in 2 suites

Beautifully restored historic inn located in Pennsylvania Dutch Country. Country setting. Victorian-style architecture and furnishings. Individually decorated deluxe rooms.

BLOOMSBURG

The Inn at Turkey Hill
991 Central Rd., 17815
I-80 Exit 35 S
717-387-1500
Elizabeth & Andrew Pruden
All year

$$ MAP
18 rooms, 18 pb
Visa, MC, AmEx, DC •
C-yes/S-yes/P-yes/H-yes

Continental plus
Sunday brunch, dinner
Bar service
library, fax machine
tennis courts nearby

Nestled amid Pennsylvania's rolling hills & farmlands, the inn extends warmth, comfort, charm & hospitality. The inn is, as one guest says, "an unexpected find." AAA 4 diamond

Irondale Inn B&B
100 Irondale Ave., 17815
717-784-1977
Bob & Linda Wink
All year

$$$ B&B
4 rooms
C-10+/S-ltd/P-no/H-no

Full breakfast
Comp. wine, snacks, tea
Lunch & dinner on requ.
sitting room, sun porch
library, patio, gardens

Walking distance to Bloomsburg University. Just off of Route 80. Seven fireplaces, sun porch, lush lawns, gardens, great food. Dinner upon request. Circa 1838.

CANADENSIS

Dreamy Acres
P.O. Box 7, 18325
Rt. 447 & Seese Hill Rd.
717-595-7115
William & Esther Pickett
All year

$ B&B
6 rooms, 4 pb
C-6+/S-yes/P-no/H-no

Continental plus
Sitting room, piano
color cable TV, VCRs
air-conditioning

Dreamy Acres is situated in the "Heart of the Pocono Mountain Vacationland" close to stores, gift shops, churches and recreational facilities.

Nearbrook B&B
RD 1, Box 630, 18325
717-595-3152
Barb & Dick Robinson
All year

$ B&B
3 rooms, 1 pb
C-yes/P-ask/H-no

Full breakfast
Wooden train set
games, piano, sleds
art lessons

Rock garden paths, roses, woods and a mountain stream. Relaxing breakfast on outdoor porch. 7 restaurants within 4 miles. Hiking and skiing. Weekly rates. Parties for groups.

CANADENSIS

Old Village Inn
RR 1, Box 404, 18325
Rt. 390 N, N. Skytop Rd.
717-595-2120
Otto & Vera Lissfeld
All year

$$$ B&B
11 rooms, 9 pb
Visa, MC, AmEx, Diners •
C-12+/P-no/H-no
German, French

Full breakfast
Restaurant, bar
Maid, turndown, porch
lawn games, near golf
tennis, hiking, skiing

Quiet elegance in the fine European tradition. Rooms and suites tastefully decorated with antiques. Charming, intimate restaurant offering superb American and ethnic cuisine.

Pine Knob Inn
Route 447, Box 275, 18325
717-595-2532
Annie & Scott Frankel
All year

$$ MAP
27 rooms, 18 pb
Visa, MC •
C-5+/S-no/P-no/H-no

Full breakfast
Dinner, bar
Sitting room, tennis
Steinway grand piano
swimming pool, hiking

The inn is in a lovely country setting in the Pocono Mountains. Antiques and art abound. Nightly turndown service. Best of all, the food is scrumptious!

Pump House Inn Inc.
RR1 Box 430, Skytop Rd., 18325
717-595-7501
John Keeney
All year exc. January

$$ B&B
6 rooms, 6 pb
Visa, MC, AmEx, DC
C-yes/S-yes/P-no/H-no

Continental breakfast
Dinner, bar
Private sitting rooms
piano

Relax at this charming inn surrounded by the beauty and quietude that is the Poconos. Enjoy exquisite gourmet French dining.

CHRISTIANA

Winding Glen Farm Home
107 Noble Rd., 17509
215-593-5535
Minnie & Robert Metzler
All year

$ B&B
5 rooms
C-yes/S-ltd/P-no/H-ltd

Full breakfast
Sitting room
piano
slide shows

Working dairy farm situated in beautiful valley. Stores and quilt shops nearby. Handcrafted furniture made on premises.

CLARK

Tara — A Country Inn
3665 Valley View Rd., 16113
412-962-3535 800-782-2803
Donna & Jim Winner
All year

$$$ B&B/MAP
27 rooms, 27 pb
Visa, MC, Disc •
C-no/S-ltd/P-no/H-no

Full breakfast
Restaurant, bar
Aftn. tea, comp. wine
sitting room, library
hot tubs, pool, spa

Relive the grace and grandeur of "Gone With The Wind". Three distinct restaurants—gourmet, tavern, family-style. Antiques and golfing in the area. Conference center.

COOKSBURG

Clarion River Lodge
P.O. Box 150, 16217
River Rd., Cook Forest
800-648-6743 814-744-8171
Ellen C. O'Day
All year

$$ B&B
20 rooms, 20 pb
Visa, MC, AmEx •
C-yes/S-yes

Continental breakfast
Restaurant
Beverage service
sitting room, library
adjacent to river

Small romantic inn along the gentle Clarion River in northwestern Pennsylvania's great forest. Year-round outdoor activities. Fine lodging, dining and spirits.

Tara—A Country Inn, Clark, PA

COOKSBURG

Gateway Lodge & Cabins
Route 36 Box 125, 16217
814-744-8017 800-843-6862
Joseph & Linda Burney
All year

$$ EP
8 rooms, 3 pb
C-ltd/S-yes/P-ltd/H-ltd

Full breakfast $
Dinner, lunch, snacks
Piano, buggy rides
sitting room, hot tubs
swimming pool, gift shop

Colonial log cabin inn with large stone fireplace. Fine dining by lantern light. Heavy quilts on hand-hewn beds. Year-round activities. Indoor heated swimming pool.

DOYLESTOWN

The Inn at Fordhook Farm
105 New Britain Rd., 18901
215-345-1766
E. Romanella, B. Burpee Dohan
All year

$$$ B&B
6 rooms, 4 pb
Visa, MC, AmEx
C-12+

Full farm breakfast
Afternoon tea
Snacks
sitting room
library

Burpee (seed) family estate with 60 acres of meadows and woodlands. 1760s home with grandfather clocks, majestic mirrors, fireplaces and balconies. On Nat'l Historic Register.

DUSHORE

Cherry Mills Lodge
RR 1, Box 1270, 18614
RR 1, Route 87 South
717-928-8978
Florence & Julio
All year

$$ EP
8 rooms, 1 pb
Visa, MC
C-yes

Full breakfast $
Packed lunches for hikes
Wine with dinner
fireplaces, porch
sauna, pond

Restored 1865-era country hotel. Secluded; by a mountain trout stream; antique furnished; superb cuisine; pond and 27 acres; hiking trails; antique shop.

EAGLES MERE

Eagles Mere Inn
P.O. Box 356, Mary Ave., 17731
717-525-3273
Susan & Peter Glaubitz
All year

$$$ MAP
17 rooms, 17 pb
Visa, MC, AmEx ●
C-ltd/S-no/P-no/H-no

Full breakfast
5-course dinner incl.
Bar, sitting room, piano
tennis, swimming pool
golf, skiing, hunting

Charming country inn located in a quiet Victorian town high in the Endless Mountains. Superb food. Beautiful lake with sandy beach nearby. Undisturbed nature.

EAGLES MERE

Shady Lane B&B	$$ B&B	Full breakfast
P.O. Box 314, 17731	8 rooms, 8 pb	Comp. wine
Allegheny Ave.	Disc •	Two sitting rooms
717-525-3394	C-yes/S-no/P-no/H-no	
Pat & Dennis Dougherty		
All year		

Picturesque mountaintop resort close to excellent hiking, swimming, fishing, skiing and tobogganing. Eagles Mere: "the town time forgot." Summer craft and antique shops.

EAST BERLIN

Bechtel Mansion Inn	$$ B&B	Continental plus
400 West King St., 17316	9 rooms, 7 pb	Complimentary tea
717-259-7760	Visa, MC, AmEx •	Sitting room, library
Ruth Spangler/C. & M. Bechtel	C-yes/S-ltd/P-no/H-no	A/C, meeting room
All year		downhill & X-C skiing

Restored Victorian mansion with fine antiques, in a Pennsylvania German National Historical District. Popular with honeymooners, Civil War and architecture buffs.

EAST STROUDSBURG

The Inn at Meadowbrook	$$ B&B	Full breakfast
RD 7, Box 7651, 18301	18 rooms, 12 pb	Dinner
Cherry Lane Rd.	Visa, MC	Sitting room
717-629-0296	C-12+/S-yes/P-no/H-no	tennis, swimming pool
Bob & Kathy Overman		bicycles
All year		

Forty acres of meadows and woods located in the heart of the Poconos. Close to skiing and major attractions.

ELM

Elm Country Inn	$ B&B	Full breakfast
P.O. Box 37, 17521	2 rooms	Coffee, cold drinks
450 Elm Road	Visa, MC •	Sitting room, porch
717-664-3623 800-245-0523	C-yes/S-no/P-no/H-no	private bath available
Betty & Mel Meck		
All year		

Charming 1860 house, warm hospitality, easy access to Amish country, Hershey and Gettysburg. Near Lititz, PA, in Lancaster County. Above average service at affordable prices.

EPHRATA

Guesthouse at Doneckers	$$ B&B	Continental plus
318-324 N. State St., 17522	31 rooms, 29 pb	Restaurant, fireplaces
301 W. Main St.	AmEx, Visa, MC, DC, CB	Comp. tea, jacuzzis
717-733-8696	C-yes/S-yes/P-no/H-yes	sitting room, library
Jan Grobengieser		porches, deck, suites
All year		

Unique getaway with country simplicity and genteel luxury. Elegance with antiques and folk art; buffet breakfast; fine dining and splendid shopping. Two carriage suites.

The Smithton Inn	$$ B&B	Full breakfast
900 W. Main St., 17522	8 rooms, 8 pb	Comp. tea, snacks
717-733-6094	Visa, MC	Sitting room, fireplaces
Dorothy Graybill	C-yes/S-no/P-ltd/H-ltd	whirlpool baths
All year		library, canopy beds

Picturesque 1763 Penn. Dutch Country Inn. Fireplaces in parlor, dining and guest rooms. Chamber music; canopy four-poster beds, refrigerator, quilts and candles in each room.

ERWINNA

Evermay on-the-Delaware
River Rd., 18920
215-294-9100
Ronald Strouse, Fred Cresson
All year exc. Dec 24

$$$ B&B
16 rooms, 16 pb
Visa, MC •
C-no/S-ltd/P-no/H-yes

Continental plus
Comp. sherry in parlor
Cordial in rm., bar, tea
restaurant (weekends)
sitting room, piano

Romantic Victorian inn on 25 acres of gardens, woodlawn paths and pastures. Elegant dinner served Friday-Sunday & holidays. Rooms face the picturesque Delaware River.

Golden Pheasant Inn
River Rd., Route 32, 18920
215-294-9595
Barbara & Michel Faure
All year

$$$ EP
5 rooms, 1 pb
Visa, MC
C-12+/S-ltd/P-no
French, Spanish, Italian

Cont. breakfast $
Restaurant, bar, canoes
Dinner (Tues-Sun)
Delaware Canal & River
wine in room, solarium

1857 fieldstone inn situated between river and canal. Five rooms furnished with incredible blend of antiques. Quiet. Plant-filled solarium for romantic candlelight dining.

FRANKLIN

Quo Vadis B&B
1501 Liberty St., 16323
814-432-4208
Kristal & Stanton Bowmer
All year

$$ B&B
6 rooms, 6 pb
Visa, MC, AmEx •
C-12+/S-no/P-no/H-no

Continental plus
Coffee, tea, cookies
Sitting room, library
TV, dining room
fine restaurants nearby

Queene Anne 1867 brick house, heirloom furnishings, quilts, and needlework. Located in Federal Registered Historic District, Franklin, America's Victorian City.

GARDENVILLE-BUCKS COUNTY

Maplewood Farm B&B
P.O. Box 239, 18926
5090 Durham Rd.
215-766-0477
Cindy & Dennis Marquis
All year

$$$ B&B
5 rooms, 5 pb
Visa, MC, AmEx •
C-ltd/S-no/P-no/H-no

Full breakfast
Afternoon tea, soda
Comp. wine, snacks
sitting room
library

Cozy circa 1826 country farmhouse featuring fabulous breakfasts; grazing sheep; chickens. Near New Hope artist colony; antiques; shopping; great restaurants.

GETTYSBURG

The Brafferton Inn
44 York St., 17325
717-337-3423
Mimi & Jim Agard
All year

$$$ B&B
11 rooms, 4 pb
Visa, MC •
C-7+/S-no/P-no/H-yes

Full breakfast
Coffee, tea, sitting rm.
Library, atrium, piano
hat collection, old mags
primitive mural

Stone and clapboard inn circa 1786 near the center square of Gettysburg. The rooms have stenciled designs, antiques. Walk to battlefield and restaurants.

Hickory Bridge Farm
96 Hickory Bridge Rd., 17353
Orrtanna
717-642-5261
Hammetts & Martins
All year

$$$ B&B
7 rooms, 6 pb
Visa, MC
C-yes/S-yes/P-no/H-no

Full breakfast
Saturday dinner
Sitting room
bicycles, fishing,
pond swimming

Hickory Bridge Farm is a quiet retreat at the foot of the South Mountains, eight miles west of Gettysburg.

GETTYSBURG

Historic Farnsworth House
401 Baltimore St., 17325
717-334-8838
Loring H. Shultz Family
All year

$$ B&B
4 rooms, 4 pb
Visa, MC, AmEx, Disc
C-yes/S-ltd/P-no/H-no

Full breakfast
Restaurant, bar
Box lunches, tea, treats
sitting room, library
garden, gallery

Enchanting blend of Victorian elegance and Civil War ambiance. Breakfast served in garden. Sharpshooters used to live here; 100 bullet holes. Civil War print and book gallery.

Keystone Inn
231 Hanover St., 17325
717-337-3888
Doris Martin
All year

$$ B&B
4 rooms, 2 pb
Visa, MC
C-yes/S-ltd/P-no

Full breakfast from menu
Lemonade, coffee, tea
Sitting room
library, antiques
tennis courts nearby

Unique decor—lots of natural chestnut and oak; comfort our priority. Area rich in history; antique lover's paradise. Country breakfast!

Tannery B&B
P.O. Box 4565, 17325
449 Baltimore St.
717-334-2454
Charlotte & Jule Swope
All year

$$ B&B
5 rooms, 5 pb
Visa, MC
C-8+/S-no/P-no/H-no

Continental plus
Comp. wine, snacks
Sitting room, library
rocking chairs on
front porch, golf nearby

Built in 1868 of Gothic structure, The Tannery is located within walking distance of historical sites, museums, and restaurants.

GETTYSBURG—GARDNERS

Goose Chase B&B
200 Blueberry Rd., 17324
717-528-8877
Marsha Lucidi
All year

$$ B&B
5 rooms, 5 pb
Visa, MC •
C-10+/S-no/P-no/H-no
some German

Full breakfast
Comp. pvt. vintage wine
Sitting room, library
walking trails, skiing
animals, mystery weekend

Unique country hideaway (circa 1759); period antiques and A/C rooms. Romantic, relaxing atmosphere close to antique area and restaurants. Gardens, vineyard, fireplaces.

GETTYSBURG—HANOVER

Beechmont Inn
315 Broadway, Route 194, 17331
717-632-3013 800-553-7009
Monna Hormel
All year

$$ B&B
7 rooms, 7 pb
Visa, MC, AmEx •
C-12+/S-ltd/P-no/H-no

Full breakfast
Comp. wine, snacks
Afternoon tea
sitting room, library
honeymoon/anniv. package

Federal period elegance; echoes of Civil War memories; a refuge from the rush of the 20th century—a bridge across time. Located near Gettysburg; antiquing nearby.

GORDONVILLE—INTERCOURSE

Osceola Mill House
313 Osceola Mill Rd., 17529
717-768-3758
Robin & Sterling Schoen
Exc. Christmas & Easter

$$$ B&B
3 rooms
C-12+/S-no/P-no/H-no
German

Full gourmet breakfast
Comp. beverages
Sitting room
bicycles nearby

Historic stone mill house built in 1766. Located in a scenic Lancaster County surrounded by Amish farms. Fireplaces and antiques throughout.

HAWLEY

Academy Street B&B
528 Academy St., 18428
717-226-3430 201-316-8148
Judith & Sheldon Lazan
May–October

$$ B&B
7 rooms, 4 pb
Visa •
C-no/S-yes/P-no/H-no

Full breakfast buffet
Comp. wine, coffee, cake
Afternoon tea
sitting room, TV
A/C in rooms

Magnificent Victorian in Poconos near Lake Wallenpaupack. European gourmet breakfast, afternoon coffee and cheesecake. Near restaurants, all activities.

Settlers Inn
4 Main Ave., 18428
717-226-2993 800-833-8527
Grant & Jeanne Genzlinger
All year

$$ B&B
18 rooms, 18 pb
Visa, MC, AmEx, DC •
C-yes/S-yes/P-ltd/H-no

Full breakfast
Lunch, dinner, bar
Eve. cheese & crackers
sitting room, library
tennis, bicycles, piano

Delightful country inn of Tudor architecture, with gift shops and art gallery. Lake Wallenpaupack and shopping are nearby. Air conditioned rooms.

HESSTON

Aunt Susie's
RD 1, Box 225, 16647
814-658-3638
John
All year

$ B&B
8 rooms, 2 pb
C-yes/S-no/P-no/H-no
French, German

Continental plus
Afternoon tea
Snacks, sitting room
houses with kitchens,
boat parking, bed linens

Experience country living in a warm friendly atmosphere; antiques, oil paintings. 28-mile-long Raystown Lake for recreation. Quaint village of Hesston. Inn, cottages & houses.

HOLICONG

Barley Sheaf Farm
P.O. Box 10, Route 202, 18928
215-794-5104
Don & Ann Mills
Exc. Xmas, wkdys to 2/14

$$$ B&B
9 rooms, 9 pb
C-8+/S-yes/P-no/H-yes
French

Full farm breakfast
Swimming pool
sitting room

30-acre working farm—raise sheep. Rooms all furnished in antiques. Good antiquing and historic sights in area.

HOLICONG–NEW HOPE

Ash Mill Farm
P.O. Box 202, 18928
5358 Old York Rd.,Rte 202
215-794-5373
Patricia & Jim Auslander
All year

$$$ B&B
4 rooms
Visa, MC •
C-ltd/S-yes/P-no/H-no

Full gourmet breakfast
Afternoon tea
Evening brandy
sitting room
near tennis & swimming

18th-century farmhouse on 10 acres of rural countryside, adjacent to Peddlers' Village and convenient to all of Bucks County. Featured in Gourmet Magazine.

JIM THORPE

Harry Packer Mansion
P.O. Box 458, 18229
Packer Hill
717-325-8566
Robert & Patricia Handwerk
All year

$$$ B&B
13 rooms, 8 pb
Visa, MC •
C-no/S-no/P-no/H-no

Full breakfast
Murder Mystery weekends
Sitting room, library
tennis, water sports

Magnificent Victorian mansion in historic district with period furnishings, original woodwork and stained glass. Gracious and friendly atmosphere with sports activities near.

362 Pennsylvania

KANE

Kane Manor B&B
230 Clay St., 16735
814-837-6522 FAX:837-6664
Laurie Anne Dalton
All year

$$$ B&B
10 rooms, 6 pb
Visa, MC, AmEx •
C-yes/S-ltd/P-no/H-yes

Full breakfast (wkends)
Continental (wkdays)
Afternoon tea
sitting room, piano
mystery weekend packages

Original Kane family home situated in the Allegheny National Forest, furnished with family furniture and artifacts. Summer recreation, cross-country skiing.

KENNETT SQUARE

Meadow Spring Farm
201 E. Street Rd., 19348
215-444-3903
Anne I. Hicks
All year

$$ B&B
6 rooms, 3 pb
AmEx •
C-yes/S-yes/P-no/H-no

Full breakfast
Dinner upon request
Comp. wine, tea, snacks
hot tubs, game room
pool, pond for fishing

1836 farmhouse on working farm with sheep, pigs & cows; filled with antiques, dolls & teddy bears. Full country breakfast served on porch, spacious dining room or by the pool.

Scarlett House B&B
503 W. State St., 19348
215-444-9592
Susan Lalli-Ascosi
All year

$$ B&B
4 rooms, 2 pb
C-no/S-no/P-no/H-no

Continental plus
Afternoon tea, snacks
Sitting room, library
Victorian parlor, piano
A/C, fireplaces, porch

Elegantly restored Victorian located minutes from Longwood Gardens, Winterthur and Brandywine Valley attractions. Old-fashioned hospitality, gracious atmosphere, antiques.

LAHASKA, BUCKS COUNTY

The Golden Plough Inn
P.O. Box 218, 18931
Routes 202 & 263
215-794-4004
Earl/Donna Jamison, R.Cassidy
All year

$$$ B&B
Visa, MC, AmEx, others •
C-yes/S-ltd/P-no/H-no

Continental plus
Champagne in room
Six restaurants, bar
rooms with jacuzzis
library

Luxurious country inn furnished in 18th-century American antiques and reproductions, lush fabrics, refrigerators. Walk to specialty shops, history, landscaped acres, New Hope.

LAMPETER

B&B — The Manor
P.O. Box 416, 17537
830 Village Rd.
717-464-9564
Jackie Curtis/MaryLou Paolini
All year

$$ B&B
5 rooms, 2 pb
Visa, MC
C-yes/S-no/P-no/H-yes

Full breakfast
Lunch, dinner
Snacks, sitting room
A/C, swimming pool
winter & group discounts

Cozy farmhouse centrally located in scenic Amish country. Deluxe inground swimming pool, full gourmet breakfast. Children welcome, group discount rates.

LANCASTER

The Apple Bin Inn
2835 Willow Street Pike, 17584
717-464-5881 800-338-4296
Barry & Debbie Hershey
All year

$$ B&B
4 rooms, 2 pb
Visa, MC •
C-yes/S-no/P-no/H-no

Full breakfast
Afternoon tea, snacks
Sitting room, patios
A/C & cable TV in rooms
bike storage and maps

Warm colonial charm with a country flavor. Antiques, reproductions. Located near Amish community, antique and craft shops, excellent restaurants and historical sites.

LANCASTER ————————————————————

Candlelite Inn B&B
2574 Lincoln Hwy East, 17572
Route 30 East, Ronks
717-299-6005
D. Simpson, R. Hartzell
February–November

$$ B&B
4 rooms, 2 pb
Visa, MC
C-12+/S-no/P-no/H-no

Full breakfast
Sitting room

1920s brick farmhouse offering 4 quiet rooms, surrounded by Amish farmlands. Antique and collectibles shop on premises. Close to attractions.

Churchtown Inn B&B
Route 23, Churchtown, 17555
M.A. 2100 Main St, Narvon
215-445-7794
H. & S. Smith, J. Kent
All year

$$ B&B
8 rooms, 6 pb
Visa, MC, AmEx
C-12+/S-ltd/P-no
German

Full 5-course breakfast
Dinner with Amish family
Glass garden room, piano
game rm., carriage house
musical innkeeper

In the heart of Pennsylvania Dutch country. Historic circa 1735 stone federal colonial. Near tourist attractions, antiquing, farm markets and outlets. Completely restored.

King's Cottage, A B&B Inn
1049 E. King St., 17602
717-397-1017 800-747-8717
Karen & Jim Owens
All year

$$$ B&B
7 rooms, 7 pb
Visa, MC •
C-12+/S-no/P-no/H-no
Spanish

Full breakfast
Afternoon tea, cordials
Sitting room, library
water garden, Dinner w/
Amish family available

Enjoy National Register award-winning architecture, elegance. Central location, near Amish farms, restaurants, antiques, outlets, quilts, historic sites. Mobil-Excellent.

Lincoln Haus Inn B&B
1687 Lincoln Hwy E., 17602
717-392-9412
Mary K. Zook
All year

$ B&B
8 rooms, 8 pb
Personal checks •
C-yes/S-no/P-no/H-ask
Dueisch, German

Full breakfast (rooms)
Sitting room
No alcohol on premises
honeymoon suite avail.
Amish crafts nearby

Unique suburban home, built in the late 1800s, with rooms and apartments. Natural oaks woodwork, antiques. Owner is a member of the old order Amish church.

Witmer's Tavern—1725 Inn
2014 Old Philadelphia, 17602
717-299-5305
Brant E. Hartung
All year

$$ B&B
5 rooms
•
C-yes/S-ltd/P-no/H-no

Continental breakfast
Popcorn and poppers
Antique shop, sitting rm
air field, canoeing
8 museums/sites nearby

Lancaster's only pre-Revolutionary inn still lodging travelers. Fireplaces, antiques, quilts & fresh flowers in all romantic rooms. On National Register.

LANCASTER–CHURCHTOWN ————————————————

Inn at Twin Linden
2092 Main St., 17555
215-445-7619
Donna & Bob Leahy
All year

$$$ B&B
6 rooms, 6 pb
Visa, MC, AmEx •
C-yes/S-ltd/P-no/H-no
some Spanish

Full breakfast
Restaurant
Afternoon sherry, tea
sitting room, hot tubs

Elegant historic estate is everything an inn should be. Exceptional candlelight dining, gourmet breakfast. Romantic getaway, antiques, jacuzzi, views.

LANCASTER—COLUMBIA

The Columbian
360 Chestnut St., 17512
717-684-5869 800-422-5869
Linda & John Straitiff All year

$$ B&B
5 rooms, 5 pb
Visa, MC •
C-12+/S-no/P-no/H-no

Full breakfast
Comp. beverages
Sitting room, A/C, TV in all
rooms, fireplace in 1,
wrap-around sun porch

Restored turn-of-the-century Colonial Revival mansion decorated with antiques in Victorian or country style. Hearty breakfast of hot main dishes, fresh fruit, homemade breads.

LANCASTER—LAMPETER

Walkabout Inn
P.O. Box 294, 17537
837 Village Rd.
717-464-0707
Richard & Margaret Mason
All year

$$ B&B
5 rooms, 5 pb
Visa, MC, AmEx, Choice •
C-yes/S-no/P-no/H-no

Full Aussie breakfast
Afternoon tea
Library, antique shop
playground/picnic area
movies on Amish culture

Country-restored 1925 Mennonite home, beautifully landscaped in a quaint village setting. Dinner and tour with Amish family arranged. Picturesque English gardens.

LANCASTER—NOTTINGHAM

Little Britain Manor
20 Brown Rd., 19362
Village of Little Britain
717-529-2862
Fred & Evelyn Crider
All year

$ B&B
4 rooms
C-yes

Full breakfast
Dinner by request
2 rooms with A/C
help with tours

A home away from home country farm furnished with antiques and country flair. See up close the unique culture of the Amish people and markets.

LEWISBURG

Pineapple Inn
439 Market St., 17837
717-524-6200
Charles & Deborah North
All year

$$ B&B
6 rooms, 2 pb
Visa, MC, DC, CB
C-ltd/S-ltd/P-no/H-no
German

Full breakfast
Comp. tea, snacks
All rooms A/C, tea room
piano, sitting room
tennis, pool nearby

This circa 1857 home of Federalist design is decorated with period antiques. Just blocks from Bucknell University. Full country breakfast. Upside-Down Shoppe.

LITITZ

Swiss Woods B&B
500 Blantz Rd., 17543
717-627-3358 800-594-8018
Werner & Debrah Mosimann
All year

$$ B&B
5 rooms, 5 pb
Visa, MC •
C-yes
German, Swiss German

Full breakfast
Lunch (picnic baskets)
Comp. tea and cake
sitting room
bicycles

A chalet nestled in the woods overlooking Speedwell Fodge Lake. Swiss specialties and European decor. Queen beds and down comforters. Two rooms with jacuzzis.

LUMBERVILLE

1740 House
River Road, 18933
215-297-5661
Robert John Vris
All year

$$ B&B
24 rooms, 24 pb
•
C-no/S-yes/P-no

Full breakfast
Restaurant, aftn. tea
Sitting room, library
bicycles, swimming pool
tennis & X-C ski

If you can't be a house guest in Buck's County, be ours—24 attractively furnished rooms overlooking the Delaware River. Horseback riding, canoeing, antiquing, etc. nearby.

MERCER

Magoffin Inn
129 S. Pitt St., 16137
412-662-4611
J. McClelland, G. Slagle
All year

$$ B&B
7 rooms, 7 pb
Visa, MC, AmEx •
C-yes/S-no/P-no/H-no

Continental plus
Lunch, dinner
Cordial, snacks
library
tennis courts, pool

1884 Queen Anne Victorian. Affordable elegance in ideal location. Outdoor activities abound: boating, fishing, golf, cross-country skiing. Near I-79 and I-80.

MERCERSBURG

The Mercersburg Inn
405 S. Main St., 17236
717-328-5231
Fran Wolfe
All year

$$$ B&B
15 rooms, 15 pb
Visa, MC, AmEx •
C-ltd/S-ltd/H-no
Swiss, German, French

Continental plus
6-course dinner wkends $
Bar service
golf course, skiing &
tennis courts nearby

Elegant, restored mansion in south central Pennsylvania. 90 minutes from Washington, D.C. Gourmet dining by candlelight. Handmade canopy beds, antiques & crackling fireplace.

MERTZTOWN

Longswamp B&B
RD2, Box 26, 19539
215-682-6197
Elsa & Dean Dimick
All year

$$ B&B
10 rooms, 6 pb
C-yes/S-ltd/P-no/H-ltd
French

Full breakfast
Comp. wine & cheese, etc
Picnics, sitting room
library, piano, bicycles
horseshoes, bocce court

Historic country farmhouse near Amish country and skiing. Tempting delicacies prepared by area chef. Book and music collection for guests' use.

MILFORD

Black Walnut B&B
RD 2 Box 9285, 18337
Fire Tower Rd.
717-296-6322
Hermien Ankersmit
All year

$$ B&B
14 rooms, 8 pb
Visa, MC, AmEx
C-ltd/S-ltd/P-no/H-no

Full breakfast
Restaurant, comp. sherry
Pool table, lawn games
piano, pond, hot tub
riding lessons, trails

Large secluded estate for an exclusive clientele. Tudor-style stone house with historic marble fireplace, charming bedrooms with antiques and brass beds. Riding stable also.

Cliff Park Inn & Golf Crs.
RR 4, Box 7200, 18337
717-296-6491 800-225-6535
Harry W. Buchanan, III
All year

$$$ B&B/MAP/AP
18 rooms, 18 pb
Visa, MC, AmEx, DC, Dis •
C-yes/S-yes/P-no/H-ltd
French, Spanish

Full breakfast
Restaurant, bar
Sitting room
library, 8 rooms with
fireplace & jacuzzi

Historic country inn surrounded by long-established golf course on secluded 600-acre estate. Cross-country skiing in the winter. Gourmet dining. Rated 3-Star by Mobil Guide.

Pine Hill Farm B&B
P.O. Box 1001, 18337
717-296-7395
Lynn & Bob Patton
Exc. Thksgvng, New Years

$$$ B&B
3 rooms, 3 pb
C-ltd/S-ltd/P-no/H-no
German

Full breakfast
Restaurants nearby
Sitting room, library
color TV, A/C, BBQtrails,
two streams

Private 268-acre mountaintop estate, circa 1875. Breakfast on terrace overlooking Delaware River. Antique-filled suites—living room, bedroom, sparkling new private bath.

MONTOURSVILLE

Carriage House—Stonegate	$$ B&B	Full breakfast
RD 1, Box 11A, 17754	2 rooms	Continental plus (summr)
717-433-4340	•	Snacks, bar service
Harold & Dena Mesaris	C-yes/S-yes/P-yes	sitting room, library
All year		bicycles

Total privacy along the banks of Mill Creek, 30 yards from the main house in the beautfiul Loyalsock Creek Valley. Tubing in creeks and hiking nearby

MONTROSE

The Montrose House	$ B&B	Full breakfast
26 S. Main St., 18801	12 rooms, 6 pb	Restaurant, lounge bar
717-278-1124	Visa, MC, AmEx, DC, Dis	200-seat banquet fac.
Frederick & Candace Rose	•	cable TV, telephones
All year	C-yes/S-yes/P-yes/H-no	

In the heart of the Endless Mountains; country inn offering cozy comfort and fine dining in Early American setting. Dining by candlelight. Close to shops and sports.

MOUNT JOY

Cedar Hill Farm	$$ B&B	Continental plus
305 Longenecker Rd., 17552	4 rooms, 4 pb	All private baths
717-653-4655	Visa, MC, AmEx	Central air-conditioning
Russel & Gladys Swarr	C-yes/S-no/P-no/H-no	porch, private balcony
All year		roam this working farm

Host born in this 1817 Fieldstone farmhouse. Quiet area overlooks stream. Near Lancaster's Amish country and Hershey. Farmer's markets and quaint villages nearby.

Hillside Farm B&B	$$ B&B	Full breakfast
607 Eby Chiques Road, 17552	4 rooms, 2 pb	Comp. wine, snacks
717-653-6697	C-10+/S-no/P-no/H-no	Sitting room, library
Gary & Deb Lintner		baby grand piano
All year		

1866 farmhouse in Amish Country, furnished with dairy farm antiques and milk bottles. Very secluded, near creek & waterfall. Biking, hiking, outlets, antique shops, wineries.

NEW HOPE

Aaron Burr House	$$$ B&B	Continental plus
80 W. Bridge St., 18938	6 rooms, 6 pb	Comp. liqueur, snacks
corner of Chestnut St.	AmEx •	Afternoon tea, library
215-862-2343	C-yes/S-no/P-no/H-yes	bicycles, tennis, pool
Nadine & Carl Glassman	French, Spanish	patio with white wicker
All year		

Discover "safe haven" in this vintage village Victorian inn — just like Aaron Burr did after his famous pistol duel with Alexander Hamilton in 1804. Innkeeping seminars.

Back Street Inn	$$$ B&B	Full gourmet breakfast
144 Old York Rd., 18938	7 rooms, 7 pb	Sitting room
215-862-9571	Visa, MC •	swimming pool
Robert Puccio, John Hein	S-yes	croquet
All year	German	

There is New Hope in Bucks County, PA, a village of vitality and romance. 10 min. stroll into center of town. Swimming pool, A/C rooms & full gourmet breakfast in garden room.

NEW HOPE

Centre Bridge Inn
Box 74 Star Route, 18938
Routes 32 & 263
215-862-9139 215-862-2048
Stephen R. DuGan
All year

$$$ B&B
9 rooms, 9 pb
Visa, MC
C-ltd/S-yes/P-no/H-no

Continental breakfast
Dinner, bar
Sitting room w/fireplace
riverside deck

Charming riverside country inn furnished with lovely period antiques; cozy Old World restaurant with walk-in fireplace and alfresco dining in season.

Hotel du Village
N. River Rd., 18938
at Phillips Mill Rd.
215-862-9911 215-862-5164
Barbara & Omar Arbani
All year

$$$ B&B
20 rooms, 20 pb
AmEx •
C-ltd/S-yes/P-no/H-yes
French, Spanish

Continental plus
Dinner, bar
Swimming pool
tennis courts
sitting room

Intimate country dining & lodging in Bucks County, Pennsylvania.

Wedgewood B&B Inn
111 W. Bridge St., 18938
215-862-2570
C. Glassman & N. Silnutzer
All year

$$ B&B
18 rooms
•
C-yes/S-ltd/P-ltd/H-ltd
Fr, Hebr, Dutch, Ger, Fr

Continental plus
Aftn. tea & refreshments
Victorian gazebo, parlor
horsedrawn carriage ride
club w/tennis, swimming

Victorian mansion in New Hope. Wedgewood china, fresh flowers & original art. Innkeepers on hand to make your stay as pleasant as the surroundings. OUR 1989 INN OF THE YEAR!

The Whitehall Inn
RD 2, Box 250, 18938
1370 Pineville Rd.
215-598-7945
Mike & Suella Wass
All year

$$$ B&B
6 rooms, 4 pb
Visa, MC, AmEx, DC •
C-no/S-no/P-no/H-no

Full candlelight brkfast
High tea, comp. sherry
Pool & rose garden
library, sun room
piano & pump organ

Experience our four-course candlelit breakfast using European china and crystal and heirloom sterling silver. Formal tea; fireplaces; working dressage horse farm.

NORTH EAST

Brown's Village Inn
51 E. Main St., 16428
814-725-5522
Rebecca Brown
All year

$ B&B
3 rooms, 3 pb
Visa, MC •
C-yes/S-yes/P-ltd
Dutch, French

Full breakfast
Lunch/dinner, restaurant
Afternoon tea, snacks
sitting room, library
golf, tennis, beach near

A restored 1832 federal-style house now is home for a fine restaurant and antique-appointed guest rooms. Only 1 mile to the Lake Erie shore. Experience a bit of yesteryear.

NORTH WALES

Joseph Ambler Inn
1005 Horsham Rd., 19454
Montgomeryville
215-362-7500
Steve & Terry Kratz
All year

$$$ B&B
28 rooms, 28 pb
Visa, MC, AmEx, DC, CB •
C-yes/S-yes/P-no/H-ltd
French, German

Full breakfast
Restaurant
3 sitting rooms
banquet/meeting room

1735 estate house set on 13 acres and furnished with antiques, four-poster beds, walk-in fireplace. Children welcome.

ORBISONIA

Salvino's Guest House
P.O. Box 116, 17243
48 Ridgely St., Rt. 522
814-447-5616
Elaine & Joe Salvino
All year

$ B&B
5 rooms
Visa, MC
C-yes/S-no/P-yes/H-no

Continental plus
Front porch w/swing
sitting room w/TV

Historic Orbisonia is home to EBT Steam Train & trolley museums & near Lake Raystown. Your hostess Elaine is an avid quilter and her Chatelaine Quilt Shop is right next door.

PARADISE

Maple Lane Farm B&B
505 Paradise Lane, 17562
717-687-7479
Edwin & Marion Rohrer
All year

$ B&B
4 rooms, 2 pb
C-yes/S-no/P-no/H-no

Continental plus
Sitting room
Organ, front porch
spacious lawns

Maple Lane Farm has air conditioning, antiques. Near Amish homesteads, museums, farmer's markets. Farm guest house plus 120-cow dairy, streams and woodland.

Neffdale Farm
604 Strasburg Rd., 17562
717-687-7837 717-687-9367
Roy/Ellen/Charles/Glenda Neff
All year

$ EP
6 rooms, 4 pb
C-yes/S-no/P-no/H-no

Coffee or tea
Picnic tables
Sitting room
fully carpeted
air conditioned rooms

200-year-old farmhouse. 160 acres of woods, meadows, crop lands. Stay on a real working farm. Amish neighbors. Close to everything in the heart of Pennsylvania Dutch country.

PHILADELPHIA

Society Hill Hotel
301 Chestnut St., 19106
215-925-1919
Jackie
All year

$$$ B&B
12 rooms, 12 pb
Visa, MC, AmEx, DC •
C-yes/S-yes/P-ltd

Continental breakfast
Restaurant
Piano bar
telephones

An "urban inn" located in the midst of Philadelphia's Historic Park. Fresh flowers, chocolates and brass double beds grace each room.

Steele Away B&B
7151 Boyer St., 19119
215-242-0722
Diane Steele
All year

$$ B&B
2 rooms
C-6+/S-no/P-no/H-no

Full breakfast (wkends)
Continental plus (wkdys)
Sitting room w/fireplace
TV, A/C, veranda
kitchen available

Guests described this weaver and architect's Victorian home as a "slice of heaven," "piece of paradise." Scandanavian furnishings, stenciling, handwoven accents.

Thomas Bond House
129 S. Second St., 19106
215-923-8523 800-845-BOND
Jerry & Lisa Dunn
All year

$$$ B&B
12 rooms, 12 pb
Visa, MC, AmEx •
C-yes/S-yes/P-no/H-no

Continental plus (wkdys)
Full breakfast (wkends)
Aftn. tea, comp. wine
Wet bar, whirlpool tubs
bikes, Murder Mysteries

Colonial period (c. 1770) guest house listed in National Register. Individually decorated rooms with hair dryers, TV, phones. Located in Independence National Historical Park.

PITTSBURGH

The Priory—A City Inn
614 Pressley St., 15212
412-231-3338 FAX:231-4838
Mary Ann Graf
All year

$$$ B&B
24 rooms, 24 pb
AmEx, Visa, MC •
C-yes/S-yes/P-no/H-yes

Continental plus
Comp. tea, port, sherry
Sitting room, library
fireplace, courtyard
comp. limo service

Newly restored historic Victorian Priory—antiques; courtyard or city view; neighborhood atmosphere; close to city. National Register district. TV and phone in rooms.

POINT PLEASANT

Tattersall Inn
P.O. Box 569, 18950
Cafferty & River Rds.
215-297-8233
Gerry & Herb Moss
All year

$$$ B&B
6 rooms, 6 pb
AmEx, Visa, MC, Disc •
C-yes/S-ltd/P-no/H-no

Continental plus
Apple cider, snacks
Library, sitting room
antique pinball machine
piano for guest use

· *Historic lilac and cream mansion of the early 1800s. B&B in a village setting. Antique phonograph collection for your enjoyment.*

POTTSTOWN

Coventry Forge Inn
RR 7—Coventryville, 19464
1.5 mi. W. of Pa100 on 23
215-469-6222
All year

$$ B&B
5 rooms, 5 pb
Visa, MC, AmEx, DC
S-yes/P-no/H-no

Continental breakfast
Restaurant, bar
Dinner available
sitting room, library

Superb French restaurant in Chester County horse country. Brandywine Valley & Amish country nearby. Excellent antiquing.

QUAKERTOWN

Sign of The Sorrel Horse
243 Old Bethlehem Road, 18951
215-536-4651
All year

$$$ EP/B&B
5 rooms, 5 pb
Visa, MC, AmEx
C-no/S-no/P-yes/H-no
French, German

Continental plus
Restaurant, bar, dinner
Comp. sherry & fruits
sitting room, bicycles
skiing, fishing, boating

Built in 1749 as a stagecoach stop; secluded on 5 manicured acres; gracious country inn; five antique-filled guest rooms. A little bit of France in Bucks County.

QUARRYVILLE

**Runnymede Farm
Guesthouse**
1030 Robert Fulton Hwy., 17566
717-786-3625
Herb & Sara Hess
All year

$ EP/B&B
3 rooms
C-yes/S-no/P-no/H-no

Full country breakfast
Snacks
Piano
sitting room

Enjoy old-fashioned hospitality when you vacation in our clean, comfortable farm home. Full country breakfast available. Bicycling, hiking, picnicking.

RIDGWAY

Faircroft B&B
Box 17 Montmorenci Rd., 15853
814-776-2539
Lois & John Shoemaker
All year

$ B&B
3 rooms, 2 pb
S-no/H-no

Full breakfast
Comp. beverages, snacks
Sitting room
hiking trails, hunting
fishing, swimming, golf

Two miles from Route 219. Warm, comfortable, 1870 farmhouse on 75 acres. Antiques, Swedish foods. Next to Allegheny National Forest.

SLIPPERY ROCK

Applebutter Inn	$$ B&B	Full gourmet
152 Applewood Lane,	11 rooms, 11 pbVisa, MC •	breakfastComp. beverages
16057412-794-1844	C-yes/S-no/P-no/H-yes	& snacks
Gary & Sandra McKnight		sitting room, library
All year		banquet/meeting room

Restored 1844 farmstead with fireplaces, canopy beds and genuine antiques; gourmet breakfasts; warm quiet atmosphere; close to university, parks.

SMOKETOWN

Homestead Lodging	$ EP	Comp. coffee, danish
184 E. Brook Rd., 17576	4 rooms, 4 pb	Gift shop, tennis court
717-393-6927	Visa, MC	Air-conditioning
Robert & Lori Kepiro	C-yes/S-yes/H-yes	color TV w/stereo radio
All year		Amish country tours

Quiet country lodging in hand-stenciled rooms. Gift shop with local handcrafts. Located beside Amish farm. Walk to restaurants and outlets.

SOLEBURY

Holly Hedge English Estate	$$$ B&B	Full breakfast
Box 213, 18963	16 rooms, 16 pb	Sunday brunch, dinner
4969 Upper York Rd.	Visa, MC •	Library, sitting room
215-862-3136	C-no/S-yes/P-no/H-yes	piano, tennis courts
Jay		swimming pool, horses
All year		

Discover the warm, friendly atmosphere and exquisite charm of Holly Hedge English Estate. Relax, enjoy the fresh air at our cozy Shangri-La.

SOMERSET

Bayberry Inn	$ B&B	Continental plus
611 N. Center Ave., 15501	11 rooms, 11 pb	Snacks
814-445-8471	Visa, MC, Disc •	Sitting room, library
Marilyn & Bob Lohr	C-12+/S-no/P-no/H-no	central A/C
All year		TV room with VCR/stereo

One and one-half blocks from turnpike exit, near Georgian Place outlet mall. Seven Springs and Hidden Valley ski resorts, whitewater rafting, "Fallingwater".

STARLIGHT

The Inn at Starlight Lake	$$$ B&B/MAP	Full breakfast
P.O. Box 27, 18461	27 rooms, 21 pb	Lunch, dinner, full bar
717-798-2519	Visa, MC •	Sitting room, piano
Judy & Jack McMahon	C-yes/S-yes/P-no/H-no	tennis courts, boating
Exc. late Mar–Apr 16		bicycles, ski trails

A beautiful clear lake; setting of pastoral tranquillity; excellent food and spirits; recreation for every season; congenial & informal atmosphere. Suite with whirlpool for 2.

STRASBURG

The Decoy	$$ B&B	Full breakfast
958 Eisenberger Rd., 17579	4 rooms, 4 pb	Sitting room
717-687-8585	•	library, A/C
Deborah & Hap Joy	C-yes/S-no/P-no/H-no	bicycles tours
All year		

Spectacular view; quiet rural location in Amish farm country. Former Amish home. Bike touring paradise. Two cats in residence!

WASHINGTON CROSSING

Woodhill Farms Inn
150 Glenwood Dr., 18977
215-493-1974
Don & MaryLou Spagnuolo
All year

$$ B&B
5 rooms, 5 pb
Visa, MC
C-6+/S-ltd/P-no/H-no
German

Full breakfast (weekend)
Continental plus (M-F)
Sitting room, piano
entertainment
use as small conf. ctr.

Nestled on ten wooded acres. Enjoy delicious breakfasts in rural, relaxing Bucks County. New York, Philadelphia, Princeton close by; New York—90 min.

WEST CHESTER

Bankhouse B&B
875 Hillsdale Rd., 19382
215-344-7388
Diana & Michael Bove
All year

$$ B&B
2 rooms

C-12+/S-no/P-no/H-no

Full breakfast
Snacks
Sitting room, porch
library
private entrances

Charming 18th-century "bankhouse" located across from a 10-acre horse farm. Convenient to Longwood Gardnes, Wynthertur, etc. Quiet country setting.

WILLIAMSPORT

The Reighard House
1323 E. 3rd St., 17701
717-326-3593
Susan L. Reighard
Exc. Christmas, New Year

$$ B&B
6 rooms, 6 pb
Visa, MC, AmEx, CD, CB
C-yes/S-no/P-no/H-no

Full breakfast
Afternoon tea
Comp. wine, beer, snacks
sitting room, library
club membership at YMCA

1905 stone and brick Victorian house; formal parlor, music room, formal dining room. Six large bedrooms with private baths, color TV, phone, carpeting, air conditioning.

WRIGHTSTOWN (BY NEW HOPE)

Hollileif B&B
677 Durham Rd., 18940
215-598-3100
Richard & Ellen Butkus
All year

$$$ B&B
4 rooms, 4 pb
Visa, MC •
C-ltd/S-no/P-no/H-no
some Spanish

Full gourmet breakfast
Comp. wine, refreshments
Afternoon tea, snacks
volleyball, croquet
badminton, horseshoes

Let us pamper you in our romantic 18th-century home; on 5.5 beautiful country acres; trees, gardens, stream; charming country furnishings; in lovely Bucks Country, PA.

WRIGHTSVILLE

Roundtop B&B
RD #2 Box 258, 17368
717-252-3169
Tyler Sloan
All year

$$ B&B
6 rooms, 1 pb
C-yes/S-yes/P-no/H-no

Full breakfast
Afternoon tea
Sitting room
library
hiking

Romantic 1880 stone home—unique setting—100 acres woodland, most spectacular view of Susquehanna River anywhere.

YORK

Briarwold B&B
RD 24, Box 462, 17406
717-252-4619
Marion Bischoff
All year

$$ B&B
3 rooms
•
C-yes/S-yes/P-no/H-no

Full breakfast
Comp. tea, coffee
Sitting room
library

1830s house of Colonial architecture, furnished with lovely antiques. 3 acres of grass and trees. Close to Amish country, Gettysburg, and many attractions. Hospitality plus.

YORK

Smyser-Bair House B&B	$$ B&B	Full breakfast
30 S. Beaver St., 17401	4 rooms, 1 pb	Afternoon tea
717-854-3411	C-7+/S-no/P-no/H-no	Large parlor, library
The King Family		player piano, A/C
All year		convenient parking

Magnificent Italianate Victorian townhouse in historic district. Antiques, warm hospitality, breakfasts made from nearby market produce. Near Lancaster and Gettysburg.

More Inns . . .

Abigail Adams B&B 1208 Walnut St., Philadelphia, 19107 215-893-9393
Alden House 62 E. Main St., Lititz, 17543 717-627-3363
Appleford Inn 218 Carlisle St., Gettysburg, 17325 717-337-1711
B&B of Valley Forge P.O. Box 562, Valley Forge, 19481 800-344-0123
Beach Lake Hotel P.O. Box 144, Beach Lake, 18405 717-729-8239
Behm's B&B 166 Waugh Ave., New Wilmington, 16142 412-946-8641
Bennett's B&B 1700 Pennsylvania Ave E, Warren, 16365 814-723-7358
Bethany Guest House 325 So. Main St., Cambridge Springs, 16403 814-398-2046
Bethlehem Inn 476 N. New St., Bethlehem, 18018 215-867-4985
Bianconi's B&B 727 East End Ave, Regent Square, 15221 412-731-2252
Bishop's Rocking Horse Inn 40 Hospital Road, Gettysburg, 17325 717-334-9530
Black Bass Hotel 3774 River Rd., Rt. 32, Lumberville, 18933 215-297-5770
Blue Lion inn 350 S. Market St., Selinsgrove, 17870 717-374-2929
Bluebird Hollow B&B RD 4, Box 217, Brookville, 15825 814-856-2858
Brandywine River Hotel P.O. Box 1058, Chadd's Ford, 19317 215-388-1200
Brenneman Farm—B&B RD 1, Box 310, Mount Joy, 17552 717-653-4213
Bridgeton House P.O. Box 167, Upper Black Eddy, 18972 215-982-5856
Brookpark Farm B&B 100 Reitz Blvd., Rt. 45, Lewisburg, 17837 717-524-7733
Brookview Manor B&B R.D. 1, Box 365, Canadensis, 18325 717-595-2451
Buck Hill Inn Buck Hill Falls, 18232 800-233-8113
Bucksville House R.D.2, Box 146, Kintnersville, 18930 215-847-8948
Buffalo Lodge R.D.1, Box 277, Buffalo Mills, 15534 814-623-2207
Buttonwood Farm 231 Pemberton Rd., Kennett Square, 19348 215-444-0278
Cameron Estate Inn RD 1, Box 305, Mount Joy, 17752 717-653-1773
Campbell House B&B 160 E. Doe Run Rd., Kennett Square, 19348 215-347-6756
Canadensis Old Village Inn P.O. Box 404, Canadensis, 18325 717-595-2120
Cedar Run Inn Cedar Run, 17727 717-353-6241
Century Inn S, Scenery Hill, 15360 412-945-6600
Chadds Ford Inn Rts. 1 & 100, Chadds Ford, 19317 215-388-1473
Cherry Mills Lodge Rt. 87 South, Rd#1, Wyomissing, 19610 717-928-8978
Clearview Farm B&B 355 Clearview Rd., Ephrata, 17522 717-733-6333
Cole's Log Cabin B&B RD 1, Box 98, Pine Bank, 15354 412-627-9151
Columbus Inn, The 400 Landmarks Bldg., Pittsburgh, 15219 412-471-5420
Conifer Ridge Farm RD 2, P.O. Box 202A, Clearville, 15535 814-784-3342
Country Road B&B HER 1, Box 9A, Grange R, Mount Pocono, 18344 717-839-9234
Country Spun Farm B&B P.O. Box 117, Loganville, 17342 717-428-1162
Cozy Comfort Inn 264 Baltimore St., Gettysburg, 17325 717-337-3997
Cranberry B&B Box 1009, Cranberry Township, 16033 412-776-1198
Crier In The Country Route 1, Glen Mills, 19342 215-358-2411
Crooked Windsor 409 S. Church St., West Chester, 19382 215-692-4896
Das Tannen-Lied Route 1, Jamestown, 16134 412-932-5029
Dilworthtown Inn Old Wilmington Pike, West Chester, 19382 215-399-1390
Dingeldein House 1105 E. King St., Lancaster, 17602 717-293-1723
Discoveries B&B RD #1, Box 42, Sigel, 15680 814-752-2632
Dobbin House Tavern Gettys 89 Steinwehr Ave., Gettysburg, 17325 717-334-2100
Donegal Mills Plantation Box 257, Mount Joy, 17552 717-653-2168
Duling Kurtz House 146 S. Whitford Rd., Exton, 19341 215-524-1830
Eagle Rock Lodge River Rd., Box 265, Shawnee-On-Delaware, 18356 717-421-2139

Eaglesmere RR 3, Box 2350, Malvern, 19355 215-296-9696
East Shore House P.O. Box 12, Beach Lake, 18405 717-729-8523
Emig Mansion Box 486, 3342 N.George, Emigsville, 17318 717-764-2226
Fairhaven RD 12 Box 445, Keller, York, 17406 717-252-3726
Fairville Inn Rt 52, Kennett Pk,Box 2, Mendenhall, 19357 215-388-5900
Fairway Farm Vaughan Rd., Pottstown, 19464 215-326-1315
Farm Fortune 204 Lime Kiln Rd., New Cumberland, 17070 717-774-2683
Fassitt Mansion 6051 Old Philadelphia, Gap, 17527 717-442-3139
Faunbrook B&B 699 W. Rosedale Ave., West Chester, 19382 215-436-5788
Fern Hall Box 1095, RD 1, Crystal, Carbondale, 18407 717-222-3676
Forge, The RD 1, Box 438, Pine Grove, 17963 717-345-8349
Franklin B&B 1501 Liberty St., Franklin, 16323 814-432-4208
Garrott's B&B RD 1, Box 73, Cowansville, 16218 412-545-2432
General Sutter Inn 14 E. Main St., Lititz, 17543 717-626-2115
Gerhart House B&B 287 Duke St., Ephrata, 17522 717-733-0263
Germantown B&B 5925 Wayne Ave., Philadelphia–Germantown, 19144 215-848-1375
Grandmaw's Place Bunk RD 2, Box 239, Benton, 17814 717-925-2630
Grant House B&B 244 W. Church St., Ligonier, 15658 412-238-5135
Green Gables B&B 2532 Willow St. Pike, Willow Street, 17584 717-464-5546
Greystone Box 280, Blue Ridge Summit, 17214 717-794-8816
Greystone, The P.O. Box 280, Blue Ridge Summit, 17214 717-794-8816
Groff Tourist Farm Home 766 Brackbill Rd., Kinzer, 17535 717-442-8223
Guest Home 1040 Lincoln Way, McKeesport, 15132 412-751-7143
Haag's Hotel Main St., Shartlesville, 19554 215-488-6692
Hacienda Inn 36 W. Mechanics St., New Hope, 18938 215-862-2078
Hackman's Country Inn 140 Hackman Rd., Ephrata, 17522 717-733-3498
Hawk Mountain Inn RD 1, Box 186, Kempton, 19529 215-756-4224
Heart of Somerset 130 W. Union St., Somerset, 15501 814-445-6782
Herb Cottage Inn Lincoln Hwy E., Rt. 30, Fayetteville, 17222 717-352-7733
Herr Farmhouse Inn 2256 Huber Dr., Manheim, 17545 717-653-9852
Herr Tavern Publick House 900 Chambersburg Rd., Gettysburg, 717-334-4332
Highland Manor B&B 855 Hillsdale Rd., West Chester, 19382 215-686-6251
Historic Cashtown Inn, The Old Route 30, Box 103, Cashtown, 17310 717-334-9722
Historic Fairfield Inn 15 W. Main St., Box 196, Fairfield, 17320 717-642-5410
Historic Gen. Sutter Inn 14 East Main St., Lititz, 17543 717-626-2115
Hollinger House B&B 2336 Hollinger Rd., Lancaster, 17602 717-464-3050
Holly Hedge Estate P.O. Box 213, Solebury, 18963 215-862-3136
Horetsky's Tourist Home 217 Cocoa Ave., Hershey, 17033 000-533-5783
Hotel La Reserve 1804 Pine St., Philadelphia, 19103 215-735-0582
Hunter House 118 S. Fifth St., Reading, 19602 215-374-6608
Huntland Farm B&B RD #9, Box 21, Greensburg, 15601 412-834-8483
Indian Mountain Inn B&B RD 1 Box 68, Brackney, 18812 717-663-2645
Inn at Centre Park 730 Centre Ave., Reading, 19601 215-374-8557
Inn at Mundis Mills RD 22, Box 15, York, 17402 717-755-2002
Inn at Phillips Mill North River Rd., New Hope, 18938 215-862-9919
Inn of Innisfree Box 108, Point Pleasant, 18950 215-297-8329
Inn on Fiddler's Tract Route 192 W., Lewisburg, 17837 717-523-7197
Jean Bonnet Tavern R.D.2, Box 724, Bedford, 15522 814-623-2250
Jefferson Inn RD 2, Box 36, Route 171, Thompson, 18465 717-727-2625
Jesse Robinson Manor 141 Main St., Wellsboro, 16901 717-724-5704
John Hayes House 8100 Limestone Rd., Oxford, 19363 215-932-5347
Kaltenbach's B&B Stony Ford Rd. 6, Wellsboro, 16901 717-724-4954
Kaufman House Box 183, Route 63, Sumneytown, 18084 215-234-4181
La Anna Guest House RD 2, Box 1051, Cresco, 18326 717-676-4225
Lafayette Inn, The 525 W. Monroe St., Easton, 215-253-4500
Lahaska Hotel Route 202, Lahaska, 18931 215-794-0440
Landyshade Farms 1801 Colebrook Rd., Lancaster, 17601 717-898-7689
Laurel Grove Inn Canadensis, 18325 717-595-7262
Lewisburg Hotel 136 Market St., Lewisburg, 19837 717-523-1216
Ligonier Country Inn P.O. Box 46, Rt. 30 E, Laughlintown, 15655 412-238-3651

Lime Valley Cottage 1107 Lime Valley Rd., Lancaster, 17602 717-687-6118
Limestone Inn B&B 33 E. Main St., Lancaster–Strasburg, 17579 717-687-8392
Line Limousin Farm Vac. 2070 Ritner Hwy, Carlisle, 17013 717-243-1281
Little House, The RD3, Box 341, Boyerton, 19512 215-689-4814
Log Cabin B&B Box 393, Rt. 11, Hallstead, 18822 717-879-4167
Logan Inn 10 W. Ferry St., New Hope, 18938 215-862-5134
Loom Room RD 1, Box 1420, Leesport, 19533 215-926-3217
Marshalton Inn Route 162, West Chester, 19380 215-692-4367
Meadowbrook School B&B 160 Engbert Rd., Johnstown, 15902 814-539-1756
Meadowview Guest House 2169 New Holland Pike, Lancaster, 17601 717-299-4017
Milheim Hotel Main St., Milheim, 16854 814-349-5994
Millstone Inn P.O. Box 279, Rt. 30, Schellsburg, 15559 814-733-4864
Mount Gretna Inn Kauffman at Pine, Mount Gretna, 17064 717-964-3234
Mountville Antiques B&B 407 E. Main St., Rt. 4, Mountville, 17554 717-285-5956
Nethercott Inn P.O. Box 26, Starrucca, 18462 717-727-2211
Nolt Farm Guest Home S. Jacob St. Farm, Mount Joy, 17552 717-653-4192
Noon-Collins Inn 114 East High St., Ebensburg, 15931 814-472-4311
Oakwood 235 Johnston Rd., Pittsburgh, 15241 412-835-9565
Overlook Inn RD 1, Box 680, Canadensis, 18325 717-595-7519
Pace One Glen Mills & Thornton, Thornton, 19373 215-459-3702
Pear & Patridge Inn Dept. NT Old Easton Rd., Doylestown, 18901 215-345-7800
Phillips 1890 House B&B 32 Eagle St., Greenville, 16125 412-588-4169
Pine Barn Inn #1 Pine Barn Pl., Danville, 17821 717-275-2071
Pine Tree Farm 2155 Lower State Rd., Doylestown, 18901 215-348-0632
Pine Wood Acres B&B Route 1, Box 634, Scottdale, 15683 412-887-5404
Pineapple Hill 1324 River Rd., New Hope, 18938 215-862-9608
Pinehurst Inn B&B 50 Northeast Dr., Hershey, 17033 717-533-2603
Point House P.O. Box 13, Waterville, 17776 717-753-8707
Rayba Acres Farm 183 Black Horse Rd., Paradise, 17562 717-687-6729
Riegelsville Hotel 10-12 Delaware Rd., Riegelsville, 18077 215-749-2469
River Inn, The 258 West Front St., Mariatta, 17547 717-426-2290
River's Edge Cafe B&B 203 Yough St., Confluence, 15424 814-395-5059
Rose Manor 124 S. Linden St., Manheim, 17545 717-664-4932
Salisbury House 910 E. Emmause Ave., Allentown, 18103 215-791-4225
Sevenoaks Farm B&B 492 New Galena Rd., Chalfont, 18914 215-822-2164
Sewickley B&B 222 Broad St., Sewickley, 15143 412-741-0107
Shady Elms Farm B&B Box 188, R.D.1, Hickory, 15340 412-356-7755
Shippen Way Inn 416-418 Bainbridge St., Philadelphia, 19147 215-627-7266
Smoketown Village Tourist 2495 Old Phila. Pike, Smoketown, 17576 717-393-5975
Sterling Inn Route 191, South Sterling, 18460 717-676-3311
Stranahan House 117 E. Market St., Mercer, 16137 412-662-4516
Strasburg Village Inn One W. Main St., Strasburg, 17579 717-687-0900
Sunbury Street B&B 310 E. Sunbury, Box 555, Millerstown, 17062 717-589-7932
Sunday's Mill Farm R.D.2, Box 419, Bernville, 19506 215-488-7821
Swinn's Lodging 31 E. Lincoln Ave., Gettysburg, 17325 717-334-5255
Tara 1 Bridgeton Hill, Upper Black Eddy, 18972 215-982-5457
Tavern Box 153, On the Square, New Wilmington, 16142 412-946-2020
Three Center Square Inn P.O. Box 428, Maytown, 17550 717-426-3036
Town House 201 S. Fairfield St., Ligonier, 15658 412-238-5451
Towne House Inn 138 Center St., Saint Marys, 15857 814-781-1556
Tressler House P.O. Box 38, New Bloomfield, 17068 717-582-2914
Twin Brook Inn Box 1042, RD 24, Kreut, York, 17409 717-757-5384
Twin Turrets Inn 11 E. Philadelphia Ave., Boyertown, 19512 215-367-4513
Tyler Hill B&B P.O. Box 62, Route 371, Tyler Hill, 18469 717-224-6418
Verdant View Farm 429 Strasburg Rd., Paradise, 17562 717-687-7353
Victorian Guest House 118 York Av., Towanda, 18848 717-265-6972
Vietersburg Inn B&B 1001 E. Main St., Berlin, 15530 814-267-3696
Village Guest House B&B 808 S. 2nd St., Philadelphia, 19147 215-755-9770
Villamayer 1027 East Lake Road, Jamestown, 16134 412-932-5194
Walnut Hill B&B 113 Walnut Hill Rd., Millersville, 17551 717-872-2283

Waltman's B&B RD 1, Box 87, New Albany, 18833 717-363-2295
White Cloud RD 1, Box 215, Newfoundland, 18445 717-676-3162
Windy Hill Bed & Breakfast Candy Rd, RD1, Box 1085, Mohnton, 19540 215-775-2755
Woodbury Inn Main St., Woodbury, 16695 814-766-3647
Woodward Inn Box 177, Woodward, 16882 814-349-8118
Wycombe Inn P.O. Box 204, Wycombe, 18980 215-598-7000
Wye Oak Farm Tourists RD #1, Box 152, Strasburg, 17579 717-687-6547
Yoder's B&B RD 1, Box 312, Huntingdon, 16652 814-643-3221

Puerto Rico

SAN JUAN

Arcade Inn Guest House
8 Taft St.—Condado, 00911
809-725-0668 809-728-7524
Aurelio & Renee Cinque
All year

$ EP
19 rooms, 18 pb
•
C-yes/S-yes/P-no/H-ltd
French, Italian, Spanish

Full breakfast $
Light lunch, bar,restrnt
Sitting room
sun deck

European-type guesthouse located in quiet area yet near everything, steps from beach. Owners are your hosts from arrival to departure.

Tres Palmas Guest House
2212 Park Blvd., 00913
Puntas Las Marias
809-727-4617 FAX:727-5434
Francis & Eileen Walsh
All year

$$ B&B
7 rooms, 5 pb
Visa, MC, AmEx •
C-ltd/S-ltd/P-no/H-no

Continental plus
refrigerators in rooms
Sitting room, cable TV
sun deck, tropical pool
beach, apartments avail.

Beachfront; casinos and gourmet restaurants five minutes away; airport and historic Old San Juan ten minutes. Daily maid service. Welcome drink on arrival.

More Inns . . .

Bananas Guesthouse P.O. Box 1300 Esperanza, Vieques, 00765 809-741-8700
Beach House 1957 Italia, Ocean Park, 00913 809-727-5482
Buena Vista by-the-Sea 2218 Gen.Del Valle, Ocean Park, Santurce, 00913 809-726-2796
Ceiba Country Inn P.O. Box 1067, Ceiba, 00635 809-885-0471
Duffys' Inn #9 Isla Verde Rd., Carolina, 00913 809-726-1415
El Canario Inn 1317 Ashford Ave., San Juan, 00907 809-722-3861
El Prado Inn 1350 Luchetti St., Condado, San Juan, 00907 809-728-5526
Green Isle Inn 36 Cale Uno—Villamar, San Juan, 00913 809-726-4330
Horned Dorset Primavera Ho Apartado 1132, Rincon, 00743 809-823-4030
Hosteria del Mar 5 Cervantes St., San Juan, 00907 809-724-8203
Hotel Caribe Playa HC 764 Buzon 8490, Patillas, 00723 809-839-6339
Jewel's by the Sea Seaview 1125-Condado, San Juan, 00907 809-725-5313
La Casa Mathiesen 14 Calle Uno, Villamar, Isla Verde, 00913 809-727-3223
La Casa del Frances Box 458, Esperanza, Vieques, 00765 809-741-3751
La Condesa Inn Cacique 2071, Ocean Park—Santurce, 00911 809-727-3698
La Playa 6 Amapola, Isla Verde, 00630 809-791-1115
Palmas del Mar P.O. Box 2020, Humacao, 00661 809-852-6000
Parador Hacienda Juanita Box 838, Maricao, 00706 809-838-2550
Parador Martorell P.O. Box 384, Luquillo, 00673 809-889-2710
Parador Oasis P.O. Box 144, San German, 00753 809-892-1175
Posada La Hamaca 68 Castelar St., Culebra, 00645 809-742-3516
Safari on the Beach Yardley Place #2, Ocean Park-San Juan, 00911 809-726-0445

San Antonio Guest House 1 Tapia, Ocean Park, San Juan, 00752 914-727-3302
Sea Gate Guest House Barriada Fuerts, Vieques, 00765 809-741-4661
Tamboo Resorts H-C 01 4433, Rincon, 00743 809-823-8550
Villa Boheme P.O. Box 218, Culebra Island, 00645 809-742-3508
Wind Chimes 53 Calle Taft, San Juan, 00911 809-727-4153

Rhode Island

BLOCK ISLAND

The 1661 Inn
P.O. Box I, Spring St., 02807
401-466-2421
R & S Draper, J & J Abrams
May–October

$$$ B&B
25 rooms, 16 pb
AmEx, Visa, MC •
C-3+/S-yes/P-no/H-yes

Full buffet breakfast
Lunch, dinner, full bar
Comp. brandy in room
ocean view deck
sitting room

Island country inn overlooking Atlantic Ocean—full buffet breakfast, wine & nibble hour, flaming coffees served on ocean view deck.

The Blue Dory Inn
Box 488, Dodge St., 02807
401-466-5891
Ann & Ed Loedy, Vin McAloon
All year

$$ B&B
13 rooms, 13 pb
Visa, MC, AmEx, DC •
C-10+/S-yes/P-no/H-ltd
Spanish, German

Continental plus
Sitting room
bicycles
ocean

Charming Victorian inn with Block Island's beautiful crescent beach at our back door. Antique furnishings. Walk to beach, shops, restaurants.

Hotel Manisses
P.O. Box I, 02807
401-466-2836 401-466-2421
J.& J. Abrams, R.& S. Draper
All year

$$ B&B
18 rooms, 18 pb
Visa, MC, Amex •
C-10+/S-yes/P-no/H-yes
Spanish, Portuguese

Full buffet breakfast
Lunch & dinner, full bar
Comp. wine, appetizers
elegant lobby, sitting
phones in all rooms

1872 Victorian hotel—fully restored—some rooms with jacuzzi. Gourmet dining, High Tea served daily. Seafood Raw Bar.

The Sheffield House
P.O. Box C-2, High St., 02807
401-466-2494
Claire & Steve McQueeny
All year

$$ B&B
7 rooms, 5 pb
Visa, MC, AmEx •
C-no/S-yes/P-no/H-yes

Continental plus
Comp. wine, snacks, tea
Bicycles & tennis nearby
beaches, hiking trails
bird sanctuaries, nature

1886 Victorian home in the historic district; walk to beach, shops, restaurants. Quiet, gracious home furnished in family antiques & collections. Breakfast in country kitchen.

CHARLESTOWN

General Stanton Inn
P.O. Box 222, 02813
4115 A Old Post Rd.
401-364-8888
Angelo & Janice Falcone
All year

$$ EP
16 rooms, 16 pb
Visa, MC, AmEx
C-yes/S-yes/P-no/H-yes

Full breakfast
Restaurant, bar
Brick ovens, fireplaces
hand hewn timbers

Real country inn. 5 minutes to beach. Fishing, boating, surfing, golfing, best beaches on the East coast. Large flea market.

CHARLESTOWN

Inn the Meadow
1045 Shannock Rd., 02813
401-789-1473
Yolanda & Michael Day
All year

$$ B&B
4 rooms
Visa, MC, Dis •
C-14+/S-no/P-no/H-no
German

Full breakfast
Afternoon tea, soda
Sitting room w/library
bicycles

Secluded country setting on five acres, yet nearby are beaches, Newport, Block Island ferry, Providence, and Mystic. A charming home base to enjoy much of New England.

MIDDLETOWN

The Country Goose
563 Greenend Ave., 02840
401-846-6308
Paula Kelley
All year

$$ B&B
3 rooms
Visa, MC
C-ask/S-yes/P-no/H-no

Continental
Wine & cheese on arrival
Sitting room, bicycles
large yard, volleyball
near tennis & beach

Country setting minutes from downtown Newport. Front porch furnished with wicker for comfortable relaxation. House decorated with family heirlooms and antiques.

MIDDLETOWN/NEWPORT

Lindsey's Guest House
6 James St., 02840
401-846-9386
Anne & Dave
All year

$ B&B
3 rooms
Visa, MC •
C-yes/H-yes

Continental plus
Sitting room
large yard, deck
ceiling fans in all rms

We are within a 10 min. walk to beaches and restaurants. One mile from Bellevue Ave. mansions. Two miles from downtown Newport harborfront. Off-street parking, large yard.

NARRAGANSETT

The Richards
144 Gibson Ave., 02882
401-789-7746
Nancy & Steven Richards
All year

$$ B&B
3 rooms, 2 pb
C-12+/S-no/P-no/H-no

Full gourmet breakfast
Comp. sherry in room
Library w/fireplace
tennis courts nearby
fireplaces in bedrooms

Gracious accommodations in a country setting. Awaken to the smell of gourmet coffee and freshly baked goods and then enjoy a refreshing walk to the beach.

Sea Gull Guest House
50 Narragansett Ave.,
02882 401-783-4636
Kimber Wheelock
All year

$ EP
5 rooms Visa, MC •
C-ltd/S-yes/P-no/H-no

Bar service
Ocean beach 1
block Tennis courts nearby

Large rooms cooled by ocean breezes. Close to everything. Swim, sun, sail and fish in comfort that you can afford.

White Rose B&B
22 Cedar Street, 02882
401-789-0181
Pat & Sylvan Vaicaitis
All year

$ B&B
4 rooms
C-8+/S-no/P-no/H-no
Some French & Spanish

Continental plus
Refrigerator, comp. wine
Sitting room with TV
bikes, 1 block to ocean
fishing, tennis nearby

A classic Victorian where the upbeat atmosphere is simple and elegant. Enjoy the breeze of the front porch or soak up the sun in our large yard.

Cliffside Inn, Newport, RI

NEWPORT

Bellevue House
14 Catherine St., 02840
401-847-1828
Joan & Vic Farmer
Late May–late October

$$ B&B
8 rooms, 6 pb
●
C-10+/S-no/P-no/H-no

Continental breakfast
Kitchen use 24 hours
Restaurant nearby
laundry, patio, parking
mid-week sail package

Centrally located on Historic Hill; easy walk to harbor front; mile to beach; combines Victorian charm, colonial history and nautical decor. Guest accommodations since 1828.

Brinley Victorian Inn
23 Brinley St., 02840
401-849-0271
Peter Carlisle
All year

$$ B&B
17 rooms, 12 pb
●
C-12+/S-yes/P-no/H-no

Continental breakfast
Wine & lobster dinner
Sitting room
landscaped courtyard
air conditioning

Romantic Victorian uniquely decorated with antiques, period wallpapers. Brick courtyard planted with Victorian garden flowers. Park & walk to historic sites and beaches.

Cliff View Cottage
4 Cliff Terrace, 02840
401-846-0885
Pauline & John Shea
May 1–November 1

$$ B&B
4 rooms, 2 pb
Visa, MC
C-yes/S-yes/P-no/H-no

Continental plus
Sitting room
piano

Two-story Victorian (circa 1871-1890). East side has view of Atlantic Ocean. Two porches, open sun deck. Walk to beach or Cliff Walk.

Cliffside Inn
2 Seaview Ave., 02840
401-847-1811
Annette King
May–October

$$$ B&B
10 rooms, 10 pb
Visa, MC ●
C-10+/S-yes/P-no/H-no

Continental breakfast
Afternoon ice tea
Guest living room
porch, piano
ceiling fans in rooms

Gracious, informal home furnished with antiques. Each room individually & tastefully decorated. Quiet home just off the Cliff Walk, 5-minute walk to beach.

The Melville House, Newport, RI

NARRAGANSETT

Harborside Inn
Christie's Landing, 02840
401-846-6600 800-421-3454
Mary Comforti
All year

$$ B&B
14 rooms, 14 pb
Visa, MC, AmEx, DC
C-yes/S-yes/P-no/H-no

Continental plus
Afternoon tea & mixers
Harbor Room
refrigerators, wet bars
TVs, decks

On Newport's historic waterfront, a new inn with each suite featuring a wet bar, refrigerator, color TV, sleeping loft, deck. Homebaked breads each morning.

Melville House
39 Clarke St., 02840
401-847-0640
Rita & Sam Rogers
March–December

$ B&B
7 rooms, 5 pb
Visa, MC, AmEx ●
C-12+/S-yes/P-no/H-no

Continental plus
Comp. sherry hour
Sitting room
library, bicycles
off-street parking

1750 colonial inn, heart of historic district, close to shops, restaurants, wharfs. Homemade granola, yogurt, and muffins for breakfast. National Register of Historic Places.

Merritt House Guests
57–2nd St., 02840
401-847-4289
Angela R. Vars
All year

$$ B&B
2 rooms, 1 pb

Full breakfast
Hot or iced tea
Sitting room
private dining room
patio, glider in yard

Historic home (circa 1850) in Point Section, two blocks from bay, 10 minutes from center of city, beaches & mansions. Nominated one of 100 Best B&B Homes in North America.

Pilgrim House Inn
123 Spring St., 02840
401-846-0040 800-525-8373
Mary Weaver Rose
All year

$$ B&B
10 rooms, 8 pb
Visa, MC
C-no/S-yes/P-no/H-no

Continental breakfast
Comp. sherry, shortbread
Deck
living room w/fireplace

Beautifully restored Victorian home in center of downtown historic district; magnificent rooftop deck with panoramic view of Newport Harbor.

380 Rhode Island

NEWPORT

Samuel Honey House
12 Francis St., 02840
401-847-2669
Roxy & Claire Ernsberger
All year

$$$ B&B
2 rooms
•
C-ask/S-yes/P-no/H-no

Continental plus
Sitting room
library

1873 Victorian summer cottage, in-town with easy access to harbor, beaches and mansions.

Villa Liberté
22 Liberty St., 02840
401-846-7444
Leigh Anne Mosco
All year exc. January

$$ B&B
15 rooms, 15 pb
Visa, MC •
C-yes/S-yes/P-no/H-no

Continental breakfast
Dinner, Tavern Fare
"Harpo's" Lounge, bar
sun deck, room service

Elegance with the intimacy of a guest house. Suites, rooms, apartments in a 1910 "House of the evening." Ideally located off Historic Bellevue Avenue in the heart of Newport.

The Willows of Newport
8 Willow St., 02840
Historic Point
401-846-5486
Pattie Murphy
February–January 3

$$$ B&B
5 rooms, 5 pb
C-no/S-ltd/P-no/H-no

Continental breakfast
Breakfast in bed
Victorian parlor
wet bar
yard

Elegant breakfast in bed—cut flowers, mints on your pillow. Private parking and private bath, air conditioning. Featured nationally on PM Magazine. (8/26/86)

PROVIDENCE

The Old Court B&B
144 Benefit St., 02903
401-751-2002
Jon Rosenblatt/Robert Shields
All year

$$$ B&B
10 rooms, 10 pb
Visa, MC, AmEx, Diners •
C-no/S-yes/P-no/H-no
French

Continental plus
Comp. tea, sitting room
Kitchen, washer/dryer
antiques, apt. available
wet bars in some rooms

Built in 1863, Italianate in design and in ornate details; combines tradition with contemporary standards of luxury; filled with antique furniture, chandeliers. Private baths.

SMITHFIELD

The Newport Collection
445 Putman Pike, 02828
800-947-4667
Annette King
May–October

$$$ B&B
10 rooms, 10 pb
Visa, MC •
C-10+/S-yes/P-no/H-no

Continental breakfast
Afternoon ice tea
Porch, piano
ceiling fans in rooms

Gracious, informal home furnished with antiques. Each room individually & tastefully decorated, alive with colors, a unique decor (and) lots of energy.

WAKEFIELD

The Larchwood Inn
521 Main St., 02879
401-783-5454
Francis & Diana Browning
All year

$ EP
19 rooms
Visa, MC, AmEx, DC, CB •
C-yes/S-yes/P-yes/H-no
Spanish, French

All meals available $
Restaurant, bar
Cocktail lounge
sitting room

Intimate country inn in New England townhouse style. Circa 1831. Conveniently located near Newport, Mystic Seaport, Block Island and Univ. of Rhode Island.

WESTERLY ───

Shelter Harbor Inn $$$ B&B   Full breakfast
10 Wagner Rd., Route 1, 02891   24 rooms, 24 pb   Lunch, dinner, bar
401-322-8883   Visa, MC, AmEx, DC •   Library, paddle tennis
Jim & Debbye Dey   C-yes/S-yes/P-no/H-no   hot tub, croquet court
All year   private beach, gardens

A charming country inn where the emphasis is on relaxation, superlative food, and a warm friendly atmosphere. Just a mile from the Rhode Island shore.

───

Woody Hill B&B $$ B&B   Full breakfast
330 Woody Hill Rd., 02891   3 rooms, 1 pb   Sitting room
401-322-0452   •   Extensive library
Ellen L. Madison   C-yes/S-no/P-no/H-ltd   porch with swing, pool
All year   winter hearth cooking

Near beaches and Mystic Seaport, yet secluded country atmosphere. Handmade quilts, antiques, wide-board floors, gardens, casual Colonial feeling.

WYOMING ───

The Cookie Jar B&B $$ B&B   Full breakfast
64 Kingston Rd., 02898   3 rooms, 1 pb   Snacks, sitting room
Route 138, just off I95   •   Library, 3 acres has
401-539-2680   C-yes/S-no/P-no/H-no   fruit trees, grape vines
Dick & Madelein Sohl   berries, grass & gardens
All year

A simple farmhouse on the outside, unusually attractive inside. Living room (1732) was a blacksmith shop and is almost in original condition. Swimming pool & golf nearby.

More Inns . . .

Aboard Commander's Quarter 54 Dixon St., Newport, 02840 401-849-8393
Admiral Benbow Inn 8 Fair St. (mailing), Newport, 02840 401-846-4256
Admiral Farragut Inn 31 Clarke St., Newport, 02840 401-846-4256
Admiral Fitzroy Inn 398 Thames St., Newport, 02840 401-846-4256
Andrea Hotel 89 Atlantic Ave., Misquamicut, 02891 401-348-8788
Anna's Victorian 5 Fowler Av., Newport, 02840 401-849-2489
Atlantic Inn Box 188, Block Island, 02807 401-466-2005
Ballyroreen 75 Stone Church Rd., Little Compton, 02837 401-635-4396
Barrington Inn P.O. Box 397, Block Island, 02807 401-466-5510
Blue Stone 33 Russell Ave., Newport, 02840 401-846-5408
Castle Keep 44 Everett, Newport, 02840 401-846-0362
Chestnut House 11 Chestnut St., Narragansett, 02882 401-789-5335
Cliff Walk Manor 82 Memorial Blvd, Newport, 02840 401-847-1300
Commodore Perry 8 Fair St., Newport, 02840 401-846-4256
Cornerstone Inn Route 1, Westerly, 02891 401-322-3020
Covell Guest House 43 Farewell St., Newport, 02840 401-847-8872
Driftwind Guests High St., Block Island, 02807 401-466-5548
Duck Harbor 295 Boston Neck Rd., Narragansett, 02882 401-783-3495
Elm Tree Cottage 336 Gibbs Av., Newport, 02840 401-849-1610
Fairfield-by-The-Sea B&B 527 Green Hill Beach Rd, Green Hill, 02879 401-789-4717
Finnegan's Inn at Shadow L 120 Miantonomi Ave., Middletown, 02840 401-847-0902
Francis Malbone House, The 392 Thames St, Newport, 02840 401-846-0392
Gables Inn P.O. Box 516, Block Island, 02807 401-466-2213
Going My Way 75 Kingstown Rd., Narragansett, 02882 401-789-3479
Gothic Inn P.O. Box 458, Block Island, 02807 401-466-2918
Grandview B&B 275 Shore Rd., Westerly, 02891 401-596-6384
Guest House P.O. Box 24, Center Rd., Block Island, 02807 401-466-2676
Guest House International 28 Weaver Ave., Newport, 02840 401-847-1501
Hedgerow B&B 1747 Mooresfield Rd., Kingston, 02881 401-783-2671

House of Snee 191 Ocean Rd., Narragansett, 02882 401-783-9494
Hydrangea House 16 Bellevue Ave, Newport, 02840 401-846-4435
Ilverthorpe Cottage 41 Robinson St., Narragansett, 02882 401-789-2392
Inn at Castle Hill Ocean Dr., Newport, 02840 401-849-3800
Inn at Old Beach 19 Old Beach Rd., Newport, 02840 401-849-3479
Inn at Watch Hill Bay St., Watch Hill, 02891 401-596-0665
Inn of Jonathan Bowen 29 Pelham St., Newport, 02840 401-846-3324
Inn on the Hill 29 Summer St., Westerly, 02891 401-596-3791
Inntowne 6 Mary St., Newport, 02840 401-846-9200
Island Manor Resort Chapel St., Block Island, 02807 401-466-5567
J. Livingston's Guesthouse 39 Weekapang Rd., Westerly, 02891 401-322-0249
Jailhouse Inn 13 Marlborough St., Newport, 02840 401-847-4638
John Banister House 56 Pelham St., Newport, 02840 401-846-0050
Joseph Reynolds House 956 Hope St., Bristol, 02809 401-254-0230
Kenyon Farms P.O. Box 648, Narragansett, 02882 401-783-7123
King Tom Farm P.O. Box 1440, Charlestown, 02807 401-364-3371
La Forge cottage 96 Pelham St., Newport, 02840 401-847-4400
Ma Gallagher's 348 Thames St., Newport, 02840 401-849-3975
Mary W. Murphy 59 Walcott Ave., Jamestown, 02835 401-423-1338
Mill Pond Cottages Old Town Rd., Block Island, 02807 401-466-2423
Mill Street Inn 75 Mill St., Newport, 02840 401-849-9500
Mon Reve 41 Gibson Ave., Narragansett, 02882 401-783-2846
Murphy's B&B 43 South Pier Road, Narragansett, 02882 401-789-1824
Narragansett Pier Inn 7 Prospect Ave., Narragansett, 02882 401-783-8090
New Shoreham House Inn P.O. Box 356, Block Island, 02807 401-466-2651
Nordic Lodge Pasquiset Pond Rd., Kenyon, 02836 401-783-4515
Ocean Cliff Ocean Dr., Newport, 02840 401-849-9000
Ocean House 2 Bluff Ave, Watch Hill, 02891 401-348-8161
Ocean View Atlantic Ave., Misquamicut Beach, 02891 401-596-7170
Old Dennis House 59 Washingon St., Newport, 02840 401-846-1324
Old Town Inn Old Town Rd, P.O. Box 3, Block Island, 02807 401-466-5958
One Bliss One Bliss Rd., Newport, 02840 401-846-5329
Open Gate Motel 840 Quaker Lane, Warwick, 02886 401-884-4490
Peckham's Guest Home 272 Paradise Av., Middletown, 02840 401-846-2382
Phoenix House 29 Gibson Ave., Narragansett, 02882 401-783-1918
Pier House Inn 113 Ocean Rd., Narragansett, 02882 401-783-4704
Queen Anne Inn 16 Clarke St., Newport, 02840 401-846-5676
Rhode Island House 77 Rhode Island Ave., Newport, 02840 401-849-7765
Rose Farm Inn Roselyn Rd., Block Island, 02807 401-466-2021
Sea Breeze Inn Spring St., Box 141, Block Island, 02807 401-466-2275
Sea Quest 9 Cliff Terrace, Newport, 02840 401-846-0227
Seacrest Inn 207 High St., Block Island, 02807 401-466-2882
Seven Granite St. B&B 7 Granite St., Westerly, 02891 401-596-6384
Southwest Wind Acres 8 Lindsley Rd., Narragansett, 02882 401-783-5860
Sparrow's Nest 470 Annaquatucket Rd., Wickford, 02852 401-295-1142
Spring Street Inn 353 Spring St., Newport, 02840 401-847-4767
State House Inn 43 Jewett St, Providence, 02908 401-785-1235
Stone Bridge Inn 1 Lawton Ave., Tiverton, 02878 401-624-6601
Stone Lea 40 Newton Ave., Narragansett, 02882 401-783-9546
Sunset Cabins 1172 W. Main Rd., Portsmouth, 02871 401-683-1874
Thames Street Inn 400 Thames St., Newport, 02840 401-847-4459
Victorian Ladies, The 63 Memorial Blvd., Newport, 02840 401-849-9960
Watch Hill Inn 50 Bay Street, Watch Hill, 02891 401-348-8912
Wayside 406 Bellevue Ave., Newport, 02840 401-847-0302
Weekapaug Inn Weekapaug, 02891 401-322-0301
Whimsey Cottage 42 Briarwood Ave, Middletown, 02840 401-841-5824
William Fludder House 30 Bellevue Ave., Newport, 02840 401-849-4220
Willow Grove P.O. Box 156, Block Island, 02807 401-466-2896
Windswept Farm Inn Rt. 1, Post Rd, Box 154, Charlestown, 02807 401-364-6292

South Carolina

BEAUFORT ──────────────────────────────────

Bay Street Inn	$$$ B&B	Full breakfast
601 Bay St., 29902	6 rooms, 6 pb	Sherry, fruit, chocolate
803-524-7720	Visa, MC ●	Library, bicycles
Gene & Kathleen Roe	C-yes/S-yes/P-no/H-no	air conditioned
All year	French	

Antebellum cotton planter's home furnished with antiques; beautiful water views and fireplaces in every room; beaches, restaurants, golf and tennis nearby.

Old Point Inn	$$ B&B	Continental plus
212 New St., 29902	4 rooms, 4 pb	Comp. wine
803-524-3177	Visa, MC, AmEx	Sitting room
Joe & Joan Carpentiere	C-yes/S-ltd	verandas
All year		

1898 Victorian with double verandas and hammock. Downtown historic residential district. River views. Delicious homemade breakfast breads. Relaxed, comfortable, friendly.

The Rhett House Inn	$$$ B&B	Full breakfast
1009 Craven St., 29902	8 rooms, 8 pb	Comp. sherry in rooms
803-524-9030	Visa, MC ●	Sitting room, library
Marianne & Stephen Harrison	C-5+/S-no/P-no/H-no	landscaped gardens
All year	Spanish	phones in room, A/C

Restored, historic antebellum mansion. Beautifully landscaped gardens. Courtyard with fountain. Walking distance to everything. Enjoy hammocks on a wide veranda.

Trescot Inn	$$ B&B	Continental breakfast
500 Washington St., 29902	6 rooms, 6 pb	Comp. sherry in room
803-522-8552	Visa, MC, AmEx	Sitting room
JoAnne Mitchell	C-12+/S-ltd/P-no/H-no	bicycles
All year		perfumed soaps

Old plantation home retains charm and hospitality of Old South while providing all modern conveniences.

TwoSuns Inn	$$$ B&B	Full breakfast
1705 Bay St., 29902	5 rooms, 5 pb	Aftn. tea, comp. wine
803-522-1122	Visa, MC, AmEx ●	Sitting room, bicycles
Carrol and Ron Kay	C-12+/S-no/P-no/H-yes	public tennis courts
All year		computer, fax, cable TV

Enjoy the bay from our veranda, explore the charm of Historic Beaufort (founded in 1711) and relax with gracious hospitality. Handwoven items available from Carrol.

CHARLESTON ──────────────────────────────────

1837 B&B & Tearoom	$$ B&B	Full gourmet breakfast
126 Wentworth St., 29401	8 rooms, 8 pb	Beer or wine avail. ($)
803-723-7166	C-ask/S-no/P-no/H-no	Comp. mint tea or coffee
Sherri Weaver, Richard Dunn	French	verandas, rocking chairs
All year		formal dining room

Gracious southern home in historic Charleston. Breakfast in the formal dining room is festive; everyone visits & enjoys each other. Convenient to plantations and Fort Sumter.

CHARLESTON

Ann Harper's B&B
56 Smith St., 29401
803-723-3947
Ann D. Harper
All year

$$ B&B
2 rooms, 1 pb
C-10+/S-ltd/P-no/H-no

Full breakfast
Small garden
off-street parking

Charming circa 1870 home located in Charleston's historic district. The owner, a retired medical technologist, enjoys serving a full Southern breakfast each morning.

Ansonborough Inn
21 Hasell St., 29401
803-723-1655 800-522-2073
Allen B. Johnson
All year

$$$ B&B
37 rooms, 37 pb
Visa, MC, AmEx ●
C-yes/S-yes/H-yes
Spanish, French

Continental plus
Comp. wine, snacks
Bar, sitting room
golf & tennis nearby
nonsmoking rooms avail.

Circa 1900 warehouse renovated and furnished in 19th-century traditional Charleston decor. All suite inn with full kitchens and private baths in suites. Conference facilities.

The Barksdale House Inn
27 George St., 29401
803-577-4800
George & Peggy Sloan
All year exc. Christmas

$$$ B&B
10 rooms, 10 pb
Visa, MC ●
C-ltd/S-yes/P-no/H-no

Continental breakfast
Comp. tea, wine
Sitting room
whirlpool baths, decks
bicycle rental

Circa 1778, elegant inn with whirlpool baths, fireplaces, built-in dry bars, elaborate furnishings and antiques; adjacent to the historic shopping district.

The Belvedere
40 Rutledge Ave., 29401
803-722-0973
Jim Spell, Fran Oniffith
All year

$$$ B&B
3 rooms, 3 pb
C-12+/S-yes/P-no/H-no

Continental breakfast
Sherry
Sitting room, newspaper
TV, A/C, bicycles
porch with lake view

We offer hospitable accommodations in our gracious mansion overlooking beautiful Colonial Lake. We provide bicycles, sherry and other extras.

Cannonboro Inn B&B
184 Ashley Ave., 29403
803-723-8572
Sally & Bud Allen
All year

$$ B&B
6 rooms, 6 pb
Visa, MC ●
C-yes/S-no/P-no/H-no

Full breakfast
Comp. wine
Sitting room, library
garden, bicycles
tennis court

Antebellum home c.1850 in Charleston's historic district. Enjoy a full breakfast served on a circular piazza overlooking a low country garden. All rooms have fireplaces.

Country Victorian B&B
105 Tradd St., 29401
803-577-0682
Diane Deardurff Weed
All year

$$ B&B
2 rooms, 2 pb
●
C-yes/S-no/P-no/H-no

Continental plus
Afternoon tea, snacks
Parking, bicycles
TV, restaurants nearby
piazzas

Private entrances, antique iron and brass beds, old quilts, antique oak and wicker furniture. Situated in the historic district. Walk to everything. Many extras.

Cannonboro Inn, Charleston, SC

CHARLESTON

The Hayne House
30 King St., 29401
803-577-2633
Ben Chapman
All year

$$$ B&B
3 rooms, 3 pb
C-yes/S-ltd/P-no/H-no

Continental plus
Comp. tea
Sitting room, library
piano, bicycles
porch with rockers

Fourth generation family home (1770/1840) in heart of residential historic district. Walking distance of downtown. Furnished with antiques. No TV, but lots of good books.

Indigo Inn
One Maiden Lane, 29401
8 Cumberland St.
803-577-5900 800-845-7639
Larry Deery
All year

$$$ B&B
40 rooms, 40 pb
Visa, MC, AmEx ●
C-yes/S-yes/P-ltd/H-yes

Continental plus
Comp. wine, snacks
Afternoon tea
sitting room, library
bicycles, hot tubs

Luxurious Old South charm furnished in 18th-century antiques and reproductions; lush open-air courtyard. Near open-air market, churches, mansions, restaurants. AAA 4-Diamond.

Jasmine House
8 Cumberland, 29401
64 Hasell St.
803-577-5900 800-845-7639
Larry Deery
All year

$$$ B&B
8 rooms, 8 pb
Visa, MC, AmEx ●
C-12+/S-yes/P-no/H-no

Continental breakfast
Aftn. tea, comp. wine
Concierge, bar
courtyard, jacuzzi
tennis and golf nearby

1840s antebellum mansion and carriage house. Canopied beds, fireplaces, lush courtyard and jacuzzi in the heart of historic Market District.

CHARLESTON ————————————————————————————————————

John Rutledge House Inn
116 Broad St., 29401
803-723-7999 800-476-9741
Linda Bishop
All year

$$$ B&B
19 rooms, 19 pb
Visa, MC, AmEx •
C-yes/S-ltd/P-no/H-yes

Continental plus
Comp. wine/brandy/sherry
Bar, sitting room
hot tubs, concierge
turndown service

John Rutledge, one of the signers of US Constitution, built this elegant home in 1763. Now you can visit and relive history. Downtown location near shopping & historic sites.

King George IV Inn
32 George St., 29401
803-723-9339 803-722-7551
Jean, B.J., Mike
All year

$ B&B
8 rooms, 8 pb
Visa, MC •
C-yes/S-no/P-ask/H-ltd

Continental breakfast
Comp. coffees & teas
Three levels of porches
parking, refrigerators
A/C, TV, television

Circa 1790s Federal-style old Charleston home. Lovely wide-planked hardwood floors, original six-ft. oak doors, 10-ft. ceilings. Short walk to King St. shopping & restaurants.

Kings Courtyard Inn
198 King Street, 29401
803-723-7000 800-845-6119
Laura Fox Howard
All year

$$$ B&B
58 rooms, 58 pb
Visa, MC, AmEx •
C-yes/S-yes/P-no/H-yes

Continental plus
Comp. wine/sherry/brandy
Sitting room
hot tub, bicycles
free parking

1853 historic inn, rooms with period furnishings, canopied beds, fireplaces, overlook two inner courtyards. Concierge service, evening turndown with brandy and chocolate.

Kitchen House (c 1732)
126 Tradd St., 29401
803-577-6362
Lois Evans
All year

$$$ B&B
3 rooms, 3 pb
Visa, MC •
C-yes/S-yes/P-no/H-no

Full breakfast
Kitchen, afternoon tea
Complimentary sherry
sitting room, cable TV
concierge service

Deluxe, restored pre-Revolutionary house in the heart of the historic district with patio & herb garden. Featured in Colonial Homes Magazine.

Maison Du Pre
317 E. Bay St., 29401
at George St.
803-723-8691 800-662-INNS
Lucille/Bob/Mark Mulholland
All year

$$$ B&B
15 rooms, 15 pb
Visa, MC, AmEx •
C-yes/S-yes/P-no/H-no

Continental breakfast
Low country tea party
(wine, hors d'oeuvres)
drawing room
porch, patio, bicycles

Ideally located in Charleston's historic district. 15 guest rooms with private baths. Antiques, carriage rides. Honeymoon suites, kitchen suites, executive suites.

Queen Victoria Inn
208 King St., 29401
803-720-2944 800-933-5464
Richard Widman
All year

$$$ B&B
16 rooms, 16 pb
Visa, MC, AmEx •
C-yes/S-ltd/P-no/H-yes

Continental plus
Bar service
some hot tubs

Victorian inn built in 1889. Document wallpapers and paint colors. Furnished with antiques and historically accurate reproductions. Located in a historic district.

CHARLESTON

Rutledge Victorian Inn
114 Rutledge Ave., 29401
803-722-7551
BJ, Jean, Mike
All year

$ EP/B&B
11 rooms
MC, Visa
C-yes/S-ltd

Continental breakfast
24-hour refrshmnt. table
Porch with rocking chair
TV, A/C, refrigerator
parking, student rates

Century-old Victorian house in Charleston's historic district. Rooms quaint, antique decor. Beautiful porch. Reasonable rates for historic district. Near all sightseeing.

Two Meeting Street Inn
2 Meeting St., 29401
Battery Park
803-723-7322
Karen M. SpellAll year

$$$ B&B
9 rooms, 9 pb
C-8+/S-ltd/P-no/H-no

Continental breakfast
eve. sherry on porch
honeymoon suites
formal Southern garden
overlooking harbor

Given as a wedding gift in 1890, this Queen Anne mansion epitomizes Southern grace and hospitality. Guests enjoy luxury with Tiffany windows, Oriental rugs, English antiques.

Villa de La Fontaine B&B
138 Wentworth St., 29401
803-577-7709
Aubrey Hancock, Bill Fontaine
All year

$$$ B&B
6 rooms, 6 pb
Visa, MC, AmEx ●
C-9+

Full breakfast
Canopy beds
Garden, terraces
tennis nearby
off-street parking

Southern colonial mansion, circa 1838, in historic district; half-acre garden; fountain and terraces. Furnished with 18th-century museum pieces. Walk to places of interest.

COLUMBIA

Claussen's Inn
2003 Greene St., 29205
803-765-0440 800-622-3382
Dan Vance
All year

$$$ B&B
29 rooms, 29 pb
●
C-yes/S-yes/P-no/H-yes

Continental plus
Comp. wine/sherry/brandy
Morning paper
turn-down service with
chocolate & brandy

Restored old bakery building close to the university, shops, dining, entertainment. Some rooms have kitchenettes.

GEORGETOWN

Ashfield Manor
3030 S. Island Rd., 29440
803-546-5111 803-546-0464
Dave & Carol Ashenfelder
All year

$ B&B
4 rooms
Visa, MC, AmEx, Disc
C-yes/S-no/P-no/H-no

Continental plus
Afternoon tea, lemonade
Sitting room

An elegant country setting. Breakfast is served in your room, the parlor, or on our 57-foot screened porch, complete with rocking chairs, overlooking our lake.

Shaw House
8 Cyprus Court, 29440
803-546-9663
Mary Shaw
All year

$ B&B
3 rooms, 3 pb
●
C-yes/S-yes/P-no/H-ltd

Full breakfast
Comp. wine, tea, coffee
Sitting room
piano
bicycles

Spacious rooms furnished with antiques. Bird-watching from glassed-in den overlooking Willowbank Marsh. Walk to Historic District. Hostess loves pleasing her guests.

LITTLE RIVER

Stella's Guest Home
P.O. Box 564, 29566
803-249-1871
Stella McLamb
All year

$ EP
4 rooms, 4 pb
C-no/S-yes/P-no/H-no

Full breakfast $
Dinner
Sitting room, piano

Old-fashioned Southern hospitality and elegance. Rooms have private entrance and color TV. Special Southern breakfast.

McCLELLANVILLE

Laurel Hill Plantation
P.O. Box 190, 29458
8913 N. Hwy 17
803-887-3708
Jackie & Lee Morrison
All year

$$$ B&B
4 rooms, 4 pb
C-6+/S-ltd/P-no/H-no

Full breakfast
Comp. wine, snacks
Sitting room
fishing boat trip
freshwater fish pond

Located with a fantastic waterfront view of Cape Romain and the Atlantic Ocean, this 1850s plantation home is furnished with country antiques.

MYRTLE BEACH

Serendipity, an Inn
407 N. 71st Ave., 29572
803-449-5268
Cos & Ellen Ficarra
March–November

$$ B&B ·
15 rooms, 15 pb
Visa, MC, AmEx ●
C-yes/S-ltd/P-no/H-no
Spanish, Italian

Continental plus
Sitting room, patio
Heated pool, bicycles
color TV & A/C in rooms
garden room, grill

Lovely Spanish mission style, surrounded by lush tropical vegetation. Winners of Myrtle Beach "Keep America Beautiful" Award. Two blocks to ocean. Daily maid service.

PENDLETON

Liberty Hall Inn
Business Hwy 28, 29670
803-646-7500
Tom & Susan Jonas
All year

$$ B&B
10 rooms, 10 pb
Visa, MC, AmEx, DC, Dis
C-ltd/S-ltd/P-no/H-no

Continental plus
Dinner, bar

Lodge and dine in this classic 1840 Piedmont home, authentically restored, furnished in period antiques. In charming Pendleton National Historic District.

SPARTANBURG

Nicholls-Crook Plantation
P.O. Box 5812, 29304
Plantation Dr.
803-583-7337
Suzanne & Jim Brown
All year

$$ B&B
3 rooms, 1 pb
●
C-ltd/S-no/P-ltd/H-no
French, Spanish, German

Full breakfast
Dinner by reservation
Comp. sherry
sitting room, AC
fireplaces

Join us in our authentically restored, rare 18th-century plantation house, on National Register. Tranquil country setting, near I-26 and I-85.

SUMTER

Sumter B&B
6 Park Avenue, 29150
803-773-2903
Bob & Merilyn Carnes
All year

$$ B&B
4 rooms, 2 pb
Visa, MC, Dis
C-yes/S-no/P-no/H-no

Continental plus
Complimentary wine
Sitting room, library
HBO, tennis court
tours & golf available

Historic District—1896 home; large front porch facing lush, green, quiet park; spacious fire-placed rooms, antiques, ancient artifacts, spinning wheel demonstration.

More Inns ...

1790 House 630 Highmarket St., Georgetown, 29440 803-546-4821
Almost Home B&B 1236 Oceanview Rd., James Island, 29412 803-795-8705
Annie's Inn P.O. Box 311, Montmorenci, 29839 803-649-6836
Battery Carriage House 20 S. Battery, Charleston, 29401 803-723-9881
Belmont Inn 106 E. Pickens St., Abbeville, 29620 803-459-9625
Cedars Inn 1325 Williston Rd., Beech Island, 29841 803-827-0248
Coosaw Plantation Dale, 29914 803-846-8225
Cox House Inn P.O. Box 486, Johnston, 29832 803-275-4552
Croft Magnolia Inn 414 Cassua St., Darlington, 29532 803-393-1908
Elliott House Inn 78 Queen St., Charleston, 29401 803-723-1855
Evergreen Inn 1109 South Main St., Anderson, 29621 803-225-1109
Fair Oaks 1308 Fair St., Camden, 29020 803-432-1499
Five Thirty Prince St. B&B 530 Prince St., Georgetown, 29440 803-527-1114
Fripp House Inn P.O. Box 857, Bridge St, Bluffton, 29910 803-757-2139
Gadsden Manor Inn Box 1710, Summerville, 29484 803-875-1710
Guilds Inn 101 Pitt St., Mount Pleasant, 29464 803-881-0510
Halcyon Harbormaster 604, Hilton Head Island, 29928 803-785-7912
Holland's Guest House 15 New St., Charleston, 29401 803-723-0090
Holley Inn 235 Richland Ave.,W., Aiken, 29801 803-648-4265
Hollie Berries Inn 1560 Powderhouse Rd. S., Aiken, 29801 803-648-9952
Holly Hill Route 1, Box 223, Landrum, 29356 803-457-4010
Inn on Broad 1308/10 Broad St., Camden, 29020 803-425-1806
John Lawton House 159 3rd St. E, Estill, 29918 803-625-3240
Lodge Alley Inn 195 E. Bay St., Charleston, 29401 800-845-1004
Magnolia Grove B&B 201 Holliday Dr., Manning, 29102 803-435-4722
Middleton Inn Ashley River Rd., Charleston, 29411 803-556-0500
New-Berry Inn B&B 240 New Berry St. SW, Aiken, 29801 803-649-2935
Palmer Home 87 Wentworth St., Charleston, 29401 803-723-1574
Palmettos P.O. Box 706, Sullivan's Island, 29482 803-883-3389
Pine Knoll Inn 305 Lancaster St. SW, Aiken, 29801 803-649-5939
Planters Inn 112 N. Market St., Charleston, 29401 803-722-2345
Spears B&B 501 Kershaw St., Cheraw, 29520 803-537-7733
Sword Gate Inn 111 Tradd St., Charleston, 29401 803-723-8518
Twelve Oaks Inn P.O. Box 4126, Beaufort, 29902 803-525-1371
Vendue Inn 19 Vendue Range, Charleston, 29401 803-577-7970
Webster's Manor 115 E. James St., Mullins, 29574 803-464-9632
Willcox Inn, The 100 Colleton Ave., Aiken, 29801 803-649-1377

South Dakota

CANOVA

Skoglund Farm	$$ MAP	Full breakfast
Route 1, Box 45, 57321	6 rooms	Dinner included
605-247-3445	●	Sitting room, piano
Alden & Delores Skoglund	C-yes/S-ltd/P-yes/H-no	bicycles, horses
All year	Swedish	

Enjoy overnight on the South Dakota prairie. Return to your childhood, get away from it all at our farm—animals, horseback riding, country walking, home-cooked meals.

CUSTER

Custer Mansion B&B
35 Centennial Dr., 57730
605-673-3333
Mill & Carole Seaman
All year

$ B&B
5 rooms, 2 pb
C-6+/S-no/P-no/H-no
Spanish

Full breakfast
Restaurant, aftn. tea
Sitting room, bicycles
tennis, golf nearby
hiking in Black Hills

Historic 1891 Victorian home on 1 acre. Beautifully restored offering Western hospitality & delicious, home-baked food. All in the unique setting of the majestic Black Hills.

INTERIOR

Prairie's Edge B&B
P.O. Box 11, 57750
605-433-5441 605-456-2836
Robert & Sheryl Trohkimoinen
June–August

3 rooms
C-4+/S-ltd/P-no

Full breakfast
Comp. tea & goodies
Full-sized beds
a variety of wildlife

Inn on banks of White River with prairie stretching west and majestic Badland buttes a short hike away; 1940s style; full-sized beds. A photographer's and artist's paradise!

RAPID CITY

Audrie's Cranbury Corner
RR 8, Box 2400, 57702
605-342-7788
Hank & Audry Kuhnhauser
All year

$$$ B&B
3 rooms, 3 pb
C-no/S-no/P-no/H-no

Full breakfast
Comp. wine, snacks
Restaurant nearby
trout fishing, hiking
bicycles, hot tubs

Each quiet room has a private patio, entrance, bath and spa. A full breakfast is served in your room.

WEBSTER

Lakeside Farm B&B
RR 2, Box 52, 57274
605-486-4430
Glenn & Joy Hagen
All year

$ B&B
2 rooms
C-yes/S-no/P-no/H-no

Full breakfast
Other meals possible
Comp. coffee, tea, snack
sitting room, bicycles
piano

Sample a bit of country life with us. A family-owned/operated dairy farm. Northeastern South Dakota lakes area. Fresh air. Open spaces. Fresh milk. Homemade cinnamon rolls.

YANKTON

Mulberry Inn
512 Mulberry St., 57078
605-665-7116
Millie Cameron
All year

$ B&B
6 rooms, 2 pb
Visa, MC
C-yes/S-yes/P-ltd

Continental breakfast
Full breakfast $
Comp. wine, snacks
parlors, fireplaces
porch, parlors

Built in 1873. Beautiful hand-carved door, high ceilings and marble fireplaces. Very warm and homey with a quiet atmosphere. Missouri River offers boating, fishing, parks.

More Inns ...

Adams House 22 Van Buren, Deadwood, 57732 605-578-3877
B&B H-D Lodge RR 8, Box 3360, Rapid City, 57702 605-341-7580
B&B Inn Box 154, Keystone, 57751 605-666-4490
Bavarian Inn P.O. Box 152, Custer, 57730 605-673-2802
Black Forest Inn HC 33, Box 3123, Rapid City, 57702 605-574-2000
Cascade Ranch B&B P.O. Box 461, Hot Springs, 57747 605-745-3397
Cheyenne Crossing B&B HC 37, Box 1220, Lead, 57754 605-584-3510
Christensen's Country Home 432 Hillsview, Spearfish, 57783 605-642-2859
Cow Creek Lodge HCR 37, Box 134, Pierre, 57501 605-264-5450
Cross Roads Inn Box 970, Jct. Hwy 18/73, Martin, 57551 605-685-1070
Elk Haven Resort Hwy 16A, Box 717K, Keystone, 57751 605-666-4856

Fitch Farms Box 8, Milesville, 57553 605-544-3227
Flying Horse B&B 630—8th St., Spearfish, 57783 605-642-1633
Harer Lodge & B&B Route 1, Box 87A, Gettysburg, 57442 605-765-2167
Heart of the Hills B&B 517 Main St., Hill City, 57745 605-574-2704
Hidden Fortune B&B Box 748, Custer, 57730 605-666-4744
Hillside Country Cottages HC 33, Box 1901, Rapid City, 57702 605-342-4121
Homestead, The Box 635, Hill City, 57745 605-574-4226
Kelly Inn 540 E. Jackson, Spearfish, 57783 605-642-7795
Landmark Country Inn HCR 77, Box 2, Murdo, 57559 605-669-2846
Luxury Lodge P.O. Box 437, Spearfish, 57783 605-642-2728
Palmer Gulch Lodge Box 295 V, Hill City, 57745 605-574-2525
Pine Crest Inn 4501 W. 12th St., Sioux Falls, 57106 605-336-3530
Pine Rest Cabins P.O. Box 377, Hill City, 57745 605-574-2416
Riverview Ridge B&B HC 69, Box 82A, Chamberlain, 57325 605-734-6084
Robins Roost Cabins HCR 87, Box 62, Hill City, 57745 605-574-2252
Rock Crest Lodge P.O. Box 687, Custer, 57730 605-673-4323
Roghair Herefords B&B HCR 74 Box 16, Okaton, 57562 605-669-2529
Spring Creek Resort 610 N. Jackson, Pierre, 57501 605-224-8336
State Game Lodge Custer, 57730 605-255-4541
Sylvan Lake Lodge Box 752, Custer, 57730 605-574-2561
Thorson's Homestead HCR 2 Box 100, Philip, 57567 605-859-2120
Triple R Dude Ranch Box 124, Keystone, 57751 605-666-4605
Western Dakota Ranch HCR 1, Wall, 57790 605-279-2198
Willow Springs Cabin HCR 39 Box 108, Rapid City, 57702 605-342-3665

Tennessee

CHATTANOOGA

Alford House B&B	$ B&B	Continental plus
2501 Lookout Mtn. Pkwy., 37419	3 rooms	Afternoon tea, snacks
Route 4	●	Sitting room, gazebo
615-821-7625	C-yes	child care service
Robert & Rhoda Alford		trails up Lake Mountain
All year		

Edge of national forest; minutes from attractions & downtown. Furnished in antiques (glass basket displayed). Coffee served at wakeup.

GATLINBURG

Buckhorn Inn	$$$ B&B	Full breakfast
Route 3, Box 3, 37738	11 rooms, 11 pb	Dinner
615-436-4668	C-ltd/S-ltd/P-no/H-no	Sitting room, fireplace
John & Connie Burns		piano, porch
All year		small conference center

Quiet hilltop overlooking landscaped lawns and breathtaking views of highest peaks of the Smokies. Nearby golf course, Great Smoky Mountains National Park within 1 mile.

Eight Gables Inn B&B	$$$ B&B	Continental plus
Rt. 4, N. Mountain Tr., 37738	10 rooms, 10 pb	Picnic lunches
615-430-3344	Visa, MC, AmEx ●	Afternoon tea
Helen Smith	C-12+/S-ltd/P-no/H-no	sitting room
All year		hot tubs

Exquisite spacious guest rooms individually decorated. Wraparound porch with rocking chairs and wicker. Gazebo and spa. TV lounge. Bountiful continental breakfast.

GREENEVILLE

Hilltop House B&B Inn
Route 7, Box 180, 37743
615-639-8202
Denise M. Ashworth
All year

$$ B&B/MAP
3 rooms, 3 pb
Visa, MC, AmEx ●
C-3+/S-no/P-no/H-no

Full breakfast
Afternoon tea
Sitting room, library
hiking trails
trout fishing, rafting

Comfortable country home with panoramic mountain views and English antiques. Visit historic towns, hike mountain trails with local hiking club. Gourmet meals.

GREENVILLE

Big Spring Inn
315 N. Main St., 37743
615-638-2917 800-245-2155
Jeanne Driese, Cheryl VanDyck
All year

$$ B&B
6 rooms, 5 pb
●
C-12+/S-yes

Full breakfast
Picnic basket, dinner
Cookies & fruit in room
2 rooms with fireplaces
sitting room, pool

A unique, three-story turn-of-the-century home in a storybook town, nestled in the hills of East Tennessee.

JACKSON

Highland Place B&B
519 N. Highland Ave., 38301
901-427-1472
Larry & Peggy Hewgley
All year

$ B&B
3 rooms, 1 pb
Visa, MC ●
C-12+/S-no/P-no/H-no

Full breakfast
Snacks, sitting room
Library, gardens
screened porch, patio
rec. room w/pool table

Highland Place is a stately 1911 home in a garden setting, furnished with antiques, offering comfortable accommodations and Southern hospitality.

JOHNSON CITY

The Hart House
207 East Holston Ave., 37601
615-926-3147
Francis & Vanessa Gingras
All year

$$ B&B
3 rooms, 3 pb
Visa, MC ●
C-yes/S-no/P-no/H-no

Full breakfast
Afternoon tea, snacks
Sitting room, library
basketball court

1910 Dutch Colonial home lovingly restored to its original grandeur. Relax on the front porch or spend an evening by the fireplace.

JONESBOROUGH

Robertson House B&B Inn
212 E. Main St., 37659
615-753-3039 800-843-4755
R.J. Robertson, J.O'Callaghan
All year

$$ B&B
3 rooms, 2 pb
●
C-yes/S-no/P-no/H-no

Full breakfast
Aftn. tea, comp. wine
Homemade breads and
preserves

Located in Jonesborough, Tennessee's oldest town. Enjoy historic tours, antique hunting, craft shopping and the best of Southern hospitality.

KNOXVILLE

Compton Manor
3747 Kingston Pike, 37919
615-523-1204
Brian & Hala Hunt
All year

$$ B&B
3 rooms, 3 pb
Visa, MC ●
C-12+/S-no/P-no/H-no
Arabic

Continental plus
Afternoon tea, solarium
Sitting room, library
tennis, pool, Eng. darts
croquet, horseshoes

Elegant 1920s English Tudor near Univ. of Tennessee. Antiques, Persian rugs, carved fireplace, leaded windows, paneled library and dining room with high tea on the terrace.

KNOXVILLE

Graustein Inn
8300 Nubbin Ridge Rd., 37923
615-690-7007
Jim & Darlene Lara
All year

$$ B&B/AP
5 rooms, 3 pb
Visa, MC •
C-13+/S-no/P-no/H-no
Spanish

Full breakfast
Lunch, dinner
Snacks
sitting room
library, game room

Located on 20 wooded acres, the inn is furnished with 17th- and 18th-century antiques. Special areas include great room, library, breakfast porch and game room.

LIMESTONE

Snapp Inn B&B
1990 Davy Crockett Rd., 37681
615-257-2482
Dan & Ruth Dorgan
All year

$$ B&B
2 rooms, 2 pb
•
C-ltd/S-no/P-yes/H-no

Full breakfast
Kitchen priv. on request
Sitting room
library
pool table

Gracious 1815 Federal home, furnished with antiques. Farm country setting, mountain views. Friendly home atmosphere. Near Jonesborough and Greeneville.

MONTEAGLE

Edgeworth Inn
Monteagle Assembly, 37356
615-924-2669
Wendy & David Adams

$$ B&B
11 rooms, 11 pb
Visa, MC, Dis •
C-ltd/S-ltd/P-no/H-ltd
French

Full breakfast
Living room, library
Garden sitting rm.
tennis, pool (summer)
Chautauqua program (sum)

A century old Victorian village is the mountaintop setting for this National Register jewel. Custom bedding, museum art. 200 feet of veranda. 120 miles of hiking trails.

MURFREESBORO

Clardy's Guest House
435 E. Main St., 37130
615-893-6030
Robert & Barbara Deaton
All year

$ B&B
4 rooms, 3 pb
C-yes/S-yes/P-no/H-no

Continental breakfast
Comp. beverages
Sitting room w/cable TV
porch

Built in 1898 during opulent and decorative times, the house is completely furnished with beautiful antiques. Murfreesboro is the South's antique center.

NASHVILLE

Monthaven B&B
1154 W. Main St., 37075
Hendersonville
615-824-6319
Hugh Waddell, Lisa Neideffer
All year

$$ B&B
2 rooms, 2 pb
Visa, MC, AmEx •
C-yes/S-no/P-yes/H-yes

Continental plus
Lunch, dinner, bar
Afternoon tea, snacks
sitting room, bicycles
tennis & pool nearby

On National Register; Monthaven offers both serene tranquillity of middle Tennessee & convenience; 15 mi. from downtown Nashville. True "Southern charm." Log cabin available.

ORLINDA

Aurora Inn—B&B
8253 Hwy. 52, 37141
615-654-4266
Mr. & Mrs. James Jernigan
All year

$$$ B&B
3 rooms, 3 pb
Visa, MC
C-no/S-no/P-no

Full breakfast
Afternoon tea, snacks
Sitting room, library
croquet, horse shoes
indoor basketball

Pre-Civil War home set on 7 acres, antique furnishings, curved walnut staircase, spacious rooms with 12 foot ceilings, 30 minutes north of Nashville.

PIGEON FORGE

Hilton's Bluff B&B Inn
2654 Valley Heights Dr., 37863
615-428-9765
Jack & Norma Hilton
All year

$$ B&B
10 rooms, 10 pb
Visa, MC, AmEx •
C-yes/S-no/P-no/H-no

Full breakfast
Lunch & dinner (groups)
Refreshments, snacks
sitting room, library
golf and swimming nearby

Elegant country living. View of Smoky Mountains. Romantic mingling of old and new. Enjoy covered decks/rockers, in-room jacuzzis. Near Dollywood, crafts and outlet shopping.

ROGERSVILLE

Hale Springs Inn
110 W. Main St., 37857
Town Square
615-272-5171
Carl & Janet Netherland-Brown
All year

$ B&B
10 rooms, 10 pb
Visa, MC, AmEx •
C-yes/S-yes/P-ltd/H-no

Continental breakfast
Restaurant, sitting room
Central A/C and heat
fireplaces, guided tours
formal gardens & gazebo

Restored 1824 brick. Fronts Village Green with other antebellum buildings. Antiques, poster beds, working fireplaces, plush large rooms—near Gatlinburg.

RUGBY

Newbury House Inn
Hwy 52, P.O. Box 8, 37733
615-628-2430
Barbara Stagg
All year

$$ B&B
8 rooms, 3 pb
Visa, MC
C-ltd/S-ltd/P-no/H-ltd

Full breakfast
Restaurant, tea & coffee
Victorian parlor
period library
games, fireplace

Unique 1880s Victorian village offers lodging in restored and antique-filled Newbury House and Pioneer Cottage, home-style restaurant; near river gorges.

SEVIERVILLE

Von-Bryan Inn
2402 Hatcher Mtn. Rd., 37862
615-453-9832 800-633-1459
D.J. & Jo Ann Vaughn
All year

$$$ B&B
7 rooms, 6 pb
Visa, MC, AmEx •
C-ask/S-ltd/P-no/H-no

Full breakfast
Lunch, beverages, snacks
Porches, decks, hot tubs
pool, garden room, views
hammocks, pool table

Lovely log home on a mountaintop near the great Smoky Mountains, offering majestic views; private relaxed atmosphere; old-fashioned hospitality. 2-bedroom chalet available.

More Inns ...

Abbey Road 1551 Abbey Rd., Brownsville, 38012 901-772-5680
Bottle Hollow Lodge P.O. Box 92, Shelbyville, 37160 615-695-5253
Branner-Hicks House Rt. 1, Box 4, Jefferson City, 37760 615-475-2302
Brown Manor 215—20th St. , Cleveland, 37311 615-476-8029
Butcher House Rt. 2 Box 750, Gatlinburg, 37738 615-436-9457
Chateau Graeme 2200 Lebanon Rd., Nashville, 37214 615-883-1687
Colonel's Lady Rt. 1, Box 273, Gatlinburg, 37738 615-436-5432
Country Inn Rt. 3, Chris Haven Dr., Seymour, 37865 615-573-7170
Cove Country Inn Route 6, Box 197, Sevierville, 37862 615-453-3997
Day Dreams Country Inn Pigeon Forge, 615-428-0370
Falls Mill Log Cabin Rt. 1 Box 44, Belvidere, 37306 615-469-7161
Flow Blue Inn P.O. Box 495, Sweetwater, 37874 615-442-2964
Fox Trot Inn 402 May St., Sweetwater, 37874 615-337-4236
Grandma's House Route #1 Pollard Rd., Kodak, 37764 615-933-3512
Granville House 229 Pulaski St., Lawrenceburg, 38464 615-762-3129
Grey Gables B&B P.O. Box 5252, Hwy. 52, Rugby, 37733 615-628-5252
Hachland Hill Inn 5396 Rawlings Rd., Nashville, 37080 615-255-1727
Hannah's House Rt. 3, Middle Creek Rd., Pigeon Forge, 37863 615-428-2192
Harmony Hill Inn Rt. 3 Box 1937, Chuckey, 37641 615-257-3893

Herbert's B&B Box 2166, Brentwood, 37027 615-373-9300
Hidden Acres Farm B&B Hwy. 67, Rt. 3, Box 39, Mountain City, 37683 615-727-6564
Historic Inn on the River P.O. Box 1417, Glen Rose, 76043 817-897-2101
Homestead House Inn P.O. Box 218, Pickwick Dam, 38365 901-689-5500
Jonesborough B&B P.O. Box 722, Jonesborough, 37659 615-753-9223
Kero Mountain Resort Route 11, Box 380, Sevierville, 37862 615-453-7514
LeConte Lodge P.O. Box 350, Gatlinburg, 37738 615-436-4473
Leawood-Williams Estate P.O. Box 24, Shiloh, 38376 901-689-5106
Lowenstein-Long House 217 N. Waldran, Memphis, 38105 901-527-7174
Lynchburg B&B P.O. Box 34, Mechanic, Lynchburg, 37352 615-759-7158
Lyric Springs Inn 7306 S. Harpeth Rd., Franklin, 37334 615-255-5714
Magnolia Manor B&B 418 N. Main St., Bolivar, 38008 901-658-6700
Manor B&B 10 Main St., Box 240, Altamont, 36301 615-692-3153
Mason Place B&B 600 Commerce St., Loudon, 37774 615-458-3921
McEwen Farm Log Cabin B&B P.O. Box 97, Bratton Ln, Duck River, 38454 615-583-2378
Middleton, The 800 West Hill Ave., Knoxville, 37902 615-524-8100
Milk & Honey Country 2803 Old Country Way, Sevierville, 37862 615-428-4858
Mill Dale Farm and B&B Route 5, Dandridge, 37725 615-397-3470
Mockingbird Country Inn 1243 Allensville Rd., Sevierville, 37862 615-428-1398
Mountain Breeze B&B 501 Mountain Breeze Ln., Knoxville, 37922 615-966-3917
Mountainbrook Inn Route 3, Box 603, Gatlinburg, 37738 800-251-2811
Nolan House Inn P.O. Box 164, Waverly, 37185 615-296-2511
North Gate Lodge Box 858, Monteagle, 37356 615-924-2799
Old Cowan Plantation B&B Rt. 9, Box 17 Boonshill, Fayetteville, 37334 615-433-0225
Parish Patch Farm & Inn P.O. Box 27, Normandy, 37360 615-857-3441
Phelp's House Inn Route 1, Box 55, Highlands, 28741 704-526-2590
Pride Hollow Route 1, Box 86, Gordonsville, 38563 615-683-6396
River Road Inn Route 1, P.O. Box 372, Loudon, 37774 615-458-4861
Scarecrow Country Inn 1720 E. Spring St., Cookeville, 38501 615-526-3431
Smoky Bear Lodge 160 Bear Lodge Dr., Townsend, 37882 615-448-6442
Sugar Fork Lodge Rt. 1, Box 19, Dandridge, 37725 615-397-7327
The Gallery House P.O. Box 5274, Sevierville, 37864 615-428-6937
Three Chimneys 1302 White Ave., Knoxville, 37916 615-521-4970
Touch of Thyme B&B 501 E. Watauga Ave., Johnson City, 37601 615-926-7570
Tullahoma B&B 308 N. Atlantic St., Tullahoma, 37388 615-455-8876
Victoria Rose Tea Room 217 Cedar St., Sevierville, 37862 615-428-0759
White Oak Creek B&B Rt. 2, Box 184, McEven, 37101 615-582-3827
Woodlee House Cumberland St. Box 310, Altamont, 37301 615-692-2368

Texas

ABILENE

Bolin's Prairie House B&B	$ B&B	Full breakfast
508 Mulberry, 79601	4 rooms	Sitting room, den
915-675-5855	Visa, MC, AmEx, DC, Dis	high ceilings
Ginny Bolin	C-12+/S-no/P-no/H-no	hardwood floors
All year		

Built in 1902. Completely renovated. Relax in spacious rooms accented with antiques. Great breakfast served on china and lace. Brochure available.

AUSTIN ———————————————————————————————————

Brook House
609 W. 33rd St., 78705
512-459-0534
Maggie & Gary Guseman
All year

$$ B&B
4 rooms, 2 pb
Visa, MC •
C-yes/S-no/P-no/H-yes

Full breakfast
Comp. wine, beverages
Sitting room, library
gazebo, screened porch
bicycles

1920s "petite" estates adjacent to University of Texas and capital. Beautifully decorated and landscaped. 2 private cottages and a friendly cat named Tony.

Carrington's Bluff B&B
1900 David St., 78705
512-479-0638
David & Gwen Fullbrook
All year

$$ B&B
5 rooms, 3 pb
AmEx •
C-yes/S-no/P-no/H-no

Full breakfast
Comp. coffee, soda
Afternoon tea
sitting room

English country inn located on tree-covered acre in the heart of the city. Antique-filled rooms and fabulous breakfasts.

The McCallum House
613 W. 32nd, 78705
512-451-6744
Roger & Nancy Danley
All year

$$ B&B
5 rooms, 5 pb
Visa, MC •
C-8+/S-no/P-no/H-no

Full breakfast
Private kitchens
Sitting area in room
some rooms w/pvt. porch

Discover beautiful Austin from this historic, antique-filled late Victorian. We're ten blocks from UT-Austin, 20 blocks from Capitol and downtown.

Peaceful Hill B&B
10817 Ranch Rd. 2222, 78730
512-338-1817 800-369-2805
Peninnah Thurmond
All year

$$ B&B
2 rooms, 2 pb
Visa, MC
C-yes/S-yes/P-ask/H-no

Full breakfast
Comp. beverages & snacks
Sitting room, library
swimming, hot tub, and
tennis at nearby club

Hill country getaway. Sumptuous breakfast on porch overlooking panoramic view of city. Birdwatcher's paradise; 18-hole golf; 15 min. to Lake Travis.

Southard-House
908 Blanco, 78703
512-474-4731
Jerry & Rejina Southard
All year

$$ B&B
5 rooms, 5 pb
Visa, MC, AmEx •
C-ltd/S-yes/P-no/H-no

Continental plus (wkdys)
Full breakfast (wkends)
Complimentary wine
sitting room, porches
garden, gazebo

Elegant historic home. Clawfoot tub, cutwork linens. Dine by a roaring fire. Caring hosts in the grand Texas style. Downtown.

Wild Flower Inn
1200 W. 22½ St., 78705
800-747-9231 512-477-9639
Kay Jackson, Claudean Schultz
All year

$$ B&B
4 rooms, 2 pb
Visa, MC, AmEx •
C-no/S-no/P-no/H-no

Full breakfast
Afternoon tea, snacks
Sitting room
nearby public tennis
hiking & biking trails

Lovely old home furnished with antiques; located on tree-shaded street; delicious full breakfast; near University of Texas and State Capitol.

CANYON

The Hudspeth House & Spa
1905–4th Ave., 79015
806-655-9800
Dave & Sally Haynie
All year

$ B&B
8 rooms, 5 pb
Visa, MC ●
C-yes/S-ltd

Full gourmet breakfast
Lunch & dinner (reserv.)
Comp. wine/tea/lemonade
gazebo, veranda, hot tub
health & fitness center

Relaxed historic 1909 B&B featuring gourmet breakfasts, antiques and original stained glass. Close to musical drama "Texas," state park, Panhandle Plains Museum and WTSU.

DALLAS

Ponda-Rowland B&B
RR1, Box 439, Dallas, TX 18612
717-639-3245
Jeanette & Cliff Rowland
All year

$$ B&B
3 rooms, 3 pb
Visa, MC
C-yes/S-no/P-no

Full candlelight breakfast
Picnics, other meals
Satellite TV, fireplace
wildlife sanctuary
walking, hiking

130-acre farm in the Endless Mountains. Beautiful mountain and forest scenery. Farm includes 30-acre wildlife refuge, with ponds for canoeing and swimming. Visit the farm animals.

ENNIS

Raphael House
500 W. Ennis Ave., 75119
214-875-1555
Danna Cody
All year

$$ B&B
6 rooms, 6 pb
Visa, MC, AmEx, DC ●
C-ltd/S-ltd/P-no/H-no
Spanish

Full 3-course breakfast
Lunch & dinner available
Afternoon tea, snacks
sitting room, library
hot tub, sauna, pool

1906 mansion with original antiques " ... perhaps the most romantic B&B in Texas," says Park Cities' People. 35 minutes from Dallas. Tennis, golf and a health club nearby.

FORT DAVIS

Hotel Limpia
Box 822, 79734
Main St. on the Square
915-426-3237
Lanna & Joe Duncan
All year

$$ EP
20 rooms, 20 pb
Visa, MC, AmEx
C-yes/S-yes/P-yes/H-yes
Spanish

Family-style restaurant
Meals can be in-rm., Bar
Sitting room, library
glassed-in verandas and
porches, rocking chairs

Historic hotel built in 1912. 1-mile high in the Davis mountains. Beautiful scenery. Close to Big Bend National Park, McDonald Observatory, museums, rafting, swimming, golf.

FORT WORTH

Miss Molly's Hotel B&B
109½ W. Exchange Ave, 76106
817-626-1522
Susan & Mark Hancock
All year

$$ B&B
8 rooms, 1 pb
Visa, MC, AmEx ●
C-yes/S-no/P-no/H-no

Continental plus
Comp. wine, tea, snacks
Sitting room, antiques
claw-foot tubs, quilts
stained glass skylight

A 1910 bordello with light "Old West" rooms located in the historic Stockyards, home of Billy Babs–World's largest honky-tonk. Many activities nearby.

FREDERICKSBURG

Country Cottage Inn
405 E. Main, 78624
512-997-8549
Ms. Jeffery Webb
All year

$$ B&B
5 rooms, 5 pb
Visa, MC ●
C-yes/S-no/P-no/H-no

Continental breakfast
Comp. wine on arrival
Fireplaces
kitchens
cable TV

Historic Texas stone home; built in 1850 by German pioneers; handcrafted woodwork, rafters, 24" walls; antique furnishings, king beds, jacuzzis; National Register.

FREDERICKSBURG

J Bar K Ranch B&B
HC 10, Box 53-A,
78624 512-669-2471
Kermit & Naomi Kothe
March–December

$$ B&B
4 rooms, 3 pb Visa, MC
C-7+/S-yes/P-no/H-no
German

Full breakfast
Comp. wine, sitting room
Tour of the ranch
private kitchen
porch with great views

Large historic German rock home on Texas hill country ranch; full country breakfast; 15 min. drive to Fredericksburg, TX, with German heritage and quaint shops.

GALVESTON

The Gilded Thistle
1805 Broadway, 77550
409-763-0194
Helen L. Hanemann
All year

$$$ B&B
●

Full breakfast
Comp. wine & cheese tray
Homemade breads
porches, garden

A well-appointed historical home; share a feeling of history and rekindle that special sense of graciousness of times gone by. Come and experience our island.

GLEN ROSE

Inn on the River
P.O. Box 1417, 76043
209 Barnard
817-897-2101
Peggy Allman, Elaine Dooley
All year

$$$ B&B
24 rooms, 24 pb
Visa, MC ●
C-no/S-no/P-no/H-yes
Spanish

Full breakfast
Bar service
Library, sitting room
swimming pool
meeting house

Restored historical structure near town square with Paluxy River frontage. Fresh homemade breads, gourmet foods. Period-decorated rooms.

HOUSTON

Durham House B&B
921 Heights Blvd., 77008
713-868-4654
Marguerite Swanson
All year

$$ B&B
5 rooms, 4 pb
Visa, MC, AmEx ●
C-12+
German

Full breakfast
Comp. wine, refreshments
Sitting room, gazebo
tandem bicycles
Murder mystery evenings

Authentic Victorian on National Register of Historic Places. Antique furnishings; gazebo. Romantic getaway and wedding location. Near downtown Houston.

The Patrician B&B Inn
1200 Southmore Ave., 77004
713-523-1114 800-553-5797
Pat Thomas
All year

$$ B&B
5 rooms, 5 pb
Visa, MC, AmEx ●
C-10+/S-no/P-no/H-no

Full breakfast
Comp. wine, snacks
Sitting room
perfect for weddings
parties or receptions

1919 mansion only minutes to downtown Houston, Texas Medical Center, Museum of Fine Arts and Rice University. Several two-room suites, claw foot tubs and fireplaces.

Sara's B&B Inn
941 Heights Blvd., 77008
713-868-1130 800-593-1130
Donna & Tillman Arledge
All year

$$ B&B
12 rooms, 3 pb
Visa, MC, AmEx, DC, CB ●
C-ltd/S-ltd/P-no/H-no

Continental plus
Cold drinks, coffee, tea
Sitting room, large deck
hot tub, bicycles

Old-time hospitality in the heart of Houston. Twelve distinctive bedrooms are furnished with antiques. Only four miles from downtown Houston.

JEFFERSON

Austin Cottage
P.O. Box 488, 75657
406 Austin St.
903-938-5941 800-874-9429
Tim & Cindy Edwards-Rinkle
All year

$$ B&B
3 rooms, 3 pb
Visa, MC, AmEx •
C-13+/S-yes

Continental breakfast
Snacks available
Full kitchen, sun room
porch with rockers
board games, A/C

Lovingly restored 1923 batten board cottage decorated with a country flair & primitive antiques; enjoy homemade breakfast breads in the sun room or on the antique brick patio.

Hale House
702 S. Line St., 75657
903-665-8877
L.D. Barringer
All year

$$$ B&B
7 rooms, 3 pb
Visa, MC
C-yes/S-no/P-no/H-no

Full breakfast
Parlor
sun porch
bicycles

1890 Victorian home, overlooks park, historic churches. Charming guest rooms, antiques, large parlor and sun porch. Gourmet southern breakfast.

JEFFERSON

Pride House
409 Broadway, 75657
214-665-2675
Ruthmary Jordan
All year

$$ B&B
10 rooms, 10 pb
Visa, MC •
C-ltd/S-yes/P-no/H-no

Full breakfast
Comp. coffee, tea
Sitting room, A/C
rooms have ceiling fans,
stained glass windows

Experience the charm of the Victorian era and the traditional legendary hospitality of the deep South in the oldest B&B in Texas. The two-story Pride House was built c. 1889.

MARBLE FALLS

La Casita B&B
1908 Redwood Dr., 78654
Granite Shoals
512-598-6443
Joanne & Roger Scarborough
All year exc. Christmas

$$ B&B
1 rooms, 1 pb
•
C-yes/S-ltd/P-no/H-yes

Full breakfast
Comp. wine on arrival
Refrigerator, sink
library, bicycle
flowers, swimming

Private, hill country cottage west of Marble Falls, wildlife and wildflowers, near Lake LBJ, Vanishing Texas River Cruise and vineyards. Restaurant nearby.

NACOGDOCHES

Llano Grande Plantation
Route 4, Box 9400, 75961
409-569-1249
Ann & Charles Phillips
All year

$$ B&B
3 rooms, 3 pb
C-ask/S-yes/P-no/H-no

Full breakfast
Private kitchen
Sitting room
historic tours

Deep in the pine woods you will find the charming 1840s restored homestead of Tol Barret, who in 1866 drilled Texas' first producing oil well.

PORT ISABEL

Yacht Club Hotel
P.O. Box 4114, 78578
700 Yturria St.
512-943-1301
Ron & Lynn Speier
All year

$ B&B
2 rooms, 1 pb
Major credit cards •
C-yes/S-yes/P-no/H-yes
Spanish

Continental breakfast
Restaurant, bar, dinner
Swimming pool
A/C & cable TV in rooms
fishing charters avail.

Port Isabel's finest accommodation. Spanish architecture with the elegance and ambiance of the 1920s. Gourmet restaurant specializing in seafood. Just 20 minutes to Mexico.

SAN ANTONIO

Bullis House Inn
P.O. Box 8059, 78208
621 Pierce St.
512-223-9426
Alma & Steve Cross
All year

$ B&B
7 rooms, 2 pb
Visa, MC, AmEx, Disc •
C-yes/S-yes/P-no/H-no
Spanish

Continental plus
Guest kitchen, snacks
Child care (fee), phones
library, veranda, pool
king/queen/full beds

Historic 3 story, white mansion, minutes from Alamo, Riverwalk, downtown. Chandeliers, fireplaces, decorative 14-ft. ceilings, geometrically patterned floors of fine woods.

Falling Pines B&B
300 W. French Place, 78212
512-733-1998 800-880-4580
Grace & Bob Daubert
All year

$$$ B&B
4 rooms, 4 pb
•
C-10+/S-no/P-no/H-no

Continental plus
Comp. wine/brandy in rm.
Sitting room, library
tennis courts
bicycles

Near downtown, riverwalk (5 minutes), three-story mansion in historic district with towering trees in parklike setting. Pristine restoration.

Norton Brackenridge House
230 Madison, 78204
512-271-3442
All year

$$$ B&B
5 rooms, 5 pb
Visa, MC, AmEx •
C-no/S-yes/P-no/H-no

Full breakfast
Veranda
off-street parking
6 blocks to downtown

Lovely blend of comfort and nostalgia. Original pine floors, double-hung windows, high ceilings and antique furniture are complemented by king and queen-size beds.

SAN MARCOS

Crystal River Inn
326 W. Hopkins, 78666
512-396-3739
Mike & Cathy Dillon
All year

$$ B&B
12 rooms, 10 pb
Visa, MC, AmEx •
C-8+/S-ltd/P-no/H-yes

Full breakfast
Comp. brandy, chocolates
Fireplaces, courtyard
piano, fountain, bikes
four 2-room suites also

Romantic, luxurious Victorian capturing matchless spirit of Texas Hill Country. Fireplaces, fountain courtyards, fresh flowers, homemade treats. Suites have many amenities.

TYLER

Mary's Attic B&B
413 S. College, 75702
417 S. College
903-592-5181
Mary Mirsky
All year

$$ B&B
3 rooms, 3 pb
Visa, MC, AmEx
C-10+/S-no/P-no/H-no

Continental plus
Antique shop next door

The completely restored 1920 bungalow and annex garage apartment are located on the brick streets in the historical district of Tyler. American and English antiques.

Rosevine Inn B&B
415 S. Vine, 75702
903-592-2221
Bert & Rebecca Powell
All year

$$ B&B
5 rooms, 5 pb
•
C-no/S-no/P-no/H-no
French

Full breakfast
Comp. wine, cheese tray
Sitting room, library
spa, outdoor hot tub
courtyard

Original bed and breakfast in the rose capital of the world. Pleasant accommodations with delicious breakfast. Friendly hosts make you feel at home.

WAXAHACHIE

Bonnynook B&B	$$ B&B	Full breakfast
414 W. Main St., 75165	4 rooms, 4 pb	Comp. wine, snacks
214-937-7207	Visa, MC, AmEx, DC ●	Picnic basket, piano
Bonnie & Vaughn Franks	C-yes/S-yes/P-no/H-no	porches, gift shop
All year		whirlpool tub in 1 room

1887 Victorian home, located near Square in a historic district. Each room is a different experience; plants and fresh flowers.

WIMBERLEY

Old Oaks Ranch B&B	$$ B&B	Continental plus
P.O. Box 912, 78676	3 rooms, 3 pb	Full breakfast (Sunday)
County Rd. 221	Visa, MC ●	Sitting room
512-847-9374	C-no/S-no/P-no/H-no	one 2-bedroom cottage
Bill & Susan Holt		Two 1-bedroom cottages
All year		

Quiet, country inn furnished with Victorian antiques. Hiking. Cows, geese, wild birds, deer. Hills and trees. Picturesque. Close to resort area. Golf & tennis available.

WIMBERLEY

Southwind B&B	$$ B&B	Full breakfast
Route 2, Box 15, 78676	2 rooms, 2 pb	Sitting room
512-847-5277	●	library, porch
Herb & Carla Felsted	C-12+/S-no/P-no/H-no	ABBA member
All year	Spanish	

Rocking chairs on porch; 25 scenic hill country acres; hearty southwestern breakfasts; homemade bread and muffins. Convenient to Austin (40 min.) and San Antonio (1 hour).

WINNSBORO

Thee Hubbell House	$$ B&B	Full breakfast
307 W. Elm, 75494	4 rooms, 4 pb	Candlelight dinner (res)
214-342-5629	Visa, MC ●	Sitting room, library
Dan & Laurel Hubbell	C-yes	veranda, gallery
All year		piano, honeymoon pckages

1888 historic Georgian home, authentically restored and furnished in period antiques. Plantation or continental breakfast. Centrally located to other tourist areas.

More Inns ...

Anglin Queen Anne 723 N. Anglin, Cleburne, 76031 817-645-5555
Annie's B&B Country Inn P.O. Box 928, Big Sandy, 75755 214-636-4355
Aquarena Springs Inn P.O. Box 2330, San Marcos, 78666 512-396-8900
B&B on the Bay 7629 Olympia Dr.Houston, Seabrook, 77586 713-861-9492
Badu House 601 Bessemer, Llano, 78643 915-247-4304
Baron's Creek Inn 110 E. Creek St., Fredericksburg, 78624 512-997-9398
Be My Guest 330 W. Main, Fredericksburg, 78624 512-997-7227
Big Thicket Guest House Box 91, Village Mills, 77663 409-834-2875
Borgman's Sunday House B&B 911 S. Main, Boerne, 78006 512-249-9563
Browning Plantation Rt. 1, Box 8, Chappell Hill, 77426 409-836-6144
Captain's Castle 403 E Walker, Jefferson, 75657 903-665-2330
Cardinal Cliff 3806 Highcliff, San Antonio, 78218 512-655-2939
Castle B&B 1403 E. Washington, Navasota, 77868 409-825-8051
Catnap Creek B&B 417 Glen Canyon Dr., Garland, 75040 214-530-0819
Cayo Del Oso B&B 6093 S. Alameda St., Corpus Christi, 78412 512-992-2711
Chain-O-Lakes P.O. Box 218, Romayor, 77368 713-592-2150
Cleburne House 201 N. Anglin, Cleburne, 76031 817-641-0085
Comfort Common 240 S. Seguin Ave., New Braunfels, 78130 512-995-3030
Cotten's Patch 703 E. Rusk, Marshall, 75670 214-938-8756

402 Texas

Country Place Hotel P.O. Box 39, Fayetteville, 78940 409-378-2712
Dickens Loft 2021 Strand, Galveston, 77550 409-762-1653
Excelsior House 211 W. Austin St., Jefferson, 75657 214-665-2513
Farlton House of 1895 211 N. Pleasant St., Hillsboro, 76645 817-582-7216
Farris 1912 201 N. McCarty, Eagle Lake, 77434 409-234-2546
Gardner Hotel 311 E. Franklin Ave., El Paso, 79901 915-532-3661
Gast Haus Lodge Box 423, 952 High St., Comfort, 78013 512-995-2304
Gastehaus Schmidt 501 W. Main St., Fredericksburg, 78624 512-997-5612
Ginger House 200 S. Rogers St., Waxahachie, 75165 214-937-3663
Gingerbread House 601 E. Jefferson, Jefferson, 75657 214-665-8994
Gingerbread House Gingerbread St., Box 94, Chireno, 75937 409-362-2365
Ginocchio Hotel 707 N. Washington St., Marshall, 75670 214-935-7635
Granny's Hse c/o Ledbetter P.O. Box 212, Ledbetter, 78946 409-249-3066
Gregg-Plumb Home 1006 E. Bowie, Marshall, 75670 214-935-3366
Gruene Mansion Inn 1275 Gruene Rd., New Braunfels, 78130 512-629-2641
Haden Edwards Inn 106 N. Lanana, Nacogdoches, 75961 409-564-9999
Harlyn House 508 Main St., Marble Falls, 78654 512-693-7651
Hazelwood House 1127 Church, Galveston, 77550 713-762-1668
Hermitage, The P.O. Box 866036, Plano, 75086 214-618-2000
High Cotton Inn 214 S. Live Oak, Bellville, 77418 800-321-9796
Highlander, The 607 Highland St., Houston, 77009 713-861-7545
Hill Country Haven 227 S. Academy St., New Braunfels, 78130 512-629-6727
Hill Top Cafe & Guesthouse Fredericksburg Rt,Bx 88, Doss, 78618 512-997-8922
Hotel Turkey Box 37, Turkey, 79261 806-423-1151
Hygeia Health Retreat 439 Main St., Yorktown, 78164 512-564-3670
Inn on Fairmount P.O. Box 190244, Dallas, 75219 214-522-2800
John C. Rogers House 416 Shebyville, Center, 75935 409-598-3971
Joy Spring Ranch B&B Route 1, Box 174-A, Hunt, 78024 512-238-4531
Key Largo 5400 Seawall Blvd., Galveston, 77550 800-833-0120
Knittel House P.O. Box 261, Buchanan Dam, 78639 512-793-6408
La Borde House 601 E. Main St., Rio Grande, 78582 512-487-5101
La Colombe d'Or 3410 Montrose Blvd., Houston, 77226 713-524-7999
La Maison Malfacon 700 E. Rusk, Marshall, 75670 214-935-6039
La Quinta Inn 1402 Seawall Blvd., Galveston, 77550 800-531-5900
Lajitas on the Rio Grande Box 400, Terlingua, 79852 915-424-3471
Landmark Inn P.O. Box 577, Castroville, 78009 512-538-2133
Lash-Up B&B 215 N. Austin, Marfa, 915-729-4487
Ledbetter Bed & Breakfast P.O. Box 212, Ledbetter, 78940 409-249-3066
Lipan Ranch Rt 1 Box 21C, Paint Rock, 76866 915-468-2571
Magnolias Inn 209 E. Broadway, Jefferson, 75657 214-665-2754
Main House 3419 Main St., Texarkana, 75503 214-793-5027
Matali B&B Inn 1727 Sealy, Galveston Island, 77550 409-763-4526
Mather-Root Home 1816 Winnie, Galveston, 77550 713-439-6253
McKay House B&B Inn 306 E. Delta St., Jefferson, 75238 214-348-1929
Meredith House 410 E. Meredith St., Marshall, 75670 214-935-7147
Michael's-A B&B Inn 1715–35th St., Galveston, 77550 409-763-3760
Mimosa Hall Route 1, Box 635, Karnack, 75661 214-679-3632
Mrs. Cauthorn's Inn 217 King William St., San Antonio, 78204 512-227-5770
New Canaan Farm P.O. Box 1173-1, Elkhart, 75839 214-764-2106
Nueces Inn P.O. Box 29, Beeville, 78104 713-362-0868
Nutt House Town Square, Granbury, 76048 817-573-5612
Patrician B&B Inn, The 1200 Southmore Ave., Houston, 77004 713-523-1114
Pfeiffer House 1802 Main St., Bastrop, 78602 512-321-2100
Pine Colony Inn 500 Shelbyville St., Center, 75935 409-598-7700
Pink Lady Inn 1307 Main St., Bastrop, 78602 512-321-6273
Prince Solms Inn 295 E. San Antonio, New Braunfels, 78130 512-625-9169
Red Rooster Square Route 3, Box 3387, Edom, 75756 214-852-6774
Reiffert-Mugge Inn 304 W. Prairie St., Cuero, 77954 512-275-2626
Rio Grande B&B P.O. Box 16, Weslaco, 78596 512-968-9646
River Bend B&B P.O. Box 158, Hunt, 78024 512-238-4681

River View Farm 145 E. Main, Fredericksburg, 78624 512-997-7227
Robin's Nest 4104 Greeley St, Houston, 77006 713-528-5821
Room with a View 821 Rim Rd., El Paso, 79902 915-534-4400
Roseville Manor 217 West Lafayette, Jefferson, 75657 800-665-7273
Sand Dollar Hospitality 3605 Mendenhall, Corpus Christi, 78415 512-853-1222
Schmidt "Barn" B&B Route 2, Box 112A3, Fredericksburg, 98624 512-997-5612
Small Inn 4815 W. Bayshore Dr., Bacliff, 77518 713-339-3489
Smith House 306 W. Aspen St., Crosbyton, 79322 806-675-2178
St. James Inn 723 St. James, Gonzales, 78629 512-672-7066
Stillwater Inn 203 E. Broadway, Jefferson, 75657 214-665-8415
Stockyards Hotel Main & Exchange Sts., Fort Worth, 76106 817-625-6427
Sunset Heights B&B Inn 717 W. Yandell Ave., El Paso, 79902 800-767-8513
Tarlton House 211 N. Pleasant St., Hillsboro, 76645 817-582-7216
Terlingua Ranch State Rd. 118, Study Butte, 915-371-2416
Terrill's B&B 242 W. Main St., Apt. A, Fredericksburg, 78624 512-997-8615
Thomas J. Rusk Hotel 105 E. Sixth St., Rusk, 75785 214-683-2556
Three Oaks B&B 609 N. Washington Ave., Marshall, 75670 903-938-6123
Tremont House 2300 Ship's Mechanic Rd, Galveston, 77550 800-874-2300
Victorian House 619 W. Main, Fredericksburg, 78624 512-997-4937
Victorian Inn 511—17th St., Galveston, 77550 409-762-3235
Weimar Country Inn P.O. Box 782, Weimar, 78962 409-725-8888
Weisman-Hirsch-Beil Home 313 S. Washington, Marshall, 75670 214-938-5504
White House Inn P.O. Box 992, Goliad, 77963 512-645-2701
William Clark House 201 W. Henderson, Jefferson, 75657 214-665-8880
Williams Point 16 Lakeside Dr., Burnet, 78611 512-756-2074

Utah

CEDAR CITY

Paxman Summer House	$$ B&B	Continental plus
170 N. 400 W., 84720	4 rooms, 4 pb	Sitting room
801-586-3755	MC ●	swimming pool
Karlene Paxman	C-yes/S-ltd/P-ltd/H-no	tennis courts
All year		

Comfortable Victorian home, one block from Utah's Shakespearean Festival. Near Zion, Dixie and Bryce National Parks. Swimming, golf and tennis.

MOAB

Canyon Country B&B	$$ B&B	Full breakfast
590 North 500 West, 84532	5 rooms, 3.5 pb	Afternoon tea
801-259-5262 800-635-1792	Visa, MC, AmEx, Dis ●	Library, bikes, walk or
C. & J. Nichols, J. Lambla	C-6+/S-no/P-no	bike to local museums
All year		shops, restaurants, etc.

Casual Southwestern home. A warm decor, freshly cut flowers in your room, a large yard with patio & travel library all combine to provide a "home away from home" atmosphere.

Castle Valley Inn	$ B&B	Full breakfast
CVSR Box 2602, 84532	8 rooms, 8 pb	Box lunches, dinner
424 Amber, Castle Valley	Visa, MC ●	VCR, outdoor hot tub
801-259-6012 800-842-6622	C-ltd/S-no/P-no/H-no	outdoor dining deck
Eric & Lynn Forbes Thomson		tour & trail planning
All year		

A "western" bed & breakfast inn with dramatic 360-degree views of Utah Canyonlands, red rock and mountain silhouettes. Six acres of maintained orchard, lawn, and fields.

PARK CITY

Old Miners' Lodge B&B
P.O. Box 2639, 84060
615 Woodside Ave.
801-645-8068 800-648-8068
Daniels, Sadowsky, Wynne
All year

$$ B&B
10 rooms, 10 pb
Visa, MC, AmEx, Disc •
C-yes/S-no/P-no/H-no

Full country breakfast
Evening refreshments
Organ, fireplace
sitting room, library
hot tub, games

An original miner's lodge—antique-filled rooms, feather beds, full breakfast, complimentary refreshments and fine hospitality; an unforgettable experience!

Washington School Inn
P.O. Box 536, 84060
543 Park Ave.
801-649-3800 800-824-1672
Nancy Beaufait
All year

$$$ B&B
15 rooms, 15 pb
Visa, MC, AmEx •
C-12+/S-ltd/P-no/H-ltd

Full breakfast
Comp. wine, tea, snacks
Sitting room
hot tub, sauna
steam showers

Original schoolhouse is now an unique country inn, antique furnishings, in the center of Park City. Many activities, including skiing.

SAINT GEORGE

Greene Gate Village
76 W. Tabernacle, 84770
801-628-6999
Mark & Barbara Greene
All year

$ B&B
12 rooms, 9 pb
Visa, MC •
C-yes/S-no/P-yes/H-yes

Full breakfast
Lunch, Dinner
Soft drinks on arrival
sitting room, hot tubs
tennis courts, pool

Restored original pioneer home in an unique village close to downtown but in a quiet neighborhood. Close to Zion, Grand Canyon.

Seven Wives Inn
217 N. 100 West, 84770
801-628-3737 800-484-1084
The Curtises and Bowcotts
All year

$ B&B
13 rooms, 13 pb
major credit cards •
C-ask/S-no/P-no/H-ltd

Full gourmet breakfast
Comp. fruit
Bicycles, hot tub, pool
sitting room, organ
golf & tennis nearby

1870s pioneer home on National Register, furnished throughout in antiques, in heart of St. George—close to national parks.

SALT LAKE CITY

Brigham Street Inn
1135 E. South Temple, 84102
801-364-4461
John & Nancy Pace
All year

$$$ B&B
9 rooms, 9 pb
Visa, MC, AmEx •
C-yes/S-yes/P-no/H-no

Continental breakfast
Comp. tea, coffee
Entertainment, piano
jacuzzi in 1 suite
sitting room, library

National historic site, served as a designers' showcase in May 1982. Winner of several architectural awards. Near 7 major ski areas. Unique executive hotel.

More Inns ...

505 Woodside, B&B Place P.O. Box 2446, Park City, 84060 801-649-4841
Blue Church Lodge 424 Park Ave., Box 1720, Park City, 84060 801-649-8009
Bluff B&B P.O. Box 158, Bluff, 84512 801-672-2220
Cedar Breaks Condos B&B Center & 4th East, Moab, 84532 801-259-7830
Center Street B&B Inn 169 E. Center St., Logan, 84321 801-752-3443
Imperial Hotel P.O. Box 1628, Park City, 84060 801-649-1904
Mansion House 298 S. State St. #13, Mount Pleasant, 84647 801-462-3031
Manti House Inn 401 N. Main St, Manti, 84642 801-835-0161
Meadeau View Lodge P.O. Box 356, Cedar City, 84762 801-682-2495

Miss Sophie's B&B 30 N. 200 W., Kanab, 84741 801-644-5952
Miss Sophie's B&B 30 North 200 West, Kanah, 84741 801-644-5952
Mountain Hollow B&B Inn P.O. Box 1841, Sandy, 84092 801-942-3428
National Historic B&B 936 E. 1700 South, Salt Lake City, 84105 801-485-3535
Pack Creek Ranch P.O. Box 1270, Moab, 84532 801-259-5505
Peterson's B&B P.O. Box 142, Monroe, 84754 801-527-4830
Pinecrest B&B 6211 Emigration Canyon, Salt Lake City, 84108 801-583-6663
Pullman B&B Inn 415 S. University Ave., Provo, 84601 801-374-8141
Quail Hills Guesthouse 3744 E. N.Little Cttnwd, Sandy, 84092 801-942-2858
Recapture Lodge & Pioneer Box 36, Bluff, 84512 801-672-2281
Saltair B&B 164 S. 900 E., Salt Lake City, 84012 801-533-8184
Saltair B&B 164 S. 900 East, Salt Lake City, 84102 801-533-8184
Snowed Inn 3770 N. Hwy 224, Park City, 84060 801-649-5713
Spruces B&B 6151 S. 900 East, Salt Lake City, 84121 801-268-8762
Sundance P.O. Box 837, Provo, 84601 801-225-4100
Westminister B&B 1156 Blaine Ave., Salt Lake City, 84105 801-467-4114
Woodbury Guest House 237 S. 300 W., Cedar City, 84720 801-586-6696
Zion House B&B Box 323, Springdale, 84767 801-772-3281
Zion Overlook B&B P.O. Box 852, La Verkin, 84745 801-877-1061

Vermont

ARLINGTON

Arlington Inn
Historic Route 7A, 05250
802-375-6532 800-443-9442
Paul & Madeline Kruzel
All year

$$ B&B
13 rooms, 13 pb
Visa, MC, AmEx •
C-yes/S-yes
French

Continental plus
Lunch (summer/fall)
Cookies and cider
Restaurant, bar
sitting rm; tennis court

Antique-filled rooms in one of Vermont's finest Greek revival homes. Located in Norman Rockwell country. Winner of 1988 Travel Holiday Dining Award & Taste of Vermont Award.

Hill Farm Inn
RR 2, Box 2015, 05250
Hill Farm Rd, Sunderland
802-375-2269 800-882-2545
George & Joanne Hardy
All year

$$ B&B13 rooms, 8 pb
Visa, MC, AmEx, Disc. •
C-yes/S-ltd/P-ltd/H-no

Full breakfastComp.
afternoon snacks
Sitting room, piano
fireplace, fruit baskets
guide to the area in rm.

1790 & 1830 farmhouses, an inn since 1905; pleasant mountain views, hearty home cooking, fish the Battenkill, hike country roads.

Inn at Sunderland
RR 2, Box 2440, 05250
Route 7A
802-362-4213 800-441-1628
Tom & Peggy Wall
All year exc. April

$$$ B&B
10 rooms, 8 pb
Visa, MC, AmEx
C-ltd/S-ltd/P-no/H-yes

Full breakfast
Afternoon cheese/cider
Sitting room, bicycles
wagon & sleigh rides
country club privileges

Country elegance in a B&B inn; beautifully restored Victorian farmhouse with antiques and fireplaces, double-decker porch with Green Mountains view. Your 4-season hideaway.

The Leslie Place, Belmont VT

ARLINGTON

Shenandoah Farm	$$ B&B	Full breakfast
Route 313, Box 3260, 05250	5 rooms, 3 pb	Comp. wine, tea
802-375-6372	●	Sitting room
Woody Masterson	C-yes/S-yes/P-no/H-no	piano, library
All year		fishing/canoeing/tubing

Beautifully restored 1820 colonial furnished with antiques, overlooking Battenkill River and rolling meadows. Near skiing, golf, tennis.

West Mountain Inn	$$$ MAP	Full breakfast
Box 481, 05250	15 rooms, 15 pb	Dinner included, bar
Route 313 & River Rd.	Visa, MC, AmEx ●	Fruit, chocolate llama
802-375-6516	C-yes/S-ltd/P-no/H-yes	sitting room, piano
Mary Ann & Wes Carlson	French	dining room, flowers
All year		

150-acre hillside estate; hike or ski woodland trails. Fish the Battenkill. Hearthside dining, charming rooms. Relax and enjoy the llamas, goats and rabbits.

BELMONT

The Leslie Place	$$ B&B	Continental plus
Box 62, 05730	4 rooms, 2 pb	Sitting room
802-259-2903	Visa, MC	Spacious rooms
Mary K. Gorman	C-yes/S-no/P-no/H-no	swimming & hiking nearby
All year		separate apt. available

New England farmhouse, peacefully set on 100 acres; mountain views and open meadows; near Weston. A perfect retreat close to ski areas, fine restaurants, theater and shops.

BELMONT

Parmenter House
PO Box 106, 05730
Healdville Rd.
802-259-2009
Jeff & Lois Predom
Memorial Day–mid-March

$$ B&B
5 rooms, 5 pb
Visa, MC ●
C-6+/S-no/P-no/H-no
French, Spanish

Continental plus
Comp. wine, refreshments
Sitting room
bicycles
lake swimming

Antique-furnished country Victorian in idyllic lakeside village. Summer sports, cross-country skiing, sleigh rides. Near Weston Priory. Group rates available.

BENNINGTON

Molly Stark Inn
1067 E. Main St., 05201
802-442-9631 800-356-3076
Reed Fendler
All year

$$ B&B
6 rooms, 6 pb
Visa, MC, AmEx, Dis ●
C-12+/S-no/P-no/H-no

Full gourmet breakfast
Champagne dinner avail.
Den with woodstove, TV
hardwood floors, antique
quilts, clawfoot tubs

Charming 1860 Victorian on Main Street, one mile from center. Decorated with country American, antiques, classical music playing. Gourmet breakfast served each morning.

BRANDON

Churchill House Inn
RD #3, Box 3265 PL, 05733
Route 73 East
802-247-3300
Roy & Lois Jackson
Exc. November & April

$$$ MAP
8 rooms, 8 pb
Visa, MC
C-yes/S-ltd/P-no/H-no

Full breakfast
Dinner included, bar
Swimming pool
library, piano
bicycles

Century-old farmhouse on the edge of the Green Mountain National Forest. Delicious home cooking, hiking, skiing, biking, inn-to-inn adventures. Some rooms with whirlpool.

BRIDGEWATER CORNERS

October Country Inn
P.O. Box 66, Upper Rd., 05035
802-672-3412
Richard Sims, Patrick Runkel
Dec–mid-April, May–Nov

$$ B&B/$$$ MAP
10 rooms, 7 pb
●
C-yes/S-no!/P-no/H-ltd

Full breakfast
Dinner (MAP)
Homebaked aftn. treats
sitting room
sun deck, pool

19th-century Vermont farmhouse. Meals include garden vegetables, freshly baked breads, desserts. Fireplace, antique wood stove, comfortable rooms, cozy living room.

BRISTOL

Long Run Inn
RD 1 Box 560, 05443
Lincoln Gap Rd.
802-453-3233
Michael & Beverly Conway
Mid-May-Oct/late Dec-Mar

$$$ B&B/MAP
8 rooms
C-yes/S-ltd/P-no/H-no

Full breakfast
Dinner, evening snack
Sitting room, antiques
old pump harmonium
swimming hole

Authentic lumberjack inn. Quiet location in center of quaint mountain village of Lincoln near Long Trail. Close to Sugarbush ski area, Middlebury College and Lake Champlain.

BROOKFIELD

Green Trails Country Inn
Main St., 05036
by the Floating Bridge
802-276-3412 800-243-3412
Pat & Peter Simpson
May–March

$$ B&B
15 rooms, 9 pb
●
C-yes/S-ltd/P-no/H-no
Swedish

Full breakfast
Dinner with notice, tea
3 sitting rms, fireplace
swimming, canoeing,
X-C skiing, biking

National Register of Historic Places. Located by the Floating Bridge. Decorated with quilts & antiques. Warm hospitality–like going home to Grandma's. Featured on Today Show.

BURLINGTON

Howden Cottage B&B
32 N. Champlain St., 05401
802-864-7198
Bruce M. Howden
All year

$ B&B
2 rooms
Visa, MC
C-no/S-no/P-no/H-no

Continental breakfast
Sitting room
sinks in rooms

Howden Cottage offers cozy lodging and warm hospitality in the atmosphere of a private home. Owned and operated by a local artist, Bruce M. Howden. Reservations, please!

CHARLOTTE

The Inn at Charlotte
RR1, Box 1188, 05445
State Park Rd.
802-425-2934
Letty Ellinger
All year

$$ B&B
6 rooms, 4 pb
Visa, MC
C-yes/S-no/P-no/H-no
Philippine (Tagalog)

Full breakfast
Picnic lunch basket
Dinner on adv. request
comp. wine, appetizers
tennis courts, pool

Beautiful courtyard with flower gardens. Spacious rooms with country furniture. Breakfast served poolside. Picnic baskets and dinner available on request.

CHELSEA

Shire Inn
8 Main St., 05038
802-685-3031
James & Mary Lee Papa
All year

$$ B&B
6 rooms, 6 pb
Visa, MC
C-7+/S-no/P-no/H-no

Full breakfast
Dinner by reservation
Sitting room
fireplaces
bicycles

Elegant country atmosphere; antique furnishings. Gracious candlelight dining. On White River with bridge to hiking trail. Cross-country skiing in winter.

CHESTER

Chester House
P.O. Box 708, 05143
Main St., Village Green
802-875-2205
Irene & Norm Wright
All year

$$ B&B
4 rooms, 4 pb
●
C-3+/S-yes

Full breakfast
Sitting room, library
jacuzzi
fireplaces in rooms

A southern Vermont B&B inn of extraordinary charm and hospitality. Beautifully restored, antique-furnished circa 1780 home in the National Register of Historic Places.

Greenleaf Inn
P.O. Box 188, Depot St., 05143
802-875-3171
Dan & Elizabeth Duffield
All year

$$ B&B
4 rooms, 4 pb
Visa, MC
C-7+/S-yes/P-no/H-no

Full breakfast
Picnic box lunch $
Beverages, art gallery
2 large living rooms
library, bicycles nearby

Lovely 1880s village inn. Comfortable, large, airy rooms. Private baths. Big, fluffy towels. Spotlessly clean. Beautifully furnished throughout. Two large living rooms.

Henry Farm Inn
P.O. Box 646, 05143
Green Mountain Trnpk
802-875-2674
J. E. Bowman
All year

$$ B&B
7 rooms, 7 pb
●
C-yes/S-ltd/P-no/H-ltd

Full breakfast
Tea, coffee, cookies
Sitting room
library
pond, hiking

1750s farmhouse in charming country setting in the glorious Green Mountains. Full country breakfast each morning. Extensive grounds available for your pleasure. Join us.

CHESTER

Hugging Bear Inn & Shoppe
Box 32, Main St., 05143
802-875-2412
The Thomases
All year

$$$ B&B
6 rooms, 6 pb
Visa, MC
C-yes/S-no/P-no/H-no
Russian

Full breakfast
Afternoon bev., snacks
Sitting room
library
bicycles

Elegant Victorian in National Historic District, on the Village Green, thousands of Teddy Bears throughout, thousands in the shoppe. (3,609 at last count!) FUN!

The Stone Hearth Inn
Route 11 W., 05143
802-875-2525
Janet & Don Strohmeyer
All year

$$ B&B
10 rooms, 10 pb
•
C-yes/S-ltd/P-no/H-ltd
Fr., Dutch, Flem., Ger.

Full breakfast
Dinner—reserv. only
Lunch, wine cellar, pub
game room, library
pianos, whirlpool spas

Lovingly restored country inn built in 1810—beams, fireplaces, wide pine floors. Attached barn has game room, cozy pub. Family atmosphere.

CHITTENDEN

Mountain Top Inn
Mountain Top Rd., 05737
802-483-2311 800-445-2100
William P. Wolfe
All year

$$$ MAP
33 rooms, 33 pb
Visa, MC, AmEx •
C-yes/S-yes/P-no/H-no
German

Full breakfast
Restaurant, bar
Lunch, dinner
tennis, hot tub, sauna
pool, boating, skiing

This warm New England country inn steeped in the area's finest tradition, has been referred to as "Vermont's Best Kept Secret."

Tulip Tree Inn
Chittenden Dam Rd., 05737
802-483-6213
Ed & Rosemary McDowell
Exc. Apr, Nov to Thksgvg

$$$ MAP
8 rooms, 8 pb
Visa, MC •
C-ltd/S-ltd/P-no/H-no
German

Full breakfast
Dinner included
Full bar & wine cellar
sitting room, library
some rooms w/jacuzzis

Small, antique-filled country inn, hidden away in the Green Mountains. Gracious dining, homemade breads and desserts, liquor license, wine list. One of Uncle Ben's 10 best.

CRAFTSBURY

Craftsbury Inn
Main St., 05826
802-586-2848 800-336-2848
Blake & Rebecca Gleason
Exc. November & April

$$ B&B
10 rooms, 6 pb
Visa, MC
C-yes/S-ltd/P-no/H-no

Full breakfast
Dinner, bar
Sitting room, piano
lake swimming

Authentic Vermont Inn located in a quiet & picturesque hill town. Renowned dining, cross-country skiing. Redecorated rooms with quilts.

CRAFTSBURY COMMON

Inn on the Common
P.O. Box 75, Main St., 05827
802-586-9619 800-521-2233
Michael & Penny Schmitt
All year

$$$ B&B/MAP
18 rooms, 18 pb
Visa, MC •
C-15+/S-yes/P-arr/H-no

Full breakfast
Dinner (MAP), bar
Sitting rooms, library
pool, sauna, tennis
walking & biking

Superbly decorated, meticulously appointed, wonderful cuisine, complete recreation facilities. For the inn connoisseur, everything you could want. AAA 4 Diamond Award.

Inn on the Common, Craftsbury Common, VT

CUTTINGSVILLE

Buckmaster Inn B&B
RR1, Box118, Shrewsbury, 05738
Lincoln Hill Rd.
802-492-3485
Sam & Grace Husselman
All year

$$ B&B
3 rooms, 1 pb
C-4+/S-ltd/P-no/H-ltd
Dutch

Full breakfast
Comp. tea & cookies
Sitting room, fireplace
porches, library
organ, bicycles

1801 historic stagecoach stop with spacious rooms, charm of family heirlooms in Green Mountains. Hike, bike, X-C skiing from door. Nature paradise, relaxing atmosphere.

Maple Crest Farm
Box 120, 05738
Lincoln Hill, Shrewsbury
802-492-3367
Donna & William Smith
All year

$$ B&B
6 rooms, 2 pb
C-yes/S-yes/P-no/H-ltd

Full breakfast
Afternoon tea
Sitting room
piano, hiking
cross-country skiing

Dairy farm located in beautiful mountain town of Shrewsbury. Lovingly preserved for five generations of Vermont tradition. Rutland area. Our 22th anniversary this year!

DANBY

Silas Griffith Inn
RR 1, Box 66F, 05739
S. Main St.
802-293-5567
Paul & Lois Dansereau
All year

$$ B&B
17 rooms, 11 pb
Visa, MC, AmEx ●
C-yes/S-yes

Full breakfast
Restaurant, bar, dinner
Aftn. beverages, cookies
sitting room, library
swimming pool

Lovingly restored Victorian mansion and carriage house. Relax in antique-filled rooms; enjoy a quiet 19th-century village. Spectacular Green Mountain views.

Maplewood Inn, Fair Haven, VT

DORSET

Barrows House
Route 30, 05251
802-867-4455
Tim & Sally Brown
All year

$$$ MAP
28 rooms, 28 pb
●
C-yes/S-yes/P-ltd/H-ltd
German

Full breakfast
Lunch, dinner, bar
Swimming pool, sauna
tennis courts, bicycles
sitting room, piano

Eight buildings on six parklike acres in picturesque Dorset, close to hiking, fishing, golf, horseback riding, shopping, cross-country ski shop.

EAST BURKE

Burke Green Guest House
RR 1, Box 81, 05832
802-467-3472
Beverly & Harland Lewin
All year

$ B&B
3 rooms, 1 pb
C-yes/S-yes/P-no/H-yes

Continental plus
Sitting room
fireplace
skiing nearby

Peaceful, comfortable home with beautiful view of Burke Mountain; 1849 farmhouse on 25 acres. Relax by the fireplace or enjoy nearby skiing, hiking and lakes.

FAIR HAVEN

Maplewood Inn
RR 1, Box 4460, 05743
Route 22A South
802-265-8039 800-253-7729
Cindy & Doug Baird
All year

$$ B&B
5 rooms, 4 pb
Visa, MC, AmEx ●
C-6+/S-ltd

Full breakfast
Comp. wine, tea, coffee
BYOB tavern, chocolates
sitting room, toiletries
library, TV room

Romantic, elegantly appointed, air conditioned rooms, suites and several common areas. Fireplace. In lakes region close to everything. We will pamper you!

FAIRLEE

Silver Maple Lodge/Cottage
RR 1, Box 8, 05045
S. Main St.
802-333-4326 800-666-1946
Scott & Sharon Wright
All year

$ B&B
15 rooms, 7 pb
Visa, MC ●
C-yes/S-yes/P-no/H-no

Continental breakfast
Cottages available
Sitting room, lawn games
picnic area
bicycle & canoe rental

Quaint country inn located in a scenic resort area; convenient to antique shops, fishing, golf, swimming, tennis and winter skiing. Ballooning packages available.

GAYSVILLE

Cobble House Inn
P.O. Box 49, 05746
Childrens Camp Rd.
802-234-5458
Beau, Phil & Sam Benson
All year

$$$ B&B
6 rooms, 6 pb
Visa, MC •
C-5+/S-no/P-no/H-ltd

Full breakfast
Romantic restaurant
Afternoon hors d'oeuvres
2 sitting rooms, river
swimming, X-C skiing

Victorian mansion, 1864. Mountain views on the White River; country breakfasts; gourmet dinners; antique furnishings; private baths. Golf tours arranged.

Laolke Lodge
P.O. Box 107, 05746
Laury Hill Rd.
802-234-9205
Olive Pratt
All year

$ MAP
5 rooms
•
C-yes/S-yes/P-ltd/H-no

Full breakfast
Evening meal
Sitting room, piano
pool, color TV, tennis
river swimming, tubing

Family-style vacations in modern, rustic log cabin. Home cooking. Near skiing, horseback riding, hunting, boating, and other Vermont attractions.

GOSHEN

Blueberry Hill
RFD 3, 05733
802-247-6735 800-448-0707
Tony Clark
2/15–3/31; 6/1–10/31

$$$ MAP
8 rooms, 8 pb
Visa, MC •
C-yes/S-ltd/P-no/H-yes
French, Spanish

Full breakfast
Dinner, tea
Sitting room
swimming pond
75km X-C ski trails

1800 charming inn, gourmet cooking, dining by candlelight. Relax in an atmosphere of elegance and leisure. Fishing, swimming, hiking, cross-country skiing.

GRAFTON

The Old Tavern at Grafton
Main St., Box 009, 05250
802-843-2231
Richard Ernst
Exc. Dec 24-25 & April

$$ B&B/MAP
Visa, MC, AmEx •
C-8+/S-ltd/P-ltd/H-yes
French, Spanish, German

Continental plus
Restaurant, bar
Lunch, dinner available
library, bicycles
tennis, pool, game room

Village inn in tiny, picture-perfect Grafton. A virtual museum of antiquity with elegant yet comfortable rooms. Easy access to sports.

GUILDHALL

Guildhall Inn B&B
P.O. Box 129, Route 102, 05905
802-676-3720
Claire & Richard Dill
All year

$ B&B
3 rooms
C-yes/S-no/P-ltd/H-no

Full breakfast
Sitting room
meadow walks

Walk by Connecticut River in inn's meadows; mountain views. Enjoy hiking, biking, canoeing, area skiing and golfing.

JAMAICA

Three Mountain
Box 180, Main St., 05343
802-874-4140
Charles & Elaine Murray
Exc. 4/15–5/15 & Nov

$$$ MAP
10 rooms, 8 pb
•
C-yes/S-yes/P-no/H-no

Full breakfast
Dinner, bar
Sitting room
bicycles
swimming pool

Small romantic 1780 Colonial Inn. Charming rooms and fine food, cross-country skiing and hiking in State Park; swimming pool; near 3 downhill ski areas.

JEFFERSONVILLE

The Smuggler's Notch Inn
Church St., Box 280, 05464
802-644-2412 800-845-3101
Virginia & Jeff Morgan
All year

$$$ MAP
11 rooms, 11 pb
Visa, MC ●
C-yes/S-yes/P-yes/H-no
French, Spanish

Full breakfast
Dinner included, bar
Sitting room, bicycles
tennis courts, pool
hot tub in guest room

Over 100 years of service to the Smugglers' Notch area. Maple floors, tin ceilings, screened porch, village setting. Enjoy our relaxing atmosphere.

JERICHO

Homeplace B&B
RR 2, Box 367, 05465
802-899-4694
Hans & Mariot Huessy
All year

$$ B&B
4 rooms
●
C-yes/S-no/P-no/H-no
German

Full breakfast
Comp. wine, beer, juice
Sitting room, library
Perenial gardens, trails
tennis courts nearby

A quiet spot in a 100-acre wood, 1.5 miles from Jericho. Our farm animals welcome you to their sprawling home, full of European antiques, Vermont craftwork and charm.

KILLINGTON

The Inn at Long Trail
P.O. Box 267, 05751
Route 4, Sherburne Pass
802-775-7181 800-325-2540
K & R McGrath, M & P McGrath
Summer, fall, winter

$$ B&B
20 rooms, 20 pb
Visa, MC ●
C-yes/S-yes/P-no/H-ltd

Full breakfast
All meals, Irish pub
Sitting room
hot tub
weekend Irish music

Historic 1938 ski lodge, woodpaneled, candlelit dining, fieldstone fireplaces, adjacent to famous Appalachian and Long Trails for summer hiking.

Mountain Meadows Lodge
RR 1 Box 4080, 05751
Thundering Brook Rd.
802-775-1010
The Stevens Family
Ex. 4/15-6/1;10/15-11/21

$$$ B&B/MAP
18 rooms, 15 pb
Visa, MC ●
C-yes/S-ltd/P-no/H-ltd

Full breakfast
Dinner, coffee, tea
Swimming pool
sitting room
mountain getaway pkges

A casual, friendly family lodge in a beautiful secluded mountain and lake setting. Complete cross-country ski center. Converted 1856 farmhouse and barn.

The Vermont Inn
Route 4, Cream Hill Rd., 05751
802-775-0708 800-541-7795
Susan & Judd Levy
Memorial Day–April 15

$$ MAP
16 rooms, 12 pb
Visa, MC, AmEx ●
C-6+/S-no/P-no/H-ltd
French, Spanish

Full breakfast (winter)
Continental plus (summ.)
Dinner included, bar
library, piano, pool
tennis, sauna, whirlpool

Award-winning cuisine; fireside dining (winter), spectacular mountain views, secluded romantic stream. Minutes to Killington and Pico ski areas.

LONDONDERRY

Highland House
Route 100, 05148
802-824-3019
Suzanne Bowser, Jack Carroll
Exc. April, Thanksgiving

$$ B&B
17 rooms, 15 pb
Visa, MC, AmEx
C-5+/S-ltd/P-no/H-yes

Full breakfast
Dinner Wed-Sun
Tea (winter), sitting rm
pool, tennis court
cross country skiing

An 1842 country inn with swimming pool and tennis court. Set on 32 acres. Classic, candlelight dining. Located in the heart of the Green Mountains.

414 Vermont

LOWER WATERFORD ──────────────────────

Rabbit Hill Inn
Route 18, 05848
802-748-5168 800-76-BUNNY
Maureen & John Magee
All year

$$$ B&B
18 rooms, 18 pb
Visa, MC •
C-no/S-no/P-no/H-no
French

Full 4-course breakfast
Restaurant, bar
Afternoon tea & pastry
lawn games, swim pond
golf, rooms w/fireplace

Stylish country inn established 1795. Peaceful, storybook 15-acre setting. Heartfelt service and commitment to detail, dining, decor and music. Internationally acclaimed.

LUDLOW ──────────────────────

Andrie Rose Inn
13 Pleasant St., 05149
802-228-4846
Rick & Carolyn Bentzinger
All year

$$$ B&B/MAP
10 rooms, 10 pb
Visa, MC, AmEx •
C-ltd/S-no/P-no/H-no

Full breakfast buffet
5-course cndlght. dinner
Comp. cheese/fruit/bread
down comforters, bar
hot tubs, bicycles

Elegant c. 1829 country village inn at base of Okemo Ski Mtn. Antique-filled rooms. Near skiing, lakes, golf, shops. 1 of top 50 Inns in the country—Inn Times 1991.

Black River Inn
100 Main St., 05149
802-228-5585
Rick & Cheryl DelMastro
All year

$$$ B&B/MAP
10 rooms, 8 pb
Visa, MC, AmEx •
C-yes/S-yes/P-no/H-no

Full breakfast
4-course dinner
Full beverage service
TV-game rm., sitting rm.
jacuzzi

A charming 1835 country inn, with 19th century antique furnished guest rooms, including family suite & brandy at bedside. Near downhill & X-C skiing, swimming, golf, fishing.

The Combes Family Inn
RFD 1, Box 275, 05149
802-228-8799
Ruth & Bill Combes
All year exc. 4/15–5/15

$$ B&B/MAP
11 rooms, 11 pb
Visa, MC, AmEx •
C-yes/S-ltd/P-ltd/H-yes
French

Full breakfast
Dinner
Sitting room, piano
bicycles

The Combes Family Inn is a century-old farmhouse located on a quiet country back road.

Governor's Inn
86 Main St., 05149
802-228-8830
Charlie & Deedy Marble
All year exc. April

$$$ B&B/MAP
8 rooms, 8 pb
Visa, MC, AmEx •
C-no/S-ltd/P-no/H-no

Full 5-course breakfast
6-course dinner, bar
Restaurant, picnic lunch
fireside hors d'oeuvres
afternoon tea, library

A stylish, romantic, Victorian inn (circa 1890). Furnished with family antiques. Beautiful fireplaces. Warm, generous hospitality in a quiet VT town. OUR 1987 INN OF THE YEAR!

The Okemo Inn
RFD #1, Box 133, Locust, 05149
Rtes. 103 & 100 N.
802-228-8834 800-328-8834
Ron & Toni Parry
All year

$$$ B&B/MAP
11 rooms, 11 pb
Visa, MC, AmEx, Disc •
C-6+/S-yes/P-no/H-no

Full country breakfast
Candlelight dinner
Fireside cocktail lounge
library, TV room, piano
pool, sauna, bicycles

Fine food and lodging—lovely 1810 country inn where antiques set the mood. Convenient to all-season sports and activities. Biking and walking tours arranged.

MANCHESTER

Birch Hill Inn
P.O. Box 346, West Rd., 05254
802-362-2761
Jim & Pat Lee
Exc. Nov–Xmas, Apr–May

$$ B&B
6 rooms, 6 pb
Visa, MC, AmEx •
C-6+/S-ltd/P-no/H-no

Full breakfast
Dinner, aftn. tea, wine
Swimming pool
sitting room, piano
trout pond

Small country inn, more than 15 kilometers of private cross-country ski trails through the woods; panoramic views, country cuisine; swimming pool; large fireplace.

MANCHESTER

Manchester Highlands Inn
P.O. Box 1754, 05255
Highland Ave.
802-362-4565
Robert & Patricia Eichorn
Exc. midweek Apr & Nov

$$$ B&B
15 rooms, 10 pb
Visa, MC, AmEx •
C-8+/S-yes/P-no/H-no

Full breakfast
Dinner by arrangement
Bar, homemade snacks
sitting rm.,piano, pool
game room, feather beds

Romantic Victorian inn with 15 charming rooms. Resident cat. Homemade country breakfast in bed. Biking, hiking, golf, tennis, skiing, antiquing. Manchester's best-kept secret!

MANCHESTER CENTER

Brook-n-Hearth
P.O. Box 508, 05255
Star Routes 11 & 30
802-362-3604
Larry & Terry Greene
Exc. early Nov & May

$$ B&B
3 rooms, 3 pb
AmEx
C-yes/S-ltd/P-no/H-no

Full breakfast
Gas BBQ grill, sodas
Sitting room, VCR
player piano
library, swimming pool

Cozy early American decor, close to everything. Wooded pastoral setting, lawn games, walking or cross-country skiing trails by brook.

MANCHESTER VILLAGE

The Inn at Manchester
Route 7A, Box 41, 05254
802-362-1793
Harriet & Stan Rosenberg
All year

$$ B&B
22 rooms, 13 pb
Visa, MC, AmEx •
C-8+/S-ltd/P-no/H-no

Full breakfast
Comp. wine (Sat. nights)
Sitting room, library
piano, swimming pool
3 lounge areas, porch

Beautiful Victorian mansion restored by owners. Furnished with antiques. Delicious breakfasts. Golf, tennis, shopping, antiquing nearby. Country elegance.

Village Country Inn
P.O. Box 408, Route 7A, 05254
802-362-1792
Anne & Jay Degen
All year

$$$ MAP
30 rooms, 30 pb
Visa, MC •
C-no/S-yes/P-no/H-ltd

Full breakfast
Candlelight dinner
Tavern, sitting room
fireplaces in common rms
tennis court, pool

"A French Auberge" located in the heart of the Green Mountains. Beautiful country French decor, antiques, baskets & flowers. gracious rooms & 13 special suites.

MIDDLEBURY

Brookside Meadows
RD 3, Box 2460, 05753
Painter Rd.
802-388-6429
Linda & Roger Cole
All year

$$ B&B
5 rooms, 4 pb
•
C-5+/S-ltd/P-ltd/H-ltd

Full breakfast
Comp. wine
Sitting room, piano
2 bedroom suite w/bath,
private entr., woodstove

Comfortable, gracious home in rural area, only 2.5 miles from town and Middlebury College. Near Shelburne Museum. Hiking, cross-country skiing on property.

MIDDLEBURY

Middlebury Inn
14 Courthouse Square, 05753
P.O. Box 798
802-388-4961 800-842-4666
Frank & Jane Emanuel
All year

$$$ EP
Visa, MC ●
C-yes/S-yes/P-ltd/H-yes

Continental breakfast
Restaurant, bar
Afternoon tea
sitting room, library
private bath, bath phone

Elegant 1827 village inn. Distinctively decorated rooms. Gracious dining. Walk to college, unique shops, historic sites in picturesque Middlebury. Year-round activities.

Swift House Inn
25 Stewart Lane, Rt. 7, 05753
802-388-9925
Andrea & John Nelson
All year

$$$ B&B
14 rooms, 14 pb
Visa, MC, AmEx, D
C-yes/S-yes/P-no/H-no

Continental breakfast
Restaurant, bar
Sitting room, library
formal gardens
whirlpool tubs in 3 rms

Warm and gracious lodging and dining in an elegant 1815 federalist estate furnished with antiques. Four of the bedrooms have working fireplaces.

MT. SNOW–WILMINGTON

The Inn at Quail Run
HCR 63, Box 28-Smith Rd, 05363
800-343-7227
Tom, Marie & Molly Martin
All year

$$$ B&B
15 rooms, 15 pb
Visa, MC ●
C-yes/S-no/P-no/H-no

Full breakfast
Sitting room, library
Game room, exercise room
sauna, pool, tennis ct.
antique store, X-C ski

Romantic country inn on 12 acres with mountain views. Antiques, brass beds & cozy comforters. Hearty country breakfast & afternoon snacks each day. A home away from home.

NEWFANE

The Four Columns Inn
P.O. Box 278, West St., 05345
802-365-7713
Pamela & Jacques Allembert
All year

$$$ EP/MAP
15 rooms, 15 pb
Visa, MC, AmEx
C-yes/S-no/P-yes/H-no
French

Continental plus
Restaurant, bar
Afternoon tea
sitting room
swimming pool

The Four Columns Inn has the only 4 diamond restaurant, rated by AAA, in Vermont. And the Inn is just as fine!

NORTH HERO

North Hero House
P.O. Box 106, Route 2, 05474
Champlain Islands
802-372-8237
John C. Apgar
June 15–October

$ EP
32 rooms, 21 pb
Credit cards accepted
C-yes/S-yes/P-no/H-yes
Spanish, French

Full breakfast $
Restaurant, coffee, tea
Lounge, sitting room
tennis, lake swimming
bicycles, sauna

Lake Champlain island inn (1890). Magnificent view of Mt. Mansfield and Green Mountains. Crystal-clear water for marvelous swimming, boating and fishing.

NORTHFIELD

Northfield Inn
27 Highland Ave., 05663
802-485-8558
Aglaia & Alan Stalb
All year

$$$ B&B
8 rooms, 8 pb
Visa, MC ●
C-no/S-no/P-no/H-no
Greek

Full breakfast
Lunch & dinner by arr.
Comp. wine, snacks
X-C & alpine skiing
bicycles, nearby tennis

Victorian comfort and congeniality. Private baths, antiques, brass beds and feather bedding. Hearty breakfast, beautiful porches, magnificent hillside setting, golden sunsets.

NORWICH

The Norwich Inn
P.O. Box 908, 05055
225 Main Street
802-649-1143
Sally A. Johnson
All year

$$ EP
22 rooms, 21 pb
Visa, MC, AmEx ●
C-yes/S-yes/H-yes

Full breakfast $
Restaurant, bar service
Sitting room
library
near Dartmouth College

Small town inn with country charm, personalized service and gourmet dining. Myriad of cultural and recreational activities. Come relax ... enjoy ... .Special packages available.

ORWELL

Historic Brookside Inn
Route 22A, Box 36, 05760
802-948-2727
Joan & Murray Korda
All year

$$$ B&B
6 rooms, 2 pb
●
C-yes/S-yes/P-no/H-yes
Fr., Sp., Ger., Ital.

Full country breakfast
Lunch, dinner, wine
Sitting room, library
music room, antique shop
X-C skiing, skating

Enjoy country elegance in our National Register Greek revival mansion, set on 300 acres and furnished in period antiques. Antique shop on premises.

PITTSFIELD

The Inn at Pittsfield
Box 675, Route 100, 05762
802-746-8943
Barbara Morris, Vikki Budasi
Exc. November & May

$$ MAP
10 rooms, 6 pb
Visa, MC ●
C-yes/S-yes/P-no/H-no

Full breakfast
Dinner included, bar
Sitting room
piano, bicycles
biking & hiking tours

Hideaway for the outdoor activities enthusiasts who do not want to compromise on the luxuries of fine food and accommodations. Two-day seminars in floral arrangements.

POULTNEY

Lake St. Catherine Inn
P.O. Box 129, 05764
Cones Point Rd.
802-287-9347 800-626-LSCI
Patricia & Raymond Endlilch
May–October

$$$ MAP
35 rooms, 35 pb
●
C-yes/S-yes/P-no/H-yes

Full breakfast
5-course dinner, bar
Piano, bicycles
free use of sailboats,
paddleboats & canoes

Rural country inn located among tall pines on the shores of Lake St. Catherine. Swimming, boating, fishing, and country dining. 3-bedroom cottage available.

PROCTORSVILLE

Golden Stage Inn
P.O. Box 218, Depot St., 05153
802-226-7744
Kirsten Murphy, Marcel Perret
Exc. April & November

$$$ MAP
10 rooms, 6 pb
Visa, MC ●
C-yes/S-yes/P-no/H-no
Swiss, German, French

Full breakfast
Candlelight dinner, bar
Hors d'oeuvres by fire
sitting room, pool
flower gardens

Country inn on 4 acres, Swiss specialties, sumptuous deserts, own baking, vegetable garden, colorful flowers, library, hiking, biking, skiing nearby.

Okemo Lantern Lodge
P.O. Box 247, 05153
Main St.
802-226-7770
Pete & Dody Button
Exc. November & April

$$$ B&B/MAP
10 rooms, 10 pb
Visa, MC, AmEx
C-8+/S-no/P-no/H-no
French

Full breakfast
Dinner, wine
Sitting room
antiques
oriental rugs

Victorian Gingerbread; comfortable antiques, flower bouquets; lace & white starched linens; raspberry pies cooling on the sill; possibly one of your fondest memories.

PUTNEY

Hickory Ridge House
RFD 3. Box 1410, 05346
Hickory Ridge Rd.
802-387-5709
J. Walker, S. Anderson
All year

$ B&B
7 rooms, 3 pb
Visa, MC
C-yes/S-no/P-no/H-yes
French, German, Russian

Full breakfast
Mulled cider in winter
Coffee, tea, cocoa
sitting room, piano
swimming hole

Gracious 1808 brick Federal with six fireplaces, rolling meadows, woods to explore on foot or skis. Our own breads, eggs, jams and honey for breakfast.

QUECHEE

Quechee Inn-Marshland Farm
P.O. Box BB, 05059
Clubhouse Rd.
802-295-3133 800-235-3133
Hal Lothrop
All year

$$$ MAP
24 rooms, 24 pb
Visa, MC, AmEx ●
C-yes/S-yes/P-no/H-ltd

Continental plus
Dinner included, bar
Wine list, sitting room
club membership (sauna,
swimming, tennis)

The beautifully restored 18th-century farmstead of Vermont's first lieutenant governor; nearby private Quechee Club for golf, tennis, swimming, boating, etc.

RICHMOND—BOLTON VALLEY

The Black Bear Inn
P.O. Box 26, 05477
Mountain Road
802-434-2126 800-395-6335
Denis & Sally Turpin
Dec—April, May—Oct

$$ EP
26 rooms, 26 pb
Visa, MC ●
C-ltd/S-yes/P-no/H-no

Poolside breakfast $
Dinner, bar, Sun. brunch
Pool, entertainment
sitting room, piano
X-C & downhill skiing

Delightful mountaintop inn, many rooms with panoramic views. Hiking, tennis, golf, swimming and skiing. Indoor sport center available year-round.

ROCHESTER

Liberty Hill Farm
Liberty Hill Rd., 05767
802-767-3926
Bob & Beth Kennett
All year

$$$ MAP
5 rooms
●
C-yes/S-yes/P-no/H-no

Full breakfast
Dinner included
Sitting room
bicycles, babysitting
cribs, highchairs

Family dairy farm in Green Mtns. bounded by National Forest and White River. Hiking, cross-country skiing from house. Major ski areas nearby. Farm breakfasts.

ROYALTON

Fox Stand Inn & Restaurant
Route 14, 05068
802-763-8437
Jean & Gary Curley
All year

$$ B&B
5 rooms
Visa, MC
C-yes/S-yes/P-no/H-no

Full breakfast
Lunch, dinner
Licensed restaurant
river swimming

Restored 1818 handsome brick building, family-owned and operated inn. Economical rates include full breakfast. Fishing, golf, cross-country skiing nearby.

SAINT JOHNSBURY

Echo Ledge Farm Inn
P.O. Box 77, Route 2, 05838
East Saint Johnsbury
802-748-4750 FAX:748-1640
Dorothy & Fred Herman
All year

$ B&B
6 rooms, 4 pb
Visa, MC
C-yes/S-ltd./P-no/H-no

Full breakfast
Tea, coffee, cookies
Sitting room
color TV

Come spend the night in the real Vermont at a farm settled in 1793. Recommended by National Geographic Traveler. Freshly papered or stenciled walls, hardwood floors.

SOUTH LONDONDERRY

Londonderry Inn Box 301-12,
Rt. 100, 05155
802-824-5226
Jim & Jean Cavanagh
All year

$ B&B25 rooms, 20 pb
•
C-yes/S-yes/P-no/H-yes

Continental plus
Dinner, bar
Swimming pool
sitting room, lounge
game room, billiards

1826 homestead near skiing and the Green Mountain National Forest. Private & shared baths. Period furniture. Families welcome.

STOCKBRIDGE

The Stockbridge Inn B&B
Route 100N, P.O. Box 45, 05772
802-746-8165
Jan Hughes
All year

$$ B&B
6 rooms, 2 pb
Visa, MC •
C-yes/S-ltd/P-no/H-no

Full breakfast
Dinner upon request
Comp. wine, snacks
sitting room, library

Share the romantic countryside of Vermont in our large Victorian home. A charming historical landmark close to skiing, golf, fishing, white-water rafting and antiquing.

STOWE

The 1860 House B&B Inn
P.O. Box 276, 05672
School St.
802-253-7351 800-248-1860
R. Hubbard, R. Matulionis
All year

$$$ B&B
5 rooms, 5 pb
Visa, MC •
C-yes/S-no/P-no/H-no
German

Continental plus
Sitting room, piano
Decks, terraces, sauna
jacuzzi, pool, bicycles
health club facilities

Charming historic village inn. Decks & terraces overlooking flower gardens. Sauna, hot tub, steam room & outdoor pool nearby. Close to skiing, tennis, golf. National Register.

Andersen Lodge
3430 Mt. Road, 05672
802-253-7336 800-336-7336
Dietmar & Trude Heiss

$$ B&B/$$$ MAP
17 rooms, 16 pb
credit cards accepted •
C-yes/S-yes/P-ltd/H-no
German, French

Full breakfast
Dinner avail, sitting rm
Piano, game room, spa
jacuzzi, tennis court
heated pool, golf nearby

Set in relaxing surroundings with lovely view of mountains. Trout fishing, horseback riding, mountain hiking. Owners and hosts of Austrian background. Austrian chef.

Brass Lantern
717 Maple St., 05672
Route 100 North
802-253-2229 800-729-2980
Mindy & Andy Aldrich
All year

$$ B&B
9 rooms, 9 pb
Visa, MC, AmEx •
C-yes/S-no/P-no/H-no

Full country breakfast
Picnic lunch, bar
Afternoon tea, snacks
sitting room with piano
library, fireplaces, A/C

1800s farmhouse and carriage barn with antiques, handmade quilts, stenciled walls, and views. 1989 Award winning restoration by innkeepers. Sports, dining, theater packages.

Butternut Inn at Stowe
Box 950, 05672
2301 Mountain Rd.
802-253-4277 800-3-BUTTER
Jim & Deborah Wimberly
6/15–10/20, 12/18–4/20

$$ B&B, $$$ MAP
18 rooms, 18 pb
Visa, MC •
C-12+/S-no/P-no/H-no

Full country breakfast
Dinner (winter)
Comp. sherry, aftn. tea
sitting rm., piano, pool
sun room, courtyard

Landscaped grounds, mountain views, by mountain stream. Hospitality is a family tradition. Country wallpaper. Poolside breakfast and fireside dining. Couples retreat.

STOWE

Edson Hill Manor
1500 Edson Hill Road, 05672
802-253-7371 800-621-0284
Jane & Eric Lande
All year

$$$ MAP
27 rooms, 22 pb
Visa, MC, AmEx •
C-yes/S-yes/P-no/H-no

Continental (ex. summer)
Dinner/Lunch (ex. summr)
Swimming pool
sitting room
horseback riding all yr.

Country estate on 400 secluded acres. Cross-country skiing; gorgeous swimming pool, outdoor games, barbeques, horseback riding, hiking in summer. Sleigh rides.

Fiddler's Green Inn
4859 Mountain Rd., 05672
Route 108
802-253-8124 800-882-5346
Bud & Carol McKeon
All year

$ B&B
7 rooms, 6 pb
Visa, MC, AmEx •
C-yes/S-yes/P-no/H-no

Full breakfast
Dinner in ski season
beverages & snacks
guest living room
tennis nearby

Cozy New England inn situated on Vermont babbling brook. Hearty country breakfast. Hiking in Green Mountains or cross-country skiing from our doorstep. Near golf & antiquing.

The Gables Inn
1457 Mt. Rd., 05672
802-253-7730
Lynn & Sol Baumrind
All year

$$ EP/$$$ MAP
16 rooms, 16 pb
•
C-yes/S-yes/P-ltd/H-no

Full breakfast
Winter MAP, Summer EP
Sitting room, fireplace
piano, swimming pool
hot tub, jacuzzis, A/C

Classic country inn—antiques, wide plank floors, panoramic view. Outstanding breakfast on lawn or porch (summer). Near golf, hiking, skiing, tennis, bicycling.

Golden Kitz Lodge
1965 Mountain Rd., 05672
Route 108
802-253-4217 800-KITS-LOV
The Jones Family
All year

$ EP
16 rooms, 8 pb
Visa, MC, AmEx, CB, Dis
•
C-yes/S-ltd/P-ltd/H-ltd

Full breakfast $
Apres-ski wine/cheese
Sitting room, porch
piano, art studio
bicycles, riverside path

Share legendary Old World antique family treasures in cozy caring comfort. International 1747 Room. Yummy & chummy breakfasts. Unkink frazzled nerves fireside.

Green Mountain Inn
Main St., P.O. Box 60, 05672
802-253-7301 800-445-6629
Patti Clark
All year

$$ EP
54 rooms, 54 pb
Visa, MC, AmEx •
C-yes/S-yes/P-yes/H-ltd
French

Restaurant, bar
Lunch, dinner, snacks
Full service health club
pool, massage, aerobics
beauty salon, shops

Beautifully renovated 1833 inn listed in the Register of Historic Places. Antique furnished guest rooms with every modern convenience. Heart of Stowe Village.

Raspberry Patch B&B
606 Randolph Rd., 05672
802-253-4145
Linda V. Jones
All year

$$ B&B
4 rooms, 3 pb
Visa, MC •
C-yes/S-ltd/P-ltd

Full breakfast
Comp. tea
Snacks, grills, A/C
bicycles, sitting
roomcroquet, badminton

Friendly hospitality, a peaceful mountain view. Immaculate, cozy rooms with antiques and down comforters await you at the Raspberry Patch.

STOWE

The Siebeness
3681 Mountain Rd., 05672
802-253-8942 800-426-9001
Sue & Nils Andersen
All year

$$ B&B
10 rooms, 10 pb
Visa, MC, AmEx, DC, Dis •
C-yes/S-yes/P-no/H-no

Full breakfast
Comp. beverages & snacks
Lounge, hot tub
pool, X-C skiing
golf & tennis nearby

Charming country inn, newly renovated with antiques and quilts. Outstanding food served with mountain view. X-C skiing from door, near golf, tennis, skiing, recreation path.

Ski Inn
Route 108, Mountain Rd., 05672
802-253-4050
The Heyer Family
All year

$ B&B/$$$ MAP
10 rooms, 5 pb
•
C-yes/S-yes/P-ltd/H-no
some French

Continental breakfast
Full breakfast (winter)
Dinner (winter MAP)

This comfortable inn, noted for good food and good conversation, is a great gathering place for interesting people. MAP available in the winter.

Ten Acres Lodge
14 Barrows Road, 05672
802-253-7638 800-327-7357
Curt & Cathy Dann
All year

$$$ B&B
12 rooms, 9 pb
Visa, MC, AmEx, DC •
C-yes/S-ltd/P-ltd/H-no

Full breakfast
Iced tea, spiced cider
Dinner, bar
tennis court, sitting rm
swimming pool, hot tub

Stowe's favorite country inn and restaurant for over forty years. Close to ski trails, hiking, golf in New England ski capital. Hill house and cottages available.

Timberhölm Inn
452 Cottage Club Rd., 05672
RR 1 Box 810
802-253-7603 800-753-7603
Kay & Richard Hildebrand
All year

$$ B&B
10 rooms, 10 pb
Visa, MC •
C-yes/S-ltd/P-no/H-no

Full breakfast
Comp. wine, tea
Aftn. soups/refreshments
sitting room, library
A/C, hot tub

Country inn tucked in the woods. Beautiful mountain setting. Close to ski slopes, town of Stowe, shopping, activities. Rooms are tastefully decorated with antiques and quilts.

Ye Olde England Inne
Mountain Rd., Box 320, 05672
802-253-7558 802-253-7064
Christopher & Linda Francis
All year

$$ B&B
23 rooms, 23 pb
Visa, MC •
C-yes/S-yes/P-ltd/H-no
French, Arabic

Full breakfast, aftn tea
Dinner, valet parking
Library, piano, pool
pub, murder mystery wknd
polo & gliding packages

Classic English luxury, Lara Ashley rooms/cottages. Four posters, fireplaces & jacuzzi's. Gourmet dining in Copperfield's. Mr. Pickwick's Polo Pub, 150 beers/ales/rare wines

THETFORD HILL

Fahrenbrae Hilltop Retreat
Box 129, 05074
802-785-4304
F. Wooten, D. Marks, K. Finch
All year

$$$ EP
3 rooms, 3 pb
C-yes/S-no/P-yes/H-no

Three wonderful homes
For 4 and 6 people
Fully equipped kitchens
color TV, stereo, porch
washer/dryer, sun decks

10 minutes from Hanover, NH, and Dartmouth College. Incredible views, meticulously appointed interiors; extraordinarily restful. Some of the most private & dramatic lodging.

VERGENNES

Strong House Inn
RD1, Box 1003, 05491
82 W. Main St., (Rt. 22A)
802-877-3337
Michelle & Ron Bring
Ex. Nov/mid Mar–mid Apr

$$ B&B
7 rooms, 2 pb
Visa, MC, AmEx •
C-yes/S-ltd/P-ltd/H-ltd

Full country breakfast
Dinner with notice
Aftn. beverage & snack
sitting room w/fireplace
piano, catering avail.

Comfortably elegant lodging in a tastefully decorated historic home. Wonderful breakfasts. Convenient to Middlebury, Burlington, Lake Champlain. Superb cycling.

WAITSFIELD

Hyde Away
RR 1, Box 65, 05673
Route 17
802-496-2322 800-777-HYDE
Bruce Hyde
All year

$$ B&B/MAP
16 rooms, 3 pb
Visa, MC, AmEx •
C-yes/S-yes/P-no/H-no

Full breakfast $
Restaurant, bar
Afternoon tea, snacks
sitting room, library
bicycles, skiing

Comfortable, cozy, rustic circa 1820 converted farmstead. Families encouraged. Toy area, mountain bike touring center. Outrageous downhill and cross-country skiing.

Inn at Round Barn Farm
RR 1, Box 247, 05673
E. Warren Rd.
802-496-2276
Jack, Doreen, AnneMarie Simko
All year

$$$ B&B
6 rooms, 6 pb
Visa, MC, AmEx •
C-no/S-no/P-no/H-no
Hungarian

Full breakfast
Comp. wine, tea, snacks
Sitting room, library
bicycles, 60-ft lap pool
jacuzzi in rooms

Sugarbush's most noted landmark; elegant inn; 85 acres for quiet walks, gourmet picnics, Bach, Mozart, and simple pleasures of unspoiled Vermont.

Knoll Farm Country Inn
RFD 1, Box 179, 05673
Bragg Hill Rd.
802-496-3939 802-496-3527
Ann Day
Exc. April & November

$$ B&B/$$$ MAP
4 rooms
C-yes/S-no/P-no/H-no
some Spanish

Full breakfast
Dinner, lunch, teas
Sitting room, library
swimming pond, hiking
farm animals, 150 acres

Unique combination of inn and farm; pond, spectacular views; peaceful, away from highway; delicious family-style farm grown meals; 150 acres of nature.

Lareau Farm Country Inn
Box 563, Route 100, 05673
802-496-4949 800-833-0766
Dan & Susan Easley
All year

$$ B&B
14 rooms, 10 pb
Visa, MC •
C-ltd/S-ltd/P-no/H-no

Full breakfast
Apres-ski hors d'oeuvres
Dinner, wine & beer $
sitting room, fireplace
porches, picnic lunches

Picturesque Vermont farmhouse, now an inn, nestled in a picturesque meadow beside the Mad River, our 150-year-old farmhouse is minutes from skiing and shopping.

Millbrook
RFD Box 62, Route 17, 05673
802-496-2405
Joan & Thom Gorman
All year exc. April-May

$$ B&B\$$$ MAP
7 rooms, 4 pb
Visa, MC, AmEx •
C-ltd/S-ltd/P-ask/H-ltd

Full breakfast from menu
Full dinner from rest.
Comp. refreshments
3 sitting rooms, piano

Charming hand-stenciled guest rooms with handmade quilts, country gourmet dining in our small candlelit restaurant, friendly, unhurried atmosphere.

Newton's 1824 House Inn, Waitsfield, VT

WAITSFIELD

Newton's 1824 House Inn
Route 100, Box 159, 05673
802-496-7555
Nick & Joyce Newton
All year

$$$ B&B
6 rooms, 6 pb
Visa, MC, AmEx ●
C-yes/S-no/P-no/H-no
Spanish

Full gourmet breakfast
Dinner by special order
Comp. sherry, tea
library, swimming hole
cross country skiing

Relaxed elegance, pristine countryside, oriental rugs, chandeliers, fireplaces. "Best breakfast" say our guests! Near Sugarbush Resort, golf, tennis, horseback riding.

WARREN

Beaver Pond Farm Inn
RD Box 306, 05674
Golf Course Rd.
802-583-2861
Betty & Bob Hansen
All year exc. May

$$ B&B
6 rooms, 4 pb
Visa, MC, AmEx ●
C-yes/S-yes/P-no/H-no
French

Full breakfast
Comp. sherry, brandy
Sitting room, library
weddings, Thanksg. pack.
golf and skiing packages

Beautifully restored Vermont farmhouse adjacent to golf course. Hiking, swimming and skiing nearby. Spectacular views from spacious deck; hearty breakfasts.

Sugartree—A Country Inn
RR Box 38, 05674
Sugarbush Valley
802-583-3211 800-666-8907
Howard & Janice Chapman
All year

$$$ B&B
10 rooms, 10 pb
Visa, MC, AmEx ●
C-5+/S-yes/P-no/H-yes

Full country breakfast
Living room w/fireplace
all rooms have brass,
antiques, or canopy beds

Beautifully decorated with unique country flair and antiques. Enchanting gazebo amid flower gardens. Breathtaking views of ski slopes or fall foliage.

WATERBURY

Grünberg Haus B&B
RR 2, Box 1595, 05675
Route 100 South, Duxbury
802-244-7726 800-800-7760
C. Sellers, M. Frohman
All year

$$ B&B
10 rooms, 5 pb
Visa, MC, AmEx, Enr ●
C-yes/S-no/P-no/H-no

Full breakfast
Dinner, comp. wine
Self-serve pub, piano
tennis court, jacuzzi
sauna, flock of chickens

Hand-built Tyrolian chalet secluded on 10 acres in Green Mountains where guests are treated as friends. Hiking trails, gardens, decks. Feed our chickens! Creative breakfasts.

WATERBURY

Inn at Blush Hill	$$ B&B	Full breakfast
RR 1, Box 1266, 05676	6 rooms, 6 pb	Aftn. tea, sitting room
Blush Hill Rd.	Visa, MC, AmEx, Enroute	Library, fireplaces
802-244-7529 800-736-7522	•	piano, lawn games
Pamela & Gary Gosselin	C-6+/S-ltd/P-no/H-ltd	electric mattress pads
All year		

Cozy, country, 1790s brick farmhouse, located across from 9-hole golf course, fifteen minutes to Sugarbush, Bolton, Stowe. Fireplaces, antiques. Swimming and boating nearby.

Thatcher Brook Inn	$$$ MAP	Continental breakfast
RD 2 Box 62, 05676	24 rooms, 24 pb	Dinner packages ($), pub
Route 100 North	Visa, MC, AmEx •	Restaurant, library
802-244-5911 800-292-5911	C-5+/S-ltd/P-no/H-yes	whirlpools, fireplaces
Kelly & Peter Varty	French	bicycles, gazebo porches
All year		

Beautifully restored 1899 country Victorian mansion. Centrally located between renowned resorts of Stowe and Sugarbush. Exquisite lodging and superb gourmet dining!

WATERBURY CENTER

Black Locust Inn	$$ B&B	Full breakfast
RR 1, Box 715, 05677	6 rooms, 6 pb	Afternoon tea
802-244-7490 800-366-5592	Visa, MC •	Comp. wine, snacks
George & Anita Gajdos	C-6+/S-no/P-no/H-ltd	sitting room, library
All year	Hungarian	lawn games, croquet

Beautifully decorated 1832 farmhouse set on hill surrounded by Green Mountains and Worcester Range. Cross-country skiing, hiking, biking, fishing and antiquing nearby.

WEATHERSFIELD

Inn at Weathersfield	$$$ MAP	Full breakfast
P.O. Box 165, 05151	12 rooms, 12 pb	High tea & dinner incl.
Route 106, Perkinsville	Visa, MC, AmEx •	5 sitting rooms, piano
802-263-9217 800-477-4828	C-8+/S-ltd/P-no/H-ltd	library, sauna, bicycles
Mary Louise, Ron Thorburn	German	sleigh/carriage rides
All year		

Set back 400 feet from the road on maple-lined drive. Breakfast in bed on English butler's tray. Hot wassail on open hearth all winter.

WEST DOVER

Austin Hill Inn	$$$ B&B	Full breakfast
P.O. Box 859, Route 100, 05356	12 rooms, 12 pb	Dinner, bar service
802-464-5281 800-332RELAX	Visa, MC, AmEx •	Afternoon tea, snacks
Robbie Sweeney	C-8+/S-ltd/P-no/H-no	sitting room, library
All year		swimming pool, bicycles

Escape to "timeless relaxation"; casual elegance and gracious service—antiques, wine list, fine dining. The comfort and fond memories of our guests are a primary tradition.

Shield Inn	$$ B&B/MAP	Full breakfast
Box 366, Route 100, 05356	11 rooms, 11 pb	Dinner (winter), tea
802-464-3984 802-464-6585	Visa, MC, AmEx	Sitting rooms w/cable TV
John & Marijke Sims	C-yes/S-yes/P-no/H-no	fireplaces, whirlpools
All year	Dutch, German	near tennis/pool/skiing

A true country inn experienced in relaxed elegance. Antiques delight each superbly decorated room. Rooms available with fireplaces & whirlpool baths.

Silver Fox Inn, West Rutland, VT

WEST DOVER

Snow Den Inn & Gallery
Route 100, Box 625, 05356
802-464-9355 800-852-9240
Andrew & Marjorie Trautwein
June–April

$$$ B&B
8 rooms, 8 pb
Visa, MC, AmEx ●
C-10+/S-yes/P-no/H-no

Full breakfast
Comp. wine, beer, sodas
Sitting room, fireplaces
color cable TV
art gallery–local/nat'l

Lovely country inn filled with antiques–fireplaces in five rooms. Close to golfing, swimming, tennis, skiing, hiking, antiquing, skating, boating.

Weathervane Lodge B&B
HCR 63, Box 57, 05356
Dorr Fitch Rd.
802-464-5426
Liz & Ernie Chabot
All year

$$ B&B
11 rooms, 5 pb
●
C-yes/S-yes/P-no/H-no
French

Full breakfast
Comp. beverages, snacks
BYOB bar, sitting room
lounge, piano, fireplc's
Bike & walking trails

Mountainous country inn: Colonial antiques, lounge, recreation rooms with fireplaces. X-C skiing, tennis, golf, swimming; bring children. A home away from home.

West Dover Inn
P.O. Box 506, Route 100, 05356
802-464-5207
Don & Madeline Mitchell
All year exc. Apr–June

$$$ B&B
10 rooms, 10 pb
Visa, MC, AmEx ●
C-8+/S-yes/P-no/H-no

Full breakfast
Dinner plan (exc. Wed.)
Bar, lounge, library
2 suites w/fireplace
bicycles, organ

Historic inn. Handsomely appointed guest rooms with cozy quilts, antiques. Fine country dining. Golf, skiing, swimming, antiquing nearby. Register of Historic Places.

WEST RUTLAND

Silver Fox Inn
RFD 1, Box 1222, 05777
Route 133, Clarendon Ave.
802-438-5555
Pam & Gerry Bliss
May–March

$$$ B&B/MAP
7 rooms, 7 pb
Visa, MC, AmEx, DC ●
C-yes/S-ltd/P-no/H-yes

Full breakfast
Restaurant, bar, dinner
Snacks, sherry in room
sitting room, library
bicycles, tennis nearby

Country elegance in a 1768 farmhouse. Mountain views galore. Hiking, fishing, biking, cross-country skiing, golf nearby. 20 minutes to Killington-Pico.

WEST TOWNSHEND

Windham Hill Inn	$$$ MAP	Full breakfast
RR 1, Box 44, 05359	15 rooms, 15 pb	6-course dinner, cordial
off Route 30	Visa, MC ●	Bar, 3 sitting rooms
802-874-4080	C-12+/S-no/P-no/H-ltd	library, swimming pond
Ken & Linda Busteed		hiking, ski trails
Ex. Apr & Nov (open Thgv)		

Carefully restored 1825 farmhouse & barn offering warm, distinctive guest & public rooms, elegant dining, secluded hilltop setting. 1988 & 1989 One of Ten Best Inns—Innsider.

WESTON

1830 Inn on the Green	$$ B&B	Full breakfast
Route 100, Box 104, 05161	4 rooms, 3 pb	Afternoon tea
802-824-6789	Visa, MC	Comp. wine
Sandy & Dave Granger	C-14+/S-ltd	bedtime sweets
All year		sitting room

A small, romantic inn located on the Village Green. Recognized by the National Register of Historic Places.

Colonial House	$$ B&B	Full breakfast
RR 1, Box 138 IG, 05161	15 rooms, 9 pb	Dinner
Route 100	Visa, MC	Tea, coffee, baked goods
800-639-5033 802-824-6286	C-yes/S-ltd/P-ltd/H-ltd	sitting room
John & Betty Nunnikhoven		
All year		

Your country cousins are waiting with a warm welcome, old-fashioned meals and a relaxing living room for you while you visit the attractions of southern Vermont.

The Darling Family Inn	$$$ B&B	Full breakfast
Route 100, 05161	7 rooms, 7 pb	Dinner with notice
802-824-3223	C-ltd/S-yes/P-ltd/H-no	Comp. wine, refreshments
Chapin & Joan Darling		sitting room, cottages
All year		swimming pool

Restored Colonial in farmland and mountain setting with American and English country antiques. Closest inn to the famous Weston Priory.

Inn at Weston	$$ MAP	Full breakfast
Route 100, P.O. Box 56, 05161	20 rooms, 13 pb	Dinner included
802-824-5804	C-yes/S-yes/P-no/H-yes	Pub, tea/cider in winter
Jeanne & Bob		dining room
All year		game room, piano

1848 converted farmhouse. Creative country cuisine. Featured in Gourmet Magazine. Stroll to Weston shops. 11 years making memories. "Where Friendships Begin."

WILLIAMSTOWN

Rosewood Inn	$$ B&B	Full gourmet breakfast
P.O. Box 31, 05679	5 rooms, 1 pb	Afternoon tea
Main St., Route 14	Visa, MC, AmEx ●	Sitting room
802-433-5822	C-yes/S-yes/P-no/H-no	bicycles
Elaine & John Laveroni		
All year		

Elegant Victorian mansion. Charming country village. Awake to the aroma of our gourmet breakfast. Skiing, hunting, fishing all nearby.

WILMINGTON

Hermitage Inn & Brookbound
P.O. Box 457, 05363
Coldbrook Rd.
802-464-3511
Jim McGovern
All year

$$ MAP
29 rooms, 25 pb
AmEx, Visa, MC, DC
C-yes/S-yes/P-no/H-no
French, Spanish

Full breakfast
Dinner included, bar
Sitting room, piano
entertainment, swimming
sauna, tennis courts

Specializing in home-raised gamebirds. Over 1,200 selections on our award-winning wine list. Individually decorated guest rooms with fireplaces. 55 km. of X-C skiing trails.

Nutmeg Inn
P.O. Box 818, Route 9W, 05363
Molly Stark Trail
802-464-3351
Del & Charlotte Lawrence
All year

$$$ B&B
16 rooms, 16 pb
AmEx
C-8+/S-ltd/P-no/H-ltd

Full breakfast from menu
Dinner, 3 dining rooms
Sitting room, piano
2-room suites w/firepl.
king bedrooms w/firepl.

"Charming and cozy" early American farmhouse with informal homelike atmosphere. Spotless guest rooms—delicious "country-style" meals. Enjoy complimentary afternoon tea/coffee

Red Shutter Inn
P.O. Box 636, 05363
Route 9 West
802-464-3768
Max & Carolyn Hopkins
Exc. early Nov & April

$$$ B&B
9 rooms, 9 pb
Visa, MC
C-14+/S-yes

Full breakfast
Restaurant, bar service
Snacks, alfresco dining
fireplaces, guest suites
whirlpool bath

Congenial hillside inn and renovated Carriage House at the village edge featuring candlelight dining. Fireplace suites, whirlpool. Golf, hike, ski amid mountains and valleys.

Trail's End, A Country Inn
Smith Rd., 05363
802-464-2727
Bill & Mary Kilburn
Exc. late Apr, early Nov

$$ B&B
22 rooms, 22 pb
C-yes/S-yes/P-no/H-no

Full breakfast
Comp. sherry, beverages
Snacks, library, pool
fireplace/jacuzzi suites
clay tennis court

Friendly inn tucked along a country road with English flower gardens, hiking trails, trout pond. Dramatic 2-story fireplace and loft. Skiing and golf nearby.

WOLCOTT

Golden Maple Inn
P.O. Box 35, 05680
Route 15, Wolcott Village
802-888-6614
Dick & Jo Wall
All year

$$ B&B
3 rooms, 1 pb
Visa, MC ●
C-12+/S-no/P-no/H-no

Full breakfast
Comp. tea, sweets
Library, sitting room
alpine, X-C skiing near
river trout fishing

Enjoy exceptional accommodations in this 1865 country inn on the Lamoille River. Spacious rooms in unique themes, all with antiques and cozy down comforters.

WOODSTOCK

Kedron Valley Inn
Route 106, S. Woodstock, 05071
802-457-1473
Max & Merrily Comins
All year

$$$ B&B/MAP
29 rooms, 29 pb
Visa, MC, DC ●
C-yes/S-yes/P-yes/H-yes
French, Spanish

Full country breakfast
Dinner, bar
Sitting room, swim pond
piano, TV's, quilts

Distinguished inn built in 1822 in gentle valley. Full riding stables, hiking, X-C skiing. Nouvelle cuisine with local Vermont products. Canopy beds, fireplaces. OUR 1991 INN OF THE YEAR.

Golden Maple Inn, Wolcott, VT

WOODSTOCK

Lincoln Covered Bridge Inn
RR 2, Box 40, Route 4, 05091
802-457-3312
Harry & Pat Francis
All year

$$$ B&B/MAP
6 rooms, 6 pb
Visa, MC, AmEx ●
C-no/S-yes/P-no/H-no

Full breakfast
Restaurant, bar
Sitting room, library
gazebo overlooking river
horses, golf nearby

200 year old farmhouse on 6 acres of private park along the bank of the Ottauquechee river. Fireside dining. 15 minutes from Killington.

Woodstocker B&B
61 River St., Route 4, 05091
802-457-3896
L. Deignan, R. Formichella
All year exc. April

$$ B&B
7 rooms, 7 pb
Visa, MC ●
C-ltd/S-yes/P-no/H-yes

Continental plus
Afternoon tea
Sitting room
hot tub
library

We enjoy making our guests feel at home. Within easy walking distance of shops and restaurants. Cross-country and downhill skiing close by.

More Inns ...

1811 House P.O. Box 39, Route 7A, Manchester, 05254 802-362-1811
A Century Past P.O. Box 186, Route 5, Newbury, 05051 802-866-3358
Abel Barron House 37 Main, P.O. Box 532, Quechee Village, 05059 802-295-1337
Aloha Manor Lake Morey, Fairlee, 05045 802-333-4478
Alpenrose Inn P.O. Box 187, Bondville, 05340 802-297-2750
Arches Country Inn 53 Park St., Route 73-E, Brandon, 05733 802-247-8200
Auberge Alburg RD 1, Box 3, Alburg, 05440 802-796-3169
Austria Haus Box 2, Austria Haus Rd., Mount Holly, 05758 802-259-2441
Beauchamp Place US Route 7, Brandon, 05733 802-247-3905
Bellevue 9 Parsons Lane, Saint Albans, 05478 802-527-1115
Berkson Farms RFD 1, Enosburg Falls, 05450 802-933-2522
Black Lantern Inn Route 118, Montgomery Village, 05470 802-326-4507

Blue Gentian Lodge Box 129 RR #1, Londonderry, 05148 802-824-5908
Brandon Inn 20 Park Green, Brandon, 05733 802-247-5766
Brick House Box 128, East Hardwick, 05836 802-472-5512
Bromley View Inn Route 30, Bondville, 05340 802-297-1459
Brook Bound Building Coldbrook Rd., Wilmington, 05363 802-464-3511
Carriage House B&B Woodstock, 05091 802-457-4322
Castle Inn Box 157, Proctorsville, 05153 802-226-7222
Charleston House Inn 21 Pleasant St., Woodstock, 05091 802-457-3843
Charlies Northland Lodge Route 2, Box 88, North Hero, 05474 802-372-8822
Chipman Inn, The Route 125, Ripton, 05766 802-388-2390
Cooper Hill Inn Cooper Hill Rd., Box 14, East Dover, 05341 802-348-6333
Cornucopia of Dorset Route 30, Dorset, 05251 802-867-5751
Country Hare Rt. 11 & Magic Mtn Rd., Londonderry, 05148 802-824-3131
Darcroft's Schoolhouse Rt. 100, Wilmington, 05363 802-464-2631
Deer Brook Inn HCR 68, Box 443, Rt. 4W, Woodstock, 05091 802-672-3713
Deerhill Inn & Restaurant P.O. Box 397, West Dover, 05356 802-464-3100
Derby Village Inn B&B 46 Main St., Derby Line, 05830 802-873-3604
Doveberry Inn HCR 63 Box 9, Dover, 05356 802-464-5652
Dovetail Inn Route 30, Main St., Dorset, 05251 802-867-5747
Eastwood House River St., Bethel, 05032 802-234-9686
Eaton House B&B P.O. Box 139, Jericho, 05465 802-899-2354
Echo Lake Inn Route 100, 05056, Tyson, 05149 802-228-8602
Emersons' Guest House 82 Main St., Vergennes, 05491 802-877-3293
Evergreen Sandgate, Box 2480, Arlington, 05250 802-375-2272
Fair Haven Inn Fair Haven, 05743 802-265-3833
Farmhouse 'Round the Bend P.O. Box 57, Grafton, 05146 802-843-2515
Fitch Hill Inn RFD 1, Box 1879, Hyde Park, 05655 802-888-5941
Fjord Gate Inn & Farm Higley Hill Road, Wilmington, 05363 802-464-2783
Flower Cottage Lower Waterford, 05848 802-748-8441
Fontain B&B Route 100, Box 2480, Stowe, 05672 802-253-9285
Four Chimneys Inn 21 West Rd., Bennington, 05201 802-447-3500
Fox Bros. Farm Corn Hill Rd., Pittsford, 05763 802-483-2870
Foxfire Inn RR2, Box 2180, Stowe, 05672 802-253-4887
Garrison Inn P.O. Box 177, East Burke, 05832 802-626-8329
Gazebo Inn 25 Grove St., Route 7, Brandon, 05733 802-247-3235
Green Meadows B&B Mt. Philo Rd., POB 1300, Charlotte, 05445 802-425-3059
Green Mountain Tea Room RR 1 Box 400, Route 7, South Wallingford, 05773 802-446-2611
Greenhurst Inn RD2, Box 60, Bethel, 05032 802-234-9474
Grey Bonnet Inn Killington, 05751 800-342-2086
Grey Fox Inn Stowe, 05672 802-253-8921
Guesthouse Christel Horman RR #1 Box 1635, Stowe, 05672 802-253-4846
Gwendolyn's Route 106, P.O. Box 225, Perkinsville, 05151 802-263-5248
Hartness House Inn 30 Orchard St., Springfield, 05156 802-885-2115
Harveys Mt. View Inn Rochester, 05767 802-767-4273
Haven, est. 1948 One Fourth St., Fair Haven, 05743 802-265-3373
Hayes House Grafton, 05146 802-843-2461
Henry M. Field House RR 2, Box 395, Jericho, 05465 802-899-3984
Highland Lodge RR 1, Box 1290, Greensboro, 05841 802-533-2647
Hillside RR #1, Box 196, Andover, 05143 802-875-3844
Hob Knob Inn Mountain Rd., Stowe, 05672 802-253-8549
Honeysuckle's Inn P.O. Box 828, Waitsfield, 05673 802-496-6200
Hound's Folly Box 591, Mount Holly, 05758 802-259-2718
Hunts' Hideaway RR 1, Box 570, West Charleston, 05872 802-895-4432
Inn at Long Last Box 589, Chester, 05143 802-875-2444
Inn at Montpelier 147 Main St., Montpelier, 05602 802-223-2727
Inn at Sawmill Farm Box 8 (#100), West Dover, 05356 802-464-8131
Inn at South Newfane Dover Rd., South Newfane, 05351 802-348-7191
Inn at Tiffany Corner RD 3, Blof Course Rd., Brandon, 05733 802-247-6571
Inn at Willow Pond P.O. Box 1429, Route 7, Manchester Center, 05255 802-362-4733
Inn at Woodchuck Hill Farm Middletown Rd., Grafton, 05146 802-843-2398

Innsburck Inn RR1, Box 1570, Stowe, 05672 802-253-8582
Inwood Manor RD 1 Box 127, East Barnet, 05821 802-633-4047
Jackson House at Woodstock Route 4 West, Woodstock, 05091 802-457-2065
Jay Village Inn Route 242, Mountain Rd, Jay, 05859 802-988-2643
Johnny Seesaw's P.O. Box 68, Route 11, Peru, 05152 802-824-5533
Juniper Hill Inn RR 1, Box 79, Windsor, 05089 802-674-5273
Kahagon at Nichols Pond Box 728, Hardwick, 05843 802-472-6446
Kincraft Inn P.O. Box 96, Hancock, 05748 802-767-3734
Lake House Inn Route 244, P.O. Box 65, Post Mills, 05058 802-333-4025
Lindenwood–A Country Inn 916 Shelburne Rd., South Burlington, 05403 802-862-2144
Little Lodge at Dorset P.O. Box 673, Dorset, 05251 802-867-4040
Logwood Inn & Chalets Box 2290, Route 1, Stowe, 05672 800-426-6697
Longwood Inn Route 9, P.O. Box 86, Marlboro, 05344 802-257-1545
Mad River Barn P.O. Box 88, Route 17, Waitsfield, 05673 802-496-3310
Maplewood Colonial Inn Route 30, P.O. Box 1200, Dorset, 05251 802-867-4470
Marble West Inn Box 22, West Rd., Dorset, 05251 802-867-4155
Merry Meadow Farm Lower Plain, Route 5, Bradford, 05033 802-222-4412
Middletown Springs Inn Box 1068, Middletown Springs, 05757 802-235-2198
Mill Brook B&B & Gallery P.O. Box 410, Brownsville, 05037 802-484-7283
Misty Mountain Lodge Wilmington, 05356 802-464-3961
Moffett House B&B 69 Park St., Brandon, 05733 802-247-3843
Mountain View Inn Route 17, RFD Box 69, Waitsfield, 05673 802-496-2426
Mt. Anthony Guest House 226 Main St., Bennington, 05201 802-447-7396
New Homestead Rochester, 05767 802-767-4751
Nichols Lodge Box 1098, Stowe, 05672 802-253-7683
Nordic Hills Lodge Wilmington, 05356 802-464-5130
Nordic Inn Rt. 11, P.O. Box 96, Landgrove, 05148 802-824-6444
Nunts Hideaway Route 111, Morgan, 05872 802-895-4432
Old Coach Inn RR 1 Box 260, Readsboro, 05350 802-423-5394
Old Cutter Inn Burke Mt. Access Rd., East Burke, 05832 802-626-5152
Old Newfane Inn P.O. Box 101, Newfane, 05345 802-365-4427
Old Town Farm Inn Route 10, Gassetts, 05143 802-875-2346
On the Rocks Lodge Wilmington, 05363 802-464-8364
Parker House 16 Main St., Box 0780, Quechee, 05059 802-295-6077
Partridge Hill P.O. Box 52, Williston, 05495 802-878-4741
Peeping Cow Inn Route 106, P.O. Box 47, Reading, 05062 802-484-5036
Poplar Manor RD 2, Rts. 12 & 107, Bethel, 05032 802-234-5426
Quail's Nest B&B Inn P.O. Box 221, Main St., Danby, 05739 802-293-5099
Red Clover Inn RR 2, Woodward Rd., Mendon, 05701 802-775-2290
Red Door 7 Pleasant St., Ludlow, 05149 802-228-2376
Reluctant Panther Inn Box 678, West Rd., Manchester, 05254 802-362-2568
Rowell's Inn RR 1, Box 267D, Chester, 05143 802-875-3658
Salt Ash Inn Jct. Rts. 100 & 100A, Plymouth Union, 05056 802-672-3748
Saxon Inn RR2, Box 4295, S. Orr, Jericho, 05465 802-899-3015
Saxtons River Inn Main St., Saxtons River, 05154 802-869-2110
Scandinavia Inn & Chalet Stowe, 05672 802-253-8555
Scarborough Inn Rt. 100 HCR 65 Box 23, Stockbridge, 05772 802-746-8141
Schneider Haus Route 100, Duxbury, 05676 802-244-7726
Seymour Lake Lodge Route 111, Morgan, 05853 802-895-2752
Shoreham Inn Route 74W, Main St., Shoreham Village, 05770 802-897-5081
Sky Line Inn Box 325, Manchester, 05254 802-362-1113
Snowy Owl Lodge HCR 70, Rt 100A, Box106, Plymouth, 05056 802-672-5018
Snuggery Inn Box 65, RR#1, Waitsfield, 05673 802-496-2322
South Shire Inn 124 Elm St., Bennington, 05201 802-447-3839
Spruce Pond Inn Stowe, 05672 802-253-4828
Stone House Inn Box 47, Route 5, North Thetford, 05054 802-333-9124
Stonebridge Inn Route 30, Poultney, 05764 802-287-9849
Stowehof Inn P.O. Box 1108, Stowe, 05672 802-253-9722
Stronghold Inn HCR 40, Route 121, Grafton, 05146 802-843-2203
Sun & Ski Motor Inn Mountain Rd., Stowe, 05672 802-253-7159

Swiss Farm Lodge P.O. Box 630, Pittsfield, 05762 802-748-8341
Sycamore Inn RD 2, Box 2485, Rt. 7A, Arlington, 05250 802-362-2284
Thomas Hill Farm B&B Rose Hill, Woodstock, 05091 802-457-1067
Three Church Street B&B 3 Church St., Woodstock, 05091 802-457-1925
Three Stallion Inn RD #2 Stock Farm Rd., Randolph, 05060 802-728-5575
Truax Tourist Home 32 University Terrace, Burlington, 05401 802-862-0809
Tucker Hill Lodge RD 1, Box 147 (Rt. 17), Waitsfield, 05673 802-496-3983
Tyler Place-Lake Champlain P.O. Box 45, Highgate Springs, 05460 802-868-3301
Valley House Inn 4 Memorial Square, Orleans, 05860 802-754-6665
Valley Inn Route 100, RR 1, Box 8, Waitsfield, 05673 802-496-3450
Vermont Marble Inn 12 W. Park Place, Fair Haven, 05743 802-265-4736
Village Auberge P.O. Box 970, Dorset, 05251 802-867-5715
Village Inn RFD Landgrove, Londonderry, 05148 802-824-6673
Village Inn Rt. 242, Jay, 05859 802-988-2643
Village Inn of Bradford P.O. Box 354, Bradford, 05033 802-222-9303
Village Inn of Woodstock 41 Pleasant St., Woodstock, 05091 802-457-1255
Waitsfield Inn Route 100, P.O. Box 969, Waitsfield, 05673 802-496-3979
Waitsfield Inn Rt. 100 Box 969, Waitsfield, 05673 802-496-3979
Waldwinkel Inn West Dover, 05356 802-464-5281
Wallingford Inn 9 N. Main St., Wallingford, 05773 802-446-2849
Watercours Way Route 132, South Strafford, 05070 802-765-4314
Waybury Inn Route 125, East Middlebury, 05740 802-388-4015
West River Lodge RR 1, Box 693, Newfane, 05345 802-365-7745
Whispering Pines East Fairfield, 05448 802-827-3827
White House of Wilmington Route 9, Box 757, Wilmington, 05363 802-464-2135
White Rocks Inn RR1, Box 297, Wallingford, 05773 802-446-2077
Wilder Homestead Inn RR1, Box 106D, Weston, 05161 802-824-8172
Wildflower Inn Darling Hill Rd., Lyndonville, 05851 802-626-8310
Wiley Inn Route 11, P.O. Box 37, Peru, 05152 802-824-6600
Windridge Inn B&B Main St., Rt. 15 & 108, Jeffersonville, 05464 802-644-8281
Woodruff House 13 East St., Barre, 05641 802-476-7745
Woodshed Lodge Jay, 05859 802-988-4444
Woodstock Inn & Resort 14 The Green, Woodstock, 05091 800-448-7900
Yankee's Northview B&B Lightening Ridge Rd., Calais, 05667 802-454-7191

Virgin Islands

SAINT THOMAS

Danish Chalet Inn	$$ B&B	Continental breakfast
P.O. Box 4319, 00803	15 rooms, 6 pb	Bar service ($1 drinks)
9E-9J Nordseidevj	Visa, MC •	Sitting room, library
809-774-5764 800-635-1531	C-yes/S-yes/P-no/H-no	spa, jacuzzi, sun deck
Frank & Mary Davis	English	beach towels
All year		

Family inn overlooking Charlotte Amalie harbor, 5-minute walk to town, duty-free shops, restaurants. Cool breezes, honor bar, sun deck, jacuzzi. 15 min. to beaches.

Galleon House Hotel	$$ B&B	Continental plus
P.O. Box 6577, 00804	14 rooms, 7 pb	Refrigerators
31 Kongens Gade	•	A/C in rooms, pool
800-524-2052 809-774-6952	C-yes/S-yes/P-no/H-no	snorkel gear/windsurfing
John & Donna Slone	English	veranda, beach towels
All year		

Visit historical Danish town. Superb view of harbor with city charm close to everything. Duty-free shopping, beach activities in 85-degree weather.

SAINT THOMAS ————————————————————————

Island View Guest House	$$ B&B	Continental breakfast
P.O. Box 1903, 00803	15 rooms, 13 pb	Hors d'oeuvres (Friday)
11-1C Contant	●	Sandwiches, bar, gallery
809-774-4270 800-524-2023	C-14+/S-yes/P-no/H-no	freshwater swimming pool
Barbara Cooper, Norman Leader		
All year		

Overlooking St. Thomas harbor, free continental breakfast, honor bar and freshwater pool. Spectacular harbor view from all rooms. Convenient to town and airport.

More Inns . . .

Cruz Inn Box 566, Cruz Bay, Saint John, 00830 809-776-7688
Estate Zootenvaal Hurricane Hole, Saint John, 00830 809-776-6321
Gallows Point Box 58, Saint John, 00830 809-776-6434
Heritage Manor P.O. Box 90, Saint Thomas, 00804 809-774-3003
Hotel 1829 P.O. Box 1567, Saint Thomas, 00801 809-774-1829
Inn at Mandahl P.O. Box 2483, Saint Thomas, 00803 809-775-2100
Intimate Inn of St. John P.O. Box 432, Cruz Bay, Saint John, 00830 809-776-6133
Kyalami Estate Elizabeth No. 27, Saint Thomas, 11837 809-774-9980
Mafolie Hotel P.O. Box 1506, Saint Thomas, 00801 809-774-2790
Maison Greaux Guest House P.O. Box 1856, Saint Thomas, 00803 809-774-0063
Mark Saint Thomas, The Blackbeard's Hill, Charlotte Amalie, 00802 809-774-5511
Pavilions & Pools Hotel Route 6, Saint Thomas, 00802 800-524-2001
Pelican Beach Club Box 8387, Saint Thomas, 00801 809-775-6855
Pink Fancy Hotel 27 Prince St., Christiansted—St. Croix, 00820 800-524-2045
Raintree Inn Box 566, Saint John, 00830 809-776-7449
Selene's P.O. Box 30, Cruz Bay, Saint John, 00830 809-776-7850
Twiins Guest House 5 Garden St,Charlotte A, Saint Thomas, 00801 809-776-0131
Villa Elaine 66 Water Island, Saint Thomas, 00802 809-774-0290
Villa Madeleine P.O. Box 24190, Gallows Bay, St. Croix, 00824 800-548-4461

Virginia

ARLINGTON ————————————————————————

Crystal B&B	$$ B&B	Full breakfast (wkends)
2620 S. Fern St., 22202	3 rooms	Continental plus (wkdys)
703-548-7652		Tea, baked goods, fruit
Susan Swain	●	TV room, gardens
All year	C-yes/S-yes/P-no/H-no	handmade quilts each rm.

Country in the city; breakfast served in lovely garden; country motif decor. Walk to subway; many restaurants nearby. 20 minutes to heart of D.C.; near Historic Alexandria.

Memory House	$$ B&B	Continental plus
6404 N. Washington Blvd, 22205	2 rooms, 1 pb	Beverage on arrival
703-534-4607		Two sitting rooms
John & Marlys McGrath	●	one block from subway
All year	C-no/S-no/P-no/H-no	

Ornate 1899 Victorian decorated with antiques and collectibles. Convenient base for exploring nation's capitol. Two blocks from I-66. Notable house—featured on tours.

BOYCE

The River House
Route 2, Box 135, 22620
703-837-1476
Cornelia & Donald Niemann
All year

$$ B&B
5 rooms, 5 pb
Visa, MC ●
C-yes/S-yes/P-yes/H-yes
French

Full breakfast
Cheese, fruit, beverages
After dinner liqueurs
sitting room, library
special comedy weekends

1780 Fieldstone rural getaway, convenient to scenic, historical, recreational areas; near superb restaurants. Houseparties; small workshops; family reunions.

CHARLES CITY

Edgewood Plantation
4800 John Tyler Hwy., 23030
Route 5
804-829-2962
Dot & Juilian Boulware
All year

$$$ B&B
6 rooms, 2 pb
Visa, MC ●
C-10+/S-yes

Full breakfast
Comp. refreshments
Antique and gift shops
formal gardens, gazebo
hot tubs, pool, fishing

Sweetness, romance, uniqueness and charm fill each large antique bedroom. Breakfast in formal dining room or country kitchen. Pre-Civil War 1849 house filled with history.

North Bend Plantation B&B
Route 1, Box 13A, 23030
12200 Weyanoke Rd.
804-829-5176
George & Ridgely Copland
All year

$$$ B&B
3 rooms
●
C-6+
some French

Full breakfast
Comp. wine, lemonade
Sitting room, library
game room w/pool table
piano, swimming pool

Virginia Historic Landmark circa 1819 located in the James River Plantation area. 25 min. to historic Williamsburg. Private, peaceful, surrounded by 250 acres of farmland.

CHARLOTTESVILLE

Clifton—The Country Inn
Route 13, Box 26, 22901
804-971-1800
Steven & Donna Boehmfeldt
All year

$$$ B&B
9 rooms, 9 pb
Visa, MC
C-yes/S-yes/P-no/H-no
French

3-course full breakfast
Gourmet kitchen
Comp. wine, snacks, bar
library, bicycles, pool
tennis, fishing, croquet

Sumptuous 18th-century Jeffersonian estate. Pine floors, paneled walls. Every room has fireplace and private bath. Close to Monticello and University. Gourmet kitchen.

The Inn at Monticello
Route 19, Box 112, 22902
804-979-3593
Carol & Larry Engel
All year except X-mas

$$$ B&B
5 rooms, 5 pb
Visa, MC ●
C-8+/S-no/P-no/H-no
some French

Full breakfast
Comp. wine, aftn. tea
Sitting room, hammock
covered porch, croquet
tennis court nearby

19th century manor, perfectly located 2 miles from Thomas Jefferson's beloved "Monticello". Antiques, canopy beds, fireplaces. Golf, tennis, canoeing, wine-tasting nearby.

Palmer Country Manor
Route 2, Box 1390, 22963
Northside of Route 640
800-253-4306
Gregory & Kathleen Palmer
Exc. last 2 weeks in Dec

$$$ B&B
12 rooms, 10 pb
Visa, MC, AmEx ●
C-yes/S-ltd/P-no/H-no
Spanish

Full breakfast
Comp. tea, snacks
Restaurant, sitting rm
library, pool, fish pond
trails, balloon rides

Beautifully restored 1834 plantation. Enjoy manicured gardens, acres of woods, pond fishing, river rafting, a heated pool, and hot air ballooning. A country resort.

CHARLOTTESVILLE

Woodstock Hall
Route 3, Box 40, 22903
804-293-8977
Jean Wheby, MaryAnn Elder
All year

$$$ B&B
4 rooms, 4 pb
•
C-8+/S-no/P-no/H-no

Full breakfast
Afternoon tea
Dinner by prior arrange.
sitting room, croquet
hiking, horseshoes

Historic landmark built circa 1757-1808. Perfect for a relaxing, romantic getaway. Period furnishings; private baths; fireplaces; central air; full gourmet breakfasts.

CHINCOTEAGUE

Miss Molly's Inn
113 N. Main St., 23336
804-336-6686
Dr. & Mrs. James Stam
April–November

$$ B&B
7 rooms, 1 pb
•
C-12+/S-yes

Full breakfast
Afternoon tea
Sitting room

Charming Victorian B&B inn over the bay. All rooms are air-conditioned & furnished with period antiques. Marguerite Henry stayed here while writing "Misty of Chincoteague."

CHINCOTEAGUE ISLAND

Channel Bass Inn
100 Church St., 23336
804-336-6148
James S. Hanretta
All year

$$$ EP
11 rooms, 11 pb
Visa, MC, AmEx, DC •
C-no/S-yes/P-no/H-no

Full breakfast $
Dinner by reservation
Basque cuisine, bar
room service, sitting rm
Suite w/whirlpool avail.

Near Assateague seashore; elegant colonial atmosphere; all oversized beds; superb continental and classical cuisine. Art gallery specializing in 19th-century paintings.

CLARKSVILLE

Needmoor Inn
P.O. Box 629, 23927
801 Virginia Ave.
804-374-2866
Lucy & Buddy Hairston
All year

$$ B&B
4 rooms, 3 pb
C-yes/S-ltd/P-ltd/H-no

Full gourmet breakfast
Aftn. tea, snacks
Comp. wine, bicycles
library, airport pickup
therapeutic massage

Heartfelt hospitality in the heart of Virginia's Lake Country. 1889 homestead amid 1.5 acres of fruit trees and herb garden. Three blocks away from all water sports.

CLUSTER SPRINGS

Oak Grove Plantation B&B
P.O. Box 45, Hwy 658, 24535
804-575-7137
Pickett Craddock
May–September

$$ B&B
2 rooms
•
C-yes/S-no/P-no/H-no
Spanish

Full breakfast
Dinner
Sitting room
library
bicycles

Come, enjoy our antebellum country home built by our ancestors in 1820. 400 acres with trails, creeks and wildlife. Gourmet breakfast. Children welcome.

COVINGTON

Milton Hall B&B Inn
RR 3, 24426
703-965-0196
John & Vera Eckert
All year

$$$ B&B
6 rooms, 5 pb
Visa, MC •
C-yes/S-yes/P-yes/H-no

Full breakfast
Dinner, box lunch
Bar service, comp. wine
aftn. tea, sitting room
library, patio, jacuzzi

English country manor c. 1874 set on 44 wooded acres with gardens. This Historic Landmark adjoins National Forest, mountains, lakes, springs/baths. Hunting & fishing nearby.

The Bailiwick Inn, Fairfax, VA

CULPEPPER

Fountain Hall B&B Inn
609 S. East St., 22701
703-825-8200 800-476-2944
The Walker Family
All year

$$ B&B
5 rooms, 5 pb
Visa, MC, AmEx ●
C-ltd/S-no/P-no/H-ltd

Continental plus
Comp. refreshments
3 sitting rooms, books
fireplaces, VCR, porches
golf nearby, bicycles

Gracious accommodations for business and leisure travelers. Centrally located in quaint historic Culpepper, between Washington, D.C., Charlottesville & Skyline Drive.

EDINBURG

Mary's Country Inn
Rt. 2, Box 4, 22824
218 S. Main St.
703-984-8286
Mary & Jim Clark
All year exc. January

$$ B&B
6 rooms, 3 pb
Visa, MC ●
C-yes/S-yes

Continental plus
Comp. iced tea, lemonade
Restaurant (next-door)
wrap-around porch
antique books, magazines

Country Victorian with turn-of-the-century charm and hospitality. Bright, airy rooms decorated with antiques. Bountiful country-fresh breakfast.

FAIRFAX

Bailiwick Inn
4023 Chain Bridge Rd., 22030
703-691-2266 800-366-7666
Anne & Ray Smith
All year

$$$ B&B
14 rooms, 14 pb
Visa, MC, AmEx ●
C-yes/S-no/P-no/H-yes

Full breakfast
Comp. wine, tea, treats
Fireplaces, jacuzzis
gardens, feather beds
Murder Mystery weekends

The first B&B in the historic city of Fairfax. Fourteen rooms from Virginia mansions. Fireplaces, jacuzzis, colonial brick-walled garden, bridal suite. 15 miles from D.C.

FLINT HILL

Caledonia Farm B&B	$$ B&B	Full breakfast
Route 1, Box 2080, 22627	3 rooms, 1 pb	Comp. wine, social hour
703-675-3693	Visa, MC ●	Bikes, lawn games, VCR
Phil Irwin	C-12+/S-no/P-ask/H-yes	evening fun hayrides
All year	German, Danish	68 miles to D.C.

Beautifully restored 1812 stone farm home adjacent to Shenandoah National Park/Blue Ridge Mountains. Virginia Landmark, on National Register. Year-round hospitality.

FREDERICKSBURG

Fredericksburg Colonial	$$ B&B	Continental breakfast
1707 Princess Anne St., 22401	32 rooms, 32 pb	Conference room avail.
703-371-5666	Visa, MC ●	honeymoon/anniversary
Robert S. Myers	C-yes/S-yes/P-yes/H-yes	Colonial suites
All year		

Rooms furnished in Victorian decor. Enjoy our antiques, prints, and museum. Inn located in historic district. Antique shops, restaurants nearby.

Kenmore Inn	$$$ B&B	Continental plus
1200 Princess Anne St., 22401	13 rooms, 12 pb	Restaurant, wine tasting
703-371-7622	Visa, MC ●	Patio garden for dining
Ed & Alice Bannan	C-yes/S-yes/P-ltd/H-yes	sitting room, lounge
All year		antiques, bicycles

On the historic walking tour, elegant guest rooms with bath & air-conditioning, considered to be among Virginia's 5 most exclusive restaurants.

La Vista Plantation	$$$ B&B	Full breakfast
4420 Guinea Station Rd., 22408	2 rooms, 2 pb	Comp. soda and juice
703-898-8444	Visa, MC ●	Sitting room, library
Michele & Edward Schiesser	C-yes/S-no/P-ltd/H-no	bicycles, A/C, kitchen
All year		TV, phone, wicker furn.

Lovely 1838 classical revival country home on 10 acres outside historic Fredericksburg. Antiques; fireplaces; old trees; pond. In the center of Virginia's historic triangle.

FRONT ROYAL

Chester House	$$ B&B	Continental plus
43 Chester St., 22630	6 rooms, 2 pb	Comp. wine, snacks
703-635-3937 800-621-0441	Visa, MC ●	Living & dining room
Bill & Ann Wilson	C-12+/S-ltd/P-no/H-no	lawns, gardens
All year		television parlor

Quiet, elegant, relaxed atmosphere home reminiscent of a bygone era. Amidst formal boxwood garden and shade trees. Golf, tennis, horseback riding, hiking, canoeing nearby.

Constant Spring Inn	$$ B&B	Full breakfast
413 S. Royal Ave., 22630	9 rooms, 9 pb	Comp. beverages
703-635-7010	Visa, MC ●	Sitting room, bicycles
Mary Ann, Charles Wood	C-yes/S-yes/P-no/H-ltd	conf. room, FAX, copying
Exc. 2 weeks in Jan		fitness studio

Three blocks from Skyline Drive; parklike setting; heart of history land. Located atop a hill with a view of the countryside. 80 minutes to Washington, D.C. Country cooking.

GORDONSVILLE

Sleepy Hollow Farm B&B
16280 Blue Ridge Turnpk, 22942
703-832-5555
Beverley Allison/Dorsey Comer
All year

$$ B&B
7 rooms, 6 pb
Visa, MC •
C-yes/S-yes/P-ask/H-no
Spanish, French

Full breakfast
Comp. wine, beverages
Sitting room, conf. room
croquet field, gazebo
pond fishing & swimming

Old farmhouse and cottage furnished in antiques, eclectic accessories. One bdrm with fireplace & jacuzzi. Located in beautiful countryside, near James Madison's Montpelier.

HILLSVILLE

Bray's Manor B&B Inn
Route 3, Box 210, 24343
703-728-7901
Dick & Helen Bray
March–January

$ B&B
4 rooms, 2 pb
Visa, MC •
C-yes/S-no/P-no/H-no

Full breakfast
Snacks, soft drinks
Sitting room with TV
parlor, library

Beautiful southwest Virginia; 12 miles north of Blue Ridge Parkway; croquet; badminton; rambling porch for sitting, sipping; near golf and crafts.

LEESBURG

Fleetwood Farm B&B
Route 1, Box 306-A, 22075
703-327-4325
Bill & Carol Chamberlin
All year

$$$ B&B
2 rooms, 2 pb
C-12+/S-no

Full country breakfast
Comp. wine, snacks, tea
Living room w/TV, stereo
library, games, jacuzzi
cook-out fac., canoe

1745 hunt country manor house. Beautiful rooms each with private baths, air-conditioning, fireplaces, antiques. Horseback riding nearby. A Virginia Historic Landmark.

LEXINGTON

Fassifern B&B
Route 5, Box 87, 24450
State Rte. 39W & Rte. 750
703-463-1013
Ann Carol & Arthur Perry
All year

$$$ B&B
5 rooms, 5 pb
Visa, MC, AmEx
S-ltd/P-no/H-no

Continental plus
Comp. snacks
Living room
pond & lawn chairs

Comfortable 1867 manor house with antique furnishings in beautiful Shenandoah Valley near historic sites, Virginia Horse Ctr, and Blue Ridge Pkwy. Ambiance is our trademark.

Llewellyn Lodge–Lexington
603 S. Main St., 24450
703-463-3235
Ellen & John Roberts
All year

$$ B&B
6 rooms, 6 pb
Visa, MC, Choice •
C-yes/S-yes/P-no/H-no

Full breakfast
Comp. beverages
Sitting room
tennis courts, pool, and golf
nearby

Charming half-century-old colonial with a warm friendly atmosphere, where guests can relax after visiting this historic Shenandoah town. Gourmet breakfast.

LYNCHBURG

The Madison House B&B
413 Madison Street, 24504
804-528-1503
Irene & Dale Smith
All year

$$ B&B
3 rooms, 3 pb
•
C-no/S-no/P-no/H-no

Full breakfast
Afternoon tea
Complimentary snacks
sitting room
library

Lynchburg's finest Victorian B&B, 1880 antique-filled elegant mansion. Historic District known as "quality row". Wonderful breakfast and English high tea.

MANASSAS

Sunrise Hill Farm B&B
5513 Sudley Road, 22110
703-754-8309
Frank & Sue Boberek
All year

$$ B&B
2 rooms, 1 pb
Visa, MC •
C-10+/P-no/H-no

Full gourmet breakfast
Sitting room, library
near hiking, antiquing
tennis, golf, horses

Civil War treasure located within the heart of 6500 acre Manassas/Bull Run National Battlefields just 35 minutes west of Washington D.C.

MATHEWS

Ravenswood Inn
P.O. Box 250, 23109
Poplar Grove Lane
804-725-7272
Marshall & Linda Warner
Mid-Feb—early Dec

$$$ MAP/B&B
5 rooms, 5 pb
•
C-no/S-ltd/P-no/H-no
Spanish

Full breakfast,
5-course French dinner
Comp. wine, living room
hot tub, library
sailboats, bicycles

Five-acre hideaway on Chesapeake's East River with focus on fine food and nesting; restored 1913 manor house with beautiful river views. A/C in all rooms.

MIDDLETOWN

Wayside Inn Since 1797
7783 Main St., 22645
703-869-1797 FAX:869-6038
Maggie Edwards
All year

$$ B&B
22 rooms, 22 pb
Visa, MC, AmEx, DC, CB •
C-yes/S-yes/P-no/H-yes

Full breakfast
Lunch, dinner appetizers
Bar service
sitting room, piano
entertainment

In Shenandoah Valley, offering Civil War history with southern cooking. Rooms are decorated in different historic styles with antiques for sale. Colonial cuisine.

MOLLUSK

Greenvale Manor
Route 354, Box 70, 22517
804-462-5995
Pam & Walt Smith
All year

$$ B&B
6 rooms, 6 pb
C-no/S-ltd/P-no

Full breakfast
Saturday summer cookouts
Sitting room, library
veranda, pool, beach
docks, boating, bicycles

Historical 1840 waterfront manor house with antiques, privacy, pool, dock, private beach, gorgeous sunsets and guest houses on a 13-acre peninsula. Charter boat available.

MONTEREY

Highland Inn
P.O. Box 40, Main St., 24465
703-468-2143
Michael Strand & Cynthia Peel
All year

$ B&B
18 rooms, 18 pb
Visa, MC •
C-yes/S-yes/P-no

Continental breakfast
Breakfast, lunch, dinner
Restaurant, bar
porches
library

Relaxing country getaway with wraparound porches, antiques, private baths, country cooking, and a tavern. Lots of charm. Fishing (fresh trout), hunting and skiing.

MONTROSS

Inn at Montross
P.O. Box 908, 22520
Courthouse Sqaure
804-493-9097
Eileen & Michael Longman
All year

$$ B&B/$$$ MAP
6 rooms, 6 pb
Visa, MC, Disc •
C-ask/S-yes/P-no/H-no

Continental plus
Restaurant, English pub
Bedside brandy, truffles
games, piano, tennis
phone & cable TV in rms

Country inn dating back in part to 1683, offers antiques, fine dining, and elegant accommodations. Located in historic area near Stratford Hall.

MOUNT JACKSON

Widow Kip's Shenandoah Inn
Route 1, Box 117, 22842
703-477-2400
Rosemary Kip
All year

$$ B&B
7 rooms, 7 pb
●
C-yes/S-yes/P-no/H-no

Full breakfast
Comp. sherry
Picnics & snacks
sitting room, VCR
bicycles, swimming pool

1830 gracious colonial on 7 acres overlooking Shenandoah. Seven fireplaces. Chock-full of antiques and memories. Like visiting a grandmother's house. Near skiing.

NELLYSFORD

Meander Inn
Rts. 612 & 613, POB 443, 22958
804-361-1121
Kathy & Rick Cornelius
All year

$$$ B&B
5 rooms, 3 pb
Visa, MC ●
C-yes/S-no/P-no/H-no
French

Full breakfast
Sitting room
Library, hot tub
fishing, hiking, skiing
golf, tennis nearby

Peaceful, romantic hideaway alongside Rockfish River. Splendid views of Blue Ridge. Nearby Wintergreen Resort offers skiing, golf, tennis, swimming, horseback riding.

Sunset Hill
Route 1, Box 375, 22958
Route 151 & 613 West
804-361-1101
Elena Woodard
All year

$$$ B&B
10 rooms, 10 pb
personal checks ●
C-yes/S-no/P-no/H-yes
some French & Spanish

Continental plus
Lunch baskets & dinner
Comp. tea, snacks, wine
Sitting rm, pvt. jacuzzi
bikes, lawn games

Near historic Charlottesville, scenic Skyline Dr. Beautifully restored, antique appointed. Romantic, peaceful getaway, breathtaking view of Blue Ridge Mountains.

Trillium House
P.O. Box 280, 22958
Wintergreen Drive
804-325-9126 800-325-9126
Ed & Betty Dinwiddie
All year

$$$ B&B
12 rooms, 12 pb
Visa, MC ●
C-yes/S-yes/P-no/H-yes

Full breakfast
Afternoon tea, bar
Dinner Fri & Sat
sitting room, library
near tennis, pool, golf

Birds entertain at breakfast at this owner-designed inn in year-round Wintergreen Resort. Fall and spring foliage are specialties.

Inn at Montross, Montross, VA

NEW MARKET

A Touch of Country
9329 Congress St., 22844
703-740-8030
Dawn Kasow, Jean Schoellig
All year

$$ B&B
6 rooms, 6 pb
Visa, MC •
C-12+/S-ltd/P-no/H-no

Full breakfast
Comp. beverages
Sitting room with TV

A comfortable 1870s restored home decorated with antiques, collectibles, and a country flavor. Located in the beautiful Shenandoah Valley.

NORTH GARDEN

Inn at the Crossroads
RR 692, Rt. 2, Box 6, 22959
804-979-6452
Lynn L. Neville
All year

$$ B&B
5 rooms, 1 pb
Visa, MC •
C-8+/S-no/P-no/H-no

Full breakfast
Catered supper or dinner
Two sitting rooms

Landmark 1820s tavern nestled in foothills of mountains; close to historic Charlottesville, U.Va., Monticello. All types of outdoor activities nearby. Wonderful breakfasts.

ONANCOCK

Colonial Manor Inn
P.O. Box 94, 23417
84 Market St.
804-787-3521
June & Jerry Evans
All year

$ EP
14 rooms, 5 pb
C-yes/S-yes/P-no/H-no

Morning coffee
Sitting room
Glass-enclosed porch
Victorian gazebo
cable TV, A/C

Family-owned business since 1936. Cozy, at-home kind of friendly atmosphere in a historic little town on the water; fine restaurants nearby.

ORANGE

Hidden Inn
249 Caroline St., 22960
703-672-3625
Ray & Barbara Lonick
All year

$$$ B&B/MAP
10 rooms, 10 pb
Visa, MC •
C-yes/S-no/P-no/H-no

Full country breakfast
Aftn. tea, lunch (Tu-Sa)
Dinner by reservation
sitting room, jacuzzi
air conditioned

Comfortably furnished country inn tucked away in rural community. Convenient to D.C., Charlottesville, Blue Ridge Mountains. Super breakfasts!

Mayhurst Inn B&B
P.O. Box 707, 22960
US Route 15 S.
703-672-5597
Stephen & Shirley Ramsey
February 15–December 31

$$$ B&B
8 rooms, 8 pb
•
C-ltd/S-no/P-ask/H-no

Full breakfast
Dinner served Sat. eves
Comp. wine, sitting room
fireplaces in rooms
pond, 2 cottages

Exciting Italianate villa on 36 acres of pasture land. Rooftop gazebo, balconies for guests. Antique furniture. Special weekend packages available.

PETERSBURG

Folly Castle Inn B&B
323 W. Washington St., 23803
804-733-6463
Cliff Houghton
All year

$$ B&B
3 rooms, 3 pb
C-16+/S-ltd/P-no/H-no

Continental plus
Complimentary wine
Tea, snacks, library
porches overlooking pvt.
botwood/flower garden

Elegant Georgian mansion filled with art and antiques. Large rooms feature comfortable furniture. Nearby Civil War sites, antique shops.

PETERSBURG

Mayfield Inn
P.O. Box 2265, 23804
3348 W. Washington St.
804-861-6775 804-733-0866
Jamie & Dot Caudle
All year

$$ B&B
4 rooms, 4 pb
Visa, MC, Choice ●
C-yes/S-ltd/P-no/H-no

Full breakfast
Afternoon tea
Two sitting rooms
swimming pool

A 1750 house that has been completely and very beautifully restored, set on four tranquil acres. Close to historic Petersburg and battlefields.

RAPHINE

Oak Spring Farm & Vineyard
Route 1, Box 356, Ra, 24472
US 11 & County Rd. 706
703-377-2398
Jim & Pat Tichenor
All year

$$ B&B
3 rooms, 3 pb
Visa, MC
C-16+/S-no/P-no/H-no
some French & German

Continental plus
Comp. refreshments
Sitting room
hiking trails, animals
near swimming, skiing

Oak Spring Farm is a working farm and vineyard. The old plantation house (c. 1826) is filled with antiques and views. This is a special place where guests will feel relaxed.

RICHMOND

Emmaneul Hotzler House
2036 Monument Ave., 23220
804-353-6900
Lyn M. Benson
All year

$$$ B&B
4 rooms, 4 pb
Visa, MC ●
C-12+/S-no/P-no/H-no

Full breakfast
Natural cereals
Living room, library
fireplace in 2 of rooms
jacuzzi in large room

Elegant 1914 Italian Renaissance in historic district with natural mahogany raised paneling, wainscoting, leaded glass windows, coffered ceilings with dropped beams.

Mr. Patrick Henry's Inn
2300 E. Broad St., 23223
804-644-1322
Lynn & Jim News
All year

$$$ B&B
4 rooms, 4 pb
Visa, MC, AmEx, DC
C-yes/S-yes/P-no/H-no

Full breakfast
Restaurant, bar
Lunch, dinner
sitting room, fireplaces
kitchenettes, balconies

A pre-Civil War inn. Walking distance to many tourist attractions. Featuring a gourmet restaurant, English pub and garden patio. Suites include fireplaces & full breakfast.

The William Catlin House
2304 E. Broad St., 23223
804-780-3746
Robert & Josephine Martin
All year

$$$ B&B
5 rooms, 4 pb
Visa, MC, AmEx ●
C-13+/S-yes/P-no/H-no

Full breakfast
Comp. sherry & mints
Fireplaces, antiques
oriental rugs
crystal chandeliers

Retire in a four-poster bed in front of a romantic, burning fireplace—wake up to freshly brewed coffee served in your room.

ROANOKE

The Mary Bladon House
381 Washington Ave. SW, 24016
703-344-5361
Bill & Sheri Bestpitch
All year

$$$ B&B
4 rooms, 4 pb
Visa, MC ●
C-yes/S-no/P-no/H-no

Full breakfast
Afternoon tea
Sitting room
A/C in rooms
24 hr answering service

Romantic Victorian setting with period antiques and local arts and crafts. Walking distance to historic downtown area, shops and restaurants.

SCOTTSVILLE ————————————————

Chester B&B	$$ B&B	Full breakfast
Route 4, Box 57, 24590	5 rooms, 1 pb	Dinner available
James River Road, Rt. 726	AmEx ●	Aftn. tea, comp. wine
804-286-3960	C-9+/S-yes/P-yes/H-ask	sitting room, library
Gordon Anderson, Dick Shaffer		bicycles
All year		

Historic 1847 Greek Revival Mansion; 7 acres of tree-shaded lawns; furnished with antiques and orientals. Featured on 1991 Historic Virginia Garden Week.

High Meadows Vineyard Inn	$$$ B&B/MAP	Full breakfast
Route 4, Box 6, 24590	6 rooms, 6 pb	Candlelight dinner
Route 20 South	●	Nightly winetasting
804-286-2218	C-8+/S-ltd/P-ltd/H-no	library, hot tub, pond
Peter Sushka, Mary Jae Abbitt	French	gazebo, bikes, vineyard
All year		

Enchanting historical landmark south of Charlottesville. Large, tastefully appointed rooms; fireplaces; period antiques. Private 23 acres for walking & picnics. Wine-tasting.

SMITH MOUNTAIN LAKE ————————————————

Holland-Duncan House	$ B&B	Full gourmet breakfast
Route 5, Box 681, 24121	4 rooms, 3 pb	Comp. wine, log cabins
Route 122, Moneta	C-yes/S-ltd/P-ask/H-no	Library, sitting room
703-721-8510		tennis courts, boating
Clint & Kathryn Shay		swimming, fishing, golf
February–November		

This charming, historic antebellum mansion and its outbuildings are situated in a lake resort. It is a beautiful blend of old and new. Authentic log cabin also available.

Manor at Taylor's Store	$$ B&B	Full breakfast
Route 1, Box 533, 24184	6 rooms, 4 pb	Comp. tea, kitchen
Route 122, Wirtz	Visa, MC ●	Parlor, piano, library
703-721-3951	C-ltd/S-ltd/P-no/H-ltd	exercise room, swimming
Lee & Mary Lynn Tucker	some German	hot tub, fishing, hiking
All year		

Explore 120 acres of private paradise and delight in all luxury amenities. Elegant accommodations in antique-filled mansion. This country inn is a very special place!

SMITHFIELD ————————————————

Isle of Wight Inn	$$ B&B	Full breakfast
1607 S. Church St., 23430	10 rooms, 10 pb	Snacks, tea, soft drinks
804-357-3176	Visa, MC, AmEx ●	Sitting room, bicycles
The Hart's, The Earl's	C-yes/S-ltd/P-no/H-yes	jacuzzi, walking tour
All year		golf and fishing nearby

Luxurious inn and antiques shop. Famous for Smithfield hams and old homes dating from 1750. Saint Lukes church 1632. Near Colonial Williamsburg and Jamestown.

STAFFORD ————————————————

Rennaisance Manor B&B	$$ B&B	Continental plus
2247 Courthouse Rd., 22554	4 rooms, 2 pb	Aftn. tea, comp. sherry
703-720-3785	Visa, MC ●	Sitting room
The Bernard's & The Houser's	C-yes/S-no/P-no/H-no	library
All year	German	

Resembles Mount Vernon in architecture, decor and charm. Afternoon tea or homemade ice cream and wonderful expanded continental breakfasts.

STANLEY

Jordan Hollow Farm Inn
Route 2, Box 375, 22851
703-778-2285 703-778-2209
Marley & Jetze Beers
All year

$$$ EP
16 rooms, 16 pb
Visa, MC, DC ●
C-yes/S-yes/P-yes/H-no
Dutch, German, French

Full breakfast $
Restaurant & bar
Sitting room, game room
library, canoeing
horseback trail riding

A 200-year-old restored colonial horse farm. Friendly, informal atmosphere with spectacular views. Neaby Luray Caverns, Skyline Drive, canoeing. Carriage rides!

STAUNTON

Ashton Country House
1205 Middlebrook Road, 24401
703-885-7819
S. Kennedy, S. Polanski
All year

$$ B&B
4 rooms, 4 pb
C-16+/S-no/P-ask/H-no

Full breakfast
Afternoon tea, snacks
Sitting room
live piano music often
accompanies tea

1860's Greek Revival on 20 aces. One mile from town. Professional musician & professional chef entertain and care for you. Delicious! Delightful!

Frederick House
P.O. Box 1387, 24401
Frederick and New Streets
703-885-4220 800-334-5575
Joe & Evy Harman
All year

$ B&B
14 rooms, 14 pb
Visa, MC, AmEx, DC ●
C-yes/S-no/P-no/H-no

Full breakfast
Sitting room
library
conference facilities

Located in the oldest city west of the Blue Ridge Mountains of Virginia. Historic Staunton contains Woodrow Wilson birthplace, shops and restaurants.

STAUNTON

The Sampson Eagon Inn
238 East Beverley St., 24401
703-886-8200 FAX:886-8200
Laura & Frank Mattingly
All year

$$$ B&B
4 rooms, 4 pb
C-12+/S-no/P-no

Full breakfast
Sitting room
TV/VCR and sitting area
in each accommodation

An elegant alternative in in-town historic lodging. The inn features spacious, air-conditioned, antique furnished accommodations complemented by gracious personal service.

STRASBURG

Hotel Strasburg
201 S. Holliday St., 22601
703-465-9191
Gary Rutherford
All year

$$ B&B
24 rooms, 24 pb
Visa, MC, AmEx, DC ●
C-yes/S-yes/P-no/H-no

Continental breakfast
Restaurant, bar service
Snacks, meeting rooms
sitting room, near beach
jacuzzi in some rooms

Charming Victorian restoration, all rooms period antiques, some jacuzzi suites. Great food & atmosphere. Antique capital of Virginia, 11 miles to Skyline Drive.

TREVILIANS

Prospect Hill Plantation
Route 3, Box 430, 23093
Highway 613
703-967-0844 800-277-0844
Bill & Michael Sheehan
All year

$$$ B&B/MAP
10 rooms, 10 pb
Visa, MC ●
C-yes/S-yes/P-no/H-no

Full breakfast in bed
Dinner, afternoon tea
Comp. wine or cider
library, fireplaces
jacuzzi, pool, bicycles

1732 plantation. Bedrooms with fireplaces in manor house and grooms' quarters. Fifteen miles east of Charlottesville. Continental dining, peace & quiet in the country.

Hotel Strasburg, Strasburg, VA

VIRGINIA BEACH

Angie's Guest Cottage
302–24th St., 23451
804-428-4690
Barbara G. Yates
April–September

$ B&B
7 rooms, 1 pb
C-ltd/S-ltd/P-ltd/H-no

Continental plus
Kitchens
Sitting room, sun deck
BBQ pit, picnic tables
shaded porch, library

Located in the heart of the resort area by Atlantic Ocean. Guests have opportunity to meet visitors from other countries staying at our youth hostel.

WARM SPRINGS

Inn at Gristmill Square
Box 359, Route 645, 24484
703-839-2231
The McWilliams Family
All year exc. March 1-15

$$$ B&B
14 rooms, 14 pb
Visa, MC ●
C-yes/S-yes/P-yes/H-ltd

Continental breakfast
Lunch, dinner, bar
Sauna
swimming pool
tennis courts

Casual country hideaway, historic original mill site dating from 1800s. Each room individually decorated. Fine dining and distinguished wine cellar.

WASHINGTON

The Foster-Harris House
P.O. Box 333, Main St., 22747
703-675-3757 800-666-0153
Camille Harris & Pat Foster
All year

$$ B&B
3 rooms, 3 pb
Visa, MC ●
C-yes/S-yes/P-ltd/H-no
Spanish, German

Full breakfast
Comp. sweets & beverages
Sitting room, queen beds
fireplace stove, kennel
baby-sitting, whirlpool

Restored Victorian (circa 1900) house in historic "Little" Washington, Virginia. Antiques, fresh flowers, mountain views, three blocks from 5-star restaurant.

WASHINGTON

Heritage House
P.O. Box 427, Main St., 22747
703-675-3207
Al & Polly Erickson
All year

$$$ B&B
4 rooms, 4 pb
Visa, MC
C-yes/S-no/P-no/H-yes

Full breakfast
Comp. sweets
Sitting room
walk to restaurant
Scandinavian heritage

153-year-old Colonial home in quaint village George Washington surveyed as a 17-year-old. 12 miles from Skyline Dr.; near vineyards, antiques. Unique candlelight breakfasts!

WHITE POST

L'Auberge Provencale
P.O. Box 119, 22663
Rt. 1, Box 203, Boyce
703-837-1375 FAX:837-2004
Chef Alain & Celeste Borel
Exc. Jan–mid-Feb

$$$ B&B
10 rooms, 10 pb
Visa, MC, AmEx, DC
C-10+/S-yes/P-no/H-no
French

Full gourmet breakfast
Dinner, bar service
Refreshments, flowers
library, sitting room
bicycles, gardens

4th generation master chef Alain Borel, from Avignon, France, prepares nationally acclaimed cuisine moderne. Elegant overnight accommodations. Extensive wine list.

WILLIAMSBURG

Applewood Colonial B&B
605 Richmond Rd., 23185
804-229-0205 800-899-2753
Fred Strout
All year

$$ B&B
4 rooms, 4 pb
Visa, MC ●
C-yes

Continental plus
Afternoon tea
Sitting room
fireplaces

Elegant colonial decor. Walking distance to colonial Williamsburg & College of William and Mary. Fireplaces, antiques, apple collection and lots of comfort.

The Cedars
616 Jamestown Rd., 23185
804-229-3591
Deborah Howard
All year

$$ B&B
9 rooms, 4 pb
●
C-yes/S-ltd/P-no/H-yes

Continental breakfast
Afternoon tea
Screened porch
parlor with fireplace

Brick Georgian colonial house, air-conditioned, antiques and canopy beds. Room for 22 guests, plus brick cottage with fully equipped kitchen for 6-8.

Colonial Capital B&B
501 Richmond Rd., 23185
800-776-0570
Barbara & Phil Craig
All year

$$$ B&B
5 rooms, 5 pb
●
C-6+/S-ltd/P-no/H-no

Full breakfast
Aftn. tea, comp. wine
Parlor, books, solarium
games, videos, bicycles
near Virginia plantation

Colonial Revival home circa 1926; 3 blocks from Virginia's Colonial Capital restoration. Canopy beds, antique furnishings, screened porch, patio. Attentive and gracious hosts.

Legacy of Williamsburg
930 Jamestown Rd., 23185
804-220-0524 800-WMBGS-BB
Ed & Mary Ann Lucas
All year

$$$ B&B
3 rooms, 3 pb
Visa, MC, AmEx
C-13+

Full breakfast
Comp. wine
Bar service
library, billiards
6 fireplaces, bicycles

Step back in time to the romantic 18th century. Tall poster curtained canopied beds. Fireplaces. Private baths. Unforgettable breakfast. Walk to historic Williamsburg.

WILLIAMSBURG ─────────────

Liberty Rose B&B
1022 Jamestown Rd., 23185
804-253-1260
Brad & Sandri Hirz
All year

$$$ B&B
5 rooms, 5 pb
Visa, MC
C-ltd

Full breakfast
Comp. beverages, snacks
Sitting room, gift shop
Suite w/many amenities
available, touring bikes

"Williamsburg's most romantic B&B." Charming old home renovated and decorated in perfect detail. On an acre of magnificent trees. Delightful antiques, wallpapers, lace.

Newport House
710 S. Henry St., 23185
804-229-1775
John & Cathy Millar
All year

$$$ B&B
2 rooms, 2 pb
•
C-yes/S-no/P-no/H-no
French

Full breakfast
Sitting room
Library, Harpischord
Ballroom for receptions

Designed in 1756. Completely furnished in period. 5 minute walk from historic area. Colonial dancing every Tuesday evening.

Piney Grove at Southall's
P.O. Box 1359, 23187
Charles City
804-829-2480
The Gordineers
All year

$$$ B&B
6 rooms, 4 pb
•
C-yes/S-no/P-no/H-no
German

Full breakfast
Picnic lunches (request)
Comp. wine, mint juleps
sitting room, library
swimming pool

National Registry property in James River Plantation Country—20 miles from Williamsburg. Two authentically restored and antique-filled antebellum houses.

Williamsburg Sampler B&B
922 Jamestown Rd., 23185
804-253-0398 800-722-1169
Helen & Ike Sisane
All year

$$$ B&B
4 rooms, 4 pb
•
C-10+/S-no/P-no/H-no

Full breakfast
Beautiful garden w/ 18th
century carriage house
parking, antiques/pewter
samplers, 4-poster beds

Williamsburg's finest plantation style colonial home. Richly furnished. Guests have included great granddaughter of Charles Dickens and decendents of John Quincy Adams.

WOODSTOCK ─────────────

Azalea House B&B
551 S. Main St., 22664
703-459-3500
Margaret & Price McDonald
All year

$ B&B
3 rooms, 1 pb
Visa, MC
C-12+/S-no/P-no/H-no

Full breakfast
Snacks
Sitting room
library

Attractive, comfortable rooms with mountain viewing. Located in the rolling hills of the Shenandoah Valley. Nearby restaurants, vineyards, caverns, hiking.

Inn at Narrow Passage
P.O. Box 608, US 11 S., 22664
703-459-8000
Ellen & Ed Markel
All year

$$ B&B
12 rooms, 8 pb
Visa, MC •
C-yes/S-ltd/P-no/H-no

Full breakfast
Small conference fac.
Sitting room
fireplace, swimming
fishing, rafting

Historic 1740 log inn on the Shenandoah River. Fireplaces, colonial charm, close to vineyards. Civil War sites, hiking, fishing and caverns.

WOODSTOCK

River'd Inn	$$ B&B/MAP	Full breakfast
Route 1, Box 217A1, 22664	8 rooms, 6 pb	Restaurant, bar
703-459-5369	Visa, MC •	Sitting room
Rick & Cyndi Moss	C-12+/S-yes/P-no/H-no	swimming pool
All year	French	hot tubs

Located at the base of the Massanutten Mountains, down a country road, on one of the famous bends of the 7 bends of the Shenandoah River in the heart of the Shenandoah Valley.

More Inns . . .

1763 Inn Rt. 1 Box 19 D, Upperville, 22176 703-592-3848
200 South Street Inn 200 South St., Charlottesville, 22901 804-979-0200
Abbie Hill B&B P.O. Box 4503, Richmond, 23220 804-355-5855
Alexander-Withrow House 3 W. Washington, Lexington, 24450 703-463-2044
Alexandria Lodgings 10 Sunset Dr., Alexandria, 22313 703-836-5575
Ashby Inn Route 1, Box 2/A, Paris, 22130 703-592-3900
B&B Larchmont 1112 Buckingham Ave., Norfolk, 23508 804-489-8449
Belle Grae Inn 515 W. Frederick St., Staunton, 24401 703-886-5151
Blue Knoll Farm Route 1, Box 141, Castleton, 22716 703-937-5234
Boxwood Hill 128 South Court, Luray, 22835 703-743-9484
Brass Lantern Lodge 1782 Jamestown Rd., Williamsburg, 23185 804-229-9089
Brookfield Inn P.O. Box 341, Floyd, 24091 703-763-3363
Buckhorn Inn E Star Route, Box 139, Churchville, 24421 703-337-6900
Candlewick Inn 127 N. Church St., Woodstock, 22664 703-459-8008
Conyers House Route 1, Box 157, Sperryville, 22740 703-987-8025
Country Antiques B&B Route 2, Box 85, Charles City, 23030 804-829-5638
Country Fare 402 N. Main St., Woodstock, 22664 703-459-4828
Doubleday Inn 104 Doubleday Ave., Gettysburg, 17325 717-334-9119
Evans Farm Inn 1696 Chain Bridge Rd., McLean, 22101 703-356-8000
Fort Lewis Lodge Millboro, 24460 703-925-2314
Fox Grape of Williamsburg 701 Monumental Ave., Williamsburg, 23185 804-229-6914
Fox Hill Inn 16 S., P.O. Box 88, Troutdale, 24378 703-677-3313
Garden & The Sea Inn P.O. Box 275, New Church, 23415 804-824-0672
Gibson Hall Inn P.O. Box 25, Upperville, 22176 703-592-3514
Grave's Mountain Lodge Syria, 22743 703-923-4231
Hamilton Garden Inn 353 W. Colonial Highway, Hamilton, 22068 703-338-3693
Hawksbill Lodge Luray, 22835 703-281-0548
High Street Inn 405 High St., Petersburg, 23803 804-733-0505
Hyde Park Farm Route 2, Box 38, Burkeville, 23922 804-645-8431
Inn at Levelfields P.O. Box 216, Lancaster, 22503 804-435-6887
Inn at Little Washington Box 300, Middle & Main, Washington, 22747 703-675-3800
Irish Gap Inns Rt. 1, Box 40, Vesuvius, Irish Gap, 24483 804-922-7701
Irvington House Box 361, Irvington, 22480 804-438-6705
Joshua Wilton House 412 S. Main St., Harrisonburg, 22801 703-434-4464
Kinderton Manor RR 1, Box 19A, Clarksville, 23927 804-374-4439
King Carter Inn P.O. Box 425, Irvington, 22480 804-438-6053
Lambsgate B&B Route 1, Box 63, Swoope, 24479 703-337-6929
Laurel Brigade Inn 20 W. Market St., Leesburg, 22075 703-777-1010
Little River Inn P.O. Box 116, Rt. 50, Aldie, 22001 703-327-6742
Little Traveller Inn 112 N. Main St., Chincoteague, 23336 804-336-6686
Little's B&B 105 Goodwyn St., Emporia, 23847 804-634-2590
Luck House P.O. Box 919, Middleburg, 22117 703-687-5387
Lynchburg Mansion Inn 405 Madison St., Lynchburg, 24504 804-528-5400
Main Street House P.O. Box 126, Chincoteague, 23336 804-336-6030
Maple Hall 11 N. Main St., Lexington, 24450 703-463-2044
McCampbell Inn 11 N. Main St., Lexington, 24450 703-463-2044
McGrath House 225 Princess Anne St., Fredericksburg, 22401 703-371-4363
Meadow Lane Lodge Route 1, Box 110, Warm Springs, 24484 703-839-5959

Milton House P.O. Box 366, Main St., Stanley, 22851 703-778-3451
Nethers Mill Route 1, Box 62, Sperryville, 22740 703-987-8625
Norris House Inn 108 Loudoun St. SW, Leesburg, 22075 703-777-1806
Oaks, The 311 E. Main St., Christiansburg, 24073 703-381-1500
Olive Mill Bed & Breakfast Route 231, Banco, Madison City, 22711 703-923-4664
Peaks of Otter Lodge P.O. Box 489, Bedford, 24523 703-586-1081
Pumpkin House Inn, Ltd. Route 2, Box 155, Mount Crawford, 22841 703-434-6963
Red Fox Inn & Tavern P.O. Box 385, Middleburg, 22117 703-687-6301
Richard Johnston Inn 711 Caroline St., Fredericksburg, 22401 703-899-7606
Riverfront House B&B P.O. Box 310, Rt. 14 E., Mathews, 23109 804-725-9975
Rockledge Mansion 1758 410 Mill St., Occoquan, 22125 703-690-3377
Rose Hummingbird Inn P.O. Box 70, Goshen, 24439 703-997-9065
Ruffner House Inn, The Box 620, Route 4, Luray, 22835 703-743-7855
Shadows B&B Inn Route 1, Box 535, Orange, 22960 703-672-5057
Shenandoah Valley Farm Route 1, Box 142, McGaheysville, 22840 703-289-5402
Silver Thatch Inn 3001 Hollymead Rd., Charlottesville, 22901 804-978-4686
Sims-Mitchell House B&B 242 Whittle St. Box 429, Chatham, 24531 804-432-0595
Sky Chalet Country Inn Route 263 West, Basye, 22810 703-856-2147
Spangler B&B Route 2, Box 108, Meadows of Dan, 24120 703-952-2454
Stuartfield Hearth Route 1, Box 199, Mitchells, 22729 703-825-8132
Sugar Tree Inn P.O. Box 548, Hwy 56, Vesuvius, 24483 703-377-2197
Summerfield Inn 101 W. Valley St., Abingdon, 24210 703-628-5905
Surrey House Surrey, 23883 804-294-3191
Swift Run Gap B&B Skyline Dr. & Rt. 33 E., Stanardsville, 22973 804-985-2740
Sycamore Hill House Route 1, Box 978, Washington, 22747 703-675-3046
Thistle Hill Route 1, Box 291, Boston, 22713 703-987-9142
Thornrose House 531 Thornrose Ave., Staunton, 24401 703-885-7026
Three Hills Inn P.O. Box 99, Warm Springs, 24484 703-839-5381
Tipton House P.O.Box 753, Hillsville, 24343 703-728-2351
Victorian Inn 105 Clark St., Chincoteaque, 23336 804-336-1161
Vine Cottage Inn P.O. Box 918, Rt. 220, Hot Springs, 24445 703-839-2422
Watson House, The 302 N. Main St., Chincoteague, 23336 804-336-1564
Welbourne Route 743, Middleburg, 22117 703-687-3201
Wood's Guest Home 1208 Stewart Dr., Williamsburg, 23185 804-229-3376
Woods Edge Guest Cottage Route 2, Box 645, Troutville, 24175 703-473-2992
Year of the Horse Inn 600 S. Main St., Chincoteuque, 23336 804-336-3221

Washington

ANACORTES

Albatross B&B	$$ B&B	Full breakfast
5708 Kingsway W., 98221	4 rooms, 4 pb	Restaurant 1 block away
Fidalgo Island	Visa, MC •	King & queen beds
206-293-0677	C-ltd/S-ltd/P-ltd/H-yes	Library
Cecil & Marilyn Short	Spanish, some French	Washington travel videos
All year		

Marina across the street from this Cape Cod-style house. Large deck with a view. Charter boats, fine fishing, crabbing. Close to Washington Park and Sunset Beach

Channel House	$$ B&B	Full breakfast
2902 Oakes Ave., 98221	6 rooms, 4 pb	Coffee/tea/cocoa/cookies
206-293-9382	Visa, MC •	Sitting room
Dennis & Patricia McIntyre	C-12+/S-no/P-no/H-no	library, hot tub
All year		bicycle rentals

Gateway to the San Juan Islands; built in 1902; Victorian-style mansion; all antiques throughout. All rooms view San Juans and Puget Sound. Separate Rose Cottage.

ANACORTES

Nantucket Inn
3402 Commercial Ave., 98221
206-293-6007
Sallie Lingwood
All year

$ EP
6 rooms, 1 pb
C-yes/S-no/P-no/H-no

Comp. tea
Sitting room

One of the finest old homes in the area, furnished in antiques, handmade quilts and petitpoint pieces done by innkeeper.

ASHFORD

Mountain Meadows Inn B&B
28912 SR 706E, 98304
206-569-2788
Chad Darrah
All year

$$ B&B
3 rooms, 3 pb
Visa •
C-yes/S-no/P-no/H-yes

Full country breakfast
Tea, coffee, s'mores
Library, VCR, pvt. lake
rooms with kitchens
6 mi. to Mt. Rainier Prk

Quiet country elegance; full veranda porch; pondside relaxation and atmosphere; campfire by night; reflection all day; hearty mountain breakfast; hiking, fishing.

BELLINGHAM

North Garden Inn
1014 N. Garden, 98225
800-367-1676 800-922-6414
Barb & Frank DeFreytas
All year

$$ B&B
10 rooms, 2 pb
Visa, MC •
C-yes
French

Continental plus
Comp. tea
2 sitting rooms

North Garden Inn is a Queen Anne Victorian with a sweeping view of Bellingham Bay and the San Juan Islands.

Schnauzer Crossing B&B
4421 Lakeway Dr., 98226
206-733-0055 206-734-2808
Vermont & Donna McAllister
All year

$$$ B&B
3 rooms, 3 pb
Visa, MC
C-yes/P-ltd
Some Fr., Span., Ger.

Full gourmet breakfast
Outdoor spa, deck
Sitting room, lake view
library, tennis court
canoe for Lake Whatcom

A luxury bed & breakfast set amidst tall evergreens overlooking Lake Whatcom. Master suite with jacuzzi. Cottage has fireplace, VCR, private deck, jacuzzi, skylights.

BREMERTON

Willcox House
2390 Tekiu Rd., 98312
206-830-4492
Cecilia & Phillip Hughes
All year

$$$ B&B
5 rooms, 5 pb
Visa, MC •
C-15+/S-no/P-no/H-no

Full breakfast
Lunch, dinner
Comp. wine and cheese
library, game room
with pool table

Secluded 1930s estate on Hood Canal; quiet relaxation in an elegant, historic mansion with landscaped grounds, private pier and beach.

CATHLAMET

Country Keeper B&B Inn
P.O. Box 35, 98612
61 Main St.
800-551-1691
Barbara & Tony West
All year

$$ B&B
4 rooms
Visa, MC •
C-yes/S-no/P-no/H-no

Full breakfast
Complimentary wine
Tea & coffee
sitting room, library
golf, tennis & pool near

Our stately 1907 home overlooks the scenic Columbia River and Puget Island. Candlelit breakfasts in elegant dining room. Historic area. Marina, ferry, and game reserve nearby.

CATHLAMET

The Gallery B&B	$$ B&B	Full breakfast
Little Cape Horn, 98612	4 rooms, 2 pb	Complimentary cookies
206-425-7395	AmEx •	Sitting room
Carolyn & Eric Feasey	C-ask/S-no/P-ask/H-no	hot tub, beach
All year		windsurfing, fishing

Very private country elegance. Contemporary home on private beach. Breakfast served overlooking fascinating ship channel of Columbia River.

COUPEVILLE

Captain Whidbey Inn	$$ B&B	Continental breakfast
2072 W. Capt. Whidbey, 98239	34 rooms, 21 pb	All meals, bar
206-678-4097 800-366-4097	Visa, MC, AmEx, CB, DC •	Sitting room, piano
Capt. John & Geoff Stone	C-ltd/S-ltd/P-ltd/H-no	bicycles, library
All year	French, German, Spanish	sailboats & rowboats

Historic log inn, est. 1907. On the shores of Penn Cove. Antique furnished. Fine restaurant and quaint bar. Sailboats, rowboats & bikes.

Colonel Crockett Farm B&B	$$ B&B	Full breakfast
1012 S. Fort Casey Road, 98239	5 rooms, 5 pb	Private dining tables
206-678-3711	Visa, MC •	Afternoon tea
Robert & Beulah Whitlow	C-14+/S-no/P-no/H-no	sitting room, library
All year		solarium

With a change of pace and a feeling of openness, the inn provides 135 years of Victorian/Edwardian serenity in a farm-quiet island setting.

DEER HARBOR

Palmer's Chart House	$$ B&B	Full breakfast
P.O. Box 51, Orcas Isl., 98243	2 rooms, 2 pb	Day & overnight sails
206-376-4231	•	Library, private deck
Majean & Donald Palmer	C-ltd/S-ltd/P-no/H-no	travel slide shows
All year	Spanish	flower beds, gardens

Quiet, intimate and informal atmosphere. Your hosts know how to pamper you. Fishing, hiking, golf, biking nearby. Day sails and overnight sails on a private 33-foot yacht.

EASTSOUND

Kangaroo House B&B	$$ B&B	Full breakfast
P.O. Box 334, 98245	5 rooms	Comp. beverages & snacks
5 N. Beach Rd.	Visa, MC	Sitting room
206-376-2175	C-yes/S-ltd/P-no/H-no	fireplace
Jan & Mike Russillo		
All year		

Small country inn; stone fireplace in sitting room; gourmet breakfast in sunny dining room. Furnished in antiques. Close to town and beach.

Outlook Inn on Orcas Isle	$$ EP	Continental breakfast
P.O. Box 210, Main St., 98245	29 rooms, 11 pb	some private phones
206-376-2200	Visa, MC, AmEx •	
Carol Cheney	C-yes/S-yes/P-no/H-no	
All year		

Lovely turn-of-the-century inn completely refurbished, full of memorabilia. Home-style dining. Perfect island hideaway.

Anderson House, Ferndale, WA

EASTSOUND

Turtleback Farm Inn
Route 1, Box 650, 98245
Crow Valley Rd, Orcas Isl
206-376-4914
William & Susan Fletcher
All year

$$ B&B
7 rooms, 7 pb
Visa, MC •
C-ask/S-no/P-no/H-yes

Full breakfast
Comp. tea & coffee
Bar, comp. sherry
games, living room
fireplace

Charming country inn. 80 acres of meadows, forests and ponds. Furnished with fine antiques. Quiet comfort and warm hospitality. On Orcas Island.

FERNDALE

Anderson House B&B
P.O. Box 1547, 98248
2140 Main St.
206-384-3450
Dave & Kelly Anderson
All year

$ B&B
5 rooms, 3 pb
Visa, MC •
C-8+/S-no/P-no/H-no

Full Northwest breakfast
Comp. sherry
Sitting room
golf courses
Canada within 15 miles

It is 1897 at the finest home of its time. You are enjoying Northwest hospitality at its best. Perfect jumpoff for a two-nation vacation.

FRIDAY HARBOR

Duffy House
760 Pear Point Rd., 98250
206-378-5604
Jeffrey K. Beeston
All year

$$ B&B
6 rooms
Visa, MC •
C-10+/S-no/P-no/H-no

Full breakfast
Sitting room
beach cabin
private beach

Located on 116 acres including two thousand feet of water front, this 1928 Tudor remains in impeccable condition. The atmosphere is unmatched in the San Juans—guaranteed!

GREENBANK

Guest House Cottages
835 E. Christenson Rd., 98253
Whidbey Island
206-678-3115
Mary Jane & Don Creger
All year

$$$ B&B
7 rooms, 7 pb
Visa, MC, AmEx, Disc •
C-no/S-no/P-no/H-ltd

Continental plus
5 cottages & 2 houses
Exercise room, pool, spa
retreat & honeymoon spot
rated 4 diamond by AAA

An unique, romantic experience—we aren't your usual B&B—very pvt. & secluded on 25 acres wooded & pastoral. Jacuzzi, TV/VCR, full kitchen & feather bed in all accomodations.

ISSAQUAH

Wildflower B&B Inn
25237 SE Issaquah Rd., 98027
Fall City Rd.
206-392-1196
Laureita Caldwell
All year

$$ B&B
4 rooms, 3 pb
•
C-12+

Full breakfast
Afternoon tea, coffee
Snacks

Lovely log home in acres of evergreens offers quiet, relaxing country charm of years gone by. Delightful suburb of Seattle.

KIRKLAND

Shumway Mansion
11410–99th Place NE, 98033
206-823-2303
Richard & Salli Harris
All year

$$ B&B
7 rooms, 7 pb
Visa, MC •
C-12+/S-no/P-no/H-ltd

Full breakfast
Evening snack, drinks
Sitting room, piano
athletic club privileges
weddings, receptions

Four-story mansion circa 1910. Beautiful views of lake and bay. Delicious breakfasts and afternoon treats. Walk to beach, shops, galleries.

LA CONNER–MOUNT VERNON

White Swan Guest House
1388 Moore Rd., 98273
206-445-6805
Peter Goldfarb
All year

$$ B&B
3 rooms
•
C-ltd/S-no/P-no/H-no

Continental plus
Cookies
Sitting room
library
private garden cottage

A "storybook" Victorian farmhouse six miles from the historic waterfront village of La Conner. 1 hour north of Seattle. English gardens, farmland. A perfect romantic getaway.

LANGLEY

Log Castle B&B
3273 E. Saratoga Rd., 98260
206-321-5483
Senator Jack & Norma Metcalf
All year

$$$ B&B
4 rooms, 4 pb
Visa, MC •
C-no/S-no/P-no/H-no

Full breakfast
Cider, homemade cookies
Sitting room
guest canoe & rowboat

Unique waterfront log lodge on Whidbey Island. Turret bedrooms, secluded beach, fantastic view of mountains, 50 miles north of Seattle.

Lone Lake Cottage & Bkfst.
5206 S. Bayview Rd., 98260
206-321-5325
Dolores & Ward Meeks
All year

$$$ B&B
3 rooms, 3 pb
Visa, MC
C-no/S-no/P-no/H-no

Continental plus
Private beach, bicycles
VCR films, Jacuzzi tub
paddle tennis court
canoes, 14' sailboat

Whidbey's "Shangri-la"! Romantic, lovely cottages, one a 40-foot house boat. Fireplaces, kitchens, beautiful beach. Boat and canoe rides. Excellent fishing and biking.

LEAVENWORTH

Haus Rohrbach Pension
12882 Ranger Rd., 98826
509-548-7024
Robert & Kathryn Harrild
Nov–Thanksgiving Fri

$$ B&B
10 rooms, 3 pb
Visa, MC •
C-yes/S-ltd/P-no/H-no

Full breakfast
Desserts offered
Sitting room
swimming pool
hot tub

One-of-a-kind, European-style country inn, unequaled in the Pacific Northwest. Alpine-setting pool and hot tub. Year-round outdoor activities. Suites w/fireplace and whirlpool

LOPEZ ISLAND

Edenwild Inn
Box 271, Lopez Road, 98261
206-468-3238
Sue Aran
All year

$$$ B&B
7 rooms, 7 pb
Visa, MC •
C-yes/S-no/P-no/H-yes

Full breakfast
Comp. wine, aftn. tea
Dinner October-April
bicycles, volleyball
croquet, kayaking

Elegant country inn located in the heart of Lopez village on Lopez island in the San Juans. Gourmet breakfasts, English gardens, summer patio, beautiful bay sunsets.

Inn at Swifts Bay
Route 2, Box 3402, 98261
206-468-3636
R. Herrman, C. Brandmeir
All year

$$$ B&B
4 rooms, 2 pb
Visa, MC •
Portuguese, some Ger, Sp

Full breakfast
Comp. sherry, min. water
Sitting room
video library, hot tub
bicycle rentals

English country comfort in the San Juan Islands. Private separate beach. Delightful breakfasts. Bald eagles, Orca whales. Pastoral and restful.

MONTESANO

Sylvan Haus
P.O. Box 416, 98563
417 Wilder Hill Drive
206-249-3453
Jo Anne & Mike Murphy
Exc. Nov–Apr (hike in)

$$ B&B
3 rooms, 2 pb
C-no/S-no/P-no

Full gourmet breakfast
Country kitchen, snacks
Restaurant nearby
hot tub, decks, boating
swimming, hiking

A gracious family home surrounded by towering evergreens; secluded high hill overlooking valley. Dining room; 5 decks; hot tub; gourmet breakfast. 1 hour from Sea Tac Airport.

OLYMPIA

Harbinger Inn
1136 E. Bay Dr., 98506
206-754-0389
Marisa & Terrell Williams
All year

$$ B&B
4 rooms, 1 pb
Visa, MC, AmEx
C-ltd/S-no/P-no/H-no

Continental plus
Comp. wine
Sitting room
library

Restored turn-of-the-century home with beautiful water view; period furnishings; conveniently located for boating, bicycling, business and entertainment.

Puget View Guesthouse B&B
7924–61st Ave. NE, 98506
206-459-1676
Dick & Barbara Yunker
All year

$$$ B&B
2 rooms, 1 pb
Visa, MC
C-yes/S-yes/P-ask/H-no

Continental plus
Suite sleeps 4
Private dining area/deck
books, games, canoe
100-acre park next door

Charming waterfront guest cottage suite next to host's log home. Breakfast to your cottage. Peaceful. Picturesque. A "NW Best Places" since 1984. Puget Sound 5 min. off I-5.

ORCAS

Orcas Hotel
P.O. Box 155, 98280
at the Ferry Landing
206-376-4300 206-376-4306
Barbara & John Jamieson
All year

$$ B&B
12 rooms, 3 pb
AmEx, Visa, MC •
C-yes/S-yes/P-no/H-ltd
French, Spanish

Continental breakfast
Restaurant & bar
Sitting room, library
bicycle storage
music Saturday, Sunday

Beautifully restored Victorian inn above ferry landing, gorgeous view, fine dining, local seafood, cocktails, "White Pickets & Wicker," garden, antiques.

PORT ANGELES

Tudor Inn
1108 S. Oak, 98362
206-452-3138
Jane & Jerry Glass
All year

$$ B&B
5 rooms, 1 pb
Visa, MC •
C-9+/S-ltd/P-no/H-no

Full breakfast
Afternoon tea
Sitting room, TV

European antiques, water/mountain views, winter cross-country ski package, salmon, steelhead fishing, ferry to Victoria, BC. Free brochure.

PORT TOWNSEND

Ann Starrett Mansion B&B
744 Clay St., 98368
206-385-3205 800-321-0644
Edel & Bob Sokol
All year

$$$ B&B
10 rooms, 10 pb
Visa, MC •
C-8+/S-yes/P-no/H-ltd

Full breakfast
Comp.sherry, tea
Sitting room
player/baby grand pianos
jacuzzi, hot tub

Port Townsend's only full-service Victorian inn. Internationally renowned for its classic Victorian architecture, frescoed ceilings & free hung three-tiered spiral staircase.

Bishop Victorian Suites
714 Washington St., 98368
206-385-6122 800-822-8696
Lloyd & Marlene Cahoon
All year

$$$ B&B
12 rooms, 12 pb
Visa, MC, AmEx
C-yes/S-yes/P-yes/H-no

Continental breakfast
Coffee, tea
Sitting room
parking lot

Downtown, Victorian-era hotel; beautifully restored. Gracious suites. Mountain and water views. Walk to Port Townsend, Washington's historic Victorian seaport.

Heritage House Inn
305 Pierce St., 98368
206-385-6800
P & J Broughton, B & C Ellis
All year

$$ B&B
6 rooms, 3 pb
Dis •
C-8+/S-no/P-no/H-ltd

Full breakfast
Coffee/tea/fresh cookies
Victorian parlor
bicycles

Unique combination of Victorian setting, unparalleled view of the bay, classic Italianate inn, quaint charm, warm traditional attention to comfort.

Holly Hill House
611 Polk, 98368
206-385-5619
Bill & Laurie Medlicott
All year

$$$ B&B
4 rooms, 4 pb
Visa, MC •
C-12+/S-no/P-no/H-no

Full breakfast
Sitting room
library
queen-size beds

Beautifully maintained 1872 Victorian home, in historic uptown. Walking distance to downtown. Bountiful breakfast. Enjoy our Victorian waterfront community.

PORT TOWNSEND

James House
1238 Washington St., 98368
206-385-1238
Carol McGough, Anne Tiernan
All year

$$ B&B
12 rooms, 4 pb
Visa, MC
C-12+/S-no/P-no/H-ltd

Continental plus
Comp. tea, sherry
Sitting parlors
player piano, fireplaces
porch with swing

1889 Queen Anne Victorian mansion featuring unsurpassed water and mountain views, period antiques. First B&B in the Northwest, still the finest.

The Lincoln Inn
538 Lincoln St., 98368
206-385-6677 800-477-4667
Joanie & Robert Allen
Easter-Thanksgiving

$$ B&B
6 rooms, 6 pb
Visa, MC •
C-no/S-ltd/P-ltd/H-no
French, German

Full gourmet breakfast
Dinner, stocked fridge
Comp. wine, sitting rm.
workout facilities
bicycles, tennis court

A small personally run inn offering an unique Victorian atmosphere and hospitality. Victorian antiques in all rooms. Leave the world behind you.

Lizzie's Victorian B&B
731 Pierce St., 98368
206-385-4168
Bill & Patti Wickline
All year

$$ B&B
7 rooms, 4 pb
Visa, MC
C-10+

Full breakfast
Coffee, tea
Sitting room
tennis courts nearby

Victorian comfort and hospitality amid elegance and class. Close to town, beach and mountains.

Manresa Castle
P.O. Box 564, 98368
7th & Sheridan Sts.
206-385-5750 800-732-1281
Ronald & Carol Smith
All year

$$ EP
Visa, MC, AmEx •
C-yes/S-yes/P-no/H-ltd

Lobby
player piano
cable TV, phones

Restored castle; altered only to provide modern conveniences. A historical landmark. Victorian decor. Spectacular views of bay, mountains and Victorian Port Townsend.

Old Consulate Inn/Hastings
313 Walker St., 98368
at Washington St.
206-385-6753
Rob & Joanna Jackson
All year

$$ B&B
8 rooms, 8 pb
Visa, MC •
C-8+/S-no/P-no/H-no

Full breakfast
Refreshments, aftn. tea
Formal dining room
parlors, grand piano
library, billiard room

Victorian decor that creates a nostalgia for great-grandmother's house! Cluttered elegance, romantic bedrooms—quiet and peaceful.

SEATTLE

Beech Tree Manor
1405 Queen Anne Ave. N., 98109
206-281-7037
Virginia Lucero
All year

$$ B&B
6 rooms, 3 pb
Visa, MC •
C-yes/S-no/P-no/H-no

Full breakfast
Antique linen shop
Sitting room
library
porch with wicker chairs

1904 mansion, near City Center, yet quiet; scrumptious breakfasts; original art in all rooms; luxuriously comfortable.

Chambered Nautilus, Seattle, WA

SEATTLE

Broadway Guest House
959 Broadway East, 98102
206-329-1864
H. Lee Vennes
All year

$$$ B&B
3 rooms, 3 pb
AmEx •
C-yes

Continental plus
Sitting room
library
conference facilities

One of Capitol Hill's gracious mansions circa 1909. Luxury antique-filled rooms, hand-carved woodwork.

Capitol Hill Inn
1713 Belmont Ave., 98122
206-323-1955
Katie & Joanne Godmintz
All year

$$ B&B
5 rooms, 3 pb
AmEx
C-no/S-no/P-no/H-no

Full breakfast
Espresso bar
Sitting room
European antiques

Victorian ambiance within walking distance of Convention Center, downtown, Broadway shops & restaurants. All rooms furnished in European antiques, brass beds & down comforters

---

**Chambered Nautilus
B&B Inn**
5005 22nd Ave. NE, 98105
206-522-2536
Bunny & Bill Hagemeyer
All year

$$$ B&B
9 rooms, 7 pb
Visa, MC, AmEx, DC, CB
•
C-10+/S-ltd/P-no/H-no
German

Full gourmet breakfast
Tea & homemade lollypops
Sitting room with phone
desks in rooms
Fireplaces, grand piano

"Seattle's Finest". Gracious historic in-city retreat close to downtown & University of Washington. National Award-winning family-style breakfasts.

SEATTLE ———————

Chelsea Station B&B Inn
4915 Linden Ave. N, 98103
206-547-6077
Dick & MaryLou Jones
All year

$$$ B&B
5 rooms, 5 pb
Visa, MC, AmEx, DC, Dis •
C-12+/S-no/P-no/H-no

Full breakfast
Eve. snack, comp. tea
Kitchen suite
sitting room
pump organ, hot tub

Old World charm and tranquil country setting amidst the city's activity. Each room is a very private answer to a quiet getaway. Banana batter French toast: "Best in the West."

Mildred's B&B Inn
1202 15th Ave. E, 98112
206-325-6072
Mildred J. Sarver
All year

$$ B&B
4 rooms, 1 pb
•
C-yes/S-ltd/P-no/H-no

Full breakfast
Afternoon tea or coffee
Sitting room
library, veranda
grand piano

1890 Victorian. Wraparound veranda, lace curtains, red carpets, grand piano, fireplace. City location near bus, electric trolley, park, art museum, flower conservatory.

Prince of Wales B&B
133 13th Ave. E., 98102
206-325-9692
Naomi Reed, Bert Brun
All year

$$ B&B
4 rooms, 2 pb
Visa, MC •
C-13+/S-no/P-no/H-no

Full breakfast
Morning coffee to room
Sitting room
fireplaces, garden
attic suite w/prvt. deck

Downtown 1.5 miles away; on bus line; walk to convention center; turn-of-the-century ambiance; panoramic views of city skyline, Puget Sound and the Olympic Mountains.

Salisbury House
750 16th Ave. E., 98112
206-328-8682
Cathryn & Mary Wiese
All year

$$ B&B
4 rooms, 2 pb
Visa, MC, AmEx
C-13+/S-no/P-no/H-no
Spanish

Full breakfast
Comp. tea, lemonade
Sitting room, library
porch, down comforters
croquet, badminton

Elegant Capitol Hill home. Ideal location for business or pleasure. Take advantage of Seattle's excellent transit system. Minutes to downtown, Univ. of WA, Seattle Univ.

Seattle B&B
2442 NW Market #300, 98107
206-784-0539
Inge Pokrandt
All year

$ EP/B&B
3 rooms, 2 pb
Visa, MC, AmEx •
C-ltd/S-no/P-no/H-yes
German

Some staple foods
Comp. tea, wine
Sitting rm, maid service
color cable TV, phone
kitchen, prvt. entrance

Private suite and cottage near downtown, parks, University. Relaxed atmosphere. Lots of tourist books/materials—hostess knowledgeable about area; a most hospitable home.

Tugboat Challenger
809 Fairview Place N., 98109
206-340-1201 FAX:621-9208
Jerry Brown
All year

$$ B&B
7 rooms, 4 pb
•
C-yes/S-yes/P-no/H-yes

Full gourmet breakfast
Soft drinks
Sitting room, library
bicycles, fireplace
small boats

On board a fully functional, exceptionally clean, restored tugboat. Near downtown Seattle. Closed circuit TV. Carpeted throughout. Nautical antiques.

458 Washington

SEATTLE —————————————————————————————

Williams House B&B
1505–4th Ave. N., 98109
206-285-0810
Ruth McGill
All year

$$ B&B
5 rooms, 1 pb
Visa, MC, AmEx
C-yes/S-ltd/P-no/H-no

Full breakfast
Coffee, tea, cookies
Sitting room
piano

Views of Seattle, Puget Sound, mountains. One of Seattle's oldest neighborhoods. Very close to Seattle activities, parks, lakes.

SEQUIM —————————————————————————————

Greywolf Inn
177 Keeler Rd., 98382
206-683-5889 206-683-1487
Peggy Melang
All year

$ B&B
5 rooms, 5 pb
Visa, MC, AmEx
C-no/S-no/P-no

Continental breakfast
Sitting room
Library, fireplace
patio, decks
trees, fields, stream

Five-acre rural retreat overlooking Sequim. Near golfing, John Wayne Marina, Dungeness Spit Wildlife Refuge, Olympic Mtns., Victoria Ferry. Come "Sequim" with us.

Margie's Inn on the Bay
120 Forrest Road, 98382
206-683-7011
Margie Vorhies
March–October

$$ B&B
6 rooms, 6 pb
Visa, MC •
C-12+/S-no/P-no/H-yes

Full breakfast
Comp. sherry
Sitting room
tennis courts
VCR, TV, boats

Country hideaway: large modern ranch-style home on the water. Full breakfast. Golf, fish, hike. Close to John Wayne marina.

SNOHOMISH —————————————————————————————

Countryman B&B
119 Cedar, 98290
206-568-9622
Larry & Sandy Countryman
All year

$$ B&B
3 rooms, 3 pb
Visa, MC •
C-yes/S-no/P-yes/H-no
German

Full breakfast
Afternoon tea
Sitting room
bicycles

1896 Queen Anne Victorian in National Historic district. One block from 300 antique dealers. The inn with the extras.

SOUTH CLE ELUM —————————————————————————————

Moore House Country Inn
P.O. Box 861, 98943
526 Marie St.
509-674-5939 800-22-TWAIN
Monty & Connie Moore
All year

$ B&B
12 rooms, 4 pb
Visa, MC, AmEx •
C-yes/S-ltd/P-no/H-no

Full breakfast
Lunch, dinner, hot tubs
Sitting room, bicycles
caboose unit with bath
winter sleigh rides

Old railroad hotel adjacent to Iron Horse State Park. Mountain location makes four seasons of activities possible from our doorstep. Group dinners, receptions, weddings.

SPOKANE —————————————————————————————

Fotheringham House
2128 W. 2nd Ave., 99204
509-838-4363
Howard & Phyllis Ball
All year

$$ B&B
8 rooms, 5 pb
AmEx, Visa, MC •
C-12+/S-no/P-no/H-no

Continental plus
Comp. tea, cookies
Living room, library
A/C in rooms
near tennis & park

Victorian home located in historic Spokane District. Antique furnishings, queen beds, park across street. Next to restaurant in Victorian mansion.

SUNNYSIDE

Sunnyside Inn B&B
800 Edison Ave., 98944
509-839-5557
Karen & Donavon Vlieger
All year

$ B&B
8 rooms, 8 pb
Visa, MC, AmEx •
C-yes/S-no/P-no/H-no

Full breakfast
Snacks, hot tubs
Sitting room
near tennis, golf, and
wineries

Eight luxurious rooms, all with private baths, 7 with private jacuzzi tubs. In the heart of Washington wine country.

VASHON ISLAND

The Swallow's Nest
6030 SW 248th St., 98070
Maury Island
206-463-2646
Kathryn & Robert Keller
All year

$$ EP
5 rooms, 3 pb
Visa, MC •
C-yes/S-no/P-ltd/H-ltd

Breakfast ($–arrange)
Coffee, tea, cocoa
Hot tubs & fireplaces
golf nearby

Get away to comfortable country cottages on the bluffs overlooking Puget Sound and Mt. Rainier. Optional breakfast brought to your cottage.

WHITE SALMON

Inn of the White Salmon
P.O. Box 1549, 98672
172 W. Jewett
509-493-2335
Janet & Roger Holen
All year

$$$ B&B
18 rooms, 18 pb
Major CC •
C-yes/S-ltd/P-ask

Full breakfast
Restaurant nearby
Sitting room, hot tub
phone, TV, A/C in rooms

Columbia River Gorge, "the quiet side". Built as an hotel in 1937. Furnished with antiques. World famous breakfast. Windsurfing, hiking, skiing.

More Inns ...

Abel House B&B 117 Fleet St. S., Montesano, 98563 206-249-6002
Admiral's Hideaway 1318–30th St., Anacortes, 98221 206-293-0106
Alexander's Country Inn Hwy. 706, Ashford, 98304 206-569-2300
American Hearth B&B 7506 Soundview Dr., Gig Harbor, 98335 206-851-2196
Amy's Manor B&B P.O. Box 411, Pateros, 98846 509-923-2334
Anderson Creek Lodge 5602 Mission Rd., Bellingham, 98226 206-966-2126
Apple Tree Inn 43317 SE N. Bend Way, North Bend, 98045 206-888-3572
Arcadia Country Inn 1891 S. Jacob Miller Rd, Port Townsend, 98368 206-385-5245
Ashford Mansion Box G, Ashford, 98304 206-569-2739
Bavarian Meadows B&B 11097 Eagle Creek Rd., Leavenworth, 98826 509-548-4449
Beach Cottage 5831 Ward Ave., , Bainbridge Island, 98110 206-842-6081
Beach House 7338 S. Maxwelton Rd., Clinton, 98236 206-321-4335
Bear Creek Inn 19520 N.E. 144th Place, Woodinville, 98072 206-881-2978
Bellevue B&B 830–100th Ave. SE, Bellevue, 98004 206-453-1048
Bennett House B&B 325 E. 6th, Port Angeles, 98362 206-457-0870
Betty's Place P.O. Box 86, Lopez, 98261 206-468-2470
Blair House B&B 345 Blair Ave., Friday Harbor, 98250 206-378-5907
Blakely Estate B&B E. 7710 Hodin Dr., Spokane, 99212 509-926-9426
Blue Heron Route 1, Box 64, Eastsound, 98245 206-376-2954
Blue House Inn & B&B 513 Anthes, Langley, 98260 206-221-8392
Bombay House 8490 Beck Rd., Bainbridge Island, 98110 206-842-3926
Brown's Farm B&B 11150 Hwy 209, Leavenworth, 98826 509-548-7863
Burrow's Bay B&B 4911 MacBeth Dr., Anacortes, 98221 206-293-4792
Burton House P.O. Box 9902, Seattle, 98109 206-285-5945
Bush House P.O. Box 58, Index, 98256 206-793-2312
Carson Hot Springs Hotel P.O. Box 370, Carson, 98610 509-427-8292
Cascade Mountain Inn 3840 Pioneer Lane, Concrete-Birdsview, 98237 206-826-4333
Castle, The 1103–15th, Bellingham, 98225 206-676-0974

Cathlamet Hotel 67-69 Main St, Cathlamet, 98612 800-446-0454
Cathy Robinson P.O. Box 1604, Friday Harbor, 98250 206-378-3830
Cedarym, A Colonial B&B 1011–240th Ave. , Redmond, 98053 206-868-4159
Century House B&B 401 S. B.C. Ave., Lynden, 98264 206-354-2439
Circle F 2399 Mt. Baker Hwy, Bellingham, 98226 206-733-2509
Cliff House 5440 Windmill Rd., Freeland, 98249 206-321-1566
College Inn Guest House 4000 University Way , Seattle, 98105 206-633-4441
Collins House 225 "A" St., Friday Harbor, 98250 206-378-5834
Country Manner B&B 1120 First St., Snohowish, 98290 206-568-8254
De Cann House B&B 2610 Eldridge Ave, Bellingham, 98225 206-734-9172
Desert Rose P.O. Box 166, Moxee City, 98936 509-542-2237
Downey House B&B, The 1880 Chilberg Rd., LaConner, 98257 206-466-3207
Eagles Nest Inn 3236 E. Saratoga Rd., Langley, 98260 206-321-5331
Ecologic Place 10 Beach Dr., Nordland, 98358 206-385-3077
Edel Haus Pension 320 Ninth St., Leavenworth, 98826 509-548-4412
Edson House Route 3, P.O. Box 221, Vashon Island, 98070 206-463-2646
Em's B&B Inn P.O. Box 206, Chelan, 98816 509-682-4149
Flying L Ranch Inn 25 Flying L Lane, Glenwood, 98619 509-364-3488
Forget-Me-Not B&B 1133 Washington St., Wenatchee, 98801 509-663-6114
Fort Casey Inn 1124 S. Engle Rd., Coupeville, 98239 206-678-8792
French House B&B 206 W. Warren, Pateros, 98846 509-923-2626
Galer Place B&B 318 W. Galer St., Seattle, 98119 206-282-5339
Garden Path Inn, The 111 First St., Box 575, Langley, 98260 206-321-5121
Glen Mar by the Sea 318 N. Eunice, Port Angeles, 98362 206-457-6110
Grand Old House P.O. Box 667, Hwy. 14, Bingen, 98605 509-493-2838
Green Gables Inn 922 Bonsella, Walla Walla, 99362 509-525-5501
Groveland Cottage 1673 Sequin-Dungeuess, Dunqeuess, 98382 206-683-3565
Growly B&B 37311 SR 706, Ashford, 98304 206-569-2339
Hanford Castle, The Box 23, Oakesdale, 99158 509-285-4120
Hanson House B&B 1526 Palm Ave. SW, Seattle, 98116 206-937-4157
Harrison House 210 Sunset Ave., Edmonds, 98020 206-776-4748
Heather House 1011 "B" Ave., Edmonds, 98020 206-778-7233
Heaven Can Wait Lodge 12385 Shugart Flats Rd., Leavenworth, 98826 206-881-5350
Heron in La Conner Box 716, 117 Maple St., La Conner, 98257 206-466-4626
Hill Top B&B 5832 Church Rd., Ferndale, 98248 206-384-3619
Hillside House 365 Carter Ave., Friday Harbor, 98250 206-378-4730
Hillside House E. 1729 18th Ave., Spokane, 99203 509-534-1426
Hillwood Gardens B&B 41812 S. E. 142nd St., North Bend, 98045 206-888-0799
Home by the Sea 2388 E Sunlight Beach R, Clinton, 98236 206-221-2964
Hopkinson House 862 Bumping River Rd., Goose Prairie, 98929 509-248-2264
Hotel Europa 833 Front St., Leavenworth, 98826 509-548-5221
Hotel de Haro/Resort 4950 Tarte Mem. Dr., Roche Harbor, 98250 206-378-2155
Hudgrens Haven 9313–190th, SW, Edmonds, 98020 206-776-2202
Idyl Inn on the River 4548 Tolt River Rd., Carnation, 98014 206-333-4262
Inn At Burg's Landing 8808 Villa Beach Rd., Anderson Island, 98303 206-884-9185
Inn New England 400 N. Bend, Box 1349, North Bend, 98045 206-888-3879
Inn at Ilwaco 120 Williams St. N.E, Ilwaco, 98624 206-642-8686
Inn at Langley P.O. Box 835, Langley, 98260 206-221-3033
Inn at Penn Cove P.O. Box 85, Coupeville, 98239 206-678-6990
Irish Acres P.O. Box 466, Port Townsend, 98368 206-385-4485
Island Inn B&B Route 1, Box 950, Vashon Island, 98070 206-567-4832
Jasmer's Guest House 30005 SR 706 E, Ashford, 98304 206-569-2682
Kalaloch Lodge HC 80, Box 1100, Kalaloch, 98331 206-962-2271
Katy's Inn 503 S. 3rd, Box 304, La Conner, 98257 206-466-3366
Kennedy's Bed & Breakfast 322 E. 5th, Port Angeles, 98362 206-457-3628
Kimbrough House 505 Maiden Lane, Pullman, 99163 509-334-3866
La Conner Country Inn P.O. Box 573, La Conner, 98257 206-466-3101
Lake Chelan River House Route 1, Box 614, Chelan, 98816 509-682-5122
Lake Crescent Lodge Star Route 1, Port Angeles, 98362 206-928-3211
Lake Quinault Lodge P.O. Box 7, S. Shore Rd., Quinault, 98575 206-288-2571

Lakeside Manor B&B 2425 Pend Oreille Lakes, Colville, 99114 509-684-8741
Le Cocq House 719 W. Edson, Lynden, 98264 206-354-3032
Lions B&B 803—92nd Ave. N.E., Bellevue, 98004 206-455-1018
Llama Ranch B&B 1980 Hwy 141, White Salmon, 98672 509-395-2264
Lowman House B&B 701 "K" Ave., Anacortes, 98221 206-293-0590
MacKaye Harbor Inn Route 1, Box 1940, Lopez Island, 98261 206-468-2253
Manitou Lodge P.O. Box 600, Forks, 98331 206-374-6295
Manor Farm Inn 26069 Big Valley Rd., Poulsbo, 98370 206-779-4628
Maple Valley B&B 20020 S.E. 228th, Maple Valley, 98038 206-432-1409
Marit's B&B 6208 Palatine Ave. N., Seattle, 98103 206-782-7900
Mary Kay's Whaley Mansion Route 1, Box 693, Chelan, 98816 509-682-5735
Mazawa Country Inn Mazawa, 98833 509-996-2681
Meadows, The 1980 Cattle Point Rd., Friday Harbor, 98250 206-378-4004
Miller Tree Inn P.O. Box 953, Forks, 98331 206-374-6806
Mio Amore Pensione P.O. Box 208, Trout Lake, 98650 509-395-2264
Moon & Sixpence 3021 Beaverton Valley, Friday Harbor, 98250 206-378-4138
Murphy's Country B&B Route 1, Box 400, Ellensburg, 98926 509-925-7986
Murray House NW 108 Parkwood Blvd., Pullman, 99163 509-332-4569
National Park Inn Longmire, 98398 206-569-2565
Noris House 312 Ave. D, Snohomish, 98290 206-568-3825
North Bay Inn B&B East 2520 Hwy 302, Belfair, 98528 206-275-5378
North Cascades Lodge P.O. Box W, Chelan, 98816 509-682-4711
Oceanfront Lodge N. Ocean Shores Blvd., Ocean Shores, 98569 206-289-3036
Ogle's B&B 1307 Dogwood Hill S.W., Port Orchard, 98366 206-876-9170
Olalla Orchard B&B 12530 Orchard Ave. S.E., Olalla, 98359 206-857-5915
Old Blewett Pass B&B 3470 Highway 97, Leavenworth, 98826 509-548-4475
Old Brick Silo B&B 9028 E. Leavenworth Rd., Leavenworth, 98826 509-548-4772
Old Brook Inn 530 Old Brook Lane, Anacortes, 98221 206-293-4768
Old Honey Farm Country Inn 8910 384th Ave. S.E., Snoqualmie, 98065 206-888-9399
Old Mill House B&B P.O. Box 543, Eatonville, 98328 206-832-6506
Olde Glencove Hotel 9418 Glencove Rd., Gig Harbor, 98335 206-884-2835
Olympic Lights 4531A Cattle Point Rd., Friday Harbor, 98250 206-378-3186
Olympic View B&B 15415 Harvey Rd., NE Bainbridge Island, 98110 206-842-4671
Orchard 619 3rd St., Langley, 98260 206-221-7880
Orchard Hill Inn Route 2, Box 130, White Salmon, 98672 509-493-3024
Otter's Nest 2724 N. Nugent Rd., Lummi Island, 98262 206-758-2667
Packwood Hotel Route 256, Packwood, 98361 206-494-5431
Palace Hotel 1004 Water St., Port Townsend, 98368 206-385-0773
Petersen B&B 10228 S.E. 8th, Bellevue, 98004 206-454-9334
Phippen's B&B 1226 Front St., Leavenworth, 98826 800-666-9806
Pillars By The Sea 1367 E. Bayview, Freeland, 98249 206-221-7738
Pinkham's Pillow, Ltd. 202 3rd Ave. S., Edmonds, 98020 206-774-3406
R.C. McCroskey House Box 95, Garfield, 99130 509-635-1459
Rainbow Inn B&B 1075 Chilberg, Box 1600, La Conner, 98257 206-466-4578
Ramage House 1306 Franklin St., Port Townsend, 98368 206-385-1086
Ramblin' Rose 102 W. Railroad, Cle Elum, 98922 509-674-5224
Ravenscroft Inn Ltd. 533 Quincy St., Port Townsend, 98368 206-385-2784
Rees Mansion Inn 260 E. Birch St., Walla Walla, 99362 509-529-7845
River Bend Inn Route 2 Box 943, Usk, 99180 509-445-1476
River Inn Route 3, Box 3858 D, Forks, 98331 206-374-6526
River Valley B&B Box 158, Acme, 98220 206-595-2686
Rosario Resort Hotel Eastsound, 98245 206-376-2222
Run of the River B&B 9308 E. Leavenworth Rd., Leavenworth, 98826 509-548-7171
San Juan Inn P.O. Box 776, Harbor, 98250 206-378-2070
Saratoga Inn Langley, 98260 206-221-7526
Secret Garden 1807 Lakeway Dr., Bellingham, 98226 206-671-7850
Shelburne Country Inn P.O. Box 250, Seaview, 98644 206-642-2442
Shirlin Inn, The 105 Patton St., Richland, 99352 509-375-0720
Shorebird House 2654 N. Nugent Rd, Lummi Island, 98262 206-758-2177
Smith House B&B 307 Maple St., Hamilton, 98255 206-826-4214

Summer House 2603 Center Rd., Chimacum, 98325 206-732-4017
Summer Song B&B P.O. Box 82, Seabeck, 98380 206-830-5089
Syndicate Hill B&B 403 S. 6th St., Dayton, 99328 509-382-2688
Three Creeks Lodge 2120 Hwy 97 Satus Pass, Goldendale, 98620 509-773-4026
Tokeland Hotel P.O. Box 117, Tokeland, 98590 206-267-7700
Town & Country Cottage B&B N7620 Fox Point Dr., Spokane, 99208 509-466-7559
Tucker House B&B 260 "B" St., Friday Harbor, 98250 206-378-2783
Tulin House, The S. 812 Main St., Colfax, 99111 509-397-3312
Twin River Ranch B&B E 5730 Hwy 3, Shelton, 98584 206-426-1023
Unicorn's Rest 316 E. 10th St., Olympia, 98501 206-754-9613
Villa Heidelberg 4845—45th Ave. S.W., Seattle, 98116 206-938-3658
Walton House 12340 Seabeck Hwy NW, Seabeck, 98380 206-830-4498
Waverly Place B&B W 709 Waverly Place, Spokane, 99205 509-328-1856
Westwinds Bed & Breakfast 4909 N. Hannah Hghlnds, Friday Harbor, 98250 206-378-5283
Whaley Mansion 415 Third St., Lake Cheelan, 98816 509-682-5735
Whidbey Inn P.O. Box 156, Langley, 98260 206-221-7115
Whispering Pines B&B E. 7504—44th Ave., Spokane, 99223 509-448-1433
White Gull 420 Commercial, Anacortes, 98221 206-293-7011
Willows Inn B&B 2579 W. Shore Dr., Lummi Island, 98262 206-758-2620
Woodsong B&B P.O. Box 32, Orcas, 98280 206-376-2340

West Virginia

BERKELEY SPRINGS

Highlawn Inn	$$ B&B	Full country breakfast
304 Market St., 25411	6 rooms, 6 pb	Dinner by reservation
304-258-5700	Visa, MC	Catering, weddings
Sandra Kauffman	C-no/S-yes/P-no/H-ltd	TV, veranda, porch swing
All year		golf, tennis, hiking

Restored Victorian; luxurious touches, solitude and antiques in quiet mountain town. Minutes from famous mineral baths. Winter Victorian escape packages. Thanksgiving feast.

CHARLES TOWN

Cottonwood Inn	$$$ B&B	Full breakfast
RR 2, Box 61-S, 25414	7 rooms, 7 pb	Comp. tea, coffee, wine
Mill Lane & Kable Town Rd	Visa, MC, Choice	Picnic lunch, dinner
304-725-3371	C-yes/S-yes/P-no/H-no	sitting room, library
Colin & Eleanor Simpson		trout stream
All year		

Quiet country setting, stocked trout stream, near Harper's Ferry in historic Shenandoah Valley. Bountiful breakfast. Guest rooms have TV and air-conditioning.

Gilbert House B&B	$$$ B&B	Full gourmet breakfast
P.O. Box 1104, 25414	3 rooms, 3 pb	Tea/wine/champagne/fruit
Middleway Historic Dist.	Visa, MC ●	Sitting room, library
304-725-0637	C-no/S-ltd/P-no/H-no	piano, fireplaces
Jean & Bernie Heiler	German, Spanish	walking tour of village
All year		

Near Harper's Ferry, magnificent stone house on National Register in 18th-century village. Tasteful antiques, art treasures. Leisurely breakfast. Romantic.

CHARLES TOWN

Hillbrook Inn
Route 2, Box 152, 25414
Rte. 13, Summit Point Rd.
304-725-4223
Gretchen Carroll
All year

$$$ B&B
5 rooms, 5 pb
Visa, MC •
C-no/S-ltd/P-no/H-no
French

Full breakfast
Restaurant, bar service
Afternoon tea, snacks
sitting room, library
antiques, art collection

Award winning country inn in the European style. Intimate dining room serves 7-course dinner. Dining terrace w/fountain. Sweeping lawns, gardens, woodlands, streams & ponds.

ELKINS

Post House
306 Robert E. Lee Ave., 26241
304-636-1792
Jo Ann Post Barlow
All year

$ B&B
3 rooms, 1 pb
Visa
C-yes/S-no/P-no/H-no

Continental plus
Afternoon tea
AMTA certified massage
near 5 ski resorts

Surrounded by mountain and park recreation, yet in town. Parklike backyard with children's playhouse. Handmade quilts for sale, and certified massage on premises.

Retreat at Buffalo Run
214 Harpertown Rd., 26241
304-636-2960
Kathleen, Bertha & Earl Rhoad
All year

$ B&B
7 rooms
C-yes/S-no/P-no/H-no

Full breakfast
Gateway to Monongahela
short walk to tennis and
swimming pool

Gracious turn-of-the-century home surrounded by oaks, hemlock and rhododendron groves. Near Monongahela National Forest and unspoiled wilderness. Walk to festival & downtown.

Tunnel Mountain B&B
Route 1, Box 59-1, 26241
304-636-1684
Anne & Paul Beardslee
All year

$ B&B
3 rooms, 3 pb
C-10+/S-no/P-no/H-no

Full breakfast
Restaurant nearby
Sitting room w/fireplace
patio, wooded paths, A/C
scenic views, cable TV

Romantic country fieldstone B&B nestled in the scenic West Virginia. Mountains next to National Forest and recreational areas. Antiques, fireplaces, warm hospitality.

MARTINSBURG

Dunn Country Inn
Route 3, Box 33J, 25401
304-263-8646
Prince & Dianna Dunn
All year

$$$ B&B
5 rooms, 2 pb
Visa, MC
C-12+/S-no/P-no/H-ltd

Full breakfast
Comp. wine, snacks
Sitting room

Country inn providing a tranquil setting—a welcome retreat from the city. Scrumptious and hearty breakfast. 1805 Home on National Register.

ROMNEY

Hampshire House 1884
165 N. Grafton St., 26757
304-822-7171
Jane & Scott Simmons
All year

$$ B&B/MAP/AP
5 rooms, 5 pb
Visa, MC, AmEx, DC •
C-yes/S-no/P-no/H-no

Full breakfast
Lunch, dinner
Comp. wine, snacks
sitting room, library
bikes, near tennis, pool

Completely renovated 1884 home. Period furniture, lamps, fireplaces. Gourmet dining. Quiet. Central heat and air. Therapeutic massage available.

SHEPHERDSTOWN

Thomas Shepherd Inn
P.O. Box 1162, 25443
300 W. German St. at Duke
304-876-3715
Margaret Perry
All year

$$$ B&B
6 rooms, 4 pb
Visa, MC, AmEx
C-12+/S-ltd/P-no/H-no

Full breakfast
Sherry, coffee, tea
Living room w/fireplace
bicycles & picnics

1868 restored stately home in quaint historic Civil War town. Period antiques, very special breakfasts, fireside beverage, excellent restaurants.

SUMMIT POINT

Countryside
P.O. Box 57, 25446
Hawthorn Ave.
304-725-2614
Lisa & Daniel Hileman
All year

$$ B&B
2 rooms, 2 pb
Visa, MC
C-yes/S-yes/P-yes/H-no

Continental breakfast
Afternoon tea & cookies
Sitting room, bicycles
down comforters
feather beds

Near historic Harper's Ferry; quiet and cozy country inn; hiking, cycling, antiquing, sightseeing. For romantic getaways, honeymoons, anniversary and birthday celebrations.

WHEELING

Yesterdays Ltd.
827 Main St., 26003
304-232-0864
Bill & Nancy Fields
All year

$$ B&B
26 rooms, 22 pb
Visa, MC •
C-yes/S-no/P-no/H-no

Full breakfast
Restaurant, lunch
Dinner, afternoon tea
sitting room
whirlpool suites

Lovingly restored Victorian townhouses in historic district overlooking river. Antiques. Breakfast served on elegant china, crystal and silver. Walk to downtown and events.

WHITE SULPHUR SPRINGS

James Wylie House B&B
208 E. Main St., 24986
304-536-9444
Cheryl & Joe Griffith
All year

$$ B&B
3 rooms, 3 pb
Visa, MC, AmEx
C-yes/S-no/P-no/H-no

Full breakfast
Comp. wine
Sitting room, antiques
library, bicycles
volleyball, croquet

Georgian Colonial-style dwelling c.1819 accented with antiques. near famous resort, The Greenbrier. State parks, state fair and ski resorts nearby.

More Inns ...

Bavarian Inn & Lodge Route 1, Box 30, Shepherdstown, 25443 304-876-2551
Beekeeper Inn Helvetia, 26224 304-924-6435
Bright Morning Route 32, William Ave., Davis, 26260 304-259-2719
Cabin Lodge Box 355, Route 50, Aurora, 26705 304-735-3563
Cardinal Inn B&B Route 1 Box 1, Rt. 219, Huttonsville, 26273 304-335-6149
Carriage Inn 417 E. Washington St., Charles Town, 25414 304-728-8003
Cheat Mountain Club P.O. Box 28, Durbin, 26264 304-456-4627
Cheat River Lodge Route 1, Box 116, Elkins, 26241 304-636-2301
Chestnut Ridge School B&B Morgantown, 304-598-2262
Cobblestone-on-the-Ohio 103 Charles St., Sistersville, 26175 304-652-1206
Country Inn 207 S. Washington St., Berkeley Springs, 25411 304-258-2210
Crawford's Country Corner Box 112, Lost Creek, 26385 304-745-3017
Current, The HC 64, Box 135, Hillsboro, 24946 304-653-4722
Elk River Touring Center Slatyfork, 26291 304-572-3771
Fillmore Street B&B Box 34, Harpers Ferry, 25245 301-337-8633
Folkestone B&B Route 2, Box 404, Berkeley Springs, 25411 304-258-3743
Fuss 'N Feathers Box 1088, 210 W. German, Shepherdstown, 25443 304-876-6469
Garvey House B&B P.O. Box 98, Winona, 25942 304-574-3235

General Lewis Inn 301 E. Washington St., Lewisburg, 24901 304-645-2600
Glen Ferris Inn US Route 60, Glen Ferris, 25090 304-632-1111
Greenbrier River Inn US Rt.60 nr Lewisburg, Caldwell, 24925 304-647-5652
Guest House Low-Gap, Lost River, 26811 304-897-5707
Hickory Hill Farm Route 1, Box 355, Moorefield, 26836 304-538-2511
Kilmarnock Farms Route 1 Box 91, Orlando, 26412 304-452-8319
Little Inn P.O. Box 219, Shepherdstown, 25443 304-876-2208
Manor P.O. Box 342, Berkeley Springs, 25411 304-258-1552
Maria's Garden & Inn 201 Independence St., Berkeley Springs, 25411 304-258-2021
Maxwell B&B Route 12, Box 197, Morgantown, 26505 304-594-3041
McMechen House B&B 109 N. Main St., Moorefield, 26836 304-538-2417
Mecklenberg Inn 128 E. German St,Box 16, Shepherdstown, 25443 304-876-2126
Morgan Orchard Route 2, Box 114, Sinks Grove, 24976 304-772-3638
Oak Knoll B&B Crawley, Greenbrier County, 24931 304-392-6903
Pennbrooke Farm B&B Granny-she Run, Chloe, 25235 304-655-7367
Prospect Hill B&B P.O. Box 135, Gerrardstown, 25420 304-229-3346
Shang-Ra-La B&B Route 1, Box 156, Shepherdstown, 25443 304-876-2391
Shelly's Homestead Route 1, Box 1-A, Burlington, 26710 304-289-3941
Stratford Springs Inn 355 Oglebay Dr., Wheeling, 26003 304-233-5100
Thomas Shepherd Inn P.O. Box 1162, Shepherdstown, 25443 304-876-3715
Twisted Thistle B&B P.O Box 480, Fourth St., Davis, 26260 304-259-5389
Valley View Farm Route 1, Box 467, Mathias, 26812 304-897-5229
Wells Inn 316 Charles St., Sistersville, 26175 304-652-3111
West Fork Inn Route 2, Box 212, Jane Lew, 26378 304-745-4893

Wisconsin

BARABOO

The Barrister's House	$$ B&B	Continental plus
226—9th Ave., 53913	4 rooms, 4 pb	Comp. wine/bedside mints
608-356-3344	C-6+/S-no/P-no/H-no	Lemonade, iced tea, soda
Glen & Mary Schulz		sitting room, library
Exc. weekdays Nov—Apr		piano, veranda, terrace

Colonial charm and simple elegance in a parklike setting. Unique guest rooms, paneled library, fireplaces, screened porch and sitting room with game table and piano.

BELLEVILLE

Abendruh B&B Swisstyle	$ B&B	Full Swiss breakfast
7019 Gehin Rd., 53508	3 rooms, 2 pb	Afternoon tea, wine
608-424-3808	Visa, MC •	Comp. hors d'oeuvres
Franz & Mathilde Jaggi	German, French, Swiss	sitting room, library
All year		hot tub

True European hospitality. Beautiful, quiet country getaway. Fireplaces, central A/C. Near cross-country skiing, biking, nature trails. Many tourist attractions nearby.

BURLINGTON

Hillcrest B&B Inn	$$ B&B	Full breakfast
540 Storle Ave., 53105	3 rooms, 1 pb	Afternoon tea
414-763-4706	Visa, MC	Comp. wine, snacks
Dick & Karen Granholm	C-12+/S-no/P-no/H-no	sitting room
All year		bicycles, gardens

Historic 4-acre grand estate with spectacular view and lovely flower gardens. Meticulously restored, showcasing mahogany and walnut woodwork. Furnished with antiques.

Hillcrest B&B, Burlington, WI

CEDARBURG

Stagecoach Inn B&B	$$ B&B	Continental plus
W61 N520 Washington Ave,	13 rooms, 13 pb	Full bar, restored pub
53012	Visa, MC, AmEx	Library, sitting room
414-375-0208	C-no/S-no/P-no/H-no	whirlpools, antiques
Brook & Liz Brown		tennis court nearby
All year		

Restored 1853 stone inn furnished with antiques and Laura Ashley comforters. Historic pub and chocolate shop on the first floor.

Washington House Inn	$$ B&B	Continental plus
W62 N573 Washington Ave,	29 rooms, 29 pb	Afternoon social
53012	●	Sitting room, fireplaces
414-375-3550 800-369-4088	C-yes/S-yes/P-no/H-yes	whirlpool baths, sauna
Wendy Porterfield		wet bars, bicycles
All year		

A country inn in the center of historical district. Breakfast served in charming gathering room. Shopping, golf, winter sports. Whirlpool baths and wet bars in each room.

EAGLE

Eagle Centre House	$$ B&B	Full breakfast
W370, S9590 Hwy 67, 53119	4 rooms, 4 pb	Comp. wine, cider, etc.
414-363-4700	call about credit cards	Parlor, tap room
Riene Wells, Dean Herriges	C-yes/S-no/P-no/H-no	air-conditioning
All year exc. Christmas		hiking, riding, skiing

Greek Revival Inn features period antiques. In scenic Kettle Moraine Forest. Half mile from "Old World Wisconsin" Historic Site. Near Milwaukee.

ELLISON BAY

Griffin Inn & Cottages
11976 Mink River Rd., 54210
414-854-4306
Laurie & Jim Roberts
All year

$$ B&B
10 rooms, 4 pb
C-7+/S-ltd/P-no/H-no

Full country breakfast
Lunch & dinner by request
Evening popcorn/beverage
gathering rooms, library
bicycles, tennis court

A New England-style country inn on the Door County Peninsula, since 1910. Handmade quilts on antique beds. Full country breakfasts. Set on five lovely acres. Winter packages.

EPHRAIM

Eagle Harbor Inn
P.O. Box 72, 54211
9914 Water St.
414-854-2121
Ronald & Barbara Schultz
All year

$$ B&B
21 rooms, 21 pb
Visa, MC •
C-15+/P-no/H-yes

Full breakfast
9 inn rooms, 12 cottages
Sitting rooms
cottages have TV & grill
200 yds to sandy beach

An intimate New England-styled country inn. Antique-filled, period wallpapers. Close to boating, beaches, golf course, parks. 12 private cottages. Queen-size or double beds.

Hillside Hotel
P.O. Box 17, 54211
9980 Hwy 42
414-854-2417 800-423-7023
David & Karen McNeil
May–October, Jan–Feb

$$ B&B/MAP
12 rooms
Visa, MC, AmEx, Disc
C-yes/S-no/P-no/H-no

Full breakfast
6-course dinner
Full restaurant
private beach, mooring
charcoaler for picnics

Country-Victorian hotel with harbor view, private beach, specialty breakfasts, gourmet dinners, original furnishings, spectacular views; near galleries, shops; in resort area.

FISH CREEK

Thorp House Inn & Cottages
P.O. Box 490, 54212
4135 Bluff Rd.
414-868-2444
C. & S. Falck-Pedersen
All year

$$ B&B
4 rooms, 4 pb
C-no/S-no
Norwegian

Continental plus
7 private cottages
Sitting room w/fireplace
library, bicycles

Antique-filled historic home backed by wooded bluff, overlooking bay. Walk to beach, park, shops and restaurants. Winter: cross-country skiing.

HARTLAND

Monches Mill House
W301 N9430 Hwy E, 53029
414-966-7546
Elaine Taylor
May–December

$ B&B
4 rooms, 2 pb
C-yes/S-yes/P-yes/H-yes
French

Continental plus
Sitting room
hot tub, bicycles
tennis, canoeing, hiking

House built in 1842, located on the bank of the mill pond, furnished in antiques, choice of patio, porch or gallery for breakfast enjoyment.

JANESVILLE

Jackson Street Inn B&B
210 S. Jackson St., 53545
608-754-7250
Ilah & Bob Sessler
All year

$$ B&B
4 rooms, 2 pb
Visa, MC •
C-yes/S-yes/P-no/H-no

Full breakfast
Comp. beverages
Sitting room, library
fireplace, shuffleboard
cable TV, putting green

Near I-90, home has spacious rooms, Old World charm. Full gourmet breakfast. Great golf, biking, ski trails. Brochure available.

KENOSHA

The Manor House	$$$ B&B	Continental breakfast
6536—3rd Ave., 53140	4 rooms, 4 pb	Meals upon arrangement
414-658-0014	Visa, MC,AmEx •	Sitting room, library
Ron & Mary Rzeplinski	C-12+/S-ltd/P-no/H-no	piano, bicycles
All year	French	fireplaces in 2 rooms

Georgian mansion overlooking Lake Michigan. Furnished with 18th-century antiques. Formal landscaped grounds. Between Chicago and Milwaukee. On National Register.

LACROSSE

The Martindale House B&B	$$$ B&B	Full breakfast
237 S. 10th St., 54601	4 rooms, 4 pb	Complimentary snacks
608-782-4224	Visa, MC	Central air-conditioning
Anita & Tim Philbrook	C-ask/S-no/P-no/H-no	antiques, bike trails
March 1–November 15	Norwegian/German/	near restaurants
	Swedish	

On the National Registry. 4 elegant guest rooms with antiques & private baths. Close to downtown LaCrosse, Amish Country riverfront, river cruises, antique shops.

LAC DU FLAMBEAU

Ty-Bach	$$ B&B	Full breakfast
3104 Simpson Lane, 54538	2 rooms, 2 pb	Sitting room, library
715-588-7851	•	80 acres of woods
Janet & Kermit Bekkum	C-no/S-no/P-ask/H-no	bicycles, lake—swim
All year		fish, paddleboat, canoe

Secluded northwoods lake home; large guest area; private entrance; relax on the decks; explore wooded eighty acres; many local attractions.

LAKE DELTON

The Swallow's Nest B&B	$$ B&B	Full breakfast
P.O. Box 418, 53940	4 rooms, 4 pb	Afternoon tea, beverages
141 Sarrington	Visa, MC	Two-story atrium
608-254-6900	C-12+/S-no/P-no/H-no	decks, gallery
Mary Ann & Rod Stemo		library, photo studio
All year		

Beautifully sited new home with cathedral windows and ceilings offers quiet seclusion. Relax on screened deck, in library or by fireplace. Golf, boating & restaurants nearby.

LAKE GENEVA

The Geneva Inn	$$$ B&B	Continental plus
804 S. Lake Shore Drive, 53147	37 rooms, 37 pb	Restaurant, lunch/dinner
414-248-5680	Visa, MC, AmEx, DC	Turndown cognac & choc.
Mr. Richard B. Treptow	C-yes/S-yes/P-no/H-yes	whirlpools, gift shop
All year	German, French, Spanish	atrium, lake swimming

A relaxing retreat on the shores of Lake Geneva. Deluxe accommodations touched with English charm. Restaurant and lounge. Banquet/meeting facilities; marina; gift shop.

T.C. Smith Historic Inn	$$ B&B	Continental plus buffet
865 Main St., 53147	9 rooms, 5 pb	Afternoon tea, snacks
414-248-1097	Visa, MC, AmEx	Sitting room, library
The Marks Family	C-yes/S-yes/P-yes/H-no	bicycles, gift shoppeA/C,
All year		TV, bicycle rentals

Relax by the fireplaces to experience the romance and warmth of the Grand Victorian era in this downtown lakeview mansion of 1845. Listed on National Register.

MADISON

Annie's Hill House
2117 Sheridan Dr., 53704
608-244-2224
Annie & Larry Stuart
All year

$$ B&B
4 rooms, 2 pb
•
C-yes/S-ltd/P-ltd/H-no

Full breakfast
Snacks on arrival
Library, whirlpool, A/C
tennis, fishing, jogging
boat rentals, X-C skiing

Beautiful country garden setting in the city, complete with romantic gazebo. Full recreational facilities. 10 min. to downtown and campus. Woodland whirlpool room for 2 avail.

Collins House B&B
704 E. Gorham St., 53703
608-255-4230
Barb & Mike Pratzel
All year

$$ B&B
5 rooms, 5 pb
Visa, MC
C-yes/S-ltd/P-yes/H-no

Full breakfast (wkends)
Comp. chocolate truffles
Sitting room w/fireplace
library, movies on video

Restored prairie school style. Overlooks Lake Mendota, near university and state capitol. Elegant rooms, wonderful gourmet breakfasts and pastries.

The Lake House On Monona
4027 Monona Drive, 53716
608-222-4601 800-657-5147
Gordon & Carol Kowing
All year

$ B&B
4 rooms, 3 pb
Visa, MC
C-12+/S-no/P-no/H-no

Full breakfast
Comp. wine, snacks
Coffee to rm, sitting rm
porch, bicycles, lake,
fishing, canoe pier

Gracious 1947 Lannon stone home. Enjoy spectacular Madison skyline from canoe pier or boathouse deck. Lovely antique-filled home. Down comforters. Delicious hearty breakfasts.

Mansion Hill Inn
424 N. Pinckney St., 53703
608-255-3999 800-798-9070
Polly Elder
All year

$$$ B&B
11 rooms, 11 pb
Visa, MC, AmEx •
C-12+/S-yes/P-no/H-no

Continental plus
Afternoon tea, snacks
Comp. wine, bar service
sitting room, hot tubs
sauna, valet service

Victorian elegance abounds in our antique-filled guest rooms. Fireplaces, private baths with whirlpools, valet service. We await your pleasure.

Plough Inn
3402 Monroe St., 53711
608-238-2981
R. Ganser, K. Naherny
All year

$$ B&B
3 rooms, 3 pb
Visa, MC
C-no/S-no/P-no/H-no

Continental (weekdays)
Full breakfast (wkends)
New "tap" room added
sitting room

Historic 1850s inn with 3 charming, spacious rooms. Arborview room has fireplace and whirlpool bath. Across from arboretum, near university campus.

MERRILL

Candlewick Inn
700 W. Main St., 54452
715-536-7744
Dan & Loretta Zimmerman
All year

$$ B&B
5 rooms, 3 pb
Visa, MC •
C-12+/S-ltd/P-no/H-no

Full breakfast
Complimentary snacks
Restaurant nearby
sitting room, library
bicycles, gift shop

Elegantly restored century-old mansion, appointed with fine antiques, and four fireplaces. Golf, water sports, downhill and cross-country skiing nearby.

Candlewick Inn, Merrill, WI

NORWALK

Lonesome Jake's Ranch
Route 2, Box 108A, 54648
County Highway T
608-823-7585
Lone Jake, Pretty Kitty Menn
All year

$$ B&B
3 rooms
•
C-yes/S-no/P-no/H-no
Spanish

Full breakfast
Complimentary wine
Picnic area under pines
sitting room, porch
near Amish settlement

Turn-of-the-century farm house with beautiful grounds bordered by towering pines on 2,000 acre ranch.

PLYMOUTH

B. L. Nutt Inn
632 E. Main St., 53073
414-892-8566
Doris Buckman
All year

$ B&B
2 rooms
C-yes/S-no/P-no/H-no

Continental plus
Complimentary snacks
Sitting room
Renaissance style open
staircase, porches

1875 Italianate landmarked home, quietly located along Mullet River. Close to Road America race track, Kettle Moraine State Forest and Lake Michigan. Delicious homemade treats

POYNETTE

Jamieson House
407 N. Franklin St., 53955
608-635-4100
Heidi Hutchison
All year

$$ B&B
10 rooms, 10 pb
AmEx, DC •
C-ltd/S-ltd/P-ltd/H-no

Full breakfast
Restaurant, bar
Garden room
piano, bicycles

The Jamieson House features intimate gourmet dining amid quiet Victorian elegance. Guest rooms have sumptuous velvet couches, sunken baths, antiques.

RACINE

Lochnaiar Inn
1121 Lake Ave., 53403
414-633-3300
Dawn Weisbrod
All year

$$$ B&B
8 rooms, 8 pb
Visa, MC, AmEx
C-yes/S-ltd/P-no/H-yes

Full breakfast
Comp. wine, beer, juice, soda
sitting room, library
bicycles, near tennis

Elegant English Tudor guest inn on Lake Michigan; wood floors, four-poster beds, 6 fireplaces, suites, meeting rooms; near 900-slip marina. Close to Chicago and Milwaukee.

SISTER BAY

The White Apron
414 Maple Dr., 54234
414-854-5107
Jim & Mary Werner
May-Nov, Jan-Mar

$$ B&B
5 rooms, 5 pb
Visa, MC, AmEx
C-no/S-yes/P-no/H-no

Full breakfast
Lunch, dinner
Restaurant
snacks
sitting room

Turn-of-the-century inn boasts chef as its host and an elegant creole dining room. Snug, pleasant rooms.

SPARTA

The Franklin Victorian
220 E. Franklin St., 54656
608-269-3894 800-845-8767
Jane & Lloyd Larson
All year

$$ B&B
4 rooms, 2 pb
C-10+

Full 3-course breakfast
Afternoon tea, snacks
Sitting room
library
canoe rental

Relax in quiet, gracious comfort—spacious rooms, fine woods. Delectable breakfasts. Surrounding area abounds with beauty. Recreation all four seasons. Near famous bike trail.

Just-N-Trails B&B/Farm
Route 1, Box 274, 54656
608-269-4522 800-488-4521
Donald & Donna Justin
All year

$$ B&B
3 rooms
Visa, MC ●
C-yes/S-no/P-no/H-no

Full breakfast
Lemonade, apple cider
Specialize in recreation,
relaxation & romance
log cabin available

Roam on a 200-acre dairy farm, daydream by a pond. Ride on nearby Elroy-Sparta bike trail, cross-country ski or hike our 20 km. of trails. Relax in our charming country home.

STURGEON BAY

The Gray Goose B&B
4258 Bay Shore Dr., 54235
414-743-9100
Jack & Jessie Burkhardt
All year

$$ B&B
4 rooms
Visa, MC, AmEx
C-15+/S-ltd/P-no/H-no

Full country breakfast
Refreshments, sitting rm
Beautiful dining room
full covered porch
cable TV, games, books

Comfortable Civil War home; spacious rooms; ceiling fans; antiques. Quiet, wooded setting north of city. Water view. Personal attention. Queen-, double- and twin-bed rooms.

Inn at Cedar Crossing
336 Louisiana St., 54235
414-743-4200
Terry Wulf
All year

$$ B&B
9 rooms, 9 pb
Visa, MC, DC
C-6+/S-ltd/P-no/H-no

Continental plus
Restaurant, pub
Comp. beverages, cookies
dining rms., sitting rm.
Whirlpool in some rooms

1884 inn is situated in historic district close to shops, restaurants, museum, beaches. Country antique decor, fireplaces, whirlpools, common room.

STURGEON BAY

White Lace Inn	$$ B&B	Continental plus
16 N. 5th Ave., 54235	15 rooms, 15 pb	Tea, coffee, chocolate
414-743-1105	Visa, MC	Sitting room
Bonnie & Dennis Statz	C-no/S-ltd/P-no/H-ltd	tandem bicycles
All year		fireplaces, whirlpools

A Victorian country inn with romantic decor; 15 charming guest rooms, all with fine antiques, authentic Victorian or poster bed; 10 w/fireplace, 7 w/whirlpool and fireplace.

TWO RIVERS

Red Forest B&B	$$ B&B	Full breakfast
1421–25th St., 54241	3 rooms	Snacks
414-793-1794	•	Sitting room, fireplace
Kay & Alan Rodewald	C-yes/S-ltd/P-no/H-no	sun porch, near golf,
All year		skiing & hiking

1907 Shingle-style home filled with warmth and family heirloom antiques. Located along WI East Coast. Excellent hiking, fishing, golf nearby. Midway to Door County Peninsula.

WHITEWATER

Greene House Country Inn	$ B&B	Full breakfast
Box 214, Rt. 2, Hwy 12, 53190	7 rooms, 2 pb	Restaurant, bar
414-495-8771 800-468-1959	Visa, MC, AmEx, Dis •	Afternoon tea, snacks
Lynn & Mayner Greene	C-yes/S-ltd/P-no/H-no	sitting room, library
All year		game & exercise room

1848 country inn near State Park area of hiking, bicycling, horseback riding; antiquing. Quiet countryside. Great food. Short drive from Chicago. Guitar gallery at the inn.

More Inns ...

52 Stafford (Irish House) P.O. Box 217, Plymouth, 53073 414-893-0552
Albany Guest House 405 S. Mill St., Albany, 53502 608-862-3636
Amberwood 320 McKenney St, St. Croix Falls, 54024 715-483-9355
Bay Shore Inn 4205 Bay Shore Dr., Sturgeon Bay, 54235 414-743-4551
Bayberry Inn 265 S. Main St., Lake Mills, 53551 414-648-3654
Bettinger House B&B 855 Wachter Ave.,, Plain, 53577 608-546-2951
Birch Creek Inn 2263 Birch Creek Rd., De Pere, 54115 414-336-7084
Bluebell Inn 122 Hewett St., Neillsville, 54456 715-743-2929
Boyden House 727 Third St, Hudson, 54016 715-386-7435
Breese Waye B&B 816 Macfarlane Rd., Portage, 53901 608-742-5281
Brick House B&B, The 108 S. Cleveland St., Merrill, 54452 715-536-3230
By the Okeag 446 Wisconsin St., Columbus, 53925 414-623-3007
Chateau Madeleine P.O. Box 27, La Pointe, 54850 715-747-2463
Chesterfield Inn 20 Commerce St., Mineral Point, 53565 608-987-3682
Chippewa Lodge 3525 Chippewa Lodge Trl, Lac du Flambeau, 54538 715-588-3297
Circle B Bed & Breakfast 3804 Vinburn Rd., DeForest, 53532 608-846-3481
ClearView Hills B&B Route 2, Box 87, Colfax, 54730 715-235-7180
Convent House Route 1, Box 160, Cashton, 54619 608-823-7906
Cooper Hill House P.O. Box 1288, Bayfield, 54814 715-779-5060
Country Aire Route 2 Box 175, Portage, 53901 608-742-5716
Country Gardens B&B 6421 Hwy. 42, Egg Harbor, 54209 414-743-7434
Creamery Box 22, Downsville, 54735 715-664-8354
Crystal River B&B E1369 Rural Rd., Waupaca, 54980 715-258-5333
Cunningham House 110 Market St., Platteville, 53818 608-348-5532
De Winters of Hazel Green 22nd at Main St., Hazel Green, 53811 608-854-2768
Dorshel's B&B Guest House W140 N7616 Lilly Rd., Menomonee Falls, 53051 414-255-7866
Duke House B&B 618 Maiden St., Mineral Point, 53565 608-987-2821
Duvall House 815 Milwaukee St., Kewaunee, 54216 414-388-0501
Edward's Estates N4775 22nd Ave., Mauston, 53948 608-847-5246
Eleven Gables Inn 493 Wrigley Dr., Lake Geneva, 53147 414-248-8393

Elizabethian Inn 463 Wrigley Dr., Lake Geneva, 53147 414-248-9131
Emerald View House B&B P.O. Box 322, Fontana-On-Geneva Lake, 53125 414-275-2266
Fanny Hill Inn 3919 Crescent Ave., Eau Claire, 54703 715-836-8184
Fargo Mansion Inn 406 Mulberry St., Lake Mills, 53551 414-648-3654
Firefly House Kingstown Box 349, Saint Vincent, 809-458-4621
Foxmoor B&B Fox River Rd., Wilmot, 53192 414-862-6161
French Country Inn 3052 Spruce Ln, Box 129, Ephraim, 54211 414-854-4001
Frenchtown B&B Inn 822 S.Tomahawk, Box 121, Tomahawk, 54487 715-453-3499
Gallery House 215 N. Main St., Box 55, Alma, 54610 608-685-4975
Gandt's Haus und Hof 2962 Lake Forest Park, Sturgeon Bay, 54235 414-743-1238
Geiger House 401 Denniston, Cassville, 53806 608-725-5419
Gollmar Guest House, The 422 Third St., Baraboo, 53913 608-356-9432
Grand Inn, The 832 W. Grand Ave, Port Washington, 53074 414-284-6719
Grandpa's Gate B&B E13841 Lower DL, Merrimac, 53561 608-493-2755
Greene House of 819 819 N. Cass St., Milwaukee, 53202 414-271-1979
Greunke's Inn 17 Rittenhouse, Bayfield, 54814 715-779-5480
Greystone Farms B*B 770 Adam's Church Rd., East Troy, 53120 414-495-8485
Halfway House B&B Route 2, Box 80, Oxford, 53952 608-586-5489
Haus Zur Gemutlichkeit 1052 Berry Lane N., Ellison Bay, 54210 414-854-4848
Hazelhurst Inn 6941 Hwy 51, Hazelhurst, 54531 715-356-6571
Hill Street B&B 353 Hill St., Spring Green, 53588 608-588-7751
Historic Bennett House 825 Oak St., Wisconsin Dells, 53965 608-254-2500
Homestead, The 1916 W. Donges Bay Rd., Mequon, 53092 414-242-4174
House of Seven Gables Box 204, Baraboo, 53913 608-356-8387
House on River Road 922 River Rd., Wisconsin Dells, 53965 608-253-5573
Inn 30 Wisconsin Ave., Montreal, 54550 715-561-5180
Inn at Wildcat Mountain P.O. Box 112, Ontario, 54651 608-337-4352
James Wylie House B&B 208 E. Main St., White Sulphur Springs, 24986 304-536-9444
Jefferson-Day House 1109–3rd St., Hudson, 54016 715-386-7111
Jordan House 81 S. Main St., Hartford, 53027 414-673-5643
Journey's End P.O. Box 185, Amherst, 54406 715-824-3970
King Olaf's Pub & Inn Hwy 42, Algoma, 54201 414-487-2090
Knapp Haus 1117 Main St., La Crosse, 54601 608-784-5272
Kraemer House B&B Inn, The 1190 Spruce St., Plain, 53577 608-546-3161
Lake House RR 2, Box 217, Strum, 54770 715-695-3519
Laue House Inn Box 176, Alma, 54610 608-685-4923
Limberlost Inn 2483 Hwy 17, Phelps, 54554 715-545-2685
Mansion 323 S. Central, Richland Center, 53581 608-647-2808
Marybrooke Inn 705 W. New York Ave., Oshkosh, 54901 414-426-4761
Mascione's Hidden Valley Route 2, Box 74, Hillsboro, 54634 608-489-3443
McConnell Inn 497 S. Lawson Dr.,Box 6, Greenlake, 54941 414-294-6430
Mustard Seed B&B, The 205 California, Hayward, 54843 715-634-2908
Nash House 1020 Oak St., Wisconsin Rapids, 54494 715-424-2001
Neumann House B&B 121 N. Michigan St., Prairie du Chien, 53821 608-326-8104
O'Reilly House B&B 7509 Stiger Rd., Potosi, 53802 608-763-2386
OJ's Victorian Village P.O. Box 98, Hwy 12, Lake Delton, 53940 608-254-6568
Oak Hill Farm 9850 Highway 80, Livingston, 53554 608-943-6006
Oak Street Inn 506 Oak St., Prescott, 54021 715-262-4110
Ogden House 2237 N. Lake Dr., Milwaukee, 53202 414-272-2740
Old Oak Inn & Acorn Lodge Hwy 131 South, Box 1500, Soldiers Grove, 54655 608-624-5217
Old Parsonage 508 Central Ave., Coon Valley, 54623 608-452-3833
Old Rittenhouse Inn P.O. Box 584, Bayfield, 54814 715-779-5111
Open Window B&B Route 5, Box 5194, Hayward, 54843 715-462-3033
Otter Creek Inn 2536 Hwy 12, Eau Claire, 54701 715-832-2945
Pahl's Bed & Breakfast 608 Railroad St., Wilton, 54670 608-435-6434
Palmquist Farm River Rd., Brantwood, 54513 715-564-2558
Parkview B&B 211 N. Park St., Reedsburg, 53959 608-534-4333
Parson's Inn B&B Rock School Rd., Glen Haven, 53810 608-794-2491
Pederson Victorian B&B 1782 Hwy. 120 N., Lake Geneva, 53147 414-248-9110
Pfister Hotel 424 E. Wisconsin Ave., Milwaukee, 53202 414-273-8222

Phipps Inn 1005 Third St, Hudson, 54016 715-386-0800
Pine Ridge B&B 1152 Scout Rd., East Troy, 53120 414-594-3269
Pinehurst Inn Hwy 13, P.O. Box 222, Bayfield, 54814 715-779-3676
Proud Mary P.O. Box 193, Fish Creek, 54212 414-868-3442
Queen Anne B&B 837 E. College Ave., Appleton, 54911 414-739-7966
Rambling Hills Tree Farm 8825 Willever Lane, Newton, 53063 414-726-4388
Red House Inn B&B 512 Wells St., Lake Geneva, 53147 414-248-1009
Riley Bed-n-Breakfast Inn 8205 Klevenville-Riley, Verona, 53593 608-845-9150
Rosenberry Inn 511 Franklin St., Wausau, 54401 715-842-5733
Sandy Scott 1520 State St., La Crosse, 54601 608-784-7145
Serendipity Farm Route 3 Box 162, Viroqua, 54665 608-637-7708
Seven Pines Lodge Lewis, 54851 715-653-2323
Shady Ridge Farm 410 Highland View, Houlton, 54082 715-549-6258
Sherman House 930 River Rd., Box 397, Wisconsin Dells, 53965 608-253-2721
Son Ne Vale Farm B&B Route 1, Box 132, Colfax, 54730 715-962-4342
Sonnenhof Inn 13907 N Port Washington, Mequon, 53092 414-375-4294
St. Croix River Inn 305 River St., Osceola, 54020 715-294-4248
St. Germain B&B 6255 Hwy 70 E, Box 6, Saint Germain, 54558 715-479-8007
Stokstad's B&B 305 Hwy 51, Stoughton, 53589 608-884-4941
Stonewood Haus 894 Riverdale Dr., Oneida, 54155 414-499-3786
Strawberry Hill Route 1, Box 524-D, Green Lake, 54941 414-294-3450
Taylor House B&B 210 E. Iola St., Iola, 54945 715-445-2204
Tiffany Inn 206 Algoma Blvd, Oshkosh, 54901 414-426-1000
Trillium Route 2, Box 121, La Farge, 54639 608-625-4492
Ty-Bach 2817, Beloit, 53511 608-365-1039
Victorian Swan on Water 1716 Water St., Stevens Point, 54481 715-345-0595
Victorian Treasure B&B 115 Prairie St., Lodi, 53555 608-592-5199
Viroqua Heritage Inn B&B 220 E. Jefferson St., Viroqua, 54665 608-637-3306
Westby House State St., Westby, 54667 608-634-4112
Westlin Winds 3508 Halsey St., Eau Claire, 54701 715-832-1110
Whip-Poor-Will Inn P.O. Box 64, Star Lake, 54561 715-542-3600
Whistling Swan Inn P.O. Box 193, Main St., Fish Creek, 54212 414-868-3442
White Gull Inn Box 175, Fish Creek, 54212 414-868-3517
Willson House 320 Superior St., Chippewa Falls, 54729 715-723-0055
Wilson House Inn 110 Dodge St., Mineral Point, 53565 608-987-3600
Wisconsin House Stagecoach 2105 E. Main, Hazel Green, 53811 608-854-2233
Wm. A. Jones House 215 Ridge St., Hwy 1, Mineral Point, 53565 608-987-2337
Wolf River Lodge Star Route Hwys 55 & 64, White Lake, 54491 715-882-2182
Wolfway Farm Rural Route 1, Box 18, West Salem, 54669 608-486-2686
Woods Manor 165 Front St., Box 7, La Pointe, 54850 715-747-3102
Ye Olde Manor House B&B R.R. 5, Box 390, Elkhorn, 53121 414-742-2450

Wyoming

BIG HORN ――――――――――――――――――――――――――――――――――――――

Spahn's Big Horn Mountain	$$ B&B	Full breakfast
P.O. Box 579, 82833	3 rooms, 3 pb	Lunch, dinner available
70 Upper Hideaway Lane	●	Library, sitting room
307-674-8150	C-yes/S-ltd/P-yes/H-no	hot tub, baby-sitting
Ron & Bobbie Spahn		fishing
All year		

Secluded handcrafted log lodge on a high, pine-forested mountainside. Hundred-mile vista, hiking trails, deer and moose. Close to Interstate 90 and Sheridan.

CHEYENNE

Drummonds Ranch Recreation
399 Happy Jack Rd., 82007
307-634-6042
Kent & Taydie Drummond
All year

$$ B&B
2 rooms, 1 pb
C-yes/S-no/P-yes/H-no
French

Full breakfast
Lunch, dinner, snacks
Sitting room, library
hot tubs, riding arena
boarding for horses

Near I-80. Adjacent to state park; National Forest. Relax, X-C ski, fish, hike, mountain bike, rock climb. Bring your horse. Very peaceful!

CODY

Lockhart B&B Inn
109 W. Yellowstone Ave., 82414
307-587-6074
Cindy Baldwin
All year

$$ B&B
7 rooms, 7 pb
Visa, MC, CB, Diners •
C-4+/S-ltd/P-no/H-no

All-you-can-eat breakfst
Comp. brandy, coffee
Sack lunch, sitting room
cable color TV
phones

Historic home of famous western author Caroline Lockhart—featuring antiques, old-style comfort and hearty all-you-can-eat breakfast. Western hospitality. AAA-rated inn.

JACKSON

Wildflower Inn
P.O. Box 3724, 83001
3725 Teton Village Rd.
307-733-4710
Sherri & Ken Jern
All year

$$$ B&B
5 rooms, 5 pb
Visa, MC
C-yes/S-no/P-no/H-no

Full breakfast
Comp. wine, tea, coffee
Sitting room
library, hot tubs
solarium, deck

Lovely log home situated on 3 acres of aspens, cottonwoods, and of course, wildflowers. 5 sunny guest rooms, some with private decks. Near racquet club, golf club, ski area.

JACKSON HOLE

Teton Tree House
P.O. Box 550, Wilson, 83014
6159 Heck of a Hill Rd.
307-733-3233
Chris & Denny Becker
All year

$$$ B&B
6 rooms, 6 pb
Visa, MC, Disc •
C-yes/S-no/P-no/H-no

Full breakfast
Comp. wine, beer, juice
Sitting room, fireplace
library
slide shows

Helpful longtime mountain and river guides offer a rustic but elegant 4-story open-beam home on a forested, wildflower-covered mountainside. Breakfast is low cholesterol.

JACKSON HOLE (WILSON)

Fish Creek B&B
P.O. Box 366, 83014
2455 N. Fish Creek Rd.
307-733-2586
Putzi & John Harrington
All year

$$$ B&B
3 rooms, 3 pb
Visa, MC •
C-ask/S-no/P-no/H-yes
French, German, Spanish

Full breakfast
Sitting room, hot tubs
private fly-fishing
cozy log home

Secluded country hideaway, private baths and entrances. Fishing, hiking, skiing and hot-tubbing. Gourmet breakfasts beside beautiful Fish Creek.

LARAMIE

Annie Moore's Guest House
819 University, 82070
307-721-4177 800-552-8992
Ann Acuff & Joe Bundy
All year

$$ B&B
6 rooms
Visa, MC, AmEx •
C-no/S-no/P-no/H-no

Continental plus
Comp. juice, coffee, tea
Sitting room
sun deck
Florida room

Beautifully renovated post-Victorian Queen Anne. Cheerful parlor and second-story sun deck. Close to university, museums, downtown. Rocky Mountain recreational delight.

RAWLINS

Ferris Mansion B&B
607 W. Maple, 82301
307-324-3961
Janice M. Lubbers
All year

$ B&B
4 rooms, 4 pb
C-10+/S-no/P-no/H-no

Continental plus
Sitting room, fireplaces
Library, porch & swing
parlour, private baths
remote control TV in rm

Step back into history! 1903 Victorian mansion (National Register) has grand stairway leading to large, elegant, antique-filled bedrooms. Guests say: "Best B&B!"

SARATOGA

Wolf Hotel
P.O. Box 1298, 82331
101 E. Bridge
307-326-5525
Doug & Kathleen Campbell
All year

$ EP
11 rooms, 7 pb
Visa, MC, AmEx, DC, CB
C-yes/S-yes/P-no/H-no

Restaurant, bar
Breakfast, lunch, dinner
Luxury suite available

Hotel built in 1893 as a stage stop. Listed in National Register. Blue Ribbon fishing, golf, hot springs nearby. Dining room (AAA approved) & lounge redone in Victorian style.

More Inns . . .

Akers Ranch B&B 81 Inez Rd., Douglas, 82633 307-358-3741
Bar X Ranch 109 Rd 8 WC, Clark, Powell, 82435 307-645-3231
Bessemer Bend B&B 6905 Speas Rd., Casper, 82604 307-265-6819
Big Mountain Inn P.O. Box 7453, Jackson, 83001 307-733-1981
Box K Ranch Box 110, Moran, 83013 307-543-2407
Bunkhouse P.O. Box 384, Moose, 83012 307-733-7283
Cottonwood Ranch B&B 951 Missouri Valley Rd., Riverton, 82501 307-856-3064
Country Fare B&B 904 Main St., Lander, 82520 307-332-9604
Elephant Head Lodge 1170 Yellowstone Hwy, Wapiti, 82450 307-587-3980
Fir Creek Ranch P.O. Box 190, Moran, 83013 307-543-2416
Fort William Recreat. Area P.O. Box 1081, Pinedale, 82941 307-367-6353
Goff Creek Lodge P.O. Box 155, Cody, 82414 307-587-3753
Heck of A Hill Homestead P.O. Box 105, Wilson, 83014 307-733-8023
Hidden Valley Ranch 153 Rd., 6MF, S. Fork R, Cody, 82414 307-587-5090
Hotel Higgins P.O. Box 741, Glenrock, 82637 307-436-9212
Lorraine's B&B Lodge Box 312, Encampment, 82325 307-327-5200
Mountain Shadows Ranch Box 110BB, Wapiti, 82450 307-587-2143
Paradise Guest Ranch P.O. Box 790, Buffalo, 82834 307-684-7876
Powderhorn Ranch P.O. Box 7400, Jackson Hole, 83001 307-733-3845
Rancho Alegre 3600 S. Parkloop Rd., Jackson Hole, 83001 307-733-7988
Savery Creek Thoroughbred Ranch, Box 24, Savery, 82332 307-383-7840
Shoshone Lodge Resort P.O. Box 790BB, Cody, 82414 307-587-4044
Snow Job P.O. Box 371, Wilson, 83014 307-739-9695
Spring Creek Ranch Box 3154, Jackson, 83001 307-733-8833
Sundance Inn 135 W. Broadway, Jackson, 83001 307-733-3444
Teton View B&B P.O. Box 652, Wilson, 83014 307-733-7954
Y L Hideaway Holiday P.O. Box 24, Savery, 82332 307-383-7840

Alberta

BLAIRMORE

Bedside Manor
Box 1088, T0K OEO
403-628-3954
William & Shirley Sara
All year

$$ B&B
2 rooms
C-yes/S-yes/P-no/H-no

Full breakfast
Lunch, dinner available
Complimentary wine
afternoon tea, snacks
sitting room

Working ranch straddling Crowsnest River class "A" trout stream. Turn of the century home with period furnishings on secluded river frontage.

CLARESHOLM

Anola's B&B
P.O. Box 340, T0L 0T0
9 mi. east on Hwy 520
403-625-4389
Anola & Gordon Laing
All year

$ B&B
3 rooms, 2 pb
●
C-yes/S-no/P-no/H-yes

Full breakfast
Evening tea & muffins
Comp. wine with cottage
library, bikes, hot tub
museum, grain farm

Relax in our country cottage guest house. Perfect for honeymooners. Antique furnishings and Franklin stove. Visit Granddad's museum. Close to Head-Smashed-Inn Buffalo Jump.

DIDSBURY

Ausen Hus B&B
RR 2, T0M 0W0
403-335-4736
Cal & Bev Ausenhus
All year

$$ B&B
2 rooms
Visa
C-12+/S-no/P-ask/H-no

Full breakfast
Dinner, aftn. tea
Sitting room, library
bike rental, X-C skiing,
walking & biking trails

Comfortable luxury in a country setting. Gourmet breakfasts feature locally grown produce. Good food, warm hospitality. One suite sleeps 4.

SEEBE

Brewster's Kananaskis Rnch
General Delivery, T0L 1X0
403-673-3737 FAX:762-3953
The Brewster Family
May–October 15

$$$ B&B
27 rooms, 27 pb
Visa, MC ●
C-yes/S-yes/P-no/H-yes

Full breakfast
Lic. dining room, lounge
Seminar facility, golf
whirlpool, horses
Western barbecues

Turn-of-the-century guest ranch; private cabins & chalet units; antique furniture. Operated by 5th-generation Brewsters. 45 miles west of Calgary, 30 miles east of Banff.

More Inns ...

Back Porch B&B 266 Northumberland St., Fredericton, E3B 3J6 506-454-6875
Black Cat Guest Ranch P.O. Box 6267, Hinton, T7V 1X6 403-865-3618
Blue Mountain Lodge P.O. Box 2763, Banff, T0L OCO 403-762-5134
Broadview Farm RR #2, Millet, T0C 1Z0 403-387-4963
Canadian Rocky Mountain Box 95, Canmore, T0L 0M0 403-678-6777
Crazee Akerz Farm RR #1, Bentley, T0C 0J0 403-843-6444
Edmonton Hostel 10422–91st St., Edmonton, T0L 0M0 403-429-0140
Gwynalta Farm Gwynne, T0C 1L0 403-352-3587
Haus Alpenrose Lodge 629–9th St., Box 723, Canmore, T0L 0M0 403-678-4134
Mesa Creek Ranch Vacation General Delivery, Millarville, T0L 1K0 403-931-3573
Rafter Six Ranch Resort Seebe, T0L 1X0 403-673-3622
Scenic Waters B&B Box 33, Site 20, RR 2, Calgary, T2P 2G5 403-286-4348
Spring Creek B&B Box 172, Canmore, T0L 0M0 403-678-6726
Timber Ridge Homestead Box 94, Nanton, T0L 1R0 403-646-5683

British Columbia

CAMPBELL RIVER

Campbell River Lodge
1760 Island Hwy., V9W 2E7
604-287-7446 800-663-7212
Ted Arbour, Brian Clarkson
All year

$$ B&B
30 rooms, 30 pb
Visa, MC, EnRoute •
C-yes/S-yes/P-sml/H-no

Continental breakfast
Lunch, dinner, pub
Sitting room, piano
phones, laundry
sauna

The BIG little fishing resort on the famous Campbell River. Restaurant and pub. Very experienced saltwater salmon and freshwater guides. Est. 1948.

FORT STEELE

Wild Horse Farm
Box 7, Hwy 93/95, V0B 1N0
604-426-6000
Bob & Orma Termuende
May–October

$ B&B
3 rooms, 3 pb
•
C-no/S-ltd/P-ltd/H-no

Full breakfast
Antiques
Sitting room
player piano
games table

Spacious early 1900s log-faced country manor nestled in the Rocky Mountains; extensive lawns, gardens, trees on grounds. Across from Fort Steele Historic Park.

GALIANO ISLAND

Woodstone Country Inn
RR#1, Georgeson Bay Rd., V0N 1P0
604-539-2022
Rosemary Walker
All year

$$$ B&B
12 rooms, 12 pb
Visa, MC •
C-10+/S-no/P-no/H-yes
French

Full breakfast
Picnic lunch, aftn. tea
Restaurant, dinner
sailing, fishing, riding
swimming, kayaking, golf

Casual, elegant country inn on most beautiful of Gulf Islands. Guest rooms with wood burning fireplaces, wonderful beds. Superb dining.

GANGES

Beach House B&B Inn
930 Sunset Dr., RR 1, V0S 1E0
604-537-2879 FAX:537-4747
March–October

$$$ B&B
4 rooms, 4 pb
Visa, MC •
C-no/S-no/P-no/H-no
Italian

Full breakfast
Tea & coffee on arrival
Sitting room, library
bicycles
tennis courts

Luxury waterfront hideaway. Two cottages, two large suites with private entrances. Salmon fishing, gourmet breakfasts, sherry in room, tennis and golf.

GIBSON'S

Ocean View Cottage B&B
RR 2, Site 46, C10, V0N 1V0
1927 Grandview Road
604-886-7943
Bert & Dianne Verzyl
All year

$$ B&B
3 rooms, 2 pb
C-yes/S-no/P-no/H-no
French, Dutch

Full gourmet breakfast
Comp. coffee, tea, snacks
sun room dining
self-contained cottage

Set on 3-acres in quiet, rural setting overlooking Vancouver Island and Georgia Strait. Golf, fishing, hiking, sandy beaches, scenic cruises nearby.

HALFMOON BAY

Lord Jim's Resort Hotel
RR 1, Ole's Cove Rd., V0N 1Y0
604-885-7038 604-681-6168
Susan Parker
All year

$$$ EP
25 rooms, 25 pb
Visa, MC, AmEx •
C-yes/S-yes/P-no/H-yes

Full breakfast
Restaurant, bar ($)
Afternoon tea, snacks
swimming pool, sauna
waterviews, fishing

Rustic cabins. Lodge rooms on 9 scenic waterfront acres. Gourmet dining, lounge, game room. Fishing charters, conference facilities.

KELOWNA

View to Remember B&B
1090 Trevor Dr., V1Z 2J8
604-769-4028
Celia & Robin Jarman
All year

$$ B&B
2 rooms
C-yes/S-no/P-no/H-yes
some German & French

Full breakfast
Comp. beverage
Sitting rm., babysitting
patio overlooking
beautiful view

Fabulous view, peaceful area. Elegant, spacious guest rooms, antiques. Gourmet breakfast. Well-travelled hosts, originally from Australia, enjoy sharing with guests.

MILL BAY

Billion $ View B&B
610 Shorewood Rd.,
RR#1, V0R 2P0
Vancouver Island
604-743-2387
All year

$$ B&B
3 rooms, 2 pb
C-yes/S-no/P-no/H-yes
German, Spanish, Italian

Full gourmet breakfast
Television
Hot tub

View of bay, Mt. Baker, Gulf Islands. Beautiful flower garden. Beach in Provincial Park—5 Km—ocean access from house. Contemporary house—3 years old.

Pinelodge Farm B&B
3191 Mutter Rd., V0R 2P0
604-743-4083
Clifford & Barbara Clarke
All year

$$ B&B
7 rooms, 7 pb
•
C-yes/S-ltd/P-no/H-no

Full farm breakfast
Sitting room
2 bedroom cottage avail.
antique sales, museum

Our lodge is on a 30-acre farm with panoramic ocean views. Each room is furnished with exquisite antiques and stained glass windows. Museum open to public. Antique sales.

NANOOSE BAY

The Lookout B&B
3381 Dolphin Drive, V0R 2R0
604-468-9796
Marj & Herb Wilkie
All year

$$ B&B
4 rooms, 3 pb
•
C-7+/S-no/P-no/H-ltd
Australian, English

Full breakfast
Comp. wine (sometimes)
Sitting room, library
fishing charter avail.
suite available by week

Spectacular views of Georgia Strait, watch boats, eagles, cruise ships, maybe even Orca whales. Country breakfast on wrap around deck. Golf, fishing, marina nearby. Quiet.

Oceanside B&B
Box 26, RR2, Blueback,
V0R 2R0
3161 Dolphin Dr.
604-468-9241
Lee & Leone Chapman
April–October

$ B&B
4 rooms, 1.5 pb
C-yes/S-ltd/P-no/H-no

Full breakfast
Sitting room
Salmon fishing charters
complimentary row boat
ocean swimming, beach

Scenic country setting. King & Queen bedrooms on main. Oceanview suite with kitchen, living room, fireplace, deck, king & twin bedrooms, pull-out, crib & cot.

NORTH PENDER ISLAND

Hummingbird Hollow B&B
36125 Galleon Way, VON 2MO
604-629-6392
Doreen Ball & Chuck Harris
All year

$$ B&B
3 rooms, 3 pb
●
C-no/S-no/P-no/H-no
Some French

Full 3-course breakfast
Tea, coffee available
Refrigerator in room
dining & sitting rooms
cable TV, VCR

Friendly sunny Gulf Island lakeside retreat with country garden. Private lakeview sunrooms and balconies. Quiet, natural—walkers', birdwatchers' paradise. 2 day minimum.

NORTH VANCOUVER

Grouse Mountain B&B
900 Clements Ave., V7R 2K7
604-986-9630
Lyne & John Armstrong
All year

$$ B&B
2 rooms, 1 pb
●
C-yes/S-no/P-yes/H-no
French, German

Full gourmet breakfast
Tea & coffee in room
Sitting room
piano

Nestled in the foothills of Grouse Mountain, our comfortable, modern home awaits you. Features include large private rooms, warm hospitality.

Helen's B&B
302 E. 5th St., V7L 1L1
604-985-4869
Helen Boire
All year

$$ B&B
3 rooms, 1 pb
●
C-no/S-yes/P-no/H-no
French

Full 3-course breakfast
Comp. wine
Sitting room
game room, color TV

Lovely, comfortable Victorian home. Views to ocean and city. Only five blocks to sea. Near all transport and attractions. Grouse Mountain skiing nearby.

The Nelsons'
470 West St. James Rd., VTN 2P5
604-985-1178
Roy & Charlotte Nelson
March–November

$$ B&B
3 rooms, 3 pb
C-yes/S-no/P-no/H-no

Full breakfast
Afternoon tea
Sitting room
swimming pool

Gracious residence offering seclusion and relaxation in garden setting. Easily accessible to Vancouver attractions and island ferries.

Platt's B&B
4393 Quinton Place, V7R 4A8
604-987-4100
Nancy & Elwood Platt
All year

$ B&B
2 rooms, 1 pb
C-no/S-no/P-no/H-no
English

Full breakfast
Homemade bread & jams

Quiet parklike area, homemade bread and jams. 15 minutes to heart of town and our famous Stanley Park.

Sue's Victorian B&B
152 E. 3rd, V7L 1E6
604-985-1523
Sue Chalmers
All year

$ EP/$$ B&B
3 rooms, 1 pb
C-yes/S-no/P-no/H-no
English

Cont. & Full breakfast
Kitchen privileges
Piano, laundry, parking
phone & TV in room
baby-sitting available

This lovely restored 1904 home, just four blocks from the harbor is centrally located for transportation, shopping, restaurants and tourist attractions.

NORTH VANCOUVER

VickeRidge B&B
3638 Loraine Ave., V7R 4B8
604-985-0338
Barrie & Connie Vickers
All year

$ B&B/MAP
3 rooms, 1 pb
●
C-yes/S-no/P-no/H-no
French

Full breakfast
Dinner by prior arrang.
Comp. wine, snacks
sitting room, library
honeymoon package

Gracious accommodations, superb breakfasts, quiet alpine village, convenient to downtown, cruise ships, other destinations, cultural, recreational, business activities.

SALT SPRING ISLE—GANGES

Cranberry Ridge B&B
C16, 269 Don Ore Rd,RR2, V0S
1E0
604-537-4854
Gloria Callison Lutz
All year

$$$ B&B
2 rooms
Visa, MC ●
C-no/S-no/P-no/H-no

Full breakfast
In-room sitting room
4-6 person hot tub
large sun deck
magnificent views

Two large rooms with private powder rooms and private entrances. Fantastic views from both rooms. Great Canadian hospitality. Full home-cooked breakfast with homebaked goods.

SIDNEY

Graham's Cedar House
1825 Landsend Rd., V8L 3X9
604-655-3699 FAX:655-1422
Kay & Dennis Graham
All year

$$$ B&B
3 rooms, 3 pb
●
C-10+/S-no/P-no/H-no

Full breakfast
Afternoon tea, snacks
Sitting room
private entrances, decks
sitting area, TV, bath

Chalet luxury on woodsy country acreage is minutes from Victoria. Close to Butchart Gardens, U.S., BC Ferries, Victoria Airport and charming Sidney-By-The-Sea.

VANCOUVER

Diana's Luxury B&B
1019 E. 38th Ave., V5W 1J4
604-321-2855
Diana & Danny
All year

$$ B&B
8 rooms, 2 pb
●
C-no/S-yes/P-yes/H-yes
Polish,Russ,Yugos,Czech

Continental breakfast
Comp. tea, coffee
Sitting room, patio
jacuzzi, garden
TV, games, bicycles

Luxury home in a central area. Free airport pickup. Comfortable, friendly atmosphere. Accommodation right in downtown Vancouver also available. Babysitting available.

Kenya Court Guest House
2230 Cornwall Ave., V6K 1B5
604-738-7085
D. M. Williams
All year

$$$ B&B
5 rooms, 3 pb
US Cheque
C-10+/S-no/P-no/H-no
Italian, French, German

Full breakfast
Comp. tea, coffee
Sitting room, library
tennis courts
glass solarium

Heritage guest house overlooking Kitsiland Beach, mountains, English Bay. Gourmet breakfast served in glass solarium with panoramic view. Minutes from downtown, Granville Isl.

Rose Guest House
3453 Prince Albert St., V5V 4H6
604-876-4419 604-872-1800
Kathryne Holm
All year

$$ B&B
2 rooms
Visa ●
C-yes/S-no/P-no/H-no

Full breakfast
Tea and snacks
Sitting room
library

This gracious, licensed home, located in a residential area, is close to exciting downtown. Your travel-certified Vancouver-born hostess is eager to help you plan excursions.

482 British Columbia

VANCOUVER

West End Guest House
1362 Haro Street, V6E 1G2
604-681-2889
Evan Penner
All year

$$$ B&B
7 rooms, 7 pb
Visa, MC
C-no/S-no/P-no/H-no
English, French

Continental plus
Bedside sherry (5–7pm)
Sitting room, library
parking, TV in lounge
piano, phones in rooms

Walk to Stanley Park, beaches, Robson Street shops and restaurants; then enjoy the quiet ambiance of our comfortable historic inn. Popular with romantic couples.

VANCOUVER (DELTA)

John & Mary Parker
11149 Prospect Dr., V4E 2R4
604-594-1832
John & Mary Parker
May–October

$$ B&B
2 rooms, 2 pb
C-yes/S-no/P-no/H-no

Full breakfast
Afternoon tea
Sitting room, library
hot tubs, pool
3 golf clubs nearby

Spacious rooms in one of Vancouver's loveliest suburbs, the Sunshine Hills. 20 minutes from U.S. border, Vancouver Island ferry, airport, downtown. Host is author and actor.

VICTORIA

Abigail's Hotel
906 McClure St., V8V 3E7
604-388-5363
Hazel Prior
All year

$$$ B&B
16 rooms, 16 pb
Visa, MC, AmEx ●
C-yes/S-no/P-no/H-no

Full breakfast
Comp. sherry
Social hour, library
sitting room, bicycles
Jacuzzi in some rooms

Completely updated classic Tudor building. Private jacuzzi tubs, fireplaces and goose down comforters. Walk to downtown. Delicious breakfast. First-class smiling hospitality.

Battery Street Guest House
670 Battery St., V8V 1E5
604-385-4632
Pamela Verduyn
All year

$$ B&B
6 rooms, 2 pb
C-ltd/S-no/P-no/H-no
Dutch

Full breakfast
Sitting room
walk to park and ocean

Comfortable guest house (1898) in downtown Victoria. Centrally located; walk to town, sites, Beacon Hill Park, ocean. Ample breakfast. Host speaks Dutch as a first language.

The Beaconsfield Inn
998 Humboldt St., V8V 2Z8
604-384-4044
Hazel Prior
All year

$$$ B&B
15 rooms, 15 pb
Visa, MC, AmEx ●
C-yes/S-no/P-no/H-no

Full breakfast
Comp. sherry
Social hour, sun room
library, piano
bicycles

Award-winning restoration of an English mansion. Walk to downtown. Antiques throughout; rich textures, velvets, leather, warm woods. Delicious breakfast. Pampering service.

Captain's Palace
309 Belleville St., V8V 1X2
604-388-9191
Florence Prior, Helen Beirnes
All year

$$ B&B
14 rooms, 14 pb
Visa, MC, AmEx ●
C-no/S-no/P-no/H-no

Full breakfast from menu
Comp. wine, coffee

1897 mansion with crystal chandeliers, stained glass, antiques and restaurant; near heart of Victoria; full view of Inner Harbor; Christmas shop & chocolate factory to visit.

VICTORIA

Elk Lake Lodge

5259 Patricia Bay Hwy, V8Y 1S8
604-658-8879
Marie McQuade
All year

$$ B&B
5 rooms, 5 pb
Visa, MC •
C-6+/S-ltd/P-ltd/H-no

Full breakfast
Afternoon tea, coffee
Library and T.V.
large lounge
hot tub on patio

Formerly a unique 1910 monastery and church. Antique furnishings with bedrooms and living room overlooking Elk Lake. Ten minutes from the city center, ferries.

Heritage House B&B

P.O. Box 3189, V8Z 7A7
3808 Heritage Lane
604-479-0892
Larry & Sandra Gray
All year

$$ B&B
5 rooms
Visa, MC
C-no/S-no/P-no/H-no

Full breakfast
Afternoon tea
Comp. wine
sitting room, library
2-day minimum stay

1910 Craftsman-style heritage house among giant Douglas firs. Large veranda and gardens. Three miles from city center on private road. Convenient to ferries and highways.

Hibernia B&B

747 Helvetia Crescent, V8Y 1M1
604-658-5519
Aideen Lydon
All year

$$ B&B
3 rooms
MC, Visa •
C-yes/S-no/P-no/H-yes
French, Spanish, Gaelic

Full Irish breakfast
Wine, tea, coffee
Sitting room with TV
grand piano, library
large lawn with trees

Peaceful. 15 minutes from Victoria, ferries, airport, Butchart Gardens, cul-de-sac; 5 minutes off Highway 17. Full Irish breakfast. Antique furnishings.

Holland House Inn

595 Michigan St., V8V 1S7
604-389-1279
L. Austin-Olsen, R. Birsner
All year

$$$ B&B
19 rooms, 19 pb
Visa, MC, AmEx, DC •
C-yes/S-no/P-no/H-yes

Full breakfast
Sherry, tea, coffee, etc
Sitting room
library
fresh flowers

A unique 19-room luxury inn furnished throughout with eclectic furnishings and original, contemporary art. Winter months include string quartets once a month.

Oak Bay Guest House

1052 Newport Ave., V8S 5E3
Oak Bay
604-598-3812
Dave & Pam Vandy
March — October

$$$ B&B
11 rooms, 9 pb
Visa, MC
C-no/S-no/P-no/H-no

Full breakfast
Sitting room
library

Charming, peaceful character home furnished with antiques. Beautiful gardens, close to scenic walks, beaches, golf and minute's drive into Victoria.

"Our Home on the Hill" B&B

546 Delora Dr., V9C 3R8
604-474-4507
Grace Holman
All year

$ B&B
3 rooms, 1 pb
•
C-yes/S-no/P-no/H-no

Full breakfast
Comp. coffee, tea
Sitting room
hot tub

Enjoy peaceful seclusion; cozy, antique-accented bedrooms; a hearty breakfast; near beaches, parks and trails, 20 minutes from Victoria. A warm welcome awaits you.

VICTORIA ───────────────────────────

Portage Inlet House B&B
993 Portage Rd., V8Z 1K9
604-479-4594
Jim & Pat Baillie
All year

$$ B&B
4 rooms, 3 pb
Visa, MC
C-yes/S-ltd/P-no/H-yes

Full English breakfast
Organically grown food
Private entrances
garden, water views
"honeymoon" cottage

Acre of waterfront, 3 miles from city centre, located at mouth of salmon stream. Organic food; hearty breakfast. Ducks, swans, eagles, heron and other wildlife on property.

Prior House B&B Inn
620 St. Charles St., V8S 3N7
604-592-8847
Candis L. Cooperrider
All year

$$ B&B
5 rooms, 5 pb
Visa, MC ●
C-yes/S-no/P-no/H-no

Full breakfast
Afternoon tea
Comp. wine
sitting room
library

Grand English manor built for king's representative. Fireplaces, antiques, ocean vistas and gardens. Recapture romance in elegant beauty.

Sealake House B&B
5152 Santa Clara Ave., V84 1W4
604-658-5208
Ann & Charlie Laidman
All year

$$ B&B
3 rooms
C-yes/S-no/P-no/H-yes

Full breakfast
Afternoon tea
Sitting room
½ acre of gardens
bicycles

1905 character home overlooking beautiful Elk Lake. Quiet, charming guest & sitting rooms. Quaint dining rm., elegant breakfast. Enjoy cycling, running, hiking & water sports.

Sunnymeade House Inn
1002 Fenn Ave., V8Y 1P3
Cordova Bay by the Sea
604-658-1414
Jack & Nancy Thompson
All year

$$ B&B
5 rooms, 1 pb
Visa, MC
C-no/S-no/P-no

Full breakfast
Restaurant, bar
Afternoon tea
sitting room, flowers
garden, tennis courts

Village by the Sea. Walk to shops, restaurants, beach. Country-style B&B inn. Beautiful decor and furnishings; modern conveniences. 15 minutes to Butchart Gardens and Ferry.

Swallow Hill Farm B&B
4910 William Head Rd., V8X 3W9
RR#1
604-474-4042
Gini & Peter Walsh
All year

$$ B&B
2 rooms, 2 pb
Visa, MC
C-yes/S-no/P-no/H-no

Full breakfast
Comp. tea/coffee, snacks
Sitting room, library
books & games for guests
many activity brochures

The natural getaway—country setting minutes from Victoria. Charming private suite, queen bed, delicious farm breakfasts, spectacular views, central to S. Vancouver Island.

Top O' Triangle Mountain
3442 Karger Terrace, V9C 3K5
604-478-7853 FAX:478-2245
Henry & Pat Hansen
All year

$$ B&B
3 rooms, 3 pb
Visa, MC ●
C-yes/S-ltd/P-no/H-yes
Danish

Full breakfast
Refreshments on arrival
Sitting room
2 room suite avail.
near golf, fishing

Warm, solid cedar home tucked in among the firs. Breathtaking view. Clean, comfortable beds. Hospitality and good food are our specialties. We make guests "at home."

VICTORIA

Wellington B&B
66 Wellington Ave., V8V 4H5
604-383-5976
Inge & Sue Ranzinger
All year

$$ B&B
4 rooms, 4 pb
MC •
C-12+/S-no/P-no/H-no
German, Spanish

Full breakfast
Refrigerator, ice
Sitting room, library
sun porch, sun deck
tennis court nearby

A touch of class! Quiet street, close to ocean, park and downtown. Beautifully designed bright rooms with queen & king beds.

Wooded Acres B&B
4907 Rocky Point Rd, V98 5B4
RR#2
604-478-8172
Elva & Skip Kennedy
All year

$$$ B&B
2 rooms, 2 pb
•
C-10+/S-ltd/P-no/H-no

Full country breakfast
Ice box, tea, snacks
Sitting room, library
bicycles, fishing & golf
beaches & arts nearby

Our log home is tastefully decorated with antiques. Enjoy our romantic country atmosphere with private hot tub, candlelight and a touch of wilderness. Many activities nearby.

WEST VANCOUVER

Creekside B&B
1515 Palmerston Ave., V7V 4S9
604-926-1861 604-328-9400
John Boden & Donna Hawrelko
All year

$$$ B&B
2 rooms, 2 pb
Visa, MC •
C-12+/S-no/P-no/H-no
Ukrainian

Full breakfast
Complimentary wine
Color TV, fireplace
2 person jacuzzi tubs
private parking

Private, natural, woodsy creekside hideaway. Close to parks, skiing, beaches and ocean. Honeymoon suite available. Complimentary toiletries. 2 day minimum.

WHISTLER

Golden Dreams B&B
Box 692, 6412 Easy St., V0N 1B0
604-932-2667
Ann & Terry Myette-Spence
All year

$$ B&B
2 rooms
Visa, MC •
C-yes/S-no/P-no/H-no

Full breakfast
Comp. sherry
Jacuzzi, TV, VCR
theme rooms: Aztec, etc.
golf practice tee

Attentively catered; nutritious home cooking; tastefully decorated home in heart of valley. Walk on trail along golf course to village, downhill & X-C skiing, hiking, lakes.

More Inns . . .

Aguilar House Bamfield, V0R 1B0 604-728-3323
April Point Lodge Box 1, 900 April Pt. Rd, Campbell River, V9W 4Z9 604-285-2222
B&B at Laburnum Cottage 1388 Terrace Ave., North Vancouver, V7R 1B4 604-988-4877
B&B for Visitors 10356 Skagit Dr., North Delta, V4C 2K9 604-588-8866
Beachside B&B 4208 Evergreen Ave., West Vancouver, V7V 1H1 604-922-7773
Blair House 1299 Rodondo Place, Kelowna, V1V 1G6 604-762-5090
Bobbing Boats Box 88, 7212 Peden Ln., Brentwood Bay, V0S 1A0 604-652-9828
Bradshaw's Minac Lodge On Canim Lake, Eagle Creek, V0K 1L0 604-397-2416
Brentwood Bay B&B Box 403, Brentwood Bay, V0S 1A0 604-652-2012
Brown House B&B, The 3020 Dolphin Dr, Nanoose Bay, V0N 2J0 604-468-7804
Burley's Lodge Box 193, Ucluelet, V0R 3A0 604-726-4444
Camelot P O Box 5038, Stn. B, Victoria, V8R 6N3 604-592-8589
Castle on the Mountain 8227 Silver Star Rd., Vernon, V1T 8L6 604-542-4593
Cat's Meow 5299 Chute Lake Rd., Kelowna, V1Y 7R3 604-764-7407
Chilanko Lodge & Resort Gen. Delivery, Hwy 20, Kleena Kleene, V0L 1M0 604-Kleena K
Cindosa B&B 3951–40th St. NE, Salmon Arm, V1E 4M4 604-832-3342
Clayoquot Lodge P.O. Box 188, Tofino, V0R 2Z0 604-725-3284
Corbett House Corbett Rd., Pender Island, V0N 2M0 604-629-6305
Corbett House B&B Corbett Rd., Pender Island, VON 2MO 604-629-6305
Country Gardens B&B 1665 Grant Rd., RR 5, Duncan, V9L 4T6 604-748-5865

Craigmyle B&B 1037 Craigdorroch Rd., Victoria, V8S 2A5 604-595-5411
Denman Island Guest House Box 9, Denman Rd., Denman Island, V0R 1T0 604-335-2688
Dogwoods 302 Birch St., Campbell River, V9W 2S6 604-287-4213
Durlocher Hof P.O. Box 1125, Whistler, V0N 1B0 604-932-1924
Dutch-Canadian B&B 201 East 7th Ave, New Westminster, V3L 4H5 604-521-7404
Emilie's Bed & Breakfast 1570 Rockland Ave., Victoria, V8S 1W5 604-598-8881
Fairburn Farm RR 7, Duncan, V9L 4W4 604-746-4637
Feathered Paddle B&B 7 Queesto Dr., Port Renfrew, V0S 1K0 604-647-5433
Fen Mor Manor Box 453, Sicamous, V0E 2V0 604-836-4994
Fernhill Lodge Box 140, Mayne Island, V0N 2J0 604-539-2544
Five Junipers 3704—24th Ave., Vernon, V1T 1L9 604-549-3615
Gables Country Inn 2405 Bering Rd/Box 1153, Kelowna, V1Y 7P8 604-768-4468
Gingerbread House Campbell Bay Rd., Mayne Island, V0N 2J0 604-539-3133
Gisela's Bed & Breakfast 3907 17th Ave., Vernon, V1T 6Z1 604-542-5977
Great-Snoring-On-Sea 10858 Madrona Dr., RR1, Sidney, V8L 3R9 604-659-9549
Greystone Manor RR 6, Site 684/C2, Courtenay, V9N 8H9 604-338-1422
Grove Hall Estate B&B 6159 Lakes Rd., Duncan, V9L 4J6 604-746-6152
Haida Inn 1342 Island Hwy, Campbell River, V9W 2E1 604-287-7402
Hastings House Box 1110, Ganges, Salt Spring Island, V0S 1E0 800-661-9255
Haynes Point Lakeside 3619—87th St., Osoyoos, V0H 1V0 604-495-7443
Heritage Inn 422 Vernon St., Nelson, V1L 5P4 604-352-5331
Hirsch's Place 10336-145 A St., Surrey, V3R 3S1 604-588-3326
Hotel 129 W. Third St., Kelowna, V1Y 7R3 507-452-5460
Humboldt House 867 Humboldt St., Victoria, V8V 2Z6 604-384-8422
Hummingbird Inn Sturdies Bay Rd., Galiano Island, V0N 1P0 604-539-5472
Joan Brown's B&B 834 Pemberton Rd., Victoria, V8S 3R4 604-592-5929
La Berengerie Montague Harbor Bl., Galiano Island, V0N 1P0 604-539-5392
Lakewoods B&B Site 339, C5, RR 3, Port Alberni, V9Y 7L7 604-723-2310
Manana Lodge Box 9 RR 1, Ladysmith, V0R 2E0 604-245-2312
Nelson House 977 Broughton St., Vancouver, V6G 2A4 604-684-9793
Nolan House Box 135, Atlin, V0B 1A0 604-651-7585
Ocean Wilderness 109 W. Coast Rd., RR2, Sooke, V0S 1N0 604-646-2116
Oceanwood Country 22 Dinner Bay Rd., Mayne Island, V0N 2J0 604-539-5074
Oceanwood Country Inn 630 Dinner Bay Road, Mayne Island, V0N 2J0 604-539-3002
Olde England Inn 429 Lampson St., Victoria, V8S 2A5 604-388-4353
Oxford Castle Inn 133 George Rd., East, Victoria, V9A 1L1 604-388-6431
Park Place B&B 1689 Birch St., Prince George, V2L 1B3 604-563-6326
Quilchena Hotel Quilchena, V0E 2R0 604-378-2611
Ram's Head Inn Red Mt. Ski Area Box 63, Rossland, V0G 1Y0 604-362-9577
Raven Tree Iris Gardens 1853 Connie Rd., Victoria, V9B 5B4 604-642-5248
Sabey House Box 341, Whistler, V0N 1B0 604-932-3498
Schroth Farm Site 6, Comp 25, R.R.8, Vernon, V1T 8L6 604-545-0010
Sea Breeze Lodge Hornby Island, V0R 1Z0 604-335-2321
Silver Creek Guest House 6820—30th Ave. SW, Salmon Arm, V1E 4M1 604-832-8870
Sooke Harbour House 1528 Whiffen Spit Rd., Sooke, V0S 1N0 604-642-3421
Surf Lodge Ltd. RR1, Site 1, Gabriola Island, V0R 1X0 604-247-9231
Taliesin Guest House B&B Box 101, Parson, V0A 1L0 604-348-2247
The Cabin 7603 Westkal Rd., Vernon, V1B 1Y4 000-542-3021
Thom's Bed & Breakfast 615 W. 23rd St., North Vancouver, V7M 2C2 604-986-2168
Three Pines Lodge S. 85, RR 2, Summerland, V0H 1Z0 604-494-1661
Tucker's B&B 5373 Pat Bay Hwy. #2, Victoria, V8Y 1S9 604-658-8404
Twin Willows By The Lake Site 10, Comp 16, RR 4, Vernon, V1T 6L7 604-542-8293
Wayward Wind Lodge Box 300, Sointula, V0N 3E0 604-973-6307
Weathervane B&B, The 1633 Rockland Ave., Victoria, V8S 1W6 604-592-0493
West Coast Contemporary 784 Terrien Way, Parksville, V0R 2S0 604-248-2585
Whyte House 155 Randall St., Victoria, V8V 2E3 604-389-1598
Wilcuma Resort RR 3, Cobble Hill, V0R 1L0 604-748-8737
Willow Point Lodge RR 1, Nelson, V1L 5P4 604-825-9411
Windmill House S 19A, C2, RR 1, Vernon, V1T 6L4 604-549-2804
Yellow Point Lodge RR 3, Ladysmith, V0R 2E0 604-245-7422

Manitoba

Chestnut House	$ B&B	Full breakfast
209 Chestnut St., R36 1R8	4 rooms	Sitting room
204-772-9788	●	
John & Louise Clark	C-yes/S-no	
All year		

Restored home in historic location, furnished with antiques. Close to downtown facilities, restaurants, antique shops. Full breakfast complemented by home baking.

More Inns ...

Bannerman East 99 Bannerman Avenue, Winnipeg, R2W 0T1 204-589-6449
Beulah Land Box 26, Treherne, R0G 2V0 204-723-2828
Casa Maley 1605 Victoria Ave., Brandon, R7A 1C1 204-728-0812
Deerbank Farm Box 23, RR 2, Morris, R0G 1K0 204-746-8395
Edna O'Hara 242 Amherst Street, Winnipeg, R3J 1Y6 204-888-6848
Ernie & Tina Dyck Box 1001, Boissevain, R0K 0E0 204-534-2563
Nancy & Geoff Tidmarch 330 Waverly St., Winnipeg, R3M 3L3 204-284-3689
Paul & Trudy Johnson 455 Wallasey Street, Winnipeg, R3J 3C5 204-837-3368
Thomas & Marie Wiebe 25 Valley View Drive, Winnipeg, R2Y 0R5 204-888-0910

New Brunswick

Reid Farms Tourist Home	$ B&B/MAP	Full breakfast
RR 1, E0J 1H0	4 rooms, 2 pb	Lunch, tea, dinner
506-276-4787	C-yes/S-no/P-no/H-ltd	Sitting room, bicycles
Ken & Shirley Reid		log cabin near lake
All year		fishing, skiing, golfing

Enjoy a rural atmosphere and old-fashioned hospitality down on the farm. We have a lake stocked with trout. Also log cabin in the woods with 5 miles of cross-country trails.

Happy Apple Acres	$$ B&B	Full breakfast
RR 4, Hwy 105, E3B 4X5	4 rooms, 3 pb	Afternoon tea, snacks
½ m. past Douglas School	C-yes/S-ltd/P-ask/H-yes	Sitting room, library
506-472-1819	some French	sauna, funny pool
Margaret & Angus Hamilton		whirlpool in one room
All year		

Enjoy peace and tranquillity in a rural setting just minutes from all the tourist attractions of the Fredericton area. Comfortable bedrooms, welcome snack, gourmet breakfast.

RIVERSIDE

Cailswick Babbling Brook
Albert Co., Route 114, E0A 2R0
506-882-2079
Eunice Cail
All year

$ B&B
5 rooms, 2 pb
C-yes/S-no/P-no/H-no
French

Full country breakfast
Evening snack
Beverages, sweets
sitting room, television

Country living. Quiet, serene and restful. Home-cooked meals. Century-old Victorian overlooking Shepardy Bay, running brooks, lovely grounds. Near Fundy National Park.

ROTHESAY

Shadow Lawn Inn
P.O. Box 41, E0G 2W0
3180 Rothesay Rd.
506-847-7539
Patrick & Margaret Gallagher
All year

$$ EP
8 rooms, 5 pb
●
C-yes/S-yes/P-yes/H-no
French

Full breakfast $
Dinner by reservation
Bar service
sitting room, piano
tennis courts

Shadow Lawn in the village of Rothesay—next to golf, tennis, sailing. Gourmet dining, with silver service.

More Inns ...

A Touch of Country 61 Pleasant St., Saint Stephen, E3L 1A6 506-466-5056
Andersons Holiday Farm Sussex RR 2, Sussex, E0E 1P0 506-433-3786
Chez Prime B&B RR 3, S. 32, Losier St., Tracadie, E0C 2B0 506-395-6884
Compass Rose North Head, Grand Manan, E0G 2M0 506-662-8570
Cross Tree Guest House Seal Cove, Grand Manan, E0G 3B0 506-536-1291
Different Drummer Box 188, Sackville, E0A 3C0 506-536-1291
Dutch Treat Farm RR 1, Shepody, Hopewell Cape, E0A 1Y0 506-882-2552
Eveleigh Hotel Evandale, RR1, Hampstead, E0G 1Y0 506-425-9993
Ferry Wharf Inn North Head, Grand Manan, E0G 2M0 506-662-8588
Florentine Manor RR 2, Albert, E0A 1A0 506-882-2271
Governor's Mansion Main St., Nelson, E0C 1T0 506-622-3036
Grand Harbour Inn Box 73, Grand Harbour, Grand Manan, E0G 1X0 506-662-8681
Ingle-Neuk Lodge B&B RR 3 Box 1180, Bathurst, E2A 4G8 506-546-5758
Mactaquac B&B Mactaquac RR1, Mactaquac, E0H 1N0 506-363-3630
Manan Island Inn & Spa P.O. Box 15, Grand Manan, E0G 2M0 506-662-8624
Marshlands Inn Box 1440, Sackville, E0A 3C0 506-536-0170
Northern Wilderness Lodge Box 571, Plaster Rock, E0J 1W0 506-356-8327
Pansy Patch P.O. Box 349, Saint Andrews, E0G 2X0 506-529-3834
Poplars—Les Peupliers RR1 Site 11 Box 16, Beresford, E0B 1H0 506-546-5271
Puff'Inn P.O. Box 135, Saint Andrews, E0G 2X0 506-529-4191
Shiretown Inn Town Square, Saint Andrews, E0G 2X0 506-529-8877
Shorecrest Lodge North Head, Grand Manan Island, E0G 2M0 506-662-3216
Victoriana Rose B&B 193 Church St., Fredericton, E3B 4E1 506-454-0994
Woodsview II B&B RR 5, Hartland, E0J 1N0 506-375-4637

Newfoundland

More Inns ...

Chaulk's Tourist Home P.O. Box 339, Lewisporte, A0J 3A0 709-535-6305
Village Inn, Trinity, A0C 2S0 709-464-3269

Northwest Territories

More Inns ...

Harbour House Box 54, 1 Lakeshore Dr., Hay River, X0E 0R0 403-874-2233

Nova Scotia

AMHERST

Amherst Shore Country Inn
RR #2, B4H 3X9
Hwy. 366 at Lorneville
902-667-4800 902-542-2291
Donna & Jim Laceby
May—Can. Thanksgiving

$ EP
6 rooms, 4 pb
Visa, MC ●
C-ltd/S-no/P-ltd/H-no

Full breakfast ($)
Gourmet dinner, bar
Sitting room, piano
clay tennis court
bicycles, private beach

Beautiful panoramic view of the Northumberland Strait. Donna is renowned for the 4-course dinner she serves each evening by reservation only.

ANNAPOLIS ROYAL

Milford House
RR #4, South Milford, B0S 1A0
902-532-2617 902-462-8106
Robert & Dawn Howell
June—September

$$$ MAP
27 rooms
●
C-yes/S-yes/P-yes/H-yes

Full breakfast
Dinner, maid service
27 cottages along shores
of two lakes, swimming
croquet, canoes, tennis

Old-fashioned country resort situated at the head of a chain of lakes which lead into the wilderness of Nova Scotia.

CHESTER

Mecklenburgh Inn
78 Queen St., B0J 1J0
902-275-4638
Suzan Fraser
June 1 — October 31

$$ B&B
4 rooms
Visa ●
C-yes/S-ltd/P-no/H-no
French

Full breakfast
Picnic lunch
Sitting room, bicycles
near tennis, golf
Yacht Club, restaurants

Circa 1890 inn in heart of seaside village. Period furnishing; breakfast served before an open fire by young cordonbleu hostess.

HEBRON

Manor Inn
P.O. Box 56, R.R. 1, B0W 1X0
Yarmouth Co.
902-742-2487 FAX:742-8094
Bev & Terry Grandy
May—December

$ EP/B&B
Visa, MC, AmEx ●
C-yes/S-yes/P-ltd/H-no
French

Breakfast $
Lunch, dinner, bar
Entertainment
tennis courts, pool
putting green, croquet

Nine acres of landscaped grounds, formal rose garden, 3,000 feet of lake front. Magnificent old mansion and 24-unit motel. Boating, swimming, lawn games.

PUGWASH

The Blue Heron Inn
Box 405, B0K 1L0
Route 6, Durham St.
902-243-2900 902-243-2516
Bonnie Bond & John Caraberis
June–September 7

$ B&B
5 rooms, 2 pb
Visa
C-yes/S-yes/P-no/H-no

Continental breakfast
Lounge, color TV
sitting room, piano
tennis nearby

A renovated home in the Village of Pugwash furnished with many antiques. Close to beaches, golf course and craft shops.

WOLFVILLE

Blomidon Inn
P.O. Box 839, B0P 1X0
127 Main St.
902-542-2291 FAX:542-7461
Jim Laceby
All year

$$ B&B
27 rooms, 25 pb
Visa, MC ●
C-yes/S-yes/P-ltd/H-yes

Continental plus
Lunch, dinner
Afternoon tea sitting room
tennis, shuffleboard

A tastefully restored 19th-century sea captain's mansion near the land of Evangeline. Gracious cuisine with fresh offerings from the fertile valley and bountiful sea.

Ontario

ALTON

Cataract Inn
1490 Cataract St., RR#2, L0N 1A0
519-927-3033 FAX:927-5779
Rodney Hough
All year

$$$ B&B
5 rooms
Visa, MC, AmEx
C-no/S-yes/P-no/H-no

Continental plus
Restaurant, bar
Lunch, dinner
catering for weddings
tennis, fishing, golfing

Sound sleep ... sunshine ... birds singing.... Smell the coffee and homemade muffins? Late riser? No hurry. We'll wait for you.

BAYFIELD

Little Inn of Bayfield Ltd
P.O. Box 100, N0M 1G0
519-565-2611
Pat & Gayle Waters
All year

$$$ EP
31 rooms, 31 pb
credit cards accepted ●
C-yes/S-yes/P-no/H-yes
French, German, Polish

Lunch, dinner, bar
Sitting room
sauna/whirlpool
cottage

Ontario's oldest continuously operating Inn–since 1832. Antique-filled bedrooms and quiet parlors. Award-winning dining room. Cross-country ski trails.

BRAMPTON

Creditview B&B
RR 10, Creditvw Rd 7650, L6V 3N2
416-451-6271
Karl & Anna DeRooy

$$ B&B
1 rooms, 1 pb

Full breakfast
Complimentary wine
Kitchen & dining room
color TV, walk-out deck
near golf & "Go train"

Comfortable private cottage surrounded by trees in peaceful country atmosphere. Features 2 bedrooms, full bath, dining room, kitchen, deck & TV. Close to downtown Toronto.

COBOURG —————————————

Northumberland Heights Inn $$ EP
RR 5, K9A 4J8
Northumberland Heights Rd
416-372-7500 FAX:372-4574
Mike & Veronica Thiele
All year

14 rooms, 14 pb
Visa, MC, AmEx ●
C-yes/S-yes/P-no/H-yes
German, French, Dutch

Full breakfast $
Lunch, dinner, bar
Hot tub, sauna
swimming pool
sitting room, piano

Situated on 100 acres of rolling countryside. Relaxing patio areas, miniature golf, outdoor checkers, trout pond, cross-country skiing, skating. Two-night "Plan" available.

COLDWATER —————————————

Graymore Inn
2 Sturgeon Bay Rd., L0K 1E0
705-686-7676
Joyce & Herb Irvine
All year

$$ B&B
6 rooms, 6 pb
Visa, MC
C-5+/S-no/P-no/H-no

Continental plus
Afternoon tea, snacks
Sitting room, library
fireplaces, whirlpool
TVs, golf & ski packages

A large limestone estate. Architecturally unique and elegantly restored. Situated on picturesque Coldwater River. Excellent year-round recreation. 75 minutes from Toronto.

ELMIRA —————————————

Teddy Bear B&B Inn
RR #1, N3B 2Z1
519-669-2379
Gerrie & Vivian Smith
All year

$ B&B
3 rooms, 2 pb
Visa, MC
C-yes/S-no/P-no/H-no

Full breakfast
Dinner with reservation
Comp. coffee anytime
sitting room, library
bicycles

Hospitality abounds in this outstandingly beautiful countryside inn with Mennonite quilts, crafts, and antiques. Close to Elora, St. Jacob's, and Stratford.

GORE'S LANDING —————————————

The Victoria Inn
County Rd. 18, K0K 2E0
416-342-3261
Mid-May–mid-October

$$ EP
9 rooms, 9 pb
Visa, MC, AmEx ●
C-ltd/S-yes/P-no/H-yes

Full breakfast $
Lunch, dinner, bar
Sitting room, piano
boat rental
swimming pool

Restful waterfront estate, stained glass windows, fireplaces highlight quaint rooms. Veranda dining room with panoramic view of Rice Lake. Boat dockage.

LEAMINGTON —————————————

Home Suite Home
115 Erie St. South, N8H 3B5
519-326-7169
Agatha & Harry Tiessen
Feb 15–Dec 31

$ B&B
4 rooms, 1 pb
●
C-yes/S-no/P-no/H-no
German

Full elaborate breakfast
Coffee or tea on request
Sitting room, A/C
sunporch, swimming pool
hand-made quilts on beds

Enjoy warm hospitality in a turn-of-the-century distinctive & spacious home. Decorated in Victorian and country. Large in-ground pool. Excellent bird watching at Point Pelee.

McKELLER —————————————

The Inn at Manitou
McKellar Center Road, P0G 1C0
251 Davenport Rd. M5R 1J9
416-967-3466 705-389-2171
Ben & Sheila Wise
May–October

$$$ AP
Visa, Mc, AmEx ●
C-yes/S-ltd
French

Full breakfast
Lunch & French dinner
Stocked library, saunas
lake, hot tubs, pool
13 tennis courts

Five star lakeside sophisticated Relais and Chateaux resort. Thirteen tennis courts, luxurious suites featuring skylit sumptuous washrooms with whirlpool baths and sauna.

MERRICKVILLE

Sam Jakes Inn
46 Cartier St., K0G 1N0
118 Main St. East
613-269-3711
Gary B. Clarke
All year

$$$ B&B
30 rooms, 30 pb
Visa, MC, AmEx, EnRoute
●
C-12+/S-no/P-no/H-yes

Full breakfast
Restaurant, tavern
Afternoon tea, snacks
sitting room, gardens
whirlpool, exercise room

Canalside country inn, once home of a prominent village merchant, lets you relive the 1860s in a historic town setting! Inquire about our tours.

NIAGARA FALLS

A Rose & Kangaroo
5239 River Rd., L2E 3G9
Niagara Parkway
416-374-6999
Laurence & Virginia Furnell
All year

$ B&B
4 rooms, 3 pb
●
C-yes/S-ltd/P-ltd/H-no
some French, Ukrainian

Full breakfast
Afternoon tea
Sitting room, BBQ facil.
bicycles, tennis
jogging & biking trail

A perfect retreat, overlooking the Niagara River, yet within walking distance to the Falls and attractions. A home as unique as its name.

OTTAWA

Albert House
478 Albert St., K1R 5B5
613-236-4479 800-267-1982
John & Cathy Delroy
All year

$$ B&B
17 rooms, 17 pb
Visa, MC, AmEx
C-12+/S-yes/P-no/H-no
French, English

Full English breakfast
Tea, coffee, juices
Sitting room
color cable TV in rooms
telephones

Fine restored Victorian residence designed by Thomas Seaton Scott in post-Confederate period. Complimentary breakfast, parking.

Australis Guest House
35 Marlborough Ave., K1N 8E6
613-235-8461
Carol & Brian Waters
All year

$$ B&B
3 rooms, 1 pb
C-yes/S-yes/P-no/H-no

Full breakfast
Afternoon tea
Sitting room, piano
bicycles
off-street parking

An older renovated antique-filled downtown home close to all attractions in an area of embassies, parks and the river. Family suite available.

Cartier House Inn
46 Cartier St., K2P 1J3
613-236-4667
Barbara LaFlamme
All year

$$$ B&B
11 rooms, 11 pb
Visa,MC, AmEx, DC, Enr ●
C-8+/S-ltd/P-no/H-no
French, Chinese, Dutch

Continental plus
Afternoon tea
Jacuzzis in suites
morning paper, TVs
Relais du Silence member

A "grand luxe" European inn which has been offering tranquillity and an attentive staff since the turn of the century. Near the Parliament, shops, restaurants, nightlife.

Gasthaus Switzerland Inn
89 Daly Ave., K1N 6E6
613-237-0335 800-267-8788
Josef & Sabina Sauter
All year

$$ B&B
25 rooms, 21 pb
Visa, MC ●
C-yes/S-no/P-no/H-no
German, Serb., French

Swiss country breakfast
Comp. wine, tea, cafe
Sitting room, TV room
air-conditioned
barbecue, garden

Warm Swiss atmosphere in Canada's beautiful capital; clean, cozy rooms; full Swiss-continental breakfast; close to tourist attractions; free parking. Warm, clean & cheery!

OTTAWA

O'Connor House B&B
172 O'Connor St., K2P 1T5
613-236-4221 800-268-2104
Donna Bradley
All year

$$ B&B
34 rooms
Visa, MC, AmEx, En, DC ●
C-yes/S-yes/P-no/H-no
French

Full buffet breakfast
Afternoon tea, snacks
Sitting room, bicycles
ice skates (winter)
tennis packages, A/C

The most centrally located B&B in Ottawa. Friendly, comfortable accommodations. Full all-you-can-eat Canadian breakfast. Free use of bicycles and ice skates.

Rideau View Inn
177 Frank St., K2P 0X4
613-236-9309 FAX:237-6842
George W. Hartsgrove
All year

$$ B&B
7 rooms
Visa, MC, AmEx ●
C-ltd/S-no/P-no/H-no
English, French

Full breakfast
Coffee, tea, soft drinks
Sitting room
tennis nearby

Large 1907 Edwardian home with very well appointed guest rooms. Walking distance to Parliament Hill, Rideau Canal, fine restaurants, shopping and public transport.

Westminster Guest House
446 Westminster Ave., K2A 2T8
613-729-2707
B. Deavy, K. Mikoski
All year

$ B&B
3 rooms, 1 pb
C-ltd/S-ltd/P-ltd/H-no
French

Full breakfast
Box lunch, dinner
Evening refreshments
sitting room, piano
fireplace

A turn-of-the-century home in a peaceful setting just a short drive from Parliament Hill. Close to bicycle and walking trails along Ottawa River.

OWEN SOUND

Sunset Farms B&B
RR 6, N4K 5N8
519-371-4559
Bill & Cecilie Moses
All year

$ B&B
3 rooms, 1 pb
C-yes/S-no/P-no/H-ltd

Full breakfast
Comp. tea, cofee
Sitting room
nearby restaurants
creek, pond, many birds

Country estate setting. Antiques, wood fires. Tourpoint for Manitoulin, Georgian Bay, Bruce Trail. Skiing, golf, beaches, nature lovers' paradise.

PORT CARLING

Sherwood Inn
P.O. Box 400, P0B 1J0
Sherwood Rd, Glen Orchard
705-765-3131 800-461-4233
John & Eva Heineck
All year

$$$ MAP
29 rooms, 27 pb
Visa, MC, AmEx, DC ●
C-yes/S-yes/P-no/H-ltd
German

Full breakfast
Dinner included, lunch
Bar, sitting room
piano, tennis court
landscaped grounds

A charming country inn but also a luxury resort with just the right touches of elegance and privacy. Among towering pines and at the edge of beautiful Lake Joseph.

PORTLAND-ON-THE-RIDEAU

Gallagher House
Box 99, West Water St., K0G 1V0
613-272-2895
Eleanor & Patrick Dickey
All year

$$ B&B
12 rooms, 4 pb
Visa, MC, AmEx, DC, Enr ●
C-yes/S-yes/P-no/H-yes
some French

Full breakfast
Restaurant, bar
Sitting room, library
bikes, hot tubs, sauna
on the lake

Historic homes on Rideau Waterway (circa 1830-1910). Country inn meals and ambience. Boating, golf, conservation hiking, antiques, golf at our door. "Big Rideau hospitality."

Gallagher House, Portland-on-the-Rideau, Ontario, Canada

ROCKPORT

Houseboat Amaryllis Inn
General Delivery, K0E 1V0
613-659-3513
Peter Bergen, Janet Rodier
June–October 15

$$ B&B
3 rooms, 3 pb
Visa, AmEx •
C-yes/S-no/P-no/H-no
Spanish, French

Full breakfast
Dinner, picnic baskets
Sitting room
river, picnic tours in
sailing packages avail.

Inn is a double-deck houseboat on its own 7.5-acre island. Enjoy fishing and abundant wild-life. Private baths. Gourmet meals.

SAINT JACOBS

Jakobstettel Guest House
16 Isabella St., N0B 2N0
519-664-2208
Ella Brubacher
All year

$$$ B&B
12 rooms, 12 pb
Visa, MC, AmEx
C-yes/S-no/P-no/H-no
Pennsylvania German

Continental plus
Tea, coffee, snacks
Swimming pool, trail
tennis courts, bicycles
sitting room, library

Luxurious privacy set amidst 5 acres w/trees. Each room decorated with its own charm and Victorian features. Local artisan shops within walking distance.

TORONTO

Ashleigh Heritage Home
Box 235, Station E, M6H 4E2
42 Delaware Ave.
416-535-4000
Gwen Lee
All year

$$ B&B
4 rooms
Visa •
C-yes/S-ltd/P-no/H-no

Continental plus
Coffee and tea
Sitting room, piano
bicycles, library
parking

Restored 1910 home with interesting architectural details and a large garden. Just minutes from the University, the museum and government offices.

TORONTO

Bonnevue Manor B&B Place

33 Beaty Ave., M6K 3B3	$$ B&B	Continental plus
416-536-1455 800-661-1847	6 rooms, 1 pb	Sunday brunch, snacks
Glenn & Dorothy Dodds	Visa, MC, AmEx •	Restaurant, sitting room
All year	C-yes/S-yes/P-no/H-no	bicycles, BBQ area
		sundeck, kitchenettes

Victorian-style heritage mansion located on lovely treelined boulevard near parks, museums, shopping, restaurants, downtown Toronto. Impeccable service and affordable prices.

Burken Guest House

322 Palmerston Blvd., M6G 2N6	$$ B&B	Continental plus
416-920-7842 FAX:960-9529	8 rooms	Deck, garden
Burke & Ken	Visa, MC •	TV lounge
All year	C-yes/S-no/P-no/H-no	parking
	German, French	

Very attractive home in charming downtown residential area. Period furniture, close to Eaton Centre. Nearby public transportation to downtown. Friendly Old World atmosphere.

More Inns ...

Al Leclerc's Residence 253-McLeod St., Ottawa, K2P 1A1 613-234-7577
Angel Inn, Est. 1828 224 Regent St., Niagara-On-The-Lake, L0S 1J0 416-468-3411
Arrowwood Lodge P.O. Box 125, Port Severn, L0K 1S0 705-538-2354
At-Home-In-The-Beach 237 Lee Ave., Toronto, M4E 2P4 416-690-9688
Auberge Ambiance 330 Nepean, Ottawa, K1R 5G6 613-563-0421
Aurel & Marj Armstrong B&B RR4, Kincardine, N2Z 2X5 519-395-3301
Ayr-Wyn Farms RR3, Hanover, N4N 3B9 519-364-1540
B&B Macpine Farms Box 51, Lancaster, K0C 1N0 613-347-2003
Bea's B&B House Box 133, Maynooth, K0L 2S0 613-338-2239
Beatrice Lyon Guest House 479 Slater St., Ottawa, K1R 5C2 613-236-3904
Blue Spruces B&B 187 Glebe Ave., Ottawa, K1S 2C6 613-236-8521
Breadelbane Inn 487 St. Andrew St. W., Fergus, N1M 1P2 519-843-4770
Burnside Guest Home 139 William St., Stratford, N5A 4X9 519-271-7076
Caledon Inn Caledon East, L0N 1E0 416-584-2891
Cataract Inn Rt. 2, Alton, L0N 1A0 519-927-3033
Cedarlane Farm B&B R.R. 2, Iroquois, K0E 1K0 613-652-4267
Chantry House Inn 118 High St., Southampton, N0H 2L0 519-797-2646
Chestnut Inn 9 Queen St., Cookstown, L0L 1L0 705-458-9751
Constance House B&B 62 Sweetland Ave., Ottawa, K1N 7T6 613-235-8888
Cornerbrook Farms RR2, Cargill, N0G 1J0 519-366-2629
Country Guest Home RR 2, Bradford, L3Z 2A5 416-775-3576
Crescent Manor 48 Albert Street N., Southampton, N0H 2L0 519-797-5637
Doral Inn Hotel 486 Albert St., Ottawa, K1R 5B5 613-230-8055
Fillimchuk B&B R.R. #1, Simcoe, N3Y 4J9 519-428-5165
Flora House 282 Flora St., Ottawa, K1R 5S3 613-230-2152
Glenroy Farm RR 1, Braeside, K0A 1G0 613-432-6248
Gowanlock Farm RR2, Port Elgin, N0H 2C0 519-389-5256
Gwen's Guest Home 2071 Riverside Dr., Ottawa, K1H 7X2 613-737-4129
Hart Country Estate RR #4, Lansdowne, K0E 1L0 613-659-2873
Hatties's Hideaway RR2, Dobbinton, N0H 1L0 519-363-6543
Haydon House 18 Queen Elizabeth Drwy, Ottawa, K2P 1C6 613-230-2697
Hillcrest B&B 394 Gould St., Wiarton, N0H 2T0 519-534-2262
Holiday House Inn P.O. Box 1139, Bracebridge, P0B 1C0 705-645-2245
Hollingborne House 48 Grey Street N., Southampton, N0H 2L0 519-797-3202
Horseshoe Inn RR 2, Alton, L0N 1A0 519-927-5779
Hudson House B&B 7 Lorne St., Carleton Place, K7C 2J9 613-257-8547
Ivy Lea Inn 1000 Isl. Pkwy., Lansdowne, K0E 1L0 613-659-2329
Kettle Creek Inn Main St., Port Stanley, N0L 2A0 519-782-3388
Kiely House Inn P.O. Box 1642, Niagara-On-The-Lake, L0S 1J0 416-468-4588

Lambert House B&B 231 Cathcart St., London, N6C 3M8 519-672-8996
Lamont Guest Home Kimberley, N0C 1G0 519-599-5905
Landfall Farm RR1, Blackstock, L0B 1B0 416-986-5588
Lonesome Pines 192–12th Ave., Hanover, N4N 3B9 519-364-2982
Lucky Lancione's 635 Metler Rd. RR3, Fenwick, L0S 1C0 416-892-8104
MacPine Farm's B&B Box 51, Lancaster, K0C 1N0 613-347-2003
Maplehurst 277 Frank Street, Wiarton, N0H 2T0 519-534-1210
Margaret's Guest House 510 Raglan St. S., Renfrew, K7V 4A4 613-432-3897
McGee's Inn 185 Daly Ave., Ottawa, K1N 6E8 613-237-6089
McIvor House RR4, Wiarton, N0H 2T0 519-534-1769
McMillen's B&B 41 Church St. E., Burgessville, N0J 1C0 519-424-9834
Minden House P.O. Box 789, Minden, K0M 2K0 705-286-3263
Moffat Inn 60 Picton St., Box 578, Niagara-On-The-Lake, L0S 1J0 416-468-4116
Moses Sunset Farms B&B RR6, Owen Sound, N4K 5N8 519-371-4559
Mrs. Mitchell's Violet Hill, L0N 1S0 819-925-3672
Oban Inn 160 Front St., Niagara-on-the-Lake, L0S 1J0 416-468-2165
Old Bridge Inn Young's Point, K0L 3G0 705-652-8507
Orchard View B&B 92 Orchard View Blvd., Toronto, M4R 1C2 416-488-6826
Paines' B&B Carling Bay Rd., RR1, Nobel, P0G 1G0 705-342-9266
Prince George Hotel 200 Ontario St., Kingston, K7L 2Y9 613-549-5440
Queensborough Hotel Group Box 8, RR#2, Madoc, K0K 2K0 613-473-5454
Rebecca's B&B 4058 Petrolia St., Petrolia, N0N 1R0 519-882-0118
Rose House, The 526 Dufferin Ave., London, N6B 2A2 519-433-9978
Shrewsbury Manor 30 Shrewsbury St., Stratford, N5A 2V5 519-271-8520
Sir Sam's Inn Eagle Lake P.O., Eagle Lake, K0M 1M0 705-754-2188
Ste. Anne's Inn RR1, Grafton, K0K 2G0 416-349-2493
Sterling Lodge Newboro, K0G 1P0 613-272-2435
Unicorn Inn & Restaurant RR# 1, South Gillies, Thunder Bay, P0T 2V0 807-475-4200
Union Hotel B&B, Main St. Box 38, RR 1, Normandale, N0E 1W0 519-426-5568
Waterlot Inn 17 Huron St., New Hamburg, N0B 2G0 519-662-2020
Willi-Joy Farm RR #3, Norwich, N0J 1P0 519-424-2113
Windermere House Windermere, P0B 1P0 705-769-3611

Prince Edward Island

CHARLOTTETOWN ───────────────────────

Barachois Inn
P.O. Box 1022, C1A 7M4
Church Rd., Route 243
902-963-2194
Judy & Gary MacDonald
May–October

$ EP
6 rooms, 1 pb
C-yes/S-no/P-no/H-no
English, French

Full breakfast $
Comp. tea or coffee
Sitting room
pump organ

Victorian house offers lovely views of bay, river and countryside. Antique furnishings and modern comforts. Walk to seashore.

COXEHEAD

Stanhope by the Sea
Route 25, C01 1P0
Stanhope
902-672-2047 902-892-6008
Dr. Alfy Tadros
June–August

$$ EP
Visa, MC ●
C-yes/S-yes/P-yes/H-no
French

Full breakfast from menu
Lunch, dinner, bar
Sitting room, piano
entertainment, tennis
bikes, golf, surfing

Furnished with period antiques, resort setting, National Park beaches, sand dunes, windsurfing, bicycle packages and all-you-can-eat lobster smorgasbord daily.

DALVAY AREA

Dalvay By The Sea Hotel
P.O. Box 8, C0A IP0
East End National Park
902-672-2048
David R. Thompson
June 1–Oct. 1

$$$ B&B/MAP
26 rooms, 26 pb
Visa, MC, AmEx ●
C-yes/H-yes
French, Spanish

lunch, dinner
Restaurant, bar service
Sitting room, library
bicycles, tennis court
croquet green, canoes

Victorian inn located 200 yards from a spectacular beach. Very relaxing, romantic atmosphere. Excellent cuisine.

MONTAGUE

Partridges' B&B
Panmure Island, RR2, C0A 1R0
902-838-4687
Gertrude Partridge
All year

$ B&B
7 rooms, 5 pb
Visa ●
C-yes/S-no/P-yes/H-yes

Full breakfast
Sitting room, library
guests may use bicycles
canoe and row boat

Five minute walk to a beautiful, clean, quiet beach of white sand. Grocery stores, excellent restaurants, lobster fishing & golf all nearby.

MURRAY RIVER

Bayberry Cliff Inn B&B
RR 4, Little Sands, C0A 1W0
902-962-3395
Nancy & Don Perkins
May 15–September

$ B&B
7 rooms
Visa, MC
C-yes
Spanish

Full breakfast
Sitting room
Library, craft shop
stairs down 40-ft. cliff to
shore

Two remodeled post & beam barns 50 feet from edge of cliff. Furnishings: antiques, marine paintings. 8 minutes to W.I.'s ferry. Five levels. Perfect for honeymooners.

SUMMERSIDE

Silver Fox Inn
61 Granville St., C1N 2Z3
902-436-4033
Julie Simmons
All year

$$ B&B
6 rooms, 6 pb
Visa, MC, AmEx ●
C-no/S-yes/P-no/H-no

Continental plus
Sitting room
piano

Restored 1892 house with antique furnishings. Sun room, sitting room with fireplace, and balcony for guests. Breakfast with homemade muffins, jams, farm eggs.

VERNON RIVER

Lea's Hobby Farm B&B
C0A 2E0
902-651-2501 902-651-2051
Ralph & Dora Lea
All year

$ EP
5 rooms, 1 pb
C-yes/S-yes/P-no/H-no

Full breakfast $3.25
Continental plus $2
Hot tub
sitting room, piano

Small farm with beef cattle, pheasants, rabbits and a bird dog called Tipsy. Bedrooms with two double beds, some with one double bed. Country breakfasts.

More Inns ...

Allix's B&B 11 Johnson Av., Charlottetown, C1A 3H7 902-892-2643
Amber Lights B&B P.O. Box 14, Route 26, York, C0A 1P0 902-894-5868
Anchors Aweigh B&B 45 Queen Elizabeth Dr., Charlottetown, C1A 3A8 902-892-4319
Bayberry Cliff Inn B&B RR 4, Little Sands, Murray River, C0A IW0 902-962-3395
Beach Point View Inn RR 5, Kensington, C0B 1M0 902-836-5260
Blakeney's B&B 15 MacLean Ave., Box 17, Kensington, C0B 1M0 902-836-3254
Brydon's B&B Heatherdale RR 1, Montague, C0A 1R0 902-838-4747
Carr's Corner Farm Tourist Route 12, Miscouche, C0B 1T0 902-436-6287
Chez-Nous B&B Ferry Rd., RR 4, Corwan, C0A 1H0 902-566-2779
Churchill Farm T.H. RR3, Bonshaw, C0A 1C0 902-675-2481
Creekside Farm B&B Stanley Bridge, C0A 1E0 902-886-2713
Doctor's Inn B&B Tyne Valley, C0B 2C0 902-831-2164
Dundee Arms Inn 200 Pownal St., Charlottetown, C1A 3W8 902-892-2496
Dyment Bed & Breakfast Summerside RR#, Wilmot Valley, C1N 4J9 902-436-9893
Elmwood P.O. Box 3128, Charlottetown, CIA 7N8 902-368-3310
Enman's Farm B&B P.O. RR 2 Vernon Bridge, Vernon Bridge, C0A 2E0 902-651-2427
Faye & Eric's B&B 380 Mac Ewen Road, Summerside, C1N 4X8 902-436-6847
Fralor Farm Tourist Home RR 1, Kensington, Darnley, C0B 1M0 902-836-5300
Green Valley B&B Box 714, Kensington, Spring Valley, C0B 1M0 902-836-5667
Gulf Breeze Stanley Bridge, C0A 1E0 902-886-2678
Harbour Lights T. H. RR #2, Tignish, C0B 2B0 902-882-2479
Harbourview B&B RR 1, Murray Harbour, C0A 1V0 902-962-2565
Joyce's Tourist Home North Rustico, C0A 1X0 902-963-2257
Just Folks B&B RR 5, Charlottetown, C1A 7J8 902-569-2089
Kelly's Bed & Breakfast Box 20, Morell, C0A 1S0 902-961-2389
Laine Acres B&B Cornwall RR2, Nine Mile Creek, C0A 1H0 902-675-2402
Lazydays Farm B&B RR1, Belfast, C0A 1A0 902-659-2267
Linden Lodge RR 3, Belfast, C0A 1A0 902-659-2716
MacCallum's B&B Route 2, Saint Peters Bay, C0A 2A0 902-961-2957
MacLeod's Farm B&B UIGG, Vernon P.O., Vernon, C0A 2E0 902-651-2303
Manor House B&B 65 Main St. South, Montague, C0A 1R0 902-838-2224
Murphy's Sea View B&B Route 20, Kensington, C0B 1M0 902-836-5456
Obanlea Farm Tourist Home RR 4 North River PO, Cornwall, C0A 1H0 902-566-3067
Redcliffe Farm B&B RR1, Montague, Brooklyn, C0A 1R0 902-838-2476
Rosevale Farm B&B Marshfield, RR 3, Charlottetown, C1A 7J7 902-894-7821
Senator's House P.O. Box 63, Tyne Vally, Port Hill, C0B 2C0 902-831-2071
Shaw's Hotel & Cottages Brackley Beach, C0A 2H0 902-672-2022
Sherwood Acres Guest Home RR 1, Kensington, C0B 1M0 902-836-5430
Shore Farm B&B Borden RR1, Augustine Cove, C0B 1X0 902-855-2871
Smallman's B&B Knutsford, RR 1, O'Leary, C0B 1V0 902-859-3469
Stanhope by the Sea P.O. Box 2109, Stanhope, C0B 1M0 902-672-2047
Strathgartney Country Inn RR #3, Bonshaw, C0A 1C0 902-675-4711
Thomas Bed & Breakfast O'Leary RR 3, Mill River, C0B 1V0 902-859-3209
Victoria Village Inn Victoria-By-The-Sea, C0A 2G0 902-658-2288
Waugh's Farm B&B Lower Bedeque, C0B 1C0 902-887-2320
West Island Inn Box 24, Tyne Valley, C0B 2C0 902-831-2495
Windsong Farm Route 6, RR 1, Winsloe, Brackley Beach, C0A 2H0 902-672-2874
Woodington's Country Inn Sea View, RR 2, Kensington, C0B 1M0 902-836-5518

Province of Quebec

AYER'S CLIFF

Ripple Cove Inn
700 Ripple Cove Rd., J0B 1C0
819-838-4296
Debra & Jeffrey Stafford
All year

$$$ MAP
24 rooms, 24 pb
Visa, MC, AmEx ●
C-yes/S-yes/P-no/H-no
French

Full breakfast, Dinner
Restaurant, bar
Comp. wine, sitting room
tennis, pool, sailing
canoes, water skiing

A charming lakeside inn on 12 private acres. Refined French cuisine. 24 deluxe rooms and suites, many with fireplaces and whirlpool bath. All water sports, tennis, X-C skiing.

MONTREAL

Armor Inn
151 Sherbrooke E., H2X 1C7
514-285-0140
Horvan Annick
All year

$ B&B
14 rooms, 7 pb
●
C-yes/S-yes/P-no/H-no
French

Continental breakfast
Comp. coffee

Once a fine Victorian townhouse in downtown Montreal. Fine woodwork in foyer and some guest rooms.

Auberge De La Fontaine
1301 E. Rachel St., H1L 6K9
514-597-0166
Celine Boudreau, Jean Lamothe
All year

$$$ B&B
21 rooms, 21 pb
Visa, MC, AmEx ●
C-12+/S-yes/P-no/H-yes
French

Continental plus buffet
Afternoon tea
Whirlpool in some rooms

Facing Parc La Fontaine (84 acres), located near downtown area. A charming inn where you are welcomed as friends. Public transportation nearby. Warm and friendly staff.

Downtown B&B
3523 Rue Jeanne-Mance, H2X 2K2
514-845-0431
Bruno Bernard
All year

$$ B&B
3 rooms
●
C-8+/S-yes/P-no/H-no
French

Continental plus
Bicycles
color TV

In the heart of downtown, residential. Color TV, phone, ventilation, limited parking, access to a different kitchen for guests. Very friendly and intimate.

Lola's B&B
5 Burton Ave., H3Z 1J6
514-483-6555
Lola Gordon
All year

$$ B&B
2 rooms
●
C-yes/S-no/P-no/H-no
French

Full breakfast
Afternoon tea, wine
Sitting room

One double, one twin in upper duplex one mile from heart of downtown and all tourist attractions. Close to metro and bus, shops, restaurants, yet very quiet.

Manoir Ambrose
3422 Stanley St., H3A 1R8
514-288-6922 FAX:288-5757
Lucie Seguin
All year

$ B&B
22 rooms, 17 pb
Visa, MC ●
C-yes/S-yes/P-no/H-no
Eng., Fr., Span., Ger.

Continental breakfast
Phone in each room
cable TV, sitting room
air conditioning

Perfect location of this Victorian-style lodge close to McGill University, musee, restaurants, shopping center. Quiet surroundings and friendly home atmosphere.

NEW CARLISLE

Bay View Manor	$ B&B	Full breakfast
P.O. Box 21, G0C 1Z0	6 rooms, 2 pb	Lunch, dinner
395 Fauvel, Route 132	C-yes/P-no	Sitting room, library
418-752-2725 418-752-6718	French	tennis courts, pool
Helen Sawyer		near golf, cottage avail
All year		

Seaside country haven, yet on a main highway. Fresh farm produce. August Folk Festival. Quilts, handicrafts and home-baking on sale. Cottage at $250 per week also available.

NOTRE DAME DES ANGES

Batiscan River's Domain	$$ B&B/$$$ AP	Full breakfast
974 Rte Rousseau Rd., G0X 1N0	3 rooms	Dinner (by request) ·
418-336-2619	C-yes/S-yes/P-yes/H-no	Aftn. tea, comp. wine
F. Lavoie, F. Beaulieu	French	library, bicycles, river
All year		sandy beach, footpath

In heart of Quebec, on shores of Batiscan River, our log house will charm you. Visit our Maple orchard, beaches, 300-acre property. Green in summer, white in winter. Welcome!

POINTE-AU-PIC

Auberge Donohue	$$ B&B	Continental plus
145 Principale, CP 211, G0T 1M0	17 rooms, 17 pb	Afternoon tea, piano
418-665-4377	●	Sitting room, pool
Aumont Orval	C-ltd/S-yes/P-no/H-no	fireplaces, garden
All year	French	whirlpool/frplce. avail.

Cozy house situated right by the St. Lawrence River. Very large living room with fireplace. Every room has private bath; most rooms have view of the river.

QUEBEC CITY

Chateau de la Terrasse	$$ EP
6 Terrasse Dufferin, G1R 4N5	18 rooms, 18 pb
418-694-9472	C-yes/S-yes/P-no/H-no
C. Detcheverry	French, English
February–November	

Located inside the walls of Old Quebec, on the boardwalk. Front rooms overlook St. Lawrence River

Le Chateau De Pierre Inc.	$$$ EP	Kitchenettes in 2 units
17 Ave. Ste-Genevieve, G1R 4A8	15 rooms, 15 pb	Color cable TVs
418-694-0429	Visa, MC ●	air-conditioned
Lily & Richard Couturier	C-yes/S-ltd/P-no/H-no	garage parking
All year	French, Spanish	

Old English colonial mansion with colonial charm. Fine appointments and distinctive atmosphere. Located in Old Quebec Uppertown. Walk to Citadell, shopping, historical points.

Maison Marie Rollet	$$ EP
81, rue Ste-Anne, G1R 3X4	10 rooms, 10 pb
418-694-9271	Visa ●
Fernand Blouin	C-yes/S-yes/P-no/H-no
All year	French

Well situated, in the center of Old Quebec facing the City Hall. Parking across the street. Quiet Victorian house.

QUEBEC CITY

Manoir Ste Genevieve
13 Ave. Ste-Genevieve, G1R 4A7
418-694-1666
Marguerite Corriveau
All year

$$$ EP
9 rooms, 9 pb
C-yes/S-yes/P-no/H-no
French

Continental plus ($)
Fresh flowers
window boxes

Manor with modern facilities, furnished with antiques. Friendly and comfortable. Located behind Chateau Frontenac, on the St. Lawrence River. Walk to all points of interest.

SAINT ANTOINE DE TILLY

Auberge Manoir de Tilly
3854 Chemin de Tilly, G0S 2C0
418-886-2407 FAX:886-2595
Jocelyne & Majella Gagnon
All year

$$$ B&B
32 rooms, 32 pb
Visa, MC, AmEx, EnRoute
●
C-yes/S-ltd/P-no/H-ltd
French, English

Full breakfast
Dinner available
Piano, swimming pool
bicycles, shuffleboard
golf, tennis nearby

200-year-old manor on St. Lawrence River shores. Furnished in antiques. Fifteen miles from Quebec Bridge (gate of Old City). Antique stores nearby. Whirlpools in some rooms.

ST-MARC-SUR-RICHELIEU

Auberge Handfield Inn
555 Richelieu, J0L 2E0
514-584-2226
Conrad Handfield
All year

$$ EP/MAP (wint)
53 rooms, 53 pb
Visa, MC, AmEx, DC ●
C-yes/S-yes/P-no/H-yes
French

Full breakfast $
Restaurant, bar service
Aftn. tea, snacks
pool, horseback riding
tennis courts, marina

Country inn on the River Sibe. Ancestral house, 165 years old. All rooms decorated with antiques. Marina available for traveling sailors.

SUTTON

Auberge Schweizer
357 Schweizer Rd., J0E 2K0
514-538-2129
Heidi or Pauline

$ MAP

Full breakfast
Dinner

Simple lodging; two persons per room; beautiful 3 bedroom house available. Quiet mountain farm setting. Meals are just great—vegetarian food on request.

More Inns ...

Antonio Costa 101 Northview, Montreal, H4X 1C9 514-486-6910
Au Chateau Fleur de Lis 15 Ave. Ste. Genevieve, Quebec City, G1R 4A8 418-694-1884
Au Petit Hotel 3 Ruelle des Ursulines, Vieux–Quebec, G1R 3Y6 418-694-0965
Auberge De La Chouette 71 Rue D'Auteuil, Quebec City, G1K 5Y4 418-694-0232
Auberge Du Lac Des Sables 230 St. Venant, C.P.213, Ste.-Agathe, J8C 2A3 819-326-7016
Auberge Hollandaise Route 329, Morin Heights, G0R 1H0 514-226-2009
Auberge La Goeliche Inn 22 Rue du Quai, Sainte Petronille, G0A 4C0 418-828-2248
Auberge La Martre La Martre, Comte de Mantane, G0E 2H0 418-288-5533
Auberge La Pinsonniere 124 St. Raphael, Cap-A-L'aigh, G0T 1B0 418-665-4431
Auberge Laketree RR 2, Stage Coach Rd., Knowlton, J0E 1V0 514-243-6604
Auberge Le Coin Du Banc Route 132, Coin du Banc-Perce, G0C 2L0 418-645-2907
Auberge Sauvignon Route 327, Mont Tremblant, J0T 1Z0 819-425-2658
Auberge St-Denis 61, St-Denis, CP 1229, Saint Sauveur Des Monts, J0R 1R0 514-227-4766
Auberge du Vieux Foyer 3167 Doncaster, Val David, J0T 2N0 819-322-2686
Chalet Caribou Lodge Lac Superieur, J0T 1P0 819-688-5201
Chateau Beauvallon, Inc. 616 Montee Ryan, Box138, Mont Tremblant, J0T 1Z0
819-425-7275
Chateau de la Terrasse 6 Terrasse Dufferin, Quebec City, G1R 4N5 418-694-9472
Chez les Dumas 1415 Chemin Royal, St., Ile d'Orleans, G0A 3Z0 418-828-9442
Edale Place Edale Pl., Portneuf, G0A 2Y0 418-286-3168

France Beaulieu House 211 Chemin dela Travers, Portneuf, G0A 2Y0 418-336-2724
Georgeville Country Inn CP P.O. Box 17, Georgeville, J0B 1T0 819-843-8683
Gite du Mont Albert Case Postale 1150, Saint Anne des Mont, G0E 2G0 418-763-2288
Gite du Passant B&B 81 Ave. Morel, Kamouraska, G0L 1M0 418-492-2921
Hatley Inn P.O. Box 330, North Hatley, J0B 2C0 819-842-2451
Hazelbrae Farm 1650 English River Rd., Howick, J0S 1G0 514-825-2390
Henry House 105 DuParc, St. Simeon, Gaspesie, G0C 3A0 418-534-2115
Hostellerie Les Trois Till 290 rue Richelieu, St.-Marc-Sur-Richelieu, J0L 2E0 514-584-2231
Hostellerie Rive Gauche 1810 boul. Richelieu, Beloeil, J3G 4S4 514-467-4650
Hotel la Normandie P.O. Box 129, Perce, Gaspe Peninsula, G0G 2L0 418-782-2112
Hovey Manor P.O. Box 60, North Hatley, J0B 2C0 819-842-2421
La Maison Otis 23 R. St. Jean Baptiste, Baie Saint Paul, G0A 1B0 418-435-2255
La Muse 39, St-Jean-Baptiste, Baie St-Paule, GOA 1BO 418-435-6939
Le Breton 1609 St. Hubert, Montreal East, H2L 3Z1 514-524-7273
Leduc 1128CH Riviere de Guerr, Huntington, J0S 1M0 514-264-6533
Maison sous les Arbres 145 Chemin Royal, Saint Laurent, G0A 3Z0 418-828-9442
Manoir des Erables 220 Du Manoir, Montmagny, G54 V1G 418-248-0100
Maplewood Malenfant Rd., Dunham, J0E 1M0 514-295-2519
Memory Lane Farm RR #1, Quyon, J0X 2V0 819-458-2479
Otter Lake Haus C.S. 29, CH Trudel, Huberdeau, J0T 1G0 819-687-2767
Parker's Lodge 1340 Lac Paquin, Val David, J0T 2N0 819-322-2026
Pelletier House 334 de la Seigneurie, Saint Roch Des Aulnaies, G0R 4E0 418-354-2450
Perras 1552 RR 1, Waterloo, J0E 1N0 514-539-2983
Steiner Family 266 Montee Steiner, Thurso, J0X 3B0 819-985-2359
Willow Inn 208 Main Rd., Como, J0P 1A0 514-458-7006
Willow Place Inn 208 Main St., Hudson, J0P 1A0 514-458-7006

Saskatchewan

More Inns ...

B & J's B&B 2066 Ottawa St., Regina, S4P 1P8 306-522-4575
Bonshaw House Box 67, Grenfell, S0G 2B0 306-697-2654
Dee Bar One Box 51, Truax, S0H 4A0 306-868-4614
Eastons' Farm Box 58, Wawota, S0G 5A0 306-739-2910
Ellis Farm Box 84, Balcarres, S0G 0C0 306-334-2238
Lakeside Leisure Farm P.O. Box 1, Meota, S0M 1X0 306-892-2145
Moldenhauer's Farm Box 214, Allan, S0K 0C0 306-257-3578
Pipestone View Ranch General Delivery, Percival, S0G 3Y0 306-735-2858
Pleasant Vista Angus Farm Box 194, Wawota, S0G 5A0 306-739-2915
Prairie Acres B&B Box 1658, Tisdale, S0E 1T0 306-873-2272
Sargent's Holiday Farm Box 204, Borden, S0K 0N0 306-997-2230
Silent Hollow Farms Box 25, Meskanaw, S0K 2W0 306-864-3728
Sugden Simmental Vacation Box 2, Peebles, S0G 3V0 306-697-3169
Sweetgrass Farms B&B Box 218, Rose Valley, S0E 1M0 306-322-2217
Tiger Lily Farm Box 135, Burstall, S0N 0H0 306-679-4709
Turgeon International Hse 2310 McIntyre St., Regina, S4P 2S2 306-522-4200
Vereshagin's Country Place Box 89, Blaine Lake, S0J 0J0 306-497-2782

Reservation Service Organizations

These are businesses through which you can reserve a room in thousands of private homes. In many cases, rooms in homes are available where there may not be an inn. Also, guest houses are quite inexpensive. RSOs operate in different ways. Some represent a single city or state. Others cover the entire country. Some require a small membership fee. Others sell a list of their host homes. Many will attempt to match you with just the type of accomodations you're seeking and you may pay the RSO directly for your lodging.

Reservation Service Organization by Region—See main RSO listings under the state headings in this section for full description.

NORTHEAST

B&B International
San Francisco, CA

New Hampshire B&B
Guilford, CT

Bed & Breakfast, Ltd.
New Haven, CT

Covered Bridge B&B Reserv. Serv.
Norfolk, CT

Nutmeg B&B Agency
West Hartford, CT

B&B League/Sweet Dreams & Toast
Washington, DC

Bed 'n' Breakfast Ltd.
Washington, DC

B&B of Delaware
Wilmington, DE

A B&B Above the Rest
Boston, MA

A B&B Agency of Boston
Boston, MA

B&B Associates Bay Colony, Ltd.
Boston, MA

Host Homes of Boston
Boston, MA

Greater Boston Hospitality
Brookline, MA

B&B Cambridge & Gtr Boston
Cambridge, MA

Pineapple Hospitality Inc.
New Bedford, MA

New England B&B
Newton Center, MA

House Guests Cape Cod & Islands
Orleans, MA

Be Our Guest B&B, Ltd.
Plymouth, MA

Bed & Breakfast USA
South Egremont, MA

Bed & Breakfast Cape Cod
West Hyannisport, MA

Berkshire Bed & Breakfast Homes
Williamsburg, MA

Traveller in Maryland
Annapolis, MD

Amanda's B&B Reservation
Baltimore, MD

Bed & Breakfast Down East, Ltd.
Eastbrook, ME

B&B Adventures
Midland Park, NJ

B&B of Princeton
Princeton, NJ

Bed & Breakfast USA, Ltd.
Croton-on-Hudson, NY

American Country Collection B&B
Del Mar, NY

Elaine's B&B & Inn Reservation
Elbridge, NY

...Aaah! B&B #1
New York, NY

Abode Bed & Breakfast, Ltd.
New York, NY

At Home in New York
New York, NY

B&B Network of New York
New York, NY

Bed & Breakfast (& Books)
New York, NY

City Lights B&B, Ltd.
New York, NY

New World Bed & Breakfast
New York, NY

Urban Ventures, Inc.
New York, NY

American Country Collection
Schenectady, NY

B&B Connection NY
Vernon, NY

B&B of Chester County
Kennett Square, PA

B&B of Philadelphia
Philadelphia, PA

All About Town - B&B Philadelphia
Valley Forge, PA

Guesthouses, Inc.
West Chester, PA

Anna's Victorian Connection
Newport, RI

B&B of Rhode Island
Newport, RI

Blue Ridge B&B
Berryville, VA

SOUTHEAST

Bed & Breakfast Atlanta
Atlanta, GA

Savannah Historic Inns
Savannah, GA

Quail Country B&B, Ltd.
Thomasville, GA

Bed & Breakfast USA
South Egremont, MA

Amanda's B&B Reservation
Baltimore, MD

Charleston Society B&B
Charleston, SC

Historic Charleston B&B
Charleston, SC

Charleston East B&B League
Mount Pleasant, SC

Princely B&B Ltd.
Alexandria, VA

Blue Ridge B&B
Berryville, VA

Guesthouses B&B, Inc.
Charlottesville, VA

Bensonhouse Reservation Service
Richmond, VA

NORTH CENTRAL

B&B International
San Francisco, CA

Bed & Breakfast/Chicago
Chicago, IL

B&B NW Suburban—Chicago
Hoffman Estates, IL

Bluegrass Bed & Breakfast
Versailles, KY

Ozark Mountain Country B&B
Branson, MO

B&B Kansas City
Lenexa, KS, MO

B&B Western Adventure
Billings, MT

Bed & Breakfast USA, Ltd.
Croton-on-Hudson, NY

Columbus Bed & Breakfast
Columbus, OH

B&B of Milwaukee, Inc.
South Milwaukee, WI

South Central

Bed & Breakfast Montgomery
Montgomery, AL

Arkansas Ozarks B&B Reservation
Calico Rock, AR

New Orleans B&B
Metairie, LA

Ozark Mountain Country B&B
Branson, MO

Lincoln, Ltd. Mississippi Reserv.
Meridian, MS

Natchez Pilgrimage Tours
Natchez, MS

B&B — Tennessee
Nashville, TN

B&B of Fredericksburg
Fredericksburg, TX

Gästhaus Schmidt Reserv. Serv.
Fredericksburg, TX

B&B Society of Texas
Houston, TX

B&B Hosts of San Antonio
San Antonio, TX

NORTHWEST

Alaska Private Lodgings
Anchorage, AK

Alaska B&B Association
Juneau, AK

Kodiak Bed & Breakfast
Kodiak, AK

Bed & Breakfast of Idaho
Boise, ID

B&B Western Adventure
Billings, MT

Ashland's B&B Network
Ashland, OR

Country Host Registry
Myrtle Creek, OR

Pacific B&B Agency
Seattle, WA

SOUTHWEST

Bed & Breakfast In Arizona
Scottsdale, AZ

Mi Casa Su Casa
Tempe, AZ

Old Pueblo Homestays B&B
Tucson, AZ

Eye Openers B&B Reservations
Altadena, CA

Bed & Breakfast Exchange
Calistoga, CA

B&B of Southern California
Fullerton, CA

S.S. Seafoam Lodge
Mendocino, CA

American Family Inn-B&B SF
San Francisco, CA

B&B International
San Francisco, CA

B&B of Los Angeles
Westlake Village, CA

CoHost, America's B&B
Whittier, CA

Bed & Breakfast Colorado
Boulder, CO

B&B - Rocky Mountains, Inc.
Denver, CO

Bed & Breakfast Vail/Ski Areas
Vail, CO

Go Native. .Hawaii
Hilo, HI

B&B Honolulu & Statewide
Honolulu, HI

All Islands B&B
Kailua, Oahu, HI

Pacific-Hawaii B&B
Kailua, Oahu, HI

Bed & Breakfast Hawaii
Kapaa, Kauai, HI

B&B of New Mexico
Santa Fe, NM

EASTERN CANADA

Niagara Regional/On The Lake
Niagara Falls, ON

Ottawa Area B&B
Ottawa, ON

Downtown Toronto Assoc. of B&Bs
Toronto, ON

Toronto Bed & Breakfast Inc.
Toronto, ON

A Bed & Breakfast
Montreal, PQ

B&B Relais Montreal Hospitality
Montreal, PQ

B&B Bonjour Québec
Quebec, PQ

WESTERN CANADA

A.A. Accommodations West
Victoria, BC

All Seasons B&B Agency, Inc.
Victoria, BC

B&B of Manitoba
Winnipeg, MB

Canada-West Accommodations
North Vancouver, BC

Old English B&B Registry
North Vancouver, BC

Town & Country B&B in B.C.
Vancouver, BC

INTERNATIONAL

CoHost, America's B&B
Whittier, CA

Bed & Breakfast Vail/Ski Areas
Vail, CO

Go Native. .Hawaii
Hilo, HI

Traveller in Maryland
Annapolis, MD

B&B Adventures
Midland Park, NJ

... Aaah! B&B #1
New York, NY

At Home in New York
New York, NY

City Lights B&B, Ltd.
New York, NY

Urban Ventures, Inc.
New York, NY

Guesthouses, Inc.
West Chester, PA

B&B Bonjour Québec
Quebec, PQ

Charleston East B&B League
Mount Pleasant, SC

B&B — Tennessee
Nashville, TN

ALABAMA

Bed & Breakfast Montgomery P.O. Box 1026 Montgomery, AL 36101	205-264-0056 FAX: 205-262-1872 $ Dep. $20	Free brochure Montgomery, AL 8am-10pm 7 days

ALASKA

Alaska Private Lodgings P.O. Box 200047-PL Anchorage, AK 99520	907-248-2292 $ Dep. 1 night Ger,Fr,Sp	Brochure $2.50 Alaska 8am-5pm (M-F)
Alaska B&B Association P.O. Box 21890 Juneau, AK 99801	907-586-2959 FAX: 907-463-6788 $$ Visa, MC, AmEx Ger,Tlinget	Free brochure Alaska 8am-5pm M-F
Kodiak Bed & Breakfast 308 Cope St. Kodiak, AK 99615	907-486-5367 $$ Dep. $10 Visa, MC Sp	Brochure Alaska Evenings

More RSOs ...

Accomodations Alaska Style, 3605 Arctic Blvd Box173, Anchorage, AK, 99503 907-344-4006

Fairbanks Bed & Breakfast, P.O. Box 74573, Fairbanks, AK, 99707 907-452-4967

Ketchikan Bed & Breakfast, P.O. Box 7735, Ketchikan, AK, 99801 907-225-3860

Sourdough Bed & Breakfast, 339-BW Cardigan Circle, Anchorage, AK, 99503

ARIZONA

| **Mi Casa Su Casa**
P.O. Box 950
Tempe, AZ 85281 | 602-990-0682
800-456-0682
$
Dep. $25 or 1 night
Fr,Ger,Sp,It,Port,Rom,Ch | Directory $5
Arizona/NM/Ut
8am-8pm 7 days |

More RSOs...
Arizona Assoc. of B&B Inns, 3661 N. Campbell, Tucson, AZ, 85719
Florence A. Ejrup RSO, 941 W. Calle Dadivoso, Tucson, AZ, 85704
Inter-Bed, 5708 N. Via Lozana, Tucson, AZ, 85715 602-323-4045
Valley o' the Sun B&B, P.O. Box 2214, Scottsdale, AZ, 85252 602-941-1281

ARKANSAS

| **Arkansas Ozarks B&B**
Reservation
HC 61, Box 72
Calico Rock, AR 72519 | 501-297-8764
501-297-8211
$
Dep. 1 night
Visa, MC
Fr | Brochure SASE
Arkansas
8am-6pm Mon-Sat |

More RSOs...
B&B Reservation Services, 11 Singleton, Eureka Springs, AR, 72632 501-253-9111

CALIFORNIA

| **Eye Openers B&B**
Reservations
P.O. Box 694
Altadena, CA 91003 | 213-684-4428
818-797-2055
$
Dep. $25
Visa, MC
Sp,Fr,Ger,Hun,Rus,Heb | List $1 with SASE
California
9am-6pm M-F |

| **Bed & Breakfast Exchange**
1458 Lincoln Ave. Suite 3
Calistoga, CA 94515 | 707-942-2924
800-942-2924
$$
Dep. 1 night
Visa, MC
Sw,Ger,Fin,Lith | Northern CA
8:30am-5pm M-F |

| **B&B of Southern California**
1943 Sunny Crest, Suite 304
Fullerton, CA 92635 | 714-738-8361
FAX: 714-525-0702
$$$
Dep. 20%
Directory $5
Sp,Fr,Ger,Du,It,ASL,Lith | Directory $5
Brochure SASE
California
8:30-4:30 M-Th |

| **S.S. Seafoam Lodge**
P.O. Box 68
Mendocino, CA 95460 | 707-937-1827
$$$
Visa, MC | Brochure SASE
California
9am-9pm daily |

| **B&B International**
P.O. Box 282910
San Francisco, CA 94128 | 415-696-1690
FAX: 415-696-1699
$$
Dep. $25
Visa/MC/AmEx/DC
Fr,Ger,It,Ch,Jap,Sp, | SASE brochure
CA/HI/NV/IL/NY
9am-5pm M-F |

B&B of Los Angeles 32074 Waterside Lane Westlake Village, CA 91361	818-889-8870 $ Dep 20% or CrCd Visa, MC	Brochure $2 California 9am-8pm M-F
CoHost, America's B&B P.O. Box 9302 Whittier, CA 90608	213-699-8427 $$ Dep. $25 Free brochure	Free brochure Listing $3 CA/Can/Jp/Ger/UK 7am-7pm daily

More RSOs...

B&B Approved Hosts, 10890 Galvin, Ventura, CA, 93004 805-647-0651
B&B Exchange of Marin, 45 Entrata Ave., San Anselmo, CA, 94960 415-485-1971
B&B Hospitality, 823 La Mirada Ave., Leucadia, CA, 92024 619-436-6850
B&B Laguna Beach, P.O. Box 388, San Juan Capistrano, CA, 92693 714-496-7050
B&B/Monterey Peninsula, P.O. Box 1193, Pebble Beach, CA, 93953 408-372-7425
Bed & Breakfast Almanac, P.O. Box 295, Saint Helena, CA, 94574 707-963-0852
Bed & Breakfast Homestay, P.O. Box 326, Cambria, CA, 93428 805-927-4613
Calif. Houseguests Int'l., P.O. Box 643, Tarzana, CA, 91356 818-344-7878
Carolyn's B&B Homes, 416 Third Ave., Chula Vista, CA, 92010 619-422-7009
El Camino Real B&B, P.O. Box 7155, Northridge, CA, 91327 818-363-6753
Hospitality Plus, P.O. Box 388, San Juan Capistrano, CA, 92693 714-496-7050
Megan's Friends B&B Res., 1776 Royal Way, San Luis Obispo, CA, 93401 805-544-4406
Mendocino Coast Reserv., 1001 Main St., Box 1034, Mendocino, CA, 95460 707-937-1913
Napa Valley's Finest Ldgs., 1557 Madrid Ct., Napa, CA, 94559 707-224-4667
Paradise Vacation Rentals, 45005 Ukiah St, Box 208, Mendocino, CA, 95460
Pilots International B&B, PO Box 1847, Columbia, CA, 95310
Place to Stay, 14497 New Jersey, San Jose, CA, 95124
Rent A Room B&B, 11531 Varna St., Garden Grove, CA, 92640 714-638-1406
Reservations Plus, 1141 Merrimac Dr., Sunnyvale, CA, 94807
Unique Housing, 81 Plaza Dr., Berkeley, CA, 94705 415-658-3494
Visitor's Advisory Service, P.O. Box 1753, Alameda, CA, 94510
Wine Country B&B, P.O. Box 3211, Santa Rosa, CA, 95403 707-578-1661

COLORADO —

B&B - Rocky Mountains, Inc. 906 S. Pearl St. Denver, CO 80209	719-630-3433 $ Dep. 1 night Visa, MC Free small broch.	Free small broch. Directory $4.50 CO, Utah, NM 9:30am-5:30pm M-F
Bed & Breakfast Vail/Ski Areas P.O. Box 491 Vail, CO 81658	303-949-1212 800-748-2666 $$ Dep. or CrCd Visa, MC Ger,Sp	Brochure $2 CO, Worlwide 9am-5pm M-F

More RSOs ...

B&B Cambridge Club, 1550 Sherman St., Denver, CO, 80903

CONNECTICUT —

New Hampshire B&B 329 Lake Dr. Guilford, CT 06437	603-279-8348 $ Dep. 1 night Fr,Sp,Gr	List $2 New Hampshire 9am-8pm 7 days

Bed & Breakfast, Ltd. P.O. Box 216 New Haven, CT 06513	203-469-3260 $$ Dep. 20% Travelers checks Fr,Sp,Ger	Free list SASE CT, MA, RI 5-9:30pm Sept-Jun
Covered Bridge B&B Reserv. **Serv.** P.O. Box 447, 69 Maple Ave. Norfolk, CT 06058	203-542-5944 800-488-5690 $$ Dep. full Visa, MC, AmEx Free listing SASE Fr	Free listing SASE Booklet $3 CT, MA, NY, RI/VT 9am-6pm M-F
Nutmeg B&B Agency P.O. Box 1117 West Hartford, CT 06127	203-236-6698 800-727-7592 $$ Dep. or CrCd Visa, MC, AmEx	Brochure $5 CT, NY, MA, RI 9:30am-5pm M-F

More RSOs...
Alexander's B&B Res. Serv., P.O. Box 1182, Sharon, CT, 06069 203-364-0505
Four Seasons Int'l B&B, 11 Bridlepath Rd., West Simsbury, CT, 06092 203-651-3045
Nautilus Bed & Breakfast, 133 Phoenix Drive, Groton, CT, 06340 203-448-1538
Seacoast Landings, 133 Neptune Drive, Groton, CT, 06340 203-442-1940

DISTRICT OF COLUMBIA

B&B League/Sweet Dreams **& Toast** P.O. Box 9490 Washington, DC 20016	202-363-7767 $$ Dep. $25 Visa/MC/AmEx/DC	Free brochure Washington, D.C., 9am-5pm M-Th
Bed 'n' Breakfast Ltd. P.O. Box 12011 Washington, DC 20005	202-328-3510 $$ Dep. $50 Visa/MC/AmEx/DC Fr,Sp	Free brochure Washington, D.C. 10am-5pm M-F

FLORIDA

More RSOs...
A & A B&B of Florida, P.O. Box 1316, Winter Park, FL, 32790 305-628-3233
B&B Company—Tropical Florida, P.O. Box 262, South Miami, FL, 33243 305-661-3270
B&B Homestays of Florida, 8690 Gulf Blvd., Saint Pete Beach, FL, 33706 813-360-1753
B&B of the Florida Keys, 5 Man-O-War Dr., Marathon, FL, 33050 305-743-4118
Central Florida B&B, 719 SE 4th St., Ocala, FL, 32671 904-351-1167
Key West Reservation Service, 628 Fleming St., P.O. Box 1689, Key West, FL, 33041
800-327-4831
Magic Bed & Breakfast, 8328 Curry Ford Rd., Orlando, FL, 32822 407-277-6602
Open House B&B Registry, P.O. Box 3025, Palm Beach, FL, 33480 407-842-5190

GEORGIA

Bed & Breakfast Atlanta 1801 Piedmont NE, Suite 208 Atlanta, GA 30324	404-875-0525 404-875-9672 $ Dep. $40 Visa/MC/AmEx/DC Heb,Fr,Ger,Yid	Brochure SASE GA, Metro Atla. 9am-5pm M-F

Quail Country B&B, Ltd. 1104 Old Monticello Rd. Thomasville, GA 31792	912-226-7218 912-226-6882 $ Dep. $25	Free brochure Thomasville, GA 9am-9pm 7 days

More RSOs...

Atlanta Hospitality, 2472 Lauderdale Dr., Atlanta, GA, 30345 404-493-1930
Bed & Breakfast Inns, 117 West Gordon St., Savannah, GA, 31401 912-238-0518
R.S.V.P. Savannah B&B, 417 E. Charlton St., Savannah, GA, 31401 912-232-7787
Savannah Area Visitors, 222 W. Oglethorpe Ave., Savannah, GA, 31499 912-944-0444

HAWAII

Go Native ... Hawaii P.O. Box 11418 Hilo, HI 96721	808-935-4178 800-662-8483 $$ Dep. 20% Directory $2 Ger,Sp,Sw,Jap,Kor	Directory $2 Free brochure HI, US. Worldwide 8am-6pm M-Sat
B&B Honolulu & Statewide 3242 Kaohinani Dr. Honolulu, HI 96817	808-595-7533 800-288-4666 $ Dep. 3 days or 50% Visa, MC	Free brochure Hawaiian Islands 8am-5pm M-F
All Islands B&B 823 Kainui Dr. Kailua, Oahu, HI 96734	800-542-0344 808-263-2342 $ Dep. 20% Visa, MC, AmEx	Free brochure Hawaii 8am-5pm M-F
Bed & Breakfast Hawaii P.O. Box 449 Kapaa, Kauai, HI 96746	808-822-7771 800-733-1632 $$ Dep. 20% Visa, MC Free brochure Ger,Fr,Hun,Swiss	Free brochure Guide book $6 Hawaii all island 8:30-4:30 Mon-Fri

More RSOs ...

B&B Maui Style, P.O. Box 98, Puunene, HI, 96753 808-879-7865

ILLINOIS

Bed & Breakfast/Chicago P.O. Box 14088 Chicago, IL 60614	312-951-0085 $$ Dep. $25 or CrCd Visa, MC, AmEx Fr,Sp,Aussy,Persian	Brochure SASE Downtown Chicago 9am-5pm M-F
B&B NW Suburban—Chicago P.O. Box 95503 Hoffman Estates, IL 60195	708-310-9010 $ Dep. $40 Visa, MC, Disc	Brochure $ Illinois 9am-9pm 7 days

IDAHO

More RSOs...
Bed & Breakfast Inland Northwest, P.O. Box 2502, Coeur d'Alene, ID, 83814

INDIANA

More RSOs...
Indiana Amish Country B&B, 1600 W. Market St., Nappanee, IN, 46550 219-773-4188
Indiana B&B Association, P.O. Box 1127, Goshen, IN, 46526
InnServ Nationwide Res., Route 1, Box 68, Redkey, IN, 47373 317-369-2245
Tammy Galm Bed & Breakfast, P.O. Box 546, Nashville, IN, 47448

IOWA

More RSOs...
Bed & Breakfast In Iowa, P.O. Box 430, Preston, IA, 52069 319-689-4222

KENTUCKY

More RSOs...
Ohio Valley B&B, Inc., 6876 Taylor Mill Rd., Independence, KY, 41051 606-356-7865

LOUISIANA

New Orleans B&B	504-838-0071	Brochure SASE
671 Rosa Ave., Suite 201	504-838-0072	Louisiana
Metairie, LA 70005	$	8am-5pm M-F
	Dep. 20%	
	Visa, MC, AmEx	
	Ger,Fr,Rus	

More RSOs...
B&B Reservation Services, P.O. Box 14797, Baton Rouge, LA, 70898 504-346-1928
B&B of Louisiana, P.O. Box 8128, New Orleans, LA, 70182
Bed & Breakfast, Inc., 1021 Moss St., Box 52257, New Orleans, LA, 70152 504-488-4640
New Orleans Bed, Bath & Breakfast, P.O. Box 52466, New Orleans, LA, 70152 504-897-3867
Southern Comfort B&B Res., 2856 Hundred Oaks, Baton Rouge, LA, 70808 504-346-1928

MAINE

Bed & Breakfast Down East, Ltd.	207-565-3517	Directory $4
	$	Free brochure
Box 547, Macomber Mill Rd.	Dep 50% or 1 night	Maine
Eastbrook, ME 04634	Visa, MC, AmEx	9am-5pm M-F
	Directory $4	
	Fr,Ger,It	

More RSOs...
Bed & Breakfast of Maine, 32 Colonial Village, Falmouth, ME, 04105 207-781-4528
Nova Scotia Tourist Info., 129 Commercial St., Portland, ME, 04101

MARYLAND

Traveller in Maryland	301-269-6232	Brochure $3
P.O. Box 2277	800-736-4667 RESV	Maryland, London
Annapolis, MD 21404	$$	9-5 M-Th, 9-1pm F
	Dep. 1 night	
	Visa, MC, AmEx	

More RSOs...
Annapolis Bed & Breakfast, 235 Prince George St., Annapolis, MD, 21401
Green Street B&B, 161 Green St., Annapolis, MD, 21401

MASSACHUSETTS

A B&B Above the Rest
50 Boatswains Way #105
Boston, MA 02150

617-884-7748
800-677-2262
$$
Dep. 25%
Visa/MC/AmEx/DC

Brochure SASE
North East
8am-8pm M-F

A B&B Agency of Boston
47 Commercial Wharf
Boston, MA 02110

617-720-3540
800-CITY-BNB
$$
Dep. 30%
Visa, MC
Fr,Sp,Ger,Arab,It

Free brochure
MA, Camb., Boston
9am-9pm 7 days

B&B Associates Bay Colony, Ltd.
P.O. Box 57166, Babson Park
Boston, MA 02157

617-449-5302
FAX: 617-449-5958
$$
Dep. 30%
Visa/MC/AmEx/DC
Directory $6
Fr,Ger,It,Nor,Sp,Gr,Rus

Directory $6
Free brochure
Massachusetts
10am-5pm M-F

Host Homes of Boston
P.O. Box 117, Waban Branch
Boston, MA 02168

617-244-1308
FAX: 617-244-5156
$$
Dep. 1 night
Visa, MC, AmEx
Fr,Ger,Sp,Gr,Jap,Rus

Free brochure
MA, Bost. Cape Cd
9am-noon and

Greater Boston Hospitality
P.O. Box 1142
Brookline, MA 02146

617-277-5430
$$
Dep. 1 night
Visa, MC, AmEx
Sp,Fr,Heb,Ger,It,Pol

Brochure SASE
Massachusetts
8:30am-5:30pm M-F

House Guests Cape Cod & Islands
P.O. Box 1881
Orleans, MA 02653

800-666-HOST
617-896-7053
$
Dep. 1 night
Visa, MC, AmEx

Listing $3.95
Massachusetts
9am-7pm 7 days

Be Our Guest B&B, Ltd.
P.O. Box 1333
Plymouth, MA 02362

617-837-9867
$$
Dep. $25 or 25%
Visa, MC, AmEx
Fr

Brochure $1
Massachusetts
10am-8pm 7 days

Bed & Breakfast USA
P.O. Box 418, Old Sheffield Rd.
South Egremont, MA 01258

800-255-7213
413-528-2113
$
Dep. full
Visa, MC, AmEx
Fr,Ger,Jap,Rom,Heb

Directory $5.25
NY, NH, MA, VT,CT
10am-5pm M-F

Bed & Breakfast Cape Cod P.O. Box 341 West Hyannisport, MA 02672	508-775-2772 FAX: 508-775-2884 $$ Dep. 25% Visa, MC, AmEx	Brochure SASE MA/Cape Cd/Islnds 8:30am-6pm 7 days
Berkshire Bed & Breakfast Homes P.O. Box 211 Williamsburg, MA 01096	413-268-7244 $ Dep. 1 night Visa, MC, AmEx	Listing SASE MA, VT, NY, CT 9am-6pm Mon-Fri

More RSOs...

B&B Accom. by Guest House, P.O. Box 8, Dennis, MA, 02360
B&B Brookline/Boston, Box 732, Brookline, MA, 02146 617-277-2292
B&B House Guests—Cape Cod, Box AR, Dennis, MA, 02638 617-398-0787
B&B Marblehead/Northshore, P.O. Box 35, Newtonville, MA, 02160 508-921-1336
B&B in New England, Main Street, Williamsburg, MA, 01096 413-268-7244
B&B/The National Network, Box 4616, Springfield, MA, 01101
Battina's Bed & Breakfast, P.O. Box 585, Cambridge, MA, 02238
Dukes County Reserv. Serv., P.O. Box 2370, Oak Bluffs, MA, 02557
Educators Inn, P.O. Box 603, Lynnfield, MA, 01940 617-334-6144
Greater Springfield B&B, 25 Bellevue Avenue, Springfield, MA, 01108
Hampshire Hills B&B, P.O. Box 307, Williamsburg, MA, 01096 413-634-5529
Martha's Vineyard Reserv., P.O. Box 1769, Vineyard Haven, MA, 02568
Massachusetts B&B Hdqrtrs, P.O. Box 1703, Cotuit, MA, 02635
Nantucket Accommodations, Box 426, Nantucket, MA, 02554
Orleans B&B Associates, P.O. Box 1312, Orleans, MA, 02653 617-255-3824
University Bed & Breakfast, 12 Churchill Street, Brookline, MA, 02146
Yankee B&B of New England, 8 Brewster Rd., Hingham, MA, 02043 617-749-5007
Historic Inns of Rockport, P.O. Box 812, Rockport, MA, 01966 800-762-5778

MICHIGAN

More RSOs...

B&B in Michigan, P.O. Box 1731, Dearborn, MI, 48121 313-561-6041
B&B of Grand Rapids, 344 College S.E., Grand Rapids, MI, 49503 616-451-4849
Betsy Ross Bed & Breakfast, 701 E. Ludington Ave., Ludington, MI, 49431 313-561-6041
Capital Bed & Breakfast, 5150 Corey Rd., Williamston, MI, 48895 517-468-3434
Frankenmuth Area B&B, 337 Trinklein St., Frankenmuth, MI, 48734 517-652-8897

MINNESOTA

More RSOs...

B&B Registry Ltd., P.O. Box 8174, Saint Paul, MN, 55108 612-646-4238
Uptown Lake District B&B, 2301 Bryant Ave., Minneapolis, MN, 55405 612-872-7884

MISSISSIPPI

Lincoln, Ltd. Mississippi Reserv. P.O. Box 3479, 2303 23rd Ave Meridian, MS 39303	601-482-5483 800-633-MISS (RS) $$ Dep. 1 night Visa, MC, AmEx Fr,Ger	List $3.50 MS, AL, TN, LA 9am-5pm M-F

More RSOs...

Creative Travel B&B Center, Canal Street Depot, Natchez, MS, 39120 800-824-0355

MISSOURI

Ozark Mountain Country B&B P.O. Box 295 Branson, MO 65616	800-695-1546 417-334-4720 $ Dep. 1 night Visa, MC, AmEx	Free broch. SASE SW MO, NW AR 7:30am-10:30pm
B&B Kansas City P.O. Box 14781 Lenexa, KS, MO 66215	913-888-3636 $ Dep. 20% Visa, MC	Free list SASE Missouri, Kansas 8am-11pm

More RSOs . . .

Lexington Bed & Breakfast, 115 N. 18th St., Lexington, MO, 64067
River Country of MO & IL, #1 Grandview Heights, Saint Louis, MO, 63131 314-965-4328
Truman Country B&B, 424 N. Pleasant, Independence, MO, 64050 816-254-6657

MONTANA

B&B Western Adventure P.O. Box 20972, 806 Poly Dr. Billings, MT 59104	406-259-7993 $ Dep. 1 night or 50% Visa, MC Free brochure	Free brochure Directory $5 Mt/Wy/Id/SD 8am-5pm summer

NEBRASKA

More RSOs . . .

B&B of the Great Plains, P.O. Box 2333, Lincoln, NE, 68502 402-423-3480
Swede Hospitality B&B, 1617 Avenue A, Gothenburg, NE, 69138 308-537-2680

NEW HAMPSHIRE

More RSOs . . .

Valley Bed & Breakfast, P.O. Box 1190, Conway, NH, 03818 207-935-3799

NEW JERSEY

B&B Adventures 103 Godwin Ave., Suite 132 Midland Park, NJ 07432	800-992-2632 201-444-7409 $$ Full deposit Visa, MC, AmEx Free broch. SASE Sp,Fr,It,Ge,Ar,Sw,Yi,Lux	Free broch. SASE Directory $10 NY, NJ, PA 9:30am-4:30pm M-F
B&B of Princeton P.O. Box 571 Princeton, NJ 08540	609-924-3189 $$ Dep. 1 night	Listing SASE Princeton, NJ 24 hr. ans. mach.

More RSOs...

Cape Associates, 340 46th Place, Sea Isle, NJ, 08243
InnNovations, Inc., 118 South Ave. E, 3rd. Floor, Cranford, NJ, 07016 201-272-3600
Northern New Jersey B&B, 11 Sunset Trail, Denville, NJ, 07834

NEW MEXICO

B&B of New Mexico P.O. Box 2805 Santa Fe, NM 87504	505-982-3332 800-648-0513 $$ Dep. 50% Visa, MC	Brochure SASE New Mexico 9am-5pm M.S.T.

More RSOs...
B&B of the Southwest, P.O. Box 1357, Ruidoso, NM, 88345

NEW YORK

American Country Collection B&B 4 Greenwood Lane Del Mar, NY 12054	518-439-7001 $ Dep. 1 night or 50% Visa, MC, AmEx Free brochure	Free brochure Directory $3 VT, W. MA, E. NY 10am-1pm/2:30-5pm
Elaine's B&B & Inn Reservation 4987 Kingston Rd. Elbridge, NY 13060	315-689-2082 $$ Dep. 1 night or 50%	List SASE Central NY/W MA 10am-8pm daily
....Aaah! B&B #1 P.O. Box 200 New York, NY 10108	212-246-4000 800-776-4001 $$ Dep. 25% MC	Free brochure NY/London/Paris 9am-5pm M-F
Abode Bed & Breakfast, Ltd. P.O. Box 20022 New York, NY 10028	212-472-2000 $$$ Dep. 25%, 2 ngt min AmEx	Free brochure NY: Manh/Pk Slope 9am-5pm M-F,
At Home in New York P.O. Box 407, 140 W. 55th St. #9A New York, NY 10185	212-956-3125 FAX: 212-247-3294 $$ Dep. 25% Visa, MC, AmEx Fr,Sp,Ger	NY, Nat./Internat 9am-5pm M-F
B&B Network of New York 134 W. 32nd St, Ste 602 New York, NY 10001	212-645-8134 $$ Dep. 25%	Free brochure New York 8am-6pm M-F
Bed & Breakfast (& Books) 35 West 92nd St. New York, NY 10025	212-865-8740 $$$ Dep. 1 night or 25% Fr,Ger	Free list SASE New York City 9:30am-5pm M-F
City Lights B&B, Ltd. P.O. Box 20355, Cherokee Station New York, NY 10028	212-737-7049 FAX: 212-535-2755 $$ Dep. 25% Visa, MC, AmEx	Free brochure NYC and outer/USA 9am-5pm M-F 9am-12 Sat.
New World Bed & Breakfast 150 5th Ave., Suite 711 New York, NY 10011	212-675-5600 800-443-3800 $$ Dep. 25% Visa/MC/AmEx/DC	Free brochure Manhattan, NY 9am-5pm M-F

Urban Ventures, Inc.	212-594-5650	Free list SASE
306 West 38th St., 6th floor	FAX: 212-947-9320	NY/Eng/Fr/Belg/It
New York, NY 10018	$$	9am-5pm M-F
	Dep. 1 night	
	All mayor CrCd	

More RSOs...

A Reasonable Alternative, 117 Spring St. Ste 100, Port Jefferson, NY, 11777 516-928-4034
Alternative Lodging, P.O. Box 1782, East Hampton, NY, 11937 516-324-9449
B&B Res. Ser. of Gtr. NY, P O Box 1015, Pearl River, NY, 10965 914-735-4857
B&B Reservation Service, 162 Hook Rd., Macedon, NY, 14502 315-986-4536
B&B Western New York, 40 Maple Ave., Franklinville, NY, 14737 716-676-5704
B&B of Central New York, 4336 Fay Rd., Syracuse, NY, 13204
B&B of Columbia County, Box 122, Spencertown, NY, 12165 518-392-2358
B&B of Long Island, P.O. Box 392, Old Westbury, NY, 11568 516-334-6231
B&B of Niagara Frontier, 440 LeBrun Rd., Buffalo, NY, 14226
Blue Heron B&B Reservations W.W., 384 Pleasant Valley Rd., Groton, NY, 13073 607-803-3814
Cherry Valley Ventures, 6119 Cherry Vlley Tnpke, Lafayette, NY, 13084 315-677-9723
East End B&B, Inc., P.O. Box 178, West Hampton, NY, 11977
Finger Lakes B&B Assoc., Box 6576, Ithaca, NY, 14851
Host Homes of North Fork, Box 333, Peconic, NY, 11958 516-765-5762
House Minders & Finders, 53 University Ave., Hamilton, NY, 13346 315-824-2311
Island B&B Registry, 5 Exeter Court, Northport, NY, 11768 516-757-7398
Lodgings Plus B&B, Box 279, 319 Gerald Dr., East Hampton, NY, 11937 212-858-9589
Mid-Island B&B Res. Serv., 518 Mid-Island Plaza, Hicksville, NY, 11801 516-931-1234
North Country B&B Reserv., P.O. Box 286, Lake Placid, NY, 12946 518-523-9474
Rainbow Hospitality, 9348 Hennepin Avenue, Niagara Falls, NY, 14304 716-283-4794
Seaway Trail B&B Assoc., Box 101, Alton, NY, 14413
Tobin's B&B Guide, Rd. 2, Box 64, Rhinebeck, NY, 12572
US Virgin Isl. Gov't Trvl, 1270 Av of the Americas, New York, NY, 10020

NORTH CAROLINA

More RSOs...

B&B in the Albemarle, P. O. Box 248, Everetts, NC, 27825 919-792-4584

NORTH DAKOTA

More RSOs ...

Old West B&B Reserv. Serv., Box 211, Regent, ND, 58650

OHIO

More RSOs ...

Buckeye Bed & Breakfast, P.O. Box 130, Powell, OH, 43065 614-548-4555
Private Lodgings, Inc., P.O. Box 18590, Cleveland, OH, 44118 216-321-0400

OKLAHOMA

More RSOs...

B&B Oklahoma Style, PO Box 32045, Oklahoma City, OK, 73123 405-946-2894
Oklahoma B&B Innkeepers, 100 W. Oklahoma, Guthrie, OK, 73044

OREGON

Ashland's B&B Network	503-482-BEDS	Brochure SASE
P.O. Box 1051	Dep. 1 night	Oregon
Ashland, OR 97520	Visa, MC	9:30am-7pm daily

| Country Host Registry
901 NW Chadwick Lane
Myrtle Creek, OR 97457 | 503-863-5168
$
Visa, MC | Free brochure
Oregon/Washg.
8am-8pm |

More RSOs...
B&B Accom.–Oregon Plus, 5733 S.W. Dickinson St., Portland, OR, 97219 503-245-0642
Bend Bed & Breakfast, 19838 Ponderosa Dr., Bend, OR, 97702 503-388-3007
Gallucci Hosts Hostels B&B, P.O. Box 1303, Lake Oswego, OR, 97035 503-636-6933
Inn Formation, PO Box 1376, Ashland, OR, 97520
Northwest Bed & Breakfast, 610 SW Broadway, Portland, OR, 97205 503-243-7616
Roomservice, no business by mail, Ashland, OR, 503-488-0338
Southern Oregon Res. Ctr., PO Box 477, Ashland, OR, 97520

PENNSYLVANIA

| B&B of Chester County
P.O. Box 825
Kennett Square, PA 19348 | 215-444-1367
$
Dep. 20%
Fr,Sp,Du,Ger,It | Free brochure
Penn/Delaware
24 hours |

| B&B of Philadelphia
1616 Walnut St., Suite 1120
Philadelphia, PA 19103 | 800-220-1917
$
Dep. 1 night
Visa, MC, AmEx | Free brochure
Penn/New Jersey
9am-5pm M-F |

| All About Town - B&B
Philadelphia
P.O. Box 562
Valley Forge, PA 19481 | 215-783-7783
800-344-0123
$
Dep. 1 night
Visa/MC/AmEx/DC
Sp,Fr,It,Dutch,Ger | Free broch. SASE
Pennsylvania
9am-9pm 7 days |

| Guesthouses, Inc.
P.O. Box 2137
West Chester, PA 19380 | 800-950-9130
215-692-4575
$$
Dep. 1 night
Visa, MC, AmEx
Fr | No Fee
Free brochure
PA/DE/NJ/MD
Noon-4pm M-F |

More RSOs...
B&B Center City, 1804 Pine St., Philadelphia, PA, 19103 215-735-1137
B&B Connections, P.O. Box 21, Devon, PA, 19333 215-687-3565
B&B Lancaster County, P.O. Box 19, Mountville, PA, 17554 717-285-7200
B&B of SE Pennsylvania, 146 W. Philadelphia Ave, Boyertown, PA, 19512 215-367-4688
B&B-Lancaster Harrisburg, 463 N. Market St., Elizabethtown, PA, 17022 717-367-9408
Magic Forests Travel Bureau, RD 3, Box 256, Clarion, PA, 16214 800-348-9393
Nissly's Olde Home Inns, 624-632 West Chestnut St., Lancaster, PA, 17603 717-392-2311
Pennsylvania Travel Council, 902 N. Second St., Harrisburg, PA, 17102 717-232-8880
Rest & Repast B&B Service, P.O. Box 126, Pine Grove Mills, PA, 16868 814-238-1484

RHODE ISLAND

| Anna's Victorian Connection
5 Fowler Ave.
Newport, RI 02840 | 401-849-2489
$
Dep. 50%
All mayor CrCd
Fr | Brochure SASE
RI, Ma, SE
8am-10pm 7 days |

More RSOs...

Access to Accommodations, 9 Broadway, Newport, RI, 02840
At Home in New England, Box 25, Saunderstown, RI, 02874
B&B International, 21 Dearborn St., Newport, RI, 02840
B&B Registry-Castlekeep, 44 Everett St., Newport, RI, 02840
Bed & Breakfast, Newport, 33 Russell Ave., Newport, RI, 02840 401-846-5408
Newport Historic Inns, P.O. Box 981, Newport, RI, 02840 401-846-ROOM
Newport Reservation Serv., P.O. Box 518, Newport, RI, 02840 401-847-8878

SOUTH CAROLINA

Charleston Society B&B 84 Murray Blvd. Charleston, SC 29401	803-723-4948 $$$ Dep. 1 night	Free brochure South Carolina 9am-5pm M-F
Historic Charleston B&B 43 Legare St. Charleston, SC 29401	803-722-6606 $$ Dep. 1 night Visa, MC Fr,Sp	Free broch. SASE South Carolina 9:30am-6pm M-F
Charleston East B&B League 1031 Tall Pine Rd. Mount Pleasant, SC 29464	803-884-8208 $ Dep. 20%	List $1 South Carolina 10am-6pm

More RSOs...

Bay Street Accomodations, 601 Bay St., Beaufort, SC, 29902

SOUTH DAKOTA

More RSOs...

Old West & Badlands B&B Assoc., HCR 02, Box 100A, Philip, SD, 57567 605-859-2120

TENNESSEE

B&B – Tennessee P.O. Box 110227 Nashville, TN 37222	615-331-5244 800-458-2421 $$ Full deposit All mayor CrCd Sp,Fr,Ger	Brochure $4 TN/Nat./Internat 9am-4pm M-F

More RSOs...

Bed & Breakfast in Memphis, P.O. Box 41621, Memphis, TN, 38174 901-726-5920
Jonesborough B&B, P.O. Box 722, Jonesborough, TN, 37659 615-753-9223

TEXAS

B&B of Fredericksburg 102 S. Cherry St. Fredericksburg, TX 78624	512-997-4712 $$ Dep. or CrCd Visa, MC	Free brochure Texas 9am-7pm M-Sat
Gästhaus Schmidt Reserv. Serv. 501 W. Main St. Fredericksburg, TX 78624	512-997-5612 $$ Dep. 1 ngt or CrCd Visa/MC/AmEx/Dis	Booklet $3 Fredericksburg,TX 10am-6pm M-Sat

More RSOs...

B & B Society of Houston, 4432 Holt St., Bellaire, TX, 77401 713-666-6372

B&B Country Style, Box 1100, 1160 N Hwy 19, Canton, TX, 7513 214-567-2899
B&B Society of Austin, 1702 Gaywood Cove, Austin, TX, 78704
B&B Texas Style, 4224 W. Red Bird Lane, Dallas, TX, 75237 214-298-8586
B&B of Wimberley Texas, P.O. Box 589, Wimberley, TX, 78676 512-847-9666
Bed & Breakfast-Galveston, 1805 Broadway, Galveston, TX, 77550
NRSO, P.O. Box 850653, Richardson, TX, 75085
Sand Dollar Hospitality, 3605 Mendenhall Dr., Corpus Christi, TX, 78415 512-853-1222

UTAH

More RSOs...
Bed & Breakfast Inns of Utah, P.O. Box 3066, Dept. I, Park City, UT, 84060 801-645-8068

VERMONT

More RSOs...
American B&B—New England, Box 983, Saint Albans, VT, 05478
Vermont Bed & Breakfast, P.O. Box 1, East Fairfield, VT, 05448 802-827-3827
Vermont Travel Info. Serv., Pond Village, Brookfield, VT, 05036 802-276-3120

VIRGINIA

Princely B&B Ltd. 819 Prince St. Alexandria, VA 22314	703-683-2159 $$$ Dep. 1 night Fr,Sp,Ger	Alexandria, VA 10am-6pm M-F
Guesthouses B&B, Inc. P.O. Box 5737 Charlottesville, VA 22905	804-979-7264 $$ Dep. 25% + tax Visa, MC, AmEx Fr,Ger	List $1 SASE Virginia Noon-5pm M-F
Bensonhouse Reservation Service 2036 Monument Ave. Richmond, VA 23220	804-353-6900 $$ Dep. 1 night or 50% Visa, MC	List $1.50 Virginia 11am-6pm M-F

More RSOs...
B&B of Roanoke Valley, 1708 Arlington Rd., Roanoke, VA, 24015
B&B of Tidewater Virginia, P.O. Box 3343, Norfolk, VA, 23514 804-627-1983
B&B on the Hill, 2304 East Broad Street, Richmond, VA, 23223 804-780-3746
Rockbridge Reservations, Sleepy Hollow, Box 76, Brownsburg, VA, 24415 703-348-5698
Shenandoah Valley B&B Reserv., P.O. Box 634, Woodstock, VA, 22664 703-459-8241
Travel Tree, P.O. Box 838, Williamsburg, VA, 23187 804-253-1571

WASHINGTON

Pacific B&B Agency 701 N.W. 60th St. Seattle, WA 98107	206-784-0539 FAX: 206-782-4036 $$ Dep. $25 Visa, MC, AmEx Free brochure Ger,Fr,Dan,Nor,Du	Free brochure List $5 SASE Washington/BC 9am-5pm M-F

More RSOs...
B&B Guild—Whatcom County, 2610 Eldridge Ave., Bellingham, WA, 98225 206-676-4560
B&B Service (BABS), 400 W. Lake Samish Dr., Bellingham, WA, 98227 206-733-8642
INNterlodging Co-op Serv., P.O. Box 7044, Tacoma, WA, 98407 206-756-0343
RSVP B&B Reserv. Station, P.O. Box 778, Ferndale, WA, 98248 206-384-6586

Travellers' B&B, P.O. Box 492, Mercer Island, WA, 98040 206-232-2345
West Coast B&B, 11304 20th Place S.W., Seattle, WA, 98146
Whidbey Island B&B Assoc., P.O. Box 259, Langley, WA, 98260 206-321-6272

WEST VIRGINIA

More RSOs...

Countryside Accommodations, P.O. Box 57, Summit Point, WV, 25446 304-725-2614

WISCONSIN

B&B of Milwaukee, Inc. 727 Hawthorne Ave. South Milwaukee, WI 53172	414-571-0780 $ Dep. 1 night Visa, MC, AmEx Sp,Fr,Port	Free brochure Wisc/Canada/USA 9am-9pm daily

More RSOs...

B&B Guest Homes, Route 2, 698 County U, Algoma, WI, 54201 414-743-9742
B&B Info. Serv.–Wisconsin, 458 Glenway St., Madison, WI, 53711 608-238-6776

WYOMING

More RSOs...

Hosts & Guests, Inc., Box 6798 FDR Station, Wy, WY, 10150 212-874-4308

ALBERTA

More RSOs...

AAA Bed West, 207-35A St. S.W., Calgary, AB, T3C 1P6
Alberta Hostelling, 10926 - 88th Ave., Edmonton, AB, T6G 0Z1 403-433-7798
B&B Bureau Canadian Care, Box 7094, Post Sta. E, Calgary, AB, T3C 3L8 403-242-5555
Banff/Jasper Central Res., 204 Caribou, Box 1628, Banff, AB, T0L 0C0
Big Country B&B Agency, P.O. Box 1027, Duinheller, AB, T0J 0Y0
Welcome West Vacation Ltd., 1320 Kerwood Cres. SW, Calgary, AB, T2V 2N6

BRITISH COLUMBIA

Canada-West **Accommodations** P.O. Box 86607 North Vancouver, BC V7L 4L2	604-929-1424 800-873-7976 $$ Dep. 25% Visa, MC, AmEx Immediate booking	Immediate booking Free brochure Vanc/Vic/Whis/Oka 8am-10pm daily
Old English B&B Registry P.O. Box 86818 North Vancouver, BC V7L 1J3	604-986-5069 $$ Dep. or CrCd Visa, MC	Free brochure British Columbia 9am-6pm
Town & Country B&B in B.C. P.O. Box 46544, Stn. G Vancouver, BC V6R 4G8	604-731-5942 $$ Dep. 1 night Fr,Ger,Sp	Guide $10.50 BC. Victoria 9am-4:30pm M-F
A.A. Accommodations West 660 Jones Terrace Victoria, BC V8Z 2L7	604-479-1986 $ Dep. or CrCd Visa, MC, AmEx Fr,Ger,Sp,Wel,Dan,Jap,Cz	BC, Vanc. Isl. 7am-11pm daily

All Seasons B&B Agency, Inc.	604-595-2337	Free brochure
P.O. Box 5511, Stn. B	604-655-7173	Book $6
Victoria, BC V8R 6S4	$$	British Columbia
	Dep. 20%	10am-5pm M-F Sum.
	Visa, MC	
	Free brochure	
	Fr,Du,Ger	

More RSOs...
A B & C B&B of Vancouver, 4390 Frances St., Vancouver, BC, V5C 2R3 604-298-8815
AAA Bed & Breakfast, 658 E. 29th Ave., Vancouver, BC, V5V 2R9 604-875-8888
Alberta & Pacific Bed & Breakfast, P.O. Box 15477, M.P.O., Vancouver, BC, V6B 5B2
604-944-1793
Bairich Bed & Breakfast, 7241 Cambie St. #804, Vancouver, BC, V6P 3H3
Born Free B&B of B.C. Ltd., 4390 Frances St., Burnaby, BC, V5C 2R3 604-298-8815
Campbell River B&B Agency, 302 Birch St., Campbell River, BC, V9W 2S6
Home Away From Home B&B, 1441 Howard Ave., Burnaby, BC, V5B 3S2 604-294-1760
Traveller's B&B, 1840 Midgard Ave., Victoria, BC, V8P 2Y9 604-477-3069
VIP Bed & Breakfast, 1786 Teakwood Road, Victoria, BC, V8N 1E2 604-477-5604
Vancouver B&B Ltd., 1685 Ingleton Ave., Burnaby, BC, V5C 4L8 604-291-6147
Western Comfort B&B Regis., 1890 E. Carisbrooke Rd., North Vancouver, BC, V7N 1M9

MANITOBA

More RSOs...
Manitoba Farm Vacations, 525 Kylemore Ave., Winnipeg, MB, R3L 1B5

NEW BRUNSWICK

More RSOs...
New Brunswick Tourism, P.O. Box 12345, Frederick, NB, E3B 5C3

NEWFOUNDLAND

More RSOs...
Tourist Services Division, Box 2061, Saint John's, NF, A1C 5R8

ONTARIO

Niagara Regional/On The Lake	416-358-8988	Free brochure
4917 River Rd.	$$	Ont/Niag. Pen.
Niagara Falls, ON L2E 3G5	Ask about deposit	7 days
	Visa, MC, AmEx	
	Ger,Pol,Ukr,Fr	

Downtown Toronto Assoc. of B&Bs	416-977-6841	Free brochure
P.O. Box 190 Station B	416-598-4562	Ontario
Toronto, ON M5T 2W1	$$	9:15am-2pm daily
	Dep. 50%	
	Visa (to hold rm)	
	Sp,It,Fr	

Toronto Bed & Breakfast Inc.	416-588-8800	Free brochure
Box 269, 253 College St	$$	Tor/Ont/Ott/Mont
Toronto, ON M5T 1R5	Dep. 1 night	9-noon, 2-7pm M-F
	Visa, MC, DC	
	Fr,Ger,It,Pol,Uk,Jap,Swe	

More RSOs...
All Seasons B&B Assoc., 383 Mississauga Valley, Mississauga, ON, L5A 1Y9 416-276-4572

B&B Prince Edward County, Box 1500, Picton, ON, K0K 2T0 613-476-6798
B&B Registry of Peterborough, P.O. Box 2264, Peterborough, ON, K9J 7Y8
Beachburg & Area B&B Assoc, Box 146, Beachburg, ON, K0J 1C0 613-582-3585
Bed & Breakfast Burlington, 5435 Stratton Rd., Burlington, ON, L7L 2Z1 416-637-0329
Brighton Area B&B Assoc., 61 Simpson St. Box 1106, Brighton, ON, K0K 1H0 613-475-0538
Capital B&B Assoc. Ottawa, 2071 Riverside Dr., Ottawa, ON, K1H 7X2 613-737-4129
Country Host - Year Round, RR #1, Palgrave, ON, L0N 1P0 519-941-7633
Eastern Ontario Cntry B&B, c/o Roduner Farm RR1, Cardinal, ON, K0E 1E0 613-657-4830
Fergus/Elora B&B Assoc., 550 Saint Andrew St. E., Fergus, ON, N1M 1R6 519-843-2747
Flesherton & Beaver Valley, Box 119, Flesherton, ON, N0C 1E0 519-924-2675
Grey Bruce B&B Association, 435 Wellington, Port Elgin, ON, N0H 2T0 519-832-5520
Hamilton-Wentworth B&B, 61 E 43rd St., Hamilton, ON, L8T 3B7 416-648-0461
Kingston Area Bed & Breakfast, P.O. Box 37, 10 Westview Rd., Kingston, ON, K7M 4V6 613-542-0214
Metropolitan B&B Registry, 615 Mt. Pleasant, # 269, Toronto, ON, M4S 3C5 416-964-2566
Muskoka B&B Association, Box 1431, Gravenhurst, ON, P0C 1G0 705-687-4395
Niagara-on-the-Lake B&B, P.O. Box 1515, Niagara-on-the-Lake, ON, L0S 1J0 416-358-8988
Ontario Vacation Farms Assoc., Box 9, Alma, ON, N0B 1A0 519-846-9788
Orillia & District B&B, RR 2, Lakeshore Rd., Hawkestone, ON, L0L 1T0 705-487-7191
Parry Sound & District B&B, P.O. Box 71, Parry Sound, ON, P2A 2X2 705-342-9266
Pelee Island B&B Assoc., c/o Lynn Tiessen, Pelee Island, ON, N0R 1M0 519-724-2068
Penetanguishene Area B&B, C.P. 1270, 63 rue Main, Penetanguishene, ON, L0K 1P0 705-549-3116
Point Pelee B&B Association, 115 Erie St. S., Leamington, ON, N8H 3B5 519-326-7169
Port Stanley & Sparta Area, 324 Smith St. Box 852, Port Stanley, ON, N0L 2A0 519-782-4173
Prince Edward County B&B, 299 Main St., Wellington, ON, K0K 3L0 613-399-2569
SW Ontario Countryside Vac, RR #1, Millbank, ON, N0K 1L0 519-595-4604
Sarnia-Lambton B&B, #503 - 201 Front St. N, Sarnia, ON, N7T 7T9 519-332-1820
Seaway Valley B&B Assoc., P.O. Box 884, Cornwall, ON, K6J 1Z3 613-932-0299
Serena's Place, 720 Headley Dr., London, ON, N6H 3V6 519-471-6228
South Renfrew County B&B, c/o B.Collins, Box 67, Calabogie, ON, K0J 1H0 613-752-2201
St. Catharines B&B Assoc., 489 Carlton St., Saint Catharines, ON, L2M 4W9 416-937-2422
Stratford Area Visitors, 38 Albert St., Stratford, ON, N5A 3K3 519-271-5140
Stratford B&B Two, 208 Church St., Stratford, ON, N5A 2R6 519-273-4840
Upper Canada B&B, P.O. Box 247, Morrisburg, ON, K0C 1X0
B&B Across The City Registry, 1823 Foleyet Cres., Toronto, ON, L1V 2X8 416-837-0024

PRINCE EDWARD ISLAND

More RSOs ...

Kensington Area Tourist, RR 1, Kensington, PEI, C0B 1M0 902-436-6847
Visitors Services Division, P.O. Box 940, Charlottetown, PEI, C1A 7MJ

PROVINCE OF QUEBEC

B&B Relais Montreal Hospitality 3977 Ave Laval Montreal, PQ H2W 2H9	514-287-9635 $ Dep. 1 night Visa, MC	Montreal 8am-6pm
B&B Bonjour Québec 3765, Bd. Monaco Quebec, PQ G1P 3J3	418-527-1465 $ Dep. 1 night	Free brochure Québec City 9am-7pm daily

More RSOs...

Bed & Breakfast Montreal, 4912 Victoria, Montreal, PQ, H3W 2N1 514-738-9410
Gite Quebec, 3729 Ave. le Corbusier, St-Foy, PQ, G1W 4R8 418-651-1860
Mont–Royal Chez Soi, Inc., 5151 Cote-St-Antoine, Montreal, PQ, H4A 1P1
Tourism Quebec, CP 20 000, Quebec, PQ, G1K 7X2

SASKATCHEWAN ———————————————————————

More RSOs...
 Saskatchewan Country Vaca., Box 89, Blaine Lake, SA, S0J 0J0 306-497-2782

YUKON TERRITORY ———————————————————————

More RSOs...
 Northern Network of B&B's, Box 302, Dawson City, YU, Y0B 1G0 403-993-5772
 Tourism Yukon, Box 2703, Whitehorse, YU, Y1A 2C6
 Yukon Bed & Breakfast, 102-302 Steele St., Whitehorse, YU, Y1A 2C5 403-668-2999

B&B Inns with Special Features

Antiques

Many of the inns we list are graced by antiques. These inns have put a special emphasis on antiques and period decor.

Patton House B&B Inn
Wooster, AR

The Greenway House
Bisbee, AZ

Eastlake Victorian Inn
Los Angeles, CA

Whitegate Inn
Mendocino, CA

Beazley House
Napa, CA

The Martine Inn
Pacific Grove, CA

Heritage Park B&B Inn
San Diego, CA

Holden House—1902 B&B Inn
Colorado Springs, CO

Butternut Farm
Glastonbury, CT

Queen Anne Inn
New London, CT

Jesse Mount House
Savannah, GA

Redstone Inn
Dubuque, IA

Lafitte Guest House
New Orleans, LA

Cyrus Kent House Inn
Chatham, MA

Inn on Sea Street
Hyannis, MA

Addison Choate Inn
Rockport, MA

Isaiah Jones Homestead
Sandwich, MA

Spring Bank—A B&B Inn
Frederick, MD

Spencer—Silver Mansion
Havre De Grace, MD

National Pike Inn
New Market, MD

Manor House Inn
Bar Harbor, ME

The Hammons House
Bethel, ME

English Meadows Inn
Kennebunkport, ME

Maine Stay Inn & Cottages
Kennebunkport, ME

Garth Woodside Mansion
Hannibal, MO

Harding House B&B
Saint Joseph, MO

Rosswood Plantation
Lorman, MS

Cedar Crest Victorian Inn
Asheville, NC

The Morehead Inn
Charlotte, NC

Bungay Jar B&B
Franconia, NH

Josiah Reeve House B&B
Alloway, NJ

Bedford Inn
Cape May, NJ

Carriage House B&B
Las Vegas, NM

Rosewood Inn
Corning, NY

Strathmont — A B&B
Elmira, NY

Chestnut Tree Inn
Saratoga Springs, NY

Cobbler Shop B&B Inn
Zoar, OH

Adamstown Inn
Adamstown, PA

Hotel Manisses
Block Island, RI

Country Victorian B&B
Charleston, SC

Seven Wives Inn
Saint George, UT

Mayhurst Inn B&B
Orange, VA

Legacy of Williamsburg
Williamsburg, VA

Inn at Narrow Passage
Woodstock, VA

Governor's Inn
Ludlow, VT

Historic Brookside Inn
Orwell, VT

Thorp House Inn & Cottages
Fish Creek, WI

The Manor House
Kenosha, WI

Yesterdays Ltd.
Wheeling, WV

Pinelodge Farm B&B
Mill Bay, BC

Auberge Manoir de Tilly
Saint Antoine de Tilly, PQ

Comfort

Old-fashioned comfort and friendly staff are important to every lodging. These inns have these qualities in abundance.

Saddle Rock Ranch B&B
Sedona, AZ

Pelican Cove Inn
Carlsbad, CA

Forbestown Inn
Lakeport, CA

Grandmere's Inn
Nevada City, CA

The LITTLE INN on the Bay
Newport Beach, CA

Heart's Desire Inn
Occidental, CA

Gatehouse Inn
Pacific Grove, CA

Cinnamon Bear B&B
Saint Helena, CA

524 Special Features

The Balboa Park Inn
San Diego, CA

Arroyo Village Inn
San Luis Obispo, CA

Old Yacht Club Inn
Santa Barbara, CA

Spring Garden
Laurel, DE

A Small Wonder B&B
Wilmington, DE

The Kenwood Inn
Saint Augustine, FL

Victoria Place
Lawai, Kauai, HI

Harrison House B&B
Naperville, IL

Davis House
Crawfordsville, IN

Mimi's House
Washington, IN

The RidgeRunner
Middlesborough, KY

Windfields Farm
Cummington, MA

Point Way Inn
Edgartown, MA

Village Green Inn
Falmouth, MA

Grafton Inn
Falmouth — Cape Cod, MA

Haus Andreas
Lee, MA

Walker House Inn
Lenox, MA

Whistler's Inn
Lenox, MA

The Bayberry
Martha's Vineyard Island,
MA

Corner House
Nantucket, MA

Northfield Country House
Northfield, MA

Rocky Shores
Inn/Cottages
Rockport, MA

Coach House Inn
Salem, MA

Honeysuckle Hill
West Barnstable, MA

Kemp House Inn
Saint Michaels, MD

Castlemaine Inn
Bar Harbor, ME

Hearthside B&B
Bar Harbor, ME

Windward House B&B
Camden, ME

The Dock Square Inn
Kennebunkport, ME

Inn at Harbor Head
Kennebunkport, ME

Old Fort Inn
Kennebunkport, ME

The Cape Neddick House
York—Cape Neddick, ME

Doanleigh Wallagh Inn
Kansas City, MO

Mountain High
Glenville, NC

New Berne House Inn
B&B
New Bern, NC

Colonel Ludlow Inn
Winston—Salem, NC

Haverhill Inn
Haverhill, NH

The Forest—A Country Inn
Intervale, NH

Benjamin Prescott Inn
Jaffrey, NH

Crab Apple Inn
Plymouth, NH

Mountain Laurel Inn
Wentworth, NH

Conover's Bay Head Inn
Bay Head, NJ

Normandy Inn
Spring Lake, NJ

Sea Crest By The Sea
Spring Lake, NJ

Austin Manor
Ithaca—Groton, NY

The Lamplight Inn B&B
Lake Luzerne, NY

The Smithton Inn
Ephrata, PA

Tattersall Inn
Point Pleasant, PA

Tres Palmas Guest House
San Juan, PR

Compton Manor
Knoxville, TN

Edgeworth Inn
Monteagle, TN

Old Miners' Lodge B&B
Park City, UT

Fassifern B&B
Lexington, VA

Cobble House Inn
Gaysville, VT

Golden Kitz Lodge
Stowe, VT

Raspberry Patch B&B
Stowe, VT

Nutmeg Inn
Wilmington, VT

North Garden Inn
Bellingham, WA

Schnauzer Crossing B&B
Bellingham, WA

Palmer's Chart House
Deer Harbor, WA

Chelsea Station B&B Inn
Seattle, WA

The Swallow's Nest
Vashon Island, WA

Abendruh B&B Swisstyle
Belleville, WI

Conference

Small conferences can be very productive when held in the inns listed below, all of which have the facilities you need and the quiet and opportunity, too, for the fellowship you require.

Power's Mansion Inn
Auburn, CA

Cobblestone Inn
Carmel, CA

Valley Lodge
Carmel Valley, CA

San Benito House
Half Moon Bay, CA

Gosby House Inn
Pacific Grove, CA

Old St. Angela Inn
Pacific Grove, CA

Edward II B&B Inn
San Francisco, CA

Jackson Court
San Francisco, CA

Petite Auberge
San Francisco, CA

The Queen Anne Hotel
San Francisco, CA

The Hensley House
San Jose, CA

Madison Street Inn
Santa Clara, CA

St. George Hotel
Volcano, CA

English Manor Inns
Clayton, GA

Manoa Valley Inn
Honolulu, Oahu, HI

Walden Inn
Greencastle, IN

Heritage House
Topeka, KS

Max Paul...An Inn
Wichita, KS

Yankee Clipper Inn
Rockport, MA

Colonial House Inn
Yarmouth Port, MA

Gibson's Lodgings
Annapolis, MD

The Strawberry Inn
New Market, MD

Robert Morris Inn
Oxford, MD

High Meadows B&B
Eliot, ME

East Wind Inn
Tenants Harbor, ME

York Harbor Inn
York Harbor, ME

Yelton Manor
South Haven, MI

Schwegmann House B&B Inn
Washington, MO

Richmond Hill Inn
Asheville, NC

The Jefferson Inn
Jefferson, NH

The Lyme Inn
Lyme, NH

New London Inn
New London, NH

Whistling Swan Inn
Stanhope, NJ

Troutbeck Country Inn
Amenia, NY

Brae Loch Inn
Cazenovia, NY

The Inn at Cooperstown
Cooperstown, NY

The Genesee Country Inn
Mumford, NY

Ansonborough Inn
Charleston, SC

Fountain Hall B&B Inn
Culpepper, VA

Frederick House
Staunton, VA

Ten Acres Lodge
Stowe, VT

Hermitage Inn & Brookbound
Wilmington, VT

Kedron Valley Inn
Woodstock, VT

Moore House Country Inn
South Cle Elum, WA

Jakobstettel Guest House
Saint Jacobs, ON

Decor

Distinctive decor and unusual architure are always a pleasure. Enjoy them in these inns.

The Marks House Inn
Prescott, AZ

Baywood B&B Inn
Baywood Park, CA

Mount View Hotel
Calistoga, CA

Hope-Merrill/Bosworth
Geyserville, CA

Blackthorne Inn
Inverness, CA

Bluebelle House B&B
Lake Arrowhead, CA

Old World Inn
Napa, CA

Centrella Hotel
Pacific Grove, CA

Buttons and Bows B&B
Red Bluff, CA

Alamo Square Inn
San Francisco, CA

The Inn at Union Square
San Francisco, CA

Inn on Castro
San Francisco, CA

The Monte Cristo
San Francisco, CA

The Bayberry Inn B&B
Santa Barbara, CA

Casa Madrona Hotel
Sausalito, CA

Oleander House
Yountville, CA

The Lovelander B&B Inn
Loveland, CO

Chimney Crest Manor B&B
Bristol, CT

The Palmer Inn
Mystic, CT

The Watson House
Key West, FL

Wedgwood B&B
Hamilton, GA

The Richards House
Dubuque, IA

Chateau des Fleurs
Winnetka, IL

The Rock House
Morgantown, IN

A Hotel—The Frenchmen
New Orleans, LA

Ashley Manor
Cape Cod—Barnstable, MA

Bradford Inn & Motel
Chatham, MA

The Farmhouse
East Orleans, MA

Colonial Inn of Marthas
Edgartown, MA

Mostly Hall B&B Inn
Falmouth, MA

The Gables Inn
Lenox, MA

Amelia Payson Guest House
Salem, MA

Cleftstone Manor
Bar Harbor, ME

Brannon-Bunker Inn
Damariscotta, ME

Kemah Guest House
Saugatuck, MI

Coachlight B&B
Saint Louis, MO

Winter House
Saint Louis, MO

Walnut Street Inn
Springfield, MO

Wright Inn/Carriage House
Asheville, NC

Shield House
Clinton, NC

The Manor on Golden Pond
Holderness, NH

Bay Head Sands B&B
Bay Head, NJ

The Gingerbread House
Cape May, NJ

Leith Hall
Cape May, NJ

Allen Villa B&B
Troy, OH

Spring House
Airville, PA

The Old Court B&B
Providence, RI

Villa de La Fontaine B&B
Charleston, SC

The William Catlin House
Richmond, VA

The Inn at Manchester
Manchester Village, VT

Eagle Harbor Inn
Ephraim, WI

Lochnaiar Inn
Racine, WI

The Franklin Victorian
Sparta, WI

The Gray Goose B&B
Sturgeon Bay, WI

Hampshire House 1884
Romney, WV

Jakobstettel Guest House
Saint Jacobs, ON

Family Fun

Be sure to check this list if you're travelling with your brood of six. The inns below are ideal for a family fun vacation.

Harbor Breeze
Harwich Port, MA

Gosnold Arms
New Harbor, ME

Goose Cove Lodge
Sunset, ME

B&B at Ludington
Ludington, MI

Down Over Inn
Arrow Rock, MO

Lone Mountain Ranch
Big Sky, MT

Earthshine Mountain Lodge
Lake Toxaway, NC

Franconia Inn
Franconia, NH

Cordova
Orange Grove, NJ

Country Spread B&B
Richfield Springs, NY

Angie's Guest Cottage
Virginia Beach, VA

Hugging Bear Inn & Shoppe
Chester, VT

Liberty Hill Farm
Rochester, VT

Hyde Away
Waitsfield, VT

Teton Tree House
Jackson Hole, WY

Milford House
Annapolis Royal, NS

Farm Vacations

The inns listed below are working farms.

Lynx Creek Farm B&B
Prescott, AZ

DeHaven Valley Farm
Westport, CA

Howard Creek Ranch
Westport, CA

Double M Ranch B&B
Zolfo Springs, FL

Wingscorton Farm Inn
East Sandwich, MA

Wood Farm
Townsend, MA

Ellis River House
Jackson, NH

Litco Farms B&B
Cooperstown, NY

Sonka's Sheep Station Inn
Myrtle Creek, OR

Ponda-Rowland B&B
Beaumont, PA

Winding Glen Farm Home
Christiana, PA

Barley Sheaf Farm
Holicong, PA

Meadow Spring Farm
Kennett Square, PA

Cedar Hill Farm
Mount Joy, PA

The Whitehall Inn
New Hope, PA

Skoglund Farm
Canova, SD

Lakeside Farm B&B
Webster, SD

Caledonia Farm B&B
Flint Hill, VA

Fleetwood Farm B&B
Leesburg, VA

Oak Spring Farm &
Vineyard
Raphine, VA

Echo Ledge Farm Inn
Saint Johnsbury, VT

Knoll Farm Country Inn
Waitsfield, VT

Just-N-Trails B&B/Farm
Sparta, WI

Reid Farms Tourist Home
Centreville, NB

Lea's Hobby Farm B&B
Vernon River, PEI

Fishing

Nothing like a good catch. These inns are near the haunts of the really big ones. Fishing over, head back to the inn and tell tales to fellow enthusiasts.

Glacier Bay Country Inn
Gustavus, AK

Gustavus Inn
Gustavus, AK

The Matlick House
Bishop, CA

Sorensen's Resort
Hope Valley, CA

Requa Inn
Klamath, CA

Jean Pratt's Riverside
B&B
Oroville, CA

River Rock Inn
Placerville, CA

The Faulkner House
Red Bluff, CA

Pleasure Point Inn
Santa Cruz, CA

The Biggerstaff House
B&B
Carbondale, CO

Mary Lawrence Inn
Gunnison, CO

Charley's Harbour Inne
Mystic, CT

Colonial River House
Cocoa, FL

Hopp-Inn Guest House
Marathon, FL

McBride's B&B
Guesthouse
Irwin, ID

Black Friar Inn
Bar Harbor, ME

Dockside Guest Quarters
York, ME

Raymond House Inn
Port Sanilac, MI

Langdon House
Beaufort, NC

The Gingerbread Inn
Chimney Rock, NC

Blue Boar Lodge
Robbinsville, NC

Inn at Coit Mountain
Newport, NH

Mountain Laurel Inn
Wentworth, NH

Thousand Islands Inn
Clayton—1000 Islands, NY

Highland Inn
Monterey, VA

West Mountain Inn
Arlington, VT

Churchill House Inn
Brandon, VT

North Hero House
North Hero, VT

Lake St. Catherine Inn
Poultney, VT

Lareau Farm Country Inn
Waitsfield, VT

Tudor Inn
Port Angeles, WA

Griffin Inn & Cottages
Ellison Bay, WI

Fish Creek B&B
Jackson Hole (Wilson),
WY

Wolf Hotel
Saratoga, WY

Campbell River Lodge
Campbell River, BC

Lord Jim's Resort Hotel
Halfmoon Bay, BC

The Lookout B&B
Nanoose Bay, BC

Reid Farms Tourist Home
Centreville, NB

Gardens

Ah, to while away an hour in a lovely garden. What could be more relaxing? These inns are renowned for their lush gardens.

Calistoga Wayside Inn
Calistoga, CA

Holiday House
Carmel, CA

Sandpiper
Inn-At-the-Beach
Carmel, CA

Vintage Towers B&B Inn
Cloverdale, CA

Mill Rose Inn
Half Moon Bay, CA

The B&B Inn at La Jolla
La Jolla, CA

The Victorian Farmhouse
Little River, CA

Brewery Gulch Inn
Mendocino, CA

Jabberwock
Monterey, CA

Country Garden Inn
Napa, CA

Villa Royale Inn
Palm Springs, CA

The Feather Bed
Quincy, CA

Harvest Inn
Saint Helena, CA

Monets Garden
San Diego, CA

Seal Beach Inn & Gardens
Seal Beach, CA

Victorian Garden Inn
Sonoma, CA

Barretta Gardens Inn
Sonora, CA

Country House Inn
Templeton, CA

Howard Creek Ranch
Westport, CA

Blue Lake Ranch
Durango, CO

Clark Cottage, Wintergreen
Pomfret, CT

Merlinn Guesthouse
Key West, FL

Wicker Guesthouse
Key West, FL

Shiverick Inn
Edgartown, MA

Bradford Gardens Inn
Provincetown, MA

Hartwell House
Ogunquit, ME

Hope Farm
Natchez, MS

Cedar Grove Mansion-Inn
Vicksburg, MS

The Blooming Garden Inn
Durham, NC

Martin Hill Inn
Portsmouth, NH

Woolverton Inn
Stockton, NJ

Back of the Beyond
Colden, NY

Inn at Cowger House #9
Zoar, OH

Back Street Inn
New Hope, PA

The Rhett House Inn
Beaufort, SC

Villa de La Fontaine B&B
Charleston, SC

Trail's End, A Country Inn
Wilmington, VT

Sunnymeade House Inn
Victoria, BC

Golf

Tee off, walk and relax, then head back to your cozy inn. What could be nicer?

Kinter House Inn
Corydon, IN

Teetor House
Hagerstown, IN

Old Hoosier House
Knightstown, IN

Fairhaven Inn
Bath, ME

Chebeague Island Inn
Chebeague Island, ME

The 1802 House B&B Inn
Kennebunkport, ME

Red Dog B&B
Saugatuck, MI

Buttonwood Inn
Franklin, NC

The Old Edwards Inn
Highlands, NC

The Greystone Inn
Lake Toxaway, NC

Pine Ridge Inn
Mount Airy, NC

Pine Cone Manor B&B
Pinebluff, NC

The Fairway Inn
Spruce Pine, NC

Pine Crest Inn
Tryon, NC

Cliff Park Inn & Golf Crs.
Milford, PA

The Inn at Manchester
Manchester Village, VT

The 1860 House B&B Inn
Stowe, VT

Beaver Pond Farm Inn
Warren, VT

Red Shutter Inn
Wilmington, VT

Gourmet

An excellent meal can add a lot to your stay. The inns listed here are particularly celebrated for their fine cuisine.

Harbor House Inn
Elk, CA

The Hotel Carter
Eureka, CA

The Old Milano Hotel
Gualala, CA

Madrona Manor—Country Inn
Healdsburg, CA

McCloud Guest House
McCloud, CA

Copper Beech Inn
Ivorytown, CT

Old Lyme Inn
Old Lyme, CT

Chalet Suzanne Country Inn
Lake Wales, FL

The Stovall House
Sautee, GA

The Veranda
Senoia, GA

La Corsette Maison Inn
Newton, IA

Columns Hotel
New Orleans, LA

Bramble Inn
Brewster, MA

The Old Manse Inn
Brewster, MA

Quaker House Inn & Rest.
Nantucket, MA

The Old Inn on the Green
New Marlborough, MA

The Harrington Farm
Princeton, MA

Camden Harbour Inn
Camden, ME

White Barn Inn
Kennebunkport, ME

The Newcastle Inn
Newcastle, ME

Schumacher's New Prague
New Prague, MN

Blake House Inn
Asheville, NC

Randolph House Country Inn
Bryson City, NC

Grandview Lodge
Waynesville, NC

The Bradford Inn
Bradford, NH

The Inn at Crystal Lake
Eaton Center, NH

Colby Hill Inn
Henniker, NH

New London Inn
New London, NH

Stonehurst Manor
North Conway, NH

Woodstock Inn
North Woodstock, NH

The Inn at Sunapee
Sunapee, NH

Chesterfield Inn
West Chesterfield, NH

Barnard-Good House
Cape May, NJ

Stockton Inn, "Colligan's"
Stockton, NJ

Ananas Hus B&B
Averill Park, NY

Crabtree's Kittle House
Chappaqua, NY

Balsam House
Chestertown, NY

Swiss Hutte
Hillsdale, NY

Rose Inn
Ithaca, NY

Taughannock Farms Inn
Trumansburg, NY

Golden Pheasant Inn
Erwinna, PA

Academy Street B&B
Hawley, PA

Longswamp B&B
Mertztown, PA

The Montrose House
Montrose, PA

Centre Bridge Inn
New Hope, PA

Shelter Harbor Inn
Westerly, RI

Inn on the River
Glen Rose, TX

Clifton—The Country Inn
Charlottesville, VA

Channel Bass Inn
Chincoteague Island, VA

Kenmore Inn
Fredericksburg, VA

Inn at Montross
Montross, VA

L'Auberge Provencale
White Post, VA

Arlington Inn
Arlington, VT

Craftsbury Inn
Craftsbury, VT

The Vermont Inn
Killington, VT

Governor's Inn
Ludlow, VT

The Norwich Inn
Norwich, VT

Millbrook
Waitsfield, VT

Inn at Weston
Weston, VT

Inn at Swifts Bay
Lopez Island, WA

The Geneva Inn
Lake Geneva, WI

Woodstone Country Inn
Galiano Island, BC

Historic

Inns situated in historic buildings or locales hold a special appeal for many people. The following is a sampling.

Webster House B&B Inn
Alameda, CA

Mine House Inn
Amador City, CA

Power's Mansion Inn
Auburn, CA

The Coloma Country Inn
Coloma, CA

City Hotel
Columbia, CA

Fallon Hotel
Columbia, CA

The Heirloom
Ione, CA

Julian Gold Rush Hotel
Julian, CA

The Victorian Farmhouse
Little River, CA

Eastlake Victorian Inn
Los Angeles, CA

Meadow Creek Ranch B&B Inn
Mariposa, CA

The Headlands Inn
Mendocino, CA

The Ink House B&B
Saint Helena, CA

The Washington Square Inn
San Francisco, CA

Abriendo Inn
Pueblo, CO

Teller House Hotel
Silverton, CO

Red Brook Inn
Mystic, CT

French Renaissance House
Plainfield, CT

Spring Garden
Laurel, DE

David Finney Inn
New Castle, DE

William Penn Guest House
New Castle, DE

Historic Island Hotel
Cedar Key, FL

St. Francis Inn
Saint Augustine, FL

Shellmont B&B Lodge
Atlanta, GA

Bed & Breakfast Inn
Savannah, GA

Almeda's B&B Inn
Tonganoxie, KS

Talbot Tavern/McLean House
Bardstown, KY

530 Special Features

Taylor-Compton House
Frankfort, KY

Thomas Huckins House
Barnstable, MA

Hawthorne Inn
Concord, MA

Penny House Inn
Eastham–North, MA

Edgartown Inn
Edgartown, MA

Perryville Inn
Rehoboth, MA

Lion's Head Inn
West Harwich, MA

Colonial House Inn
Yarmouth Port, MA

The White Swan Tavern
Chestertown, MD

Glenburn
Taneytown, MD

The Jeweled Turret Inn
Belfast, ME

Lincoln House Country Inn
Dennysville, ME

Todd House
Eastport, ME

High Meadows B&B
Eliot, ME

Bagley House
Freeport, ME

Borgman's B&B
Arrow Rock, MO

Amzi Love B&B
Columbus, MS

Millsaps Buie House
Jackson, MS

Rosswood Plantation
Lorman, MS

The Briars Inn
Natchez, MS

Hope Farm
Natchez, MS

Oak Square Plantation
Port Gibson, MS

Inn at Brevard
Brevard, NC

The King's Arms Inn
New Bern, NC

Oakwood Inn
Raleigh, NC

Six Chimneys
Plymouth, East Hebron, NH

The Cable House
Rye, NH

Captain Mey's Inn
Cape May, NJ

Ashling Cottage
Spring Lake, NJ

Preston House
Santa Fe, NM

The Bird & Bottle Inn
Garrison, NY

The Westchester House
Saratoga Springs, NY

The Inn at Fordhook Farm
Doylestown, PA

Quo Vadis B&B
Franklin, PA

Historic Farnsworth House
Gettysburg, PA

Beechmont Inn
Gettysburg–Hanover, PA

Osceola Mill House
Gordonville–Intercourse, PA

Ash Mill Farm
Holicong–New Hope, PA

Witmer's Tavern–1725 Inn
Lancaster, PA

Salvino's Guest House
Orbisonia, PA

Bellevue House
Newport, RI

Melville House
Newport, RI

Bay Street Inn
Beaufort, SC

Maison Du Pre
Charleston, SC

Nicholls-Crook Plantation
Spartanburg, SC

Hale Springs Inn
Rogersville, TN

Country Cottage Inn
Fredericksburg, TX

North Bend Plantation B&B
Charles City, VA

Bailiwick Inn
Fairfax, VA

La Vista Plantation
Fredericksburg, VA

Wayside Inn Since 1797
Middletown, VA

High Meadows Vineyard Inn
Scottsville, VA

Isle of Wight Inn
Smithfield, VA

Chester House
Chester, VT

Swift House Inn
Middlebury, VT

West Dover Inn
West Dover, VT

Plough Inn
Madison, WI

Gilbert House B&B
Charles Town, WV

Annie Moore's Guest House
Laramie, WY

Stanhope by the Sea
Coxehead, PEI

Low Price

The following lodgings are particularly noted for modest pricing. It is possible to obtain a room for $35 or less.

Stoney Brook Inn
McCloud, CA

Casa Cody B&B Country Inn
Palm Springs, CA

Junction Country Inn B&B
Grand Junction, CO

Midwest Country Inn
Limon, CO

The Alma House
Silverton, CO

Teller House Hotel
Silverton, CO

Curtis House, Inc.
Woodbury, CT

Die Heimat Country Inn
Homestead, IA

Smith House B&B
Shoup, ID

Meriwether House B&B
Columbus, KS

Crystle's B&B
Concordia, KS

Almeda's B&B Inn
Tonganoxie, KS

Captain Isaiah's House
Bass River, MA

Anthony's Town House
Brookline, MA

Avon House B&B
Flint, MI

Evelo's B&B
Minneapolis, MN

Cordova
Orange Grove, NJ

The Plum Tree B&B
Pilar, NM

Spencertown Guests
Spencertown, NY

Zane Trace B&B
Old Washington, OH

Dreamy Acres
Canadensis, PA

Winding Glen Farm Home
Christiana, PA

Neffdale Farm
Paradise, PA

**Runnymede Farm
Guesthouse**
Quarryville, PA

Homestead Lodging
Smoketown, PA

Stella's Guest Home
Little River, SC

Lakeside Farm B&B
Webster, SD

Clardy's Guest House
Murfreesboro, TN

Yacht Club Hotel
Port Isabel, TX

Seven Wives Inn
Saint George, UT

Ski Inn
Stowe, VT

Wolf Hotel
Saratoga, WY

The Blue Heron Inn
Pugwash, NS

Bayberry Cliff Inn B&B
Murray River, PEI

Lea's Hobby Farm B&B
Vernon River, PEI

Armor Inn
Montreal, PQ

Luxury

These establishments are famed for their luxurious appointments and special attention to creature comforts and style.

Gingerbread Mansion
Ferndale, CA

Carriage House
Laguna Beach, CA

Mountain Home Inn
Mill Valley, CA

Doryman's Inn
Newport Beach, CA

Seven Gables Inn
Pacific Grove, CA

Archbishop's Mansion Inn
San Francisco, CA

Jackson Court
San Francisco, CA

West Lane Inn
Ridgefield, CT

1842 Inn
Macon, GA

Ballastone Inn
Savannah, GA

Foley House Inn
Savannah, GA

The Gastonian
Savannah, GA

Lamothe House
New Orleans, LA

Soniat House
New Orleans, LA

Harraseeket Inn
Freeport, ME

The Captain Lord Mansion
Kennebunkport, ME

Mainstay Inn & Cottage
Cape May, NJ

Preston House
Santa Fe, NM

Historic James R. Webster
Waterloo, NY

Guesthouse at Doneckers
Ephrata, PA

Kings Courtyard Inn
Charleston, SC

Clifton—The Country Inn
Charlottesville, VA

Andrie Rose Inn
Ludlow, VT

Mansion Hill Inn
Madison, WI

Captain's Palace
Victoria, BC

**Northumberland Heights
Inn**
Cobourg, ON

The Inn at Manitou
McKeller, ON

Le Chateau De Pierre Inc.
Quebec City, PQ

Nature

Nature lovers, alert! Whether your fancy is ornithology or whale watching, these inns will speak to your heart.

Briar Patch Inn
Sedona, AZ

Graham's B&B Inn
Sedona, AZ

Cazanoma Lodge
Cazadero, CA

Elk Cove Inn
Elk, CA

Karen's B&B Yosemite Inn
Fish Camp, CA

Grey Whale Inn
Fort Bragg, CA

Sorensen's Resort
Hope Valley, CA

Marsh Cottage
Inverness (Pt.Reyes Stn), CA

Requa Inn
Klamath, CA

Meadow Creek Ranch B&B Inn
Mariposa, CA

Joanie's B&B
McCloud, CA

The Red Castle Inn
Nevada City, CA

Inn at Shallow Creek Farm
Orland, CA

River Rock Inn
Placerville, CA

Rancho San Gregorio
San Gregorio, CA

Oak Hill Ranch B&B
Sonora, CA

Twain Harte's B&B
Twain Harte, CA

Little St. Simons Island
Saint Simons Island, GA

Holmes Retreat B&B
Pocatello, ID

The Inn at Duck Creeke
Wellfleet, MA

Wades Point Inn On The Bay
Saint Michaels, MD

Manor House Inn
Bar Harbor, ME

The Anchor Watch
Boothbay Harbor, ME

Tarry-a-While B&B Resort
Bridgton, ME

Breezemere Farm Inn
Brooksville, ME

Lincoln House Country Inn
Dennysville, ME

Kawanhee Inn Lakeside
Weld, ME

Sunset House
West Gouldsboro, ME

Pincushion Mountain B&B
Grand Marais, MN

Cedarcroft Farm B&B
Warrensburg, MO

Burggraf's Countrylane B&B
Bigfork, MT

Willows Inn
Red Lodge, MT

Folkestone Inn
Bryson City, NC

Trestle House Inn
Edenton, NC

Havenshire Inn
Hendersonville, NC

Berkley Center Country Inn
Ocracoke, NC

Key Falls Inn
Pisgah Forest, NC

The Pines Country Inn
Pisgah Forest, NC

Heath Lodge
Waynesville, NC

Country Inn at Bartlett
Bartlett, NH

Province Inn
Strafford, NH

De Bruce Country Inn
De Bruce, NY

R.M. Farm
Livingston Manor, NY

Taughannock Farms Inn
Trumansburg, NY

Adirondack Mountain Chalet
Wells, NY

Holmes Sea Cove B&B
Brookings, OR

Captain's Quarters B&B
Coos Bay, OR

Secluded B&B
Newberg, OR

Swiss Woods B&B
Lititz, PA

Woodhill Farms Inn
Washington Crossing, PA

Alford House B&B
Chattanooga, TN

Trillium House
Nellysford, VA

Three Mountain
Jamaica, VT

The Inn at Long Trail
Killington, VT

Lareau Farm Country Inn
Waitsfield, VT

Mountain Meadows Inn B&B
Ashford, WA

Puget View Guesthouse B&B
Olympia, WA

Spahn's Big Horn Mountain
Big Horn, WY

Teton Tree House
Jackson Hole, WY

Outstanding

Ah, romance! These inns offer a hideaway, a peaceful space in which to be together and let the world go by.

Dairy Hollow House
Eureka Springs, AR

Williams House B&B Inn
Hot Springs Nat'l Park, AR

Graham's B&B Inn
Sedona, AZ

Carter House
Eureka, CA

Gingerbread Mansion
Ferndale, CA

Grey Whale Inn
Fort Bragg, CA

Dunbar House, 1880
Murphys, CA

Beazley House
Napa, CA

The Britt House 1887
San Diego, CA

The Mansions Hotel
San Francisco, CA

Seal Beach Inn & Gardens
Seal Beach, CA

Queen Anne Inn
Denver, CO

San Sophia
Telluride, CO

Bishopsgate Inn
East Haddam, CT

Old Lyme Inn
Old Lyme, CT

The Kalorama Guest
House
Washington, DC

The Veranda
Senoia, GA

Soniat House
New Orleans, LA

Captains House of
Chatham
Chatham, MA

The Whalewalk Inn
Eastham, MA

Seacrest Manor
Rockport, MA

Stephen Daniels House
Salem, MA

Schumacher's New Prague
New Prague, MN

Havenshire Inn
Hendersonville, NC

The Swag
Waynesville, NC

Snowvillage Inn
Snowville, NH

The Abbey
Cape May, NJ

Barnard-Good House
Cape May, NJ

Mainstay Inn & Cottage
Cape May, NJ

Grant Corner Inn
Santa Fe, NM

Troutbeck Country Inn
Amenia, NY

B&B on the Park
Brooklyn, NY

Rose Inn
Ithaca, NY

Adelphi Hotel
Saratoga Springs, NY

Historic James R. Webster
Waterloo, NY

Chanticleer Inn
Ashland, OR

Coachaus
Allentown, PA

The Inn at Turkey Hill
Bloomsburg, PA

Wedgewood B&B Inn
New Hope, PA

Indigo Inn
Charleston, SC

Two Meeting Street Inn
Charleston, SC

Edgewood Plantation
Charles City, VA

Green Trails Country Inn
Brookfield, VT

Tulip Tree Inn
Chittenden, VT

Inn on the Common
Craftsbury Common, VT

Rabbit Hill Inn
Lower Waterford, VT

Black River Inn
Ludlow, VT

Governor's Inn
Ludlow, VT

Windham Hill Inn
West Townshend, VT

Outstanding—54
'

Dairy Hollow House
Eureka Springs, AR

Vintage Comfort B&B Inn
Hot Springs, AR

Knickerbocker Mansion
Big Bear Lake, CA

Happy Landing Inn
Carmel, CA

Elk Cove Inn
Elk, CA

Murphy's Jenner Inn
Jenner, CA

Channel Road Inn
Los Angeles, CA

Green Gables Inn
Pacific Grove, CA

Seven Gables Inn
Pacific Grove, CA

Jasmine Cottage
Point Reyes, CA

Cricket Cottage
Point Reyes Station, CA

Bartels Ranch/Country
Inn
Saint Helena, CA

Deer Run Inn
Saint Helena, CA

Simpson House Inn
Santa Barbara, CA

Babbling Brook Inn
Santa Cruz, CA

Cliff Crest B&B Inn
Santa Cruz, CA

The Darling House
Santa Cruz, CA

Holden House—1902 B&B
Inn
Colorado Springs, CO

Queen Anne Inn
Denver, CO

Eagle River Inn
Minturn, CO

Manor House
Norfolk, CT

Simsbury 1820 House
Simsbury, CT

Liberty Inn 1834
Savannah, GA

The Veranda
Senoia, GA

Chateau des Fleurs
Winnetka, IL

Cornstalk Hotel
New Orleans, LA

Old Sea Pines Inn
Brewster, MA

Dunscroft By-the-Sea
Harwich Port, Cape Cod,
MA

Thorncroft Inn
Martha's Vineyard Island,
MA

Wedgewood Inn
Yarmouth Port, MA

Graycote Inn
Bar Harbor, ME

Ledgelawn Inn
Bar Harbor, ME

The Victorian Villa Inn
Union City, MI

Schumacher's New Prague
New Prague, MN

Rowan Oak House
Salisbury, NC

Greenfield B&B Inn
Greenfield, NH

Cabbage Rose Inn
Flemington, NJ

Hacienda Del Sol
Taos, NM

La Posada de Taos
Taos, NM

**Interlaken
Inn—Restaurant**
Lake Placid, NY

Oliver Loud's Inn
Pittsford, NY

Sandlake Country Inn
Sandlake, OR

Spring House
Airville, PA

Clarion River Lodge
Cooksburg, PA

Brinley Victorian Inn
Newport, RI

The Willows of Newport
Newport, RI

Durham House B&B
Houston, TX

Ravenswood Inn
Mathews, VA

Liberty Rose B&B
Williamsburg, VA

Village Country Inn
Manchester Village, VT

Turtleback Farm Inn
Eastsound, WA

Guest House Cottages
Greenbank, WA

White Lace Inn
Sturgeon Bay, WI

West End Guest House
Vancouver, BC

Skiing

These inns share a proximity to downhill or cross-country skiing. Nothing like coming back from an exhilarating day on the slopes to a warm, cozy fire.

**Gold Mountain Manor
B&B**
Big Bear City, CA

Sorensen's Resort
Hope Valley, CA

Snow Goose Inn
Mammoth Lakes, CA

The Captain's Alpenhaus
Tahoma, CA

**Snow Queen Victorian
Lodge**
Aspen, CO

Ullr Lodge
Aspen, CO

Lark B&B
Frisco, CO

Mary Lawrence Inn
Gunnison, CO

San Sophia
Telluride, CO

Turning Point Inn
Great Barrington, MA

Birchwood Inn
Lenox, MA

Cornell Inn
Lenox, MA

The Noble House
Bridgton, ME

Maine Stay Inn & Cottages
Kennebunkport, ME

The Herbert
Kingfield, ME

Kandahar Lodge
Whitefish, MT

Country Inn at Bartlett
Bartlett, NH

The Bradford Inn
Bradford, NH

Mountain Fare Inn
Campton, NH

Darby Field Inn
Conway, NH

Franconia Inn
Franconia, NH

Haverhill Inn
Haverhill, NH

Meeting House Inn
Henniker, NH

Dana Place Inn
Jackson, NH

Inn at Thorn Hill
Jackson, NH

The Village House
Jackson, NH

The 1785 Inn
North Conway, NH

Old Red Inn & Cottages
North Conway, NH

Sunny Side Inn
North Conway, NH

Haus Edelweiss B&B
Sunapee, NH

The Historic Taos Inn
Taos, NM

Salsa del Salto B&B Inn
Taos, NM

Back of the Beyond
Colden, NY

Mount Tremper Inn
Mount Tremper, NY

Garnet Hill Lodge
North River, NY

Washington School Inn
Park City, UT

Shire Inn
Chelsea, VT

Greenleaf Inn
Chester, VT

Blueberry Hill
Goshen, VT

The Inn at Long Trail
Killington, VT

Mountain Meadows Lodge
Killington, VT

Andrie Rose Inn
Ludlow, VT

Brookside Meadows
Middlebury, VT

Golden Stage Inn
Proctorsville, VT

Liberty Hill Farm
Rochester, VT

Hyde Away
Waitsfield, VT

Sugartree—A Country Inn
Warren, VT

Shield Inn
West Dover, VT

Weathervane Lodge B&B
West Dover, VT

Colonial House
Weston, VT

Tudor Inn
Port Angeles, WA

Amherst Shore Country Inn
Amherst, NS

Little Inn of Bayfield Ltd
Bayfield, ON

Spas

Hot mineral waters are nature's own relaxant. These inns are close to, or are, spas!

"Culver's," A Country Inn
Calistoga, CA

Scarlett's Country Inn
Calistoga, CA

White Sulphur Springs B&B
Clio, CA

Palisades Paradise B&B
Redding, CA

Arroyo Village Inn
San Luis Obispo, CA

Howard Creek Ranch
Westport, CA

Wilbur Hot Springs
Williams, CA

St. Elmo Hotel
Ouray, CO

Six Sisters B&B
Saratoga Springs, NY

Abed & Breakfast at Sparks
Corvallis, OR

The Hudspeth House & Spa
Canyon, TX

Highlawn Inn
Berkeley Springs, WV

Special

These inns all have an extra special, out-of-the-ordinary something that distinguishes them. We hope you'll agree.

Lynx Creek Farm B&B
Prescott, AZ

Seacrest Manor
Rockport, MA

Wildwood Inn
Ware, MA

The Keeper's House
Isle Au Haut, ME

Mansion Hill Country Inn
St. Louis—Bonne Terre, MO

Casita Chamisa B&B
Albuquerque, NM

Brae Loch Inn
Cazenovia, NY

The Teepee
Gowanda, NY

The Inn on Bacon Hill
Saratoga Springs, NY

Harry Packer Mansion
Jim Thorpe, PA

Pineapple Inn
Lewisburg, PA

Crystal River Inn
San Marcos, TX

Jordan Hollow Farm Inn
Stanley, VA

Hugging Bear Inn & Shoppe
Chester, VT

Sports

Sports are an integral part of many people's vacation plans. These inns are noted for their sporting facilities or locales. Be sure to call ahead to see if they have the special facilities you require.

Westways "Private" Resort
Phoenix, AZ

North Coast Country Inn
Gualala, CA

Tucker Hill Inn
Middlebury, CT

Charley's Harbour Inne
Mystic, CT

The Inn on Lake Waramaug
New Preston, CT

1735 House
Amelia Island, FL

Habersham Hollow Inn
Clarkesville, GA

Center Lovell Inn
Center Lovell, ME

Savanna Portage Inn
McGregor, MN

Jack's Fork Country Inn
Mountain View, MO

Greenwood B&B
Greensboro, NC

Ye Olde Cherokee Inn
Kill Devil Hills, NC

The Notchland Inn
Bartlett, NH

Cranmore Mountain Lodge
North Conway, NH

Nereledge Inn
North Conway, NH

Snowvillage Inn
Snowville, NH

Sunset House
Santa Fe, NM

Mountainaire Adventures
Wevertown, NY

Gateway Lodge & Cabins
Cooksburg, PA

Eagles Mere Inn
Eagles Mere, PA

The Inn at Starlight Lake
Starlight, PA

Old Miners' Lodge B&B
Park City, UT

Hill Farm Inn
Arlington, VT

Parmenter House
Belmont, VT

Churchill House Inn
Brandon, VT

October Country Inn
Bridgewater Corners, VT

Barrows House
Dorset, VT

The Vermont Inn
Killington, VT

The Okemo Inn
Ludlow, VT

Manchester Highlands Inn
Manchester, VT

Northfield Inn
Northfield, VT

Quechee Inn-Marshland Farm
Quechee, VT

The Black Bear Inn
Richmond–Bolton Valley, VT

Londonderry Inn
South Londonderry, VT

Brass Lantern
Stowe, VT

The Gables Inn
Stowe, VT

The Siebeness
Stowe, VT

Snow Den Inn & Gallery
West Dover, VT

Palmer's Chart House
Deer Harbor, WA

Red Forest B&B
Two Rivers, WI

Wildflower Inn
Jackson, WY

Shadow Lawn Inn
Rothesay, NB

Sherwood Inn
Port Carling, ON

Vegetarian

Inns where vegetarian meals are prepared for guests.

Peppertrees B&B Inn
Tucson, AZ

The Red Castle Inn
Nevada City, CA

Historic Island Hotel
Cedar Key, FL

The Veranda
Senoia, GA

Turning Point Inn
Great Barrington, MA

Chatsworth B&B
Saint Paul, MN

Grandview Lodge
Waynesville, NC

Corrales Inn B&B
Corrales, NM

Auberge Schweizer
Sutton, PQ

ON BECOMING AN INNKEEPER

Do you dream of being an innkeeper, meeting and making friends with interesting guests and regaling them with your own special brand of hospitality? Make no mistake, innkeeping is hard work, but can be very rewarding.

We have prepared a packet of information on resources for prospective innkeepers which we will send to you free of charge.

Many people prefer to buy an established inn. If you are interested in buying an inn you may wish to contact the editor of this guide regarding information we have on inns for sale. To receive the resource packet or information on inns for sale, please send your request and a legal size, stamped, self-addressed envelope to:

The Complete Guide to Bed & Breakfasts, Inns & Guesthouses
P.O. Box 20467
Oakland, CA 94620

Lanier Travel Guides
In Book Stores Everywhere!

Lanier Travel Guides have set the standard for the industry:

"All necessary information about facilities, prices, pets, children, amenities, credit cards and the like. Like France's Michelin...."—*New York Times.*

"Provides a wealth of the kinds of information needed to make a wise choice."—*American Council on Consumer Interest.*

Golf Courses
The Complete Guide

It's about time for a definitive directory and travel guide for the nation's 30 million avid golf players, 7 million of whom make golf vacations an annual event. This comprehensive guide includes over 8,000 golf courses in the United States that are open to the public. Complete details, greens fees, and information on the clubhouse facilities is augmented by a description of each of the golf courses' best features. A beautiful gift and companion to *Golf Resorts—The Complete Guide.* Introduction by Arthur Jack Snyder.

Golf Resorts International

A wish book and travel guide for the wandering golfer. This guide, written in much the same spirit as the bestselling *Elegant Small Hotels,* reviews the creme de la creme of golf resorts all over the world. Beautifully illustrated, it includes all pertinent details regarding hotel facilities and amenities. Wonderful narrative on each hotel's special charm, superb cuisine and most importantly, those fabulous golf courses. Written from a golfer's viewpoint, it looks at the challenges and pitfalls of each course. For the non-golfer, there is ample information about other activities available in the area, such as on-site health spas, nearby shopping, and more.

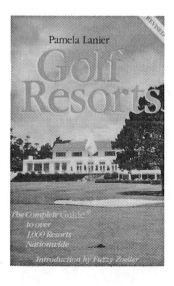

Golf Resorts
— The Complete Guide

The first ever comprehensive guide to over 1,000 golf resorts coast to coast. Includes complete details of each resort facility and golf course particulars. "The Complete Guide to Golf Resorts is a wonderful golf destination guide." — LPGA   Introduction by Fuzzy Zoeller.

Elegant Small Hotels
— A Connoiseur's Guide

This selective guide for discriminating travelers describes over 200 of America's finest hotels characterized by exquisite rooms, fine dining, and perfect service par excellence. Introduction by Peter Duchin. "Elegant Small Hotels makes a seductive volume for window shopping." — *Chicago Sun Times*.

All-Suite Hotel Guide
— The Definitive Directory

The only guide to the all suite hotel industry features over 1,200 hotels nation-wide and abroad. There is a special bonus list of temporary office facilities. A perfect choice for business travelers and much appreciated by families who enjoy the additional privacy provided by two rooms.

Condo Vacations—
The Complete Guide

The popularity of Condo Vacations has grown exponentially. In this national guide, details are provided on over 3,000 Condo resorts in an easy to read format with valuable descriptive write-ups. The perfect vacation option for families and a great money saver!

AVAILABLE IN BOOK STORES EVERYWHERE

VOTE

FOR YOUR CHOICE OF
INN OF THE YEAR

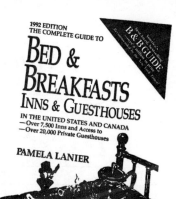

To the editors of **The Complete Guide to Bed & Breakfasts, Inns and Guesthouses in the U.S. and Canada:**

I cast my vote for "Inn of the Year" for:

Name of Inn _____

Address _____

_____

Phone _____

Reasons _____

_____

_____

I would also like to (please check one):

___ Recommend a new Inn   ___ Comment
___ Critique   ___ Suggest

Name of Inn _____

Address _____

_____

Phone _____

Comment _____

_____

Please send your entries to:
The Complete Guide to Bed & Breakfast Inns
P.O. Box 20467
Oakland, CA 94620-0467

Travel Books from
LANIER GUIDES

ORDER FORM

QTY.	TITLE	EACH	TOTAL
	Golf Courses—The Complete Guide	$14.95	
	Golf Resorts—The Complete Guide	$14.95	
	Golf Resorts International	$19.95	
	Condo Vacations—The Complete Guide	$14.95	
	Elegant Small Hotels	$19.95	
	All-Suite Hotel Guide	$14.95	
	The Complete Guide to Bed & Breakfasts, Inns & Guesthouses	$16.95	
	Sub-Total		$
	Shipping		$2.00 each
	TOTAL ENCLOSED		$

Send your order to:
TEN SPEED PRESS
P.O. Box 7123
Berkeley, California 94707

Allow 3 to 4 weeks for delivery

Please send my order to:

_____

_____

_____ STATE _____ ZIP_____